Sheldon B. Rothbell, Esq.
6 Split Rail Lane
East Setauket, N.Y. 11733-1835

Subscription Service Filing Record

RELEASE NUMBER 6

October 2005

has been filed in

INTERNATIONAL LITIGATION:
A Guide to Jurisdiction, Practice, and Strategy
(Third Edition)

Filed ____________________ Date ____________________

NOTE: In order to assist subscribers in assuring themselves that their looseleaf sets are and continue to be complete and up to date, the Publisher has instituted a system of sequential numbering of all subscription service releases for each publication. The accompanying material is designated "Release Number 6" for INTERNATIONAL LITIGATION—THIRD EDITION. Subsequent releases, in sequence, will each call for a check of the preceding Service Filing Record sheet to ensure the continuity of filing releases.

For information or assistance in connection with service for this volume please contact:

Transnational Publishers, Inc.
410 Saw Mill River Road
Ardsley, NY 10502
(914) 693-5100

FILE THIS SHEET IN THE VERY FRONT OF YOUR VOLUME, RETAIN THIS RECORD IN YOUR VOLUME FOR FUTURE REFERENCE UNTIL RELEASE NUMBER 7 IS ISSUED.

This book is dedicated with gratefulness, love, and appreciation to Arlene, Jennifer, Sarah, Susannah, Bobbi Jo, Scott, Devon, Davis, and Selden.

NOTICE

As every lawyer knows, each case turns on the specific facts involved. The material covered in these chapters should not be interpreted as fact-specific; the book is intended to provide only general background material and guidance to the reader. This book is not intended to, nor does it purport to, provide legal advice. Such advice can only be provided by counsel that is familiar with the specific situations of parties to cases that may be pertinent to the material covered in this book.

The views presented in this book are the personal views of the authors, not those of the United States Department of Justice, its clients, or the law firms of Crowell & Moring, Rountree, Losee & Baldwin, L.L.P., or their clients.

CONTENTS

Chapter 3
ADVICE TO THE PROSPECTIVE LITIGANT

Chapter 4
SERVICE OF PROCESS

Chapter 5
SELECTED LIMITATIONS ON THE JURISDICTION OF U.S. COURTS

Chapter 6
SELECTED ISSUES OF PERSONAL JURISDICTION OR JURISDICTION TO ADJUDICATE AND LIMITATIONS

Chapter 7
THE FOREIGN SOVEREIGN IMMUNITIES ACT

Chapter 8
THE ACT OF STATE DOCTRINE

Chapter 9
PROVING FOREIGN LAW AND DETERMINING WHAT LAW APPLIES

Chapter 10
OBTAINING THE EVIDENCE

Chapter 11
ENFORCEMENT OF JUDGMENTS

Chapter 12
USE OF THE COURTS IN SUPPORT OF INTERNATIONAL ARBITRATION

APPENDICES

ABOUT THE AUTHORS

David Epstein has a private practice specializing in international litigation. He is the former Director of the Office of Foreign Litigation in the Civil Division of the U.S. Department of Justice. In that capacity, he was responsible for the worldwide supervision of cases involving the United States in foreign courts. He received his law degree from the Georgetown University Law Center (LL.B., 1961) and a Masters in Law degree (LL.M.) from the same institution in 1966. He is admitted to practice in the District of Columbia. He is currently an Adjunct Professor at the Washington College of Law, American University, teaching courses on International Litigation and Arbitration.

Jeffrey L. Snyder is a partner in the International Trade Group in the Washington, D.C. office of Crowell & Moring, the international law firm. He is the author of numerous articles and columns on international trade and business, and speaks frequently on international trade export matters. Mr. Snyder has been a lecturer at the Washington College of Law, American University, teaching a course on International Trade in Services and Telecommunications, and has also taught legal research and writing techniques. He received his J.D., *cum laude,* from Washington College of Law, American University, and his LL.M. from Columbia University School of Law.

Charles S. Baldwin, IV, is a litigation and international trade partner at Rountree, Losee & Baldwin, L.L.P. in Wilmington, North Carolina. He has prosecuted international trade and arbitration cases in federal and state courts and is the author of ''Protecting Confidential and Proprietary Commercial Information in International Arbitration,'' 31 *Tex. Int'l L.J.* 451 (1996). Mr. Baldwin received his J.D. from American University, where he was a Note & Comment Editor on the Law Review. He also holds an M.A. in Law and International Affairs from American University School of International Service and an LL.M., *with distinction,* in international and comparative law from Georgetown

University. Mr. Baldwin welcomes comments at Cbaldwin@rlblawfirm.com or P.O. Box 1409, Wilmington, North Carolina 28402.

PREFACE

This Third Edition is the product of a significant amount of revising and updating. The subjects covered in this Guide span a wide range of areas and legal issues. We have made every effort to maintain and in fact expand our ''practical'' approach to the issues involved, and have added practical tips, strategies, and advice in many more places. Many format changes have been made, appendices added, citations expanded, forms included, and so on, all designed to make the material more accessible and the Guide more helpful.

We have received many comments from readers and welcome them from you. The best way for us to make this Guide work for you is to learn how you use it and what would make it better.

David Epstein
Jeffrey L. Snyder
Washington, D.C.
August 1998

Charles S. Baldwin, IV
Wilmington, N.C.
August 1998

ACKNOWLEDGMENTS

We thank our families for once again enduring all of the late evenings and weekends devoted to this project. Their patience and support keeps us going.

Chapter 1

OVERVIEW OF TRANSNATIONAL LITIGATION

§ 1.01 INTRODUCTION

The growth in transnational litigation has been attributed to the steady increase in foreign trade and industry in the United States. During the last several decades, the globalization of the economy has led to an expanded demand in the United States for foreign goods and services and strong competition between domestic and foreign companies for their share of the U.S. market. As we enter the next century, whatever theories economists have on how the changing world economy will impact on foreign trade in the United States, foreign companies will no doubt continue to control a sizeable share of the U.S. market. Correspondingly, the need will continue for U.S. lawyers to become more familiar with and better prepared to handle transnational litigation in U.S. courts.

Modern technological changes, especially in the areas of transportation and communication, have also contributed to the need for U.S. lawyers to understand foreign laws and procedures. It is not unusual for a U.S. attorney to engage in legal activities in another country, such as interviewing witnesses, reviewing documents, serving papers, obtaining evidence, etc. When engaged in legal activities in other countries, many U.S. lawyers are often surprised to discover that the extraterritorial application of U.S. laws and procedures is non-existent. In addition, U.S. lawyers are incredulous when confronted with the differences between foreign laws and procedures and the U.S. legal system they have been trained to understand. Those dealing with transnational issues soon learn that U.S. trial practice has no precise counterpart anywhere in the world. The purposes of this book are two-fold: (1) to educate the lawyer in the handling of transnational litigation issues under U.S. law and procedure; and (2) to contribute to the lawyer's understanding of international law and practice from a global perspective.

Both sides to a transnational dispute need to explore fully at the earliest stage how modern concepts of jurisdiction apply to the case and affect their positions. Plaintiff, of course, has the important preliminary task of determining whether jurisdiction can be maintained in a United States forum. Before undergoing needless time and expense, plaintiff should analyze the links which can be classified as "reasonable" in deciding whether the U.S. forum is to be preferred over other possible choices.

From the foreign defendant's perspective, decisions may involve whether to appear in the U.S. proceeding and to challenge jurisdiction or to risk entry of a default judgment. If the latter course is chosen, defendant must consider its chances of defeating the foreign enforcement action on grounds of lack of jurisdiction by the U.S. court.[1]

Although large gaps still exist between the understanding and treatment of domestic law issues versus transnational issues in U.S. courts, recent Supreme Court decisions discuss the needs of the foreign litigant. In *Asahi Metal Indus. Co. v. Superior Court*,[2] the Supreme Court stressed the need to evaluate whether jurisdiction over the foreign resident would be "reasonable."[3] To satisfy a showing of "reasonableness" the interests of the plaintiff's forum state must be more than minimal in order to outweigh any serious burdens imposed by the assertion of jurisdiction on the foreign defendant. The Court emphasized the burdens that would be placed on the foreign litigant by requiring it to travel to California to litigate the dispute and to submit the dispute to a foreign legal system.

In addressing the foreign interests involved, the Court stated:

> The procedural and substantive interests of other nations in a state court's assertion of jurisdiction over an alien defendant will differ from case to case. In every case, however, those interests, as well as the Federal Government's interest in its foreign relations policies, will be best served by a careful inquiry into the reasonableness of the assertion of jurisdiction in the particular case, and an unwillingness to find the serious burdens on an alien defendant outweighed by minimal interest on the part of the plaintiff or the forum State. Great care and reserve should be exercised when extending our notions of personal jurisdiction into the international field.[4]

The Court concluded that, considering the international context and the heavy burden on the alien defendant which outweighed the minimal interest of the plaintiff and the forum state, personal jurisdiction over *Asahi* would be unreasonable and unfair.

Sensitivity to the same concerns expressed by the Supreme Court in *Asahi* may also be found in the Restatement (Third) of Foreign Relations Law (1987). Sections 421 and 403 of the Restatement have

---

1. For a discussion of the various jurisdictional hurdles present under U.S. law, *see infra* Chapters 5 and 6.

2. 480 U.S. 102 (1987).

3. *Id.* at 115. *But see* Hartford Fire Ins. Co. v. California, 509 U.S. 764 (1993) (declining to find rule of reason invoked in absence of "true conflict of law"). *See infra* § 5.07[2] (addressing jurisdictional rule of reason).

4. 480 U.S. at 115 (citation omitted).

adopted a similar principle of "reasonableness" as a basis for a state's exercise of jurisdiction. From an international law standpoint, such factors as the ownership of property within the state, activity which causes injury within the state, or defendant's residence in the state may be classified as "reasonable" in nature. Under the factors set forth in the Restatement, it is important for both domestic and foreign parties to evaluate the type of links which can be established to the forum state and whether they would be classified as "reasonable" or "exorbitant" under modern concepts of jurisdiction.[5]

The Supreme Court further recognized the special discovery problems faced by foreign litigants in U.S. litigation in *Societe Nationale Industrielle Aerospatiale v. United States Dist. Court.*[6] In *Aerospatiale*, the Court considered whether the Hague Evidence Convention supplanted the Federal Rules of Civil Procedure in obtaining discovery abroad from a party over whom the U.S. court had jurisdiction. In rejecting a first use requirement of the Convention before the imposition of U.S. procedural rules, the Court declined to provide guidance to the lower courts on when the Convention should be employed.[7] Nevertheless, the Court was mindful of possible discovery abuse of foreign litigants. In this connection, the Court stated:

> American courts, in supervising pretrial proceedings, should exercise special vigilance to protect foreign litigants from the danger that unnecessary, or unduly burdensome, discovery may place them in a disadvantageous position. Judicial supervision of discovery should always seek to minimize its costs and inconvenience and to prevent improper uses of discovery requests. When it is necessary to seek evidence abroad, however, the District Court must supervise pretrial proceedings particularly closely to prevent discovery abuses . . . . Objections to "abusive" discovery that foreign litigants advance should therefore receive the most careful consideration. . . . American courts should therefore take care to demonstrate due respect for any special problem confronted by the foreign litigant on account of its nationality or the location of its operations, and for any sovereign interest expressed by a foreign state. We do not articulate specific rules to guide this delicate task of adjudication.[8]

---

5. *See infra* § 5.07[2].

6. 482 U.S. 522 (1987).

7. *Id.* at 544. *See infra* § 10.11 (discussing *Aerospatiale*); § 10.10 (addressing Hague Evidence Convention).

8. 482 U.S. at 546.

Special considerations in the case of foreign discovery requests are also recognized in Section 442 of the Restatement (Third) of Foreign Relations Law. Section 442 contemplates that, where foreign interests are involved, U.S. courts should use pretrial conferences, as provided under Rule 16 of the Federal Rules of Civil Procedure, to control discovery practice from the outset of the litigation. The aim of Section 442 of the Restatement is to encourage the court to scrutinize a foreign discovery request more closely than a comparable discovery request for information located in the United States. In the explanatory notes, it is suggested that foreign discovery requests should be limited to information that is directly relevant and material to the action.

Despite repeated criticisms that the Supreme Court in *Aerospatiale* ignored obligations imposed by international comity, there appears to be, at least, a growing awareness that U.S. courts should subject foreign discovery requests to close examination. Counsel for foreign parties should bring unique foreign discovery requests to the attention of the court for appropriate guidance and supervision.

On the other hand, the Supreme Court in *Aerospatiale* emphasized that foreign litigants did not enjoy any double standard or procedural advantage over domestic parties in U.S. courts. The Supreme Court stated that an interpretation of exclusivity of the Hague Evidence Convention would lead to this result. In this connection, the Supreme Court stated:

> The opposite conclusion of exclusivity would create three unacceptable asymmetries. First, within any lawsuit between a national of the United States and a national of another contracting Party, the foreign party could obtain discovery under the Federal Rules of Civil Procedure, while the domestic party would be required to resort first to the procedures of the Hague Convention.
>
> Second, a rule of exclusivity would enable a company which is a citizen of another contracting State to compete with a domestic company on uneven terms, since the foreign company would be subject to less extensive discovery procedures in the event that both companies were sued in an American court. Petitioners made a voluntary decision to market their products in the United States. They are entitled to compete on equal terms with other companies operating in this market. But because the district court unquestionably has personal jurisdiction over petitioners, they are subject to the same legal constraints, including the burdens associated with American judicial procedures, as their American competitors. A general rule according foreign nationals a preferred position in pretrial proceed-

> ings in our courts would conflict with the principle of equal opportunity that governs the market they elected to enter.
>
> Third, since a rule of first use of the Hague Convention would apply to cases in which a foreign party is a national of a contracting State, but not to cases in which a foreign party is a national of any other foreign state, the rule would confer an unwarranted advantage on some domestic litigants over others similarly situated.[9]

Counsel representing foreign parties in U.S. litigation should pay close attention to this dictum and advise their clients that they will be litigating on an equal footing with their domestic counterparts.

When parties need to be served in other countries, counsel involved in transnational disputes should be aware of special procedures pertaining to service of process abroad. In *Volkswagenwerk Aktiengesellschaft v. Schlunk*,[10] the Supreme Court, in reaffirming the mandatory nature of the Hague Service Convention, noted the special sensitivities in this area and the practical considerations involved in insuring that proper service methods are employed. The Hague Service Convention is the first multilateral treaty on service procedures and is intended to establish formalized procedures to reconcile the different service of process practices of civil and common law countries. In *Schlunk*, the Supreme Court held that the Hague Service Convention did not apply when service of process could be made on a foreign corporation in the United States under state service rules and in accordance with due process requirements.[11] The *Schlunk* decision did not disturb the mandatory application of the Convention "when it applies."

Insofar as the *Schlunk* decision may be interpreted as an exception to the mandatory application of the Convention, the scope of the exception seems limited. More importantly, the Supreme Court noted the practical necessity of serving under the Convention, even where the *Schlunk* exception was applicable. In this connection, the Supreme Court cautioned that those choosing to serve outside Convention provisions might later determine that the Convention was the exclusive means of service in the foreign country involved. In addition, those serving under the Convention might find it easier to enforce their

9. *Id.* at 540.

10. 486 U.S. 694 (1988).

11. *Id.* at 707–708. *See infra* § 4.04[5] (discussing exclusivity of Hague Service Convention).

judgments abroad.[12] Foreign sensitivities to the manner in which service is made, as well as evidence obtained, are important elements in the proper handling of transnational disputes. As pointed out in *Schlunk*, the client should be advised of the long term ramifications of proper performance of these acts.

§ 1.02 ATTRACTIVENESS OF THE U.S. FORUM

The U.S. forum provides procedural advantages to any plaintiff over other jurisdictions. Even where the contacts or links to the U.S. forum seem tenuous, many plaintiffs will engage in forum shopping in order to avail themselves of benefits, both procedural and substantive, available in U.S. courts. The jury system makes the U.S. forum attractive in litigating certain types of actions, especially tort suits (such as product liability cases). Juries are viewed as plaintiff-oriented and the availability of a jury trial is virtually non-existent in similar civil cases in civil law countries. In addition, plaintiffs can take advantage of the different choice of law rules in the fifty state jurisdictions and of various standards of liability which may not be available in other countries.

The U.S. forum further provides plaintiffs with the opportunity of presenting a myriad of damage theories in suits, especially in the tort area, which are unrecognized or considered as novel in other jurisdictions. Damage awards rendered by U.S. courts are the highest in the world. In addition, the ability to award punitive damages contributes to the potential for excessive awards in tort cases. This has had a negative effect on U.S. efforts to negotiate bilateral treaties with our trading partners concerning the mutual enforcement of judgments. With the advent of greater unification of Europe, this places the United States at a real disadvantage with our European allies, all of whom are members of multilateral conventions on enforcement.

In 1996 President Clinton issued Executive Order Number 12988,[13] recommending changes to the U.S. civil justice system. The reforms adopted should be of considerable interest to foreign companies and others likely to become ensnared in the U.S. legal system.

The Executive Order establishes reforms which specifically address aspects of litigation in U.S. courts that are often criticized by U.S. trading partners. The Order concentrates on pretrial discovery and

12. *Id.* at 706.

13. Exec. Order No. 12998 [of Feb. 5, 1996], 61 Fed. Reg. 4729 WL 4665 (Pres.)

reforms aimed at encouraging good faith litigation and early settlement of disputes. The reforms do not apply to litigation brought by or against the United States in foreign courts or tribunals. The mandates of the Order are applicable to all federal agencies in the Executive Branch.

The reforms set forth guidelines to promote just and efficient civil litigation involving the Federal Government. This includes a pre-filing notice requirement. Prior to the filing of any lawsuit, litigation counsel must make a reasonable effort to notify all parties about the nature of the dispute and to attempt to achieve a settlement.

Litigation counsel are encouraged to evaluate settlement possibilities and make reasonable efforts to settle the litigation. These efforts include offering to participate in a settlement conference or requesting that the court convene a conference pursuant to Rule 16 of the Federal Rules of Civil Procedure. Litigation counsel are also expected to use alternative methods, i.e., ADR techniques or processes of resolving the dispute in litigation, before proceeding to trial.

The Executive Order also covers reforms in the discovery process. Litigation counsel are encouraged to make every reasonable effort to streamline and expedite discovery. Each agency is mandated to establish a coordinated procedure for the conduct and review of document discovery undertaken in litigation directly by that agency. This procedure includes a review by a senior lawyer prior to service or filing of the request in litigation to determine that the request is not unreasonable or burdensome while taking into account the amount in controversy and the importance of the issues at stake in the litigation.

The Order further seeks to encourage the resolution of discovery disputes. Before filing a discovery motion or seeking sanctions for discovery abuses, litigation counsel are required to attempt to resolve the dispute with opposing counsel. If a discovery motion is filed, litigation counsel should state in the motion that any attempt at resolution was unsuccessful or impracticable under the circumstances.

The Order establishes a procedure whereby sanctions are sought against opposing counsel for abusive practices. Prior to filing a motion for sanctions, litigation counsel are required to submit the motion for review to the sanctions officer within the litigation counsel's agency. The litigation officer is also responsible for reviewing motions for sanctions that are filed against the litigation counsel or the agency involved.

The Order also establishes guidelines for expediting civil litigation under the litigation counsel's supervision and control. These include making reasonable efforts to stipulate to facts that are not in dispute, narrowing pleadings and other filings to reflect the results of discovery, requesting early trial dates where practicable, and encouraging the filing of motions for summary judgment where the movant is likely to prevail or where the motion is likely to narrow the issues to be tried.

The concept of punitive damages is not recognized in civil law systems. The reluctance of U.S. courts to limit punitive damage awards has become an issue in international trade discussions among the U.S. and its major trading partners. For example, the German law of torts does not provide for punitive damages even where gross negligence or intentional torts are involved.[14] This poses difficulties for U.S. plaintiffs seeking recognition and enforcement of a judgment of a U.S. court in Germany which includes an award of punitive damages. In a recent decision, the German Supreme Court refused to recognize the portion of a judgment of a California court on the punitive damage count.[15] The German court ruled that such damage awards were not enforceable in Germany because they violated German *ordre public*. The judgment of the California court was recognized only to the extent of the amount representing compensatory damages.

In *BMW of North America, Inc. v. Gore*,[16] the Supreme Court ruled that a punitive damage award was ''grossly excessive'' and thus violative of the Due Process Clause of the Fourteenth Amendment. The Court stated that the assessment of punitive damages must be related to the State's interests in punishing unlawful conduct.[17] In order to insure that a party received notice that the conduct at issue was unlawful and punishable by punitive damages under established notions of fairness, the Court established the following three guideposts: (1) the degree of reprehensibility of the defendant's conduct; (2) the ratio between the plaintiff's compensatory damages and the amount of the punitive damages; and (3) the difference between the punitive damages award and the civil or criminal sanctions that could be imposed for comparable misconduct.[18]

The *BMW v. Gore* decision will undoubtedly serve to limit punitive damage awards in future cases. As a consequence, application of the

14. Andre R. Fiebig, *The Recognition and Enforcement of Punitive Damage Awards in Germany: Recent Developments*, 22 Ga. J. Int'l & Comp. L. 635 (1992).

15. Judgment of June 4, 1992, BGH 46 Westpapier-Mitteihunger 1451, 1461 (1992).

16. 517 U.S. 559 (1996).

17. *Id.* at 568.

18. *Id.* at 574–575.

''excessiveness'' guidelines articulated by the Supreme Court will be of obvious interest to foreign companies trading in the United States.

As an additional safeguard in this area, the Supreme Court recently held, in *Cooper Industries, Inc. v. Leatherman Tool Group, Inc.,*[18.1] that courts of appeals should apply a *de novo* standard of appellate review to a district court's resolution of issues of the constitutionality of punitive damages. The Court determined that ''abuse of discretion'' was the wrong standard to apply to such situations.

In reaffirming its earlier ruling in the *BMW* case, the Supreme Court held, in *State Farm Mutual Automobile Insurance Co. v. Campbell,*[18.2] that punitive damage awards must be reasonable and proportionate to the harm and general damages suffered by plaintiff. While not imposing a ''bright line'' ratio, the Court suggested that punitive damage awards that exceeded compensatory damages in the same case by more than a single-digit ratio might not satisfy Constitutional due process requirements.

§ 1.03 FORUM NON CONVENIENS

The doctrine of forum non conveniens presents significant obstacles to plaintiffs with only a minimal interest in litigating in the United States.[19] The two principal Supreme Court cases which have refined this doctrine are *Gulf Oil Corp. v. Gilbert,*[20] and *Piper Aircraft Co. v. Reyno.*[21] These cases vest the trial court with considerable discretion in determining whether to exercise jurisdiction in a given case or dismiss the case when the U.S. forum is inconvenient. In *Gilbert*, the Court established a balancing test consisting of private and public interest factors which should be considered in determining whether to grant the motion to dismiss on forum non conveniens grounds. The private interest factors include the following: relative ease of access to sources of proof; availability of compulsory process for attendance of unwilling witnesses; the cost of obtaining the attendance of willing witnesses at the trial; and other trial-related factors. The public interest factors include the following: administrative problems such as congested court dockets; whether there is a local interest in the controversy; and the governing

18.1. 121 S. Ct. 1678 (2001).
18.2. 123 S. Ct. 1513 (2003).
19. *See infra* § 5.06 (discussing forum non conveniens).
20. 330 U.S. 501 (1947).
21. 454 U.S. 235 (1981).

law in the case. Under *Gilbert*, the presumption in balancing these factors is in plaintiff's favor. In this connection, the Court stated "unless the balance is strongly in favor of the defendant, the plaintiff's choice of forum should rarely be disturbed."[22]

With several modifications, the Supreme Court's decision in *Piper Aircraft Co. v. Reyno* basically left the *Gilbert* balancing test intact. The Court reaffirmed the trial court's broad discretion in this area and stated that, in the absence of an abuse of discretion, there was no basis for reversal. The Court cautioned that there must be some minimally adequate remedy to the plaintiff. However, the trial court could not consider whether the plaintiff would be subject to less favorable law on liability or damages. The Court in *Gilbert* recognized that if it could not dismiss on forum non conveniens grounds, where dismissal might lead to an unfavorable change in law, the U.S. courts would become even more attractive to foreign litigants. The Court summarized the attractiveness of the U.S. forum in tort cases as follows:

> First, all but 6 of the 50 American states . . . offer strict liability. . . . [S]trict liability remains primarily an American innovation. Second, the tort plaintiff may choose, at least potentially, from among 50 jurisdictions if he decides to file suit in the United States. Each of these jurisdictions applies its own set of malleable choice-of-law rules. Third, jury trials are almost always available in the United States, while they are never provided in civil law jurisdictions. . . . Even in the United Kingdom, most civil actions are not tried before a jury. . . . Fourth, unlike most foreign jurisdictions, American courts allow contingent attorney's fees, and do not tax losing parties with their opponents' attorney's fees. . . . Fifth, discovery is more extensive in American than in foreign courts.[23]

Subsequent to *Gilbert*, some courts have commented that due to modern technological advances, no forum is "as inconvenient as it was in 1947."[24] Courts have noted that these changes should be factored into the balancing of public and private interests set forth in *Gilbert* and *Piper Aircraft*. As stated in *Calavo Growers of California v. Generali Belgium*:

> [T]he assessment of whether the balance of public and private interests strongly overcomes the plaintiff's choice of forum must be made in

22. 330 U.S. at 508.
23. 454 U.S. at 252 n.18.
24. Fitzgerald v. Texaco, Inc., 521 F.2d 448, 457 (2d Cir. 1975) (Oakes, J., dissenting).

> light of the realities of modern transportation and communications. A forum is not necessarily inconvenient because of its distances from pertinent parties or places if it is readily accessible in a few hours of air travel. It will often be quicker and less expensive to transfer a witness or a document than to transfer a lawsuit. Jet travel and satellite communications have significantly altered the meaning of "non conveniens."[25]

In this connection, where the major factor of inconvenience of the U.S. forum is the location of a witness, the court, in its discretion, may require plaintiff to transport witnesses to the United States at its own expense or pay counsel fees for the taking of their depositions abroad.[26]

A contemporary approach to forum non conveniens may be found in the litigation arising out of the disaster in Bhopal, India.[27] The district court opinion examined in detail the private and public interest factors analyzed by the Supreme Court in *Piper* and *Gilbert* and found India's interest in the litigation far greater than that of the U.S. forum. The most interesting part of the opinion was the court's discussion of the adequacy and ability of the Indian courts to conduct the Bhopal litigation. As the district court stated:

> The Court thus finds itself faced with a paradox. In the Court's view, to retain the litigation in this forum, as plaintiffs request, would be yet another example of imperialism, another situation in which an established sovereign inflicted its rules, its standards and values on a developing nation. This Court declines to play such a role. The Union of India is a world power in 1986, and its courts have the proven capacity to mete out fair and equal justice. To deprive the Indian judiciary of this opportunity to stand tall before the world and to pass judgment on behalf of its own people would be to revive a history of subservience and subjugation from which India has emerged. India and its people can and must vindicate their claims before the independent and legitimate judiciary created there since the Independence of 1947.[28]

In dismissing the case on the grounds of forum non conveniens, the court imposed unique conditions on Union Carbide: (1) consent to the jurisdiction of the courts of India and waiver of defenses based upon

---

25. 632 F.2d 963, 969 (2d Cir. 1980) (Newman, J., concurring).

26. *See* Manu Int'l, S.A. v. Avon Prods., Inc., 641 F.2d 62, 64 (2d Cir. 1981).

27. *See In re* Union Carbide Corp. Gas Plant Disaster, 634 F. Supp. 842 (S.D.N.Y. 1986), *aff'd*, 809 F.2d 195 (2d Cir.), *cert. denied*, 484 U.S. 871 (1987).

28. 634 F. Supp. at 867.

the statute of limitations; (2) agreement to satisfy any judgment rendered against it by an Indian court; and (3) discovery under the model of the Federal Rules of Civil Procedure after appropriate demand by plaintiffs. The court of appeals held that dismissal on forum non conveniens grounds was proper. While the court of appeals ruled that defendant was properly required to agree to submit to the jurisdiction of the Indian courts and to waive statute of limitations defenses, it was error to require defendant to agree to enforcement of the Indian judgment and to abide by the discovery provisions of the Federal Rules of Civil Procedure.[29]

The court of appeals further determined that the district court had proceeded on the erroneous assumption that the plaintiff might not be able to enforce an Indian judgment against Union Carbide in the United States. However, the court of appeals determined that, under New York Law, a foreign-country money judgment would be recognized and enforceable.[30] In addition, the court of appeals removed the discovery condition, so as to permit reciprocal discovery of both parties under the applicable discovery rules of India.[31]

§ 1.04 PRO-FORUM BIAS OF U.S. COURTS

To properly handle transnational litigation issues, lawyers need to be aware of the ability of U.S. courts to act in this area. In other words, are foreign law issues and considerations easily understood and quickly grasped by U.S. judges; do U.S. judges fairly treat the interests of foreign nations and foreign legal systems? The view has been expressed that U.S. judges are inexperienced in the international area and insensitive to the outcome of legal disputes which may be offensive to foreign nations and incompatible with foreign legal systems. Such judicial inexperience increases the difficulties of the lawyer representing a foreign client in U.S. litigation. In addition to gaining a proper understanding of the transnational issues involved in a dispute, the lawyer has the added responsibility of educating the judge so that the issue is evaluated in the proper context.

United States judges have noted the pro-forum bias of U.S. courts when faced with the balancing of interests of foreign nations with domestic ones. In *Societe Nationale Industrielle Aerospatiale v. United*

---

29. *In re* Union Carbide Gas Plant Disaster, 809 F.2d 195, 205 (2d Cir.), *cert. denied*, 484 U.S. 871 (1987).

30. 809 F.2d at 204.

31. *Id.* at 205.

States Dist. Court, Justice Blackmun, in his dissenting opinion, commented on the pro-forum bias of U.S. courts as follows:

> [C]ourts are generally ill-equipped to assume the role of balancing the interests of foreign nations with that of our own. Although transnational litigation is increasing, relatively few judges are experienced in the area and the procedures of foreign legal systems are often poorly understood. . . . As this Court recently stated, it has "little competence in determining precisely when foreign nations will be offended by particular acts."[32] A pro-forum bias is likely to creep into the supposedly neutral balancing process and courts not surprisingly often will turn to the more familiar procedures established by their local rules.[33]

In *Aerospatiale*, the Court was unwilling to articulate a particularized comity test to guide lower courts in assessing when it should apply the Hague Evidence Convention in place of the federal discovery rules. Nevertheless, the Court emphasized that U.S. courts, in supervising pretrial proceedings, should exercise special vigilance, to protect foreign litigants from burdensome discovery. Lower courts were also encouraged to consider comity demands imposed by special interests of the foreign state involved. Despite these encouragements, lower courts have almost uniformly found the Court's comity analysis unhelpful and have not required first use of the Convention to obtain discovery from a litigant.[34]

Furthermore, in the post-*Aerospatiale* context, commentators have noted the absence of any detailed comity approach in lower court rulings which identified and balanced the foreign and U.S. interests involved. This apparent presumption by lower courts that the Convention should be ignored has led to criticisms that district courts lack the ability to properly undertake a comity-based test and are guilty of a pro-forum bias.[35] As the court of appeals stated in *Laker Airways, Ltd. v. Sabena Belgian World Airlines*,[36] "[D]omestic courts do not sit as internationally constituted tribunals. . . . The courts of most developed countries follow international law only to the extent it is not overridden by national law. Those courts inherently find it difficult to neutrally balance

32. Container Corp. v. Franchise Tax Bd., 463 U.S. 75, 194 (1983).

33. 482 U.S. at 553.

34. Gary B. Born & Scott Hoing, *Comity and the Lower Courts: Post Aerospatiale Applications of the Hague Evidence Convention*, 24 Int'l Law. 393 (1990).

35. *Id.* at 403.

36. 731 F.2d 909, 951 (D.C. Cir. 1984).

competing foreign interests. When there is a doubt, national interests will tend to be favored over foreign interests.''[37]

Section 442(1)(c) of the Restatement (Third) of Foreign Relations Law provides another example of a balancing test of U.S. and foreign interests. This provision suggests that the trial court consider the use of a comity test in deciding whether to issue a foreign discovery order. In framing such an order, the court should use the following factors:

(1) the importance to the . . . litigation of the documents or other information requested;

(2) the degree of specificity of the request;

(3) whether the information originated in the United States;

(4) the availability of alternative means of securing the information; and

(5) the extent to which noncompliance with the request would undermine important interests of the United States, or compliance with the request would undermine important interests of the state where the information is located.

Section 442(1)(c) incorporates the principle of reasonableness in balancing both foreign and domestic interests. While there has been notable hostility to United States discovery practices, U.S. courts have shown a reluctance to impose less stringent discovery obligations on foreign companies doing business in the United States.[38] The Restatement supports the Supreme Court's approach in rejecting the imposition of a double standard with respect to persons who do business in the United States or otherwise subject themselves to U.S. jurisdiction.[39] According to the Restatement, such persons should be subject to the burdens as well as the benefits of U.S. law, including the laws on discovery. The only accommodation proposed by the Restatement is that the principle of reasonableness should be applied to foreign discovery requests.[40] Furthermore, the Restatement suggests closer supervision of foreign discovery by U.S. courts in order to further the comity

37. *Id. See, e.g.*, Hartford Fire Ins. Co. v. California, 509 U.S. 764 (1993) (imposing U.S. antitrust laws on British reinsurance market).

38. *See* Societé Nationale Industrielle Aerospatiale v. United States Dist. Court, 482 U.S. at 540 n.25.

39. RESTATEMENT (THIRD) FOREIGN RELATIONS LAW § 442 (1987), reporter's note 1.

40. *Id.*

considerations set forth in Section 442(1)(c) and in order to facilitate compliance with the Hague Evidence Convention.

Because of the international controversy surrounding U.S. discovery abroad, many foreign states have enacted blocking statutes or bank and business secrecy laws in an effort to restrict U.S. efforts to obtain the production of documents located outside of the United States.[41] Such statutes generally prohibit the disclosure or removal of documents from the territory of the state where they are located unless authorized by the foreign authorities involved. In *Aerospatiale*, the Supreme Court summarily rejected extraterritorial application of such statutes in U.S. litigation where such statutes were designed to frustrate compliance with U.S. discovery orders. According to the Supreme Court:

> It is well-settled that such statutes do not deprive an American court of the power to order a party subject to its jurisdiction to produce evidence even though the act of production may violate that statute. Nor can the enactment of such a statute by a foreign nation require American courts to engraft a rule of first resort onto the Hague Convention, or otherwise to provide the nationals of such a country with a preferred status in our courts. It is clear that American courts are not required to adhere blindly to the directives of such a statute. Indeed, the language of the statute, if taken literally, would appear to represent an extraordinary exercise of legislative jurisdiction by the Republic of France over a United States District Judge, forbidding him or her from ordering any discovery from a party of French nationality, even simple requests for admissions or interrogatories that the party could respond to on the basis of personal knowledge.[42]

The Supreme Court stated that the relevance of blocking statutes in a particularized comity analysis would depend on "the extent that its terms and its enforcement identify the nature of the sovereign interests in nondisclosure of specific kinds of material."[43]

The balancing of domestic and foreign interests has factored into many U.S. decisions where foreign nondisclosure laws have been raised as a defense to compliance with U.S. discovery orders or the imposition of sanctions for noncompliance with such orders. In general, U.S. courts have tended to favor U.S. domestic considerations, especially where

41. *See infra* § 10.25 (discussing secrecy and blocking statutes).
42. 482 U.S. at 544 n.29 (citation omitted).
43. *Id.*

strong U.S. governmental interests in securing the information have been demonstrated.[44]

In particular, U.S. courts have upheld the interests of the U.S. forum in connection with grand jury subpoenas for bank records concerning investigations into drug-related crimes.[45] On the other hand, where U.S. governmental interests have not been of paramount importance, various U.S. courts have deferred to foreign states' interests in protection of their nondisclosure and banking secrecy laws.[46]

§ 1.05 PRE-LITIGATION CONSIDERATIONS

The first important task in handling an international litigation case is to organize the relevant material. In the typical situation, both domestic and foreign law material will be involved. Before starting the legal research involved, a preliminary check list of resources may save time. Various governmental agencies may have relevant material. If the case will involve serving papers or obtaining evidence overseas, the State Department's Bureau of Consular Affairs may be able to advise attorneys concerning the correct procedures to be used in the particular country involved.[47] That office also has information on the proper authentication of foreign legal documents, as well as hints for hiring overseas lawyers. The Bureau has a list of foreign attorneys broken down country-by-country and in the larger countries, city-by-city. Foreign law firms are also listed in the *Martindale-Hubbell International Law Digest*.[48] The Justice Department's Office of International Judicial Assistance, which is housed in the Civil Division, can also advise on the

---

44. *See, e.g.*, Richmark Corp. v. Timber Falling Consultants, 959 F.2d 1468 (9th Cir. 1992), *cert. dismissed*, 113 S. Ct. 454 (1993); United States v. Vetco, Inc., 691 F.2d 1281 (9th Cir. 1981), *cert. denied*, 454 U.S. 1098 (1981); United States v. Field, 532 F.2d 404 (5th Cir. 1976), *cert. denied*, 429 U.S. 940 (1976); United States v. First Nat'l City Bank, 396 F.2d 897 (2d Cir. 1968).

45. *See, e.g.*, United States v. Bank of Nova Scotia II, 740 F.2d 817 (11th Cir. 1984), *cert. denied*, 469 U.S. 1106 (1985); United States v. Bank of Nova Scotia I, 691 F.2d 1384 (11th Cir. 1982), *cert. denied*, 462 U.S. 1119 (1983).

46. *See, e.g.*, Cochran Consulting, Inc. v. Uwatec USA, Inc., 102 F.3d 1224 (Fed. Cir. 1996); Volkswagen A.G. v. Valdez, 909 S.W.2d 900 (Sup. Ct. Tex. 1995); Reinsurance Co. of Am., Inc. v. Administratia Asigurarilor de Stat, 902 F.2d 1275 (7th Cir. 1990); *In re* Sealed Cases, 825 F.2d 494 (D.C. Cir.), *cert. denied*, 484 U.S. 963 (1987); United States v. First Nat'l Bank of Chicago, 699 F.2d 341 (7th Cir. 1983); Ings v. Ferguson, 282 F.2d 149 (2d Cir. 1960).

47. Bureau of Consular Affairs, U.S. Department of State, Washington, D.C. 20520; telephone: (202) 647–5226. *See* Appendix 21, *infra*.

48. Sources of information on foreign lawyers and considerations in hiring and working with a foreign lawyer are discussed *infra* §§ 2.10–2.13.

proper procedures for service and evidence. This office is the U.S. Central Authority for the Hague Service Convention, Hague Evidence Convention, and the Inter-American Convention on Letters Rogatory.

To be informed on current developments in the international law issues involved in a case, the lawyer may wish to consult international legal periodicals published in the United States.[49] Two of the most informative and useful periodicals are *The International Lawyer* and *The American Journal of International Law*.[50] *The International Lawyer* concentrates mostly on articles dealing with private or business law topics. *The American Journal of International Law*, which is published by the American Society of International Law, concentrates mainly on public international law topics. Articles in these periodicals may be found in the *Index to Legal Periodicals* and the *Index to Foreign Legal Periodicals*. There are also a growing number of international law journals published by such law schools as Harvard, Cornell, the University of Virginia, George Washington University Law School, and the Washington College of Law (the American University).

Another useful resource and research tool is the Restatement (Third) of the Law of Foreign Relations. While it is not intended to be an official document of the United States, it provides a summary of the foreign relations law of the United States and the practice of international law under relevant U.S. domestic law. The rules of the Restatement are often relied on in U.S. court decisions as the standard to be applied in resolving international law disputes.[51]

If the interpretation of a treaty is involved in the law suit, its history in the ratification process before the United States Senate as well as the pre-ratification history must be thoroughly studied. *International Legal Materials*, which is published by the American Society of International Law, publishes treaties and other international documents before they appear in the official treaty series. *United States Treaties and Other International Agreements Series* is now the official publication of treaties and agreements to which the United States is a party. The full text of the treaty is included, as well as a translation in its official language. In some cases, it is important to study the official language of the treaty since the meaning of certain words or provisions may differ

49. The Internet allows cost-effective access to an ever-increasing body of international legal materials, as discussed *infra* §§ 2.02.

50. These and the following legal materials are also considered *infra* §§ 2.02.

51. For several caveats on the use of the Restatement as authority in determining international law, *see* United States v. Yousef, 2003 WL 1786882, ** 17, 18 (2d Cir. (N.Y.)).

from the English version. In any judicial interpretation of the treaty, courts are bound to apply the meaning as defined in the official language version. The most comprehensive treaty collection series is in *Treaties and Other International Agreements of the United States of America, 1776–1949 (Bevins)*. In order to locate a particular treaty, the lawyer should consult the publication entitled, *Treaties in Force: A List of Treaties and Other International Agreements of the United States*, which is published by the Government Printing Office. This is a useful reference guide since it lists all treaties and international agreements to which the United States is a party which are currently in force. This volume cites to the texts of treaties in the official treaty series.

If foreign law is involved, it may be helpful to employ the services of a foreign lawyer or foreign law expert.[52] The following considerations may be pertinent to that decision:

(1) Is the foreign law understandable? Would the foreign lawyer be helpful in explaining it and in obtaining the necessary translations?

(2) Where is the foreign law located? Can it be obtained in the United States? Can the foreign lawyer assist in obtaining the necessary material?

(3) Who has custody and control of the foreign material? Will the production of documents be an issue in the litigation? Are defenses available to the production of documents located in foreign countries? In other words, it may be necessary to analyze the legal relationship between the U.S. party and the party which has custody of the documents (e.g., parent/subsidiary). In addition, are there foreign laws (blocking and secrecy laws, etc.) which prevent disclosure? If foreign documents form an important part of the case, the services of a foreign lawyer may be indispensable.

(4) Would the services of a foreign lawyer be helpful in gaining a better preliminary assessment of the case? The U.S. parties may want certain issues addressed at an early stage, such as the procedures for obtaining service of process and evidence in the foreign country involved, and the substantive law of the foreign country, if choice of law considerations will be involved in the

52. *See infra* §§ 2.09–2.13 (discussing employing foreign attorneys).

> determination of the issues. Furthermore, it may be of considerable importance for both parties to be informed of the likelihood of enforceability of the U.S. judgment in another country. In addition, if related foreign legal proceedings are involved, it will be important to know their status as well as their effect on the U.S. litigation.

Another important consideration in deciding whether to employ the services of a foreign lawyer or expert, is whether foreign law has to be proven in the U.S. case, and if so, how.[53] Any party intending to rely on foreign law should be familiar with the provisions of Rule 44.1 of the Federal Rules of Civil Procedure. Rule 44.1 requires a party to give notice of the foreign law materials as soon as possible in order to avoid ''unfair surprise.'' The pleader is thus obligated to specify the issues governed by the foreign law and to identify the applicable legal system involved. The court ''may consider any relevant material or source'' of foreign law under Rule 44.1. This may include extracts from foreign written sources such as affidavits, briefs, and opinion letters of foreign counsel. A common method of proving foreign law is by deposition or oral testimony of an acknowledged expert of the law of the foreign country. However, affidavits and other written statements concerning foreign law are more common methods of proof than oral testimony.

The themes introduced in this introductory chapter are explored in greater detail throughout this book. These themes—the complexity of transnational litigation, limitations of litigation in resolving international disputes, the attractiveness of the U.S. forum, and others—are signals to counsel that involvement in transnational litigation presents new challenges not frequently encountered in purely domestic litigation. Reliance on the traditional characteristics of counsel; tenacity, resourcefulness, and the tireless pursuit of the client's interests, while armed with a knowledge of the special considerations implicated by transnational litigation, will best serve you and your client. The purpose of this work is to contribute to these ends.

53. *See infra* Chapter 9, ''Proving Foreign Law and Determining What Law Applies.''

Chapter 2

RESEARCHING THE INTERNATIONAL CASE AND OTHER RESPONSIBILITIES OF THE INTERNATIONAL LAWYER

§ 2.01 INTRODUCTION

This chapter describes the problems faced by a lawyer who undertakes to handle an "international case" or a case that has issues involving the law or parties of more than one country. The research tools involved in exploring the international law issues in the case may be unfamiliar to the U.S. lawyer. This chapter sets forth the basic source materials which generally will be used in handling international assignments.

The first query faced by the U.S. attorney is whether the attorney is competent to undertake the international aspects of the matter. When foreign law issues are present, is the responsibility owed to the client any different from a purely domestic case? If so, should the U.S. lawyer turn the case over to a specialist or seek advice from a foreign lawyer who is familiar with the laws of the other country involved in the assignment? Finally, the U.S. lawyer needs to know where to look for assistance in hiring a lawyer abroad who is qualified to handle the job and to be aware of the pitfalls involved in dealing with a foreign lawyer.

§ 2.02 RESEARCHING THE INTERNATIONAL CASE

For a U.S. lawyer, researching issues pertaining to international law in general can be a difficult and frustrating exercise. This subject is only lightly touched on in most American law schools and, compared to domestic law materials, international materials are unorganized and difficult to find. Lawyers should reestablish themselves with international legal research concepts and systems of documentation before embarking on the research assignment.[1]

While it remains true that certain international legal materials may be difficult to find, the Internet is providing a cost-effective and ever-expanding means of accessing foreign law. The law libraries of many law schools are now online and provide both information about their own foreign legal resources and links to Web sites containing international legal resources.[2] Numerous other Web sites contain or may assist

1. Three good sources for this study are: L. O'Connor, *International and Foreign Legal Research: Tips, Tricks, and Sources*, 28 CORNELL INT'L L.J. 417 (1995); *Guide to International Legal Research*, GEO. WASH. J. INT'L L. & ECON. (vol. 20, nos. 1 & 2) (1986); and COHEN, HOW TO FIND THE LAW 412–45 (1976).

2. Cornell (http://www.law.cornell.edu/) and Emory (http://www.law.emory.edu/) Universities are examples.

in locating foreign legal materials.[3] Like printed legal materials, electronic legal materials must be relied on with caution. Two litmus tests are: (1) the credibility of the organization maintaining the Web site; and (2) the frequency with which the site is updated.

Law libraries of major law schools and collections housed in libraries located in large, metropolitan areas are an obvious source of international legal materials. One of the largest collections of international legal materials is housed in the International Law Library of the Library of Congress in Washington, D.C. International law sections of local, state, and national bar associations should be contacted for information as to the location of nearby source material. Insuring that the research is current can be a problem. Some of the best current material can be obtained at seminars and lectures sponsored by bar associations and international law societies. In this connection, contact should be made with such organizations as the American Bar Association's Section of International Law, the American Society of International Law and Practice, the Inter-American Bar Association, and the Practicing Law Institute for a list of their publications.[4]

An additional source for international legal research is the *Martindake-Hubbell Law Directory*. The Directory contains the text of selected international treaties and also law digest for many foreign nations.[5] The Directory is available in the offices of many law firms.

Periodicals are a good way to keep abreast of international law developments. General services such as the *Index to Legal Periodicals* and the *Index to Foreign Legal Periodicals* are useful in gaining access to articles. Two of the leading international legal periodicals are *The International Lawyer* and *The American Journal of International Law*. *The International Lawyer*, which is published by the International Law and Practice Section of the American Bar Association, contains articles,

---

3. *See, e.g.*, U.S. House of Representatives Internet Law Library Treaties and International Law (http://law.house.gov/52.htm); U.S. Department of State Private International Law Database (http://www.his.com/~pildb/); State Dep't Office of Legal Adviser (*www.state.gov/www/global/legal_affairs/legal_advisor.htm*); Hieros Gamos, containing information, forums, and links to other sites regarding international law (http://www.hg.org); Europa, providing information on the laws and institutions of the European Union (http://europa.eu.int/index.htm); Findlaw, devoted entirely to legal research and containing "LawCrawler" search engine (http://www.findlaw.com/); and YAHOO!, containing search engine and links to law Web sites (http://www.yahoo.com/).

4. *See Guide to International Legal Research, supra* note 1, at 24–29.

5. MARTINDALE–HUBBELL INTERNATIONAL LAW DIRECTORY, ARGENTINA–VIETNAM LAW DIGESTS; SELECTED INTERNATIONAL CONVENTIONS (1997).

notes, and comments dealing primarily with private or business law topics. *The American Journal of International Law* is published by the American Society of International Law, headquartered in Washington, D.C., and covers mostly public international law topics and other scholarly matters. *International Legal Materials* is published six times a year by the American Society of International Law. It publishes the texts of treaties and other international documents before they appear in other collections. Student-edited journals that specialize in international law topics are also worth noting. These include the *Columbia Journal of Transnational Law*, the *Cornell International Law Journal*, the *Harvard International Law Journal*, the *Journal of International Law and Economics* (George Washington University), the *Virginia Journal of International Law*, and the *American University International Law Review* (formerly *Journal of International Law and Policy*).[6]

§ 2.03 SOURCES OF INTERNATIONAL LAW

Sources of international law include international conventions, international custom, general principles of law recognized by civilized nations, judicial decisions and scholarly writings.[7] These sources must be considered in researching any international law issue. In beginning any research assignment in international law, it is useful to look for a general treatment of the subject under study. For some time, the Department of State has been issuing the *Digest of International Law*, a series, which discusses international law topics, foreign policy and the law of diplomacy, and treaty matters. In this series, the Whiteman Digest covers the years 1963–1973. This series has been supplemented by a new series, *Digest of United States Practice in International Law*, which has been published by the Department of State since 1973.

The Restatement (Third) of the Law of Foreign Relations is a valuable resource tool for practically any international law issue. The Restatement is published in two volumes by the American Law Institute and is a summary of United States practice in international law. Rather than a digest of international law, the Restatement is intended to be a

6. *See* COHEN, *supra* note 1, at 431.

7. STATUTE OF THE INTERNATIONAL COURT OF JUSTICE, Art. 38(1) (setting forth above-described list and generally regarded as most authoritative listing of sources of international law); RESTATEMENT (THIRD) OF FOREIGN RELATIONS LAW, § 102 (commenting on sources of international law); *See* COHEN, *supra* note 1, at 413–414. The use of foreign court decisions as a source of law should also be considered. *See* Lawrence v. Texas, 71 U.S.L.W. 4574 (U.S. June 26, 2003).

statement of the foreign relations law of the United States. It is not meant to be an official document of the United States. As defined in the Restatement, the foreign relations law of the United States consists of international law as applied in the United States under relevant domestic law. The domestic component in the Restatement is derived from federal law as defined in the Constitution, statutes and case law. The international law component in the Restatement emanates from customary international law and international agreements to which the United States is a party. The Restatement contains a comprehensive treatment of the relevant source material from which the law is derived. In the United States, this may include legislative and executive action, including international agreements, as well as judicial decisions in the United States and decisions of other national and international tribunals. The rules of the Restatement are often cited in American judicial decisions and relied on in many cases as the established norm or practice.[8] However, over-reliance should not be placed on the Restatement as an official source of international law doctrine. In the Supreme Court decision of *United States v. Stuart*,[9] Justice Scalia noted in his concurring opinion that the Restatement provision relied on in the Court's interpretation of the treaty at issue in the case ''must be regarded as a proposal for change rather than a restatement of existing doctrine.''[10]

Similarly, in *United States v. Yousef*,[10.1] the Court of Appeals described the use of the Restatement as authority in determining international law as follows:

> The Restatement (Third) a kind of treatise or commentary, is not a *primary* source of authority upon which, standing alone, courts may rely for propositions of customary international law. Such works at most provide evidence of the practice of States, and then only insofar as they rest on factual and accurate descriptions of the past practices of states, not on projections of future trends or the advocacy of the ''better rule.''

8. *See, e.g.*, Banco Nacional de Cuba v. Sabbatino, 376 U.S. 398, 430 (1964).
9. 489 U.S. 353 (1988).
10. *Id.* at 375.
10.1. 2003 WL 1786882, **17, 18 (2d Cir. (N.Y.)).

The Court of Appeals held that the Restatement can not be relied on as a primary source of law where it advocates expanding the law beyond the scope presently recognized by the community of states.[10.2]

§ 2.04 RESEARCHING THE TREATY

Treaty interpretation is prominently involved in international cases. Lawyers often encounter research difficulties in this area.

If a treaty provision is involved, it is necessary to research its history in the ratification process before the United States Senate as well as the preparatory work before the treaty was signed.[11] After tracing the treaty history, judicial application and interpretation of the treaty should be researched. Secondary sources, such as scholarly writings, may be used in support of a particular interpretation of the treaty.[12] In researching the treaty's ratification history, pertinent Senate documents including committee reports and debates should be studied. Some of the committee reports are summarized or reprinted in full in the *U.S. Code Congressional and Administrative News*. Senate debates of the treaty can be found in the *Congressional Record*. Preparatory work which took place during the actual negotiations of the treaty provisions should also be studied. This may include the official proceedings of the conference or the international organization which formulated the treaty. It should be determined whether the official documents of the conference have been published in book form. In the United States, it is also important to look at ratification materials prepared by the State Department and relevant government agencies and the transmittal documents forwarded by the President to the Senate.

The United States has an extensive treaty document system. The office of the Assistant Legal Adviser for Treaty Affairs, United States Department of State, is responsible for collecting the treaties to which the United States is a party. That office should be contacted if one is unable to locate a treaty or is uncertain as to the present status of the treaty. One of the most useful treaty publications is *Treaties in Force: A List of Treaties and Other International Agreements of the United States*,[12.1] which is published by the Government Printing Office. This publication, which is prepared annually by the Department of State, lists

10.2. *Id.* 17, 18.

11. *See* COHEN, *supra* note 1, at 418–25.

12. *See id.*, at 414.

12.1. Also available at http://www.state.gov/www/global/legal_affairs/t:findex.html.

all treaties and international agreements to which the United States is a party and which are in force at the beginning of each year. This volume cites to the texts of the treaties in major treaty collections, and lists bilateral agreements, which are arranged by country and subject, and multilateral agreements, which are arranged by subject.

United States treaties and international agreements were published by Congress in *Statutes At Large* until the 1950–51 Congressional session. *United States Treaties and Other International Agreements* is now the official publication of treaties and agreements to which the United States is a party. This series, cited as U.S.T. and Stat., are admissible evidence in all federal and state court cases. The full text of each treaty is included as well as a translation in its official language. The series also includes relevant documents for each treaty, such as preparatory documents from conferences. The treaties are arranged in chronological order in each volume and there is an index by subject matter and country. The most comprehensive treaty collection is in *Treaties and Other International Agreements of the United States of America, 1776–1949 (Bevins)*. This series is a compilation of all treaties and international agreements entered into by the United States from 1776 to 1949, including those which are not presently in force.[12.2]

§ 2.05 JUDICIAL INTERPRETATION OF TREATIES

The Supreme Court's decision in *United States v. Stuart*,[13] provides an interesting example of judicial interpretation of treaties and certain pitfalls in researching in this area. The case involved the interpretation of the Convention Respecting Double Taxation Between the United States and Canada,[14] which obligates the United States, when requested and consistent with United States revenue laws, to obtain information for Canadian authorities to assist in determining the income tax liability of a Canadian taxpayer. The issue involved was whether the U.S. Internal Revenue Service could issue an administrative summons pursuant to a request by Canadian authorities only if it first determined that the Canadian tax investigation had not reached the equivalent stage of a

12.2. *See* Comparative Chart on Selected Private International Law Treaties (CH–1) following the Appendices, *infra*. For an overview of the multilateral treaties drawn up by The Hague Conference on Private International Law, consult the web site at http://www.hcch.net/e/conventions/index.html.

13. 489 U.S. 353 (1989).

14. Mar. 4, 1942, 56 Stat. 1405–1406, T.S. No. 983.

domestic tax investigation referred to the Justice Department for criminal prosecution. The Court held that neither the Convention nor domestic legislation imposed this precondition to issuance of an administrative summons.[15]

In interpreting the treaty, the majority opinion of the Court relied on the maxim that ''[t]he clear impact of treaty language controls unless 'application of the words of the treaty according to their obvious meanings effects a result inconsistent with the intent or expectations of its signatories.' ''[16] The Court concluded that the specific articles of the Convention involved in the dispute on their face did not support respondent's position.[17]

The Court noted that the Solicitor General, in his brief, relied on the pre-ratification Senate debate of the Convention. The Court found that reliance on such non-textual sources as pre-ratification debates and reports often assist in ''giving effect to the intent of the treaty parties,'' but could find nothing in the Convention's ratification which reinforced respondents' claim.[18]

In his concurring opinion, Justice Scalia rejected the use of pre-ratification material.[19] First, Justice Scalia determined that because the text of the Convention was completely dispositive of petitioner's argument, there was no need to inquire into the intent of the treaty

(*Text continued on page 2-9*)

15. 489 U.S. at 360–68.
16. *Id.* at 365–66 (citation omitted).
17. *Id.* at 366–70.
18. *Id.* at 366.
19. *Id.* at 371–77; United States v. Swiss American Bank Ltd., 189 F.3d 30 (1st Cir. 1999).

parties.[20] He stated that it is only when a treaty provision is ambiguous that it is appropriate to give effect to extra-textual materials.[21] Justice Scalia emphatically noted that use of pre-ratification Senate floor debate material was unprecedented.[22] According to his research, not a single case could be discovered where the Court had consulted the Senate debate, committee hearings, or committee reports.[23] He suggested that the use of such materials would promote reliance on unilateral understanding of what the legislature thought it was agreeing to, rather than the mutual understanding (as, for example, extant in the negotiating history) of the treaty parties.[24]

Justice Scalia's views on proper judicial interpretation of treaties have prompted discussion on research problems in this area.[25] It has been pointed out that, with careful research, the missing category of Supreme Court cases noted by Justice Scalia that relied on pre-ratification Senate materials could have been discovered.[26] Some of the ways suggested of locating this material are the use of modern technology such as LEXIS or WESTLAW and the traditional approach of reading treaty interpretation cases of the Supreme Court until one finds opinions that use Senate materials.[27] Regardless of the methods used, every lawyer should employ tactics in researching treaties that are resourceful, creative, and above all, exhaustive.

Another case illustrative of judicial interpretation of treaties is *Banco de Credito Indus., S.A. v. Tesoreria General.*[28] In *Banco de Credito Indus., S.A.*, the Fifth Circuit was required to interpret Spanish law pertaining to maritime liens under the International Convention for the Unification of Certain Rules Related to Maritime Liens and Mortgages ("Brussels Convention").[29] The court of appeals observed that, as the Spanish legal system was civil in nature, the role of positive

---

20. *Id.* at 371.
21. *Id.* at 372–73.
22. *Id.* at 373.
23. *Id.*
24. *Id.* at 374.
25. *See, e.g.*, Detlev F. Vagts, *Senate Materials and Treaty Interpretation: Some Research Hints for the Supreme Court*, 83 AM. J. INT'L L. 546 (1989).
26. *Id.* at 547–550.
27. *Id.* at 547–548.
28. 990 F.2d 827 (5th Cir. 1993), *cert. denied*, 114 S. Ct. 877 (1994).
29. *Done* 1926, 100 L.N.T.S. 187, *reprinted in*, 6A BENEDICT ON ADMIRALTY 8–17 (7th ed. 1993).

legislation was emphasized over *stare decisis*.[30] Therefore, in determining Spanish law concerning maritime liens, the court looked first to the language of the treaty itself and then to the legislation of other signatory nations, including France, concerning the treaty.[31] The court then looked to Spanish internal law on maritime liens.[32] Finding that the parties had failed to conclusively establish foreign law, the court undertook an analysis of domestic U.S. law "to fill in any gaps."[33]

§ 2.06 LAWYER'S RESPONSIBILITY FOR FOREIGN LAW

Despite their unfamiliarity with foreign law, lawyers who undertake the representation of a client in an international case which involves the laws of more than one nation will be held responsible to that client for capable and effective representation. Failure to adequately protect the interests of the client because of ignorance of the foreign law may result in civil liability or possible disciplinary proceedings.

The issue of the responsibility of the U.S. attorney for foreign law arose over half a century ago in *Degan v. Steinbrink*.[34] In *Degan*, the defendants, a New York law firm, represented the plaintiff's assignor in preparing an agreement of guarantee and three chattel mortgages for property used to secure a loan. The property was located in three states: New York, New Jersey, and Connecticut. When the borrower subsequently was petitioned into bankruptcy, plaintiff's assignor again retained the defendants to protect his interests. The referee in bankruptcy held that the chattel mortgages were invalid because of defendants' failure to abide by technicalities in all three states when preparing the mortgages and, as a result, the assignor/lender, treated as a general creditor, received a sum below the value of the loan.

Relying on the theory that New York lawyers were not presumed to know the laws of other states, the referee held that the defendants were only liable for their failure to properly execute the New York mortgage. The appellate division reversed, noting that:

30. 990 F.2d at 833.
31. *Id.* at 833–36.
32. *Id.* at 836.
33. *Id.*
34. 202 A.D. 477, 195 N.Y.S. 810 (App. Div. 1922), *aff'd*, 236 N.Y. 669, 142 N.E. 328 (1923).

> When a lawyer undertakes to prepare papers to be filed in a state foreign to his place of practice, it is his duty, if he has not knowledge of the statutes, to inform himself, for, like any artisan, by undertaking the work, he represents that he is capable of performing it in a skillful manner.[35]

The decision in *Degan* was subsequently cited with approval in *In Re Roel*,[36] a case involving the illegal practice of law by a Mexican attorney who was not licensed in New York. Although *Degan* was cited primarily for the principle that the conduct of attorneys admitted in New York can be regulated by New York courts, the court's *dicta* is evidence that the rule of *Degan* is firmly established. In this connection, the court of appeals held:

> When counsel who are admitted to the Bar of this State are retained in a matter involving foreign law, they are responsible to the client for the proper conduct of the matter, and may not claim that they are not required to know the law of the foreign State.[37]

Thus, the court of appeals refused to allow ignorance of the foreign law to operate as an excuse for incompetent representation. Following *Roel*, it is established that the "law" contemplated by New York statutes dealing with the unlawful practice of law extends to rendering advice on foreign law.[38]

§ 2.07 PROFESSIONAL AND ETHICAL CONSIDERATIONS

Case law in this area primarily relates to the lawyer's responsibility to correctly apply the laws of other states and jurisdictions within the United States. Nevertheless, the duty to provide effective representation requires equal, if not greater, care when the laws of foreign nations are involved.

Canon 6 of the American Bar Association's Code of Professional Responsibility[39] requires the lawyer to "represent a client competent-

---

35. *Id.*, 202 A.D. at 481, 195 N.Y.S. at 813. *See also* Rekeweg v. Federal Mutual Ins. Co., 27 F.R.D. 431 (N.D. Ind. 1961), *aff'd*, 324 F.2d 150 (1963), *cert. denied*, 376 U.S. 943 (1964).

36. 3 N.Y.2d 224, 144 N.E.2d 24, 165 N.Y.S.2d 31, 37 (1957), *appeal dismissed*, 355 U.S. 604 (1958).

37. *Id.*, 3 N.Y.2d at 232, 144 N.E.2d at 28, 165 N.Y.S.2d at 37.

38. *See* El Gemayel v. Seaman, 72 N.Y.2d 701, 706, 533 N.E.2d 245, 248, 536 N.Y.S.2d 406, 409 (1988).

39. Model Code of Professional Responsibility, Canon 6 (1980).

ly." Thus, attorneys who agree to represent a client in litigation involving foreign law have a duty to familiarize themselves with the relevant foreign law pertinent to the litigation. Canon 6 states, further, that an attorney may accept employment in an area of law in which the attorney is not qualified only:

> *if he expects to become qualified through study and investigation*, as long as such preparation would not result in unreasonable delay or expense to his client . . . [and] if he does not expect to become so qualified should either decline the employment or, with the consent of his client, accept the employment and associate a lawyer who is competent in the matter.[40]

Failure to prepare "adequate [to] the circumstances" in the handling of a legal matter may subject attorneys to disciplinary proceedings.[41] Preparation "adequate [to] the circumstances" may entail extensive research, in order to become familiar with the law of an unfamiliar jurisdiction. It is of vital importance that attorneys carefully examine the nature of their undertaking, not only to provide competent representation, but also to eliminate unnecessary expense to the client. It is the lawyer's duty to identify the foreign law questions and alert the client to those aspects of foreign law which need to be explored. Lawyers must next determine how the foreign law questions will be handled. It must be decided, within the purview of Canon 6, whether they will deal with the problem or advise the client that other foreign or domestic counsel should be retained for the foreign law aspects of the case.[42] This type of appraisal will help to insure that the requirements of Canon 6 are satisfied.

A few examples illustrate the type of problem faced by U.S. lawyers in deciding whether they have the competence to handle the particular foreign law question involved. A common question in U.S. litigation is how to effect service of process on a defendant in a foreign country or obtain testimony from a foreign witness. The lawyer must first determine whether domestic or foreign law (or both) applies to the situation. This type of question may be sufficiently basic for U.S. attorneys to engage in their own research of foreign law questions without fear of "unreasonable delay or expense" to the client.

40. *Id.* at 6–3.

41. MODEL CODE OF PROFESSIONAL RESPONSIBILITY, DR 6–101(A)(2) (1980).

42. *See* Janis, *The Lawyer's Responsibility for Foreign Law and Foreign Lawyers*, 16 INT'L LAW. 693 (1982).

However, if the question were more substantive or complicated, such as enforceability of a potential judgment in a foreign country, foreign counsel would be better able to advise on foreign law and it would be prudent, as well as economical, to suggest this approach to the client. One cautionary note is that the U.S. lawyer may be held responsible for the selection and supervision of foreign counsel.[43] This requires U.S. attorneys to take the proper steps, in a due care sense, to satisfy themselves that foreign counsel is competent to do the job.

§ 2.08 ROLE OF THE FOREIGN LAWYER IN THE UNITED STATES

Virtually all states have restrictions against the practice of law by persons who have not been admitted to the local bar. In the U.S., these restrictions apply to attorneys who are licensed in another state, as well as to attorneys who are licensed, practicing lawyers or barristers in their country of origin. Attorneys licensed in a foreign nation or even a neighboring state may be found guilty of violating penal statutes for the unlicensed practice of law and for giving legal advice in a state where they are not members of the bar.

In *In re Roel*,[44] New York's highest court affirmed a ruling of criminal contempt against a Mexican lawyer who offered legal advice on Mexican divorce law. The court ruled that advising on foreign law constituted the practice of law within the meaning of the New York penal code and enjoined Roel from the practice of law. Roel, who was admitted to practice law in Mexico, argued that he gave no advice on New York law, but merely prepared divorce papers and other legal documents pertaining to the laws of Mexico. He noted, further, that he advised clients to consult a competent local lawyer as well, and that his retainer included a disclaimer as to the legal validity or effect of Mexican divorces outside of Mexico. In rejecting his claim, the court acknowledged that Roel "renders only specialized services dealing with a field in which he claims to be peculiarly competent," but that "the competence of [Roel] is not dispositive of the case before us."[45]

---

43. *See, e.g.*, Tormo v. Yormark, 398 F. Supp. 1159 (D.N.J. 1975); Bluestein v. State Bar of California, 13 Cal. 3d 162, 529 P.2d 599, 118 Cal. Rptr. 175 (1974).

44. 3 N.Y.2d 224, 144 N.E.2d 24, 165 N.Y.S.2d 31 (1957), *appeal dismissed*, 355 U.S. 604 (1958).

45. 3 N.Y.2d at 230, 144 N.E.2d at 28, 165 N.Y.S.2d at 36.

There are a number of reasons for the requirement that attorneys be licensed in the state in which they wish to practice their profession. These include the interest that the state bar has in maintaining high standards for its profession and its desire to admit only those persons who have a knowledge of the local laws and procedures. State bars also have a legitimate interest in limiting the number of lawyers who practice in their state. It is not surprising, therefore, that there has been much resistance to the lowering of admission requirements for foreign attorneys who wish to practice law in the United States.[46] State requirements which hold that a member of the bar be the graduate of an ABA accredited law school make it difficult for the foreign attorney to meet admission standards. These requirements may compel foreign lawyers or persons knowledgeable in the laws of a foreign country to seek admission to a United States law school and, on the completion of their legal education, to take the bar exam.

Until 1973, a majority of states excluded aliens from the practice of law by requiring United States citizenship for bar membership.[47] In that year, however, the Supreme Court, in *In re Griffiths*,[48] held that the rule in Connecticut barring resident aliens from admission to the state bar violated the equal protection clause of the fourteenth amendment. As a result of the ruling, persons who are not United States citizens are eligible to take the bar examination and become members of the bar in all fifty states and the District of Columbia.

The ruling in *Griffiths* has not resulted in a flood of resident aliens seeking bar membership, however. Most states still require that their bar members complete their legal education at an ABA accredited law school and successfully complete the bar examination.[49] New York, alone, has held that an attorney who is licensed to practice law in a foreign country whose jurisprudence is based upon the principles of the

---

46. *See* Comment, *Providing Legal Services in Foreign Countries: Making Room for the American Attorney*, 83 COLUM. L. REV. 1767, 1795–96 (1983).

47. In 1972, 38 states and the District of Columbia had bar admission requirements which excluded non-citizens from the practice of law. Knoppke-Wetzel, *Employment Restrictions and the Practice of Law by Aliens in the United States and Abroad*, 1974 DUKE L.J. 871, 891.

48. 413 U.S. 717, 737 (1973).

49. *See generally Comprehensive Guide to Bar Admission Requirements (1993–94)*, American Bar Association & National Conference of Bar Examiners (1993) (providing, often in helpful chart form, extremely detailed information on state bar admission requirements, including categories of admission, educational and practice requirements, foreign law school graduates, test scores, filing deadlines, and fees).

English common law (Pakistan) is entitled to be admitted to the state bar without examination.[50]

§ 2.09 FOREIGN LAWYERS' PRACTICE AS FOREIGN LEGAL CONSULTANTS

A number of states now allow foreign lawyers to practice as "foreign legal consultants" without taking the state bar examination. In the 1980's, a substantial number of foreign firms opened branch offices in the United States.[51] This increase was due, in large part, to changes in local bar requirements (or proposed rules) which authorize the licensing of "foreign legal consultants." For example, New York changed its bar requirements to authorize foreign legal consultants in order to satisfy the demand for their services in areas such as international finance.[52] The New York bar regulations were also motivated by the desire to promote reciprocal practices in favor of attorneys from the United States practicing in foreign countries.[53] In the United States, Alaska, California, Connecticut, the District of Columbia, Florida, Georgia, Hawaii, Illinois, Michigan, New Jersey, New York, Ohio, Oregon, Texas, and Washington allow foreign lawyers to practice as consultants.[54]

In essence, these local bar rules allow foreign attorneys who have been specially licensed by the local bar to work as foreign legal consultants and to render professional advice on the law of the foreign country in which they are admitted to practice. The basic provisions of local court rules for foreign legal consultant licensing tend to be almost identical, and provide that the litigant must have actually practiced and be in good standing for a requisite period of time prior to licensing

50. *See, e.g.*, Shaikh v. Appellate Div. of Supreme Court, 39 N.Y.2d 676, 385 N.Y.S.2d 514, 350 N.E.2d 902 (1976). *But see* Application of Spyropoulos, 34 A.D.2d 565, 310 N.Y.S.2d 12 (1970) (denying admission to applicant licensed in Greece); Sodha v. New York State Board of Law Examiners, 105 Misc. 2d 159, 431 N.Y.S.2d 885 (1980) (finding failure to establish substantial educational equivalence).

51. Emily Couric, *Foreign Firms Invade the U.S.: An Asset to Bar?*, NAT. L.J., Oct. 29, 1984, at 1.

52. *See* Kosagi, *Regulation of Practice by Foreign Lawyers*, 27 AM. J. COMP. L. 678, 687 (1979).

53. *Id.* at 687.

54. *Comprehensive Guide to Bar Admission Requirements (1993–94)*, American Bar Association & National Conference of Bar Examiners (1993), at 48–49. The state registration fees for foreign legal consultants range from $ 200 (New Jersey) to $ 5,000 (Georgia). *Id.*

in the United States.[55] Some rules may require a showing of reciprocity. The District of Columbia rules, but not the New York rules, include a reciprocity provision that allows the court, in acting on an application for "special legal consultant," to consider whether a member of the District of Columbia bar could establish an office in the country where the applicant was admitted to the bar.[56]

Once attorneys are licensed as foreign legal consultants, they are authorized to practice law on a limited basis and to render professional legal advice on the law of the foreign country where they are admitted to practice. Foreign lawyers may legally hold themselves out as foreign legal consultants in that particular jurisdiction. The services they provide may range from foreign probate law to advice on the effect of foreign laws on international transactions. In this connection, foreign consultants may assist in advising on international joint ventures, foreign licensing, and international business transactions. Advice on foreign law prior to entering into these international transactions may help avoid litigation in the future.

Prior to retaining foreign legal consultants, it is important to check the specific nature of services that they are authorized to provide in the particular jurisdiction. Thus, in New York State, for example, foreign legal consultants may not prepare deeds or other instruments for the transfer of real property in the United States; prepare wills or trust documents for United States property; or administer estates.[57] New York regulations provide, in addition, that foreign legal consultants may not prepare documents relating to marital relations or child custody matters pertaining to a U.S. resident.[58] The District of Columbia provisions contain similar restrictions on scope of practice and do not allow foreign consultants to appear in court.[59] In this connection, New York provisions state that foreign legal consultants may give advice on United States law only if they base the legal advice

55. *See, e.g.*, Michigan Supreme Court Rule 5(A)(6); Hawaii Supreme Court Rule 21; Illinois Supreme Court Rule Art. VII, part A, § 712 et seq.; D.C. Ct. App. R. 46 (1986); N.Y. Jud. Law § 53.6 (McKinney 1983).

56. D.C. Ct. App. R. 46(c)(4)(C) (1986); N.Y. Comp. Codes R. & Regs., tit. 22, § 521.1(a)(1986).

57. *See* N.Y. Comp. Codes R. & Regs., tit. 22, § 521.3(b)–(d) (1986).

58. *Id.*

59. D.C. Ct. App. R. 46(c)(4)(D) (1986).

on the opinion of an attorney practicing in the United States.[60] The same rule applies in the District of Columbia.[61]

Where international issues predominate, the foreign legal consultant may be a cost-effective addition to a litigation team. In the pre-litigation stage, the consultant may be called upon to assess the viability of a claim under the applicable foreign law, and to interpret that law as it applies to the specific facts of the case at hand. Once litigation has been initiated, the consultant may continue to advise on substantive aspects of the foreign law, as well as procedural considerations, such as the complex discovery or pretrial limitations found in many nations.[62] Furthermore, the foreign legal consultant may have legal contacts in the foreign country which may be an asset in taking depositions, obtaining evidence needed for the proceeding, or handling other matters before the foreign court.

The foreign legal consultant may also be useful at trial. There, the consultant may be retained as an expert witness to advise the court of the law of the foreign jurisdiction. This testimony may often be crucial as the United States court may have little understanding of the law of the foreign nation and may need to rely on the foreign consultant in order to become educated on the foreign law involved. The consultant may also assist in preparing necessary affidavits to prove foreign law in support of summary judgment motions, etc.

§ 2.10 HIRING A LAWYER ABROAD

Frequently, during the course of international litigation, it becomes necessary to retain "local" counsel in the foreign jurisdiction. Although this can be a difficult task, there are a number of resources which offer assistance in this area. One good resource is the Office of American Citizens Services (ACS) of the Department of State.[63] On request, this office will provide a country-by-country list of attorneys who practice in the particular foreign jurisdiction together with basic biographical information, specialties of practice, and language capabilities. In larger countries, the list is sub-divided to include larger cities or districts. ACS also possesses information about process servers in many nations.

---

60. *See* N.Y. Comp. Codes R. & Regs., tit. 22, § 521.3(g) (1986).

61. *See* D.C. Ct. App. R. 46(c)(4)(D)(5) (1986).

62. *See infra* Chapter 10.

63. American Citizens Services, U.S. Department of State, Washington, D.C. 20520; telephone: (202) 647–5226.

ACS also distributes a short but practical guide to retaining and utilizing a foreign attorney. The attorneys' list is updated annually. ACS is divided into five geographical divisions: the Europe and Canada Division; the Inter-American Division; the East Asia and Pacific Division; the African Division; and the Near Eastern & South Asia Division. Those offices can be contacted directly for additional advice on specific countries. Advice disseminated by ACS is for general information only. ACS advises that any specific questions about the education and licensing of foreign attorneys in a particular foreign country be addressed to the foreign bar association or other similar local body.

Another source for identifying foreign attorneys is the *Martindale-Hubbell International Law Directory,* vols. I & II (1997). The Directory provides professional biographies and indexes of foreign counsel. As inclusion in the Directory is obtained for a fee, this source may not be quite as inclusive as the information provided by ACS. Nevertheless, it provides additional names for selection. *Martindale-Hubbell* also maintains information concerning attorneys on the Internet.[64] Searches may be run for attorneys by name, type of practice and geographic location in many nations. Lawyers may also advertise on the Internet expertise in international law. Care should be taken, however, to verify the credentials and experience of such lawyers.

If these resources are not helpful, there are local points of contact which may be pursued. These include attorneys at respected local firms, local or regional offices of foreign consulates, persons who have been involved with international business transactions, lawyers who are active in international law sections of bar associations, and law faculty members who are familiar with the international area involved.

Another option is to retain one of the major U.S. international law firms that maintains foreign branch offices. This may be one of the best solutions if your case involves international business or investment matters which may be one of the firm's areas of specialization.[65] The client may feel more at ease working through a U.S.-based office, and need not worry about language or other communication problems that can occur when a foreign lawyer, located thousands of miles away, is employed. If potential litigation is involved in the foreign country, one

64. http://lawyers.martindale.com/marhub.

65. *See generally* Note, *Foreign Branches of Law Firms: The Development of Lawyers Equipped to Handle International Practice*, 80 HARV. L. REV. 1284 (1967).

will need to employ the services of a member of the local bar. Often a U.S. attorney is not qualified to be licensed in the foreign jurisdiction. However, large U.S. law firms, maintaining foreign branch offices, will usually have a member of the bar of the foreign country in its employ or be affiliated with a local law firm.

Since World War II, U.S. lawyers have played a significant role in developing a special legal practice relating to international business transactions.[66] This has been attributed to their fluency in English, substantial experience in international business transactions, and creative lawyering skills which facilitate international business deals.[67] Because of the unique services they offer, U.S. lawyers often act as "transaction facilitators" where there are American ties to the transaction or a large business deal is involved.[68] They also may provide assistance to their client in selecting foreign lawyers to contribute their advice to the transaction.

In recent years, there has been a proliferation of law firm associations to serve clients on an international basis.[69] These associations provide immediate access to firms in other countries which can save the member from having to search for qualified foreign firms possessing the particular expertise for the job. Such associations emphasize that clients will receive quality service from firms that have been screened and reviewed or recommended by other member firms. In addition, there may be personal interchanges between member firms, including exchange programs in which lawyers from one firm work for another firm for a limited period of time. Firm associations cater to different needs, ranging from large law firm groups to those composed of smaller-sized firms. Those associations comprised of smaller firms stress the personal attention provided to clients as well as their lower fee structure as compared to larger law firms.[70] It may be possible, however, to work out lower fee arrangements with overseas

---

66. *See* Comment, *Providing Legal Services in Foreign Countries: Making Room for the American Attorney*, 83 COLUM. L. REV. 1767, 1768–69 (1983).

67. *Id.* at 1768.

68. *Id.* at 1769.

69. *See* Adam Wright, *Firm Associations Provide Network of Global Counsel*, CORP. LEGAL TIMES, Mar. 1993, at 36.; *Lex Mundi Directory of Law Firm Associations, Alliances, Clubs, and Other Affiliations*, INT'L LAW. NEWSL., vol. xv, no. 6, 1993, at 26–27; MARTINDALE-HUBBELL INTERNATIONAL LAW DIRECTORY, vols. I & II (1997).

70. David Rubenstein, *Foreign Firms Offer Quality Work at Bargain Rates*, CORP. LEGAL TIMES, Nov. 1992, at 12.

affiliates of large U.S. law firms if the client has an on-going business relationship with the firm.[71]

§ 2.11 PITFALLS OF RETAINING A FOREIGN ATTORNEY

The Office of American Citizens Services in the State Department provides general information concerning retaining the services of a private attorney for legal advice in other countries.[72] A State Department circular on retaining a foreign attorney is reprinted as Appendix 1. While the circular is directed to the public in general, it provides useful guidance for U.S. lawyers when it becomes necessary to employ foreign counsel for their clients. The circular points out the need to employ the services of foreign counsel when domestic counsel is not in a position to represent the private party's interests abroad. An example of this occurs when the laws of the foreign country require a foreign attorney to participate in foreign court proceedings. Also, when an evidentiary request is directed to a court in a civil law country, it is usually the judge who presides over the evidence gathering proceeding and questions the witness. It is advisable to have a foreign attorney present at such proceedings to insure that the party's interests are protected since a U.S. attorney may not be authorized to appear in the foreign court. The foreign attorney may be able to ask supplemental questions or even cross-examine the witness if the judge is amenable to such procedures. This insures some measure of damage control over the witness' testimony. Such precautions may prove especially helpful at a deposition for use at trial in the United States.

The State Department circular contains the following "do's" and "don'ts" in dealing with a foreign attorney. It is of primary importance to determine the attorney's qualifications and experience. Several attorneys or firms should first be interviewed and it is absolutely necessary to determine whether the attorney is fluent in the English language. The party should further understand that the representation requirements for a particular legal problem may vary from country to country. For example, in the United Kingdom, it may be necessary to employ the services of both a barrister and a solicitor. In this connection, barristers are allowed to appear in court while solicitors advise clients and prepare barristers to try cases in court. In other countries, such as France, notaries public, "notaries" and "huissiers"

---

71. *Id.*
72. *See supra* § 2.10.

perform many of the functions performed by attorneys in the United States. Foreign notaries draft instruments, wills, and conveyances, and may be empowered, together with "huissiers," to serve legal documents. Notarial functions may include not only the preparation of documents, but the administration and settlement of estates as well.

The party seeking the services of foreign counsel also needs to determine the attorney's plan of representation. The party should remember that foreign legal proceedings may take as long or longer than those in U.S. courts. It is, therefore, necessary for the party to insure that foreign counsel regularly monitors the proceedings and periodically advises the client of the status, including new developments, in the case. The circular further suggests that the client check on the fees the attorney charges and how the attorney expects to be paid.

Some of the problems regarding compensation for services performed by foreign counsel were involved in *Ackermann v. Levine.*[73] In that case, the foreign attorney sued the defendant, an American citizen, in U.S. District Court, to enforce a German default judgment for legal fees charged under a German fee statute. Under the statute, the fee charged was based on a price that reflected the value of the legal questions or financial transaction and the percentage of the total fee to be charged. The parties never discussed attorney's fees or the nature of their relationship. The judgment was found enforceable under New York public policy, except for a period of time in which the court of appeals found no evidence for any authorization to do the work specified or of the existence of any work product.[74] The case points out the need for the party engaging the foreign attorney to have a full understanding of the fee compensation arrangement under the law of the foreign country and a written agreement concerning the work authorized.

§ 2.12 DEALING WITH FOREIGN COUNSEL: DO'S AND DON'TS

This section offers some suggestions on dealing with foreign counsel.

73. 788 F.2d 830 (2d Cir. 1986).
74. *Id.* at 845.

Effective Communications

Be sensitive to cultural and language differences.

- Understand the basics of the foreign legal system involved. Be patient in learning and listen carefully.

- As a general rule, consider hiring English-speaking attorneys.

- Give careful, written instructions on what you wish to accomplish and on the limits of the authority you are conveying.

- Be clear in your instructions on reporting requirements. Establish a reporting schedule, if necessary.

- Anticipate that written materials requested (i.e., opinion letters, briefs, memoranda, etc.) may be prepared in a different style. For example, briefs may be shorter and less advocacy oriented than under U.S. legal practice.

- Make sure foreign legal advice is clear and understandable. If advice is unclear, assist foreign counsel to solve the problem (by rephrasing the questions, furnishing additional background material, clarifying translated material, providing samples, etc.).

Billings

- Determine the type of billing practices common to the jurisdiction. Evaluate what specific modifications, if any, will be required to suit your needs.

- Request an estimate of the total hours and costs of doing the work. Be clear at the outset who will be involved in the work and the fees to be charged by each participant. Determine if other attorneys or specialists need to be consulted, such as barristers.

- Establish a billing system that details your requirements. Foreign lawyers may be unaccustomed to including a description of work performed.

- Establish a periodic billing schedule to suit your needs. Foreign law firms may bill in an irregular fashion and are commonly slower to issue invoices than U.S. firms.

§ 2.13 WORKING WITH FOREIGN COUNSEL

In employing the services of a foreign lawyer, U.S. counsel should be sensitive to the cultural and language problems as well as comparative differences in the legal systems involved. As a general rule, it is advisable to look for an English-speaking lawyer. Most firms engaged in international practice will have English-speaking attorneys in the major specialties. If an English-speaking lawyer is not available, arrangements should be made in advance for a good translator to act as an effective "go-between." If the foreign lawyer does not speak English but is an expert in the field needed, this factor may outweigh any language difficulties presented.

The key element in dealing with foreign counsel is to communicate effectively your expectations and the objectives you wish to accomplish. A discussion of the legal problems to be addressed should be described in detail, with accompanying background materials and documents, etc. If the work to be performed by the foreign lawyer relates to proceedings in U.S. courts, information should be provided about applicable U.S. law and procedure. U.S. counsel should not assume that foreign counsel will be familiar with the U.S. legal system or the substantive law involved. Foreign counsel should also have no doubts as to the extent of his or her authority and should be given a full description of assigned duties and responsibilities. If, for example, foreign counsel is being engaged to provide information on specific foreign laws or to prepare an opinion letter on certain issues, the assignment should be limited to that work and the nature of the work to be performed should be clearly established at the outset.

U.S. counsel should also clearly convey the reporting requirements needed. As contrasted to U.S. practice, lawyers in many foreign countries are not accustomed to making detailed written reports. If the legal analysis has not been sufficiently developed, the foreign lawyer should be asked to supplement the material provided. If the material submitted is not understandable, you should rephrase the questions or restate the issues until the foreign lawyer can work with them. In some cases, the difficulty may stem from language or technical translation issues. Determine the source of the problem quickly and eliminate it. If you think the written briefs are too concise, be sure to check on the role and function of the document in that legal system. It may be that the evidentiary hearing is more important than the brief, for instance. More difficult, at times, is motivating the lawyer to take an aggressive,

U.S. style approach in litigation. Patience will serve you well in the process of explaining your expectations and encouraging the accommodation of your needs.

Chapter 3

ADVICE TO THE PROSPECTIVE LITIGANT

§ 3.01 ARBITRATION VERSUS LITIGATION

Once an international legal dispute arises, the parties must decide whether the dispute should be resolved by litigation or an alternate form of dispute resolution, such as fact-finding, mediation, or arbitration. Because of the differences between common law and civil law legal systems, arbitration particularly has become an attractive alternative to litigation and an increasingly effective way of resolving international legal controversies. Recent commentators have noted the popularity of arbitration and concluded that it has become the preferred means of dispute resolution.[1] When negotiating international contracts, parties should consider whether the inclusion of an arbitration clause will provide an effective mechanism for resolving the dispute. Arbitration may also be used by the parties after the dispute has arisen. An appreciation of the advantages and disadvantages of arbitration versus litigation will assist in choosing the best means of settling the dispute.

The Supreme Court has reaffirmed the strong United States policy in favoring enforcement of arbitration provisions.[2] In *Mitsubishi Motors Corp. v. Soler Chrysler-Plymouth, Inc.*,[3] the parties had entered into a sales agreement for car distribution outside of the United States. The sales agreement contained an arbitration clause providing for arbitration by the Japan Commercial Arbitration Association in all disputes arising out of certain articles of the agreement. Petitioner brought an action in court under the Federal Arbitration Act[4] and the Convention on the Recognition and Enforcement of Foreign Arbitral Awards (the "New York Convention")[5] seeking an order to compel arbitration.

---

1. Christine Lecuyer-Thieffry & Patrick Thieffry, *Negotiating Settlement of Disputes Provisions in International Business Contracts: Recent Developments in Arbitration and Other Processes*, 45 BUS. LAW. 581 (1990); Luis M. Martinez, *International Groups Report ADR Caseload Rise*, DISP. RESOL. TIMES (American Arbitration Association, Winter 1997–98) at 1 (observing increase in international case filings with arbitral tribunals).

2. *See* Scherk v. Alberto-Culver, 417 U.S. 506 (1975); Mitsubishi Motors Corp. v. Soler Chrysler-Plymouth, Inc., 473 U.S. 614 (1985).

3. 473 U.S. 614 (1985).

4. 9 U.S.C. § 1.

5. The United Nations Convention on the Recognition and Enforcement of Foreign Arbitral Awards, *done* June 10, 1958, *entered into force for the U.S.*, Dec. 29, 1970, [hereinafter New York Convention], 21 U.S.T. 2517, T.I.A.S. No. 6997, 330 U.N.T.S. 3. *See infra* Appendix 17 for the text of the Convention.

Respondent counterclaimed by raising counts under the Sherman Act and other statutes. The Supreme Court held that the Federal Arbitration Act mandated enforcement of such agreements and observed the "emphatic federal policy in favor of arbitral dispute resolution."[6] The Court determined there was no reason to depart from this presumption where the party bound by the arbitration agreement raised claims founded on statutory rights. The Supreme Court found that through the treaty mechanism of the New York Convention, and implementing legislation in the Federal Arbitration Act, the federal policy favoring arbitration in dispute resolution applied with special force in the field of international commerce.[7]

Enforcement of arbitral awards and suits to compel parties to submit to arbitration has been made easier by the New York Convention. The Convention has gained wide acceptance, with over 100 countries as signatories.[8] Under the New York Convention the courts are required to refer the parties to arbitration except in certain limited circumstances, such as where the arbitration agreement is null and void.[9] Moreover, organizations such as the United Nations Committee on International Trade Law (UNCITRAL) and the International Chamber of Commerce have developed rules of arbitration which are widely accepted in resolving different types of international commercial disputes.[10] It has been observed that the institutionalized

---

6. *Mitsubishi*, 473 U.S. at 631.

7. 473 U.S. at 631.

8. The signatories to the New York Convention are as follows: Algeria; Antigua and Barbuda; Argentina; Australia; Austria; Bahrain; Bangladesh; Barbados; Belarus; Belgium; Benin; Bolivia; Bosnia-Herzegovina; Botswana; Brunei Darussalam; Bulgaria; Burkina Faso; Byelorussian Soviet Republic; Cambodia; Cameroon; Canada; Central African Republic; Chile; China; Colombia; Costa Rica; Cote d'Ivoire; Croatia; Cuba; Cyprus; Czech Republic; Dahomey; Denmark; Djibouti; Dominica; Ecuador; Egypt; Estonia; Finland; France (withdrew, declaration effective 11/27/89); Federal Republic of Germany; Georgia; Ghana; Greece; Guatemala; Guinea; Haiti; Holy See; Hungary; India; Indonesia; Ireland; Israel; Italy; Japan; Jordan; Kampuchea; Kazakhstan; Kenya; Korea; Kuwait; Latvia; Lesotho; Lithuania; Luxembourg; Macedonia; Madagascar; Malaysia; Mali; Mauritius; Mexico; Monaco; Mongolia; Morocco; Netherlands; New Zealand; Niger; Nigeria; Norway; Panama; Peru; Philippines; Poland; Portugal; Romania; Russian Federation; San Marino; Saudi Arabia; Senegal; Singapore; Slovak Republic; Slovenia; South Africa; Spain; Sri Lanka (Ceylon); Sweden; Switzerland; Syrian Arab Republic; Tanzania; Thailand; Trinidad and Tobago; Tunisia; Turkey; Uganda; Ukraine; United Kingdom; United States; Uruguay; Uzebekistan; Venezuela; Vietnam; Yugoslavia; Zimbabwe.

9. *See infra* § 12.03 (discussing enforcement of arbitration agreements).

10. *See* Steven C. Nelson, *Alternatives to Litigation of International Disputes*, 23 INT'L LAW. 187, 194 (1989).

framework for dispute resolution by arbitration is more developed than the international judicial process.[11]

Because of the widespread recognition and acceptance of international arbitration rules, parties are encouraged to bring the dispute before the selected forum without fear that the courts will refuse to enforce an arbitral award obtained. The ability of the parties to agree to arbitrate and thereby determine in advance the forum for prosecuting a dispute prevents multiple proceedings and discourages forum shopping. There is now greater likelihood of the enforceability of arbitral awards than foreign judicial judgments.[12] The international law relating to the enforcement of judgments has not correspondingly expanded due to jurisdictional objections and notions of comity which are inconsistently applied by foreign courts.[13]

Parties seeking to resolve international disputes should compare procedural and evidentiary requirements and inherent distinctions between arbitration and litigation. The U.S. legal system is noted for pretrial discovery, technical rules of evidence, and the dilatory tactics of attorneys. Foreign companies doing business in the United States are often surprised and confused at the dissimilarities between litigation procedures in United States courts and those under civil law systems. Arbitration procedures tend to be more flexible than traditional litigation, and parties may develop a structure that is simpler and conforms more closely to their needs.[14] In addition, parties may select arbitrators who possess the requisite technical and legal expertise to deal with the specific issues involved. On the other hand, disputes in litigation may be assigned to judges who are inexperienced in dealing with issues involving international law. Issues which affect foreign relations interests or extraterritorial concerns may be complex and also detract from a speedy resolution of the controversy in national courts.

Nevertheless, arbitration may lack many of the procedural and other safeguards inherent in the U.S. litigation system. It may be an advantage for a party to rely on the full range of discovery including the right to compel production of documents and to depose recalcitrant witnesses. Procedural complexities aside, the U.S. litigation system is designed to allow each side to fully develop its own case and strategy. In addition, arbitration may not be more efficient and expeditious in

11. *Id.* at 194.
12. *See infra* § 12.06 (discussing enforcement of arbitral awards).
13. *See* Lecuyer-Thieffry & Thieffry, *supra* note 1, at 585–88.
14. *See* Nelson, *supra* note 10, at 197–98.

all cases. While parties to arbitration must submit to the whole process, a judicial trial may be short-circuited by disposition of the case on a motion to dismiss or summary judgment. Finally, on a comparative basis, the costs of arbitration may be higher since the expenses, including the fees of the arbitrators, are borne by the parties to the arbitration.[15]

§ 3.02 DIFFERENCES BETWEEN CIVIL LAW AND COMMON LAW LEGAL SYSTEMS

Where there is a choice between litigating in the United States or a foreign forum, the practitioner needs to be aware of the differences–and pitfalls–of litigating under different legal systems. As pointed out below, the procedural variations between the common law and civil law systems are considerable and should be carefully outlined and explained to the client before a decision is made where to litigate the dispute.

In adjudicating the dispute in a civil law country, courts tend to focus on laws and the codification of the law. This may include reliance on general principles based on the statutory code and analogies drawn therefrom. In common law countries, courts concentrate more on cases and *stare decisis*. Case precedent may be used in civil law systems but it is only one source of law and may not be controlling.

Common law proceedings have been described as accusatorial, i.e., a contest between two sides. Under U.S. procedural rules, the parties themselves are responsible for asserting, as well as protecting, their own interests. Therefore, their attorneys play a much more active role in the conduct of the proceeding than their civil law counterparts. In a forum in the United States, it is the duty of each side of the controversy to outline the issues and utilize sources of proof. During the pretrial phase of the case each party is responsible for developing its case and complying with the requisite procedural rules and notice requirements. The court plays a passive role during the pretrial part of the proceeding and becomes involved only where timely objections are raised by either side. The court may issue sanctions or take action against a party for violating any rules of procedure.

In civil law countries, it is the court, not the parties or their attorneys, which plays the active role. The entire proceeding is under

15. *Id.* at 203.

the court's control and authority. Of note is the absence of pretrial discovery under the civil law system. Parties in these countries do not take depositions or serve interrogatories, and the production of documents is considerably more limited.[16] Even in the common law Commonwealth countries, U.S. attorneys are generally surprised to find that pretrial discovery, including the production of documents, is not as extensive an undertaking as under the U.S. system.

An essential component of the common law system is a separate trial proceeding with examination and cross-examination of witnesses. There also is the right to a jury trial. The seventh amendment preserves the right to a jury trial in suits at common law.[17] In addition, state constitutions generally contain express guarantees of the right to trial by jury.[18] In civil law countries there are usually a series of proceedings rather than a separate trial. In addition, trials are generally conducted without juries. It is the court that decides which witnesses to call to testify, and the court, not the attorney, examines the witness.[19] In some countries, the attorney may be permitted to ask supplemental questions. However, the concept of cross-examination is not recognized or well understood. Parties are never called to testify. Witnesses do not testify under oath and there is no verbatim transcript. While testimony of ordinary witnesses is greatly relied on in common law countries, courts in civil law countries tend to rely on written statements of public officials. Nevertheless, parties do not retain their own experts, since this is exclusively within the authority of the court.[20]

United States lawyers are frequently surprised to learn of foreign notions of judicial sovereignty and foreign law proscriptions to that effect.[21] In this connection, there are restrictions in civil law countries which prevent any contact or interview between attorneys and witnesses before and during the trial. As an example, Article 271 of the Swiss Penal Code provides in pertinent part: "Whoever, on Swiss territory, without being authorized . . . takes on behalf of a foreign government any action which is solely within the province [of the Swiss authorities] . . . shall be punished or imprisoned." This would prevent

---

16. *See* Lecuyer-Thieffry & Thieffry, *supra* note 1, at 577.
17. U.S. CONST. amend. VII.
18. 47 AM. JUR. 2d *Jury* § 10 (1969).
19. Lecuyer-Thieffry & Thieffry, *supra* note 1, at 584.
20. *Id.*
21. *See infra* § 10.02.

foreign attorneys from engaging in such practices as interviewing witnesses, taking depositions, or preparing affidavits in Switzerland.[22]

§ 3.03 CHOOSING THE RIGHT FORUM

The threshold question of whether to sue in the United States or the foreign forum depends on differences in substantive law, public policy, and procedures in effect in the countries involved.[23] The cost of proceeding in a particular jurisdiction may also play an important part in forum selection. If there is jurisdiction over a dispute in the courts of two or more countries, an important consideration in selecting the right forum is the location in which sufficient assets exist to satisfy the judgment.[23.1] This is a crucial factor since enforcement of the judgment in a foreign jurisdiction may be problematic and subject to varying conditions and exceptions. If assets are located in more than one jurisdiction, a further element to be considered is the availability of preliminary remedies to maintain the status quo during the pendency of the litigation, such as preliminary injunctive relief and preliminary attachments. These are important remedies, especially where there is a threat of asset flight out of the jurisdiction prior to final adjudication of the dispute.

The issue has arisen as to whether a United States District Court has the power to issue a preliminary injunction in order to protect a potential future damages remedy, even if the usual requirements for obtaining preliminary equitable relief have been met. In *De Beers Consol. Mines v. United States*,[24] the government sought to enjoin future antitrust violations by De Beers. The government did not seek a preliminary injunction to protect any potential future damages remedy to which it might become entitled. Instead, the government sought to preserve a source of funds against which it could later threaten a contempt sanction as a practical means of enforcing whatever injunction might be granted. The Court held that the preliminary injunction

22. *See* Jones, *International Judicial Assistance: Procedural Chaos and a Program for Reform*, 62 YALE L.J. 515, 519–521 (1953).

23. *See* Nelson, *supra* note 10, at 187–88.

23.1 If a judgment is likely to be unenforceable in the country where the foreign party has assets, counsel may consider whether the agreement should provide for some other means of financial guaranty (e.g., escrow, bank guaranty, letter of credit, etc.).

24. 325 U.S. 212 (1945).

was inappropriate inasmuch as it "deal[t] with a matter wholly outside the issues in the suit."[25] In this connection, the Court stated as follows:

> To sustain the [preliminary injunction] would create a precedent of sweeping effect. This suit . . . is not to be distinguished from any other suit in equity. What applies to it applies to all such. Every suitor who resorts to chancery for any sort of relief by injunction may, on a mere statement of belief that the defendant can easily make away with or transport his money or goods, impose an injunction on him, indefinite in duration, disabling him to use so much of his funds or property as the court deems necessary for security or compliance with its possible decree. And, if so, it is difficult to see why a plaintiff in any action for a personal judgment in tort or contract may not, also, apply to the chancellor for a so-called injunction sequestering his opponent's assets pending recovery and satisfaction of a judgment in such a law action. No relief of this character has been thought justified in the long history of equity jurisprudence.[26]

In *United States v. First Nat'l City Bank*,[27] the government sought to collect taxes allegedly owed to it by a foreign corporation. Pending personal service on the foreign corporation, the government sought a preliminary injunction ordering the bank to freeze the taxpayer's accounts in its foreign branches. The Court distinguished *De Beers Consol. Mines*, and held that in the instant suit there was property which would be "the subject of the provisions of any final decree in the cause."[28] In approving the injunction, the Court stated as follows:

> The temporary injunction issued . . . seems to us to be eminently appropriate to prevent further dissipation of assets . . . If such relief were beyond the authority of the District Court, foreign taxpayers facing jeopardy assessments might either transfer assets abroad or dissipate those in foreign accounts under control of American institutions before personal service on the foreign taxpayer could be made. Such a scheme was underfoot here, the affidavits aver. Unlike *De Beers* . . . , there is here property which would be "the subject of the provisions of any final decree in the cause.". . . We conclude that this temporary injunction is "a reasonable measure to preserve the status quo. . . ."[29]

25. *Id.* at 220.
26. *Id.*
27. 379 U.S. 378 (1965).
28. *Id.* at 385.
29. *Id.*

The Court agreed that *De Beers* was inapplicable because the trial court in that case could award only injunctive relief whereas in *First Nat'l* the judgment sought was monetary relief.

In subsequent decisions, federal courts of appeals have issued conflicting holdings with respect to the propriety of the issuance of preliminary injunctive relief in order to protect a potential future damages remedy. In *Teradyne, Inc. v. Mostek Corp.*,[30] the court of appeals, relying on *Deckert v. Independence Shares Corp.*,[31] held that injunctive relief restraining the transfer of assets could be granted when the district court found that the defendant might be insolvent before a final judgment was entered. The court held that, under the circumstances presented, defendant manufacturer should be enjoined from disposing of assets sufficient to satisfy any judgment or arbitration award obtained by the supplier.[32]

However, in *In re Fredeman Litigation*,[33] the Fifth Circuit held that an injunction was inappropriate to protect a potential future damages remedy under the RICO statute involved in the case even assuming "that the defendants are scoundrels who will try to escape judgment."[34] In narrowly interpreting its inherent authority to act in this area under *De Beers*, the court of appeals found that the property of defendants which was the subject of the preliminary injunction was unrelated to the underlying claim. In analyzing the issues in the RICO actions, the Fifth Circuit determined that plaintiffs did not ultimately seek return of any particular asset or fund and that the action did not focus on any actions by defendants to secrete assets for the purpose of escaping judgment.

The court of appeals further stated that the district court's inherent power to issue preliminary injunctions under Rule 65 of the Federal Rules of Civil Procedure would not extend to orders "designed simply to aid the plaintiff in enforcing any judgment he might obtain."[35] In this connection, the court of appeals cited the additional remedy of attachment under Rule 64 of the Federal Rules of Civil Procedure as a possible protection from a defendant's schemes to avoid judgments.

30. 797 F.2d 43 (1st Cir. 1986).
31. 311 U.S. 282 (1940).
32. *Teradyne, Inc.*, 797 F.2d at 53.
33. 843 F.2d 821 (5th Cir. 1988).
34. *Id.* at 826.
35. *Id.*

In a decision presenting this issue, *Hoxworth v. Blinder, Robinson & Co.*,[36] the district court had entered a broad preliminary injunction designed to protect a potential future damages remedy in a class action alleging securities fraud and civil RICO violations. The preliminary injunction ordered defendant to repatriate some eleven million dollars transferred abroad during the course of the litigation and prohibited defendants, from, *inter alia*, transferring any funds outside the ordinary course of business and outside the country without prior approval by the district court. The district court had concluded that defendant Blinder was attempting to put his assets beyond the reach of the court and that plaintiffs were likely to suffer irreparable injury without ensuring that any potential future judgment would be satisfied.

The court of appeals rejected appellants' argument that *De Beers* should be broadly read to bar the district court's exercise of power to issue a preliminary injunction in order to protect a potential future damages remedy, even if the usual requirements for obtaining preliminary equitable relief had been met. The court of appeals noted that *De Beers* distinguished cases in which "an interlocutory injunction was granted with respect to a fund or property which could have been the subject of the provisions of any final decree in the cause,"[37] citing *Deckert v. Independence Shares Corp.*[38] The Third Circuit concluded that *De Beers*, read in light of *Deckert and First Nat'l*, established that a defendant's money might not be encumbered by a preliminary injunction when the ultimate judgment did not involve a transfer of money from defendant to plaintiffs.

The court of appeals emphasized that a preliminary injunction to protect a potential future damages remedy would not be appropriate in "a run-of-the-mill damages action" and would require close scrutiny and satisfaction of the traditional requirements for obtaining equitable relief.[39] In reviewing the scope of the district court's injunction, the court of appeals determined that there must be some reasonable attempt to relate the value of the assets encumbered to the likely value of the expected judgment. The Third Circuit concluded that the district court's

36. 903 F.2d 186 (3d Cir. 1990).
37. 325 U.S. at 220.
38. 311 U.S. 282 (1940).
39. 903 F.2d at 197.

failure to match, in some fashion, these respective values, was an abuse of discretion, requiring that the injunction be vacated.[40]

In *Grupo Mexicano de Desarrollo S.A. v. Alliance Bond Fund, Inc.,*[40.1] the Supreme Court decided the question of whether, in an action for money damages, a U.S. District Court had the power to issue a preliminary injunction preventing the defendant from transferring assets in which no lien or equitable interest is claimed. In that action plaintiff sought money damages for breach of obligations due under notes issued and guaranteed by the Mexican defendant. The District Court granted a preliminary injunction under Rule 65 of the Federal Rules of Civil Procedure restraining the defendant from transferring or encumbering other notes issued to it by the Mexican government, and the Second Circuit affirmed. In reversing the court of appeals' ruling, the Court held that the preliminary injunction in this case was beyond the District Court's equitable power and declined to create any exceptions to the general rule requiring a creditor to obtain a judgment establishing the debt before equitable remedies could be pursued.[40.2] The Court noted the extensive use of ''Mareva'' injunctions in England in similar circumstances, but left any such enlargement of the district courts' equitable powers to Congress.[40.3]

U.S. courts have also disagreed concerning their authority to order preliminary relief in aid of arbitration.[41] Recent court decisions appear more likely than their predecessors to order the attachment of property or other preliminary measures in aid of arbitration.[42]

§ 3.04 FORUM SELECTION CLAUSES

Parties to international commercial transactions may prosecute a dispute in a national court with appropriate jurisdiction or designate by agreement, either in the contract at issue or later, a particular forum for resolution of a dispute.[43] A clause which confers jurisdiction on the

---

40. *Id.* at 199.

40.1. 527 U.S. 308 (1999).

40.2. *Id.* at 326–327.

40.3. *Id.* at 330–333.

41. *See infra* § 12.04.

42. *See, e.g.*, Alvenus Shipping Co., Ltd. v. Delta Petroleum (U.S.A.) Ltd., 876 F. Supp. 482, 487 (S.D.N.Y. 1994) (ordering preliminary injunction to aid monetary recovery in London arbitration and ruling that irreparable harm for issuance of an injunction may be shown, even when the claim is for money damages, where the money judgment will go unsatisfied absent equitable relief).

43. *See generally* § 5.10[1], *infra*, (discussing forum selection clauses).

courts of a designated state but denies jurisdiction to all others is called a ''derogation'' agreement.[44] Such clauses are generally enforceable in the courts of most common law and civil law countries. Research should be done with respect to the law of the particular countries involved in the legal dispute to determine if jurisdiction is valid under the forum selection clause or whether minimum contacts with the agreed upon forum are necessary. Commentators have pointed out the convenience to the parties to the dispute of having recourse to the courts of a third country to adjudicate the controversy. This convenience has less to do with the partiality of the courts of most countries than with the likelihood that a national of a particular jurisdiction will be able to present a more convincing case than a foreigner.[45]

In European Union member states, Article 17 of the Brussels Convention[46] supersedes provisions of the member states' domestic laws as long as the jurisdiction chosen by the parties is within the territory of the European Union. Article 17–1 of the Brussels Convention provides as follows:

> If the parties, one or more of whom is domiciled in a Contracting State, have agreed that a court or the courts of a Contracting State are to have jurisdiction to settle any disputes which have arisen or which may arise in connection with a particular legislative relationship, that

(*Text continued on page 3-13*)

44. KEYES, ENCYCLOPEDIC DICTIONARY OF CONTRACT AND PROCUREMENT LAW, vol. 20 (1987).

45. Lecuyer-Thieffry & Thieffry, *supra* note 1, at 582.

46. Convention on Jurisdiction and Enforcement of Judgments in Civil and Commercial Matters at Brussels, Sept. 27, 1968, [hereinafter Brussels Convention], 8 I.L.M. 229. *See infra* Appendix 15 for the text of the Brussels Convention.

> court or those courts shall have exclusive jurisdiction. Such an agreement conferring jurisdiction shall be either in writing or evidenced in writing or, in international trade or commerce, in a form which accords with the procedures in that trade or commerce of which the parties are or ought to have been aware. Where such an agreement is concluded by the parties, none of whom is domiciled in a Contracting State, the courts of other Contracting States shall have no jurisdiction over their disputes unless the court or courts chosen have declined jurisdiction.[47]

In considering the advisability of a choice of forum provision, the U.S. party should be made aware of the marked procedural differences of litigating the case in a foreign jurisdiction under a civil law system.[48] United States parties may be reluctant to expose themselves to a system which is non-adversarial in nature and where the development of the case is not in the hands of the attorneys but largely under the control of the judge assigned to the case. Foreign parties, on the other hand, may have fears about the U.S. litigation system, particularly pretrial discovery and the considerable expenses involved.[49]

Parties should also be cognizant of the fact that United States law favors recognition of choice of forum clauses.[50] In *M/S Bremen v. Zapata Offshore Co.*,[51] the Supreme Court recognized a provision in a maritime contract that all disputes under the contract were to be adjudicated in the United Kingdom and ordered dismissal of an action brought in a federal district court in Florida. In addition, in *Scherk v. Alberto-Culver Co.*,[52] the Supreme Court gave effect to an arbitration clause by which the parties had agreed to settle their disputes by arbitration in Paris. Finally, in *Mitsubishi Motors Corp. v. Soler Chrysler-Plymouth, Inc.*,[53] the Supreme Court reemphasized the presumption in favor of the recognition of contractual choice of forum provisions.

---

47. *Id.* at Art. 17–1.
48. Section 3.02, *supra.*
49. Christine Lecuyer-Thieffry & Patrick Thieffry, *supra* note 1, at 583–85.
50. *See infra* § 5.08[1] (discussing forum selection clauses).
51. 407 U.S. 1, 10 (1972).
52. 417 U.S. 506, 519–21 (1975).
53. 473 U.S. 614, 631 (1985). *See also* Carnival Cruise Lines, Inc. v. Shute, 499 U.S. 585 (1991).

§ 3.05 PRESENCE OF PROPERTY

In determining where to sue, a logical consideration is the location of property belonging to the defendant. Section 421 of the Restatement (Third) of Foreign Relations Law sets forth international rules and guidelines for the exercise of jurisdiction to adjudicate in cases where international issues are involved.[54] Under subsection (2)(k), a state may not exercise general jurisdiction over a person on the ground that the defendant owns property in the state. However, the presence of property is sufficient to establish jurisdiction to enforce a judgment.[55]

In *Shaffer v. Heitner*,[56] the Supreme Court determined that the presence of property in a state might bear on jurisdiction by providing the necessary contacts when the claims to the property itself were the source of the underlying controversy between the parties to the suit. If the cause of action complained of was unrelated, the presence of property alone would not support the state's jurisdiction.

The holding in *Shaffer v. Heitner* is mentioned in the Restatement, which notes that judgments against nonresidents rendered on the basis of the presence of property alone would not be entitled to recognition by courts of other states. However, as the Court noted in *Shaffer*, a state in which property was located possessed jurisdiction to attach that property through its proper processes, as security for a judgment being sought in a forum where jurisdiction over the litigation was properly maintained.[57]

§ 3.06 JURISDICTION

In advising the client whether the U.S. courts provide a proper jurisdictional basis to adjudicate the dispute, the lawyer is faced with reconciling the myriad of standards and concepts developed by the Supreme Court in the past fifty-plus years since *International Shoe Co. v. Washington*.[58] Indeed, under the *International Shoe* test, it remains of fundamental importance to determine whether defendant's conduct constitutes meaningful "contacts, ties, or relations" to a jurisdiction.[59] However, the test of whether a party has "minimum contacts" for

---

54. *See infra* § 6.01 (addressing transnational jurisdictional issues).
55. *See* Restatement (Third) of Foreign Relations Law § 421, comment 1 (1987).
56. 433 U.S. 186, 211–16 (1977).
57. *Id.* at 210.
58. 326 U.S. 310 (1945).
59. *Id.* at 319.

jurisdictional purposes is subject to a number of interpretations and it has become more difficult to assess jurisdiction as a result of recent Supreme Court decisions in this area.[60]

In *World Wide Volkswagen v. Woodson*,[61] the Supreme Court defined the issue of jurisdictional contacts as whether "a corporation delivers its products into the stream of commerce with the expectation that they will be purchased by consumers in the forum state."[62] However, this standard was modified and limited in *Asahi Metal Indus. Co. v. Superior Court*.[63] In *Asahi* the issue presented was whether Asahi, a Japanese manufacturer of tire valve assemblies in Taiwan, which were incorporated into tire tubes sold in California, was amenable to suit in California for an accident caused there. The Court was faced with determining whether the awareness, on the part of Asahi, that its components would reach California in the stream of commerce constituted "minimum contacts."

The Court determined, in the context of an indemnity claim, that the Taiwanese tire maker's assertion of jurisdiction over the Japanese valve maker did not satisfy the "minimum contacts" test since there was no "action of the defendant purposefully directed toward the forum State."[64] Considering certain factors, the Court found that jurisdiction over Asahi would be unreasonable, even apart from the question of the placement of goods in the "stream of commerce."[65] The Court emphasized the severity of the burdens that would be placed on Asahi by forcing it to travel to California from Japan and by submitting the dispute to a foreign legal system. In contrast, the interests of the forum and those of the plaintiff were slight since the Taiwanese manufacturer could litigate its indemnification claim against Asahi in Taiwan or Japan. A different result might have occurred if the suit had been instituted by California residents in the United States rather than by foreign companies from two different countries.

Under the standard set forth in *Asahi* the lawyer needs to evaluate whether jurisdiction over the foreign resident would be unreasonable

---

60. *See infra* § 6.04 (discussing personal jurisdiction).
61. 444 U.S. 286 (1980).
62. *Id.* at 297–298.
63. 480 U.S. 102 (1987).
64. *Id.* at 112.
65. *Id.* at 114.

and unfair. In *Asahi*, the Supreme Court stated that the federal interest in foreign relations policies:

> will best be served by a careful inquiry into the reasonableness of the assertion of jurisdiction in the particular case, and an unwillingness to find the serious burden on an alien outweighed by the minimal interests on the part of the plaintiff or the forum State. . . .[66]

As outlined in *Asahi*, such factors as the burden on the defendant, the interests of the forum state, and the plaintiff's interest in obtaining relief should also be considered. The client should be made aware of how a U.S. court might balance the various burdens and interests involved in the dispute and the arguments to be raised by both sides in the determination of whether jurisdiction over the foreign defendant would be unreasonable and unfair. Under *Asahi*, the foreign defendant's lawyer is faced with the burden of challenging the reasonableness of the assertion of U.S. jurisdiction over the dispute. At the same time, plaintiff's lawyer is faced with the task of demonstrating conduct of the defendant sufficient to establish a "substantial connection" with the forum state.

The principle of "reasonableness" of the assertion of jurisdiction to adjudicate in an international law context is embodied in Sections 421 and 403 of the Restatement (Third) of Foreign Relations Law.[67] The Restatement points out that modern concepts of jurisdiction to adjudicate are similar to those developed under the due process clause of the Constitution. In this respect, states exercise jurisdiction to adjudicate on the basis of various links which, according to the Restatement, may be classified as "reasonable" or "exorbitant" depending on their nature. The following links are accepted as "reasonable": "the defendant's presence, conduct, or, in some cases, ownership of property within the state; conduct outside the state producing certain kinds of injury within the state; or the defendant's nationality, domicile, or residence in the state."[68]

Section 421 of the Restatement sets forth certain international rules and guidelines for the exercise of jurisdiction to adjudicate which are applicable to courts in the United States and in other states. Some of these rules may also be relevant to recognition and enforcement of foreign judgments. Section 421 provides as follows:

66. *Id.* at 115.

67. *See infra* § 5.08[2] (addressing jurisdictional rule of reason).

68. *See* Restatement (Third) of Foreign Relations Law § 421 (1987).

(1) A state may exercise jurisdiction through its courts to adjudicate with respect to a person or thing if the relationship of the state to the person or thing is such as to make the exercise of jurisdiction reasonable.

(2) In general, a state's exercise of jurisdiction to adjudicate with respect to a person or thing is reasonable if, at the time jurisdiction is asserted:

(a) the person or thing is present in the territory of the state, other than transitorily;

(b) the person, if a natural person, is domiciled in the state;

(c) the person, if a natural person, is resident in the state;

(d) the person, if a natural person, is a national of the state;

(e) the person, if a corporation or comparable juridical person, is organized pursuant to the law of the state;

(f) a ship, aircraft or other vehicle to which the adjudication relates is registered under the laws of the state;

(g) the person, whether natural or juridical, has consented to the exercise of jurisdiction;

(h) the person, whether natural or juridical, regularly carries on business in the state;

(i) the person, whether natural or juridical, had carried on activity in the state, but only in respect of such activity;

(j) the person, whether natural or juridical, had carried on outside the state an activity having a substantial, direct, and foreseeable effect within the state, but only in respect of such activity; or

(k) the thing that is the subject of adjudication is owned, possessed, or used in the state, but only in respect of a claim reasonably connected with that thing.

(3) A defense of lack of jurisdiction is generally waived by any appearance by or on behalf of a person or thing (whether as plaintiff, defendant, or third party), if the appearance is for a purpose that does not include a challenge to the exercise of jurisdiction.

These rules should be reviewed in evaluating and comparing the various jurisdictional bases for adjudicating the dispute in the courts of the United States or a foreign forum. It should be remembered, however, that these rules are in no way binding on a U.S. court and do not constitute precedent or supersede applicable case law.

§ 3.07 FOREIGN SOVEREIGN IMMUNITIES ACT

Where foreign states, agencies, or instrumentalities are named as defendants in U.S. litigation, the attorney should be familiar with the jurisdictional prerequisites of the Foreign Sovereign Immunities Act.[69] The Act provides the exclusive basis for jurisdiction over suits against foreign sovereigns in United States courts,[70] and embodies the restrictive theory of immunity, in that immunity is limited to sovereign or governmental acts and not commercial activities. Section 1605(a)(2) provides that the foreign state is not immune from the jurisdiction of courts of the United States in any case:

> . . . in which the action is based upon a commercial activity carried on in the United States by the foreign state; or upon an act performed in the United States in connection with a commercial activity of the foreign state elsewhere; or upon an act outside the territory of the United States in connection with a commercial activity of the foreign state elsewhere and that act causes a direct effect in the United States.

A commercial activity under the Act is defined in section 1603 as follows:

> (d) A "commercial activity" means either a regular course of commercial conduct or a particular commercial transaction or act. The commercial character of an activity shall be determined by reference to the nature of the course of conduct or particular transaction or act, rather than by reference to its purpose.
>
> (e) A "commercial activity" carried on in the United States by a foreign state means commercial activity carried on by such state and having substantial contact with the United States.[71]

---

69. Pub. L. No. 94–583, 90 Stat. 2891 (1976), 28 U.S.C.A. §§ 1330, 1332(a)(2), (3), and (4), 1391(f), 1441(d), 1602–1611. *See infra* Appendix 8[1] for the text of the Act and Chapter 7 (addressing Foreign Sovereign Immunities Act).

70. Argentine Republic v. Amerada Hess Shipping Corp., 488 U.S. 428, 443 (1989).

71. 28 U.S.C.A. § 1603(d), (e).

Courts have held that due process notions of minimum contacts have been incorporated into the Act.[72] This safeguard is derived from the legislative history of the Act which states that the federal long-arm provision over foreign states[73] embodies the requirements of minimum jurisdictional contacts and adequate notice.[74] Section 1330(b) provides: "[p]ersonal jurisdiction over a foreign state shall exist as to every claim for relief over which the district courts have jurisdiction under subsection (a) where service has been made under section 1608 of this title." A simple way of defining personal jurisdiction under the Act is that "subject matter jurisdiction plus service of process equals personal jurisdiction."[75] For personal jurisdiction to exist under the Act, there must be a due process scrutiny to determine proper exercise of the court's authority over a particular defendant.[76] This means that the same criteria discussed in relevant Supreme Court decisions should be evaluated in determining whether the foreign state has satisfied the traditional "minimum contacts" test.

§ 3.08 SERVICE OF PROCESS

In U.S. litigation, the plaintiff needs to be aware of the proper means of service to acquire jurisdiction under U.S. law.[77] Service also has to comport with the law of the foreign country involved in the event that subsequent enforcement of the judgment becomes necessary. A defendant needs to be advised as to whether proper service has been made and whether the court has personal jurisdiction over the action. A defendant may elect to appear and contest personal jurisdiction or risk entry of a default judgment. In the event a default judgment is entered, defendant may contest enforceability of the judgment in the foreign forum on the ground that service did not comport with foreign law requirements or that the forum state lacked personal jurisdiction over the dispute.

---

72. *See* Waukesha Engine Div. v. Banco Nacional de Fomento, 485 F. Supp. 490, 492 (E.D. Wis. 1980).

73. 28 U.S.C.A. § 1330(b).

74. H.R. Rep. No. 94–1487, 94th Cong., 2d Sess. 5 (1976), *reprinted in* 1976, U.S.C.C.A.N. 6604, 6612.

75. *See* Texas Trading & Milling Corp. v. Federal Republic of Nigeria, 647 F.2d 300, 308 (2d Cir. 1981), *cert. denied,* 454 U.S. 1148 (1982).

76. *Id.* at 308.

77. *See generally* Chapter 4, *infra,* discussing service of process.

In *Volkswagenwerk Aktiengesellschaft v. Schlunk*,[78] the Supreme Court reiterated that the terms of the Convention on Service Abroad of Judicial and Extrajudicial Documents in Civil or Commercial Matters (''Hague Service Convention'')[79] were mandatory and not optional. Even so, it was held that the Hague Service Convention did not apply where service of process was made on the agent of the parent foreign corporation under state law.[80] A problem with adhering to the exception in *Schlunk* is that there may be difficulty in enforcing the U.S. judgment in a foreign court if proper service has not been made in accordance with the laws of the foreign forum. This is particularly true in certain civil law countries which may regard service of judicial process as an exercise of judicial sovereignty.[81]

Plaintiffs in U.S. litigation often seek to avoid service pursuant to the Hague Service Convention so as not to incur the considerable translation expenses and other costs involved. Nevertheless, in the long run, it may be shortsighted to bypass the Hague Service Convention if it is foreseeable that the U.S. litigation may give rise to foreign enforcement proceedings. At a minimum, all relevant service requirements under domestic and foreign law should be considered so that an informed decision is made on the means of service at the outset of the proceeding.

If the Hague Service Convention applies, the text of the treaty, plus the declarations and reservations made by the particular country on accession to the treaty, should be reviewed in order to insure the proper methods of service are employed. These materials may be found in Martindale-Hubbell International Law Digest and in the appendix to Rule 4 of the Federal Rules of Civil Procedure.[82] The Convention allows for service of process by international registered mail and by agent. Under the Convention, the usual means of service of process are by the central authority in the receiving state by means prescribed by the state's internal law.[83] Service is accomplished by the party seeking service pursuant to a request submitted on a form USM-94, which is available at

---

78. 486 U.S. 694 (1988).

79. Hague Convention on the Service Abroad of Judicial and Extrajudicial Documents in Civil or Commercial Matters, *done* Nov. 15, 1965, 20 U.S.T. 362. A copy of the Hague Service Convention is reprinted, *infra*, as Appendix 2[1]. *See also infra* § 4.04 (addressing Hague Service Convention).

80. 486 U.S. at 707–708. *See infra* § 4.04[5] (discussing *Schlunk* and its progeny).

81. For example, Germany and Switzerland.

82. MARTINDALE-HUBBELL INTERNATIONAL LAW DIGEST, ARGENTINA-VENEZUELA & SELECTED INTERNATIONAL CONVENTIONS; FED. R. CIV. P. 4.

83. *See* Article 5 of the Hague Service Convention.

the office of any United States Marshal. Under Rule 4(c)(2)(A) of the Federal Rules of Civil Procedure, as amended, the U.S. Marshal no longer transmits form USM-94 directly to the foreign central authority. The attorney, in the capacity of an officer of the court, executes the portion of form USM-94 marked "Identity and Address of the Applicant" and the "Name and Address of the Requesting Authority" portion of the "Summary of the Document to be Served."

The Office of American Citizens Services (ACS) of the U.S. Department of State has relevant procedural and substantive information available to the public concerning service under the Hague Convention.[84] This information contains a sample "Request for Service Form" with guidelines on how to complete the form.[85] The completed form, accompanying documents, and translations should be mailed directly to the foreign central authority. The State Department circular on the Convention also includes the names and addresses of the foreign central authorities. The Department of Justice, Civil Division, Office of International Judicial Assistance, functions as the U.S. Central Authority to transmit incoming requests from the treaty countries.[86]

Article 5 of the Convention provides that the central authority serves by a method prescribed by the foreign country's internal laws. Unless the state of destination objects, Article 10 provides that the Convention shall not interfere with service by mail. Where an appropriate reservation has been made under Article 10, American courts have generally held that international mail service of civil summonses is not proper.[87] On the other hand, where the country has made no objection to the use of "postal channels" under Article 10(a), service of process by registered mail may be an appropriate method of service under the Convention.[88] Unless a particular method is requested, the document may be served by delivery to an addressee who accepts it voluntarily. This is the approach most commonly used by a substantial number of contracting states. If personal service is required, it has to be noted as the method on the "Request for Service" form.

84. The address of the Office of American Citizens Services is: U.S. Department of State, Washington, D.C. 20520. The telephone number is (202) 647–5226.

85. The State Department Circular: Hague Service Convention is reprinted *infra* in Appendix 2[2]. *See also infra* Appendix 3 (request forms).

86. Information may be obtained from the U.S. Central Authority: Office of International Judicial Assistance, Civil Division, Department of Justice, Washington, D.C. 20530. The telephone number is (202) 514–7455.

87. *See, e.g.,* Bankston v. Toyota Motor Corp., 889 F.2d 172 (8th Cir. 1989).

88. *See* Ackermann v. Levine, 788 F.2d 830, 839 (2d Cir. 1988).

Article 5 further provides that if service is made by a method prescribed by the country's internal law, the central authority may require that the documents be translated into the official language of the State addressed. No translation is required if the party accepts service voluntarily. Article 7 provides that the terms in the Request form shall be written in French or in English, or in the official language of the state in which the document originated. The corresponding blanks to be filled in by the central authority may be completed either in the language of the State addressed or in French or in English.

The Inter-American Convention and Additional Protocol[89] thereto is currently in force between the United States and the following Latin American countries: Argentina, Brazil, Chile, Columbia, Ecuador, Guatemala, Mexico, Panama, Paraguay, Peru, Uruguay, and Venezuela. The treaty provisions are similar to those contained in the Hague Service Convention. Under the Inter-American Convention, the U.S. Department of Justice, Civil Division, Office of International Judicial Assistance, functions as the central authority to transmit outgoing requests for service of process to the treaty countries, as well as to process incoming requests for service from the treaty countries. For incoming requests from treaty countries, the Office of International Judicial Assistance forwards the requests to the appropriate U.S. Marshals offices for service and processing in the same manner as those received under the Hague Service Convention. Under the Convention, use of the model forms is mandatory.[90] Information concerning the treaty and in completing the forms may be obtained from the Office of International Judicial Assistance in the Department of Justice.[91]

Absent a treaty, service should be made in accordance with domestic law requirements under federal and state rules and in a manner which conforms to the laws of the foreign country where service is to be made. The Office of American Citizens Services of the State Department

89. Inter-American Convention on Letters Rogatory, *done* Jan. 30, 1975, *entered into force for the U.S.*, Aug. 27, 1988, 14 I.L.M. 339. Additional Protocol to the Inter-American Convention on Letters Rogatory, *done* May 8, 1979, *entered into force for the U.S.*, Aug. 27, 1988, 18 I.L.M. 1238. The Inter-American Convention and Additional Protocol are reprinted, *infra*, in Appendix 5[1] and 5[2]. Forms of request for service abroad of judicial or extrajudicial documents pursuant to the Convention and Additional Protocol are reprinted, *infra*, in Appendix 6[1] and 6[2].

90. Copies of forms USM 272 and 272A are available from the U.S. Marshals Service. Forms 272 and 272A are reprinted *infra* in Appendix 3.

91. *See supra* note 86 (providing information on Office of International Judicial Assistance).

provides country-to-country assistance on the particular service methods to be employed. In many countries, service of process is a function to be performed by public and/or judicial officers. It may be an offense in many countries to employ the services of a private process server or use other means of service of process. If service by mail cannot be accomplished, it may be necessary to serve by letters of request. A letter of request is a request for judicial assistance and is addressed by the court of one state to the court of another where service is to be made. Use of letters of request would be required in countries, such as Switzerland, which do not permit service by mail and in which service of process is regarded as a sovereign act to be performed by public officials.

Depending on the particular methods prescribed by the foreign country involved, the letters of request may be sent directly by the U.S. court to the foreign court or, in situations where diplomatic service is required, routed through the Department of State.[92] Instructions for preparing letters of request and a sample form may be obtained from the Office of American Citizens Services. Finally, U.S. law provides that a U.S. court or judicial officer may receive and execute letters of request issued by a foreign court.[93]

§ 3.09 EVIDENCE

It is important to advise the client of the likely scenario and potential problems to be encountered when there is a need to obtain foreign-based evidence.[94] A checklist will be helpful in considering some of the relevant factors, such as:

(1) Where is the evidence located, and who has it?

(2) Is the evidence sought from a party or a third-party witness?

(3) If depositions are sought, is the testimony voluntary or compulsory?

(4) If the evidence is foreign based, is the country a signatory to the Hague Evidence Convention?

---

92. *See* Fed. R. Civ. P. 4 (f)(2)(A), (B); 28 U.S.C.A. § 1781(b)(2).
93. *See* 28 U.S.C.A. § 1781(b)(1).
94. *See infra* Chapter 10 (discussing obtaining evidence abroad).

The Supreme Court held, in *Societe Nationale Industrielle Aerospatiale v. United States Dist. Court,*[95] that the Hague Convention on the Taking of Evidence Abroad in Civil or Commercial Matters[96] did not provide the exclusive or mandatory procedures for obtaining documents and information located in a foreign signatory's territory. Rather, the Court concluded that the Convention was intended to establish optional procedures for obtaining evidence abroad and that it did not deprive the district court of its jurisdiction to order, under the Federal Rules of Civil Procedure, a foreign national party to produce evidence physically located within a signatory nation. Thus, the Convention is one method of seeking evidence that the court may seek to employ, and its procedures apply to the production of evidence in a litigant's possession whether or not that evidence is "abroad." While the Supreme Court cautioned that U.S. courts should protect foreign litigants from unnecessary discovery or discovery abuses, it declined to articulate special rules to guide courts in deciding when to employ Convention procedures during the discovery process.[97]

Where the U.S. court has personal jurisdiction over the foreign defendant, the party is subject to the same extensive pretrial procedures as its domestic counterpart. Because *Aerospatiale* did not adopt any fixed comity analysis in determining the use of Convention procedures, lower courts have found the case difficult to follow.[98] As a result, few U.S. courts have required litigants to forego extraterritorial discovery from foreign witnesses and resort to the Convention's procedures as a matter of first use.[99] It seems clear that the party seeking to require first use of the Convention bears the burden of demonstrating the necessity of using those procedures.[100] The Convention will be required in those situations where foreign-based evidence is sought from non-party witnesses. In addition, it will apply where the physical act of discovery

95. 482 U.S. 522 (1987).

96. Hague Evidence Convention on the Taking of Evidence Abroad in Civil or Commercial Matters, Mar. 18, 1970, 8 I.L.M. 37. A copy of the Hague Evidence Convention is reprinted, *infra,* in Appendix 14. The Convention is also reprinted in the appendices to 28 U.S.C.A. § 1782; and in MARTINDALE-HUBBELL INTERNATIONAL LAW DIGEST, ARGENTINA-VENEZUELA & SELECTED INTERNATIONAL CONVENTIONS.

97. 482 U.S. at 546.

98. *See infra* § 10.12 (addressing post-*Aerospatiale* cases); Gary B. Born & Scott Hoing, *Comity and the Lower Courts: Post-*Aerospatiale *Applications of the Hague Evidence Convention*, 24 INT'L LAW. 393 (1990).

99. *See* Born & Hoing, *supra* note 98, at 402.

100. *See* Rich v. KIS Cal., Inc., 121 F.R.D. 254, 257–258 (M.D.N.C. 1988); *In Re* Aircraft Disaster Near Roselawn, Indiana, 172 F.R.D. 295, 307–311 (N.D. Ill. 1998).

(depositions, inspection of property, etc.) is to take place on foreign soil.[101]

The Hague Evidence Convention entered into force for the United States in 1972. It is currently in force in approximately thirty-three countries including: Argentina, Australia, Barbados, China, Cyprus, Czech Republic, Denmark, Djibouti, Estonia, Finland, France, Germany, Hong Kong, Israel, Italy, Latvia, Luxembourg, Mexico, Monaco, the Netherlands, Norway, Poland, Singapore, Slovak Republic, South Africa, Spain, Sweden, Switzerland, the United Kingdom, the United States, Venezuela, and the Sovereign Base Areas of Akroteri and Dhekelia. Information on the treaty may be obtained from the Office of American Citizens Services in the U.S. State Department.[102] A circular describing the Convention and listing the names and addresses of the foreign central authorities is available to the public.[103] The circular also lists the names and telephone numbers of the appropriate geographical divisions of the Office of American Citizens Services where additional questions may be directed. Information on the Hague Evidence Convention may also be obtained from the U.S. Central Authority which is housed in the Civil Division of the Department of Justice.[104]

Each country in which the Convention is in force has made certain declarations and reservations regarding the applicability of each article of the Convention to the country.[105] The specific declarations and reservations made when the party States acceded to the Convention should be studied for the particular country where evidence is sought. Even where a witness is willing to be deposed, the country may permit the deposition only under certain limited conditions. The declarations and reservations are also important as to the procedures and restrictions on the use of consular officials and commissioners in obtaining evidence.

---

101. *See* Scotch Whiskey Ass'n v. Majestic Distilling Co., Inc., No. 88–808 (D. Md. 1988).

102. *See supra* note 84 (providing ACS contact information).

103. State Department Circular: Obtaining Evidence Abroad is reprinted *infra* at Appendix 11. *See also* MARTINDALE-HUBBELL INTERNATIONAL LAW DIGEST, ARGENTINA-VENEZUELA & SELECTED INTERNATIONAL CONVENTIONS.

104. Office of International Judicial Assistance, Civil Division, Department of Justice, Washington, D.C. 20530. The telephone number is (202) 514–7455.

105. *See infra* § 10.03 (discussing declarations and reservations of member states). *See also* MARTINDALE-HUBBELL INTERNATIONAL LAW DIGEST, ARGENTINA-VENEZUELA & SELECTED INTERNATIONAL CONVENTIONS.

Under Article 23 of the Convention, countries may limit the use of the Convention for the pretrial production of documents. Most countries party to the Convention have made specific declarations objecting to the pretrial discovery of documents. The key distinction is whether such declarations are "full" or "limited." "Full" declarations completely restrict the use of the Convention for pretrial purposes.[106] "Limited" declarations generally authorize pretrial production of documents provided they are limited in number and are reasonably related to the purposes of the trial.[107] A study of the declarations and reservations is also important in determining the translation requirements of the particular country involved.

In accordance with Convention requirements, the requesting court in the United States transmits the model letter of request and accompanying documents, in duplicate, with translations in duplicate, directly to the foreign central authority. The request should include any special procedures sought by the requesting court. This usually pertains to requests that U.S. procedures be utilized in the taking of the deposition such as obtaining verbatim transcripts or providing the opportunity for the attorney to ask supplemental questions or cross-examine the witness.

Where no treaty is involved, different considerations should be addressed. If compulsion is necessary, the traditional form for obtaining the evidence is via letters of request. The procedure is similar to the letter of request procedures under the Hague Evidence Convention, except that central authorities are not used. The letter of request is transmitted directly from the requesting court in the United States to the foreign court where the evidence is to be obtained. Letters of request are not honored as a treaty obligation but are executed on the basis of international comity or discretion on the part of the foreign judicial authorities involved. They are admissible as evidence in U.S. district court proceedings under the Federal Rules of Civil Procedure and may not be excluded merely because they depart from requirements for depositions taken within the United States under federal requirements.[108]

---

106. For example, Denmark's Article 23 reservation provides that letters of request issued for the purpose of obtaining pretrial discovery of documents may not be executed in that country.

107. For example, the reservation of the United Mexican States provides, *inter alia,* that it will process letters of request for the production of documents in which the direct relationship between the evidence sought and the pending proceeding is identified.

108. FED. R. CIV. P. 28(b).

If the witness is willing to testify voluntarily, the best procedure is to take an "American" style deposition before the U.S. consul in the foreign country.[109] The relevant procedure may vary, since some countries view the taking of even voluntary testimony as an infringement of their territorial sovereignty.[110] Information concerning the requirements of particular countries where no treaty arrangements exist may be obtained from the Office of American Citizens Services of the U.S. Department of State. In addition, a description of the role of U.S. officials in taking depositions on notice abroad and the procedures involved may be found in applicable State Department regulations.[111]

§ 3.10 FOREIGN ATTITUDES TOWARD U.S. PRETRIAL DISCOVERY PROCEDURES

It may be helpful to educate the foreign party to U.S. litigation about U.S. pretrial discovery procedures. Foreign parties have a legitimate apprehension about U.S. discovery practices, since pretrial practice is virtually unknown in civil law countries. It should be explained that the common law system is adversarial in nature and, consequently, it is the parties, and not the court, who are responsible for obtaining the evidence prior to trial. The purpose of pretrial discovery is to elicit as many facts as possible from the other side to avoid surprise at the trial. In this connection, the fundamental maxim of discovery is that "(m)utual knowledge of all the relevant facts gathered by both parties is essential to proper litigation."[112]

In the usual case, the court may not become involved in the pretrial process, unless there is a special problem or objection to the discovery request. However, where it is necessary to obtain evidence abroad, the district court should supervise pretrial proceedings closely to prevent discovery abuses.[113] In particular, the requirements of Rule 34 of the Federal Rules of Civil Procedure pertaining to the production of documents should be explained to the foreign party. Civil law countries are sensitive to wholesale discovery requests in this area, which are commonly referred to as "fishing expeditions." For example, the Federal Republic of Germany has declared, pursuant to Article 23 of the

109. 22 C.F.R. § 92.49–65. For text of regulations, *see infra* Appendix 12.
110. *See* 22 C.F.R. § 92.4(a).
111. 22 C.F.R. § 92.49–66. For text of regulations, *see infra* Appendix 12.
112. Hickman v. Taylor, 329 U.S. 495, 507 (1947).
113. *See Aerospatiale,* 482 U.S. at 546.

Hague Evidence Convention, that it will not "in its territory, execute Letters of Request for the purpose of obtaining pretrial discovery of documents as known in Common Law Countries."

It should be pointed out that the requested party has the opportunity pursuant to Rule 34(b), to object to the turning over of all or part of the request. Further, Rule 26(c) provides that upon motion and accompanying certification from a party from whom discovery is sought, the court may order that the discovery not be had or conducted only on specified terms and conditions. The motion may be based on a number of grounds, including undue burden or expense. It is possible under Rule 26(c) that the court may order that the documents be sealed to prevent disclosure of trade secrets or other confidential information.

Rule 26 may greatly assist parties to international litigation by, in the words of the Advisory Committee's Notes, "impos[ing] on parties a duty to disclose, without awaiting formal discovery requests, certain basic information that is needed in most cases to prepare for trial . . . ."[114] Unless otherwise stipulated or directed by court order or local rule, parties are required to provide:

> (A) the name, and if known, the address and telephone number of each individual likely to have discoverable information relevant to disputed facts alleged with particularity in the pleadings, identifying the subjects of the information;
>
> (B) a copy of, or a description by category and location of, all documents, data compilations, and tangible things in the possession, custody, or control of the party that are relevant to disputed facts alleged with particularity in the pleadings;
>
> (C) a computation of any category of damages claimed by the disclosing party, making available for inspection and copying as under Rule 34 the documents or other evidentiary material, not privileged or protected from disclosure, on which such computation is based, including materials bearing on the nature and extent of injuries suffered; and
>
> (D) for inspection and copying as under Rule 34 any insurance agreement under which any person carrying on an insurance business may be liable. . . .[115]

---

114. Fed. R. Civ. P. 26(a)(1).
115. *Id.*

The disclosures required under Rule 26(a)(1) must be made at or within 10 days after the meeting of the parties required under Rule 26(f).[116] Rule 26(f) provides a mechanism which, if utilized, may prove particularly well-suited to facilitating the needs of parties in international litigation and protecting foreign litigants from special problems or burdensome discovery requests. Rule 26(f) provides, unless exempted by local rule or court order, for the mandatory meeting "as soon as practicable and in any event at least 14 days before a scheduling conference" of all parties to an action.[117] It should be noted, however, that foreign parties may be exempt under local rules or by court order from the requirements of Rule 26(f). Parties subject to Rule 26(f) are required to discuss the "nature and basis of their claims and defenses and the possibilities for a prompt settlement or resolution of the case."[118] The parties are also required to formulate a proposed discovery plan which "shall indicate the parties' views and proposals concerning" the following:

> (1) what changes should be made in the timing, form, or requirement for disclosures under subdivision (a) or local rule, including a statement as to when disclosures under subdivision (a)(1) were made or will be made;
>
> (2) the subjects on which discovery may be needed, when discovery should be completed, and whether discovery should be conducted in phases or be limited to or focused upon particular issues;
>
> (3) what changes should be made in the limitations on discovery imposed under these rules or by local rule, and what other limitations should be imposed; and
>
> (4) any other orders that should be entered by the court. . . .[119]

In addition, all parties are jointly responsible for presenting a written report outlining the discovery plan to the court within 10 days of their meeting.[120] The Advisory Committee's Notes indicate that "their report will assist the court in seeing that the timing and scope of disclosures under revised Rule 26(a) and the limitations on the extent of discovery under these rules and local rules are tailored to the circumstances of the

116. *Id.*
117. Fed. R. Civ. P. 26(f).
118. *Id.*
119. *Id.*
120. *Id.*

particular case.''[121] If, however, parties fail to meet, courts are authorized to impose sanctions under Rule 37(g).[122]

Foreign parties should be aware of other rules to deal with the problem of excessive discovery. Rule 26(g)(2) imposes a certification requirement on the attorney making discovery requests. The signature of the attorney or party constitutes a certification that the signer has read the request, and based on his knowledge and belief after a reasonable inquiry, it is not interposed for any improper purpose, such as to harass or to cause unnecessary delay or needless increase in the cost of litigation, and not unreasonable or unduly burdensome or expensive. An explanation of the pretrial process and the safeguards against abusive discovery may alleviate some of the concerns about U.S. practice and procedure.

§ 3.11 ENFORCEMENT OF JUDGMENTS

An attorney needs to advise clients of the many pitfalls and problems which exist in the area of recognition and enforcement of foreign judgments.[123] First, there are no agreed upon principles governing recognition and enforcement and, in the absence of a treaty, courts generally are guided by notions of comity and fairness that may vary from country to country. In this connection, foreign courts may ask for assurances that a comparable judgment rendered by that court would be enforced in the United States and, in the absence of a showing of reciprocity, the foreign court may refuse to enforce or recognize the U.S. judgment.[124] Furthermore, in contrast to European countries, the United States is not a member of any bilateral or multilateral convention providing for the enforcement in one signatory country, under simplified terms and conditions, of judgments entered in another signatory country. It should be noted, however, that the United States, through the sponsorship of the Hague Conference on Private International Law, is currently participating in negotiations for a proposed multilateral convention on jurisdiction and enforcement of judgments.[125]

Commentators have noted the apparent unwillingness of our trading partners to enter into treaty arrangements with the United States which is

---

121. *Id.*, Advisory Committee's Notes.

122. *Id.*

123. *See infra* Chapter 11 (adressing enforcement of foreign judgments).

124. *See* Nelson, *supra* note 10, at 190.

125. *See infra* § 11.01.

due largely to the comparably high damage awards entered by U.S. courts.[126] Damages obtainable in U.S. courts may be disproportionately higher than those awarded by foreign courts, especially in negligence and products liability cases, since civil law countries do not recognize the concept of punitive damages or special remedies such as treble-damages provisions. It is likely that foreign courts would decline to recognize such judgments on the basis of conflict with their public policy, and the absence of a similar law or remedy in the foreign jurisdiction.

The lawyer needs to consider problems associated with recognition and enforcement of the judgment in selecting the best forum to litigate the dispute. There may be advantages in choosing a forum country that is a member of an international treaty providing for the recognition and enforcement of judgments rendered in a signatory state. For example, the 1968 Brussels Convention on Jurisdiction and the Enforcement of Judgments in Civil and Commercial Matters (''Brussels Convention'')[127] which is in effect in the European Union, provides for uniform procedures and limited review by the court in which enforcement of the judgment is sought. Where jurisdiction over the dispute could be obtained in a member state to the Brussels Convention, there would be minimal risk in seeking enforcement in another signatory state, in which the debtor has assets.[128]

Some of the principal defenses to enforcement of a foreign judgment are lack of jurisdiction of the foreign tribunal and denial of procedural due process. For this reason, service of process should be made in a manner which comports with applicable treaties, such as the Hague Service Convention and Inter-American Convention on Letters Rogatory, as well as notions of foreign judicial sovereignty.[129] In *Volkswagenwerk Aktiengesellschaft v. Schlunk,*[130] which involved the exclusivity of the Hague Service Convention, the Supreme Court stressed that compliance with valid methods of service under foreign law, even where not mandatory under U.S. law, would facilitate the subsequent enforcement of a judgment in that country. If enforcement of a judgment in a foreign country is likely, it may be advisable to consult with local

126. *See* Christine Lecuyer-Thieffry & Patrick Thieffry, *supra* note 1, at 587.

127. EC 46 (1978), 21 O.J. Eur. Com. (L. 304) 77. The text of the Brussels Convention is found *infra* in Appendix 15.

128. *See* Christine Lecuyer-Thieffry & Patrick Thieffry, *supra* note 1, at 587.

129. *See* discussion, *supra* § 3.08, on service of process.

130. 486 U.S. 694 (1988).

counsel in the foreign country to ascertain the best method of service. Despite the extra time and expense involved, the client should be advised of the practical importance of strict compliance with foreign law service requirements.

A fundamental consideration is whether the defendant should appear and defend the action or challenge the enforceability of the default judgment in the foreign jurisdiction. The United States treats default judgments and contested judgments similarly for enforcement purposes. On the other hand, some countries, such as Great Britain, enforce default judgments only in limited circumstances.[131] The advice of foreign counsel may be helpful in determining the differences between the enforceability of contested versus default judgments. An appearance in the foreign forum may constitute submission to the jurisdiction of the court and preclude that issue from being raised in the U.S. proceeding.[132] However, a defense to recognition and enforcement of the foreign judgment may exist if the jurisdiction of the foreign forum fails to satisfy recognized standards of due process.[133]

§ 3.12 ENFORCEMENT OF ARBITRAL AWARDS

The enforceability of arbitral awards has been greatly facilitated by the United Nations Convention on the Recognition and Enforcement of Foreign Arbitral Awards ("New York Convention"),[134] which has over 100 signatories including the United States.[135] This Convention is used both to compel arbitration and to enforce an award once it has been obtained. As a result of the Convention and implementing legislation,[136] arbitral awards are enforceable in the United States as a matter of federal law and treaty obligation. Furthermore, the Convention provides that each party must enforce arbitral awards made in the territory of another party, except under limited circumstances such as where the arbitration

---

131. *See* RESTATEMENT (THIRD) OF FOREIGN RELATIONS LAW § 481, comment 6, illus. (a) (1987).

132. *See, e.g.*, Somportex Ltd. v. Philadelphia Chewing Gum Corp., 453 F.2d 435 (3d Cir. 1971), *cert. denied*, 405 U.S. 1017 (1972).

133. *See, e.g.*, Koster v. Automark Indus., Inc., 640 F.2d 77 (7th Cir. 1981).

134. New York Convention, *supra* note 5. *See also* Chapter 12, *infra*, addressing "Use of the Courts in Support of International Arbitration."

135. *See supra* note 8 (listing signatories).

136. 9 U.S.C. § § 201–208.

agreement is invalid under the subject law, or where the losing party was not given adequate notice of the proceeding.[137]

Under article V of the New York Convention, the burden of proof is placed on the party objecting to the enforcement of the award to prove the invalidity of the award. In addition, as contrasted to the variances in the enforceability of foreign default judgments, an arbitral award rendered under the New York Convention must be recognized and enforced even after default. Commentators have also noted that it is less likely that arbitrators, in contrast to national courts, will entertain defenses based on considerations of public policy which are extrinsic to the agreement of the parties that they must enforce.[138] Finally, in conformity with the objectives of the New York Convention, the general immunity of foreign states from suits in the United States has been removed with respect to actions to enforce an arbitral agreement against a foreign state or to confirm an award made pursuant to such an agreement to arbitrate.[139]

137. *Id.* at § 201, art. V.

138. *See* Nelson, *supra* note 10, at 195.

139. 28 U.S.C.A. § 1605(a)(6). *See infra* § 7.10 (discussing arbitral award exception to foreign sovereign immunity); *and* § 8.12 (addressing arbitration exception to act of state doctrine).

Chapter 4

SERVICE OF PROCESS

§ 4.01 INTRODUCTION: LOOKING FOR ASSISTANCE

International judicial assistance refers to cooperation between countries in the areas of service of process and evidence gathering procedures. To be effective, service must comply with the law of the forum.[1] Therefore, the practitioner must be familiar with relevant federal and state provisions relating to service involving the jurisdiction where the action is pending. As with evidence gathering procedures, the party requesting service should be aware of notions of foreign judicial sovereignty if service is to take place abroad. For example, certain civil law countries such as Germany and Switzerland consider service of process on their territory to be an official function and improper service may violate foreign laws in this area.[2] The party requesting service may have various options of serving the defendant in its home country or abroad. In determining the method of service, an important factor for the plaintiff to consider is whether the judgment will only be enforced in the domestic forum or whether subsequent recognition and enforcement abroad will eventually be sought.

Multinational agreements, such as the Hague Service Convention[3] and the Inter-American Convention on Letters Rogatory[4] and Additional Protocol[5] thereto prescribe methods of service abroad of judicial documents in civil and commercial cases. The attorney seeking service in a foreign country should determine whether the country involved is a member of one of these treaties (*see* Treaties Chart *infra*) and should follow the designated procedures and terms and conditions agreed to by that country. Compliance with such procedures are material considerations in acquiring valid jurisdiction over the foreign defendant and in enforcing any subsequent judgment abroad.

---

1. *In re* Hunt's Pier Assocs., 156 Bankr. 464 (E.D. Pa. 1993); Low v. Bayerische Moteren Werke, A.G., 88 A.D.2d 504, 449 N.Y.S.2d 733 (1982).

2. *See* Vorhees v. Fischer & Krecke, 697 F.2d 574 (4th Cir. 1983) (noting German objection to service by mail); Umbenhauer v. Woog, 969 F.2d 25, 27 (3d Cir. 1992) (noting Swiss objection to service by mail).

3. Hague Convention on the Service Abroad of Judicial and Extrajudicial Documents in Civil or Commercial Matters, *done* Nov. 15, 1965, 20 U.S.T. 362 [hereinafter Hague Service Convention]. *See infra*, § 4.04 and Appendix 2[1].

4. Inter-American Convention on Letters Rogatory, *done* Jan. 30, 1975, *entered into force for the U.S.* Aug. 27, 1988, S. Treaty Doc. 98–27, 98th Cong., 2d Sess. (1984). *See infra* § 4.05 and Appendix 5[1].

5. Additional Protocol to the Inter-American Convention on Letters Rogatory, *done* May 8, 1979, *entered into force for the U.S.*, Aug. 27, 1988, S. Treaty Doc. 98–27, 98th Cong., 2d Sess. (1984). *See infra* § 4.05 and Appendix 5.

§ 4.02 U.S. STATE DEPARTMENT ASSISTANCE

Unlike evidence-gathering issues,[6] service of process abroad involving United States litigation is not a function of United States diplomatic or consular missions. Under existing regulations, consular officials are specifically prohibited from serving legal process and from appointing others to do so except when expressly authorized by the Department of State.[7] Usually, the consular officer becomes involved only in service by an agent (usually a local attorney or an attorney's agent) in which the agent may execute an affidavit of service before the consular officer and in service pursuant to a letter rogatory.

There are various governmental sources for information on service of process in foreign countries. Whether or not service is made pursuant to local procedure or treaty, the litigant will need to know the laws and procedures of the foreign country involved. For example, certain countries have informed the State Department that some methods of service constitute violations of their judicial sovereignty. In this connection, in Germany, service pursuant to the Hague Service Convention through the central authority is the sole method of service and service through postal channels should not be attempted. In ascertaining foreign laws on this subject, the practitioner may consult with the Bureau of Consular Affairs of the Department of State;[8] the Office of International Judicial Assistance which is a part of the Civil Division of the Department of Justice;[9] or, perhaps, the foreign embassy or consulate of the country involved.[10] There are also various compilations which deal with service of process and evidence gathering, and contain a country-to-country breakdown as to acceptable methods of service and particular service treaties in which the country participates.[11]

---

6. *See infra* Chapter 10, discussing obtaining evidence in foreign jurisdictions.

7. 22 C.F.R. § 92.85.

8. *See infra* note 14, providing address and phone number of the Bureau of Consular Affairs. Also, consult the State Department's Consular Home Page (http://travel.state.gov/). The Autofax number is (202) 647–3000. *See* Appendix 21, *infra.*

9. Information may be obtained from the U.S. Central Authority: Office of International Judicial Assistance, Civil Division, Department of Justice, Washington, D.C. 20530. The telephone number is (202) 514–7455.

10. Information, including the addresses and phone numbers of foreign central authorities under the Hague Service Convention is provided in State Department Circular: Hague Service Convention, *infra* Appendix 2[2]; FED. R. CIV. P. 4; MARTINDALE-HUBBELL INTERNATIONAL LAW DIGEST, ARGENTINA-VENEZUELA & SELECTED INTERNATIONAL CONVENTIONS.

11. *See infra* Treaties Chart. *See generally* Hague Conference on Private International Law, Practical Handbook on the Operation of the Hague Convention of 15 Nov. 1965 on the Service Abroad of Judicial and Extrajudicial Documents in Civil or Commercial Matters

The Bureau of Consular Affairs also has prepared circulars which contain helpful advice when service abroad is contemplated.[12] There are, in addition, American-based companies which, for a fee, will serve foreign process world-wide.[13]

28 U.S.C. § 1781(b)(2) authorizes "the transmittal of a letter rogatory or request directly from a tribunal in the United States to the foreign or international tribunal, officer, or agency to whom it is addressed and its return in the same manner." The Bureau of Consular Affairs[14] should be consulted on the various procedures for transmitting letters rogatory or letters of request and the various countries which require that these procedures be followed for valid service.

28 U.S.C. § 1608(a) sets forth relevant service provisions under the Foreign Sovereign Immunities Act.[15] This section provides that if service on a foreign state cannot be effected by other methods provided in this section, the Department of State can assist. The summons and complaint, together with a translation, are transmitted by the clerk of the court to the Director of Special Consular Services of the State Department.[16] The Secretary of State transmits the papers through diplomatic channels to the foreign state and sends to the clerk of the court a certified copy of the diplomatic note indicating when the papers were transmitted.[17]

§ 4.03 DETERMINING THE METHOD OF SERVICE: GENERAL PROVISIONS

Rule 4 of the Federal Rules of Civil Procedure has important consequences for the establishment of jurisdiction over foreign parties to litigation in U.S. courts. To ascertain the proper method of service, the

(1983); 1 BRUNO RISTAU, INTERNATIONAL JUDICIAL ASSISTANCE: CIVIL AND COMMERCIAL (1990).

12. A copy of the State Department Circular on the Hague Service Convention is reprinted *infra* in Appendix 2[2]. These documents may be obtained from the State Department's Web Site (http://travel.state.gov/) or through the automated fax system ((202)647–3000).

13. *See, e.g.*, Attorney's Process Service Int'l, Minneapolis, MN.

14. The address of the Bureau of Consular Affairs in the U.S. Department of State is 2120 C Street, N.W., Washington, D.C. 20520. The telephone number is (202) 647–5226.

15. 28 U.S.C.A. § 1608. For text of the F.S.I.A., *see infra* Appendix 8[1]. *See infra* Appendix 8[2] for Notice of Suit Under the Foreign Sovereign Immunities Act, 22 C.F.R. § 93.2.

16. 28 U.S.C.A. § 1608(a)(4).

17. *Id.*

jurisdictional basis of the proposed action should first be determined. Rule 4(k)(2) authorizes the exercise of territorial jurisdiction over the person of any defendant against whom a claim is made arising under any federal law if that person is subject to personal jurisdiction in no state.[18] This rule will facilitate the use of federal long-arm jurisdiction against defendants who cannot be served under any state law but who can be constitutionally subjected to the jurisdiction of the federal court. Rule 4(k)(1)(D) provides for service ''when authorized by a statute of the United States.''[19] The purpose of this provision is to reference federal legislation that may provide for nationwide or even world-wide service of process in cases arising under particular federal laws. The Federal Rules of Civil Procedure, however, no longer require that the method of extraterritorial service be specifically authorized by state or federal law.[20] The advisory committee's notes state that considering the number of lawsuits in federal courts involving international transactions and events, ''it is appropriate to infer a general legislative authority to effect service on defendants in a foreign country.''[21] In federal question cases, federal standards govern amenability to personal jurisdiction.[22] When a federal question case is based upon a federal statute and that statute is silent as to service of process, territorial jurisdiction over a party may be asserted even if the party is not subject to state standards of jurisdiction.[23]

Rule 4(f) provides methods of serving process in a foreign country. Rule 4(f) states:

> Unless otherwise provided by federal law, service upon an individual from whom a waiver has not been obtained and filed . . . may be effected in a place not within any judicial district of the United States:
>
> (1) by any internationally agreed means reasonably calculated to give notice, such as those means authorized by the Hague Convention on the Service Abroad of Judicial and Extrajudicial Documents; or

18. FED. R. CIV. P. 4(k)(2).

19. FED. R. CIV. P. 4(k)(1)(D). *See* Securities and Exchange Commission v. Carrillo, 115 F.3d 1540 (11th Cir. 1997); United States v. Swiss American Bank Ltd., 191 F.3d 30 (1st Cir. 1999).

20. FED. R. CIV. P. 4(f) ''Service Upon Individuals in a Foreign Country.''

21. FED. R. CIV. P. 4(f) Advisory Committee's Note.

22. United Rope Distribs., Inc. v. Seatriumph Marine Corp., 930 F.2d 532, 534 (7th Cir. 1992).

23. FED. R. CIV. P. 4(f), 4(k)(2). *See also* Fed. R. Civ. P. 4(f), (K) Advisory Committee's Notes.

(2) if there is no internationally agreed means of service or the applicable international agreement allows other means of service, provided that service is reasonably calculated to give notice:

(A) in the manner prescribed by the law of the foreign country for service in that country . . . ; or

(B) as directed by the foreign authority in response to a letter rogatory or letter of request; or

(C) unless prohibited by the law of the foreign country, by

(i) delivery to the individual personally of a copy of the summons and the complaint; or

(ii) any form of mail requiring a signed receipt, to be addressed and dispatched by the clerk of the court to the party to be served; or

(3) by other means not prohibited by international agreement or as may be directed by the court.[24]

Rule 4(f) specifically provides for service effected pursuant to treaty means, such as under the Hague Service Convention or the Inter-American Convention on Letters Rogatory.[25] The methods of service available under treaty agreements are to be employed if available and if the treaty so requires.[26] If no treaty provisions are applicable, Rule 4 provides for alternative means of service "reasonably calculated to give notice."[27] Rule 4 does not, however, require specific authorization by a state or federal statute for the method of service of process abroad.[28]

It is important that the plaintiff research the country's service laws in advance and select from the alternatives listed in Rule 4(f) the method that best satisfies foreign service requirements. Clause (A) of Rule 4(f)(2) provides that service may be made "in the manner prescribed by the law of the foreign country for service in that country."[29] Where permissible, service by process server may be an effective means since it provides adequate proof of service.[30] Clause B allows for a method which can be accomplished only upon request to the foreign court, i.e.,

24. Fed. R. Civ. P. 4.
25. Fed. R. Civ. P. 4(f)(1).
26. Fed. R. Civ. P. 4(f)(1); *see also* Fed. R. Civ. P. 4(f) Advisory Committee's Note.
27. Fed. R. Civ. P. 4(f)(2).
28. Fed. R. Civ. P. 4(f); *see also* Fed. R. Civ. P. 4(f) Advisory Committee's Note.
29. Fed. R. Civ. P. 4(f)(2)(A).
30. *See* Curtis v. Nid Pty., 248 F. Supp. 2d 836 (S.D. La. 2003).

"in response to a letter of request," which in turn directs the service to be made.[31] This is the customary method of service in many countries.[32] Under this method, the plaintiff applies to the U.S. federal court and the court requests assistance from the appropriate foreign tribunal. Clause C permits personal delivery to an individual defendant.[33] Rule 4 also allows for service by any form of mail which requires a signed receipt and is transmitted by the clerk of court to the party to be served.[34] However, in attempting service under clause C(ii), it should first be considered whether there is any reasonable probability of getting the receipt back signed for proof of service. Counsel should always inquire in advance of service of process which procedures are recognized in the foreign country. Service methods such as personal delivery or service by mail should not be considered if they are offensive to the foreign country involved.[35]

Additionally, Rule 4(f)(3) contains a catch-all provision that enables courts to devise, upon appropriate motion, a method of service not prohibited by international agreement which is responsive to the unique facts of the case.[36] In one case, where service on the Iranian government was thwarted, the court authorized substituted service by telex which insured that defendants would receive actual notice of the suits and the claims of the plaintiffs.[37] In another case, the court ordered that service be made to defendants in Saudi Arabia by regular and certified mail with a copy of the court's Memorandum and Order accompanying each mailing.[38]

In a case of first impression,[39] the 9th Circuit upheld the sufficiency of the service of process, effected via email and regular mail pursuant to

---

31. Fed. R. Civ. P. 4(f)(2)(B).

32. *See infra* § 10.09, discussing obtaining evidence by letters of request.

33. Fed. R. Civ. P. 4(f)(2)(C)(i).

34. Fed. R. Civ. P. 4(f)(2)(C)(ii). *See* Dee-K Enterprises Inc. v. Heveafil Sdn. Bhd., 174 F.R.D. 376 (E.D. Va. 1997) (service by DHL courier sufficient under laws of Indonesia and Malaysia).

35. Fed. R. Civ. P. 4(f) Advisory Committee's Note ("[s]ervice by methods that would violate foreign law is not generally authorized"); *see In re* Ski Train Fire in Kaprun, Austria, 2003 U.S. Dist. LEXIS 11961 (S.D.N.Y.).

36. Fed. R. Civ. P. 4(f)(3). *See In re* Ski Train Fire in Kaprun, Austria, 2003 U.S. Dist. LEXIS 11961 (S.D.N.Y.).

37. New England Merchants Nat'l Bank v. Iran Power Generation & Transmission Co., 508 F. Supp. 49 (S.D.N.Y. 1980).

38. Tinicum Properties v. Garnett, No. 92–C0860, 1992 WL 99590 (E.D. Pa. Apr. 29, 1992).

39. Rio Properties, Inc. v. Rio Int'l Interlink, 284 F.3d 1007 (9th Cir. 2002).

Rule 4(f)(3). The court of appeals determined, under the facts presented, that email service was reasonable since defendant, a foreign Internet business entity, had structured its business so that it could be contacted only via its email address, and on its website and print media, had designated its email address as its preferred contact information.

Rule 4(m) of the Federal Rules of Civil Procedure requires dismissal without prejudice if service is not made within 120 days after the filing of the complaint.[40] However, the rule expressly states that it "does not apply to service in a foreign country pursuant to subdivision (f) or (j)(1)."[41]

The amendments to Rule 4(d) include "waiver of service" provisions which affect the service of process abroad. Rule 4(d) suggests that to "avoid costs, the plaintiff may notify [the] defendant of the commencement of the action and request that the defendant waive service of a summons."[42] While Rule 4(d) creates a duty on the part of domestic persons or organizations subject to service of process to avoid unnecessary costs by waiving service of process, a foreign defendant need not show good cause for its failure to waive service.[43] This contrasts with suits among domestic parties, where a plaintiff may notify the defendant of the commencement of the action and request that the defendant waive formal service of summons.[44] The advisory committee's note to Rule 4(d), however, suggests that the waiver provision may be advantageous to foreign defendants who, by waiving service, may reduce the costs that may be taxed against it in an unsuccessful lawsuit.[45] It remains to be seen whether the waiver provision will conflict with current methods of transnational service, such as those under the Hague Service Convention, discussed in this chapter. Certain foreign governments may view this type of service as offensive to their notions of judicial sovereignty and there may be difficulties in these

---

40. Fed. R. Civ. P. 4(m).

41. *Id.;* Pennsylvania Orthopedic Ass'n v. Mercedes-Benz A.G., 160 F.R.D. 58 (E.D. Pa. 1995); Standard Commercial Tobacco Co. Inc. v. Mediterranean Shipping Co. S.A., 1995 WL 753901 (S.D.N.Y. Dec. 19, 1995); Kim v. Frank Mohn A/S, 909 F. Supp. 474 (S.D. Tex. 1995); Riendeau v. St. Lawrence & Atlantic Railroad Co., 167 F.R.D. 26 (D. Vt. 1996); Turpin v. Mori Seiki Co., Ltd., 56 F. Supp. 121, 128-129 (D. Mass. 1999).

42. Fed. R. Civ. P. 4(d)(2). Rule 4(d)(2)(A)–(G) sets forth in detail the procedure and methods to be followed in transmitting the notice and waiver request.

43. Fed. R. Civ. P. 4(d)(2) Advisory Committee's Note.

44. *Id.*

45. *Id.*

countries in enforcing U.S. judgments based on service under waiver provisions.[45.1]

Rule 4(d)(2)(B) allows the notice of commencement and request for waiver of service to be dispatched either by first-class mail or "other reliable means."[46] The advisory committee's note interprets "other reliable means" to include private messenger services or electronic communications, such as facsimile transmissions.[47] The advisory committee's note observes that in some countries, facsimile transmission may be the most economical and efficient means of communication. A plaintiff should maintain records of electronic transmissions to ensure proof of transmission if receipt is denied.[48]

§ 4.04 SERVICE UNDER THE HAGUE SERVICE CONVENTION

The Hague Service Convention[49] is a multinational agreement that prescribes methods of service abroad of judicial documents in civil or commercial cases.[50] The Convention, which was ratified by the United States in 1969, is in force between the United States[51] and the following countries: Anguilla, Antigua and Barbuda, Argentina, Aruba, Bahamas, Barbados, Belarus, Belgium, Belize, Bermuda, Botswana, British Virgin Islands, Bulgaria, Canada, Cayman Islands, China, Cyprus, Czech Republic, Denmark, Djibouti, Egypt, Estonia, Falkland Islands, Fiji, Finland, France, French Polynesia, Germany, Gibraltar, Greece, Guernsey, Hong Kong, Ireland, Isle of Man, Israel, Italy, Japan, Jersey,

---

45.1 See discussion of objections made by the British government to the waiver system to Rule 4(d), as originally proposed, including the assessment of costs to non-waiving defendants noted in Brockmeyer v. May, 2004 WL 1936395 (9th Cir. 2004).

46. FED. R. CIV. P. 4(d)(2)(B).

47. FED. R. CIV. P. 4(d)(2)(B) Advisory Committee's Note. However, service by electronic transmission (e-mail) is not presently recognized as a valid method of service under Rule 4. *See* WAWA, Inc. v. Christensen, 1999 U.S. Dist. LEXIS 11510, 1999 WL 557936 (E.D. Pa. July 27, 1999).

48. *Id.*

49. The Convention is reprinted *infra* Appendix 2[1], as an annotation to FED. R. CIV. P. 4, and in MARTINDALE-HUBBELL INTERNATIONAL LAW DIGEST, ARGENTINA-VENEZUELA & SELECTED INTERNATIONAL CONVENTIONS.

50. *See generally* State Department Circular: Hague Service Convention, reprinted *infra* Appendix 2[2]; Hague Conference on Private International Law, Practical Handbook on the Operation of the Hague Convention of 15 Nov. 1965 on the Service Abroad of Judicial and Extra-judicial Documents in Civil or Commercial Matters (1983); 1 BRUNO RISTAU, INTERNATIONAL JUDICIAL ASSISTANCE CIVIL AND COMMERCIAL (1990).

51. The United States extended the Convention to the District of Columbia, Guam, Puerto Rico, and the Virgin Islands, FED. R. CIV. P. 4, "Annex to the Convention."

Kiribati, Korea, Latvia, Mexico, Montserrat, Pakistan, Pitcairn, Poland, Portugal, St. Christopher, St. Lucia, St. Vincent & the Grenadines, Seychelles, Slovak Republic, Solomon Islands, Spain, Sri Lanka, St. Helena, Sweden, Switzerland, Turkey, Turks and Caico Islands, Tuvalu, Ukraine, the United Kingdom, including various possessions, and Venezuela.[52]

The Convention seeks ''to create appropriate means to ensure that judicial and extrajudicial documents to be served abroad shall be brought to the notice of the addressee in sufficient time'' and, ''to improve the organization of mutual judicial assistance.''[53] The treaty provides a simple, effective, and inexpensive mechanism for the service of legal documents which the signatories to the treaty have agreed to honor.[54] Before proceeding with service in a foreign country, the attorney should determine whether the country involved is a member of the Service Convention. The reservations and declarations of the country where service is to be made should be reviewed in order to determine the terms and conditions agreed on by that country.[55]

[1] Applicability, Form, and Execution

Article 1 provides that the Convention ''shall apply in all cases, in civil or commercial matters, where there is occasion to transmit a judicial or extrajudicial document for service abroad.''[56] In order for the Convention to apply, the address of the person to be served must be known.[57] Pursuant to Article 2, each member state designates a central

52. TREATIES IN FORCE, U.S. DEPARTMENT OF STATE 351 (1993).

53. Hague Service Convention, *supra* note 3, preamble.

54. In fiscal year 1999, the United States Central Authority processed 6,142 incoming requests for service in this country. Statistics are not available as to the number of American requests transmitted abroad because the United States Central Authority functions only with respect to incoming requests. However, it is believed that outgoing requests are also sizeable in number. The cost of service in the U.S. under the Convention for parties of non-member states is $15.00 and an international money order for this amount payable to ''Treasurer of the United States'' must accompany each service request. FED. R. CIV. P. 4, at 16, ''Annex to the Convention,'' para. 5. Effective June 1, 2003, the U.S. Department of Justice delegated the service of process function under the Hague Service Convention to a private contractor, Process Forwarding International of Seattle, Washington. The contractor is responsible for serving incoming requests under the Convention. Current charges on the party requesting service are $89 per request. *See* Appendix 21, *infra*.

55. A copy of the Convention forms and declarations of member states can be found in FED. R. CIV. P. 4, at 4–15. *See also*, MARTINDALE-HUBBELL INTERNATIONAL LAW DIGEST.

56. Hague Service Convention, *supra* note 3, Art. 1.

57. *Id.*

authority, which undertakes to ''receive requests for service coming from other contracting States'' and to process requests in conformity with the provisions of the Convention.[58] Under Article 3, the request is transmitted directly by the competent authority of the State of origin to the central authority of the State of execution. The United States central authority interprets ''[t]he authority or judicial officer'' competent to transmit such requests under Article 3 to include any court official or attorney.[59]

Article 3 requires that the request conform to the model annexed to the Convention.[60] This includes the ''Request,'' the ''Summary of the Document to be Served,'' and the ''Certificate.'' The request and the document are to be furnished in duplicate.[61] Pursuant to Article 5, the Central Authority in the state of execution arranges for service of the document by a method prescribed by its internal law or by a method requested by the applicant, provided that it is compatible with local law. This procedure allows service to be effected without utilizing the central authority provided the member nation receiving service has not objected to the method used. Thus, the Convention would not bar the use of more liberal service methods provided in the Federal Rules of Civil Procedure and state long-arm statutes, unless such procedures are incompatible with the law of the requested state.[62]

If the central authority deems that the request does not comply with the provisions of the Convention, it is required to promptly inform the applicant and specify its objections to the request.[63] Article 5 provides that if the document is served by the Central Authority, it may require the document to be written in, or translated into, the official language of

---

58. Hague Service Convention, *supra* note 3, Art 2.

59. For example, the attorney should designate in the Request form in the space provided for the ''identity and address of the Applicant'' that the applicant is duly authorized by relevant state or federal provisions to serve a summons. *See* Greene v. Le Dorze, 1998 WL 158632 (N.D. Tex. Mar. 24, 1998) in which the court determined that a process server authorized to serve process in the United States was competent to forward documents to the foreign central authority under Article 3.

60. *See infra* Appendix 2[2]. Model requests are also included in FED. R. CIV. P. 4 and MARTINDALE-HUBBELL INTERNATIONAL LAW DIGEST, *supra* note 49.

61. The forms are available to the public free of charge at all U.S. Marshals' offices. Copies of the Request forms are reprinted *infra* Appendix 3.

62. Sheets v. Yamaha Motor Co. Ltd., 891 F.2d 533 (5th Cir. 1990); Anbe v. Kikuchi, 141 F.R.D. 498 (D. Hi. 1992); Coblentz GMC/Freightliner, Inc. v. General Motors Corp., 724 F. Supp. 1364 (M.D. Ala. 1989). *See* Northrup King Co. v. C.O.P.S.A., 51 F.3d 1383, 1389 (8th Cir. 1995).

63. *See* Hague Service Convention, *supra* note 3, Art. 4.

the State addressed. Article 7 provides that "[t]he standard terms in the model annexed to the Convention shall in all cases be written either in French or in English."[64] They may also be written in the official language, or in one of the official languages, of the state in which the documents originate.[65]

It has been held that Article 5 required translation of the judicial document, and not the request form.[66] Furthermore, courts have held that the translation requirement only applied when the document was served by the Central Authority and not direct postal service or other method of service.[67] Since the translation requirement was not mandatory, it would be sufficient if the defendant had actual notice of the proceeding.[68] However, in *Teknekron Management, Inc., v. Quante Ternmeldetechnik*,[69] service in West Germany pursuant to the Convention was held defective where plaintiff failed to translate a lengthy contract which was attached as an exhibit to the complaint. West Germany required that all documents served be translated into the German language. The court reasoned that since the exhibit was considered part of the complaint under applicable state and federal law, the exhibit should have also been translated.[70] Although the service failed to conform to the requirements of the Convention, the court ruled that the action would not be dismissed until plaintiffs were given a reasonable opportunity to attempt to effect valid service of process on the defendant in a manner complying with the Hague Convention.[71]

The Convention permits other methods of service, such as through consular or diplomatic channels, so long as the receiving state does not object.[72] It is important to review the declaration and reservations of the

64. Hague Service Convention, *supra* note 3, Art. 7.

65. *Id.*, Art. 7.

66. Taylor v. Uniden Corp. of America, 622 F. Supp. 1011 (E.D. Mo. 1985).

67. Lemme v. Wine of Japan Import, Inc., 631 F. Supp. 456, 463–64 (E.D.N.Y. 1986). *See also* Greenfield v. Suzuki Motor Co., Ltd., 776 F. Supp. 698, 701–703 (E.D.N.Y. 1991); Jordan v. Septa, 708 A.2d 150 (Comm. Ct. of Pa. 1998); Taft v. Moreau, 177 F.R.D. 201 (D. Vt. 1997); Brown v. Bandai America, Inc., 2002 WL 1285265 (N.D. Tex.).

68. *Lemme*, 631 F. Supp. at 464.

69. 115 F.R.D. 175 (D. Nev. 1987).

70. *Id.* at 176–177. *See also* Vorhees v. Fischer & Krecke, 697 F.2d 274 (4th Cir. 1983); McConnell v. Transatlantic Capital Corp., 92–C5451, 1993 WL 337996 (S.D.N.Y. Aug. 31, 1993) (documents must be fully translated into German under Hague Service Convention).

71. *Id.* at 177. *See also* Cooper v. Makita, USA, Inc., 117 F.R.D. 16 (D. Me. 1987); Pennsylvania Orthopedic Ass'n v. Mercedes-Benz A.G., 160 F.R.D. 58 (E.D. Pa. 1995).

72. *See* Hague Service Convention, *supra* note 3, Arts. 8–11.

country where service is to be made to determine if alternative procedures are recognized.

[2] Proof of Service

Article 6 provides that upon effecting service, the central authority shall complete a certificate indicating that the document has been served, including the method, place, date of service, and person to whom the document was delivered. In addition, the central authority's return of a completed certificate of service is prima facie evidence that the authority's method of service complied with the convention.[73] Upon effecting service, the Central Authority completes a certificate indicating that the document has been served, including the method, place, date of service, and the person to whom the document was delivered. The Central Authority's failure to return a proper certificate should not be imputed to the plaintiff so as to vitiate the service. In *Fox v. Regie Nationale des Usines Renouet*,[74] the district court noted that under then Federal Rule of Civil Procedure 4(g), failure to make proof of service did not affect the validity of the service. In addition, under then Rule 4(i)(2), proof of service would include any evidence of delivery satisfactory to the court. The court further pointed out that while the Hague Convention articulated the procedure to be followed in perfecting service abroad, it did not prescribe the procedure for the forum court should the procedure fail. Thus, the fact that the form certificate did not include the information relating to the place at which the documentation was served should not be held against the plaintiff where it was clear that the defendant had sufficient notice of the action.[75]

[3] Service by Mail and Refusal to Serve

Article 10 includes the authority to serve persons abroad directly by mail. Many members states, however, have made declarations or reservations prohibiting service by mail in their jurisdiction. In pertinent part, Article 10 provides as follows:

---

73. *See* Northrup King Co. v. C.O.P.S.A., 51 F.3d 1383 (8th Cir. 1995); Fed. R. Civ. P. 4(1).

74. 103 F.R.D. 453 (W.D. Tenn. 1984).

75. *See also* Silverman v. Modulgranito Iberico, S.A., No. 89–C0432–OG, 1990 WL 481934 (D.D.C. Apr. 30, 1990) (entry of default judgment proper despite failure to obtain certificate of service from Central Authority in Madrid); Greene v. Le Dorze, 1998 WL 158632 (N.D. Tex. Mar. 24, 1998) (service of process valid despite failure of the French central authority to describe the method of service in the certificate).

> Provided the State of destination does not object, the present convention shall not interfere with–(a) the freedom to send judicial documents, by postal channels, directly to persons abroad. . . .[76]

Courts have been divided over whether the word ''send'' in Article 10(a) was intended to mean ''service'' and the summons was therefore among the mail-method beneficiaries.[77] This problem has become particularly acute with respect to service by mail under the Hague Convention in Japan. Although Japan objected to Article 10(b) and (c), which provide for service via the judicial officers, officials, or other competent persons of the receiving state, it did not object to Article 10(a). This has led to confusion as to whether Japan's failure to object to Article 10(a) was intended to authorize the use of mail as an effective means of service.

In *Shoei Kako Co. v. Superior Court*,[78] the California Court of Appeals concluded that the word ''send'' in Article 10(a) was intended to mean ''service.'' The court, therefore, determined that service by direct mail to the Japanese party was proper. As the court stated ''the freedom to send judicial documents by postal channels, directly to persons abroad would be superfluous unless it was related to the sending of such documents for the purpose of service.''[79] However, in a more

---

76. *See* Hague Service Convention, *supra* note 3, Art. 10.

77. *See, e.g.*, Arrogar Distribs., Inc. v. KIS Corp., 151 F.R.D. 221 (D.P.R. 1993) (''send'' means service under Article 10(a) in case involving service to France); Arco Elecs. Control Ltd. v. Core Int'l, 794 F. Supp. 1144 (S.D. Fla. 1992) (''send'' does not mean service under Article 10(a) in case involving service to Israel); Postal v. Princess Cruises, Inc., 163 F.R.D. 497 (N.D. Tex. 1995) (same as to service in the United Kingdom); Gonnuscio v. Seabrand Shipping Ltd., 908 F. Supp. 823 (D. Or. 1995) (same as to service in Greece); Chowaniec v. Heyl Truck Lines, No. 90–C07034, 1991 WL 111156 (N.D. Ill. 1991) (''send'' means service under Article 10(a) in case involving service to Canada); Quinn v. Keinicke, 700 A.2d 147 (Sup. Ct. Del. 1996) (service by mail proper as to Denmark); Riendeau v. St. Lawrence & Atlantic Railroad Co., 167 F.R.D. 26 (D. Vt. 1996) (service by mail not proper as to Canada); Dominguez v. Pyrgia Shipping Corp., 1998 WL 204798 (E.D. La. Apr. 24, 1998) (service by mail proper as to Greece); Pavia v. Club Med Inc., 1998 WL 229912 (D. Conn. Mar. 30, 1998) (service by mail proper as to France and the United Kingdom); Taft v. Moreau, 177 F.R.D. 201 (D. Vt. 1997) (service by mail proper as to Canada); Randolph v. Hendry, 50 F. Supp. 2d 572 (S.D.W.Va. 1999) (service by mail valid to Canada); WAWA, Inc. v. Christensen, 1999 U.S. Dist. LEXIS 11510 (E.D. Pa. 1999) (service by mail valid to Denmark); Johnson v. Pfizer, Inc., 2000 WL 347786 (Conn. Super. Mar. 17, 2000) (service by mail not valid to Sweden); Nuovo Pignone Spa v. M/V Storman Asia, 310 F.3d 374 (5th Cir. 2002) (service by mail not proper as to Italy); Chattem Chemicals, Inc. v. Akzo Nobel Chemicals B.V., 229 F. Supp. 2d 555 (M.D. La. 2002) (service by mail proper as to France); Brown v. Bandai America, Inc., 2002 WL 1285265 (N.D. Tex.) (service by mail proper as to Japan).

78. 33 Cal. App. 3d 808, 109 Cal. Rptr. 402 (1973).

79. 33 Cal. App. 3d at 821–22, 109 Cal. Rptr. at 411–12.

recent decision, *Suzuki Motor Co., Ltd. v. Superior Court,*[80] the California Court of Appeals ruled that service of process by mail was not one of the methods authorized by the Convention for service of process on Japanese defendants. The court stated that it was not bound by the holding in *Shoei Kako* since that case was based on a substantially different factual record. The court relied on expert testimony that Japan did not have an internal legal system which allowed service of process by registered mail and that Japan, unlike California, did not authorize attorneys or process servers to serve process by mail. Since Japan itself did not recognize a form of service equivalent to registered mail, it was unlikely that Japan's failure to object to Article 10(a) was intended to authorize the use of registered mail as an effective mode of service of process. Instead, the court viewed Japan's intent under Article 10(a) as allowing only the transmission of judicial documents, rather than service of process. The decision of the court in *Suzuki* was followed by the California Court of Appeals in *Honda Motor Co., Ltd. v. Superior Court.*[81] Observing the split at both the federal and state level courts in the interpretation of Article 10(a), the court found it "more plausible to assume that Japan did not regard subparagraph (a) as authorizing any service."[82]

In *Bankston v. Toyota Motor Corp.,*[83] the Eighth Circuit Court of Appeals held that sending a copy of the summons and complaint by registered mail to a defendant in Japan was not a proper method of service under the Hague Service Convention. In so ruling, the Court of Appeals followed a line of cases which interpreted the word "send" in Article 10(a) as not the equivalent of "service of process." The Court of Appeals reasoned that because the word "service" was specifically used in other sections of the Convention, namely Articles 10(b) and 10(c), the drafters of the Convention would have included "service" in Article 10(a) if they had intended that subsection to provide an additional manner of service of judicial documents.

In *Ackermann v. Levine,*[84] the Second Circuit Court of Appeals was faced with the issue of whether service of a summons and complaint by registered mail in the United States violated the Hague Convention. The

80. 200 Cal. App. 3d 1476, 249 Cal. Rptr. 376 (1988).

81. 10 Cal. App. 4th 1043, 12 Cal. Rptr. 2d 861 (1992).

82. *Id.* at 1047.

83. 889 F.2d 172 (8th Cir. 1989). *See also* Nuovo Pignone v. Storman Asia M/V, 310 F.3d 374 (5th Cir. 2002).

84. 788 F.2d 830 (2d Cir. 1986).

Court of Appeals determined that since the United States had made no objection to the use of ''postal channels'' under Article 10(a), service of process by registered mail was an appropriate method of service in this country under the Convention.[85] Reviewing the negotiating history of the Convention, the Court of Appeals concluded that the word ''send'' in Article 10(a) was intended to mean ''service'' and the use of ''send'' was attributable to ''careless drafting.''[86] Although the *Ackermann* court perceived a consistent line of authority on the Article 10(a) issue, the majority of courts have followed *Bankston* and concluded that direct mail service of process is not allowed under Article 10(a) of the Hague Service Convention.[87]

In *Brockmeyer v. May*,[87.1] the Ninth Circuit developed a third line of authority under Article 10(a). Following the Second Circuit, the Ninth Circuit held that ''send'' under Article 10(a) included ''serve.'' However, the Court of Appeals further determined that service in the subject proceeding was not in accordance with the law of the forum as required by Rule 4(f) of the Federal Rules of Civil Procedure. In this connection, the court of appeals reasoned that service did not comport with Hague Service Convention procedures since service by international first class mail was not permitted under the law of the United Kingdom and hence not authorized under Rule 4(f)(2)(A).

In addition, the issue has arisen whether personal service by officials included under Articles 10(b) and (c) comports with the law of the state of destination. Article 10(b) provides as follows:

---

85. *Id.* at 838–39. *See also* Curcuruto v. Cheshire, 864 F. Supp. 1410 (S.D. Ga. 1994) (direct mail service to Canada under Art. 10(a) proper); G.A. Modefine, S.A. v. Burlington Coat Factory, 164 F.R.D. 24 (S.D.N.Y. 1995) (same as to Italy); R. Griggs Group Limited v. Filanto Spa, 920 F. Supp. 1100 (D. Nev. 1996) (same).

86. 788 F.2d at 839. *See also* Turick v. Yamaha, 121 F.R.D. 32 (S.D.N.Y. 1988).

87. *See* Sheets v. Yamaha Motor Co. Ltd., 891 F.2d 533 (5th Cir. 1990) (direct mail service to Japan not permitted under Art. 10(a)); McElroy v. Yokota Cycle Co., No. 92–4517, 1993 U.S. Dist. LEXIS 3834, 1993 WL 89734 (E.D. Pa. Mar. 26, 1993) (same); Mateo v. The M/S Kiso, 805 F. Supp. 792 (N.D. Cal. 1992) (same); Anbe v. Kikuchi, 144 F.R.D. 498 (D. Hi. 1992) (same); Brand v. Mazda Motor of America, Inc., 920 F. Supp. 1169 (D. Kan. 1996) (same). *Cf.* Patty v. Toyota Motor Corp., 777 F. Supp. 956 (N.D. Ga. 1991) (service by mail to Japan under Art. 10(a) proper); Arco Electronics Control Ltd. v. Core Int'l, 794 F. Supp. 1144 (S.D. Fla. 1992) (service by mail to United States under Art. 10(a) not proper); Paradigm Entertainment v. Video System Co., Ltd., 2000 WL 251731 (N.D. Tex. Mar. 3, 2000) (service by mail to Japan under Art. 10 (a) proper); Schiffer v. Mazda Motor Corporation, 192 F.R.D. 335 (N.D. Ga. 2000) (same).

87.1. 2004 WL 1936395 (9th Cir. 2004).

> The freedom of judicial officers, officials or other competent persons of the State of origin to effect service of judicial documents directly through the judicial officers, officials or other competent persons of the State of destination.

Article 10(c) provides for "the freedom of any person interested in a judicial proceeding" to effect service. These provisions cover service by process servers.[88]

At a 1985 special Commission meeting of the Hague Conference on Private International Law on the Hague service and evidence Conventions, the Japanese delegation issued the following statement of its position on Article 10(a):

> Japan has not declared that it objects to the sending of judicial documents, by postal channels, directly to persons abroad. In this connection, Japan . . . has made it clear that no objection to the use of postal channels for sending judicial documents to persons in Japan does not necessarily imply that the sending by such a method is considered valid service in Japan; it merely indicates that Japan does not consider it as infringement of its sovereign power.[89]

It remains to be seen how American courts will interpret Japan's position statement and whether this will lead to uniformity of results on the validity of service by mail under the Service Convention in Japan.

Article 12 generally provides that there will be no charge for the service except for costs associated with the employment of a judicial officer or other competent person in the state addressed as well as the use of a particular method of service.[90] Article 13 only permits the state addressed to refuse service if it determines that compliance would infringe its sovereignty or security.[91] The state addressed may not refuse to comply with service because under its internal law it claims exclusive jurisdiction over the subject matter of the action or its law does not permit the action involved in the service request.[92] The Central

---

88. *See* Balcom v. Hiller, 46 Cal. App. 4th 1758, 54 Cal. Rptr. 2d 536 (1996) (service by process server in the United Kingdom proper under Articles 10(b) and (c)).

89. Report of the Second Meeting of the Special Commission on the Operation of the Hague Convention on the Service Abroad of Judicial and Extrajudicial Documents and the Taking of Evidence Abroad in Civil or Commercial Matters, May 28–31, 1985, 24 I.L.M. 1668. The Report is reprinted *infra* as Appendix 4.

90. Hague Service Convention, *supra* note 3, Art. 12.

91. *Id.* art. 13.

92. *Id.*

Authority must promptly inform the applicant of the refusal and the reasons for the refusal to serve.[93]

[4] Default Judgments

Articles 15 and 16 contain appropriate safeguards with respect to default judgments. Article 15 provides that where a document has been transmitted abroad for service, and the defendant has not appeared, judgment shall not be given unless–

(1) the document was served by a method prescribed by the internal law of the state addressed for the service of documents in domestic actions upon persons who are within the territory, or

(2) the document was actually delivered to the defendant or to his residence by another method provided for by this Convention.

Service must be made in sufficient time to allow defendant to defend.

Under Article 15 a state is free to declare that the judge may give judgment even if no certificate of service or delivery has been received if: (a) the document was transmitted pursuant to methods prescribed by the Convention; (b) a period of time of at least six months has passed since the date of transmission; and (c) no certificate has been received despite efforts to obtain it through the state addressed.[94]

Under Article 16, the judge has the power to relieve the defendant from the effects of the expiration of time for appeal if the defendant, without any fault on his part had no knowledge of the documents in sufficient time to defend or to appeal. The application for relief may be filed only within a reasonable time after the defendant obtains knowledge of the judgment and has shown a *prima facie* defense to the action on the merits. A state may declare that the application will not be entertained if it was not filed within a certain time from the date of judgment, but not less than one year from that date.

93. *Id.*

94. *See* Marschhauser v. Travelers Indemnity Co., 145 F.R.D. 605 (S.D. Fla. 1992) (court exercises discretion in refusing to enter default judgment under Article 15 where defendant indicates desire to contest action); Silverman v. Modulgranito Iberico, S.A., No. 89–C0432–OG, 1990 WL 481934 (D.D.C. Apr. 30, 1990) (entry of default judgment proper despite failure to obtain certificate of service from central authority in Madrid).

[5] "Exclusivity of the Convention"

Unlike the Hague Evidence Convention,[95] the Hague Service Convention provides mandatory procedures for service of documents abroad. Thus, Article 1 provides that the Convention ''shall apply in all cases, in civil or commercial matters, where there is occasion to transmit a judicial or extrajudicial document for service abroad.'' (emphasis added). As will be discussed,[96] this aspect of the Hague Service Convention contrasts with the Supreme Court's interpretation of the Hague Evidence Convention as providing only optional methods for litigants to gather evidence from foreign nationals of member countries.[97]

There has been little controversy that the Hague Service Conventions's procedures, when they apply, are generally mandatory and exclusive.[98] The United States, in briefs filed before the Supreme Court, observed that ''United States courts have consistently and properly held that litigants wishing to serve process in countries that are parties to the Service Convention must follow the procedures provided by that Convention unless the nation involved permits more liberal procedures.''[99] The Supreme Court recently made the same point in *Aerospatiale* in discussing the role of the Hague Evidence Convention in litigation in United States courts, comparing the Service Convention's use of ''mandatory language'' in its first article.[100]

The mandatory language of Article 1 applies whenever the service takes place within another nation's borders. However, the question has arisen in numerous cases as to the applicability of the Hague Service Convention where service is made pursuant to procedures under domestic and local law. Courts have been divided on the question as to whether the Convention applies in situations when the foreign corporation or its agent is located and served within the United States. There have been a wide range of results as to the extent to which the Hague

95. Discussed in Chapter 10, *infra.*

96. *See infra* § 10.11.

97. *See* Société Nationale Industrielle Aerospatiale v. United States Dist. Court, 482 U.S. 522 (1987).

98. *See* Vorhees v. Fischer & Krecke, 697 F.2d 574 (4th Cir. 1983). *See also* Volkswagenwerk, A.G. v. Schlunk, 486 U.S. 694, 699 (1988); McConnell v. Transatlantic Capital Corp., No. 92–C5451, 1993 WL 337996 (S.D.N.Y. 1993); *In re* Hunt's Pier Assocs., 156 Bankr. 464, 469–470 (E.D. Pa. 1993).

99. Brief for the United States as Amicus Curiae at 5, Volkswagenwerk, A.G. v. Falzon, 465 U.S. 1014 (1984). *See* Shenouda v. Mehanna, 203 F.R.D. 166 (D.N.J. 2001).

100. *Aerospatiale*, 482 U.S. at 534, n.15.

Service Convention preempts application of state service rules to foreign nationals and corporations.[101] In a related context, the issue had arisen as to whether the Hague Service Convention applied to indirect service pursuant to state rules through a state official, such as the state Secretary of State or other imputed agents, such as a subsidiary of a foreign corporation found within the state, who is charged with responsibility for transmitting process to the foreign corporation. Various courts had ruled in this respect that the Hague Convention's procedures were inapplicable in such situations where the foreign corporation was the alter ego, or agent under a similar agency standard, and therefore the agent of the foreign corporation in the United States for the purpose of service of process.[102] However, other courts had ruled under similar facts that the Hague Service Convention preempted the local law which permitted service of process through the state Secretary of State[103] or on a domestic subsidiary as involuntary agent for service of process.

This issue was addressed by the Supreme Court in *Schlunk v. Volkswagenwerk, A.G.*[104] In *Schlunk*, respondent filed a wrongful death action in Illinois state court. Volkswagen of America, Inc. (VWOA) was named as a defendant and petitioner Volkswagenwerk (VWAG) was later added as a defendant. VWAG is a German corporation and the sole owner of VWOA. Respondent attempted to serve the amended complaint on VWAG by serving VWAO as VWAG's agent under Illinois "alter ego" provisions. VWAG took the position that it could be served only in accordance with the Hague Service Convention and that respondent had not complied with the Convention's requirements. The Illinois court concluded that since service took place in the United States, the Convention did not apply. The Illinois court ruled that VWAO and VWAG were so closely related that VWAO was VWAG's agent for service of process as a matter of law. The Appellate Court of Illinois affirmed, ruling that the Illinois long-arm statute authorized substituted service on VWOA, which did not violate the Convention.

101. *See, e.g.*, Mommsen v. Toro Co., 108 F.R.D. 444, 445 (S.D. Iowa 1985); Low v. Bayerisch Motoren Werke, A.G., 88 A.D.2d 504, 505, 449 N.Y.S.2d 733, 734–735 (1982). *See also* Fleming v. Yamaha Motor Corp., 774 F. Supp. 992, 995 (W.D. Va. 1991); Wissmiller v. Lincoln Trail Motosports, 195 Ill. App. 3d 399, 552 N.E. 2d 295, 299–300 (1990).

102. *See, e.g., Ex parte* Volkswagenwerk, A.G., 443 So.2d 880 (Ala. 1983). *See also* Melia v. Les Grands Chais De France, 135 F.R.D. 28, 35 (D.R.I. 1991); King v. Perry & Sylva Machinery Co., 776 F. Supp. 638, 640 (N.D. Ill. 1991).

103. Cipolla v. Picard Porsche Audi, Inc., 496 A.2d 130 (R.I. 1985). *See also* Fleming v. Yamaha Motor Corp., 774 F. Supp. 992, 995 (W.D. Va. 1991).

104. 486 U.S. 694 (1988).

(Rel.6–10/05)

Reviewing the case, the Supreme Court held that the Convention does not apply when process is served on the foreign corporation's "alter ego," which under state law is the foreign corporation's involuntary agent for service of process. The Court focused its inquiry on the scope of Article 1 of the Convention which states: "[t]he present Convention shall apply in all cases, in civil or commercial matters, where there is occasion to transmit a judicial or extrajudicial document for service abroad."[105] The Court acknowledged that this language was mandatory. Therefore, under the Supremacy Clause, Article VI of the U.S. Constitution, the Convention preempted inconsistent methods of service prescribed by state law in all cases to which it applied. Based on a review of the negotiation history of the Convention, the Court stated that whether there is valid service abroad must be determined by the law of the forum state.[106] There was no evidence in the negotiating history that the Convention was intended to apply to substituted service on a subsidiary like VWOA which was so closely related to the defendant parent corporation.[107] Therefore, the Illinois long-arm statute authorized Schlunk to serve VWAG by substituted service on VWOA and did not require service abroad. The Court rejected VWAG's contention that service on VWAG was not completed until VWOA transmitted the complaint to VWAG in Germany.[108] Contrary to VWAG's position, the Court did not view the Due Process Clause as requiring an official transmission abroad every time there was service on a foreign national. Since the case did not present an "occasion to transmit" a judicial document for service abroad within the meaning of Article 1, the Court refused to apply the Convention and service was validly accomplished under state law.[109]

The concurring opinion of Justice Brennan admonished the majority's failure to impose a precise standard which could lead a forum nation to conclude that it could avoid application of the Convention by designating any type of service as "domestic."[110] The absence of an articulated standard could lead a forum nation to consider service effective upon deposit in the mailbox or, alternatively, to designate any domestic agent to accept service for any foreign defendants. However,

105. Hague Service Convention, *supra* note 3, Art. 1.

106. *Id.* at 704.

107. *Id.* at 706–08.

108. *Id.* at 707–08.

109. *Id.*

110. *Id.* at 708–16.

the majority of the Court deemed it unlikely that any country would deliberately manipulate its internal laws to circumvent the Convention where it would otherwise be appropriate to transmit judicial documents for service abroad.[111] In any event, the concurring opinion accepted the holding of the majority that the Convention did not prohibit the type of service at issue, insofar as it pertained to service on a wholly owned, closely controlled subsidiary and that under these particular facts due process standards had been satisfied.

It has been speculated that the Court's opinion will adversely affect United States commerce in that foreign courts will retaliate against U.S. companies by subordinating the Convention to the foreign nations' own internal laws.[112] The concurring opinion similarly noted potential adverse consequences on United States citizens abroad by providing inadequate notice of service of process.[113]

In post-*Schlunk* cases, courts have differed on the applicability of the Convention to substituted service provisions under state law. In a significant extension of *Schlunk*, the court in *Melia v. Les Grands Chais de France*,[114] determined that the Convention was inapplicable where it concluded that service had been effectively made on the Secretary of State under state law.[115] The court ruled that the defendant was ''carrying on business'' within the meaning of the statute for substituted service of process.[116] As there was no additional requirement that plaintiff send notice directly to defendant, service on the Secretary of State was complete and the Convention was not implicated.[117] The court applied the minimum contacts test under the substituted service provisions in concluding that defendant's business activities were sufficient to bring it within the statute.[118] In *Curcuruto v. Cheshire*,[119]

111. *Id.* at 705–6.

112. *See* Gary B. Born, *Whole World in Their Hands*, INT'L LEGAL TIMES, Aug. 29, 1988.

113. 486 U.S., at 714–16.

114. 135 F.R.D. 28 (D.R.I. 1991). *See also* Pittsburgh National Bank v. A.B. Kasir, 153 F.R.D. 1994 (W.D. Pa. 1994) (Hague Service Convention does not apply where service made on domestic agent appointed for such purpose). *But see* Rovema Verpackungsmaschinen v. Deloach, 500 S.E.2d 647 (Ct. App. Ga. 1998), in which the court rejected service of process on the registered agent of a wholly-owned domestic subsidiary of that foreign corporation where the subsidiary was not otherwise an agent for service of process of the foreign national parent corporation.

115. *Id.* at 31–32.

116. *Id.* at 35.

117. *Id.* at 35–36.

118. *Id.* at 33–35.

however, the Convention was held to apply when state law required a plaintiff both to serve the Secretary of State and to send a copy of the summons and complaint to the defendant via registered mail. In *King v. Perry & Sylva Machinery Co.*,[120] a close nexus between a foreign parent corporation and its U.S. subsidiary was found to establish an agency relationship sufficient for service of process under the Illinois long-arm statute.[121]

Some cases have focused on the proper procedure to be utilized by the state secretary of state in transmitting the papers abroad in order to complete service of process.[122] Where service by mail is required, some courts have looked to the provisions of the treaty to determine whether this means of service is permissible in the particular country involved. If service by mail is not authorized, other means, such as formal transmission to a foreign central authority may be required.

Other courts have, however, found that the Hague Convention preempted state methods of service where plaintiffs failed to comply with state statutes governing service of process. In *Fleming v. Yamaha Motor Corp.*,[123] the court distinguished the Virginia service statute from the Illinois statute at issue in *Schlunk.*[124] The court ruled that under Virginia law, service on a wholly owned subsidiary in the absence of shared corporate identities was improper and applied the Hague Convention.[125] In *Akari Imeji Co. v. Qume Corp.*,[126] the court analyzed whether a domestic corporation was properly an agent for service of process on a foreign corporation under Illinois law.[127] The court found that insufficient contacts existed between the parent corporation and its domestic subsidiary for the subsidiary to be an agent for service purposes.[128] The

---

119. 864 F. Supp. 1410 (S.D. Ga. 1994); Kim v. Frank Mohn A/S, 909 F. Supp. 475 (S.D. Tex. 1995) (same as to Texas long-arm statute); Quinn v. Keinicke, 700 A.2d 147 (Sup. Ct. Del. 1996) (same as to Delaware's motor vehicle long-arm statute).

120. 766 F. Supp. 638 (N.D. Ill. 1991).

121. *Id.* at 640.

122. *See* Gonnuscio v. Seabrand Shipping Ltd., 908 F. Supp. 823 (D. Ore. 1995); Wood v. Wood, 231 A.D.2d 713, 647 N.Y.S2d 830 (1991); Riendeau v. St. Lawrence & Atlantic Railroad Co., 167 F.R.D. 26 (D. Vt. 1996); Froland v. Yamaha Motor Co., Ltd., 2003 WL 22971360 (D. Minn. 2003) (formal transmission required under Hague Service Convention procedures).

123. 774 F. Supp. 992 (W.D. Va. 1991).

124. *Id.* at 994.

125. *Id.*

126. 748 F. Supp. 588 (N.D. Ill. 1990).

127. *Id.* at 592–93.

128. *Id.* at 595; R. Griggs Group Limited v. Filanto Spa, 920 F. Supp. 1100 (D. Nev. 1996); Chung v. Tarom, S.A., 990 F. Supp. 581 (N.D. Ill. 1998); Gilmore v. Festo KG, 1998 WL 164887 (N.D. Ill. Mar. 31, 1998).

court in *Dunakey v. American Honda Motor Co., Inc.*,[129] distinguished the Missouri service statute from the Illinois statute in *Schlunk* and held that without a showing of shared corporate identities, a domestic subsidiary was not a foreign corporation's involuntary agent for service of process.[130]

A central factor in determining the propriety of service of process under state statutes has been the degree of control exercised by the foreign parent corporation over the subsidiary. In applying state substituted service provisions, courts have been persuaded by facts evidencing control over a subsidiary, such as the parent company's ownership stake, supervisory role, use of common books and accounts, common promotional and marketing activities, and commonality of board of directors.[131] Mere ownership of a subsidiary was not sufficient to establish jurisdiction over a foreign parent corporation.[132]

Before bypassing Convention procedures, counsel should consider whether later enforcement of the judgment in a signatory state to the Convention is likely. It may be prudent in some situations to voluntarily comply with Convention service requirements.[133] Counsel should remember that in establishing the validity of service of process under the convention, the best form of proof is the certificate of service executed by the central authority in the requested state.[134]

---

129. 124 F.R.D. 638 (E.D. Mo. 1989).

130. *Id.* at 640; Davies v. Jobs & Adverts Online, GMBH, 94 F. Supp. 2d 719 (E.D. Va. 2000) (same). *See* Rhodes v. J.P. Sauer & Sohn, Inc., 98 F. Supp. 2d 746 (W.D. La. 2000), in which the court held that the Hague Service Convention applied where domestic subsidiary was not served in agency capacity; Glass v. Volkswagen of America, Inc., 172 F. Supp. 2d 743 (D. Md. 2001); Lafarge Corp. v. Altech Environment, 220 F. Supp. 2d 823 (E.D. Mich. 2002).

131. King v. Perry & Sylva Machinery Co., 766 F. Supp. 638, 640 (N.D. Ill. 1991); Gallagher v. Mazda Motor of America, 781 F. Supp. 1079, 1085 (E.D. Pa. 1992); Akari Imeji Co. v. Qume Corp., 748 F. Supp. 588, 591–93 (N.D. Ill. 1990); Dunakey v. American Honda Motor Co., Inc., 124 F.R.D. 638, 639 (E.D. Mo. 1989).

132. Gallagher v. Mazda Motor of America, 781 F. Supp. 1079, 1083 (E.D. Pa. 1992); Fleming v. Yamaha Motor Corp., 774 F. Supp. 992, 994 (W.D. Va. 1991); Dunakey v. American Honda Motor Co., Inc., 124 F.R.D. 638, 639 (E.D. Mo. 1989). Interestingly, the court in *Gallagher* also exempted holding companies from service under Pennsylvania statute. *Gallagher*, 781 F. Supp. at 1085; Glen v. Club Mediterranee, S.A., 2005 U.S. Dist. LEXIS 6838 (S.D. Fla. 2005).

133. *See infra* § 4.07.

134. *See* Northrup King Co. v. C.O.P.S.A., 51 F.3d 1383 (8th Cir. 1995).

§ 4.05 SERVICE UNDER THE INTER-AMERICAN CONVENTION ON LETTERS ROGATORY

The Inter-American Convention on Letters Rogatory[135] and the Additional Protocol[136] to the Convention were ratified by the United States Senate in October, 1986. The instrument of ratification was signed by the President on November 10, 1986. The agreement entered into force on August 27, 1988 for the United States with other countries which had already ratified it.[137] Similar in purpose to the Hague Service Convention, the Inter-American Convention and its Additional Protocol seek to facilitate the service in the territory of one contracting state of judicial documents emanating from civil and commercial proceedings in another contracting state. These agreements represent a treaty-based system of multilateral cooperation between the United States and other members of the Organization of American States (OAS). United States ratification of the Convention and Additional Protocol is subject to the reservation that treaty relations are only undertaken with respect to states which have ratified or acceded to the Convention and Additional Protocol and not the Convention alone.[138]

The Convention, which was originally adopted in 1975, has been ratified by seventeen countries and has been signed by two countries which have not yet ratified it. The countries which have ratified the treaty are Argentina, Brazil, Chile, Columbia, Costa Rica, Ecuador, El Salvador, Guatemala, Honduras, Mexico, Panama, Paraguay, Peru, Spain, United States, Uruguay and Venezuela.[139] The countries which are signatories to the treaty are Bolivia and Nicaragua. The United States did not originally sign the Convention since it believed that service of judicial documents could be more effectively accomplished if certain additional provisions were incorporated in the treaty regime. The Additional Protocol, which was proposed by the United States, was opened for signature on May 8, 1979, and both the Convention and the

---

135. Inter-American Convention on Letters Rogatory, *supra* note 4. The Inter-American Convention on Letters Rogatory and the Additional Protocol to the Inter-American Convention on Letters Rogatory are presented *infra* in Appendix 5.

136. Additional Protocol to the Inter-American Convention on Letters Rogatory, *supra* note 5.

137. Treaties in Force, U.S. Department of State 351 (1993).

138. In ratifying the Inter-American Convention and the Additional Protocol, the United States has made the reservation expressly permitted by Article 2(b) of the Convention which precludes the use of letters rogatory for the purpose of taking evidence under the Convention.

139. Treaties in Force, U.S. Department of State 351 (1993).

Additional Protocol were signed by the United States on April 15, 1980.[140] Those countries, in addition to the United States, which have ratified the Additional Protocol include Argentina, Brazil, Chile, Columbia, Ecuador, Guatemala, Mexico, Panama, Paraguay, Peru, Uruguay and Venezuela.[141] Six other countries, which are signatories to the Additional Protocol, have not yet ratified it. These include Bolivia, Costa Rica, Dominican Republic, El Salvador, Haiti, and Honduras.[142]

Article 1 of the Convention limits the applicability of the Convention to "letters rogatory," as that term is commonly understood.[143] Article 2 of the Convention, in conjunction with the Additional Protocol,[144] limits the scope of the Convention to service of judicial documents such as summonses and complaints by a judicial authority and not an administrative authority. Article 3 expressly excludes

(*Text continued on page 4-27*)

140. *Id.*

141. *Id.*

142. *Id.*

143. Letters rogatory are the "medium whereby one country, speaking through one of its courts, requests another country, acting through its own courts and by methods of court procedure peculiar thereto and entirely within the latter's control, to assist the administration of justice in the former country." BLACK'S LAW DICTIONARY (6th ed. 1994). Letters rogatory are a form of letter of request. FED. R. CIV. P. 28 Advisory Committee's Note.

144. Additional Protocol to the Inter-American Convention on Letters Rogatory, *supra* note 5, art. 1.

compulsory enforcement measures such as attachments, garnishments, restraining orders and other enforcement-oriented measures from the purview of the Convention. Articles 5, 6, and 7 of the Convention obligate contracting states to execute letters rogatory sent through the designated channels if the requisite formalities have been observed. Contracting states are not required to execute the letters rogatory unless they have been legalized. However, when they are transmitted through consular or diplomatic channels or through the Central Authority, no legalization is necessary. Article 3 of the Additional Protocol also limits the authentication requirements by providing that the seal of the requesting court shall suffice when the requests are transmitted to the state of destination by the Central Authority of the state of origin.

Among the major provisions of the Protocol are those that:

- clarify the obligation of parties to the Convention to designate the Central Authority to which requests for service would be transmitted;[145]
- simplify the authentication requirements for the documents transmitted by letters rogatory for service;
- prescribe the use of agreed forms for issuance and execution of requests; and
- establish a procedure for payments of costs for the purpose of insuring the prompt service of documents.

Pursuant to Article 18 of the Convention, the United States has informed the Secretary General of the Organization of American States that letters rogatory to be executed in the United States must be translated into the English language.

Pursuant to Article 3 of the Additional Protocol, letters rogatory are prepared on the model form annexed to the Convention.[146] Letters rogatory are accompanied by a copy of the complaint or pleading that initiated the action, as well as a translation thereof into the language of the State of destination. Documents attached to the complaint or pleading together with any rulings ordering issuance of the letter

---

145. *See* Lawrence W. Newman, *Service of Process in Latin Ametica: Potential Pitfalls,* New York Law Journal (Sept. 27, 2002), which describes deficiencies in proper implementation of the Convention in certain member countries.

146. Copies of the model forms are attached as Appendix 6[1] (English) and Appendix 6[2] (Spanish).

rogatory should also be included. The accompanying documents need not be translated. It is also necessary for the forwarding party to complete the form annexed to the Protocol which contains information on the identity and nature of the action and the addresses of the person to be served or the authority to receive the documents. There is also a form attached to the Protocol which is to be completed by the Central Authority of the State of destination attesting to execution or non-execution of the letter rogatory. Forms for submitting letters rogatory under the Convention are available at U.S. Marshals' offices.

Pursuant to Article 5 of the Protocol, processing of the letters rogatory by the State of destination is to be free of charge. However, each State party is authorized to seek payment for those services which, in accordance with local law, are required to be paid by the parties requesting execution of the letters rogatory. Article 6 of the Protocol provides that each State party either designates a schedule of costs or sets a fixed amount to cover the cost of such services. On a reciprocal basis, the State party may elect not to charge parties for the cost of providing such services.[147] The United States has declared that the fee for service of foreign judicial documents in the United States as specified in Article 6 of the Additional Protocol is $25. However, pursuant to Article 7 of the Additional Protocol, service will be made free of charge on a reciprocal basis.

Unlike the Hague Service Convention, the Inter-American Convention, in Article 4, provides that the Central Authority may process letters rogatory to the authority to which they are addressed by the interested parties. Thus, the United States Central Authority is used to process both incoming and out-going requests. The Department of Justice, in addition to its functions under the Hague Service Convention, serves as the Central Authority under the Inter-American Convention and the Additional Protocol.[148]

It has been held that the provisions of the Inter-American Convention on Letters Rogatory are not exclusive. In *Kreimerman v. Casa*

147. Additional Protocol to the Inter-American Convention on Letters Rogatory, *supra* note 5, art. 7.

148. Effective June 1, 2003, the U.S. Department of Justice delegated the service of process function under the Inter-American Convention to a private contractor, Process Forwarding International of Seattle, Washington. This covers both incoming and outgoing requests. Service under the Inter-American Convention remains free of charge. See Appendix 21, *infra.*

Veerkamp,[149] plaintiffs sued defendants for libel, civil conspiracy, and slander. Plaintiffs served process on defendants in Mexico by mail through the Texas Secretary of State under the Texas Long-Arm Statute. The court quashed this service holding that the Inter-American Convention was the exclusive means of service. In reversing the district court on this issue, the court of appeals determined that the Inter-American Convention applied only to regulating the use of letters rogatory—only one of many procedural mechanisms of serving process in other countries.[150] In so ruling, the court distinguished the mandatory effect of the Hague Service Convention which prohibits all methods of service on signatory countries that do not comply with treaty requirements.[151]

§ 4.06 SERVICE OF FOREIGN PROCESS IN THE UNITED STATES

The United States follows a liberal policy regarding the service of foreign judicial process in this country. 28 U.S.C.A. § 1696 provides that ''[t]he district court of the district in which a person resides or is found may order service upon him of any documents issued in connection with a proceeding in a foreign or international tribunal.''[152] Under Section 1696 the order may be made pursuant to a letter rogatory issued by a foreign tribunal or upon application of any interested person. Letters rogatory issued for the purpose of obtaining international judicial assistance (i.e., service of process and/or taking of testimony) should not be confused with recognition or enforcement of foreign judgments. Neither Section 1696 nor 28 U.S.C.A. §§ 1781-1782 provide for the enforcement of foreign judgments and this remedy is not available through the issuance of letters rogatory.[153]

149. 22 F.3d 634 (5th Cir. 1994).

150. *Id.* at 639–640.

151. *Id. See also* Pizzabiocche v. Vinelli, 772 F. Supp. 1245, 1249 (M.D. Fla. 1991); Skanchy v. Calcados Ortope SA, 952 P.2d 1071 (Utah 1998); Laino v. Cuprum S.A. de C.V., 663 N.Y.S.2d 275 (App. Div. 1997).

152. 28 U.S.C.A. § 1696.

153. *See* Sprague & Rhodes Commodity Corp. v. Instituto Mexicano Del Cafe, 566 F.2d 861, 863 (2d Cir. 1977); Nippon Emo-Trans Co., Ltd. v. Emo-Trans, Inc., 744 F. Supp. 1215, 1229 (E.D.N.Y. 1990); Tacul, S.A. v. Hartford Nat'l Bank & Trust Co., 693 F. Supp. 1399, 1400 (D. Conn. 1988); *In re* Civil Rogatory Letters Filed by Consulate of the United States of Mexico, 640 F. Supp. 243 (S.D. Tex. 1986); *In re* Letters Rogatory From City of Haugesund, Norway, 497 F.2d 378, 381 (9th Cir. 1974); *In re* Letter Rogatory, 2002 WL 257822 (E.D.N.Y.).

Similar to Section 1696, 28 U.S.C.A. § 1781(b)(1) states that a letter rogatory may be transmitted directly from a foreign tribunal to a tribunal in the United States to which it is addressed. Finally, Section 1696(b) provides that service of a document is not precluded by the absence of an order of court. In *Corporacion Salvadorena de Calzado v. Injection Footwear Corporation*,[154] letters rogatory issued by the foreign court were not transmitted to the U.S. District Court for service on the defendant. Instead, the letters rogatory were mailed to the defendant by the U.S. Embassy in El Salvador using certified mail. The court pointed out that while service could have been made without an order of the court pursuant to Section 1696(b), any such service must comport with Rule 4 of the Federal Rules of Civil Procedure and that the clerk of the court must send the summons or notice to the defendant to be notified in this country. Since neither requirement was satisfied, the court determined that the service of process was insufficient to support commencement of the foreign proceeding.

The Department of Justice, as the Central Authority under the Hague Service Convention, is responsible for processing incoming service requests from foreign countries under the Convention.[155] In addition, the Department of Justice also processes requests which are transmitted from non-Convention countries via diplomatic channels, i.e., under 28 U.S.C.A. § 1781. Non-Convention requests are processed and served in the same manner as Convention requests. Once received from the foreign tribunal or the Department of State, the Department of Justice transmits the documents directly to the U.S. Marshals for service. Rule 4 of the Federal Rules of Civil Procedure allows for service by mail or other means,[156] provided no local law within the state of service requires a stricter standard, such as certified mail.[157] Under the rule, if service is accomplished by first-class mail, then an acknowledgement form confirming receipt of the documents and a return envelope, postage prepaid, addressed to the sender, must be enclosed with the documents. Also, amended Rule 4(d) provides that a foreign corporation may notify a U.S. party of the commencement of an action and request the U.S. party to waive service of a summons.[158] However, the U.S. party may refuse without good cause to waive service and no costs will be imposed

154. 533 F. Supp. 290 (S.D. Fla. 1982).
155. 28 C.F.R. § 0.49.
156. Fed. R. Civ. P. 4(c)(2)(c)(ii).
157. Fed. R. Civ. P. 4(e)(1).
158. Fed. R. Civ. P. 4(d).

for the failure to waive service.[159] After service, a copy of the documents served, together with the Marshal's return of service, is returned to the requesting authority. Convention requests must be returned to the foreign requesting authority abroad. Non-Convention requests are returned to the Department of State or to a foreign embassy or consulate in this country depending on the source. Service of judicial documents under 28 U.S.C.A. § 1696 may be a slower procedure than through the Hague Service Convention. Use of the Convention procedures is more efficient since the request for service is transmitted directly to the U.S. Central Authority and the need for diplomatic channels, which may be cumbersome, is avoided.

§ 4.07 THE ROLE OF SERVICE OF PROCESS IN THE ENFORCEMENT OF JUDGMENTS

A principal ground for objecting to the enforcement of a foreign judgment is lack of proper service. In the same regard, if the party seeking enforcement of the foreign judgment has served the party in a manner deemed acceptable in the foreign jurisdiction,[160] the judgment will not be denied recognition, at least on the grounds of ineffective service, by the foreign jurisdiction.

As will be discussed in greater detail in the subsequent chapter dealing with enforcement of judgments,[161] a foreign defendant is faced with the choice of appearing and litigating the suit in the domestic forum or taking the entry of a default judgment and risking enforcement of the judgment in the foreign jurisdiction. It is therefore important for both parties to consider whether service of process is in conformity with the laws of both jurisdictions. The case of *Ackermann v. Levine*[162] illustrates how the service issue may arise in the enforcement of judgment context. In *Ackermann*, an action was brought by partners in a West German law firm to enforce a default judgment entered against a defendant in New York by a court in West Berlin. In the suit in federal district court, defendant appeared and argued, *inter alia*, that the court should decline to enforce judgment on the ground that service of process by registered mail violated the Hague Convention and due process. Reversing the

---

159. Fed. R. Civ. P. 4(d)(2).

160. Bruno Ristau, International Judicial Assistance: Civil and Commercial 56 (1990).

161. *See* Chapter 11, *infra*.

162. 788 F.2d 830 (2d Cir. 1986).

district court, the Court of Appeals upheld the use of mail service pursuant to the Convention in the United States, and refused to disallow enforcement of the foreign judgment on that ground.

The issue, in reverse, arose in *Volkswagenwerk, A.G. v. Schlunk.*[163] In that case, the issue before the Supreme Court pertained to the exclusivity of the Hague Service Convention as applied to service of a U.S. subsidiary in the United States as ''involuntary agent'' of its German principal. The Federal Republic of Germany, which filed a brief *amicus curiae*, advised the Court that the Hague Service Convention provided the exclusive means of effectuating service of process on defendants in Germany. Service upon an ''involuntary agent'' would not have the desired effect of constituting valid service for purposes of recognition and enforcement of U.S. judgments in Germany because German courts would not recognize and enforce judgments obtained in violation of the Convention.[164] According to its brief, when a foreign judgment was to be recognized and enforced in the Federal Republic of Germany, the German courts wererequired to apply the Code of Civil Procedure which provided, in relevantpart, that a judgment of a foreign court was not to be recognized if adefendant, who had not entered an appearance on the merits, raised thedefense that he was not properly served with the initial pleading (Section 328).[165] Germany contended that in interpreting the Convention, the Court should take cognizance of the greater certainty the Convention had brought to the enforcement of foreign judgments and the detrimental effects on U.S. plaintiffs of serving a domestic ''involuntary agent'' rather than through Convention means.[166] The United States similarly acknowledged in its own brief *amicus curiae* that ''we expect that respondent's failure to employ the Convention's procedures may raise serious obstacles to obtaining foreign assistance in enforcing any judgment that he might ultimately receive.''[167]

It is no doubt true that the Convention facilitates enforcement of judgments in signatory states since it establishes the basic methods of service which are recognized as valid in both the state of origin and the

163. 486 U.S. 694 (1988). *See* discussion at § 4.04[5].

164. Brief for Volkswagenwerk, A.G. at 16, Volkswagenwerk, A.G. v. Schlunk, 486 U.S. 694 (1988).

165. *Id.* at 16.

166. *Id.* at 17.

167. Brief for the United States as Amicus Curiae at 20 no. 32, Volkswagenwerk, A.G. v. Schlunk, 486 U.S. 694 (1988).

state addressed.[168] In its opinion in *Schlunk* the Court noted the practical importance of complying with the Convention even where domestic law did not so require. The Court specifically noted that those choosing to follow its procedure might find it easier to subsequently enforce their judgments abroad.[169] This would lead to voluntary use of the Convention in cases where mandatory application would not be required under the *Schlunk* rationale or local law.

168. Committee on Int'l Law, the Hague Convention on the Service Abroad of Judicial and Extrajudicial Documents in Civil or Commercial Matters, 22 *Rec. Ass'n Bar of City of N.Y.* 280, 286 (1967).

169. 486 U.S. at 705–6.

Chapter 5

SELECTED LIMITATIONS ON THE JURISDICTION OF U.S. COURTS

§ 5.01 INTRODUCTION AND OVERVIEW

In considering the transnational disputes and parties subject to U.S. jurisdiction, U.S. courts face numerous complex and difficult issues of national and international law. How far may the courts of one nation reach? Which parties are subject to the laws of a particular nation? What limits exist to prevent the courts and laws of one nation from interfering or conflicting with those of another?

Courts must first establish their jurisdiction under U.S. law, whether state or federal, and then, increasingly, they must look to principles of international law. International law both identifies valid bases for the exercise of jurisdiction and places limits on the scope of a nation's power to exercise that jurisdiction.

This chapter focuses on limitations on the authority of U.S. state and federal courts to exercise jurisdiction to prescribe (i.e., subject matter jurisdiction) in the transnational context, including questions of statutory grant of jurisdiction, the doctrine of forum non conveniens, international comity and jurisdictional rule of reason, and limitations arising out of parties' prior agreements (forum selection and related clauses). Section 5.02 provides an analysis of these issues in the context of an international case in a U.S. court, including analysis of the sort of jurisdictional issues involved in a particular problem. Section 5.03 discusses selected issues relating to the litigation of international cases in state court, while Section 5.04 focuses on jurisdiction in the federal courts. Suits by foreign sovereigns or nationals are considered in Section 5.05. This chapter then turns to selected limitations on the jurisdiction of U.S. courts, including the doctrine of forum non conveniens in Section 5.06, and the principles of international comity and reasonableness in Section 5.07. The final selected limitations, forum selection and arbitration clauses, are considered in Section 5.08. Section 5.09 concludes the chapter with a discussion of practical strategies and a checklist of jurisdictional issues.

Chapter 6 deals with jurisdiction to adjudicate, or *in personam* jurisdiction, as it is commonly known in the United States. It addresses international law and limitations—primarily constitutional—on the jurisdiction of U.S. courts to adjudicate disputes involving international issues or actors. Chapters 7 and 8 deal with specialized limitations on U.S. courts in the nature of limitations on jurisdiction. Chapter 7 deals with the Foreign Sovereign Immunities Act (FSIA), specifically, jurisdiction of United States courts with respect to foreign states and instrumentalities. The FSIA not only codifies the operation of the foreign sovereign immunity defense to jurisdiction, but is also the exclusive way to obtain jurisdiction over foreign sovereigns. Chapter 8 deals with a specialized limitation on the power of U.S. courts that is unique to the international context, the act of state doctrine. Although not truly jurisdictional, it is an important limitation on a U.S. court's ability to reach the merits of a particular international dispute.

§ 5.02 ANALYSIS OF INTERNATIONAL JURISDICTIONAL ISSUES

Jurisdictional issues under U.S. law are traditionally analyzed by considering, first, whether the court has subject matter jurisdiction, sometimes called competence or jurisdiction to prescribe, and, second, whether in personam jurisdiction or jurisdiction to adjudicate exists. The current Restatement of Foreign Relations Law states:

> [T]his Restatement deals with jurisdiction under the following headings: (1) *jurisdiction to prescribe, i.e.,* the authority of a state to make its law applicable to persons or activities; (2) *jurisdiction to adjudicate, i.e.,* the authority of a state to subject particular persons or things to its judicial process; and (3) *jurisdiction to enforce, i.e.,* the authority of a state to use the resources of government to induce or compel compliance with its law.[1]

Although these three categories could be used to analyze the actions of any nation—including the United States—under international law, under U.S. law, a court may not consider a case unless it has both subject matter and in *personam* jurisdiction. If either is absent, the court is without the authority to consider either the dispute or particular parties. For practical purposes it is important to consider these issues from the perspective of both the national and international concepts of jurisdiction involved in international cases.

The bifurcation of jurisdictional questions into subject matter and personal jurisdiction issues is a function of the U.S. Constitution. As a threshold issue, parties have two considerations in the international case. The first issue is whether U.S. law applies to the transaction, and second, whether it can be applied to the particular parties.

---

1. Restatement (Third) of Foreign Relations Law, Part IV, introductory note, at 231 (1987).

When the question is whether a U.S. court has been empowered, by constitution or statutes, to hear and decide a particular type of dispute, then the question is one of jurisdiction to prescribe (competence, or subject matter jurisdiction). When the question is whether a U.S. court can exercise that jurisdiction over the events or actors in a particular case, then the question is one of jurisdiction to adjudicate (personal jurisdiction). Once either issue is resolved, counsel must in addition consider whether any limitations imposed by U.S. or international law apply.

Under international law, a state has jurisdiction to prescribe, that is, the courts may entertain a particular dispute, when one or more of the recognized bases of national jurisdiction are present. The Restatement (Third) of Foreign Relations Law of the United States identifies these bases in section 402. The Restatement provides, subject to certain limitations discussed in Section 5.07, below, that:

> A state has jurisdiction to prescribe law with respect to
>
> (1) (a) conduct that, wholly or in substantial part, takes place within its territory;
>
> (b) the status of persons, or interests in things, present within its territory;
>
> (c) conduct outside its territory that has or is intended to have substantial effect within its territory;
>
> (2) the activities, interests, status or relations of its nationals outside as well as within its territory; and
>
> (3) certain conduct outside its territory by persons not its nationals that is directed against the security of the state or against a limited class of other state interests.[2]

Under section 402, a nation may prescribe laws only with respect to conduct that satisfies these tests. Consequently, in considering the question of jurisdiction in a particular case, counsel should always consider whether principles of international law are consistent with the issues of a particular case.

This chapter will focus primarily on section 402(1) and its three bases of territorial jurisdiction as they exist under U.S. law. The next

---

2. *Id.* § 402.

section, however, will consider the traditional analysis of jurisdiction under state law.

§ 5.03 STATE COURT JURISDICTION

[1] Generally

Although the lion's share of international litigation in the United States occurs in federal court, state courts provide an alternative forum in many instances. State courts are empowered by legislation to hear various actions and, unless federal courts have been given exclusive jurisdiction over a particular cause of action, many suits may be originally brought in state courts and litigated there. As one commentator has noted:

> In addition to a significant difference between federal and state in personam jurisdiction, . . . there is a fundamental difference in *subject matter jurisdiction.* Federal courts constituted under article III of the Constitution are limited to the subject matter jurisdiction embodied in that provision. In contrast, state courts of "general jurisdiction" are free to entertain any suit unless forbidden by state constitution or statute or, as noted below, by an act of Congress. It is significant that, generally, the areas of jurisdiction enumerated in article III are not made exclusively federal by operation of the Constitution. Broadly speaking, aside from admiralty cases, state courts have concurrent jurisdiction unless forbidden by Congress. Congressional prohibition is the exception rather than the rule.[3]

Typically, international litigation in a state court is pursued in actions in torts,[4] family law,[5] or employment law.[6] Some international commercial disputes, however, are also pursued in state courts.[7]

The basis for the exercise of U.S. state court jurisdiction under international law is described in the Restatement (Third) of Foreign Relations Law, which provides:

---

3. Graham C. Lilly, *Jurisdiction Over Domestic and Alien Defendants,* 69 VA. L. REV. 85, 123, n.142 (1983) (citations omitted) (emphasis supplied).

4. Hattori v. Peairs, 662 So. 2d 509 (La. Ct. App. 1995) (personal injury); Hayes v. Evergo Telephone Co. Ltd., 397 S.E.2d 325 (N.C. Ct. App. 1990) (product liability); *In re* Minnesota Asbestos Litigation, 540 N.W.2d 896 (Minn. Ct. App. 1995) (environmental tort).

5. Ivaldi v. Ivaldi, 672 A.2d 1226 (N.J. Super. 1996) (child custody).

6. D'Agostino v. Johnson & Johnson, 628 A.2d 305 (N.J. Super. 1993) (wrongful termination).

7. Sarieddine v. Moussa, 820 S.W.2d 837 (Tex. Ct. App. 1991) (default on stock purchase agreement).

International law normally is not concerned with how authority to exercise jurisdiction is allocated within a state's domestic constitutional order. Whether a state may exercise jurisdiction that the United States is entitled to exercise under international law is, therefore, only a question of United States law. Subject to constitutional limitations, a State may exercise jurisdiction on the basis of territoriality, including effects within the territory, and, in some respects at least, on the basis of citizenship, residence, or domicile in the State.[8]

[2] Note on Removal

If suit is commenced in state court, a foreign defendant has a right of removal to federal district court under 28 U.S.C.A. § 1441(a) and (b). Subsections (a) and (b) provide, in pertinent part:

(a) Except as otherwise expressly provided by Act of Congress, any civil action brought in a State court of which the district courts have original jurisdiction, may be removed by the defendant or the defendants, to the district court of the United States for the district and division embracing the place where such action is pending.

(b) Any civil action of which the district courts have original jurisdiction founded on a claim or right arising under the Constitution, treaties or laws of the United States shall be removable without regard to the citizenship or residence of the parties. Any other such action shall be removable only if none of the parties in interest properly joined and served as defendants is a citizen of the State in which the action is brought.

The procedures for removal are contained in section 1446, including the time limits for filing a notice of removal.[9] The removability of actions is a function of whether the federal district courts have original jurisdiction over such actions.[9.1] The next section deals with both the types of transnational actions the district courts have original jurisdiction over, and the limits placed on the jurisdictional power of the federal courts.

8. Restatement, *supra* note 1, § 402, cmt. k, pp. 241–42; reporters' note 5.

9. *See* 28 U.S.C.A. § 1446(b); Restatement, *supra* note 1, § 402. For a discussion of the removal statute in the context of foreign sovereign defendants, *see* § 7.03[2].

9.1. Procedural issues in a Court's addressing subject matter jurisdiction and personal jurisdiction concerning a case removed to federal court are addressed, *infra* § 6.02[2].

§ 5.04 FEDERAL COURT JURISDICTION

Foreign parties frequently prefer U.S. federal court over U.S. state court. Foreign parties may perceive that the national character of the federal courts facilitates impartiality and that federal judges may be more sophisticated concerning commercial and international disputes.[10] The jurisdiction of the federal courts, however, is limited and delineated by Article III of the Constitution and federal law.[11] If a specific jurisdictional grant is not present, the judicial power is absent. Consequently, the first step in analyzing any federal jurisdiction issue is identifying the specific jurisdictional grant. All federal jurisdictional authority starts with the Constitution. It provides broad categories of jurisdictional authority under which Congress provides specific legislation authorizing particular cases. Section 2 of Article III provides, in pertinent part:

> The judicial Power shall extend to all Cases, in Law and Equity arising under this Constitution, the Laws of the United States, and Treaties made, or which shall be made, under their Authority;–to all Cases affecting Ambassadors, other public Ministers and Consuls;–to all Cases of admiralty and maritime Jurisdiction;–to Controversies to which the United States shall be a Party;—to Controversies between two or more States;—between a State and Citizens of another State;—between citizens of different States;—between Citizens of the same State claiming lands under Grants of different States, and between a State, or the Citizens thereof, and foreign States, Citizens, or Subjects.

If the Constitution contains a grant of jurisdictional power encompassing a particular type of action (e.g., federal question, diversity) then the next step is generally to identify a specific statutory grant of jurisdiction. As the Supreme Court has stated: "the subject matter jurisdiction of the lower federal courts is determined by Congress, 'in the exact degree and character which to Congress may seem proper for the public good.'"[12]

---

10. *See 2d Circuit Bars Suits by "Offshore" Corporations*, NAT'L L.J., Mon., Aug. 25, 1997, at B9 (suggesting federal court bias of foreign litigants).

11. *See* Insurance Corp. of Ireland v. Compagnie des Bauxites de Guinee, 456 U.S. 694, 701 (1982) (jurisdiction of lower federal courts is "limited to those subjects encompassed within the statutory grant of jurisdiction").

12. Carry v. Curtis, 44 U.S. (3 How.) 236, 245 (1845). *See* Insurance Corp. of Ireland, Ltd. v. Compagnie Des Bauxites De Guinea, *supra* note 11; Bush v. Lucas, 462 U.S. 367, 374 (1983). *But see* Davis v. Passman, 442 U.S. 228, 246 (1979); Bell v. Hood, 327 U.S. 678, 684 (1946).

For instance, Congress has specifically authorized federal court jurisdiction over diversity actions in 28 U.S.C.A. § 1332. Section 1332(a)(2) provides for "alienage jurisdiction," or jurisdiction to hear civil cases between citizens of a state or states and of foreign states (assuming the in-excess-of-$75,000.00 amount in controversy requirement is met). Recent cases have dealt with certain issues which may arise in determining alien citizenship.[13] Section 1332(a)(3) provides that jurisdiction exists where there is diversity of citizenship between domestic U.S. parties and where foreign citizens are additional parties to either or both sides of the action.[14] Section 1332(c)(1) states that "a corporation shall be deemed to be a citizen of any State by which it has been incorporated and of the State where it has its principal place of business. . . ."[15]

Diversity jurisdiction under 28 U.S.C.A. § 1332(a) is not available, however, between a citizen of a foreign state and a citizen of the U.S. domiciled abroad at commencement of the action. The reason is that for diversity purposes a person's citizenship is determined by her domicile.[15.1] U.S. citizens domiciled abroad are therefore neither citizens of any U.S. state nor citizens or subjects of a foreign state within the requirements of § 1332. This "stateless person" bar to diversity may apply to plaintiffs or defendants. In *Cresswell v. Sullivan & Cromwell*,[15.2] the Court found it lacked diversity jurisdiction over claims of foreign plaintiffs where three of the large group of plaintiffs were U.S. residents domiciled abroad. The case was brought by foreign investors against a U.S. securities firm and the U.S. law firm that represented the securities firm. Simply dropping the claims of the three U.S. citizens

13. *See* Foy v. Schantz, 108 F.3d 1347 (11th Cir. 1997) (official permanent resident status required to avoid categorization as alien and mere intent to permanently reside in U.S. is insufficient); Singh v. Daimler-Benz, A.G., 9 F.3d 303 (3d Cir. 1993) (complete diversity of citizenship among parties Plaintiff and Defendant is not required for jurisdiction as long as U.S. citizen is in action); Lloyds Bank v. Norkin, 817 F. Supp. 414 (S.D.N.Y. 1993) (contra; requiring complete diversity of citizenship); Saadeh v. Farouki, 107 F.3d 52 (D.C. Cir. 1997) (intent of 1988 amendment to § 1332(a) was to deny jurisdiction in actions between citizen of state and permanent resident alien of same state).

14. Dresser Industries, Inc. v. Underwriters at Lloyds of London, 106 F.3d 494 (3d Cir. 1997) (diversity jurisdiction exists in suit of New York citizen against California citizen and French citizen).

15. One court has concluded "that for diversity purposes a corporation incorporated in the United States with its principal place of business abroad is solely a citizen of its 'State' of incorporation." Torres v. Southern Peru Copper Corp., 113 F.3d 540 (5th Cir. 1997).

15.1. Domicile is defined by residence-in-fact, along with intent to remain or to return when absent. Domicile is *prima facie* evidence of residency.

15.2. 922 F.2d 60 (2d Cir. 1990).

domiciled abroad would not have established diversity: The law firm had partners who were U.S. citizens domiciled abroad. A partnership is deemed to have the citizenship of each of its members.

Practice Note: Counsel seeking a federal court forum by diversity jurisdiction under 28 U.S.C.A. § 1332 should carefully investigate the domicile of all potential parties, particularly in cases where many parties may be involved or where one party is a partnership which may have U.S. citizen members domiciled abroad, such as an international law or tax firm. Diversity jurisdiction is not available where one or more parties is a U.S. citizen with permanent domicile abroad.

Congress has also specifically authorized federal court jurisdiction over federal question actions in § 1331. In *Joseph Muller Corporation Zurich v. Société Anonyme de Gérance*,[16] the court was faced with two actions between two foreign parties. One suit was a contract action, and the other was an antitrust action. The federal court decided that it had no authority to exercise jurisdiction over the contract action, stating:

> While considerations of international comity would suggest that—given the policy expressed in the Franco-Swiss treaty—United States courts should decline to exercise jurisdiction over a purely private action such as the contract suit here at issue, particularly when the contracts were entered into and were to be performed largely outside the United States, we need not rest our decision on that ground. The pleadings in this case fail to reveal any basis of federal jurisdiction. Joseph Muller's complaint asserted jurisdiction based upon diversity of citizenship. But as the pleadings clearly show, all parties are aliens, and neither the constitutional nor statutory grants of jurisdiction include such a suit.[17]

Without the power to hear the contract action, the court allowed only the antitrust claim to go forward.[18]

In addition to the Constitution, federal statutes, and treaties, federal common law has also been held to supply federal-question jurisdiction under 28 U.S.C.A. § 1331. Courts have found federal-question jurisdiction to exist with regard to issues of international relations even when the Plaintiff's complaint alleges only state law claims.[19]

---

16. 451 F.2d 727 (2d Cir. 1971) (per curiam), *cert. denied*, 406 U.S. 906 (1972).

17. *Id.* at 729 (citations omitted).

18. *Id.*

19. *See, e.g.*, Torres v. Southern Peru Copper Corp., 113 F.3d 540 (5th Cir. 1997) (finding federal-question jurisdiction regarding international relations where action involved Peru's

Practice Note: Foreign defendants often prefer a federal court over a state forum. Federal common law may provide a basis for federal court jurisdiction where diversity of citizenship or other Constitutional or other statutory bases for such jurisdiction is lacking. Federal common law jurisdiction may be found in cases which invoke issues of U.S. international relations by addressing significant political interests of a foreign sovereign. Mere foreign economic interests may be insufficient. Such jurisdictional arguments may be assisted by the filing of correspondence or an amicus brief by U.S. agencies (e.g., State Department or Justice Department) or the foreign sovereign.

In an action over a state law claim, even if the federal court finds lack of jurisdiction based on diversity of citizenship, it may be possible to pursue the claim on the grounds of pendent jurisdiction, when a related federal claim can be asserted. Pendent jurisdiction over state claims exists when the federal claim is sufficient to confer federal jurisdiction, and there is a common nucleus of operative fact between the state and federal claim.[20] The ultimate lack of merit of the federal claim does not mean that pendent jurisdiction cannot attach; the federal claim must be devoid of merit and frivolous in order to divest

(*Text continued on page 5-11*)

vital economic interests and sovereignty); Republic of Philippines v. Marcos, 806 F.2d 344 (2d Cir. 1986) (federal-question jurisdiction found in suit by foreign government against its former head of state); Marathon Oil Co. v. Ruhrgas, A.G., 115 F.3d 315 (5th Cir. 1997) (no federal-question jurisdiction where suit did not question official German policy decisions, despite filing of amicus brief and letter of protest by Germany asserting that its sovereignty was at issue).

20. United Mine Workers of Am. v. Gibbs, 383 U.S. 715, 725 (1966).

the court of pendent jurisdiction. The court may retain jurisdiction even if the federal claims over which it had original jurisdiction are dismissed. The decision to retain jurisdiction over state law claims is within the district court's discretion, weighing factors such as economy, convenience, fairness, and comity.[21]

[1] Note on Applicable Law

Because federal courts exercising diversity jurisdiction must apply state law,[22] some international cases require the federal courts to apply state law on particular issues.[23] For instance, in *Clarkson Co., Ltd. v. Shaheen*,[24] a federal court in New York was faced with a suit by a Canadian trustee in bankruptcy, appointed by a Canadian court, to obtain records located in the New York offices of bankrupt corporations. The trustee sought an order obtaining access to the records. The district court granted access, and the defendant appealed, bringing a collateral attack on the Canadian bankruptcy proceeding. The Second Circuit, in rejecting the challenge, applied the New York law of international comity.[25] Under this doctrine "New York courts recognize the statutory title of an alien trustee in bankruptcy, as long as the foreign court had jurisdiction over the bankrupt and the foreign proceeding has not resulted in injustice to New York citizens, prejudice to creditors' New York statutory remedies, or violation of the laws or public policy of the state."[26] The *Clarkson* case illustrates the application of a state law doctrine of international deference applied in a diversity suit in federal court. Counsel must be prepared for the application of state law, even in cases brought in federal court involving international issues.

21. Brady v. Brown, 51 F.3d 810 (9th Cir. 1995) (court found no diversity jurisdiction over plaintiff's state law claims, including fraud, because defendant, U.S. citizen domiciled in Mexico, was neither "citizen of a state" nor "alien"; but because of federal jurisdiction over RICO claims, court could also exercise jurisdiction over state claims).

22. Erie R.R. Co. v. Tompkins, 304 U.S. 64 (1938).

23. *See* Cornfeld v. Investors Overseas Services, Ltd., 471 F. Supp. 1255, 1259 n.5 (S.D.N.Y. 1979), *aff'd mem.*, 614 F.2d 1286 (2d Cir. 1979) (court, in diversity action, holding New York law controlling on issue of comity).

24. 544 F.2d 624 (2d Cir. 1976).

25. *Id.* at 629–30. The doctrine of comity is discussed *infra* in § 5.08.

26. *Id.* at 629 (citations omitted).

[2] The Presumption Against Extraterritoriality

Some international litigation may involve a suit brought over conduct of a defendant overseas on the grounds that the conduct is proscribed or regulated by a U.S. statute. The issue then arises whether the court can exercise its subject matter jurisdiction based on the statute. As a general rule, the answer is no, based on the doctrine known as the presumption against extraterritoriality. The Supreme Court recently reminded us that "it is a longstanding principle of American law that legislation of Congress, unless a contrary intent appears, is meant to apply only within the territorial jurisdiction of the United States."[27] The presumption serves to protect against unintended clashes between our laws and those of other nations which would result in international discord.[28] Moreover, the presumption recognizes that Congress is primarily concerned with domestic conditions when it legislates.[29]

As discussed in *Kollinas v. D&G Marine Maintenance Co.*,[30] a two-fold inquiry is required when attempting to apply the presumption in a specific factual setting. First, the court must determine if the presumption applies at all. After identifying the conduct proscribed or regulated by the particular legislation in question, the court must consider if that conduct occurred outside of the borders of the United States. Second, if the presumption is implicated, an inquiry into congressional intent must be undertaken to determine if Congress intended to extend the coverage of the relevant statute to such extraterritorial conduct.[31]

The act of Congress will not apply to conduct occurring outside the United States unless the affirmative intention of Congress is clearly expressed in the statute.[32] In *Kollinas v. D&G Marine Maintenance*, the court interpreted *Aramco* as holding that a court may consider the specific language of a statute and other indicia of Congressional intent—including legislative history and administrative interpretations—to determine if the presumption against extraterritoriality has

27. EEOC v. Arabian American Oil Co. (Aramco), 499 U.S. 244, 248 (1991), *quoting* Foley Bros., Inc. v. Folardo, 336 U.S. 281 (1949).

28. *Aramco*, 499 U.S. at 248.

29. *Id.*

30. 29 F.3d 67, 70–75 (2d Cir. 1994).

31. Gushi Bros. Co. v. Bank of Guam, 28 F.3d 1535, 1542–43 (9th Cir. 1994).

32. *Aramco*, 499 U.S. at 248 (*quoting* Benz v. Compania Naviera Hidalgo, S.A., 353 U.S. 138, 147 (1957).

been overcome.[33] In *Environmental Defense Fund v. Massey*,[34] the court enumerated three distinct categories of cases in which the presumption does not apply: (1) where the regulated conduct occurs within the United States; (2) where Congress clearly intended to extend the scope of a statute to conduct occurring within foreign nations; and (3) where the failure to extend the scope of the statute to a foreign setting will result in "adverse effects" in the United States. Under these principles, the Sherman Anti-Trust Act,[35] the Lanham Trade-Mark Act,[36] and the Securities and Exchange Act[37] have been applied extraterritorially.[38]

Although most courts discussing the "effects" exception to the presumption against extraterritoriality have required that the actor intend that its conduct result in substantial effects within the United States,[39] the ultimate touchstone of extraterritoriality consists of an ascertainment of congressional intent. The courts have not relied solely on the consequences within the United States of a failure to give a statutory scheme extraterritorial application.[40] For example, in *Aluminum Co. of America,* Judge Learned Hand, in considering the effects of the defendant's conduct within the United States stated "we are concerned only with whether Congress chose to attach liability to conduct outside the United States of persons not in allegiance to it."[41] It is therefore unclear if the domestic effects of foreign conduct, in the absence of congressional direction that a statute be applied to such conduct, is sufficient to render the presumption inapplicable and create a valid cause of action under the relevant statute.

---

33. *See also* Subafilms Ltd. v. MGM-Pathé Communications Co., 24 F.3d 1088 (9th Cir. 1994) (en banc) (court considered copyright law and other enactments to determine if copyright laws applied to conduct outside of United States), *remanded,* 31 F.3d 812 (9th Cir. 1994).

34. 986 F.2d 528, 531 (D.C. Cir. 1993).

35. U.S. v. Aluminum Co. of America, 148 F.2d 416 (2d Cir. 1945).

36. Steele v. Bulova Watch Co., 344 U.S. 280 (1952).

37. Schoenbaum v. Firstbrook, 405 F.2d 200 (2d Cir. 1968).

38. *See also* RESTATEMENT, *supra* note 1, at § 402(1)(c).

39. E.g., U.S. v. Aluminum Co. of Am., 148 F.2d at 443; Laker Airways v. Sabena, Belgian World Airlines, 731 F.2d 909, 924 (D.C. Cir. 1984).

40. *Subafilms Ltd.*, 24 F.3d at 1096.

41. 148 F.2d at 443.

§ 5.05 SELECTED ISSUES REGARDING JURISDICTION TO PRESCRIBE

[1] Securities Law

The extent of the extraterritorial application of U.S. securities laws over international fraudulent conduct has presented difficult issues for courts. In general, two jurisdictional tests have emerged, the "conduct test" and the "effects test." Under the "conduct test," a federal court has jurisdiction if a plaintiff's losses are directly caused by a defendant's wrongful act or omission within the U.S., if such misconduct was more than merely preparatory to the fraud.[42] Under the "effects test," a federal court has jurisdiction if the effects of a securities fraud taking place abroad are felt in the United States.[43] At least one Circuit has applied a combination of the two tests, finding that the combination of U.S.-based conduct and U.S.-felt effects may justify U.S. federal court jurisdiction.[44]

§ 5.06 SUITS BY FOREIGN SOVEREIGNS OR NATIONALS

In considering the jurisdiction of U.S. courts in cases involving international issues, an important question is whether non-U.S. plaintiffs are entitled to access to the judiciary. May non-U.S. parties invoke the jurisdiction of U.S. courts? There are numerous examples of foreign plaintiffs bringing suit in the United States such as *Sarieddine v. Moussa*.[45] Some limitations exist, however, on whether foreign plaintiffs may bring suit in U.S. courts.

In the federal system, in the absence of a specific statutory definition of who is entitled to invoke the court's jurisdiction, the Constitution limits access to U.S. courts. For instance, the federal courts have jurisdiction only over actions specifically set out in article

---

42. *See, e.g.*, Bersch v. Drexel Firestone, Inc., 519 F.2d 974, 987 (2d Cir. 1975), *cert. denied*, 423 U.S. 1018 (1975).

43. *See, e.g.*, Consolidated Gold Fields, PLC v. Minorco, S.A., 871 F.2d 252, 262–63 (2d Cir. 1989), *amended on other grounds*, 890 F.2d 569 (2d Cir. 1989), *cert. dismissed*, 492 U.S. 939 (1989); *In re* Marc Rich & Co., A.G., 707 F.2d 663, 666–67 (2d Cir. 1983), *cert. denied*, 463 U.S. 1215 (1983).

44. Itoba, Ltd. v. LEP Group, PLC, 54 F.3d 118 (2d Cir. 1995), *cert. denied*, 116 S. Ct. 702 (1996) (asserting U.S. court jurisdiction over securities fraud allegedly committed by U.K. corporate issuer in predominately foreign transactions).

45. 820 S.W.2d 837 (Tex. Ct. App. 1991). The *Sarieddine* case is discussed *supra* in § 5.03.

III and the federal jurisdictional statutes.[46] Because article III specifically includes suits brought by a "foreign citizen" and those involving "a foreign state," the courts are generally open to foreign plaintiffs.[47] Federal courts do not, however, have jurisdiction over suits between aliens as a general rule.[48]

[1] Alien Tort Statute

The principal exception to the general rule, that U.S. courts do not have jurisdiction over suits whose parties and subject matter are wholly foreign, is the Alien Tort Statute, 28 U.S.C.A. § 1350. The Statute provides:

> The district courts shall have original jurisdiction of any civil action by an alien for a tort only, committed in violation of the law of nations or a treaty of the United States.

The Statute, therefore, provides a private right of action concerning violations of (i) *jus cogens* (internationally recognized norms) or (ii) of a treaty of the United States.[48.1] The Statute was originally enacted in 1789 to allow U.S. courts to redress acts of piracy but has been seldom invoked.[49] The requirement under provision (i) that the violation be of "the law of nations" is extremely restrictive and, until recently, few cases met such standard.[50]

The Alien Tort Statute, however, emerged as a viable jurisdictional vehicle in *Filartiga v. Pena-Irala*.[51] In that case, Dr. Joel Filartiga, a Paraguayan citizen and dissident, obtained a $10 million judgment

---

46. *See* U.S. Const., Art. III; 28 U.S.C.A. §§ 1331 & 1332. *See generally supra* § 5.04.

47. *See, e.g.*, Iran Handicraft & Carpet Export Ctr. v. Marjan Int'l Corp., 655 F. Supp. 1275, 1281 (S.D.N.Y. 1987), *aff'd mem.*, 868 F.2d 1267 (2d Cir. 1988).

48. *See, e.g.*, Singh v. Daimler-Benz, AG, 9 F.3d 303 (1993); A.T.X. Export, Ltd. v. Mendler, 849 F. Supp. 283 (S.D.N.Y. 1994); Lloyd's Bank PLC v. Norkin, 817 F. Supp. 414 (S.D.N.Y. 1993). One exception to this general rule is the Alien Tort Statute, 28 U.S.C.A. § 1350, discussed *infra*, § 5.06[1].

48.1 Abebe-Jira v. Negewo, 72 F.3d 844, 848 (11th Cir.1996) (Alien Tort Claims Act "establishes a federal forum where courts may fashion domestic common law remedies to give effect to violations of customary international law"). Thus, the ATCA "creates both subject matter jurisdiction and a private right of action." Estate of Winston Cabello v. Fernandez-Larios, 157 F. Supp. 2d 1345 (S.D. Fla. 2001), citing *Abebe-Jira,* 72 F.3d at 848.

49. *See* Kadic v. Karadzic, 70 F.3d 232 (2d Cir. 1995), *reh'g denied*, 74 F.3d 377, *cert. denied*, 116 S. Ct. 2524 (1996) (examining legislative history and prior court decisions regarding Statute).

50. *See* Filartiga v. Pena-Irala, 630 F.2d 876, 887 (2d Cir. 1980) (observing that "Alien Tort Statute has rarely been the basis for jurisdiction during its long history . . . .").

51. 630 F.2d 876 (2d Cir. 1980).

against Paraguayan police official Americo Pena-Irala who was served with process in Brooklyn, N.Y.[52] Filartiga testified that Pena-Irala killed Filartiga's son by torture and that the Paraguayan judicial system failed to redress such act.[53] The court found subject matter and personal jurisdiction under the Alien Tort Act for violations of the law of nations.[54] The Court ruled that the right to be free from torture is "now among" the narrow list of fundamental rights conferred by international law for purposes of the Alien Tort Statute.[55]

The *Filartiga* decision was codified as the Torture Victim Protection Act.[56] The Torture Victim Protection Act establishes a civil cause of action concerning torture or extrajudicial killing committed under state authority.[57] The Act imposes an exhaustion of local remedies requirement and ten-year statute of limitation.[58] Since *Filartiga*, several courts have awarded substantial damages concerning acts of torture and extrajudicial killings by foreign government officials.[59]

Jurisdiction under the Alien Tort Statute was expanded by the Second Circuit in *Kadic v. Karadzic*.[60] Suit in *Karadzic* was brought by Croat and Muslim citizens of Bosnia-Herzegovina against defendant Radovan Karadzic, leader of a non-internationally recognized Bosnian-Serb republic within Bosnia-Herzegovina. Plaintiffs complained of acts by troops under Karadzic's command, including, among others, rape, torture, and execution.[61]

Karadzic was personally served with process while visiting in New York as an invitee of the United Nations.[62] The Second Circuit ruled

---

52. *Id.* at 878–79; *see War Crimes Suits on Tap in NYC*, NAT'L L.J., Mon., Dec. 29, 1997, at A6 (discussing *Filartiga* and current alien tort litigation).

53. 630 F.2d at 878.

54. *Id.* at 887.

55. *Id.* at 885, 890. It may also be noted that the damages awarded on remand, 577 F. Supp. 860 (E.D.N.Y. 1984), were not enforced, a common problem in cases against international tortfeasors.

56. 28 U.S.C.A. § 1350, Pub. L. No. 102–256, Mar. 12, 1992, 106 Stat. 73.

57. *Id.* at § 2(a) (rendering liable individuals who have committed torture or extrajudicial killing "under actual or apparent authority or color of law, of any foreign nation").

58. *Id.* at § 2(b), (c).

59. Abebe-Jira v. Negewo, 72 F.3d 844 (11th Cir. 1996) (suit by Ethiopian torture victims against their torturer); Xuncax v. Gramjo, 886 F. Supp. 162 (D. Mass. 1995); Paul v. Avril, 901 F. Supp. 330 (S.D. Fla. 1994).

60. 70 F.3d 232 (2d Cir. 1995), *reh'g denied*, 74 F.3d 377, *cert. denied*, 116 S. Ct. 2524 (1996).

61. *Id.* at 236–37.

62. *Id.* at 237 (finding such service of process proper as Karadzic was merely invitee of United Nations, not recognized head of state, and not otherwise entitled to immunity under several theories asserted by Karadzic).

that the Alien Tort Statute conferred jurisdiction for violations of the law of nations committed by those not acting under the authority of a recognized state and that such violations include genocide, war crimes, and crimes against humanity.[63] The Court further observed that the content of the law of nations must be judged, "not as it was in 1789, but as it has evolved and exists among the nations of the world today."[64]

It should be noted, however, that the jurisdictional standard under the Alien Tort Statute remains extremely high. Current law only supports jurisdiction where the acts involved were violative of fundamental human rights as codified by international Convention. As the *Filartiga* Court observed:

> the mere fact that every nations' municipal law may prohibit theft does not incorporate "the Eight Commandment, 'Thou Shalt not steal' . . . [into] the law of nations." It is only where the nations of the world have demonstrated that the wrong is of mutual, and not merely several, concern, by means of express international accords, that a wrong generally recognized becomes an international law violation within the meaning of the statute.[65]

The list of torts which may be encompassed within the Alien Tort Statute will continue to develop under case law. A recent case has suggested, at least at the preliminary motions stage, that the Statute may apply to denial of a union's right to associate and organize.[66] The Alien Tort Statute has been found to confer jurisdiction over corporations, as well as over individuals.[67] Commercial/property torts and air crash disasters have not provided jurisdiction under the Alien Tort Statute.[68]

---

63. *Id.* at 241–44.

64. *Id.* at 238, *quoting Filartiga*, 630 F.2d at 881.

65. 630 F.2d at 888, *citing*, Judge Friendly in ITT v. Vencap, 519 F.2d 1001, 1015 (1975).

66. Estate of Rodriquez v. Drummond Co., Inc., 256 F. Supp. 2d 1250, 1262 (N.D. Ala. 2003).

67. John Doe I v. Unocal Corp., 963 F. Supp. 880 (C.D. Cal. 1998) (acts of torture, rape, forced labor, and confiscation of property in connection with oil pipeline project); Bowoto v. Chevron, No. 99–2506 (N.D. Cal., Judge Charles Legge, Order of Apr. 7, 2000) (denying Chevron's motion to dismiss Alien Tort Claims Act suit concerning Chevron's alleged participation in Nigerian government actions to quell civil unrest in oil region). Judge Legge suggested that *forum non conveniens* motions to dismiss of defendants in ATCA suits should be viewed skeptically by courts, as the law provides expressly for U.S. jurisdiction and "is a factor that ought to be weighed in favor of the plaintiffs."

68. *See* Hamid v. Price Waterhouse, 51 F.3d 1411 (9th Cir. 1995), *cert. denied*, 116 S. Ct. 709 (claims in substance of fraud, breach of fiduciary duty and misappropriation of funds are not within ambit of Statute); Dreyfus v. von Finck, 534 F.2d 24 (2d Cir.), *cert. denied*, 429 U.S. 835 (1976) (no international consensus exists regarding forced sale of property); DeWitt

The Supreme Court in *Sosa v. Alvarez-Machain*[69] ruled that a single illegal detention, of less than one day, of a Mexican national, custody of whom was then transferred to lawful authorities in the United States for prompt arraignment, violated no norm of customary international law so well defined as to support creation of a cause of action that the district court could hear under the Alien Tort Statute.[70] The facts in *Sosa* were that Plaintiff, a Mexican national acquitted of murder after being abducted and transported to the United States to face prosecution, brought action under Alien Tort Statute (ATS) and Federal Tort Claims Act (FTCA) against United States, Drug Enforcement Agency (DEA) agents, former Mexican policeman, and Mexican civilians, alleging that his abduction violated his civil rights. Although denying the particular claims brought, the *Sosa* Court, significantly, did not preclude aliens from seeking redress of fundamental international law violations in U.S. courts under the ATS. Although the *Sosa* Court was the first Supreme Court ruling to address the ATS, the ruling does not appear to have shed much light on the applicability or interpretation of the ATS beyond the specific facts of the case.

It may also be noted that the second provision of the Alien Tort Statute, concerning violation of a treaty of the United States, has been rarely invoked.[71] As with the first provision of the Alien Tort Statute, the treaty provision is extremely narrow. As one court observed, the Statute applies only to those treaty provisions that create a ''tort'' action by their violation and not to all violations of a U.S. Treaty.[71.1]

The limitation period applicable to Alien Tort Statute claims is that of the forum state, not that of the foreign state in which the conduct causing the injury occurred.[71.2] The Torture Victim Protection Act imposes a ten-year statute of limitations.[71.3]

---

v. KLM Royal Dutch Airlines, N.V., 570 F. Supp. 613 (D.N.Y. 1983) (circumstances involved in action against former employer were not so extraordinary as to permit jurisdiction); Benjamins v. British European Airways, 572 F.2d 913 (2d Cir. 1978), *cert. denied*, 439 U.S. 1114 (1979) (willful negligence causing air disaster does not violate law of nations).

69. 542 U.S. 692, 124 S. Ct. 2739, 159 L. Ed. 2d 718 (2004).

70. *Id.*, 124 S. Ct. at 2769.

71. *See Karadzic*, 70 F.3d at 232, fn. 1 (observing that Plaintiffs in *Karadzic* and *Filartiga* did not consider alternative prong of Alien Tort Act, suits by aliens for tort committed in violation of U.S. treaty).

71.1. Xuncax v. Gramjo, 886 F. Supp. 162 (D. Mass. 1995).

71.2. Forti v. Suarez-Mason, 672 F. Supp. 1531 (N.D. Cal. 1987), *reconsideration granted in part*, 694 F. Supp. 707; *see also* Xuncax v. Gramjo, 886 F. Supp. 162 (D. Mass. 1995) (finding suit timely under Massachusetts borrowing statute when brought within three years of Defendant's entering Massachusetts but nine years from earliest alleged misconduct).

71.3. 28 U.S.C.A. § 1350, § 2(c).

Practice Note: The Alien Tort Statute confers jurisdiction over suits by aliens, in tort only, and for actions violative of the law of nations. Such actions include piracy, torture, genocide, extrajudicial killing, and war crimes, and they include other torts. It is unclear whether terrorism is on such list. It is not settled whether the defendant must commit such actions under color of state authority.[71.4] Commercial/property torts and claims concerning transportation disasters are unlikely to qualify under the Alien Tort Statute.

The Third Circuit examined procedural issues concerning the Alien Tort Statute and Torture Victim Protection Act in *Cabello v. Fernandez-Larios*.[71.5] In *Cabello*, the Estate of a 28-year-old economic consultant to Chilean President Salvador Allende, who was kidnapped, tortured and killed by a death squad in 1973, was awarded $4 million by a federal jury in the Southern District of Florida. The court affirmed the district court's denial of defendants' motion to dismiss and the judgment entered against defendants. The court held that the Torture Victim Protection Act's (TVPA's) ten-year statute of limitations could be applied retroactively to a cause of action arising under the Alien Tort Claims Act (ATCA) before the TVPA went into effect.[71.6] The court held that retroactive application of the TVPA was not impermissible as ''The TVPA creates no new liabilities nor does it impair rights. Rather, the TVPA extended the ATCA, which had been limited to aliens, to allow citizens of the United States to bring suits for torture and extrajudicial killings in United States courts.''[71.7] The court also held that the ten-year statute of limitations was equitably tolled while members of the Chilean government engaged in acts of concealment, by refusing to disclose location of grave where political prisoner was buried.[71.8] The court also held that the ATCA and TVPA permit parties injured by acts of torture, crimes against humanity and the like to pursue recovery, not only against those who are directly liable, but against those that conspired with or

71.4. Estate of Rodriquez v. Drummond Co., Inc., 256 F. Supp. 2d 1250, 1260 (N.D. Ala. 2003) (denying defendants' motion to dismiss and declining to decide whether the tort must be committed under color of state law).

71.5. 402 F. 3d 1148 (3d Cir. 2005).

71.6. *Id.* at 1153-54 (*citing* prior precedent that ''[t]he ATCA and the TVPA share the same ten-year statute of limitations,'' Arce, et al. v. Garcia, 400 F.3d 1340 (11th Cir. 2005)).

71.7. *Id.* at 1154.

71.8. *Id.* at 1155-56.

assisted those directly liable on conspiracy or accomplice liability theory.[71.9]

[2] Selected Limitations on Suits by Foreign Parties

In some situations a question arises about what is included in the definition of a "foreign state," especially in the case of a foreign

(*Text continued on page 5-19*)

71.9. *Id.* at 1157-58 (*citing* Hilao v. Estate of Marcos, 103 F.3d 767, 776-77 (9th Cir. 1996); Carmichael v. United Tech. Corp., 835 F.2d 109, 113-14 (5th Cir. 1988) and legislative history, S. Rep. No. 102-249, at 8-9 (1991)).

government unrecognized by the U.S. Government.[72] Because recognition of foreign states is a power delegated to the executive branch, the courts rely on determinations of status performed by the executive.[73] As the court in *Vietnam v. Pfizer, Inc.*,[74] stated:

> The law is well settled that a foreign government that is not recognized by the United States may not maintain suit in state or federal court. . . . The recognition of foreign governments is a function of the executive branch and is wholly outside the competence of the judiciary. . . . While executive action pertaining to the recognition or nonrecognition of a foreign government is binding on the courts, the courts are nevertheless free to determine the legal consequences of that executive action upon pending litigation. . . . On occasion, suit has been brought by a foreign government recognized by the United States and, during the pendency of the action, diplomatic recognition of the party plaintiff has been withdrawn. Under these circumstances, courts have traditionally responded by either dismissing the action or suspending it *sine die* pending recognition of a new government by the United States.[75]

In *Pfizer*, the court of appeals affirmed the district court's dismissal because, during the pendency of the action, the government of Vietnam was no longer recognized by the United States.[76]

In other cases, the court must determine whether citizens or entities of a foreign unrecognized state may maintain suit. For instance, in *Iran Handicraft & Carpet Export Ctr. v. Marjan Int'l Corp.*,[77] the court was faced with the issue of whether citizens of an unrecognized, but nevertheless existing, foreign government were eligible to maintain an

72. In general, a State is defined in international law as "an entity that has a defined territory and a permanent population, under the control of its own government, and that engages in, or has the capacity to engage in, formal relations with other such entities." Kadic v. Karadzic, 70 F.3d 232 (2d Cir. 1995), *reh'g denied*, 74 F.3d 377, *cert. denied*, 518 U.S. 1005 (1996), *quoting*, RESTATEMENT (THIRD) OF FOREIGN RELATIONS LAW, § 201.

73. *Id.* at 1277. *See generally* Mary Beth West & Sean D. Murphy, *The Impact on U.S. Litigation of Non-Recognition of Foreign Governments*, 26 STAN. J. INT'L L. 435 (1990); Marian Nash (Leich), *Contemporary Practice of the United States Relating to International Law, Unrecognized Governments: Access to U.S. Courts*, 90 AM. J. INT'L L. 263 (1996) (discussion of statement of interest in case of Liberia).

74. 556 F.2d 892 (8th Cir. 1977).

75. *Id.* at 894.

76. *Id.* at 894–895. *See also* Ministry of Defense of Islamic Republic of Iran v. Gould, Inc., 969 F.2d 764 (9th Cir. 1992); Federal Republic of Germany v. Elicofon, 358 F. Supp. 747, 757 (E.D.N.Y. 1972), *aff'd*, 478 F.2d 231 (2d Cir. 1973), *cert. denied*, 415 U.S. 931 (1974).

77. 655 F. Supp. 1275 (S.D.N.Y. 1987).

action in a U.S. court. For this purpose, the court acknowledged the "fundamental distinction between recognition of a state as an international juridical entity and recognition of a particular government."[78] The court held that even though the particular government was not recognized, for purposes of a citizen's action under section 1332, the issue turned on the international juridical status. The court stated, "The rationale for denying access to our courts is simply not implicated when a private citizen of a recognized foreign state seeks vindication of individual rights related to a purely commercial dispute with a citizen of the United States."[79]

A similar issue, the standing of a corporation organized under the laws of a non-recognized state to bring suit in U.S. federal courts, was recently addressed by the Second Circuit in *Matimak Trading Co. v. Khalily*.[80] That Court ruled that a Hong Kong corporation cannot sue a U.S. defendant in U.S. federal court under alienage jurisdiction.[81] The Court reasoned that Hong Kong, not recognized under the United States-Hong Kong Policy Act of 1992, was not a foreign state for purposes of 28 U.S.C.A. § 1332.[82] This decision creates a circuit split and may impact litigation by "offshore" entities organized in other foreign dependant territories, including the British Virgin Islands, Cayman Islands and Bermuda.[83] These offshore foreign entities maintain, however, their standing to prosecute actions in U.S. state, as opposed to federal, courts.

If a specific statutory grant of jurisdiction is involved, the courts are required to make a determination of whether a foreign state qualifies as an eligible party entitled to maintain suit. For instance, in *Pfizer, Inc. v. India*,[84] the Supreme Court considered whether a foreign state qualifies under section 4 of the Clayton Act, entitling it to maintain an action

78. *Id.* at 1277.

79. *Id.* at 1281. *See also* National Petrochemical Co. of Iran v. M/T Stolt Sheaf, 860 F.2d 551, 554 (2d Cir. 1988), *cert. denied*, 489 U.S. 1081 (1989) (holding access to U.S. courts not limited to recognized governments). *Compare* West & Murphy, *supra* note 73, at 30–40.

80. 118 F.3d 76 (2d Cir. 1997).

81. 28 U.S.C.A. § 1332 (federal court jurisdiction over actions involving U.S. party and citizen or subject of foreign state).

82. *Id.* at 82.

83. *See* Wilson v. Humphreys (Cayman) Ltd., 916 F.2d 1239 (7th Cir. 1990) (ruling that federal courts have alienage jurisdiction over Cayman Islands corporation) *2d Circuit Bars Suits by "Offshore" Corporations*, NAT'L L.J., Mon., Aug. 25, 1997, at B9 (observing circuit split and discussing implications of ruling).

84. 434 U.S. 308 (1978).

under U.S. antitrust laws. Specifically at issue was whether the government of India was a ''person'' for purposes of the antitrust laws.

The Supreme Court identified two issues that might prevent India from qualifying as a person: that it was foreign and that it was a government.[85] The Court first recognized that foreign corporations are specifically entitled to maintain an action under the antitrust laws, and that, considering the remedial purposes of the antitrust laws, India's foreign status would not prevent it from qualifying.[86] On the second issue, the Court found that, similar to an earlier finding that a state of the United States qualifies under section 4, ''a foreign nation, like a domestic State, is entitled to pursue the remedy of treble damages when it has been injured in its business or property by antitrust violations.''[87] In general, the Court noted that it ''has long recognized the rule that a foreign nation is generally entitled to prosecute any civil claim in the courts of the United States upon the same basis as a domestic corporation or individual might do.''[88]

The Fourth Circuit recently considered whether a foreign sovereign may sue to enforce treaty rights in U.S. federal court. In *Republic of Paraguay v. Allen*,[89] Paraguay sought a declaration of violation by the Commonwealth of Virginia of treaties between Paraguay and the U.S., vacatur of a capital conviction and death sentence imposed by Virginia on a Paraguayan national, and an injunction against further Treaty violations. Paraguay alleged that Virginia's agents impeded contact between Paraguayan officials and the national accused of murder and rape and violated the Vienna Convention on Consular Relations and the U.S.-Paraguay Treaty of Friendship, Commerce, and Navigation. The Fourth Circuit dismissed the action on narrow jurisdictional grounds, ruling that under the Eleventh Amendment, the Virginia officials were immune from Paraguay's claims. The Court reasoned that Paraguay's claims did not meet the exception to Eleventh Amendment immunity set forth in *Ex parte Young*,[90] where (1) the violation is ongoing and (2) the relief sought is prospective. The Court held that Paraguay alleged no ongoing Treaty violation and sought merely retrospective relief concern-

85. *Id.* at 308.
86. *Id.* at 312.
87. *Id.* at 318.
88. *Id.* at 318–319.
89. 134 F.3d 622 (4th Cir. 1998).
90. 209 U.S. 123 (1908).

ing the past criminal conviction. The Court reserved consideration of the "political-question" issue and other jurisdictional issues.

§ 5.07 SELECTED LIMITATIONS: FORUM NON CONVENIENS

As discussed in the introduction to this chapter, many important issues of subject matter jurisdiction are questions of limitation. This section and the following sections address several selected limitations on the ability of a court to hear a particular type of case.

The first such limitation is the doctrine of forum non conveniens. Under the equitable doctrine of forum non conveniens, a court faced with two possible forums for the conduct of litigation must determine where the litigation should most appropriately occur.[91] A relatively new element of United States jurisprudence, the doctrine arose in the late 1940s, and was first recognized by the Supreme Court in *Gulf Oil Co. v. Gilbert*.[92] In *Gilbert*, the Court recognized its authority to decline to exercise jurisdiction under certain circumstances,[93] explaining:

> If the combination and weight of factors requisite to given results are difficult to forecast or state, those to be considered are not difficult to name. An interest to be considered, and one likely to be most pressed, is the private interest of the litigant. Important considerations are the relative ease of access to sources of proof; availability of compulsory process for attendance of unwilling, and the cost of obtaining attendance of willing, witnesses; possibility of view of premises, if view would be appropriate to the action; and all other practical problems that make trial of a case easy, expeditious and inexpensive. There may also be questions as to the enforceability of a judgment if one is obtained. The court will weigh relative advantages and obstacles to fair trial. . . . unless the balance is strongly in favor of the defendant, the plaintiff's choice of forum should rarely be disturbed.
>
> Factors of public interest also have a place in applying the doctrine. Administrative difficulties follow for the courts when litigation is piled up in congested centers instead of being handled at its origin. Jury duty is a burden that ought not to be imposed upon the

---

91. *See* American Dredging Co. v. Miller, 510 U.S. 443 (1994); Exxon Corp. v. Chick Kam Choo, 881 S.W.2d 301 (Tex. Sup. Ct. 1994); Jacqueline Duval-Major, *One Way Ticket Home: The Federal Doctrine of Forum Non Conveniens and the International Plaintiff*, 77 CORNELL L. REV. 650 (1992).

92. 330 U.S. 501 (1947). *See generally* Margaret G. Stewart, *Forum Non Conveniens: A Doctrine in Search of a Role*, 74 CAL. L. REV. 1259 (1986).

93. *Id.* at 504.

> people of a community which has no relation to the litigation. In cases which touch the affairs of many persons, there is reason for holding the trial in their view and reach rather than in remote parts of the country where they can learn of it by report only. There is a local interest in having localized controversies decided at home. There is an appropriateness, too, in having the trial of a diversity case in the forum that is at home with the state law that must govern the case, rather than having a court in some other forum untangle problems in conflict of laws, and in law foreign to itself.[94]

Although *Gilbert* involved the choice between two U.S. forums, an issue since covered by the transfer statute under 28 U.S.C.A. § 1404(a), the doctrine remains an important consideration in transnational litigation[95] and in state cases.[96]

More recently, the Court considered the doctrine of forum non conveniens in the context of international litigation in the case of *Piper Aircraft Co. v. Reyno*.[97] At issue in *Piper* was a lawsuit brought in the United States seeking damages for deaths resulting from a plane crash in Scotland. In ruling on the defendant's forum non conveniens motion, the court was faced with the issue of whether trial of the suit in Scotland, under arguably less favorable law, would weigh in favor of denying the motion. The district court dismissed the action under the doctrine, but the court of appeals held that the adverse change in the substantive law weighed against dismissal. In reversing, the Supreme Court ruled that "[t]he possibility of a change in substantive law should ordinarily not be given conclusive, or even substantial weight in the forum non conveniens inquiry."[98]

The Court did note, however, that "if the remedy provided by the alternative forum is so clearly inadequate or unsatisfactory that it is no remedy at all, the unfavorable change in the law may be given substantial weight; the district court may conclude that dismissal would not be in the interests of justice."[99] In practice, *Piper* has come to mean that the court will not consider the relative favorableness of the law in

94. *Id.* at 508–09.

95. *See generally* Stewart, *supra* note 92.

96. *See* Sarieddine v. Moussa, 820 S.W.2d 837, 839–44 (Tex. Ct. App. 1991); Irrigation & Indus. Dev. Corp. v. Indag S.A., 37 N.Y.2d 522, 528, 337 N.E.2d 749, 751–52, 375 N.Y.S.2d 296, 299 (1975).

97. 454 U.S. 235 (1981).

98. *Id.* at 247.

99. *Id.* at 254.

each forum unless there is a question whether one forum provides any remedy at all.[100]

Practice Note: It is the defendant's responsibility to assert a motion to dismiss on forum non conveniens grounds within a reasonable time after the facts or circumstances which serve as the basis for a motion have developed and have become known or reasonably knowable to defendant. The court must give deference to plaintiff's choice of forum, so the moving defendant must establish that private and public interests weigh heavily on the side of holding trial in the foreign forum.

The analysis proceeds in two steps. First, a defendant must demonstrate the existence of an adequate alternative forum.[100.1] If that threshold requirement is met, the court must then weigh the relevant private factors of convenience and judicial efficiency and public factors of community interest as well as burden, and the conflict of laws issues, as set forth in *Gilbert.* However, the foreign plaintiff's choice of forum will be given less deference than the local plaintiff's choice of forum, as it may not be reasonable to assume that foreign plaintiff's choice was convenient.[100.2]

---

100. *See, e.g., In re* Union Carbide Corp. Gas Plant Disaster, 809 F.2d 195, 198 (2d Cir.), *cert. denied,* 484 U.S. 871 (1987); Leon v. Millon Air, Inc., 251 F.3d 1305, 1311–12 (11th Cir. 2001) (affirming *on forum non conveniens* grounds district court dismissal of suit brought by Ecuadorans over 1996 crash of Millon Air cargo plane in Ecuador and observing that ''[a]n adequate forum need not be a perfect forum,'' and ''the argument that the alternate forum is too corrupt to be adequate 'does not enjoy a particularly impressive track record' ''). *See also* Aguinda v. Texaco, Inc., 303 F.3d 470 (2d Cir. 2002) (absence of class action procedure and allegations of corruption and bias insufficient to show Ecuador is inadequate forum); Gonzalez v. Chrysler Corp., 301 F.3d 377 (5th Cir. 2002) ($2,500.00 damages cap on child's life in Mexico does not establish Mexican courts as inadequate forum).

100.1. The defendant must agree to submit to the jurisdiction of the alternate forum for that forum to be adequate. Dole Food Co. v. Watts, 393 F.3d 1104 (9th Cir. 2002); Jota v. Texaco, Inc., 157 F.3d 153 (2d Cir. 1998).

100.2. *See, e.g.,* Hyatt Int'l Corp. v. Coco, 302 F.3d 707 (7th Cir. 2002) (commenting that plaintiff's choice of forum deserves less deference in cases where plaintiff seeks only declaratory relief); Iragorri v. United Technologies Corp., 274 F.3d 65, 72-73 (2d Cir. 2001) (adopting sliding scale of deference to be given plaintiff's choice of forum, including whether choice of forum was dictated by valid reasons, such as ability to obtain evidence, as opposed to apparent forum shopping); Wiwa v. Royal Dutch Petroleum Co., 226 F.3d 88 (2d Cir. 2000) (Court should properly consider each parties' residence as factor that bears on inconvenience rather than bias in favor of U.S. residents); Evolution Online Systems, Inc. v. Koninklijke PTT Nederland, N.V., 145 F.3d 505 (2d Cir. 1998) (where there is a forum selection clause, heavy presumption favoring plaintiff's choice of forum does not apply, rather equal playing field is appropriate presumption).

The trial court has broad discretion in deciding a motion to dismiss based on forum non conveniens. On appeal, trial court decisions can be reversed only if discretion was abused.

The Eleventh Circuit, in *Honduras Aircraft Registry, Ltd. v. Gov't of Honduras*,[101] examined the propriety of exercising pendent jurisdiction over a Government/Defendant's forum non conveniens argument where the appeal was from the district court's finding a waiver of sovereign immunity under the Foreign Sovereign Immunities Act (FSIA).[102] The Circuit Court observed:

> Pendent jurisdiction depends on the exercise of this court's discretion and judicial economy considerations. In determining whether to exercise discretionary pendent jurisdiction, we do so with caution.[103]

The *Honduras* Court found persuasive the Fifth Circuit's *Walter Fuller Aircraft* decision not to exercise pendant jurisdiction:

> After considering some of the various criteria, the district court determined that the Southern District of Florida was not a forum non conveniens for this case. *Walter Fuller*, a case which also involves the FSIA and the act of state doctrine, sets forth and discusses the factors to be considered when determining whether a particular forum is a forum non conveniens, including ''the threshold question whether there exists an alternative forum.'' 965 F.2d at 1389. In our judgment the Fifth Circuit wisely concluded that it was ''inappropriate to reach out and decide the forum non conveniens issue in a case in which [its] appellate jurisdiction is carefully defined by concerns about enforcing the immunity of foreign sovereigns from litigation.'' *Id.* at 1390. The issue of forum non conveniens is ''not closely related to the considerations involved in reviewing decisions concerning either sovereign immunity or the act of state doctrine.'' *Id.* at 1389. We agree, and decline at this time to exercise our pendent jurisdiction.[104]

A notable case involving the doctrine of forum non conveniens, is that involving the Bhopal chemical disaster. In *In re Union Carbide Corp. Gas Plant Disaster*,[105] the court of appeals considered a district court's decision to grant a conditional motion to dismiss under the

101. 129 F.3d 543, *reh'g denied en banc*, 131 F.3d 157 (11th Cir. 1997).

102. The FSIA is discussed *infra* Chapter 7.

103. 129 F.3d at 545 (*citing* Walter Fuller Aircraft Sales, Inc. v. Republic of Philippines, 915 F.2d 1375, 1387, 1389 (5th Cir. 1992)).

104. *Id.* at 550.

105. 809 F.2d at 195.

doctrine of forum non conveniens, and to permit the suit for injuries resulting from the plant accident to be tried in India. The district court, applying the doctrine as articulated by the Supreme Court in *Gilbert* and *Piper*, granted the motion to dismiss, based on an analysis of the private and public interest factors that constitute the elements of the doctrine.[106] The district court ruled that under the circumstances, failing to dismiss might constitute an abuse of discretion. The court stated that ''[p]ractically all relevant factors demonstrate that transfer of the cases to India for trial and adjudication is both fair and just to the parties.''[107]

The district court, however, imposed several conditions on Union Carbide, the defendant in the suit, in the dismissal under the doctrine of forum non conveniens:

(1) Consent to the jurisdiction of the courts of India and continue to waive defenses based on the statute of limitations;

(2) Agree to satisfy any judgment rendered by an Indian court against it and upheld on appeal, provided the judgment and affirmance ''comport with minimal requirements of due process;'' and

(3) Be subject to discovery under the Federal Rules of Civil Procedure of the United States.[108]

The Second Circuit found that the first condition was a common one, and did not disturb it.[109] For instance, in *Domingo v. States Marine Lines*,[110] the court granted a motion to dismiss on the basis of forum non conveniens, but required as a condition that the defendants submit to jurisdiction in the Philippines and waive the statute of limitations defense.[111]

The court in *Union Carbide*, however, did disagree with the remaining two conditions imposed by the district court, and directed that they be deleted. On the condition that Union Carbide consent to enforceability of an Indian judgment, the Second Circuit emphatically explained that U.S. courts may not play the role Union Carbide requested:

---

106. *Id.* at 198–200.
107. *Id.* at 202.
108. *Id.* at 198.
109. *Id.* at 203–04.
110. 340 F. Supp. 811 (S.D.N.Y. 1972).
111. *Id.* at 817.

> [Union Carbide's] proposed remedy is not only impractical but evidences an abysmal ignorance of basic jurisdictional principles, so much so that it borders on the frivolous. The district court's jurisdiction is limited to the proceedings before it in this country. Once it dismisses on the grounds of forum non conveniens it ceases to have any further jurisdiction over the matter unless and until a proceeding may someday be brought to enforce here a final conclusive Indian money judgment. Nor could we, even if we attempted to retain some form of supervisory jurisdiction, impose our due process requirements upon Indian courts, which are covered by their laws, not ours. The concept of shared jurisdictions is both illusory and unrealistic. The parties cannot simultaneously submit to both jurisdictions the resolution of pretrial and trial issues when there is only one consolidated case pending in one court. Any denial by the Indian courts of due process can be raised by [Union Carbide] as a defense to the plaintiff's later attempt to enforce a resulting judgment against [Union Carbide] in this country.[112]

On the final condition—concerning discovery under the U.S. Federal Rules of Civil Procedure—the court noted that such a condition could obviously not be imposed on the other party, and was therefore not reciprocal. Although the court noted that in some cases a forum non conveniens dismissal may be conditioned on some form of discovery requirements, in this case reciprocity was paramount: "Basic justice dictates that both sides be treated equally, with each having equal access to the evidence in the possession or under control of the other."[113] The *Union Carbide* case provides an excellent example of the elements involved in a determination of the applicability of the doctrine of forum non conveniens, and the methods available to the courts to tailor dismissal to be consistent with the dictates of justice and fairness.

As a practical summary of the application of the doctrine of forum non conveniens, the District of Columbia Circuit articulated a four-part test in the recent case of *Pain v. United Technologies Corp.*:[114]

- First, determine whether there is an adequate alternative forum that can try the entire case;

112. 809 F.2d at 205.

113. *Id.*

114. 637 F.2d 775 (D.C. Cir. 1980), *cert. denied*, 454 U.S. 1128 (1981). *See also* Transamerican S.S. Corp. v. Somali Democratic Republic, 590 F. Supp. 968, 978 (D.D.C. 1984), *modified*, 767 F.2d 998 (D.C. Cir. 1985); Mercier v. Sheraton Int'l Inc., 981 F.2d 1345, 1354 (1st Cir. 1992), *cert. denied*, 113 S. Ct. 2346 (1993); Hoffman v. Goberman, 420 F.2d 423, 426–27 (3d Cir. 1970).

- Second, "consider all relevant factors of private interests, *weighing in the balance a strong presumption against disturbing plaintiffs' initial forum choice*;"

- Third, if the balance of interests is in or near "equipoise," consider whether the public interest favors a foreign forum;

- Fourth, if the balance favors a foreign forum, ensure that plaintiffs can reinstate their suit in the alternative forum without "undue inconvenience or prejudice."[115]

Despite some criticism of the doctrine stemming from the equation of dismissal under forum non conveniens to dismissal altogether, the current application of the doctrine has produced results that are consistent with the policy concerns expressed by the Supreme Court in 1947 in *Gulf Oil Co. v. Gilbert*.[116]

---

115. Pain, 637 F.2d at 784–85 (emphasis added).

116. 330 U.S. 501 (1947), *supra* § 5.07. *See generally* Piper Aircraft Co. v. Reyno, 454 U.S. 235 (1981); Pollux Holding, Ltd. v. Chase Manhattan Bank, 329 F.3d 64 (2d Cir. 2003) (affirming dismissal of suit by Liberian corporations that had purchased notes from defendant-bank in London, as part of alleged pyramid scheme); Leon v. Millon Air, Inc., 251 F.3d 1305, 1310–11 (11th Cir. 2001) (affirming on *forum non conveniens* grounds district court dismissal of suit brought by Ecuadorans over 1996 crash of Millon Air cargo plane in Ecuador and observing, "[t]he moving party must demonstrate that (1) an adequate alternative forum is available, (2) the public and private factors weigh in favor of dismissal, and (3) the plaintiff can reinstate his suit in the alternative forum without undue inconvenience or prejudice"). *See* Baumgart v. Fairchild Aircraft Corp., 981 F.2d 824, 828, 835–37 (5th Cir. 1993); Lony v. E.I. Du Pont De Nemours & Co., 935 F.2d 604, 609–14 (3d Cir. 1991); Torres v. Southern Peru Copper Corp., 113 F.3d 540 (5th Cir. 1997) (affirming district court's dismissal on forum non conveniens grounds of tort action by about 700 Peruvian citizens allegedly harmed by sulfur dioxide emissions from Defendant's copper smelting operations in Peru); Base Metal Trading, S.A. v. Russian Aluminum, 253 F.Supp.2d 681 (S.D.N.Y. 2003) (forum non conveniens finding warranted in action by Metal trading companies brought against Russian consortia, stemming from allegedly illegal takeovers of Russian aluminum and vanadium producers); Leslie v. Lloyd's of London, 1995 U.S. Dist. LEXIS 15380, 1995 WL 661090 (S.D. Tex. Aug. 25, 1995) (denying Lloyd's motion to dismiss on grounds of forum non conveniens and finding that English court would have more difficulty adjudicating legal rights of U.S. citizen under complex U.S. securities and consumer protection statutes than U.S. court would have applying English common law); Firma Melodiya v. ZYX Music GmbH, 882 F. Supp. 1306 (S.D.N.Y. 1995) (denying motion of German and Australian Defendants to dismiss on forum non conveniens grounds where Defendants failed to show existence of adequate alternative forum concerning U.S. copyright law and balance of public and private interests weighed in favor of Plaintiffs' choice of forum); Bybee v. Oper der Standt Bonn, 899 F. Supp. 1217 (S.D.N.Y. 1995) (dismissing on forum non conveniens grounds action filed by Plaintiff opera singer against German state opera company and finding suitable alternative forum existed in Germany, New York choice of law principles favored application of German law, and parties wrote contract in German).

State courts may be less likely than federal courts to grant a dismissal on forum non conveniens grounds.[116.1] For example, in Texas, a statute divests courts of the discretion to dismiss on such grounds.[116.2]

Federal courts have held that federal forum non conveniens principles pre-empt state rules in diversity cases.[116.3] An exception is that federal principles do not pre-empt otherwise applicable state forum non conveniens principles in admiralty cases originally filed in state court under the Jones Act.[116.4]

Practice Note: A plaintiff wishing to avoid a dismissal on forum non conveniens grounds should file in a favorable state court jurisdiction where possible. The plaintiff should also consider structuring the case to avoid removal to federal court.

§ 5.08 SELECTED LIMITATIONS: INTERNATIONAL COMITY AND REASONABLENESS

In disputes involving a factual setting that includes contacts with more than one jurisdiction, an important issue is whether the traditional doctrine of comity and the more recently developed doctrine of reasonableness will operate to cause a court in the United States to decline, or to decline to exercise, jurisdiction over a matter. As discussed above,[117] a nation possesses jurisdiction to prescribe laws with respect to conduct that takes place within its territory; the status of persons, or interests in things, present within its territory; and conduct outside its territory that has or is intended to have substantial effect within its territory.[118] In cases involving contacts with multiple jurisdictions, these bases for jurisdiction may permit more than one nation to resolve a dispute.

When two or more states have jurisdiction to prescribe with respect to a particular conduct or event, a situation of ''concurrent'' jurisdiction exits. Because both nations have a valid claim to regulate the activity, it becomes necessary to balance the jurisdictional power of each nation.

116.1. *See, e.g.,* Mar-Land Indus. Contrs., Inc. v. Carribbean Petroleum Ref., L.P., 777 A.2d 774 (Del. 2001).)

116.2. Texas Civil Practice and Remedies Code, § 71.031. *See also* Dow Chem. Co. v. Alfaro, 786 S.W. 2d 674 (1990).

116.3. Piper Aircraft Co., *supra*; Ikospentakis v. Thalassic S.S. Agency, 915 F.2d 176 (5th Cir. 1990).

116.4. American Dredging Co. v. Miller, 510 S. Ct. 443 (1994).

117. *See supra* § 5.02.

118. *See* RESTATEMENT, *supra* note 1, at § 402.

Traditionally, the mechanism the courts have used to perform such balancing has been the doctrine of comity.

[1] The Doctrine of Comity

Courts have declined to exercise jurisdiction over actions involving transnational issues under traditional notions of comity. International comity has been variously defined, but one recent description is as follows:

> [C]omity is the deference voluntarily displayed by one sovereign state towards another independent and sovereign nation: the rules of

(*Text continued on page 5-29*)

> politeness, convenience and goodwill observed by States in their mutual intercourse without being legally bound by them.[119]

Similarly, in *Somportex Ltd. v. Philadelphia Chewing Gum Corp.*,[120] the court explained:

> Comity is a recognition which one nation extends within its own territory to the legislative, executive, or judicial acts of another. It is not a rule of law, but one of practice, convenience, and expediency. Although more than mere courtesy and accommodation, comity does not achieve the focus of an imperative or an obligation. Rather it is a nation's expression of understanding which demonstrates due regard both to international duty and convenience and to the rights of persons protected by its own laws.[121]

Considerations of international comity provide a court with a basis to decline to exercise jurisdiction. For instance, in *Gannon v. Payne*,[122] the court was faced with a case of concurrent jurisdiction, and on the basis of comity declined to affirm the issuance of an antisuit injunction preventing the defendant in Texas from seeking declaratory relief in Canada.[123] Similarly, in *Cornfeld v. Investors Overseas Services, Ltd.*,[124] the court applied the doctrine of comity to dismiss an indemnification action brought in New York against a Canadian corporation undergoing liquidation under Canadian law. The court so held despite a choice of law clause providing that the law of New York would apply.[125] Recently, the Third Circuit in *Philadelphia Gear Corp. v. Philadelphia Gear De Mexico*,[126] held that a comity analysis must be performed to evaluate whether, in the context of parallel bankruptcy actions, "(1) the foreign bankruptcy court shares our policy of equal distribution of assets; and (2) the foreign law mandates the issuance of or

---

119. Dieter Lange & Gary Born, The Extraterritorial Application of National Laws 38–40 (1989), *citing* Oppenheim, I International Law 34 n.1 (8th ed. 1955). *See generally* Brian Pearce, *The Comity Doctrine as a Barrier to Judicial Jurisdiction: A U.S.-E.U. Comparison,* 30 Stan. J. Int'l L. 525 (1994); Joel R. Paul, *Comity in International Law,* 32 Harv. Int'l L.J. 1 (1991).

120. 453 F.2d 435 (3d Cir. 1971).

121. *Id.* at 440. *See also* Hilton v. Guyot, 159 U.S. 113, 164–65 (1895); Restatement, *supra* note 1, at § 402. *See generally* Société Nationale Industrielle Aérospatiale v. U.S. Dist. Court, 482 U.S. 522 (1987).

122. 706 S.W. 2d 304 (Tex. 1986).

123. *Id.* at 308.

124. 471 F. Supp. 1255 (S.D.N.Y. 1979).

125. *Id.* at 1261.

126. 44 F.3d 187 (3d Cir. 1994).

at least authorizes the request for the stay.''[127] In the mass tort context, the Fifth Circuit recently affirmed the district court's dismissal on comity grounds of a tort action by about 700 Peruvian citizens allegedly harmed by sulfur dioxide emissions from Defendant's copper smelting operations in Peru.[128]

The doctrine of international comity does not divest a court of jurisdiction, but rather provides a court with a rationale for not exercising jurisdiction that it possesses. This principle is illustrated in *Joseph Muller Corp. Zurich v. Société Anonyme de Gérance et D'Arment*.[129] In this case, the court was faced with a motion to dismiss, based on international comity, a contract claim between two foreign parties. The court dismissed the contract claim, not on grounds of international comity, but instead on subject matter jurisdiction grounds.[130] Although diversity jurisdiction was alleged, neither the constitutional nor statutory grant provided a basis for the court to hear the suit. In other words, the court could never properly reach the international comity issue, because it did not possess subject matter jurisdiction over the suit.

The lesson of *Joseph Muller* is that an international comity analysis is proper only after the subject matter jurisdiction of the court is established. The court must then determine whether, in the interests of international comity, exercising that jurisdiction is appropriate.[131]

A comity analysis was also undertaken in *Rivendell Forest Prods., Ltd. v. Canadian Forest Prods., Ltd.*,[132] in which the court concluded that the ''principle of comity requires this court to refuse to exercise jurisdiction in this matter.''[133] At issue in *Rivendell* was an antitrust class action brought by U.S. purchasers of Canadian softwood lumber products seeking relief under the Sherman Act. Plaintiffs claimed that alleged price fixing in Canada resulted in higher prices in the U.S. The court assumed, for purposes of the motion to dismiss, that the defendant's conduct in Canada had a ''substantial and reasonably foreseeable effect on import trade or import commerce in the United

127. *Id.* at 9.

128. Torres v. Southern Peru Copper Corp., 113 F.3d 540 (5th Cir. 1997).

129. 451 F.2d 727 (2d Cir. 1971) (per curiam), *cert. denied,* 406 U.S. 906 (1972).

130. *Id.* at 729.

131. *Id.* at 729. *See also* Industrial Inv. Dev. Corp. v. Mitsui & Co., Ltd., 671 F.2d 876, 884 & n.7 (5th Cir. 1982) (discussing distinction between subject matter jurisdiction and international comity analysis), *vacated on other grounds,* 460 U.S. 1007 (1983).

132. 810 F. Supp. 1116 (D. Co. 1993).

133. *Id.* at 1119–20.

States,''[134] and, therefore, that subject matter jurisdiction existed under the antitrust laws. The court, however, determined that ''the interests of Canada in the subject matter of this case are far more substantial than the interests of the United States in obtaining benefits for lumber wholesalers from price competition among Canadian producers of lumber products.''[135]

Courts in other contexts, however, have rejected arguments that the doctrine of comity prevents adjudication of a dispute. In *Kaepa, Inc. v. Achilles Corp.*,[136] a Texas manufacturer of athletic shoes (Kaepa) filed suit in Texas state court against its Japanese distributor (Achilles), claiming fraud and breach of the distributorship contract. Achilles removed the action to federal district court and filed a similar suit against Kaepa in Japan. The district court granted Kaepa's motion for an antisuit injunction to prevent prosecution of the Japan lawsuit. Achilles appealed, arguing that the district court failed to give proper deference to principles of international comity concerning the anti-suit injunction. The Fifth Circuit held that the district court did not abuse its discretion in issuing the antisuit injunction where simultaneous prosecution of a nearly identical case in a foreign forum would result in hardship and would delay efficient resolution of the dispute. The Court observed that the case involved no public international issue between Japan and the U.S. and the contract between the parties required dispute resolution in Texas and the application of Texas law and the English language.

In the intellectual property area, courts apply a comity analysis to determine whether to issue injunctions extraterritorially to stop infringing conduct. For instance, in *Nintendo of America v. Aeropower Co., Ltd.*,[137] the Fourth Circuit held that several factors must be considered, including the significance of the impact of the infringement in the U.S., the citizenship of the defendant, and the possibility of conflict with foreign law.[138]

The antitrust area has proved a particularly volatile ground for courts' exercise of comity limitations on jurisdiction. In *Hartford Fire*

---

134. *Id.* at 1119.

135. *Id.*

136. 76 F.3d 624 (5th Cir. 1996).

137. 34 F.3d 246 (4th Cir. 1994).

138. *Id.* at 251. *See also* Mars Inc. v. Nippon Conlux Kabushiki-Kaisha, 825 F. Supp. 73 (D. Del. 1993) (court declines to exercise jurisdiction over foreign infringement claims on comity grounds), *aff'd on other grounds,* 24 F.3d 1368 (Fed. Cir. 1994).

Ins. Co. v. California,[139] the Supreme Court considered the issue of whether the Sherman Act[140] applied to the activities of reinsurance syndicates organized at Lloyd's of London. Nineteen states and numerous other parties alleged a conspiracy by reinsurers on the London market to prevent the issuance in the United States of environmental insurance on an "occurrence" basis and to limit coverage of pollution risks.[141]

The Court found that the activities of the reinsurers were squarely within the ambit of the Sherman Act's mandate to address foreign conduct intended to produce and in fact producing a substantial effect in the United States.[142] The London reinsurers (and the British Government as *amicus curiae*), however, alleged that the district court should have declined to exercise jurisdiction on the principle of international comity. Justice Souter, writing for a five-Justice majority, determined that the only substantial comity issue presented was whether there was a "'true conflict between domestic and foreign law.'"[143] While the activities of the London reinsurers were legal under the comprehensive British scheme of insurance regulation, the majority, citing Comment *e* of the Restatement (Third) of Foreign Relations Law § 403, found that since British law did not prevent the parties from also complying with U.S. law, there was no conflict of law.[144] The Court declined to address other considerations of comity and found the district court's exercise of jurisdiction over the London reinsurers and the extraterritorial application of the Sherman Act proper.[145]

In a dissent joined by four members of the Court, Justice Scalia argued that comity considerations prevented Congress from legislating over the actions of the foreign reinsurers and, therefore, necessarily prevented a district court from exercising jurisdiction.[146] Scalia observed that "[c]omity in this sense includes the choice-of-law principle that, 'in

139. 509 U.S. 764 (1993).

140. 26 Stat. 209, as amended, 15 U.S.C. § 1.

141. *Hartford*, at 2908. The plaintiffs alleged that the reinsurers sought to coerce primary insurers into offering insurance on a claims-made basis. *Id.* Claims basis insurance covers only claims brought during the life of a policy while occurrence basis insurance covers all claims which originated from events occurring during the life of a policy, no matter when the claims are brought.

142. *Id.* at 2909.

143. *Id.* at 2910, *citing*, Société Nationale Industrielle Aérospatiale v. United States Dist. Court, 482 U.S. 522, 555 (1987) (Blackmun, J., concurring in part).

144. *Id.* at 2910–11.

145. *Id.* at 2911.

146. *Id.* at 2920.

the absence of contrary congressional direction,''' national laws are assumed not to apply extraterritorially.[147] Relying on the Restatement (Third) of Foreign Relations Law § 403, the dissent found that customary international law counseled against the extraterritorial application of U.S. antitrust law.[148] The fact that the Supreme Court in *Hartford* specifically declined to address other considerations that ''might inform decision to refrain from the exercise of jurisdiction on the grounds of international comity,''[149] has been interpreted to mean that the ruling need not apply in contexts other than antitrust.[150]

Because comity is based on the respect sovereign nations afford each other by limiting the reach of their laws, courts have naturally looked to international choice of law principles in attempting to apply the comity doctrine.[151] Comity is a traditional component of choice of law theory. Courts have adopted choice of law rules that require the application of the law of the jurisdiction having the greatest interest in the litigation. This analysis is basically the same as that set out in the Restatement (Third) of Foreign Relations Law.[152] Under the Restatement, the touchstone of a choice of law analysis is reasonableness. The factors set

147. *Id.* at 2910, *citing* Romero v. International Terminal Operating Co., 358 U.S. 354, 382–83 (1959).

148. *Id.* at 2920–22. For a useful analysis of the role and significance of the Restatement, *compare* Andreas F. Lowenfeld, *Conflict, Balancing of Interests, and the Exercise of Jurisdiction to Prescribe: Reflections on the Insurance Antitrust Case,* 89 AM. J. INT'L L. 42 (1995) with Phillip R. Trimble, *The Supreme Court and International Law: The Demise of Restatement Section* 403, 89 AM. J. INT'L L. 53 (1995).

149. *Id.* at 2911.

150. *See* Sterling Drug, Inc. v. Bayer AG, 14 F.3d 733, 746–47 (2d Cir. 1994) (holding that ''true conflict'' requirement of *Hartford* does not necessarily apply to questions of trademark law and finding that the decision in *Hartford* did not bar comity considerations arising in context of extraterritorial injunction under Lanham Act); *In re* Maxwell Communications Corp. PLC, 186 B.R. 807 (S.D.N.Y. 1995) (finding *Hartford* approach inappropriate in context of bankruptcy law and declaring that there was no basis for requirement that ''true conflict'' exist between U.S. and foreign preference laws); Joseph W. Dellapenna, *Transnational Litigation Today,* A.B.A. Section of Int'l Law & Practice, Fall/Winter Section Meeting, Panel on Resolving Commercial Disputes in the North American Market, Jan. 20, 1994, at 12–15 (discussing *Hartford* decision); Joseph P. Griffin, *U.S. Supreme Court Encourages Extraterritorial Application of U.S. Antitrust Laws,* INT'L BUS. LAW., Sept. 1993, at 389, 391–93 (addressing implications of *Hartford*); Joseph P. Griffin, *Justices Finally Tackle ''Foreign Conduct,''* NAT'L L.J., Aug. 9, 1993, at 29, 34 (suggesting that true conflicts of law will be rare as vast majority of antitrust cases involve foreign conduct legal in foreign country).

151. ''An act of Congress ought never to be construed to violate the law of nations if any other possible construction remains.'' Murray v. The Charming Betsy, 2 Cranch 64, 2 L.Ed 208 (1804) (Marshall, C.J.).

152. *See infra* § 5.07[2].

out in the Restatement that a court may consider as part of a reasonableness inquiry are focused on locating a jurisdiction whose laws and policies are the most involved with the controversy.

[2] The Jurisdictional Rule of Reason

More recently, a similar, yet distinct limitation on the power of U.S. courts to exercise jurisdiction has arisen. It is called the rule of reason, and is designed to permit only those exercises of jurisdiction which are reasonable. The rule emerged from several cases in the United States, primarily in the competition law area, and has gained acceptance in other nations. The driving force behind the development of the rule of reason is the effects portion of the territorial jurisdictional principle.[153]

The exercise of jurisdiction under the effects doctrine is one example of how concurrent jurisdiction can produce conflicts with the laws of other nations.[154] The rule of reason is designed to provide a mechanism to balance the conflicts of jurisdiction, and assist courts in making a determination whether a particular exercise of jurisdiction is reasonable.

The Restatement (Third) of Foreign Relations Law contains the most accessible articulation of the rule of reason. The rule is codified in section 403, which provides that even if one of the valid bases of jurisdiction exists,

> a state may not exercise jurisdiction to prescribe law with respect to a person or activity having connections with another state when the exercise of jurisdiction is unreasonable.

In deciding whether the exercise of jurisdiction in a particular case is unreasonable, the Restatement provides the following eight factors for evaluation:

---

153. *See* United States v. Aluminum Co. of Am., 148 F.2d 416, 443–45 (2d Cir. 1945); Foreign Trade Antitrust Improvements Act of 1982, Title IV of the Export Trading Company Act of 1982, Pub. L. No. 97–290, 96 Stat. 1246 (codified at 15 U.S.C. § 6a) (providing that Sherman Act shall not apply to foreign commerce unless it "has a direct, substantial, and reasonably foreseeable effect").

154. *See, e.g.*, Dieter Lange & Gary Born, The Extraterritorial Application of National Laws 38-40 (1989); A. J. Lowe, Extraterritorial Jurisdiction 90, 106, 156 (1983); Douglas E. Rosenthal & William M. Knighton, *National Laws and International Commerce: The Problem of Extraterritoriality* 79 (1982); Harold G. Maier, *Resolving Extraterritorial Conflicts, or "There and Back Again,"* 25 Va. J. Int'l L. 7, 33–40 (1984); Harold G. Maier, *Extraterritorial Jurisdiction at a Crossroads: An Intersection Between Public and Private International Law,* 76 Am. J. Int'l L. 280, 295 (1982); Karl M. Meesen, *Antitrust Jurisdiction Under Customary International Law,* 78 Am. J. Int'l L. 783, 783 (1984).

(a) the link of the activity to the territory of the regulating state, i.e., the extent to which the activity takes place within the territory or has substantial, direct, and foreseeable effect upon or in the territory;

(b) the connections, such as nationality, residence or economic activity, between the regulating state and the person principally responsible for the activity to be regulated, or between that state and those whom the regulation is designed to protect;

(c) the character of the activity to be regulated, the importance of the regulation to the regulating state, the extent to which other states regulate such activities, and the degree to which the desirability of such regulation is generally accepted;

(d) the existence of justified expectations that might be protected or hurt by the regulation;

(e) the importance of the regulation to the international political, legal, or economic system;

(f) the extent to which the regulation is consistent with the traditions of the international system;

(g) the extent to which another state may have an interest in regulating the activity; and

(h) the likelihood of conflict with the regulation by another state.[155]

The rule of reason has grown out of a series of cases primarily involving questions of the applicability of U.S. antitrust law to conduct outside the United States allegedly having an effect in the United States. Two of the leading cases behind the reasonableness test of section 403 are *Timberlane Lumber Co. v. Bank of America Nat'l Savings & Trust Ass'n*,[156] in which the court articulated a jurisdictional "rule of rea-

155. RESTATEMENT, *supra* note 1, at § 403. *See also* Hartford Fire Ins. Co. v. California, 509 U.S. at 764 (Scalia, J., dissenting) (applying principles of jurisdictional rule of reason set forth in § 403).

156. 549 F.2d 597 (9th Cir. 1976), *cert. denied*, 472 U.S. 1032 (1985). *See also* Hartford Fire Ins. Co. v. California, 509 U.S. at 764 (Scalia, J., dissenting) (citing *Timberlane* for proposition that reasonableness requirement of international law limits extraterritorial reach of statutes).

son,''[157] and *Mannington Mills v. Congoleum Corp.*,[158] which is one of the best illustrations of the principles involved.

The Ninth Circuit has articulated an additional test for a court's exercise of jurisdiction under the doctrine of reasonableness. A clear enunciation of the test is found in *Metro Industries, Inc. v. Sammi Corp.*[159] The inquiry requires the weighing of the answers to three questions:

(1) Does the alleged restraint affect, or was it intended to affect, the foreign commerce of the United States?

(2) Is it of such a type and magnitude as to be cognizable as a violation of the Sherman Act?

(3) As a matter of international comity and fairness, should the extraterritorial jurisdiction of the United States be asserted to cover it?

The comity question alone requires the consideration of several elements, including:

(1) the degree of conflict with foreign law or policy;

(2) the nationality and allegiance of the parties and the locations or principal place of business of corporations;

(3) the extent to which enforcement by either state can be expected to achieve compliance;

(4) the relative significance of the effects on the United States as compared to elsewhere;

(5) the extent to which there is explicit purpose to harm or affect U.S. commerce;

---

157. *Id.* at 613–14. *See also* Timberlane Lumber Co. v. Bank of Am. N.T & S.A. (*Timberlane* III), 749 F.2d 1378, at 1386 (9th Cir. 1984) (declining to exercise jurisdiction through operation of rule of reason), *cert. denied*, 472 U.S. 3514 (1985); O.N.E. Shipping, Ltd. v. Flota Mercante Grancolombiana, 830 F.2d 449, 451 (2d Cir. 1987), *cert. denied*, 488 U.S. 923 (1988) (upholding refusal to exercise jurisdiction over antitrust claims based on application of *Timberlane* factors); Star-Kist Foods, Inc. v. P.J. Rhodes & Co., 769 F.2d 1393, 1395 (9th Cir. 1985) (following *Timberlane* in application of rule of reason as rule of jurisdiction in considering extraterritorial application of the Lanham Act); Montreal Trading Ltd. v. Amax, Inc., 661 F.2d 864, 869 (10th Cir. 1981), *cert. denied*, 455 U.S. 1001 (1982) (applying *Timberlane* balancing test).

158. 595 F.2d 1287, 1297–98 (3d Cir. 1979).

159. 82 F.3d 839 (9th Cir. 1996).

(6) the foreseeability of such effect; and

(7) the relative importance of the violation charged to conduct within the United States as compared with conduct abroad.

The jurisdictional rule of reasonableness has also arisen outside the antitrust context. In *Neely v. Club Med Mgmnt. Services,*[160] the Third Circuit considered whether the federal Jones Act[161] and U.S. admiralty law should apply in a personal injury action brought by a scuba diving instructor injured while employed at Club Med resort in St. Lucia. The Defendant argued that the analysis in *Lauritzen v. Larsen*[162] and subsequent cases[163] prevented the application of U.S. maritime law and thereby deprived the district court of jurisdiction. The Court determined, however, that the choice of law issue of whether U.S. law would apply was a separate analysis from whether the court has subject matter jurisdiction. The Court observed that at a minimum, jurisdiction exists under the federal question statute[164] to determine whether the Jones Act and U.S. admiralty law apply. The Court held that the *Lauritzen* analysis in two-fold and applies when the Defendant contests the applicability of U.S. maritime law. Initially, the Plaintiff must demonstrate the existence of substantial U.S. interests, providing a basis for prescriptive jurisdiction. The Plaintiff must then show that the application of U.S. law is reasonable given all relevant factors. Once the Plaintiff shows that the choice of law is reasonable, the burden shifts to the Defendant to show that significant foreign contacts compel the conclusion that the application of U.S. law is unreasonable. The Court held that application of U.S. law was proper in the instant case, although the accident occurred in St. Lucia and the vessel was registered there, because Plaintiff was domiciled in the United States, the parties contracted in the United States, much of the resort's business originated in the United States, and the Defendant failed to produce evidence that St. Lucia law should apply.

160. 63 F.3d 166 (3d Cir. 1995) (*en banc*).

161. 46 U.S.C.A. § 688 (granting seamen same rights to sue their employers for personal injury and death as railway workers have under the Federal Employers Liability Act, 45 U.S.C.A. § 51–60).

162. 345 U.S. 571 (1953).

163. Specifically, Romero v. Int'l Terminal Operating, 358 U.S. 354 (1959) and Hellenic Lines, Ltd. v. Rhoditis, 398 U.S. 306 (1970) (all sometimes collectively called the "*Lauritzen* triad").

164. 28 U.S.C.A. § 1331.

The adherence to the rule of reason and the multi-factor approach as a mechanism to resolve such questions has not received universal acceptance. For instance, in *Laker Airways, Ltd. v. Sabena*,[165] the court rejected judicial efforts to balance foreign interests in determining whether to exercise jurisdiction.

[3] Parallel Proceedings and Anti-Suit Injunctions

Because parties to international transactions are often located in different jurisdictions, when a dispute arises, there exists the possibility of litigation on the same subject matter occurring in each jurisdiction.[166] Such concurrent litigation is known as "parallel proceedings." It has been observed:

> Three possible responses exist when proceedings, asserting the same claims, are pending before both a domestic and a foreign court:
>
> (1) stay or dismiss the domestic action;
>
> (2) enjoin the parties from proceeding in the foreign forum (referred to as an anti-suit injunction); or
>
> (3) allow both suits to proceed simultaneously, with the likely attendant race to judgment.[167]
>
> Thus the question of strategy is where to fight one's battles—here, there, or both places.[168]

Litigation concerning parallel proceedings commonly arises either: (1) on motion of a party to stay or dismiss the domestic action; or (2) on motion of a party to enjoin the foreign proceeding. Motions to stay or dismiss the domestic action will be considered first.

These motions frequently require a Court to pass upon the nature of the foreign proceedings and their adequacy. Sensitive issues of international relations and comity may, therefore, be present. The U.S.

165. 731 F.2d 909, 948–53 (D.C. Cir. 1984).

166. This likelihood is lessened, though still present, where the parties have agreed in advance concerning dispute resolution, such as through an arbitration or forum selection clause in a contract.

167. In an interesting example of a party using parallel proceedings to win the race for res judicata, a defendant sought a declaratory judgment, *before* any relief was granted to Plaintiff, that the foreign judgment being sought by Plaintiff would be unenforceable. Basic v. Fitzroy Eng'g, Ltd., 949 F. Supp. 1333 (N.D. Ill. 1996), *aff'd*, 132 F.3d 36 (7th Cir. 1997).

168. Louise Ellen Teitz, *International Litigation, I. Parallel Proceedings: Treading Carefully*, 32 INT'L LAW. 223, 223 (1998).

Supreme Court has not yet articulated the standard for determining whether to stay or dismiss an action in deference to a foreign proceeding. U.S. Courts which have addressed the issue have considered a number of factors, including:

(1) adequacy of relief available in alternative forum;

(2) issues of fairness to and convenience of parties, counsel, and witnesses;

(3) the possibility of prejudice to any of the parties; and

(4) the temporal sequence of filing of the actions.[169]

An example of a Court's addressing these issues is *Dragon Capital Partners, L.P. v. Merrill Lynch Capital Services, Inc.*[170] In *Dragon Capital*, Plaintiff Dragon Capital filed suit in Hong Kong for damages for wrongful liquidation of accounts by Merrill Lynch. Dragon Capital later filed suit in New York federal court concerning the same subject matter, and added claims for fraud and Securities Laws violations. Defendant moved the New York federal court to stay the New York action, out of deference to the Hong Kong court under the doctrine of comity; or, alternatively, to dismiss the New York action on the doctrine of forum non conveniens. The District Court observed that the term "comity" was often applied by courts to a variety of situations beyond the strict definition of "comity":

> The Defendants refer to this argument [to stay the case in deference to the Hong Kong proceeding] as International Comity. This is technically incorrect. As defined in Black's Law Dictionary . . . international comity is: "the recognition which one nation allows within its territory to the legislative, executive, or judicial acts of another nation, having due regard both to international duty and convenience and to the right of its own citizens or of other persons who are under the protection of its laws." . . . [C]ourts use the terms comity and, to a lesser extent, international abstention, to refer to the doctrine of judicial deference to pending foreign proceedings, although neither of these terms is technically appropriate. Comity refers to deference to another sovereign's definitive law or judicial decision.[171]

---

169. Caspian Investments, Ltd. v. Viacom Holdings, Ltd., 770 F. Supp. 880, 884 (S.D.N.Y. 1991).

170. 949 F. Supp. 1123 (S.D.N.Y. 1997).

171. *Id.* at 1127 n.8 (citation omitted).

The *Dragon Capital* Court then considered the motion for a stay under the four factors noted above from *Caspian Investments, Ltd. v. Viacom Holdings, Ltd.*[172] The Court placed significant weight on the fourth factor, "sequence of filing the actions," as the Plaintiff had first selected Hong Kong and then sought to file in New York, arguing that the Hong Kong forum was inadequate. The Court ruled that the factors balanced in favor of a stay in deference to the Hong Kong proceedings. The District Court also undertook a forum non conveniens analysis and found that dismissal of the action was proper under forum non conveniens, particularly in light of the factors justifying a stay. The Court, therefore, found that comity in its broad sense justified both a stay and dismissal of the action.

As noted above, an anti-suit injunction refers to the order of a domestic court purporting to stay or enjoin an action in a foreign forum.[173] As an anti-suit injunction necessarily involves a direct intrusion on the judicial process of another sovereign nation, it is proper in only extraordinary circumstances. The Second Circuit has announced five factors to consider:

(1) whether a policy of the enjoining forum is being frustrated:

(2) whether the maintenance of the action is vexatious;

(3) whether the court's jurisdiction is threatened;

(4) whether there are other equitable considerations; and

(5) the delay, inconvenience, expense, and race to judgment that would result if the injunction is not granted.[174]

The enforceability and effect of an anti-suit injunction may be uncertain as a tribunal may rebuff the attempted intrusion by an alien court.

Two principal factors have been cited as causes of parallel proceedings: lack of a multilateral convention to which the United States is a party on the enforcement of foreign judgments[175] and vexatious

---

172. 770 F. Supp. at 884.

173. George Bermann, *The Use of Anti-Suit Injunctions in International Litigation*, 28 COLUM. J. TRANSNAT'L L. 589 (1990); Note, *Antisuit Injunctions and International Comity*, 71 VA. L. REV. 1039 (1985).

174. China Trade & Development Corp. v. M/V Choong Yong, 837 F.2d 33, 36–37 (2d Cir. 1987).

175. United States efforts to enter into bilateral treaties covering the recognition and enforcement of judgments have been unsuccessful. A U.S.-sponsored multilateral convention

litigation. Lack of a U.S. Convention leads to parallel proceedings because it is uncertain whether a U.S. judgment will be enforced or whether a foreign judgment will be enforced in the United States. Faced with such uncertainty, parties may pursue actions in multiple jurisdictions. Vexatious litigation leads to parallel proceedings where parties file multiple actions or pursue separate actions for perceived strategic reasons, which may include questionable tactics of increasing the cost of the dispute or subjecting the opponent to proceedings in a distant place. Of course, parallel proceedings are not necessarily improper. A party may have well-founded, good faith reasons for filing a separate action on a common subject matter. These reasons may include, among many others, a substantial question regarding the personal or subject matter jurisdiction of a tribunal or concerning the corruption or bias of a tribunal in a state hostile to U.S. interests.

§ 5.09 SELECTED LIMITATIONS: POLITICAL QUESTION DOCTRINE

The political question doctrine arises from the separation of powers set forth in the U.S. Constitution, which establishes co-equal Legislative, Executive, and Judicial branches of government. Under the political question doctrine, U.S. courts should refrain from ruling in cases where the outcome is determined by a ''political question'' reserved to another branch of government. The mere fact that a case is political or touches on foreign policy concerns is generally insufficient to invoke the doctrine.[176] The Second Circuit has observed:

> A nonjusticiable political question would ordinarily involve one or more of the following factors:
>
> [1] a textually demonstrable constitutional commitment of the issue to a coordinate political department; or [2] a lack of judicially discoverable and manageable standards for resolving it; or [3] the impossibility of deciding without an initial policy determination of a kind clearly for nonjudicial discretion; or [4] the impossibility of a court's undertaking independent resolution without expressing lack of respect due coordinate branches of government; or [5] an unusual need for unquestioning adherence to a political decision already made; or [6] the potentiality

on this subject is currently being negotiated under the auspices of the Hague Conference on Private International Law. *See supra* § 11.01.

176. Klinghoffer v. S.N.C. Achille Lauro, 937 F.2d 44, 49 (2d Cir. 1991) (doctrine is one of ''political questions,'' not one of ''political cases'').

> of embarrassment from multifarious pronouncements by various departments on one question.[177]

Recent cases suggest that the political question doctrine may be particularly difficult to invoke in the human rights context. As stated in *Kadic v. Karadzic*:[178]

> Not every case ''touching on foreign relations'' is nonjusticiable . . . and judges should not reflexively invoke these doctrines [the political question doctrine and act of state doctrine] to avoid difficult and somewhat sensitive decisions in the context of human rights. We believe a preferable approach is to weigh carefully the relevant considerations on a case-by-case basis . . . our decision in *Filartiga*,[179] established that universally recognized norms of international law provide judicially discoverable and manageable standards for adjudicating suits brought under the Alien Tort Act, which obviates any need to make initial policy decisions of the kind normally reserved for nonjudicial discretion.

§ 5.10 SELECTED LIMITATIONS: FORUM SELECTION AND ARBITRATION CLAUSES

A set of important limitations on a court's ability to exercise jurisdiction over a particular case includes a court's deferral to the intent of the parties by giving effect to forum selection and arbitration clauses. Standard international contracts often contain provisions directing that the law of a particular nation will apply to disputes arising between the parties under the agreement, or that any disputes arising under the agreement will be resolved through arbitration. As a matter of public policy, the courts have refrained from exercising jurisdiction over such cases, in an effort to promote the use of voluntary forum selection and dispute resolution devices.

[1] Forum Selection Clauses

When parties to a transnational contract execute an agreement in today's commercial environment, they often include a designation of where any disputes arising from the agreement should be resolved. Forum selection clauses of this type will generally be given effect to

177. Kadic v. Karadzic, 70 F.3d 232, 249 (2d Cir. 1995), *reh'g denied*, 74 F.3d 377 (1996), *cert. denied*, 518 U.S. 1005 (citations omitted).

178. *Id.*

179. 630 F.2d 876 (2d Cir. 1980), discussed *supra* § 5.05[1].

provide predictability in international commerce. This policy was at the heart of the seminal Supreme Court case on this issue, *M/S Bremen v. Zapata Offshore Co.*[180] In *Bremen*, the Court held that the following forum selection clause must be given effect: "Any dispute arising must be treated before the London Court of Justice."

The court of appeals held the clause unenforceable as against public policy. Applying the elements of the doctrine of forum non conveniens,[181] the court of appeals declined to give effect to a contract "in advance of controversy whose objective is to oust the jurisdiction of the courts."[182] The Supreme Court reversed, and articulated why such clauses should be respected:

> For at least two decades, we have witnessed an expansion of overseas commercial activities by business enterprises based in the United States. The barrier of distance that once tended to confine a business concern to a modest territory no longer does so. Here we see an American company with special expertise contracting with a foreign company to tow a complex machine thousands of miles across seas and oceans. The expansion of American business and industry will hardly be encouraged if, notwithstanding solemn contracts, we insist on a parochial concept that all disputes must be resolved under our laws and in our courts. . . . We cannot have trade and commerce in world markets and international waters exclusively on our terms, governed by our laws, and resolved in our courts.[183]

As a result, the Court held that "such clauses are prima facie valid and should be enforced unless enforcement is shown by the resisting party to be 'unreasonable' under the circumstances."[184]

The Court offered two examples of what would constitute "unreasonableness," justifying nonenforcement of a forum selection clause. The first example is when "enforcement would contravene a strong public policy of the forum in which the suit is brought, whether declared by statute or judicial decision."[185] The second example is when "the chosen forum is *seriously* inconvenient for the trial of the action."[186]

---

180. 407 U.S. 1 (1972).
181. For a discussion of the doctrine of forum non conveniens, *see supra* § 5.08.
182. 407 U.S. at 6.
183. *Id.* at 8–9.
184. *Id.* at 10.
185. *Id.* at 15.
186. *Id.* at 16.

One Circuit examined the first example, concerning a "strong public policy of the forum." In *Shell v. R.W. Sturge, Ltd.*,[187] the Plaintiff members of Great Britain's Society of Lloyd's insurance syndicate alleged in an Ohio district court diversity action that Defendants violated Ohio securities laws by selling unregistered securities in Ohio. Defendants moved to dismiss the action for improper venue under Fed. R. Civ. P. 12(b)(3) based upon forum selection and choice of law clauses in the agreement among the parties which named the courts of England and English law. Plaintiffs appealed the district court's dismissal of the action, arguing that such clauses were unenforceable. The Plaintiffs noted the strong public policy of Ohio favoring the registration of securities and claimed that dismissal would deprive them of substantive rights under Ohio's securities laws. The Sixth Circuit disagreed with Plaintiffs and enforced the forum selection and choice of law clauses, affirming the dismissal. The Court stated the key inquiry regarding the international agreement as whether Plaintiffs would be deprived of any remedy or treated unfairly. The Court found no evidence of such. The Court also observed that under *The Bremen v. Zapata Off-Shore Co.*,[188] discussed above, Plaintiffs were required to show that Ohio's interest in protecting the public concerning securities registration outweighed the public policy interest in the integrity of international agreements.[189]

In another ruling on the interpretation of forum selection clauses, the Supreme Court had occasion to consider the *Zapata* "seriously inconvenient" basis for a finding of unreasonableness. In *Carnival Cruise Lines v. Shute*,[190] the Court enforced a forum selection clause on a cruise passenger's ticket because the plaintiff, from Washington State, was unable to overcome the heavy burden articulated in *Bremen* that the

---

187. 55 F.3d 1227 (6th Cir. 1995).

188. 407 U.S. 1 (1972).

189. *See contra* Leslie v. Lloyd's of London, 1995 U.S. Dist. LEXIS 15380, 1995 WL 661090 (S.D. Tex., Aug. 20, 1995) (denying motion to enforce Lloyd's forum selection clause where Plaintiff was induced to accept clause by fraud and overreaching). Litigation involving forum selection clauses in Lloyd's of London agreements has been widespread. In addition to the Sixth Circuit's decision in *R.W. Sturge, Ltd.*, six other circuits, with varying degrees of certainty, have enforced such forum selection provisions. Richards v. Lloyd's of London, 135 F.3d 1289 (9th Cir. 1998); Haynsworth v. The Corporation, 121 F.3d 956 (5th Cir. 1997); Allen v. Lloyd's of London, 94 F.3d 923 (4th Cir. 1996); Bonny v. Society of Lloyd's, 3 F.3d 156 (7th Cir. 1993), *cert. denied*, 510 U.S. 1113 (1994); Roby v. Corporation of Lloyd's, 996 F.2d 1353 (2d Cir.), *cert. denied*, 510 U.S. 945 (1993); Riley v. Kingsley Underwriting Agencies, Ltd., 969 F.2d 953 (10th Cir.), *cert. denied*, 506 U.S. 1021 (1992).

190. 499 U.S. 585 (1991).

litigation of the dispute in Florida would be so inconvenient as to be unreasonable. The clause at issue stated:

> It is agreed by and between the passenger and the Carrier that all disputes and matters whatsoever arising under, in connection with or incident to this Contract shall be litigated in and before a Court in the State of Florida, U.S.A., to the exclusion of the Courts of any other state or country.[191]

The passenger had boarded the cruise vessel in Los Angeles, and was injured in a fall when the vessel was in international waters. She brought suit in Washington State, arguing that the clause was not negotiated and would "deprive respondents of their day in court."[192]

The Supreme Court found that the clause was enforceable because it was not shown to be the product of overreaching.[193] Nor was it shown that the clause would deprive the passenger of a day in court. In a reference to the *Bremen* rationale, the Court explained that Florida is not a remote alien jurisdiction that would seriously inconvenience the passenger.[194]

The standard referred to by the Court in *Carnival Cruise Lines,* that of the "remote alien forum," came from the Court's opinion in *Bremen.* In *Bremen,* the Court evaluated a hypothetical case of unreasonableness and used as an example an "agreement between two Americans to resolve their essentially local disputes in a remote alien forum."[195]

Such a case is not entirely hypothetical. In *Spradlin v. Lear Siegler Management Services Co.,*[196] the Ninth Circuit ruled on an agreement between two U.S. parties to resolve their dispute in Saudi Arabia. An employment agreement between the parties provided:

> This Employment Agreement shall be governed by the laws of the Kingdom of Saudi Arabia. The Courts of Saudi Arabia shall have sole jurisdiction over any disputes arising out of this Employment Agreement.[197]

The Ninth Circuit found that the plaintiff did not lack sophistication and although it questioned the defendant's standard use of a Saudi Arabia

191. *Id.* at 587–88.
192. *Id.* at 588.
193. *Id.* at 595.
194. *Id.* at 594.
195. 407 U.S. at 17.
196. 926 F.2d 865 (9th Cir. 1991).
197. *Id.* at 866.

forum selection clause, the plaintiff did not demonstrate inconvenience. The court stated:

> he has not only failed to produce evidence of inconvenience he would suffer by being forced to litigate in Saudi Arabia, he has even failed to offer any specific allegations as to travel costs, availability of counsel in Saudi Arabia, location of witnesses, or his financial ability to bear such costs and inconvenience.[198]

The lesson of the *Spradlin* case as an interpretation of the *Bremen* standard, is to develop and present specific evidence of inconvenience when attempting to set aside a forum selection clause. Indeed, the Ninth Circuit seemed prepared to set aside the clause selecting Saudi Arabia, but chose not to do so because of the plaintiff's failure to demonstrate inconvenience. The *Spradlin* decision illustrates that courts will not assume inconvenience when reviewing forum selection clauses involving non-U.S. forums.

In an earlier case on the subject, *Lauro Lines SRL v. Chasser*,[199] the Supreme Court considered whether a party may appeal the denial of a motion to dismiss based on a contractual forum selection clause. At issue in *Lauro Lines* was a suit against the owners of the cruise ship ''Achille Lauro'' for damages stemming from the terrorist attack of October 1985. The actions were initiated in U.S. district court in New York, and the vessel owners moved to dismiss based on a forum selection clause printed on the passenger tickets. The trial court denied the motion, deciding that the ticket as a whole did not constitute sufficient notice that the passengers were waiving their rights to maintain suit in the United States.[200] The ticket's cover contained the following language:

> ''**IMPORTANT:** Passenger's attention is drawn to the Shipowner's terms and conditions printed inside.''[201]

Among thirty-two fine print articles on the back of the ticket was article 31, which stated:

> All controversies that may arise directly or indirectly in connection with or in relation to this passage contract must be instituted before the

---

198. *Id.* at 869. *See also* Hugel v. Corporation of Lloyd's, 999 F.2d 206, 210–11 (7th Cir. 1993).

199. 490 U.S. 495 (1989).

200. *See* Chasser v. Achille Lauro Lines, 844 F.2d 50, 51–52 (2d Cir. 1988).

201. Hodes v. S.N.C. Achille Lauro, 858 F.2d 905, 907 (3d Cir. 1988), *appeal dismissed,* 490 U.S. 1001 (1989).

> judicial authority in Naples, the jurisdiction of any other authority being expressly renounced and waived.[202]

The trial court found that the ticket did not give fair warning to the American passengers that they were waiving the opportunity to sue in a domestic forum over a contract made and delivered in the United States.[203]

The defendant sought to appeal the denial of the motion as an interlocutory order, without moving for certification of the issue for immediate appeal under 28 U.S.C.A. § 1292(b), instead arguing that the dismissal was an appealable collateral final order. The Supreme Court held that an interlocutory order denying a motion to dismiss on the basis of a contractual forum selection clause is not immediately appealable as a collateral final order.[204] The denial of the motion meant that the action had to go forward in the undesirable forum before any appeal could be taken. Although such an unfortunate result may be inevitable in some cases, planning is required to alleviate the risk of being forced to maintain the action in an undesirable forum.

In *McDonnell Douglas Corp. v. Islamic Republic of Iran*,[205] the court considered whether a change in the government of a country designated by the parties to a forum selection clause would have an impact on whether the clause would be given effect. In *McDonnell Douglas,* the parties entered into a contract in 1975, before a revolutionary change in government took place in Iran, and included a forum selection clause that provided:

> Any difference or dispute from the execution of the contract that may not be settled amicably should be settled through the Iranian courts.[206]

The court reviewed the application of *Bremen* and *Scherk v. Alberto-Culver*,[207] and determined that it was not deprived of jurisdiction by virtue of this clause because the parties before it had used the word "should" rather than "must." The court concluded that the use of the word "should" expressed only a preference between the two available

202. *Id.*
203. *Lauro Lines S.R.L.*, 490 U.S. at 497.
204. *Id.* at 501.
205. 758 F.2d 341 (8th Cir.), *cert. denied,* 474 U.S. 948 (1985).
206. *Id.* at 343.
207. 417 U.S. 512 (1974). *See infra* § 5.10[2], discussing *Scherk.*

fora.[208] In addition, the lower court acknowledged plaintiff's allegations that "the current Iranian legal system is inadequate for, and ill disposed to, fairly adjudicate the contractual dispute between the parties."[209]

In *Regis Assocs. v. Rank Hotels (Management) Ltd.*,[210] the court held that the inclusion of a forum selection clause in an agreement does not constitute a waiver of the right to removal.[211] At issue in *Regis Assocs.* was the following forum selection clause:

> The interpretation and application of this Agreement shall be governed by the law of the State of Michigan and the parties hereby submit to the jurisdiction of the Michigan Courts.[212]

Plaintiff argued that not only did this clause work to effect a choice of the Michigan forum, it also operated as a waiver of defendant's right of removal. Plaintiff contended that unless the right to go to federal court was specifically reserved in the forum selection clause, it was waived.[213] The court disagreed, noting that the right of removal is a statutory one that is absolute if certain requirements in the removal statute are satisfied.[214] It is possible to waive the right to removal, but the waiver, to be effective, must be clear and unequivocal.[215]

[2] Arbitration Clauses

Many international commercial contracts include not only a forum selection clause, but also agreements to submit disputes to arbitration rather than resolution in court. Specific legal issues, pitfalls, and drafting issues concerning arbitration clauses are discussed below, at § 12.02[4]. The insertion of arbitration provisions in international commercial contracts is often motivated by the parties' desire to avoid litigation before alien tribunals. As a result of the United States Arbitration Act,[216] the traditional opposition to arbitration was erased. As a matter of

208. *Id.* at 347.

209. McDonnell Douglas Corp. v. Islamic Republic of Iran, 591 F. Supp. 293, 303 (E.D. Mo. 1984). *See also McDonnell Douglas Corp.*, 758 F.2d at 345–46.

210. 894 F.2d 193 (6th Cir. 1990).

211. *Id.* at 196.

212. *Id.* at 194.

213. *Id.* at 195.

214. *Id.*

215. *Id. See also In re* Delta Am. v. National Distillers & Chem. Corp., 900 F.2d 890, 894 (6th Cir.), *cert. denied,* 498 U.S. 890 (1990). Waiver of removal in the FSIA context is discussed in § 7.03[2], *infra.*

216. 9 U.S.C.A. § 1 et seq.

policy, therefore, courts will encourage arbitration by giving effect to agreements to arbitrate.[217] It should be noted, however, that parties who wish to have arbitral awards confirmed should clearly indicate this intent in the agreement to arbitrate.[218] Although international law contemplates the ready enforcement of arbitral awards, U.S. courts have applied a "consent-to-confirmation" analysis which considers the intent of the parties at the time of contract formation.[219]

In addition, many of the policy reasons that support the enforcement of forum selection clauses also provide the policy foundation for the enforcement of arbitration clauses. For instance, in *Scherk v. Alberto-Culver*,[220] the Supreme Court considered an agreement to arbitrate that required "any controversy or claim arising out of the agreement or the breach thereof 'would be referred to arbitration before the International Chamber of Commerce in Paris, France, and that the laws of the State of Illinois, U.S.A. would apply to the agreement, its interpretation and performance.'"[221]

The court noted that an "agreement to arbitrate before a specified tribunal is, in effect, a specialized kind of forum selection clause that posits not only the situs of the suit but also the procedure to be used in resolving the dispute."[222] Articulating similar policy concerns as stated in *Bremen*,[223] the court stated:

> A contractual provision specifying in advance the forum in which disputes shall be litigated and the law to be applied is, therefore, an almost indispensable precondition to achievement of the orderliness and predictability essential to any international business transaction. Furthermore, such a provision obviates the danger that a dispute under the agreement might be submitted to a forum hostile to the interests of one of the parties or unfamiliar with the problem area involved.
>
> A parochial refusal by the courts of one country to enforce an international arbitration agreement would not only frustrate these purposes, but would invite unseemly and mutually destructive jockeying by the parties to secure tactical litigation advantages.[224]

---

217. *See* Scherk v. Alberto-Culver Co., 417 U.S. 506, 510–11 (1974).
218. Gerald W. Palmer, *Enforcing Arbitral Decisions*, NAT'L L.J., Feb. 7, 1994, at 25.
219. *Id.*
220. 417 U.S. 506 (1974).
221. *Id.* at 508.
222. *Id.* at 519.
223. The *Bremen* decision is discussed *supra* § 5.10[1].
224. *Scherk* at 516–17 (footnote omitted).

The court's decision in *Scherk* illustrates the strong policy in favor of arbitration, especially in international transactions.

The Supreme Court extended this policy beyond traditional limitations in the case of *Mitsubishi Motors Corp. v. Soler Chrysler-Plymouth.*[225] At issue in *Mitsubishi* was a dispute between the manufacturer of automobiles in Japan and a distributor located in Puerto Rico. To prevent the distributor from transferring unsold vehicles to other markets under the terms of the distributorship agreement, Mitsubishi sought to compel arbitration under the arbitration clause in the agreement that provided:

> All disputes, controversies or differences which may arise between [Mitsubishi] and [Soler] out of or in relation to Articles I-B through V of this Agreement or for the breach thereof, shall be finally settled by arbitration in Japan in accordance with the rules and regulations of the Japan Commercial Arbitration Association.[226]

In response, Soler alleged various claims, including several statutory ones, such as antitrust claims under the Sherman Act. The district court held that despite precedent suggesting that the statutory claims were not arbitrable, the Supreme Court's decision in *Scherk* meant that the international character of the Mitsubishi-Soler dispute "required enforcement of the agreement to arbitrate even as to the antitrust claims."[227] The court of appeals affirmed, rejecting Soler's contention that any agreement to arbitrate the antitrust claims would have to explicitly so state.[228]

The Supreme Court affirmed, holding that in the international context, the policy reasons that would otherwise compel denial of an arbitration in a purely domestic context do not apply. The Court considered several arguments against permitting arbitration of statutory issues, and especially of antitrust issues. The four standard arguments are:

(1) private antitrust suits are an important tool of government policy enforcement;

225. 473 U.S. 614 (1985).

226. *Id.* at 617.

227. *Id.* at 620–21. *Compare* Tai Ping Ins. Co. Ltd. v. M/V Warschau, 731 F.2d 1141, 1146 (5th Cir. 1984) (discussing "non-arbitrable" nature of securities and antitrust claims).

228. 473 U.S. at 621–22.

(2) some contracts giving rise to antitrust disputes are contracts of adhesion;

(3) antitrust issues are too sophisticated and complex for arbitration; and

(4) antitrust regulation of business is too important to be left to arbitrators.[229]

The Court found each of these factors unpersuasive in the international context, but focused on the primary concern, the first factor; that the objectives of the antitrust laws will not be served if they are subject to arbitration. The Court explained:

> There is no reason to assume at the outset of the dispute that international arbitration will not provide an adequate mechanism. To be sure, the international arbitral tribunal owes no prior allegiance to the legal norms of particular states; hence, it has no direct obligation to vindicate their statutory dictates. The tribunal, however, is bound to effectuate the intentions of the parties. Where the parties have agreed that the arbitral body is to decide a defined set of claims which includes, as in these cases, those arising from the application of American antitrust law, the tribunal therefore should be bound to decide that dispute in accord with the national law giving rise to the claim. . . . And so long as the prospective litigant effectively may vindicate its statutory cause of action in the arbitral forum, the statute will continue to serve both its remedial and deterrent function.[230]

The *Mitsubishi* decision illustrates the growing acceptance of the courts of the need for predictability in international commerce:

> As international trade has expanded in recent decades, so too has the use of international arbitration to resolve disputes arising in the course of that trade. The controversies that international arbitral institutions are called upon to resolve have increased in diversity as well as in complexity. Yet the potential of these tribunals for efficient disposition of legal disagreements arising from commercial relations has not yet been tested. If they are to take the central place in the international legal order, national courts will need to "shake off the old judicial hostility to arbitration, . . ." and also their customary and understandable unwillingness to cede jurisdiction of a claim arising under domestic law to a foreign or international tribunal. To this extent, at least, it will be necessary for national courts to subordinate

229. *Id.* at 636.

230. *Id.* at 636–37 (citation omitted).

domestic notions of arbitrability to the international policy favoring commercial arbitration.[231]

Parties are cautioned, however, to exercise foresight when drafting or seeking to enforce an agreement to arbitrate. While the public policy favoring the enforcement of international arbitral agreements is extremely strong,[232] such agreements may still be subject to a court's concerns of mutuality and unconscionability.[233] An example of a court's voiding an arbitration agreement as unduly oppressive, albeit in a purely domestic employment agreement, is *Stirlen v. Supercuts, Inc.*[234] In that case, the Court ruled the arbitration clause unconscionable where it had no valid commercial justification, afforded Supercuts greater remedies than would be available, and deprived Mr. Stirlen of substantial rights and remedies. Parties holding an advantage in negotiations are therefore cautioned to avoid overreaching in drafting an agreement to arbitrate. Counsel should circumspectly advise clients where enforcement of such an agreement is sought.

§ 5.11 PRACTICAL STRATEGIES AND CHECKLIST

In the area of subject matter jurisdiction, counsel must first consider whether the maintenance of the action in the United States is consistent with principles of international law.[235] Next, counsel should consider two general issues. First, what specific grant of authority enables the court to exercise jurisdiction over the particular matter? Second, are there any limitations that will cause the court to decline to exercise that grant of authority?

The following checklist presents issues counsel should consider in undertaking subject matter jurisdiction analyses:

(1) Should the suit be brought in state court?

---

231. *Id.* at 638–39, *citing* Kulukundis Shipping Co. v. Amtorg Trading Corp., 126 F.2d 978, 985 (2d Cir. 1942). *See also* Deloitte Noraudit v. Deloitte Haskins & Sells, 9 F.3d 1060, 1063–65 (2d Cir. 1993); Progressive Casualty Ins. Co. v. C.A. Reasegoadora Nacional De Venezuela, 991 F.2d 42, 48–49 (2d Cir. 1993); Riley v. Kingsley Underwriting Agencies, Ltd., 969 F.2d 953, 958–60 (10th Cir. 1992).

232. *Mitsubshi Motors Corp.*, 473 U.S. at 627; Alamria v. Telcor Int'l, Inc., 920 F. Supp. 658, 663 (D. Md. 1996).

233. *Courts Stress Importance of Clear [Arbitration] Clauses*, NAT'L L.J., Mon., Sept. 22, 1997, at B23.

234. 51 Cal. App. 4th 1519, 60 Cal. Rptr. 2d 138 (Ct. App. 1 Dist. 1997).

235. For a discussion of the relationship between suits in the United States and international law, *see supra* § 5.01.

(2) Does the state court have jurisdiction over the matter?

(3) If the suit is commenced in state court, can it be removed?

(4) Should suit be brought in federal court?

(5) What specific basis of federal jurisdiction grants the court authority over the matter?

(6) Does the doctrine of forum non conveniens apply? Is it possible to have the case dismissed, forcing resolution elsewhere?

(7) Even though the court may have jurisdiction over the matter, should the court decline to exercise that jurisdiction under the doctrine of comity? Similarly, do the restrictions contained in the doctrine of reasonableness militate toward resolution of the controversy in another forum?

(8) Have the parties included a forum selection clause in the contract? Should it be given effect? Can it be overridden? What evidence of inconvenience can be developed to demonstrate that it would be unfair to require litigation of the dispute in a non-U.S. forum?

(9) Have the parties included an arbitration clause in the contract? Should it be given effect? Can it be overridden?

The limitations described in this Chapter are a few of the most important and common limitations that will arise in the course of international litigation. Questions of personal jurisdiction, discussed in Chapter 6 must also be considered in conjunction with any subject matter jurisdictional analysis. In addition, counsel in an international case should carefully review Chapters 7 and 8, dealing with the Foreign Sovereign Immunity Act (''FSIA'') and the act of state doctrine, to determine the extent to which such issues are implicated. As a final note of caution, it may be observed that jurisdictional defenses may be waived in certain instances, if not timely presented. Jurisdictional defenses, therefore, should be promptly explored and asserted.

Chapter 6

SELECTED ISSUES OF PERSONAL JURISDICTION OR JURISDICTION TO ADJUDICATE AND LIMITATIONS

Chapter 6

§ 6.01 INTRODUCTION TO PERSONAL JURISDICTION ISSUES IN A TRANSNATIONAL CONTEXT

As described in Chapter 5, jurisdictional issues can be divided broadly into two categories. The first category, the subject of Chapter 5, is subject matter jurisdiction, or what is now often called jurisdiction to prescribe.[1] This chapter deals with the second category of jurisdiction, *in personam* jurisdiction, or in terms used in the Restatement (Third) of Foreign Relations Law, jurisdiction to adjudicate, or judicial jurisdiction.[2]

Before turning to the U.S. law on this subject, a threshold question involves the limits placed on national assertions of jurisdiction by international law.[3] The limits arising under international law are spelled out in section 421 of the Restatement (Third) of Foreign Relations Law, which provides generally that a nation may exercise jurisdiction over parties only on the basis of reasonable contacts with the forum nation.[4] The exercise of jurisdiction is reasonable in one or more of three types of contacts with the forum:

(1) If the defendant is present in the forum, whether by virtue of citizenship or corporate organization;[5]

(2) If the defendant has consented to the exercise of jurisdiction;[6] or

(3) If the defendant regularly carries on business or other activities in the forum or engages in activity outside the forum that has a substantial, direct, and foreseeable effect within the forum.[7]

Although these standards parallel in major part the standards under U.S. law,[8] they provide a yardstick for the evaluation of particular actions, and indicate when a case is consistent with international norms.

---

1. *See* Restatement (Third) of Foreign Relations Law § 421, cmt. j (1987).
2. *Id.* § 421, cmt. a. *See generally* Gary B. Born, *Reflections on Judicial Jurisdiction in International Cases,* 17 Ga. J. Int'l Comp. L. 1 (1987).
3. Restatement, *supra* note 1, § 421, reporters' note 1 ("modern concepts of jurisdiction to adjudicate under international law are similar to those developed under the due process clause of the United States Constitution").
4. *Id.*
5. *Id.* § 421(2)(a)–(e).
6. *Id.* § 421(g).
7. *Id.* § 421(h)–(k).
8. Restatement, *supra* note 1, § 421, reporters' note 1.

In most cases tried in U.S. courts, however, limits arising from international law are important, but are often secondary to constitutional limits on the jurisdictional reach of courts.[9] Under U.S. law, a court possesses *in personam* jurisdiction only if authorized by federal or state statute, and if consistent with constitutional due process requirements.[10] These two requirements establish a formula for reviewing questions of in personam jurisdiction that involves a three part inquiry into:

(1) The statute or rule authorizing the exercise of jurisdiction;

(2) The minimum contacts required under the due process clause of the Constitution; and

(3) The overall reasonableness test required by the Constitution.[11]

Jurisdiction over foreign defendants based on their contacts with the United States is the subject of the balance of this chapter. The scope of U.S. jurisdiction over U.S. citizens and foreign branches and subsidiaries of U.S. companies, although beyond the scope of this inquiry, may also become an issue. In *Blackmer v. United States*,[12] the Supreme Court held that, consistent with section 421 of the Restatement, a nation retains jurisdiction over citizens wherever they may be located:

> The jurisdiction of the United States over its absent citizen, so far as the binding effect of its legislation is concerned, is jurisdiction *in personam*, as he is personally bound to take notice of the laws that are applicable to him and to obey them. . . . But, for the exercise of judicial jurisdiction *in personam,* there must be due process, which requires appropriate notice of the judicial action and an opportunity to be heard.[13]

Similarly, questions of U.S. jurisdiction over corporate branches and subsidiaries outside the United States may also become an issue. In such cases, counsel should begin with section 414 of the Restatement (Third) of Foreign Relations Law, entitled: "Jurisdiction With Respect to

---

9. RESTATEMENT, *supra* note 1, § 421.

10. *See* Note, *Alien Corporations and Aggregate Contacts: A Genuinely Federal Jurisdictional Standard,* 95 HARV. L. REV. 470, 471 (1981) ("the overwhelming consensus among federal courts is to analyze questions of in personam jurisdiction over alien defendants by examining the relationship, the litigation and the forum under traditional *International Shoe* principles", *quoting* Superior Coal Co. v. Ruhrkohle, A.G., 83 F.R.D. 414, 419 (E.D. Pa. 1979)).

11. *See generally* RESTATEMENT, *supra* note 1, § 421.

12. 284 U.S. 421 (1932).

13. *Id.* at 438 (citations omitted).

Activities of Foreign Branches and Subsidiaries.''[14] A related issue, which is the reverse, is the question whether a foreign corporate parent or affiliate is subject to U.S. jurisdiction by virtue of the presence of a related corporation in the United States. This issue is the subject of § 6.06, below.

This chapter will primarily explore the issues raised under U.S. law with respect to *in personam* jurisdiction, or jurisdiction to adjudicate. Section 6.02 will discuss these questions as they arise in state court, and review removal procedures. Section 6.03 will review *in personam* jurisdiction in federal court. The traditional ''minimum contacts'' and due process analysis will be reviewed with respect to foreign defendants in § 6.04. Questions of waiver of objections to *in personam* jurisdiction will be considered in § 6.05, with special questions pertaining to related corporations discussed in § 6.06. Section 6.07 will discuss the so-called national contacts theory of jurisdiction over non-U.S. corporations, and § 6.08 will review venue considerations in cases involving alien defendants. Section 6.09 provides a checklist of issues relating to *in personam* jurisdiction and practical strategies.

§ 6.02 STATE COURT JURISDICTION AND REMOVAL

[1] State Court Jurisdiction

When a suit against a foreign defendant is brought in state court, the court must engage in a two-pronged inquiry. First, has the legislature specifically authorized the exercise of jurisdiction? Second, the court must consider whether such an exercise of jurisdiction is consistent with constitutional requirements of due process. As one court explained:

> [N]ot only must the requirements of due process be met before a court can properly assert *in personam* jurisdiction, but the exercise of jurisdiction must also be affirmatively authorized by the legislature.[15]

14. *See generally* Stanley J. Marcuss, *Jurisdiction With Respect to Foreign Branches and Subsidiaries: Judicial Power in the Foreign Affairs Context Under Section 414 of the Foreign Relations Restatement,* 26 INT'L LAW. 1 (1992).

15. Wells Fargo & Co. v. Wells Fargo Express Co., 556 F.2d 406, 414 (9th Cir. 1977). *See also* Covia v. Robinson, 507 N.W.2d 411, 413 (Iowa 1993); Geelhoed v. Jensen, 277 Md. 220, 224, 352 A.2d 818 (1976); Tate v. Blue Cross of Washington & Alaska, 59 Md. App. 206, 213, 474 A.2d 1353 (1984); N.E. Contract Packers v. Beverage Services, 6 Conn. L. Rptr. 582 (Conn. Super. 1992).

This section deals with the question of statutory authority in the context of a state court action. Section 6.04 focuses on due process considerations from the standpoint of both state and federal actions.

In most cases, the common statutory provision will be the state's long arm statute because the case will involve questions of specific jurisdiction. Under state law, a court must look to the statutory provisions, the so-called long-arm statutes, for the requirements that must be satisfied before jurisdiction may be exercised. For instance, the District of Columbia long-arm statute provides, in part:

> § 13–423. *Personal Jurisdiction Based on Conduct.*
>
> (a) A District of Columbia court may exercise personal jurisdiction over a person, who acts directly or by an agent, as to a claim for relief arising from the person's—
>
> (1) transacting any business in the District of Columbia;
>
> (2) contracting to supply services in the District of Columbia;
>
> (3) causing tortious injury in the District of Columbia by an act or omission in the District of Columbia;
>
> (4) causing tortious injury in the District of Columbia by an act or omission outside the District of Columbia if he regularly does or solicits business, engages in any other persistent course of conduct, or derives substantial revenue from goods used or consumed, or services rendered, in the District of Columbia. . . .
>
> ****
>
> (b) When jurisdiction over a person is based solely upon this section, only a claim for relief arising from acts enumerated in this section may be asserted against him.

The District of Columbia statute provides for jurisdiction based on the four types of relationships with the forum listed in section 13-423 and explicitly limits such jurisdiction to specific jurisdiction.[16]

The application of the District of Columbia statute is illustrated by a suit brought in the District against a German corporation. In *Liberty Mutual Ins. Co. v. American Pecco Corp.*,[17] the court asserted jurisdiction over the defendant even though the product at issue, a crane,

16. *See infra* § 6.04[2] (discussing specific jurisdiction).
17. 334 F. Supp. 522 (D.D.C. 1971).

was sold to an unrelated U.S. corporation on a F.O.B. Hamburg basis. The court found that the subsection (a)(4) requirement was satisfied by two facts: (1) the defendant derived substantial revenue from the sale of the crane; and (2) the crane was used in the District.[18] The court's decision in *Liberty Mutual* is an example of the stream of commerce theory of specific jurisdiction, a theory explored in greater detail in § 6.04 [1] below.

State long-arm statutes are often construed to extend the jurisdiction of the state's courts as far as permissible under the due process limits of the Constitution. In such cases, only the "minimum contacts" with forum state and "fair play and substantive justice" requirements must be satisfied to establish the court's jurisdiction over the person of a foreign defendant. Examples of the states whose courts interpret their long-arm statutes in this way are California,[19] Michigan,[20] Minnesota,[21] Pennsylvania,[22] and Texas.[23]

In other jurisdictions, a separate analysis of the long-arm statute is required. In New York, for example, no simple test appears to exist to determine the propriety of personal jurisdiction, and jurisdiction may be proper based on one telephone call, or impermissible based on numerous telephone calls and facsimile transmissions.[24] However, New York courts frequently evaluate the validity of *in personam* jurisdiction based on whether a clear nexus existed between business transacted by the defendant and the cause of action.[25]

18. *Id.* at 524.

19. Hirsch v. Blue Cross and Blue Shield of Kansas City, 800 F.2d 1474 (9th Cir. 1986).

20. Sifers v. Horen, 188 N.W.2d 625 (Mich. 1971); LAK, Inc. v. Deer Creek Enterprise, 885 F.2d 1293 (6th Cir. 1989).

21. Domtar, Inc. v. Niagara Fire Insurance Co., 533 N.W.2d 25 (Minn. 1995).

22. Pa. Cons. Stat. Ann. § 5322(b) (Purdon 1981); Travellers Indemnity Co. v. TEC America, Inc., 909 F. Supp. 249 (M.D. Penn. 1995).

23. Schlobohm v. Schapiro, 784 S.W.2d 355 (Tex. 1990).

24. Manhattan Life Insurance Co. v. A.J. Stratton Syndicate, 731 F. Supp. 587 (S.D.N.Y. 1990).

25. Frummer v. Hilton Hotels International, Inc., 19 N.Y. 2d 533, 277 N.E.2d 851, 281 N.Y.S.2d 41, *cert. denied,* 389 U.S. 923 (1967) (in a personal injury case arising out of an accident in London Hilton hotel, the court found that a British corporation transacted business in New York with a clear nexus to the cause of action including public relations and contacts with travel agents); *see also* Delagi v. Volkswagenwerk AG of Wolfsburg, 29 N.Y.2d 426, 278 N.E. 895, 328 N.Y.S.2d 763 (1972) (in a breach of warranty and negligence suit against a German corporation, the court found the defendant was not engaged in continuous and systematic course of doing business in New York when it exported automobiles to its wholly owned subsidiary, a New Jersey corporation, which in turn sold the cars to an unrelated New York corporation).

Under the Massachusetts long-arm statute, a court may exercise personal jurisdiction over a person who acts directly or through an agent as to a cause of action in law or equity arising from the person's transacting any business in the state.[26] This language was originally interpreted as barring a cause of action in case of injuries to state residents at out-of-state hotels.[27] This was changed in 1994 when the Supreme Judicial Court of Massachusetts ruled that when the plaintiff was injured in a slip-and-fall accident in a California hotel, the exercise of jurisdiction was proper because the reservation of a room in the hotel was the first step in the train of events that resulted in the personal injury.[28] Following this decision, the First Circuit adopted its more liberal interpretation of the state's long-arm statute.[29] Mississippi's long-arm statute subjects to jurisdiction in the state's courts any nonresident who makes a contract with a resident of the state to be performed in whole or in part in the state, or who commits a tort in the state, or who does any business in the state.[30] In a wrongful termination suit involving an employment contract performed overseas, the statute has been interpreted as not allowing personal jurisdiction over a foreign employer.[31] Similarly, Colorado courts interpret the tort provisions of the state's long-arm statute as requiring that either the tortious act or the injury resulting from the tortious act occur in state.[32] Thus, a state resident was precluded from suing a British law firm on the allegation that it affected unauthorized disbursements from plaintiff's funds in England.[33]

Suits involving foreign defendants are not, of course, limited to state court. Cases originating in state court may, in some instances, be removed to federal court, or the case may be initiated in federal court. The following subsection discusses the removal provision, and § 6.03 discusses the operation of personal jurisdiction in cases heard in federal court.

26. Mass. Gen. Laws Ann. 223A, § 3a (1985).

27. Pizarro v. Hotels Concorde International C.A., 907 F.2d 1256 (1st Cir. 1990); Marina v. Hyatt Corp., 793 F.2d 427 (1st Cir. 1986).

28. Tatro v. Manor Care, Inc., 625 N.E.2d 549 (Mass. 1994).

29. Nowak v. Tak How Investment, Ltd., 899 F. Supp. 25 (D. Mass. 1995).

30. Miss. Code Ann. § 13-3-57 (Supp. 1995).

31. Peterson v. Test International, E.C., 904 F. Supp. 574 (S.D. Miss. 1995).

32. Classic Auto Sales, Inc. v. Schochet, 832 P.2d 233 (Colo. 1992).

33. Wenz v. Memery Crystal, 55 F.3d 1503 (10th Cir. 1995).

[2] Removal of Actions to Federal Court

Cases involving foreign defendants that are originally brought in state court are often removed to federal court. Removal of actions is governed by 28 U.S.C.A. § 1441, which provides, generally, that any action that could originally have been brought in federal court may be removed if brought in state court.[33.1] Removal does not operate as a waiver of objections to the assertion of personal jurisdiction; objections are preserved and may operate in the federal forum.[34]

In *Ruhrgas, AG v. Marathon Oil Co.*,[34.1] the U.S. Supreme Court considered whether a federal court must first decide whether it has subject matter jurisdiction over a case removed from state court before determining whether it should exercise personal jurisdiction. The dispute in *Ruhrgas* stemmed from a venture to produce gas in the North Sea. Marathon Oil Co. sued Ruhrgas in Texas state court, asserting state-law claims of fraud, tortious interference with prospective business relations, breach of fiduciary duty, and civil conspiracy.

Ruhrgas removed the case to the federal District Court, asserting three bases for federal jurisdiction: diversity of citizenship under 28 U.S.C.A. § 1332, on the theory that another party (Marathon Petroleum Norge) had been fraudulently joined; federal question, because Marathon's claims raised questions of international relations under 28 U.S.C.A. § 1331; and 9 U.S.C.A. § 205, which authorizes removal of cases relating to international arbitration agreements. Ruhrgas moved to dismiss the complaint for lack of personal jurisdiction. Marathon moved to remand the case to the state court for lack of federal subject-matter jurisdiction.

The District Court granted Ruhrgas' motion to dismiss for lack of personal jurisdiction. The Texas long arm statute authorized personal jurisdiction to the extent permitted by the due process clause of the U.S. Constitution. The District Court, however, found Ruhrgas' contacts with Texas insufficient to support personal jurisdiction.

The Fifth Circuit, en banc, vacated the District Court's decision and remanded the case, ruling that, in removed cases, district courts must

---

33.1. *See supra* § 5.03[2].

34. *See* Nationwide Eng'g & Control Sys., Inc. v. Thomas, 837 F.2d 345, 347–48 (8th Cir. 1988); *see* R. CASAD, JURISDICTION IN CIVIL ACTIONS § 5.04, at 5–36 (2d ed. 1983). For a discussion of the operation of the unconditional right of removal provision in the context of cases under the Foreign Sovereign Immunities Act of 1976, *see infra* § 7.03[2].

34.1. 526 U.S. 574 (1999).

decide issues of subject matter jurisdiction first, and then determine personal jurisdiction issues only if subject matter jurisdiction is found to exist. The Fifth Circuit limited its holding to removed cases, finding the procedure it outlined necessary to prevent federal courts from usurping the jurisdiction of state courts.

A unanimous Supreme Court reversed the Fifth Circuit and remanded the case. The Court held that in cases removed from state court to federal court, as in cases originating in federal court, there is no unyielding jurisdictional hierarchy requiring the federal court to adjudicate subject matter jurisdiction before considering a challenge to personal jurisdiction. The Court ruled:

> The Fifth Circuit erred in according absolute priority to the subject-matter jurisdiction requirement on the ground that it is nonwaivable and delimits federal court power, while restrictions on a court's jurisdiction over the person are waivable and protect individual rights. Although the character of the two jurisdictional bedrocks unquestionably differs, the distinctions do not mean that subject-matter jurisdiction is ever and always the more "fundamental." Personal jurisdiction, too, is an essential element of district court jurisdiction, without which the court is powerless to proceed to an adjudication.

The Court noted, however, that "in most instances, subject-matter jurisdiction will involve no arduous inquiry, and both expedition and sensitivity to state courts' coequal stature should impel the federal court to dispose of that issue first."

§ 6.03 PERSONAL JURISDICTION IN FEDERAL COURT: USE OF STATE STATUTES AND SOME UNIQUE FEDERAL RULES

In contrast to state court actions, two separate lines of analysis for *in personam* jurisdiction in actions in federal court are required. For cases involving diversity jurisdiction, federal courts are generally limited to the scope of jurisdiction available under state provisions.[35] In federal question cases, the issue is more complex, but generally involves

35. *See* Arrowsmith v. United Press Int'l, 320 F.2d 219, 224 (2d Cir. 1963) (en banc); RESTATEMENT, *supra* note 1, § 421, reporters' note 7 ("Except where nationwide jurisdiction is conferred by statute . . . the jurisdiction of a federal court in the United States to adjudicate claims against foreign parties depends on the law of the State where the court sits. . .").

consideration of the specific statutory provisions, some of which provide for nationwide jurisdiction.[36]

In diversity cases, state law governs, and the federal court must determine whether the defendant is amenable to suit under state law.[37] For example, in *Alexander Proudfoot Co. v. Thayer*,[38] a Florida corporation sought to enforce an employment agreement in state court. The agreement contained a clause conferring personal jurisdiction over the defendant in Florida. The defendant removed the state law contract claim to federal court.

At issue was whether the court should follow federal policy, under which such contractual clauses are given effect as a waiver of jurisdiction, or whether Florida law, under which such clauses are not favored, controlled.[39] Under the established doctrine of *Erie Railroad Co. v. Tompkins*,[40] and *Hanna v. Plumer*,[41] because the federal court was exercising diversity jurisdiction, the federal court was required to apply state law.[42] Ironically, although the court found that under Florida law the clause would not be operative, under an analysis of Florida's long-arm statute, the court determined that the defendant was properly subject to suit in Florida by reason of the satisfaction of the minimum contacts due process test.[43]

In contrast, when a federal court is exercising federal question jurisdiction, state law controls in some cases, but not in others.[44] If the federal statute giving rise to the cause of action does not provide specifically for the scope of jurisdiction to be exercised, then state rules

---

36. *See* Federal Trade Comm'n v. Jim Walter Corp., 651 F.2d 251, 255–57 (5th Cir. 1981); Driver v. Helms, 577 F.2d 147, 155–57 (1st Cir. 1978); *In re* Colonial Realty Co. v. Vlerbaum, 163 B.R. 431, 432–33 (D. Conn. 1994); Cannon v. Gardner-Martin Asphalt Corp. Retirement Trust-Profit Sharing Plan, 699 F. Supp. 265, 266–268 (M.D. Fla. 1988); *In re* Prospect Hill Resources, Inc., 69 B.R. 79, 79–81 (N.D. Ga. 1986). *See also* RESTATEMENT *supra* note 1, § 421.

37. *See, e.g.*, Ellicott Machine Corp., Inc. v. John Holland Party, Ltd., 995 F.2d 474, 477 (4th Cir. 1993); Coblentz GMC/Freightliner, Inc. v. General Motors Corp., 724 F. Supp. 1364, 1368 (M.D. Ala. 1989), *aff'd*, 932 F.2d 977, 978 (11th Cir. 1991); Arrowsmith v. United Press Int'l, 320 F.2d 219, 224 (2d Cir. 1963) (en banc); *In re* Lupron Marketing and Sales Practices Litigation, 245 F. Supp. 2d 280 (D. Mass. 2003).

38. 877 F.2d 912 (11th Cir. 1989).

39. *Id.* at 916.

40. 304 U.S. 64 (1938).

41. 380 U.S. 460 (1965).

42. *Alexander Proudfoot*, 877 F.2d at 919.

43. *Id.* at 920.

44. *See generally* Note, *Alien Corporations and Aggregate Contacts: A Genuinely Federal Jurisdictional Standard, supra* note 10.

apply, just as in a diversity case.[45] However, if the state long-arm statute is silent on jurisdiction concerning the particular federal claim, the Federal Rules of Civil Procedure now contain a stop-gap provision for the assertion of personal jurisdiction. Rule 4(k)(2) provides that "[i]f the exercise of jurisdiction is consistent with the Constitution and laws of the United States, serving a summons or filing a waiver of service is also effective, with respect to claims arising under federal law, to establish personal jurisdiction over the person of any defendant who is not subject to the jurisdiction of the courts of general jurisdiction of any state."[46] Therefore, if jurisdiction over a party concerning a federal claim comports with due process but is not specifically provided for under federal or state law, jurisdiction may be asserted. Such a circumstance arises when the defendant is a nonresident of the United States and has contacts with the U.S. sufficient to justify the application of U.S. law and to satisfy federal standards of forum selection, but has insufficient contacts with any one state to support jurisdiction under the state long arm statute or meet the requirements of the fourteenth amendment limitation on state court territorial jurisdiction.[47] It may also be noted that if personal jurisdiction is established for a federal claim under Rule 4(k)(2), then 28 U.S.C. § 1367(a) provides supplemental jurisdiction over related federal and state claims, subject to the court's discretion to decline to exercise that jurisdiction under 28 U.S.C. § 1367(c).[48]

In some special cases, federal statutes do specifically delineate the scope of jurisdiction to be exercised.[49] For instance, U.S. securities law (Securities Exchange Act), antitrust law (Clayton Act), and bankruptcy law (Bankruptcy Rule 7004(d)) provide for nationwide jurisdiction over foreign defendants. On the other hand, the False Claims Act (as amended 1986) limits the jurisdiction for an action brought pursuant to the Act to the judicial districts where any defendant can be found, resides, transacts business, or in which any conduct prescribed by the

---

45. Omni Capital Int'l v. Rudolf Wolff & Co., Ltd., 484 U.S. 97, 108 (1987); Aviles v. Kunkle, 978 F.2d 201, 203-04 (5th Cir. 1992), *reh'g denied*, 1993 U.S. Dist. LEXIS 2362 (5th Cir. Jan. 28, 1993). *See* Robert A. Lusardi, *Nationwide Service of Process: Due Process Limitations on the Power of the Sovereign*, 33 VILL. L. REV. 1, 2 (1988).

46. FED. R. CIV. P. 4(k)(2) & Advisory Committee's Notes.

47. *Id.*

48. *Id.*

49. *See, e.g.*, RESTATEMENT, *supra* note 1, § 421, reporters' note 9.

Act occurred,[50] while the patent laws[51] authorize the assertion of personal jurisdiction over a nonresident owner of a U.S. patent only by the District Court for the District of Columbia in cases respecting the patent,[52] unless pendent jurisdiction can be asserted over the defendant based on a cause of action allowing nationwide service of process.[53]

§ 6.04 "MINIMUM CONTACTS," DUE PROCESS AND ALIEN DEFENDANTS

Determining whether a court possesses *in personam* jurisdiction over a foreign defendant is a two-pronged inquiry. First, the forum state's jurisdictional statute must confer personal jurisdiction.[54] Second, the exercise of jurisdiction must accord with the constitutional requirements of due process.[55] Under the Constitution, state court jurisdiction is limited by the Fourteenth Amendment,[56] and the scope of federal jurisdiction is limited by the due process clause of the Fifth Amendment.[57] This section deals with the second aspect of this test, and reviews the issues particularly important in an international context.

[1] Minimum Contacts and Due Process

Any consideration of the due process question must begin with *International Shoe Co. v. Washington*,[58] and the Supreme Court's articulation of the classic formulation of the minimum contacts test. Under the *International Shoe* test, due process requires that the requisite "minimum contacts" with the forum exist such that the exercise of jurisdiction "does not offend 'traditional notions of fair play and substantial justice.'"[59] The *International Shoe* test has been interpreted as a two-part test. First, the court must determine whether the defendant has certain "minimum contacts" with the forum. Second, the court must

---

50. Thistlethwaiste v. Dowty Woodville Polymer, Ltd., 911 F. Supp. 130 (S.D.N.Y. 1996).

51. 35 U.S.C.A. § 293.

52. National Patent Dev. v. T.J. Smith and Nephew, Ltd., 877 F.2d 1003 (D.C. Cir. 1989).

53. Miller Pipeline Corp. v. British Gas, Plc, 901 F. Supp. 1416 (S.D. Ind. 1995).

54. Ellicott Machine Corp., Inc. v. John Holland Party, Ltd., 995 F.2d 474, 477 (4th Cir. 1993); Mylan Labs. v. Akzo, N.V., 2 F.3d 56, 60 (4th Cir. 1993).

55. *Id.;* RESTATEMENT, *supra* note 1, § 421, reporters' note 2.

56. World-Wide Volkswagen Corp. v. Woodson, 444 U.S. 286, 291 (1980).

57. Omni Capital Int'l v. Rudolf Wolff & Co., Ltd., 484 U.S. 97, 103–04 (1987), *citing* Insurance Corp. of Ireland v. Compagnie des Bauxites de Guinée, 456 U.S. 694, 702 (1982).

58. 326 U.S. 310 (1945).

59. *Id.* at 316.

evaluate whether the exercise of that jurisdiction is consistent with constitutional requirements of reasonableness.[60]

In *International Shoe,* the minimum contacts test was applied to a domestic corporation, not a foreign one, and the issue was whether the defendant's contacts were sufficient to satisfy the due process requirement of the Fourteenth Amendment. Nonetheless, the *International Shoe* standard is applicable to both foreign and domestic defendants, with the difference that proper constitutional focus shifts from one of due process under the Fourteenth Amendment, which concerns a state's exercise of jurisdiction, to that of due process under the Fifth Amendment.[61]

Since *International Shoe,* courts have striven to determine what constitutes minimum contacts and to determine when the exercise of jurisdiction is consistent with constitutional requirements of reasonableness.[62]

Practice Note: Discovery is available on the issue of personal jurisdiction. Consider whether discovery could enhance the court's determination.[63]

When considering a challenge to its jurisdiction, a court may receive and weigh affidavits. During this preliminary process, the burden of proof rests on the party asserting jurisdiction. If the court's decision is based on submission of written materials, the burden of proof is usually met by a prima facie showing that personal jurisdiction is conferred under the relevant jurisdictional scheme. Later in the proceeding, if a motion to dismiss for lack of personal jurisdiction is filed after the parties have taken discovery and the court has conducted an evidentiary hearing on the motion, the plaintiff must establish jurisdiction by a preponderance of the evidence. However, any factual disputes will be resolved in the plaintiff's favor and any uncontroverted allegations in the complaint will be treated as true.

To establish personal jurisdiction, valid service of process is generally required. The validity of service of process can often be challenged,

---

60. *See* Burger King Corp. v. Rudzewicz, 471 U.S. 462, 477–78 (1985); Ellicott Machine Corp., Inc. v. John Holland Party, Ltd., 995 F.2d 474, 477 (4th Cir. 1993).

61. Mathews v. Diaz, 426 U.S. 67 (1976) (aliens are afforded protection under Fifth Amendment); Wong Wing v. U.S., 163 U.S. 228 (1896) (same).

62. *See* Note, *Asahi Metal Industry Co. v. Superior Court: Effect of State Court Jurisdiction on International Trade,* Am. U. J. Int'l L. Pol'y 197, 204–208 (1988).

63. *See, e.g.,* Renner v. Lanard Toys Ltd., 33 F.3d 277 (3d Cir. 1994).

especially in cases involving foreign defendants. The plaintiff bears the burden of proving that proper service was effected.[64]

In the many cases applying the minimum contacts analysis, a multitude of factual circumstances have been considered. The subjectiveness of the standard does not lend itself to a formulation that will invariably apply in any case. The Restatement (Third) of Foreign Relations Law, for instance, provides a list of the common categories of contacts, including regularly carrying on business in the forum, activity in the forum giving rise to a cause of action,[65] and activity outside the forum that has a "substantial, direct, and foreseeable effect within the state."[66] The Restatement does not, however, resolve the various disparate approaches adopted by courts in their efforts to balance the policy interests inherent in determinations of personal jurisdiction over alien corporations, approaches that involve a synthesis of a multitude of precedents, and in which uncertainty may have a disruptive effect on commercial relations. Despite the Supreme Court's numerous attempts to identify the minimum contacts required to establish personal jurisdiction, a definitive standard remains elusive. In part, this void is caused by the fact-bound nature of jurisdictional inquiry and the unsuitability of talismanic formulas.[67]

In *World-Wide Volkswagen Corp. v. Woodson*,[68] the Court found that a principal purpose of the minimum contacts requirement was to protect the defendant from unfair surprise. The Court has held that to satisfy the requirement, the defendant must be shown to have "purposefully directed" his activities toward the forum state, such that it could reasonably anticipate being hauled into court there, and the litigation results from injuries that arise from or relate to those activities.[69] The requirement has also been held to mean that "the defendant must have purposefully availed itself of the privilege of conducting activities within the jurisdiction."[70] The Court then considers five factors in determining if the exercise of personal jurisdiction meets the minimum contacts requirement: (1) the quantity of contacts with the forum state, (2) the

64. Fredrick v. Hydro-Aluminium, S.A., 153 F.R.D. 120 (E.D. Mich. 1994).

65. *See* Coblentz GMC/Freightliner, Inc. v. General Motors Corp., 724 F. Supp. 1364, 1370–72 (M.D. Ala. 1989), *aff'd,* 932 F.2d 977, 978 (11th Cir. 1991).

66. Restatement, *supra* note 1, § 421.

67. Burger King Corp. v. Rudzewicz, 471 U.S. 462 (1985).

68. 444 U.S. 286 (1980).

69. Burger King Corp. v. Rudzewicz, 471 U.S. 462 (1985).

70. Hanson v. Denckla, 357 U.S. 235 (1958).

nature and quality of contacts, (3) the source and connection of the cause of action with these contacts, (4) the interest of the state in providing a forum, and (5) the convenience of the parties.[71] The first three factors are given more weight in the final determination. When the above test is used, the

(*Text continued on page 6-15*)

71. World-Wide Volkswagen Corp. v. Woodson, 444 U.S. 286 (1980); Rostad v.On-Deck, Inc., 372 N.W.2d 717, 719–720 (Minn. 1985).

courts often establish the first two factors (quantity and quality of contacts) through the so-called stream of commerce theory.[72]

In an oft-cited decision on minimum contacts in the context of alien defendants, the Supreme Court has explored, but not significantly clarified, the application of the *International Shoe* doctrine. In *Asahi Metal Indus. Co., Ltd. v. Superior Court*,[73] the Court held that California could not exercise jurisdiction over a component parts supplier in Japan, but a splintered court resulted in a mixed message on the standard to be applied in future cases.

At issue in *Asahi* was a suit against the manufacturer of a motorcycle tire. The tire gave way on the road, injuring the driver and killing the passenger. The manufacturer, Cheng Shin, a Taiwan corporation, had purchased valve stem assemblies from a manufacturer in Japan, Asahi Metal Industry Co. When Cheng Shin was named in the suit, it filed a cross-complaint, seeking indemnification from Asahi on the grounds that the valve stem assembly was the cause of the accident. The Supreme Court was faced with a ruling by the California Supreme Court that personal jurisdiction over Asahi on the cross-claim was appropriate under the California statute and the Constitution. The Supreme Court reversed, and found that jurisdiction could not be maintained over Asahi consistent with the Constitution.

Although the Court was unanimous in its finding that jurisdiction over Asahi was not appropriate, the rationale for the result generated substantial disagreement. The Court agreed in general that the two-part *International Shoe* test applied, and therefore there must be both a finding of minimum contacts, and that the exercise of jurisdiction did not offend the Constitution.[74] The primary difference between the members of the Court was over the first issue, specifically over what standard should be applied to determine whether the requisite minimum contacts exist.

On one side, in a plurality opinion joined only by Chief Justice Rehnquist and Justices Powell and Scalia, Justice O'Connor found that the "stream of commerce" theory alone was insufficient for purposes of establishing jurisdiction.[75] The stream of commerce theory had arisen

72. Travellers Indemnity Co. v. TEC America, Inc., 909 F. Supp. 249 (M.D. Pa. 1995).
73. 480 U.S. 102 (1987).
74. *Id.* at 109.
75. *Id.* at 112.

in *World-Wide Volkswagen*,[76] in which the Court "rejected the assertion that a *consumer's* unilateral act of bringing the defendant's product into the forum State was a sufficient constitutional basis for personal jurisdiction over the defendant."[77] Justice O'Connor noted that *International Shoe* and its progeny have focused on actions of the defendant in availing itself of the forum.[78] Under the O'Connor formulation, on the other hand, a finding of minimum contacts requires a "substantial connection" that arises from "*an action of the defendant purposefully directed toward the forum State.*"[79] Justice O'Connor articulated the purposeful direction standard as follows:

> The placement of a product into the stream of commerce, without more, is not an act of the defendant purposefully directed toward the forum State. Additional conduct of the defendant may indicate an intent or purpose to serve the market in the forum state, for example, designing the product for the market in the forum State, advertising in the forum State, establishing channels for providing regular advice to customers, or marketing the product through a distributor who has agreed to serve as the sales agent in the forum State. But a defendant's awareness that the stream of commerce may or will sweep the product into the forum State does not convert the mere act of placing the product into the stream into an act purposefully directed toward the forum state.[80]

The affirmation of the "purposeful direction" standard by the plurality is limited in its impact by the divergence of the Court not only on the proper standard to be applied but on whether the articulation was even necessary to decide the case.

In contrast to the plurality opinion, Justice Brennan's formulation, in which Justices White, Marshall, and Blackmun joined, focused on the stream of commerce theory and its underlying policy rationale to find that additional conduct is not necessary to support jurisdiction.[81] As Justice Brennan explained:

> I see no need for such a showing, however. The stream of commerce refers not to unpredictable currents or eddies, but to the regular and

76. 444 U.S. 286 (1980).

77. *Asahi*, 480 U.S. at 109 (emphasis in original).

78. *Asahi*, *supra* note 73, at 109–12; Burger King Corp. v. Rudzewicz, 471 U.S. 462 (1985); Hanson v. Denckla, 357 U.S. 235 (1958); McGee v. International Life Ins. Co., 355 U.S. 220 (1957).

79. *Asahi*, 480 U.S. at 112 (emphasis in original).

80. *Id.*

81. *Id.* at 116.

> anticipated flow of products from manufacture to distribution to retail sale. As long as a participant in this process is aware that the final product is being marketed in the forum State, the possibility of a lawsuit there cannot come as a surprise. Nor will the litigation present a burden for which there is no corresponding benefit. A defendant who has placed goods in the stream of commerce benefits economically from the retail sale of the final product in the forum State, and indirectly benefits from the State's laws that regulate and facilitate commercial activity.[82]

Although, to a certain extent, the controversy is one of semantics, since those who disagreed considered the stream of commerce theory to include activities that could be characterized as purposeful direction, the standard did not receive unequivocal support. Clarification of the appropriate standard must await a case that squarely presents the issue for determination. As commentators have observed,[83] the issue was whether California was the appropriate forum for the indemnification action by Cheng Sin. If the plaintiff had originally named Asahi, then perhaps the policy issue would have been more squarely presented and the outcome reversed. Ultimate resolution of the issue must await such a case.

Due to the Supreme Court's lack of consensus, federal circuits and state jurisdictions have also split on what actions by the defendant will satisfy the minimum contacts requirement. Some circuits have elected not to follow the stream of commerce doctrine.[84] In other circuits, the

---

82. *Id at* 117.

83. *See, e.g.*, RESTATEMENT, *supra* note 1, § 421, reporters' note 2, at 310 ("[t]he result might have been different if the suit had involved a claim by the California accident victims themselves . . . or if the suit had involved parties from two States of the United States other than California, rather than from two foreign countries") (citation omitted); Note, *Jurisdiction: Personal Jurisdiction Over Alien Corporations,* 29 HARV. INT'L L.J. 207, 213–214 (1988).

84. E.g., D'Almeida v. Stork Brabant, B.V., 71 F.3d 50 (1st Cir. 1995), *cert. denied,* 116 S. Ct. 1570 (1996) (finding that "traditional notions of fair play and substantial justice, as applied in *Asahi Metal Indus.*" would be violated by maintaining indemnity and contribution action against third-party Netherlands machinery manufacturer, where contract between named defendant and manufacturer called for Netherlands forum for resolving disputes and because compensation of Massachusetts citizen was not at issue); Lesnick v. Hallingsworth Vose Co., 35 F.3d 939 (4th Cir. 1994) (adopting Justice O'Connor's position that additional conduct purposefully directed at forum state is necessary to assert personal jurisdiction); Tobin v. Astra Pharmaceutical Prod., 993 F.2d 528 (6th Cir. 1993); Renner v. Lanard Toys, Ltd., 33 F.3d 277 (3d Cir. 1994) (even under Justice Brennan's view, the mere knowledge or awareness that one's product will end up in the forum state without some regularity of shipment would not be enough; the contact must be purposeful rather than incidental, because the "stream of commerce" does not refer to unpredictable currents or eddies).

liberal interpretation of the stream of commerce theory has been adopted.[85] The Fifth Circuit has applied the "stream of commerce" doctrine to contract disputes.[86] However, it should be noted that the "stream of commerce" test is applicable primarily in tort cases since the forum state has a great interest in protecting its citizens by providing a local forum in product liability and other tort cases, and the forum has a lesser interest in protecting a corporation embroiled in a commercial dispute, especially when the corporation has left the state to solicit and secure the contract.[87]

When the "stream of commerce" theory cannot be applied, a foreseeability argument can sometimes be made. The Supreme Court has stated that "the foreseeability that is critical to the due process analysis is that the defendant's conduct and connection with the forum state are such that he should reasonably anticipate being hailed to court here."[88] For example, the concept of foreseeability has been applied in the context of a bankruptcy proceeding seeking to recover preferential transfers from a foreign defendant, where the court stated:

> A foreign company cannot enter into a major debtor-creditor commercial relationship with a United States corporation and be entitled to use advantages that our bankruptcy system provides for all creditors without submitting itself to jurisdiction when the result may be detrimental to it.[89]

Other courts have declined to assert jurisdiction, saying that mere foreseeability is not enough. In *Pawluczyk v. Global Upholstery Co., Ltd.*,[90] the court rejected an assertion of general jurisdiction over a Canadian defendant, finding that the "mere foreseeability that a product placed in the stream of commerce in Canada might enter Pennsylvania is not sufficient."[91]

---

85. E.g., Dehmlow v. Austin Fireworks, 963 F.2d 941 (7th Cir. 1992) (knowledge by the manufacturer that a product that ultimately caused an injury will reach a forum gave a court in that forum personal jurisdiction over the manufacturer); Irving v. Owens-Corning Fiberglass Corp., 864 F.2d 383 (5th Cir. 1989); Stanek v. API, Inc., 474 N.W.2d 829 (Minn. App. 1991); Keen v. Ashot Ashkelon, Ltd., 748 S.W.2d 91 (Tex. 1988).

86. Gulf Consolidated Services v. Corinth Pipeworks, S.A., 898 F.2d 1071 (5th Cir. 1990); Ruston Gas Turbines v. Donaldson, 9 F.3d 415 (5th Cir. 1993).

87. *In re* Schwinn Bicycle Co., 192 B.R. 461 (Bankr. N.D. Ill. 1996) *citing* Lakeside Bridge & Steel Co. v. Mountain State Constr. Co., Inc., 597 F.2d 596 (7th Cir. 1979).

88. World-Wide Volkswagen v. Woodson, 444 U.S. at 297.

89. *In re* Schwinn Bicycle Co., 192 B.R. 461 (Bankr. N.D. Ill. 1996).

90. 854 F. Supp. 364 (E.D. Pa. 1994).

91. *Id.* at 366.

If minimum contacts exist, then the court considers whether its exercise of personal jurisdiction over the defendant "accords with the notions of fair play and substantial justice."[92] The factors relevant to

(*Text continued on page 6-19*)

92. International Shoe Co. v. Washington, 326 U.S. 310 (1945); Grand Entertainment Group Ltd. v. Star Media Sales, Inc., 988 F.2d 476 (3d Cir. 1993).

the determination are: (1) burden on the defendant in litigating in the forum state; (2) the interests of the forum state; (3) the plaintiff's interest in obtaining relief; (4) the interstate judicial system's interest in obtaining the most efficient resolution of controversies; and (5) the shared interest of the several states in furthering fundamental substantive social policies.[93] Once ''minimum contacts'' with the forum state are determined, there is a strong presumption of reasonableness of jurisdiction and the defendant bears the burden of proof that such is not the case. In determining if the defendant's burden of proof has been met, a sliding scale approach is used: The weaker the plaintiff's showing of the first prong of jurisdictional inquiry, the less the defendant has to show in terms of unreasonableness to defeat jurisdiction.[94] Although the burden of proof of unreasonableness of jurisdiction is heavy, the Supreme Court, in *Asahi,* noted that the ''unique burdens placed upon one who must defend oneself in a foreign legal system should have significant weight in assessing the reasonableness of stretching the long-arm of personal jurisdiction over national borders,'' and further admonished that ''great care and reserve should be exercised when extending our notions of personal jurisdiction into the international field.''[95]

The following alternative set of factors relevant to a ''fair and reasonable'' jurisdictional analysis has been applied in international cases:

(1) the defendant's burden of defending in the forum;

(2) the extent of conflict with the sovereignty of defendant's state;

(3) the forum's interest in adjudicating a dispute;

(4) the most efficient judicial resolution of the controversy;

(5) the importance of the forum to plaintiff's interest in adjudicating a dispute; and

(6) the existence of an alternative forum.[96]

---

93. Asahi Metal Industry Co. v. Superior Court, 480 U.S. 102 (1987); Burger King Corp. v. Rudzewicz, 471 U.S. 462 (1985).

94. Ticketmaster-New York, Inc. v. Alioto, 26 F.3d 201 (1st Cir. 1994).

95. 480 U.S. at 114.

96. Nordberg v. Granfinanciera, 835 F.2d 1341, 1345 (11th Cir. 1988); Adden v. Middlebrooks, 688 F.2d 1147, 1158 (7th Cir. 1982); Federal Deposit Ins. Corp. v. British-American Ins. Co., Ltd., 828 F.2d 1439 (9th Cir. 1987).

A very common formulation of jurisdictional analysis, found particularly in the Ninth Circuit, but also in other circuits, is a three-part test that combines the above elements of "minimum contacts" and "fair play and substantial justice" requirements:

(1) The nonresident defendant must do some act by which he purposefully avails himself of the privilege of conducting activities in the forum,

(2) The claim must arise out of or result from the defendant's forum-related activities; and

(3) The exercise of jurisdiction must be reasonable.[97]

One court recently observed that the international commercial context of litigation in U.S. cases involving an analysis of personal jurisdiction are likely to increase, echoing the Supreme Court's observations in *World-Wide Volkswagen*.[98] The court stated:

> Although a generation has not quite passed since *World-Wide Volkswagen* was decided, the acceleration in the internationalization of commerce is apparent. In this age of NAFTA and GATT, one can expect further globalization of commerce, and it is only reasonable for companies who distribute allegedly defective products through regional distributors in this country to anticipate being haled into court by plaintiffs in their home states.[99]

In *Yahoo! Inc. v. La Lique Contre le Racisme et l'Antiesemitisme*,[99.1] a French anti-racism group obtained an order from a French court to block French customers' access to Nazi memorabilia and material offered for sale on Yahoo!'s U.S. website. Yahoo!'s French website already blocked such material. Yahoo! filed suit in the Northern District of California for a declaratory judgment that the French court's order was unconstitutional with respect to the U.S. website. The French parties moved to dismiss for lack of personal jurisdiction. The U.S. district court declined to dismiss and asserted personal jurisdiction over the French parties, holding that the French parties' actions constituted a "purposeful availment" of California law and could negatively affect Yahoo!'s Constitutional rights.

---

97. Omeluk v. Langsten Slip & Batbyggeri, A.S., 52 F.3d 267 (9th Cir. 1995); Disk Data, Inc. v. Systems Technology Assoc., 557 F.2d 1280 (9th Cir. 1977).

98. 444 U.S. 286, 293 (1980) (noting growth in international commerce).

99. Barone v. Rich Brothers Interstate Fireworks Co., 25 F.3d 610, 615 (8th Cir. 1994).

99.1. 2001 WL 640418 (N.D. Cal.).

[2] General and Specific Jurisdiction

Another common issue in cases involving foreign defendants is the distinction between specific and general jurisdiction, which are two forms of *in personam,* or judicial, jurisdiction.[100] The distinction arose as an analytical device to distinguish the degree of contact with the forum in any given case.[101] The distinction is important because it provides an indication of the range of conduct for which a defendant may be sued upon in the forum. One commentator has described the distinction as follows:

> A court has general jurisdiction when the contacts (or affiliating circumstances) between the defendant and the forum are of such a nature and quality as to enable the court to entertain any action against the defendant, even when the claim does not arise from the contacts. Specific jurisdiction refers to the situation in which the court can adjudicate claims intimately related to the defendant's contacts with the state, but not other claims. The traditional bases of personal jurisdiction over individuals—presence, consent, and domicile—permitted assertion of general jurisdiction. Jurisdiction exercised under typical long arm statutes is illustrative of specific jurisdiction.[102]

The distinction was also described in a case involving a foreign defendant in federal court in California. In *Meyers v. ASICS Corp., Ltd.,*[103] the court explained that:

> Personal jurisdiction over [a foreign defendant] may be established in one of two forms—general or specific. Where contacts are substantial, systematic, or continuous, a party may be subject to suit in a forum on any topic, even if the suit is unrelated to the activities which it conducts in the forum. Even without general jurisdiction, a court may have specific jurisdiction over a party where its activities in the forum relate to the injury sued upon.[104]

Of interest in the international context, the Supreme Court has adopted the distinction, and applies it without respect to the identity of

---

100. *See* RESTATEMENT, *supra* note 1, § 421 reporters' note 3. *See generally* Giotis v. Apollo of the Ozarks, Inc., 800 F.2d 660, 666 n.3 (7th Cir. 1986) (explaining concepts).

101. *See, e.g.,* Mary Twitchell, *The Myth of General Jurisdiction,* 101 HARV. L. REV. 610, 611 (1988); von Mehren & Trautman, *Jurisdiction to Adjudicate, A Suggested Analysis,* 79 HARV. L. REV. 1121 (1966).

102. R. CASAD, *supra* note 34, at 1–10 through 1–11. *See* RESTATEMENT, *supra* note 1, § 421, reporters' note 3 (discussing distinction between general and specific jurisdiction).

103. 711 F. Supp. 1001 (C.D. Cal. 1989).

104. *Id.* at 1003.

the defendant. The Court distinguishes between specific jurisdiction, in which the cause of action arises from the defendant's contacts with the forum, and general jurisdiction, in which the cause of action does not arise from the defendant's activities in the forum, but the defendant's activities constitute "continuous and systematic general business contacts."[105] Many have argued that the Court should adopt a higher or lower jurisdictional standard with respect to alien defendants for various policy reasons, including the promotion of international trade or the fear that low standards could bring reprisals against U.S. corporations in foreign forums.[106]

Although many cases involving foreign defendants are based on the application of specific jurisdiction, the distinction is important because at some point the defendant's activities in a forum will rise above a specific level and provide general jurisdiction over the defendant. The line between general and specific jurisdiction is obviously not a bright one, and the question will require a case-by-case analysis of the particular statutory grant of jurisdiction and the facts of each case.[107]

[3] A Note on Transient Jurisdiction

Under section 421 of the Restatement (Third) of Foreign Relations Law, "a state's exercise of jurisdiction to adjudicate with respect to a person or thing is reasonable if, at the time the jurisdiction is asserted . . . the person or thing is present in the territory of the state, *other than transitorily*." The Restatement notes that jurisdiction based on transitory presence is insufficient under international law, but has not been ultimately resolved under U.S. law.

Although problematic in modern jurisprudence, the validity of transitory jurisdiction has not been extinguished. Although some cases and commentators have interpreted *Shaffer v. Heitner*[108] as having departed completely from the territorial power theory of jurisdiction,[109] others have interpreted *Shaffer* as having preserved certain types of

105. Helicopteros Nacionales De Colombia, S.A. v. Hall, 466 U.S. 408, 416 (1984).

106. *See* Charles A. Friedrich, Note, *Jurisdiction: Personal Jurisdiction Over an Alien Corporation,* 26 HARV. INT'L L.J. 630, 634–635 (1985).

107. *See, e.g.,* Laitram Corp. v. Oki Electric Indus. Co., Ltd., No. 93–0908, 1994 U.S. Dist. LEXIS 421, * 5, 1994 WL 43823 (E.D. La. Jan. 18, 1994); Charas v. Sand Technol. Sys. Int'l, Inc., No. 90 Civ. 5638, 1992 U.S. Dist. LEXIS 15227, * 12–17, 1992 WL 296406 (S.D.N.Y. Oct. 7, 1992).

108. 433 U.S. 186 (1977).

109. *See* R. CASAD, *supra* note 34, at 1–11, 2–50.

transitory jurisdiction, particularly when the plaintiff is a resident of the forum state[110] or when the defendant has incurred liability in the United States.[111] In *Burnham v. Superior Court*,[112] the Supreme Court held that the due process clause of the fourteenth amendment is not a *per se* bar to a state court exercising personal jurisdiction over a defendant who is served with process while physically but transitorily in the state.[113] As there are no necessary grounds for distinguishing the fifth amendment from the fourteenth amendment for transient jurisdiction purposes, it is likely that a federal court could exercise jurisdiction under Rule 4(k)(2) over a foreign defendant temporarily present anywhere in the United States. However, under Rule 4(k)(2), transient or "tag" jurisdiction in federal courts would only be proper in instances where the person is not otherwise "subject to the jurisdiction of the courts of general jurisdiction of any state."[114] The few transitory jurisdiction cases, such as *Grace v. MacArthur*,[115] in which the court found that service of process on defendant while on an airplane flying over the state was sufficient to give Arkansas courts jurisdiction over the defendant, or *Aluminal Indus., Inc. v. Newtown Commercial Assocs.*,[116] testify to a continued validity. In *Amusement Equip., Inc., v. Mordelt*,[117] the court observed that transitory jurisdiction survives, and may in some cases provide the basis for *in personam* jurisdiction under U.S. law.[118] The invalidity of so-called "tag" jurisdiction under international law, however, provides an opportunity for challenge if transitory jurisdiction is the basis of a particular jurisdictional assertion.

---

110. Amusement Equip., Inc. v. Mordelt, 779 F.2d 264, 268-71 (5th Cir. 1985); Scholz Research & Dev., Inc. v. Kurzke, 720 F. Supp. 710, 711 (N.D. Ill. 1989); Opert v. Schmid, 535 F. Supp. 591, 594 (S.D.N.Y. 1982); Humphrey v. Langford, 246 Ga. 732, 734–35, 273 S.E.2d 22, 24 (1980). *Cf.* Harold M. Pitman Co. v. Typecraft Software, Ltd., 626 F. Supp. 305, 313–14 (N.D. Ill. 1986).

111. *In re* Grand Jury Proceedings, United States v. Field, 532 F.2d 404, 409–10 (5th Cir.), *cert. denied*, 429 U.S. 940 (1976); Restatement, *supra* note 1, § 421, reporters' note 5.

112. 495 U.S. 604 (1990).

113. *Id.* at 631.

114. Fed. R. Civ. P. 4(k)(2).

115. 170 F. Supp. 442, 447–48 (E.D. Ark. 1959).

116. 89 F.R.D. 326, 329 (S.D.N.Y. 1980).

117. 779 F.2d 264 (5th Cir. 1985).

118. *Id.* at 270–71. *See also* Rittenhouse v. Mabry, 832 F.2d 1380, 1388–89 (5th Cir. 1987). *See generally* Restatement, *supra* note 1, reporters' note 5, at 310.

[4] "Virtual Jurisdiction": Personal Jurisdiction Based on Electronic Contacts

The growing use of the "Internet" or "World-Wide Web" for communication and commercial purposes has forced U.S. courts to consider the circumstances in which purely electronic contacts with a jurisdiction may lead to the assertion of personal jurisdiction over a party. At least three federal Appellate Courts have now addressed this issue, as discussed below.

In *Compuserve, Inc. v. Patterson,*[119] the Sixth Circuit found the Defendant's purely electronic contacts with the forum state sufficient to confer jurisdiction. Compuserve was a computer information service headquartered in Ohio. Defendant Patterson, a resident of Texas, entered into several agreements via the Internet with Compuserve. Patterson subscribed to Compuserve and also entered a Shareware Registration Agreement ("SRA") with Compuserve. Pursuant to the SRA, Patterson electronically transferred 32 software files to Compuserve and also sold his software products to various purchasers, including approximately 12 in Ohio.[120] The SRA also provided that it was entered in Ohio and subject to Ohio laws.[121] When Patterson complained via the Internet to Compuserve that Compuserve was violating certain of his trademarks, Compuserve filed a declaratory judgment action in Ohio concerning the parties' respective trademark rights and sought personal jurisdiction over Patterson.

Patterson filed a motion to dismiss under Rule 12(b)(6), Fed. R. Civ. P., and the Court framed its inquiry as, "Did Compuserve make a prima facie showing that Patterson's contacts with Ohio, which have been almost entirely electronic in nature, are sufficient, under the Due Process Clause [of the U.S. Constitution], to support the district court's exercise of personal jurisdiction over him?"[122] The Court observed that the "crucial federal constitutional inquiry" is whether the nonresident defendant has sufficient contacts with the forum state that the court's exercise of jurisdiction comports with the "traditional notions of fair play and substantial justice" set forth in *International Shoe Co. v. Washington*[123] and its offspring.[124]

119. 89 F.3d 1257 (6th Cir. 1996).
120. *Id.* at 1260–61.
121. *Id.* at 1260.
122. *Id.* at 1262.
123. 326 U.S. 310 (1945).
124. 89 F.3d at 1263.

The Court defined the constitutional inquiry as:

> First, the defendant must purposely avail himself of the privilege of acting in the forum state or causing a consequence in the forum state. Second, the cause of action must arise from the defendant's activities there. Finally, the acts of the defendant or consequences caused by the defendant must have a substantial enough connection with the forum to make the exercise of jurisdiction over the defendant reasonable.[125]

The *Compuserve* Court then applied the facts of the case to each of these three criteria. The Court concluded that in the context of a 12(b)(6) motion, where the Court must view the facts in the light most favorable to Compuserve, Patterson's purposefully contracting with

(*Text continued on page 6-25*)

125. *Id.*

Compuserve to market Patterson's software in other states made it reasonable to subject Patterson to suit in Ohio, the forum state of Compuserve's headquarters.[126] The Court expressly noted, however, that it did not pass judgment on whether personal jurisdiction based upon purely electronic contacts with a forum would be proper in other contexts.[127]

In *Bensusan Restaurant Corp. v. King*,[128] the Second Circuit considered whether an internet web site advertising a small Missouri jazz cabaret was sufficient contact with the State of New York for the Court to assert jurisdiction under the New York long-arm statute in a Trademark infringement case. Plaintiff Bensusan Restaurant Corporation claimed that the individual Defendant Richard B. King's internet advertisement for his cabaret "The Blue Note" violated "The Blue Note" trademark of Plaintiff's "enormously successful jazz club in New York City."[129] The Court analyzed the specific provisions of the state long-arm statute[130] and determined that the conduct complained of did not satisfy the statutory provisions.

The Court first considered whether Defendant had committed a tort within the state for purposes of jurisdiction under CPLR § 302(a)(2). The Court found particularly significant the facts that the acts giving rise to the lawsuit, including the authorization and creation of King's web site, were performed by persons physically present in Missouri and not in New York.[131] The Court, therefore, ruled that Defendant's conduct did not satisfy the "within the state" criteria, which the Court interpreted to require an act physically within the state.[132]

The Court then considered whether jurisdiction was proper under CPLR 302(a)(3), which applies "to persons who expect or should reasonably expect the tortious act to have consequences in the state and in addition derive substantial revenue from interstate commerce."[133]

---

126. *Id.*
127. *Id.* at 1268.
128. 126 F.3d 25 (2d Cir. 1997).
129. *Id.* at 26.
130. CPLR § 302(a)(2), (a)(3).
131. 126 F.3d at 29.
132. *Id.*
133. *Id.*

The Court ruled that these criteria were also unsatisfied, as Defendant King did not derive substantial revenue from interstate commerce.[134]

The *Bensusan* Court, therefore, engaged in a very narrow, technical reading of the long-arm statute, rather than a Constitutional analysis, to decline to exercise jurisdiction. It is unclear how the Court would have ruled if the Defendant's web site had been interactive, such as one offering goods for sale, rather than being a purely "passive" informational site.

The Ninth Circuit was faced with a case factually similar to *Bensusan* in *Cybersell, Inc. v. Cybersell, Inc.*[135] The Court addressed the issue of whether the allegedly infringing use of a service mark in a home page on the World Wide Web suffices for personal jurisdiction in the state where the holder of the mark has its principal place of business. The Plaintiff in *Cybersell* was an Arizona corporation that advertised for commercial services under the registered trademark "Cybersell." The Defendant was a Florida corporation that offered web page construction services under the "Cybersell" name. Like the Second Circuit in *Bensusan,* the Ninth Circuit in *Cybersell* declined to exercise jurisdiction over the out of state Defendant where the web site was passive in nature.

Unlike the New York long-arm statute at issue in *Bensusan,* however, Arizona Rule of Civil Procedure 4.2(a) allowed personal jurisdiction over a nonresident to the maximum extent allowed by the federal Constitution.[136] The *Cybersell* Court, therefore, applied a constitutional "minimum contacts" analysis and ruled that "it would not comport with 'traditional notions of fair play and substantial justice' . . . for Arizona to exercise personal jurisdiction over an allegedly infringing Florida web site advertiser who has no contacts with Arizona other than maintaining a home page that is accessible to Arizonians, and everyone else, over the Internet."[137] In dicta, however, the Court did not foreclose the possibility that jurisdiction based upon electronic contacts may be proper in some contexts:

> In sum, the common thread [in Internet jurisdictional case law], . . . is that "the likelihood that personal jurisdiction can be constitutionally

---

134. *Id.*
135. 130 F.3d 414 (9th Cir. 1997).
136. *Id.* at 416.
137. *Id.* at 415 (citations omitted).

exercised is directly proportionate to the nature and quality of commercial activity that an entity conducts over the Internet.''[138]

In *Christian Science Board of Directors v. Nolan*,[138.1] the Fourth Circuit considered whether a North Carolina federal court may assert jurisdiction over an individual defendant, resident of Arizona, with respect to the content of Defendant's internet site, which was housed on a California computer server. The court found the assertion of jurisdiction proper where the defendant had hired a North Carolina resident to assist defendant to establish and maintain the site and upload the site to the California computer server. The court found the use of a webmaster or de facto webmaster in the forum state satisfied constitutional standards of due process for the assertion of jurisdiction.

None of the foregoing Circuit Courts set forth bright-line tests for when personal jurisdiction is proper, based upon purely electronic contacts with a forum. In fact, the *Compuserve* and *Cybersell* Courts suggested in dicta that electronic jurisdiction will continue to be analyzed according to the traditional Constitutional notions set forth in *International Shoe Co.* and its progeny.[139] It is also likely that Courts will draw analogies to familiar, non-electronic conduct, such as the entry into paper contracts and physical acts and presence in a forum.

Practice Note: The foregoing cases suggest, but do not require, a distinction between merely passive websites which advertise or communicate information and interactive websites by which a person may order products or services. Significant factors in the personal jurisdictional analysis, therefore, may include:

- whether a web site is passive or active, although mere interactivity is likely not enough to confer jurisdiction as advancing technology has made many sites interactive;[139.1]

---

138. *Id.* at 419, *quoting* Zippo Mfg. Co. v. Zippo Dot Com, Inc., 953 F. Supp. 1119, 1124 (W.D. Pa. 1997).

138.1. 259 F.3d 209 (2001).

139. *Compuserve*, 89 F.3d at 1263; *Cybersell*, 130 F.3d at 416, 420.

139.1. Toys ''R'' Us, Inc. v. Step Two, S.A., 318 F.3d 446 (3rd Cir. 2003) (defendant's maintenance of interactive, commercial web sites in Spain and its two sales to New Jersey residents did not establish minimum contacts sufficient to support exercise of personal jurisdiction); GTE New Media Services, Inc. v. BellSouth Corp., 199 F.3d 1343 (D.C. Cir. 2000) (mere accessibility to an interactive Web site by users within a forum is not enough to establish the minimum contacts needed for personal jurisdiction in that forum).

- whether there is a pattern of sales or conduct directed at the forum state;
- whether an electronic contract was entered;
- whether such contract sets forth the applicable jurisdiction or law; and
- Whether the defendant used the services of a webmaster or de facto webmaster in the forum jurisdiction.

§ 6.05 WAIVER OF PERSONAL JURISDICTION REQUIREMENT

From a practical perspective, an important feature of *in personam* or judicial jurisdiction is that it can be waived. Unlike subject matter jurisdiction, which a court must always establish, personal jurisdiction may be conferred upon the court by the parties.[140] As the Supreme Court explained in *Insurance Corp. of Ireland v. Compagnie Des Bauxites De Guinee*,[141] subject matter jurisdiction cannot be waived, or conferred upon a court. The Court explained that:

> None of this is true with respect to personal jurisdiction. The requirement that a court have personal jurisdiction flows not from Art. III, but from the Due Process Clause. The personal jurisdiction requirement recognizes and protects an individual liberty interest. It represents a restriction on judicial power not as a matter of sovereignty, but as a matter of individual liberty. . . . Because the requirement of personal jurisdiction represents first of all an individual right, it can, like other such rights, be waived.[142]

The Restatement (Third) of Foreign Relations Law notes that under international law, the exercise of jurisdiction to adjudicate is reasonable if the party consents.[143] Most commonly, parties confer *in personam* jurisdiction on the court by waiving any objections or consenting to the exercise of jurisdiction. Waivers can be either explicit or implicit.

---

140. *See* Insurance Corp. of Ireland v. Compagnie Des Bauxites De Guinee, 456 U.S. 694, 703 (1982) (''no action of the parties can confer subject matter jurisdiction upon a federal court'').

141. *Id.*

142. *Id.* at 702–703 (footnote omitted). *See also* Creighton Ltd. v. Gov't of State of Qatar, 181 F.3d 118 (D.C. Cir. July 2, 1999, *reh'g en banc denied*, Sept. 7, 1999) (discussing waiver of personal jurisdiction in context of suit against foreign government under the U.S. Foreign Sovereign Immunities Act).

143. Restatement, *supra* note 1, § 421(2)(g).

Explicit waivers are typically included in agreements between parties and are commonly enforced by the courts. For instance, in *National Equip. Rental, Ltd. v. Szukhent*,[144] the Supreme Court held that "parties to a contract may agree in advance to submit to the jurisdiction of a given court."[145] Forum selection clauses can also operate to grant a court *in personam* or judicial jurisdiction over foreign defendants.[146]

In some circumstances, waivers can also be implicit. In the leading case on implicit or constructive waiver, the Supreme Court in *Insurance Corp. of Ireland v. Compagnie Des Bauxites De Guinee*,[147] considered whether the sanction of a finding of personal jurisdiction was appropriate for failure to respond to discovery requests. The Court noted that "the failure to enter a timely objection to personal jurisdiction constitutes, under Rule 12(h)(1), a waiver of the objection. A sanction

(*Text continued on page 6-29*)

144. 375 U.S. 311 (1964).

145. *Id.* at 316. *See also* Alexander Proudfoot World Headquarters v. Thayer, 877 F.2d 912 (11th Cir. 1989).

146. Sarieddine v. Moussa, 820 S.W.2d 837, 839 (Tex. Ct. App. 1991). RESTATEMENT, *supra* note 1, § 421, reporters' note 6, at 311. For a full discussion of the operation of forum selection clauses, *see supra* § 5.08 [1].

147. 456 U.S. 694 (1982).

under Rule 37(b)(2)(A) consisting of a finding of personal jurisdiction has precisely the same effect.''[148]

An interesting and unresolved question is whether Fifth Amendment due process protections apply to foreign states concerning the exercise of personal jurisdiction. The D.C. Circuit, in *Creighton Ltd. v. Gov't of State of Qatar*,[148.1] noted the Circuit's prior findings ''that the requirements of the FSIA for personal jurisdiction . . . 'do not affect the constitutional *in personam* jurisdiction requirement [of] the due process clause of the Fifth Amendment.'''[148.2] The *Creighton* Court observed that ''[m]ore recently, however, the Supreme Court questioned whether the personal jurisdiction requirement of the due process clause applies at all to foreign states, citing its prior holding that a State of the Union is not a ''person'' for purposes of that clause.''[148.3] The Court further observed that ''the district court in turn has held that the requirement of personal jurisdiction does not apply to a foreign state.''[148.4]

Consent to jurisdiction provides opportunities for planning. It is almost axiomatic in modern practice that an agreement specify the law to be applied, the forum for resolution of disputes, and the consent to jurisdiction in that forum. Inclusion of such provisions is necessary to avoid the intricate process of establishing general or specific *in personam* or judicial jurisdiction over the defendant.

§ 6.06 PERSONAL JURISDICTION OVER RELATED CORPORATIONS

Special jurisdictional rules apply when a foreign corporation is related to another entity, either through the establishment of a branch or subsidiary in the United States, or through other agency or ownership

148. *Id.* at 705. *See also* Von Pein v. Bonucci, No. 92–4310, 1993 U.S. Dist. LEXIS 13055, * 7, 1993 WL 276487 (E.D. Penn. July 8, 1993); Babitt v. Frum, 606 F. Supp. 680, 681–82 (S.D.N.Y. 1985).

148.1. 181 F.3d 118 (D.C. Cir. July 2, 1999, *reh'g en banc denied*, Sept. 7, 1999).

148.2. *Id., citing Foremost-McKesson*, 905 F.2d at 442 n.10; *see also* Maritime Int'l Nominees Estab. v. Republic of Guinea, 693 F.2d 1094, at 1105 n.18 (''Of course, a finding of FSIA personal jurisdiction, which would rest in part on a finding of non-immunity, must comport with the demands of due process, and Congress intended that the Act satisfy those demands''), *cert. denied*, 464 U.S. 815 (1984); Gilson v. Republic of Ireland, 682 F.2d 1022, 1028 (D.C. Cir. 1982) (''a statute cannot grant personal jurisdiction where the Constitution forbids it'').

148.3. *Id., citing* Republic of Argentina v. Weltover, Inc., 504 U.S. 607, 619 (1992).

148.4. *Id., citing* Flatova v. Islamic Republic of Iran, 999 F. Supp. 1, 19–21 (D.D.C. 1998).

relationships. The important question in such situations is whether a sufficient connection between the two entities permits a court to exercise jurisdiction over the parent corporation. In such cases, the courts have examined the nature of the relationship between the two corporate entities to determine whether an assertion of jurisdiction is reasonable.[149]

For instance, in *Andrulonis v. United States*,[150] a federal district court in New York in a diversity action was faced with the question of whether it could exercise jurisdiction over a German corporation by virtue of a subsidiary organized under the laws of New York. The German parent manufactured and sold specialized air encapsulation machines. The products were distributed in the United States by a New York corporation, which although not formally a subsidiary, had 85 percent of its stock owned by the sole shareholder of the German corporation. In examining the relationship between the two corporations, the court reviewed the applicable tests under New York law.

Citing *Frummer v. Hilton Hotels Int'l Inc.*,[151] the court found that under New York law, "the cases clearly indicate that the systematic activities of a subsidiary or agent in New York may subject a foreign principal to personal jurisdiction."[152] The court noted that the agency relationship itself is not sufficient, and that "additional factors" are necessary before personal jurisdiction can be established.[153] Under New York law, two tests were developed to evaluate whether jurisdiction over the parent is possible because of the activities of the local representative:[154]

> [f]irst, if the relationship between the foreign and local corporations gives rise to a "valid inference" of an agency relationship; and second, if control by the foreign company over the local affiliate is so complete that the latter is, in fact, merely a department of the

149. *See generally* Mylan Labs. v. Akzo, N.V., 2 F.3d 56 (4th Cir. 1993); Laitram Corp. v. Oki Electric Indus. Co., Ltd., No. 93–0908, 1994 U.S. Dist. LEXIS 421, 1994 WL 43823 (E.D. La. Jan. 18, 1994); Hill v. Showa Denko, K.K., 425 S.E.2d 609 (W. Va. 1992).

150. 536 F. Supp. 183 (N.D.N.Y. 1981).

151. 19 N.Y.2d 533, 227 N.E.2d 851, 281 N.Y.S.2d 41, *cert. denied,* 389 U.S. 923 (1967). The *Frummer* case is discussed in § 6.02, *supra.*

152. 536 F. Supp. at 187.

153. *Id.*

154. *Id.* at 188.

> former. . . . Both tests look to economic realities, not formal relationships.[155]

Based on this test, the court found that jurisdiction over the German corporation was fair and reasonable because of the close relationship between the two. The court's analysis began with a finding that an agency relationship of broad scope existed between the two corporations.[156] The court then found that:

(1) the two corporations shared officers and directors;

(2) the two corporations were mutually dependent for sales and profits (the German corporation derived over a quarter of its revenues from U.S. sales);

(3) the German corporation trained some of the U.S. employees;

(4) the U.S. corporation placed orders with the German corporation immediately upon receiving an order;

(5) the common shareholder extended loans to the U.S. corporation;

(6) the accounting systems of the two corporations were correlated;

(7) because of narrow product lines, the two corporations were highly integrated, and tight control was maintained over the sales affiliate in the United States;

(8) the U.S. corporation was dependent on the German corporation and the resulting organization was "monocentrist"; and

(9) the U.S. corporation was involved in the sale at issue of the allegedly defective product manufactured by the German corporation.

After reviewing these factors, the court determined that "it would be unfair for the [German corporation] to be able to reap the benefits of increased sales yet escape jurisdiction."[157] Thus, for jurisdictional purposes, the primary issue is how much control the parent has over the subsidiary. A finding of personal jurisdiction over the parent, based on the activities of the subsidiary, is appropriate only when the parent exerts

155. *Id. See also* Nippon Emo-Trans Co., Ltd. v. Emo-Trans, Inc., 744 F. Supp. 1215, 1230 (E.D.N.Y. 1990).

156. *Andrulonis*, 536 F. Supp. at 188.

157. *Id.* at 190.

substantial control over the day-to-day activities of the subsidiary. Such control is typically found in situations where a manufacturer/parent directs the sales and services of a distributor/subsidiary. Such day-to-day control with cross-over in business operations is less likely in the context of a holding company.[158]

In *Meyers v. ASICS Corp.*,[159] the court considered the issue of jurisdiction over a foreign parent corporation by virtue of a U.S. subsidiary. At issue was a patent infringement suit by a U.S. plaintiff, Meyers, against a Japanese shoe manufacturer, ASICS. After failing to obtain jurisdiction over ASICS in New York, Meyers refiled in California, alleging that ASICS had the requisite contacts there.[160] In assessing whether jurisdiction existed over the Japanese defendant, the court reviewed the applicable standard of jurisdiction in the Ninth Circuit, which is a three-part test:

> (1) the nonresident must do some act or consummate some transaction with the forum by which he purposefully avails himself of the privilege of conducting activities in the forum, thereby invoking the benefits and protections of its laws;
>
> (2) the claim must arise out of or result from its forum related activities; and
>
> (3) the exercise of jurisdiction must be reasonable.[161]

Under this standard, the court looked to whether the establishment of a subsidiary constituted purposeful availment for purposes of jurisdiction.[162] The court first recognized that a parent is not automatically subject to jurisdiction merely by virtue of its subsidiary, but that actions of the parent in the forum through the subsidiary will often suffice. In *Meyers,* the court found that the "wholly owned subsidiary was a mere part of an overall marketing plan, which purposefully availed itself of the privilege of doing business in California."[163]

---

158. Integrated Business Information Services, Ltd. v. Dun & Bradstreet Corp., 714 F. Supp. 296, 300–301 (N.D. Ill. 1989).

159. 711 F. Supp. 1001 (C.D. Cal. 1989).

160. *Id.* at 1003.

161. *Id. See also* United States v. Toyota Motor Corp., 561 F. Supp. 354 (C.D. Cal. 1983). Cf. § 6.04[1].

162. *Meyers,* 711 F. Supp. at 1004.

163. *Id.*

On the issue of the nature of the contacts with California, the court employed the liberal "but for" test adopted by the Ninth Circuit.[164] Under this formulation of the contacts analysis, the court considers whether the alleged violation of the law would have occurred "but for" the sales.[165]

The "but for" test was explicitly adopted in an earlier Ninth Circuit case, *Shute v. Carnival Cruise Lines*,[166] which relied on the "but for" test in determining "whether a cause of action arises from a defendant's forum-related activities."[167] The court in *Shute* found the "but for" test to be:

> consistent with the basic functioning of the "arising out of" requirement—it preserves the essential distinction between general and specific jurisdiction. Under this test, a defendant cannot be hailed into court for activities unrelated to the cause of action in the absence of a showing of substantial and continuous contacts sufficient to establish general jurisdiction. . . . The "but for" test preserves the requirement that there be some nexus between the cause of action and the defendant's activities in the forum.[168]

On the final issue of reasonableness, the court in *Meyers* applied a seven part test similar to that employed by the Supreme Court in *Asahi*.[169] The seven factors, drawn largely from the Restatement (Third) of Foreign Relations Law, are:

(1) the extent of purposeful injection;

(2) the burden on the defendant;

(3) the extent of the conflict with the sovereignty of defendant's state;

(4) the forum state's interest in the dispute;

(5) the most efficient forum for resolution of the matter;

(6) the importance of the chosen forum to the plaintiff's interest in convenient and effective relief; and

164. *Id.* at 1006. *See, e.g.*, Shute v. Carnival Cruise Lines, 863 F.2d 1437 (9th Cir. 1988), *rev'd on other grounds*, 499 U.S. 585 (1991).

165. *Meyers*, 711 F. Supp. at 1006.

166. 863 F.2d 1437 (9th Cir. 1988), *rev'd on other grounds*, 499 U.S. 585 (1991).

167. *Id.* at 1444.

168. *Id.* at 1445 (citations omitted).

169. Asahi Metal Indus. Co., Ltd. v. Superior Court, 480 U.S. 102, 113 (1987). *See supra* § 6.04 (discussing *Asahi*).

(7) the existence of an alternative forum.[170]

In analyzing the reasonableness of the assertion of jurisdiction, the court primarily relied on the fact that "California is apparently the only state with which ASICS has sufficient contacts to establish jurisdiction."[171]

Practice Note: As the decisions in *Frummer, Delagi, Andrulonis*, and *Meyers* illustrate, corporate relationships may often provide the basis for jurisdiction over foreign defendants. Corporations selling to the United States must be aware of the rules and common bases of jurisdiction over foreign corporations. Given the liberality of tests such as the "but for" and others, foreign corporations deriving benefit from the United States must carefully consider whether they will be subject to U.S. jurisdiction.[172]

§ 6.07 PERSONAL JURISDICTION IN FEDERAL QUESTION CASES BASED ON AGGREGATED OR NATIONAL CONTACTS

[1] The National or Aggregate Contacts Doctrine

As discussed in §§ 6.02 and 6.03, *in personam* or judicial jurisdiction refers to power over a particular defendant based on a relationship or contacts with the forum. In most instances that forum is a state of the United States. This rule of United States law is a function of the federal system in the United States. In the past, unless a federal statute specifically authorized nationwide jurisdiction, courts generally limited their analysis of jurisdiction to a defendant's contacts with a particular state rather than with the United States as a whole.[173] For

170. *Meyers*, 711 F. Supp. at 1007.

171. *Id.*

172. *See, e.g.*, Anderson v. Dassault Aviation, 361 F.3d 449 (8th Cir.), *cert. denied*, 125 S. Ct. 606 (2004) (reversing district court's dismissal of case for lack of personal jurisdiction and finding French plane maker had sufficient minimum contacts with Arkansas where plane maker had close ties to Arkansas subsidiary and two entities shared Web site, directors and unified marketing strategy); Mylan Labs. v. Akzo, N.V., 2 F.3d 56, 61–64 (4th Cir. 1993); Laitram Corp. v. Oki Electric Indus. Co., Ltd., No. 93–0908, 1994 U.S. Dist. LEXIS 421, * 7–17, 1994 WL 43823 (E.D. La. Jan. 18, 1994); Loral Fairchild Corp. v. Victor Co. of Japan, Ltd., 803 F. Supp. 626, 630–36 (E.D.N.Y. 1992); Hill v. Showa Denko, K.K., 425 S.E.2d 609, 616 (W. Va. 1992).

173. *See* Omni Capital Int'l v. Rudolf Wolff & Co., Ltd., 484 U.S. 97, 108 (1987); Aviles v. Kunkle, 978 F.2d 201, 203–04 (1992), *reh'g denied*, 1993 U.S. App. LEXIS 2362 (5th Cir. Jan. 28, 1993); United Rope Distribs., Inc. v. Seatriumph Marine Corp., 930 F.2d 532, 535, *reh'g denied*, 1991 U.S. App. LEXIS 8983 (7th Cir. May 9, 1991); *In re* Atteberry v. Barclays

instance, in *Omni Capital Int'l v. Rudolf Wolff & Co., Ltd.*,[174] the Supreme Court confronted the jurisdictional issue of whether nationwide service of process could be made by commodities futures investors against marketers of a trading program. The Court rejected plaintiffs' argument that district court jurisdiction is proper if not contrary to the fifth amendment.[175] The Court observed:

> Before a federal court may exercise personal jurisdiction over a defendant, the procedural requirement of service of summons must be satisfied . . . . Thus, before a court may exercise personal jurisdiction over a defendant, there must be more than notice to the defendant and a constitutionally sufficient relationship between the defendant and the forum. There also must be a basis for the defendant's amenability to service of summons. Absent consent, this means there must be authorization for service of summons on the defendant.''[176]

The Court found that since neither the Commodity Exchange Act nor the Louisiana long-arm statute under former Federal Rule of Civil Procedure 4(e) provided for service on the marketers of the trading program, service was improper and the district court lacked jurisdiction over the defendants.[177]

As observed by the Advisory Commitee's Notes:

> [A] problem was presented when the defendant was a non-resident of the United States having contacts with the United States sufficient to justify the application of United States law and to satisfy federal standards of forum selection, but having insufficient contact with any one state to support jurisdiction under state long-arm legislation, or meet the requirements of the Fourteenth Amendment limitation on state court territorial jurisdiction. In such cases, the defendant was shielded from the enforcement of federal law by the fortuity of a favorable limitation on the power of state courts which was incorporated into federal practice by the former rule [4].[178]

However, amendments to the Federal Rules of Civil Procedure providing for national or aggregate contacts analysis in federal question cases took effect December 1, 1993.[179] Rule 4(k)(2) provides that:

---

174. 484 U.S. 97 (1987).
175. *Id.* at 104.
176. *Id.*
177. *Id.* at 111.
178. Fed. R. Civ. P. 4(k)(2) Advisory Committee's Notes.
179. Fed. R. Civ. P. 1.

> [i]f the exercise of jurisdiction is consistent with the Constitution and laws of the United States, serving a summons or filing a waiver of service is also effective, with respect to claims arising under federal law, to establish personal jurisdiction over the person of any defendant who is not subject to the jurisdiction of the courts of general jurisdiction of any state.[180]

Therefore, if jurisdiction over a party concerning a federal claim comports with due process but is not specifically provided for under federal law or the state long-arm statute, jurisdiction may be asserted. Such a circumstance arises when the defendant is a non-resident of the United States and has contacts with the U.S. sufficient to justify the application of U.S. law and to satisfy federal standards of forum selection, but has insufficient contacts with any one state to support jurisdiction under the state long-arm statute.[181]

The proper test for applying Rule 4(k)(2) was recently addressed by the First Circuit in *U.S. v. Swiss American Bank, Ltd.*[181.1] The Court ruled that to meet its initial burden of showing the applicability of Rule 4(k)(2), the Plaintiff must show that "the putative defendant's contacts with the nation as a whole suffice to satisfy the applicable constitutional requirements," and must certify that, based upon the information available to the Plaintiff, the Defendant is not subject to the jurisdiction of any one state. This test does not require Plaintiff to show that the long arm statutes of all 50 states are inapplicable. Rather, if Plaintiff satisfies these initial requirements, the burden shifts to the Defendant to show: (1) that its contacts with the United States are constitutionally insufficient for the assertion of personal jurisdiction; or (2) that it is subject to personal jurisdiction under the long arm acts of one or more states. While the limited scope of Rule 4(k)(2)'s applicability has limited its use, it remains an open question whether it may soon be found to have broader applicability in the context of electronic commerce.[181.2] It may also be noted that if personal jurisdiction is established for a federal claim under Rule 4(k)(2), then 28 U.S.C. § 1367(a) provides supplemental jurisdiction over related federal and state claims, subject to the

180. FED. R. CIV. P. 4(k)(2) & Advisory Committee's Notes.

181. FED. R. CIV. P. 4(k)(2) Advisory Committee's Notes.

181.1. 191 F.3d 30 (1st Cir. 1999).

181.2. Richard F. Ziegler, *Litigation: A Rule Comes of Age*, NAT'L L.J., Oct. 25, 1999, at B9 (positing that "a foreign defendant's Web site, though inadequate to warrant jurisdiction in any one state, nonetheless could be held to satisfy the due process standard when applied to the nation as a whole").

court's discretion to decline to exercise that jurisdiction under 28 U.S.C. § 1367(c).[182] In general, however, the Advisory Committee's Notes point out that Rule 4(k)(2) does not establish personal jurisdiction "if the only claims are those arising under state law or the law of another country, even though there might be diversity or alienage subject matter jurisdiction as to such claims."[183]

[2] National Contacts Precedent

In several cases, the courts have confronted the question of whether the aggregation of national contacts will provide a basis for jurisdiction that is consistent with the Constitution. For example, in *Go-Video, Inc. v. Akai Elec. Co., Ltd.*,[184] the Ninth Circuit held that under the Clayton Act "personal jurisdiction may be established in any district, given the existence of sufficient national contacts."[185] The basis of the *Go-Video* decision is the long-arm provision of the Clayton Act, which provides:

> Any suit, action, or proceeding under the antitrust laws against a corporation may be brought not only in the judicial district whereof it is an inhabitant, but also in any district wherein it may be found or transacts any business; and all process in such cases may be served in the district of which it is an inhabitant, or wherever it may be found.[186]

Given the breadth of the authorization under the Clayton Act's long-arm provision, the court then turned to whether a national contacts analysis was appropriate.[187] The court relied on an earlier national contacts case under the securities law, *Securities Investor Protection Corp. v. Vigman*,[188] in which the court found that "so long as a

---

182. *Id.*

183. *Id.*

184. 885 F.2d 1406 (9th Cir. 1989).

185. *Id.* at 1415. *See also* Busch v. Buchman, Buchman & O'Brien, Law Firm, 11 F.3d 1255, 1258 (5th Cir. 1994); United Liberty Life Ins. Co. v. Ryan, 985 F.2d 1320, 1330 (6th Cir. 1993); United Elec., Radio & Machine Workers of Am. v. 163 Pleasant St. Corp., 960 F.2d 1080, 1085 (1st Cir. 1992); Lisak v. Mercantile Bancorp, Inc., 834 F.2d 668, 671–72 (7th Cir. 1987), *cert. denied*, 485 U.S. 1007 (1988); Securities Investor Protection Corp. v. Vigman, 764 F.2d 1309, 1315–16 (9th Cir. 1985), *rev'd on other grounds sub nom.*, Holmes v. Securities Investor Protection Corp., 503 U.S. 258 (1992); Hirsch v. Vlerbaum, 163 B.R. 431, 432–33 (D. Conn. 1994); *In re* Atteberry v. Barclays Bank, PLC, 159 B.R. 1, 5–6 (D. Kan. 1993).

186. Section 12 of the Clayton Act, 15 U.S.C. § 22.

187. *Id.* at 1414.

188. 764 F.2d 1309 (9th Cir. 1985), *rev'd on other grounds sub nom.*, Holmes v. Securities Investor Protection Corp., 503 U.S. 258 (1992).

defendant has minimum contacts with the United States, Section 27 of the [Securities Exchange] Act confers personal jurisdiction over the defendant in any federal district court.''[189] On this basis, the Ninth Circuit in *Go-Video* found that ''a federal statute which permits the service of process beyond the boundaries of the forum state broadens the authorized scope of personal jurisdiction.''[190] By its terms, the

(*Text continued on page 6-37*)

189. *Id.* at 1316.
190. *Go-Video,* 885 F.2d at 1414.

holding in *Go-Video* is limited to cases involving federal statutes authorizing a national contacts analysis.

Practice Note: Amendments to the Federal Rules of Civil Procedure open up a broader category of cases to the use of the national contacts theory of jurisdiction.

§ 6.08 ALIEN VENUE CONSIDERATIONS

A final consideration in a case involving foreign defendants is the question of the proper venue for the action. Although not strictly a jurisdictional issue,[191] the question of appropriate venue also arises in transnational cases.[192] The federal venue statute is found in 28 U.S.C.A. § 1391(d), and is refreshingly simple: "An alien may be sued in any district."

Two cases involving an analysis of the alien venue statute illustrate its operation. First, in *Brunette Machine Works, Ltd. v. Kockum Indus., Inc.*,[193] the Supreme Court held that section 1391(d) is the only provision governing venue in an action against an alien, even in a patent infringement action.[194] In *Brunette,* the defendant argued that the special venue provision in patent infringement actions, 28 U.S.C.A. § 1400(b), which limits venue to either the district in which the defendant resides or in which the alleged infringement occurred, controlled. The Court reviewed the origin and development of the venue provisions and held that in section 1391(d) Congress was "stating a principle of broad and overriding application" that the alien venue statute is a "declaration of the long-established rule that suits against aliens are wholly outside the operation of all of the federal venue laws, general and special."[195]

Second, in *Go-Video, Inc. v. Akai Elec. Co., Ltd.*,[196] the Ninth Circuit considered whether the venue provision of the Clayton Act was exclusive in actions under the antitrust laws against alien defen-

---

191. *See generally* Brunette Machine Works, Ltd. v. Kockum Indus., Inc., 406 U.S. 706 (1972); Victor & Hood, *Personal Jurisdiction, Venue, and Service of Process in Antitrust Cases Involving International Trade: Amenability of Alien Corporations To Suit*, 46 ANTITRUST L.J. 1063 (1978).

192. *See, e.g.*, Go-Video, Inc. v. Akai Elec. Co., Ltd., 885 F.2d 1406 (9th Cir. 1989).

193. 406 U.S. 706 (1972).

194. *Id.* at 714.

195. *Id.*

196. 885 F.2d 1406 (9th Cir. 1989). For a discussion of the *Go-Video* case, *see* § 6.07, *supra*.

dants.[197] After reviewing the Clayton Act venue statute and the analysis, *inter alia,* of the Supreme Court's decision in *Brunette,* the Ninth Circuit determined that the Clayton Act's venue provision was not exclusive, and that venue was proper under section 1391(d).[198]

Although the Ninth Circuit did not have occasion to decide the issue, it noted that many commentators have concluded that the Clayton Act venue provisions, at least in the case of alien defendants, are "wholly redundant."[199] In any event, the broad scope of section 1391(d) and its application in cases such as *Brunette* and *Go-Video* illustrate that, as a practical matter, the establishment of appropriate venue in federal cases will not be a significant hurdle for plaintiffs suing alien defendants. Alien defendants, however, may be forced to defend actions in very inconvenient forums, given the growth in acceptance of the national contacts theory and the broad application of the federal venue statute.

§ 6.09 PRACTICAL STRATEGIES AND CHECKLIST

[1] General Review and Checklist

Many practical questions are implicated by the various issues of *in personam* or judicial jurisdiction. Because *in personam,* or judicial, jurisdictional issues are closely related to issues of subject matter, or adjudicatory, jurisdiction,[200] the two areas must be considered together in any jurisdictional analysis in a case with international aspects.

In analyzing personal jurisdiction issues in cases with international aspects, the overriding issue is whether the exercise of personal jurisdiction is consistent with the United States Constitution. From this core issue, the analysis proceeds to consider the various features of federal and state court jurisdiction, and the practical questions of waiver, removal, and venue.

From the perspective of representing an alien corporation, and, implicitly, the perspective of bringing suit against an alien corporation, the starting point for analysis is the law of the forum at issue.[201] Consider the specific statutory grant of jurisdiction applicable, and

197. *Id.* at 1408.

198. *Id.* at 1413.

199. *Id.* at 1413, *citing* 15 Charles A. Wright & Arthur R. Miller, Federal Practice & Procedure § 3818, at 110 (1986).

200. *See supra* Chapter 5, addressing adjudicatory jurisdiction.

201. *See supra* § 6.01.

determine whether its terms are satisfied. Is the jurisdictional basis one of general or systematic contacts with the forum, or is it based on the more narrow specific jurisdiction?[202] This question has important implications for the range of conduct subject to scrutiny in the United States.

Is the action removable to federal court? Is it the type of action that could originally have been brought in federal court?[203] Once in federal court, is the court's jurisdiction based on diversity or federal question jurisdiction?[204] If it is based on diversity, then the court will be limited to the range of jurisdiction under state law.[205] If the jurisdictional basis is a federal question, does the federal statute specifically provide for nationwide jurisdiction, or must the court rely on state authority?[206] Will the court apply the national contacts theory, and aggregate the foreign defendant's contacts with the United States?[207]

Does the defendant have the requisite minimum contacts with the forum, whether state or national, sufficient to subject it to jurisdiction in the United States?[208] Is the exercise of jurisdiction reasonable and consistent with the Constitution?[209] More generally, is the exercise of jurisdiction consistent with international law?[210]

Has the defendant waived, either explicitly or constructively, any objections to the exercise of jurisdiction over it by a United States court?[211] Can the court exercise jurisdiction over a foreign corporation by virtue of a related corporation in the United States?[212] Finally, is venue proper in the forum?[213]

[2] Practical Strategies

When advising parties to transnational transactions, counsel must be aware of the numerous opportunities and pitfalls of the scope of jurisdiction under U.S. law. In addition to the issues and concepts

202. *See supra* § 6.04[2].
203. *See supra* § 6.02[2].
204. *See supra* § 6.03 and Chapter 5.
205. *See supra* § 6.03.
206. *See supra* § 6.03.
207. *See supra* § 6.07.
208. *See supra* § 6.04[1].
209. *See* § 6.04[1] and [2].
210. *See* § 6.04[3].
211. *See supra* § 6.05.
212. *See supra* § 6.06.
213. *See supra* § 6.08.

explored in this chapter, counsel should be familiar with the rules developed in chapter 5, dealing with subject matter jurisdiction.

Planning opportunities commonly arise in the jurisdictional area. For instance, when advising U.S. parties to international transactions, counsel should seek to establish the best forum for resolution of any disputes. When this forum is the United States, it is important to obtain unequivocal expressions of the parties' intent in the documentation of the transaction. If a U.S. plaintiff that is not a party to any form of agreement has nevertheless suffered injury because of the conduct of a foreign person or corporation, counsel should explore how and when U.S. courts will assert *in personam* jurisdiction. Often, obtaining a favorable jurisdictional ruling can have a significant impact on the ultimate resolution of the case. If the foreign party is forced to litigate in the U.S., settlement discussions may be more fruitful. Conversely, if a U.S. party learns that it must travel great distances at great expense to litigate a matter, it may not pursue its remedies as aggressively.

Foreign parties trading with the United States or who are engaged in transactions with U.S. parties must also be advised by counsel of the many pitfalls lurking in U.S. law on jurisdiction. In general, parties can voluntarily submit to jurisdiction in the United States or they can have jurisdiction asserted over their objections. U.S. parties will generally always seek to include the U.S. forum in any agreement for reasons of convenience and expense. Non-U.S. parties should be aware of the significance of accession to such a clause and extract appropriate concessions from the U.S. party in return. A non-U.S. party's intent to consent to U.S. jurisdiction need not be explicit, but may be implied from the circumstances of the transaction. Care should be taken, therefore, in drafting the agreement to ensure that intentions are clearly expressed.

Finally, as numerous cases illustrate, even parties who never considered themselves subject to U.S. jurisdiction have been called into U.S. forums because of their conduct abroad. Parties engaged in trade with the U.S. must evaluate the benefits of the U.S. market with the potential drawback of being subject to U.S. jurisdiction.

Chapter 7

THE FOREIGN SOVEREIGN IMMUNITIES ACT

Bank, PLC, 159 B.R. 1 (D. Kan. 1993) (nationwide service authorized by Bankruptcy Rule 7004(d)).

§ 7.01 INTRODUCTION

With the passage of the Foreign Sovereign Immunities Act of 1976[1] ("FSIA") the United States codified what is known as the restrictive theory of sovereign immunity, and adopted a jurisdictional and procedural framework for suits against foreign sovereigns and instrumentalities. Because virtually all aspects of a suit against a foreign sovereign—from service of process to execution of a judgment—are covered by the FSIA, it is the primary tool for counsel bringing or defending such litigation.

FSIA issues arise both in a counselling context and in a practice context. In a counselling context, any relationships with foreign sovereigns or their instrumentalities must be structured to avoid later frustration by the immunity defense. In a practice context, the intricacies of the FSIA offer opportunities for the prudent, and traps for the unwary.

Before enactment of the FSIA, the question whether a defendant was entitled to immunity was resolved by the courts with guidance from the Executive, not the Congress.[2] Until the mid-20th century, the courts of the United States followed the so-called "absolute" theory of sovereign immunity, which accords broad immunity to foreign states.[3] International comity and the need for peaceful relations between sovereigns justified U.S. application of the doctrine.[4]

In the early 1950s, U.S. policy began to shift toward the "restrictive" theory of sovereign immunity.[5] Under the restrictive theory,

1. The Foreign Sovereign Immunities Act of 1976, Pub. L. No. 94–583, 90 Stat. 2891 (1976), 28 U.S.C.A. §§ 1330, 1332(a)(2), (3), and (4), 1391(f), 1441(d), 1602–1611 (1994), *reprinted in,* 71 AM. J. INT'L L. 595 (1977), 15 I.L.M. 1388 (1976). The primary legislative history of the FSIA relied upon in this Chapter is the Report of the House Judiciary Committee, H.R. Rep. No. 1487, 94th Cong., 2d Sess. (1976) [hereinafter cited as House Report], *reprinted in,* 1976 U.S.C.C.A.N. 6604. The text of the FSIA is reprinted *infra* in Appendix 8[1].

2. *See* House Report, *supra* note 1, at 7; von Mehren, *The Foreign Sovereign Immunities Act of 1976,* 17 COLUM J. TRANSNAT'L L. 33, 36–43 (1978).

3. *See generally* von Mehren, *supra* note 2, at 36–37 (discussing erosion of absolute theory of sovereign immunity). The nominal absoluteness of the doctrine belies several built in exceptions, such as those for actions relating to certain property, such as gifts and immovables, that existed even before the adoption of the restrictive theory. *See infra* § 7.08.

4. The Schooner Exchange v. McFaddon, 11 U.S. (7 Cranch) 116 (1812).

5. Letter from Jack B. Tate, Acting Legal Advisor of Department of State, to Phillip Perlman, Acting U.S. Attorney General (May 19, 1952), *reprinted in,* 26 DEP'T STATE BULL. 984 (1952); also *reprinted in,* Alfred Dunhill of London, Inc. v. Republic of Cuba, 425 U.S. 682, 712–15 app. 2 (1976).

foreign states retain their traditional immunity for governmental acts ("de jure imperii"), but are denied immunity for private or commercial acts ("de jure gestionis").[6] The rationale for the restrictive theory was well-articulated by a British court in 1977:

> Governments everywhere engage in activities which although incidental in one way or another to the business of government are in themselves essentially commercial in their nature. To apply a universal doctrine of sovereign immunity to such activities is much more likely to disserve than to conserve the comity of nations on the preservation of which the doctrine is founded. It is no longer necessary or desirable that what are truly matters of trading rather than of sovereignty should be hedged about with special exonerations and fenced off from the processes of the law by the attribution of a perverse and inappropriate notion of sovereign dignity.[7]

This excerpt illustrates some of the considerations behind the U.S. shift to the restrictive theory.[8] The restrictive theory furthered a U.S. policy to protect American citizens in transactions with foreign states. Another consideration was the desire to bring U.S. policy into conformance with the general practice of other foreign states at the time, including Austria, Belgium, Canada, England, Egypt, France, Germany, Greece, Italy, Pakistan, the Philippines, and Yugoslavia.[9]

Abandoning the absolute theory in the mid-1950s was only the first step toward today's complex set of legal rules. The Executive still remained responsible for deciding immunity questions on a case-by-case basis, respecting, among other considerations, the foreign policy ramifications of denying a foreign state immunity.[10] Questions left unanswered in the shift to the restrictive theory, particularly those regarding the analysis involved in determining whether an act was of a

---

6. *Id.* at 985; RESTATEMENT (THIRD) OF FOREIGN RELATIONS LAW OF THE UNITED STATES § 451, cmt. a (1987) [hereinafter cited as RESTATEMENT (THIRD)].

7. Trendtex Trading Corp. v. Central Bank of Nigeria, [1977] 2 W.L.R. 356, 386 (C.A.), *reprinted in* 16 I.L.M. 471, 498 (1977).

8. *See generally* House Report, *supra* note 1, at 6–8.

9. Alfred Dunhill of London, Inc. v. Cuba, 425 U.S. 682, 702 n.15 (1976). *See, e.g.*, United States v. Public Serv. Alliance of Canada, 32 I.L.M. 1 (1993) (applying restrictive theory under Canada's State Immunity Act).

10. *See* Monroe Leigh, *Sovereign Immunity—The Case of the* Imias, 68 AM. J. INT'L L. 280, 280–81 (1974).

public or commercial nature,[11] motivated Congress to attempt to resolve the matter by means of the legislative process.[12]

Although the enactment of the FSIA was the culmination of many years of legislative effort, it marked the beginning of judicial attempts to grapple with the provisions of the Act. Issues requiring interpretation abound in the FSIA. The law not only sets forth comprehensive rules governing "the jurisdiction of United States district courts in cases involving foreign states," it sets out "procedures for commencing a lawsuit against foreign states in both federal and state courts."[13] If a case proceeds to the merits of the dispute and a judgment is entered, the FSIA provides the exclusive remedies for attachment and execution. How the FSIA reaches its objectives in each of these categories—as interpreted by the courts—is the subject of this chapter.

The United States has also supported the efforts of the U.N. International Law Commission in developing a draft set of articles on Jurisdictional Immunities of States and Their Property. The State Department published the draft articles in the Federal Register for public comment.[14] The draft Convention reflects the restrictive theory of sovereign immunity, but does not parallel in all respects the FSIA.[15]

In the spring of 1996, the FSIA was amended to provide a new exception to immunity. Section 221 of the Antiterrorism and Effective Death Penalty Act of 1996 [Pub. L. No. 132, 104th Cong., 2d Sess.] amended 28 U.S.C. § 1605 to add a seventh exception to immunity. It provides, with certain limitations, that a sovereign will not be immune in an action "in which money damages are sought against a foreign state for personal injury or death that was caused by an act of torture, extrajudicial killing, aircraft sabotage, hostage taking, or the provision of material support or resources."[16]

---

11. *See, e.g.,* Victory Transport, Inc. v. Comisaria General de Abastecimientos y Transportes, 336 F.2d 354, 359 (2d Cir. 1964), *cert. denied,* 381 U.S. 934 (1965).

12. *See, e.g.,* Georges R. Delaume, *Public Debt and Sovereign Immunity: Some Considerations Pertinent to S. 556,* 67 Am. J. Int'l L. 745, 745–47 (1973). *See generally* House Report, *supra* note 1, at 1 ("It was also designed to bring U.S. practice into conformity with that of most other nations by leaving sovereign immunity decisions exclusively to the courts, thereby discontinuing the practice of judicial deference to 'suggestions of immunity' from the Executive Branch").

13. *See* House Report, *supra* note 1, at 12.

14. Office of the Legal Advisor, *Draft Convention on Sovereign Immunity,* 58 Fed. Reg. 16729 (Mar. 30, 1993). A copy of this Notice with the draft Convention is reprinted *infra* as Appendix 7.

15. *Id.* at 16730.

16. 28 U.S.C.A. § 1605(a)(7). The terrorist act exception to immunity is discussed *supra* § 7.11.

§ 7.02 ANALYZING FOREIGN SOVEREIGN IMMUNITY ISSUES

Many of the issues involved in a FSIA case can be considered in the chronological sequence in which they would be approached by counsel representing either a plaintiff or a foreign sovereign defendant. From the first contact with the party, counsel must analyze the structure of the Act and its provisions, beginning with the preliminary issues of a party's status and characterization of the defendant's acts, through issues surrounding execution and attachment. This section provides a chronological narrative analytical approach to the issues facing an attorney with little familiarity with the FSIA and its operation.

[1] Analyzing FSIA Issues: Steps in the Process

Step 1. Determine whether the potential defendant is a foreign state or instrumentality.[17] Separate rules in certain instances—venue, service, attachment—turn on the distinction between state and instrumentality, so identification issues must be resolved in the early stages of the case. If the proposed defendant is neither a state nor instrumentality, then the FSIA is not relevant to the case.

If the proposed defendant does satisfy one of the definitions in section 1603, then the FSIA is the exclusive means to pursue a judgment.[18] Since the Supreme Court's decision in *Argentine Republic v. Amerada Hess Shipping Corp.*,[19] the Alien Tort Claims Act, or federal statutes other than the FSIA, may not form the basis for a suit against a foreign state or instrumentality.

Suits against foreign sovereign defendants may be brought only under the FSIA in either state or federal court. Suits in state court are commenced under and governed by the FSIA.[20] All suits under the FSIA are tried to a judge; no jury trials are available under the FSIA.[21] Moreover, punitive damages are not available in suits against foreign states, but may be available in suits against instrumentalities.[22] If initiated in state court, the defendant has an unconditional right of

17. Counsel should refer to the definitions in § 1603 of the FSIA, and to the discussion at § 7.03[1], *infra*.

18. *See infra* § 7.03.

19. 488 U.S. 428, 443 (1989).

20. *See infra* § 7.03[2].

21. *See infra* § 7.03[3].

22. *Id.*

removal under 28 U.S.C.A. § 1441(f).[23] If in federal court, special separate venue issues under 28 U.S.C.A. § 1391(d) exist for states and instrumentalities.

Step 2. Once the preliminary status issues are resolved, consideration must turn to the basic questions of jurisdiction. Under the FSIA, subject matter and personal jurisdictional questions are linked with immunity questions. Section 1330(a) provides jurisdiction over non-immune in personam claims. Under section 1604, the general rule is that foreign states and instrumentalities are immune from the jurisdiction of United States courts unless a statutory exception is satisfied, a burden that rests with the court in the absence of an appearance.[24]

Accordingly, examination of whether jurisdiction exists is an examination of whether one of the following nine enumerated exceptions to immunity are satisfied.[25]

- First, under section 1605(a)(1), did the defendant waive immunity, either explicitly or implicitly?[26]
- Second, under section 1605(a)(2), is the action based on a commercial act of the defendant that satisfies one of the three clauses?[27]
- Third, under section 1605(a)(3), is the action based on a taking of property in violation of international law?[28]
- Fourth, under section 1605(a)(4), does the case involve gifts or immovable property?[29]
- Fifth, under section 1605(a)(5), does it involve a noncommercial tort?[30]

---

23. *See infra* § 7.03[2].

24. *See* Verlinden B.V. v. Central Bank of Nigeria, 461 U.S. 480, 493 (1983); RESTATEMENT (THIRD), *supra* note 6, introductory note, Chapter 5, at 394 n.15. *See generally infra* § 7.03.

25. *See infra* § 7.04. *See* Princz v. Federal Republic of Germany, 813 F. Supp. 22, 27 (D.D.C. 1992) (finding jurisdiction despite absence of application of any of the FSIA's exceptions), *rev'd,* 26 F.3d 1166 (D.C. Cir. 1994).

26. *See infra* § 7.05.

27. *See infra* § 7.06.

28. *See infra* § 7.07.

29. *See infra* § 7.08.

30. *See infra* § 7.09.

- Sixth, under section 1605(a)(6), does it involve enforcement of an arbitral award?[31]

- Seventh, under section 1605(a)(7), is the case for monetary damages concerning a terrorist act?[32]

- Eighth, under section 1605(b), does it involve a maritime lien?[33]

- Ninth, under section 1607, does the claim against the foreign state arise in the form of a counterclaim?[34]

Step 3. If one or more exceptions are satisfied, obtaining in personam jurisdiction over the defendant is the next issue. Under the FSIA, section 1330(b) confers personal jurisdiction if one of the enumerated jurisdictional exceptions to immunity is satisfied *and* service is perfected on the defendant.[35] Section 1608 provides exclusive service rules to perfect process on both foreign states and instrumentalities.[36]

[2] Analyzing Procedural Issues

If the FSIA's subject matter and personal jurisdiction requirements are satisfied, special problems arise if the foreign state wants to appeal a trial court's denial of immunity, or if the defendant does not appear, or does not comply with discovery orders.[37] Obtaining necessary discovery about the nature and acts of a foreign sovereign entity, particularly to address a preliminary jurisdictional motion, may present additional obstacles to a litigant.[37.1]

[3] Attachment and Enforcement of Judgments Issues

If a judgment is obtained against a foreign state or instrumentality, attachment and enforcement issues become important. The FSIA provides the exclusive procedural mechanism for the enforcement of

---

31. *See infra* § 7.12. *See generally* Charles N. Brower, *Jurisdiction Over Foreign Sovereigns: Litigation v. Arbitration,* 17 INT'L LAW. 681 (1983).
32. *See infra* § 7.11.
33. *See infra* § 7.12.
34. *See infra* § 7.13.
35. *See infra* § 7.14.
36. *See infra* § 7.15.
37. These and similar issues are discussed *infra* § 7.16.
37.1. Discovery-related issues are addressed *infra* § 7.16.

judgments against foreign states and instrumentalities.[38] Generally, the property of foreign states and instrumentalities is immune from attachment or execution on the same principles as immunity in the first instance from jurisdiction.

In § 7.18 of this chapter, a set of practical strategies and a checklist summarizes the provisions of the FSIA discussed in this chapter.

§ 7.03 SPECIAL THRESHOLD ISSUES UNDER THE FSIA

Although the FSIA created a wholly statutory process for suits against foreign states and instrumentalities, many important procedural issues were addressed only in passing or not at all. These issues are peculiar to cases under the FSIA and are important to the judicial development of a body of precedent for actions under the FSIA. Because they are important threshold issues in actions under the FSIA, this section will discuss the miscellaneous issues—such as the distinction between a state and an instrumentality, exclusivity of the FSIA, federal versus state court jurisdiction and removal, the absence of the availability of jury trials and punitive damages, and venue—important in assessing the prospects for success when counselling clients in FSIA actions.[39] These issues will also be discussed in subsequent sections when they are relevant to developments under other sections of the FSIA.

[1] States and Instrumentalities Under the FSIA

One of the first issues in analyzing any FSIA case is the determination of whether the potential defendant is indeed the type of defendant for which the FSIA provides the exclusive mechanism for suit. The threshold status determination begins with section 1603(a) of the Act, which provides that a foreign state "includes a political subdivision of a foreign state or an agency or instrumentality of a foreign state. . . ," except for purposes of service under section 1608.[40] Because agencies and instrumentalities are included within the definition of a

38. These issues are discussed *infra* § 7.17.

39. A rare but important qualification to the use of the FSIA by U.S. litigants is the President's authority to suspend claims by virtue of the foreign affairs power. *See, e.g.*, Dames & Moore v. Regan, 453 U.S. 654 (1981).

40. 28 U.S.C.A. § 1603(a). Separate service rules for states and instrumentalities are discussed *infra* § 7.15.

foreign state for purposes of immunity, the general rules of immunity apply to them as if they were a state.[41]

The question of categorizing an entity for FSIA purposes has often arisen in a variety of contexts, including those discussed below.

[a] *Definition of "State," "Officical Capacity," Immunities, Timing of Determinations, and Selected Other Issues Affecting the FSIA Analysis*

Whether a foreign state is a state for FSIA purposes, i.e., one that is recognized and has diplomatic relations with the United States, is a rare, but important question.

Another issue that has arisen is whether suits against foreign heads of state and government officials are governed by the FSIA. The text of the FSIA does not address the applicability of the Act to individuals.[42] However, because the FSIA provides the sole basis of jurisdiction in claims against an "agency or instrumentality of a foreign state,"[43] it has been held that suits against individuals acting in their official capacities are governed by the FSIA.[44] Several cases have addressed the issue of whether government officials were acting within the scope of their official capacities, thus triggering application of the FSIA. For instance, in *In re Estate of Ferdinand E. Marcos Human Rights Litigation*,[45] the court found that the actions of the daughter of Ferdinand Marcos in ordering the torture and murder of an individual while she was head of the Philippine military police, "cannot have been the acts of an agent or instrumentality of a foreign state within the meaning of the FSIA."[46] The FSIA, therefore, was held inapplicable.[47]

However, in contrast to the "official capacity" analysis which is used to determine the applicability of the FSIA to acts of foreign agents or instrumentalities, the immunity of heads of state is not governed by reference to provisions of the FSIA. Courts defer to case-by-case

41. *Id.*

42. 28 U.S.C.A. § 1603 (defining foreign state); Lafontant v. Aristide, 844 F. Supp. 128 (E.D.N.Y. 1994).

43. Argentine Republic v. Amerada Hess Shipping Corp., 488 U.S. 428, 434 (1989). *See infra* § 7.04[2] (discussing exclusivity of jurisdiction under FSIA).

44. *See* Chuidian v. Philippine Nat'l Bank, 912 F.2d 1095, 1099–1103 (9th Cir. 1990).

45. 978 F.2d 493, (9th Cir. 1992), *cert. denied,* 113 S. Ct. 2960 (1993).

46. *Id.* at 498.

47. *Id. See also* Siderman v. Republic of Argentina, 965 F.2d 699, 705 (9th Cir. 1992); McKeel v. Islamic Republic of Iran, 722 F.2d 582, 588 (9th Cir. 1983), *cert. denied,* 469 U.S. 880 (1984); Paul v. Avril, 812 F. Supp. 207, 210–13 (S.D. Fla. 1993).

guidance from the U.S. Department of State in determining whether to grant immunity to individuals under common-law head of state immunity.[48]

It should also be noted that the immunity of foreign diplomats for their actions in the United States is governed by the Vienna Convention on Diplomatic Relations,[49] not the FSIA.[50] The Vienna Convention grants nearly absolute immunity to diplomats concerning criminal prosecution and protection from most civil and administrative actions.[51] An exception to diplomatic immunity is liabilities "relating to any professional or commercial activity exercised by the diplomatic agent in the receiving State outside his official functions."[52] However, this exception is narrowly construed by the United States State Department, which views that "commercial activity . . . focuses on the pursuit of trade or business activity; it does not encompass contractual relationships for goods and services incidental to the daily life of the diplomat and family in the receiving State."[53] Moreover, cases involving the commercial activity exception to diplomatic immunity should be rare, as Diplomats, by the express terms of the Vienna Convention, "shall not . . . practice for personal profit any professional or commercial activity."[54]

Under section 1603(b), an agency or instrumentality of a foreign state is defined to include any entity (1) which is a separate legal person, corporate or otherwise, and (2) which is an organ of a foreign state or political subdivision thereof, or a majority of whose shares or other

---

48. *See generally* Lafontant v. Aristide, 844 F. Supp. 128 (E.D.N.Y. 1994) (finding Jean-Bertrand Aristide immune under head of state doctrine from claim arising from ordered execution of leader of unsuccessful Haitian coup and providing detailed analysis of head of state immunity and its relation to FSIA).

49. Apr. 18, 1961, 23 U.S.T. 3227, T.I.A.S. No. 7502.

50. *See* Tabion v. Mufti, 73 F.3d 535, 539 (4th Cir. 1996) (holding that Vienna Convention bars suit by former domestic servant against diplomat for alleged illegal employment practices). Another potential source of immunity of foreign persons in U.S. courts is the International Organizations Immunities Act, § 7a(b), *amended and codified at*, 22 U.S.C.A. § 288d(b). *See* Rendell-Speranza v. Nassim, 107 F.3d 913 (D.C. Cir. 1997) (finding employee of international organization immune from liability for battery under Immunities Act where alleged battery was in employee's official capacity, but holding that immunity does not extend to Supervisor, whose alleged assaults and batteries were outside scope of employment).

51. *Id.* at 537.

52. Vienna Convention, Art. 31(1)(c), 23 U.S.T. at 3241.

53. 73 F.3d at 538.

54. Vienna Convention, Art. 42, 23 U.S.T. at 3247.

ownership interest is owned by a foreign state or political subdivision thereof.[55]

Because of the myriad forms of political and commercial organizations operating today,[56] a determination of a particular entity's status can often be a troublesome proposition. In recent years the question of the timing of the determination of status has arisen. If a defendant is a government entity at the time of the events giving rise to the action, but is subsequently privatized, does the FSIA provide a basis for jurisdiction? Courts considering this issue had uniformly ruled that the change in status does not affect the application of the FSIA.[57] The U.S. Supreme Court recently decided this issue in the opposite. In *Dole Food Co. v. Patrickson*,[57.1] the Court ruled that the determination of whether a corporation is an instrumentality of a foreign state is made at the time suit is filed, not as of the time of the conduct giving rise to the action.[57.2] Whether a particular entity is actually part of a foreign state or a separate instrumentality is important for determining many subsequent FSIA issues.[58] For instance, in *Transaero, Inc. v. La Fuerza Aerea Boliviana*,[59] the court was faced with the question whether the Bolivian Air Force is a foreign state or an instrumentality of a foreign state. The

55. 28 U.S.C.A. § 1603(b).

56. For instance, in Mangattu v. M/V Ibn Hayyan, 35 F.3d 205 (5th Cir. 1994), the court found that United Arab Shipping, an entity owned by six foreign states, qualifies as "agency or instrumentality" under the FSIA based on a "pooling" of interests. *Compare* Gardiner Stone Hunter Int'l v. Iberia Lineas Aereas de Espana, 896 F. Supp. 125 (S.D.N.Y. 1995) (finding pooling inappropriate when interests owned by different governments), *with*, Gates v. Victor Fine Foods, 54 F.3d 1457 (9th Cir. 1995) (denying instrumentality status to entities owned by instrumentalities). *See generally* Darryl Van Duch, *When Does a Sovereign State Control a Company?*, NAT'L L.J., Apr. 1, 1996 (discussing theories of pooling and tiering of foreign interests).

57. General Electric Capital Corp. v. Grossman, 991 F.2d 1376 (8th Cir. 1993); Gould, Inc. v. Pechiney Ugine Kuhlmann, 853 F.2d 445 (6th Cir. 1988); Leith v. Lufthansa German Airlines, 897 F. Supp. 1115 (N.D. Ill. 1995). A related question, only recently addressed, is whether the status of an entity is evaluated at the time the events giving rise to the case occur or at the time the case is filed. In General Electric Capital Corp. v. Grossman, 991 F.2d 1376 (1993), the court held status was evaluated at the time of the events giving rise to the case, not at the time of suit. *Id.* at 1380–82. *See generally* Richard A. Kaplan, Jay N. Fastow & Lawrence J. Reina, *A Foreign Company Can Be a 'Sovereign State,' If the Timing Is Right*, NAT'L L.J., Jan. 13, 1994, at C12.

57.1. 123 S. Ct. 1655, 155 L. Ed. 2d 643 (2003).

57.2. *Id.*, 123 S. Ct. at 1662.

58. *See* Gray v. Permanent Mission, 443 F. Supp. 816, 820 (S.D.N.Y. 1978) (holding foreign state's mission to United Nations is foreign state, not agency or instrumentality), *aff'd mem.*, 508 F.2d 1044 (2d Cir. 1978).

59. 30 F.3d 148 (D.C. Cir. 1994).

question was relevant because the FSIA service procedures are different for the two. In this case, the plaintiff had performed service as if the Air Force were an instrumentality. The court, however, held that the Air Force was a foreign state and must be served as a foreign state. The court in *Transaero* began its analysis by noting that the issue was whether the Bolivian Air Force is a "separate legal person, corporate or otherwise" under § 1603(b)(1).[60]

The court noted that three tests have emerged in this analysis. First, a balancing test has been used in which the three characteristics of separate legal status are evaluated: (1) to sue and be sued in its own

(*Text continued on page 7-13*)

60. *Id.* at 151.

name; (2) to contract in its own name; and (3) to hold property in its own name.[61]

The second test identified is the so-called "categorical test" articulated by the court in *Segni v. Commercial Office of Spain*.[62] Under the second test, the question is "whether the defendant is the type of entity 'that is an integral part of a foreign state's political structure, [or rather] an entity whose structure and function is predominately commercial.' "[63]

The third test is one proposed by the U.S. Government, the "core function test."[64] The court saw the second and third tests as similar, and combined them in its holding. The court re-stated the issue as "whether the core functions of the armed forces of a foreign sovereign are governmental or commercial."[65] The court then held: "armed forces are as a rule so closely bound up with the structure of the state that they must in all cases be considered as the foreign state itself, rather than a separate 'agency or instrumentality' of the state." The "powers to declare and wage war" are among the "necessary concomitants" of sovereignty.[66] "We hold that the armed forces of a foreign sovereign are the 'foreign state' and must be served under § 1608(a)."[67]

Recent courts have continued to test the distinctions between political subdivisions and agencies and instrumentalities. In *Hyatt Corp. v. Stanton*,[68] the court adopted a "legal characteristics" test of whether the entity is a "political subdivision" or an "agency or instrumentality." The Court suggested that "political subdivisions should be read to refer to all governmental units that cannot act and are not suable in their own name, while agencies and instrumentalities would denote governmental units which act and are suable in their own name."[69]

---

61. *Id.* (citing Bowers v. Transportes Navieros Ecuadorianos, 719 F. Supp. 398, 400 (E.D. Va. 1984)).

62. 650 F. Supp. 1040, 1041–42 (N.D. Ill. 1988).

63. 30 F.3d 148 (citing *Segni*, 650 F. Supp. at 1041–42).

64. *Id.*

65. *Id.* at 153.

66. *Id.*

67. *Id.*

68. 945 F. Supp. 675 (S.D.N.Y. 1996).

69. *See also*, Transaero v. La Fuerza Aera Boliviana, 30 F.3d 148 (D.C. Cir. 1994) (setting forth "core-function" test which the Court in Hyatt Corp. v. Stanton, 945 F. Supp. 675 (S.D.N.Y. 1996), declined to follow).

If the entity's categorization is not immediately apparent, consultations should be initiated with U.S. government agencies, including the country desks at the Departments of State and Commerce, to learn whether information concerning status is readily available. Consultation with counsel in the foreign country may also be necessary.[70]

If counsel has a difficult time establishing the defendant's character or status, it is likely that special forms of proof may be required to satisfy the court of the defendant's character. In addition, a foreign defendant may need to establish the sovereign nature of an instrumentality. In such cases, the courts have several mechanisms available. For instance, in *Jet Line Servs., Inc. v. M/V Marsa El Hariga*,[71] the Libyan government sought to establish the nature of the entity at issue through affidavits and other submissions. In addition, the court took judicial notice of previous judicial considerations of the entity, and of the entity's "sovereign character."[72] After consideration of the evidence submitted, the court found that the defendant had produced such prima facie evidence as to shift the burden of showing no right to immunity to the plaintiff; absent such evidence, the court found that defendant had satisfied the requirements of section 1603 of the FSIA.[73]

In enacting the FSIA, Congress did not intend to alter the substantive law of liability of foreign states and instrumentalities, including the attribution of liability between states and instrumentalities.[74] The House Report explains:

> The bill is not intended to affect the substantive law of liability. Nor is it intended to affect . . . *the attribution of responsibility between or among entities of a foreign state;* for example, whether the proper entity of a foreign state has been sued, or whether an entity sued is liable in whole or in part for the claimed wrong.[75]

---

70. *See supra* Chapter 2. *See generally* Gould v. Pechiney Ugine Kulhmann & Trefimetaux, 853 F.2d 445, 450 (6th Cir. 1988) (determination of status as "foreign state" made as of date events occurred).

71. 462 F. Supp. 1165 (D. Md. 1978).

72. *Id.* at 1172 (citing Puente v. Spanish National State, 116 F.2d 43 (2d Cir. 1940), *cert. denied*, 314 U.S. 627 (1941)). The court in *Jet Line* also cited to Rule 902(3) of the Federal Rules of Evidence. On issues of proof of foreign law, *see infra* Chapter 9.

73. *Id.* at 1176–78.

74. House Report, *supra* note 1, at 12; *see also* Ronald D. Lee, Note, *Jurisdiction over Foreign States for Acts of Their Instrumentalities: A Model for Attributing Liability*, 94 YALE L.J. 394, 398 & n.23 (1984).

75. House Report, *supra* note 1, at 12 (emphasis supplied).

Consequently, any attribution of liability is performed just as it was before the FSIA, based on international or federal common law, on a case-by-case basis.[76] The issue has arisen frequently since enactment of the FSIA, and as a result of a combination of FSIA issues, several notable decisions have produced some guidance in this area.[77]

[b] Attributing Liability Among Instrumentalities and States

The issue of when a foreign state can be sued for the acts of an instrumentality, and vice versa, is important because of the great number and variety of nominally separate government instrumentalities, such as banks and state trading corporations.[78] These instrumentalities are often legally separate from the foreign government. As a practical matter, however, the foreign state often directly or indirectly owns and/or finances these instrumentalities. If abused, the instrumentality form permits the foreign state to escape liability for the commercial activities of an instrumentality, activities for which the foreign state itself, under the FSIA, might be held accountable. In response, the courts have faced plaintiffs' attempts to attribute the liability of the instrumentality to the foreign state.

As a general rule of international common law, separate juridical entities which are distinct from a sovereign are routinely presumed to enjoy independent status, despite the fact that they may operate openly as government instrumentalities.[79] The leading case on this issue is a Supreme Court decision attributing liability for the actions of the state to the instrumentality. In *First Nat'l City Bank v. Banco Para El Comercio Exterior de Cuba*,[80] the Supreme Court held that the presumption of independence "may be overcome. . . , where giving effect to the corporate form would permit a foreign state to be the sole beneficiary of a claim pursued in the United States courts while

76. *See* Note, *supra* note 74, at 398–99.

77. *See* Foremost-McKesson, Inc. v. Islamic Republic of Iran, 905 F.2d 438, 446–48 (D.C. Cir. 1990); Federal Ins. Co. v. Richard I. Rubin & Co., Inc., 12 F.3d 1270, 1286–92 (3d Cir. 1993). *See generally* Goekjian, *Jurisdiction Over Iran Under the FSIA and the Algiers Accord, A Loose Application:* Foremost-McKesson, Inc. v. Islamic Republic of Iran, 59 GEO. WASH. L. REV. 1311 (1991).

78. *See* Note, *supra* note 74, at 394.

79. *See* RESTATEMENT (THIRD), *supra* note 6, § 451. *see generally* Note, *supra* note 74.

80. 462 U.S. 611 (1983).

escaping liability to the opposing party imposed by international law."[81]

The instrumentality at the center of the controversy was Bancec, the Cuban government's official autonomous credit union for foreign trade. Bancec, established in 1960, was state-owned but had independent juridical status. Following the Cuban government's seizure and nationalization of the First National City Bank's Cuban assets, Bancec filed a suit in a United States federal district court seeking to collect on a letter of credit which had been issued by First National. First National then entered a counterclaim against Cuba and sought to set off the amount of its seized assets against the debt for which Bancec had demanded payment. First National asked the court to pierce the corporate veil between Bancec and the Cuban government and thereby allow the right to setoff. Following Bancec's filing of its claim against First National, but before First National had entered its counterclaim, Bancec was dissolved by the Cuban government, its capital divided between Cuba's central bank and other foreign trade entities under the Cuban Ministry of Foreign Trade.

The district court, noting that First National's seized assets exceeded the amount of the debt claimed by Bancec, held that First National should be granted the right of setoff.[82] The district court was not persuaded by Bancec's argument that its separate juridical status protected it from being held liable for the actions of the Cuban government in the seizure and nationalization of First National's assets.[83] The court of appeals, however, reversed, finding that Bancec could not be held liable for the actions of the Cuban government for the purposes of First National's counterclaim.[84]

The Supreme Court, in a decision that agreed with the district court, held that First National Bank could apply the setoff, and rejected Bancec's contention that the FSIA prohibits holding a foreign instrumentality, owned and controlled by a foreign government, liable for the acts of that government.[85] In preface, the Court stated that: "The language and history of the FSIA clearly establish that the Act was not intended to affect the substantive law determining the liability of a foreign state or instrumentality, or the attribution of liability among

81. *Id.* at 614.
82. 505 F. Supp. 412, 442 (S.D.N.Y. 1980).
83. *Id.*
84. 658 F.2d 913, 920 (2d Cir. 1981).
85. 462 U.S. at 633 (1983).

instrumentalities of a foreign state.''[86] The Court noted that ordinarily, government instrumentalities established as distinct and independent juridical entities should be treated as separate from their sovereign. ''During its deliberation, Congress clearly expressed its intention that duly created instrumentalities of a foreign state are to be accorded a presumption of independent status.''[87]

Nevertheless, the Court recognized that principles of equity allow this presumption to be overcome in certain circumstances. On the facts in *Bancec*, the Court concluded that allowing the presumption to operate would permit a gross injustice, because it would allow the Cuban government to obtain relief in the courts of the United States while avoiding responsibility for the seizure of First National's assets, a seizure which the court of appeals had deemed violative of international law.[88]

The *Bancec* decision does not, however, provide formulaic guidance for determinations about attribution of liability to instrumentalities. The Court stated:

> Our decision today announces no mechanical formula for determining the circumstances under which the normally separate juridical status of a government instrumentality is to be disregarded. Instead, it is the product of the application of internationally recognized equitable principles to avoid the injustice that would result from permitting a foreign state to reap the benefits of our courts while avoiding the obligations of international law.[89]

Although the *Bancec* decision offers little predictability it does provide opportunities for advocacy that the operation of the presumption in a particular case is inequitable.[90]

Alternatively, the issue has arisen of when a foreign sovereign will be liable for acts of instrumentalities. In *Gibbons v. Republic of Ireland*,[91] the court granted Ireland's motion for summary judgment on the ground that on the facts presented, Ireland was not subject to suit for the

---

86. *Id.* at 626.

87. *Id.* at 628.

88. *Id.* at 633–34.

89. *Id.*

90. *Compare* Hercaire Int'l, Inc. v. Argentina, 821 F.2d 559, 564–65 (11th Cir. 1987) (instrumentality not subject to liability for acts of foreign sovereign) *with* Letelier v. Republic of Chile, 748 F.2d 790, 794–95 (2d Cir. 1984) (holding instrumentality subject to liability for acts of foreign sovereign).

91. 532 F. Supp. 668 (D.D.C. 1982).

alleged wrongdoings of instrumentalities.[92] In an analysis that is similar to but distinct from the *Bancec* analysis, the court found that the instrumentalities possessed independent indicia of existence, and there was no evidence of knowledge or participation in any alleged wrongdoings of the instrumentalities.[93] Other courts faced with similar issues have found the foreign sovereign liable for the acts of instrumentalities, but on what the court in *Gibbons* called "stronger" indications of involvement by the foreign sovereign.[94]

[c] Foreign Government-Owned Business Entities

The question of whether a foreign government-owned business entity qualifies as an agency or instrumentality for purposes of application of the FSIA has troubled courts.[95] Under section 1603(b), an agency or instrumentality of a foreign state is defined to include any entity (1) which is a separate legal person, corporate or otherwise, and (2) which is an organ of a foreign state or political subdivision thereof, or a majority of whose shares or other ownership interest is owned by a foreign state or political subdivision thereof.[96] The threshold for foreign government ownership to trigger the FSIA's application, including "tiering," the ownership of an entity which in turn owns an interest in the entity subject of the dispute was recently settled by the U.S. Supreme Court in *Dole Food Co. v. Patrickson*.[96.1] The Court held that a foreign state must itself directly own a majority of the shares of a corporation if the corporation is to be deemed an instrumentality of the state under the FSIA. In *Dole Food Co.*, ownership of the defendant company was at various times separated from the State of Israel by one or more corporate layers, each of which intervening companies was at least majority-owned by the State of Israel. The Court ruled that "only direct ownership of a majority of shares by the foreign state satisfies the statutory requirement." This ruling effectively ends the issue of "tiering." Whether States can now avoid liability under the FSIA by

92. *Id.* at 670.

93. *Id.*

94. *See* American Int'l Group, Inc. v. Islamic Republic of Iran, 493 F. Supp. 522, 524–26 (D.D.C. 1980), *vacated on other grounds*, 657 F.2d 430 (D.C. Cir. 1981); United Euram Corp. v. Union of Soviet Socialist Republics, 461 F. Supp. 609, 610–12 (S.D.N.Y. 1978).

95. *Compare* In re Air Crash Disaster Near Roselawn, Indiana, 96 F.3d 932 (7th Cir. 1996) *with* Gates v. Victor Fine Foods, 54 F.3d 1457 (9th Cir. 1995), *cert. denied*, 116 S.Ct. 187; Hyatt Corp. v. Stanton, 945 F. Supp. 675 (S.D.N.Y. 1996).

96. 28 U.S.C.A. § 1603(b).

96.1. 123 S. Ct. 1655, 155 L. Ed. 2d 643 (2003).

merely acting through at least two levels of subsidiaries may produce unfair results and be revisited by courts or Congress.

Prior to *Dole Foods*, in *Gates v. Victor Fine Foods*,[97] the Court analyzed the FSIA's applicability to certain Canadian agricultural entities, Alberta Pork Producers Development Corporation (''Alberta Pork'') and its 100 percent-owned subsidiary, Fletcher's Fine Foods (''FFF''). Observing that Alberta Pork was the marketing board established pursuant to Canadian law to advance hog exports from Alberta and under active government supervision, the Court ruled that such entity was an agency or instrumentality of a foreign state.[98] The Court found guidance in the FSIA's legislative history that a state trading company and an export

(*Text continued on page 7-19*)

97. 54 F.3d 1457 (9th Cir. 1995), *cert. denied*, 516 U.S. 869.
98. *Id.* at 1460.

association can be organs of a foreign state. The Court opined that "an entity's involvement in commercial affairs does not automatically render the entity non-governmental."[99]

The Court then considered whether Alberta Pork's wholly owned subsidiary, FFF, a pork-processing plant in British Columbia, was majority-owned by a foreign state or political subdivision thereof for purposes of the FSIA's application. The Court concluded that, although Alberta Pork was an agency or instrumentality of a foreign state, Alberta Pork was not "a foreign state or political subdivision" as required by the Statute's majority share ownership provision.[100] The Court, therefore, rejected the FSIA's application to FFF. The Court stated:

> As it is written, the Act provides potential immunity to entities that are either organs of a foreign state or political subdivision thereof or have a majority of shares owned by the foreign state or political subdivision. To add to that list entities that are owned by an agency or instrumentality would expand the potential immunity considerably because it would provide potential immunity for every subsidiary in a corporate chain, no matter how far down the line, so long as the first corporation is an organ of the foreign state or political subdivision or has a majority of its shares owned by the foreign state or political subdivision.[101]

While thus applying the FSIA's protections to Alberta Pork, the Court rejected such protection to FFF, Alberta Pork's wholly-owned subsidiary.

Similarly, in *Hyatt Corp. v. Stanton*,[102] the Court ruled that a bank whose majority owner was the Finnish Government was not entitled to FSIA protection. While the Court determined that the majority shareholder of the bank, a Government Guarantee Fund ("GCF"), was a government agency or instrumentality, it ruled that mere majority ownership of the bank by GCF did not make the bank itself an agency or instrumentality. The Court also opined that the "prevailing international rule" is to not accord sovereign immunity to indirectly government-owned entities as "many corporations with distant government investments, even if far removed, would be covered."

---

99. *Id.*
100. *Id.* at 1461.
101. *Id.*
102. 945 F. Supp. 675 (S.D.N.Y. 1996).

In contrast, the Court in *In re Air Crash Disaster Near Roselawn, Indiana*,[103] ruled that the FSIA governed suits arising from an aircrash against an aircraft manufacturer owned indirectly by the French and Italian governments. The entity, Avions de Transport Regional, was created as a French corporation and owned 50 percent by a French Company and 50 percent by an Italian Company.[104] In turn, the French Company was 92 percent owned by the French Government and the Italian Company was 62 percent owned by an Italian Government-owned holding company.[105] The Court held that the language and legislative history of the FSIA dictate that the FSIA be broadly applied to foreign entities.[106]

Practice Note: In summary, an important threshold matter in approaching FSIA issues is the status of the defendant as a foreign sovereign or an instrumentality. The importance of this threshold issue is highlighted in several provisions of the FSIA that provide differential treatment for states and instrumentalities. Several other important threshold questions will be addressed in the subsequent sections.

[2] FSIA Removal and Venue Provisions

The FSIA does not vest exclusive jurisdiction in the federal courts; it contemplates suits against foreign sovereigns or instrumentalities in state courts.[107] If a case is brought in state court, it may only be commenced and maintained in accordance with the FSIA: ''All the defenses and immunities provided by the FSIA are applicable to actions against foreign states in State courts.''[108]

If suit is commenced in state court, the foreign sovereign has an unconditional right of removal to federal district court under 28 U.S.C.A. § 1441(d). Section 1441(d) provides, in pertinent part:

---

103. 96 F.3d 932 (7th Cir. 1996).

104. *Id.* at 935–36.

105. *Id.*

106. *Id.* at 941; *cf.*, Mexicana de Servicios Maritimos, S.A. de C.V. v. The M/T Respect, 89 F.3d 650 (9th Cir. 1996) (applying *Gates v. Victor Fine Foods* test and concluding that Pemex-Refining, Mexican government-owned oil refining company, qualified for application of the FSIA as agency or instrumentality of foreign state); Supra Medical Corp. v. McGonigle, 955 F. Supp. 374 (E.D. Pa. 1997) (applying Court's analysis in *Mexicana de Servicios Maritimos, S.A. de C.V. v. The M/T Respect* but concluding that two British medical schools were not agencies or instrumentalities of foreign state).

107. *See* House Report, *supra* note 1, at 13.

108. *See* Restatement (Third), *supra* note 6, § 458 & cmt. a.

> Any civil action brought in a State court against a foreign state as defined in section 1603(a) of this title may be removed by the foreign state to the district court of the United States for the district and division embracing the place where such action is pending. Upon removal the action shall be tried by the court without jury. Where removal is based on this subsection, the time limitations of section 1446(b) [sixty days] may be enlarged at any time for cause shown.

FSIA defendants are not tightly restricted by the standard time limits placed on removal.[109] The rationale for the unconditional removal provision is explained in the legislative history:

> In view of the potential sensitivity of actions against foreign states and the importance of developing a uniform body of law in this area, it is important to give foreign states clear authority to remove to a Federal forum actions brought against them in the State courts. New subsection (d) of section 1441 permits the removal of any such action at the discretion of the foreign state, *even if there are multiple defendants and some of these defendants desire not to remove the action* or are citizens of the State in which the action is brought.[110]

Waiver of the right of removal will not be implied; a waiver must be explicit.[111] The operation of the removal rule is well-illustrated in *Arango v. Guzman Travel Advisors Corp.*,[112] a case in which a foreign state defendant invoked the removal provision. The court held that Congress intended that the provision "should operate to remove the entire action pending in state court against all defendants, private and domestic, as well as the foreign sovereign."[113]

In contrast, the court in *Laughlin v. Dow Chem. Co.*[114] held that, in a case involving multiple actions, some of which did not involve foreign states, a removal motion operated to remove only the action against the

---

109. *See* Talbot v. Saipem, A.G., 835 F. Supp. 352, 354–55 (S.D. Tex. 1993). *But see* Steadman v. Sinclair, 1996 WL 257664 (S.D.N.Y. May 16, 1996) (holding no extension of time for removal). The absence of a jury trial after removal is discussed *infra* in § 7.03[3].

110. House Report, *supra* note 1, at 32 (emphasis supplied).

111. *See* In re Delta America Reinsurance Co., 900 F.2d 890, 894 (6th Cir.), *cert. denied,* 498 U.S. 890 (1990).

112. 621 F.2d 1371 (5th Cir. 1980).

113. *Id.* at 1377. *See also In re* Disaster at Riyadh Airport, 540 F. Supp. 1141, 1143 (D.D.C. 1982) (holding section 1441(d) requires "removal of the entire action against all defendants"); *accord* Tucker v. Whitaker Travel, Ltd., 620 F. Supp. 578, 581–82 (E.D. Pa. 1985) (following *Arango* and finding no assent to removal required of non-sovereign defendants for removal to operate), *aff'd mem.*, 800 F.2d 1140 (3d Cir.), *cert. denied,* 479 U.S. 986 (1986).

114. 563 F. Supp. 271 (S.D. Tex. 1983).

foreign sovereign defendants.[115] The court specifically declined to apply *Arango* because it "would unduly expand the reach of § 1441(d) and would result in an unwarranted injustice to the plaintiffs."[116] The court distinguished *Arango* on its facts, citing *Alifieris v. American Airlines, Inc.*,[117] in which the court permitted removal of a third party action, including a claim against a foreign state, but did not permit removal of the primary action.[118]

Practice Note: Despite the right of removal to federal court, state choice of law rules provide guidance on the applicable law. For instance, in *Barkanic v. General Admin. of Civil Aviation of the PRC*,[119] the court applied the law of the People's Republic of China to limit recovery to $20,000 for the wrongful death of a non-Chinese citizen killed in a plane crash in China.[120] Counsel preparing to bring suit against a foreign sovereign defendant must, therefore, carefully evaluate the impact of the choice of law rules applicable in the jurisdiction where the suit is brought.

In *Walpex Trading v. Yacimientos Petroliferos*,[121] the court addressed the question of which law should apply to a suit over contract formation. Plaintiff argued that under § 1606 of the FSIA the defendant is liable "in the same manner and to the same extent as a private individual under like circumstances," and therefore the provision of Bolivia law governing contract formation by governmental entities should not apply. In *Walpex,* the court noted that New York state choice of law rules point to Bolivian law, which:

> establishes different rules of primary conduct for governmental agencies and similarly situated individuals. . . . Thus, while formation of a contract with an instrumentality of the Bolivian government requires certain formalities, including a witnessed, notarized writing that is recorded as a public deed and choice of law and forum clauses, Walpex argues that § 1606 requires that court to disregard these rules

115. *Id.* at 272–73.
116. *Id.* at 273.
117. 523 F. Supp 1189, 1193 (E.D.N.Y. 1981).
118. *Laughlin,* 563 F. Supp. at 272.
119. 923 F.2d 957 (2d Cir. 1991).
120. *Id.* at 960.
121. 789 F. Supp. 1268 (S.D.N.Y. 1992).

> of primary conduct and treat [the defendant] as though it were a Bolivian individual.[122]

The court reviewed the structure and legislative history of § 1606, noting that despite plaintiff's reading, in enacting § 1606 Congress said that the FSIA was "not intended to affect the substantive law of liability."[123] The court held that "section 1606 is concerned with the liability of a foreign state for damages, and does not alter basic rules of primary conduct that govern contract formation. . . . this conclusion is consistent both with the language and purpose of the FSIA and with basic contract principles, which establish that the issue of contract formation precedes, and is distinct from, the issue of liability for breach."[124]

Venue in FSIA cases is controlled by 28 U.S.C.A. § 1391(f), which provides:

> (f) A civil action against a foreign state as defined in section 1603(a) of this title may be brought—
>
> (1) in any judicial district in which a substantial part of the event or omissions giving rise to the claim occurred, or a substantial part of the property that is the subject of the action is situated;
>
> (2) in any judicial district in which the vessel or cargo of a foreign state is situated, if the claim is asserted under section 1605(b) of this section;
>
> (3) in any judicial district in which the agency or instrumentality is licensed to do business or is doing business, if the action is brought against an agency or instrumentality of a foreign state as defined in section 1603(b) of this title; or
>
> (4) in the United States District Court for the District of Columbia if the action is brought against a foreign state or political subdivision thereof.

The four subsections provide separate rules for different types of defendants and actions under the FSIA.

As to claims against foreign states or political subdivisions, venue is proper in both the District of Columbia under subsection (f)(4) and for commercial or tort actions in the appropriate forum under subsection

122. *Id.* at 1276.
123. *Id.*
124. *Id.* at 1277 (citations omitted).

(f)(1). As to claims against instrumentalities of foreign states, subsection (f)(3) provides that venue is proper only where the instrumentality is licensed to do or is doing business. Finally, in admiralty cases under section 1605(b) of the FSIA, venue is proper only where the vessel or cargo is located.[125]

Practice Note: In contracts with parties that may be eligible to avail themselves of the FSIA in any litigation arising from the contract, a waiver of any objections to venue—especially by instrumentalities—should be considered. Although section 1391(f) does not explicitly provide for waiver, as with venue in general, the legislative history of the FSIA explains that "venue in any court could be waived by a foreign state, such as by failing to object to improper venue in a timely manner."[126] Given the relatively more restrictive venue provisions for instrumentalities, advance planning on this issue could make any eventual litigation more convenient for the parties.

The operation of the venue provision as to foreign state defendants is illustrated by the court's decision in *Tifa Ltd. v. Republic of Ghana.*[127] At issue in *Tifa* was whether venue in a suit against Ghana was proper in a forum convenient to the plaintiff, New Jersey, under the act or omission provision of subsection (f)(1) of the FSIA venue rule, or in the District of Columbia under subsection (f)(4).[128] After reviewing the contacts alleged to exist with New Jersey, the court held that venue was improper under subsection (f)(1) because "a substantial part of the acts or omissions which give rise to this action did not occur in New Jersey . . . ."[129] Consequently, the court granted Ghana's motion to transfer the action to the District of Columbia.[130]

In reviewing the precedent under the FSIA venue provision, the court in *Tifa* noted that "extensive events or omissions giving rise to a claim" are required before venue can be proper,[131] and observed that the

125. *See* Restatement (Third), *supra* note 6, § 457, cmt. d.

126. House Report, *supra* note 1, at 32.

127. 692 F. Supp. 393 (D.N.J. 1988).

128. *Id.* at 405.

129. *Id.* at 406.

130. *Id.* at 407.

131. *Id.* at 405 (citing Schmidt v. Polish People's Republic, 579 F. Supp. 23, 28 (S.D.N.Y. 1983), *aff'd,* 742 F.2d 67 (2d Cir. 1984) (finding extensive contacts justified venue in New York under § 1391(f)(1)); Translinear, Inc. v. Republic of Haiti, 538 F. Supp. 141, 144–45 (D.D.C. 1982) (finding extensive contacts justified venue in Texas under § 1391(f)(1)).

mere presence of plaintiff's corporate headquarters is insufficient to satisfy the requirements for venue under subsection (f)(1).[132]

[3] Absence of Jury Trials and Limitation of Damages Under the FSIA

An important feature of litigation as opposed to arbitration or other means of international dispute resolution is the role of the jury. To plaintiffs, the jury can be an important feature of resolution of a dispute in court as opposed to arbitration. In drafting the FSIA, Congress explicitly granted the federal courts jurisdiction over "non-jury civil action[s] against a foreign state. . . ."[133] Moreover, section 1441(d), the FSIA removal provision, provides that "upon removal, the action shall be tried by the court without a jury."[134] The legislative history explains that the reason for Congress' jury trial prohibition is twofold; first, it parallels treatment of the U.S. Government in litigation; second, it "will tend to promote a uniformity in decision where foreign governments are involved."[135]

Several other issues have arisen in relation to the jury trial prohibition that have resulted in several important decisions under the FSIA. In an effort to avoid the "non-jury" jurisdictional grant of section 1330(a), plaintiffs have asserted jurisdiction over actions against foreign states under section 1332, which does not bar jury trials. In perhaps the leading case on the issue, *Ruggerio v. Compania Peruana De Vapores*,[136] the court rejected the section 1332 alternative, and explained that:

> The courts must learn to accept that, in place of the familiar dichotomy of federal question and diversity jurisdiction, the Immunities Act has created a tripartite division—federal question cases, diversity cases and actions against foreign states. If a case falls within the third division, there is to be no jury trial even if it might also come within one of the other two.[137]

---

132. *Tifa*, at 405 (citing Falcoal, Inc. v. Turkiye Komur Isletmelori Kurumu, 660 F. Supp. 1536, 1543 (S.D. Tex. 1987) (finding plaintiff's headquarters insufficient for venue purposes if defendant has insufficient contacts with forum)).

133. 28 U.S.C.A. § 1330(a) (1994).

134. For a discussion of the FSIA removal provision, *see infra* § 7.03[2].

135. House Report, *supra* note 1, at 13.

136. 639 F.2d 872 (2d Cir. 1981).

137. *Id.* at 876. *See also* Rex v. Pervana De Vapores, S.A., 660 F.2d 61, 69 (3d Cir. 1981), *cert. denied*, 456 U.S. 926 (1982); Williams v. Shipping Corp. of India, 653 F.2d 875,

Following *Ruggerio,* the courts have consistently found that a jury trial is not available under the FSIA.[138] For instance, in *Kraikeman v. Sabena Belgian World Airlines,*[139] the court considered an action against Sabena (an instrumentality of a foreign state) under the Age Discrimination in Employment Act (ADEA). The court held that although a jury trial is available under the ADEA, it is not available if the ADEA suit is against a foreign state or instrumentality.[140] The court found that, "Because of the limited grant of jurisdiction in 28 U.S.C. § 1330, there is no jury trial in actions against foreign states . . . in federal courts, regardless of whether the basis of jurisdiction is diversity of citizenship or a federal question."[141] "The law regarding actions against foreign sovereigns is *sui generis* . . . and there is no reason to suppose that Congress intended to alter it by the 1978 amendment specifying jury trials of ADEA actions against private employers and local and state governments."[142]

In addition to the absence of a jury trial, punitive damages are not available in tort suits under the FSIA against foreign states. Section 1606 of the FSIA provides that a "foreign state shall be liable in the same manner and to the same extent as a private individual under like circumstances; *but a foreign state except for an agency or instrumentality thereof shall not be liable for punitive damages.*"[143] Specifically excepted from the rule are agencies and instrumentalities defined under section 1603(b), against whom punitive damages may be enforced. The legislative history explains that, as a matter of "current international practice, punitive damages are usually not assessed against foreign states."[144]

881–83 (4th Cir. 1981), *cert. denied,* 455 U.S. 982 (1982); Herman v. El Al Israel Airlines, Ltd., 502 F. Supp. 277, 280 (S.D.N.Y. 1980), *cert. denied,* 455 U.S. 982 (1982).

138. *See, e.g.,* Universal Consol. Cos., Inc.v. Bank of China, 35 F.3d 243 (6th Cir. 1994) (no jury trial available in suit against Bank of China, instrumentality of foreign state). Note that the rule does not apply to the U.S. subsidiary of a foreign company owned by a foreign state. *See* Gould v. Aerospatiale Helicopter Corp., 40 F.3d 1033 (9th Cir. 1994).

139. 674 F. Supp. 136 (S.D.N.Y. 1987).

140. *Id.* at 137.

141. *Id.* (citing *Ruggerio,* 689 F.2d 872 (2d Cir. 1981)).

142. *Id.* at 138. *See also* Compagnie Nationale Air France, 699 F. Supp. 1016, 1017 (D.P.R. 1988) (granting motion to strike jury trial in action against instrumentality of foreign state, noting that "Congress was not required to allow jury trials because, at common law, no civil actions were allowed against foreign states, and thus the Seventh Amendment is inapplicable").

143. 28 U.S.C.A. § 1606 (emphasis added).

144. House Report, *supra* note 1, at 22.

§ 7.04 IMMUNITY AND JURISDICTION UNDER THE FSIA

[1] Special Nature of Jurisdiction Under the FSIA

In *Verlinden B.V. v. Central Bank of Nigeria*,[145] the Supreme Court held that the FSIA's grant of jurisdiction to the federal courts over suits between aliens and foreign states was constitutional. This important ruling on the scope of jurisdiction under the FSIA also contains important observations on the nature of immunity and jurisdiction under the FSIA. First, the Supreme Court described the analysis of jurisdictional issues:

> Under the Act . . . both statutory subject matter jurisdiction (otherwise known as ''competence'') and personal jurisdiction turn on application of the substantive provisions of the Act. . . . . Thus, if none of the exceptions to sovereign immunity set forth in the Act applies, the District Court lacks both subject matter jurisdiction and personal jurisdiction.[146]

In addition, the Court clarified that the burden of establishing the existence of jurisdiction through an exception to immunity rests with the court in the absence of an appearance by the foreign state, ''even if the foreign state does not enter an appearance to assert an immunity defense, a district court must still determine that immunity is unavailable under the Act.''[147]

Under the FSIA, immunity is not merely a defense, it goes to jurisdiction itself, the power of the court to adjudicate the action. For example, the legislative history explains:

> A judgment dismissing the action for lack of jurisdiction because the foreign state is entitled to sovereign immunity would be determinative of the question of sovereign immunity. Thus, a private party, who lost on the question of jurisdiction, could not bring the same case in a state court claiming that the federal court's decision extended only to the question of federal jurisdiction and not to sovereign immunity.[148]

On this issue, the District of Columbia Circuit has noted that ''[s]overeign Immunity under the FSIA is thus a gateway issue, not

145. 461 U.S. 480 (1983).

146. *Id.* at 485 n.5. *But see* Princz v. Federal Republic of Germany, 813 F. Supp. 22, 27 (D.D.C. 1992) (finding jurisdiction despite absence of any exceptions to immunity), *rev'd*, 26 F.3d 1166 (D.C. Cir. 1994).

147. 461 U.S. 480, at 493 n.20.

148. House Report, *supra* note 1, at 13.

simply a plea in defense to a claim: if the foreign state is entitled to immunity with respect to the claim asserted, then the district court lacks both subject matter and personal jurisdiction, and must dismiss the case.''[149] Conversely, where one of the FSIA exceptions to immunity applies, the U.S. court has personal jurisdiction over the Defendant. The legislative history of the FSIA suggests that constitutional due process requirements of personal jurisdiction are satisfied under the exceptions.[149.1]

[2] Exclusivity of Jurisdiction Under the FSIA

A lingering question following the enactment of the FSIA was whether the revised jurisdictional provisions in section 1330(a) provided the exclusive basis for jurisdiction over suits against foreign sovereigns. The question arose in at least two contexts. The first involved cases in which plaintiffs sought to avoid the FSIA's jury trial bar, and attempted to rely on diversity jurisdiction, which carries no such bar.[150] The second context in which the exclusivity issue arose was whether suit could be maintained against a foreign state under the Alien Tort Claims Act (''Alien Tort Statute'').[151]

In *Argentine Republic v. Amerada Hess Shipping Corp.*,[152] the Supreme Court held that the FSIA provides the exclusive basis of federal jurisdiction over suits against foreign states.[153] At issue in *Amerada Hess* was whether a suit for an alleged tort committed by a foreign sovereign, Argentina, could be maintained in federal court under the Alien Tort Statute, or ''ATS.'' The ATS confers ''original jurisdiction of any civil action by an alien for a tort only, committed in violation of the law of nations or a treaty of the United States.''[154] The district court

---

149. Practical Concepts, Inc. v. Republic of Bolivia, 811 F.2d 1543, 1544–45 (D.C. Cir. 1987).

149.1 H.R. Rep. No. 1487, 94th Cong., 2d Sess., *reprinted in* 1976 U.S. Code Admin. News at 6613 (''Significantly, each of the immunity provisions in the bill, sections 1605-1607, requires some connection between the lawsuit and the United States. These immunity provisions, prescribe the necessary contacts which must exist before our courts can exercise personal jurisdiction''). *See also* Altmann v. Republic of Austria, 142 F. Supp. 2d 1187, 1206 (C.D. Cal. 2001) (analyzing case law on this issue).

150. *See* Herman v. El Al Israel Airlines, Ltd., 502 F. Supp. 277, 279 (S.D.N.Y. 1980). The FSIA jury trial issue is discussed *supra* in § 7.03[3].

151. 28 U.S.C.A. § 1350.

152. 488 U.S. 428 (1989).

153. *Id.* at 443.

154. 28 U.S.C.A. § 1350.

granted Argentina's motion to dismiss the claims as barred by the FSIA.[155]

On appeal, the Second Circuit reversed, holding that in enacting the FSIA, Congress did not intend to supplant "existing remedies in United States Courts for violations of international law" by foreign states under the Alien Tort Statute.[156] The Second Circuit reasoned that the FSIA's focus on "commercial concerns" and Congress' failure to explicitly repeal the ATS signalled its design to permit continued jurisdiction over eligible suits against foreign states separate from the FSIA.[157]

The Supreme Court reversed, holding that the FSIA provides the exclusive basis of jurisdiction over suits against foreign states.[158] The Court stated that "the text and structure of the FSIA demonstrate Congress' intention that the FSIA be the sole basis for obtaining jurisdiction over a foreign state in our courts."[159] Although jurisdiction under the ATS remains for suits against non-sovereign defendants,[160] the Court held that "immunity is granted in those cases involving illegal violations of international law that do not come within one of the FSIA's exceptions."[161]

After concluding that any ATS grant of jurisdiction over foreign sovereigns did not survive the FSIA,[162] the Court examined whether the suit could proceed under the FSIA, that is, whether any of the FSIA's enumerated exceptions applied.[163] After review of the claims and the facts, the Court agreed with the district court that "none of the FSIA's exceptions" was applicable.[164]

The *Amerada Hess* decision establishes the exclusivity of the FSIA as a jurisdictional basis in suits against foreign states. Under *Amerada*

155. 638 F. Supp. 73, 77 (S.D.N.Y. 1986).

156. 830 F.2d 421, 426 (2d Cir. 1987).

157. *Id.* at 426–27. For a cogent analysis of several of the failings of the Second Circuit's analysis that are not fully revealed in the Supreme Court opinion, *see* Frederic L. Kirgis, *Alien Tort Claims, Sovereign Immunity and International Law in U.S. Courts*, 82 AM. J. INT'L L. 323 (1988).

158. 488 U.S. at 443.

159. *Id.* at 434.

160. *Id.* at 438 (observing "same effect after the passage of the FSIA as before with respect to defendants other than foreign states").

161. *Id.*

162. The Court noted that only one reported case found jurisdiction over a foreign state under the ATS, a case decided after the enactment of the FSIA. *Id.* at 436 (citing Von Dardel v. Union of Soviet Socialist Republics, 623 F. Supp. 246 (D.D.C. 1985)).

163. *Id.* at 439.

164. *Id.*

Hess, the Court has strengthened the FSIA by removing any question of the scope or overlap of other jurisdictional grants in cases involving suits against foreign states.[165]

[3] Retroactivity of the FSIA

As a general proposition, the enactment of the FSIA does not ''affect the substantive law of liability;''[166] the merits of a particular claim will be decided according to the applicable law—including choice of law rules—of the forum jurisdiction.[167] This feature of the FSIA was reflected in several cases in which courts held that the FSIA did not operate ''retroactively'' to re-activate claims that may have existed but were then barred prior to the enactment of the FSIA.[168] Some courts concluded that the FSIA did apply retroactively.[169]

165. *See* Saudi Arabia v. Nelson, 507 U.S. 349 (1993); Republic of Argentina v. Weltover, Inc., 504 U.S. 607 (1992); Commercial Bank of Kuwait v. Rafidain Bank, 15 F.3d 238, 240 (2d Cir. 1994); Gould, Inc. v. Mitsui Mining & Smelting Co., Ltd., 750 F. Supp. 838, 844 (N.D. Ohio 1990) (holding RICO inapplicable in action against foreign state instrumentality). *See generally* Peter D. Trooboff, *International Decisions*, 83 Am. J. Int'l L. 565 (1989) (discussing *Amerada Hess*).

166. House Report, *supra* note 1, at 12. *See also* First Nat'l City Bank v. Banco Para El Comercio Exterior De Cuba, 462 U.S. 611, 620 (1983).

167. *Id.*

168. *See, e.g.*, Carl Marks & Co., Inc. v. Union of Soviet Socialist Republics, 841 F.2d 26, 27 (2d Cir. 1988) (FSIA inapplicable to claims arising before 1952 adoption of restrictive theory), *cert. denied*, 487 U.S. 1219 (1988); Jackson v. People's Republic of China, 794 F.2d 1490, 1499 (11th Cir. 1986) (finding no retroactive application of FSIA to repudiation of debt occurring prior to 1952), *cert. denied*, 480 U.S. 917 (1987); Slade v. United States of Mexico, 617 F. Supp. 351, 358 (D.D.C. 1985) (''retroactive application of the Act would repudiate the immunity of foreign sovereigns for transactions predating 1952 and thus be inconsistent with Congress' intent not to affect the substantive law of liability''), *aff'd mem.*, 790 F.2d 163 (D.C. Cir. 1986), *cert. denied*, 479 U.S. 1032 (1987); Schmidt v. Polish People's Republic, 742 F.2d 67, 71 (2d Cir. 1984) (''nothing . . . [in FSIA] indicates that . . . wholesale reactivation of ancient claims was intended''); Corporacion Venezolana de Fomento v. Vintero Sales Corp., 629 F.2d 786, 791 (2d Cir. 1980) (holding FSIA does not provide basis for jurisdiction in case pending at time Act became law); Djordjevich v. Bundesminister Der Finanzen, 827 F. Supp. 814, 816–17 (D.D.C. 1993) (finding FSIA not retroactive to event that occurred in 1941); Ye-Shih Lin v. Government of Japan, 1994 U.S. Dist. LEXIS 6061, at 3 (D.D.C. May 6, 1994) (FSIA does not apply retroactively to permit suit for conduct prior to the FSIA; plaintiffs sought to collect on obligations held by Japan in 1924; court held that ''Prior to May 1952, Japan would not have anticipated being sued in a United States court. Retroactive liability cannot be imposed under these circumstances.''). *See also* Princz v. Federal Republic of Germany, 23 F.3d 1166, 1170–71 (D.C. Cir. 1994) (discussion of retroactivity issue).

169. *See, e.g., Princz,* note 169, *supra*, 26 F.3d at 1170 (''[t]here is a strong argument in favor of applying the FSIA retroactively''); Crist v. Republic of Turkey, 995 F. Supp. 5 (D.D.C. 1998) (''this court is satisfied that Congress intended the FSIA to be applied retroactively'').

The debate over retroactivity of the FSIA was resolved in *Republic of Austria v. Altmann.*[170] The facts in *Altmann* concerned liability of Austria for valuable art stolen by the Nazis in World War Two from Ms. Altmann's ancestors. The Court affirmed the 9th Circuit and ruled that the FSIA applies to all claims, including Ms. Altmann's, regardless of when the conduct at issue occurred. The Court ruled that retroactive application of the FSIA was not impermissible and violated no dictate of Congress.[171] The Court found clear evidence that Congress intended the Act to apply to pre-enactment conduct.:

> . . . the preamble of the FSIA expresses Congress' understanding that the Act would apply to all postenactment claims of sovereign immunity. That section provides: ''*Claims* of foreign states to immunity should *henceforth* be decided by courts of the United States and of the States in conformity with the principles set forth in this chapter.''[172]

Summary & Practice Note: This Chapter is organized in an order roughly comparable to that in which counsel should consider issues under the FSIA as the case is prepared. After addressing the general jurisdictional and immunity issues discussed in § 7.04, counsel should turn to the specific provisions establishing the presence or absence of an exception to immunity. The jurisdictional calculus under section 1605 of the FSIA involves analysis of the eight categories under which a foreign state will not be entitled to immunity. If one or more exceptions are satisfied, jurisdiction exists and the case moves to the merits. In § 7.05, each exception is examined in turn.[173]

§ 7.05 EXCEPTION ONE: WAIVER OF IMMUNITY

[1] The FSIA Waiver Provision

The first exception to sovereign immunity under the FSIA is satisfied when a foreign sovereign waives its right to immunity. As one court stated: ''Unlike other questions of subject matter jurisdiction . . .

170. 541 U.S. 677, 124 S. Ct. 2240, 159 L. Ed 2d 1 (2004).
171. 124 S. Ct. at 2252-53.
172. *Id.*, 124 S. Ct. at 2252-53 (*quoting* 28 U.S.C. § 1602).
173. *See* § 7.14, *infra*, for a discussion of personal jurisdiction issues under the FSIA.

the defense can be waived 'either explicitly or by implication.' "[174] Waivers of immunity cannot be revoked unilaterally.[175]

The text of the waiver exception is contained in section 1605(a)(1) of the FSIA, which provides:

> (a) A foreign state shall not be immune from the jurisdiction of courts of the United States or of the States in any case-(1) in which the foreign state has waived its immunity either explicitly or by implication, notwithstanding any withdrawal of the waiver which the foreign state may purport to effect except in accordance with the terms of the waiver.

In conformance with the dichotomy in the statute between explicit and implicit waivers of immunity, they are discussed below in turn.

An important conceptual distinction in analyzing waivers is the separate treatment under the FSIA of the issues of immunity from jurisdiction and immunity from attachment and execution.[176] A waiver analysis must be performed for both types of immunity, as a waiver of either will generally not suffice to waive the other. Cases discussing this issue are included below.

[2] Explicit Waiver of Immunity Under the FSIA

Section 1605(a)(1) provides an exception to jurisdictional immunity if the foreign sovereign explicitly waives its sovereign immunity. In describing what it contemplated would qualify as an explicit waiver, Congress explained that:

> [a] foreign state may renounce its immunity by treaty, as has been done by the United States with respect to commercial and other activities in a series of treaties of friendship, commerce, and navigation, or a foreign state may waive its immunity in a contract with a private party . . . .[177]

One of the best examples of an explicit waiver of immunity in a contract is that considered in *Proyecfin de Venezuela, S.A. v. Banco*

174. Canadian Overseas Ores Ltd. v. Compania De Acero del Pacifico S.A., 727 F.2d 274, 277 (2d Cir. 1984). In Marlowe v. Argentine Naval Comm'n, 604 F. Supp. 703 (D.D.C. 1985), the court explicitly rejected the argument that jurisdiction must still be found if a waiver has occurred. *Id.* at 709–710.

175. House Report, *supra* note 1, at 18.

176. *Compare* 28 U.S.C.A. § 1605 *with* 28 U.S.C.A. § 1610.

177. House Report, *supra* note 1, at 18.

Industrial de Venezuela.[178] Proyecfin, a privately owned Venezuelan development corporation, had entered into a loan agreement with a Venezuelan bank. The agreement included a ''Supervisory Contract'' which clearly stated that ''the foregoing waiver of immunity shall have effect under and be construed in accordance with the United States Sovereign Immunities Act [of] 1976.''[179-181] A waiver this unambiguous is rarely litigated, and need not be so explicit to be considered effective. It is clear, however, that merely entering into a contract with a foreign state

(*Text continued on page 7-33*)

178. 760 F.2d 390 (2d Cir. 1985).
179-181. *Id.* at 393.

does not constitute an express waiver of immunity.[182] When a waiver is included in the contract the terminology expressing the waiver, whether found in a treaty or in a contract, must be precise.[183] As one court noted, the waiver must be an "intentional and knowing relinquishment of the legal right."[184]

Under the FSIA, explicit waiver can also occur by virtue of provisions contained in an international agreement. For instance, in *Harris Corp. v. National Iranian Radio & Television*,[185] the court considered whether a clause in the Treaty of Amity, Economic Relations, and Consular Rights Between the United States and Iran operated as an explicit waiver of immunity. In pertinent part, the clause stated:

> No enterprise of either high contracting party, including corporations, associations, and government agencies and instrumentalities, which is publicly owned or controlled shall, if it engages in commercial, industrial, shipping or other business activities, within the territories of the other high contracting party, claim or enjoy for either itself or for its property, immunity therein from taxation, suit, execution or judgment or other liability in which privately owned and controlled enterprises are subject therein.[186]

The court found this clause sufficient to constitute an explicit waiver of immunity by the defendant.[187]

In contrast, in *O'Connell Machinery Co. v. M.V. Americana*,[188] the Second Circuit refused to find an explicit waiver of immunity from prejudgment attachment pursuant to a Treaty of Friendship, Commerce and Navigation between the United States and Italy. The language used, in what are commonly called FCNs, was deemed to be too narrow to constitute an explicit waiver of immunity to prejudgment attachment.

---

182. Friedar v. Government of Israel, 614 F. Supp. 395 (S.D.N.Y. 1985).

183. Waivers of immunity found in treaties may not be interpreted as waiving immunity from prejudgment attachment. *See* S & S Machinery Co. v. Masinexportimport, 706 F.2d 411, 417 (2d Cir. 1983), *cert. denied,* 464 U.S. 856 (1984); O'Connell Machinery Co., Inc. v. M.V. Americana, 566 F. Supp. 1381, 1384 (S.D.N.Y. 1983), *aff'd,* 734 F.2d 115 (2d Cir.), *cert. denied,* 469 U.S. 1086 (1984). On the issue of waivers effective for attachment and execution purposes, *see infra* § 7.17.

184. Castro v. Saudi Arabia, 510 F. Supp. 309, 312 (W.D. Tex. 1980) (citing Mitchell v. Aetna, 579 F.2d 342, 347 (5th Cir. 1978)).

185. 691 F.2d 1344 (11th Cir. 1982).

186. *Id.* at 1350.

187. *Harris,* 691 F.2d at 1350–51.

188. 734 F.2d 115 (2d Cir.), *cert. denied,* 469 U.S. 1086 (1984).

The words used in the Treaty, that the parties "shall [not] . . . claim . . . immunity . . . from any other liability", were held not to be an express waiver of immunity under section 1605(a)(1).[189] The court was particularly concerned with a perceived attempt on the part of the plaintiffs to obtain jurisdiction by means of a prejudgment attachment.

On the issue of prejudgment attachment and explicit waiver,[190] it is important to note the court's finding that "prejudgment attachment is permitted only where the foreign state explicitly has waived its immunity. . . ."[191] A waiver of attachment may not be sufficient for purposes of jurisdiction; prudent counsel will seek to include both in any agreements with FSIA parties.

Practice Note: Counsel should not be distracted by the text of the FSIA which seems to contain what could be considered waiver provisions in other sections. For instance, there is qualifying language to the jurisdictional grants in section 1330(a) ("under any applicable international agreement") and section 1604 ("subject to existing international agreements to which the United States is a party at the time of enactment of this Act"). These provisos have been interpreted by the courts to have been subsumed in the explicit waiver provision of section 1605(a)(1).[192] Because the purpose of the existing agreements language was intended to demonstrate Congress' desire not to undermine any existing agreements,[193] courts have not generally read an expansive grant of jurisdiction into the provisos that exceeds the specific exception to immunity contained in section 1605(a)(1).[194]

In an example of an explicit waiver not specifically contemplated by the legislative history, the court in *Hercaire Int'l, Inc. v. Argentina*,[195] found that in its answer to the complaint, the foreign sovereign

---

189. *Id.* at 117–18. *See also* S & S Machinery Co. v. Masinexportimport, 706 F.2d 411, 417 (2d Cir. 1983), *cert. denied*, 464 U.S. 856 (1984); Foremost-McKesson v. Islamic Republic of Iran, 905 F.2d 438, 451–52 (D.C. Cir. 1990). *But see* Calgarth Investments, Ltd. v. Bank Saderat Iran, 1996 WL 204470 (S.D.N.Y. 1996) (finding waiver of immunity by treaty).

190. *See infra* § 7.17.

191. *O'Connell*, 734 F.2d, at 117.

192. *Compare* Harris Corp. v. National Iranian Radio & Television, 691 F.2d 1344, 1350 n.11 (11th Cir. 1982) (discussing overlap of §§ 1330(a) and 1605(a)(1) with Colonial Bank v. CGMF, 645 F. Supp. 1457, 1460–61 (S.D.N.Y. 1986) (analyzing preexisting treaty under §§ 1604 and 1605(a)(1)).

193. *See* House Report, *supra* note 1, at 12 (expressing intent not to override or preempt preexisting agreements as to immunity).

194. *See supra* note 179 and accompanying text.

195. 642 F. Supp. 126 (S.D. Fla. 1986), *rev'd*, 821 F.2d 559, 565 (11th Cir. 1987).

"explicitly waived its sovereign immunity *and that of its agencies.*"[196] At issue in *Hercaire* was whether the explicit waiver as to jurisdiction operated as an implicit waiver as to attachment.[197] Although the district court found that Congress contemplated implicit waivers in such circumstances,[198] the court of appeals reversed, holding that an explicit waiver as to jurisdiction did not operate as an implicit waiver as to execution.[199] The Court of Appeals' ruling reinforces the need for counsel representing non-sovereign parties to seek explicit waivers of both jurisdiction and attachment in commercial agreements.[200]

[3] Implicit Waiver of Immunity Under the FSIA

Section 1605(a)(1) also contemplates implicit waivers of sovereign immunity from jurisdiction. The legislative history specifies three situations in which a waiver of sovereign immunity may be implied. These include situations in which the foreign defendant has appeared in the court (or filed a responsive pleading in an action without raising the defense of immunity),[201] or agreed to arbitrate in another country,[202] or allowed the law of a particular country to govern a contract.[203] The House Report states:

> With respect to implicit waivers, the courts have found such waivers in cases where a foreign state has agreed to arbitration in another country or where a foreign state has agreed that the law of a particular country should govern a contract. An implicit waiver would also include a

---

196. *Id.* at 128 (emphasis in original).

197. *Id.*

198. The district court stated:

> When a foreign state or agency willingly consents to suit in the courts of the United States, files a counterclaim against the Plaintiff, and subjects the court to a full-scale trial on the merits, it cannot, when it discovers it has lost the suit, invoke its sovereign immunity with respect to execution. *Id.* at 129, *rev'd,* 821 F.2d 559, 565 (11th Cir. 1987).

199. 821 F.2d 559, 565 (11th Cir. 1987).

200. *See* Georges R. Delaume, *The Foreign Sovereign Immunities Act and Public Debt Litigation: Some Fifteen Years Later,* 88 AM. J. INT'L L. 257, 267 (1994).

201. *See generally* Canadian Overseas Ores, Ltd. v. Compania de Acero del Pacifico S.A., 727 F.2d 274 (2d Cir. 1984). *But see* Drexel Burnham Lambert Group, Inc. v. Committee of Receivers, 12 F.3d 317, 327 (2d Cir. 1993).

202. *See generally* Birch Shipping Corp. v. Embassy of United Republic of Tanzania, 507 F. Supp. 311 (D.D.C. 1980).

203. *See generally* Marlowe v. Argentine Naval Comm'n, 604 F. Supp. 703 (D.D.C. 1985).

situation where a foreign state has filed a responsive pleading in an action without raising the defense of sovereign immunity.[204]

Courts have been reluctant to find implicit waivers in circumstances other than those identified in the legislative history and absent definite and precise language, but have confronted actions involving allegations of all three forms of implicit waivers contemplated by Congress. The D.C. Circuit recently concluded that the case precedents are "virtually unanimous . . . construing the implied waiver provision narrowly."[205] The *Creighton* Court further observed "that implicit in § 1605(a)(1) is the requirement that the foreign state have intended to waive its sovereign immunity.[206]

With respect to an implied waiver by virtue of an arbitration agreement, contracts with foreign states and instrumentalities often contain agreements stipulating that disputes arising from the transaction shall be submitted to arbitration.

Because of the frequent use of arbitration clauses and strict construction of the implied waiver provision, courts have held that merely agreeing to arbitrate does not waive immunity. As noted by the D.C. Circuit in *Creighton*:[207]

> [I]f the language of the legislative history [were] applied literally, a foreign government would be subject to the United States's jurisdiction simply because it agreed to have the contract governed by another country's laws, or agreed to arbitrate in a country other than itself, even though the agreement made no reference to the United States. Such an interpretation of §§ 1605(a)(1)'s "implicit waiver" exception would vastly increase the jurisdiction of the federal courts over matters involving sensitive foreign relations.

In *Creighton*, therefore, the Court found that Qatar did not implicitly waive immunity where Qatar merely agreed to arbitrate in France.[207.1] If,

204. House Report, *supra* note 1, at 18.

205. Creighton Ltd. v. Gov't of State of Qatar, 181 F.3d 118 (D.C. Cir. July 2, 1999, *reh'g en banc denied*, Sept. 7, 1999) (citation omitted).

206. *Id.*, *citing* Princz v. Federal Republic of Germany, 26 F.3d 1166, 1174 (D.C. Cir. 1994); Foremost-McKesson, Inc. v. Islamic Republic of Iran, 905 F.2d 438, 444 (D.C. Cir. 1990).

207. *Supra* note 205.

207.1. Although France is a signatory to the N.Y. Convention, Qatar is not. Nor is Qatar a signatory to another agreement with the U.S. to enforce an arbitral award. Other courts have found an implied waiver of immunity irrespective of the State-Defendant's treaty status. *Cf.* M.B.L. Int'l Contractors v. Republic of Trinidad & Tobago, 725 F. Supp. 52, 54–55 (D.D.C. 1989); Ipitrade Int'l S.A. v. Federal Republic of Nigeria, 465 F. Supp. 824, 826 (D.D.C. 1978).

however, Qatar had been a signatory to the New York Convention[207.2] or other agreement with the United States to enforce foreign arbitral awards, an implied waiver of immunity may have been found.

> In *Seetransport* the Second Circuit reasoned, correctly we think, that "when a country becomes a signatory to the Convention, by the very provisions of the Convention, the signatory state must have contemplated enforcement actions in other signatory states." 989 F.2d at 578.[207.3]

In *Maritime Int'l Nominees Estab. v.*

(*Text continued on page 7-37*)

Id. See Seetransport Wiking Trader Schiffarhtgesellschaft MBH & Co. v. Navimpex Centrala Navala, 989 F.2d 572, 577 (2d Cir. 1993) (implicit waiver generally does not occur merely by entering into contract naming a third country for arbitration or choosing which law applies; however, when arbitration had already occurred with knowledge the enforcement was possible, waiver occurred); *cf.* Shapiro v. Republic of Bolivia, 930 F.2d 1013, 1017 (2d Cir. 1991). *See also* Birch Shipping Corp. v. Embassy of United Republic of Tanzania, 507 F. Supp. 311 (D.D.C. 1980).

207.2. The New York Convention on the Recognition and Enforcement of Foreign Arbitral Awards is discussed *infra* § 12.06.)

207.3. *Creighton, supra* note 205.

Republic of Guinea,[208] a commercial contract between Maritime International and the Republic of Guinea stipulated that all disputes resulting from the contract would be settled by arbitration conducted by the International Center for the Settlement of Investment Disputes (ICSID). The plaintiff argued that designating the ICSID implicitly designated Washington, D.C., because ICSID is located in Washington, D.C.[209] Despite ICSID's location in Washington, D.C., the court held that it was not foreseeable that traditional United States courts would become involved in dispute resolution.[210] Plaintiff's contention that an implicit waiver of sovereign immunity by Guinea had occurred was therefore rejected.[211]

The second form of implied waiver contemplated by Congress involves the designation of a particular law as governing any disputes arising from the contract. Such a recognition operates as an acceptance of the submission of the dispute to legal resolution, and may constitute an implied waiver of immunity. For instance, in *Marlowe v. Argentine Naval Comm'n*,[212] the court held that a choice of law clause constituted an implied waiver of immunity.[213] In the agreement at issue, the choice of law clause provided that the contract "shall be governed by and construed in accordance with the laws of the District of Columbia."[214] The court found that precedent on the issue was clear: "if the parties to a contract agree that the laws of one country will govern contractual interpretations, they have implicitly waived the defense of sovereign immunity."[215]

208. 693 F.2d 1094 (D.C. Cir. 1982), *cert. denied*, 464 U.S. 815 (1984).

209. *Id.* at 1100.

210. *Id.* at 1104.

211. *Id.*

212. 604 F. Supp. 703 (D.D.C. 1985).

213. *Id.* at 708–09.

214. *Id.* at 708.

215. *Id.* at 709 (citing Resource Dynamics Int'l Ltd. v. General People's Committee, 593 F. Supp. 572, 575 (N.D. Ga. 1984) (finding implicit waiver by choice of Virginia law); Ohntrup v. Firearms Center, Inc., 516 F. Supp. 1281, 1284–85 (E.D. Pa. 1981) (dicta on rationale for implicit waiver by choice of law clause); Ipitrade Int'l, S.A. v. Federal Republic of Nigeria, 465 F. Supp. 824, 826 (D.D.C. 1978) (finding waiver by choice of Swiss law); Eckert International Inc. v. Government of Fiji, 32 F.2d 77 (4th Cir. 1994) (Fiji's execution of agreement designating the law of Virginia constituted implicit waiver of immunity); Berdakin v. Consulado de La Republica de El Salvador, 912 F. Supp. 458 (C.D. Cal. 1995) (finding implicit waiver from agreement to application of California law). *But see* Eaglet Corporation Limited v. Banco Central de Nicaragua, 839 F. Supp. 232, 234–235 (S.D.N.Y. 1993) (holding that executing agreement providing for application of English law not a waiver).

The final form of implicit waiver of immunity contemplated by Congress involves an implicit waiver through a foreign sovereign defendant's participation in litigation without invoking immunity.[216] At issue in such a case is whether responsive pleadings or an appearance in court constitutes waiver of sovereign immunity by a foreign defendant.[217]

In *Canadian Overseas Ores, Ltd. v. Compania De Acero del Pacifico S.A.*,[218] the court was faced with the issue of whether the defendant had implicitly waived its immunity by failing to raise the defense until after it had filed several motions and participated in limited discovery.[219] The court found that the defendant had not waived immunity because the motions were not pleadings as contemplated by Congress in designing the waiver provision, and certain types of participation do not automatically result in waiver.[220] The court issued a warning, however, to all FSIA defendants:

> We emphasize that our affirmance here in no way detracts from the discretionary authority of the district courts to effect an earlier resolution of the issue by requiring . . . assertion or abandonment of the defense prior to a responsive pleading. Nor do we wish to encourage parties considering assertion of the defense of sovereign immunity to procrastinate. Security lies either in the early assertion of the defense or in securing a deadline from the district court for its assertion.[221]

Other cases have dealt with other forms of implicit waivers, including for example, whether an implicit waiver can result from participation in international agreements such as the United Nations Charter and the Helsinki Accords. In *Frolova v. Union of Soviet Socialist Republics*,[222] a U.S. citizen sought to recover damages from the Soviet Union stemming from the Soviet Union's refusal to allow plaintiff's husband

216. House Report, *supra* note 1, at 18.

217. *See* Drexel Burnham Lambert Group, Inc. v. Committee of Receivers, 12 F.3d 317, 326 (2d Cir. 1993); Shapiro v. Republic of Bolivia, 930 F.2d 1013, 1017 (2d Cir. 1991); Hercaire Int'l, Inc. v. Argentina, 821 F.2d 559, 564–65 (11th Cir. 1987); *In re* Rio Grande Transport, Inc., 516 F. Supp. 1155, 1159 (S.D.N.Y. 1981); Castro v. Saudi Arabia, 510 F. Supp. 309, 311–12 (W.D. Tex. 1980); *In re* Oil Spill by Amoco Cadiz Off Coast of France, 491 F. Supp. 161, 169 (N.D. Ill. 1979).

218. 727 F.2d 274 (2d Cir. 1984).

219. *Id.* at 277.

220. *Id.* at 277–78.

221. *Id.* at 278.

222. 761 F.2d 370 (7th Cir. 1985).

to emigrate expeditiously. The plaintiff asserted that the Soviet Union's signing of the United Nations Charter and the Helsinki Accords constituted an implied waiver for purposes of the FSIA. The court, however, disagreed, stating that there was:

> absolutely no evidence from the language, structure or history of the agreements at issue that implies a waiver of the U.S.S.R.'s sovereign immunity. There is no basis for finding a waiver from the vague, general language of the agreements nor is there any reason to conclude that the nations that are parties to these agreements anticipated when signing them that American courts would be the means by which the documents' provisions would be enforced.... To the contrary..., the countries that agreed to the United Nations Charter and the Helsinki Accords retained considerable discretion in implementing the provisions on which Frolova's suit is based. . . .[223]

The court in *Frolova* also noted that "[c]ourts have generally required convincing evidence that a treaty was intended to waive sovereign immunity before holding that a foreign state may be sued in this country."[224]

In *Drexel Burnham Lambert v. Committee of Receivers*,[225] the court found that the defendant had not waived immunity by its participation in the litigation. The court held that the proper standard is that "the filing of a responsive pleading is the *last chance* to assert FSIA immunity if the defense has not been previously asserted."[226] In contrast, in *Talbot v. Saipem*,[227] the court found a waiver by conduct:

> By filing both an answer and amended answer to this lawsuit in state court and opposing this motion to remand without asserting the defense of sovereign immunity, Saipem has permanently waived any possibility of raising the issue at a later date.[228]

Although courts have confronted a number of other possible forms of implied waiver—finding that endowing an instrumentality with the

223. *Id.* at 378.

224. *Id. See also* Von Dardel v. Union of Soviet Socialist Republics, 736 F. Supp. 1, 4 (D.D.C. 1990); Berkovitz v. Islamic Republic of Iran, 735 F.2d 329, 333 (9th Cir. 1984); Skeen v. Federative Republic of Brazil, 566 F. Supp. 1414, 1419–20 (D.D.C. 1983).

225. 12 F.3d 317 (2d Cir. 1993).

226. *Id.* at 326.

227. 835 F. Supp. 352 (S.D. Tex. 1993).

228. *Id.* at 354. *See also* Rodriguez v. Transnave, Inc., 810 F. Supp. 194 (S.D. Tex. 1993) (finding waiver by conduct because defendant participated in litigation for more than two years before moving on immunity grounds).

ability to sue and to be sued,[229] merely entering into a contract,[230] and participating in an AID contract,[231] do not constitute implied waivers—the issue remains an active one under the FSIA.

Practice Note: Implicit waiver issues present opportunities for counsel familiar with precedent. Despite a reluctance to go beyond the specific examples cited by Congress in the legislative history, new forms of implied waivers are a matter of demonstrating consent, the underlying policy of the exception. Because consent to suit is the key to waiver, advocacy should turn on a demonstration that the foreign sovereign was aware of and accepted the possible assertion of jurisdiction by U.S. courts.

§ 7.06 EXCEPTION TWO: COMMERCIAL ACTIVITY

[1] Introduction and Background

The commercial activity exception is the second exception to immunity under the FSIA. The commercial activity exception has received attention from the courts far more than any other exception.[232] The often fact-specific precedent is legion,[233] and can be bewildering on first approach. Rather than attempt to reconcile often irreconcilable precedent, or catalog the myriad types of commercial activities considered by the courts since enactment of the FSIA, this section will focus on the analytical questions involved in a commercial activity case, and provide examples of important decisions illustrating the principles involved.

229. Dayton v. Czechoslovak Socialist Republic, 834 F.2d 203, 205 (D.C. Cir.) ("no intelligent waiver of a foreign sovereign's immunity is fairly extracted from endowment of a state trading company with the capacity to sue and be sued"), *cert. denied,* 486 U.S. 1054 (1987). *See also* Arriba Ltd. v. Petroleos Mexicanos, 962 F.2d 528, 538 (5th Cir.), *cert. denied,* 113 S. Ct. 413 (1992).

230. Castro v. Saudi Arabia, 510 F. Supp. 309, 312 (W.D. Tex. 1980) ("[a] foreign state does not waive its sovereign immunity by merely entering into a contract with another nation").

231. *See* Transamerican S.S. Corp. v. Somali Democratic Republic, 590 F. Supp. 968, 973–74 (D.D.C. 1984), *modified,* 767 F.2d 998 (D.C. Cir. 1985).

232. *See, e.g.,* Note, *Two Faces of the Trader: Guidelines for Distinguishing Between Governmental and Commercial Acts Under the Foreign Sovereign Immunities Act of 1976,* 23 TEX. INT'L L.J. 465 (1988); Note, *Effects Jurisdiction Under the Foreign Sovereign Immunities Act: How Far Does the Long Arm Reach?,* 20 L. & POL'Y INT'L BUS. 463 (1988).

233. *See generally,* Note, *Jurisdiction Over Foreign Governments: A Comprehensive Review of the Foreign Sovereign Immunities Act,* 19 VAND. J. TRANSNAT'L L. 119 (1986).

As background, Congress deliberately left the contours of the commercial activity exception vague, and placed reliance on the courts to interpret and apply the provisions.[234] The House Report anticipated that the "courts would have a great deal of latitude in determining what is a 'commercial activity' for the purposes of this bill."[235] The exception was described as "the most important single issue which remains open. . . ." after the passage of the FSIA.[236] Consequently, the courts have played an important role in the development of the substance of the commercial activity exception under the FSIA.

[2] Statutory Overview

Despite the role of the courts, the starting point in an analysis of the commercial activity exception is the statute itself. The relevant statutory provisions are section 1605(a)(2), which provides an exception to immunity, and the definitional provisions in section 1603(d) & (e), which provide the statute's only definition of commercial activity.

Section 1605(a)(2), which provides the exception to immunity, is divided into three clauses, each of which provides a different basis for jurisdiction over a commercial act. Because each clause operates to provide an independent jurisdictional grant, cases under section 1605(a)(2) can be categorized usefully under each, for instance, as a "clause 1 case," and so on.[237] Section 1605(a)(2) provides that immunity will not be granted to a foreign state:

> in any case in which the action is [clause 1] based upon a commercial activity carried on in the United States by the foreign state; or [clause 2] upon an act performed in the United States in connection with a commercial activity of the foreign state elsewhere; or [clause 3] upon an act outside the territory of the United States in connection with a commercial activity of the foreign state elsewhere and that act causes a direct effect in the United States.

---

234. *See* House Report, *supra* note 1, at 16; Texas Trading & Milling Corp. v. Federal Republic of Nigeria, 647 F.2d 300, 308–309 (2d Cir. 1981), *cert. denied,* 454 U.S. 1148 (1982).

235. House Report, *supra* note 1, at 16.

236. von Mehren, *The Foreign Sovereign Immunities Act of 1976,* 17 COLUM. J. TRANSNAT'L L. 33, 48 (1978); House Report, *supra* note 1, at 18 (describing commercial activity exception as "probably the most important instance in which foreign states are denied immunity").

237. *See generally* Georges R. Delaume, *Long-Arm Jurisdiction Under the Foreign Sovereign Immunities Act,* 74 AM. J. INT'L L. 640 (1980).

To fit within section 1605(a)(2), the facts of a case must fall within the framework established by one of the three clauses. The clauses each provide a formula for jurisdiction, based on the variables of where the act at issue occurs, where the commercial activity occurs, and most importantly, the connection, or nexus, between the act and the commercial activity and the United States.

[3] Definition of Commercial Activity

Cases interpreting each of the three clauses are discussed below, but an issue common to all three, and a threshold question under section 1605(a)(2), is what kind of activity is commercial. The definitional section of the FSIA, section 1603, contains two important subsections dealing with commercial activity. Subsection (d) defines a "commercial activity" as:

> either a regular course of commercial conduct or a particular commercial transaction or act. The commercial character of an activity shall be determined by reference to the nature of the course of conduct or particular transaction or act, rather than by reference to its purpose.

This definition is important for all three clauses of section 1605(a)(2). Subsection (e) contains a definition relevant primarily to clause 1; it specifies that " 'a commercial activity carried on in the United States by a foreign state' means commercial activity carried on by such state and having substantial contact with the United States."

Under this statutory framework, the analytical process begins with determining whether the act giving rise to the cause of action is commercial. If the act is a commercial one, which of the three clauses covers the relationship at issue? The following discussion is divided into an examination of how the courts have applied this framework, first by reviewing illustrative decisions on the definition of commercial activity under the FSIA, and then by examining cases under the three clauses.

In *Republic of Argentina v. Weltover, Inc.*,[238] the Supreme Court considered whether the issuance of bonds by the Argentine government constituted a commercial activity under the FSIA. In reviewing the definition of commercial activity in the FSIA, the Court noted that:

> This definition, however, leaves the critical term "commercial" largely undefined: The first sentence simply establishes that the commercial nature of an activity does *not* depend upon whether it is a

238. 504 U.S. at 607.

single act or a regular course of conduct, and the second sentence merely specifies what element of the conduct determines commerciality (i.e., nature rather than purpose), but still without saying what "commercial" means.[239]

The Court reviewed the status of the restrictive theory of immunity, codified in the FSIA, and reviewed its decision in *Alfred Dunhill of London, Inc. v. Republic of Cuba*,[240] decided very near to the time of the enactment of the FSIA. The *Dunhill* decision addressed the issue of a commercial act exception to the act of state doctrine[241] and explored the contours of the term "commercial" that were the basis for the enactment of the FSIA.[242] Based on this review, the Court found that Argentina's issuance of bonds constituted a commercial act for purposes of the FSIA.[243] It stated:

> [W]e conclude that when a foreign government acts, not as a regulator of a market, but in the manner of a private player within it, the foreign sovereign's actions are "commercial" within the meaning of the FSIA.[244]

The Court suggested that central to the analysis of commercial activity is whether a state engaged in activity where it exercised powers that could also be exercised by private citizens or whether the powers exercised were peculiar to sovereigns.[245] Argentina argued that the nature–purpose distinction is not appropriate because the "essence of an act is defined by its purpose."[246] Once and for all, the Court rejected this line of argument:

> We think that this line of argument is squarely foreclosed by the language of the FSIA. However difficult it may be in some cases to separate "purpose" (i.e., the *reason* why the foreign state engages in the activity) from "nature" (i.e., the outward form of the conduct that

239. *Id.* at 2165 (emphasis supplied).

240. 425 U.S. 682 (1976).

241. *See infra* § 8.10.

242. 504 U.S. at 612–15.

243. *Id.* at 2166. *See generally* Georges R. Delaume, *The Foreign Sovereign Immunities Act and Public Debt Litigation: Some Fifteen Years Later*, 88 AM. J. INT'L L. 257 (1994).

244. *Weltover* at 614.

245. *Id., citing Dunhill,* 425 U.S. at 704.

246. *Id.* at 617, *citing*, De Sanchez v. Banco Central de Nicaragua, 770 F.2d 1385, 1393 (5th Cir. 1985).

the foreign state performs or agrees to perform) . . . the statute unmistakably commands that to be done.[247]

In contrast to the Supreme Court's decision in *Weltover* is the Supreme Court's decision in *Saudi Arabia v. Nelson*,[248] where the Court also had the opportunity to review the definition of commercial activity under section 1605(a)(2) of the FSIA. Applying the sovereign or public acts (jure imperii) versus private or commercial acts (jure gestionis) analysis established by *Weltover,* the *Nelson* Court characterized the detention and torture in Saudi Arabia of a United States citizen-employee of a Saudi Arabian hospital as sovereign police conduct.[249] Although the plaintiff, Nelson, had been recruited in the U.S., signed an employment contract in the U.S., had undergone processing and orientation in the U.S., and had been arrested in the hospital as the result of a dispute with the hospital, the Court declined to view the conduct of Saudi Arabia as involving the commercial activity of Nelson's recruitment and hiring in the United States or the running of the Saudi Arabian hospital.[250] One *amicus* even observed that the Saudi Government commonly used detainment and torture to resolve commercial disputes.[251] Distinguishing *Weltover,* the Court stated that the conduct at issue in *Nelson* was solely the wrongful arrest, imprisonment, and torture of Nelson.[252] The Court held that such police activity was noncommercial and that a foreign state's exercise of the police power is understood under the restrictive theory of sovereign immunity (which the FSIA codified) as peculiarly sovereign in nature.[253] In so ruling, the Supreme Court reversed the court of appeals, which had found that the detention and torture of Nelson were intertwined with his employment at the hospital.[254] The Supreme Court did suggest, however, that its narrow interpretation of commercial activity in *Nelson* was limited to cases where the claim rests "entirely upon activities sovereign in character"

247. *Id.* at 617, *citing* 28 U.S.C.A. § 1603(d) (emphasis in original). In some instances, the purpose test persists. *See, e.g.,* MCI Telecommunications Corp. v. Alhadood, 82 F.3d 658 (5th Cir. 1996) (finding absence of commercial activity in agreement to pay debts).

248. 507 U.S. 349, 113 S. Ct. 1471 (1993). *See generally* Danny A. Hoek, *Foreign Sovereign Immunity and Saudi Arabia v. Nelson: A Practical Guide,* 18 HASTINGS INT'L COMP. L. REV. 617 (1995).

249. *Id.* at 1479.

250. *Id.* at 1475, 1479.

251. *Id.* at 1480.

252. *Id.* at 1479.

253. *Id.*

254. *Id.* at 1476.

(police activity here) and not to cases where the claim consists of "both commercial and sovereign elements."[255]

In one of the leading cases on the commercial activity exception, *Texas Trading & Milling Corp. v. Federal Republic of Nigeria*,[256] the court was faced with litigation arising out of Nigeria's anticipatory breach of over 100 contracts for the purchase of cement. In an exhaustive analysis of whether the breaches constituted commercial acts, the court referred to three sources of assistance which are still commonly looked to by courts confronted with commercial activity questions. The first such source is the legislative history.[257] The second source of assistance is the body of precedent focused on the commercial activity exception at the time of the passage of the FSIA, and for our purposes, since the passage of the Act. The third source is "current standards of international law concerning sovereign immunity [which] add content to the 'commercial activity' phrase of the FSIA."[258] Under all three sources, Nigeria's conduct qualified as commercial.[259]

Addressing the last of these sources first, international law was a specific basis for enactment of the FSIA. The House Report stated that the FSIA "incorporates standards recognized under international law."[260] The court in *Texas Trading* ruled that "there can be little doubt that international law follows the restrictive theory [of sovereign immunity]."[261]

The second source of assistance in the interpretation of the phrase "commercial activity" identified by the court in *Texas Trading* was the legislative history of the FSIA.[262] Congress intended section 1603(d) to be developed primarily by judicial interpretation. The House Report states that "section 1603 defines the term 'commercial activity' as including a broad spectrum of endeavor, from an individual commercial transaction or act to a regular course of commercial conduct."[263] Examples of activities that Congress considered commercial acts include contracts entered into by a foreign state to buy provisions or equipment for its military, to construct a government building or to make repairs on

---

255. *Id.* at 1478 n.4 (parenthetical added).
256. 647 F.2d 300 (2d Cir. 1981), *cert. denied,* 454 U.S. 1148 (1982).
257. *Id.* at 309–10.
258. *Id.* at 310.
259. *Id.*
260. House Report, *supra* note 1, at 14.
261. 647 F.2d at 310.
262. *Id.* at 308.
263. House Report, *supra* note 1, at 15.

an embassy facility. The House Report stipulates that these activities, despite having the purpose of furthering a public function, are of a commercial nature. In contrast, however, the House Report states that "a foreign state's mere participation in a foreign assistance program administered by the Agency for International Development is an activity whose essential nature is public or governmental, and it would not itself constitute a commercial activity."[264]

The third source of interpretive guidance in defining the term "commercial activity" identified by the court in *Texas Trading* is the precedent on the issue at the time of enactment of the FSIA.[265] With the guidance of the legislative history, the courts have since inquired, among other things, about the nature of the act rather than its purpose,[266] whether the act at issue was one that only a sovereign could perform,[267] and whether the act involves peculiarly sovereign concerns.[268] Such questions are, however, merely a starting point in the analysis. One court explained the difficult process of characterizing activity engaged in by sovereigns:

> The principal obstacle in determining whether an activity is commercial or sovereign in nature is that the same activity can often be characterized in a number of different ways. A federal trial, for example, could be characterized in the broadest generic terms as a form of dispute resolution, or more specifically as government sponsored adjudication. But whereas the broad category of dispute resolution encompasses activities that might be considered commercial, such as paid-for arbitration, the narrower category of adjudication defines an intrinsically public activity, invested with the sovereign authority of the state.[269]

This case excerpt illustrates the analytical difficulties facing courts in commercial activity cases.[270]

The difficulty experienced by the lower courts may result in large measure from the absence of guidance in the FSIA concerning the level

---

264. *Id.* at 16.

265. 647 F.2d at 309.

266. *See Weltover,* 504 U.S. at 617. Cf. De Sanchez v. Banco Central de Nicaragua, 770 F.2d 1385, 1393–94 (5th Cir. 1985).

267. *See* Friedar v. Government of Israel, 614 F. Supp. 395, 399 (S.D.N.Y. 1985).

268. *See In re* Sedco, Inc., 543 F. Supp. 561, 566 (S.D. Tex. 1982).

269. De Sanchez v. Banco Central de Nicaragua, 770 F.2d 1385, 1392 (5th Cir. 1985).

270. *See generally* Note, *Jurisdiction Over Foreign Governments: A Comprehensive Review of the Foreign Sovereign Immunities Act,* 19 VAND. J. TRANSNAT'L L. 119, 129–145 (1986).

on which the activities of foreign sovereigns are to be characterized. Activities viewed on their most specific level are apt to appear as activities individuals could carry out, e.g., issuing bonds as opposed to carrying out economic policy.[271] In contrast, activities viewed on their most general level are apt to resemble governmental activities, e.g., regulating natural resources as opposed to drilling oil wells.[272]

In a case that illustrates well how a sovereign can act in a commercial, private capacity, the court asked whether the foreign state's activities were governmental in nature, or more similar to activities in which private individuals or corporations engage. In *Transamerican S.S. Corp. v. Somali Democratic Republic*,[273] the issue was the character of actions taken by the Somali Embassy in seeking to collect monies from a shipping corporation commissioned by the United States to ship grain from Texas to Somalia pursuant to a famine relief program. The court concluded that the Embassy's actions in attempting to secure payment for taxes and duties on the delivered grain bore more resemblance to actions of a debt collection agency or a private bank than they did to any sovereign function. The court stated, "it is a normal commercial function to act for another in collecting and holding funds and advising a principal as to their receipt; private banks and collection agencies do this routinely."[274] Similarly, allegations in *American Bonded Warehouse Corp. v. Air France*,[275] of a scheme implemented by the defendant "to eliminate its competition in the freight forwarding industry in violation of RICO" subjected the defendant to jurisdiction under the commercial activity exception.[276]

In a case involving an action based on an activity that only a sovereign can perform, the court in *Friedar v. Government of Israel*,[277] ruled that the commercial activity exception did not apply. In *Friedar* a United States plaintiff brought suit against Israel for compensation for injuries sustained while active in the Israeli army. The court reasoned that only a sovereign could engage in the activities at issue: "Unlike the purchase of supplies that eventually may be used for military purposes,

271. *See generally* Republic of Argentina v. Weltover, 504 U.S. at 607.
272. *See generally In re* Sedco, Inc., 543 F. Supp. 561 (S.D. Tex. 1982).
273. 767 F.2d 998 (D.C. Cir. 1985).
274. *Id.* at 1003.
275. 653 F. Supp. 861 (N.D. Ill. 1987).
276. *Id.* at 864.
277. 614 F. Supp. 395 (S.D.N.Y. 1985).

recruiting soldiers and determining eligibility for veteran's benefits are activities conducted only by sovereigns.''[278]

In cases involving contracts with foreign sovereigns, courts have developed a rebuttable presumption that "a contract between a foreign state and a private party for the purchase of goods or services" is a commercial activity.[279] For instance, in *Segni v. Commercial Office of Spain*,[280] the court found the firing of plaintiff, who had been hired to perform services in the United States, to be a commercial activity. The court explained:

> The nature of the act of the Commercial Office in this case was contractual. Mr. Segni was employed by the Commercial Office to develop the marketing of Spanish wines in the midwestern United States. Mr. Segni was terminated during the term of his contract and brought suit to recover damages. There is no indication in the pleadings that Mr. Segni's termination had anything to do with a Spanish Government policy, or was in any way governmental.[281]

Characterization of the contract in another case, *Practical Concepts, Inc. v. Republic of Bolivia*,[282] was more difficult, because the contract contained certain provisions—such as tax exemption and diplomatic privileges—to which only a sovereign could agree.[283] Although the district court found these provisions determinative, and held that Bolivia was entitled to immunity,[284] on appeal the D.C. Circuit disagreed.[285]

The D.C. Circuit ruled that the inclusion of such terms was not determinative if they were incidental or auxiliary to the basic exchange.[286] The district court erred, it found, by focusing on:

> auxiliary provisions rather than on the agreement's core to classify the contract at issue as "governmental rather than commercial." It is more sensible, and faithful to the probable intent of Congress, we believe, generally to center on the basic exchange (e.g., the sale of goods or

278. *Id.* at 399. *See also* Practical Concepts v. Republic of Bolivia, 615 F. Supp. 92, 94 (D.C. Cir. 1985), *vacated,* 811 F.2d 1543 (D.C. Cir. 1987).

279. Practical Concepts, Inc. v. Republic of Bolivia, 811 F.2d 1543, 1549 (D.C. Cir. 1987).

280. 650 F. Supp. 1042 (N.D. Ill. 1986), *aff'd,* 835 F.2d 160 (1987).

281. *Id.* at 1044 (citation omitted).

282. 811 F.2d 1543 (D.C. Cir. 1987).

283. *Practical Concepts,* 615 F. Supp. 92, 94 (D.D.C. 1986), *vacated,* 811 F.2d 1543 (D.C. Cir. 1987).

284. 615 F. Supp. 92 (D.D.C. 1986).

285. 811 F.2d 1543 (D.C. Cir. 1987).

286. *Id.* at 1550.

services), not on the facilitating features (e.g., expediting entrance of personnel and supplies), in determining whether an obligation qualifies as a 'commercial activity' for FSIA purposes.[287]

The court, however, specifically reserved the issue of whether such an act would be sovereign or commercial if the suit involved failure to provide a benefit under the contract that could only be provided by a sovereign.[288] In *Janini v. Kuwait University*,[289] the court held that unilateral termination of an employment contract is a commercial, and not a sovereign, act even if the termination is in the form of a governmental decree.[290] Relying on the Supreme Court's decision in *Weltover,* the court noted that "Kuwait's reasons for terminating the contracts are immaterial to our inquiry . . . . so long as the act of termination is a commercial one, of the sort in which 'private players' routinely engage—as we have found it to be—it is subject to the § 1605(a)(2) commercial activity exceptions."[291]

Additional concerns arise when the contract at issue involves or relates to the natural resources of a foreign sovereign. For instance, at issue in *MOL, Inc. v. Peoples Republic of Bangladesh*,[292] was the defendant's alleged breach of a licensing agreement for the export of rhesus monkeys. The Ninth Circuit affirmed characterization of the activity as sovereign, not subject to consideration under the FSIA.[293] The court of appeals reasoned that "Bangladesh was terminating an agreement that only a sovereign could have made. . . . It concerned Bangladesh's right to regulate imports and exports, a sovereign prerogative. . . . It concerned Bangladesh's right to regulate its natural resources, also a uniquely sovereign function."[294] The court concluded that Bangladesh was immune from suit under the FSIA because "the licensing agreement was a sovereign act, not just a commercial transaction. . . . Its revocation was sovereign by nature, not commercial."[295]

When the issue of natural resources has arisen outside the context of a contract, the courts have also generally found the activity to be

---

287. *Id.* at 1548 (footnote omitted).
288. *Id.* at 1548 n.9.
289. 43 F.3d 1534 (D.C. Cir. 1995).
290. *Id.* at 1537.
291. *Id.*
292. 736 F.2d 1326 (9th Cir. 1984), *cert. denied,* 469 U.S. 1037 (1984).
293. *Id.* at 1329.
294. *Id.*
295. *Id.*

sovereign. For instance, in *In re Sedco, Inc.*,[296] the issue was whether jurisdiction under the commercial activity exception existed for suits against a foreign sovereign for injury resulting from an oil well accident during exploratory drilling. In explaining why the commercial activity exception did not apply, the court articulated the natural wealth rationale:

> The court must regard carefully a sovereign's conduct with respect to its natural wealth. A very basic attribute of sovereignty is the control over natural resources, and short of actually selling these resources on the world market, decisions and conduct concerning them are uniquely governmental in nature.[297]

Practice Note: Following the *MOL, Inc.* and *Sedco* cases, it is apparent courts are unlikely to find that an act is commercial if it involves natural resources. In such contracts, counsel representing private parties should therefore be wary of any reliance on the commercial activity exception, and should rely instead on express waivers of immunity and attachment.

Foreign central banking activity is another illustration of the difficult issues involved in the characterization of commercial activity. Although it is clear that a foreign sovereign's borrowing of funds is a commercial act,[298] characterization of a central bank's conduct involves a more intricate analysis. For instance, in *Wolf v. Banco Nacional de Mexico*,[299] and *West v. Multibanco Comermex*,[300] the sale of certificates of deposit were considered commercial activity. In contrast, the court in *De Sanchez v. Banco Central De Nicaragua*,[301] found that failure to honor a check issued to the purchaser of a certificate of deposit was a sovereign act. The court acknowledged the "quandary" it faced:

> Banco Central's issuance of the check could be characterized either as a sale of foreign currency or as the regulation and supervision of Nicaragua's foreign exchange reserves. The former is a commercial activity: Private banks often sell foreign currency to one another, particularly if they have a correspondent-bank relation. The regulation and supervision of a nation's foreign exchange reserves, however, is a

296. 543 F. Supp. 561 (S.D. Tex. 1982).

297. *Id.* at 565.

298. *See* House Report, *supra* note 1, at 16; Morgan Guaranty Trust Co. v. Republic of Palau, 657 F. Supp. 1475, 1477–78 (S.D.N.Y. 1987).

299. 739 F.2d 1458 (9th Cir. 1984), *cert. denied,* 469 U.S. 1108 (1985).

300. 807 F.2d 820 (9th Cir. 1987); *accord* Callejo v. Bancomer, 764 F.2d 1101, 1107 (5th Cir. 1985).

301. 770 F.2d 1385 (5th Cir. 1985).

sovereign activity. It is one aspect of a government's sovereign function of regulating the monetary system.[302]

Courts have also considered the nature of acts which constitute commercial activity for purposes of the exception to sovereign immunity contained in 28 U.S.C.A. § 1605(a)(2).[302.1]

Practice Note: This brief review of precedent on the issue of what constitutes a commercial activity under section 1605(a)(2) reveals no ''golden thread'' or overriding principle. Each fact pattern must be evaluated in the matrix of the legislative history and the variety of decided cases. The determination of whether a particular act is commercial, however, despite its difficulty, is only the first step in an analysis under section 1605(a)(2). The particular act must have the requisite nexus with the United States, expressed in each of the three clauses of section 1605(a)(2). Only if an act is commercial and satisfies one of the three clauses, is the commercial activity exception satisfied.

[4] Clause 1: Commercial Activity in the United States

Clause 1 of section 1605(a)(2) provides jurisdiction over cases in which the action is ''based on a commercial activity carried on in the United States by a foreign state.'' This phrase is further defined in section 1603(e) to mean ''commercial activity carried on by such state and having substantial contact with the United States.'' Because the language of clause 1 is susceptible to a variety of readings, decisions have not been ''consistent.''[303] In one of the leading cases under clause 1, the court in *Vencendora Oceanica Navigacion v. Compagnie Nationale Algerienne De Navigation,*[304] found that although the defendant had a continuing business contact with the United States, the action did not arise from the continuing business.[305] Consequently, the

302. *Id.* at 1392–93 (footnote omitted).

302.1. *See, e.g.*, Velasco v. Indonesia, 370 F.3d 392 (4th Cir. 2004) (commercial activity exception of FSIA can only be invoked when government official acts with actual authority; *ultra vires* acts are not subject to commercial activity exception to immunity); Phaneuf v. Republic of Indonesia, 106 F.3d 302 (9th Cir. 1997) (commercial activity exception does not apply to acts of agent of foreign state outside her authority); Hirsch v. Israel, 962 F.2d 377, 382 (S.D.N.Y. 1997) (commercial activity exception does not apply to contract to pay war reparations—it is ''difficult to conceive of activities more quintessentially governmental that the payment of reparations to Holocaust survivors pursuant to a treaty between two nations'').

303. Vencendora Oceanica Navigacion v. Compagnie Nationale Algerienne de Navigation, 730 F.2d 195, 199–200 (5th Cir. 1984).

304. 730 F.2d 195 (5th Cir. 1984). *See also* Barkanic v. CAAC, 822 F.2d 11, 13 (2d Cir. 1987).

305. *Id.* at 201.

court concluded that jurisdiction was not available under clause 1 of section 1605(a)(2) because there was no "nexus" between the act at issue and the continuing business of the defendant in the United States.[306]

The court in *Vencendora* adopted the nexus test only after reviewing the "widely varying formulations of the jurisdictional scope" of clause 1 reached by different courts,[307] and found that no less than four approaches were discernable.[308] First is the "literal" reading of clause 1, which would require that the cause of action be based directly on the commercial activity, not merely in connection with the commercial activity.[309] The literal approach has not garnered support in the courts.[310]

The second formulation of the jurisdictional scope of clause 1 is the bifurcated literal nexus approach. Under this formulation, jurisdiction exists if a "direct causal connection" exists between the act and the commercial activity.[311] The third formulation is the "doing business" test, the broadest reading of the language in clause 1.[312] Under the doing business test, clause 1 is satisfied if the defendant is engaged in a regular course of commercial conduct in the United States, regardless of whether the particular act giving rise to the cause of action relates to that regular course of conduct.

Choosing a reading of clause 1 that falls in between the literal and the doing business test, the court in *Vencendora* adopted the fourth approach, the nexus test.[313] The nexus approach does not require a causal connection, but instead a nexus between the act and the commercial activity.

---

306. *Id.*

307. *Id.* at 200.

308. *Id.*

309. *Id.*

310. *Id.* (citing Gemini Shipping v. Foreign Trade Org. for Chemical & Foodstuffs, 647 F.2d 317, 319 (2d Cir. 1981)); Sugarman v. Aeromexico, 626 F.2d 270 (3d Cir. 1980); Gibbons v. Udaras, 549 F. Supp. 1094 (S.D.N.Y. 1982)). *But see* Saudi Arabia v. Nelson, 507 U.S. 349 (1993); Federal Ins. Co. v. Richard I. Rubin & Co., Inc., 12 F.3d 1270, 1289 (3d Cir. 1993) (stating *Nelson* "makes clear that the commercial activity undertaken by the defendant must be directly connected to the cause of action alleged by the plaintiff").

311. 730 F.2d at 200 (citing Gilson v. Republic of Ireland, 682 F.2d 1022 (D.C. Cir. 1982)).

312. 730 F.2d at 201 (citing Rio Grande Transport, Inc., 516 F. Supp. 1155 (S.D.N.Y. 1981)).

313. *Id.* at 202. *See also* Arriba Ltd. v. Petroleos Mexicanos, 962 F.2d 528, 533 (5th Cir.), *cert. denied*, 506 U.S. 956 (1992); Stena Rederi AB v. Comision de Contratos del Comite, 923 F.2d 380, 387 (5th Cir. 1991).

An illustration of the nexus approach is the court's decision in *Sugarman v. Aeromexico*,[314] in which the court found that although the defendant carried on commercial activity in the United States, the activity giving rise to the cause of action occurred in Mexico. Nevertheless, because there was a nexus between the two activities, jurisdiction under clause 1 existed.[315] Similarly, in *Velidor v. L/P/G Benghazi*,[316] the court articulated an application of the nexus test:

> It is immaterial that the acts constituting breach of contract may have taken place outside the United States, because under § 1605(a)(2) the alleged misconduct does not have to occur in this country *if the claim arises out of a course of commercial conduct here*.[317]

In *Vencendora*, the court adopted the nexus test out of a concern that any broader reading, especially that of the doing business test, undermined the legislative intent.[318]

A recent Circuit Court to address section 1605(a)(2) conduct did not expressly state the formulation of jurisdictional scope it applied. The Eleventh Circuit, in *Honduras Aircraft Registry, Ltd. v. Gov't of Honduras*,[318.1] simply found that Honduras had acted as a private party in the marketplace and waived its immunity by contracting for the provision of goods and services in the United States to assist in implementing a Honduran civil aircraft registry. The Court found that the underlying activities of providing know-how, training, resources, etc., were commercial in nature and of the type negotiable among private parties. The Court observed that "[o]nly the 'nature' of the act, not the 'purpose' or 'motivation' for the act, is determinative. . . . [I[t is irrelevant that . . . Honduras may have intended only to fulfill its unique sovereign objectives."[318.2] In considering whether a particular fact pattern will satisfy clause 1, counsel should consider the various formulations described above. Clause 1, under all formulations, requires a regular course of commercial conduct in the United States by the defendant. In considering whether the act is sufficiently related to that conduct, counsel should examine whether the connection satisfies the literal, nexus or doing business tests. If only the latter, counsel would be

314. 626 F.2d 270 (3d Cir. 1980).
315. *Id.* at 273.
316. 653 F.2d 812 (3d Cir. 1981), *cert. denied*, 455 U.S. 929 (1982).
317. *Id.* at 820 (emphasis supplied).
318. 730 F.2d at 203. *But see* Saudi Arabia v. Nelson, 507 U.S. 349 (1993).
318.1. 131 F.3d 157 (11th Cir. 1997).
318.2. *Id.* (citations omitted).

well advised to examine the jurisdictional scope of the other clauses under section 1605(a)(2).

In *Saudi Arabia v. Nelson,*[319] the Supreme Court reversed the Eleventh Circuit's finding of a nexus, and addressed the operation of the "based upon" phrase in clause 1. At issue in *Nelson* was a claim by Nelson, an American citizen who responded to an advertisement for a medical systems engineer position at a hospital in Saudi Arabia. The recruiting was conducted by a U.S. company on behalf of the King Faisal Specialist Hospital in Riyadh, owned and operated by the Kingdom of Saudi Arabia. Nelson took the position and began work at the Hospital in Saudi Arabia. Nelson alleged that when he tried to report safety hazards, he was arrested, tortured, and imprisoned for 39 days. He brought suit under the FSIA, asserting jurisdiction based on clause 1. The district court dismissed the complaint for lack of subject matter jurisdiction, holding that the defendant's activity did not amount to commercial activity carried on in the United States, and that there was no nexus between the recruitment that occurred in the U.S. and Nelson's injuries.[320] The court of appeals reversed, finding both commercial activity and a nexus.[321]

The Supreme Court reversed, first addressing the phrase "based upon" in clause 1. The Court stated:

> In denoting conduct that forms the 'basis' or 'foundation' for a claim, . . . the phrase is read most naturally to mean those elements of a claim that, if proven, would entitle a plaintiff to relief under his theory of the case"[322]

The Court found, therefore, that the phrase "based upon" is one that "calls for something more than a mere connection with or relation to commercial activity."[323] Under this reading of the phrase "based upon" the Court determined that Nelson's allegations were insufficient to support jurisdiction under clause 1.[324]

---

319. 507 U.S. 349 (1993).
320. *Id.* at 1476.
321. *Id.*
322. *Id.* at 1477 (citations omitted).
323. *Id.* at 1478 (citation omitted).
324. *Id.* at 1481. *See* Goodman Holdings v. Rafidain Bank, 26 F.3d 1143, 1146 (D.C. Cir. 1994) (following *Nelson*).

[5] Clause 2: Commercial Activity Outside the United States

Relatively few cases have interpreted clause 2 of section 1605(a)(2), as compared with clauses 1 and 3. Under clause 2, jurisdiction exists if the action is "based upon an act performed in the United States in connection with a commercial activity of the foreign state elsewhere." The House Report explains that clause 2:

> looks to conduct of the foreign state in the United States which relates either to a regular course of commercial conduct elsewhere or to a particular commercial transaction concluded or carried out in part elsewhere. Examples of this type of situation might include: a representation in the United States by an agent of a foreign state that leads to an action for restitution based on unjust enrichment; an act in the United States that violates U.S. securities laws or regulations; the wrongful discharge in the United States of an employee of the foreign state who has been employed in connection with a commercial activity carried on in some third country.[325]

The Committee recognized that activities under clause 2 might be covered under a broad interpretation of clause 1's "commercial activity carried on in the United States" language, but nevertheless decided "to provide expressly for the case where a claim arises out of a specific act in the United States which is commercial or private in nature and which relates to a commercial activity abroad. . . . It should be noted that the acts (or omissions) encompassed in this category are limited to those which in and of themselves are sufficient to form the basis of a cause of action."[326]

Illuminating the legislative history is one of the rare cases finding jurisdiction under clause 2. In *Gilson v. Republic of Ireland*,[327] the action involved an alleged breach of a contract between a U.S. engineer and instrumentalities of Ireland. The court found that the complaint alleged "an unbroken chain of events" beginning when plaintiff contracted with one of the defendants in the U.S. and "involving the active collusion of all defendants to entice plaintiff to leave the United States for Ireland."[328] The court held that the events surrounding the

---

325. House Report, *supra* note 1, at 19.

326. *Id.* at 19. *See generally* East European Domestic Int'l Sales Corp. v. Terra, 467 F. Supp. 383, 388 (S.D.N.Y. 1979) (discussing jurisdiction under clause 2).

327. 682 F.2d 1022 (D.C. Cir. 1982).

328. *Id.* at 1027.

enticement and occurring in the U.S. were sufficient to provide jurisdiction under clause 2.[329]

A remaining unsettled question under clause 2 is the nature of the nexus requirement. The court in *Gilson* did not specifically rule on the nexus requirement, but assumed that "plaintiff will be able to demonstrate that the required nexus exists as to all defendants between their commercial activity and the subsequent wrong."[330] The court referred to nexus cases decided under clause 1,[331] and in dicta suggested that the nexus requirement under clause 2 would be satisfied if the plaintiff could show "a direct causal connection between" the act in the U.S. and the acts elsewhere, or the act in the U.S. is "an" element of the cause of action under whatever law governs the claims.[332]

[6] Clause 3: Direct Effect in the United States

The final jurisdictional clause under section 1605(a)(2) is clause 3, which provides jurisdiction over actions based upon "an act outside the territory of the United States in connection with a commercial activity of the foreign state elsewhere and that act causes a direct effect in the United States." In contrast to the dearth of precedent under clause 2, many courts have struggled with what constitutes a "direct effect" sufficient for jurisdiction under clause 3.[333] The legislative history provides that clause 3 "would embrace commercial conduct abroad having direct effects within the United States which would subject such conduct to the exercise of jurisdiction consistent with principles set forth in section 18, Restatement of the Law, Second, Foreign Relations Law of the United States (1965)."[334]

Although the Restatement is now in a revised Third edition with effects jurisdiction covered in §§ 402 & 403,[335] section 18 of the Second Restatement, at the time of enactment of the FSIA provided:

329. *Id.*

330. *Id.* at n.22.

331. *Id.* at 1027 (citing Velidor v. L/P/G Benghazi, 653 F.2d 812, 820 (3d Cir. 1981), *petition for cert. dismissed,* 455 U.S. 929 (1982); Gemini Shipping, Inc. v. Foreign Trade Org. for Chemicals & Foodstuffs, 647 F.2d 317, 319 (2d Cir. 1981); Sugarman v. Aeromexico, Inc., 626 F.2d 270, 272–73 (3d Cir. 1980)).

332. *Id.* For a discussion of the direct causal connection nexus standard, *see supra* § 7.06[4].

333. *See, e.g.,* Four Corners Helicopters, Inc. v. Turbomeca, 677 F. Supp. 1096, 1101 (D. Colo. 1988) (discussing cases and trends under clause 3).

334. House Report, *supra* note 1, at 19.

335. *See supra* Chapter 5.

A state has jurisdiction to prescribe a rule of law attaching legal consequences to conduct that occurs outside its territory and causes an effect within its territory, if either

(a) the conduct and its effect are generally recognized as constituent elements of a crime or tort under the law of states that have reasonably developed legal systems, or

(b) (i) the conduct and its effect are constituent elements of activity to which the rule applies; (ii) the effect within the territory is substantial; (iii) it occurs as a direct and foreseeable result of the conduct outside the territory; and (iv) the rule is not inconsistent with the principles of justice generally recognized by states that have reasonably developed legal systems.

In interpreting clause 3, as amplified by section 18 of the Second Restatement, the courts have developed guidelines for the application of the direct effect standard, often including a requirement that the effect be substantial, direct, and foreseeable.[336] Although terms such as substantial and foreseeable have long been susceptible of interpretation, one court articulated what has become a standard definition of directness under the FSIA: "The common sense interpretation of a 'direct effect' is one which has no intervening element, but, rather, flows in a straight line without deviation or interruption."[337]

In the only Supreme Court decision on the meaning and operation of the direct effect standard, the Court in *Republic of Argentina v. Weltover, Inc.*[338] noted that Congress' reference to section 18 is a "non sequitur."[339] The Court explained that section 18 "deals with jurisdiction to *legislate* rather than jurisdiction to *adjudicate*," which is the subject of section 1605(a)(2).[340]

The Court in *Weltover* rejected the interpretation that section 1605(a)(2) "contains any unexpressed requirement of 'substantiality' or 'foreseeability.' "[341] Instead, the Court adopted the interpretation of the court of appeals: "an effect is 'direct' if it follows 'as an immediate

---

336. *See, e.g.*, Zedan v. Kingdom of Saudi Arabia, 849 F.2d 1511, 1515 (D.C. Cir. 1988) (finding no direct effect but discussing precedent); *see also* United World Trade v. Mangyshlakneft Oil Production Ass'n, 33 F.3d 1232 (10th Cir. 1994).

337. Upton v. Empire of Iran, 459 F. Supp. 264, 266 (D.D.C. 1978), *aff'd*, 607 F.2d 494 (D.C. Cir. 1979).

338. 504 U.S. 607, 112 S. Ct. 2160 (1992).

339. *Id.* at 2168 (citing *Texas Trading*, 647 F.2d 300, at 311).

340. *Id.* at 2168 (emphasis in original).

341. *Id.* at 2168.

consequence of the defendant's . . . activity.' "[342] Using the "immediate consequence" interpretation of the direct effect clause, the Court in *Weltover* determined that Argentina's unilateral rescheduling of the maturity dates of bonds it issued in commercial activity had a direct effect in the United States for purposes of section 1605(a)(2).[343]

Many of the cases under clause 3 fall into one of two categories, those involving consideration of direct effect in the context of a personal injury[343.1] or in the context of financial damage. For instance, in *Ohntrup v. Firearms Center, Inc.*,[344] the court found jurisdiction under Clause 3 for an action involving injury resulting from a malfunctioning firearm manufactured by a firm wholly owned by the Turkish government. The injury was a substantial and foreseeable result of the defendant's actions because the sales agreement specifically envisioned sales in the United States.[345] In contrast, the court in *Zernicek v. Brown & Root, Inc.*,[346] held that "the eventual effect in the United States of the personal injury or death of an American citizen while abroad is not direct within the meaning of the Act even if the foreign government agency might foresee that a United States citizen might be injured while travelling or working within its territory."[347]

In cases of financial damage, a circuit split exists concerning whether some legally sufficient act, not just the damage, must have occurred in the United States. For instance, in *Zedan v. Kingdom of Saudi Arabia*,[348] the court held that the injury occurred in Saudi Arabia, where the alleged breach of contract occurred, and although it continued, the fact that the plaintiff returned to the United States was insufficient to

---

342. *Id.* at 2168, citing 941 F.2d at 152.

343. *Id. See also* Goodman Holdings v. Rafidain Bank, 26 F.3d 1143, 1147 (D.C. Cir. 1994) (following *Weltover*).

343.1. *See* Aldy v. Valmet Paper Machinery, Inc., 74 F.3d 72 (5th Cir. 1996) (upholding jurisdiction under third clause of commercial activities exception regarding wrongful death, faulty design and construction, and failure to warn claims against Finnish-government owned machinery manufacturing company concerning paper machinery accident in Louisiana). The *Valmet* court found that the suits appeared to be "classic design and manufacturing defect suits, which the third clause of the commercial activities exception is broad enough to cover." *Id.* at 75.

344. 516 F. Supp. 1281 (E.D. Pa. 1981), *aff'd*, 760 F.2d 259 (3d Cir. 1985).

345. *Id.* at 1286. *See also* Vermeulen v. Renault, U.S.A., Inc., 985 F.2d 1534, 1545 (11th Cir. 1993).

346. 826 F.2d 415, 417 (5th Cir. 1987), *cert. denied*, 484 U.S. 1043 (1988).

347. *Id.* at 418. *Accord* Martin v. Republic of South Africa, 836 F.2d 91, 95 (2d Cir. 1987) (finding no jurisdiction under clause 3 for injuries sustained as result of defendant's failure to provide prompt medical care).

348. 849 F.2d 1511 (D.C. Cir. 1988).

constitute a direct effect under clause 3.[349] In contrast, the court in *Voest-Alpine v. Bank of China*,[350] held that the Bank of China's refusal to honor a letter of credit abroad created a direct effect in the United States where the U.S. plaintiff suffered financial loss. The Court declined to require that the act giving rise to the direct effect be "legally significant."[351]

Whether a matter of personal injury or financial damage, the nexus requirement under clause 3 remains a difficult issue. In *Four Corners Helicopters, Inc. v. Turbomeca*,[352] the court was presented with a case of first impression in the Tenth Circuit on the meaning of clause 3's direct effect standard.[353] The case involved an action for damages resulting from the crash of an aircraft in Colorado. The defendant manufacturer argued that jurisdiction did not exist under clause 3 because although it had manufactured the hull, the hull had been salvaged after a crash in Europe, transferred to the U.S., fitted with a new engine, and sold to plaintiff, all without the knowledge or participation of the defendant.[354] The court found that the "complaint does not provide any basis for inferring the effect in this country was foreseeable or the immediate causal effect of an act of defendant . . . or was substantial. If anything, it actually outlines the very intervening elements which preclude the

349. *Id.* at 1515. *See also* Hanil Bank v. PT Bank Negara Indonesia, 148 F.3d 127 (2d Cir. 1998) (finding "legally significant act" requirement still applicable); Doe v. Unocal, 963 F. Supp. 880 (C.D. Cal. 1997) (finding "direct effect" lacking where competitive advantage in U.S. gas market was alleged to result from human rights abuses concerning construction of gas pipeline in Burma).

350. 142 F.3d 887 (5th Cir. 1998).

351. *See also* Transamerican Steamship Corp. v. Somali Democratic Republic, 767 F.2d 998 (D.C. Cir. 1985) (finding that foreign sovereign's actions abroad that caused the plaintiff to transfer funds from one U.S. bank to another, and to incur debts in the U.S., were sufficiently direct for purposes of the clause); WMW Mach. Inc. v. Werkzeugmaschinenhendel, GmbH, 960 F. Supp. 734 (S.D.N.Y. 1997) (denying foreign agency's summary judgment motion where alleged failure of East German state agency to protect New Jersey distributor's rights during privatization after reunification of East and West Germany caused distributor financial damages). *Compare* Harris Corp. v. Nat'l Iranian Radio, 691 F.2d 1344 (11th Cir. 1982); Texas Trading & Milling Corp. v. Republic of Nigeria, 647 F.2d 300 (2d Cir. 1981), *cert. denied*, 454 U.S. 1148 (1982); Wyle v. Bank Melli of Iran, 577 F. Supp. 1148 (N.D. Cal. 1983); *In re* Rio Grande Transport, Inc., 516 F. Supp. 1155, 1163 (S.D.N.Y. 1981); *with* International Housing, Ltd. v. Rafidain Bank Iraq, 893 F.2d 8 (2d Cir. 1990) (holding plaintiff foreign corporation did not suffer direct effect in U.S.); Colonial Bank v. CGMF, 645 F. Supp. 1457 (S.D.N.Y. 1986); Carey v. National Oil Corp., 592 F. Supp. 673 (2d Cir. 1979); New Hampshire Ins. Co. v. Wellesley Capital Partners, Inc., 612 N.Y.S.2d 407 (1994).

352. 677 F. Supp. 1096 (D. Colo. 1988).

353. *Id.* at 1110.

354. *Id.* at 1098–99.

inference of a 'direct effect' as that term has been judicially interpreted.''[355]

In so holding, the court reviewed the various decisions under clause 3, and noted two distinct approaches used in determining what constitutes a direct effect. The first approach, the court noted ''involves examining the nature of the injury allegedly occurring in this country and determining from this whether such injury has had a sufficient impact in the United States to warrant haling the foreign sovereign into court.''[356] The court found this approach unsatisfactory because it is based ''upon rigid categorization of injury and plaintiff status. . . .''[357]

The court found the second approach preferable. It focuses ''not on the nature of the injury sustained, but instead on the strength of the nexus between the allegedly unlawful act and the United States. . . ,'' and involves a causal analysis, not an ''itemization or classification of the damage sustained.''[358] In support of its preference, the court looked to the function of the direct effect test:

> In requiring the commercial activity of the foreign sovereign to have a direct effect in the United States, the statute clearly contemplates and demands a nexus between the allegedly unlawful activity and the damage sustained which is conceptually distinct from the traditional private law rules of causation.[359]

In summary, the court's decision in *Four Corners Helicopters* provides an overview of the approaches to determining the nexus requirement for purposes of a direct effect under clause 3 of section 1605(a)(2). As the court's decision illustrates, different approaches result in different decisions, an important feature for future development of precedent under clause 3.

Summary & Practice Note: The FSIA's commercial activity exception remains one of the most complex provisions of the FSIA. Step-by-step analysis of the issues presented in a particular case provides a method for determining whether the exception is applicable to a particular

---

355. *Id.* at 1101.

356. *Id.* at 1100 (citing Australian Gov't Aircraft Factories v. Lynne, 743 F.2d 672 (9th Cir. 1984), *cert. denied,* 469 U.S. 1214 (1985); Texas Trading v. Republic of Nigeria, 647 F.2d 300 (2d Cir. 1981), *cert. denied,* 454 U.S. 1148 (1982)).

357. 677 F. Supp. at 1100.

358. *Id.*

359. *Id.*

dispute. Because of the sheer volume of reported precedent on the issue and its fact specific nature, however, many unsettled issues remain.

§ 7.07 EXCEPTION THREE: EXPROPRIATION

During Congress' consideration of legislation on the issue of foreign sovereign immunity, efforts were made to include provisions to alter the act of state doctrine as administered by U.S courts.[360] The act of state doctrine[361] operates to bar consideration by U.S. courts of acts of a foreign sovereign taken within its own territory.[362] Although such amendments have been proposed since passage of the FSIA in 1976,[363] in its current form the FSIA does not affect the substance of the U.S. act of state doctrine.[364] As the legislative history explains, the FSIA "in no way affects existing law on the extent to which, if at all, the 'act of state' doctrine may be applicable."[365] The House Committee "found it unnecessary to address the act of state doctrine in this legislation since decisions such as that in the *Alfred Dunhill of London, Inc. v. Republic of Cuba*[366] case demonstrate that our courts already have considerable guidance enabling them to reject improper assertions of the act of state doctrine."[367] Although the timing of the enactment of the FSIA and the Supreme Court's decision in the *Dunhill* case on a potential commercial activity exception to the act of state doctrine may have persuaded the Committee to defer action on the doctrine, the contours of such an exception remain undefined.[368]

What the FSIA does do is to provide an exception to sovereign immunity in certain so-called expropriation cases. Section 1605(a)(3) of the FSIA provides an exception from immunity in any case:

> in which rights in property taken in violation of international law are in issue and that property or any property exchanged for such property is present in the United States in connection with a commercial activity carried on in the United States by the foreign state; or that property or

360. *See, e.g.*, Timothy B. Atkeson & Stephen D. Ramsey, *Proposed Amendment to the Foreign Sovereign Immunities Act*, 79 AM. J. INT'L L. 770 (1985).

361. *See infra* Chapter 8.

362. *Id.*

363. *See* Atkeson & Ramsey, *supra* note 360.

364. House Report, *supra* note 1, at 19–20.

365. *Id.* at 20 (citation and footnote omitted).

366. 425 U.S. 682 (1976).

367. House Report, *supra* note 1, at 20.

368. *See infra* § 8.10.

> any property exchanged for such property is owned or operated by an agency or instrumentality of the foreign state and that agency or instrumentality is engaged in a commercial activity in the United States.[369]

Section 1605(a)(3) creates two exceptions to the general rule of immunity for foreign sovereigns, if the property is "taken in violation of international law." The legislative history defines this phrase to include "nationalization or expropriation of property without payment of the prompt adequate and effective compensation required by international law. . . . It would also include takings which are arbitrary or discriminatory in nature."[370] A taking in violation of international law does not occur where three requisites are met: First, the taking must serve a public purpose; second, aliens must not be discriminated against; and third, payment of just compensation must be made.[370.1] A plaintiff must exhaust her remedies in the foreign jurisdiction to seek compensation for the taking prior to commencing an action in U.S. court. The exhaustion requirement may be excused where the remedies are a sham, inadequate, or would be unreasonably prolonged.[370.2]

If the action falls into this category, then the first exception involves cases in which the taken property (or property exchanged for it) is *present* in the United States, and that presence is in connection with a commercial activity[371] carried on in the United States by the foreign sovereign or an instrumentality. The second exception involves cases in which the taken property (again, or any property exchanged for such property) is *owned or operated*, but not necessarily present in the United States, by an agency or instrumentality that is engaged in a commercial activity in the United States.

In one of the few cases exercising FSIA jurisdiction under section 1605(a)(3), the court in *De Sanchez v. Banco Central De Nicaragua*[372]

---

369. 28 U.S.C.A. § 1605(a)(3).

370. House Report, *supra* note 1, at 19–20. "Under international law, the date of taking is fixed by the date of the expropriation decrees and/or the date of physical seizure, and not by a subsequent date of repudiation of an undertaking to provide compensation." Letter from Richard Fairbanks, Asst. Sec'y of State, (Oct. 2, 1981), *reprinted in* S. Rep. No. 211, 97th Cong., 1st Sess. 4-5 (1981), and *quoted in* Dayton v. Czechoslovak Socialist Republic, 834 F.2d 203, 206-06 (D.C. Cir. 1987).

370.1. Siderman de Blake v. Republic of Argentina, 965 F.2d 699, 711-12 (9th Cir. 1992), *cert. denied*, 113 S.Ct. 1812 (1993).

370.2. Restatement (Third) of Foreign Relations Law, § 713, cmt. f.

371. *See supra* § 7.06.

372. 515 F. Supp. 900 (E.D. La. 1981).

relied on the second expropriation exception.[373] The court found that the defendant instrumentality of the Nicaraguan government was engaged in commercial activity in the United States through the holding of funds in a U.S. bank for the facilitation of currency exchanges.[374] Consequently, the court exercised jurisdiction over the claim, and denied the defendant's motion to dismiss for lack of jurisdiction.[375] Moreover, because the alleged activity fell within the territorial exception to the act of state doctrine,[376] the court in *De Sanchez* also reasoned that the act of state doctrine would not operate to bar consideration of the plaintiff's

(*Text continued on page 7-63*)

373. *Id.* at 910.
374. *Id.* at 911.
375. *Id.* at 914.
376. *See infra* § 8.06.

claim.[377] The *De Sanchez* case illustrates a relatively rare fact pattern that satisfies the third exception to immunity under the FSIA.

The court's decision in *Vencedora Oceanica Navigacion v. Compagnie Nationale Alegerienne de Navigation*,[378] interpreted the second exception, in a claim involving consideration of property "operated" by an instrumentality. The court explained that:

> Although no court has interpreted "owned or operated," the legislative history of the FSIA indicates that section 1603(a)(3) was intended to subject to United States jurisdiction any foreign agency or instrumentality that has nationalized or expropriated property without compensation, or that is *using expropriated property taken by another branch of the state.*[379]

The court reviewed the factual allegations and without considering the fact that it was unclear whether the property was "taken in violation of international law," concluded that no evidence existed that an instrumentality had "assumed control" of the property and "used it" for the benefit of the government.[380]

The *De Sanchez* and *Vencedora* decisions, as two of the few opinions to examine the expropriation exception, provide an indication of some of the considerations that are involved in its application. Future decisions will continue this process.[381]

§ 7.08 EXCEPTION FOUR: GIFTS AND IMMOVABLE PROPERTY

The fourth exception to sovereign immunity provided by the FSIA is actually a codification in the statute of a preexisting exception that even predates the adoption of the restrictive theory of sovereign immunity.[382] In what has come to be commonly referred to as the Tate Letter, in which the United States adopted the restrictive theory of sovereign immunity, the United States acknowledged that under both the absolute and restrictive theories, "sovereign immunity should not be claimed or granted in actions with respect to real property (diplomatic and perhaps consular property excepted) or with respect to the disposition of the

---

377. 515 F. Supp. at 910 n.10.

378. 730 F.2d 195 (5th Cir. 1984).

379. *Id.* at 204.

380. *Id. See also* Gabay v. Mostazafan Foundation of Iran, 151 F.R.D. 250 (S.D.N.Y. 1993) (permitting discovery on factual issues that would be predicate for expropriation exception).

381. *See* von Mehren, *supra* note 2, at 57–60.

382. *See* Tate Letter, *supra* note 5.

property of a deceased person even though a foreign sovereign is the beneficiary.''[383] This exception was codified in section 1605(a)(4) of the FSIA.[384]

Section 1605(a)(4) provides an exception to immunity in cases ''in which rights in property in the United States acquired by succession or gift or rights in immovable property situated in the United States are in issue.''[385] As to gifts or succession, the legislative history explains that immunity should not be granted because ''in claiming rights in a decedent's estate or obtained by gift, the foreign state claims the same right which is enjoyed by private persons.''[386] With respect to immovable property, the legislative history notes that whether the property is used for public or commercial purposes is of no import, and concludes that ''a foreign state cannot deny to the local state the right to adjudicate questions of ownership, rent, servitudes, and similar matters, as long as the foreign state's possession of the premises is not disturbed.''[387]

In *Asociacion de Reclamantes v. United Mexican States*,[388] one of the few cases interpreting the immovable property exception,[389] the court provided some of the contours of the exception. At issue in *Asociacion de Reclamantes* was ''whether Congress, in enacting the FSIA, intended the phrase 'rights in immovable property' to be broad enough to encompass rights to compensation traceable historically to disputes over title to American land, which disputes have been settled by international agreement.''[390] The court held that Congress did not so intend because the ''principal state interest that underlies the real property exception to sovereign immunity is . . . not implicated,'' and affirmed the district court's dismissal for lack of jurisdiction under section 1605(a)(4) of the FSIA.[391]

383. *Id.*

384. 28 U.S.C.A. § 1605(a)(4).

385. *Id.*

386. House Report, *supra* note 1, at 20.

387. *Id.*

388. 735 F.2d 1517 (D.C. Cir. 1984), *cert. denied,* 470 U.S. 1057 (1985).

389. In *Asociacion,* the court cites and quotes an unreported district court case: County Board v. German Democratic Republic, Civil No. 78–293–A (E.D. Va. Sept. 6, 1978), *reprinted in* 17 INT'L LEGAL MATERIALS 1404 (1978).

390. *Id.* at 1520.

391. *Id.* at 1521. *See also* MacArthur Area Citizen's Ass'n v. Republic of Peru, 809 F.2d 918, 920–21 (D.C. Cir. 1987) (finding § 1605(a)(4) inapplicable to claim for wrongful conversion of residence into chancery because action sounded in nuisance, not real property); 767 Third Ave. Assocs. v. Consulate General of Socialist Federal Republic of Yugoslavia, 218

§ 7.09 EXCEPTION FIVE: TORTIOUS CONDUCT

Section 1605(a)(5) of the FSIA contains the fifth limitation on the ability of foreign states to claim sovereign immunity. This section specifically declares that a foreign state will not be granted immunity from the jurisdiction of the courts of the United States in an action:

> in which money damages are sought against a foreign state for personal injury or death, or damage to or loss of property, occurring in the United States and caused by the tortious act or omission of that foreign state or of any official or employee of that foreign state while acting within the scope of his office or employment.[392]

Section 1605(a)(5) specifically exempts any actions based on the performance of discretionary functions, or claims arising out of certain specified torts, including: "malicious prosecution, abuse of process, libel, slander, misrepresentation, deceit, or interference with contract rights."[393]

However, at least one Circuit Court has narrowly construed the jurisdictional bar contained in 28 U.S.C.A. § 1605(a)(5)(B) concerning the enumerated torts and, particularly, interference with contract rights. In *Export Group v. Reef Industries, Inc.*,[393.1] the Ninth Circuit reversed the district court and ruled that notwithstanding § 1605(a)(5)(B), a plaintiff may sue for interference with contract rights where the claim may be characterized as arising under the commercial activity exception

F.3d 152, 162 (2d Cir. 2000) (refuting plaintiff/landlords' argument in case concerning lease of office space to the former Socialist Federal Republic of Yugoslavia (SFRY), which had ceased to exist, for use as consular offices, that 28 U.S.C.A. § 1605(a)(4) "eliminates any concern regarding justiciability" because it concerns acquisition of "rights in property" by a foreign state through "succession or gift" and stating, "[a]s is clear both from the language of the statute and the legislative history, however, that section governs acquisition of property through bequests or gifts (as opposed to a commercial transaction"), and in no way refers to state succession"); Rodriguez v. Republic of Costa Rica, 139 F. Supp. 2d 173, 195 (D.P.R. 2001) (finding exception not applicable in suit by private landowner against Republic of Costa Rica arising from breach of rental contract concerning use of residence as Consulate and stating "[d]espite ambiguous statements in the FSIA's legislative history, precedent clearly denotes that, where the right to actual possession or title is not at stake, compensation rights "are not remotely 'rights in immovable property' within the meaning of § 1605(a)(4)''' and *citing Asociacion de Reclamantes*, *supra* note 388).

392. 28 U.S.C.A. § 1605(a)(5). *See* House Report, *supra* note 1, at 20.

393. 28 U.S.C.A. § 1605(a)(5)(A) & (B). *See* Bryks v. CBC, 906 F. Supp. 204 (S.D.N.Y. 1996) (defamation is excluded from tortious act exception; party cannot seek application of commercial activity exception for conduct excluded under § 1605(a)(5)).

393.1. 54 F.3d 1466 (9th Cir. 1995).

to immunity contained in § 1605(a)(2).[393.2] The Court stated, "[t]he clear statutory language of section 1605(a)(5) indicates that both this exception and the restrictions upon this exception are intended to apply only to torts 'not otherwise encompassed in [section 1605(a)(2)].'"[393.3] The Export Group brought claims for business torts, including interference with contractual relations, against a Mexican Government Agency. An employee of the government agency allegedly leaked the details of Export Group's bid on a contract, resulting in Export Group's loss of the contract and approximately $2 million. In reaching its decision, the Court distinguished *Gregorian v. Izvestia*,[393.4] which ruled to the contrary, that foreign states are immune from claims for the enumerated torts in § 1605(a)(5)(B), even when those torts arise from the foreign state's commercial activities. Rather, the *Export Group* Court appeared to rely on its own statutory interpretation and cases in other contexts which suggested that § 1605(a)(2) and § 1605(a)(5) are mutually exclusive.

Courts have also confronted the issue of whether a particular action by a foreign sovereign is discretionary.[394] For instance, in *MacArthur Area Citizen's Ass'n v. Republic of Peru*,[395] the court found that Peru's conversion of a residence into a chancery was a discretionary act, and therefore immune form consideration under section 1605(a)(5).[396] *In Olsen v. Government of Mexico*,[397] the court found that although the transport of prisoners pursuant to an exchange agreement with the United States was a discretionary act, acts or omissions contributing to the death of prisoners were not.[398] The court reviewed the interpretation

---

393.2. *See supra* § 7.06[2], providing overview of commercial activity exception provided in 28 U.S.C.A. § 1605(a)(2).

393.3. *Id., quoting* Joseph v. Office of Consulate General of Nigeria, 830 F.2d 1018, 1025 (9th Cir. 1987), *cert. denied,* 108 S. Ct. 1077 (1988).

393.4. 658 F. Supp. 1224, 1234-35 (C.D. Cal. 1987), *aff'd in part, rev'd in part,* 871 F.2d 1515 (9th Cir.), *cert. denied,* 110 S. Ct. 237 (1989).

394. *See, e.g.,* MacArthur Area Citizen's Ass'n v. Republic of Peru, 809 F.2d 918, 921–22 (D.C. Cir. 1987); Olsen v. Government of Mexico, 729 F.2d 641, 647 (9th Cir. 1984). In Skeen v. Federative Republic of Brazil, 566 F. Supp. 1414, 1420 (D.D.C. 1983), the court held that FSIA jurisdiction did not exist over an action for assault committed by the child of an ambassador.

395. 809 F.2d 918 (D.C. Cir. 1987).

396. *Id.* at 921–22.

397. 729 F.2d 641 (9th Cir. 1984), *cert. denied,* 469 U.S. 917 (1984).

398. *Id.* at 647.

of the term "discretionary" under a similar exception in the Federal Tort Claims Act.[399]

If the action does not involve a discretionary act or any of the enumerated torts excluded from section 1605(a)(5), courts have generated guidance on the sorts of tortious acts or omissions that are subject to action under the FSIA.[400] The interpretive question under section 1605(a)(5) is the language that requires some portion of the tortious acts or omissions to occur in the United States. The legislative history states that "the tortious act or omission must occur within the jurisdiction of the United States. . . ."[401] In combination, the statutory language and the legislative history have resulted in cases focusing on the location of the acts at issue.

Several cases finding jurisdiction under the tortious act provision have been those in which both the tort and the injury occurred in the United States.[402] For instance, the court in *Olsen v. Government of Mexico*,[403] suggests that if a plaintiff is able to "allege at least one entire tort occurring in the United States," the claim can be maintained under section 1605(a)(5). At issue in *Olsen* was an unusual fact pattern in which a plane carrying prisoners travelling from Mexico to the United States as part of a prisoner exchange arrangement between the two nations was rerouted due to poor weather conditions. The rerouting took the plane over U.S. air space temporarily where it crashed, less than one mile inside U.S. territory. The court found the "territorial" requirement of the FSIA satisfied, and denied immunity.[404]

Other cases denying jurisdiction under section 1605(a)(5) have involved acts or injury that occurred outside the United States.[405] *In*

---

399. *Id.* (citing 28 U.S.C. § 2680(a)).

400. *See, e.g.*, De Sanchez v. Banco Central de Nicaragua, 770 F.2d 1385 (5th Cir. 1985); Asociacion de Reclamantes v. United Mexican States, 735 F.2d 1517 (D.C. Cir. 1984), *cert. denied*, 470 U.S. 1057 (1985); Persinger v. Islamic Republic of Iran, 729 F.2d 835 (D.C. Cir.), *cert. denied*, 469 U.S. 881 (1984); Olsen v. Government of Mexico, 729 F.2d 641 (9th Cir.), *cert. denied*, 469 U.S. 917 (1984); Kline v. Republic of El Salvador, 603 F. Supp. 1313 (D.D.C. 1985); *In re* Sedco, Inc., 543 F. Supp. 561 (S.D. Tex. 1982); Castro v. Saudi Arabia, 510 F. Supp. 309 (W.D. Tex. 1980); Letelier v. Republic of Chile, 488 F. Supp. 665 (D.D.C. 1980).

401. House Report, *supra* note 1, at 21.

402. *See, e.g.*, De Sanchez v. Banco Central de Nicaragua, 770 F.2d 1385 (5th Cir. 1985); Olsen v. Government of Mexico, 729 F.2d 641 (9th Cir. 1984); Letelier v. Republic of Chile, 488 F. Supp. 665 (D.D.C. 1980).

403. 729 F.2d 641, 646 (9th Cir. 1984).

404. *Id.* at 646.

405. Asociacion de Reclamantes v. United Mexican States, 735 F.2d 1517 (D.C. Cir. 1984), *cert. denied*, 470 U.S. 1057 (1985); Persinger v. Islamic Republic of Iran, 729 F.2d 835

Persinger v. Islamic Republic of Iran,[406] for example, the D.C. Circuit construed the tortious act exception to the FSIA in a case involving a claim against Iran following the taking of American hostages in Teheran on November 4, 1979. The court concluded that the American Embassy in Teheran could not be considered part of the "United States" for purposes of section 1605(a)(5). Consequently, the tortious act and injury arose outside the United States and Iran was entitled to immunity. The court held that the tortious act exception applied only when both the tort and injury occurred in the United States.[407]

A similar case involved the alleged murder of an American citizen in Central America. In *Kline v. Republic of El Salvador,*[408] the parents of the victim brought suit against El Salvador for the tort of intentional infliction of emotional distress. The court, following *Persinger,* held that El Salvador was immune from the suit since the tortious act did not occur within the United States.[409] The plaintiffs, therefore, could not utilize the exception to immunity under section 1605(a)(5).

Practice Note: In summary, the tortious act exception to the FSIA provides an exception to immunity for certain torts that are not discretionary acts, if substantially all of the tortious acts or omissions, and the resulting injury, occur in the United States.

§ 7.10 EXCEPTION SIX: ENFORCEMENT OF ARBITRAL AWARDS

Added by amendment to the FSIA in 1988,[410] section 1605(a)(6) provides an additional exception from immunity for the enforcement of arbitral awards. The property of a foreign state "used for a commercial activity in the United States" is not immune from execution if it is based on a judgment confirming an arbitral award under section 1605(a)(6).[411] Under the amendment, U.S. courts may enforce an award, if:

(D.C. Cir.), *cert. denied,* 469 U.S. 881 (1984); Kline v. Republic of El Salvador, 603 F. Supp. 1313 (D.D.C. 1985).

406. 729 F.2d 835 (D.C. Cir.), *cert. denied,* 469 U.S. 881 (1984).

407. *Id.* at 842. *See also* Cicippio v. Islamic Republic of Iran, 30 F.3d 164, 169 (D.C. Cir. 1994) (affirming dismissal of hostage's suit against Iran following *Persinger* because neither act nor injury occurred in the United States).

408. 603 F. Supp. 1313 (D.D.C. 1985).

409. *Id.* at 1316.

410. Pub. L. No. 100–669, 102 Stat. 3969 (1988).

411. 28 U.S.C.A. § 1610(a)(6). *See infra* § 7.17.

> (A) the arbitration takes place . . . in the United States, [or] (B) the agreement or award is or may be governed by a treaty or other international agreement in force for the United States calling for the recognition and enforcement of arbitral awards, [or] (C) the underlying claim, save for the agreement to arbitrate, could have been brought in a United States court. . . .[412]

These changes are expected to enhance the enforcement of arbitral awards in U.S. courts, especially because it permits execution upon property owned by a foreign state that is not necessarily held in the U.S. in connection with the commercial activity upon which the arbitral decision was based.[413]

A finding of waiver of immunity, however, does not necessarily confer jurisdiction in the United States. In *Creighton Ltd. v. Gov't of State of Qatar*,[413.1] the D.C. Circuit found that Quatar had waived immunity under section 1605(a)(6) by participating in arbitration administered by the International Chamber of Commerce in France, a signatory State to the New York Convention.[413.2] The Court, however, found that Qatar had not waived its objection to the Court's asserting personal jurisdiction and that Qatar lacked sufficient minimum contacts for the exercise of jurisdiction.

---

412. 28 U.S.C.A. § 1605(a)(6).

413. 28 U.S.C.A. § 1610(a)(6) (requiring only that property be "used for a commercial activity in the United States"). For discussion of the enforcement of arbitral awards in a non-FSIA context, *see infra* Chapter 11.

413.1. 181 F.3d 118 (D.C. Cir. July 2, 1999, *reh'g en banc denied*, Sept. 7, 1999).

413.2. The New York Convention on the Recognition and Enforcement of Foreign Arbitral Awards is discussed *infra* § 12.06. In Skandia American Reinsurance Corp. v. Caja Nacional de Ahorro y Segoro, 1997 WL 278054 (S.D.N.Y. May 21, 1997), the court examined the interrelation between the N.Y. Convention on the Recognition and Enforcement of Foreign Arbitral Awards and the FSIA. In that case, a U.S. insurance company brought a proceeding to confirm an arbitration award against the defendant, an instrumentality of Argentina. The U.S. plaintiff moved the court to require the defendant to post security to secure payment of any final judgment. The Court analogized such request as an order of attachment under the FSIA. The Court observed that the FSIA restricts the availability of prejudgment attachment to certain circumstances not present here. The Court ruled that the security sought by the plaintiff was proper under the FSIA, however, because the FSIA is expressly subject to N.Y. Convention requirements. The N.Y. Convention expressly addresses in article VI the posting of security where a defendant seeks to set aside or suspend an arbitral award.

§ 7.11 EXCEPTION SEVEN: MONETARY DAMAGES ACTION CONCERNING TERRORIST ACTIVITY

The Antiterrorism and Effective Death Penalty Act of 1996,[414] added a new exception to sovereign immunity concerning certain terrorist acts carried out by official action of a foreign state.[415] Section 1605(a)(7) provides that a foreign state is not immune from the jurisdiction of the courts of the United States where:

> money damages are sought against a foreign state for personal injury or death that was caused by an act of torture, extrajudicial killing, aircraft sabotage, [or] hostage taking, or the provision of material support or resources . . . for such an act if such act or provision of material support is engaged in by an official, employee, or agent of such foreign state while acting within the scope of his or her office, employment, or agency. . . .[416]

The Statute imposes, however, several limitations. The defendant-foreign state must be officially designated as a "state sponsor of terrorism" at the time the act complained of occurred or later so designated because of such act.[417] Also, the claimant must have allowed reasonable opportunity for the foreign state to "arbitrate the claim in accordance with accepted international rules of arbitration," where the complained of act occurred in the foreign states' territory.[418] Also, the claimant must have been a U.S. national when the act occurred.[419]

The Statute defines the terms "torture," "hostage taking," and "aircraft sabotage."[420] The Statute also imposes a ten year limitation period.[421] Such limitation period, however, is presently toothless as the period is subject to "equitable tolling, including the period during which the foreign state was immune from suit. . . ."[422] Additionally, discovery may be curtailed where the U.S. Attorney General certifies that the

414. Pub. L. No. 104–132, Title II, § 221(a), Apr. 24, 1996, 110 Stat. 1241.
415. 28 U.S.C.A. § 1605(a)(7), (e)–(g).
416. 28 U.S.C.A. § 1605(a)(7).
417. *Id.* § 1605(a)(7)(A).
418. *Id.* § 1605(a)(7)(B)(i).
419. *Id.* § 1605(a)(7)(B)(ii).
420. *Id.* § 1605(e)(1)–(3).
421. *Id.* § 1605(f).
422. *Id.*

discovery would significantly interfere with a criminal investigation or national security operation.[423]

Enforcement of a judgment under § 1605(a)(7) is facilitated by § 1610(a)(7), which provides that property of the foreign state or its agency or instrumentality in the U.S. "used for commercial activity in the United States" may be attached and judgment thereupon executed.[424]

Several courts have now addressed the state-sponsored terrorism exception to sovereign immunity.[424.1]

§ 7.12 EXCEPTION EIGHT: ENFORCEMENT OF MARITIME LIENS

In admiralty cases, a very specialized area of law, counsel should be aware of an exception to sovereign immunity contained in section 1605(b) of the FSIA for cases involving maritime liens.[425] Section 1605(b) provides an exception—under certain conditions—from immunity in suits in admiralty to enforce maritime liens against a vessel or cargo of a foreign state, if the liens are based on a commercial activity of a foreign state.[426] The conditions are intricate, and the procedures for initiation of a suit must be carefully followed.[427] As one court explained:

> One of the purposes of the FSIA was to eliminate the need for attaching the vessel of a foreign government for the purpose of obtaining jurisdiction. . . . To discourage this practice, the statute provides that the notice of suit will not be deemed effective if the plaintiff improperly has arrested a foreign vessel for the purpose of in rem jurisdiction. . . . Prejudgment attachment is permitted only where the foreign state explicitly has waived its immunity and the purposes of the attachment is not to obtain jurisdiction.[428]

---

423. *Id.* § 1605(g).

424. 28 U.S.C.A. § 1610(a)(7), (b)(2).

424.1 *See, e.g.*, Flatow v. Islamic Republic of Iran, 999 F. Supp. 1 (D.D.C. 1998) (suit against Iran by parents of U.S. citizen killed in Israel by Iran-sponsored terrorist group); Rein v. Socialist People's Libyan Arab Jamahirya, 995 F. Supp. 325 (E.D.N.Y. 1998); Alejandre v. Republic of Cuba, 996 F. Supp. 1239 (S.D. Fla. 1997) (claims arising from 1996 Cuban Air Force's downing of two unarmed planes outside Cuban air space).

425. 28 U.S.C.A. § 1605(b).

426. *Id. See* RESTATEMENT (THIRD), *supra* note 6, § 455.

427. *See, e.g.*, Jet Line Servs., Inc. v. M/V Marsa El Hariga, 462 F. Supp. 1165 (D. Md. 1978).

428. O'Connell Machinery Co. v. M/V Americana, 734 F.2d 115, 117 (2d Cir.) (citations omitted), *cert. denied*, 469 U.S. 1086 (1984).

Recent amendments to the FSIA have made the notice process less draconian, but the liability under section 1605(b) remains limited by its terms to the value of the vessel or cargo.

Because the FSIA eliminated *in rem* actions involving the attachment or arrest of a vessel as a basis for establishing jurisdiction,[429] the procedures under section 1605(b) require that notice and service occur to commence an in personam action under the FSIA.[430] Under the FSIA as originally enacted, if the plaintiff was unaware of the interest of a foreign state in the vessel or the cargo, and arrest of the vessel took place, plaintiff lost the right to its in personam action, and the foreign state could rely on its immunity.[431] In amendments to the FSIA in 1988, Congress recognized the unfairness of this consequence of section 1605(b) and added the following language: "but the party bringing the suit shall be liable for any damages sustained by the foreign state as a result of the arrest if the party bringing suit had actual or constructive knowledge that the vessel or cargo of a foreign state was involved."[432] Even with the 1988 amendments, section 1605(b) remains an intricate provision; care should be exercised to determine whether a foreign state has an interest in the vessel or the cargo prior to any action being taken.

§ 7.13 EXCEPTION NINE: JURISDICTION OVER COUNTERCLAIMS

Unusual immunity questions are presented when a foreign state or instrumentality voluntarily subjects itself to the jurisdiction of U.S. courts, whether by initiating litigation, or intervening in ongoing litigation in the United States. Because the purposes of the FSIA are often not implicated, the FSIA denies immunity to foreign states on certain counterclaims asserted against them in a number of situations. The three situations in which jurisdiction over counterclaims may be upheld, and immunity denied to the foreign state, are specified in section 1607 of the FSIA.[433] It is almost axiomatic that section 1607 may not

429. *See* House Report, *supra* note 1, at 8.

430. *See* China Nat'l Chem. Import & Export Corp. v. M/V Lago Hualaihue, 504 F. Supp. 684, 687 (D. Md. 1981).

431. *See* O'Connell Machinery Co. v. M/V Americana, 734 F.2d 115, 117 (2d Cir. 1984).

432. 28 U.S.C.A. § 1605(b)(1); Pub. L. No. 100–640, 102 Stat. 3333, § 1 (1988).

433. *See generally* First Nat'l City Bank v. Banco Para El Comercio Exterior de Cuba, 462 U.S. 611 (1983); Ministry of Supply, Cairo v. Universe Tankships, Inc., 708 F.2d 80 (2d Cir. 1983).

provide a basis for jurisdiction unless the foreign state initiates the action or intervenes.[434]

In three subsections, section 1607 provides that a foreign state is not entitled to immunity:

> [W]ith respect to any counterclaim
>
> (a) for which a foreign state would not be entitled to immunity under section 1605 of this chapter had such claim been brought in a separate action against the foreign state; or
>
> (b) arising out of the transaction or occurrence that is the subject matter of the claim of the foreign state; or
>
> (c) to the extent that the counterclaim does not seek relief exceeding in amount or differing in kind from that sought by the foreign state.[435]

The first case in which a foreign state will not be granted immunity with respect to a counterclaim is when the foreign state would not be entitled to immunity under section 1605 had the claim been brought in a separate action against the foreign state.[436] Although arguably unnecessary, the first counterclaim exception explicitly prevents a claim of immunity if the defendant could have brought the suit under the FSIA, but for the coincidence of the foreign state initiating the action.

The second subsection denies the foreign state immunity with respect to any counterclaim which arises out of "the transaction or occurrence that is the subject matter of the claim of the foreign state."[437] As the legislative history explains, even if the action is not one that would fall within an exception under section 1605, "if a foreign state brings or intervenes in an action based on a particular transaction or occurrence, it should not obtain the benefits of litigation before U.S. courts while avoiding any legal liabilities claimed against it and arising from that same transaction or occurrence."[438] In *In re Oil Spill by*

434. *See, e.g.*, Alberti v. Empresa Nicaraguenese De La Carne, 705 F.2d 250, 254 (7th Cir. 1983) (holding § 1607 may not be used to seek declaratory judgment of right to offset should foreign sovereign initiate suit or intervene).

435. 28 U.S.C.A. § 1607.

436. 28 U.S.C.A. § 1607(a).

437. 28 U.S.C.A. § 1607(b). *See* Ministry of Supply, Cairo v. Universe Tankships, Inc., 708 F.2d 80 (2d Cir. 1983).

438. House Report, *supra* note 1, at 23 (citing Alfred Dunhill of London, Inc. v. Cuba, 425 U.S. 682 (1976)); *see also* Chapter 8 (addressing Act of State doctrine).

Amoco Cadiz Off Coast of France,[439] the court interpreted the phrase "transaction or occurrence" to permit both counterclaims and third-party claims to overcome assertions of immunity.[440]

The final exception under section 1607 denies immunity "to the extent that the counterclaim does not seek relief exceeding in amount or differing in kind from that sought by the foreign state."[441] This is the so-called "setoff" exception to immunity in cases of a counterclaim: "notwithstanding that the foreign state may be immune under subsections (a) and (b), the foreign state would not be immune from a setoff."[442] As the Legislative history explains, subsection (c) essentially codifies the rule articulated by the Supreme Court in *National Bank v. Republic of China.*[443] In *Republic of China,* the Court held that "the consideration of fair dealing which allows a setoff or counterclaim based on the same subject matter" prevented China from claiming immunity on a counterclaim.[444] These considerations resulted in an exception to immunity that predated the FSIA, and was codified in its enactment.[445]

Practice Note: The counterclaim exception to sovereign immunity is the final basis for jurisdiction discussed in this chapter. Counsel should now turn to the other important issues under the FSIA presented once subject matter jurisdiction is established: personal jurisdiction, service of process, and attachment and execution.

§ 7.14 IN PERSONAM JURISDICTION UNDER THE FSIA

Although under the FSIA subject matter and personal jurisdiction are rarely analyzed separately, they are two distinct questions, both of which must be addressed. One of the reasons for the dearth of judicial analysis is the structure of the FSIA.[446] The Act provides for the exercise of personal jurisdiction under section 1330(b). This section is satisfied,

---

439. 491 F. Supp. 161 (N.D. Ill. 1979).

440. *Id.* at 168.

441. 28 U.S.C.A. 1607(c).

442. House Report, *supra* note 1, at 23.

443. 348 U.S. 356 (1955). *See also* First Nat'l City Bank v. Banco Para el Comercio Exterior de Cuba, 462 U.S. 611 (1983).

444. *Id.* at 365.

445. *See infra* § 8.09 (discussing setoff/counterclaim exception to act of state doctrine).

446. *See, e.g.,* RESTATEMENT (THIRD), *supra* note 6, § 453, cmt. c (analyzing minimum contacts issues as adjunct to question of subject matter jurisdiction).

however, if subject matter jurisdiction exists,[447] and if service is perfected under section 1608 of the Act.[448]

Practice Note: An analysis of personal jurisdiction issues is often subsumed under the examination of whether subject matter jurisdiction exists. Nevertheless, in personam jurisdiction must either be established or waived before a case may proceed to the merits. Counsel should exercise caution in this area and treat each of the jurisdictional issues separately, if only for analytical purposes, to avoid failing to establish personal jurisdiction.

The legislative history contemplates satisfaction of personal jurisdiction as a distinct issue, and explains that it embodies the "requirements of minimum jurisdictional contacts and adequate notice."[449] As the House Report explains:

> For personal jurisdiction to exist under section 1330(b), the claim must first of all be one over which the district courts have original jurisdiction under section 1330(a), meaning a claim for which the foreign state is not entitled to immunity. Significantly, each of the immunity provisions in the bill, sections 1605–1607, requires some connection between the lawsuit and the United States, or an express or implied waiver by the foreign state of its immunity from jurisdiction. Besides incorporating these jurisdictional contacts by reference, section 1330(b) also satisfies the due process requirement of adequate notice by prescribing that proper service be made under section 1608 of the bill.[450]

As the House Report describes, the notice requirement is satisfied by service pursuant to section 1608.[451]

The other due process element of section 1330(b) requires a determination of whether the exercise of personal jurisdiction over the particular defendant comports with the traditional safeguards of constitutional due process.[452] As the court stated in *Texas Trading & Milling*

---

447. *See supra* § 7.04.

448. *See infra* § 7.16.

449. House Report, *supra* note 1, at 13.

450. *Id.* at 13–14.

451. For a discussion of the service provisions of the FSIA, as they relate to both states and instrumentalities, *see infra* § 7.16.

452. *Id.* at 13. *See* International Shoe v. Washington, 326 U.S. 310 (1945). *See also* Chapters 5 and 6 for a discussion of jurisdiction in a non-FSIA context.

Corp. v. Federal Republic of Nigeria,[453] "each finding of personal jurisdiction under the FSIA requires . . a due process scrutiny of the court's power to exercise its authority over a particular defendant."[454] The minimum contacts test of *International Shoe Co. v. Washington*,[455] and its progeny,[456] are controlling in the determination of whether foreign sovereign defendants are subject to the jurisdiction of United States courts pursuant to section 1330(b) of the FSIA.[457]

Several courts have specifically analyzed the personal jurisdiction issues arising under section 1330(b) of the FSIA. For instance, in one of the first such cases, a district court found personal jurisdiction lacking in a case involving a U.S corporate plaintiff and a Mexican banking institution defendant. In *Waukesha Engine Div. v. Banco Nacional de Fomento Cooperativo*,[458] the Mexican bank (Banfoco) had entered into a contract with the plaintiff corporation for the manufacture of marine engines, to be produced in Wisconsin. In addition, Banfoco had sent an officer of the Bank to Wisconsin to conduct an inspection of the engines. When Banfoco subsequently repudiated the contract, the Wisconsin corporation brought suit. Despite the existence of the contract and the visit of the Banfoco officer to Wisconsin, the court held that there were not sufficient contacts on which to base the exercise of personal jurisdiction over the foreign defendant.[459]

Shortly after the *Waukesha* decision, the Second Circuit addressed the issue of the exercise of personal jurisdiction over a foreign sovereign pursuant to the FSIA in *Texas Trading & Milling Corp. v. Federal*

453. 647 F.2d. 300 (2d Cir. 1981), *cert. denied*, 454 U.S. 1148 (1982).

454. *Id.* at 308. *See also* Thos. P. Gonzalez Corp. v. Consejo Nactional de Produccion de Costa Rica, 614 F.2d 1247, 1255 (9th Cir. 1980) (personal jurisdiction under the FSIA "requires satisfaction of the traditional minimum contacts standard"); Maritime Int'l Nominees Estab. v. Republic of Guinea, 693 F.2d 1094, 1105 & n.18 (D.C. Cir. 1982), *cert. denied*, 464 U.S. 815 (1983).

455. 326 U.S. 310 (1945).

456. *See* Asahi Metal Indus. Co., Ltd. v. Superior Court, 480 U.S. 102 (1987); Burger King Corp. v. Rudzewicz, 471 U.S. 462 (1985); Helicopteros Nacionales de Colombia, S.A. v. Hall, 466 U.S. 408 (1984); Rush v. Savchuk, 444 U.S. 320 (1980); World-Wide Volkswagen Corp. v. Woodson, 444 U.S. 286 (1980); Kulko v. Superior Court, 436 U.S. 84 (1978); Shaffer v. Heitner, 433 U.S. 186 (1977); Hanson v. Denckla, 357 U.S. 235 (1958); McGee v. International Life Ins. Co., 355 U.S. 220 (1957). For a discussion of in personam jurisdiction in a non-FSIA context, *see supra* Chapter 6.

457. *E.g.*, Verlinden B.V. v. Central Bank of Nigeria, 461 U.S. 480 (1983); RESTATEMENT (THIRD), *supra* note 6, § 453 reporters' note 3.

458. 485 F. Supp. 490 (E.D. Wis. 1980).

459. *Id.* at 493.

Republic of Nigeria.[460] The court analyzed various contacts that it deemed sufficient to exercise personal jurisdiction over the Nigerian government.[461] The court considered various details including the fact that the defendant benefitted from the privileges provided by doing business in the United States, that litigation was a foreseeable consequence of such activity, and that the United States had a legitimate interest in having the case heard in its courts.[462]

More recently, courts analyzing FSIA in personam jurisdiction issues have begun to rely on the general and specific theories of jurisdiction.[463] Under an analysis of specific, or limited, jurisdiction, the court examines the defendant's contacts that are related to the cause of action.[464] Under the general theory, the court must determine whether the defendant's contacts with the United States are "substantial," or "continuous and systematic."[465] For instance, in *Meadows v. Dominican Republic,*[466] the court found the exercise of in personam jurisdiction constitutional based on an examination of the defendant's contacts with the United States as a whole, including contacts unrelated to the cause of action.[467] More recently, the Ninth Circuit reaffirmed the "national contacts" test under the FSIA in *Richmark Corp. v. Timber Falling Consultants, Inc.*[468]

Practice Note: In summary, the requirement of section 1330(b) of the FSIA that personal jurisdiction exist must be analyzed separately from the issue of subject matter jurisdiction. If subsumed within the subject matter analysis, important features are likely to be overlooked and create vulnerability.

460. 647 F.2d. 300 (2d Cir. 1981), *cert. denied,* 454 U.S. 1148 (1982).
461. *Id.* at 308.
462. *Id.* at 313.
463. *See, e.g.,* Olsen v. Government of Mexico, 729 F.2d 641 (9th Cir.), *cert. denied,* 469 U.S. 917 (1984).
464. *Id.* at 648–49.
465. *Id.* at 648.
466. 628 F. Supp. 599 (N.D. Ca. 1986).
467. *Id.* at 607. *See also* Crimson Semiconductor v. Electronum, 629 F. Supp. 903 (S.D.N.Y. 1986).
468. 937 F.2d 1444, 1446–47 (9th Cir. 1991), 959 F.2d 1468 (9th Cir. 1992), *cert. dismissed,* 506 U.S. 948 (1993).

§ 7.15 SERVICE OF PROCESS ON FOREIGN STATES AND INSTRUMENTALITIES UNDER THE FSIA

[1] The FSIA Service Provisions

Under section 1330(b) of the FSIA, a court has personal jurisdiction over a particular foreign sovereign defendant if two conditions are satisfied. First, an exception to sovereign immunity must exist under sections 1605 or 1607.[469] Second, personal jurisdiction under the FSIA requires service of process and a due process analysis.[470] In section 1608 of the FSIA, Congress provided the exclusive means of service of process on foreign states and instrumentalities as a means of commencing suit.[471]

Because the FSIA provides different methods of service for a foreign state (or political subdivision thereof) as opposed to an agency or instrumentality of a foreign state, a threshold issue is one of identification and definition.[472] In either case the FSIA and the legislative history mandate that its service provisions are the "exclusive" means of serving an FSIA defendant.[473] Methods used prior to the enactment of the FSIA—such as service upon an embassy—are now clearly prohibited.[474]

The identification of the defendant's character is therefore a pivotal service of process issue under the FSIA. If the defendant is a foreign state, one set of rules applies, those under section 1608(a). If the defendant is an agency or instrumentality, another set applies, those under section 1608(b). This distinction was graphically illustrated in *Transaero, Inc. v. La Fuerza Aerea Boliviana*,[475] in which the court was faced with the question of whether the Bolivian Air Force was a foreign state or an instrumentality of a foreign state. Plaintiff had performed

469. *See supra* §§ 7.04–7.13 (addressing exceptions to immunity).

470. *See supra* § 7.14.

471. House Report, *supra* note 1, at 8. An excellent, detailed discussion of FSIA service provisions and procedure can be found on the World Wide Web: U.S. State Department, Bureau of Consular Affairs, "Foreign Sovereign Immunities Act" (http://travel.state.gov/fsia.html). *See generally* Velidor v. L/P/G Benghazi, 653 F.2d 812, 821 (3d Cir. 1981) (comparing service rules for instrumentalities and maritime liens; holding ship's master "agent" for purposes of service under § 1608(b)(2)). Special rules also exist for FSIA claims involving maritime liens, and will not be discussed in this section. *See supra* § 7.12.

472. *See supra* § 7.03[1] for a discussion of the process of distinguishing between states and instrumentalities.

473. House Report, *supra* note 1, at 23–25.

474. *Id.* at 26; Alberti v. Empresa Nicaraguense De La Carne, 705 F.2d 250, 253 (7th Cir. 1983) (service on ambassador insufficient under FSIA).

475. 30 F.3d 148 (D.C. Cir. 1994).

service as if the Air Force were an instrumentality. The court, however, held that the Air Force was a foreign state and must be served as a foreign state.[476] If the defendant's character cannot be definitively determined prior to the institution of proceedings, one option is to perform service according to both sets of provisions.[477]

[2] Service on Foreign States Under the FSIA

Section 1608(a)(1)–(4) provides four methods of service of process in a hierarchical manner.[477.1] The first method requires delivery of a copy of the summons and complaint pursuant to any "special arrangement" for service agreed upon between the plaintiff and the foreign state.[478] The purpose of this provision, according to the legislative history, "is to encourage potential plaintiffs and foreign states to agree to a procedure on service."[479] Although no reported cases have yet ruled on the contents of any "special arrangements,"[480] prudent counsel should consider inclusion of service procedures in any agreements with foreign states.[481]

In the absence of a private arrangement pursuant to section 1608(a)(1), subsection (a)(2) directs that a copy of the summons and complaint be delivered pursuant to an international convention in force between both nations addressing the service of judicial documents.[482]

If service is not possible under either of the first two methods, the third is the most common method of service and is based on former Rule 4(i)(2)(d) of the Federal Rules of Civil Procedure. Under the third method, the plaintiff must send a copy of the summons and complaint as well as a Notice of Suit with a translation of each in the official language

476. *Id.* at 151. *See also* § 7.03[1].

477. *See generally* George, *A Practical and Theoretical Analysis of Process Under the Foreign Sovereign Immunities Act,* 19 INT'L LAW. 49, 51 (1985).

477.1. *See* http://travel.state.gov/fsia.html, *supra* note 471 (detailing FSIA service provisions and procedure).

478. 28 U.S.C.A. § 1608(a)(1).

479. House Report, *supra* note 1, at 24.

480. George, *supra* note 477, at 52.

481. *Id.* at 52 ("It is advisable for the drafting attorney to provide for a method of service if convenience in litigation is likely to be in the client's interest.").

482. 28 U.S.C.A. § 1608(a)(2). The legislative history notes that the Hague Convention on Service Abroad of Judicial and Extrajudicial Documents, 20 U.S.T. 361, T.I.A.S. No. 6638 (1969), is the only such convention to which the United States is a party. House Report, *supra* note 1, at 24. For a discussion of service under the procedures established by international conventions, *see supra* Chapter 4. The text of the Hague Service Convention is reprinted *infra* Appendix 2[1].

of the foreign state, utilizing any form of return receipt mail, sent by the court clerk to the head of the ministry of foreign affairs of the foreign state involved.[483] Commentators have suggested that counsel for plaintiff consult Publication 42 of the United States Postal Service to determine whether the defendant foreign state has the requisite special mail service available.[484]

The legislative history explains the operation and nature of the notice of suit required under the third method:

> A "notice of suit" . . . would advise a foreign state of the legal proceeding, it would explain the legal significance of the summons, complaint and service, and it would indicate what steps are available under or required by U.S. law in order to defend the action. In short, it would provide an introductory explanation to the foreign state that may be unfamiliar with U.S. law or procedures.[485]

Regulations issued by the Department of State[486] provide the form and contents of a Notice of Suit required by section 1608, a copy of which is reproduced *infra* in Appendix 8[2].

If a foreign state which is a party to the Hague Service Convention formally objected to service by mail when it acceded to the Convention, service under section 1608(a)(3) should not be attempted, and the plaintiff should proceed to service under section 1608(a)(4). The Plaintiff should cite in the cover letter to the Department of State, Office of Overseas Citizens Services the foreign state's objection to service by mail as noted in the foreign state's accession to the Hague Service Convention.

If method three does not produce a signed receipt within thirty days, the FSIA provides for a final, fourth method. Under this method, the plaintiff must send two copies of the summons, complaint, and the notice of suit described above, again, each translated into the official language of the foreign state concerned, by return receipt mail by the court clerk to the State Department's Director of Overseas Citizens

---

483. 28 U.S.C.A. § 1608(a)(3). *See* Straub v. AP Green, Inc., 38 F.3d 448 (9th Cir. 1994) (applying "substantial compliance" test and finding that failure to have Clerk of Court mail process does not invalidate service under FSIA where actual notice of suit is received); Gerritsen v. Consulado General de Mexico, 989 F.2d 340, 345 (9th Cir. 1993) (having the court clerk send untranslated copy of the complaint to the president of Mexico by registered mail insufficient to qualify as service on foreign state).

484. *See* Asencio & Dry, *An Assessment of the Service Provisions of the Foreign Sovereign Immunities Act of 1976*, 8 J. Legis. 237–38 (1981).

485. House Report, *supra* note 1, at 24–25.

486. 22 C.F.R. § 93.2.

Services.[487] The Director of Overseas Citizens Services will examine the documents for sufficiency, and advise the court clerk of any missing items.[488] If sufficient, the Director will then send one set of copies to the foreign state via diplomatic channels, returning to the court clerk "a certified copy of the diplomatic note indicating when the papers were transmitted."[489]

In an interesting opinion involving service under the FSIA on countries with which the United States does not maintain diplomatic relations, the court in *New England Merchants Nat'l Bank v. Iran Power Generation & Transmission Co.*,[490] the court fashioned a fifth method of service on a foreign state permissible under the FSIA. Because "Congress did not seek to cover the problem of effecting service upon a foreign government should diplomatic channels be closed. . . ." the court decided to "fashion a mode of extraterritorial service."[491] Although the court recognized the unusual nature of its exercise, equitable considerations compelled its action.[492]

[3] Service on an Instrumentality Under the FSIA

The FSIA provision for service upon an agency or instrumentality contains much the same hierarchical framework as the provisions for service upon a foreign state.[493] The first method of service on an instrumentality is that of a special arrangement for service in an agreement between the parties.[494]

If no special arrangement is contained in the agreement, the second method delineates two alternative procedures.[495] First, service may be effected by "delivery of a copy of the summons and complaint either to an officer, a managing or general agent, or to any other agent authorized by appointment or by law to receive service of process in the United

487. *See* 22 C.F.R. § 93.1.
488. *Id.* § 93.1(b).
489. 28 U.S.C.A. § 1608(a)(4).
490. 495 F. Supp. 73 (S.D.N.Y. 1980).
491. *Id.* at 79.
492. *Id.* at 80–81.
493. 28 U.S.C.A. § 1608(b).
494. 28 U.S.C.A. § 1608(b)(1). *See generally* George, *supra* note 477, at 55 ("It should be easier to come to such an agreement with an agency or instrumentality than with the foreign state itself because most such entities operate as private commercial entities and often waive immunity to suit as a condition to a transaction. In the context of such a waiver, providing for a method of service is not a significant concession and is normally done.").
495. 28 U.S.C.A. § 1608(b)(2).

States'' for the agency or instrumentality.[496] Alternatively, service may be effected in accordance with an applicable international convention on service of documents, as provided for in section 1608(a)(2).[497]

If service cannot be effected on the instrumentality under either the first or second method, the third method provides three different procedures. Counsel should not attempt service under § 1608(b)(3) if service under the first two methods is possible.[497.1] Each must be ''reasonably calculated to give actual notice'' to the instrumentality defendant to comport with constitutional due process.[498] First, a copy of the summons and complaint, with translation attached, may be delivered ''as directed by an authority of a foreign state or political subdivision in response to a letter rogatory or request.''[499] Second, a plaintiff may make delivery of the same by ''any form of mail requiring a signed receipt, to be addressed and dispatched by the clerk of the court to the agency or instrumentality to be served.''[500] Third, copies of the same documents may be delivered ''as directed by order of the court consistent with the law of the place where service is to be made.''[501]

Notably, none of these three procedures for delivery requires that a notice of suit, as described above, be sent in addition to the summons and complaint. Because the second method is the simplest—because it does not require participation of the foreign state nor does it require obtaining a court order—it is the most frequently used of the three.[502]

---

496. *Id.*

497. *Id.* According to one commentator, ''serving the officer or agent in the United States . . . is preferable from a strategic standpoint because it is easier and less expensive, and actual receipt of the document is more likely.'' George, *supra* note 477, at 55.

497.1 Bybee v. Oper der Standt Bonn, 899 F. Supp. 1217 (S.D.N.Y. 1995) (Section 1608(b)(3) applies only where service cannot be made under either 1608(b)(1) or (b)(2) and finding absence of personal jurisdiction where service was improper under FSIA).

498. 28 U.S.C.A. § 1608(b)(3).

499. *Id.* § 1608(b)(3)(A).

500. *Id.* § 1608(b)(3)(B). *See* Straub v. AP Green, Inc., 38 F.3d 448 (9th Cir. 1994) (applying ''substantial compliance'' test and finding that failure to have Clerk of Court mail process does not invalidate service under FSIA § 1608(b)(3) where actual notice of suit is received).

501. *Id.* § 1608(b)(3)(C).

502. ''Service by court order [method 3] must be regarded as a last resort because it calls for the exercise of discretion, causes uncertainty, and may irritate foreign states, even though the method chosen is not prohibited by its law. When this option is used, counsel should examine the possibility of requesting service pursuant to state law, Federal Rule 4, or local rules of service developed under the authority of Federal Rule 83.'' George, *supra* note 477, at 56.

The Ninth Circuit reviewed the procedures for service under the FSIA on instrumentalities in *Richmark Corp. v. Timber Falling Consultants, Inc.*[503] In that case, the plaintiff followed section 1608(b)(3)(B) and served a copy of the summons and complaint by DHL Worldwide Express Courier, and obtained a return receipt. Although acknowledging receipt of service, the defendant contended that service under section 1608(b)(3)(B) was improper on several grounds. First, the instrumentality argued that service should have been made by letter rogatory under section 1608(b)(3)(A). The court noted that section 1608(b)(3) permits service under (A) or (B) or (C). Second, the defendant contended that service under subsection (3)(B) was improper because service can only be made under (3)(B) if it cannot be perfected under subsections (1) and (2). In support of this argument, the defendant cited the Consular Convention Between the United States and the People's Republic of China.[504] The court rejected the second argument as well, noting that the Convention was not "an applicable international convention on the service of judicial documents" under section 1608(b)(2). Consequently, because a special arrangement did not exist under subsection (1), and the Convention did not apply under subsection (2), service under subsection (3) via DHL was appropriate.[505]

In *Magness v. Russian Federation*,[505.1] the Court held that "substantial compliance" was sufficient to perfect service of process on an agency or instrumentality so long as "actual notice" is effected. The Court, however, held that "substantial compliance" was insufficient to effect service of process on a foreign state and that the FSIA requirements of 28 U.S.C. § 1608(a) must be strictly followed. The Court vacated the Plaintiff Magness family's default judgment against the Russian Federation concerning the expropriation of the family mansion and piano factory in St. Petersburg during the 1918 Bolshevik Revolution.

When unraveling and implementing the complex service provisions in section 1608 of the FSIA, counsel should consider subsection 1608(c), which addresses the issue of when service is deemed to have been made. With the exception of the method provided in section 1608(a)(4), service will be considered to have been effective "as of the date of receipt

503. 937 F.2d 1444, 1447 (9th Cir. 1991), 959 F.2d 1468 (9th Cir. 1992), *cert. dismissed*, 506 U.S. 948 (1993).

504. Feb. 19, 1982, Art. 29, 33 U.S.T. 2973, 2998, T.I.A.S. No. 10209.

505. 937 F.2d at 1448.

505.1. 247 F.3d 609 (5th Cir. 2001).

indicated in the certification, signed and returned postal receipt, or other proof of service applicable to the method of service employed.''[506] For service made pursuant to the method prescribed in (a)(4), the service will be considered made "as of the date of transmittal indicated in the certified copy of the diplomatic note.''[507] Subsection (c) is important because it provides clear guidance on what is necessary to demonstrate that service has been perfected. This proof may be necessary for statute of limitations purposes and in determining the deadline for the filing of an answer or reply, not to mention the necessary foundation for entry of a default judgment under the FSIA.[508]

An answer or other responsive pleading must be filed by the defendant under the FSIA within sixty (60) days after service has been affected under section 1608(c).[509] Although this is triple the amount of time allowed to defendants in non-FSIA cases, it is equal to the amount of time that the U.S. government has to respond to a suit in which it is named as a defendant.[510] The sixty (60) day period is an important factor to be included in both the summons and the notice of suit, where required. Failure to mention the deadline may result in ineffective service.[511]

If service is perfected, and the deadline for response has elapsed, plaintiff's counsel must consider moving for a default judgment. Under the FSIA, default judgments are available, but the procedures vary slightly from those in non-FSIA cases. According to section 1608(e), a default judgment will be entered only after the plaintiff has established the right to relief by evidence satisfactory to the court.[512] Unlike some of the other service provisions, the default judgment rule applies to foreign states and instrumentalities alike. Separate from the procedures used in

506. 28 U.S.C.A. § 1608(c)(2).

507. *Id.*

508. *See infra* § 7.16.

509. 28 U.S.C.A. § 1608(d).

510. *See* Fed R. Civ. Pro. 12(a)(1)(A). (allowing defendant 20 days to file answer or other responsive pleading); House Report, *supra* note 1, at 25.

511. *See* Jackson v. People's Republic of China, 550 F. Supp. 869 (N.D. Ala. 1982), *vacated,* 790 F.2d 1490 (11th Cir. 1986), *cert. denied,* 480 U.S. 917 (1987). One commentator has suggested that this extended response time was intended "in part to make the suit less offensive and to give the defendant state time to formulate any sovereign immunity defense." George, *supra* note 477, at 56–57.

512. 28 U.S.C.A. § 1608(e). For a description of the process of proof of entitlement to default judgment, *see* Letelier v. Republic of Chile, 488 F. Supp. 665, 667 n.2 & 674 (D.D.C. 1980)

the execution of judgments,[513] section 1608(e) requires that a copy of the default judgment be served upon the defendant consistent with the methods for service prescribed in section 1608.

Practice Note: Although relatively few decisions have interpreted the service provisions of the FSIA, those that have illustrate the need for advance planning by counsel representing potential plaintiffs and for compliance with the service provisions of the FSIA.[514] In *Harris Corp. v. National Iranian Radio*,[515] the court dismissed some technical objections by the defendant to the service performed because of unusual circumstances and the fact that actual notice was received.[516] The court nevertheless warned potential FSIA plaintiffs:

> Though we find service adequate here, we admonish those seeking to invoke the FSIA to follow the service provisions it contains. Congress has carefully established a flexible framework so that American plaintiffs will have a variety of acceptable methods of service, even when relations with the foreign country in question are strained; at the same time, the framework is designed to insure that foreign defendants will get notice. There is no excuse for departure from the dictates of the statute.[517]

§ 7.16 DEFAULT JUDGMENTS, SANCTIONS, AND DISCOVERY UNDER THE FSIA

Because actions under the FSIA present complex and sensitive issues, courts have faced difficult decisions about whether sovereign defendants should be accorded treatment in U.S. courts similar to non-sovereign defendants. These issues have arisen most acutely in the area of sanctions and default judgments,[518] but have also included issues of

513. *See infra* § 7.17.

514. *See, e.g.*, Alberti v. Empresa Nicaraguanse de la Carne, 705 F.2d 250 (7th Cir. 1983); 40 D 6262 Realty Corp. v. United Arab Emirates, 447 F. Supp. 710 (S.D.N.Y. 1978); Gray v. Permanent Mission, 443 F.Supp. 816 (S.D.N.Y. 1978), *aff'd mem.*, 508 F.2d 1044 (2d Cir. 1978).

515. 691 F.2d 1344 (11th Cir. 1982).

516. *Id.* at 1352.

517. *Id.* at 1352 n.16; *see also* George, *supra* note 477, at 61 (''Except for cases involving exceptional facts, the courts have required strict compliance with the terms of the FSIA's service provisions. This result appears proper because tolerating less than full compliance threatens the uniformity of results that Congress sought to achieve and risks the type of foreign relations complications that Congress sought to eliminate when passing the statute.'').

518. *See, e.g.*, Gregorian v. Isvestia, 871 F.2d 1515 (9th Cir. 1989); Marian N. Leich, *Judicial Determinations of Immunity and the Department of State's Role*, 81 AM. J. INT'L L. 643 (1987) (discussing *Gregorian* and *Von Dardel*).

discovery for purposes of establishing jurisdiction under the FSIA,[519] and the appealability of a denial of immunity under the FSIA.[520]

In *Segni v. Commercial Office of Spain*,[521] the district court considered the defendant's claim to immunity under the FSIA, but ruled that the exception to immunity under section 1605(a)(2) for commercial acts was satisfied.[522] Consequently, the court denied Spain's motion to dismiss for lack of jurisdiction,[523] and permitted the action to proceed. Disappointed with the denial of its motion the defendant sought to appeal the district court's determination as a collateral order.[524] The Seventh Circuit noted that the "question whether an order denying immunity under the Foreign Sovereign Immunities Act is collateral is one of first impression."[525] Acknowledging that one of the FSIA's purposes is to protect foreign states from having to litigate claims based on acts for which they are immune, the court found that:

> A foreign government should not be put to the expense of defending what may be a protracted lawsuit without an opportunity to obtain an authoritative determination of its amenability to suit at the earliest possible opportunity.[526]

The Seventh Circuit's decision in *Segni* represents an encouraging trend in the treatment of immunity questions. Rather than not appear, risk default, move to set it aside and then appeal, FSIA defendants have the

---

519. *See, e.g.*, Millicom v. Int'l Cellular, S.A. v. Republic of Costa Rica, 1997 WL 527340 (D.D.C. Aug. 18, 1997) ("plaintiffs who are facing a motion to dismiss on the basis of foreign sovereign immunity have a right to conduct preliminary discovery, as long as it is reasonably calculated to elucidate whether an F.S.I.A. jurisdictional exception applies"); *c.f.* Papandreou v. Marra, 139 F.3d 247 (D.C. Cir. 1998) (inappropriate to compel depositions of foreign cabinet-level officials to establish applicability of FSIA exception to immunity absent demonstration of particular need and lack of alternatives); Richmark Corp. v. Timber Falling Consultants, 959 F.2d 1468 (9th Cir. 1992), *cert. dismissed,* 506 U.S. 948 (1993) (finding contempt appropriate sanction for failure of defendant to participate in discovery of assets); Tifa Ltd. v. Republic of Ghana, 692 F. Supp. 393, 405 (D.N.J. 1988) (permitting discovery for purposes of determining existence of exception to immunity under FSIA); Ruiz v. Transportes Aereos Militares Ecuadorianos, 103 F.R.D. 459 (D.D.C. 1984).

520. *See, e.g.*, Segni v. Commercial Office of Spain, 816 F.2d 345, 347 (7th Cir. 1987) (holding denial of immunity appealable as collateral order).

521. 650 F. Supp. 1042 (N.D. Ill. 1986), *appeal granted,* 816 F.2d 345 (7th Cir. 1987).

522. *Id.* at 1045.

523. *Id.*

524. 816 F.2d 345, 347 (7th Cir. 1987).

525. *Id.*

526. *Id.* at 347. The court explicitly ruled, however, that the reverse is not true. That is, dismissal of a foreign sovereign defendant "is not appealable immediately as a collateral order." *Id.*

option of appealing denials of immunity before the case, with all its expense and burden, proceeds to the merits.

In the *Segni* case, the defendant participated in the original determination of immunity through an appearance and the filing of a motion to dismiss. In other cases, foreign sovereigns have chosen not to appear and participate, whether out of a lack of familiarity with the operation of the FSIA or a conscious decision not to submit to the court's jurisdiction, even for purposes of contesting jurisdiction. Although it is the position of the U.S. government to encourage foreign states to appear and present their defenses to the court,[527] courts have faced ex parte FSIA proceedings.

Under section 1608(e) of the FSIA, no default judgment may be entered against a foreign sovereign defendant "unless the claimant establishes his claim or right to relief by evidence satisfactory to the court."[528] In *Gulf Arab Media-Arab American Film Co. v. Faisal Foundation*,[529] the Ninth Circuit held that the burden under section 1603(e) is not met by the plaintiff's declaration of conclusory allegations.[530] On the other hand, section 1603(e) does not require the plaintiff to submit what would be required if discovery were available. For instance, in *Dibrell Bros. Tobacco, Inc. v. Rafidain Bank*,[531] the court explained that

> The Act requires, in addition to service and no-response, that plaintiffs must establish their right to judgment 'by evidence satisfactory to the court.' This burden of proof is less than if defendants had participated in discovery. 'To conclude otherwise would have the effect of rewarding foreign governments for shirking their internationally-recognized duty to defend properly-filed cases.'[532]

527. *See* Jackson v. People's Republic of China, 794 F.2d 1490 (11th Cir. 1986), *cert. denied*, 480 U.S. 917 (1987).

528. 28 U.S.C.A. § 1608(e); House Report, *supra* note 1, at 25–26.

529. 811 F.2d 1260 (9th Cir. 1987) (per curiam).

530. *Id.* at 1262. For instance, in Murphy v. Republic of Panama, 751 F. Supp. 1540 (S.D. Fla. 1990), the court found that the plaintiff failed to make any evidentiary showing whatsoever. "The plaintiff may file and serve a motion for summary judgment in which he will have the opportunity to produce evidence sufficient to establish that he is entitled to the relief he seeks. The amount of evidence necessary to satisfy the standard will remain within the discretion of this Court. . . . However, in light of the Ninth Circuit's opinion in *Faisal Foundation*, . . . the plaintiff is reminded that he needs more than conclusory allegations to satisfy the evidentiary burden." *Id.* at 1541.

531. 1994 U.S. Dist. LEXIS 8271, 1994 WL 324331 (11th Cir. June 15, 1994).

532. *Id.* (quoting Ohntrup v. Makina ve Kimya Endustrisi Kurumu, No. 76–142, 1993 WL 315636 (E.D. Pa. Aug. 18, 1993)).

The court in *Commercial Bank of Kuwait v. Rafidain Bank,*[533] noted that although defaults are not favored under the FSIA, they are available pursuant to section 1608(e).[534] The court then noted that the FSIA treatment of foreign sovereigns in a default case is parallel to the treatment of the federal government under Rule 55(e) of the Federal Rules of Civil Procedure.[535] The court stated that "when the United States or a foreign sovereign defaults, the court must determine whether plaintiff's allegations are supported by evidence. While in some cases this will require a hearing . . . we do not believe that § 1608(e) requires evidentiary hearings or explicit findings where the record shows that the plaintiff provided sufficient evidence in support of its claims."[536]

Counsel should also be aware that § 1608(e) of the FSIA requires that any judgment against agencies or instrumentalities of a foreign state be sent to the foreign state. As a practical matter, if service of process attempts were unsuccessful using the other methods set forth in section 1608(a), thereby requiring service under section 1608(a)(4) through the diplomatic channel, when service of a default judgment on the Foreign State becomes necessary, plaintiffs may transmit the request for service through the diplomatic channel to the Department of State, Overseas Citizens Services without repeating efforts at service under section 1608(a)(1)–(3). At least one appellate court has held that if copies of a default judgment are not served in accordance with § 1608(e), the judgment may be void or voidable. In *Antoine v. Atlas Turner, Inc.,*[536.1] default judgments were obtained in four asbestos personal injury cases against a corporation that was an instrumentality of Canada.[536.2] Plaintiffs served the default judgments on the Defendant's attorney of record during the litigation. Such attorney, however, had filed a Notice of Withdrawal and notified other counsel of record of such withdrawal prior to service of the default judgments. The Appellate court ruled that whether the default judgments were void or voidable depended on whether the Defendant had actual notice of the judgments.

When a foreign state fails to appear and a default judgment consistent with section 1608(e) is entered, courts have been faced with

533. 15 F.3d 238 (2d. Cir. 1994).

534. *Id.* at 242.

535. *Id.* (noting that "neither Rule 55(e) nor § 1608(e) relieves the sovereign from the duty to defend cases and to obey court orders").

536. *Id.* (finding evidence in form of affidavits and exhibits sufficient for entry of default under § 1603(e)).

536.1. 66 F.3d 105 (6th Cir. 1995).

536.2. 28 U.S.C.A. § 1603.

the issue of whether setting aside the default judgment is appropriate.[537] In *Meadows v. Dominican Republic*,[538] the Ninth Circuit considered whether the district court had erred in denying the defendant's motion to set aside a default judgment. In denying the defendant's motion, the district court found that defendant's culpable conduct led to the entry of the default under Rule 60(b)(1) of the Federal Rules of Civil Procedure.[539] The Ninth Circuit affirmed the finding of culpable conduct, ruling that ''conduct is culpable if [the defendant] has received actual or constructive notice of the filing of the action and failed to answer.''[540] The court found that the defendant not only had knowledge of the particular suit at issue, but, more generally, was familiar with FSIA actions, having participated in earlier actions.[541] In *Dadesho v. Gov't of Iraq*,[541.1] the Ninth Circuit considered Iraq's argument that the FSIA evinces a policy of affording foreign governments the same procedural protections afforded the U.S. government. Iraq argued that it should be entitled to 60 days to appeal the district court's entry of a default judgment against it, as is the U.S. government under Fed. R. App. P. 4(a)(1). The Court determined:

> We find no basis for extending to foreign governments all the procedural protections our laws accord our own government. We need not, and do not, treat other governments exactly as we treat our own. Section 1608(d)[, 28 U.S.C.A.] shows that Congress knows how to provide specific safeguards when it wants to. It has not provided the protection Iraq seeks; [Iraq's] appeal is therefore untimely.

In contrast, in *Gregorian v. Izvestia*,[542] the court found that the defendant's belief that jurisdiction did not exist over the claims at issue constituted excusable neglect, and warranted setting aside of the judgment.[543]

If the foreign state appears, but does not cooperate with the court, the court must consider imposing sanctions on the foreign sovereign

537. *See, e.g.*, 28 U.S.C.A. § 1608(e) (1994); Jackson v. People's Republic of China, 794 F.2d 1490 (11th Cir. 1986), *cert. denied*, 480 U.S. 917 (1987); RESTATEMENT (THIRD), *supra* note 6, § 459, cmt. d.

538. 817 F.2d 517 (9th Cir. 1987).

539. *Id.* at 521.

540. *Id.*

541. *Id.* at 522.

541.1. 139 F.3d 766 (9th Cir. 1998)

542. 871 F.2d 1515 (9th Cir. 1989).

543. *Id. See also* Practical Concepts, Inc. v. Republic of Bolivia, 811 F.2d 1543 (D.C. Cir. 1987) (affirming grant of motion to set aside judgment).

defendant. Congress, in the legislative history of the FSIA, expressly contemplated the possibility of sanctions being imposed on foreign sovereign defendants, stating that ''appropriate remedies would be available under Rule 37 F.R. Civ. P. for an unjustifiable failure to make discovery.''[544] In *Wyle v. Bank Melli of Tehran, Iran*,[545] the court entered a preclusion order against a foreign sovereign instrumentality as a sanction for failure to comply with discovery rules, previous orders, and plaintiff's ''reasonable discovery requests.''[546] The preclusion order had the effect of establishing the plaintiff's factual contentions against the instrumentality.[547]

A number of courts have considered the availability of so-called ''jurisdictional discovery,'' i.e., discovery against the foreign state by a party-plaintiff to establish an exception to immunity under the FSIA. In general, jurisdictional discovery should not be ordered when to do so would frustrate the benefit of sovereign immunity afforded to sovereigns by the FSIA.[547.1] A natural tension therefore exists between discovery, which should be afforded a party-plaintiff to establish its statutory claim, and a sovereign's legitimate claim to immunity from suit.[547.2] Courts have therefore limited the availability of jurisdictional discovery to instances where the discovery is narrowly tailored to verify allegations of specific facts.[547.3] Where a party plaintiff's theory of jurisdiction under the FSIA is not supported by specific facts, but only conjecture and speculation, Courts have denied fishing-expedition type requests for discovery.[547.4]

Practice Note: In summary, these cases illustrate that the special sovereign nature of the defendants, which forms the very purpose of the FSIA, may have an impact on the court's treatment of the foreign sovereign party. Consideration of how the court will react to arguments or strategy by a foreign sovereign should be tempered by this fact.

544. House Report, *supra* note 1, at 23.
545. 577 F. Supp. 1148, 1153 (N.D. Cal. 1983).
546. *Id.*
547. *Id.*
547.1. El-Fadl v. Central Bank of Jordan, 75 F.3d 668, 671 (D.C. Cir. 1996).
547.2. Arriba, Ltd. v. Petroleos Mexicanos, 962 F.2d 528, 534 (5th Cir. 1992).
547.3. *Arriba*, *supra* note 547.2, 962 F.2d at 534; Crist v. Republic of Turkey, 995 F. Supp. 5, 12-13 (D.D.C. 1998).
547.4. *Id.*

§ 7.17 ATTACHMENT AND EXECUTION

Once a judgment has been obtained, whether by default or on the merits, one of the most essential questions facing any attorney is how that judgment may be enforced. Under the FSIA, compared with attachment and execution in a non-FSIA context,[548] special rules restrict the options available for attachment and execution.[549] The attachment and execution provisions are some of the most important provisions of the FSIA, because they represent one of the most significant departures from pre-FSIA jurisprudence.[550] The legislative history of the FSIA noted that the FSIA renders ''unnecessary the practice of seizing and attaching the property of a foreign government for the purpose of

(*Text continued on page 7-91*)

548. *See infra* Chapter 11 for a discussion of the enforcement of judgments in a non-FSIA context.

549. *See generally* Crawford, *Execution of Judgments and Foreign Sovereign Immunity*, 75 AM. J. INT'L L. 820 (1981); Richard W. Cutler, *Executing Judgments Under the FSIA: Winning Isn't Everything*, N.Y.L.J. (Aug. 17, 1995).

550. *See* Feldman, *Foreign Sovereign Immunity in the United States Courts 1976–1986*, 19 VAND. J. TRANSNAT'L L. 19, 40 (1986) (''[t]he provisions for execution of judgment in sections 1609–1611 of the FSIA include some of the most problematic texts in the Act'').

obtaining jurisdiction,'' and seeks ''to restrict [the] broad immunity from execution.''[551]

To implement the first of these purposes, section 1609 provides for the immunity of foreign state property from ''attachment arrest and execution,'' unless one of the exceptions in sections 1610 or 1611 applies.[552] This prohibits the attachment of property of a foreign state for the purpose of obtaining jurisdiction over it.[553] To implement the second purpose, the FSIA commences with a presumption that the property of the foreign state and instrumentalities is immune from attachment and execution. From this general premise, Congress carved out various categories of property and made them susceptible to attachment and execution. In short, with the adoption of section 1610, ''Congress . . . excepted from this immunity certain property of the foreign state itself, and property of the agencies and instrumentalities of foreign states, under differing rules ultimately based on the commercial nature of the property.''[554] Next, in section 1611, the FSIA ''preserves the immunity of certain classes of property notwithstanding its possession of the requisite commercial nexus.''[555]

Turning to the heart of the FSIA's attachment and execution provisions, section 1610 is divided into five subsections. Subsection (a) provides seven exceptions to the general rule of immunity from attachment and execution for the property of states and instrumentalities that generally track the jurisdictional immunity provisions in section 1605 (i.e., waiver; commercial activity; expropriation; succession, gift, or immovable property; automobile or other casualty or liability insurance; enforcement of arbitral awards; and terrorist acts). If the property at issue falls into one of these categories, then the foreign state or its agency or instrumentality is not immune from attachment in aid of execution or satisfaction of a judgment, so long as the notice and time period provided for in subsection (c) have been satisfied.

Subsection (b) provides additional exceptions for certain property held by foreign instrumentalities engaged in commercial activity in the United States. If the instrumentality is engaged in a commercial activity, then any of its property is subject to execution if it has waived its

---

551. House Report, *supra* note 1, at 8.

552. 28 U.S.C.A. § 1609.

553. *See* House Report, *supra* note 1, at 27; 28 U.S.C.A. § 1610(d)(2).

554. Joesph W. Dellapenna, *Suing Foreign Governments and Their Corporations,* COM. L.J. 298, 301 (Aug./Sept. 1980).

555. *Id.* at 301.

immunity, or if the judgment is based on an action for which an exception to jurisdictional immunity was found under certain sections of 1605(a) or (b). As one commentator has described it:

> For these defendants, both the commercial use and the nexus to the claim in question are eliminated. Thus, so long as the agency or instrumentality is engaged in a commercial activity in the United States, any of its property can be executed upon if there has been an effective waiver, or if the defendant is found liable and not immune for a commercial act, a taking in violation of international law, a non-commercial tort, or for certain maritime claims.[556]

Practice Note: It is important to note that a waiver of immunity from attachment is insufficient to waive immunity from jurisdiction, and vice versa.[557] Prudent counsel will seek to include both waivers in any agreements with sovereign parties.

In *Libra Bank Ltd. v. Banco Nacional de Costa Rica*,[558] the court ruled on the contours of the FSIA requirements for an effective waiver of pre-judgment attachment.[559] At issue was a waiver clause reading:

> The Borrower hereby irrevocably and unconditionally waives any right or immunity from legal proceedings including suit judgment and execution on grounds of sovereignty which it or its property may now or hereafter enjoy.[560]

The court held that the FSIA is designed only to "preclude inadvertent, implied, or constructive waiver where the intent of the foreign state is equivocal or ambiguous. . . . Under this interpretation of the statute, Banco Nacional's waiver was clearly explicit."[561] Similarly, in *Atwood Turnkey Drilling, Inc. v. Petroleo Brasileiro, S.A.*,[562] the court found an

---

556. *Id.* at 302.

557. *See* Restatement (Third), *supra* note 6, § 456, cmt. e (stating parties cannot establish jurisdiction by waiving attachment). One commentator notes that "a waiver for the purposes of suit is not necessarily a waiver for purposes of execution." Dellapenna, *supra* note 554, at 301 (citing Behring Int'l, Inc. v. Imperial Iranian Air Force, 475 F. Supp. 396, 406 (D.N.J. 1979)).

558. 676 F.2d 47 (2d Cir. 1982).

559. *Id.* at 49. *See also* Concord Reinsurance Co., Ltd. v. Caja Nacionalde Ahorro Seguro, 1994 U.S. Dist. LEXIS 2964, 1994 WL 86401 (S.D.N.Y. Mar. 15, 1994) (no waiver under § 1610(d)).

560. *Id.*

561. *Id.*

562. 875 F.2d 1174 (5th Cir. 1989).

explicit waiver of immunity to pre-judgment attachment based on the following clause:

> The Borrower . . . expressly and irrevocably waives any such right of immunity (including any immunity from the jurisdiction of any court or *from any execution or attachment in and of execution prior to judgment or otherwise*) or claim thereto which may now or hereafter exist, and agrees not to assert any such right or claim in any such action or proceeding, whether in the United States or otherwise.[563]

Additionally, even if a waiver or other exception to immunity allows attachment, the FSIA permits attachment in the aid of execution, that is, only upon order of the court.[564] This provision mandates that the court be involved to ensure that notice has been provided of the judgment pursuant to section 1608(e) and that a reasonable time has elapsed following the entry of judgment.[565]

It is worthy of note that neither subsection 1610(a) nor (b) contain the tort exception to attachment and execution that is present in section 1605(a)(5). For this reason, waiver presents the only option for enforcement of a tort judgment obtained under the FSIA against property of the foreign state in the United States.[566] However, section 1610(b)(2) expressly provides that the property of a foreign states' agency or instrumentality is subject to execution to enforce a tort award under section 1605(a)(5).

Where the claim is based upon a terrorist act, enforcement of a judgment under section 1605(a)(7) is facilitated by section 1610(a)(7). That section provides that property of the foreign state or its agency or instrumentality in the U.S. "used for commercial activity in the United States" may be attached and judgment thereupon executed.[567]

Section 1610(d) provides that a foreign state's property used for a commercial activity in the U.S. is not immune from pre-judgment attachment if two conditions are met:

---

563. *Id.* at 1177 (emphasis in original).

564. 28 U.S.C.A. § 1610(c).

565. *Id.*

566. For instance, in the *Letelier* case, discussed at § 7.09, *supra* , the district court ordered execution of a tort judgment against the property of the foreign state, in this case the property being the assets of the state-owned airline. *See* Feldman, *supra* note 550, at 41. On appeal, the court stated that execution against the assets of the instrumentality was impermissible because the airline was a separate juridical entity. The court admonished Congress for failing to provide for such situations, essentially resulting in creation of "a right without a remedy." Letelier v. Republic of Chile, 748 F.2d 790, 798 (2d Cir. 1984).

567. 28 U.S.C.A. § 1610(a)(7), (b)(2).

(1) the foreign state has explicitly waived its immunity from attachment; and

(2) the purpose of the attachment is to secure satisfaction of a judgment, and not to obtain jurisdiction.[568]

Section 1610(e) allows vessel attachments in actions to foreclose a preferred mortgage.

The last attachment and execution provision, which overrides any exceptions in section 1610, covers those classes of property for which immunity is preserved, regardless of their commercial nature. Section 1611 of the FSIA outlines three types of property that are always entitled to immunity from execution, unless there has been a valid waiver.[569] The first category is for property belonging to international organizations "designated by the President as being entitled to enjoy the privileges, exemptions, and immunities provided by the International Organizations Immunities Act."[570] The second category exempts property of "a foreign central bank or monetary authority held for its own account."[571] The final category includes property that "is, or is intended to be, used in connection with a military activity and (A) is of a military character, or (B) is under the control of a military authority or defense agency."[572]

568. 28 U.S.C.A. § 1610(d)(1), (2).

569. In Western Compagnie de Finance et D'Investment, S.A. v. La Republica del Ecuador, 823 F. Supp. 1106 (S.D.N.Y. 1993), the court squarely addressed for the first time whether the immunity provided by § 1611(b)(1) from *pre-judgment* attachment can be waived. The court reviewed the anomalous statutory language and noted that § 1611(b)(1)'s waiver provision omits any reference to pre-judgment attachments. As a result, a foreign state cannot waive immunity to pre-judgment attachment "because the statute does not provide for, or contemplate, such a waiver." *Id.* at 1111. *See* Georges R. Delaume, Note, 88 AM. J. INT'L L. 340 (1994).

570. 28 U.S.C.A. § 1611(a).

571. *Id.* § 1611(b)(1). *See* Banque Compafina v. Banco de Guatemala, 583 F. Supp. 320 (S.D.N.Y. 1984); *see generally* Patrikis, *Foreign Central Bank Property: Immunity From Attachment in the United States,* 1982 U. ILL. L. REV. 265. *See supra* note 569.

572. 28 U.S.C.A. § 1611(b)(2). *See* All American Trading Corp. v. Cuartel General Fuerza Aerea Guardia Nacional De Nicaragua, 818 F. Supp. 1552, 1555 (S.D. Fla. 1993) (aircraft sent by defendant to U.S. for repairs were immune from seizure under § 1611(b)(2) because defendant demonstrated that aircraft were for military use); Behring Int'l, Inc. v. Imperial Iranian Air Force, 475 F. Supp. 396 (D.N.J. 1979).

§ 7.18 ANALYZING FSIA ISSUES: PRACTICAL STRATEGIES AND CHECKLIST

[1] Practical Strategies

This section provides some practical and strategic considerations for counsel handling an FSIA case, or involved in counselling parties to transactions with foreign sovereigns, whether states or instrumentalities. Because FSIA issues involve a complex statutory framework, and often overwhelming precedent, familiarity with these materials is essential.

Long before a case ever gets to the pleading stage, counsel involved in representing parties in transactions involving foreign states or instrumentalities should be aware of the contours of the FSIA in structuring the relationships involved. From the perspective of the non-sovereign party, waivers are the most crucial. Because of their importance in any litigation, waivers by foreign sovereign defendants should be high on the list of priorities in negotiations. Obtaining agreement to waivers during the original negotiations should be relatively easier than later, when the transaction involves a dispute.

The important waivers, for FSIA purposes, are of four types: (1) immunity;[573] (2) attachment;[574] (3) personal jurisdiction;[575] and (4) venue.[576] For service purposes, counsel should also consider a special arrangement for service of process to avoid the often technical service rules under the FSIA. If the parties have agreed to a service procedure,[577] then its provisions will govern how service is perfected and should prove more convenient than compliance with the FSIA procedures in section 1608.

[2] FSIA Checklist

In summarizing the analytical process under the FSIA, the following checklist identifies some of the major features of the statute as interpreted by the courts.

(1) Is the potential defendant a foreign state or instrumentality? Check the definitions in section 1603.[578] If so, then the FSIA is

573. *See supra* § 7.05.
574. *See supra* § 7.17.
575. *See supra* § 7.14.
576. *See supra* § 7.03[2].
577. *See supra* § 7.15.
578. *See supra* § 7.03[1].

the exclusive means for suit involving that party.[579] FSIA actions may be maintained *either* in federal or state court,[580] and in all FSIA cases, no jury trial is available.[581] No punitive damages are available against a foreign state, though they may be sought from an instrumentality.[582] If the case is initiated in state court, the foreign sovereign defendant has an unconditional right of removal, and for cases brought in federal court, venue issues are governed by section 1391(d).[583]

(2) What special discovery and other procedural matters are posed by the fact that a litigant is a sovereign entity?

(3) Once threshold status and venue issues are settled, FSIA jurisdictional questions arise under section 1330(a) and section 1604, which provide subject matter jurisdiction over actions involving non-immune in personam claims against foreign sovereign defendants.[584] Jurisdiction under the statutory formulation turns on the presence of one or more exceptions under sections 1605 and 1607.

(4) The first exception, under section 1605(a)(1), covers situations in which the defendant has explicitly or implicitly waived any immunity.[585]

(5) The second exception, under section 1605(a)(2), covers one of the most difficult FSIA issues, situations in which the defendant is engaged in commercial activity. Under section 1605(a)(2), Congress set out three specific jurisdictional clauses requiring both commercial activity and a nexus or connection with the United States.[586]

(6) The third exception, under section 1605(a)(3), involves situations in which the action is based on a taking by a foreign state in violation of international law.[587]

579. *See supra* § 7.04.
580. *See supra* § 7.03.
581. *See supra* § 7.03[3].
582. *See supra* § 7.03[3].
583. *See supra* § 7.03[2].
584. *See supra* § 7.04.
585. *See supra* § 7.05.
586. *See supra* § 7.06.
587. *See supra* § 7.07.

(7) The fourth exception, under section 1605(a)(4), covers situations in which the action involves gifts or immovable property.[588]

(8) The fifth exception, under section 1605(a)(5), involves situations in which the action is based on certain non-commercial torts.[589]

(9) The sixth exception, under section 1605(a)(6) provides an exception to immunity incases involving the enforcement of arbitral awards.[590]

(10) The seventh exception, under new section 1605(a)(7) provides immunity where monetary damages are sought against a State concerning a terrorist act.[591]

(11) The eighth exception, under section 1605(b), covers actions involving certain maritime liens.[592]

(12) The ninth exception, under section 1607, provides jurisdiction over counterclaims by non-sovereign parties when a foreign sovereign defendant initiates the action.[593]

(13) If one or more of the nine exceptions to immunity under section 1605 or 1607 are satisfied, then section 1330(b) confers personal jurisdiction if service is perfected under section 1608.[594]

(14) To perfect service, section 1608 of the FSIA provides the exclusive service rules for states and instrumentalities.[595]

(15) If subject matter and personal jurisdiction under the FSIA are obtained, several options remain open to the foreign sovereign defendant. For instance, it may decide not to participate, or to do so on a limited basis. Questions of the appealability of

588. *See supra* § 7.08.
589. *See supra* § 7.09.
590. *See supra* § 7.10.
591. *See supra* § 7.11.
592. *See supra* § 7.12.
593. *See supra* § 7.13.
594. *See supra* § 7.14.
595. *See supra* § 7.15.

denials of immunity, default judgments, and sanctions must be considered.[596]

(16) As a final matter, if a judgment is obtained, under section 1609, the property of a foreign state is immune from attachment and execution under certain conditions. The FSIA provides the exclusive means for the attachment and execution in sections 1610 and 1611.[597]

596. *See supra* § 7.16.
597. *See supra* § 7.17.

Chapter 8

THE ACT OF STATE DOCTRINE

§ 8.01 INTRODUCTION AND OVERVIEW

[1] Introduction

The act of state doctrine is one of the most controversial and confused defenses available to certain litigants in international cases. Because the doctrine has the potential for producing unpopular results, it has generated substantial criticism and opposition, including partial legislative limitation. Despite this criticism and opposition, the doctrine remains an important consideration in international cases. Indeed, the relative frequency with which the issue arises has spawned numerous interpretations of the basic court-fashioned doctrine that provide a rich and complex set of rules for litigants in cases involving dealings with foreign governments. Much of the development of the doctrine is explained by the tension between the important considerations underlying the application of the doctrine on the one hand and the seemingly unjust or illogical results that it produces in a particular case on the other. Accordingly, the nature, operation, and effect of the doctrine are apparent from the attempts to limit or avoid the application of the doctrine. This chapter first discusses the origin and purposes of the court-made doctrine and then considers the various exceptions and other limitations on the application of the doctrine that have arisen.

[2] Historical Overview

With origins in 18th and 19th century jurisprudence, the act of state doctrine arose as a judicially-created recognition that certain types of disputes involving foreign sovereigns are not appropriately considered by the courts. Over the years, the doctrine has grown to serve various masters, at once a rule of abstention, deference to the Executive, and procedurally, a choice of law rule. Although some argue that the doctrine has outlived its usefulness, or should never have been created in the first place, the doctrine remains viable.

[3] Act of State Doctrine Defined

By way of overview, the act of state doctrine is a special choice of law rule, created by the courts, that prevents judicial consideration of the validity of acts taken by a foreign sovereign in its own territory with respect to tangible or intangible property located in that territory.[1] For the doctrine to apply, effectively preventing U.S. courts from sitting in judgment on certain acts of foreign sovereigns, several basic elements must be satisfied, and none of the generally recognized or emerging exceptions can be present.[2]

Conceptually, the act of state doctrine is distinct from sovereign immunity.[3] If the jurisdictional analysis of the status of a transaction under the Foreign Sovereign Immunities Act ("FSIA")[4] yields a finding that the suit may proceed, it does not necessarily follow that the act of state doctrine will permit it to proceed.

An essential element of the basic rule that must be satisfied is the so-called public governmental act requirement,[5] which means simply that the doctrine applies only to public governmental acts—official acts of foreign states—not to the purely private acts of foreign individuals. The burden of proof is on the proponent of the doctrine and special methods of proof may be necessary.[6]

Next, the property, tangible or intangible, allegedly the subject of the act of state, must be located within the territory of the foreign sovereign at the time of the taking.[7] If the property is not located within the territory, then, generally, the foreign sovereign's act is not given extraterritorial effect and the forum state will consider the validity of the act under forum law and policy without applying the act of state doctrine.

The final basic element of the doctrine, a built in exception is that there must be no treaty obligations or otherwise controlling legal standards available for resolution of the issue involved.[8] If a treaty, such as a treaty of friendship, commerce and navigation ("FCN"),

---

1. *See* Frederic L. Kirgis, *Editorial Comment: Understanding the Act of State Doctrine's Effect,* 82 AM. J. INT'L L. 58 (1988). One commentator observed:

> The act of state doctrine contains elements of both choice of law and separation of powers analysis. The doctrine is invoked with far greater frequency than it is actually applied. When the courts do apply the doctrine, they are essentially deferring to the executive branch of the government in the conduct of foreign affairs. Prakash Rajamani, *International Litigation: Act of State,* 32 INT'L LAW. 223, 252 (1998).

2. The exceptions are discussed *infra* in §§ 8.07 to 8.13.

3. For a discussion of the distinction between sovereign immunity and the act of state doctrine, *see infra* § 8.05.

4. *See supra* Chapter 7.

5. For a discussion of the public governmental act requirement, *see infra* § 8.04.

6. *See infra* § 8.04.

7. *See infra* § 8.06.

8. *See infra* § 8.07.

contains clear and controlling guidance, the courts will not apply the act of state doctrine to bar consideration of a claim.

Once the basic elements of the doctrine have been considered, all exceptions to the doctrine must be explored before determining

(*Text continued on page 8-5*)

whether the doctrine applies. For instance, because one of the primary rationales of the doctrine is a desire to avoid interference with the Executive, if the Executive advises the court that application of the doctrine is unnecessary, the courts will generally not apply it. This is the so-called *Bernstein* exception to the doctrine, and reflects the often difficult balance between cooperative branches of government.[9] Although several other exceptions are emerging, they are still in development and cannot properly be said to have the force of law. First, there is the so-called counterclaim or setoff exception,[10] in which the doctrine will not bar consideration of an act of state if the foreign sovereign enters the U.S. court as a plaintiff and the challenge to the legality of its acts is raised by way of a counterclaim. The circumstances under which this exception has been applied do not permit the conclusion that it is a fully formed exception to the doctrine,[11] but it is an important element in the calculus of whether the doctrine will apply in a particular case.

Second, there is the so-called commercial act exception.[12] Although a less formal exception than the counterclaim/setoff exception, the emerging commercial act exception is an important one because it reflects the result of the basic tensions underlying the doctrine and the considerations that led to the adoption of the restrictive theory of foreign sovereign immunity in the FSIA.[13] The commercial act exception could potentially lead to the merger or convergence of the two doctrines on commercial acts.

Next, although severely restricted to narrow circumstances by judicial interpretation, there is the so-called Hickenlooper amendment,[14] a legislative exception to the act of state doctrine. In opposition to the Supreme Court's decision in *Banco Nacional de Cuba v. Sabbatino*,[15] Congress sought to limit the scope of the doctrine's effect. Litigants pursuing claims against foreign states should be familiar with the amendment and its limitations.

---

9. *See infra* § 8.08.

10. *See infra* § 8.09.

11. As discussed *infra*, § 8.09, the cases establishing the counterclaim or set-off exception are fact specific determinations that do not easily lend themselves to application in other circumstances.

12. *See infra* § 8.10.

13. *See supra* § 7.01 for a discussion of the rationale behind the adoption of the restrictive theory of sovereign immunity.

14. *See infra* § 8.11.

15. 376 U.S. 398 (1964).

Also, Congress, in 1988, enacted legislation amending the federal arbitration provisions to eliminate the act of state defense in suits based on arbitration agreements or awards. Finally, where antitrust or market-policing issues exist, some courts have ruled the act of state doctrine inapplicable in what is sometimes termed the corruption exception.[16]

This chapter examines these elements of, and exceptions to, the act of state doctrine. Where applicable, practical guidance and strategic considerations are also discussed.

§ 8.02 ORIGINS AND PURPOSES OF THE ACT OF STATE DOCTRINE

[1] Origins of the Act of State Doctrine

In what is generally believed to be the earliest statement of the modern act of state doctrine, the Supreme Court in an 1897 decision, *Underhill v. Hernandez*,[17] stated:

> Every sovereign State is bound to respect the independence of every other sovereign State, and the courts of one country will not sit in judgment on the acts of the government of another done within its own territory. Redress of grievance by reason of such acts must be obtained through the means open to be availed of by sovereign powers as between themselves.[18]

The *Underhill* case identifies a rule-oriented approach to the act of state doctrine and provides the source of one of the purposes of the doctrine: comity.[19] The direction that such disputes should be resolved in intergovernmental forums reflects the recognition that the issues in an act of state case often are inappropriate for resolution in court.

[2] Purposes of the Act of State Doctrine

Although the rule has endured,[20] its stated purposes have developed to encompass not only respect for sovereignty, but also to

16. *See infra* §§ 8.12–8.13.
17. 168 U.S. 250 (1897).
18. *Id.* at 252.
19. *See* Restatement (Third) Foreign Relations Law § 443, cmt. a (1987).
20. *See infra* § 8.03 for a discussion of the endurance of the doctrine.

preserve territorial choice of law principles,[21] and to avoid conflict because adjudication could "imperil the amicable relations between governments and vex the peace of nations."[22] In later cases such as *Banco Nacional de Cuba v. Sabbatino,*[23] *First Nat'l City Bank v. Banco Nacional de Cuba,*[24] and *Alfred Dunhill of London, Inc. v. Republic of Cuba,*[25] the Court has articulated additional, balancing approach rationales. For instance, in *Sabbatino,* the Court stated that the doctrine was not compelled by comity, international law, or the U.S. Constitution,[26] but does have what it termed "constitutional underpinnings." The Court stated:

> It arises out of the basic relationships between branches of government in a system of separation of powers. It concerns the competency of dissimilar institutions to make and implement particular kinds of decisions in the area of international relations. The doctrine as formulated in past decisions expresses the strong sense of the Judicial Branch that its engagement in the task of passing on the validity of foreign acts of state may hinder rather than further this country's pursuit of goals both for itself and for the community of nations as a whole in the international sphere.[27]

In *Sabbatino,* the Court also stated another rationale for the doctrine: the inability of the U.S. courts to discover, analyze, and apply international law. The doctrine avoids having the courts engage in "the sensitive task of establishing a principle not inconsistent with the national interest or with international justice."[28] Despite these additional rationales, the primary basis for the rule was found to be the avoidance of conflict with the Executive.[29]

In *First Nat'l City Bank v. Banco Nacional de Cuba,*[30] the Court reaffirmed that the doctrine has "roots . . . in the notion of comity" but "is also buttressed by judicial deference to the exclusive power of the

---

21. *See* Oetjen v. Central Leather Co., 246 U.S. 297, 303 (1918); Ricaud v. American Metal, 246 U.S. 297, 304 (1918).
22. Underhill v. Hernandez, 65 F. 577, 579 (2d Cir. 1895), *aff'd,* 168 U.S. 250 (1897).
23. 376 U.S. 398 (1964).
24. 406 U.S. 759 (1972).
25. 425 U.S. 682 (1976).
26. 376 U.S. 398, 421–25 (1964).
27. *Id.* at 423.
28. *Id.* at 428.
29. *Id.* at 435–37.
30. 406 U.S. 759 (1972).

Executive over conduct of relations with other sovereign powers."[31] The accretion of the separation of powers rationale for the doctrine (i.e., avoidance of Executive Branch embarrassment) has led to a growing tension with the distinct choice of law rationale for the doctrine.[32]

The value of considering the purpose of the doctrine is to illustrate how to pursue arguments that a court should or should not apply it in a particular case, and to predict how a court will approach the doctrine. For instance, if a particular case presents no threat to comity, does not intrude on the domain of the Executive, and does not threaten to interfere with the conduct of foreign relations, then the basis for application of the doctrine may not exist. This conclusion is illustrated in the recent litigation involving the Republic of the Philippines' suits against former President Marcos.[33]

The Ninth Circuit, in an *en banc* decision, found that the act of state doctrine did not bar consideration by U.S. courts of the alleged illegal acts of former President Marcos.[34] The court stated that "[t]he purpose of the device is to keep the judiciary from embroiling the courts and the country in the affairs of the foreign nation whose acts are challenged."[35] The court found that this purpose would not be satisfied by the doctrine's application in the *Marcos* case:

> *A fortiori,* when a ruler's former domain has turned against him and seeks the recovery of what it claims he has stolen, the classification has little or no applicability. The act of state doctrine is supple, flexible, ad hoc. The doctrine is meant to facilitate the foreign relations of the United States, not to furnish the equivalent of sovereign immunity to a deposed leader.
>
> In the instant case the Marcoses offered no evidence whatsoever to support the classification of their acts as acts of state. The burden of proving acts of state rested upon them. . . . The United States, invited by this court to address this matter as an amicus, assures us that the Executive does not at present see the applicability of this defense. . . .

31. *Id.* at 765.
32. *See* Kirgis, *supra* note 1, at 61.
33. *See generally* Republic of Philippines v. Marcos, 862 F.2d 1355 (9th Cir. 1988) (en banc).
34. *Id.* at 1360–61.
35. *Id.* at 1360.

> The act of state doctrine, the Executive declares, has "no bearing" on this case as it stands.[36]

As the court's statement explains, none of the purposes of the act of state doctrine would be served by the application of the doctrine to bar consideration of the claims against the Marcoses.[37]

[3] The Supreme Court's *Kirkpatrick* Decision

In the Supreme Court's most recent discussion of the act of state doctrine, *W.S. Kirkpatrick & Co., Inc. v. Environmental Tectonics Corp., Int'l*,[38] Justice Scalia, for a unanimous court, found that the doctrine did not apply on the facts of the case,[39] but issued a wide ranging review of the doctrine and signalled its range of applicability. The Court stated: "Act of state issues only arise when a court *must decide*—that is when the outcome of the case turns upon—the effect of official action by a foreign sovereign. When that question is not in the case, neither is the act of state doctrine."[40]

At issue in *Kirkpatrick* was a suit by an unsuccessful bidder on a construction and supply contract with the Nigerian Government.[41] The unsuccessful bidder brought a RICO action, alleging that the successful bidder obtained the contract through a bribe paid to the Nigerian officials, an act stipulated to be illegal under Nigerian law. The defendant moved to dismiss, arguing that the suit was barred by the act of state doctrine.[42] The district court held the suit barred by the

---

36. *Id.* at 1361.

37. *Accord* Republic of Philippines v. Marcos, 806 F.2d 344 (2d Cir. 1986), *cert. denied sub nom.*, New York Land Co. v. Republic of Philippines, 481 U.S. 1048 (1987). *See also In re* Oil Spill by Amoco Cadiz Off Coast of France, 491 F. Supp. 161, 169 (N.D. Ill. 1979) (finding "[a] judicially fashioned doctrine should not be applied to work an injustice, particularly where the application of the doctrine would not serve the interests it was fashioned to protect").

38. 493 U.S. 400 (1990). *See generally* Trooboff, *International Decisions*, 84 AM. J. INT'L L. 550 (1990); Swanson, *A Threshold Test for Validity: The Supreme Court Narrows the Act of State Doctrine*, 23 VAND. J. TRANSNAT'L L. 889 (1991); Note, Environmental Tectonics Corp v. W.S. Kirkpatrick, Inc.: *The Act of State Doctrine and the Problem of Judicial Inconsistency*, 14 N.C. J. INT'L L. & COM. REG. 495 (1989) (analyzing court of appeals decision).

39. 493 U.S. at 409–10.

40. *Id.* at 406 (emphasis in original). *See* Grupo Protexa, S.A. v. All American Marine Slip, 20 F.3d 1224 (3d Cir. 1994). *See generally*, Comment, Grupo Protexa, S.A. v. All American Marine Slip *and the Decline of the Act of State Doctrine*, 20 N.C. J. INT'L LAW & COM. REG. 355 (1995).

41. *Id.* at 402.

42. *Id.*

doctrine,[43] but the Third Circuit reversed, finding persuasive the advice of the Executive that the purpose of the doctrine would not be compromised by judicial resolution of the case.[44]

The Supreme Court agreed, and explained that although the doctrine originated in an expression by the Court that rested upon "the highest considerations of international comity and expediency,"[45] the doctrine has since become "a consequence of domestic separation of powers."[46] The Court's reiteration of the separation of powers rationale for the doctrine came in its determination that the "factual predicate" for the doctrine's application did not exist:

> Regardless of what the [district] court's factual findings may suggest as to the legality of the Nigerian contract, its legality is simply not a question to be decided in the present suit, and there is thus no occasion to apply the rule of decision that the act of state doctrine requires.[47]

The *Kirkpatrick* decision's discussion of the act of state doctrine, although primarily dicta, is important because it is the most recent Supreme Court statement on the nature of the doctrine and provides a source for lower courts in their attempts to grapple with the application of the doctrine.[48] In the subsequent sections of this chapter, the elements of the doctrine and its exceptions are explored. In considering the various aspects of the doctrine, its purposes are important factors in reconciling the various decisions and principles, and remain important features in how the doctrine is likely to develop in future cases.

§ 8.03 THE NATURE AND OPERATION OF THE BASIC DOCTRINE

The act of state doctrine originated primarily in the Supreme Court's decision in *Underhill v. Hernandez*.[49] The doctrine has been applied or discussed in at least eight more-recent Supreme Court

43. 659 F. Supp. 1381, 1393 (D.N.J. 1987), *rev'd*, 847 F.2d 1052 (3d Cir. 1988), *aff'd*, 493 U.S. 400 (1990).

44. 847 F.2d 1052 (3d Cir. 1988), *aff'd*, 493 U.S. 400 (1990).

45. *Id.* at 404, *quoting*, Oetjen v. Central Leather Co., 246 U.S. 297, 303–04 (1918).

46. *Id.*

47. *Id.* at 406.

48. *See generally* Fox, *Reexamining the Act of State Doctrine: An Integrated Conflicts Approach*, 33 Harv. Int'l L.J. 521 (1992).

49. 168 U.S. 250 (1897).

decisions and numerous other federal and state decisions.[50] The act of state doctrine is distinct from the jurisdictional basis of foreign sovereign immunity and operates differently.[51] In the *Sabbatino* decision, the Court held that, in a diversity case, "an issue concerned with a basic choice regarding the competence and function of the Judiciary and the National Executive in ordering our relationships with other members of the international community must be treated as an aspect of federal law."[52] Elsewhere, the Court in *Sabbatino* described the doctrine as "a principle of decision binding on federal and state courts."[53]

In considering the nature of the act of state doctrine, courts often manifest curiosity not about whether the doctrine is or is not a rule or principle of decision, but rather just what sort of rule or principle it is. As one commentator has noted, the doctrine "has been variously described as a doctrine of judicial prudence, deference, judicial restraint, judicial abstention, issue preclusion, conflict of law, and choice of law."[54] Because the doctrine often has strong political overtones, perhaps the most effective and useful characterization of the doctrine is as a choice of law rule.[55] The Restatement reporters explain:

> In most cases, the act of state doctrine may be seen as a special rule of conflict of laws. The normal rule of choice of law in most act of state cases would point to application of the rule of the state where the act took place; that rule may be disregarded in certain instances where the law thus chosen would violate the strong public policy of the forum, e.g., a policy against expropriation without compensation. . . . The act

---

50. *See* RESTATEMENT, *supra* note 19, § 443 cmt. j. *See generally* Swanson, *A Threshold Test for Validity: The Supreme Court Narrows the Act of State Doctrine*, 23 VAND. J. TRANSNAT'L L. 889 (1991); Leigh, Sabbatino's *Silver Anniversary and the Restatement: No Cause for Celebration*, 24 INT'L LAW. 1 (1990); Leacock, *The Commercial Activity Exception to the Act of State Doctrine Revisited: Evolution of a Concept*, 13 N.C. J. INT'L L. & COM. REG. 1 (1988).

51. *See, e.g.*, Banco Nacional de Cuba v. Sabbatino, 376 U.S. 398, 438 (1964) (discussing differences between sovereign immunity and act of state). *See also infra* § 8.05 (discussing distinction of doctrine from sovereign immunity).

52. *Id.* at 425.

53. *Id.* at 427.

54. Bazyler, *Abolishing the Act of State Doctrine*, 134 U. PENN. L. REV. 325, 327–28 (1986) (footnotes omitted).

55. *See* Henkin, *Act of State Today: Recollections in Tranquility*, 6 COLUM. J. TRANSNAT'L L. 175 (1967); Kirgis, *Act of State Exceptions and Choice of Law*, 44 U. COLO. L. REV. 173, 178–88 (1972); Leigh & Sandler, *Dunhill: Toward a Reconsideration of* Sabbatino, 16 VA. J. INT'L L. 685, 713–715 (1976).

of state doctrine requires the court to disregard that public policy and give effect to the foreign law.[56]

Although the nature of the doctrine may be a fertile subject for scholarly debate,[57] regardless of its nature, the doctrine has the same practical effect.

Whether as a choice of law rule, an issue preclusion device,[58] or as a principle of judicial abstention,[59] the doctrine operates to prevent courts in the U.S. from deciding a case in which the issue is whether the public governmental act of a foreign sovereign taken within its territory is valid, legal, or proper. Most recently, in the *Kirkpatrick* decision,[60] the Supreme Court explained that the doctrine applies only when the case requires a U.S. court "to declare invalid, and thus ineffective as 'a rule of decision for the courts of this country' . . . the official act of a foreign sovereign."[61]

In *Banco Nacional de Cuba v. Sabbatino*,[62] the Court declined to establish a general rule but held "only that the Judicial Branch will not examine the validity of a taking of property within its own territory by a foreign sovereign government, extant and recognized by this country at the time of suit, in the absence of a treaty or other unambiguous agreement regarding controlling legal principles, even if the complaint alleges that the taking violates customary international law."[63] Because the courts may not sit in judgment of the foreign act, they are powerless to evaluate it, and must, perhaps as an unintentional coincidence, give effect to it, regardless of its legality or offence to the U.S. policy.[64]

---

56. Restatement, *supra* note 19, § 443, reporters' note 1.

57. *See, e.g.*, Halberstam, Sabbatino *Resurrected: The Act of State Doctrine in the Revised Restatement of Foreign Relations Law*, 79 Am. J. Int'l L. 68, 74 (1985) ("[t]he act of state doctrine is not a doctrine of judicial self-restraint or abstention, comparable to the political question doctrine . . . . The court in *Sabbatino* did not dismiss the case, as it does when the case involves a political question. Instead, the Court proceeded to enforce the Cuban decree. . . . Thus the effect of the Supreme Court decision in *Sabbatino* . . . is to require U.S. courts to enforce a foreign act of state . . .").

58. Arango v. Guzman Travel Advisors Corp., 621 F.2d 1371 (5th Cir. 1980).

59. *See* Bazyler, *supra* note 54, at 327.

60. 110 S. Ct. 701 (1990). The *Kirkpatrick* decision is discussed *supra* in § 8.02[3].

61. *Kirkpatrick*, 493 U.S. at 405, *quoting*, Ricaud v. American Metal Co., 246 U.S. 304, 310 (1918). *See also* Walter Fuller Aircraft Sales v. Republic of Philippines, 965 F.2d 1375, 1388 (5th Cir. 1992).

62. 376 U.S. 398 (1964).

63. *Id.* at 428.

64. *See Sabbatino*, 376 U.S. at 439 (White, J., dissenting); Halberstam, *supra* note 57, at 75.

The operation of the doctrine can be illustrated with a simple example. In evaluating a foreign act, an important consideration is whether the property taken was located within the territory of the foreign sovereign at the time of the taking.[65] In *Republic of Iraq v. First Nat'l City Bank*,[66] the court ruled that "when property confiscated is within the United States at the time of attempted confiscation, our courts will give effect to acts of state only if they are consistent with the policy and law of the United States."[67] Accordingly, whether under the territorial exception or some other, if the doctrine does not apply, the foreign act is subject to scrutiny under the standards of U.S. law and policy, which may include international law. If the doctrine does apply, then the act is not subject to scrutiny and must be given effect without question.

The doctrine's effect and operation have yielded frustration and often produced opposition to it. Its ambiguous nature has produced confused and inconsistent interpretations. The application of the doctrine in numerous cases has produced the variety of conditions, limitations, and exceptions that are the subject of the remainder of this chapter.

As a final preliminary note about the operation of the act of state doctrine, counsel should be aware of the defense often referred to as foreign sovereign compulsion. Of recent vintage compared to the doctrine, the defense has grown in importance as a result of the increase of transnational activity.[68] The purpose of the defense is to avoid punishing conduct that might otherwise be a violation of law, if it is compelled by a foreign sovereign.[69] The defense was first mentioned in *Continental Ore Co. v. Union Carbide & Carbon Corp.*,[70] which involved antitrust issues. The defendants relied on the defense of

---

65. The territorial (or perhaps more precisely, the extraterritorial) exception to the doctrine is discussed *infra* in § 8.06.

66. 353 F.2d 47 (2d Cir. 1965), *cert. denied*, 382 U.S. 1027 (1966).

67. *Id.* at 51.

68. *See generally* Don Wallace, Jr. and Joseph P. Griffin, *The Restatement and Foreign Sovereign Compulsion: A Plea for Due Process*, 29 INT'L LAW. 63–74 (1989), and A.D. NEALE AND M.L. STEPHENS, INTERNATIONAL BUSINESS AND NATIONAL JURISDICTION (Clarendon Press 1988), at 94–98.

69. *See* RESTATEMENT (THIRD) OF FOREIGN RELATIONS LAW § 441 (addressing the defense of foreign state compulsion in relation to regulation of activities generally) and § 442 (setting forth the law of the United States on foreign state compulsion in relation to requests for disclosure of information located in one state and sought in connection with legal proceedings in another).

70. 370 U.S. 690 (1962).

compulsion. The Supreme Court held that although the defendants were acting as the Canadian government's agents, they could not invoke the defense because there was no Canadian law compelling the acts in question.[71] Similarly, in the *Swiss Watchmakers* case,[72] the court restated the compulsion requirement as a necessary condition to the application of the defense.[73] An ongoing issue is the meaning of compulsion in this context.

Conduct must be required by a foreign law in order to satisfy the requirement.[74] Sanctions for nonperformance are the deciding factor.[75] Foreign governmental approval or delegation of authority are acts that do not meet the compulsion requirement; the defense requires more than a favorable government action.[76]

> Where governmental action raises no higher than mere approval, the compulsion defense will not be recognized. It is necessary that the foreign law must have coerced the defendant into violating American antitrust law. . . . The defense is not available if the defendant could have legally refused to accede to the foreign power's wishes.[77]

In some cases, merely the threat of severe sanctions can create compulsion.[78] The test to determine whether a sanction is severe enough to create compulsion is subjective and can usually be demonstrated by showing that the violation carries sanctions in the form of either criminal or civil liability.[79]

---

71. *Id.* at 704–705.

72. United States v. Watchmakers of Switzerland Information Center, 1963 Trade Cas. (CCH) ¶ 70,600 (S.D.N.Y. 1962).

73. *See also* Matsushita Elec. Indus. Co. v. Zenith Radio Corp., 475 U.S. 574 (1986); Société Internationale v. Rogers, 357 U.S. 197 (1958); Mannington Mills, Inc. v. Congoleum Corp. 595 F.2d 1287 (3d Cir. 1979); Interamerican Refining Corp. v. Texaco Maracaibo Inc., 307 F. Supp. 291 (D. Del. 1970); United States v. General Electric Co., 82 F. Supp. 753 (D.N.J. 1949).

74. United States v. Watchmakers of Switzerland Information Center, *supra* note 72, at ¶ 77,456.

75. Sanctions can be either civil, economic, criminal or some substantial equivalent. Don Wallace, Jr. and Joseph P. Griffin, *The Restatement and Foreign Sovereign Compulsion: A Plea for Due Process*, 29 INT'L LAW. 69 (1989).

76. *See* Continental Ore Co. v. Union Carbide & Carbon Corp., 370 U.S. 690 (1962); Timberlane Lumber Co. v. Bank of America, 549 F.2d 597 (9th Cir. 1976); United States v. Watchmakers of Switzerland Information Center, *supra* note 72, at ¶ 77,456.

77. Mannington Mills, Inc. v. Congoleum Corp. 595 F.2d 1287, 1293 (3d Cir. 1979).

78. Interamerican Refining Corp. v. Texaco Maracaibo Inc., 307 F. Supp. 291 (D. Del. 1970).

79. *Id. See also* United States v. First Nat'l City Bank, 396 F.2d 897 (2d Cir. 1968), and Société Internationale v. Rogers, 357 U.S. 197 (1958).

The defense has arisen most commonly in antitrust cases in which a foreign government compelled a private party to engage in conduct having anticompetitive effects on U.S. commerce.[80] The Department of Justice has recognized the defense to an antitrust suit when two conditions are satisfied. First, the foreign government must have compelled the anticompetitive conduct in circumstances in which a refusal to comply would give rise to the imposition of "significant penalties" or to the denial of "specific substantial benefits."[81] Second, the compelled conduct must not have plainly occurred wholly or primarily in the United States.[82]

§ 8.04 THE PUBLIC GOVERNMENTAL ACT REQUIREMENT

In the classic statement of the act of state doctrine in *Underhill v. Hernandez*,[83] the Supreme Court stated that "the courts of one country will not sit in judgment on the *acts of the government* of another."[84] Under this statement, only governmental acts qualify for application of the doctrine.[85] Because only certain types of acts qualify for application of the doctrine, a threshold issue in any evaluation of whether the doctrine bars consideration of the *validity* of an act is whether the act is that of a foreign government.[86]

As a practical matter, the party asserting the applicability of the doctrine carries the burden of establishing that the act in question qualifies as an act of state.[87] The courts may conduct a preliminary

80. *See generally* U.S. Department of Justice, Antitrust Guide for International Operation (1977), and A.B.A., Section of Antitrust Law, *Task Force Report: The Antitrust Guide for International Operations Revisited,* 54 Antitrust L.J. 839 (1985).

81. U.S. Department of Justice, *Antitrust Enforcement Guidelines for International Operations* (CCH) Nov. 10, 1988.

82. *Id.* Businesses may obtain substantial certainty concerning their liability for anticompetitive conduct conforming to an order of a foreign government by seeking to obtain an opinion from the Department of Justice under its business review procedure. 28 C.F.R. § 50.6.

83. 168 U.S. 250 (1897).

84. *Id.* at 252 (emphasis added).

85. *See* Comment, *The Act of State Doctrine: A History of Judicial Limitations and Exceptions,* 18 Harv. Int'l L.J. 677, 680–683 (1977).

86. *See* Restatement, *supra* note 19, § 443 cmt. i. *See* A.D. Belgrade v. Sidex Int'l Furniture Corp., 2 F. Supp. 2d 407 (S.D.N.Y. 1998) (denying act of state defense asserted by banking corporation organized under laws of Federal Republic of Yugoslavia where U.S. did not recognize Federal Republic of Yugoslavia as foreign state).

87. *See* Alfred Dunhill of London, Inc. v. Republic of Cuba, 425 U.S. 682, 692 (1976) (observing proponents carried "burden to prove that act"). *See also* Allstate Ins. Co. v.

examination of the alleged act or exceptions,[88] and the issue may be raised by the court *sua sponte*.[89]

Methods of proof of a particular act as an act of state include judicial notice or perhaps the introduction of evidence demonstrating the character and terms of the act.[90] In this context, Rule 44.1 of the Federal Rules of Civil Procedure, which requires the proponent of foreign law to provide notice to the court, is relevant.[91]

For purposes of application of the doctrine, the types of acts qualifying as acts of state range widely in their formality, but all require some form of demonstration that the act is official and governmental. As the Restatement reporters explain:

> The act of state doctrine applies to acts such as constitutional amendments, statutes, decrees and proclamations, and in certain circumstances to physical acts, such as occupation of an estate by the state's armed forces in an application of state policy. An official pronouncement by a foreign government describing a certain act as governmental is ordinarily conclusive evidence of its official character. An action or declaration by an official may qualify as an act of state, but only upon showing (ordinarily by the party raising the issue) that the official had the authority to act for and bind the state.[92]

Administratia Asigurarilor de Stat, 962 F. Supp. 420 (S.D.N.Y. 1997) (denying summary judgment motion and finding that Romanian insurance company failed to meet its burden of establishing act of state defense where neither affidavit submitted nor any of such defendant's submissions addressed crucial subject of Romanian or U.S. foreign interests involved).

88. Restatement, *supra* note 19, § 443 cmt. i.

89. *Id.*

90. *Id.*

91. *Id.*

92. *Id.* In Riggs Nat'l Corp. v. Comm'n of IRS, 163 F.3d 1363 (D.C. Cir. 1999), the Court considered the act of state doctrine in a case involving the application of U.S. tax laws to transactions affected by certain financial orders of the Government of Brazil, including the Brazilian Minister of Finance's interpretation of Brazilian law. The Court observed:

> The government suggests that a foreign administrative official's interpretation of foreign law is not the type of act of state contemplated by the doctrine. To be sure, the doctrine has been applied principally to more "tangible" acts. *See, e.g., Sabbatino,* 376 U.S. at 403–04 (expropriation of property); *Ricaud v. American Metal Co.,* 246 U.S. 304, 310 (1918) (same); *Underhill v. Hernandez,* 168 U.S. 250, 254 (1897) (detention of person by sovereign official); *Credit Suisse v. United States Dist. Court for the Cent. Dist. of Calif.,* 130 F.3d 1342, 1347 (9th Cir. 1997) (asset freeze orders); *Callejo v. Bancomer, S.A.,* 764 F.2d 1101, 1114 (5th Cir. 1985) (promulgation of exchange control regulations). That we are unaware of cases treating an interpretation of law as an act of state, of course, does not foreclose the doctrine's applicability. We are, however, hesitant to treat an interpretation of law as an act of state, for such a view might be in tension with rules of procedure directing U.S. courts to conduct a *de novo* review of foreign law when an issue of foreign law is raised. *See* Fed. R. Civ. P. 44.1; Tax Court R. 146.

At the other end of the spectrum, the Court in *Dunhill* held that mere repudiation of a debt by a foreign sovereign, as reiterated by counsel in court, does not qualify as an act of state.[93] The Court stated:

> No statute, decree, order, or resolution of the Cuban Government itself was offered in evidence indicating that Cuba had repudiated its obligations in general or any class thereof or that it had as a sovereign matter determined to confiscate the amounts due the foreign importers.[94]

The issue of whether particular acts qualify as acts of state under the doctrine is well illustrated in the cases involving the Republic of the Philippines' suits against former President Marcos. In *Republic of Philippines v. Marcos*,[95] the Second Circuit considered whether the act of state doctrine would bar adjudication of the legality of former President Marcos' acts as head of state.[96] The court rejected the applicability of the doctrine and held:

> Appellants simply fail to make the crucial distinction between acts of Marcos as head of state, which may be protected from judicial scrutiny even if illegal under Philippine law, and his purely private acts. . . . Since the burden of proof is on the party invoking the act of state defense, . . . appellants must ultimately demonstrate that the challenged acts of Marcos were in fact public acts.[97]

In addition, the court noted that Marcos was no longer in power and, accordingly, little risk was presented that the adjudication would interfere with the Executive's conduct of foreign affairs.[98] The court also found support in the fact that the current government of the Philippines had come into court itself, thereby eliminating any concern that adjudication of the case could offend the foreign state, one of the rationales of the act of the state doctrine.[99]

---

93. Dunhill, 425 U.S. at 694–95.

94. *Id.* at 695. *See also* Galu v. Swissair, 873 F.2d 650, 653–54 (2d Cir. 1989); Millen Indus., Inc. v. Coordination Council for N. Am. Affairs, 855 F.2d 879, 882 (D.C. Cir. 1988).

95. 806 F.2d 344 (2d Cir. 1986), *cert. dismissed,* 480 U.S. 942 (1987), *cert. denied sub nom.,* New York Land Co. v. Republic of Philippines, 481 U.S. 1048 (1987).

96. *Id.* at 357.

97. *Id.* at 359.

98. *Id.*

99. *Id.*

In a subsequent Ninth Circuit decision in *Republic of Philippines v. Marcos*,[100] a three judge panel considered many of the same factors, but held that "adjudication will be barred by the act of state doctrine, the political question doctrine or both."[101] On rehearing *en banc*, the Ninth Circuit vacated the panel decision and found that the doctrine would not, at least at that point in the litigation, bar consideration of the alleged illegal acts by the Marcoses.[102] The court stated:

> *A fortiori*, when a ruler's former domain has turned against him and seeks the recovery of what it claims he has stolen, the classification [act of state] has little or no applicability. The act of state doctrine is supple, flexible, ad hoc. The doctrine is meant to facilitate the foreign relations of the United States, not to furnish the equivalent of sovereign immunity to a deposed leader.[103]

On the issue of the character of the alleged acts, the court specifically rejected Marcos' claim that they were acts of state:

> In the instant case, the Marcoses offered no evidence whatsoever to support the classification of their acts as acts of state. The burden of proving acts of state rested upon them. . . . They did not even undertake the proof. . . . As the doctrine is a pragmatic one we cannot exclude the possibility that, at some later point in the development of this litigation, the Marcoses might produce evidence that would warrant its application. On the present record, the defense does not apply.[104]

Practice Note: As the *Marcos* litigation illustrates, the characterization of particular acts as acts of state is a crucial element in securing the application of the doctrine. Careful and informed pleading, followed by evidence of the acts' official nature, is necessary to ensure that the public governmental act requirement of the act of state doctrine is satisfied.

Characterization by Defendants of human rights abuses as acts of state has proved difficult. The Second Circuit opined in *Kadic v. Karadzic*:[104.1]

---

100. 818 F.2d 1473 (9th Cir. 1987).

101. *Id.* at 1490.

102. Republic of Philippines v. Marcos, 862 F.2d 1355, 1360–61 (9th Cir. 1988) (*en banc*).

103. *Id.* at 1360–61.

104. *Id.* at 1361 (citations omitted).

104.1. 70 F.3d 232, 250 (2d Cir. 1995), *reh'g denied*, 74 F.3d 377, *cert. denied*, 518 U.S. 1005 (1996).

> The act of state doctrine, under which courts generally refrain from judging the acts of a foreign state within its territory . . . might be implicated in some cases arising under [28 U.S.C.A. § 1350 (Alien Tort Statute)].[104.2] However, as in *Filartiga,* 630 F.2d at 889,[104.3] we doubt that the acts of even a state official, taken in violation of a nation's fundamental law and wholly unratified by that nation's government, could properly be characterized as an act of state.[104.4]

§ 8.05 AS DISTINCT FROM SOVEREIGN IMMUNITY

As discussed in Chapter 7, foreign states are entitled to immunity from suit in U.S. courts if the terms of the Foreign Sovereign Immunities Act[105] are satisfied. The act of state doctrine is analytically distinct from the doctrine of sovereign immunity despite some similarities. In *Sabbatino,* a decision prior to the FSIA of 1976, but nevertheless instructive on this point, the Supreme Court explained the difference between the act of state doctrine and sovereign immunity:

> immunity relates to the prerogative right not to have sovereign property subject to suit; fairness has been thought to require that when the sovereign seeks recovery, it be subject to legitimate counterclaims against it. The act of state doctrine, however, although it shares with the immunity doctrine a respect for sovereign states, concerns the limits for determining the validity of an otherwise applicable rule of law. It is plain that if a recognized government sued on a contract with a United States citizen, concededly legitimate by the locus of its making, performance, and most significant contacts, the forum would not apply its own substantive law of contracts. Since the act of state doctrine reflects the desirability of presuming the relevant transaction

104.2. The Alien Tort Statute is discussed *supra* § 5.06[1].

104.3. *See supra* § 5.06[1] for discussion of *Filartiga.*

104.4. *See also* Flatow v. Islamic Republic of Iran, 999 F. Supp. 1 (D.D.C. 1998) (denying Iran's act of state defense to claims arising from alleged sponsorship of terrorist group that carried out suicide bombing of tourist bus in Israel); Burma v. Unocal, Inc., 176 F.R.D. 329, 357 (C.D. Cal. 1997) (declining to apply act of state doctrine to bar claims concerning alleged human rights abuses of torture and forced labor where there was no "public interest" justification for the alleged misconduct); Republic of Haiti v. Duvalier, 626 N.Y.S.2d 472 (N.Y. App. Div. 1995) (act of state doctrine inapplicable in litigation brought by Republic of Haiti to recover from wife of deposed dictator bank funds allegedly embezzled where foreign sovereign was itself Plaintiff, regime that committed acts was no longer in power, and U.S. government supported Plaintiff's position).

105. 28 U.S.C. §§ 1330, 1332(a)(2)–(a)(4), 1391(f), 1441(d), & 1602–11 ("FSIA"). The text of the FSIA is reprinted *infra* Appendix 8[1].

> valid, the same result follows; the forum may not apply its local law regarding foreign expropriations.[106]

The Court's discussion illustrates the distinction between the justiciability concerns of the act of state doctrine and jurisdictional underpinnings of immunity issues and identifies the choice of law rationale for the act of state doctrine.[107]

The Eleventh Circuit recently distinguished the Court's analysis of the act of state doctrine from the FSIA analysis. The Circuit Court succinctly observed:

> The act of state doctrine limits, for prudential rather than jurisdictional reasons, the courts in this country from inquiring into the validity of a recognized foreign sovereign's public acts committed within its own territory. . . . Accepting jurisdiction of this issue, our standard of review is different from that applied under the FSIA in the denial of the motion to dismiss. More is involved than accepting what the complaint alleges as true. The act of state doctrine does not limit courts' jurisdiction as the FSIA does, but it is flexibly designed to avoid judicial action in sensitive areas.[107.1]

In *Honduras*, the Court found a waiver of sovereign immunity by Honduras under the FSIA, but vacated and remanded for further analysis the district court's finding that Honduras' act of state doctrine argument was without merit. "[T]here is no commercial exception to the act of state doctrine as there is under the FSIA."[107.2]

Because act of state and immunity are separate considerations, it is possible to have an affirmative finding as to one but not the other. For instance, it may be that the particular act in question is a commercial one, not eligible for sovereign immunity under section 1605(a)(2) of the FSIA, but at the same time an act of state barred from judicial examination by the act of state doctrine.[108]

---

106. *Sabbatino,* 376 U.S. at 438; *see infra* § 8.11.

107. *See supra* § 8.03.

107.1. Honduras Aircraft Registry, Ltd. v. Gov't of Honduras, 129 F.3d 543, *reh'g denied en banc*, 131 F.3d 157 (11th Cir. 1997) (citations omitted).

107.2. *Id.* The *Honduras* case is discussed *supra* § 7.06[4].

108. *See Honduras, supra* note 107.1; Braka v. Bancomer, S.N.C., 762 F.2d 222, 225 (2d Cir. 1985) (finding activity commercial under § 1605(a)(2), but holding consideration of merits barred by act of state doctrine); Friedar v. Government of Israel, 614 F. Supp. 395, 399 (S.D.N.Y. 1985) (dismissing under FSIA and in dicta citing *Braka* and indicating that dismissal on act of state grounds was warranted as well).

Under the FSIA, a foreign sovereign is granted immunity unless one of the enumerated exceptions applies. If no exceptions apply, the court does not have jurisdiction to consider the claim against that defendant. The act of state doctrine, on the other hand, operates to preclude justiciability of the claim. As the Restatement reporters explain:

> [T]he doctrine of sovereign immunity is addressed essentially to the jurisdiction of the courts; the act of state doctrine is addressed to the permissible scope of inquiry by courts into particular issues presented. . . . Jurisdiction, including any defense of immunity, should be decided first; a determination that the defendant state is not entitled to immunity is not dispositive of applicability of the act of state doctrine.[109]

A broader Executive Branch role in decisions whether to exercise jurisdiction over a particular defendant may have been signalled in *Republic of Austria v. Altmann.*[109.1] Although the case solely concerned the FSIA and not the Act of State Doctrine, the Court in dicta observed: ". . . should the State Department choose to express its opinion on the implications of exercising jurisdiction over particular petitioners in connection with their alleged conduct, that opinion might well be entitled to deference as the considered judgment of the Executive on a particular question of foreign policy."[109.2] The Court, ultimately, did not decide the issue, stating, "We express no opinion on the question whether such deference should be granted in cases covered by the FSIA."[109.3]

In terms of rules of civil procedure, a foreign state's motion to dismiss under the FSIA would be brought pursuant to Rule 12(b)(1) for lack of subject matter jurisdiction. A foreign state's motion to dismiss the action on the basis of the act of state doctrine would be a motion pursuant to Rule 12(b)(6) for failure to state a claim for which relief may be granted. Despite the distinction between the two defenses, some opinions and criticism have suggested the possible eventual convergence of the two defenses, at least with respect to commercial activities.[110]

---

109. RESTATEMENT, *supra* note 19, § 443, reporters' note 10.

109.1. 541 U.S. 677, 124 S. Ct. 2240, 159 L. Ed 2d 1 (2004).

109.2. 124 S. Ct. at 2255-56 (*citing Verlinden*, 461 U.S. at 486, 103 S.Ct. 1962; American Ins. Assn. v. Garamendi, 539 U.S. 396, 414, 123 S.Ct. 2374, 156 L.Ed.2d 376 (2003) (discussing the President's "vast share of responsibility for the conduct of our foreign relations")).

109.3. *Id.*

110. *See, e.g.*, Alfred Dunhill of London, Inc. v. Republic of Cuba, 425 U.S. 682 (1976) (Opinion of White, J.); Leigh & Sandler, *Dunhill: Toward a Reconsideration of* Sabbatino, 16 VA. J. INT'L L. 685, 716 (1976).

This view reflects a perception that the absence of a commercial act exception to the act of state doctrine "emasculates" the restrictive theory of sovereign immunity now codified in the FSIA.[111]

Any attempts by litigants to invoke a commercial act exception to the act of state doctrine must be pursued with knowledge of the tension between the theoretical foundation of the two doctrines.[112] Because, as the Court stated in *Sabbatino*, they spring from different sources, different considerations are at stake.

§ 8.06 THE TERRITORIAL LIMITATION AND THE SITUS PROBLEM

[1] The Territorial Limitation

The Court in *Banco Nacional de Cuba v. Sabbatino* held only that the act of state doctrine barred examination of "the validity of a taking of property *within its own territory* by a foreign sovereign government."[113] This portion of the *Sabbatino* holding is derived directly from the Court's earlier decision in *Underhill v. Hernandez*,[114] in which the Court stated that the doctrine applies to foreign acts "done within its [the foreign government's] own territory." This condition on the holding in *Sabbatino* has come to be termed the territorial limitation on the act of state doctrine. Under this limitation, U.S. courts may evaluate what would otherwise be an act of state, if the property affected is located outside the foreign state's territory at the time of the taking.[115] If the property is not located within the territory of the foreign sovereign at the time of the taking, then the act of state doctrine does not bar consideration of the state's action under the rules of law applicable in the forum.[116]

---

111. Leigh & Sandler, *supra* note 110, at 716.

112. The commercial act exception to the act of state doctrine is discussed *infra* in § 8.10.

113. *Sabbatino*, 376 U.S. at 428 (emphasis supplied).

114. 168 U.S. 250, 252.

115. *See* Restatement, *supra* note 19, § 443, cmt. b & reporters' note 4. *See also* Department of Justice, *Guidelines for International Operations* 32 n.169 (1988) ("[i]n the Department's view, [the act of state] doctrine applies only if the specific conduct complained of is a public act of the foreign sovereign within its territorial jurisdiction on matters pertaining to its governmental sovereignty").

116. *See* Henkin, *supra* note 55; Kirgis, *supra* note 55.

[2] The Situs Problem

Under the territorial limitation on the doctrine an often troublesome issue arises as to the situs of intangible property.[117] The general

(*Text continued on page 8-21*)

117. *See generally* Knight, *International Debt and the Act of State Doctrine: Judicial Abstention Reconsidered*, 13 N.C. J. INT'L L. & COM. REG. 35 (1988).

rule under the act of state doctrine is that the reach of a foreign sovereign does not extend beyond its borders.[118] If, however, the item purported to have been taken is intangible property, the determination of that item's situs could be determinative as to the application *vel non* of the act of state doctrine.[119]

For instance, in *Republic of Iraq v. First Nat'l City Bank*,[120] the Second Circuit considered whether the act of state doctrine barred consideration of Iraq's taking of all of the property of a former king, some of which was held in the form of assets in the custody of First National City Bank. The Court held that if the "property confiscated is within the United States at the time of attempted confiscation, our courts will give effect to acts of state only if they are consistent with the policy and law of the United States."[121]

As one commentator has explained:

> A debt is an intangible asset that has no actual, physical location. Determining the situs of intangible property is a difficult task involving abstract principles. Intangible property can only be 'located' within a single jurisdiction as a matter of legal fiction. For act of state purposes, courts consider a debt located within the state that has the ability to enforce or collect the debt. The ability of a state to enforce or collect a debt depends on jurisdiction over the debtor. To determine whether the expropriating state has jurisdiction over the debtor for act of state purposes, United States courts employ one of three legal fictions: the domicile test, the complete fruition test, or the incidents of the debt test.[122]

The domicile test derives from *Harris v. Balk*,[123] in which the Supreme Court held (in a non-act of state context) that the situs of debt is the jurisdiction in which that debt is domiciled: "[T]he expropriating country is the situs of the expropriated deposit, and the act of state doctrine applies if the branch is still operating in that country at the

---

118. *See* Airline Pilots Ass'n, Int'l v. TACA Int'l Airlines, S.A., 748 F.2d 965, 970–71 (5th Cir. 1984).

119. *See* Republic of Iraq v. First Nat'l City Bank, 241 F. Supp. 567 (S.D.N.Y. 1965), *aff'd*, 353 F.2d 47 (2d Cir. 1965), *cert. denied*, 382 U.S. 1027 (1966).

120. 353 F.2d 47 (2d Cir. 1965), *cert. denied*, 382 U.S. 1027 (1966).

121. *Id.* at 51.

122. Filzer, *The Continued Validity of the Act of State Doctrine in Foreign Branch Bank Expropriation Cases*, 3 AM. U.J. INT'L L. & POL'Y 99, 116–117 (1988).

123. 198 U.S. 215 (1905).

time of the expropriation."[124] The complete fruition test looks to the issue of whether the expropriation comes to "complete fruition" in the expropriating state.[125] The final test is the incidents of the debt test, which considers a variety of issues designed to balance the interests of the taking state and the forum state.[126] Under the incidents of the debt test, courts examine whether the debtor is subject to U.S. jurisdiction, the governing law, the currency in which the debt is payable, the site of the banks lending the funds, and the relative interests of the jurisdictions involved.[127]

Because the situs issue has generated confusion and inconsistent results,[128] the Restatement reporters point to a trend away from situs determinations in favor of a broader analysis that recognizes the purpose of the inquiry:

> In principle, it might be preferable to approach the applicability of the act of state doctrine to intangible assets not by searching for an imaginary situs for property that has no real situs, but by determining how the act of the foreign state in the particular circumstances fits within the reasons for the act of state doctrine and for the territorial limitation.[129]

Under current practice, the approach that a particular court will take on issues of situs determination will depend on precedent in that jurisdiction, but may be subject to influence by effective advocacy illustrating the appropriateness of a particular test. Use of the Restatement proposal provides greater opportunity for counsel as it permits a broader inquiry into the purposes and operation of the doctrine as applied to a particular set of facts.

---

124. Filzer, *supra* note 122, at 117.

125. *See* Allied Bank Int'l v. Banco Credito Agricola de Cartago, 757 F.2d 516, 521 (2d Cir. 1985), *citing*, Tabacalera Severiano Jorge, S.A. v. Standard Cigar Co., 392 F.2d 706, 715–16 (5th Cir.), *cert. denied*, 393 U.S. 924 (1968).

126. Callejo v. Bancomer, S.A., 764 F.2d 1101, 1123–24 (5th Cir. 1985). *See generally* Knight, *International Debt and the Act of State Doctrine: Judicial Abstention Reconsidered*, 13 N.C. J. INT'L L. & COM. REG. 35, 55 (1988) (describing incidents of debt test applied in Libra Bank Ltd. v. Banco Nacional de Costa Rica, 570 F. Supp 870 (S.D.N.Y. 1983)).

127. *Id.*

128. *See* Filzer, *supra* note 122; Note, *The Act of State Doctrine: Resolving Debt Situs Confusion*, 86 COLUM. L. REV. 594 (1986).

129. RESTATEMENT, *supra* note 19, § 443, reporters' note 4.

§ 8.07 THE TREATY EXCEPTION TO THE ACT OF STATE DOCTRINE

In *Sabbatino,* the Court's statement of the act of state doctrine included the condition that the doctrine might not apply in the case of the existence of "a treaty or other unambiguous agreement regarding controlling legal principles."[130] This portion of the act of state doctrine has been termed the treaty exception, and is based on the fact that at the time of the *Sabbatino* decision, the Court found that no controlling international legal standard for the evaluation of the foreign state's act was available to U.S. courts.[131] The exception, generated by the *Sabbatino* holding, provides an opportunity for plaintiffs to allege the existence of a controlling legal standard, and thereby avoid application of the act of state doctrine.

Just such a case arose in *Kalamazoo Spice Extraction Co. v. Government of Socialist Ethiopia.*[132] In *Kalamazoo Spice,* Kalamazoo counterclaimed for an expropriation and alleged that the Treaty of Amity between the U.S. and Ethiopia provided an unambiguous and controlling legal standard as contemplated by the Court in *Sabbatino.* The district court, however, held that the treaty was "so inherently general, doubtful, and susceptible of multiple interpretation" that it could not serve as a basis under *Sabbatino* for not applying the act of state doctrine.[133] Because the district court perceived the avoidance of potential conflict with the Executive as the purpose of the doctrine, a potential presented by the "ambiguous" language of the Treaty of Amity, it held that the treaty could not displace the act of state doctrine.[134]

On appeal, the U.S Court of Appeals for the Sixth Circuit reversed, and specifically held the Treaty of Amity to be a "controlling legal standard in the area of international law."[135] Because the Treaty of Amity contained the "prompt, just and effective compensation" standard commonly employed in treaties, a standard applied in cases

---

130. *Sabbatino, supra* note 15, 376 U.S. at 428.

131. *Id.* at 428–431.

132. 729 F.2d 422 (6th Cir. 1984).

133. 543 F. Supp. 1224 (W.D. Mich. 1982).

134. *Id.* at 1230.

135. 729 F.2d 422, 426 (6th Cir. 1984) (citing American Int'l Group v. Islamic Republic of Iran, 493 F. Supp. 522 (D.D.C. 1980)) (holding Treaty of Amity with Iran satisfied treaty exception to act of state doctrine), *vacated on other grounds,* 657 F.2d 430 (D.C. Cir. 1981)).

such as *Banco Nacional de Cuba v. Chase Manhattan Bank*,[136] the Sixth Circuit held that "the standard of compensation provided for in the Treaty of Amity between Ethiopia and the United States can provide a basis for determining the extent of compensation to which Kal-Spice may be entitled."[137]

The court went on to note that the district court was also incorrect in placing such significance on the potential for interference with any efforts by the Executive Branch to resolve the dispute. Specifically, the court noted that the State Department had, with the Departments of Treasury and Justice, intervened in the case and filed an amicus brief advocating the application of the treaty exception to the act of state doctrine.[138]

Despite the *Kalamazoo* holding, the Fifth Circuit, in the 1985 decision of *Callejo v. Bancomer, S.A.*,[139] held "that the treaty exception does not render the act of state doctrine inapplicable."[140] The court in *Cajello* noted that the Supreme Court's holding in *Sabbatino* stated only that where there is no treaty the act of state doctrine does not apply; *Sabbatino* "did not state the converse, namely that if a treaty exists then the act of state doctrine does not apply."[141] This technical reading of *Sabbatino* is apparently inconsistent with the *Kalamazoo* holding, although different facts and treaties were involved that may explain the inconsistency.

Practice Note: The *Kalamazoo Spice* case, however, indicates that the treaty exception to the act of state doctrine remains a strong argument. Its success will depend on the particular treaty and factual situation. The first step for counsel is to review the treaties in force between the U.S. and the foreign country at issue.[142] The treaties should be reviewed for their applicability in the case and to determine whether

---

136. 658 F.2d 875 (2d Cir. 1981).

137. *Id.* at 427; *see also* Dayton v. Czechoslovak Socialist Republic, 834 F.2d 203, 206–207 (D.C. Cir. 1987) (holding naturalized U.S. [former Czech] citizens not U.S. "nationals" under FCN treaty, so treaty exception inapplicable).

138. *Id.* at 427.

139. 764 F.2d 1101 (5th Cir. 1985).

140. *Id.* at 1121.

141. *Id.* at 1118 n.22.

142. Counsel should explore the various treaties in force that may be applicable in a dispute, a process described in Chapter 2, which discusses researching international law. In particular, counsel may want to begin with the Treaties Chart *infra*, and then refer to the publication, TREATIES IN FORCE, which identifies by title and date all treaties to which the U.S. is a party.

they would support an argument that the act of state doctrine does not apply because of the operation of the treaty exception. For instance, in *Faysound, Ltd. v. Walter Fuller Aircraft Sales, Inc.*,[143] the court found that the treaty exception applied to permit a decision.[144] The court relied on the Geneva Convention, stating that "[both] the United States and the Philippines are signatories to the Geneva Convention, which covers property rights in aircraft along with other aviation subjects."[145] *Faysound* illustrates the operation of the treaty exception in a decision subsequent to *Callejo.*

§ 8.08 THE *BERNSTEIN* EXCEPTION

[1] The Origins and Operation of the *Bernstein* Exception

In some cases involving an act of state that would otherwise be barred by the doctrine, the courts have declined to apply the act of state doctrine in deference to the views of the Executive Branch. The original case involving this exception gives it its name: *Bernstein v. N.V. Nederlandsche-Amerikaansche Stoomvaart-Maatschaapij.*[146] At issue in *Bernstein* was a suit to recover damages for property expropriated in Nazi Germany. After application of the act of state doctrine resulted in an initially unsuccessful round of litigation,[147] the court indicated that the views of the Executive could make a difference. In the subsequent case, a letter from the Acting Legal Advisor of the Department of State was sent to the court. It stated:

> The policy of the Executive, with respect to claims asserted in the United States for the restitution of identifiable property (or compensation in lieu thereof) lost through force, coercion, or duress as a result of Nazi persecution in Germany, is to relieve American courts from any restraint upon the exercise of their jurisdiction to pass upon the validity of the acts of Nazi officials.[148]

The letter did make a difference; the court followed the advice of the State Department and instructed the lower court by "striking out all

143. 748 F. Supp. 1365 (E.D. Ark. 1990), *appeal dismissed,* 940 F.2d 339 (8th Cir. 1991).

144. *Id.* at 1370.

145. *Id.*

146. 210 F.2d 375 (2d Cir. 1954).

147. Bernstein v. Van Heyghen Freres, S.A., 163 F.2d 246 (2d Cir.), *cert. denied,* 332 U.S. 772 (1947).

148. *Reprinted* at 210 F.2d 376.

restraints based on the inability of the courts to pass on acts of officials in Germany during the period in question."[149]

The continued vitality of the *Bernstein* exception in U.S. law is subject to some debate, but the exception has not been specifically rejected.[150] In *First Nat'l City Bank v. Banco Nacional de Cuba*,[151] five Justices voted to reverse an act of state determination, but only three did so on the grounds of the *Bernstein* exception. The remaining two Justices voted to reverse on other grounds. The four dissenting Justices specifically rejected the *Bernstein* exception. Against this background, the Court's decision in *First Nat'l City Bank* cannot be read as an affirmation of the *Bernstein* exception, but the Court has not recently been confronted with such a case, and the strategy of obtaining a *Bernstein* letter from the Executive in a case remains an important consideration. For instance, in subsequent cases interpreting the doctrine and the Supreme Court's *First Nat'l City Bank* decision, lower courts have held that a *Bernstein* letter can be influential.[152]

The term "*Bernstein* letter" has arisen to refer to a letter from the Department of State to the court where the case is pending expressing the views of the Executive Branch. Attorneys involved in a case that presents act of state issues should, at the earliest opportunity, evaluate whether it is in their client's interests to obtain a *Bernstein* letter, and, if so, to begin consultations with the State Department's Office of the Legal Advisor.

[2] The Reverse *Bernstein* Exception

A separate issue is what has been termed the reverse-*Bernstein* exception. In *Kalamazoo Spice Extraction Co. v. Government of Socialist Ethiopia*,[153] a case involving a challenge to the taking of property in Ethiopia, the Executive wrote a *Bernstein* letter that has suggested the so-called "reverse" *Bernstein* exception to the act of state doctrine. Because the general rule following the *Bernstein* case could be described as calling for the application of the doctrine unless the Executive communicated to the court that the doctrine should not

149. *Id.* at 376.

150. Restatement, *supra* note 19, § 443, reporters' note 8.

151. 406 U.S. 759 (1972).

152. *See, e.g.*, Banco Nacional de Cuba v. Chase Manhattan Bank, 658 F.2d 875 (2d Cir. 1981); Empresa Cubana Exportadora de Azucar y Sus Derivados v. Lamborn & Co. Inc., 652 F.2d 231 (2d Cir. 1981).

153. 729 F.2d 422 (6th Cir. 1984). This case is also discussed in § 8.07, *supra*.

apply, the reverse-*Bernstein* exception has been characterized as a rebuttable presumption of application of the doctrine.

The so-called "reverse" *Bernstein* exception to the act of state doctrine involves a presumption that the doctrine does not apply unless the Executive specifically communicates to the court advising that application of the doctrine is necessary to safeguard the foreign policy interests of the United States.[154] In the *Bernstein* letter filed in the *Kalamazoo* case, the Executive suggested a reverse-*Bernstein* presumption in certain circumstances. Specifically, the letter in *Kalamazoo* suggested that in cases in which there is a controlling legal standard for compensation, the courts should presume that the act of state doctrine is inapplicable unless the State Department notifies the court to the contrary.

The November 19, 1982, Letter From Davis R. Robinson, Legal Advisor, Department of State, to Rex T. Lee, Solicitor General, stated in part:

> [W]e believe that a broad inflexible rule of abstention in expropriation cases is not necessary to safeguard our foreign policy interests. When . . . there is a controlling legal standard for compensation, we believe that the presumption should be that adjudication would not be inconsistent with foreign policy interests under the Act of State Doctrine.
>
> If, however, the Department of State determines in a given case that judicial abstention is necessary for foreign policy reasons, it will request the Department of Justice to communicate that determination to the appropriate court. . . . If we indicate that adjudication would be inconsistent with foreign policy interests of the United States, we trust that the court will give appropriate weight to our views. As a general rule, however, where there is a controlling legal standard for compensation we would not plan to inform the courts of the absence of foreign policy objections to adjudication of expropriation claims. Therefore, we would anticipate that silence on the part of the Executive in such cases would not be relied upon as a basis for judicial abstention under the Act of State Doctrine.[155]

The State Department's *Bernstein* letter in the *Kalamazoo* case reflected the adoption of a policy toward the act of state doctrine that recognizes that, in the case of a treaty or other controlling legal

154. *See* Leigh & Sandler, *supra* note 110, at 699.
155. J. Lacey, Act of State and Extraterritorial Reach, app. G (1983).

standard, the need for the doctrine is not present and the doctrine should not apply. This practice leaves the courts free to consider the act of state doctrine's applicability and places a greater burden on counsel proposing the doctrine's use in a particular case.

[3] Summary of the *Bernstein* Exception

In summary, the *Bernstein* exception remains an important feature of the operation of the act of state doctrine. The Restatement reporters summarized the state of the practice as follows:

> It seems that if the State Department issues a letter requesting that the courts not review the validity of a particular act, such a letter will be highly persuasive if not binding. . . . If the State Department issues a letter stating that it has no objection to adjudication of the validity of a given act of a foreign state, courts in the United States will make their own determination as to whether to apply the act of state doctrine, taking the view of the Executive Branch into account but not being bound by it.[156]

§ 8.09 THE COUNTERCLAIM/SETOFF EXCEPTION

The courts have recognized that the scope of the act of state doctrine may not be quite so broad if the foreign sovereign initiates the action in a U.S. court, and the consideration of the doctrine occurs in the context of a counterclaim.[157] For instance, although the Court's decision in *First Nat'l City Bank v. Banco Nacional de Cuba*,[158] is arguably an effective example of the operation of the counterclaim/setoff exception to the doctrine, it involved an exception to the defense of sovereign immunity, despite one Justice's identification of parallel policy concerns.[159] The Court was faced with the issue whether the act of state doctrine would bar consideration of recovery on a counterclaim against Cuba's national bank, when the bank had initiated suit to recover excess proceeds from City Bank's sale of collateral securing a loan to the bank.[160] City Bank counterclaimed (up to the amount of the excess proceeds) for losses incurred when Cuba

156. RESTATEMENT, *supra* note 19, § 443, cmt. 8, at 381.

157. Comment, *The Act of State Doctrine: A History of Judicial Limitations and Exceptions*, 18 HARV. INT'L L.J. 677, 696 (1977).

158. 406 U.S. 759 (1972). *See also* National City Bank v. Republic of China, 348 U.S. 356 (1955).

159. *See* First Nat'l City Bank, 406 U.S. 759, at 770–772 (Douglas, J., concurring).

160. 406 U.S. at 760–61.

nationalized City Bank assets in Cuba. The procedural stance of the case is complicated by the Executive's *Bernstein* letter,[161] and a splintered Supreme Court. No single rationale commanded a majority, but five Justices voted to reverse.[162]

Although the Court did not specifically hold that courts were free to examine the validity of a foreign act if the issue arose in response to a counterclaim, the effect of the Court's decision resulted in the creation of what has been termed the counterclaim/setoff exception.[163]

In *Banco Nacional de Cuba v. Chase Manhattan Bank*,[164] the Second Circuit cumulated the views of the various Justices in *First Nat'l City Bank* and articulated the following rule:

> Where (1) the Executive Branch has provided a *Bernstein* letter advising the courts that it believes act of state doctrine need not be applied, (2) there is no showing that an adjudication of the claim will interfere with delicate foreign relations, and (3) the claim against the foreign sovereign is asserted by way of counterclaim and does not exceed the value of the sovereign's claim, adjudication of the counterclaim for expropriation of the defendant's property is not barred by the act of state doctrine.[165]

Because all three conditions must be satisfied—*Bernstein* letter (or its equivalent),[166] a negative showing as to foreign relations impact, *and* a counterclaim/setoff—the exception should more appropriately be termed a *Bernstein plus* counterclaim exception.[167] In practical effect, the counterclaim exception can be viewed as an application of the *Bernstein* exception, given the irrelevance to the purposes of the doctrine of the procedural coincidence in which the issue arises.

That the counterclaim exception is really a counterclaim *plus Bernstein* exception to the act of state doctrine is evident from the Second Circuit's decision in *Empresa Cubana Exportadora de Azucara y Sus Derivados v. Lamborn & Co., Inc.*[168] In *Lamborn*, the Second

161. *See supra* § 8.08.

162. 406 U.S. at 759.

163. RESTATEMENT (THIRD) OF FOREIGN RELATIONS LAW § 443, reporters' note 9.

164. 658 F.2d 875 (2d Cir. 1981).

165. *Id.* at 884 (footnote omitted); *accord* Banco Nacional de Cuba v. Chemical Bank, 658 F.2d 903, 911 (2d Cir. 1981) ("Chemical I").

166. *See* Banco Nacional de Cuba v. Chemical Bank, 822 F.2d 230, 236 (2d Cir. 1987) ("Chemical II") (holding three requirements satisfied).

167. *Cf.* RESTATEMENT, *supra* note 19, § 443.

168. 652 F.2d 231 (2d Cir. 1981) (decided two months prior to *Chase Manhattan*, 658 F.2d 875, at 884 n.12).

Circuit held that the act of state doctrine barred consideration of the expropriation claim, despite the fact that the issue arose in the context of a counterclaim.[169] The court examined but did not find support for the *Bernstein* exception, and held that the mandate of *Sabbatino* controlled.[170] The court stated: ''otherwise applicable policy considerations require that the act of state doctrine not be abandoned merely because the sovereign appears as a plaintiff.''[171]

Practice Note: The lesson of the *Chase Manhattan and Lamborn* decisions is that litigants seeking to avoid the application of the act of state doctrine must consider multiple exceptions. It remains a common feature of act of state cases that a counterclaim may, in conjunction with other exceptions, justify consideration of expropriation claims that would otherwise be barred by the act of state defense. Under these circumstances, the opportunity of pursuing a counterclaim may be preferable to an affirmative action against a foreign sovereign on an expropriation claim.

§ 8.10 THE COMMERCIAL ACT EXCEPTION

Courts and commentators alike have debated whether a commercial act exception exists to the act of state doctrine.[172] Such an exception would not merely redefine the types of acts qualifying as acts of state,[173] but instead would exempt commercial acts of state from the scope of the doctrine. In increasingly appears that the flexible, discretionary nature of the act of state doctrine, which permits courts to avoid intervening in certain types of cases, counsels against a rigid commercial act exception, even where the court would have jurisdiction over a commercial act under the Foreign Sovereign Immunities Act.

The basis for the debate over a commercial act exception is Part III of the Supreme Court's decision in *Alfred Dunhill of London, Inc. v.*

169. 652 F.2d at 237 (noting that facts of *Sabbatino* involved counterclaim).

170. *Id.* at 239.

171. *Id.*

172. *See* Restatement, *supra* note 19, § 443, reporters' note 6. *See also supra* § 8.05 (discussing emergence of commercial act exception); Leacock, *The Commercial Activity Exception to the Act of State Doctrine: Evolution of a Concept*, 13 N.C. J. Int'l L. & Com. Reg. 1 (1988).

173. *See* § 8.04; Comment, *The Act of State Doctrine: A History of Judicial Limitations and Exceptions*, 18 Harv. Int'l L.J. 677, 692–93 (1977) (terming redefinition ''an exercise in semantics'').

Republic of Cuba,[174] a part of Justice White's opinion that commanded the support of only three other Justices.[175] The four Justices in Part III agreed that "the concept of the act of state doctrine should not be extended to include the repudiation of a purely commercial obligation owed by a foreign sovereign or by one of its commercial instrumentalities."[176]

Justice White reviewed the similarity of concerns underpinning the act of state doctrine and foreign sovereign immunity and stated that: "For all the reasons which led the Executive Branch to adopt the restrictive theory of sovereign immunity, we hold that the mere assertion of sovereignty as a defense to a claim arising out of purely commercial acts by a foreign sovereign is no more effective if given the label 'Act of State' than if it is given the label 'sovereign immunity.' "[177] Of interest to Justice White was the Executive's *Bernstein* letter in the case that not only advocated the commercial act exception, but also the counterclaim exception and even the overruling of *Sabbatino*.[178] Given the similarity of concerns leading to the restrictive theory of sovereign immunity and the Executive's views, the Court laid the foundation for, but did not create, a commercial act exception.

Circuit courts appear to be skeptical whether there is a commercial act exception to the act of state doctrine. In *International Association of Machinists and Aerospace Workers, (IAM) v. OPEC*,[178.1] Judge Choy concluded that carving a broad commercial act exception would undercut the act of state doctrine's purpose to permit U.S. courts the flexibility to avoid, where appropriate, deciding politically sensitive cases involving sovereign prerogatives. The court, in essence, distinguished sovereign immunity from act of state by noting that the sovereign immunity act focuses on the nature of the act (i.e., whether a statutory exception exists under the FSIA) and the act of state doctrine focuses on the purpose (i.e., sovereign prerogative) of the act.[178.2]

---

174. 425 U.S. 682, 96 S. Ct. 1854, 48 L. Ed. 2d 301 (1976).

175. *Id.* at 684 (Burger, C.J., and Powell and Rhenquist, JJ.).

176. *Id.* at 659.

177. *Id.* at 705 (footnote omitted).

178. *Id.* at 696–97 & n.12. The full text of the Executive's letter is reprinted as Appendix 1 to the *Dunhill* opinion.

178.1. 649 F.2d 1354 (9th Cir. 1981), *cert denied*, 102 S. Ct. 1036 (1982).

178.2. *See also* Honduras Aircraft Registry v. Gov't of Honduras, 129 F.3d 543, 550 (11th Cir. 1997) ("there is no commercial exception to the act of state doctrine as there is under the FSIA"); Braka v. Bancomer, 762 F.2d 222, 225 (2d Cir. 1985) ("We leave for another day consideration of the possible existence in this Circuit of a commercial exception to the act of state doctrine under Dunhill); Kalamazoo Spice Extraction Co. v. Ethiopia, 729 F.2d

Some lower courts have expressed support for the commercial act exception[179] —and at least one has interpreted *Dunhill* as so holding—but the exception does not appear to have been dispositive in any case.[180] Moreover, although several commentators have concluded that the *Dunhill* decision created a commercial act exception to the act of state doctrine,[181] the exception does not explicitly benefit from Supreme Court precedent.[182] Counsel have an enhanced opportunity to assist the courts in fashioning the contours of any commercial act exception. The demonstration that the purposes of the act of state doctrine are inapplicable to a given set of facts provides fertile ground for argument.

§ 8.11 THE HICKENLOOPER (*SABBATINO*) AMENDMENT

In response to the Supreme Court's decision in *Banco Nacional de Cuba v. Sabbatino*,[183] in 1964, Congress enacted the so-called second Hickenlooper amendment to the Foreign Assistance Act of 1961.[184] The first portion of the amendment would have denied foreign assistance to those nations taking the property of U.S. citizens in violation of international law. Invoked only once,[185] and subsequently repealed, the

---

422, 425 (6th Cir. 1984) (finding that while commercial act exception may exist by virtue of Alfred Dunhill ruling, the exception is "of doubtful precedential value"); Clayco Petroleum Corp. v. Occidental Petroleum Corp., 712 F.2d 404, 408 (9th Cir. 1983) ("we need not reach the question whether to adopt an exception to the act of state doctrine for purely commercial activity"), *cert. denied*, 464 U.S. 1040, 104 S. Ct. 703, 79 L. Ed. 2d 168 (1984).

179. *See, e.g.*, Texas Trading & Milling Corp. v. Federal Republic of Nigeria, 647 F.2d 300, 316 n.38 (2d Cir. 1981), *cert. denied*, 454 U.S. 1148 (1982); Hunt v. Mobil Oil Corp., 550 F.2d 68, 72–73 (2d Cir.), *cert. denied*, 434 U.S. 984 (1977); Dominicus Americana Bohio v. Gulf & Western Industries, Inc., 473 F. Supp. 680, 689–90 (S.D.N.Y. 1979). *But see* Braka v. Bancomer, S.N.C, 762 F.2d 222, 225 (2d Cir. 1985) (dismissing as dicta the support expressed in *Texas Trading* and *Hunt*).

180. Behring Int'l v. Imperial Iranian Air Force, 475 F. Supp. 396, 401 (D.N.J. 1979) ("The [act of state] doctrine . . . distinguishes between the public and governmental acts of sovereign states and their private and commercial acts"). *See also* National Am. Corp. v. Federal Republic of Nigeria, 448 F. Supp. 622, 640 (S.D.N.Y. 1978).

181. Carl, *Suing Foreign Governments in American Courts: The United States Foreign Sovereign Immunities Act in Practice*, 33 Sw. L.J. 1009, 1054 (1979); Note, *An Analysis of the Act of State Doctrine*, 22 N.Y.L. Sch. L. Rev. 995, 1008 (1977).

182. *See* Restatement, *supra* note 19, § 443 reporters' note 6.

183. 376 U.S. 398 (1964).

184. 22 U.S.C.A. § 2370(e)(2). *See* Libyan Am. Oil Co. v. Socialist People's Libyan Arab Jamahirya, 482 F. Supp. 1175, 1178–79 (D.D.C. 1980). *See generally* Lowenfeld, *The Sabbatino Amendment—International Law Meets Civil Procedure*, 59 Am. J. Int'l L. 89 (1965).

185. *See* Sweeney, Oliver Leech, The International Legal System 392 (1981) ("[s]ubsection (e)(1), actually, has only been used once, against Sri Lanka, with no discernable results. In all other cases, quiet diplomacy has been the vehicle of settlement").

first portion of the amendment provided the compensation standard of "speedy compensation for such property in convertible foreign exchange, equivalent to the full value thereof," but otherwise is of historical interest only.[186]

The second portion of the amendment, subsection (2), the so-called *Sabbatino*, or second Hickenlooper amendment, however, remains in force as an important limitation on the act of state doctrine. The legislation provides:

> Notwithstanding any other provision of law, no court in the United States shall decline on the ground of the federal act of state doctrine to make a determination on the merits giving effect to the principles of international law in a case in which a claim of title or other right to property is asserted by any party including a foreign state (or a party claiming through such state) based upon (or traced through) a confiscation or other taking after January 1, 1959, by an act of that state in violation of the principles of international law, including the

(*Text continued on page 8-33*)

186. *See* Lillich, *Requiem for Hickenlooper*, 69 AM. J. INT'L L. 97 (1975).

principles of compensation and the other standards set out in this subsection [the repealed portion]: *Provided,* That this subparagraph shall not be applicable (1) in any case in which an act of a foreign state is not contrary to international law or with respect to a claim of title or other right to property acquired pursuant to an irrevocable letter of credit of not more than 180 days duration issued in good faith prior to the time of the confiscation or other taking, or (2) in any case with respect to which the President determines that application of the act of state doctrine is required in that particular case by the foreign policy interests of the United States and a suggestion to this effect is filed on his behalf in that case with the court.[187]

The *Sabbatino* amendment creates a different sort of analysis of whether the act of state doctrine bars consideration of a claim by a U.S. court. The Restatement version of the limitation is contained in section 444, and provides:

In the absence of a Presidential determination to the contrary, the act of state doctrine will not be applied in a case involving a claim of title or other right to property, when the claim is based on the assertion that a foreign state confiscated the property in violation of international law.[188]

As an exception to the "rule" of the *Sabbatino* decision, the amendment directs the courts to examine the validity of a taking unless the President indicates that such an examination could jeopardize foreign affairs, or the taking is consistent with international law. The first proviso is an attempt to reverse the presumption of silence on the part of the executive.[189]

This reversal of the presumption was a specific goal of the amendment, as the legislative history reflects:

The effect of the amendment is to achieve a reversal of presumptions. Under the *Sabbatino* decision, the courts would presume that any adjudication as to the lawfulness under international law of the act of a foreign state would embarrass the conduct of foreign policy unless the President says it would not. Under the amendment, the court would presume that it may so proceed with an adjudication on the merits

187. 22 U.S.C.A. § 2370(e)(2).

188. RESTATEMENT, *supra* note 19, § 444. For a view critical of the Restatement's treatment of the *Sabbatino* amendment, *see* Leigh, Sabbatino's *Silver Anniversary and the Restatement: No Cause for Celebration,* 24 INT'L LAW. 1, 6–8 (1990).

189. *See also supra,* § 8.08[2] (discussing reverse *Bernstein* exception).

unless the President states officially that such an adjudication in the particular case would embarrass the conduct of foreign policy.[190]

In *Banco Nacional de Cuba v. Farr*,[191] following remand from the Supreme Court in *Sabbatino,* the Second Circuit applied the intervening second Hickenlooper amendment and did not apply the act of state doctrine to bar consideration of the claim.[192]

After *Banco Nacional de Cuba v. Farr,* the second Hickenlooper amendment was narrowly interpreted in *Banco National de Cuba v. First Nat'l City Bank*,[193] to apply "only to cases in which the expropriated property has found its way back into the United States."[194] Under this interpretation, the second Hickenlooper amendment only prevents the courts from applying the act of state doctrine in cases in which the claim of illegal taking relates to the specific property before the court, and would not prevent the doctrine from applying to bar a claim as to generalized assets of the foreign sovereign. Because this interpretation severely limits the scope of the amendment, it has been applied in very few cases.

For example, the Supreme Court of Texas, in *Hunt v. Coastal States Gas Producing Co.*,[195] stated the three prerequisites to the amendment's application:

> 1. Expropriated property must come within the territorial jurisdiction of the United States. 2. The act of the expropriating nation must be in violation of international law. 3. The asserted claim must be a claim of title or other right to property.[196]

The operation of the second Hickenlooper amendment was illustrated by the 1987 decision of *West v. Multibanco Comermex S.A.*,[197] in which the Ninth Circuit held that the legislation permitted the court to examine certain acts of the Mexican government. The court determined

---

190. S. Rep. No. 1188, Part I, 88th Cong., 2d Sess. 24 (1964), *as cited in* Banco Nacional de Cuba v. Farr, 383 F.2d 166, 174 (2d Cir. 1967), *cert. denied,* 390 U.S. 956 (1968).

191. 383 F.2d 166 (2d Cir. 1967), *cert. denied,* 390 U.S. 956 (1968).

192. 383 F.2d at 183; *see generally* Henkin, *Act of State Today: Recollections in Tranquility,* 6 COLUM. J. TRANSNT'L L. 175, 177 (1967) (discussing questionable application of amendment).

193. 431 F.2d 394 (2d Cir. 1970), *rev'd on other grounds,* 406 U.S. 759 (1972).

194. Empresa Cubana Exportadora, Inc. v. Lamborn & Co., Inc., 652 F.2d 231, 237 (2d Cir. 1981).

195. 583 S.W.2d 322 (1979).

196. *Id. But see* Ramirez de Arellano v. Weinberger, 745 F.2d 1500, 1541 n.180 (D.C. Cir. 1984) (rejecting limitation), *vacated on other grounds,* 471 U.S. 1113 (1985).

197. 807 F.2d 820 (9th Cir.), *cert. denied,* 482 U.S. 906 (1987).

that the act of state doctrine barred it from considering certain claims related to compliance with Mexican law by Mexican officials, but that the second Hickenlooper amendment permitted the court to examine plaintiff's claim of an illegal expropriation.[198] The court held that, "when Hickenlooper governs, courts are barred from invoking the judicially created doctrine under which we refrain from consideration of cases involving acts of foreign governments or foreign officials."[199]

The impact of the second Hickenlooper amendment has been limited to these cases, but the recent use in the *West* decision signals a willingness of the courts to give an expansive reading to the amendment, a reading the court in *West* held was necessary to give effect to the purpose of the amendment that "the protection afforded U.S. investments [is] to be broad in scope."[200] The *West* decision provides support for continued use of the second Hickenlooper amendment in cases in which litigants oppose the application of the act of state doctrine.

§ 8.12 THE ARBITRATION EXCEPTION

Because parties to arbitration agreements with foreign states must sometimes resort to judicial forums to resolve questions relating to the agreement or its enforcement, the act of state doctrine presents a potential obstacle to realization of the object of the arbitration agreement. Recognizing this, Congress amended the federal arbitration provisions in 1988 to add a new section on the act of state doctrine. The new section provides:

> Enforcement of arbitral agreements, confirmation of arbitral awards, and execution upon judgments based on orders confirming such awards shall not be refused on the basis of the act of state doctrine.[201]

Although no decisions have yet been reported applying the new provision, it is expected to enhance the effectiveness of arbitration as a means of dispute resolution involving foreign states. Under the amendment, courts may not interpose the act of state doctrine to decline to enforce an agreement to arbitrate, nor to decline to enforce an otherwise valid arbitral award.[202]

198. *Id.* at 829–831.

199. *Id.* at 829 (footnote omitted).

200. 807 F.2d at 830.

201. Pub. L. No. 100–669, 102 Stat. 3969 § 1 (1988) (codified at 9 U.S.C. § 15).

202. *See* Allied-Bruce Terminex Companies, Inc. v. Michael Dobson, 513 U.S. 265 (1995) (noting adoption of § 15 as "extending, not retracting, the scope of arbitration.").

§ 8.13 THE CORRUPTION EXCEPTION

[1] Introduction

A less well known and perhaps less formal exception to the act of state doctrine is the so-called corruption exception. It is not so much an exception as it is a reflection of the terms of the doctrine itself. It is, however, how the issue is often described. This section discusses this issue and reviews the origins and current operation of the exception.

[2] Background

As international competition for contracts with foreign governments intensifies—particularly in formerly communist nations or in newly industrialized nations with extensive privatization programs—corruption issues have taken on renewed importance. For U.S. companies, the restrictions of the Foreign Corrupt Practices Act, or FCPA, are a unilateral burden not shared by competitors from other nations. When the competition is among U.S. companies, however, and corruption is involved, the courts have faced a variety of legal issues. Courts have held that there is no implied private right of action under the FCPA.[203] This means that they must look to other remedies, such as RICO, or other causes of actions.

A perennial obstacle has in such cases been the act of state doctrine. Concerned about embarrassing foreign governments and compromising U.S. foreign policy, courts have in some cases been reluctant to examine the facts underlying the claims of disappointed U.S. companies.[204] The result has been to deny a remedy to a disappointed company. Other courts have determined that the act of state doctrine should not apply and therefore permit suit to go forward.[205] A split in the precedent led to the Supreme Court case of *W.S. Kirkpatrick*,[206] in which the Supreme Court held that the act of state doctrine should not bar consideration of an inquiry into the motivation of a foreign governmental act.[207] This

203. Lamb v. Phillip Morris, Inc., 915 F.2d 1924, 1927–30 (6th Cir. 1990); Clayco Petroleum Corp. v. Occidental Petroleum Corp., 712 F.2d 404, 408–9 (9th Cir. 1983).

204. *See, e.g.*, Clayco Petroleum Corp. v. Occidental Petroleum Corp., 712 F.2d 404 (9th Cir. 1983).

205. *See, e.g.*, Sage International Ltd. v. Cadillac Gage Co., 534 F. Supp. 896 (E.D. Mich. 1981).

206. W.S. Kirkpatrick & Co., Inc. v. Environmental Tectonics Corp. Int'l, 493 U.S. 400 (1990).

207. *Id.*

decision served to reinvigorate the so-called corruption exception to the act of state doctrine. It appears that a broad corruption exception to the doctrine is consistent with the purposes and objectives of U.S. law and policy in the form of the FCPA and does not undermine the goals of the act of state doctrine.[208]

[3] Early Cases

Two pre-*Kirkpatrick* decisions delineated a divergent approach to the corruption exception. In *Clayco Petroleum Corp. v. Occidental Petroleum Corp.*,[209] plaintiff brought an antitrust action charging defendant with making secret payments to foreign officials to obtain unlawfully an offshore oil concession. The district court dismissed the suit on the basis of the act of state doctrine and, when Clayco appealed the case, the Ninth Circuit agreed with the district court's analysis by adopting a mechanical approach to the act of state doctrine.

The court in *Clayco* refused to recognize a corruption exception to the act of state doctrine for private lawsuits.[210] The court found that because the underlying dispute involved a sovereign decision about the allocation of national resources, the act of state doctrine precluded judicial review.[211] Also, the court reasoned that the act of state doctrine prevents suits by private citizens, even if they allege corrupt behavior, when a government is exercising powers peculiar to sovereigns.[212]

The corruption exception was also analyzed in *Sage International, Ltd. v. Cadillac Gage Co.*[213] In this case, the district court decided that it would not follow a mechanical interpretation of the act of state doctrine; instead, the court chose to balance the policy concerns underlying the doctrine with the possibility of injury to the individual parties. In *Sage*, plaintiff claimed that Cadillac Gage had violated antitrust legislation by unlawfully instituting "sham" litigation and by participating in an

---

208. *See generally* Veronica Ann Deberardine, *Foreign Corrupt Practices: Creating an Exception to the Act of State Doctrine*, AM. U.L. REV., Vol. 34:203, 203 (1984); Maureen A. Dowd and Theodore B. Eichelberger, *Recent Decision: International Law—Act Of State Doctrine: An Emerging Corruption Exception in Antitrust Cases?*, 59 NOTRE DAME L. REV. 455 (1984).

209. Clayco Petroleum Corp. v. Occidental Petroleum Corp., 712 F.2d 404 (9th Cir. 1983).

210. *Id.*

211. *Id.* at 406.

212. *Id.* at 408.

213. 534 F. Supp. 896 (E.D. Mich. 1981).

illegal kickback scheme to prevent Sage International from entering the armed-car market in fifteen foreign countries.[214]

In determining that the act of state doctrine would not preclude Sage International from proving its claims, the court reasoned that the act of state doctrine is less relevant in a situation where antitrust laws have been invoked and where it is contended that an act of state was improperly induced by a non-sovereign defendant for anticompetitive purposes.[215] In addition, the court found that the act of state analysis in cases involving antitrust claims calls for consideration of factors distinct from those presented by non-antitrust claims arising from confiscatory or other similar sovereign acts.[216] As a result, a balancing of interests and policy-related factors is required to resolve the question of when a court properly may involve itself in adjudicating disputes relating to acts of state.[217]

[4] *Kirkpatrick*

The Supreme Court first discussed this issue in *W.S. Kirkpatrick*,[218] and held that the act of state doctrine should not bar consideration of an inquiry into the motivation, as opposed to validity, of a foreign governmental act. The Court found that the act of state doctrine does not apply unless the validity of a foreign sovereign act is at issue.[219] The Court explained that "the act of state doctrine does not establish an exception for causes and controversies that may embarrass foreign governments, but merely requires that, in the process of deciding, the act of foreign governments taken within their own jurisdiction shall be deemed valid."[220] In reaching this conclusion and in permitting the plaintiffs' claim to go forward, Justice Scalia's opinion for the unanimous Court held that the act of state doctrine does not bar a court in the United States from entertaining a cause of action that requires imputing to foreign officials an unlawful motivation (obtaining bribes) in the performance of an official act.[221]

---

214. *Id.* at 898.
215. *Id.* at 901.
216. *Id.*
217. *Id.* at 903.
218. W.S. Kirkpatrick & Co., Inc. v. Environmental Tectonics Corp. Int'l, 493 U.S. 400 (1990).
219. *Id.* at 409.
220. *Id.* at 410.
221. *Id.* at 401.

One possible consequence of *Kirkpatrick* is that lawsuits involving claims of foreign governmental corruption may be more readily maintained in U.S. courts. And, as a matter of fact, in *Lamb v. Philip Morris, Inc.*,[222] the first such decision after *Kirkpatrick*, the U.S. Court of Appeals for the Sixth Circuit determined that the act of state doctrine did not bar an action by domestic tobacco growers against tobacco importers alleging violations of the federal antitrust law.[223] The Court of Appeals held that the act of state doctrine did not bar the suit because the antitrust claims merely call into question the contracting parties' motivations and the resulting anti-competitive effects of their agreement, not the validity of any foreign sovereign act.[224]

§ 8.14 ANALYZING ACT OF STATE ISSUES: PRACTICAL STRATEGIES AND CHECKLIST

[1] Checklist of Issues

From the perspective of representing a party opposed to the application of the act of state doctrine, the following step-by-step checklist is one way to consider whether the doctrine will apply. References to sections in this chapter discussing the topic are provided.

(1) Has the proponent of the doctrine identified a public governmental act and not a private one?[225]

(2) Has the proponent satisfied the burden of demonstrating the character of the act and the act itself, including compliance with FED. R. CIV. P. 44.1?[226]

(3) If so, was the property or object of the act located within the foreign territory at the time of the taking?[227] If not, the doctrine does not apply.

222. Lamb v. Philip Morris, Inc., 915 F.2d 1924 (6th Cir. 1990).

223. *Id.* at 1027. The suit was based upon an alleged agreement between Philip Morris' subsidiaries and a Venezuelan charitable foundation, whose president was the wife of the then President of Venezuela. The agreement allegedly involved periodic contributions by the subsidiaries to the foundation in return for substantial economic benefit. *Id.* at 1025.

224. *Id.* at 1027. The court also found that no private right of action is available under the FCPA. Id. at 1024.

225. *See supra* § 8.04.

226. *See supra* § 8.04.

227. *See supra* § 8.06.

(4) If the property was in the foreign territory at the time of the taking, has it subsequently come into the U.S.? If so, the second Hickenlooper/*Sabbatino* amendment may apply to prevent application of the doctrine.[228]

(5) If the public governmental act requirement and territorial condition are satisfied, then the question is whether an exception is relevant.[229]

(6) Is there a treaty or other agreement in place, either bi- or multi-lateral, that provides an unambiguous controlling legal standard for consideration of the issues?[230]

(7) What are the views of the Executive Branch? After consultation with officials, is a *Bernstein* letter available in the case?[231]

(8) If not, does the case present strong facts for the possible application of the setoff/counterclaim exception?[232] Although this exception is primarily employed only in conjunction with the *Bernstein* exception, if the facts are strong enough, it may motivate executive action.

(9) Does the case present compelling facts for the application of the emerging commercial act exception to the act of state doctrine?[233] If the case strongly illustrates the need for a commercial act exception, assistance from the Executive, bar associations, or other organizations may be available.

(10) Does the case arise from or involve arbitration? [234] If so, the doctrine may be barred by statute.

(11) Finally, if none of the previous conditions, limitations, or exceptions apply (or even if they do) always consider a presentation that demonstrates that application of the doctrine in this particular case would be inconsistent with the purposes and rationale of the doctrine.[235] Because courts are sensitive to

228. *See supra* § 8.11.
229. *See supra* § 8.03.
230. *See supra* § 8.07.
231. *See supra* § 8.08.
232. *See supra* § 8.09.
233. *See supra* § 8.10.
234. *See supra* § 8.12
235. *See supra* § 8.02.

the purposes of the doctrine, that subject must be considered an important element of the presentation.

[2] Practical Strategies

Because act of state cases involve complex issues, it is crucial to gather support and assistance at an early stage in the litigation, regardless of which side is being presented. Whether you are the proponent or opponent of the doctrine's application, several practical steps should be considered:

(1) Know the doctrine's origins and purposes.[236] Know the conditions, limitations, and exceptions to the doctrine.[237] Can facts be developed that support one of the exceptions to the doctrine? Can specific precedent be found?

(2) Know how to plead and prove foreign law.[238] Whether proposing or opposing the application of the doctrine, know the burden the proponent carries and how to establish it or beat it.[239] If the character of the act itself is not conclusive, can you obtain official ratification or official disavowal?

(3) Know when and how to contact the Executive Branch for assistance or to learn of its views.[240] In any case involving even the potential for an act of state issue to arise, the Office of the Legal Advisor at the State Department must be contacted at a very early stage to address the foreign relations interests at issue. Cooperation is often possible, but early action is crucial, especially if an amicus brief—on either side—is desired.

(4) Be prepared to educate the decision maker, not just on the facts, but on this complex and intricate area of law. Even though many act of state cases have been decided, they are not common, and, in some jurisdictions, may never have been considered. Under these circumstances, counsel's role will be important in providing the court with information on the doctrine, as well as on the client's position. The role of counsel in an act of state case is enhanced because given the confused

236. *See supra* § 8.02.
237. *See supra* §§ 8.03–8.12.
238. *See supra* Chapter 2 & *infra* Chapter 9.
239. *See supra* § 8.04.
240. *See supra* § 8.08.

nature and varied purposes of the doctrine, greater latitude for creative approaches exists than in more well-settled areas of law.

(5) An important counselling issue for U.S. companies going abroad is the impact that the doctrine could have on their investment. Although catastrophic events are difficult to predict, they must be prepared for. One issue is whether the foreign state will "waive" the defense.[241] Although not conclusive, "waiver" can help demonstrate to the court that the purposes of the doctrine would not be served by its application.

---

241. *See* RESTATEMENT, *supra* note 19, § 443, cmt. e; Dayton v. Czechoslovak Socialist Republic, 834 F.2d 203 (D.C. Cir. 1987) (citing RESTATEMENT).

Chapter 9

PROVING FOREIGN LAW AND DETERMINING WHAT LAW APPLIES

§ 9.01 INTRODUCTION

Any party intending to rely on foreign law as part of the proof of its case must be familiar with the requirement of Rule 44.1 of the Federal Rules of Civil Procedure. That rule provides as follows:

> A party who intends to raise an issue concerning the law of a foreign country shall give notice in his pleadings or other reasonable written notice. The court, in determining foreign law, may consider any relevant material or source, including testimony, whether or not submitted by a party or admissible under the Federal Rules of Evidence. The court's determination shall be treated as a ruling on a question of law.

Rule 44.1, which was adopted in 1966, is an endeavor to furnish the federal courts with a uniform and effective procedure for raising and determining an issue concerning the law of a foreign country.[1] Prior to 1966, foreign law questions were regarded as questions of fact which had to be proved as such.[2] Treating foreign law considerations as a question of fact meant that foreign law issues had to be raised in the pleadings and proven in accordance with the rules of evidence. It further encouraged courts to regard juries as the appropriate body to ascertain questions of foreign law, thus limiting appellate review of determinations of foreign law. Even under the more liberal standards of Rule 44.1, however, it is essential that parties, while preparing for litigation, first consider whether they intend to rely on foreign law as part of their case and then determine how they intend to prove foreign law in accordance with the requirements of Rule 44.1.

§ 9.02 REASONABLE NOTICE

Rule 44.1 provides that a "party who intends to raise an issue concerning the law of a foreign country shall give notice in his pleadings or other reasonable written notice."

The notes of the Advisory Committee on Rules state:

> In some situations the pertinence of foreign law is apparent from the outset; accordingly the necessary investigation of that law will have been accomplished by the party at the pleading stage, and the notice can be given conveniently in the pleadings.[3]

---

1. Fed. R. Civ. P. 44.1 advisory committee's note, 39 F.R.D. 69, 117 (1966).
2. 9 Charles A. Wright & Arthur R. Miller, Federal Practice & Procedure § 2441 (1971).
3. Fed. R. Civ. P. 44.1 advisory committee's note, 39 F.R.D. 69, 117 (1966).

The pleader, however, does not have to commit to the application of foreign law before pretrial discovery. In *Grice v. Mowinckels*,[4] defendant filed a Rule 12(b)(6) motion to dismiss on the ground that plaintiff had failed to allege whether foreign law was applicable and hence the complaint failed to state a claim upon which relief could be granted. The court stated that while the purpose of Rule 44.1 was to avoid surprise, it would be unfair to require plaintiff, in order to survive a Rule 12(b)(6) motion, to set out in its complaint the identity and substance of the applicable law involved.[5] Similarly, where defendant raised the applicability of foreign law in a motion to dismiss, the district court in *Hodson v. A. H. Robins Co., Inc.*,[6] stated as follows:

> Certainly there is no risk of surprise present in the cases, for it is the defendants who have raised the question of the relevance of British law. . . . [w]here the applicability of foreign law is not obvious at the outset and is a matter of some contention among the parties, the "reasonable written notice," if required at all under Rule 44.1, may come at any time sufficient to give the court and the defendants adequate notice of the need to research the foreign rules.[7]

Where a party is provided with ample opportunity to present its own position as to the applicability of foreign law in the suit, however, it cannot be heard to complain that it lacked reasonable notice under Rule 44.1.[8]

Any form of notice is sufficient provided there is no issue of "unfair surprise."[9] Although foreign law materials may be considered at any time, a party should submit such evidence as early in the proceeding as possible, preferably in the district court and not at the appellate stage. In this connection it has been held that plaintiffs waived their right to rely on foreign law because the issue was not raised for the first time until the plaintiffs' motion for reconsideration.[10]

---

4. 477 F. Supp. 365 (S.D. Ala. 1979).

5. *Id.* at 367.

6. 528 F. Supp. 809 (E.D. Va. 1981), *aff'd*, 715 F.2d 142 (4th Cir. 1983).

7. *Id.* at 824.

8. *See* Cunard S.S. Co. v. Salen Reefer Services AB, 773 F.2d 452, 461 (2d Cir. 1985).

9. *See* Laminoirs-Trefileries-Cableries de Lens, S.A. v. Southwire Co., 484 F. Supp. 1063, 1067 (N.D. Ga. 1980); Nakano v. Jamie Sadock Inc., 2000 WL 680365,*4 (S.D.N.Y.) (notice insufficient where raised after disposition of summary judgment on that issue); DP Aviation v. Smith Industries Aerospace and Defense Systems Ltd., 268 F.3d 829 (9th Cir. 2001) (absent extenuating circumstances, notice of application of foreign law should be given in pretrial order).

10. Frietsch v. Refco, Inc., 56 F.3d 825, 828 (7th Cir. 1995); Whirlpool Financial Corp. v. Sevaux, 96 F.3d 216, 220 (7th Cir. 1996).

Some courts have held that if a party fails to give reasonable written notice in the district court, it is precluded from raising the issue of foreign law on appeal.[11] Other courts have held that, absent special circumstances, the parties should present issues of foreign law in their appellate briefs at the latest.[12] Similarly, where a party fails to raise a foreign law issue prior to the issuance of a final order, it may have waived the foreign law issue on remand of the case to the trial court.[13] The same ''reasonable written notice'' requirement where a party intends to raise an issue concerning the laws of a foreign country applies as well to criminal proceedings.[14]

§ 9.03 MATERIAL THE COURT MAY CONSIDER

Rule 44.1 permits the court, in determining foreign law, to consider any relevant material or source, including testimony, without regard to whether the material considered would be admissible under the rules of evidence. This liberal standard of proof is intended to make the process of determining foreign law identical, to the extent possible, with the methods of ascertaining domestic law.[15] Thus, the court is free to accept any material presented by the parties, including extracts from foreign written sources and written or oral expert testimony, and to give whatever probative value, in the court's opinion, is deserved. Moreover, a determination of foreign law in a related case does not preclude a court in a separate proceeding from considering the same issue of foreign law under Rule 44.1 in light of both evidence admitted and the court's own research and interpretation.[16]

Since, under Rule 44.1, foreign law sources are exempt from the hearsay rule, courts may consider such materials as affidavits, briefs and arguments of counsel, and opinion letters.[17]

---

11. *See* Ruff v. St. Paul Mercury Ins. Co., 393 F.2d 500, 502 (2d Cir. 1968).

12. *See* Stuart v. United States, 813 F.2d 243, 251 (9th Cir. 1987), *rev'd on other grounds*, 489 U.S. 353 (1988).

13. Thyssen Steel Co. v. M/V Kavo Yerakas, 911 F. Supp. 263, 267–268 (S.D. Tex. 1996).

14. United States v. Kearney, 560 F.2d 1358 (9th Cir. 1977).

15. 9 Charles A. Wright & Arthur R. Miller, Federal Practice & Procedure § 2441 (1971).

16. *See* Ackermann v. Levine, 788 F.2d 830, 838 n. 7 (2d Cir. 1986).

17. *See* Kalmich v. Bruno, 553 F.2d 549, 555 (7th Cir.), *cert. denied*, 434 U.S. 940 (1977); Banco de Credito Industrial, S.A. v. Tesoreria General, 990 F.2d 827, 832 n.11–12 (5th Cir. 1993); United States v. Pre-Columbian Artifacts, 845 F. Supp. 544 (N.D. Ill. 1993). *See also* John R. Schmertz, *A Modern Procedural Framework for Establishing the Law of a*

In *United States v. Mitchell*,[18] the court summarized the different sources and materials considered by U.S. courts in the determination of foreign law. The court stated:

> In determining questions of foreign law, courts have turned to a wide variety of sources, including affidavits and expert testimony from an Australian Federal Judge. . . , a Peruvian Minister of Agriculture. . . , and a South African attorney. . . , certified translations of Bolivian Supreme Decrees. . . , foreign case law, a student note in a Philippine law review. . . , information obtained by a law clerk in a telephone conversation with the Hong Kong Trade Office and presented ex parte to the court. . . , and the court's "own independent analysis of" a Yugoslavian law.[19]

In considering what discovery is permitted before a Rule 44.1 determination, courts are bound by the limits of relevancy. In *Republic of Turkey v. OKS Partners*,[20] the court ruled that discovery preliminary to a Rule 44.1 hearing should be limited to those materials which the courts of the foreign country would examine if called upon to make the determination, absent a showing, supported by expert testimony, of the necessity of obtaining additional materials.[21]

In considering "any relevant material or source . . . whether or not submitted by a party" under Rule 44.1, a court has the choice of conducting its own research or insisting that counsel fully engage in this task. According to the advisory committee note to Rule 44.1:

> In further recognition of the peculiar nature of the issue of foreign law, the new rule provides that in determining this law the court is not limited by material presented by the parties; it may engage in its own research and consider any relevant material thus found. The court may have at its disposal better foreign law materials than counsel have presented, or may wish to reexamine and amplify material that has been presented by counsel in partisan fashion or in insufficient detail. On the other hand, the court is free to insist on a complete presentation by counsel.[22]

Foreign Country, 28 PRAC. LAW., vol. 6, 63, 69 (1982). *See generally* John R. Brown, *44.1 Ways to Prove Foreign Law*, 9 MAR. LAW. 179 (1984).

18. 985 F.2d 1275 (4th Cir. 1993).

19. *Id.* at 1280 (citations omitted). *See also* National Group for Communications and Computers Ltd. v. Lucent Technologies Int'l Inc., 331 F. Supp. 2d 290 (D.N.J. 2004) (application of Saudi Arabian law to limit permissible damages in contract dispute).

20. 146 F.R.D. 24 (D. Mass. 1993).

21. *Id.* at 29.

22. 39 F.R.D. 69, 117 (1966). *See* Anglo American Insurance Group v. Calfed, Inc., 899 F. Supp. 1070, 1076–1077 (S.D.N.Y. 1995); Compania Sud Americana De Vapores, S.A. v. I.T.O. Corp. of Baltimore *et al.*, 940 F. Supp. 855, 860 (D. Md. 1996).

Expert testimony is not a necessity in establishing foreign law, and a court may reach different conclusions based on an individual examination of foreign legal authorities.[23] In *Chantier Naval Voisin v. M/Y Daybreak*,[24] the district court stated that while it could accept evidence submitted by the parties regarding the substance of the foreign law, it was not bound by the testimony of the expert witnesses presented. In that case, the court rejected the testimony of plaintiff's expert witness and made its own investigation concerning the foreign law involved.[25] In this connection, in *United States v. First Nat'l Bank of Chicago*,[26] the court of appeals stated that a sworn statement by an attorney—a written expert opinion—was not a prerequisite to proving foreign law and that the district court was entitled to consider letters, affidavits, and translations and to base its determination on a combination of that evidence.

The use of affidavits or other written statements to present expert testimony on foreign law is more common than oral testimony in federal courts.[27] Generally, translated copies of the relevant foreign law upon which the expert relies are attached to the affidavit.[28]

The case of *Bing v. Halstead*,[29] illustrates the use of written affidavits to prove foreign law. In that case, plaintiff, a New York citizen who resided in Costa Rica, sued defendant for damages for intentional infliction of emotional distress. Defendant moved for summary judgment on the ground that Costa Rican law, which the court decided should determine the right to recover, did not recognize such a tort. Both plaintiff and defendant submitted affidavits from Costa Rican attorneys reciting the foreign law based on decisions from Costa Rican courts, including an analysis of relevant portions of the criminal code. On the basis of the written submissions of the foreign law question, the court

---

23. *See infra* note 32 and accompanying text.

24. 677 F. Supp. 1563, 1567 (S.D. Fla. 1988).

25. *Id.*

26. 699 F.2d 341, 343 (7th Cir. 1983).

27. Stephen L. Sass, *Foreign Law in Federal Courts*, 29 AM. J. COMP. L. 97, 108 (1981); Adrien K. Wing, *Pleading and Proof of Foreign Law in American Courts: A Selected Bibliography*, 19 STAN. J. INT'L L. 175 (1983). *See* Trinidad Foundry & Fabricating, Ltd. v. M/V K.A.S. Camilla, 966 F.2d 613 (11th Cir. 1992); Grynberg Prod. Corp. v. British Gas, PLC, 817 F. Supp. 1338, 1351 (E.D. Tex. 1993); Oil Shipping B.V. v. Royal Bank of Scotland, PLC, 817 F. Supp. 1254, 1259 (E.D. Pa. 1993); N.F.L. Ins., Ltd. v. B & B Holdings, Inc., 91-C8580, 1993 U.S. Dist. LEXIS 3312, *9, 1993 WL 78090 (S.D.N.Y. Mar. 18, 1993).

28. *See* Stephen L. Sass, *supra* note 27, at 108. *See generally* John R. Brown, *44.1 Ways to Prove Foreign Law*, 9 MAR. LAW. 179 (1984).

29. 495 F. Supp. 517, 522 (S.D.N.Y. 1980).

entered summary judgment for the defendant.[30] Pursuant to Rule 44.1, the court's determination of foreign law was treated as a ruling on a question of law. *Bing v. Halstead* illustrates the relative ease with which courts can resolve disputes of foreign law in summary judgment situations under Rule 44.1.[31]

The best method of proving foreign law (i.e, by documents or foreign law experts) undoubtedly depends on the availability of foreign law sources and the nature of the foreign law issue to be addressed. Although the assistance of foreign law experts is often essential, the need to use them in every case has been questioned. As such, experts are not required to meet any special qualifications, and federal courts are not bound by their testimony and may reject their conclusions.[32] Some authorities have urged that parties brief and argue the foreign law in the same manner as with domestic law and that the use of documentary authorities (translated copies of judicial decisions, etc.) may be more effective than the oral testimony of a foreign law expert.[33]

In determining whether or not to conduct its own research, some authorities have taken the view that the court has the duty to take into account such factors as ''the importance of foreign law to the case, the complexity of the foreign law issue, and how best to meet the needs of and be fair to the litigants.''[34] In *Twohy v. First Nat'l Bank of Chicago*,[35] the court of appeals stated that in order to effectuate Rule 44.1's inherent policy that foreign law questions be decided on the merits, district courts should take an active role in the process of ascertaining foreign law.[36] In noting the inadequacy of the lower court's investigation of Spanish law, the court of appeals stated that the district court had not fully met its duty to ascertain foreign law under Rule 44.1. The court of appeals admonished the lower court for not requiring a more ''complete presentation by counsel'' on the difficult foreign law

30. *Id.* at 521.

31. *See also* Kashfi v. Phibro-Solomon, Inc., 628 F. Supp. 727, 737 (S.D.N.Y. 1986).

32. *See* Grynberg Prod. Corp. v. British Gas, PLC, 817 F. Supp. 1338, 1360 (E.D. Tex. 1993); N.F.L. Ins. v. B & B Holdings, 91–C8580, 1993 U.S. Dist. LEXIS 3312, *9 (S.D.N.Y. 1993); Pfizer, Inc. v. Elan Pharmaceutical Research Corp., 812 F. Supp. 1352, 1360 (D. Del. 1993).

33. *See* Milton Pollack, *Proof of Foreign Law*, 26 AM. J. COMP. L. 470 (1978).

34. 9 CHARLES A. WRIGHT & ARTHUR R. MILLER, FEDERAL PRACTICE & PROCEDURE § 2444 (1971).

35. 758 F.2d 1185 (7th Cir. 1985).

36. *Id.* at 1193. *See also* Roger Miner, *The Reception of Foreign Law in the U.S. Federal Courts*, 43 AM. J. COMP. L. 581 (1995).

issue involved in the case.[37] However, the view that district courts should play an active role under Rule 44.1 is not universally held. Some commentators have suggested that it is reasonable to place most, if not all, of the burden of proving foreign law on the parties, and not the court. They have pointed out the difficulties inherent in researching foreign law and have concluded that there should be no greater judicial time spent in cases involving foreign law than in those which entail the interpretation of domestic law.[38]

Finally, Rule 44.1 imposes no duty on the court to notify the parties of its independent examination of foreign law issues or its intention to decide an issue of foreign law on the basis of its own research. However, some states, such as California, require the court to inform the parties of any source of information not received in open court which is of substantial consequence to the determination of the action and to allow them a reasonable opportunity to respond to such information before judicial notice is taken.[39]

Where the parties have not sought to prove the application of the foreign law or assert that it is in conflict with the domestic law, the court will apply the law of the forum.[40] The parties' failure to raise the foreign law issue in pleadings or otherwise may be viewed as a waiver of this issue, and acquiescence in the application of the law of the forum may be presumed.[41] Moreover, notice alone of reliance on foreign law will not prevent the application of the law of the forum where the parties fail to brief or produce evidence of the substance or effect of the foreign law on the case.[42]

Failure to prove the applicable foreign law should rarely result in dismissal of the underlying claim. It has been suggested that courts should be reluctant to dismiss a claim for this reason since:

---

37. *Id. See also* Trans Container Serv. v. Security Forwarders, Inc., 752 F.2d 483, 486 (9th Cir. 1985); Riffe v. Magushi, 859 F. Supp. 220 (S.D. W.Va. 1994).

38. *See* Milton Pollack, *Proof of Foreign Law*, 26 AM. J. COMP. LAW 470, 471–472 (1978).

39. CAL. EVID. CODE § 455(b) (West 1966). *See also* TEX. EVID. CODE ANN. § 203 (West 1993).

40. *See* Corporacion Venezualana de Fomento v. Vintero Sales Corp., 452 F. Supp. 1108, 1112 (S.D.N.Y. 1978); Fairmont Shipping Corp. v. Chevron Int'l Oil Co., 511 F.2d 1252, 1261 n.16 (2d Cir. 1975).

41. *See* Wachs v. Winter, 569 F. Supp. 1438, 1442–43 (E.D.N.Y. 1983). *See* Stephen L. Sass, *supra* note 27, at 104.

42. *See* Bowman v. Grolsche Bierbrouwerij B.V., 474 F. Supp. 725, 730 (D. Conn. 1979); Riffe v. Magushi, 859 F. Supp. 220 (S.D. W.Va. 1994).

> The rare case in which there is a failure of proof [of foreign law] would be an especially unappealing case for holding that the party whose claim or defense is based on foreign law must lose, because this would be a case in which the foreign law could not be ascertained despite the diligent efforts of both counsel and the trial judge. It simply is not fair to bar a party from recovering when neither his attorney nor the court is able to conjure up the content of governing law.[43]

§ 9.04 FOREIGN LAW AS QUESTION OF LAW

The third element of Rule 44.1 is that the court's determination of the issue of foreign law shall be treated as a ruling on a question of law. Since appellate review is limited to questions of law and not fact, it is not narrowly confined by the "clearly erroneous" standard of Rule 52(a) of the Federal Rules of Civil Procedure. Since these issues are "freely reviewable," appellate courts may make determinations of foreign law based on their own independent research and analysis of foreign law questions.[44]

§ 9.05 CHOICE OF LAW CONSIDERATIONS

It is generally accepted that in international transactions, a choice of law provision will be enforced, absent a showing of unreasonableness.[44.1]

Choice of law is distinguishable from pleading and proof of foreign law. Even before the practitioner is faced with the determination of how to plead and prove foreign law, he must first determine whether foreign law or the law of the forum applies to the case. This is essentially a conflict of laws exercise and may be governed by choice of law rules of the forum. Traditional conflict of laws rules for contracts and torts have been reexamined and replaced in many states by more flexible contemporary standards. In preparing the case the attorney should be familiar with local choice of law rules applicable to each substantive issue.

---

43. 9 CHARLES A. WRIGHT & ARTHUR R. MILLER, *supra* note 2, § 2447. *See also* Twohy v. First Nat'l Bank of Chicago, 758 F.2d 1185, 1193 (7th Cir. 1985); Vishipco Line v. Chase Manhattan Bank, 660 F.2d 854, 860 (2d Cir. 1981); Hodson v. A.H. Robins Co., Inc., 528 F. Supp. 809, 824 (E.D.Va. 1981), *aff'd*, 715 F.2d 142 (4th Cir. 1983).

44. *See* United States v. First Nat'l Bank of Chicago, 699 F.2d 341, 344 (7th Cir. 1983); Twohy v. First Nat'l Bank of Chicago, 758 F.2d 1185, 1193 (7th Cir. 1983); Ackermann v. Levine, 788 F.2d 830 (2d Cir. 1986); Grupo Protexa v. All American Marine Slip, 20 F.3d 1224 (3d Cir. 1994).

44.1. *See In re* Millenium Seacarriers, Inc., 292 B.R. 25 (S.D.N.Y. 2003).

What are the consequences of a party's failure to provide evidence of foreign law where local choice of law rules provide that the case is governed by foreign law? This was one of the issues presented in

(*Text continued on page 9-11*)

Vishipco Line v. Chase Manhattan Bank,[45] which involved the bank's failure to honor plaintiff's certificate of deposit contracts after closing its branch in Vietnam. The court of appeals determined that the outcome of this issue depended on whether the forum's choice of law rules were mandatory rather than permissive. The court of appeals cited the movement away from the "vested rights" theory and mandatory application of the forum's choice of law rules toward the adoption of a discretionary rule.[46] It was noted that, while under Rule 44.1 a court is still permitted to apply foreign law even if not requested to do so by a party, Rule 44.1 would allow the application of the law of the forum, where the parties had not asserted at trial that the foreign law applied with respect to underlying obligations involved on the part of the defendant.[47] The law of the forum applied despite the fact that the forum's choice of law rules called for the application of foreign law. The mandatory/permissive nature of choice of law rules should first be analyzed in determining whether plaintiff's claims may be dismissed under the standards of Rule 44.1 for failure to provide evidence of foreign law.

Will the court honor the parties' stipulation that the law of a foreign country applies? In *Twohy v. First Nat'l Bank of Chicago*,[48] counsel for one of the parties stipulated in the lower court that the law of Spain controlled the action. The suit was brought by a stockholder of a Spanish corporation based on tort and contract against a bank for injury to the corporation. Plaintiff contended before the lower court that counsel's stipulation was inadvertent and that he intended at all times to bring the action under the laws of the United States. The court of appeals noted that plaintiff had consistently relied on foreign law in the lower court, including the filing of counter-affidavits of foreign law experts pursuant to FED. R. CIV. P. 44.1. The court of appeals decided that reasonable stipulations of the litigants as to choice of law in tort and contract cases should be honored.[49] According to the court's rationale, choice of law stipulations that violate public policy or call into question the court's subject matter jurisdiction would not be honored.[50] In *Twohy*, however, the court found that the foreign law

45. 660 F.2d 854, 838 n.7 (2d Cir. 1981), *cert. denied*, 459 U.S. 976 (1982).
46. *Id.* at 860.
47. *Id. See* Whirlpool Financial Corp. v. Sevaux, 96 F.3d 216, 221 (7th Cir. 1996).
48. 758 F.2d 1185, 1189 (7th Cir. 1985).
49. *Id.* at 1191.
50. *Id.* at 1190.

had a reasonable relationship to the alleged transaction and injury in question.[51] Based on *Twohy,* courts will be reluctant to allow litigants to back away from choice of law stipulations where the party's position as to the controlling law would fail under foreign law and there is reasonable indication that the party intended to rely on the foreign law involved in determining the outcome of the controversy.

An example of a modern approach to conflicts of laws analysis is *Liew v. Official Receiver & Liquidator.*[52] The issue on appeal involved whether the district court had applied the proper choice of law in evaluating the validity of an assignment of contract rights against a banking institution. Since jurisdiction was based on diversity, the district court applied the choice of law rules of California, where the action was brought. The court of appeals summarized this approach, the "governmental interest" analysis, as follows:

(1) To examine the substantive law relating to assignments in Singapore and in California, to determine if the laws in the two jurisdictions differ as applied to this assignment transaction;

(2) If they do differ, then to determine whether both jurisdictions have an interest in having their laws applied. If only one jurisdiction has such an interest, then we do not have a "true conflict" and we apply the law of that jurisdiction;

(3) If there is a "true conflict" then we proceed, under the "comparative impairment" approach, to determine which jurisdiction's interest would be more impaired if its policy were subordinated to the policy of the other. The conflict should be resolved by applying the law of the jurisdiction whose interest would be more impaired if its laws were not applied.[53]

In applying this analysis, the district court previously found that the law of the forum should apply since the receiver, the party seeking the application of foreign law, had made no actual showing of Singapore's interest in having its law applied, or of how such an interest would be

51. *Id.* at 1191.
52. 685 F.2d 1192, 1195 (9th Cir. 1982).
53. *Id.* at 1196.

impaired by California law.[54] However, the court of appeals ruled that under the governmental interest approach in California, the burden was not placed on the party relying on foreign law and the receiver had satisfactorily raised the issue of foreign law and advanced policy reasons for its application.[55] Where the jurisdiction has adopted this type of choice of law analysis, the party relying on foreign law is advised to:

(1) follow Rule 44.1;

(2) be familiar with the substantive foreign law involved; and

(3) be prepared to argue why a foreign jurisdiction has the greater interest in having its law applied.

In *Wells Fargo Asia, Ltd. v. Citibank, N.A.*,[56] a depositor brought an action against Citibank in the United States to recover the balance due on funds deposited in the Philippine branch after the branch bank refused payment as a result of a Philippine government decree. The court stated that, regardless of whether state or federal common law choice of law tests should be used, New York law should be applied to evaluate the primary issue of whether Citibank's worldwide assets were available for repayment of the deposits.[57] The court emphasized that since New York is a financial capital of the world, New York law should be applied uniformly to international transactions to perfect the expectations of the parties to the contract.[58] Under New York law, the court of appeals determined that Citibank was not excused from making repayment. The court rejected Citibank's attempt to show a conflict between New York law and federal law which would have justified the creation of a federal common law rule on the subject. In the absence of an agreement between the depositor and the institution governing payment of deposits outside the United States, no conflict existed between state and federal law.[59]

54. *Id.*
55. *Id.* at 1197.
56. 936 F.2d 723 (2d Cir. 1991), *cert. denied,* 112 S. Ct. 2990 (1992).
57. *Id.* at 726.
58. *Id.* at 726.
59. *Id.* at 727. *See also In re* Korlag, Controle Et Revision, 961 F.2d 341, 350–51 (2d Cir. 1992).

§ 9.06 CHOICE OF LAW RULES

In a diversity case, a federal district court will look to the law of the forum, including its choice-of-law provisions.[60] This applies to both the substantive law as well as the conflict of laws rules of the forum.[61] A choice of law analysis depends upon the particular issue involved and may lead to varying applications of domestic or foreign law in a single case. One commentator observed:

> there is at least one point on which there seems to be general agreement in the United States. This is that choice of the applicable law should frequently depend upon the issue involved. The search in these instances is not for the state whose law will be applicable to govern all issues in a case; rather it is for the rule of law that can most appropriately be applied to govern the particular issue. As a result, situations do arise where the court must decide whether it should apply the rules of different states to determine different issues in a single case.[62]

The ''pick and choose'' approach is evident in choice of law rules which recognize the law of the state having the ''greatest interest or more significant relationship to the transaction and the parties.''[63] Under the pick and choose analysis, a variety of factors are considered, including the interest of the foreign state; the relevant policies of the forum; the protection of justified expectations; the basic policies underlying the particular field of law, certainty, predictability and uniformity of result; and ease in the determination and application of the law to be applied.[64]

The Restatement (Second) of Conflict of Laws generally applies to foreign conflicts as well as interstate conflicts, although ''[t]here may . . . be factors in a particular international case which call for a result different from that which would be reached in an interstate case.''[65] However, in applying relevant factors under a ''significant state

60. Klaxon Co. v. Stentor Elec. Mfg. Co., 313 U.S. 487 (1941); Erie R.R. Co. v. Tompkins, 304 U.S. 64 (1938).

61. Her Majesty, The Queen in Right of Province of B. C. v. Gilbertson, 597 F.2d 1161, 1163 (9th Cir. 1979).

62. Reese, *Depacage: A Common Phenomenon in Choice of Law,* 73 COLUM. L. REV. 58 (1973). *See, e.g.,* Arno v. Club Med Boutique Inc., 134 F.3d 1424 (9th Cir. 1998).

63. Index Funds, Inc. v. Ins. Co. of N. A., 580 F.2d 1158, 1162 (2d Cir. 1978); Garcia v. Kubbar, 4 F. Supp. 2d 99 (N.D.N.Y. 1998) (federal maritime choice of law test).

64. RESTATEMENT (SECOND) CONFLICTS OF LAW § 6 (1971); *see also* De Aguilar v. Boling Company, 47 F.3d 1404, 1414 (5th Cir. 1995).

65. RESTATEMENT (SECOND) CONFLICTS OF LAW § 10 (1971).

interest'' analysis, courts may reach different results in resolving similar international conflicts issues. In a case involving an aircraft accident, *Ciprari v. Servicos Aereos Cruzeiro*,[66] the district court applied Brazilian law which limited the liability of the Brazilian air carrier. The court determined under the local choice of law rule that Brazil's interest in the limitation of damages was greater and more direct then New York's.[67] However, in a personal injury case, *Panicotto v. Sociedade de Safaris de Mocambigue, S.A.R.L.*,[68] the district court, distinguishing *Ciprari*, refused to apply the law of Mozambique which limited liability for travel accidents. The court determined that the foreign law was unreasonable and contrary to Illinois public policy and that, unlike *Ciprari*, there was no ''exceptional national concern'' which justified its application.[69]

Finally, in *McDaniel v. Petroleum Helicopters, Inc.*,[70] the court of appeals reversed the lower court, which refused to apply Colombian law restricting the amount recoverable for loss of love and affection in wrongful death cases. Analyzing the case under the state's lex loci rule, the court of appeals refused to apply any public policy exception against enforcement of the foreign law.[71] *Pancotto* and *Ciprari* also illustrate the need to isolate the substantive legal issues for choice of law analysis since both involved multiple issues, including liability and measure of damages.

A further consideration under a typical choice of law analysis is whether the law to be applied is procedural or substantive. As previously stated, in diversity cases, a federal court applies the substantive law of the state in which it sits. In many cases the procedural/substantive distinction is not a critical problem in deciding whether to apply local law or foreign law. However, a difficult issue in terms of procedure versus substance is whether local or foreign statutes of limitations should be applied under a choice of law analysis. The basic choice of law rule is that statutes of limitations are procedural in nature.[72] Thus, the statute of limitations of the forum will usually apply, even though the course of action may be governed by the law of the foreign jurisdiction.

66. 245 F. Supp. 819, 823 (S.D.N.Y. 1965), *aff'd*, 359 F.2d 855 (2d Cir. 1966).

67. *Id. See also* Value Partners S.A. v. Bain & Co., 2003 WL 253197 (D. Mass.).

68. 422 F. Supp. 405 (N.D. Ill. 1976).

69. *Id.* at 411.

70. 455 F.2d 137, 140 (5th Cir. 1972).

71. *Id.*

72. *See* Chevron Oil Co. v. Huson, 404 U.S. 97, 112 (1971); Kalmich v. Bruno, 553 F.2d 549, 553 (7th Cir. 1977).

An exception to the application of the forum's statute of limitations is recognized where the foreign cause of action is created by statute. In general, courts will follow a foreign prescriptive period if the time period within which suit is to be brought is contained in the statute which creates the right or otherwise conditions the right of action. A majority of courts have held that where the foreign limitation period is based on the assertion of the statutorily created right, it is a matter of substantive as distinguished from procedural law.[73] Courts following the choice of law approach have stated that if the time element in the foreign law is devoted "specifically" to the right sought to be enforced, the foreign limitation period is substantive rather than procedural.[74]

§ 9.07 AUTHENTICATION OF FOREIGN DOCUMENTS

In addition to proof of foreign law, it is important to be aware of the proper procedures for authenticating foreign records and general requirements for their admissibility in U.S. courts.

Under federal law in 28 U.S.C. § 1741, a copy, summary or excerpt of a foreign official record or document may be admitted if properly authenticated under the Federal Rules of Civil Procedure. The provisions for proving official records, "when admissible for any purpose," are set forth in Rule 44(a)(2), which provides that a foreign official record may be evidenced by official publications or a copy of an official publication attested to by a person authorized to make the attestation. The document must be accompanied by a final certification as to the genuineness of the signature and official position of the attesting person or of any foreign official who can attest to the genuineness of the chain of certificates of authenticity of the documents. A final certification may be made by a diplomatic or consular official of the United States or diplomatic or consular official of the foreign country who is assigned or accredited to the United States. Under a 1991 amendment to Rule 44(a)(2), the final certification by diplomatic officers is unnecessary when the United States and the foreign country where the record is located are parties to a treaty or convention that abolishes that requirement. In that event the treaty or convention is to be followed.

Rule 44(a)(2) further provides that, if reasonable opportunity has been given to all parties to investigate the authenticity and accuracy of the documents, the court may, upon a showing of good cause, admit an

73. *See id.;* Ramsey v. Boeing Company, 432 F.2d 592, 602 (5th Cir. 1970).
74. *See* Bournias v. Atlantic Maritime Co., 220 F.2d 152, 156 (2d Cir. 1955).

attested copy without a formal certification or permit the document to be evidenced by an attested summary with or without a final certification. This exception has been applied in cases where the plaintiff made diligent efforts to obtain a final certification and the defendants had a reasonable opportunity to investigate the authenticity and accuracy of the document.[75] The trial court's discretion to admit a foreign official record lacking final certification has also been upheld where the party has raised no objection to the absence of good cause.[76] Finally, Rule 44(b) states that a written statement may be admissible for purposes of proving that, after a diligent search, no record was found to exist.[77]

Similar to Rule 44(a)(2), Federal Rule of Evidence 902 also provides for self-authentication of foreign public documents when the document is executed by a person so authorized pursuant to the laws of a foreign country. The document must also be accompanied by a final certification as to the genuineness of the signature and official position of the executing or attesting person or of any foreign official who can attest to the genuineness of the chain of certificates of authenticity of the documents. Rule 902 sets forth similar requirements to Rule 44 of the Federal Rules of Civil Procedure as to the persons entitled to make the final certification and the good cause showing necessary to admit the document as presumptively authentic without final certification.

The admission of documents under the business records exception to the hearsay rule is found in the Federal Business Records Act.[78] Under the Act, the person who actually makes the record is not required to testify. However, the requisite foundation for its admission must be made through the testimony of a person who is sufficiently familiar with the business practice involved to testify that the record was made in the regular course of business. In *United States v. Leal*,[79] appellant Leal contended that no proper foundation was laid for admission of certain hotel records since the Government did not call anyone connected with the hotel to testify to its record-keeping practices. Instead, the

---

75. *See* Italusa Corp. v. M/V Thalassini Kyra, 733 F. Supp. 209, 212 (S.D.N.Y. 1990); Ins. Co. of N. A. v. S/S Italica, 567 F. Supp. 59, 61 n.1 (S.D.N.Y. 1983); United States v. Leal, 509 F.2d 122, 126 (9th Cir. 1975); Haarhuis v. Kunnan Enterprises, Ltd., 177 F.3d 1007, 1014–1015 (D.C. Cir. 1999).

76. *See* United States v. Pacheco-Lovio, 463 F.2d 232, 234 (9th Cir. 1972); United States v. Rodriguez Serrate, 534 F.2d 7, 10 (1st Cir. 1976); Construction Drilling Inc. v. Chusid, 63 F. Supp.2d 509, 514–515 (D.N.J. 1999).

77. *See* Fed. R. Evid. 803(10).

78. 28 U.S.C. § 1732. *See also* Fed. R. Evid. 803(b), 901.

79. 509 F.2d 122, 127 (9th Cir. 1975).

Government had followed the Rule 44(a)(2) procedure for proving foreign official records. An employee of the hotel gave a sworn statement before the United States Vice Consul in Hong Kong stating that documents had been prepared in the normal course of business of the hotel. The court of appeals held that the government's action in obtaining the affidavit was justified and the documents properly admitted. The court of appeals stated that the procedure followed by the Government for proving business records contained the same "guarantees of trustworthiness" as are present in Rule 44(a)(2).[80]

Other methods to authenticate foreign business records or public documents may be summarized as follows:

(1) stipulate to the authenticity of the documents by pretrial stipulation;

(2) seek testimony of the witness at trial in the United States in order to authenticate the records;

(3) seek authenticity testimony by deposition abroad. If a deposition is not possible, request the witness to prepare a sworn statement before a U.S. consular official indicating an unavailability to appear as a witness in the United States, describing the contents of the documents, attesting that the witness is the official custodian thereof, and, if business records, stating that the records were prepared in the normal course of business.

The United States and other countries are parties to the Hague Convention Abolishing the Requirement of Legalization for Foreign Public Documents.[81] The Convention entered into force for the United States on October 15, 1981.[82] The purpose of the Convention is to abolish the requirement of diplomatic and consular legalization for public documents originating in one Convention country and intended for use in another.

The Convention applies to public documents which include:

---

80. 509 F.2d at 127.

81. Oct. 15, 1981, T.I.A.S. 10072, U.N.T.S. 189. The Convention is reprinted *infra* in Appendix 9; in 28 U.S.C.A., FED. R. CIV. P. 44; and in MARTINDALE-HUBBELL INT'L LAW DIGEST, "ARGENTINA-VENEZUELA & SELECTED INTERNATIONAL CONVENTIONS."

82. Other member countries to the Convention are listed in 28 U.S.C.A., FED. R. CIV. P. 44; MARTINDALE-HUBBELL INT'L LAW DIGEST, "ARGENTINA-VENEZUELA & SELECTED INTERNATIONAL CONVENTIONS.".

(1) documents emanating from an authority or an official connected with the courts or tribunals of the state, including those emanating from a public prosecutor, a clerk of court or a process server;

(2) administrative documents;

(3) notarial acts; and

(4) official certificates which are placed on documents signed by persons in their private capacity, such as official certificates recording the registration of a document or the fact that it was in existence on a certain date and official and notarial authentications of signatures.

The Convention does not apply to documents executed by diplomatic or consular agents or administrative documents dealing directly with commercial or customs operations.

The Convention abolishes requirements of chain authentications and the need for diplomatic or consular authentication. As defined in Rule 44(a)(2) of the Federal Rules of Civil Procedure, the traditional chain authentication is a series of procedural formalities which must be complied with in order to prove the authenticity and genuineness of a public document. The only formality required under the Convention is a standard certificate called an "apostille" and the use of a single signature by a designated certifying officer.[83]

The competent authority which affixes the apostille on the document is the central authority in each member country. In the United States, the competent authorities are as follows:

(1) federal, executive and administrative agencies—Authentication Office, U.S. Department of State;

(2) United States courts—clerks and deputy clerks of the federal court system; and

(3) states and territories—state Secretary of State or official counterpart.

A list of competent federal and state authorities is presented in 28 U.S.C.A., FED. R. CIV. P. 44, and in Martindale-Hubbell Int'l Law Digest, "Argentina-Venezuela & Selected International Conventions."

83. A model certificate (apostille) is included *infra* as Appendix 10.

If a document is to be legalized in another Convention country, the nearest United States embassy or consulate should be contacted for the name of the competent local authority in that country who is authorized to affix the apostille.[84]

84. Foreign central authorities are also listed in 28 U.S.C.A., Fed. R. Civ. P. 44; and in Martindale-Hubbell Int'l Law Digest, "Argentina-Venezuela & Selected International Conventions.".

Chapter 10

OBTAINING THE EVIDENCE

§ 10.01 INTRODUCTION

Obtaining evidence abroad is one of the most troublesome and controversial aspects of transnational litigation in United States courts. American lawyers inexperienced in the area tend to view foreign evidence gathering solely under American procedural requirements of state practice and the Federal Rules of Civil Procedure. On the other hand, foreign parties resisting discovery often raise applicable treaties and different procedural requirements under foreign law. There are a wide range of options available to United States courts in imposing requirements under applicable law where foreign-based evidence is to be obtained. This is due to the court's power to order the production of evidence where there is *in personam* jurisdiction over the parties. At the same time, in considering foreign evidence requests, courts may be sensitive to comity and judicial sovereignty factors which may constitute valid defenses to discovery requests. In understanding this topic the practitioner must focus on the type of discovery sought, whether the discovery is voluntary or compulsory, and whether the discovery is being sought under applicable treaties or traditional letters of request (letters rogatory).[1]

§ 10.02 JUDICIAL SOVEREIGNTY

A United States court may order a foreign national, subject to the court's jurisdiction, to produce evidence located abroad.[2] However, such orders may conflict with different notions of gathering evidence in foreign nations. The evidentiary procedures of most civil law countries restrict a litigant's authority to collect evidence. This is totally different from procedures for gathering evidence in common law countries such as the United States, where discovery is largely in the hands of the parties and not the courts.

In civil law countries, the gathering of evidence by the courts is described as an exercise of "judicial sovereignty."[3] Consequently, if a

---

1. *See* FED. R. CIV. P. 28 advisory committee's note (letter rogatory is form of letter of request).

2. Pain v. United Technologies Corp., 637 F.2d 775 (D.C. Cir. 1980), *cert. denied,* 454 U.S. 1128 (1981); Roberts v. Heim, 130 F.R.D. 430, 439–40 (N.D. Cal. 1990); *In re* Honda American Motor Co., Inc. Dealership Relations Litigation, 168 F.R.D. 535 (D. Md. 1996).

3. *See* Société Internationale Industrielle Aerospatiale v. United States Dist. Court, 482 U.S. 522, 557–558 (1987) (Blackmun, J., concurring in part); *In re* Perrier Bottled Water Litigation, 138 F.R.D. 348, 352 (D. Conn. 1991). *See* Bernard H. Oxman, *The Choice*

foreign person attempts to perform the act of obtaining evidence in a civil law country, it may be unauthorized, unless the governmental authorities participate or give their consent.[4] For example, foreign attorneys attempting to secure a deposition or examine property in a civil law country might violate penal proscriptions of that country. This would be true, for example, under certain laws of France and Switzerland.[5] This would also include unauthorized interviews of witnesses on foreign territory.[6] In addition, many civil law countries object to a foreigner's taking evidence from a willing witness unless the proceeding takes place before a foreign consul authorized to take evidence.[7] American lawyers should carefully examine the effect of foreign criminal law when engaging in extraterritorial discovery.

§ 10.03 FOREIGN ATTITUDE TOWARD PRETRIAL DISCOVERY

Certain U.S. discovery procedures are not commonly accepted in civil law countries. In this connection, the scope of United States discovery orders is unparalleled even in comparison with other common law jurisdictions such as the United Kingdom. The standard of relevance under Rule 26 of the Federal Rules of Civil Procedure is broad and permits discovery that is "reasonably calculated to lead to the discovery of admissible evidence."[8] Thus, the use of pretrial discovery allows discovery of documents and other evidence that may not necessarily be used at trial. Also, the evidence-gathering in this country is conducted by the parties themselves, rather than the court.

Between Direct Discovery and Other Means of Obtaining Evidence Abroad: The Impact of the Hague Evidence Convention, 37 U. MIAMI L.R. 733, 761–65 (1983).

4. *See* Société Internationale Industrielle Aerospatiale v. United States Dist. Court, 482 U.S. 522, 557–558 (1987) (Blackmun, J., concurring in part); *Perrier, supra* note 3, at 355. *See* Jacques Borel & Stephen M. Boyd, *Opportunities for and Obstacles to Obtaining Evidence in France for Use in Litigation in the United States*, 13 INT'L LAW. 35, 45 (1979).

5. Art. 1A FRENCH PENAL CODE LAW (C. PEN.) No. 80–538 (providing in France that "subject to treaties or international agreements and applicable laws and regulations, it is prohibited for any party to request, seek or disclose, in writing, orally or otherwise, economic, commercial, industrial, financial or technical documents or information leading to the constitution of evidence with a view to foreign judicial or administrative proceedings or in connection therewith"); Art. 273 SWISS CRIM. CODE (Cp) (criminalizing act of revealing Swiss manufacturing or business secrets to public or private foreign authority or its agents).

6. *Aerospatiale, supra* note 3, at 526 n.6, 557–58 (Blackmun, J., concurring in part); Perrier, *supra* note 3, at 352.

7. *Aerospatiale, supra* note 3, at 557–58 (Blackmun, J., concurring in part); Perrier, *supra* note 3, at 355. *See* Oxman, *supra* note 3, at 764 n.64.

8. FED. R. CIV. P. 26(b)(1).

Civil law countries have shown a wide-spread misunderstanding of the term "pretrial" discovery and the U.S. discovery system in general. This stems from confusion as to whether "pretrial" means "prior to the institution of suit" and the meaning of that term as used in the Hague Evidence Convention.[9] Likewise, other countries, including English Commonwealth jurisdictions, object to "fishing expeditions" and the production of unlimited numbers of documents.[10]

There is notable hostility in civil law countries to U.S. pretrial discovery of documents. In this connection, Article 23 of the Hague Evidence Convention permits a contracting state to declare that it will not execute a letter of request issued "for the purpose of obtaining pretrial discovery of documents as known in Common Law countries."[11] Most of the signatory states to the Hague Evidence Convention have executed declarations under Article 23 of the Convention restricting, in whole or in part, pretrial discovery of documents.[12]

Countries that have made no declaration under Article 23 include: Barbados, the Czech Republic, Israel, the Slovak Republic and the United States. Others have made "limited" reservations where the documents sought have been specifically identified in the request. These include China, Cyprus, Estonia, Finland, France, Mexico, the Netherlands, Norway, Singapore, and the United Kingdom. The Article 23 reservations of Argentina, Australia, Denmark, Germany, Italy, Luxembourg, Monaco, Poland, Portugal, South Africa, Spain, and Sweden state that these countries will not execute letters of request for pretrial discovery purposes.

---

9. Hague Evidence Convention on the Taking of Evidence Abroad in Civil or Commercial Matters, Mar. 18, 1970, 8 I.L.M. 37 [hereinafter Hague Evidence Convention]; Report of the United States Delegation, 17 I.L.M. 1417, 1421 (1978). The text of the Convention is reprinted *infra* in Appendix 14.

10. Illustrative of problems in this area is the "Westinghouse Uranium Litigation." *See In re* Westinghouse Electric Corp. Uranium Contracts Litigation, 563 F.2d 992 (10th Cir. 1977); *In re* Uranium Antitrust Litigation, 480 F. Supp. 1138 (N.D. Ill. 1979). For a global review of foreign courts' approach to the subject of letters rogatory and attitudes toward U.S. pre-trial discovery request, *see Ask and You May Receive*, INT'L COM. LIT. at 14–23 (Mar. 1998).

11. Hague Evidence Convention, *supra* note 9, Art. 23.

12. *See* 28 U.S.C.A. § 1781, at 126–141 (reservations and declarations of member states).

§ 10.04 GATHERING EVIDENCE IN CIVIL LAW COUNTRIES

When compulsory evidence is obtained in a foreign country, the laws and procedures of the host country control. Thus, even when discovery is permitted to proceed in a civil law country, the scope and type of evidence normally expected from an American-style deposition might be restricted due to the applicable foreign procedures.[13] In civil-law countries, the searching out of evidence for use at trial is generally a function of the judge and not the parties. It is the judge who has the initial authority to determine the witnesses to question, the questions to ask, and the documents to be produced.[14] Moreover, the judge would have the absolute discretion to control the scope of oral examination and the extent of discovery.[15]

Ordinarily, a U.S. attorney will not be permitted to participate in such a proceeding. An attorney in the host country may attend the proceeding but full participation of counsel might not be allowed. For example, Germany permits attorneys to attend depositions and engage in cross-examination of a witness "under the control of the requested judge."[16] The judge usually questions the witness and there is no oath-taking requirement. In some cases, the judge may permit the foreign attorney to put additional questions to the witness.

In addition, many civil law countries do not utilize the services of court reporters or provide verbatim transcripts. The presiding judge may dictate his recollection of the witnesses' responses in summary form. The foreign state's procedures might also limit or foreclose cross-examination. The scope of foreign privilege might also prove to be broader under the letter of request procedure than under U.S. law.[17] Finally, in some cases, official translations might be required for each

---

13. *See* Pain v. United Technologies Corp., 637 F.2d 775, 789–90 (D.C. Cir. 1980), *cert. denied,* 454 U.S. 1128 (1981). *See* also *Aerospatiale, supra* note 3, at 546; *Perrier, supra* note 3, at 353.

14. *Aerospatiale, supra* note 3, at 543; *Perrier, supra* note 3, at 353. *See* Work v. Bier, 106 F.R.D. 45, 55 (D.D.C. 1985).

15. Work v. Bier, *supra* note 14, at 55.

16. Report on the Second Meeting of the Special Commission on the Operation of the Hague Convention of 18 March, 1970, on the Taking of Evidence Abroad in Civil or Commercial Matters, 24 I.L.M. 1668, 1674 (1985). *See generally,* Donald R. Shemanski, *Obtaining Evidence in the Federal Republic of Germany: The Impact of the Hague Evidence Convention on German-American Judicial Cooperation,* 17 INT'L LAW. 465, 475 (1983).

17. Novamont North America, Inc. v. Warner-Lambert Co., 91-C6482, 1992 WL 114507 (S.D.N.Y. 1992).

piece of paper involved.[18] This could add considerable cost to the litigants employing such procedures.

§ 10.05 LOOKING FOR ASSISTANCE; OFFICE OF AMERICAN CITIZENS SERVICES

The Office of American Citizens Services (ACS), which is part of the State Department, provides assistance in obtaining evidence overseas for domestic litigation.[19] ACS maintains information pertaining to international judicial assistance, such as cooperation between nations involving the transmission of judicial documents and the gathering of evidence. The office provides information pertaining to the laws and procedures of a particular country for taking depositions of willing witnesses, compelling the testimony of an unwilling witness, and obtaining documentary and physical evidence. For specific information on the laws of a particular country, litigants should consult with foreign counsel.

ACS also advises whether consular officials in particular countries are able to preside at depositions. ACS is divided into geographic divisions (for example, European and Canadian Division, African, etc.) and has particular information for the country needed. The assistance provided by ACS applies primarily where evidence is to be obtained abroad through voluntary agreement between the parties, rather than through treaty means such as the Hague Evidence Convention.[20]

§ 10.06 VOLUNTARY VERSUS COMPULSORY DISCOVERY

Foreign-based testimony may be obtained without the aid of foreign authorities only if the witness is willing to testify voluntarily and the laws of the foreign country do not prohibit the providing of such testimony. Rule 29 of the Federal Rules of Civil Procedure states that the parties may, by written stipulation, provide that depositions "be taken before any person, at any time or place, upon any notice, and

18. Pain v. United Technologies Corp., 637 F.2d 775, 789–90 (D.C. Cir. 1980).

19. The address of the Office of American Citizens Services is U.S. Department of State, 2120 C Street, N.W., Washington, D.C. 20520. The telephone number is (202) 647–5226. A State Department Circular providing guidance on the subject of obtaining evidence abroad is reprinted *infra* as Appendix 11. Information on international judicial assistance may be obtained from the State Department's web site (http://travel.state.gov/). The autofax number for this service is (202) 647–3000.

20. *See infra* § 10.10 (addressing Hague Evidence Convention).

in any manner."[21] Depositions by voluntary agreement between the parties provide the most effective means of taking testimony abroad since the participation of the foreign government is not required and the testimony can be taken in a manner compatible with U.S. discovery and evidentiary standards. In civil law countries, the parties have no power to compel the attendance of an unwilling witness. Therefore, if the prospective witness will not cooperate voluntarily, the testimony must be compelled by letters rogatory or by treaty means.

The lawyer should develop a checklist in determining how to proceed with discovery in each situation. The following factors should be considered:

(1) Is the deponent a party or non-party witness?

(2) Is the deposition voluntary or compulsory?

(3) Are American-style depositions before the U.S. consul permitted under the laws of the country where the witness resides?

(4) If so, what arrangements must be made before the deposition may be taken?

If the witness is a "party," as defined in Rule 10(b) of the Federal Rules of Civil Procedure, or similar state rules, there is a reasonable basis for reaching voluntary agreement for the taking of the evidence. If a party witness refuses to voluntarily cooperate, that person could be compelled to return to the United States to be deposed.[22] On the other hand, where there is no *in personam* jurisdiction over witnesses, such as third party witnesses, expert witnesses, etc., compulsory means will be used in most cases in obtaining the evidence.[23]

---

21. FED. R. CIV. P. 29. *See* Popular Imports, Inc. v. Wong's Int'l, Inc., 166 F.R.D. 276, 278 (E.D.N.Y. 1996).

22. *See* Roberts v. Heim, 130 F.R.D. 430, 437 (N.D. Cal. 1990); *In re* Anschuetz & Co., GmbH, 754 F.2d 602, 615 (5th Cir. 1985); *In re* Honda American Motor Co., Inc. Dealership Relations Litigation, 168 F.R.D. 535 (D. Md. 1996).

23. *See* The Gap, Inc. v. Stone Int'l Trading, Inc., 93–C0638, WL 670020 (S.D.N.Y. 1994) (observing that "Hague Convention provides the only means to request documents or testimony from foreign non-parties over whom the court has no personal jurisdiction and who are beyond the subpoena power of the court"); 4 MOORE'S FEDERAL PRACTICE, §§ 28.03–.06 (2d ed. 1991). *See* PKFinans Int'l Corp. v. UBJ Schroder Leasing Corp., 1996 WL 5911213 (S.D.N.Y. 1996).

§ 10.07 ROLE OF THE UNITED STATES CONSUL

Evidence obtained abroad must be taken in accordance with the laws of the foreign jurisdiction in order to avoid violating the judicial sovereignty of that country. U.S. consular regulations provide, where there is no treaty, that consular officers may take depositions only if the laws or authorities of the foreign government permit them to do so.[24] ACS has information as to those countries which prohibit depositions before consular officers as to United States citizens, host country nationals, and third country nationals. In countries where the taking of depositions is not permitted, consular officials who receive notice or commissions for taking depositions are instructed to return the documents with an appropriate explanation and indicate available methods for obtaining the depositions, whether by letters rogatory or otherwise.[25]

Rule 28(b)(3) of the Federal Rules of Civil Procedure provides for taking of depositions "on notice before a person authorized to administer oaths in the place in which the examination is held, either by the law thereof or by the law of the United States." U.S. consular officials are authorized pursuant to 22 U.S.C.A. § 4221 to administer and to take from any person an oath, affirmation, affidavit or deposition, and to perform notarial acts. Under 28 U.S.C.A. § 4221 every such oath, affirmation, affidavit, deposition or notarial act, when certified by the consular officer, is as valid as if administered before any other person within the United States. Section 4221 further states that if any person commits perjury in any such oath, affirmation, etc., within the meaning of any Act of Congress, the offender may be dealt with in any district of the United States in the same manner as if the offense is committed in the United States. State statutes also permit the taking of consular depositions for use in state courts.[26] Since this method obviates the need for court intervention (either foreign or domestic), it offers a simple and effective means of obtaining foreign-based testimony for use in a United States court.

The attorney should inquire in advance as to the availability of the officer and whether physical facilities can be made available. In certain posts, where the consular officer's availability may be a problem, depositions may have to be scheduled several months in advance. In

24. 22 C.F.R. § 92.55(c). The State Department Regulations on Depositions and Letters Rogatory are reprinted *infra* in Appendix 12.

25. *Id.*

26. *See, e.g.,* COLO. R. CIV. P. 28(b).

addition, certain foreign governments may require official notification in advance of the scheduled deposition.[27] Technically, the host country can refuse to allow the deposition to proceed if appropriate clearance or permission is not obtained in advance. This is an important requirement for the attorney scheduling the deposition to remember. ACS has information concerning notification requirements in effect in the country in which the deposition is to be taken.

In notifying the party of the consular proceedings, the notice provisions of Rules 30(b) or 31(a) of the Federal Rules of Civil Procedure should be followed depending on whether oral depositions are sought or depositions on written questions.[28] In addition, litigants considering the use of consular proceedings should become familiar with the applicable State Department procedures set forth in 22 C.F.R. § 92.49–92.71.[29] It is necessary for the attorney to make arrangements for taking depositions by communicating with the consular section of the Embassy or consulate. The following information should be provided in the request:

(1) name, address, and telephone numbers of requesting counsel;

(2) description of case;

(3) purpose of deposition;

(4) suggested dates;

(5) names of persons to be deposed and their citizenship;

(6) statement that witness' appearance is voluntary;

(7) method of taking deposition (i.e., oral questions or written interrogatories);

(8) request for court reporters, translator, interpreter, if needed;

(9) list of counsel and other persons who will attend depositions;

(10) need of consular officer to be present during entire proceeding or only for oath taking purposes;

---

27. For example, France and Germany.

28. *See also* 22 C.F.R. § 92.52.

29. State Department Regulations covering depositions and letters rogatory are reprinted *infra* in Appendix 12.

(11) attach check as a deposit to cover necessary fees and expenses (additional fees and expenses will be billed to requesting counsel).[30]

Attorneys for the moving party should communicate with prospective witnesses, arrange for their presence, and employ translators and reporters. It is counsel's responsibility to make separate arrangements with the witness to insure his or her appearance for the deposition (travel fees, witness fees, etc.). Video-taping is not permitted in many foreign countries. However, if counsel intends to utilize video-tape equipment for recording the deposition, special customs clearances must be obtained from the foreign country or the equipment may be confiscated by the foreign authorities or denied entry. American-made equipment may also need special adapters to function on different foreign electrical currents. ACS has information as to video-tape or special technical requirements of particular foreign countries. In connection with the taking of depositions, the consular officer requests the witnesses whose testimony is needed to appear before him as well as designated persons who have needed records or documents.[31] The consular officer may act as interpreter or translator or may make necessary arrangements for a qualified person to act in this capacity.

The consular officer is authorized to administer oaths to the witnesses, stenographers and any interpreters. He examines the witness in accordance with the procedures set forth in U.S. consular regulations,[32] and insures that the testimony of the witnesses is recorded in accordance with the Federal Rules of Civil Procedure.[33] The consular officer is required to preside at the entire examination of the witness unless, by stipulation of the parties, he needs to be present only at the administering of the oath. The consular officer insures that the transcript is prepared by the stenographer and given to the witness for correction. This requirement can be waived by agreement of counsel. Finally, the consular officer prepares a certificate that the witnesses were duly sworn and that the deposition is a true record of the testimony given by the witness.

30. *See* 22 C.F.R. §§ 22.1; 92.68–70.

31. Since certain consular offices are busy and depositions must be scheduled well in advance, litigants should determine whether other options exist, such as permitting depositions to be taken before local attorneys, notaries, etc.

32. 28 C.F.R. §§ 92.57–92.60.

33. *See* FED. R. CIV. P. 30(c), 31(b).

§ 10.08 DEPOSITIONS BY COMMISSION

Rule 28(b)(4) of the Federal Rules of Civil Procedure provides that depositions may be taken abroad ''before a person commissioned by the court, and a person so commissioned shall have the power by virtue of the commission to administer any necessary oath and take testimony.'' As defined by U.S. consular regulations, a ''commission to take depositions'' is a written authority issued by a court giving power to take the testimony of witnesses who cannot appear personally to be examined in the court.[34] A commission to take depositions is issued on application and notice, indicating the action or hearing in which the depositions are intended to be used, and the person required to take the depositions. Normally a commission is accompanied by detailed instructions for its execution. Any U.S. consular officer may be designated to execute a commission to take depositions. Where not in conflict with the law of the state of execution, the commission procedure may also be used in criminal proceedings.[35]

Although a commission to take depositions can be issued by a court to a foreign official or to a private person in a foreign country, it is common practice for commissions to be issued to U.S. consular officers.[36] A commission identifies the officer who is to take the depositions by his official title in the following manner: ''Any Consul or Vice Consul of the United States of America at [name of locality].'' When the documents are drawn in this manner, the consular officer executes the commission, provided local law does not preclude such action. However, when the officer is designated by name as well as by title, only the officer so designated may take the depositions. In acting as a commissioner, a consular officer complies with any special instructions which accompany the request for a deposition on notice or the commission, and otherwise proceeds in the same manner in taking the depositions as in the deposition by notice procedure. Once the testimony has been taken, the commissioner certifies the answers given by the witness and the deposition is returned in accordance with any special instructions which may accompany the commission.

An order appointing a commissioner may provide that the deposition be taken by oral examination or written interrogatories. The commission procedure differs from the notice procedure only in that it requires the

34. 22 C.F.R. § 92.53.

35. *See* Fed. R. Crim. P. 15(d). *See also* 18 U.S.C.A. §§ 3491–94.

36. *See* 22 C.F.R. § 92.55.

court to appoint the person before whom the testimony is to be taken. This distinction may be important in those countries where notice procedures before consular officials are not permitted. ACS has complete information as to those countries which permit the use of commissions. It should be emphasized that, with respect to the stipulation and notice procedure, deposition by commission applies only where the testimony can be voluntarily obtained. Thus, taking depositions under commission has the advantage of conforming to U.S. procedural requirements. In those countries in which the taking of testimony is regarded as a sovereign function, the use of the commission is not permitted.

§ 10.09 OBTAINING EVIDENCE BY LETTERS OF REQUEST

When the foreign country prohibits the taking of depositions, regardless of the nationality or voluntary cooperation of the witness, the evidence must be obtained pursuant to a letter of request.[37] In order to obtain evidence from an unwilling witness or where the stipulation, notice and commission procedures are unavailable, it may be necessary to proceed by way of a letter of request. The term "letter of request" may be defined as a letter of request from a court in the United States in which an action is pending, addressed to a foreign court to perform some judicial act.[38] Letters of request may include requests for taking evidence, or serving a summons, subpoena, or other legal notice. No showing need be made that the evidence cannot be obtained in any other manner before a letter of request is issued.[39] In order to successfully apply to a U.S. court for the issuance of letters of request to a court in a foreign country, the person to be examined must be subject to the foreign court's jurisdiction.[40]

The court has inherent authority to issue letters of request.[41] As opposed to compulsory procedures, i.e., treaty obligations, letters of

---

37. Letter of request is synonymous with "letter rogatory" and is preferred in modern usage. *See* BLACK'S LAW DICTIONARY (6th ed. 1994), FED. R. CIV. P. 4(f)(2)(B) advisory committee's note.

38. 22 C.F.R. § 92.54.

39. *In re* Complaint of Bankers Trust Co., 752 F.2d 874, 889–90 (3d Cir. 1984); Zassenhous v. Evening Star Newspaper Co., 404 F.2d 1361 (D.C. Cir. 1968).

40. *See* 8 CHARLES A. WRIGHT & ARTHUR R. MILLER, FEDERAL PRACTICE & PROCEDURE § 2083 (1970).

41. *See* DBMS Consultants, Ltd. v. Computer Assocs. Int'l, Inc., 131 F.R.D. 367, 369 (D. Mass. 1990); United States v. Reagan, 453 F.2d 165 (6th Cir. 1971), *cert. denied*, 406 U.S. 946 (1972).

request are honored on the basis of comity between the courts addressed.[42]

Rule 28(b)(2) of the Federal Rules of Civil Procedure provides that depositions may be taken, *inter alia,* pursuant to a letter of request. This section permits depositions by letters of request without a showing that other methods are impractical or inconvenient.[43]

The letter of request should be directed to a named foreign court or, if the identity is not known, to "The Appropriate Authority in (name of country)".[44] The letter of request should include a summary of the nature of the judicial proceeding for which the evidence is being sought and a description of the parties.[45] The language of the request should be clear and drafted in language which will be understood by a foreign civil law court. The nature of the request should be specifically stated, that is, documents should be precisely identified and all written questions to be provided to the witness should be included in the request.

In many countries, letters of request will not be honored for pretrial discovery purposes. Assurance should also be given that the evidence is reasonably related to the trial of the case. Language should be avoided which suggests that the letter of request is to be used for "fishing expeditions." Thus, the request should avoid such phrases as "any and all documents" and any uncertainty as to the existence of the evidence sought.

The evidence obtained in response to a letter of request need not conform to requirements for depositions under the Federal Rules of Civil Procedure.[46] Special requirements such as verbatim transcripts, testimony under oath, etc., should be specified in the request. In addition, the foreign court may be requested to permit a designated representative to participate in the evidence-taking proceeding, usually by asking supplementary questions after the judge has examined the witness.

The following factors should be considered in preparing a letter of request:

---

42. *See DBMS Consultants, Ltd., supra* note 41, at 369; Wright & Miller, *supra* note 40; Philadelphia Gear Corp. v. Philadelphia Gear de Mexico S.A., 1994 WL 716893 (3d Cir. 1994).

43. *In re* Complaint of Bankers Trust Company, 752 F.2d 874, 889 (3d Cir. 1984); B & L Drilling Electronics, Ltd. v. Totco Corp., 87 F.R.D. 543, 545 (W.D. Okla. 1978).

44. Fed. R. Civ. P. 28(b).

45. *See* 2A Bender's Federal Practice Forms, Fed. R. Civ. P. 28(b) (1991).

46. Fed. R. Civ. P. 28(b).

(1) Does the request for evidence emanate from a state or federal court?

(2) Is the letter of request signed by the court and certified by the clerk of the court?

(3) Has the letter of request been translated into the appropriate foreign language?

(4) Has a duplicate set of the request and accompanying documents been provided?

(5) Does the request reflect the name of the case, docket number and mailing address of the clerk to whom the executed request should be returned?

(6) Is the request accompanied by a check or money order in the proper amount to cover costs incident to the execution of the letters of request?

(7) Does the request specify the name and address of the person from whom evidence is to be obtained?

(8) Does the request provide for assurance of reciprocal assistance in similar cases?

In some countries which do not permit the taking of depositions of willing witnesses, letters of request are the only method of obtaining evidence. ACS possesses information as to the procedures and requirements of the particular foreign country and should be contacted in advance of preparation of the letters of request.[47]

Even though letters of request may often be sent directly from court to court, some foreign governments require that these requests be submitted through diplomatic channels. Under 28 U.S.C.A. § 1781(a)(2), the *transmission of such requests* through State Department (*i.e.*, diplomatic) channels is authorized. The State Department is also authorized to receive and return letters of request after execution. The diplomatic route involves the transmission of the request from the U.S. court to the Department of State to the U.S. embassy to the Foreign Ministry which will execute the request. Once the letter of request is transmitted to the U.S. embassy in the foreign country, it may be useful

---

47. *See* 4 JAMES W. MOORE ET AL., MOORE'S FEDERAL PRACTICE §§ 28.05–08 (2d ed. 1991). A State Department Circular providing guidance on the preparation of letters rogatory is attached as Appendix 13.

to telephone the embassy or the consulate and request advice and assistance. ACS or the respective American embassies and legations in foreign capitals can be helpful and furnish relevant information as to customary procedural requirements in given countries. Letters of request executed by foreign officials are returned through the same channels by which they were transmitted.[48] Requests which emanate from a U.S. court are returned to the court in which the action is pending.[49]

§ 10.10 HAGUE EVIDENCE CONVENTION

The Hague Evidence Convention on the Taking of Evidence Abroad in Civil or Commercial Matters[50] is a multi-lateral treaty which prescribes methods of obtaining evidence abroad in civil and commercial transnational disputes. It is intended to alleviate the procedural obstacles encountered when litigants seek evidence in a foreign country that has a different legal system and evidence-gathering methods.[51]

The Convention, which was ratified by the United States, is in force between the United States and the following countries: Anguilla, Argentina, Aruba, Australia, Barbados, Belarus, Bulgaria, Cayman Islands, China, Cyprus, Czech Republic, Denmark, Djibouti, Estonia, Falkland Islands, Finland, France, French Guiana, French Polynesia, Germany, Gibraltar, Guadeloupe, Guernsey, Hong Kong, Isle of Man, Israel, Italy, Jersey, Latvia, Lithuania, Luxembourg, Macao, Martinique, Mexico, Monaco, Netherlands, Norway, Poland, Portugal, Saint Pierre and Miquelon, Singapore, Slovak Republic, Slovenia, South Africa, Spain, Sri Lanka, Sweden, Switzerland, Ukraine, United Kingdom, Venezuela, and the Sovereign Base Areas of Akroteri and Dhekelia.

The Convention is intended to encourage evidence-gathering methods that are both ''tolerable'' in the state of execution and ''utilizable'' in the forum of the state of origin where the action is pending.[52]

There are three alternative methods for obtaining evidence abroad under the Convention.

48. *See* 22 C.F.R. § 92.66(c)(1).

49. 28 U.S.C.A. § 1781(b)(2).

50. Hague Evidence Convention, *supra* note 9. A copy of the Convention is reprinted *infra* as Appendix 14.

51. *See* S. Exec. Rep. 95, 92nd Cong., 2d Sess. 1 (1972); Report of United States Delegation to Eleventh Session of Hague Conference on Private International Law, 8 I.L.M., 785, 806 (1969).

52. *See generally*, Symposium, *Compelling Discovery in Transnational Litigation*, 16 N.Y.U.J. Int'l L. & Pol. 957 (1984).

[1] Letter of Request

First, a litigant may request the court where the action is pending to transmit a "Letter of Request" to the "Central Authority" in the country where the evidence is to be obtained.[53] The central authority, which is designated by the foreign government, transmits the request to the appropriate foreign court, which conducts an evidentiary proceeding under procedures of the foreign country.[54]

[2] Diplomatic or Consular Officer

Under the second procedure, the litigant may request that the evidence be taken before a diplomatic or consular officer in the country where the action is pending.[55] Under the Convention, a contracting state may reserve the right not to allow the taking of evidence before a diplomatic or consular officer.[56]

[3] Commissioners

Under the third method, the litigant may request that a specially appointed commissioner take evidence in the foreign country.[57] The three methods under the Convention are similar to the procedures specified in Rule 28(b) of the Federal Rules of Civil Procedure.[58]

[4] Use of Hague Evidence Convention

Of the three procedures discussed above, the letter of request is the most useful. First, it is the only method which applies to compulsory evidentiary proceedings. Furthermore, the other two methods are subject to limitations in the Convention, and many signatories to the Convention have taken a variety of exceptions regarding the use of these latter two procedures.[59] In this connection, the requesting party should study the declarations and reservations of each contracting state to determine the

53. *See* Hague Evidence Convention, *supra* note 9, arts. 1–2.

54. *Id.*, arts. 5–13.

55. *Id.* arts. 15–16.

56. *Id.* arts. 33, 35.

57. *Id.* art. 17.

58. *See* Fed. R. Civ. P. 28(b) advisory committee's note.

59. For example, the declarations to the Convention contain restrictions on the use of diplomatic officers or consular agents to take evidence. In this connection, Denmark will not accept the taking of evidence by commissioners. *See* 28 U.S.C.A. § 1781, at 126–141 (reservations and declarations of member states and sample forms).

extent to which consular officers and court-appointed commissioners are authorized to act on evidence-gathering procedures in the state of execution.[60]

Article 1 of the Convention provides that the assistance to be rendered is limited to "civil or commercial matters." These terms are not defined in the Convention or the treaty history. Based on the nature of the cause of action and the relief sought, the requested state has discretion in determining whether a request pertains to "civil or commercial matters." Article 1 further limits the issuance of a letter of request to judicial authorities of the state of origin. Therefore, the request must emanate from a court and not a legislative or administrative body. The letter of request is to be used "to obtain evidence, or to perform some other judicial act."[61] In general, this would include acts which fall within judicial functions in the state of origin.

Article 2 of the Convention requires each contracting state to designate a central authority to receive letters of request emanating from a judicial authority of another state and to transmit them to the authority competent to execute them. In the United States, the Department of Justice has been designated as the central authority and performs those functions in a "receiving" capacity only.[62] Requests for evidence in connection with United States judicial proceedings are transmitted directly to the foreign central authority in the state of execution.

Article 3 sets forth the contents of a letter of request. These provisions must be followed and the central authority may reject the request under Article 5 for failure to comply with the provisions of the Convention. Under Article 3, paragraph (h), the requesting party must specify any requirement that the evidence is to be given on oath or affirmation and any special form to be used. Otherwise, the executing authority will take the testimony in accordance with its own domestic law, which may not require the taking of any oath or affirmation. In addition, under paragraph (i) of Article 3, the request shall specify "any special method or procedure" to be followed by the executing authority. This provision should be read together with Article 9, which provides that the executing authority shall apply its own law as to the

60. *Id. See also* MARTINDALE-HUBBELL INT'L LAW DIGEST, "ARGENTINA-VENEZUELA & SELECTED INT'L CONVENTIONS" (reservations and declarations of member nations and sample forms).

61. Hague Evidence Convention, *supra* note 9, art. 1.

62. *See* 28 C.F.R. § 0.49(a).

methods and procedures to be followed unless the requesting authority requests that special methods or procedures be followed. Under Article 9, the judicial authority executing the request need not observe any special methods or procedures if they are incompatible with internal law in the state of execution. American parties may request that examination and cross-examination of the witness by counsel be allowed. However, executing authorities in civil law countries may refuse to substitute this procedure in place of the usual method of examination by the judge.

Article 4 requires that the letter of request be written in the language of the state of execution or accompanied by a translation into that language. This is subject to Article 4, paragraph 2, which provides that the contracting state shall accept a letter of request in either English or French unless a reservation has been made under Article 33. Article 7 provides that the requesting authority shall, if it so desires, be informed of the time and place of the proceedings so that the parties, and their attorneys, may be present.

Under Article 10, the executing state may apply appropriate measures of compulsion in requiring the witness to answer questions or produce documents, etc. The law of the requested state is applied in determining whether compulsion will be used. Article 11 allows the person examined to invoke any applicable privilege under the law of the state of execution or the law of the state of origin. In the latter situation, the letter of request should include a statement of the privilege or duty. Article 12 states that the execution of a letter of request may be refused only to the extent that: (a) the request does not fall within the functions of the judiciary in the state of execution; or (b) the state of execution considers that sovereignty or security would be prejudiced. Execution may not be refused on the ground that the state of execution claims exclusive jurisdiction over the subject matter of the action or that its internal law does not recognize the same cause of action.

Article 14 generally states that no costs shall be assessed in executing the letter of request. However, under Article 14, the state of execution is permitted to seek reimbursement of the fees paid to experts and interpreters and other special costs.

§ 10.11 "EXCLUSIVITY" OF THE CONVENTION

In order to determine whether Convention procedures must be utilized, it is necessary to consider whether the Convention operates exclusive of domestic law procedures, such as state or federal rules, or is optional. The "exclusivity" question was resolved by the Supreme Court in *Societe Nationale Industrielle Aerospatiale v. United States Dist. Court.*[63] The question presented in the case, a products liability action, concerned the extent to which a federal district court must employ the procedures set forth in the Convention when litigants seek answers to interrogatories, the production of documents, and admissions from a French adversary over whom the court had personal jurisdiction. Based on the language and negotiating history of the Convention, the Court rejected any interpretation of the Convention as exclusive. The Court found that the treaty did not speak in mandatory terms which would purport to describe the procedures for all permissible transnational discovery and exclude all other existing practices. As the Court stated, "[t]he text of the Evidence Convention itself does not modify the law of any contracting state, require any contracting state to use the Convention procedures, either in requesting evidence or in responding to such requests, or compel any contracting state to change its own evidence-gathering procedures."[64]

In concluding that the Convention was intended as a permissive supplement, and not a mandatory replacement for other means of obtaining evidence located abroad, the Court cited Article 23 which expressly authorizes a contracting state to declare that it will not execute any letter of request in aid of pretrial discovery in a common law country. The Court found the existence of this provision inconsistent with any intent of the Convention to replace completely the broad discovery powers that the common law courts in the United States previously exercised over foreign litigants subject to their jurisdiction.[65]

Rather, the Court concluded that the Convention was intended to establish optional procedures that would facilitate the taking of evidence abroad.[66] Interpreting the Convention as exclusive would lead to the unacceptable result, the Court determined, that interrogatories, document requests, and routine pretrial proceedings would be subject to the law of the Contracting State involved. The Court reasoned that this imbalance would hinder the parties' goal in discovery of obtaining knowledge of all the relevant facts; enable

63. 482 U.S. 522 (1987).
64. *Id.* at 534.
65. *Id.* at 536–37.
66. *Id.* at 538.

foreign companies to be subject to less extensive discovery procedures than domestic companies when both were sued in a United States court; and allow foreign parties who were nationals of a contracting State to enjoy an unwarranted advantage over other domestic litigants similarly situated.[67]

The Court further determined that although the Convention procedures were not mandatory, the treaty did apply to the production of evidence in a litigant's possession in the sense that it was one method of seeking evidence that a court may elect to employ. Thus, in terms of use, the Convention was an optional measure. In terms of the applicability of this Convention, the Court drew no distinction between evidence obtained from third parties and that obtained from the litigants themselves as well as between evidence that is "abroad" and evidence that is within the control of a party subject to the jurisdiction of the requesting court.[68]

Furthermore, the Court rejected the application of any general rule requiring first resort to Convention procedures whenever discovery was sought from a foreign litigant. Rather than a general rule, the Court observed that under the concept of international comity there should be "prior scrutiny in each case of the particular facts, sovereign interests, and likelihood that resort to those procedures will prove effective."[69] However, the Court declined to articulate any specific rules to guide lower courts in this task.

In objecting to the discovery sought, the foreign party had stated that under the French "blocking statute," petitioners could not respond to discovery requests that did not comply with the Convention.[70] The Court, however, ruled that the French "blocking statute," which was intended to restrict the outflow of "economic" information, did not alter its conclusion. The Court stated that if taken literally, the "blocking statute" could operate to prevent a United States district judge from ordering any discovery from a party of French nationality. Thus, under the Court's reasoning, the "blocking statute" was relevant to a court's particularized comity analysis only to the extent that the

67. *Id.* at 540 n.25.
68. *Id.* at 540–41.
69. *Id.* at 544.
70. *Id.* at 526 n.6.

nature of the sovereign interests in nondisclosure of specific kinds of material could be identified.[71]

The Court cited as relevant to any comity analysis, the factors suggested by the Restatement of Foreign Relations Law of the United States (Revised) § 437(1)(c):

> (1) the importance to the . . . litigation of the documents or other information requested;
>
> (2) the degree of specificity of the request;
>
> (3) whether the information originated in the United States;
>
> (4) the availability of alternative means of securing the information; and
>
> (5) the extent to which noncompliance with the request would undermine important interests of the United States, or compliance with the request would undermine important interests of the state where the information is located.[72]

In his separate opinion, concurring and dissenting in part, Justice Blackmun objected to the Court's relegation of the Convention to an optional status.[73] His dissent was based, in part, on a refusal to accept the Court's case-by-case comity approach on use of the Convention's procedures and the lack of any meaningful guidance for conducting that inquiry. Justice Blackmun's opinion recognized a general presumption requiring that courts resort first to the Convention unless utilization of the Convention would be futile or unhelpful.[74] The concurring opinions suggested that in attempting to reconcile a conflict between domestic and foreign law, a court "should perform a tripartite analyses that considers the foreign interests, the interests of the United States, and the mutual interests of all nations in a smoothly functioning international legal regime."[75]

---

71. *Id.* at 544–45 n. 29.

72. *Id.* at 544 n. 28. The comity analysis factors in RESTATEMENT OF FOREIGN RELATIONS LAW OF THE UNITED STATES (REVISED) § 437(1)(c) are presently found in RESTATEMENT (THIRD) OF FOREIGN RELATIONS LAW OF THE UNITED STATES § 442(1)(c) (1987).

73. *Id.* at 547–568 (1987) (Blackmun, J., concurring in part).

74. *Id.* at 548–49.

75. *Id.* at 555.

The majority of post-*Aerospatiale* decisions have failed to invoke convention procedures and have relied on discovery orders pursuant to the Federal Rules of Civil Procedure. This result was predictable since the Court in *Aerospatiale* failed to formulate any fixed criteria to assist in case-by-case comity analyses or otherwise provide lower courts with any meaningful guidance for carrying out that inquiry.

Aerospatiale clearly places the burden of invoking the procedures of the Convention on the foreign party. If certain discovery procedures are deemed to be intrusive in a nation, the producing party should demonstrate that use of the Convention is necessary under the circumstances. In this regard, the Court emphasized that United States courts should closely supervise pretrial proceedings in order to protect foreign litigants from unduly burdensome discovery and improper use of discovery requests. The foreign litigant faced with ''abusive'' discovery or any other special problem should seek a protective order, request a special order for extraterritorial discovery pursuant to the procedures in § 437 of the Restatement,[76] or seek judicial supervision of discovery pursuant to Rule 16 of the Federal Rules of Civil Procedure. Regardless of the methods used by the producing party in opposing discovery pursuant to the Federal Rules of Civil Procedure, the trial court in applying the *Aerospatiale* decision has considerable discretion in determining whether Convention procedures should be utilized.

§ 10.12 POST-*AEROSPATIALE* CASES

In applying the neutral balancing test employed in *Aerospatiale*, lower courts have shown a pro-forum bias toward U.S. discovery rules and placed the burden of proving the effectiveness of the Convention on the party seeking its use.[77] Moreover, lower courts have given little or

---

76. The provisions of § 437 of the RESTATEMENT (REVISED) are currently found in § 442 of the RESTATEMENT (THIRD) FOREIGN RELATIONS LAW (1987). *See also* RESTATEMENT (THIRD) FOREIGN RELATIONS LAW § 442, cmt. a. at 350 (1987) (stating that ''it is ordinarily reasonable [for a court] to limit foreign discovery to information necessary to the action . . . typically, evidence not otherwise readily obtainable . . . and directly relevant and material''); McKesson Corp. v. Islamic Republic of Iran, 138 F.R.D. 1, 4 (D.D.C. 1991).

77. Dorster v. Carl Schenk, A.G., 141 F.R.D. 50, 51, 54–55 (M.D.N.C. 1991); Great Lakes Dredge & Dock Co. v. Harnischfeger Corp., 734 F. Supp. 334 (N.D. Ill. 1990); Roberts v. Heim, 130 F.R.D. 430, 438 (N.D. Cal. 1990); Haynes v. Kleinwefers, 119 F.R.D. 335, 339 (E.D.N.Y. 1988). *See* Joseph P. Griffin & Mark N. Bravin, *Beyond* Aerospatiale: *A Commentary on the Foreign Discovery Provisions of the Restatement (Third) and Proposed Amendments to the Federal Rules of Civil Procedure*, 25 INT'L LAW. 331, 336–40 (1991).

no effect to international comity concerns discussed in *Aerospatiale*.[78] Consequently, courts applying the *Aerospatiale* majority's analysis have rarely required use of the Convention.[79] In *In re Automotive Refinishing Paint Antitrust Litig.*,[80] the Third Circuit Court of Appeals affirmed a lower court ruling rejecting application of any first use of the Hague Evidence Convention procedures to discovery requests concerning threshold personal jurisdiction issues as to foreign defendants.

However, in *Hudson v. Pfauter*,[81] the first post-*Aerospatiale* decision, the district court was guided by Justice Blackmun's tripartite analysis in determining, at least in the first instance, whether to defer to the provisions of the Convention. Applying the analysis suggested by Blackmun's dissenting opinion, the court held that Convention procedures should be used in seeking the information requested in plaintiffs' interrogatories. The court, placing the burden of proof on the party opposing the use of the Convention's procedures,[82] determined that plaintiffs had not sustained that burden under the circumstances presented.[83]

Weighing the foreign interests implicated against the plaintiff's desire to proceed with discovery under the Federal Rules rather than the Convention, the court found that using the Convention's procedures to conduct discovery in a civil law country would be less of an intrusion on that state's sovereignty than following the discovery procedures set forth in the Federal Rules of Civil Procedure.[84] The second prong involved consideration of the interests of the United States. Arguably, the United

---

78. *Id;* Haynes v. Kleinwefers, 119 F.R.D. 335, 339 (E.D.N.Y. 1988); Alcon Int'l Ltd. v. U.S.A. Day Mfg. Co., Inc., 1996 WL 622690 (W.D.N.Y.).

79. Great Lakes Dredge & Dock Co. v. Harnischfeger Corp., 734 F. Supp. 334 (N.D. Ill. 1990); Roberts v. Heim, 130 F.R.D. 430, 438 (N.D. Cal. 1990); Fishel v. BASF Group, 1997 WL 587003, at *2–4 (S.D. Iowa); *In re* Aircraft Disaster Near Roselawn, Indiana, 172 F.R.D. 295, 307–11 (N.D. Ill. 1998). *Cf. In re* Perrier Bottled Water Litigation, 138 F.R.D. 348, 353–56 (D. Conn. 1991); Madanes v. Madanes, 199 F.R.D. 135, 139-141 (S.D.N.Y. 2001); *In re* Vitamins Antitrust Litigation, 2001 WL 1049433 (D.D.C.) (merits discovery); American Home Assurance Co. v. Societe Commerciale Toutelectric, 128 Cal. Rptr. 2d 430 (Cal. Ct. App. Dist. 1, 2003); IDT Corp. v. Telefonica, 2003 WL 230894 (S.D.N.Y.); International Insurance Co. v. Caja Nacional De Ahorro Y Seguro, 2004 U.S. Dist. LEXIS 4280 (N.D. Ill. 2004).

80. 358 F.3d 288 (3d Cir. 2004). *See also* Adams v. Unione Mediterranea di Sicurta, 2002 U.S. Dist. LEXIS 5789 (E.D. La.); In re Vitamins Antitrust Litigation, 2001 WL 1049433 (D.D.C.).

81. 117 F.R.D. 33 (N.D.N.Y. 1987).

82. *Id.* at 38.

83. *Id.* at 40.

84. *Id.*

States had an important interest in ensuring that foreign citizens and corporations doing business here could be held accountable in American courts.[85] However, the Court maintained that use of the Convention procedures would, in all likelihood, yield satisfactory results.[86] In any event, if the Convention proved to be fruitless, the court would be able to compel discovery through the Federal Rules of Civil Procedure.[87] In considering the factor of the mutual interest of all nations, the court found that Convention procedures which did not violate the sovereign laws of a particular state would foster international cooperation and the development of an ordered international system.[88] It is interesting to speculate whether the court would have reached the same result had the discovery involved depositions or documentary evidence. Since the Federal Republic of Germany adheres to an unqualified Article 23 declaration, which prohibits the pretrial production of documents, the court could have easily found that use of the Convention for that purpose would be futile.

Several courts, however, have criticized the decision in *Hudson.* In *Benton Graphics v. Uddenholm Corp.*,[89] the District Court of New Jersey refused to follow *Hudson.* In *Benton Graphics*, Swedish corporations opposed the motion to compel responses to interrogatories and production of documents. The district court criticized the *Hudson* decision, contending that the court placed more emphasis on Blackmun's concurring and dissenting opinion in *Aerospatiale* than it did on the majority view.[90]

The court in *Benton Graphics* agreed with the majority in *Aerospatiale* that the Hague Convention was an optional procedure that might be utilized by the district court after considering: (1) the particular facts of the case; (2) the sovereign interests involved; and (3) the likelihood that resort to the Convention would be an effective discovery device.[91] Applying *Aerospatiale*, the court held that foreign parties seeking resort to the Convention had the burden of proof of supporting use of the Convention.[92] The court held that the defendants had failed to clearly

85. *Id.* at 38.
86. *Id.*
87. *Id.* at 39.
88. *Id.* at 40.
89. 118 F.R.D. 386 (D.N.J. 1987).
90. *Id.* at 389.
91. *Id.* at 388.
92. *Id.* at 389.

articulate reasons why the discovery sought was overbroad and burdensome or how specific sovereign interests of Sweden would be implicated.[93]

In *Haynes v. Kleinwefers*,[94] plaintiff had served various discovery requests, including document demands, on defendant, a West German corporation. The court in *Haynes* found that Hague Evidence Convention procedures would ''of necessity be more costly and time-consuming'' than discovery under the Federal Rules of Civil Procedure.[95] Distinguishing *Hudson*, the court held, in light of Germany's declaration under Article 23 of the Convention that it would not execute letters of request for documents, that it was uncertain whether plaintiff would obtain the information sought through use of Convention procedures.

In *In re Anschuetz & Co., GmbH*,[96] the court of appeals reconsidered its previous ruling[97] in light of *Aerospatiale*. Contrary to the urgings of petitioner Anschuetz, a German company, the court of appeals declined to issue a ''presumptive rule'' that district courts first employ the Hague Convention procedures or adopt a similar analysis to that advanced in Justice Blackmun's dissent.[98] The court of appeals cautioned, however, that in the exercise of its wide discretionary authority in this area, the district court should ''be sensitive to interests expressed in the Hague Convention''.[99]

In *In re Perrier Bottled Water Litigation*,[100] the court applied the three-pronged balancing test in Justice Blackmun's concurring and dissenting opinion in *Aerospatiale* and required first use of the Convention in connection with discovery sought from a French corporation. The court reasoned that the taking of evidence would violate the judicial sovereignty of a civil law country if performed by a person unauthorized to take discovery in that country.[101] Finally, the court ruled that France's sovereign interest in applying the Convention's

---

93. *Id.* at 390–391.

94. 119 F.R.D. 335 (E.D.N.Y. 1988).

95. *Id.* at 339. *See also In re* Meta Systems, 111 F.3d 142 (Fed. Cir. 1997); First American Corp. v. Price Waterhouse LLP, 154 F.3d 16 (2d Cir. 1998).

96. 838 F.2d 1362 (5th Cir. 1988).

97. *In re* Anschuetz & Co., 754 F.2d 602 (5th Cir. 1985).

98. 838 F.2d at 1364.

99. *Id.*

100. 138 F.R.D. 348 (D. Conn. 1991).

101. *Id.* at 352, 355.

procedures should prevail over plaintiff's concerns that its use of Convention procedures would be costly and inefficient.[102]

§ 10.13 PROVIDING INTERNATIONAL JUDICIAL ASSISTANCE TO FOREIGN COURTS

Litigants in foreign countries which are parties to the Hague Evidence Convention may obtain evidence in the United States pursuant to the treaty procedures. Usually, the letter of request is transmitted from the requesting court or the foreign central authority directly to the United States Central Authority.[103] The Central Authority in the United States for processing letters of request in civil and commercial matters is the Civil Division of the Department of Justice.[104] After reviewing the request, the Department of Justice transmits the letter of request for execution to the United States Attorney for the judicial district in which the witness resides or in which the evidence is located.

Federal courts provide international judicial assistance to foreign courts pursuant to 28 U.S.C. § 1782. The statute provides, in pertinent part, as follows:

> § 1782. Assistance to foreign and international tribunals and to litigants before such tribunals.
>
> a) The district court of the district in which a person resides or is found may order him to give his testimony or statement or to produce a document or other thing for use in a proceeding in a foreign or international tribunal. The order may be made pursuant to a letter rogatory issued, or request made, by a foreign or international tribunal or upon the application of any interested person. . . .
>
> A person may not be compelled to give his testimony or statement or to produce a document or other thing in violation of any legally applicable privilege.
>
> b) This chapter does not preclude a person within the States from voluntarily giving his testimony or statement, or producing a

---

102. *Id.* at 355. *See also* Geo-Culture, Inc. v. Siam Inv. Management S.A., 936 P.2d 1063, 1067 (Or. Ct. App. 1997); Husa v. Laboratoires Servier SA *et al.*, 326 N.J. Super. 150; 740 A.2d 1092 (App. Div. 1999); *In re* Daimler Chrysler AG Securities Litig., 2003 WL 21698358 (E.D. Mich.); Tulip Computers Int'l BV v. Dell Computer Corp., 254 F. Supp. 2d 409 (D. Del. 2003); Motorola Credit Corp. v. Vaan, 2003 WL 203011 (S.D.N.Y.).

103. *See* Hague Evidence Convention, *supra* note 9, art. 2.

104. *See* 28 C.F.R. § 0.49(a).

> document or other thing, for use in a proceeding in a foreign or international tribunal before any person and in any manner acceptable to him.

The Justice Department's Civil Division acts as the transmitting office for letters of request received pursuant to 28 U.S.C. § 1782 from foreign countries which are not signatories to the Hague Convention. The letters of request are processed in the same manner as letters of request under the Hague Evidence Convention, i.e., to the appropriate United States attorney's office.

Under 28 U.S.C. § 1781, the Department of State has the power to receive letters rogatory from foreign or international tribunals and to forward them to appropriate courts or officials in the United States for execution. Requests are received from foreign countries pursuant to section 1781 which require, as part of their judicial procedures, that letters rogatory be transmitted via diplomatic channels. Letters rogatory which are referred to the Department of Justice through diplomatic channels under section 1781(a)(1) are honored on the basis of international comity. Requests received under the Hague Evidence Convention are executed as United States treaty obligations. The Department of State forwards all letters of request to the Department of Justice for execution.

Once the request is transmitted to the appropriate United States Attorney, that office is encouraged, whenever possible, to obtain a witness' testimony through voluntary cooperation.[105] This is because in the United States, as opposed to the practice in civil law countries, district court judges do not themselves examine witnesses as part of their judicial function. If a witness agrees, the testimony is furnished in affidavit form and no court order is required. This voluntary procedure, authorized under section 1782(b), is used in the majority of cases. In order to conform to procedures in civil law countries, U.S. Attorneys do not use court stenographers or prepare verbatim transcripts unless requested to do so by the requesting court. The transcript and all pertinent documents, together with bills for any fees or expenses, are forwarded to the Department of Justice for return to the requesting country.

If the witness refuses to cooperate voluntarily, or when documents cannot be obtained without a subpoena, application may be made to the district court for an order under section 1782(a) compelling the witness

---

105. *See* 28 U.S.C.A. § 1782(b).

to appear or compelling the production of documents or other things. Applications for such orders are made ex parte.[106] The order usually designates as ''commissioner'' a U.S. Magistrate or the Assistant U.S. Attorney.[107] The commissioner subpoenas the witness and advises the witness of the nature of the proceedings and any applicable rights and privileges. It should be noted that under section 1782(a), a person may not be compelled to give testimony in violation of any legally applicable privilege. Article 11 of the Hague Evidence Convention similarly provides that the person examined may claim a privilege not to give the evidence under the law of the state of execution or under the law of the state of origin.[108] The requesting party should specify the privilege under the law of the state of origin in the Letter of Request and, for convenience of the witness, attach translated copies of the privilege to the request. The commissioner records the witness' answers to the questions and certifies the transcript.

§ 10.14 DEFENSES TO REQUESTS FOR JUDICIAL ASSISTANCE TO FOREIGN COURTS

A party against whom the requested information is to be used has standing to challenge the validity of the request on the theory that it is not authorized by or exceeds section 1782's provisions. For example, it has been held that requests for international judicial assistance pursuant to section 1782 are an incorrect vehicle to enforce a foreign judgment.[109] This statute has been interpreted to apply to criminal as well as civil proceedings.[110] Under section 1782, testimony may be taken in compliance with foreign practice and procedure and used against the witness in that proceeding.[111] If the court fails to prescribe the

106. *See In re* Request for Judicial Assistance from Seoul Dist. Criminal Court, Seoul, Korea, 555 F.2d 720 (9th Cir. 1977); *In re* Letters of Request from Supreme Court of Hong Kong, 821 F. Supp. 204, 210 (S.D.N.Y. 1993).

107. *Id.* at 211.

108. *See* Hague Evidence Convention, *supra* note 9, art. 11.

109. Osario v. Harza Eng'g Co., 890 F. Supp. 750 (N.D. Ill. 1995).

110. *See In re* Request for Assistance from Ministry of Legal Affairs of Trin. & Tobago, 848 F.2d 1151, 1156 (11th Cir. 1988), *cert. denied sub nom.*, Azar v. Minister of Legal Affairs of Trin. & Tobago, 488 U.S. 1005 (1989); *In re* Request for Judicial Assistance from Seoul Dist. Criminal Court, Seoul, Korea, 555 F.2d 720 (9th Cir. 1977); *In re* Letters Rogatory from Tokyo Dist., Tokyo, Japan, 539 F.2d 1216 (9th Cir. 1976); *In re* Letter Rogatory from Justice Court, Dist. of Montreal, Can., 523 F.2d 562, 565–66 (6th Cir. 1975); *In re* Letters of Request from Supreme Court of Hong Kong, 821 F. Supp. 204, 209 (S.D.N.Y. 1993).

111. *In re* Letter Rogatory from Justice Court, Dist. of Montreal, Can., 523 F.2d 562, 566 (6th Cir. 1975); *In re* Letters of Request from Supreme Court of Hong Kong, 821 F. Supp. 204, 209 (S.D.N.Y. 1993).

procedure, the provisions of the Federal Rules of Civil Procedure are to be followed, regardless of whether the foreign proceeding is civil or criminal in nature.[112]

Section 1782 affords the district courts wide discretion in responding to requests for assistance in proceedings before foreign tribunals.[113] In *Al Fayed v. United States*,[114] the court of appeals sustained the district court's denial of the issuance of a subpoena duces tecum to the National Security Agency (NSA) as potentially causing "grave damage to the national security."[115] The court of appeals stated that in exercising its discretion under section 1782, the district court should be guided by the statute's "twin aims of providing efficient means of assistance to participants in international litigation in our federal courts and encouraging foreign countries by example to provide similar means of assistance to our courts."[116]

In a recent decision, *Intel Corp. v. Advanced Micro Devices, Inc.*,[117] the Supreme Court endorsed a broad interpretation of 1782's provisions. In this case Advanced Micro Devices (AMD) filed an antitrust complaint against petitioner Intel with the Directorate-General for Competition of the Commission of the European Communities. The issue concerned whether 1782 authorized discovery sought by Intel to produce potentially relevant documents in connection with the foreign investigation. The Supreme Court resolved four issues in Intel involving the validity of the 1782 application. First, the Court determined that a complainant before the European Commission, such as AMD, qualified as an "interested person" within the meaning of the statute. The Court ruled that an "interested person" was not limited to party litigants but included those persons who possessed a reasonable interest in obtaining the assistance. The Court determined that a complainant who triggered a European Commission investigation had the right to submit evidence before the Commission and the right to appeal the ultimate decision and therefore qualified as an "interested person."

The second issue was whether AMD's request was for evidence intended "for use in a foreign or international tribunal" under 1782. The Court held that assistance provided pursuant to 1782 extended to

112. *In re* Letters of Request from Supreme Court of Hong Kong, *supra* note 109, at 209.
113. *See* United Kingdom v. United States, 238 F.3d 1312, 1318 (11th Cir. 2001).
114. 210 F.3d 421 (4th Cir. 2000).
115. *Id.* at 423.
116. *Id.* at 424.
117. 542 U.S. 241 (2004).

administrative and quasi-judicial proceedings abroad, such as those before the European Commission. Although the proceeding was still in the investigative stage, AMD could "use" evidence in the reviewing courts only by submitting it to the Commission in the current stage of the proceeding. The Court further rejected any requirement that assistance could only be provided under 1782 when foreign adjudicative proceedings were "pending" or "imminent." The Court ruled that it was sufficient if the dispositive ruling by the Commission was within reasonable contemplation.

The major issue presented was whether 1782 barred a district court from ordering production of documents when the foreign tribunal or "interested person" would not be able to obtain the documents if they were located in the foreign jurisdiction. The so-called "discoverability requirement" had previously split the circuit courts of appeals. The Court noted that neither the text of the statute nor its legislative history indicated an intent to impose a foreign-discoverability rule on the provision of assistance. The Court emphasized the lower courts' broad discretion to grant or reject 1782 applications and impose necessary conditions on any exercise of its authority. The Court noted, however, that the need for assistance was generally greater as to non-parties than parties to the foreign proceeding. It was further observed that in considering a 1782 request the District Court may take into account such factors as the nature of the foreign tribunal, the character of the foreign proceeding, and the receptivity of the foreign court or government to U.S. judicial assistance. However, the Court declined to impose any supervisory rules on consideration of 1782 applications by lower courts.

District Courts retain considerable discretion in responding to requests for assistance in proceedings before foreign tribunals.[118] Considering the factors noted above, the District Court on remand in the Intel proceedings rejected in full AMD's 1782 application.[119] In *Schmitz v. Bernstein Liebhard & Lifshitz, LLP*,[120] the Second Circuit Court of Appeals relied on factors considered by the Supreme Court in Intel. In affirming the lower court's denial of the 1782 application, the Court of Appeals emphasized consideration of the receptivity of the foreign

118. *See In re* Phillips, 2004 U.S. Dist. LEXIS 16426 (S.D.N.Y. 2004); *In re* Linerboard Antitrust Litig., 333 F.Supp.2d 333 (E.D. Pa. 2004); *In re* Procter & Gamble Co., 334 F. Supp. 2d 1112 (E.D. Wisc. 2004); *In re* Servicio Pan Americano de Proteccion, CA, 354 F. Supp. 2d 269 (S.D.N.Y. 2004).

119. 2004 WL 2282320 (N.D.Cal.).

120. 376 F.3d 79 (2d Cir. 2004).

government to the judicial assistance sought. In this connection, the Court of Appeals noted that the German Government had opposed the application on the grounds that production of the documents sought in the request would have compromised an ongoing criminal investigation in Germany.[121]

Courts have not considered a private commercial arbitration as a ''proceeding in a foreign or international tribunal.''[122] In addition, a party to a foreign proceeding cannot use section 1782 to obtain documents held by a person outside of the United States.[123]

Nevertheless, for purposes of section 1782, a distinction can be made between documentary evidence and depositions. In *In re Edelman*,[124] the Second Circuit held that the person was ''found'' in the district when he was served with the subpoena for deposition testimony after the section 1782 order was entered while physically present within the district.

In terms of providing evidence, it has been held that the section 1782 reference to a ''person'' does not include the sovereign and, by extension, a federal agency such as the Central Intelligence Agency (CIA).[125]

Requests for assistance under section 1782 incorporate by reference the scope of discovery permitted by the Federal Rules of Civil Procedure.[126] Thus, assistance may be denied where the information sought was ''unreasonably cumulative'' under Rule 26(b)(2) of the Federal Rules of Civil Procedure.[127]

§ 10.15 COMPULSORY DISCOVERY AND SUBPOENAS

It is increasingly likely that a U.S. attorney will need to conduct discovery of, or defend against discovery of, a non-party witness. In cases involving international transactions, it is common for an American entity to be subpoenaed to produce documents located abroad from its foreign office. This type of discovery is often complicated by the fact that the foreign country in which the witness or documents are located

121. 376 F.3d at 84-85.

122. National Broadcasting Company, Inc. v. Bear Stearns & Co., Inc., 165 F.3d 184 (2d Cir. 1999); Republic of Kazakhstan v. Biedermann Int'l, 168 F.3d 88 (5th Cir. 1999).

123. *In re* Application of Sarrio, S.A., 119 F.3d 143, 147 (2d Cir. 1997).

124. 295 F.2d 171 (2d Cir. 2002). *See also In re* Michael Schmitz, 2003 WL 1961183 (S.D.N.Y.).

125 *See In re* Al Fayed, 91 F. Supp. 137, *aff'd* 229 F.3d 272 (D.C. Cir. 2000).

126. Bayer AG v. Betachem, Inc., 173 F.3d 188 (3d Cir. 1999).

127. *Id.* at 192.

has bank secrecy laws, or even blocking statutes, passed for the purpose of thwarting U.S. courts from obtaining the type of documents or information sought through pretrial discovery.[128] Some fifteen nations have passed blocking statutes as a response to foreign hostility toward U.S. antitrust laws and the civil procedure discovery rules relevant thereto.[129]

Typical bank secrecy laws authorize numbered accounts with civil and/or criminal penalties for employees, lawyers, or others who disclose the true owner without permission of the customer. Countries known for bank secrecy regulations include the Cayman Islands, Channel Islands, Bahamas, Antigua, Bermuda, the Netherlands Antilles, Germany, Greece, Hong Kong, Liechtenstein, Luxembourg, Monaco, Panama, Singapore, and Switzerland.[130]

Section 442 of the Restatement (Third) of Foreign Relations Law sets forth factors to be considered when courts are faced with conflicting U.S. and foreign laws. Restatement § 442 provides:

> (1)(c) In deciding whether to issue an order directing production of information located abroad . . . a court . . . of the United States should take into account:
>
> (i) the importance to the investigation or litigation of the documents or other information requested;
>
> (ii) the degree of specificity of the request;
>
> (iii) whether the information originated in the United States;
>
> (iv) the availability of alternative means of securing the information; and
>
> (v) the extent to which compliance with the request would undermine important interests of the United States, or compliance with the request would undermine important interests of the state where the information is located.[131]

---

128. *See infra* § 10.23, entitled "Secrecy and Blocking Statutes as Enforcement Defenses."

129. *See* Restatement (Third) Foreign Relations Law § 442, reporter's note 1 (1987).

130. *See generally* S. Rep. No. 21, 98th Cong., 1st Sess. 6–7 (1983) (Permanent Subcommittee on Investigations of the Committee on Governmental Affairs, *Staff Study of Crime and Secrecy: The Use of Offshore Banks and Companies*).

131. Restatement (Third) Foreign Relations Law § 442(1)(c) (1987) (numbers added). *See also* Société Internationale Industrielle Aérospatiale v. United States Dist. Court, 482 U.S. 522, 544 n.28 (1987) (applying § 442 balancing test); Richmark Corp. v. Timber

In *United States v. First Nat'l Bank of Chicago*,[132] the first court of appeals decision to apply the new factors, the case was remanded to the district court for an order to determine whether to require the defendant to make a good faith effort, including seeking permission from the foreign authorities under applicable law, to produce the information specified in the summons. The court of appeals noted that while the United States had a strong interest in collecting taxes, the interest of Greece, served by its bank secrecy law, was entitled to equal weight.[133] Since defendant had adequately demonstrated that compliance would subject its employees to criminal penalties under Greek law, the court of appeals held that a balancing of relevant competing interests weighed against compelling disclosure.[134]

Furthermore, the factors set forth in section 442 are not exhaustive.[135] Other relevant factors include the extent and nature of the hardship that inconsistent enforcement would impose upon a party and the extent to which enforcement by action of either state can be expected to achieve compliance with the rule prescribed by that state.[136] It has been observed, however, that the balance of national interests prong of section 442 is the most important factor of analysis.[137] The law is unsettled concerning when the balancing test favors enforcement of U.S. discovery rules.[138] When compared to U.S. national interests in SEC, antitrust, patent, or tax evasion cases, however, foreign secrecy or trade secret interests may be found to not outweigh U.S. interests.[139]

Falling Consultants, 959 F.2d 1468, 1475–79 (9th Cir. 1992), *cert. dismissed*, 506 U.S. 948 (1993) (same); Reinsurance Co. of Am., Inc. v. Administratia Asigurarilor de Stat, 902 F.2d 1275, 1281–83 (7th Cir. 1990) (same); McKesson Corp. v. Islamic Republic of Iran, 138 F.R.D. 1, 3 (S.D.N.Y. 1991) (same); AG Volkswagen v. Court of Cameron County, Texas, 897 S.W.2d 458 (Tex. Ct. App. 1995); Volkswagen A.G. v. Valdez, 909 S.W.2d 900 (Tex. Sup. Ct. 1995).

132. 699 F.2d 341 (7th Cir. 1983).

133. *Id.* at 346.

134. *Id.*

135. *Aerospatiale*, 482 U.S. at 544.

136. *See* Richmark Corp. v. Timber Falling Consultants, 959 F.2d 1468, 1475 (9th Cir. 1992), *cert. dismissed*, 506 U.S. 948 (1993); United States v. Vetco, Inc., 691 F.2d 1281, 1288 (9th Cir.), *cert. denied*, 454 U.S. 1098 (1981); Restatement (Second) Foreign Relations Law § 40 (1971).

137. *See* Richmark Corp. v. Timber Falling Consultants, 959 F.2d 1468, 1476 (9th Cir. 1992), *cert. dismissed*, 506 U.S. 948 (1993).

138. *See Aerospatiale*, 482 U.S. at 544; *Richmark Corp.*, 959 F.2d at 1474. *Cf. In re* Sealed Case, 825 F.2d 494, 498–99 (D.C. Cir.), *cert. denied*, 484 U.S. 963 (1987).

139. SEC v. Banca Della Svizzera Italiana, 92 F.R.D. 111, 117 (S.D.N.Y. 1981) (securities laws); *In re* Uranium Antitrust Litigation, 480 F. Supp. 1138, 1149 (N.D. Ill. 1978) (antitrust laws); Graco, Inc. v. Kremlin, Inc., 101 F.R.D. 503 (N.D. Ill. 1984) (patent laws);

However, in several recent cases, U.S. courts have indicated a reluctance to order the foreign party to violate foreign law.[140]

§ 10.16 BAD FAITH, CONTEMPT, AND SANCTIONS FOR DISCOVERY

Courts have applied the good faith test in *Societe Internationale Pour Participations Industrielles et Commerciales, S.A. v. Rogers*,[141] in determining whether sanctions should be applied for non-compliance with disclosure orders.[142] The good faith test addressed in *Rogers* concerns whether a party has undertaken all efforts of a reasonable person in the circumstances to comply with a production order.[143] Courts usually engage in a full comity analysis at the sanctions stage of the discovery controversy.[144] In applying the "good faith" test, courts generally order discovery despite a litigant's showing that there exists a conflict with foreign laws.[145] In fact, courts have required a litigant to seek relief from foreign nondisclosure laws and use diligent efforts to comply.[146]

United States v. Vetco, Inc., 691 F.2d 1281, 1289–91 (9th Cir. 1981) (tax laws); Garpeg, Ltd. v. United States, 583 F. Supp. 789, 796 (S.D.N.Y. 1984) (same). *But see* Reinsurance Co. of Am., Inc. v. Administratia Asigurarilor de Stat, 902 F.2d 1275, 1283 (7th Cir. 1990); *In re* Sealed Case, 825 F.2d 494, 498–99 (D.C. Cir.), *cert. denied*, 484 U.S. 963 (1987); Minpeco, S.A. v. Conti Commodity Servs., Inc., 118 F.R.D. 331, 334–35 (S.D.N.Y. 1988). *See generally* United States v. Davis, 767 F.2d 1025, 1032–36 (2d Cir. 1985); United States v. Bank of Nova Scotia, 691 F.2d 1384 (11th Cir. 1982); Anderson v. Finesilver, 570 F.2d 1370 (10th Cir. 1978).

140. *In re* Sealed Case, 825 F.2d 494, 498–99 (D.C. Cir.), *cert. denied*, 484 U.S. 963 (1987); Reinsurance Co. of Am., Inc. v. Administratia Asigurarilor de Stat, 902 F.2d 1275, 1283 (7th Cir. 1990). Cf. Richmark Corp. v. Timber Falling Consultants, 959 F.2d 1468, 1477–78 (9th Cir. 1992), *cert. dismissed*, 506 U.S. 948 (1993).

141. 357 U.S. 197 (1958).

142. *See* Richmark Corp. v. Timber Falling Consultants, 959 F.2d 1468, 1474 (9th Cir. 1992), *cert. dismissed*, 506 U.S. 948 (1993); *In re* Westinghouse Electric Corp. Uranium Contracts Litigation, 563 F.2d 992, 997 (10th Cir. 1977); *In re* Uranium Antitrust Litigation, 480 F. Supp. 1138 (N.D. Ill. 1979).

143. *Rogers*, 357 U.S. at 201.

144. Richmark Corp. v. Timber Falling Consultants, 959 F.2d 1468, 1476 (9th Cir. 1992); Cochran Consultings, Inc. v. Uwatech USA, Inc., 102 F.3d 1224 (Fed. Cir. 1996).

145. *See* Société Internationale Industrielle Aerospatiale v. United States Dist. Court, 482 U.S. 522, 544 (1987); United States v. Bank of Nova Scotia I, 691 F.2d 1384, 1388–89 (11th Cir. 1982); United States v. Vetco, Inc., 691 F.2d 1281, 1287 (9th Cir.), *cert. denied*, 454 U.S. 1098 (1981). Cf. Reinsurance Co. of Am., Inc. v. Administratia Asigurarilor de Stat, 902 F.2d 1275, 1283 (7th Cir. 1990); Alfadda v. Fenn, 149 F.R.D. 28 (S.D.N.Y. 1993).

146. *Vetco*, *supra* note 145, at 1289–90.

The Restatement (Third) of Foreign Relations Law specifically provides in § 442 that:

> (2) If disclosure of information located outside the United States is prohibited by law . . . of the state in which the information is located, . . . (a) a court . . . may require the person to whom the order is directed to make a good faith effort to secure permission from the foreign authorities to make the information available.[147]

In *Richmark Corp. v. Timber Falling Consultants*,[148] the Ninth Circuit found that where a Chinese corporation could have avoided the hardship of discovery sanctions and a contempt order by posting a bond, sanctions of $10,000 a day were warranted.[149] In *Richmark*, disclosure of financial information was impeded by a foreign secrecy law.[150] In *Remington Products, Inc. v. North American Phillips Corporation, N.V.*,[151] the court ordered the largest company in the Netherlands to seek a waiver from Article 39 of the Dutch blocking statute.[152] Similarly, in *Compagnie Francaise D'Assurance Pour Le Commerce Exterieur v. Phillips Petroleum Co.*,[153] the court granted defendant's motion to compel production of all documents for which plaintiff had invoked the French blocking statute as a defense.[154] In addition, in *Coca-Cola Foods v. Empresa Comercial Internacional de Frutas S.A.*,[155] the court awarded sanctions against defendants for non-compliance with plaintiff's jurisdictional discovery request. Although defendants alleged that the requested discovery would violate Art. 271 of the Swiss Penal Code, the court ruled there was no showing that requiring witnesses to be deposed in the United States violated Art. 271 which pertains to acts "on Swiss territories."

---

147. Restatement (Third) Foreign Relations Law § 442 (1987). *See also id.*, § 442, Comment h.

148. 959 F.2d 1468 (9th Cir. 1992).

149. *Id.* at 1477–78.

150. *Id.* at 1478.

151. 107 F.R.D. 642 (D. Conn. 1985).

152. *Id.* at 646.

153. 105 F.R.D. 16 (S.D.N.Y. 1984).

154. *Id.* at 30.

155. 1997 WL 370121 (M.D. Fla.).

Any lack of diligent efforts to comply with disclosure orders may be interpreted as bad faith warranting the imposition of severe sanctions.[156] Bad faith has been found where a party purposefully removed records to a foreign country, and "deliberately courted legal impediments to production."[157]

In *In re Sealed Cases*,[158] the court of appeals upheld a finding of contempt against the manager of a foreign bank for refusal to testify and produce documents relating to banking transactions before the grand jury.[159] The manager invoked a Fifth Amendment claim based solely on the threat of foreign prosecution if he complied with the subpoena. The court of appeals noted that, while the Supreme Court had not yet determined whether fear of prosecution by a foreign country was sufficient to invoke the Fifth Amendment, the threat was not real since the manager could be prosecuted for the offense only if he were to return to that country voluntarily. The Fifth Amendment provided no protection "against damages voluntarily assumed."[160]

It should also be noted that a writ directed to a corporation is equally a command to corporate officers and directors.[161] The failure of officers and directors to carry out their corporate duties in complying with a court order may result in individual sanctions or punishment for contempt.[162]

§ 10.17 JURISDICTION AS PREREQUISITE TO ORDERING PRODUCTION OF EVIDENCE

Where jurisdiction over the requested party has been clearly established, a court may order compliance with a discovery request without a full comity inquiry. For instance, United States banks are usually ordered to produce information from a foreign branch of a bank,

---

156. *See* United States v. Bank of Nova Scotia, 740 F.2d 817 (11th Cir. 1984), *cert. denied*, 469 U.S. 1106 (1985); Ohio v. Arthur Andersen & Co., 570 F.2d 1370 (10th Cir. 1978), *cert. denied*, 439 U.S. 833 (1978); Ohio v. Crofters, Inc., 75 F.R.D. 12 (D. Colo. 1977); Hyde & Drath v. Baker, 24 F.3d 1162 (9th Cir. 1994).

157. *See, e.g.*, United Nuclear Corp. v. General Atomic Co., 629 P.2d 231, 306 (N.M. 1980), *appeal dismissed*, 451 U.S. 901 (1981); General Atomic Co. v. Exxon Nuclear Co., Inc., 90 F.R.D. 290 (S.D. Cal. 1981).

158. 825 F.2d 494 (D.C. Cir. 1987).

159. *Id.* at 497.

160. *Id.*

161. Wilson v. United States, 221 U.S. 361, 376 (1911).

162. *Id.;* Gerling Int'l Ins. Co. v. Comm'r of Internal Revenue, 839 F.2d 131, 138 (3d Cir. 1987).

despite the fact that the bank may not be a party and may be subject to criminal penalties under foreign nondisclosure laws.[163] Foreign banks having United States branches are likewise compelled to produce evidence on the grounds that, by operating in the United States, they too come under the jurisdiction of United States courts.[164]

§ 10.18 TAX INFORMATION EXCHANGE AGREEMENTS AND OTHER TREATIES

Since grand jury or IRS subpoenas to banks and accounting firms are the most common examples of discovery abroad directed at non-parties, attorneys representing such entities need to be aware that there are treaties, executive agreements, and other information exchange arrangements in existence between the United States and foreign countries. Also, in criminal cases, United States law enforcement officials make use of mutual legal assistance treaties (MLATs), narcotics agreements and other arrangements to obtain evidence and assistance abroad.[165] Note also that the United States has entered into Tax Information Exchange Agreements (TIEAs) with many countries including Mexico, Japan, and those in the Caribbean Basin such as Barbados, Costa Rica, and the Dominican Republic.[166] In *United States v. Toyota Motor Corp.*,[167] the court ordered enforcement of an IRS summons only after the IRS produced evidence showing the unavailability of alternative methods under treaty requests for obtaining the information requested.[168]

§ 10.19 COMPELLED CONSENT AND OTHER DISCLOSURE ISSUES

Where banks are doing business in the United States, they may be ordered to perform certain acts abroad in order to comply with subpoena

163. United States v. First Nat'l City Bank, 396 F.2d 897, 900 (2d Cir. 1968).

164. United States v. Bank of Nova Scotia I, 691 F.2d 1384, 1388–89 (11th Cir. 1982).

165. *See* James P. Springer, *An Overview of International Evidence and Asset Gathering in Civil and Criminal Tax Cases*, 22 GEO. WASH. J. INT'L L. & ECON. 277–330 (1988), and Appendix 20, which lists MLAT arrangements. *In re* Commissioner's Subpoenas, 2003 WL 1645236 (11th Cir.) (non-applicability of foreign discoverability requirement under section 1782 to Canadian/U.S. MLAT treaty request).

166. *See generally* Barquero v. United States, 18 F.3d 1311 (5th Cir. 1994).

167. 569 F. Supp. 1158, 1163 (C.D. Cal. 1983).

168. *See* Convention for the Avoidance of Double Taxation and the Prevention of Fiscal Evasion with Respect to Taxes on Income, Aug. 14, 1962, U.S.–Japan, 23 U.S.T. 969.

requests. In *United States v. Ghidoni*,[169] a subpoena was issued to a foreign bank for records kept in foreign branches, via service through a United States branch in Miami. The district court had ordered a United States citizen depositor having an account with the foreign branch in the Cayman Islands to sign a consent to disclosure. The court of appeals rejected the position that any constitutional privilege against self-incrimination was violated and reasoned that the defendant was not being ordered to produce the records themselves (in any case documents and papers have no Fifth Amendment protection) but merely to remove obstacles to their production.[170]

In *Doe v. United States*,[171] the Supreme Court resolved the question of whether the compelled execution of a consent form directing the disclosure of foreign bank records violated the Fifth Amendment's privilege against self-incrimination. The consent form did not identify the documents or acknowledge their existence. Petitioner, who was the target of a federal grand jury investigation, contended that his execution of the consent form had independent testimonial significance that would incriminate him by directing the bank to release records as to which the banks believed he had the right of withdrawal. The Court focused on the question of whether the act of executing the form was a "testimonial communication." The Court recognized that, in order to be testimonial, an accused's communication must itself "release a factual assertion or describe information."[172] The Court determined that neither the form nor its execution communicated any factual assertions or conveyed any information to the Government.[173] The form did not acknowledge that an account in a foreign financial institution was in existence or that documents or information relating to petitioner were present at an identified foreign bank. By signing the form, petitioner did not admit to the authenticity of any records produced by the bank or consent to the release of bank records.[174] The Supreme Court compared this directive to the production of a handwriting sample or voice example in that both are non-testimonial acts.[175]

---

169. 732 F.2d 814 (11th Cir. 1984), *cert. denied*, 469 U.S. 932 (1984).
170. *Accord* California Bankers Ass'n v. Schultz, 416 U.S. 21, 55 (1974).
171. 487 U.S. 201 (1988).
172. *Id.* at 210.
173. *Id.* at 214–19.
174. *Id.* at 216.
175. *Id.* at 217.

In *United States v. Davis*,[176] the court of appeals ordered a United States citizen depositor to direct a Cayman Island bank to comply with a United States court subpoena of bank records.[177] In addition, the court affirmed the district court in ordering the defendant to terminate litigation he had initiated in a foreign court to enjoin the bank from disclosing his bank records.[178] Defendant's foreign suit had been successful in thwarting United States efforts to obtain the records via diplomatic and international judicial assistance channels.

Where an American bank has been the subject of inconsistent enforcement actions, United States courts have been disinclined to enjoin enforcement of the foreign proceedings. In *Garpeg, Ltd. v. United States*,[179] the Hong Kong branch of Chase Manhattan Bank was under an interim order of a Hong Kong court enjoining it from complying with an IRS summons directed to a Hong Kong corporation's bank records. The district court denied Chase Manhattan's motion to quash the IRS summons and to enjoin the Hong Kong corporation from pursuing any action against Chase in Hong Kong courts.[180] The court held that:

(1) there was not an adjudication of the same issue between the parties in two separate actions;

(2) when separate rights arose and were enforceable only through the laws of a foreign country, the determination of a United States court was not dispositive of litigation abroad; and

(3) disputes between a foreign customer (the corporation) and a foreign branch of an American bank with respect to overseas accounts were properly adjudicated before the foreign courts.[181]

§ 10.20 SUBPOENA OF UNITED STATES NATIONALS OR RESIDENTS ABROAD

28 U.S.C.A. § 1783(a) empowers federal courts to "order the issuance of a subpoena requiring the appearance as a witness before it . . . of a national or resident of the United States who is in a foreign country . . . or requiring the production of a specified document or other thing."

176. 767 F.2d 1025 (2d Cir. 1985).
177. *Id.* at 1039–40.
178. *Id.* at 1039.
179. 583 F. Supp. 789 (S.D.N.Y. 1984).
180. *Id.* at 799.
181. *Id.* at 797–99.

The court must find that the particular testimony, or document or other tangible evidence "is necessary in the interest of justice."[182] In *Blackmer v. United States*,[183] the Supreme Court, interpreting customary international law, determined that a sovereign has the power to compel one of its citizens residing abroad to return to give testimony. Section 1783(a) applies only to a citizen of the United States or a resident and under customary international law a United States court would have no power to compel a nonresident alien to respond to an American subpoena.[184] Under *Blackmer*, witnesses who fail to comply with a subpoena served on them abroad under section 1783 are subject to contempt proceedings.[185] If the witness is found in contempt, the court may fine the person not more than $100,000, and any property of the person within the United States may be seized or sold to satisfy a judgment rendered against the person under this section.[186] The provisions of 28 U.S.C.A. § 1783(a) apply to both civil and criminal cases.

A subpoena to be served abroad may be issued in a civil case if the court finds, in addition, "that it is not possible to obtain his testimony in admissible form without his personal appearance or to obtain the production of the document or other thing in any other manner."[187] If the court determines that the interest of justice may be served by not compelling the personal appearance of the witness, it may, in its discretion, deny the subpoena.

State Department Consular regulations provide that foreign service officers may serve a subpoena issued by a United States court on a national or resident of the United States "unless such action is prohibited by the law of the foreign country."[188] In this connection, United States courts have cautioned that the service of compulsory process in a foreign country must be minimally intrusive since the act of service itself constitutes the exercise of one nation's sovereignty within the territory of another sovereign.[189]

---

182. 28 U.S.C.A. § 1783(a) (1992).

183. 284 U.S. 421, 437–38 (1932).

184. *Id.* at 437.

185. *Id.* at 438; *see* 28 U.S.C.A. § 1784 (1992); 18 U.S.C.A. § 401 (1992) (criminal sanctions).

186. *Blackmer*, 284 U.S. at 438.

187. *See* 28 U.S.C.A. § 1783(a) (1992).

188. *See* 22 C.F.R. § 92.86 (1993).

189. *See* F.T.C. v. Compagnie de Saint-Gobain-Pont-A-Mousson, 636 F.2d 1300, 1312–1314 (D.C. Cir. 1980).

Subsection (b) of section 1783 provides that service of the subpoena shall be effected in accordance with provisions of the Federal Rules of Civil Procedure relating to service of process on a person in a foreign country.[190] As described in subsection (g), the person serving the subpoena must tender to the witness his estimated necessary travel and attendance expenses.[191]

§ 10.21 LACK OF CONTROL OVER DOCUMENTS AS A DEFENSE TO DISCOVERY

As a general rule, a court has the power to order a person subject to its jurisdiction to perform an act in another state.[192] As a precondition to the exercise of this power, the court must have personal jurisdiction over the person.[193] If there is no personal jurisdiction in an *International Shoe* minimum contacts sense,[194] the court lacks authority to subject a foreign corporation to civil process or grand jury subpoena. For either purpose, the mere maintenance of a bank account or the transfer of funds in and out of that account is insufficient to subject a foreign corporation to *in personam* jurisdiction.[195]

In addition, in order for a court to order a person to produce documents located abroad, that person must have custody or control over the documents.[196] Documents need not be in the possession of a party to be discoverable provided there is the requisite custody or control by a party.[197] Furthermore, the fact that the documents are situated in a foreign country does not bar their discovery.[198] Courts apply certain

---

190. *See* Fed. R. Civ. P. 4(f).

191. 28 U.S.C.A. § 1783(b) (1992).

192. Restatement (Third) Foreign Relations Law, § 442 (1)(a) (1987).

193. *In re* Uranium Antitrust Litigation, 480 F. Supp 1138, 1148 (N.D. Ill. 1979). *See also In re* Matter of Tax Liabilities of John Does, No. C–88–0137, 1991 U.S. Dist. LEXIS 9704, *6 (N.D. Cal. 1991).

194. Int'l Shoe Co. v. Washington, 326 U.S. 310 (1945).

195. In the Matter of Arawak Trust Co. (Cayman) Ltd., 489 F. Supp. 162 (E.D.N.Y. 1980).

196. *See also In re* Uranium Antitrust Litigation, *supra* note 193, at 1144.

197. Gerling Int'l Ins. Co. v. Comm'r of Internal Revenue, 839 F.2d 131, 141 (3d Cir. 1987); Cooper Industries, Inc. v. British Aerospace, Inc., 102 F.R.D. 918, 919 (S.D.N.Y. 1984).

198. Compagnie Francaise D'Assurance Pour le Commerce Exterier v. Phillips Petroleum Co., 105 F.R.D. 16, 35 (S.D.N.Y. 1984); Golden Trade, S.r.L. v. Lee Apparel Co., 143 F.R.D. 514, 525 (S.D.N.Y. 1992); *Cooper Industries, Inc., supra* note 197, 102 F.R.D. at 920; Marc Rich & Co. v. United States, 707 F.2d 663, 667 (2d Cir. 1983), *cert. denied*, 463 U.S. 1215 (1983); Japan Halon Co., Ltd., v. Great Lakes Chemical Corporation, 155 F.R.D. 626 (N.D. Ind. 1993).

corollary principles in deciding the issue of control in situations involving multinational corporations. The test for determining whether a U.S. court can order a domestic parent corporation to produce the documents of its foreign subsidiary depends on whether the corporation has power to elect a majority of the directors of the other corporation,[199] regardless of the formalities of corporate organization.[200] Similarly, the issue of control will determine whether the production of documents sought from the foreign parent corporation can be compelled from its wholly-owned domestic subsidiary.[201]

Where the court has jurisdiction over the parent corporation and that party has control over its subsidiaries, that party may be required to produce discovery from its wholly-owned subsidiary, wherever the subsidiary is located, under applicable civil procedure rules.[202]

§ 10.22 SECRECY AND BLOCKING STATUTES AS ENFORCEMENT DEFENSES

In addition to the concerns of foreign judicial sovereignty, secrecy or blocking statutes of a foreign country may prohibit the disclosure of information sought in connection with United States proceedings. As a result, the attorney representing the foreign witness or party will have to analyze the conflicting obligations of both jurisdictions and determine whether the nondisclosure of the information sought pursuant to the foreign laws is reasonable under the circumstances presented and provides a "good faith" defense to his client. All blocking statutes provide for civil or criminal sanctions for violations.

[1] Secrecy Laws

Secrecy laws pertain to prohibitions which arise from the particular relationship between the custodian of information and some other person. Secrecy laws include banking statutes which prohibit the disclosure of confidential information in banking records.[203] Other

---

199. *In re* Uranium Antitrust Litigation, *supra* note 193, at 1152; *In re* Investigation of World Arrangements, 13 F.R.D. 280, 285 (D.D.C. 1952).

200. *In re* Uranium Antitrust Litigation, *supra* note 193, at 1145; Cooper Industries, Inc., 102 F.R.D. at 919.

201. *See* Choice-Intersil Microsystems, Inc. v. Agere Sys., Inc., 224 F.R.D. 471 (N.D. Cal. 2004).

202 *See* Bank of Tokyo-Mitsubishi, Ltd. v. Kvaerner, 671 N.Y.S.2d 902 (Sup. Ct. 1998).

203. *See, e.g.*, Alfadda v. Fenn, 149 F.R.D. 28, 33 (S.D.N.Y. 1993); Société Internationale Pour Participations Industrielles et Commerciales v. Rogers, 357 U.S. 197, 200 (1958).

secrecy laws are classified pursuant to the type of information or subject matter involved.[204] In this connection, numerous foreign laws have been enacted in reaction to American discovery requests in antitrust cases.[205] One clear purpose of these statutes has been to thwart United States antitrust and securities investigations.[206]

The first Supreme Court case to discuss the relationship between U.S. discovery and foreign nondisclosure laws was *Societe Internationale Pour Participations Industrielles et Commerciales, S.A. v. Rogers*.[207] In that case a Swiss holding company sought recovery of assets which had been seized by the Alien Property Custodian as enemy-owned property under the Trading With the Enemy Act during World War II. The United States sought a production order, pursuant to Rule 34 of the Federal Rules of Civil Procedure, requiring the claimant to make available a large number of banking records in a Swiss bank. In opposing discovery, the claimant maintained that disclosure of these records would violate certain provisions of the Swiss Penal Code and the Swiss Banking Law. Despite the district court's finding of good faith in the claimant's efforts to comply with the production order, it dismissed the complaint on the ground that there was no adequate defense under foreign law for failure to comply with the discovery order.[208]

The Supreme Court reversed the order of dismissal, citing the petitioner's extensive efforts of compliance. The Court stated that petitioner's failure to satisfy the production order ''was due to inability fostered neither by its own conduct nor by circumstances within its control. . . . It is hardly debatable that fear of criminal prosecution constitutes a weighty excuse for nonproduction.''[209] In remanding the case, the Court pointed out that, in the absence of complete disclosure by the petitioner, the district court would be justified in drawing unfavorable inferences to the petitioner as to particular events.[210] The Court's decision in *Societe Internationale* has created confusion among lower

---

204. *See* Richmark Corp. v. Timber Falling Consultants, 959 F.2d 1468, 1472 (9th Cir. 1992), *cert. dismissed*, 113 S. Ct. 454 (1993) (state secrecy laws); Reinsurance Co. of Am., Inc. v. Administratia Asigurarilor de Stat, 902 F.2d 1275, 1283 (7th Cir. 1990) (same).

205. *See, e.g.*, Foreign Proceedings (Prohibition of Certain Evidence) Act No. 121 (1976) (Australia), Uranium Information Security Regulations, Stat. O&R, 76–644 (1976) (Canada); Economic Competition Act, art. 39 (Netherlands Antilles).

206. *In re* Uranium Antitrust Litigation, 480 F. Supp. 1138, 1143 (N.D. Ill. 1979).

207. 357 U.S. 197 (1958).

208. *Id.* at 201–02.

209. *Id.* at 211.

210. *Id.* at 212–13.

federal courts in resolving conflicts between discovery orders and blocking statutes. Courts have focused on such factors as the requirement of good faith of the party from whom discovery is sought and the interests of the foreign and domestic forum. Courts engage in a comity analysis, often using the factors outlined in the Restatement (Third) of Foreign Relations Law § 442.[211]

[2] Blocking Statutes

Blocking statutes generally forbid foreign citizens to produce evidence abroad. For example, the French blocking statute provides: ''Subject to treaties or international agreement and applicable laws and regulations, it is prohibited for any party to request, seek or disclose, in writing, orally or otherwise, economic, commercial, industrial, financial or technical documents or information leading to the constitution of evidence with a view to foreign judicial or administrative proceedings or in connection therewith.''[212] The law prohibits French nationals from disclosing information when it will be used to assist foreign discovery requests. The French statute has been interpreted as expressing hostility to United States antitrust laws and judicial procedures.[213]

In *Societe Internationale Industrielle Aerospatiale v. United States District Court*,[214] the Supreme Court discussed the relevance of the French blocking statute in ruling that the Hague Evidence Convention did not provide exclusive or mandatory procedures for obtaining documents and information located in a foreign signatory's territory. Petitioner, a French corporation, had resisted discovery on grounds that the Hague Convention dictated the exclusive procedures for pretrial discovery and that under French penal law, petitioners could not respond to discovery requests that did not comply with the Convention. The Court concluded that the existence of the French blocking statute could

211. *See infra* § 10.16 (addressing § 442); Société Internationale Industrielle Aerospatiale v. United States Dist. Court, 482 U.S. 522, 544 n.28 (1987); Richmark Corp. v. Timber Falling Consultants, 959 F.2d 1468, 1475–79 (9th Cir. 1992), *cert. dismissed*, 113 S. Ct. 454 (1993); Reinsurance Co. of Am., Inc. v. Administratia Asigurarilor de Stat, 902 F.2d 1275, 1281–83 (7th Cir. 1990). *See* also Lenore B. Browne, *Extraterritorial Discovery: An Analysis Based on Good Faith*, 83 Colum. L. Rev. 1320 (1983).

212. Art. 1A French Penal Code Law (C. Pen.) No. 80–538.

213. *See* Bate C. Toms, *The French Response to Extraterritorial Application of United States Antitrust Laws*, 15 Int'l Law. 585 (1981); Brigette Ecolivet Herzog, *The 1980 French Law on Documents and Information*, 75 A.J.I.L. 382 (1981).

214. 482 U.S. 522 (1987); *see supra*, § 10.11 (''Exclusivity'' of the Convention).

not be used to require first resort to the Hague Convention or otherwise provide French nationals with a preferred status in U.S. courts.[215]

In analyzing the interplay between pretrial discovery and the French blocking statute, the Court observed that:

> It is clear that American courts are not required to adhere blindly to the directives of such a statute. The language of the statute, if taken literally, would appear to represent an extraordinary exercise of legislative jurisdiction by the Republic of France over a United States District Judge, forbidding him or her from ordering any discovery from a party of French nationality, even simple requests for admissions or interrogatories that the party could respond to on the basis of personal knowledge.[216]

The Court concluded that the blocking statute was relevant to the lower court's particularized comity analysis "only to the extent that its enforcement identif[ied] the nature of the sovereign interests in nondisclosure of specific kinds of material."[217]

The Court's treatment of the French blocking statute in *Aerospatiale* demonstrates that foreign law objections founded on hostility to U.S. law will be approached by U.S. courts with caution and skepticism. The Supreme Court noted the expression of this concern in the Restatement (Third) of the Foreign Relations Law of the United States (Revised). The Restatement's view of the interplay of blocking statutes and discovery orders is summarized as follows:

> [W]hen a state has jurisdiction to prescribe and its courts have jurisdiction to adjudicate, adjudication should (subject to generally applicable rules of evidence) take place on the basis of the best information available. . .[Blocking] statutes that frustrate this goal need not be given the same deference by courts of the United States as substantive rules of law at variance with the law of the United States.[218]

On the other hand, foreign nations may have specific interests that warrant accommodation by U.S. courts.[219] These nondisclosure laws may pertain to the protection of business or trade secrets or testimonial

215. 482 U.S. at 544–45, n. 29.

216. *Id.*

217. *Id.*

218. *See* Restatement (Third) Foreign Relations Law, § 442, reporter's note 5 (1987).

219. *See* Reinsurance Co. of Am., Inc. v. Administratia Asigurarilor de Stat, 902 F.2d 1275, 1281–83 (7th Cir. 1990).

privileges absent from American judicial processes.[220] However, based on *Aerospatiale*, it will be difficult for foreign parties toconvince American courts that blocking statutes or similar foreign nondisclosure laws should be given particular weight in any comity analysis of the respective interests involved.[221]

§ 10.23 DEPOSITIONS BY TELEPHONE OR REMOTE ELECTRONIC MEANS

Rule 30(b)(7) of the Federal Rules of Civil Procedure provides that "a deposition [may] be taken by telephone or other remote electronic means."[222] Other electronic means includes satellite television.[223] While, in general, Rule 30(b) was amended to liberalize the methods of taking depositions, taking of depositions by telephone or other electronic means requires the written stipulation of the parties or a court order upon motion.[224]

It should further be noted that a telephonic deposition is to be taken "in the district and at the place where the deponent is to answer questions"[225] rather than where the questions are pronounced. This has been interpreted to require that in order to comply with the provisions of Fed. R. Civ. P. 28(b)(3) which governs the taking of depositions abroad, the oath must be administered by an official where the witness is located and not in the location where the questions were propounded.[226] However, Rule 29 allows the deposition to be taken before any person, at any time or place, in any manner, if the parties so stipulate.[227] Locating a person to administer the deposition abroad should not prove problematic, therefore. Further, Rule 29 provides that parties may by stipulation modify procedures governing discovery.[228] Whether parties

---

220. *In re* Jenoptik AG, 109 F.3d 721 (Fed. Cir. 1997) (confidentiality/non-discoverability of trade secrets under German law).

221. *See* Richmark Corp. v. Timber Falling Consultants, 959 F.2d 1468, 1475–79 (9th Cir. 1992), *cert. dismissed*, 113 S. Ct. 454 (1995).

222. Fed. R. Civ. P. 30(b)(7). Counsel should be aware, however, that in civil law nations, conducting pretrial discovery without the permission of foreign authorities may violate foreign law. *See supra*, § 10.02.

223. Fed. R. Civ. P. 30(b)(7) advisory committee's note.

224. Fed. R. Civ. P. 30(b)(7).

225. *Id.*

226. *See* Loucas G. Mateas Salvage & Towage Maritime Co. v. M/T Cold Spring I, 1997 WL 102491 (E.D. La.).

227. Fed. R. Civ. P. 29.

228. Fed. R. Civ. P. 29.

may stipulate to taking a deposition by telephone at the place where the questions are pronounced is unclear, but would not constitute a clear violation of the spirit of Rule 29.[229]

Where a court order may be required to perform a telephonic deposition, it should be noted that courts prior to the 1993 amendments to the Federal Rules of Civil Procedure were reluctant to order depositions by telephone. In noting the exclusion of Rule 28(b), governing depositions in foreign countries, from Rule 30(b)(7), one court questioned its authority to order telephonic depositions in a foreign country.[230] Under prior rules, courts generally disallowed telephonic depositions to be conducted abroad and have been disinclined to depart from the traditional means specified in Rule 28(b), without a showing of extreme hardship.[231] It is uncertain what effect the new rules will have on the use of telephonic depositions abroad.

As to laying a foundation to admit a telephone conversation into evidence, the sufficiency of the identities of the participants is crucial. Since, in many depositions abroad, a translator may be involved, both the deponent and the translator should acknowledge the accuracy and completeness of the transcript of the deposition. The deponent and translator should also certify the time and place the deposition was held, which can then be verified by phone records. The procedures for the taking of a deposition set forth in Rule 30(b)(4) should be followed.

While a deposition abroad by telephone may be tape-recorded to reduce stenographic costs, attorneys should consider the evidentiary issues involved in admitting a tape recording of the telephonic deposition. In *Alva v. Peninsula Gen. Hosp.*,[232] the court held that where the deponents had heavy foreign accents, stenographic transcripts of the depositions might be preferable. However, a court may express a preference for tape recordings of telephone conversations over stenographic transcripts to allow the jury to evaluate the inflection and tone of voice.[233]

229. Fed. R. Civ. P. 29 advisory committee's notes.

230. Jahr v. IU Int'l Corp., 109 F.R.D. 429, 432 (M.D.N.C. 1986).

231. *See* Daly v. Delta Airlines, Inc., No. 90–C5700, 1991 U.S. Dist. LEXIS 2762, *4 (S.D.N.Y. 1991); Clem v. Allied Van Lines Int'l Corp., 102 F.R.D. 938 (S.D.N.Y. 1984); Southern Seas Shipping Co., Ltd. v. Blue Anchor, Inc., No. 83–3851 (E.D. Pa. Apr. 5, 1985). Cf. Rehau, Inc. v. Colortech, Inc., 145 F.R.D. 444, 446–47 (W.D. Mich. 1993).

232. 68 App. Div. 2d 875, 875, 414 N.Y.S.2d 43, 43 (1979).

233. People v. Williams, 109 Ill. 2d 327, 337–38, 487 N.E.2d 613, 618 (1985); People v. Harding, 44 App. Div. 2d 800, 801, 355 N.Y.S.2d 394, 397 (1974).

Attorneys should also consider the practical and logistic difficulties presented by a telephonic deposition. Primarily, parties are unable to examine the demeanor of opponents and may be impeded in the scope of their questioning by an inability to use exhibits. One court, albeit in a domestic context, has suggested that fax machines be utilized should it become necessary for counsel to send documents to opposing parties during a deposition by telephone.[234]

§ 10.24 TAKING DEPOSITIONS BY AUDIO-VISUAL MEANS

Audio or audio-visual depositions are useful in international litigation since witnesses may be in remote locations from the place of trial.[235] Also, there may be other advantages in audio or audio-visual testimony as compared to reading stenographically-transcribed depositions into evidence. In particular, audio-visual recordings, such as videotapes, serve to present the appearance and demeanor of witnesses. However, where witness demeanor is a key factor, a videotaped deposition may not be an adequate substitute for live testimony.[236]

Under Rule 30(b)(2) of the Federal Rules of Civil Procedure, parties have substantial authority to control the means of taking depositions. Unless the court orders otherwise, the deposition may be "recorded by sound, sound-and-visual, or stenographic means."[237] Amended Rule 30 departs from the previous rule and allows parties to record deposition testimony by non-stenographic means without obtaining the prior permission of the court or opposing counsel.[238]

Counsel should consult Rule 30(b)(4), which sets forth procedures to be followed in taking depositions. The Rule provides for authentication, identification of persons present, administration of oath or affirmation, and other formalities. In addition, Rule 30(b)(4) provides that if videotape or other non-stenographic methods are employed, the "appearance or demeanor of deponents or attorneys shall not be distorted through camera or sound-recording techniques."[239]

---

234. Bywaters v. Bywaters, 123 F.R.D. 175, 176 (E.D. Pa. 1988).

235. Counsel should be aware, however, that in civil law nations, conducting pretrial discovery without the permission of foreign authorities may violate foreign law. *See supra*, § 10.02.

236. *See* Kultur Films v. Covent Garden, 860 F. Supp. 1055, 1066–1067 (D.N.J. 1994).

237. Fed. R. Civ. P. 30(b)(2) advisory committee's notes, Subdivision (b).

238. *Id.*

239. Fed. R. Civ. P. 30(b)(4).

Attorneys utilizing videotape equipment abroad should also be aware of special technical considerations such as locating skilled operators, and recording on tapes compatible with equipment in U.S. courts. In addition, the practitioner may find that transporting video equipment from the United States may lead to customs problems in the country where the deposition is to take place. Before proceeding overseas to take a videotape deposition, counsel should consult with the United States State Department's Office of American Citizens Services for information as to which countries prohibit importation of video equipment or otherwise restrict this type of deposition.[240]

---

240. *See* note 19, *supra*, presenting address and phone number of Office of American Citizens Services.

Chapter 11

ENFORCEMENT OF JUDGMENTS

(Rel.1–8/98)

§ 11.01 INTRODUCTION

An understanding of the rules and concepts of enforcement of judgments will enable the lawyer handling transnational issues to better advise clients at the pre-litigation stage of the dispute. If the judgment obtained in a United States court is not enforceable in a foreign forum, litigation in this country may prove to be an enormous waste of time and money, and thus the subject of enforcement of judgments has important ramifications for both plaintiffs and defendants. The plaintiff may need to be advised whether the suit should be filed in the United States or a foreign forum. The decision where to sue usually depends on jurisdictional considerations and the determination of where the defendant owns sufficient assets to satisfy any potential judgment. The defendant, in turn, may need advice on whether to appear and defend an action filed in a foreign court and the enforceability of a foreign default judgment in the United States.

Unlike our European trading partners, the subject of recognition and enforcement of judgments in the United States is not dealt with by treaty or covered by federal statute. The only pertinent codification under United States law is the Uniform Foreign Money-Judgments Recognition Act,[1] which some states have adopted and put into law.[2] U.S. efforts to enter into bilateral treaties covering the recognition and enforcement of judgments have been unsuccessful. In the 1970's, the United States and Great Britain entered into discussions on a bilateral treaty on mutual recognition and enforcement of judgments, but the agreement was never signed.[3]

Among the obstacles between the United States and Great Britain was a reluctance to recognize decrees of United States courts in negligence suits, particularly products liability cases, with high damage awards. The liberality and size of American damage awards in tort suits and other cases would no doubt prove to be an impediment to the United States in entering into bilateral treaties with other countries or becoming parties to multilateral treaties currently in force or proposed. This puts the U.S. at a disadvantage with European countries where numerous bilateral arrangements exist.

---

1. Uniform Foreign Money-Judgments Recognition Act, 13 U.L.A. 261 (1986).
2. *See infra* § 11.09.
3. *See generally* Smit, *The Proposed United States–United Kingdom Convention on Recognition and Enforcement of Judgments: A Prototype for the Future?*, 17 VA. J. INT'L L. 443 (1977).

In 1993, the Hague Conference on Private International Law placed on its negotiating agenda the preparation of a convention on the recognition and enforcement of judgments. The proposal suggested by the U.S. delegation and experts from other countries would regulate the assertion of jurisdiction of signatory states as well as require the recognition and enforcement of judgments from signatory states.[4] The convention would deal with permissible and impermissible bases of jurisdiction and would require the recognition and enforcement in party countries of all judgments founded on required bases of jurisdiction. Formal negotiations began in 1996. After the adoption of several draft texts, it became clear that a consensus could not be reached on a ''mixed convention'' regulating both jurisdiction as well as recognition and enforcement of judgments. Negotiations recently resumed to consider a more limited convention which would require recognition and enforcement of judgments in civil and commercial cases rendered by a court which was designated in an exclusive choice of court agreement.

In addition, there are three major multilateral conventions currently in force among European countries: the EEC Convention Relating to the Jurisdiction of the Courts and the Enforcement of Judgments in Civil and Commercial Matters (the Brussels Convention);[5] the Convention for the Reciprocal Recognition and Enforcement of Judgments in Civil and Commercial Matters (the Hague Convention or 1960 Convention), July 14, 1960;[6] and the Convention on Jurisdiction and Enforcement of Judgments in Civil and Commercial Matters (the Lugano Convention), September 16, 1988.[7] These treaties tend to promote recognition and enforcement of foreign judgments.

§ 11.02 COMITY CONSIDERATIONS IN ENFORCING FOREIGN JUDGMENT AWARDS

United States courts are not bound by agreed principles or procedures in the enforcement of foreign judgments. It is usually

4. *See* Eric C. Fastiff, *The Proposed Hague Convention on the Recognition and Enforcement of Civil and Commercial Judgments: A Solution to Butch Reynolds' Jurisdiction and Enforcement Problems*, 28 Cornell Int'l L.J. 469 (1995).

5. 1978 O.J. (L 304) 77. A copy of the text of the Brussels Convention is included *infra* Appendix 15.

6. 414 U.N.T.S. 144.

7. Convention on Jurisdiction and the Enforcement of Judgments in Civil and Commercial Matters, *done* September 16, 1988, 28 I.L.M. 620 [hereinafter cited as Lugano Convention]. A copy of the Lugano Convention is included *infra* Appendix 16.

necessary for the judgment creditor to institute civil recovery and establish a jurisdictional basis over the judgment debtor to execute the foreign decree. Courts have generally held, in this regard, that in the absence of a federal statute, the effect of foreign court judgments in terms of recognition and enforceability should be determined by state rather than federal law.[8]

In determining the extent of recognition and enforceability of foreign court judgments, United States courts follow the principle of international comity. The rationale for the granting of comity is based on the principle of *res judicata* that "litigation should end after the parties have had an opportunity to present their cases fully and fairly to a court of competent jurisdiction."[9] The leading case on the principles of comity is *Hilton v. Guyot*,[10] where comity was described as:

> the recognition which one nation allows within its territory to the legislative, executive, or judicial acts of another nation, having due regard both to international duty and convenience, and to the rights of its own citizens, or of other persons who are under the protection of its laws.[11]

The Supreme Court decided that the doctrine of international comity should be followed in those cases:

> where there has been opportunity for a full and fair trial abroad before a court of competent jurisdiction, conducting the trial upon regular proceedings, after due citation or voluntary appearance of the defendant, and under a system of jurisprudence likely to secure an impartial administration of justice between the citizens of its own country and those of other countries, and there is nothing to show either prejudice in the court, or in the system of laws under which it was sitting, or fraud in procuring the judgment, or any other special reason why the comity of this nation should not allow it full effect.[12]

Where these factors are present in an action upon the judgment, there need not be a new trial of the merits of the case if the party asserts that the judgment was erroneous in law or in fact. However, the case is not ripe for recognition and enforcement until a judgment is rendered by the

8. Restatement (Third) Foreign Relations Law § 481a (1987).

9. Cunard Steamship Co., Ltd. v. Salen Reefer Services AB, 773 F.2d 452, 457 (2d Cir. 1985).

10. 159 U.S. 113 (1895).

11. *Id.* at 164.

12. *Id.* at 202.

foreign court. In this connection, a declaratory judgment action seeking to disclose that a pending case would be invalid and unenforceable does not present an actual case or controversy.[13]

§ 11.03 DUE PROCESS AND JURISDICTIONAL CONSIDERATIONS

In determining whether the foreign court has obtained personal jurisdiction over the defendant for enforcement purposes, United States courts look to our concept of due process, i.e., fundamental standards of procedural fairness. In this connection, the Restatement (Second) of Conflict of Laws[14] states that enforcement of a foreign judgment should not be "repugnant to fundamental notions of what is decent and just in the State where enforcement is sought." Where the foreign procedure comports with our standards of due process, comity should not be refused.

In *Kohn v. American Metal Climax, Inc.*,[15] the court of appeals analyzed the conduct of the foreign proceeding under the selected criteria discussed in *Hilton v. Guyot* in determining whether a full and fair trial abroad had been conducted. These criteria were summarized as follows:

(1) Opportunity for a full and fair trial abroad;

(2) Trial before a court of competent jurisdiction;

(3) Trial conducted upon regular proceedings;

(4) Proceedings following due citation or voluntary appearance of adversary parties;

(5) Trial under a system of jurisprudence likely to secure an impartial administration of justice between the citizens of its own country and those of other countries;

(6) No evidence to demonstrate

  (a) prejudice in the court,

  (b) prejudice in the system of laws in which the court was sitting;

---

13. *See* Basic v. Fitzroy Engineering, Ltd., 132 F.2d 36 (7th Cir. 1997).
14. Restatement (Second) Conflicts of Law § 117, cmt. c (1971).
15. 458 F.2d 255, 303–05 (3d Cir.), *cert. denied*, 409 U.S. 874 (1972).

(c) fraud in procuring the judgment; or

(d) any other special reason why the comity of this nation should not allow full effect.[16]

In general, if the court is reasonably convinced that the foreign country's judgment contains the traditional safeguards of fairness and due process outlined above, comity will be followed.[17] Judgments rendered by a judicial system that fails to be impartial or to conform its procedures to due process are not enforceable.[17.1]

As a general rule, the issue of whether the foreign court had personal jurisdiction over the defendant is determined under United States jurisprudence and not foreign law.[18] In *Cherun v. Frishman*,[19] the district court stated that:

> in the interest of affording United States courts a reasonable degree of certainty as to when our own courts will, under principles of comity, enforce a judgment rendered against such citizens in foreign courts, the issue of whether the foreign country had jurisdiction over the United States national should be determined by our own standards of judicial power as promulgated by the Supreme Court under the due process clause of the Fourteenth Amendment.[20]

In this connection, in *Koster v. Automark Industries, Inc.*,[21] the court of appeals applied the due process ''minimum contacts'' test in determining that defendant did not have sufficient contact with the foreign forum to support enforcement of the foreign default judgment in Illinois. In *Koster*, the document at issue was executed in Italy and involved the purchase of goods manufactured in Switzerland. The defendant's only contacts with the foreign forum in the Netherlands

---

16. *Id.* at 302.

17. *See, e.g.*, Mata v. American Life Ins. Co., 771 F. Supp. 1375, 1381 (D. Del. 1991); *In re* Enercons Virginia, Inc., 812 F.2d 1469, 1472–1473 (4th Cir. 1987); British Midland Airways Ltd. v. Int'l Travel, Inc., 497 F.2d 869, 871 (9th Cir. 1974); Society of Lloyds v. Ashenden, 233 F.3d 473, 477 (7th Cir. 2000); Kam-Tech Systems, Ltd. v. Yardeni, 774 A.2d 644, 648–51 (N.J. Super. A.D. 2001); Society of Lloyd's v. Turner, 303 F.3d 325 (5th Cir. 2002).

17.1. Bridgeway Corporation v. Citibank, 201 F.3d 134, 140–144 (2d Cir. 2000); International Transactions, Ltd. v. Embotelladora Agral Regiomontana, S.A., 347 F.3d 589, 593-597 (5th Cir. 2003).

18. *See* Mata v. American Life Ins. Co., 771 F. Supp. 1375, 1384 (D. Del. 1991); Kam-Tech Systems, Ltd. v. Yardeni, *supra* note 17, at 651–53.

19. 236 F. Supp. 292 (D.D.C. 1964).

20. *Id.* at 296.

21. 640 F.2d 77 (7th Cir. 1981).

were communications by letter, telegram and telephone preliminary to a meeting in Italy. The court of appeals concluded that such communications failed to satisfy due process standards and were insufficient to vest the Dutch court with personal jurisdiction over the defendant corporation. The rationale of *Koster* lies in the court's statement that:

> The Netherlands lacks an adequate relationship to defendant's presence and conduct to justify trial of the case in that country. The interests of international business are better served by protecting potential international purchasers from being unreasonably called to defend suits commenced in foreign courts which lack jurisdiction according to our recognized standards of due process.[22]

As a collateral matter, the court of appeals in *Koster* further determined that defendant had not been provided with adequate notice of the suit to comport with United States due process requirements. The Dutch statute requires that when a foreign defendant is named in a case in the Netherlands, process notifying the defendant must be served on the Dutch Department of Foreign Affairs. However, the statute did not further require the Department to follow up by serving notice to the foreign defendant. Defendant contended that it had never received notice of the Dutch lawsuit and was therefore unable to defend its interests in the case. Although plaintiff urged that the Dutch Department, as a matter of practice, served process on foreign defendants, the court of appeals ruled that the terms relating to the sending of notice would have to be checked by the statute to satisfy due process standards.[23]

In *Mata v. American Life Ins. Co.*,[24] defendant also challenged the validity of service of process which had been made in connection with a foreign proceeding. In *Mata*, service upon a former agent who no longer owed any duties to a company was held not "notice reasonably calculated under all the circumstances" to apprise the defendant of the lawsuit and provide an opportunity to defend.[25] The *Mata* court found that the service failed to "comport with American . . . notions of due process" and rendered the foreign judgment unenforceable.[26] However, in determining whether the defendant has had an opportunity to appear and defend the foreign proceeding, U.S. courts do not require adherence

22. *Id.* at 80. *See also* Bank Melli Iran v. Pahlavi, 58 F.3d 1406 (9th Cir. 1995).
23. *Id.* at 81 n.3.
24. 771 F. Supp. 1375 (D. Del. 1991).
25. *Id.* at 1388.
26. *Id.* at 1389.

to the provisions of the Federal Rules of Civil Procedure. In *Tahan v. Hodgson*,[27] defendant asserted that a judgment of an Israeli court was not enforceable because it had not been provided with a second notice prior to a hearing on an application for default judgment, as would be required by Rule 55(b)(2) of the Federal Rules of Civil Procedure. In concluding that the Israeli procedure satisfied our notions of fairness and due process, the court of appeals observed that:

> it would be a mistake to find failure to follow the Federal Rules by a foreign nation to be *ipso facto* a violation of American public policy. It would be unrealistic for the United States to require all foreign judicial systems to adhere to the Federal Rules of Civil Procedure.[28]

It is important to provide proper advice to the client who is sued in a foreign court in recommending whether to appear and defend the action. The client should be informed that where the foreign court has personal jurisdiction, failure to appear may subsequently result in an enforceable default judgment. On the other hand, an appearance in the foreign proceeding may be tantamount to the submission to the jurisdiction of the court and waiver of the opportunity to later contest enforcement on that ground. Whether or not to appear in the foreign proceeding depends on the presence of assets in the foreign jurisdiction and the likelihood that any default judgment would be enforced in another forum.[29]

In *Somportex Ltd. v. Philadelphia Chewing Gum Corp.*,[30] defendant chose not to contest the English court's jurisdiction over the dispute even though it had been provided with that opportunity. Defendant had initially entered a conditional appearance but subsequently withdrew its appearance altogether so as not to submit to the foreign court's jurisdiction. In upholding enforcement of the English proceeding, the court of appeals held that the defendant was precluded from choosing which forum to test the factual basis of jurisdiction under English law and that its failure to contest jurisdiction in the foreign proceeding constituted a waiver.[31]

As to the finality of the default judgment, the court of appeals in *Somportex* stated that ''[i]n the absence of fraud or collusion, a default

27. 662 F.2d 862, 866 (D.C. Cir. 1981); CIBC Mellon Trust Co. v. Mora Hotel Corp., N.V., 100 N.Y.2d 215, 792 N.E.2d 155, *cert. denied*, 124 S. Ct. 399 (2003).

28. *Id.* at 866; *See also*, Roy v. Buckley, 698 A.2d 497 (Me. 1997).

29. *See* Dart v. Balaam, 953 S.W.2d 478 (Tex. App. 1997); CIBC Mellon Trust Co. v. Mora Hotel Corp., N.V., 100 N.Y.2d 215, 792 N.E.2d 155, *cert. denied*, 124 S. Ct. 399 (2003).

30. 453 F.2d 435, 438 (3d Cir. 1971), *cert. denied*, 405 U.S. 1017 (1972).

31. *Id.* at 441.

judgment is as conclusive an adjudication between the parties as when rendered after answer and complete contest in the open courtroom.''[32] A similar result was reached in *British Midland Airways Ltd. v. International Travel Inc.*,[33] where the defendant had initially agreed to be bound by British law but voluntarily chose not to pursue the matter on appeal or to interpose the conditional defense allowed. Citing Somportex, the court of appeals observed that ''we not only look with skepticism, but we flatly reject the due process complaint of a party who was given, and . . . waived, the opportunity of making the adequate presentation in the English court.''[34] Accordingly, it would be prudent to advise a party of the risks of not appearing to defend the action in a foreign court. Before failing to appear, the party should be convinced that there are other legal grounds for contesting the default judgment or that assets are not present to satisfy the judgment in another forum.

Where United States courts have had no experience with foreign proceedings and procedures, the party seeking to deny the extension of comity should be afforded reasonable discovery to determine the fairness of the foreign proceeding. In *Drexel Burnham Lambert Group, Inc. v. Galadari*,[35] the court of appeals was faced with the enforceability of a foreign bankruptcy decree. The case involved the country of Dubai's first attempt at framing an insolvency law and the United States courts had not previously dealt with that country's bankruptcy practice and procedures. Under such circumstances, the court of appeals held that the party resisting enforcement was entitled to reasonable discovery and an evidentiary hearing as to the fairness of the foreign proceeding.[36] Moreover, to justify a hearing, the party objecting to recognition of the foreign judgment should raise specific issues which warrant a factual inquiry and not rely on summary or conclusory reasons.[37] These questions should be developed to elicit facts relating to the foreign proceeding and its relationship to domestic law and public policy.

32. *Id.* at 442.
33. 497 F.2d 869 (9th Cir. 1974).
34. *Id.* at 871.
35. 777 F.2d 877 (2d Cir. 1985).
36. *Id.* at 880.
37. *See* Ingersoll Milling Machine Co. v. Granger, 833 F.2d 680, 690 (7th Cir. 1987).

§ 11.04 PROPER SERVICE AS PREREQUISITE TO ENFORCEMENT OF UNITED STATES DECREES

United States courts have cautioned that their decrees may not be recognized or enforced by foreign courts if defendants have not been properly served under that country's notion of judicial sovereignty. In *Volkswagenwerk Aktiengelsellschaft v. Schlunk*,[38] which involved the issue of the exclusivity of the Hague Service Convention, the Federal Republic of Germany informed the Supreme Court in an *amicus* brief

(*Text continued on page 11-11*)

38. 486 U.S. 694 (1988).

that, because the Hague Service Convention was regarded as the exclusive means of service on defendants residing in Germany, German courts would not recognize and enforce judgments obtained in violation of the Convention. The United States, in its *amicus* brief, similarly noted that respondent's failure to follow the service methods of the Convention would adversely affect the enforcement of any judgment in Germany. In *Schlunk* the Supreme Court noted the importance of following the method of service recognized as valid under foreign law in terms of facilitating the subsequent enforcement of any judgment in that country.[39]

Service by mail on defendants residing in Japan may also be an obstacle to subsequent recognition and enforcement of the foreign judgment in that country. United States courts have divided on the issue of whether service by mail pursuant to the Hague Service Convention is valid in Japan.[40] Article 10(a) of the Convention governs service via postal channels, and Japan has not formally objected to Article 10(a). However, at a meeting of the Hague Conference on Private International Law Special Commission in 1989, concerning the operation of the Convention, Japan issued the following statement of position:

> Japan has not declared that it objects to the sending of judicial documents, by postal channels, directly to persons abroad. In this connection, Japan . . . has made it clear that no objection to the use of postal channels for sending judicial documents to persons in Japan does not necessarily imply that the sending by such a method is considered valid service in Japan; it merely indicates that Japan does not consider it as an infringement of its sovereign power.[41]

This statement is an acknowledgment that while service by mail is not a violation of Japanese sovereignty, any subsequent enforcement of a foreign judgment may be unenforceable for improper service. Article 200 of the Japanese Code of Civil Procedure imposes the condition of adequate service of process on Japanese defendants and is based on the requirement of justice, fairness, and due process.[42] It is likely that a

39. *Id.* at 700.

40. *See supra* Chapter 4, § 4.04[3] (discussing service by mail to Japan).

41. Hague Conference on Private Int'l Law: Special Commission Report on the Operation of the Hague Service Convention and the Hague Evidence Convention, Apr. 1989, 28 I.L.M. 1556, reprinted *infra* in Appendix 4.

42. *See* Sawaki, *Recognition and Enforcement of Foreign Judgments in Japan*, 23 INT'L LAW. 29, 33–34 (1989).

Japanese court would refuse to enforce a foreign judgment where service of process on the Japanese defendant was by mail.

It is important to advise potential parties-plaintiff of the practical importance of strict compliance with service methods under foreign law even where domestic requirements may be less stringent. For example, in *Bankston v. Toyota Motor Corp.*[43] the plaintiff insisted on service by mail because of the translation costs to be incurred in serving under Hague Service Convention procedures. While foreign service methods may be onerous, the extra time and expense in complying with such procedures may make it easier to subsequently enforce any judgment in the foreign country. In advising potential defendants, it is necessary to point out the effect of service on recognition and enforcement of foreign judgments under the law of the country where the defendant resides so that the client is in a position to make wise choices in terms of appearing and defending the suit in the United States.

§ 11.05 ENFORCEMENT OF FOREIGN JUDGMENTS OBTAINED BY FRAUD

Courts will refuse to honor the foreign judgment if it was obtained through fraud. A distinction is drawn in this respect between extrinsic fraud and intrinsic fraud. Fraud is regarded as extrinsic where it prevents a party from presenting his case or defense, whereas intrinsic fraud occurs when the judgment is founded on a fraudulent instrument or perjured evidence.[44] Extrinsic fraud will always operate as a bar to the enforceability of a foreign judgment.[45] Intrinsic fraud, however, generally does not provide a basis for collateral attack.[46] It should be noted, however, that several jurisdictions have abolished any distinctions between extrinsic and intrinsic fraud.[47] In these jurisdictions, either type of fraud is grounds for a court to examine a previous

---

43. Bankston v. Toyota Motor Corp., 889 F.2d 172 (8th Cir. 1989).

44. *See* Mata v. American Life Ins. Co., 771 F. Supp. 1375, 1389 (D. Del. 1991); Alleghany Corp. v. Kirby, 218 F. Supp. 164, 183–84 (S.D.N.Y. 1963), *aff'd*, 333 F.2d 327 (2d Cir. 1964), *cert. dismissed,* 384 U.S. 28 (1966).

45. *Id.* See also Standard S.S. Owners' Protection & Indem. Ass'n v. C & G Marine Servs., Inc., No. Civ. A.92–0144, 1992 WL 111186, *3 (E.D. La. May 13, 1992).

46. *See* John Sanderson & Co. v. Jute, 569 F.2d 696, 697–98 (1st Cir. 1978).

47. Mata v. American Life Ins. Co., 771 F. Supp. 1375, 1389 (D. Del. 1991); Bandai America, Inc. v. Bally Midway Mfg. Co., 775 F.2d 70, 73 (3d Cir. 1985), *cert. denied,* 475 U.S. 1047 (1986).

judgment.[48] According to the Restatement of Foreign Relations Law, the definition of fraud for enforcement purposes is normally the definition applicable in the state where recognition is sought, even if the judgment could not be set aside on that ground in the rendering state.[49] In appropriate cases, the United States court should stay the enforcement action to permit the judgment debtor an opportunity to petition the rendering state to set the judgment aside.[50]

§ 11.06 RECIPROCITY IN EXTENDING COMITY

Proof of reciprocity is not essential for the granting of comity. However, as will be discussed later in this chapter, reciprocity may be a relevant consideration in evaluating whether recognition and enforcement are compatible with U.S. public policy.[51] In *Hilton v. Guyot*,[52] the Supreme Court extended a degree of recognition to the rule of reciprocity in the enforcement of foreign judgments in other countries. However, the rule has fallen into disfavor and is not considered to be a part of American jurisprudence.[53] In the view of many U.S. courts, the judgment creditor should not be blamed for the refusal of the state rendering a decision to give conclusive effect to U.S. judgments.[54]

While not a condition precedent to recognition and enforcement, the domestic forum may consider whether the foreign court would extend comity to a similar U.S. decree. In *Matter of Colorado Corp.*,[55] the court of appeals held that the U.S. bankruptcy court had abused its discretion in denying comity to certain foreign bankruptcy decrees. The court of appeals ruled that proof of reciprocity was not determinative and, in any event, no evidence had been introduced that the foreign bankruptcy court involved would deny comity in a similar context.[56] Similarly, in *Cunard Co. S.S. v. Salen Reefer Services AB*,[57] the court of appeals considered conflicting evidence submitted by the

48. *Id.*

49. Restatement (Third) Foreign Relations Law, § 482 (1987).

50. *Id.*

51. *See* § 11.07.

52. 159 U.S. 113, 125–27 (1895).

53. *See* Direction der Disconto-Gesellschaft v. U.S. Steel Corp., 300 F. 741, 747 (S.D.N.Y. 1924), *aff'd*, 267 U.S. 22 (1925); Restatement (Second) Conflict of Laws § 98 (1971).

54. *See* Restatement (Third) Foreign Relations Law § 481 reporters' notes.

55. 531 F.2d 463, 469 (10th Cir. 1976).

56. *Id.*

57. 773 F.2d 452 (2d Cir. 1985).

parties as to whether American bankruptcy proceedings would be recognized by a Swedish court. Viewing the Swedish system of justice as compatible with our notions of procedural due process and justice, the court of appeals impliedly assumed United States bankruptcy decrees would be accorded deference there.[58]

In *Mata v. American Life Ins. Co.*,[59] the district court ruled that, in order for a U.S. court to extend comity, a party need not demonstrate reciprocity on the part of foreign courts. The court observed that the reciprocity requirement prevented the enforcement of American judgments abroad by causing nations to believe that their judgments would not be enforced in the United States.[60]

The precise weight, if any, to be accorded reciprocity in the comity analysis is not clear. However, in considering U.S. public policy, courts may place particular emphasis on the reciprocity factor in the enforcement of certain decrees, such as those involving the revenue and penal laws of a foreign state. In *Her Majesty, Queen in Right, of the Provence of British Columbia v. Gilbertson*,[61] the court of appeals refused to enforce a judgment for taxes rendered by courts of a foreign state. Revenue and penal laws of a foreign state are generally unenforceable in United States courts "since no country has an obligation to further the governmental interests of a foreign sovereign."[62] Although the plaintiff in *Gilbertson* had urged the court of appeals not to follow reciprocity, it was deemed an important requirement within the context of the tax laws.[63] After reviewing similar state laws' requirements as to the enforcement of a sister state's tax laws, the court determined that reciprocity should have equal effect when enforcement of a foreign country's tax laws was sought in our courts.[64]

Finally, in *Tahan v. Hodgson*,[65] the court of appeals viewed the reciprocity doctrine as a political issue and relevant, if at all, only if required by local or national legislation.

58. *Id.* at 459.
59. 771 F. Supp. 1375, 1383 (D. Del. 1991).
60. *Id.*
61. 597 F.2d 1161 (9th Cir. 1979).
62. *Id.* at 1165.
63. *Id.* at 1165–66.
64. *Id.* at 1166.
65. 662 F.2d 862, 868 (D.C. Cir. 1981).

§ 11.07 THE PUBLIC POLICY EXCEPTION

Foreign judgments will not be enforced where violative of U.S. public policy. In the language of the Restatement (Second) of Conflict of Laws, the judgment must be "repugnant to fundamental notions of what is decent and just in the State where enforcement is sought."[66] As described by the court of appeals in *Ackermann v. Levine,* "[t]he standard is high, and infrequently met."[67]

United States courts have been reluctant to deny recognition to foreign judgments under the public policy exception because of a mere difference in procedure. Thus, in *Tahan v. Hodgson,*[68] the court of appeals determined that inconsistency between the foreign law procedure and the Federal Rules of Civil Procedure did not *ipso facto* result in a violation of U.S. public policy.[69]

The public policy exception will be applied if recognition of the foreign judgment would result in prejudice to United States citizens who refused to participate in the foreign proceeding. However, it must be clearly demonstrated that the party resisting enforcement would have been unjustly treated by the foreign court.[70] The party relying on the unfairness of the foreign proceeding bears the burden of proof and must introduce specific evidence as to why comity should be denied.[71]

The intricacies of the application of the public policy exception are shown in *Ackermann v. Levine.*[72] In that case, the dispute centered on the amount of attorney's fees charged by a foreign lawyer hired by a U.S. client to perform services in Germany. Defendant contested the foreign judgment awarding the fees as violative of U.S. public policy. The court of appeals held that a defendant who chose to default in a foreign action had not thereby waived the right to contest the enforceability of the foreign judgment on grounds of public policy.[73] The court of appeals rejected the defendant-appellant's contention that

66. Restatement (Second) Conflicts of Law § 117, cmt. c (1971). *See also* Restatement (Third) Foreign Relations Law § 482 (1987); Hilton v. Guyot, 159 U.S. 113, 164–67 (1895); Matusevitch v. Telnikoff, 877 F. Supp. 1, 2–5 (D.D.C. 1995); In re Hashim, 213 F.3d 1169 (9th Cir. 2000).

67. 788 F.2d 830, 841 (2d Cir. 1986).

68. 662 F.2d 862 (D.C. Cir. 1981).

69. *Id.* at 866. *See also* Somportex Ltd. v. Philadelphia Chewing Gum Corp., 453 F.2d 435, 443 (3d Cir. 1971).

70. *See* Cunard Steamship Co., Ltd. v. Salen Reefer Services, AB, 773 F.2d at 459–60.

71. *See In re* Colorado Corp., 531 F.2d 463, 459–60 (10th Cir. 1976).

72. 788 F.2d 830 (2d Cir. 1986).

73. *Id.* at 842.

public policy interests required the disclosure of fees by attorneys to their clients.[74] However, the portion of the foreign attorney's fee award which could not be supported by any evidence of work product was deemed to be violative of public policy.[75] It was held that a court should not be limited "to recognizing a judgment entirely or not at all."[76] Where a foreign judgment contained discrete components, the enforcing court should endeavor to discern the appropriate "extent of recognition."[77] The court of appeals was guided by the principle that:

> The increasing internationalization of commerce requires "that American courts recognize and respect the judgments entered by foreign courts to the greatest extent consistent with our own ideals of justice and fair play."[78]

In *Telnikoff v. Matusevitch,*[79] the Maryland Court of Appeals refused to enforce an English libel judgment on public policy grounds. The court noted material differences between United States and English libel law, including that under English defamation law, "it is unnecessary for the plaintiff to establish fault, either in the form of conscious wrongdoing or negligence. . . . Moreover, . . . defamatory statements are presumed to be false unless a defendant proves them to be true." The court concluded that inasmuch as English defamation was so contrary to Maryland defamation law and the policy of freedom of the press underlying Maryland law, that the English judgment should be denied recognition on principles of comity.[80]

As shown in *Her Majesty, Queen in Right of the Provence of British Columbia v. Gilbertson,*[81] United States courts, under the rubric of public policy, generally refuse to recognize or enforce governmental decrees rendered by a foreign court relating to penal or fiscal matters. This includes criminal fines, penalties and forfeitures. In the fiscal area, cases involving taxes or customs duties also would not be enforceable. United States courts also will not enforce foreign

74. *Id.* at 843.

75. *Id.* at 844.

76. *Id.*

77. *Id.*

78. *Id.* at 845.

79. 702 A.2d 230 (Md. 1997), *answer to certified question conformed to* Matusevitch v. Telnikoff, 159 F.3d 636 (D.C. Cir. 1998).

80. *Id.*

81. 597 F.2d 1161, 1166. *But see* Bullen v. Her Majesty's Government of the United Kingdom, 553 So.2d 1344 (Fla. Dist. Ct. App. 1989); Chase Manhattan Bank v. Hoffman, 665 F. Supp. 73 (D. Mass. 1987).

judgments on public policy grounds where the judgment creditor has violated U.S. laws or is a fugitive from justice.[82] Similarly, foreign courts are likely to refuse enforcement of U.S. court judgments falling within these same categories. In addition, foreign courts would no doubt closely scrutinize high damage awards rendered by United States courts, especially in tort and product liability suits. It is likely that foreign courts would refuse to recognize or enforce judgments for punitive damages where such awards are not recognized and are viewed as inconsistent with notions of public policy.[83]

§ 11.08 APPLICATION OF CHOICE OF LAW PRINCIPLES

Any action to enforce a foreign judgment may involve a myriad of choice of law issues as to each claim presented. Where jurisdiction is based solely on diversity, the law of the forum with respect to comity should be applied.[84] Where U.S. state policy and procedure recognize foreign judgments, state law will generally prevail "in the absence of interference with the federal regulatory scheme."[85]

Cases involving the enforcement of foreign arbitral awards and judgments confirming arbitral awards frequently present choice of law issues. In *Island Territory of Curacao v. Solitron Devices, Inc.*,[86] the court of appeals held that the New York Convention on the Recognition and Enforcement of Foreign Arbitral Awards,[87] preempted state law only with respect to the enforcement of a foreign arbitral award and was not intended to prevent states from enforcing foreign money judgments whether they pertain to the enforcement of arbitral awards or otherwise. As to the foreign money judgment confirming the award, the court ruled that New York state law on the subject was not preempted because a comprehensive procedure for the enforcement of foreign money

---

82. *See* Jaffe v. Snow, 610 So.2d 482 (Fla. Dist. Ct. App. 1992), *reh'g denied*, 621 So.2d 432 (Fla. 1993), *cert. denied*, 114 S. Ct. 2724 (1994).

83. *See Recognition and Enforcement in Switzerland of U.S. Judgments Containing an Award of Punitive Damages*, INT'L BUS. LAW. (June 1994).

84. *See* Banque Libanaise Pour le Commerce v. Khreich, 915 F.2d 1000, 1003 (5th Cir. 1990); Somportex Limited v. Philadelphia Chewing Gum Corp., 453 F.2d 435, 440 (3d Cir. 1971).

85. Island Territory of Curacao v. Solitron Devices, Inc., 489 F.2d 1313, 1319 (2d Cir. 1973), *cert. denied*, 416 U.S. 986 (1974).

86. 489 F.2d 1313, 1319 (2d Cir. 1973).

87. 9 U.S.C.A. § 201 (1992) [hereinafter New York Convention]. A copy of the New York Convention is reprinted *infra* in Appendix 17.

judgments had been established by the Uniform Foreign Money-Judgment Recognition Act.[88]

In *Victrix Steamship Co. S.A. v. Salem Dry Cargo A.B.*,[89] the court of appeals was faced with similar choice of law issues pertaining to the enforcement of a foreign arbitration award and enforcement of a foreign money judgment confirming the award. With respect to the claim for enforcement of the arbitration award which was founded on the New York Convention, the court of appeals determined that federal law applied.[90] It stated that the New York Convention was a treaty of the United States governing the enforcement of foreign arbitration awards and that United States obligations under the Convention would be undermined if not determined according to federal law.[91] Consequently, the court of appeals viewed the Convention as preempting state law as to the entire subject of the enforcement of arbitral awards.[92]

As in *Island Territory of Curacao,* the court of appeals in *Victrix* viewed the enforceability of foreign money judgments as governed by New York state law on the subject, i.e., the Recognition of Foreign Country Money Judgments law.[93] While the court of appeals did not necessarily view enforcement of the foreign maritime judgment also in issue in the case as governed by federal law and principles of comity, it did not determine which law applied because the application of federal and state law on the subject would have led to the same result.[94]

These cases illustrate that a choice of law analysis must be applied to each claim presented. As shown in *Victrix,*[95] courts will not displace state law unless there is a need for ''controlling federal rules'' or the federal law principles of comity set forth in *Hilton v. Guyot*[96] apply. In this connection, where state law establishes a procedure for enforcement of the foreign judgment, the state policy recognizing foreign judgments

---

88. *Id.* at 1323. *See* Uniform Foreign Money-Judgments Recognition Act, *supra* note 1.
89. 825 F.2d 709 (2d Cir. 1987).
90. *Id.* at 712–13.
91. *Id.* at 712.
92. *Id.*
93. *Id.* at 715; N.Y. Civ. Prac. L. & R. 5301 (McKinney 1978). *See also* Island Territory of Curacao v. Solitron Devices, Inc., *supra* note 85, at 1323; Pariente v. Scott Meredith Literary Agency, Inc., 771 F. Supp. 609, 615–16 (S.D.N.Y. 1991).
94. 825 F.2d at 713.
95. *Id.*
96. 159 U.S. 113 (1895). *See supra* § 11.02.

will prevail ''in the absence of interference with the federal regulatory scheme.''[97]

Counsel should also be careful to observe particular provisions of state law. In *Vagenas v. Continental Gin Co.*,[98] the court held that since Alabama law did not provide a specific limitations period for actions seeking enforcement of foreign nation money judgments, a two-year residual statute of limitations applied.[99]

§ 11.09 UNIFORM FOREIGN MONEY-JUDGMENTS RECOGNITION ACT

In 1962, the National Conference of Commissioners on Uniform State Laws adopted the Uniform Foreign Money-Judgments Recognition Act.[100] One of its primary purposes was to codify state rules on the recognition of money-judgments rendered in a foreign court to assist in the reciprocal recognition of a state's judgments abroad.[101] The Act codifies state rules that have been applied by many U.S. courts. It is based on general common law requirements followed in *Hilton v. Guyot*,[102] with minor variations in substantive standards and procedural elements.[103] ''The Act supplies a statutory basis for enforcing foreign judgments, a basis that was missing in *Hilton*, and represents and important progressive step in the recognition and enforcement in this country of money judgments of the courts of other nations.''[103.1] The Act does not prescribe a uniform enforcement procedure but provides that a judgment entitled to recognition will be enforceable in the same manner as the judgment of a court of a sister state which is entitled to full faith and credit.[104] States that have enacted the Uniform Act include: Alaska, California, Colorado, Connecticut, Georgia, Idaho, Illinois, Iowa, Maryland, Massachusetts, Michigan, Minnesota, Missouri, New

97. Island Territory of Curacao v. Solitron Devices, Inc., 489 F.2d 1313, 1319 (2d Cir. 1973).

98. 789 F. Supp. 1137 (M.D. Ala. 1992).

99. *Id.* at 1140.

100. 13 U.L.A. 261 (1986).

101. *Id.* at 261.

102. 159 U.S. 113 (1895).

103. *See* §§ 4–5 of the Uniform Foreign Money-Judgments Recognition Act.

103.1. Kam-Tech Systems, Ltd. v. Yardeni, 774 A.2d 644, 648 (N.J. Super. A.D. 2001) (citing this work).

104. 13 U.L.A. 261 (1986). *See* La Société Anonyme Goro v. Accessories, Inc., 677 N.E.2d 30 (Ill. App. Ct. 1997), applying same Illinois statute of limitations period applicable to enforcement of a sister-state judgment to enforcement of foreign judgments.

Mexico, New York, North Carolina, Ohio, Oklahoma, Oregon, Pennsylvania, Texas, Virgin Islands, Virginia, and Washington.[105]

The Uniform Foreign Money-Judgments Recognition Act, rather than the Uniform Enforcement of Foreign Judgments Act,[106] governs the enforcement of foreign country judgments because the latter applies only to foreign judgments of sister states.[107] For this reason, it has been held that a judgment of a foreign country cannot be registered under the Uniform Enforcement of Foreign Judgments Act by the mere filing of the foreign country judgment.[108] State requirements under both of these statutes should be studied to insure that the correct procedure is followed. However, the institution of a new suit will usually be required before a foreign country judgment is entitled to recognition and enforcement.[109]

Section 1 of the Uniform Foreign Money-Judgments Act defines "foreign judgment" as "any judgment of a foreign state granting or denying recovery of a sum of money, other than a judgment for taxes, a fine or other penalty, or a judgment for support in matrimonial or family matters." The Act applies to any foreign judgment that is final and conclusive and enforceable even though an appeal is pending.[110] A foreign judgment under Section 3 of the Act is conclusive between the parties to the extent that it grants or denies recovery of a sum of money. Sections 4 and 5 provide, respectively, for commonly recognized grounds for nonrecognition and personal jurisdiction.[111]

The case of *Ingersoll Milling Machine Co. v. Granger*,[112] illustrates the issues presented in the enforcement of a foreign judgment under a state statute implementing the Act. In that case an Illinois corporation

---

105. 13 U.L.A. 261 (1986 & West Supp. 1993).

106. 13 U.L.A. 150 (1986).

107. *See* Van Kooten Holding, B.V. v. Dumarco Corp., 670 F. Supp. 227, 229 (N.D. Ill. 1987); Matusevitch v. Telnikoff, 877 F. Supp. 1, 3 (D.D.C. 1995); Reading & Bates Construction Co. v. Baker Energy Resources Corporation, 976 S.W.2d 702, 712–714 (Tex. Ct. App. 1998).

108. *See* id., at 228; Hennessy v. Marshall, 682 S.W.2d 340, 345 (Tex. Ct. App. 1984).

109. *See* Allstate Insurance Co. v. Administratia Asigurarilor de Stat, 962 F. Supp. 420 (S.D.N.Y. 1997). *See In Re* Letter Rogatory, 2002 WL 257822 (E.D.N.Y.).

110. Uniform Foreign Money-Judgments Act § 2.

111. *See* Ronald A. Brand, *Enforcement of Foreign Money-Judgments in the United States: In Search of Uniformity and International Acceptance*, 67 NOTRE DAME L. REV. 253, 267 (1991) (providing chart of grounds for non-recognition). *See* K & R Robinson Enterprises Ltd. v. Asian Export Material Supply Co., 178 F.R.D. 332 (D. Mass. 1998) (factual issues concerning personal jurisdiction precluded granting of summary judgment under UFCMJRA).

112. 833 F.2d 680 (7th Cir. 1987).

brought an action seeking a declaratory judgment that a former employee was not entitled to termination benefits and sought recovery of additional expenses advanced by the corporation. The former employee counterclaimed for enforcement of a Belgian judgment and dismissal of the corporation's claims. The corporation contended that the Belgian judgment was not entitled to recognition under the Uniform Act as adopted in Illinois.

The court of appeals determined that the Belgian judgment satisfied the basic requirements of the Act. First, the court found that the Belgian judgment was one which ''grants or denies recovery of a sum of money.''[113] Because the judgment was presented to the district court after the completion of all appellate review in Belgium, it therefore was ''final and conclusive and enforceable where rendered.''[114] Appellant conceded that the court had personal jurisdiction over it.[115] Nor was there a serious dispute concerning subject matter jurisdiction because the controversy centered on defendant's employment duties which had been performed in Belgium.

The court further rejected appellant's contention that ''the judgment was rendered under a system which does not provide impartial tribunals or procedures compatible with the requirements of due process of law.''[116] The court relied on the basic fairness of the foreign procedures noting that the Act did not require that the foreign and U.S. procedures be identical but only that the procedures be ''compatible with the requirements of due process of law.''[117] Finally, the court rejected various optional contentions raised by appellant as requiring denial of recognition of the foreign judgment. These included the point that the foreign cause of action was ''repugnant to the public policy of Illinois;'' that the proceeding in Belgium was ''contrary to an agreement between the parties under which the dispute in question was to be settled otherwise than by proceedings in that Court;'' and that the Belgian court was a seriously inconvenient forum for the trial of the action.[118]

---

113. *Id.* at 686. *See* Nicor Int'l Corp. v. El Paso Corp., 292 F. Supp. 2d 1357 (S.D. Fla. 2003) (foreign judgment did not award or deny a ''specific sum of money'' as required by the Uniform Act in force in Florida).

114. *Id.*

115. *Id.*

116. *Id.* at 687.

117. *Id.*

118. *Id.* at 688–89. *See also* Pariente v. Scott Meredith Literary Agency, Inc., 771 F. Supp. 609, 615–18 (S.D.N.Y. 1991); Bank of Nova Scotia v. Tschabold Equipment, Ltd., 51 Wash. App. 749, 759, 754 P.2d 1290, 1296 (1988); Reading & Bates Construction Co. v.

Similarly, in *Guinness PLC v. Ward*,[119] the Fourth Circuit enforced a *Mareva* injunction issued by a British court under the Act. The court of appeals held, *inter alia*, that the judgment debtor was estopped from raising a post-judgment settlement in the enforcement proceeding since he pursued the appeal in the British courts without informing the courts of the breach of the settlement.[120] The court of appeals further rejected appellant's contention that the *Mareva* injunction procedures were violative of the requirements of due process.[121]

Specific provisions of a state's Uniform Foreign Country Money-Judgments Recognition Act, however, may serve to bar enforcement of a foreign judgment. For instance, in *Banque Libanaise Pour le Commerce v. Khreich*,[122] the court refused to recognize an Abu Dhabi judgment upon finding that the reciprocity requirement of the Texas Act had not been met.[123] The court, however, placed the burden of proving noncompliance with the state Act on the party contesting enforcement of the judgment.[124]

Baker Energy Resources Corporation, 976 S.W.2d 702 (Tex. Ct. App. 1998) (issue as to appropriate measure of damages in a Canadian patent infringement suit does not impact the public policy of Texas); VF Jeanswear Ltd. v. Molina, 320 F. Supp. 2d 412 (M.D.N.C. 2004) (district court not required to recognize the foreign judgment pursuant to the North Carolina Foreign Money Judgments Recognition Act where proceedings in the foreign court were contrary to the binding agreement of the parties); Nicor Int'l Corp. v. El Paso Corp., 292 F. Supp. 2d 1357 (S.D. Fla. 2003) (foreign judgment contrary to the arbitration provision in an agreement between the parties).

119. 955 F.2d 875 (4th Cir. 1992).

120. *Id.* at 898.

121. *Id.* at 901.

122. 915 F.2d 1000 (5th Cir. 1990).

123. *Id.* at 1006. *See* TEX. CIV. PRAC. REM. CODE ANN. § 36.005(b)(7) (West 1993). *But see* Reading & Bates Construction Co. v. Baker Energy Resources Corporation, 976 S.W.2d 702 (Tex. Ct. App. 1998) (proof of lack of reciprocity under UFCMJRA concerning potential enforcement by Canadian court of Texas damage award in patent infringement suit not established).

124. *Id.* at 1005.

Chapter 12

USE OF THE COURTS IN SUPPORT OF INTERNATIONAL ARBITRATION

§ 12.01 INTRODUCTION AND OVERVIEW

With the increasing use of arbitration[1] and other forms of alternative dispute resolution[2] in international business, counsel must be familiar with litigation issues that relate to international arbitration. This chapter focuses on the use of United States courts in support of international arbitration and attempts to assist counsel in identifying and planning strategic issues in international dispute resolution.

This chapter begins with a brief introduction to arbitration planning issues. By focusing on one of the most important questions facing any lawyer with an international dispute—is the result enforceable?—this section identifies some of the strategic planning issues to be considered in arbitration, should the courts ever become involved.

Next, this chapter will address the circumstances in which courts most often become involved in international arbitration: enforcement of an agreement to arbitrate. When parties include an arbitration clause in an international commercial agreement, questions may arise as to the scope or enforceability of the clause. Courts are often called upon to enforce or invalidate such clauses.

While less common, participants in international arbitration have also sought some form of provisional remedy in aid of the arbitration process. They may seek judicial assistance to preserve evidence, to maintain the status quo, or to make use of the court's power of injunctive relief.

With increasing frequency, parties to international arbitration seek the assistance of U.S. courts to gather evidence in the United States for use in the arbitration proceeding. Recent cases indicate a developing set of rules.

This chapter also addresses the use of the courts to enforce an award issued in an arbitration proceeding. What factors the courts take into account in evaluating arbitral awards and the operation of the New York Convention[2.1] are key issues for any party handling questions related to enforcement of awards.

1. "Arbitration" has been defined as "submission of controversies, by agreement of the parties thereto, to persons chosen by themselves for determination. . . ." 6 C.J.S. Arbitration § 1 (1975).

2. Common forms of alternative dispute resolution include conciliation, mediation, and fact-finding.

2.1. *See infra* note 5.

The final section of the chapter provides a review of issues and offers practical suggestions for counsel dealing with the courts in support of international arbitration.

§ 12.02 SELECTED INTERNATIONAL ARBITRATION PLANNING ISSUES

[1] Introduction

A full consideration of arbitration planning issues is well beyond the scope of this chapter. There are, however, a number of critical issues that counsel advising international business clients should be aware of and consider. Alternative dispute resolution (ADR) is growing in popularity, for many of the reasons addressed elsewhere in this book such as the expense, complexity, and unpredictability of international litigation in the United States and other nations. Although this chapter focuses on arbitration, counsel should not limit their imagination and creativity to this form of ADR in developing solutions to a particular problem. Arbitration can be a formal, lengthy, and costly process. When working with companies seeking arbitration that will continue to do business together, prepare them for the possibility that the relationship may not be the same after arbitration. If, however, binding resolution is sought, then arbitration may be the best solution among a number of alternatives including mediation, conciliation, or litigation. Be sure to also consider other, less formal mechanisms. Use of the so-called wise person approach may be useful in some cases.

[2] Arbitration Versus Litigation

Is arbitration always preferable to litigation? The question suggests its own answer. No, not in all cases. There are a variety of factors to consider. Because of the differences between common law and civil law legal systems, arbitration has become an attractive alternative to litigation and an increasingly effective way of resolving international legal controversies. When negotiating international contracts, parties should consider whether the inclusion of an arbitration clause will provide an effective mechanism for resolving potential disputes. In the absence of an arbitration clause, arbitration may also be used by the parties after the dispute has arisen. An appreciation of the advantages and disadvantages of arbitration versus litigation will assist in choosing the best means of settling the dispute.

Three threshold issues include (1) costs; (2) timing; and (3) whether the arbitration agreement and any award would be enforceable in a given jurisdiction. Arbitration may be more expensive than litigation since the expenses, including the fees of the arbitrators are borne by the parties.[3] The parties may also be required to pay fees regarding the arbitral tribunal itself, if a tribunal is selected. For instance, the American Arbitration Association (''AAA'') International Arbitration Rules presently provide for a $2,000 minimum filing fee for three-member arbitral panels and a $7,000 filing fee for controversies in the $1 million to $5 million range.[4] The International Chamber of Commerce, Paris (''ICC'') Administrative fee schedule for disputes of over $1 million to $2 million is 0.60 percent of the amount in dispute. Further, the ICC arbitrator's fees are between 0.5 percent and 2.5 percent for disputes of $1 million to $2 million.[4.1] Other potential costs of arbitration include travel to and from the selected forum site and retention of counsel in such jurisdiction.

Practice Note: Contract and compromise clause drafters beware, the rules of the AAA, ICC and other arbitral bodies state that electing their rules requires them to ADMINISTER the arbitration. Administration fees are expensive and are requested in advance.

Further, unless the arbitration agreement provides otherwise, arbitration, unlike litigation in national courts, usually affords no predetermined timelines for dispute resolution. Arbitration, therefore, has the potential to be either quicker or longer than dispute resolution in national courts. Of course, arbitrating parties can shorten or lengthen such process by agreement at any time.

Moreover, whether an award rendered in a particular forum would be enforceable against the parties must be carefully considered. It would be undesirable for a party to undertake the effort and expense of arbitration and then realize that the award obtained is unenforceable against another party in that party's home jurisdiction.

As discussed below, international conventions exist which generally provide for widespread national enforcement of arbitral awards. How-

---

3. *See* Steven C. Nelson, *Alternatives to Litigation of International Disputes,* 23 INT'L LAW. 187, 203 (1989).

4. The International Arbitration Rules, fee schedules, and information concerning arbitration may be located at the AAA website, http://www.adr.org.

4.1. The ICC Rules, fee schedules, and other information on arbitration are available at the ICC website, http://www.iccwbo.org.

ever, national requirements for enforcement of awards must be investigated. The United States, for instance, requires that for enforcement of an agreement to arbitrate or of an award under the New York Convention, the corresponding jurisdiction must be a Convention member and enforce U.S. awards reciprocally.[5] Many, but not all, nations are parties to the New York Convention.[6]

The Supreme Court has repeatedly affirmed the strong United States policy favoring enforcement of arbitration provisions.[7] In *Mitsubishi Motors Corp. v. Soler Chrysler-Plymouth, Inc.*, the parties had entered into a sales agreement for car distribution outside of the United States. The sales agreement contained an arbitration clause providing for arbitration by the Japan Commercial Arbitration Association of all disputes arising out of certain articles of the agreement. Petitioner brought an action in court under the Federal Arbitration Act[8] and the Convention on the Recognition and Enforcement of Foreign Arbitral Awards[9] (the "New York Convention") seeking an order to compel arbitration.

Respondent counterclaimed by raising counts under the Sherman Act and other statutes. The Supreme Court held that the Federal Arbitration Act manifested enforcement of such agreements and noted the "liberal federal policy favoring arbitration agreements."[10] The Court determined there was no reason to depart from this presumption where the party bound by the arbitration agreement raised claims founded on statutory rights. The Supreme Court found that, through the treaty mechanism of the New York Convention and implementing legislation in the Federal Arbitration Act, the federal policy favoring

5. The United Nations Convention on the Recognition and Enforcement of Foreign Arbitral Awards, *done* June 10, 1958, 7 I.L.M. 1046 (implemented at 9 U.S.C. §§ 201–208), entered into force for the U.S. Dec. 29, 1970 [hereinafter New York Convention], 21 U.S.T. 2517, T.I.A.S. No. 6997, 330 U.N.T.S. 3. "The United States of America will apply the Convention, on the basis of reciprocity, to the recognition and enforcement of only those awards made in the territory of another Contracting State." U.S. Reservations, 9 U.S.C.A. § 201.

6. A list of signatory nations may be found in the Treaties Chart, *infra*, and following 9 U.S.C.A. § 201.

7. *See* Mitsubishi Motors Corp. v. Soler Chrysler-Plymouth, Inc., 473 U.S. 614 (1985); Scherk v. Alberto-Culver, 417 U.S. 506 (1975).

8. 9 U.S.C. § 1.

9. *See supra* note 5. The text of the New York Convention may be found in 9 U.S.C.A. § 201, at 511–514 (West 1999) and is reprinted *infra* Appendix 17.

10. 473 U.S. at 625.

arbitration in dispute resolution applied with special force in the field of international commerce.[11]

Suits to compel parties to submit to arbitration and for the enforcement of arbitral awards have been simplified through adherence to the New York Convention. The Convention has gained wide acceptance.[12] Under the New York Convention, national courts are required to refer the parties to arbitration except where the agreement is null and void. Moreover, the United Nations Committee on International Trade Law (UNCITRAL) and the International Chamber of Commerce (ICC) have developed rules of arbitration that are widely accepted in resolving different types of international commercial disputes.[13] It has been observed that the institutionalized framework for dispute resolution by arbitration is more developed than the international judicial process.[14]

Several international arbitration conventions have gained widespread acceptance. These include, without limitation, United Nations Convention on the Recognition and Enforcement of Foreign Arbitral Awards ("New York Convention");[14.1] European Convention on International Commercial Arbitration;[14.2] Agreement Relating to the Application of the European Convention on International Commercial Arbitration;[14.3] Convention on the Settlement of Investment Disputes Between States and Nationals of Other States Establishing the International Centre for the Settlement of Investment Disputes ("ICSID");[14.4] Inter-American Convention on International Commercial Arbitration;[14.5] and North American Free Trade Agreement.[14.6]

Because of the widespread recognition and acceptance of the UNCITRAL rules, parties are encouraged to bring disputes before the selected forum without fear that the courts will refuse to exercise

---

11. 473 U.S. at 631.

12. The signatories to the New York Convention are listed *infra* in the Treaties Chart, and following 9 U.S.C.A. § 201.

13. *See* Steven C. Nelson, *Alternatives to Litigation of International Disputes,* 23 INT'L LAW. 187, 194 (1989).

14. *Id.* at 194.

14.1. *See supra* note 5.

14.2. Apr. 21, 1961, 484 U.N.T.S. 364.

14.3. Dec. 17, 1962, 523 U.N.T.S. 94.

14.4. 1965, 17 U.S.T. 1270, 575 U.N.T.S. 159.

14.5. *Done* Jan. 30, 1975, 104 Stat. 449, 42 O.A.S.T.S. 1, *reprinted in* 14 I.L.M. 336, *implemented for the U.S. in* 9 U.S.C.A. §§ 301–307.

14.6. Dec. 17, 1992, entered into force Jan. 1, 1994, *reprinted in* 32 I.L.M. 289, 605 (1993) (signatories: Canada, Mexico, United States).

jurisdiction. The ability to select an available forum for recognition and enforcement of the arbitral award prevents multiple proceedings and discourages forum shopping. There is now greater likelihood of the enforceability of arbitral awards than foreign judicial judgments. The international law relating to the enforcement of judgments has not correspondingly expanded due to jurisdictional objections and notions of comity which are inconsistently applied by foreign courts.[15]

Parties seeking to resolve international disputes should compare procedural and evidentiary requirements and inherent distinctions between arbitration and litigation. The American legal system is notorious for extended pre-trial discovery, technical rules of evidence, and dilatory tactics of attorneys. Foreign companies doing business in the United States are often surprised and confused at the dissimilarities between litigation procedures in United States courts and those under the civil law system. Arbitration procedures tend to be more flexible than traditional litigation, and parties may develop a structure that is simpler and conforms more closely to their needs.[16] In addition, parties may select arbitrators who possess the requisite technical and legal expertise to deal with the specific issues involved; disputes in litigation may be assigned to judges who are inexperienced in dealing with technical or international law issues. Issues that affect foreign relations interests or extraterritorial concerns may be complex and detract from the speedy resolution of a commercial controversy.

Nevertheless, arbitration may lack many of the procedural and other safeguards inherent in the U.S. litigation system. An arbitral award is final, and unlike in litigation, there is no right to appellate review of the merits. Also, it may be an advantage for a party to rely on the full range of discovery procedures available in U.S. courts, including the right to compel production of documents and to depose recalcitrant witnesses. The nature and scope of evidence the arbitral tribunal may hear should also factor into a parties' decision to arbitrate. Arbitrators generally have wide discretion concerning the conduct of proceedings and admission of evidence.[16.1] The U.S. litigation system is designed to allow each side to

---

15. *See* 45 Bus. Law. at 585–588.

16. *See* 23 Int'l Law., *supra* note 13, at 197–198.

16.1. "While statutory and Convention provisions, applicable rules of an administering organization, case law and the parties' agreement are helpful when an arbitrator must rule on issues of evidence exclusion, alas, the final determination generally resides within the arbitrator's discretion." Julie A. Klein, *Arbitration Law: Agreeing or Refusing to Hear Evidence*, N.Y.L.J., Feb. 2, 1998.

fully develop its case. In addition, arbitration may not be more efficient and expeditious in all cases. While parties to arbitration must submit to the whole process, a judicial trial may be short-circuited by disposition of the case on a motion to dismiss or summary judgment.

[3] NAFTA ADR Provisions

Alternative dispute resolution in general has received a big boost recently. For instance, parties to the North American Free Trade Agreement (NAFTA)[16.2] envisioned the need for resolution of three types of disputes: (1) private commercial disputes between private parties; (2) investor-state disputes; and (3) trade disputes between governments. Of primary interest here is the first type, which is contained in article 2022, entitled Alternative Dispute Resolution. Article 2022 has four parts:

(1) Each Party shall, to the maximum extent possible, encourage and facilitate the use of arbitration and other means of alternative dispute resolution for the settlement of international commercial disputes between private parties in the free trade area.

(2) To this end, each Party shall provide for appropriate procedures to ensure observance of agreements to arbitrate and for the recognition and enforcement of arbitral awards in such disputes.

(3) A Party shall be deemed to be in compliance with paragraph 2 if it is a party and is in compliance with the New York Convention or the Inter-American Convention.

(4) The Commission shall establish an Advisory Committee on Private Commercial Disputes comprising persons with expertise or experience in the resolution of private international commercial disputes. The Committee shall report and provide

16.2. Dec. 17, 1992, entered into force Jan. 1, 1994, *reprinted in* 32 I.L.M. 289, 605 (1993) (signatories: Canada, Mexico, United States) (Chapter 11: Investment Dispute Provisions). NAFTA references a previously less-used multilateral arbitration treaty known as ICSID. Convention on the Settlement of Investment Disputes Between States and Nationals of Other States Establishing the International Centre for the Settlement of Investment Disputes, 1965, 17 U.S.T. 1270, 575 U.N.T.S. 159. NAFTA expressly provides that any investment dispute between a NAFTA state and a citizen of another NAFTA state may be brought before an ICSID tribunal, even absent an arbitration agreement among the parties to such dispute.

> recommendations to the Commission respecting the availability, use and effectiveness of arbitration and other procedures for the resolution of such disputes in the free trade area.

NAFTA, therefore, facilitates and expressly institutionalizes a policy favoring ADR. The effectiveness of the NAFTA provisions in encouraging the use of ADR to resolve commercial disputes remains to be seen.

[4] Selected Arbitration Clause Recommendations

If arbitration is chosen after weighing its relative merits over litigation, prudent counsel will take steps to include an effective and complete arbitration clause in the commercial documentation. Model clauses are available from many sources,[17] but should only be the starting point. The strategic development of an arbitration clause will take into account many factors, and will be based on a thorough understanding of the transaction and the parties' relationship. In many ways, the negotiation of an arbitration clause implicates the full range of issues that should be addressed between the parties. For instance, parties should consider the location of the arbitration, the language it will be conducted in, what leverage various alternatives would provide, and the convenience to the parties. A deficient arbitration clause can be expensive. Quarreling over whether a particular dispute is subject to arbitration, especially when the quarrel takes place in court, can escalate the costs of a dispute rapidly.

Practice Note: It is NOT necessarily essential to the conduct of a successful arbitration that either a set of institutional rules be selected or that a tribunal administer the proceedings. Parties should avoid the common practice of selecting institutional rules or naming international tribunals in arbitral clauses, e.g., "arbitration to be conducted pursuant to ICC Rules (or by the ICC, Paris)," without considering the many significant implications of such choice. Where, however, a dispute may involve complex matters, multiple parties or high value claims, administration by an established tribunal may be preferable.

Institutional rules should be selected only after a careful reading of the CURRENT version of the Rules. Considerations may include what law is to be applied? Who has the burden of proof? What are the discovery

17. *See* Gary B. Born, International Commercial Arbitration in the United States (1994).

or award procedures? Do provisions exist for interim measures, such as injunctions, orders for attaching property or orders for posting security? What are the timelines?

Practical considerations also exist. Where is the institution located? Where will the arbitration be conducted? Who are its arbitrators? What are the administrative fees and costs?

Consider from the outset how the clause will look to the courts that may be called upon to enforce the agreement. In the words of one commentator, a clause

> must speak to four very different sorts of persons. It must speak first to the parties who are negotiating the contract the clause will govern, then to the arbitrators who will resolve disputes under the authority of that clause. While an arbitration is taking place, it must speak to the judges of courts that might interfere with those arbitrators; and finally, when the arbitrators render their award, the clause must speak to the judges of the courts that will enforce it.[18]

Keep in mind that courts become involved in a variety of ways in arbitration—most commonly by: (1) addressing issues of arbitrability (what is the proper subject of the arbitration); (2) dealing with interim remedies and discovery-related issues; and (3) enforcing any resulting award. To anticipate these issues, counsel may consider some or all of the following non-exhaustive list of topics:

(1) Know who the parties are, where they and their assets are located, who the principals are of business entity and organization parties, and identify all such parties clearly and by their full and exact names in the applicable contract or arbitration agreement.

(2) Specify whether arbitration clause shall apply to subsidiaries, parent entities, affiliates or third-parties.

(3) Avoid ''boilerplate'' style and vague clauses; they may create more trouble than they solve.[19]

---

18. Murphy, *The Four Languages of Charles V, Resolving Commercial Disputes Without Trial*, Houston, Mar. 1992, *reprinted in* INT'L Q.

19. *Courts Stress Importance of Clear [Arbitration] Clauses*, NAT'L L.J., Monday, Sept. 22, 1997, at B23 (observing courts' concerns of mutuality and unconscionability in enforcing arbitration agreements); Stirlen v. Supercuts, Inc., 51 Cal. App. 4th 1519, 60 Cal. Rptr. 2d 138 (Ct. App. 1 Dist. 1997) (ruling arbitration clause unconscionable where it had no valid

(4) Consider, to save costs, providing for arbitration before one neutral, experienced arbitrator, perhaps selected randomly from a list maintained by a legal U.S. court or other reputable dispute resolution organization.

(5) Do not use imprecise names or identify obsolete institutions.

(6) Address the scope of what is subject to arbitration: what disputes and issues will or will not be arbitrable?

(7) If relevant, address the language of the arbitration.[19.1]

(8) Address the location of the arbitration.

(9) Specify the institution, if an institution is desired.[19.2] Select institutions with established track records, such as the American Arbitration Association, the International Chamber of Commerce, or the London Court of International Arbitration. Avoid selecting organizations located in a parties' home country or whose arbitrators must be chosen from a list of local persons in such country.[20]

(9.1) Consider NOT selecting an arbitral institution in order to avoid expensive administrative and arbitrator fees and delays that may result from institutional arbitration.[20.1] Where, however, a

---

commercial justification, afforded Supercuts greater remedies than would be available, and deprived Mr. Stirlen of substantial rights and remedies).

19.1. Choice of language may be highly important, not just for the strategic necessity of understanding the proceedings but because translation costs in a complex proceeding may be enormous. Charles R. Ragan, ''Arbitration in Japan: Caveat Drafter and Other Lessons from an American Perspective on Trans-Pacific Dispute Resolution,'' *Private Investments Abroad*, at 12–20 (Matthew Bender & Co., Inc. 1996) (revealing translation costs of about $100,000 in single Japanese commercial arbitration).

19.2. An interesting comparison is that between the International Rules of the AAA and of the ICC. The AAA International Rules are more ''Americanized,'' in that they require each party to prove its relied upon facts. AAA International Rules, Art. 19(1). The ICC Rules require the tribunal to ''establish the facts.'' ICC Rules, Art. 20(1). The rules of certain arbitral institutions may be accessed from the AAA website, www.adr.org, and from the ICC website, www.iccwbo.org.

20. For instance, the Japan Commercial Arbitration Association is known for strict application of rules and procedures which may appear complex and inefficient to western legal practitioners, for rules resulting in the appointment of Japanese arbitrators, and for lengthy proceedings. Ragan, *supra* note 19.1, at 12–1.

20.1. A sample clause may read: ''While the ______ Rules (name particular institutional arbitration rules with specificity) may generally be applied to the conduct of the proceedings, the tribunal shall not administer the proceeding, which shall be conducted as a private dispute resolution among the parties.''

dispute may involve complex issues or multiple parties, it may be prudent to provide for formal administration by an established tribunal.

(10) Specify the applicable rules with precision. Established tribunals such as the AAA and ICC have specialized sets of arbitration rules for different disputes: international, maritime, commercial, employment, etc. Simply naming "the AAA (or ICC) Rules" may be insufficient. Go online (see note 19.2, above) and compare the Rules; select the Rules best suited to the transaction or dispute at issue. Make an affirmative selection of the rules to be applied to avoid the application of rules by default as provided under certain international agreements and institutional rules.[20.2]

(11) Specify the applicable law for each purpose (merits of the claim, the agreement itself,[20.3] provisional measures, the conduct of the proceedings).

(12) Define the qualifications and number of arbitrators; consider their nationality, expertise, potential conflicts, and biases.

(12.1)If more than one arbitrator is required, shall the other arbitrators be neutral or party-appointed non-neutrals? Clauses should be carefully scrutinized which permit each of two parties to appoint a non-neutral who then select a third arbitrator.[20.4]

(13) Address the issue of confidentiality of the proceedings, of records, of evidence, and other related issues.

20.2 *See, e.g.*, Inter-American Convention, Art. 3 (applying rules of procedure of Inter-American Commercial Arbitration Commission in absence of contrary express agreement of parties); Japan-American Trade Arbitration Agreement of Sept. 16, 1952 (requiring that rules of Japan Commercial Arbitration Assoc. apply to any arbitration conducted in Japan pursuant to such Agreement); American Arbitration Association (AAA) International Rules, Art. 1 (applying AAA rules in absence of express agreement).

20.3. As a note of caution, in Pepsico v. Oficina Central de Asesoria, 945 F. Supp. 69 (S.D.N.Y. 1996), a confusing choice of law clause led a federal district court to stay proceedings to compel arbitration so that courts in Caracas could examine the validity of an arbitration clause under Venezuelan law.

20.4. Requiring all arbitrators to be neutral may minimize acrimony on the panel, such as may arise where a non-neutral arbitrator is too closely aligned to its appointing party. Arbitral rules and typical clauses provide little guidance concerning how closely a non-neutral may be aligned with its appointing party.

(14) Define the scope of discovery, the discovery timetable, and the powers of the tribunal and national courts to compel and manage the production of evidence.

(15) Address the scope and availability of provisional remedies before the tribunal and national courts.

(16) Consider defining the nature and scope of evidence which may be considered by the tribunal—Live testimony? Third-party witnesses? Written submissions only? Cross-examination of witnesses to be conducted by tribunal or parties? Other matters?

(17) If relevant, address the issue of multiple parties and their treatment in the arbitration and the consolidation of multiple actions.

(18) Consider, where relevant, whether every party to the arbitration agreement, including any which do not participate in the arbitration, shall be bound by the award.

(19) Address the issue of costs, interest and attorneys' fees.

(20) Determine the scope of damages awardable. May the tribunal award special, consequential or punitive damages?

(21) Consider including an explicit waiver of immunity from jurisdiction and attachment if one party is a sovereign.[20.5]

(22) Specify the currency of any award (and, if necessary, the rate of exchange).

(23) Where relevant, consider provisions for the availability of interest, the interest rate, and the term.

(24) Specify the form of the award, including (a) whether the reasoning of the arbitrators should be presented in writing; (b) the means of disclosing any award to the public (e.g., allowing acknowledgment of an award, specific rationale, or amount

---

20.5. Consider language providing for consent to personal and subject matter jurisdiction in any court where enforcement of an award may be sought, including the courts of the United States. *See* Creighton Ltd. v. Government of State of Qatar, 181 F.3d 118 (D.C. Cir. July 2, 1999, *reh'g en banc denied,* Sept. 7, 1999) (denying enforcement of award against sovereign party where party lacked sufficient minimum contacts to confer personal jurisdiction and party had not waived its objection to personal jurisdiction under Foreign Sovereign Immunities Act).

only to the extent necessary for enforcement or to establish certain claims and defenses); (c) whether the tribunal should enter a confidentiality order concerning the arbitration's existence or information presented in the arbitration; and (d) any agreement of the parties and the tribunal that a confidentiality order may be requested from a national court concerning all information related to the award and its confirmation or use in subsequent proceedings.

(25) Consider provisions to further the final and binding nature of the award. Appropriate language may include: "The award shall be final and binding on the Parties and neither Party shall seek recourse to the courts of any state to appeal the award. The expenses, including costs and reasonable attorneys' fees, incurred in enforcing the award shall be paid by the Party resisting the enforcement of the award. The award may be enforced by any court of competent jurisdiction."

[5] Protecting Confidential and Proprietary Information in International Arbitration

In structuring a compromisory clause or arbitration agreement or participating in an arbitration, parties who seek to protect confidential and proprietary information should be aware that, unlike in a court proceeding, a party to an arbitration may not obtain protective orders for such information which would automatically be enforced by a subsequent court or tribunal. This fact may become critical when a party seeks to prevent the disclosure, in a subsequent proceeding, of information produced in an international arbitration. The disclosure of information from a previous arbitration may have an extremely detrimental impact on a client's position in a current proceeding and, perhaps, the client's ability to compete in the marketplace. In fact, confidentiality in arbitration may be more important to a party than speed or cost considerations.[21]

Parties should also note that the rules of most international arbitral tribunals do not provide protection for confidential information, other than from disclosure by the arbitral tribunal itself. For instance, Article

21. Philip Rothman, *PSSST, Please Keep It Confidential,* 49 Disp. Resol. J. 69, 71 (1994).

34 of the American Arbitration Association International Arbitration Rules,[22] merely states that:

> Confidential information disclosed during the proceedings by the parties or by witnesses shall not be divulged by an arbitrator or by the administrator. Unless otherwise agreed by the parties, or required by applicable law, the members of the tribunal and the administrator shall keep confidential all matters relating to the arbitration or the award.[23]

Stated differently, information produced in an international arbitration would likely be discoverable in a subsequent litigation or proceeding, regardless of what privileges or doctrines may have applied to the information prior to the arbitration.[24]

Numerous means exist, however, for parties, through their own initiative, to protect confidential and proprietary information, while benefitting from the advantages that arbitration may offer over litigation in certain circumstances, advantages such as speed, informality, reduced likelihood of damage to ongoing business relationships, increased suitability to international problems, the infrequency of large punitive damage awards by arbitrators, and the availability of arbitrators who are experts in the subject matter of the dispute.[25] Agreements between the

---

22. (Apr. 1, 1997) [hereinafter AAA International Rules], available at www.adr.org. WL 495827 (A.A.A.).

23. This provision is substantively identical to that of the International Arbitration Rules of the Asia/Pacific Center for the Resolution of International Business Disputes (Nov. 1993), Art. 35 [hereinafter APC Rules]. In addition, Art. 21(4) of the APC rules provides that "[h]earings are private unless the parties agree otherwise or the law provides to the contrary."

24. United States v. Panhandle Eastern Corp., 118 F.R.D. 346, 350 (D. Del. 1988) (refusing to exclude documents from prior arbitration on grounds of confidentiality where parties and tribunal expressed no intent concerning confidentiality of documents); Esso Austl. Resources Ltd. v. Plowman, Case No. 95/014, High Court (Apr. 7, 1995) (ruling that no absolute duty of confidentiality is imposed upon arbitration participants under Australian law). British law, in contrast, may provide for confidentiality in the identical circumstances. *See* Insurance Co. v. Lloyd's Syndicate, Queen's Bench Division, Commercial Court (Mr. Justice Colman) (Oct. 27, 1994).

25. *See* Robert M. Smith, *Saving Ourselves From Being Lawyered to Death,* WASH. POST, Sept. 24, 1995 at C4 (describing potential advantages of arbitration over litigation); Tom Arnold, *et al., Patent Litigation 1990: Alternative Dispute Resolution,* 300 PLI/Pat 213 (1990) (same); Introduction, American Arbitration Association Patent Arbitration Rules (Aug. 1, 1989). Because of the New York Convention, *supra* note 5, codified in 9 U.S.C.A. §§ 201–208, arbitration awards are more easily enforced worldwide in national courts than are foreign court judgments. Also, it has been suggested that arbitration may be less formal than litigation and may require fewer attorneys and paralegals. Smith, *supra.* Arbitration, however, can involve the large-scale production of documents, with the attendant costs and legal concerns. One observer suggests that, in a complex case, an election for three arbitrators rather than one, for International Chamber of Commerce administration rather than ad hoc

parties and orders of arbitrators may be utilized to preserve confidentiality.[26]

Parties to an international arbitration, therefore, should provide for confidentiality through careful attention to the arbitration agreement and informed selection of the arbitral forum, institutional or ad hoc arbitration rules, and national law.[27] Additional proactive devices exist for parties to provide the needed level of confidentiality, such as confidentiality stipulations between the parties, seeking confidentiality orders from the tribunal,[28] the use of legend paper,[29] discovery

---

arbitration, and for a reasoned award, may cost an additional $100,000 and take an additional year. Tom Arnold, *Suggested Form of Contract to Arbitrate a Patent or Other Commercial Dispute, Annotated,* 2 TEX. INTELL. PROP. L.J. 205, 207 (1994). It is also observed, however, that a well-planned U.S. arbitration may allow a party in a complex patent infringement suit to obtain a judgment and permanent injunction within one year, whereas litigation in court would take over six years. *Id.* at 208.

26. *See generally* Charles S. Baldwin IV, *Protecting Confidential and Proprietary Commercial Information in International Arbitration,* 31 TEX. INT'L L.J. 451 (1996).

27. For instance, under British law, information produced in an arbitration would be protected from disclosure in subsequent proceedings, as an undertaking of confidentiality is implied in law. Hassneh Ins. Co. of Isr. v. Mew [1993], 2 Lloyd's Rep. 243, 247 (Q.B.); Insurance Co. v. Lloyd's Syndicate, Queen's Bench Division, Commercial Court (Mr. Justice Colman) (Oct. 27, 1994). Under United States and Australian law, however, documents produced in an arbitration would likely be discoverable in a subsequent proceeding, in the absence of a confidentiality agreement among the parties or confidentiality order by the original arbitral tribunal. *See* United States v. Panhandle Eastern Corp., 118 F.R.D. 346, 350 (D. Del. 1988); Esso Austl. Resources Ltd. v. Plowman [1994], 1 V.R. 1, 34 (Vict.). It may also be noted that where documents were not produced in an arbitration, the documents may retain applicable privileges and doctrines in subsequent actions. United States courts have held that "[s]ince arbitrations are adversarial in nature and can be fairly characterized as 'litigation' within the meaning of Rule 26(b)(3), documents prepared by or for a party in connection with arbitrations should ordinarily be protected by the work product doctrine." *see* Samuels v. Mitchell, 155 F.R.D. 195, 200 (N.D. Cal. 1994); International Ins. Co. v. Peabody Int'l Corp., 1988 U.S. Dist. LEXIS 5109, *14, 1988 WL 58611 (N.D. Ill. 1988).

28. The confidentiality stipulation or tribunal confidentiality order may provide explicit instructions concerning the treatment during and after the arbitration of either all information or specific information received. Stipulations or orders can be initiated by agreement of the parties or at the request of one party and direction of the arbitrator. As the stipulation is a contract between the parties, violation of the stipulation renders the violator liable for damages for breach of contract. *See* S & D Foods, Inc. v. Consolidated Pet Foods, Inc., 144 Bankr. Rptr. 121, 161 (D. Colo. 1992) (finding breach of confidentiality agreement protecting confidential or proprietary information). Additionally, the stipulation may be subject to an order for specific performance. *See* Klockner-Humboldt-Deutz Aktiengesellschaft v. Hewitt-Robins Div. of Litton Sys., 486 F. Supp. 283, 288 (D.S.C. 1978) (issuing preliminary injunction to ensure confidentiality of information covered by confidentiality agreement). Also, if a protective order is granted by the arbitrator, violation of the order may result in the preclusion of certain evidence or the assessment of fees against the violating party. *See* AAA Commercial rules, Art. 43. The decision to issue a protective order, however, is solely the arbitrator's.

agreements,[30] consolidation agreements,[31] joint defense and sharing agreements,[32] settlement agreement clauses, and final orders of arbitral tribunals.[33] Attention to these issues would allow parties to protect their confidential and proprietary information while benefitting from arbitration's usually touted advantages over litigation.

However, the issuance of protective orders ensuring confidentiality in discovery or covering the release of other information is becoming more frequent. *See* Rothman, *supra* note 21.

29. Legend paper is paper bearing a superimposed legend, such as the name of the proceeding and tribunal. Information copied onto legend paper is plainly visible. However, if a copy is made of a legend-paper page, the parts on the page beneath the legend appear blacked-out on the copy. The use of legend paper, therefore, discourages the unauthorized dissemination of information. Legend paper has been used extensively in U.S. tobacco litigation.

30. Discovery agreements, or discovery orders by the tribunal, may protect confidential information by setting forth the applicable rules, scope, and timetables for discovery.

31. As arbitration is private dispute resolution, strangers are normally excluded from the arbitration. *See* AAA Commercial Rules, Art. 25 (''arbitrator shall maintain the privacy of the hearings unless the law provides to the contrary''); Michael Collins, *Privacy and Confidentiality in Arbitration Proceedings,* 30 Tex. Int'l L.J. 121 (1995) (observing that ''[t]he right to privacy is recognized in English law as an implied right which attaches to all agreements to arbitrate as an incident of such contract''); Esso Austl. Resources Ltd. v. Plowman [1994], 1 V.R. 1, 1 (Australia) (observing that ''arbitrations should be heard in private in the sense of the absence of strangers''). However, the privacy of the proceedings and use of confidential information therein may be effected if separate arbitral proceedings involving additional parties are consolidated or identical testimony and evidence are introduced into separate proceedings. Consolidation agreements may be reached to address whether separate actions may be consolidated in arbitration and what evidence may be presented in overlapping proceedings.

32. Joint defense and sharing agreements are consensual agreements between parties to a proceeding to provide for the sharing of information to establish joint defenses necessary to the proceeding and not thereby waive applicable privileges and doctrines. *See* United States v. Moss, 9 F.3d 543 (6th Cir. 1993), *reh'g denied,* 1994 U.S. App. LEXIS 1612 (Jan. 28, 1994); Haines v. Liggett Group, Inc., 975 F.2d 81 (3d Cir.), *reh'g denied,* 1992 U.S. App. LEXIS 26004 (Oct. 8, 1992); *In re* Grand Jury Subpoenas 89–3 and 89–4, 902 F.2d 244 (4th Cir. 1990).

33. Arbitrating parties may want to provide in the arbitration agreement, settlement agreement, or final order that the arbitrators (or arbitral institution, if a need later arises) set forth means of disclosing any award to the public; e.g., allowing acknowledgment of an award, specific rationale, or amount only to the extent necessary for enforcement or to establish certain claims and defenses. The parties may, further, agree that a confidentiality order be requested from a national court concerning all information related to the award and its confirmation or use in subsequent proceedings. *See generally* Baldwin, *supra* note 26.

§ 12.03 ENFORCING AN AGREEMENT TO ARBITRATE

[1] Enforcing an Agreement to Arbitrate Under Federal Law

Many international commercial contracts include agreements to submit disputes to arbitration rather than to seek resolution in court. As a result of the United States Federal Arbitration Act (FAA),[34] the traditional judicial opposition to arbitration was erased. As a matter of policy, therefore, courts will encourage arbitration by giving effect to agreements to arbitrate.[35] By statute, a U.S. Court having jurisdiction over an arbitral dispute subject to the New York Convention may direct that arbitration be held and may appoint arbitrators, in accordance with the arbitral agreement.[36] There are a number of policy reasons supporting the enforcement of arbitration clauses. For instance, in *Scherk v. Alberto-Culver*,[37] the Supreme Court considered an agreement to arbitrate that read:

> Any controversy or claim [that] shall arise out of this agreement or the breach thereof would be referred to arbitration before the International Chamber of Commerce in Paris, France, and that the laws of the State of Illinois, U.S.A. shall apply and govern this agreement, its interpretation and performance.[38]

The court noted that an "agreement to arbitrate before a specified tribunal is, in effect, a specialized kind of forum selection clause that posits not only the situs of the suit but also the procedure to be used in resolving the dispute."[39] Articulating similar policy concerns as stated in *Bremen*,[40] the Court stated:

> A contractual provision specifying in advance the forum in which disputes shall be litigated and the law to be applied is, therefore, an

34. 9 U.S.C. § 1 *et seq.*

35. *See* Scherk v. Alberto-Culver Co., 417 U.S. 512, 510–11 (1974); Alamria Telcor Int'l, Inc., 920 F. Supp. 658, 663 (D. Md. 1996) (noting that "special solicitude for arbitration agreements involving international trade derives from 'concerns of international comity, respect for the capacities of foreign and transnational tribunals, and sensitivity to the need of the international commercial system for predictability in the resolution of disputes[,]' " *citing*, Mitsubishi Motors Corp. v. Soler Chrysler-Plymouth, *supra* note 7, 473 U.S. at 629, 105 S. Ct. at 3355).

36. 9 U.S.C.A. § 206. U.S. courts have similar powers concerning the Inter-American Convention on International Commercial Arbitration. 9 U.S.C.A. § 303.

37. 417 U.S. 506 (1975).

38. *Id.* at 509.

39. *Id.* at 519.

40. The *Bremen* decision is discussed *supra* in § 5.10[1].

> almost indispensable precondition to achievement of orderliness and predictability essential to any international business transaction. Furthermore, such a provision obviates the danger that a dispute under the agreement might be submitted to a forum hostile to the interests of one of the parties or unfamiliar with the problem area involved.
>
> A parochial refusal by the courts of one country to enforce an international arbitration agreement would not only frustrate these purposes, but would invite unseemly and mutually destructive jockeying by the parties to secure tactical litigation advantages.[41]

The Court's decision in *Scherk* illustrates the strong policy in favor of arbitration, especially in international transactions.

The Supreme Court recently extended this policy beyond traditional limitations in the case of *Mitsubishi Motors Corp. v. Soler Chrysler-Plymouth.*[42] At issue in *Mitsubishi* was a dispute between the manufacturer of automobiles in Japan and a distributor located in Puerto Rico. To prevent the distributor from transferring unsold vehicles to other markets under the terms of the distributorship agreement, Mitsubishi sought to compel arbitration under the arbitration clause in the agreement that provided:

> All disputes, controversies or differences which may arise between [Mitsubishi] and [Soler] out of or in relation to Articles I-B through V of this Agreement or for the breach thereof, shall be finally settled by arbitration in Japan in accordance with the rules and regulations of the Japan Commercial Arbitration Association.[43]

In response, Soler alleged various claims, including several statutory claims, such as antitrust claims under the Sherman Act. The district court held that despite precedent suggesting that the statutory claims were not arbitrable, the Supreme Court's decision in *Scherk* meant that the international character of the Mitsubishi-Soler dispute "required enforcement of the agreement to arbitrate even as to the antitrust claims."[44] The court of appeals affirmed, rejecting Soler's contention that any agreement to arbitrate the antitrust claims would have to explicitly so state.[45]

---

41. *Id.* at 516–17 (footnote omitted).

42. 473 U.S. 614 (1985).

43. *Id.* at 617.

44. *Id.* at 620–31. *Compare* Tai Ping Insurance Co. v. M/V Warschau, 731 F.2d 1141 (5th Cir. 1984) (discussing "non-arbitrable" nature of securities and antitrust claims).

45. 473 U.S. at 621–22.

The Supreme Court affirmed, holding that, in the international context, the policy reasons that would otherwise compel denial of an arbitration in a purely domestic context do not apply. The Court considered several arguments against permitting arbitration of statutory issues, and especially of antitrust issues. The four standard arguments were:

(1) private antitrust suits are an important tool of government policy enforcement;

(2) some contracts giving rise to antitrust disputes are contracts of adhesion;

(3) antitrust issues are too sophisticated and complex for arbitration; and

(4) antitrust regulation of business is too important to be left to arbitrators.[46]

The Court found each of these factors unpersuasive in the international context, but focused on the primary concern, the first factor: that the objectives of the antitrust laws will not be served if they are subject to arbitration. The Court explained:

> There is no reason to assume at the outset of the dispute that international arbitration will not provide an adequate mechanism. To be sure, the international arbitral tribunal owes no prior allegiance to the legal norms of particular states; hence, it has no direct obligation to vindicate their statutory dictates. The tribunal, however, is bound to effectuate the intentions of the parties. Where the parties have agreed that the arbitral body is to decide a defined set of claims which includes, as in these cases, those arising from the application of American antitrust law, the tribunal therefore should be bound to decide that dispute in accord with the national law giving rise to the claim. . . . And so long as the prospective litigant effectively may vindicate its statutory cause of action in the arbitral forum, the statute will continue to serve both its remedial and deterrent function.[47]

The *Mitsubishi* decision illustrates the courts' growing acceptance of the need for predictability in international commerce:

> As international trade has expanded in recent decades, so too has the use of international arbitration to resolve disputes arising in the course of that trade. The controversies that international arbitral institutions are called upon to resolve have increased in diversity as

46. *Id.* at 636.
47. *Id.* at 636–37 (citation omitted).

> well as in complexity. Yet the potential of these tribunals for efficient disposition of legal disagreements arising from commercial relations has not yet been tested. If they are to take the central place in the international legal order, national courts will need to "shake off the old judicial hostility to arbitration, . . ." and also their customary and understandable unwillingness to cede jurisdiction of a claim arising under domestic law to a foreign or international tribunal. To this extent, at least, it will be necessary for national courts to subordinate domestic notions of arbitrability to the international policy favoring commercial arbitration.[48]

The Supreme Court, construing the Federal Arbitration Act, therefore, has clearly evidenced a judicial preference that agreements to arbitrate are to be enforced.

Federal District and Circuit Courts have applied the Supreme Court's mandate that international arbitration agreements be enforced in various factual scenarios and have developed approaches, including for determining the scope of arbitral issues[49] and for determining when a non-signatory or parent corporation may be bound by an arbitration agreement.[50] Federal courts appear to construe arbitration provisions broadly in light of the strong policy favoring international arbitration.[51] For instance, in *J.J. Ryan and Sons, Inc. v. Rhone Poulenc Textile, S.A.*,[52] the Court observed such strong federal policy and instructed that "[t]o decide whether an arbitration agreement encompasses a dispute a court must determine whether the factual allegations underlying the claim are within the scope of the arbitration clause, regardless of the legal label assigned to the claim." The Court affirmed the district court's

48. *Id.* at 638–39, *citing* Kulukundis Shipping Co. v. Amtorg Trading Corp., 126 F.2d 978, 985 (2d Cir. 1942).

49. J.J. Ryan and Sons, Inc. v. Rhone Poulenc Textile, S.A., 863 F.2d 315, 319 (4th Cir. 1988).

50. Intergen, N.V. v. Grina, 2003 344 F.3d 134 (1st Cir. 2003) (finding agreement to arbitrate unenforceable as to third parties but containing thorough analysis of theories by which non-signatories may be bound to arbitration agreement); Alamria v. Telcor Int'l, Inc., 920 F. Supp. 658, 669 (D. Md. 1996); Thomson-CSF, S.A. v. American Arbitration Ass'n, 64 F.3d 773, 776 (2d Cir. 1995); Unisys Corp.v. Ceska Sporitelna A.S., 116 F.3d 467 (3d Cir. 1997), *cert. denied*, 522 U.S. 1069 (1998). In *Unisys Corp.*, the Third Circuit rejected the argument of Defendant Unisys that Plaintiff should be required to arbitrate its $155 million fraud claim, as the nature of Plaintiff's claims and an arbitration agreement entered among the Plaintiff Czech Bank and a Unisys subsidiary were allegedly "intertwined." The Court ruled that Unisys was not entitled to compel arbitration. In most cases on the issue, it is the Plaintiff seeking to enforce an arbitration agreement against a corporate parent or affiliate, rather than the reverse, as in *Unisys*.

51. *Alamria, supra* note 50, at 664.

52. *Supra* note 49, at 319.

referral of claims to arbitration, including unfair trade practices, intentional and tortious interference with contract, conversion, abuse of process, libel, defamation, and injurious falsehood and additionally ordered to arbitration a claim for civil conspiracy to destroy the importer's business and goodwill.[53]

[2] Enforcing an Agreement to Arbitrate Under State Arbitration Acts

In the United States, several states have adopted arbitration acts that may provide an independent ground to enforce an arbitration agreement. One example of such a statute is the North Carolina Uniform Arbitration Act.[54] The Uniform Act provides that "[o]n application of a party showing an [arbitration agreement], and the opposing party's refusal to arbitrate, the court shall order the parties to proceed with arbitration. . . ."[55]

Under these state statutes, the court's sole function, if a party should deny the existence of an arbitration agreement, is to "proceed summarily to the determination of the [arbitration] issue so raised and [a court] shall order arbitration if found for the moving party. . . ."[56] A trial court or tribunal, therefore, should not properly entertain discovery or other judicial process prior to a ruling on a motion to compel arbitration and stay the action.[57]

§ 12.04 U.S. COURT ENFORCEMENT OF PROVISIONAL MEASURES

It may be possible to obtain the assistance of United States or other national courts in securing provisional measures, either prior to or during an international arbitration.[58] A provisional measure may be defined as a

---

53. *Id.*

54. N.C.G.S. § 1–567.1 *et seq.*

55. N.C.G.S. § 1–567.3(a).

56. *Id.*

57. *See* Henderson v. Herman, 104 N.C. App. 482, 486, 409 S.E. 2d 739, *cert. denied,* 330 N.C. 851, 413 S.E. 2d 551 (1992).

58. In certain instances, arbitral tribunals have themselves ordered provisional remedies, though, as a practical matter, as it may take several months to impanel the tribunal, seeking provisional remedies from the arbitral tribunal would often be futile. *See generally* Sperry Int'l Trade, Inc. v. Government of Israel, 689 F.2d 301 (2d Cir. 1982) (enforcing arbitral tribunal-ordered provisional measures); Medika Int'l, Inc. v. Scanlan, Int'l, Inc., 830 F. Supp. 81, 88 (D.P.R. 1993) (holding that availability of injunctive relief provided by Puerto Rican law should be determined by arbitrator); Charles Constr. Co. v. Derderian, 586 N.E. 2d 992 (Mass.

temporary process available to a party in a civil action, which secures against loss, irreparable injury, dissipation of property or evidence, or other events, while the arbitration is in progress. Provisional measures or remedies typically include injunctions, sequestration orders, orders for posting security, attachment of funds or property, or the appointment of third parties to perform inspections or other tasks.

It should be noted, however, that the issues involved in obtaining provisional measures in aid of arbitration are often complex and are guided by considerations including (1) any applicable international arbitration convention; (2) applicable national law; (3) the parties' arbitration agreement;[59] and (4) the rules of the arbitral tribunal.[60]

In general, courts may be cautious about granting provisional measure requests in aid of arbitration, as the grant of such remedies, in the absence of their express provision in the pertinent arbitration rules or agreement of the parties, may violate the parties' choice of arbitration, as opposed to litigation, or national arbitration statutes. However, it has also been recognized that the inability of a party to obtain injunctive and other provisional relief may render an ultimate arbitration award ineffective.[61] U.S. courts are divided on their ability to grant provisional relief in aid of international arbitration.[62]

1992) (holding that American Arbitration Association rules did not provide for particular provisional measures ordered by arbitral tribunal but observing that "in the absence of an agreement or statute to the contrary, an arbitrator has inherent authority to order a party to provide security while the arbitration in continuing"). *See also* UNCITRAL Arbitration Rules, Art. 26 (providing authority of tribunal to take interim measures); London Court of International Arbitration (LCIA) Rules, Art. 13 (same); AAA International Rules, Art. 21 (same); ICC Rules, Art. 23 (same).

59. For suggested specific language providing for provisional measures in the arbitration agreement, *see* Baldwin, *supra* note 26.

60. *See generally* Gary B. Born, International Commercial Arbitration in the United States, Chapter 8, Provisional Measures in Arbitration (1994).

61. Rogers, Burgun, Shahine & Deschler, Inc. v. Dongsan Constr. Co., 598 F. Supp. 754 (S.D.N.Y. 1984). *See also* Alvenus Shipping Co., Ltd. v. Delta Petroleum (U.S.A.) Ltd., 876 F. Supp. 482, 487 (S.D.N.Y. 1994).

62. *See* Alvenus Shipping Co., Ltd. v. Delta Petroleum (U.S.A.) Ltd., *id.* at 487–88 (distinguishing earlier negative case law and finding federal and state legal grounds to support issuance of equitable relief in aid of London arbitration). *See contra* ContiChem LPG v. Parsons Shipping Co., Ltd., 229 F.3d 426 (2d Cir. 2000) (denying provisional remedy of attachment in support of international maritime arbitration pending in London); National Broadcasting Co., Inc. v. Bear Stearns & Co., Inc., 165 F.3d 184 (2d Cir. 1999) (holding that 28 U.S.C.A. § 1782 does not authorize federal courts to compel discovery in aid of private international commercial arbitration). Additional barriers parties may face to obtaining provisional relief in aid of arbitration are the high applicable legal standards. An illustrative case is Eastman Kodak Co. v. Cetus Corp., 1991 WL 255936 (Del. Ch.). In *Eastman Kodak*

[1] The Effect of the New York Convention and Other International Agreements on Obtaining Provisional Measures

Negative case law exists, and it is uncertain whether a U.S. court would order provisional measures in aid of arbitration under the New York Convention.[63] The Convention and its U.S. implementing legislation, 9 U.S.C. § 201–208 are silent concerning provisional relief. In Article II(3) the Convention states:

> The court of a Contracting State, when seized of an action in a matter in respect of which the parties have made an agreement within the meaning of this article, shall, at the request of one of the parties, refer the parties to arbitration, unless it finds that the said agreement is null and void, inoperative or incapable of being performed.

Whether granting provisional measures prior to arbitration would violate the requirement of Article II(3) that the matter be referred to arbitration is unclear. Some U.S. courts have held that the Article forbids granting provisional measures prior to arbitration.[64] Other U.S. courts and nearly all foreign courts have ruled that ordering provisional measures prior to arbitration is consistent with the New York Convention.[65] Also, where the New York Convention has been found

---

Co., Kodak sought injunctive relief before the Delaware Court of Chancery in aid of a California Arbitration. *Id.* at 2. Kodak sought to enjoin the sale of contested rights by the other arbitrating party to a third party. *Id.* The court found that Kodak would not be threatened by imminent irreparable harm as a result of the sale. *Id.* at 20–21. The court conditionally denied the injunctive relief sought, stating that the harm sought to be avoided may be addressed by the third party agreeing to be bound by the decision of the arbitrators. *Id.* at 21. A contrary result was reached in Alvenus Shipping Co., Ltd. v. Delta Petroleum (U.S.A.) Ltd. There, the Court observed the legal standards applicable for issuance of an injunction under Rule 65, FED. R. CIV. P., but ruled that irreparable harm may be shown even when the claim is for money damages where the money judgment will go unsatisfied absent equitable relief. *Id.* at 487.

63. The New York Convention is codified at 9 U.S.C. §§ 201–208. *See* Alvenus Shipping Co., Ltd. v. Delta Petroleum (U.S.A.) Ltd., *supra* note 61, at 487–88 (ordering preliminary injunction to aid monetary recovery concerning London arbitration).

64. *See* I.A.T.D. Assoc., Inc. v. Podar Bros., 636 F.2d 75 (4th Cir. 1981); McCreary Tire & Rubber Co. v. CEAT SpA., 501 F.2d 1032 (3d Cir. 1974); Cooper v. Ateliers de la Motobécane, S.A., 57 N.Y.2d 408, 456 N.Y.S.2d 728, 442 N.E.2d 1239 (N.Y. Ct. App. 1982); ContiChem LPG v. Parsons Shipping Co., Ltd., 229 F.3d 426, 433 (2d Cir. 2000) (finding that granting provisional remedies under state law would violate New York Convention).

65. *See* Alvenus Shipping Co., Ltd. v. Delta Petroleum (U.S.A.) Ltd., *supra* note 61, at 487; Carolina Power & Light Co. v. Uranex, 451 F. Supp. 1044 (N.D. Cal. 1977); Borden, Inc. v. Meiji Milk Prods. Co., 919 F.2d 822 (2d Cir. 1990), *cert. denied,* 500 U.S. 953 (1991); Castelan v. M/V Mercantil Parati, 1991 U.S. Dist. LEXIS 6472, *5–6 1991 WL 83129 (D.N.J. May 8, 1991); Filantro SpA. v. Chilewich Int'l Corp., 789 F. Supp. 1229 (S.D.N.Y. 1992), *appeal dismissed,* 984 F.2d 58 (2d Cir. 1993); Rhône Mediterranée v. Lauro, 555 F. Supp. 481

inapplicable, some courts have granted pre-arbitration provisional relief.[66]

If an arbitration involves a maritime claim,[66.1] U.S. federal courts may allow attachment and garnishment of goods, chattels, credits and effects of the Respondent which may be found within the district.[66.2]

[2] The Effect of National Law on Obtaining Provisional Measures

In general, national law defines whether and in what circumstances a court may grant provisional measures and what form of relief is proper. Both federal and state law may affect the availability of provisional measures in United States courts.

[a] Federal Law

The U.S. Federal Arbitration Act (FAA),[66.3] does not address a court's jurisdiction to award or enforce provisional measures in aid of

(D.V.I. 1982); Atlas Chartering Services, Inc. v. World Trade Group, Inc., 453 F. Supp. 861 (S.D.N.Y. 1978) (finding no conflict between provisional remedy of attachment and dictates of New York Convention).

66. Intermar Overseas, Inc. v. Argocean S.A., 503 N.Y.S.2d 736 (App. Div. 1986); MCT Shipping Corp. v. Sabet, 497 F. Supp. 1078 (S.D.N.Y. 1980).

66.1. 9 U.S.C.A. § 1 defines "maritime transactions" as "charter parties, bills of lading of water carriers, agreements relating to wharfage, supplies furnished vessels or repairs to vessels, collisions, or any other matters in foreign commerce which, if the subject of controversy, would be embraced within admiralty jurisdiction."

66.2. Result Shipping Co. v. Ferruzzi Trading USA, Inc., 56 F.3d 394, 1995 A.M.C. 2446 (2d Cir. 1995) (Court has discretion to award security and countersecurity in maritime case, notwithstanding arbitrability of dispute); Unitramp, Ltd. Mediterranean Brokerage & Agents, S.A.S., 1993 WL 386298, 1994 A.M.C. 476 (E.D. La. Sept. 13, 1993) (attachment for security is not precluded by prior commencement of arbitration and motivation to obtain security rather than jurisdiction); Castelan v. Mercantil Parati, 1991 WL 83129, 1991 A.M.C. 2141 (D.N.J. May 8, 1991) (New York Convention does not forbid pre-arbitration arrest in maritime cases). *See also* 9 U.S.C.A. § 8 (after seizure of vessel or property in admiralty case, court shall direct parties to proceed with arbitration and shall retain jurisdiction to enter its decree upon the award); Fed. R. Civ. P., Supplemental Rules for Certain Admiralty and Maritime Claims. It is an unresolved question whether a federal court would have jurisdiction (or should decline to exercise jurisdiction under the doctrine of international comity) to order attachment or garnishment concerning a foreign arbitral proceeding upon the unilateral request of a party where the arbitral tribunal has been empanelled and has not sought the Court's assistance or awarded any relief to the party. The answer would necessarily involve the interplay of the Parties' arbitration agreement, the rules of the particular tribunal, and the Court's interpretation of its jurisdiction under the New York Convention and Federal Arbitration Act.

66.3. 9 U.S.C.A. § 1–16.

arbitration. United States courts have divided on whether the FAA[67] divests them of jurisdiction to order provisional measures in aid of arbitration. Some recent courts have ruled that the "fact [a] dispute is to be arbitrated does not deprive the Court of its authority to provide provisional remedies."[68] Other courts have held that granting provisional relief is contrary to the FAA's mandate that disputes be arbitrated.[69]

United States courts have also considered whether they are the proper forum to grant provisional measures. In *Borden, Inc. v. Meiji Milk Prods. Co., Ltd.*,[70] the court considered the propriety of injunctive relief where arbitration concerning an alleged breach of a licensing agreement in Japan between Borden, a domestic company, and Meiji, a Japanese company, was to commence at an undetermined situs. The court, in undertaking a forum non conveniens analysis, determined that an adequate alternative remedy was available to Borden in the Japanese courts.[71] The court observed that it was not necessary that Japan "provide precisely the same remedies and in the same time-frame."[72] The court, however, stated that Borden would be unduly prejudiced if it were forced to wait "years or even months" to have a Japanese court review its application for temporary relief.[73] The court, therefore, denied an immediate grant of provisional relief and conditionally dismissed the action on forum non conveniens grounds, but ruled that "Borden may reapply for a preliminary injunction . . . if the Japanese court does not decide Borden's application within 60 days after it is submitted."[74]

It also appears that Rule 65, Fed. R. Civ. P. legal standards concerning preliminary injunctions apply to federal court injunctions in aid of international arbitration.[75] In general, therefore, a movant must show irreparable harm and the likelihood of success on the merits.[76] It

67. 9 U.S.C.A. § 1 *et seq.*

68. Rogers, Burgun, Shahine & Deschler, Inc. v. Dongsan Constr. Co., 598 F. Supp. 754 (S.D.N.Y. 1984); Teradyne, Inc. v. Mostek Corp., 797 F.2d 43, 51 (1st Cir. 1986); Borden, Inc. v. Meiji Milk Prods. Co., Ltd., 919 F.2d 822 (2d Cir. 1990), *cert. denied,* 500 U.S. 953 (1991); Medika Int'l, Inc. v. Scanlan, Int'l, Inc., 830 F. Supp. 81, 88 (D.P.R. 1993); Speedee Oil Change Sys. v. State St. Capital, Inc., 727 F. Supp. 289, 290 (E.D. La. 1989).

69. *See* Merrill Lynch, Pierce, Fenner & Smith, Inc. v. Hovey, 726 F.2d 1286 (8th Cir. 1984); Jab Indus., Inc. v. Silex SpA., 601 F. Supp. 971 (S.D.N.Y. 1985).

70. 919 F.2d 822 (2d Cir. 1990), *cert. denied,* 500 U.S. 953 (1991).

71. *Id.* at 829.

72. *Id.*

73. *Id.*

74. *Id.*

75. Alvenus Shipping Co., Ltd. v. Delta Petroleum (U.S.A.) Ltd., *supra* note 61, at 487.

76. *Id.*

has also been held that irreparable harm may exist where a money judgment will go unsatisfied absent equitable relief.[77]

[b] State Law

In the United States, a growing number of states have adopted statutes based on the UNCITRAL Rules to foster international arbitration.[78] Several of the state international arbitration acts address the availability of provisional remedies in aid of arbitration, in the absence of a contrary agreement by the parties.[79]

Florida Statute section 684.16 provides that an arbitral tribunal may grant any appropriate interim relief without prejudice to the right of a party to request interim relief directly from a court or other tribunal.[80] Section 684.16 also provides that a request for interim relief is not incompatible with the agreement to arbitrate.[81] The statute authorizes the arbitral tribunal itself to apply to any court or tribunal for interim relief.[82]

In its international arbitration act, North Carolina has also authorized arbitral tribunals and the courts to grant interim relief in aid of arbitration.[83] The North Carolina act, however, limits the ability of

---

77. *Id.*

78. N.C.G.S. § 1–567.30; FL. STAT. ANN. § 684.02; *see also* TEX. CIV. ST. ART. 249–1 *et seq.* (setting forth Texas Arbitration and Conciliation of International Commercial Disputes Act).

79. State law provisional remedies may be applicable to federal courts through Rule 64, FED. R. CIV. P.

80. Fl. Stat. Ann. § 684.16(1).

81. *Id.*

82. *Id.* at § 684.16(2).

83. N.C.G.S. § 1–567.39 (setting forth procedures regarding interim relief and the enforcement of interim measures). The statute provides, in part:

> (a) In the case of an arbitration where the arbitrator or arbitrators have not been appointed, or where the arbitrator or arbitrators are unavailable, a party may seek interim relief directly from the superior court as provided in subsection (c). Enforcement shall be granted as provided by the law applicable to the type of interim relief sought.
>
> (b) In all other cases, a party shall seek interim measures under G.S. 1–567.47 from the arbitral tribunal and shall have no right to seek interim relief from the superior court, except that a party to an arbitration governed by this Article may request from the superior court enforcement of an order of an arbitral tribunal granting interim measures under G.S. 1–567.47.
>
> (c) In connection with an agreement to arbitrate or a pending arbitration, the superior court may grant, pursuant to subsection (a) of this section:
>
> (1) An order of attachment of garnishment;
>
> (2) A temporary restraining order or preliminary injunction;

courts to grant interim relief in aid of arbitration to instances where the arbitrators have not been appointed or are unavailable.[84] In all other instances, parties are required to seek interim relief from the arbitral tribunal.[85] The arbitral tribunal is empowered to order any interim measure it deems necessary.[86]

New York, while not adopting an international arbitration act, has also specifically adopted a statute setting forth the circumstances in which provisional relief in aid of arbitration may be granted. New York Civil Practice Law, section 7502(c) states:

> Provisional Remedies. The supreme court in the county in which an arbitration is pending, or, if not yet commenced, in a county specified [in § 7502(a)], may entertain an application for an order of attachment or for a preliminary injunction in connection with an arbitrable controversy, but only upon the ground that the award to which the applicant may be entitled may be rendered ineffectual without such provisional relief. . . . The provisions of article 62 and 63 of this chapter shall apply to the application, including those relating to undertakings and to the time for commencement of an action (arbitration shall be deemed an action for this purpose) if the application is made before commencement, except that the sole ground for the granting of the remedy shall be as stated above.

Section 7502 was cited as one basis for a court to grant provisional relief in aid of international arbitration in *Alvenus Shipping Co., Ltd. v.*

---

(3) An order for claim and delivery;

(4) The appointment of a receiver;

(5) Delivery of money or other property into court;

(6) Any other order that may be necessary to ensure the preservation or availability either of assets or of documents, the destruction or absence of which would be likely to prejudice the conduct or effectiveness of the arbitration. . . .

(f) The availability of interim relief under this section may be limited by prior written agreement of the parties.

84. *Id.* at § 1–567.39(a).

85. *Id.* at § 1–567.39(b).

86. N.C.G.S. § 1–567.47 provides that:

Unless otherwise agreed by the parties, the arbitral tribunal may, at the request of a party, order any party to take such interim measure of protection as the arbitral tribunal may consider necessary in respect of the subject matter of the dispute, including an interim measure analogous to any type of interim relief specified in G.S. 1–567.39(c). The arbitral tribunal may require any party to provide appropriate security, including security for costs as provided in G.S. 1–567.61(h)(2), in connection with such measure.

Delta Petroleum (U.S.A.) Ltd.[87] The court observed, "In permitting injunctions in aid of arbitration, CPLR § 7502 brings New York State in line with every signatory of the United Nations Convention on the Recognition and Enforcement of Foreign Arbitral Awards."[88]

In a case which interestingly did not discuss *Alvenus Shipping Co.*, the Second Circuit appears to have foreclosed the applicability of section 7502 in aid of international arbitration. In *ContiChem LPG v. Parsons Shipping Co., Ltd.*,[89] the Court cited the state court case of *Cooper v. Ateliers de la Motobecane, S.A.*,[90] for the proposition that the New York Convention prevents section 7502 from applying to international arbitration.[90.1] Because the court in *Cooper v. Ateliers de la Motobecane* noted that federal arbitration law "specifically permits attachment to be used in admirality cases,"[90.2] the *ContiChem* Court considered whether section 7502 would permit attachment in support of an international maritime arbitration and concluded that section 7502 was inapplicable:

> In sum, we conclude that although this case involves a maritime attachment, and *Cooper* is therefore not necessarily a bar to relief, ContiChem nevertheless is not entitled to provisional remedies in aid of arbitration under C.P.L.R. 7502(c) because this is not a domestic arbitration. The charter party in this case specifically provided for arbitration of disputes in London, and Rule 7502 by its terms applies only to domestic arbitrations. Therefore, we reject ContiChem's attempt to expand the purview of this statute beyond the limits of its language and affirm the district court's conclusion that C.P.L.R. 7502(c) does not permit provisional remedies in aid of a maritime arbitration in London.[90.3]

[3] Applying the Arbitral Tribunal Rules and the Parties' Arbitration Agreement in Obtaining Provisional Measures

Rules of certain arbitral tribunals expressly address the issue of provisional remedies. Article 26(1) of the UNCITRAL Rules states that "[a]t the request of either party, the arbitral tribunal may take any

87. *Supra* note 61, at 487–88.

88. *Id.* at 488. For a case granting § 7502(c) remedies in aid of an international arbitration, *see* Borden, Inc. v. Meiji Milk Prods. Co., Ltd., 919 F.2d 822 (2d Cir. 1990), *cert. denied,* 500 U.S. 953 (1991).

89. 229 F.3d 426 (2d Cir. 2000).

90. 57 N.Y.2d 408, 456 N.Y.S.2d 728, 442 N.E. 2d 1239 (1982).

90.1. *ContiChem*, 229 F.3d at 431.

90.2. *Cooper*, 57 N.Y.2d at 415.

90.3. *ContiChem*, 229 F.3d at 433.

interim measures it deems necessary in respect of the subject matter of the dispute. . . .''[91] The article mandates that ''[a] request for interim measures addressed by any party to a judicial authority shall not be deemed incompatible with the agreement to arbitrate, or as a waiver of that agreement.''[92]

The rules of other arbitral tribunals also address the grant of interim relief.[93] It should be noted, however, that the tribunal cannot award interim relief until it has been selected, confirmed, and convened, and until other timelines provided by the rules are met. Moreover, the award of provisional relief is in the tribunal's discretion.

Practice Note: The parties' arbitration agreement should specifically address issues concerning provisional measures. The parties' written agreement concerning when provisional measures are available, what tribunals may enforce such remedies, the scope of anticipated remedies, etc., may greatly influence the ruling of a court or tribunal on such issues.

The rules of the arbitral tribunal may also provide whether and in what circumstances applying to a national court for provisional relief is appropriate. For instance, the ICC Rules state ''[b]efore the file is transmitted to the Arbitral Tribunal, and in appropriate circumstances even thereafter, the parties may apply to any competent judicial authority for interim or conservatory measures.''[94]

§ 12.05 OBTAINING EVIDENCE FOR USE IN INTERNATIONAL ARBITRAL PROCEEDINGS

[1] Obtaining Evidence Through U.S. Courts

As discussed below, recent Circuit Court decisions have ruled that parties to a foreign arbitration may not use 28 U.S.C. § 1782 to obtain

91. UNCITRAL Rules, Art. 26(1).

92. UNCITRAL Rules, Art. 26(3). *See also* APC Rules, *supra* note 23, Art. 22 (substantially adopting UNCITRAL provisions); IACAC Rules, Art. 26 (same).

93. AAA International Rules, Art. 21 (''At the request of any party, the tribunal may take whatever interim measures it deems necessary, including injunctive relief and measures for the protection or conservation of property''); ICC Rules, Art. 23 (''Arbitral Tribunal may, at the request of a party, order any interim or conservatory measure it deems appropriate''). *See also* London Ct. Int'l Arb. (LCIA), Art. 25.

94. ICC Rules, Art. 23(2). *See also* AAA Int'l Rules, Art. 21(3) (''A request for interim measures addressed by a party to a judicial authority shall not be deemed incompatible with the agreement to arbitrate or a waiver of the right to arbitrate'').

U.S. court assistance with discovery (i.e., to compel the production of documents or testimony). However, other avenues may exist for a U.S. court to assist with discovery in aid of foreign arbitration, including under the New York Convention, Inter-American Convention, or other international Convention on Commercial Arbitration; under the Federal Arbitration Act, 9 U.S.C.A. § 7; under State Arbitration Acts; or, less certainly, under the applicable arbitral tribunal rules or the parties' arbitration agreement.

In general, when one of the parties to a foreign judicial proceeding (not arbitration) is from the United States or when witnesses or evidence are located in the United States, other parties may seek to obtain evidence in the U.S. for use in a foreign proceeding. In 1958, Congress created the statutory authority for this practice by enacting 28 U.S.C. § 1782, "Assistance to Foreign and International Tribunals and to Litigants before such Tribunals," which provides, in pertinent part:

> (a) The district court of the district in which a person resides or is found may order him to give his testimony or statement or to produce a document or other thing for use in a proceeding in a foreign or international tribunal. The order may be made pursuant to a letter rogatory issued, or request made, by a foreign or international tribunal or upon the application of any interested person and may direct that the testimony or statement be given, or the document or other thing produced, before a person appointed by the court. By virtue of his appointment, the person appointed has power to administer any necessary oath and take the testimony or statement. The order may prescribe the practice and procedure of the foreign country or the international tribunal, for taking the testimony or statement or producing the document or other thing. To the extent that the order does not prescribe otherwise, the testimony or statement shall be taken, and the document or other thing produced, in accordance with the Federal Rules of Civil Procedure.

Courts interpreting section 1782 have faced several difficult interpretive questions. These questions have arisen concerning the threshold requirements, imposed by some U.S. courts, that: (1) the "tribunal" must be of an adjudicative nature; (2) the foreign proceeding must actually be contemplated; (3) the request must emanate from the tribunal itself, and not a party; and (4) the materials sought must be discoverable in the foreign proceeding.

The first threshold requirement, that the foreign tribunal be adjudicative in nature, was recently addressed by the Second Circuit in *National Broadcasting Co., Inc. v. Bear Stearns & Co., Inc.* (hereinafter

''*NBC*'').[95] In that case, the Court read section 1782 narrowly and ruled that the statute does not apply to private commercial arbitration.

The *NBC* decision concerned a private commercial arbitration administered by the International Chamber of Commerce (''ICC''), a private organization based in Paris, France, and to occur under ICC rules and Mexican law. The dispute concerned the attempted exercise by NBC of an option to purchase shares in a Mexican television broadcasting company (TV Azteca S.A. de C.V.) pursuant to a programming services agreement. Prior to the appointment of the arbitral tribunal, NBC applied *ex parte* to the District Court for the Southern District of New York for authorization to serve document subpoenas on six third-party financial institutions engaged by Azteca, including Appellee Bear Stearns & Co. The District Court granted the application and the subpoenas were served.

Azteca, Bear Stearns and others then moved to quash the subpoenas. Such motion to quash was granted by the District Court, which held that section 1782 does not encompass private international commercial arbitration. The Second Circuit *NBC* Court reviewed the District Court's interpretation of section 1782 *de novo* and affirmed such decision.

The *NBC* Court appeared swayed by its perception of policy concerning international arbitration and legislative history. The Court observed, ''Ordinarily, because commercial arbitration is a creature of contract, only the parties to the arbitration contract are bound to participate.'' The Court also noted, the ''popularity of arbitration rests in considerable part on its asserted efficiency and cost-effectiveness-characteristics said to be at odds with full-scale litigation in the courts, and especially at odds with the broad-ranging discovery made possible by the Federal Rules of Civil Procedure.''

The Court stated, ''The absence [in the legislative history] of any reference to private dispute resolution proceedings such as arbitration strongly suggests that Congress did not consider them in drafting [section 1782]. . . . In sum, the legislative history reveals that when Congress in 1964 enacted the modern version of section 1782, it intended to cover governmental or intergovernmental arbitral tribunals and conventional courts and other state-sponsored adjudicatory bodies.'' The Court, therefore, concluded that ''policy considerations of some

95. 165 F.3d 184 (2d Cir. 1999).

magnitude reinforce our conclusion . . . that Congress did not intend for that statute to apply to an arbitral body established by private parties.''[96]

A similar result was reached in *Republic of Kazakhstan v. Biedermann International*,[97] in which a foreign nation engaged in private international arbitration with a United States corporation brought an action for discovery assistance. The United States District Court for the Southern District of Texas granted the request, and denied the corporation's request for reconsideration but the Corporation appealed. The Court of Appeals, citing *NBC*, held that the statute authorizing district courts to assist discovery efforts of litigants before ''foreign and international tribunals'' did not apply to private international arbitration.

In light of the sweeping language of the *NBC* and *Kazakhstan* decisions, it is questionable whether parties to a private international commercial arbitration could provide by agreement for a U.S. district court (at least in the Second Circuit) to compel broad discovery. Absent the application of section 1782, it is doubtful whether a district court would have the authority to compel such discovery. Although not deciding the issue, the *NBC* Court did raise the possibility that 9 U.S.C.A. § 7 (Federal Arbitration Act) may provide a means by which a district court could compel the production of witnesses and documents in the limited circumstances set forth therein for an arbitral proceeding occurring in a country party to the New York Convention or Inter-American Convention on International Commercial Arbitration.[98] Section 7, 9 U.S.C.A. provides in part, ''The arbitrators selected either as prescribed in this title or otherwise, or a majority of them, may summon in writing any person to attend before them or any of them as a witness and in a proper case to bring with him or them any book, record, document, or paper which may be deemed material as evidence in the case.'' The ''material evidence'' requirement of section 7 is much more restrictive than either 28 U.S.C.A. § 1782 or Rule 26, Fed. R. Civ. P. Further precedent for a district court to compel the production of

96. Finding that § 1782 is inapplicable to private international arbitral panels, the Court avoided ruling on the issue of whether 9 U.S.C.A. § 7 (not § 1782) is the exclusive means by which a district court could compel the production of evidence for an arbitral proceeding occurring in countries party to the New York Convention or Inter-American Convention on International Commercial Arbitration.

97. 168 F. 3d 880 (5th Cir.1999).

98. 9 U.S.C.A. § 208 provides that Chapter 1 of the Federal Arbitration Act (9 U.S.C.A. §§ 1–16) applies to actions and proceedings regarding foreign commercial arbitration under the New York Convention. A similar provision concerning the Inter-American Convention exists in 9 U.S.C.A. § 307.

documents or the attendance of witnesses may also be found by Convention[99] and under rules of an established arbitral organization.[100]

Section 1782 remains available should an arbitral tribunal request the assistance of a ''real tribunal,'' such as a foreign court, in requesting that discovery be compelled in the United States[101] Query whether such requirement of enlisting the aid of a foreign court to request discovery in the United States, likely with unclear procedures and timetables, complies with the timeliness and efficiency qualities often attributed to arbitration.[102]

The *NBC* and *Kazakhstan* courts emphasized the private and commercial nature of the arbitration at issue in finding that section 1782 did not apply. The *Kazakhstan* court went so far as to determine that section 1782 did not apply even where one party to the arbitration was a foreign government itself, at least where the arbitration was private commercial arbitration. This result seems inapposite to the Supreme Court's ruling in *Intel Corp. v. Advanced Micro Devices, Inc.*[103] In *Intel Corp.*, the Court found section 1782 applicable to a request for documents to aid an administrative anti-trust investigation of the European Commission. This result clearly stretches the section 1782 definition of ''tribunal'' and requirement that a proceeding be ''contemplated'', as no adjudicative action was pending, merely a governmental investigation.[104] The Court did not, however, rule that the discovery must be allowed. Rather it stressed the discretion vested in the district court and articulated several factors relevant to the determination, including:

(1) whether the information is sought from one of the litigants in the foreign proceeding or from a third-party;

(2) the nature of the foreign tribunal;

---

99. *See supra* § 12.04[1] (discussing obtaining provisional measures by Convention).

100. *See supra* § 12.04[3] (discussing arbitral tribunal rules in provisional measures context); Inter-American Convention on International Commercial Arbitration, Art. 3 (stating rules applicable to arbitration under IAC); 9 U.S.C.A. § 306 (implementing IAC rules provision).

101. In re Application of Medway Power, Ltd., 985 F. Supp. 402 (S.D.N.Y. 1997).

102. *See NBC, supra* note 94 (the ''popularity of arbitration rests in considerable part on its asserted efficiency and cost-effectiveness-characteristics said to be at odds with full-scale litigation in the courts. . . .'').

103. 542 U.S. 241, 124 S. Ct. 2466, 159 L.Ed.2d 355 (2004).

104. The Court labeled the administrative investigation ''quasi-judicial'' in nature and noted it may lead to further legal proceedings. 124 S. Ct. at 2470.

(3) the character of the proceedings underway abroad;

(4) comity; i.e., the receptivity of the foreign government or the court or agency abroad to U.S. federal court judicial assistance;

(5) "end run"; i.e., whether the section 1782 application is an attempt to circumvent foreign discovery limitations or other policies of a foreign country or the U.S.;

(6) "reciprocity"; i.e., whether the party making the request is itself subject to similar discovery. If not, the district judge might condition relief upon that party's reciprocal exchange of information; and

(7) "burdensomeness"; unduly intrusive or burdensome requests may be denied or limited.[105]

Under *Kazakhstan*, it is even questionable whether section 1782 procedures would be available where the tribunal is inter-governmental in nature, such as the Iran-U.S. Claims Tribunal. Arguably, an inter-governmental tribunal, such as the Iran-US Claims Tribunal, would be more governmental in nature than the private commercial arbitration at issue in *Kazakhstan*.

The Second Circuit's decision in *NBC* directly conflicts with and supersedes the earlier Southern District of New York decision in *In re Application of Technostroyexport*.[106] In *Technostroyexport*, a district court in New York found that an international arbitrator or panel is a tribunal for purposes of section 1782. In *In re Application of Technostroyexport*,[107] the court considered the discovery application of Technostroyexport, a Russian company that initiated an arbitration in Moscow against a New York company, International Development and Trade Services (IDTS). In turn, IDTS initiated arbitration in Sweden. Technostroyexport sought to take depositions of principals of IDTS for use in the arbitration proceedings. The court first found that section 1782 was applicable in an arbitration, as "an arbitrator or arbitration panel is a 'tribunal' under section 1782."[108]

105. 124 S. Ct. at 2471-72.

106. 853 F. Supp. 695 (S.D.N.Y. 1994).

107. 853 F. Supp. 695, 697 (S.D.N.Y. 1994). *See generally* Fuerstman and Thomas, *Implications of the Technostroyexport Decision*, Int'l Bus. Law., Sept. 1994, at 364.

108. *Id.* at 697.

Requests found not to emanate from an adjudicative body for § 1782 purposes may include requests for evidence made by prosecuting or tax authorities preliminarily investigating wrongdoing.[109] However, the Ninth Circuit has granted section 1782 assistance concerning preliminary criminal investigations.[110] Further, one scholar involved with the formulation of the 1964 legislative amendments wrote, "The term 'tribunal' embraces all bodies exercising adjudicatory powers, and includes investigating magistrates, administrative and arbitral tribunals, and quasi-judicial agencies, as well as conventional civil, commercial, criminal, and administrative courts."[111]

Concerning the second threshold requirement, that the foreign proceeding be actually contemplated, U.S. courts had divided on the requisite status of the foreign proceeding. It is likely that proceedings need not be formally pending for section 1782 to apply. Such was the ruling of *Intel Corp. v. Advanced Micro Devices, Inc.*[112] In *Intel Corp.*, the Court held that "[t]he 'proceeding' for which discovery is sought under § 1782(a) must be within reasonable contemplation, but need not be 'pending' or 'imminent.' "[113] The Court rejected Intel's argument that the European Commission anti-trust investigation launched by AMD's complaint did not qualify for § 1782(a) assistance.[114]

The *Intel* ruling clarified disparate Circuit Court rulings. The Second Circuit had required that the adjudicative proceeding be "imminent—very likely to occur and very soon to occur."[115] In contrast, the Ninth Circuit granted section 1782 assistance in discovery requests concerning preliminary criminal investigations.[116] The Eleventh Circuit merely required that the requested evidence "will likely be of use in a judicial

109. Fonseca v. Blumenthal, 620 F.2d 322 (2d Cir. 1980); *In re* Letters Rogatory Issued by the Director of Inspection of the Government of India, 385 F.2d 1017 (2d Cir. 1967); *In re* Letters of Request to Examine Witnesses from the Court of Queen's Bench for Manitoba, Canada, 59 F.R.D. 625 (N.D. Cal.), *aff'd*, 488 F.2d 511 (9th Cir. 1973).

110. *In re* Letters Rogatory from the Tokyo District Prosecutors' Office, 16 F.3d 1016 (9th Cir. 1994).

111. Hans Smit, *International Litigation Under the United States Code*, 65 Colum. L. Rev. 1015, 1026 n. 71 (1965).

112. 542 U.S. 241, 124 S. Ct. 2466, 159 L.Ed.2d 355 (2004).

113. 124 S. Ct. at 2470.

114. *Id.*

115. *In re* International Judicial Assistance for the Federal Republic of Brazil, 936 F.2d 702 (2d Cir. 1991); *In re* Letter of Request from the Government of Switzerland, 1994 U.S. Dist. LEXIS 350, 1994 WL 17942 (S.D.N.Y. Jan. 13, 1994).

116. *In re* Letters Rogatory from the Tokyo District Prosecutors Office, 16 F.3d 1016 (9th Cir. 1994).

proceeding.''[117] The D.C. Circuit formulated the equally vague (but as it turns out, correct) test that the proceedings for which the evidence is sought be ''within reasonable contemplation.''[118]

Evidence may also be sought under section 1782 for foreign appellate proceedings, when the appellate body allows the parties to present new evidence.[119]

Prior to *Intel*, Courts had divided on the third threshold issue, whether the discovery request must emanate from a foreign tribunal itself or whether a private litigant could make the request.[120] The *Intel* decision makes clear that not only may a foreign court or agency seek assistance under 1782 but so may litigants and other ''interested persons'', such as complainants who commence a foreign agency investigation that may lead to a legal proceeding before a court or tribunal.[121]

Prior to *Intel*, Courts had also divided on the fourth threshold issue, whether the discovery sought must be permissible under the law of the forum where the tribunal sits; i.e., whether the materials are discoverable in the foreign proceeding.[122] The *Intel* Court ruled that no discoverability requirement exists. ''Section 1782(a) does not impose a foreign-

117. *In re* Request for Assistance from Ministry of Legal Affairs of Trinidad and Tobago, 848 F.2d 1155 (11th Cir. 1988).

118. *In re* Letter of Request from Crown Prosecution Service of the United Kingdom, 870 F.2d 686 (D.C. Cir. 1989).

119. *In re* Application of Euromepa, S.A., 51 F.3d 1095 (2d Cir. 1995); *In re* Request for Judicial Assistance from the Seoul District Criminal Court, Seoul, Korea, 555 F.2d 720 (9th Cir. 1977).

120. *Compare* Technostroyexport, 853 F. Supp. 695, 697-99 (S.D.N.Y. 1994) (denying application of private party where party did not first obtain discovery order from arbitrator or arbitration panel) *with In re* Malev Hungarian Airlines, 964 F. 2d 97 (2d Cir. 1992) (requiring interested person to foreign litigation to first seek discovery from foreign tribunal is at odds with purposes of section 1782).

121. 124 S. Ct. at 2469 (''A complainant before the Commission, such as AMD, qualifies as an 'interested person' within § 1782(a)'s compass. The Court rejects Intel's contention that 'interested person[s]' does not include complainant AMD, but encompasses only litigants, foreign sovereigns, and a sovereign's designated agents.'')

122. *Compare In re* Application of Asta Medica, S.A., 981 F.2d 1, 6 (1st Cir. 1992) (requiring showing of foreign discoverability on theory that ''Congress did not seek to place itself on a collision course with foreign tribunals and legislatures''); *with* Euromepa, S.A. v. R. Esmerian, Inc., 154 F. 3d 24 (2d Cir. 1998) (no foreign discovery requirement under twin aims of statute to provide efficient means of assistance to litigants and to encourage reciprocal assistance by foreign countries to U.S. courts); *with In re* Letter Rogatory from the First Court of First Instance in Civil Matters, Caracas, Venezuela, 42 F. 3d 308, 310-11 (5th Cir. 1995) (dispensing with discoverability requirement where requesting party is foreign court or government, rather than private litigant).

discoverability requirement. Although § 1782(a) expressly shields from discovery matters protected by legally applicable privileges, nothing in § 1782(a)'s text limits a district court's production-order authority to materials discoverable in the foreign jurisdiction if located there. Nor does the legislative history suggest that Congress intended to impose a blanket foreign-discoverability rule on § 1782(a) assistance.''[123]

Practice Note: Recent Circuit Court decisions have ruled that 28 U.S.C. § 1782 may not be used by arbitrating parties to obtain discovery through U.S. federal court assistance. If court assisitance is sought under other federal or state law (such as an international arbitration Convention; Federal Arbitration Act, 9 U.S.C.A. § 7; or state arbitration act), counsel handling international arbitration matters and seeking discovery in the United States should consider obtaining an order from the arbitrator(s) before applying for assistance to a U.S. court. This also suggests that care should be employed in compromise clauses and arbitration agreements in addressing the scope and nature of discovery that the parties would prefer, and what rules would apply under specified or various arbitral tribunals. Counsel may also seek an order of a foreign court in aid of arbitration to trigger the application of § 1782.

U.S. and foreign witnesses, however, may argue that they are prohibited by foreign law from either testifying or providing physical evidence. Faced with such a conflict, a U.S. court may apply the balancing test set forth in § 437 of the Restatement (Third) Foreign Relations Law to determine whether the testimony or production of evidence should nevertheless be ordered.[124]

[2] Comments on Discovery in Arbitration

An inherent tension exists between discovery, which may be costly and time-consuming, and arbitration's goals of resolving disputes in an efficient and timely manner. However, tribunals are charged with the duty of ensuring that parties' due process rights are protected. Such rights necessarily involve rights to obtain and present evidence.

---

123. 124 S. Ct. at 2470.

124. *See* Société Internationale Industrielle Aérospatiale v. United States District Court, 482 U.S. 522, 544 n. 28 (1987) (discussing effects of foreign law on U.S. discovery requests in context of exclusivity of Hague Evidence Convention and analyzing § 437 of Restatement (Third) of Foreign Relations Law). *See also, supra* §§ 10.10–10.12, 10.16 (discussing effect of conflicts of law on obtaining discovery assistance from U.S. courts).

The rules of the major private organizations which administer international commercial arbitrations appear to be granting the arbitrator/tribunal increasing authority and discretion regarding the performance of discovery and information exchange by the parties.[125] There has been observed "a convergence in the global approach to administering international cases."[126]

The AAA International Rules provide in Article 19, "Evidence":

1. Each party shall have the burden of proving the facts relied on to support its claim or defense.

2. The tribunal may order a party to deliver to the tribunal and to the other parties a summary of the documents and other evidence which that party intends to present in support of its claim, counterclaim or defense.

3. At any time during the proceedings, the tribunal may order parties to produce other documents, exhibits or other evidence it deems necessary or appropriate.

The rules are more "Americanized," in that they more closely resemble the procedures employed in U.S. courts, than those of certain other international bodies, such as the ICC, discussed below. Rule 19(1) places the burden on the parties to prove, presumably by adequate documents or other evidence, their claims or defenses. Rule 19(3) permits to tribunal, likely upon the motion of an opposing party, to direct the production of documents or other items.

ICC Rules require the Arbitral Tribunal "within as short a time as possible to establish the facts of the case by all appropriate means."[127] The burden of directing and obtaining the production of evidence, therefore, rests with the tribunal, as is common in litigation in civil code nations. This provision is not without teeth. Article 20(5) provides: "At any time during the proceedings, the Arbitral Tribunal may summon any party to provide additional evidence." The rules of many arbitral institutions, therefore, provide for early involvement of the case administrator and tribunal and the issuance of pre-hearing orders by the

125. The AAA International Rules and the rules of other international arbitral tribunals may be found at the AAA website, www.adr.org., or at the ICC website, www.iccwbo.org.

126. Michael F. Hoellering, *Administering International Arbitration Proceedings*, Disp. Resol. J. 64, 67 (AAA, Feb. 1998).

127. ICC Rules, Art. 20(1).

Tribunal concerning procedural matters, such as discovery.[128] For instance, Article 16 of the American Arbitration Association (''AAA'') International Rules provides that the tribunal may conduct the arbitration in whatever manner it deems proper, so long as the parties are treated fairly and provided due process. The AAA Rules anticipate that the case administrator will conduct a conference with the parties very early in the proceedings to address procedural and discovery matters.[129] The AAA Rules also contemplate a pre-hearing conference (by phone if necessary) among the Tribunal, case administrator, and parties to address procedural, discovery, and evidentiary matters, and the attendance of witnesses.[130] The Tribunal may issue orders concerning the matters addressed at such conferences. Such fora provide meaningful opportunities for arbitral parties to seek the tribunal's assistance in obtaining information and the attendance of witnesses, wherever located.

Discovery is largely, if not entirely, within the discretion of the arbitrator/tribunal. In addition to other powers which may be available to it,[131] the Tribunal itself may coerce information by threatening to construe a party's refusal to provide requested information in the negative or to impose other appropriate sanctions. The rules of arbitral tribunals often vest the nature and scope of discovery in the discretion of the arbitrator/tribunal. Similar to the AAA rules, the International Chamber of Commerce (''ICC'') Rules allow for the Tribunal, at an early stage, to formulate an understanding of the Terms of Reference to arbitration and to issue rulings on procedural and discovery matters.[132] Moreover, in instances where the rules of an established arbitral body are not used, discovery and information exchange are within the arbitrator's discretion. Parties should, therefore, consider certain principles regarding discovery issues.

The standard for discovery in arbitration differs from that of litigation under Rule 26, Federal Rules of Civil Procedure. Rule 26(b) grants an absolute entitlement to discovery of information concerning

---

128. *See generally* Howard M. Holtzmann, ''Balancing the Need for Certainty and Flexibility in International Arbitration Procedures'' *International Arbitration in the 21st Century: Towards ''Judicialization'' and Uniformity?* (Transnational Publishers, Inc., 1994).

129. Hoellering, *supra* at 66.

130. *Id.* at 67.

131. *See supra* § 12.05[1] (discussing availability of judicial assistance in obtaining evidence for arbitral proceedings).

132. ICC Rule 18, ''Terms of Reference; Procedural Timetable''; ICC Rule 20, ''Establishing the Facts of the Case.'' The ICC Rules may be found at the ICC website, www.iccwbo.org.

any relevant matter and "reasonably calculated to lead to the discovery of admissible evidence." Moreover, the Federal Rules of Civil Procedure offer many specific and effective means of obtaining discovery; interrogatories, requests for production and inspection, requests for admission, etc.

There is no such entitlement and there are no such procedures in arbitration. In order to invoke the higher threshold of the "due process" standard in arbitration, it must be shown that the information sought is *necessary*, not just that the information is relevant or may lead to admissible evidence. Moreover, the means of obtaining or compelling the information, if any, are within the arbitrator's discretion.

The arbitral tribunal may have difficulty obtaining assistance of U.S. courts to enforce a discovery subpoena. In *Hay Group, Inc. v. E.B.S. Acquisition Corp.*,[133] a third-party accounting firm, PriceWaterhouse-Coopers, LLP, objected to a discovery subpoena requiring it to produce documents prior to the arbitration hearing itself. The Third Circuit agreed and ruled that under the Federal Arbitration Act, 9 U.S.C. 7, a non-party witness may be compelled to bring documents to an arbitration proceeding but may not simply be subpoenaed to produce documents.[134] It may be noted that the *Hay Group* case concerned domestic, rather than international, arbitration. The New York Convention, applicable to international arbitration, provides that "[a] court having jurisdiction under this chapter may direct that arbitration be held in accordance with the agreement at any place therein provided for. . . ."[135] If the parties' agreement to arbitrate specifically provides for pre-hearing discovery, then presumably the federal courts would have the authority to enforce the agreement under the New York Convention. Further, as a treaty, the New York Convention would prevail over inconsistent domestic law.

133. 360 F.3d 404 (3rd Cir. 2004).

134. *Id.* at 406. *See also* COMSAT Corp. v. Nat'l Science Foundation, 190 F.3d 269, 275 (4th Cir. 1999) ("Nowhere does the FAA grant an arbitrator the authority to order non-parties to appear at depositions, or the authority to demand that non-parties provide the litigating parties with documents during pre-hearing discovery. By its own terms, the FAA's subpoena authority is defined as the power of the arbitration panel to compel non-parties to appear 'before them;' that is, to compel testimony by non-parties at the arbitration hearing"). In *dicta*, however, the *COMSAT* court suggested that an arbitration panel might be able to subpoena a non-party for pre-hearing discovery "under unusual circumstances" and "upon a showing of special need or hardship." *Id.* at 276. Query whether international arbitration would present such "unusual circumstances" or "special need or hardship."

135. 9 U.S.C. § 206.

An experienced arbitrator has suggested four questions for determining what is "necessary to a full and fair exploration of the issues in dispute, consistent with the expedited nature of arbitration":

- Is the information sought likely to lead to the discovery of admissible or relevant evidence?
- Will granting the request for discovery help avoid surprise at the hearing?
- Will granting the discovery request serve to expedite the hearing?
- Is the information sought necessary to ensure the parties' due process rights and to guarantee a fair hearing?[136]

Consideration of these issues may help the arbitrator/tribunal address issues concerning the discovery of information in a fair, efficient, and timely manner, while protecting the due process rights of the parties.

§ 12.06 ENFORCING ARBITRATION AWARDS; NEW YORK CONVENTION

[1] Enforcing Arbitration Awards Under Federal Law

In enforcing foreign arbitral awards, United States courts are guided by the provisions of the New York Convention.[137] Because the Convention was negotiated pursuant to the Constitution's treaty power, it must be enforced according to its terms over all inconsistent rules of law.[138] Its treaty status has enabled courts in the United States to follow

136. Alfred G. Feliu, "Discovery in Arbitration: How Much is Enough?," *ADR Currents*, Mar. 1999; *reprinted in* N.C. LAWYERS WEEKLY, Sept. 13, 1999, pp. 11–12.

137. *See supra* note 5. Numerous other multilateral and bilateral arbitration conventions exist concerning the United States. Such conventions include, for example, the Inter-American Convention on International Commercial Arbitration, Jan. 30, 1975, entered into force for the U.S., Oct. 27, 1990, Pub. L. No. 101–369, § 1, Aug. 15, 1990, 104 Stat. 448; and a United States-Argentina Investment Treaty of 1991. *See* NAT'L L.J., Nov. 17, 1997, at A12, col. 1 (discussing recent first use of U.S.-Argentina Investment Treaty arbitration provision). The members of the Inter-American Convention are set forth in the Appendix Treaties Chart, *infra*, and following 9 U.S.C.A. § 301. Procedures concerning court orders to compel arbitration and enforcement of awards under the Inter-American Convention are codified at 9 U.S.C.A. § 301, *et seq.*

138. *See* Sedco, Inc. v. Petroleos Mexicanos Mexican Nat'l Oil Co., 767 F.2d 1140, 1149 (5th Cir. 1985).

a more uniform approach in the enforcement of arbitral awards than with respect to foreign judgments.[139]

U.S. Courts, however, will not enforce foreign arbitral awards under the Convention where the award was made in a State which is not a party to the Convention or does not reciprocally enforce U.S. awards.[140] In order to broadly apply the Convention, mere accession to the Convention and not *de facto* reciprocity appears to be the test. U.S. Courts will also not enforce foreign arbitral awards under the Convention where the differences at issue do not arise from ''commercial relationships'' as defined by U.S. law.[141]

Two court decisions suggest an additional ''minimum contacts'' hurdle to the enforcement of an arbitration award against a foreign sovereign. In *Creighton Ltd. v. Government of State of Qatar,*[142] the D.C. Circuit denied enforcement of an award against a sovereign party, Qatar. The Court ruled that by consenting to arbitration, Qatar was not entitled to immunity under the Foreign Sovereign Immunities Act (''FSIA'') with respect to subject matter jurisdiction.[143] The Court, however, concluded that Qatar had not expressly or impliedly waived its immunity under FSIA section 1605(a)(1).[144] The Court, concluded that while section 1605(a)(6) conferred subject matter jurisdiction, that

139. *See* David Westin, *Enforcing Foreign Commercial Judgments and Arbitral Awards in the United States, West Germany, and England*, 19 LAW & POL'Y INT'L BUS. 325, 351–56 (1987); *see* generally Gerald W. Palmer, *Enforcing Arbitral Decisions*, NAT'L L.J., Feb. 7, 1994, at 33.

140. Fertilizer Corp. of India v. IDI Mgt., Inc., 517 F. Supp. 948, 952–53 (S.D. Ohio 1981), *reh'g denied*, 530 F. Supp. 542 (S.D. Ohio 1982) (rejecting reciprocity defense regarding alleged ''evasive devices'' employed by India in denying enforcement of awards adverse to its nationals). *See also* note 5, *supra*, and related text, discussing U.S. Reservations, 9 U.S.C.A. § 201. The Second Circuit held that the district court had jurisdiction to hear a motion to compel arbitration of a dispute between parties who were not citizens of signatories to the New York Convention, because the arbitration agreement provided for arbitration in a signatory nation. Smith/Enron Cogeneration, L.P. v. Smith Cogeneration Int'l, Inc., 198 F.3d 88 (2d Cir. 1999) (finding that only state that must be signatory is state where arbitration is to take place and that under Article II of Convention, citizenship of parties and location of disputed subject matter are not controlling).

141. *See* Sumitomo Corp. v. Parakopi Compania Maritima, S.A., 477 F. Supp. 737, 741 (S.D.N.Y. 1979), *aff'd*, 620 F.2d 286 (2d Cir. 1980) (holding that definition of ''commerce'' under Federal Arbitration Act cannot be applied to limit application of New York Convention). U.S. Reservations, 9 U.S.C.A. § 201.

142. 181 F.3d 118 (D.C. Cir. July 2, 1999, *reh'g en banc denied*, Sept. 7, 1999).

143. 28 U.S.C.A. §§ 1330, 1605(a)(6).

144. The Court indicated that a waiver may have been found if Qatar was a signatory to the New York Convention.

section does not necessarily provide for personal jurisdiction.[145] The Court determined that because Qatar had not waived its objection to personal jurisdiction, and because it lacked sufficient "minimum contacts" with the United States for the assertion of personal jurisdiction to comport with the Constitution's due process clause, personal jurisdiction did not exist.

In *Seetransport Wiking Trader Schiffarhtsgesellschaft MBH & Co. v. Navimpex Centrala Vavala*,[146] the Second Circuit considered the fact that Romania was a party to the New York Convention in determining that it had subject matter jurisdiction under FSIA section 1605(a)(1) to enforce a French award against a Romanian state entity. The Court also found a waiver of immunity under FSIA section 1605(a)(6). Despite finding two grounds for the waiver of immunity, the Court additionally held that "[o]ur inquiry does not end there. . . . Indeed the [FSIA] cannot create personal jurisdiction where the Constitution forbids it."[147] Unlike the result in *Creighton*, the *Seetransport* Court found sufficient minimum contacts to assert personal jurisdiction over the Romanian sovereign entity.

Practice Note: In light of the *Creighton* and *Seetransport* decisions, Parties negotiating an arbitration agreement with a foreign sovereign should consider including an express consent to personal and subject matter jurisdiction concerning the enforcement of an award in national courts, including those of the United States.

For the Convention to apply, an award must also satisfy either of two additional criteria: (1) The award was made in the territory of another state than the state where enforcement is sought; or (2) the award is not considered as "domestic" in the state where enforcement is sought.[148] Whether an award is "non-domestic" for purposes of the Convention was addressed in *Bergesen v. Joseph Muller Corp.*[149] The Court ruled that an award made in New York State was non-domestic for Convention purposes where the parties were a Swiss corporation and a Norwegian shipowner. The Court determined that the Convention's

145. Interestingly, the court found that a waiver of immunity under FSIA § 1605(a)(1), which waiver may be express or implied, would confer personal jurisdiction as such waiver would have had some element of "intentionality."

146. 989 F.2d 572 (2d Cir. 1993).

147. *Id.* 989 F.2d at 580 (citation omitted).

148. New York Convention, Art. I(1), 9 U.S.C.A. § 201.

149. 710 F.2d 928 (2d Cir. 1983).

failure to define a non-domestic award was intentional, "in order to cover as wide a variety of eligible awards as possible, while permitting the enforcing authority to supply its own definition of 'non-domestic' in conformity with its own national law." The Court also construed the Federal Arbitration Act's silence on awards rendered in the U.S. between two foreign parties as intended to expand the Convention's applicability. On a related issue, the Court in *Lander Co. v. MMP Investments, Inc.* held an award to be "non-domestic" and within the scope of the Convention where it was rendered in the U.S. concerning two U.S. companies but where the underlying contract merely called for partial performance in a foreign country.[150]

The United States has implemented the provisions of the New York Convention in 9 U.S.C.A. §§ 201–208. Under 9 U.S.C.A. § 208, the provisions of the Federal Arbitration Act[151] apply to the enforcement of foreign awards except to the extent the latter conflicts with the Convention. The purpose of the Convention was to liberalize procedures for enforcing foreign arbitral awards.[152] The Convention shifted the burden of proof to the party defending against enforcement and limited enforcement defenses to seven, as set forth in Article V(1). These include:

(a) Invalidity of the agreement under the law to which the parties have subjected it or under the law where the award was made;[153]

(b) The party against whom the award is invoked was not given notice of the arbitration proceedings or was unable to present his/her case;[154]

---

150. 107 F.3d 476 (7th Cir.), *cert. denied*, 118 S. Ct. 55 (1997) (agreement to distribute shampoo products in Poland).

151. 9 U.S.C.A. §§ 1–14.

152. *See* Parsons & Whittemore Overseas Inc. v. Société Générale de L'Industrie Du Papier (RAKTA), 508 F.2d 969, 973 (2d Cir. 1974).

153. *See* Prima Paint Corp. v. Flood & Conklin Mfg., 388 U.S. 395, 403–04, (1967) (ruling in domestic arbitration context that validity of contract generally, as opposed to arbitration clause itself, was for arbitrator's [not reviewing court's] sole determination and court was to review only arbitration clause concerning arbitrability of dispute).

154. *See* Biotronik Mess-und Therapiegerate GmbH & Co. v. Medford Medical Instr. Co., 415 F. Supp. 133, 140–41 (D.N.J. 1976) (rejecting Art. V(1)(b) argument against enforcement that rights and liabilities under agreement had not matured and that such circumstance therefore prevented presentation of case); Generica Ltd. v. Pharmaceutical Basics, Inc., 125 F.3d 1123 (7th Cir. 1997) (rejecting Art. V(1)(b) argument that arbitrator's discretionary refusal to permit continued cross-examination of a witness denied party due process). The *Generica Ltd.* Court defined a fair hearing as one that "meets 'the minimal requirements of

(c) The award deals with matters not falling within the terms for submission to arbitration;[155]

(d) The arbitral procedure was not in accordance with the agreement of the parties or the law of the country where the arbitration took place;[156] and

(e) The award has not yet become binding on the parties, or has been set aside or suspended by a competent authority of the country in which, or under the law of which, the award was made.[157]

---

fairness'—adequate notice, a hearing on the evidence, and an impartial decision by the arbitrator.'' *Id.* (citation omitted).

155. Such subparagraph suggests a bias favoring enforcement of awards, as non-arbitral matters may be separated and awards enforced concerning matters properly submitted to arbitration. *See generally* Ramona Martinez, *Recognition and Enforcement of International Arbitral Awards Under the United Nations Convention of 1958: The ''Refusal'' Provisions*, 24 INT'L LAW. 487, 501–02 (1990).

156. *See* AAOT Foreign Econ. Assoc. Technostroyexport v. Int'l Dev. and Trade Services, Inc., 139 F.3d 980 (2d Cir. 1998) (finding that law precludes attacks on qualifications of arbitrators on grounds previously known by party but not raised until after award was rendered and holding that party waived right to object to award on grounds of alleged corruption); Imperial Ethiopian Gov. v. Baruch-Foster Corp., 535 F.2d 334, 335–37 (5th Cir. 1976) (finding waiver of enforcement objection regarding tribunal composition where allegations that tribunal member had previously drafted civil code for prevailing party Ethiopian Government were deemed unsubstantiated).

157. *See* Fertilizer Corp. of India v. IDI Mgmt, Inc., 517 F. Supp. 948, 958 (S.D. Ohio 1981), *reh'g denied*, 530 F. Supp. 542 (S.D. Ohio 1982) (ruling that pending appeal in India court did not change ''binding'' nature of award for Convention enforcement purposes). *Compare* Chromalloy Aeroservices v. Egypt, 939 F. Supp. 907 (D.D.C. 1996) (confirming Egyptian award previously annulled by Egyptian Court and therefore unenforceable under Convention as a matter of U.S. domestic law under FAA) *with* Spier v. Calzaturificio Tecnica, S.p.A., 71 F. Supp. 2d 279 (S.D.N.Y. 1999) (finding that arbitration award rendered in Italy and vacated by Italian courts was not entitled to enforcement under New York Convention and further refusing to enforce the award under the FAA because no basis for applying U.S. national law existed where the contract was entered in a foreign state and required arbitration there, the contract did not reference U.S. law, and nothing suggested the parties intended U.S. domestic arbitral law to govern). *See also* Baker Marine, Inc. v. Chevron, 191 F.3d 194 (2d Cir. 1999) (distinguishing *Chromalloy*); Four Seasons Hotels and Resorts, B.V. v. Consorcio Barr, S.A., 267 F.Supp.2d 1335 (S.D. Fla. 2003) (post-arbitration ruling by Venezuelan courts that arbitration agreements were invalid did not bar enforcement of award).

U.S. courts, like the courts of other nations concerning awards made in their territory, are free to tailor the grounds for vacatur of awards made in the U.S. Yusuf Ahmed Alghanim & Sons, W.L.L. v. Toys 'R' Us Inc., 126 F.3d 15, 23 (2d Cir.), *cert. denied*, 118 S. Ct. 1042 (1997) (finding that country where award is rendered is ''free to set aside or modify an award in accordance with [such country's] full panoply of express or implied grounds for relief''); Broome & Wellington v. Levcor Intern., Inc., 2003 WL 21032008 (S.D.N.Y., May 07, 2003) (affirming arbitral award despite contentions that arbitrators acted in manifest disregard of law and engaged in other misconduct). Under the Federal Arbitration Act (the ''FAA''), a court

Under Article V, recognition and enforcement of an arbitral award may also be refused if:

(a) The subject matter of the difference is not capable of settlement by arbitration under the law of the country where recognition and enforcement is sought;[158] or

(b) The recognition or enforcement of the award would be contrary to the public policy of that country.[159]

The case of *Parsons & Whittemore Overseas Inc. v. Société Générale de L'Industrie Du Papier (RAKTA)*[160] illustrates the application of defenses under Article V to a suit for confirmation of a foreign arbitral award holding plaintiff liable to defendant for breach of contract. The court of appeals noted that four of the defenses to the counterclaim seeking confirmation of the foreign arbitral award were based on the express language of the New York Convention and one was arguably

---

must confirm an award upon proper application unless the award is vacated, modified or corrected on grounds specified in the statute. *See* 9 U.S.C.A. § 10(a). In addition, the Second Circuit has recognized that a court may vacate an arbitration award that was rendered in ''manifest disregard of the law.'' Greenberg v. Bear, Stearns & Co., 220 F.3d 22, 28 (2d Cir. 2000). ''[R]eview for manifest error is severely limited.'' *Id.* A determination that an arbitration award was in manifest disregard of the law requires judicial findings that: ''(1) the arbitrators knew of a governing legal principle yet refused to apply it or ignored it altogether, and (2) the law ignored by the arbitrators was well defined, explicit, and clearly applicable to the case.'' *Id.*

It remains an open question in the U.S., however, whether the parties by contract can modify the scope of judicial review. *Compare* Lapine Technology Corp. v. Kyocera, 130 F.3d 884 (9th Cir. 1997) *and* Gateway Technologies, Inc. v. MCI Telecommunications Corp., 64 F.3d 993 (5th Cir. 1995) (parties can expand judicial review to cover errors of law and/or fact) *with* Chicago Typographical Union v. Chicago Sun-Times, 935 F.2d 1501 (7th Cir. 1995) (cannot by agreement modify federal court power to review arbitral award) *and* UHC Mgmt. Co. Inc. v. Computer Sciences Corp., 148 F.3d 992, 997–98 (8th Cir. 1998) (questioning whether parties may contract for expanded judicial review of an arbitral award and stating that parties' intent to do so must be clearly and unmistakably expressed). At least one commentator has argued based on *Lapine Technology* that allowing arbitrating parties to provide by contract for wider court review (such as whether arbitrators' findings of fact are supported by substantial evidence and whether conclusions of law are erroneous) would lead to greater certainty in the conduct of arbitration by limiting the discretion of arbitrators (presumably under the spectre of national court review). Carroll E. Neeseman, *Outside Counsel: More Certainty Comes to Arbitration*, N.Y.L.J., Mar. 26, 1998.

158. *See infra* text accompanying notes 143.1 and 143.2 (discussing inapplicability of Act of State Doctrine to enforcement of arbitral award).

159. *See infra* note 131 and accompanying text (discussing public policy exception).

160. 508 F.2d 969 (2d Cir. 1974).

implicit in the Convention.[161] These included the defenses that enforcement of the award would violate the public policy of the United States; the award represented an arbitration of matters not appropriately decided by arbitration; the tribunal denied plaintiff an adequate opportunity to present its case; and the award was predicated upon a resolution of issues outside the scope of the contractual agreement to submit to arbitration.

The Convention's public policy defense, the court noted, should be construed narrowly and used as a basis to deny confirmation of the arbitral award ''only where enforcement would violate the forum state's most basic notions of morality and justice.''[162] Plaintiff sought to defend its actions as consistent with United States notions of national policy. The court rejected as irrelevant plaintiff's attempt to equate national policy with United States public policy. Plaintiff-appellant further contended that the dispute was not capable of settlement by arbitration because foreign policy issues were involved which could not ''be placed at the mercy of foreign arbitrators.''[163] The court ruled that the incidental inclusion of a national interest issue in a breach of contract claim did not make the dispute non-arbitrable.[164]

Plaintiff-appellant further defended on the ground that its due process rights had been violated by the arbitration panel's refusal to delay proceedings to accommodate the schedule of one of its witnesses. The court held that inability to produce a party's witness before an arbitration tribunal was ''a risk inherent in an agreement to submit to arbitration.''[165] In any event, the court observed that the tribunal had considered the witness' affidavit, which contained a major part of the information to which he would have testified. The court also narrowly construed appellant's defense that certain decisions had been made by the arbitration tribunal in excess of its jurisdiction, viewing such attempts as ''second-guessing the arbitrator's construction of the parties' agreement.''[166] Finally, a defense was made that the award was in ''manifest disregard'' of law. The court stated that although this defense was not a part of the New York Convention, the provisions of the

161. *Id.* at 972.
162. *Id.* at 974.
163. *Id.* at 975.
164. *Id.*
165. *Id.*
166. *Id.* at 977.

Federal Arbitration Act[167] had been interpreted to include a defense on this basis. In any event, the court refused to apply this defense as a means of reviewing the record of the arbitral proceeding for errors of fact or law.[168]

In addition, ''final and binding'' language in arbitration awards or accords of a foreign tribunal will not exclude a U.S. court from considering the defenses to enforcement provided in the New York Convention.[169] In *Iran Aircraft Industries v. Avco Corp.*,[170] the court found that a domestic corporation was denied the opportunity to meaningfully present its claim before the Iran-United States Claims Tribunal where the corporation was mislead by the tribunal concerning a proper method of proof.[171] The court in *Avco* refused to enforce the tribunal's award based on Article V(1)(b) of the New York Convention, which provides a defense where a party is ''otherwise unable to present [its] case.''[172]

Under 9 U.S.C.A. § 15, the Act of State Doctrine no longer provides a defense to enforcement of arbitral awards regarding acts such as nationalization of assets. Such legislation[173] was introduced in the wake of *Libyan American Oil Co. (LIAMCO) v. Socialist People's Libyan Arab Jamahirya*.[174] In that case the district court found that enforcement of an arbitral award regarding nationalization by Libya of an oil company's assets was barred by the Act of State Doctrine.

Also, foreign states are amenable to the jurisdiction of courts in the United States with respect to suits to enforce an arbitration agreement or to confirm an award made pursuant to such an agreement to arbitrate.[175] Claims of foreign states to immunity from the jurisdiction of United States courts are determined in accordance with the provisions of the Foreign Sovereign Immunities Act.[176] An amendment to the Act

167. 9 U.S.C.A. § 101 (1988).

168. *Parsons & Whittemore Overseas, Inc.*, 508 F.2d at 977.

169. Iran Aircraft Indus. v. Avco Corp., 980 F.2d 141, 145 (2d Cir. 1992); Fotochrome, Inc. v. Copal Co., Ltd., 517 F.2d 512, 519 (2d Cir. 1975).

170. 980 F.2d 141, 146 (2d Cir. 1992).

171. *Id.*

172. *Id.*

173. Pub. L. No. 100–669, § 1, Nov. 16, 1988, 102 Stat. 3969.

174. 482 F. Supp. 1175 (D.D.C. 1980), *vacated without op.*, 684 F.2d 1032 (D.C. Cir. 1981) (case dismissed after parties settled).

175. Cf. Monegasque de Reassurances S.A.M. v. Nak Naftogaz, 311 F.3d 488 (2d Cir. 2002) (refusing to confirm arbitral award on forum non conveniens grounds).

176. 28 U.S.C.A. § 1602 (1994).

provides that a foreign state shall not be immune from the jurisdiction of courts of the United States in any case:

> in which the action is brought, either to enforce an agreement made by the foreign State with or for the benefit of a private party to submit to arbitration all or any differences which have arisen or which may arise between the parties with respect to a defined legal relationship, whether contractual or not, concerning a subject matter capable of settlement by arbitration under the laws of the United States, or to confirm an award made pursuant to such an agreement to arbitrate, if
>
> (A) the arbitration takes place or is intended to take place in the United States,
>
> (B) the agreement or award is or may be governed by a treaty or other international agreement in force for the United States calling for the recognition and enforcement of arbitral awards,
>
> (C) the underlying claim, save for the agreement to arbitrate could have been brought in a United States court under this section or section 1607, or
>
> (D) paragraph (1) of this subsection is otherwise applicable.[177]

Clause (B) is intended to cover suits involving the recognition and enforcement of arbitral awards that are made in the territory of a state which is a party to the New York Convention or other treaties and international agreements in force for the United States. The provisions of 28 U.S.C.A. § 1610 have similarly been amended to allow for execution of assets of foreign states and foreign instrumentalities with respect to suits to enforce an arbitration agreement or to confirm an award made pursuant to such an agreement to arbitrate.

[2] Selected Procedural Issues Concerning Enforcement of Arbitral Awards

Several provisions in 9 U.S.C.A. §§ 201–208 are of particular procedural significance in the enforcement of arbitral awards under the New York Convention. Section 203 provides:

> An action or proceeding falling under the Convention shall be deemed to arise under the laws and treaties of the United States. The district courts of the United States . . . shall have original jurisdiction over such an action or proceeding, regardless of the amount in controversy.

---

177. 28 U.S.C.A. § 1605(a)(6).

U.S. District Courts, therefore, have jurisdiction to enforce awards under the Convention, regardless of the amount in controversy.

Venue for enforcement of an award under the Convention is determined by 9 U.S.C.A. § 204:

> An action or proceeding over which the district courts have jurisdiction pursuant to section 203 of this title may be brought in any such court in which save for the arbitration agreement an action or proceeding with respect to the controversy between the parties could be brought, or in such court for the district and division which embraces the place designated in the agreement as the place of arbitration if such place is within the United States.

Proper venue is therefore: (1) where a district court would have had jurisdiction in the absence of the arbitration agreement; or (2) the place within the United States named in the arbitration agreement. The first test for jurisdiction would normally invoke the US$75,000 amount in controversy requirement for diversity jurisdiction of 28 U.S.C.A. § 1332(a). It must be noted that such amount in controversy requirement is expressly abolished in 9 U.S.C.A. § 203. Venue is therefore proper where the district court could assert subject matter and *in personam* jurisdiction. Examples may include, therefore, the jurisdiction of the Respondent's principal place of business, registered office, or residence; a jurisdiction where a substantial part of the contract was performed or where a substantial part of the property at issue is situate; or ANY district where the Respondent is an alien.[178]

It should also be noted that 9 U.S.C.A. § 207 imposes a three year statute of limitation within which a party may apply to enforce an arbitral award under the Convention.[179] Also, under Article IV of the Convention, a party seeking to enforce an award must provide to the court authenticated originals or certified copies of the arbitration agreement and award, or proper translations thereof.[180] 9 U.S.C.A.

178. 28 U.S.C.A. § 1391. *See* Cortez Byrd Chips, Inc. v. Bill Harbert Construction Co., 529 U.S. 193 (2000) (reversing 11th Circuit and ruling that venue for motion to confirm, vacate, or modify arbitral award under FAA may lie in any district proper under the general venue statute, as FAA venue provisions are permissive).

179. *See* Seetransport Wiking Trader Schiffarht-gesellschaft MGH & Co. v. Navimpex Centrala Navala, 989 F.2d 572, 581 (2d Cir. 1993) (determining that under 9 U.S.C.A. § 207, time to enforce award runs from date arbitrators make decision, not from time of filing or delivery of final award).

180. 9 U.S.C.A. § 201, setting forth text of Convention.

(Rel.6–10/05)

§ 208 provides that Chapter 1 of the Federal Arbitration Act[181] applies to proceedings to enforce foreign arbitral awards under the New York Convention to the extent the FAA does not conflict with §§ 201–207 and the Convention.[182]

The New York Convention contemplates multiple, post-award enforcement proceedings in the courts of signatory nations around the world. Given this and comity considerations of respecting other nations' courts, the 5th Circuit, in *Karaha Bodas Co., L.L.C. v. Negara*,[183] reversed the district court and held that an anti-suit injunction was improperly issued. The injunction had been sought in the U.S. court to prevent the losing party to a Swiss arbitration from pursuing reversal of the award in the courts of Indonesia. The 5th Circuit did not conclude that the district court was without power to issue the anti-suit injunction but noted that the structure of the New York Convention would seldom, if ever, permit one; at least where the award had been entered in another nation or under its law. The 5th Circuit held this was so because Switzerland had primary jurisdiction over the award, which concerned arbitration in Switzerland under Swiss law. The New York Convention grants primary jurisdiction in the courts of the country in which, or under the law of which, the award is made. The U.S. and Indonesian courts merely had secondary, i.e., enforcement, jurisdiction over the award. Therefore, the stake of the U.S. court was not superior to its Indonesian counterpart nor did one proceeding necessarily interfere with the other.[184]

181. 9 U.S.C.A. §§ 1–16.

182. A similar provision is contained in 9 U.S.C.A. § 307 concerning the Inter-American Convention on International Commercial Arbitration.

183. 335 F.3d 357 (5th Cir. 2003).

184. *Id.* at 374. The court summarized its ruling: ''Although Indonesia has already purported to annul the Award, such annulment in no way affects the authority of the district court (or this court) to enforce the Award in the United States-which is, after all, the principal task of a U.S. court under the Convention. And, the Award can be enforced here with or without the district court's injunction against [Defendant]. Similarly, other enforcement jurisdictions will be forced independently to weigh the Indonesian annulment with or without awareness of a U.S. court's injunction. Inasmuch as the Convention provides for multiple proceedings and a more limited role for enforcement jurisdictions, [Defendant's] actions in Indonesia, even if spurious, are less vexatious and oppressive than they would be outside of this treaty structure. Finally, given the absence of a practical, positive effect that any injunction could have, more weighty considerations of comity dictate that the better course for U.S. courts to follow is to avoid the appearance of reaching out to interfere with the judicial proceedings in another country and to avoid stepping too far outside its limited role under the Convention.'' *Id.*

[3] Enforcing Arbitration Awards Under State Law

State statutes may also provide a basis for enforcing international arbitral awards. Certain of North Carolina's arbitration statutes are illustrative. The jurisdictional limitations of a state act should be carefully examined. With certain important exceptions, including provisions regarding petitions to a court to enforce an agreement to arbitrate and to obtain interim relief, the North Carolina International Commercial Arbitration Act only applies if the place of arbitration is in North Carolina.[185] It should also be noted that 9 U.S.C.A. § 205 expressly provides that where a state court proceeding relates to an arbitration agreement or award under the New York Convention, the proceeding may be removed to federal court of right.

The North Carolina International Commercial Arbitration Act provides:

> Subject to the relevant provisions of federal law or any applicable international agreement in force between the United States of America and any other nation or nations, upon application of a party, the superior court shall confirm an arbitral award, unless it finds grounds for modifying or vacating the award under G.S. 1–567.64. An award shall not be confirmed unless the time for correction and interpretation of awards prescribed by G.S. 1–567.63 shall have expired or been waived by all the parties. Upon the granting of an order confirming, modifying, or correcting an award, judgment or decree shall be entered in conformity therewith and enforced as any other judgment or decree. The superior court may award costs of the application and of the subsequent proceedings.[186]

North Carolina state courts, therefore, are directed to enforce international arbitral awards, subject to certain time limits and grounds. N.C.G.S. § 1–567.63 generally provides that, within 30 days of receipt of an award, a party may move the court to correct certain clerical or computational errors or to issue an interpretation of a specific point of the award.

N.C.G.S. § 1–567.64 provides that, subject to treaty or federal law, an arbitral award may be modified or vacated only for "illegality, or substantial unfairness in the conduct of the arbitral proceedings." Courts are further directed "not to engage in de novo review of the subject

185. N.C.G.S. § 1–567.31(b).
186. N.C.G.S. § 1–567.65.

matter of the dispute giving rise to the arbitration proceedings.''[187] The breadth of this review standard is, however, uncertain, as there is presently no case law on the issue.

Where a state international arbitration act is inapplicable, there may be other state law under which an international arbitral award may be enforced. North Carolina's Uniform Arbitration Act provides that a court shall confirm an arbitral award unless certain grounds for modifying, vacating, or correcting the award are present.[188] Such grounds are set forth in N.C.G.S. §§ 1–567.13 and 1–567.14 and include, among others, that there was evident partiality of an arbitrator appointed as a neutral, misconduct prejudicing the rights of a party, that the tribunal refused to postpone the hearing upon sufficient cause shown or refused to hear evidence material to the controversy, or that a mistake or miscalculation was present in the award. These grounds appear broader than the specific exceptions to enforcement of an award under the New York Convention[189] and may be unlawful to the extent they are inconsistent with a Treaty or federal law, including that implementing the New York Convention, 9 U.S.C.A. § 201 *et seq.*, or Inter-American Convention, 9 U.S.C.A. § 301 *et seq.* No case on this issue was located, however.

Practice Note: Counsel should carefully consider the advantages, if any, of attempting to enforce an arbitral agreement in a state, rather than federal, court. Given the express federal legislation on enforcement of international arbitral agreements and awards, absence of an amount in controversy requirement concerning New York Convention actions, and the potential existence of broad modification and vacation procedures and timelines under state law, a federal forum may be desirable. As removal to federal court exists of right concerning the New York Convention, commencing an action initially in federal court may also avoid the cost and delay of removal. This is not to suggest that federal courts are more knowledgeable. It is the Authors' experience that neither federal nor state courts and clerk's offices are very familiar with international arbitration law but are most interested when such issues arise and willing to be educated.

---

187. *Id.*

188. N.C.G.S. § 1–567.12.

189. *See supra* § 12.06, (discussing exceptions to enforcement of awards under the New York Convention).

§ 12.07 ANALYZING ARBITRATION ISSUES: PRACTICAL STRATEGIES

For practitioners advising clients in international arbitration, recourse to U.S. courts may be required to pursue the client's objectives. This chapter has reviewed selected issues that parties may face when seeking assistance from the courts in support of international arbitration.

Advance preparation for the possibility of litigation is always prudent. It remains so even in the area of arbitration. Planning for arbitration should include knowing how an issue will be treated in court. The arbitration provision included in any commercial agreement should, to the extent possible, address, among other issues, the issues set forth above in § 12.02[4] that affect the way courts consider arbitration questions.

To take steps to prevent a matter from being heard in court, parties preferring arbitration should include in the arbitration agreement a complete and effective clause identifying the scope of issues and disputes subject to arbitration and address in the agreement, in as much detail as possible, the selection of arbitrators, situs of the arbitration, availability of provisional measures from national courts, conduct of the proceedings, enforcement of the award, and other issues. There is, of course, a strong U.S. judicial policy favoring arbitration, but to have certainty and predictability, careful planning is required.

Appendix 1

RETAINING A FOREIGN ATTORNEY

State Department Circular

DISCLAIMER: **THE INFORMATION IN THIS CIRCULAR IS PROVIDED FOR GENERAL INFORMATION ONLY. THE DEPARTMENT OF STATE MAKES NO WARRANTY REGARDING THE ACCURACY OF THIS INFORMATION. WHILE SOME OF THE INFORMATION IS ABOUT LEGAL ISSUES, IT IS NOT LEGAL ADVICE. QUESTIONS INVOLVING INTERPRETATION OF SPECIFIC FOREIGN LAWS SHOULD BE ADDRESSED TO FOREIGN ATTORNEYS.**

PROVISO: Officers of the Department of State and U.S. Embassies and Consulates abroad are prohibited by federal regulation from acting as agents, attorneys or in a fiduciary capacity on behalf of U.S. citizens in private legal disputes abroad. (22 CFR 92.81; 10.735-206(a)(7); 72.41; 71.5.)

RECOMMENDING A FOREIGN ATTORNEY: 22 CFR 92.82 provides that Foreign Service officers shall refrain from recommending a particular foreign attorney, but may furnish names of several attorneys, or refer inquiries to foreign law directories, bar associations or other organizations.

FOREIGN ATTORNEYS REPRESENTING THE U.S. GOVERNMENT ABROAD: U.S. embassies and consulates abroad generally do not have foreign attorneys on a retainer to represent the interests of the U.S. Government. (See 22 U.S.C. 2698(a); 28 C.F.R. 0.45; Volume 2, Foreign Affairs Manual (FAM), Department of State, Sec. 283; Volume 9, Foreign Affairs Manual, Sec. 971.2.)

BACKGROUND: This information flyer was devised primarily for the lay person confronted with a private legal problem abroad. It contains general practical suggestions for dealing with a foreign attorney. General information concerning foreign legal aid is also discussed. For American lawyers facing the task of retaining foreign legal counsel, see Lewis, Selecting and Working With Foreign Counsel, The International Lawyer's Deskbook, American Bar Association, 393-410 (1996) and Epstein & Snyder, International Litigation: A Guide to Jurisdiction, Practice and Strategy, 2nd, 2.10-2.13, p. 2-17 - 2-24 (1994).

WHAT TYPE OF LAWYER WILL YOU NEED:

Barristers and Solicitors: In some foreign countries it may be necessary to retain the services of both a solicitor and a barrister. In such jurisdictions, barristers are allowed to appear in court, including trial courts and higher courts of appeal or other courts. Solicitors are allowed to advise clients and sometimes represent them in the lower courts. They may also prepare cases for barristers to try in the higher courts..**Notaries, "Notaires", "Notars", and "Huissiers"**: In some countries, notaries public, "notaires", "notars" and "huissiers" can perform many of the functions performed by attorneys in the United States. A notary in a civil law country is not comparable to a notary public in the United States. Their education and training differs from that of most notaries public in the United States. They frequently draft instruments such wills and conveyances. In some countries a notary is a public official appointed by the Ministry of Justice, whose functions include not only preparing documents, but the administration and settlement of estates. Such notaries serve as repositories for wills and are empowered to serve legal documents. In some countries "huissiers" serve documents. They are not lawyers, but are very specialized members of the foreign legal profession. They may not plead cases in court. Your foreign attorney may delegate certain functions to a notary, "notaire", "notar" or "huissier".

Foreign Legal Consultants: These are U.S. law firms with offices in foreign countries. They may or may not be licensed to practice law abroad.

Selecting an Attorney: When you receive a list of attorneys, consider contacting several attorneys, briefly describing the nature of the services you desire. Find out the attorney's qualifications and experience. Find out how the attorney plans to represent you. Ask specific questions and expect the attorney to explain legal activities in language that you can comprehend. Do not turn over documents or funds until you are satisfied that the attorney understands your problem and is willing to handle your case. Find out the rules of the foreign country concerning attorney-client confidentiality.

GUIDELINES ON HOW TO DEAL WITH YOUR FOREIGN ATTORNEY:

Understanding Your Attorney: Ask your attorney to analyze your case, giving you the positive and negative aspects and probable outcome. Do not expect your attorney to give a simple answer to a complex legal question. Be sure that you understand the technical language in any contract or other legal document prepared by your attorney before you sign it.

Fees: Find out what fees the attorney charges and how the attorney expects to be paid. In some countries fees are fixed by local law. Establish a billing schedule that meets your requirements and is acceptable to the foreign attorney. Foreign lawyers may be unaccustomed to including a description of work performed in connection with billing. Some foreign attorneys may expect to be paid in advance; some may demand payment after each action they take on your behalf and refuse to take further action until they are paid; and some may take the case on a contingency or percentage basis, collecting a pre-arranged percentage of moneys awarded to you by the foreign court. Request an estimate of the total hours and costs of doing the work. Be clear who will be involved in the work and the fees charged by each participant. Determine costs if other attorneys or specialists need to be consulted, such as barristers. See "Payment of Attorneys and Litigation Expenses in Selected Foreign Nations", U.S. Library of Congress, Law Library, Doc. LL-95-2 (March 1995) (Includes information on Australia, Canada, China, France, Germany, Great Britain, Greece, India, Italy, Japan, Mexico, Netherlands, Poland, Sweden and Taiwan.)

Method of Payment: Find out the expected means of payment (corporate check, bank check, personal check, international money order, wire transfer), specify currency and exchange rates (when and where applicable or feasible).

Progress Reports: Ask that your attorney keep you informed of the progress of your case according to a pre-established schedule. Remember that most foreign courts work rather slowly. You may, therefore, wish the attorney to send you monthly reports, even though no real developments have ensured, simply to satisfy your doubts about the progress of the case. Ask what the fee will be for progress reports.

Document Translations: If you need to provide complex or technical documents to your attorney, you may wish to consider having the documents translated into the attorney's native language. Remember that even a fundamental knowledge of English may not be enough to enable the attorney to understand technical documents you provide. Discuss with your attorney whether it is preferable to translate the documents in the U.S. or in the foreign country. Compare the costs.

Communication: Remember your responsibility to keep your attorney informed of any new developments in your case. Be honest and frank with your attorney. Tell the attorney every relevant fact in order to get the best representation of your interests. Establish how you be communicate with your foreign attorney (mail, phone, fax, Internet.)

Time: Find out how much time the attorney anticipates the case may take to complete. (Note: in some countries the courts recess for a period of several months. In addition, even if the case is resolved, currency control laws may delay the transfer of funds awarded to you from the foreign country for an indefinite period of time. Discuss these issues with your attorney to ensure there is no confusion.

Authentication and Translation of Documents: It may be helpful for you to provide foreign authorities or your attorney with authenticated, translated copies of pertinent documents. Consult your foreign attorney before going to this expense. An information flyer explaining the authentication process is available from the Office of American Citizens Services, either by mail or through our automated fax system or via our Internet Consular Affairs Home Page described below under "Additional Information". These topics include "Hague Legalization Convention" (AUTOFAX document 1053) and "General Authentication Flyer" (AUTOFAX document 1046). See also the U.S. State Department's Authentications Office Home Page at http://www.state.gov/www/authenticate/index.html.

Records: Consider requesting copies of all letters and documents prepared on your behalf. Inquire about the costs of mailing you such documents.

Complaints Against Foreign Attorneys: If the services of your foreign attorney prove unsatisfactory, in addition to notifying the U.S. Department of State and/or the consular section of the U.S. embassy or consulate abroad, you may address your complaints to the local foreign bar association. Information about foreign bar associations may be obtained from the U.S. embassy or consulate abroad. Foreign embassies and consulates in the U.S. may also have information on this subject.

Assistance of U.S. Embassies and Consulates: Should your communication with a foreign attorney prove unsatisfactory, a U.S. consular officer may, if appropriate, communicate with the attorney on your behalf. In addition, complaints against foreign attorneys whose names appear on the consular list of attorneys can result in the removal of their names from the list.

Coordination with Attorneys in the U.S.: American attorneys may not be in a position to represent your interests abroad, particularly because generally they will not be permitted to participate in foreign court proceedings under the laws of the foreign country. American attorneys experienced in international law procedure may be helpful in explaining the complex legal issues involved in your case and some may have associates abroad to whom they can refer you.

Finding A Foreign Attorney:

U.S. Department of State, Bureau of Consular Affairs, Office of American Citizens Services and Crisis Management, (CA/OCS/ACS), Room 4811A, 2201 C Street N.W., Washington, D.C. 20520; tel: 202-647-5225 or 5226. Please send a stamped, self addressed envelope, 8 1/2 x 11, to accommodate postage for 20 sheets of paper or more. These lists of attorneys are also being added to the Internet home pages of our U.S. embassies and consulates which are linked to the State Department Consular Home Page at **http://.travel.state.gov/** which can also be accessed through the main State Department Home Page at **http://www.state.gov/** under travel or consular. Lists of attorneys are prepared by U.S. embassies and consulates triennially (every three years). The lists include names, addresses, telephone numbers, etc., and information concerning the foreign attorney's educational background, areas of specialization, and language capability. When compiling the lists, U.S. consular officers send letters and questionnaires to the attorneys in their consular district in the foreign country. American attorneys licensed to practice in the foreign country or working as foreign legal consultants are also included. Local foreign bar associations are used as a resource in determining whether an attorney is in good standing. See Volume 7, Department of State Foreign Affairs Manual 990 (8/30/94) and 22 CFR 92.82.

Law Directories:

DISCLAIMER: **The Department of State assumes no responsibility for the professional ability or integrity of the firms or persons whose names appear in the attached list. The order in which they appear has no significance.**

Martindale-Hubbell Law Directory, 800-526-4902, on-line via Lexis. See also the Martindale-Hubbell Home Page on the Internet at **http://www.martindale.com/products/digests.html**.

Campbell's List - A Directory of Selected Lawyers, 407-644-8298.

Russell Law List - Legal Correspondents International, 410-820-4475.

The American Lawyer - Practice Directories, 212-973-2800.

American Bar Association, 1995 Directory of Lawyer Referral Services in the U.S. and Canada.

ABA INTERNATIONAL LIAISON SECTION: While the ABA does not provide international referrals, it can provide the names and addresses of national or local bar associations as well as the names of several reference guides. Contact the Section by e-mail at intlliaison@abanet.org or call 312-988-5107 or visit the Section's Home Page at American Bar Association, International Liaison Office, **http://www.abanet.org/liaison/home.html.**

LEGAL AID: There may be facilities in the foreign country for low cost or free legal services. If information is not included in the consular list of attorneys, ask the local foreign bar association or Ministry of Justice about the availability of legal aid. Contact the legal attach or consular section of the foreign embassy in Washington for specific guidance. Legal aid information may also be available from a local branch of the International Social Service. The agencies' headquarters are in Geneva, Switzerland, but information or assistance may be available through its New York branch at 10 W. 40th Street, New York, N.Y. 10018, 212-532-6350. See also, American Bar Association, Directory of State and Local Lawyer Assistance Programs in the U.S. and Canada.

See Also:

DISCLAIMER: **The Department of State makes no warranty or guarantee concerning the accuracy or reliability of the content of other web sites. The order in which they appear has no significance.**

ABA Standing Committee on Lawyer Referral and Information Service: **http://www.abanet.org/legalserv/lrishome.html.**

ABA Divison for Legal Services: Access to Justice: **http://www.abanet.org/legalserv/home.html**

ABA Standing Committee on Legal Aid and Indigent Defendants: **http://www.abanet.org/legalserv/sclaid.html**

ABA Resources on Legal Services for the Poor: **http://www.abanet.org/legalserv/sclaidpubs.html**

ABA Center for Pro Bono; Pro Bono Hotline: 312-988-5769; Internet: **http:www.abanet.org/legalserv/probono.html**

EU/EAA Countries: (AUSTRIA, BELGIUM, DENMARK, FINLAND, FRANCE, GERMANY, GREECE, ICELAND, IRELAND, ITALY, LUXEMBOURG, THE NETHERLANDS, NORWAY, PORTUGAL, SPAIN, SWEDEN, UNITED KINGDOM) via the Internet:
http//europa.eu.int/en/comm/spc/la/c4.htm

BAR ASSOCIATIONS:

DISCLAIMER: **The Department of State makes no warranty or guarantee concerning the accuracy or reliability of the content of other web sites. The order in which they appear has no significance.**

American Bar Association, 750 N. Lake Shore Drive, Chicago, IL 60611, 312-988-5000, home page via Internet: **http://www.abanet.org/.**

American Bar Association, Section of International Law and Practice, **http://www.abanet.org:80/intlaw/home.html.**

American Society of International Law, 2223 Massachusetts Avenue, N.W., Washington, D.C. 20008, Tel: (202) 939-6000; Fax: (202) 797-7133.

Inter-American Bar Association (IABA), 1211 Connecticut Avenue, N.W., Suite 202, Washington, D.C. 20036; tel: 202-393-1217; fax: 202-393-1241, Home Page via Internet: **http://www.erols.com/iaba/.**

International Bar Association (IBA), 2 Harewood Place, Hanover Square, London, WIR9HB, England, Tel: (011) (44) (171) 629-1206; Fax: (011) (44) (171) 409-0-456.

Inter-Pacific Bar Association (IPBA), Nashiazabu Sonic Building, 3-2-12 Nichiazabu, Minato-Ku, Tokyo, 106, Japan, Tel: (011) (81) (3) 34085079; Fax: (011) (81) (3) 334085505.

Law Association for Asia and the Pacific, 33 Barrack Street, 3rd Floor, Perth, W.A., 6000, Australia, Tel: (011) (61) (9) 221-5914.

National Asian Pacific Bar Association (NAPABA) at **www.napaba.org.**

Union Internationale des Avocats (UIA), 25 Rue de Jour, Paris, France, 75001, Tel: (011) (33) (1) 4508-8231; Fax: (011) (33) (1) 4508-8231.

World Jurist Association, 1000 Connecticut Avenue, N.W., Suite 202, Washington, D.C. 20036, Tel: (202) 466-5428; Fax: (202) 452-8540.

Other Resources:

Library of Congress Law Library, Room 240, James Madison Bldg., 101 Independence Avenue, S.E., Washington, D.C. 20540, tel: 202-707-5079 or via the Internet at **http://lcweb2.loc.gov/glin/lawhome.html.**

SELECTED REFERENCES:

American Bar Association, Report on the Regulation of Foreign Lawyers (1977).

Aranson, The United States Percentage Contingent Fee System: Ridicule and Reform From An International Perspective, 127 Texas Int'l L.J. 755-793 (1992).

Bader-Ginsburg, Chairman, The Availability of Legal Services to Poor People and People of Limited Means in Foreign Systems, 6 Int'l Law. 128 (1971).

Barrager, The Great Lawyer Lockout, The Journal of the American Chamber of Commerce in Japan, 10-18, (November 1991).

Barsade, The Effect of EC Regulations upon the Ability of U.S. Lawyers to Establish a Pan-European Practice, 28 Int'l Law. 313 (1994).

Bisconti, Reform of the Professional Law in Italy, 14 Int'l Legal Prac. 55 (1989).

Boyd, Mutual Recognition of Lawyers' Qualifications, Bus. L. Rev. 163 (June 1986).

Brown, The Foreign Lawyer in France, 59 A.B.A.J. 365 (1973).

Busch, The Right of United States Lawyers to Practice Abroad, 3 Int'l Law. 297 (January, 1971).

Busch, The Right of United States Lawyers to Practice Abroad, 3 Int'l Law. 617 (April, 1971).

Comment, Providing Legal Services in Foreign Countries: Making Room for the American Attorney, 83 Colum. L. Rev. 1767, 1768-69 (1983).

Comment: International Legal Practice Restrictions on the Migrant Attorney, 15 Harv. Int'l L.J. 298 (1974).

Comment, The Legal Services Act of the Republic of Croatia — A Guarantee of the Advocate's Independence and Autonomy, 29 Int'l Law. 209 (1995).

Dedingfield, The Contingency Fee System in America, 143 New Law Journal 1670 (Nov. 26, 1993).

Directory of Legal Aid and Advice Facilities Available Throughout the World, the International Legal Aid Association, International Bar Association, (1966).

Epstein & Snyder, International Litigation: A Guide to Jurisdiction, Practice and Strategy, 2nd, 2.10-2.13, p. 2-17 - 2-24 (1994).

Figa, The "American Rule" Has Outlived Its Usefulness; Adopt the "English Rule," 9 Nat'l L.J. 13 (1986).

Finding the Right Lawyer, American Bar Association, Law Practice Management Section, LC: 94-76852 (1995). Can be ordered via internet: **http://www.abanet.org/store/con-bandp.html.**

Friedman and Wilson, Representing Foreign Clients in Civil Discovery and Grand Jury Proceedings, 26 Va. J. of Int'l L. 327 (1986).

Georgakakis, Greece Allows Lawyers to Form Companies, Int'l Fin. L. Rev. 12 (July 1990).

Goebel, Lawyers in the European Community: Progress Towards Community-Wide Rights of Practice, 15 Fordham Int'l L. J. 556, 563 (1992).

Goebel, Professional Qualification and Educational Requirements for Law Practice in a Foreign Country: Bridging the Gap, 63 Tul. L. Rev. 443, 475 (1989).

Greiter, How to Get Your Money in Foreign Countries: A Survey of Court Costs and Lawyer's Fees in 151 Countries, (Boston, Kluwer Law and Taxation Publishers, 1988).

Harper, Bye Bye Barrister, 76 American Bar Association Journal 58-62 (Mar. 1990).

Hergen, How to Practice Family Law in Europe When You're Not European", 3 Family Advocate 25, Spring (1981).

Hieros Gamos, List of Bar Associations, **http://www.hg.org/.**

Hufbauer, Europe 1992: Opportunities and Challenges, Brookings Rev., Summer 1990 at 15; Story, supra note 12, at 18, 27.

Kenadjian, R. Wohl, S. Chemtob, & G. Fukushima, Practice By Foreign Lawyers in Japan, Fordham International Law Journal, 1989-1990, Vol. 13, No. 3, pp. 390-404.

Knoppek-Wetzel, Employment Restrictions and the Practice of Law by Aliens in the United States and Abroad, Duke L.J. 871 (1974).

Kritzer, The English Rule, 78 A.B.A.J. 54 (Nov. 1992).

Lewis, Selecting and Working With Foreign Counsel, The International Lawyer's Deskbook, American Bar Association, 393-410 (1996).

Lang, European Community Law, Irish Law and the Irish Legal Profession — Protection of the Individual and Cooperation between Member States and the Community, 5 D.U.L.J. (n.s.) 1 (June 1983).

Lex Mundi Directory of Law Firm Associations, Alliances, Clubs, and Other Affiliations, Int'l Law. Newsletter, vol. xv, no. 6, 1993, at 26-37.

Lowry, Foreign Legal Consultants in Connecticut, 16 Int'l Legal Prac. 115 (1991).

MacMullin, Foreign Attorneys in Japan: Past Policies, The New Special Measures Law and Future Expectations, Florida International Law Journal, Fall 1988, Vol. 4, No. 1, pp. 51-84.

McCrory, Reform of the English Legal Profession: An American's Perspective, 134 Solicitor's Journal 819-821 (June 1, 1990).

Napier and Armstrong, Costs After the Event (United Kingdom), 143 New Law Journal 12 (Jan. 8, 1993)

Note, Foreign Branches of Law Firms: The Development of Lawyers Equipped to Handle International Practice, 80 Harv. L. Rev. 1284 (1967).

Payment of Attorneys and Litigation Expenses in Selected Foreign Nations, U.S. Library of Congress, Law Library, Doc. LL-95-2 (March 1995).

Pfennigstorf, The European Experience With Attorney Fee Shifting (Research Contributions of the American Bar Foundation, 1984, No. 2.), reprinted from 47 Law and Contemporary Problems 37 (1984).

Ramseyer, Lawyers, Foreign Lawyers, and Lawyer-Substitutes: The Market for Regulation in Japan, Harvard International Law Journal, 1986, Vol. 27, pp. 499-539.

Roorda, The Internationalization of the Practice of Law, 28 Wake Forest L. Rev. 141, 150 (1993).

Rubenstein, Foreign Firms Offer Quality Work at Bargain Rates, Crop. Legal Times Nov. 1992, at 12.

Ryan, The Development of Representative Proceedings in the Federal Court, 11 Aust. Bar Review 131, 139 (1993).

Saunders, The EEC and the USA: Will the Gates Be Oened for American Law Firms in 1992?, 3 Temple Int'l & Comp. L.J. 191, 214 (1989).

Schutzer, An Alien's Right to Practice Law, 38 Alb. L. Rev. 888 (1974).

Scott, The Green Paper on Contingency Fees (United Kingdom), 8 Civil Justice Quarterly 97-103 (April 1989).

Section Recommendation and Report, American Bar Association Section of International Law and Practice Report to the House of Delegates: Model Rule for the Licensing of Legal Consultants, 28 Int'l Law. 207 (1994).

Sheehey, Japan's New Foreign Lawyer Law, Law and Policy in International Business, Vol. 19, No. 2, 1987, pp. 361-383.

Sokol, Reforming the French Legal Profession, 26 Int'l Law. 1025 (1992).

Spedding, Transnational Legal Practice in the EEC and the United States, 185-200 (1987).

Stewart, Is the Siesta Over for Spanish Lawyers, Int'l Fin. L. Rev. 20 (Feb. 1991).

Sydney, Are Some Lawyers More Equal than Others?, Int'l Fin. L. Rev. 16 (Aug. 1989).

Tada, Role of Corporate Legal Departments in Japan, The International Lawyer, Winter 1988, Vol. 22, No. 4, pp. 1141-1144.

The American Lawyer: When and How to Use One, American Bar Association, Public Education Division, PC: 235-0021 (1993). Can be ordered via internet: **http://www.abanet.org/store/con-bandp.html.**

The Foreign Legal Operations Manual: A Survey and Analysis of U.S. Law Firms Overseas. (s.1.) Abacus Press, Division of Sachem International Corp., 1984.

Toumlin, The Right of Barristers to Practice in the EEC, New L.J. 1309 (1990).

Toumlin, A Worldwide Common Code of Professional Ethics?, 15 Fordham Int'l L.J. 673, 685 (1991-1993).

You and Your Lawyer: A Client's Guide, American Bar Association, General Practice Section, PC: 515-0100-1102 (1994); Can be ordered via internet: **http://www.abanet.org/store/con-bandp.html.**

Vargo, The American Rule On Attorney Fee Allocation: The Injured Person's Access to Justice (U.S., U.K. & Australia), 42 American University Law Review 1567-1639 (Spring-Summer 1993).

Warren, Monahan & Duhot, Role of the Lawyer in International Business Transactions, 58 A.B.A.J. 181 (1972).

Weil, The Proposal for a Directive on the Right of Establishment for Lawyers in the European Community, 15 Fordham Int'l L.J. 699 (1991-92).

Whetley, A Way to Pay the Piper (contingency fees for U.K. lawyers are to be introduced), The Times 27 (Aug. 17, 1993).

White, Comment, The Reform of the French Legal Profession: A Comment on the Changed Status of Foreign Lawyers, 11 Colum. J. Transnat'l L. 435 (1972).

Wilson, EEC: Freedom to Provide Services for EEC Lawyers, 19 Harv. Int'l L.J. 379 (1978).
Wright, Firm Associations Provide Network of Global Counsel, Corp. Legal Times, Mar. 1993, at 36.

Zander, The Thatcher Government's Onslaught on the Lawyers: Who Won?, 24 Int'l Law. 753 (1990).

Zheng, The Evolving Role of Lawyers and Legal Practice in China, 36 American Journal of Comparative Law, 473 (1988).

ADDITIONAL INFORMATION: The Office of American Citizens Services has available general information flyers on international judicial assistance many of which are available through our automated fax system or via our Internet Consular Affairs Home Page.

Using the Autofax System:

* Dial (202) 647-3000 using the phone on your fax machine.

* Follow the prompt to obtain a printed index of judicial assistance topics. There are four indexes.

Travel Information - Index of Countries - Press 1
Passports and Visas - Index of Flyers - Press 2
Judicial Assistance - General and Country Specific - Press 3
Child Custody and Adoption - Index of Flyers - Press 4

* Enter the four digit code for the document desired as listed in the index.

* When the prompt identifies the document and asks if you want that document, enter Y (9) for yes or N (6) for no.

* If you want another document, enter the four digit code, using the same procedures noted in the previous step.

* When you finish selecting, press the # key on the phone keyboard and press the start button on your fax machine.

* After a brief delay of up to a minute, the documents will print automatically on your fax machine.

Using the Internet: Many of our judicial assistance flyers are also available on the Internet via the Department of State, Bureau of Consular Affairs Home Page at **http://travel.state.gov/** under International Legal Assistance or through the main State Department Home Page at **http://www.state.gov/** under Travel, Consular, or International Legal Assistance. See also, the Department of State, Office of the Legal Adviser for Private International Law (L/PIL) Home Page at **http://his.com/~pildb/** for information regarding private international law unification. See also the Home Pages for many of our embassies which are linked to the Consular Affairs Home Page.

Questions: Additional questions may be addressed to the U.S. Department of State, Bureau of Consular Affairs, Office of American Citizens Services at (202) 647-5225 or 202-647-5226.

Appendix 2[1]

HAGUE CONVENTION ON THE SERVICE ABROAD OF JUDICIAL AND EXTRAJUDICIAL DOCUMENTS IN CIVIL AND COMMERCIAL MATTERS

(Concluded November 15, 1965)

The States signatory to the present Convention,

Desiring to create appropriate means to ensure that judicial and extrajudicial documents to be served abroad shall be brought to the notice of the addressee in sufficient time,

Desiring to improve the organisation of mutual judicial assistance for that purpose by simplifying and expediting the procedure,

Have resolved to conclude a Convention to this effect and have agreed upon the following provisions:

Article 1

The present Convention shall apply in all cases, in civil or commercial matters, where there is occasion to transmit a judicial or extrajudicial document for service abroad.

This Convention shall not apply where the address of the person to be served with the document is not known.

Chapter I — Judicial Documents

Article 2

Each Contracting State shall designate a Central Authority which will undertake to receive requests for service coming from other Contracting States and to proceed in conformity with the provisions of Articles 3 to 6.

Each State shall organise the Central Authority in conformity with its own law.

Article 3

The authority or judicial officer competent under the law of the State in which the documents originate shall forward to the Central Authority of the State addressed a request conforming to the model annexed to the present Convention, without any requirement of legalisation or other equivalent formality.

The document to be served or a copy thereof shall be annexed to the request. The request and the document shall both be furnished in duplicate.

Article 4

If the Central Authority considers that the request does not comply with the provisions of the present Convention it shall promptly inform the applicant and specify its objections to the request.

Article 5

The Central Authority of the State addressed shall itself serve the document or shall arrange to have it served by an appropriate agency, either—

a) by a method prescribed by its internal law for the service of documents in domestic actions upon persons who are within its territory, or

b) by a particular method requested by the applicant, unless such a method is incompatible with the law of the State addressed.

Subject to sub-paragraph *(b)* of the first paragraph of this Article, the document may always be served by delivery to an addressee who accepts it voluntarily.

If the document is to be served under the first paragraph above, the Central Authority may require the document to be written in, or translated into, the official language or one of the official languages of the State addressed.

That part of the request, in the form attached to the present Convention, which contains a summary of the document to be served, shall be served with the document.

Article 6

The Central Authority of the State addressed or any authority which it may have designated for that purpose, shall complete a certificate in the form of the model annexed to the present Convention.

The certificate shall state that the document has been served and shall include the method, the place and the date of service and the person to whom the document was delivered. If the document has not been served, the certificate shall set out the reasons which have prevented service.

The applicant may require that a certificate not completed by a Central Authority or by a judicial authority shall be countersigned by one of these authorities.

The certificate shall be forwarded directly to the applicant.

Article 7

The standard terms in the model annexed to the present Convention shall in all cases be written either in French or in English. They may also be written in the official language, or in one of the official languages, of the State in which the documents originate.

The corresponding blanks shall be completed either in the language of the State addressed or in French or in English.

Article 8

Each Contracting State shall be free to effect service of judicial documents upon persons abroad, without application of any compulsion, directly through its diplomatic or consular agents.

Any State may declare that it is opposed to such service within its territory, unless the document is to be served upon a national of the State in which the documents originate.

Article 9

Each Contracting State shall be free, in addition, to use consular channels to forward documents, for the purpose of service, to those authorities of another Contracting State which are designated by the latter for this purpose.

Each Contracting State may, if exceptional circumstances so require, use diplomatic channels for the same purpose.

Article 10

Provided the State of destination does not object, the present Convention shall not interfere with—

a) the freedom to send judicial documents, by postal channels, directly to persons abroad,

b) the freedom of judicial officers, officials or other competent persons of the State of origin to effect service of judicial documents directly through the judicial officers, officials or other competent persons of the State of destination,

c) the freedom of any person interested in a judicial proceeding to effect service of judicial documents directly through the judicial officers, officials or other competent persons of the State of destination.

Article 11

The present Convention shall not prevent two or more Contracting States from agreeing to permit, for the purpose of service of judicial documents, channels of transmission other than those provided for in the preceding Articles and, in particular, direct communication between their respective authorities.

Article 12

The service of judicial documents coming from a Contracting State shall not give rise to any payment or reimbursement of taxes or costs for the services rendered by the State addressed.

The applicant shall pay or reimburse the costs occasioned by—

a) the employment of a judicial officer or of a person competent under the law of the State of destination,

b) the use of a particular method of service.

Article 13

Where a request for service complies with the terms of the present Convention, the State addressed may refuse to comply therewith only if it deems that compliance would infringe its sovereignty or security.

It may not refuse to comply solely on the ground that, under its internal law, it claims exclusive jurisdiction over the subject-matter of the action or that its internal law would not permit the action upon which the application is based.

The Central Authority shall, in case of refusal, promptly inform the applicant and state the reasons for the refusal.

Article 14

Difficulties which may arise in connection with the transmission of judicial documents for service shall be settled through diplomatic channels.

Article 15

Where a writ of summons or an equivalent document had to be transmitted abroad for the purpose of service, under the provisions of the present Convention, and the defendant has not appeared, judgment shall not be given until it is established that—

a) the document was served by a method prescribed by the internal law of the State addressed for the service of documents in domestic actions upon persons who are within its territory, or

b) the document was actually delivered to the defendant or to his residence by another method provided for by this Convention,

and that in either of these cases the service or the delivery was effected in sufficient time to enable the defendant to defend.

Each Contracting State shall be free to declare that the judge, notwithstanding the provisions of the first paragraph of this Article, may give judgment even if no certificate of service or delivery has been received, if all the following conditions are fulfilled—

a) the document was transmitted by one of the methods provided for in this Convention, *b)* a period of time of not less than six months, considered adequate by the judge in the particular case, has elapsed since the date of the transmission of the document,

c) no certificate of any kind has been received, even though every reasonable effort has been made to obtain it through the competent authorities of the State addressed.

Notwithstanding the provisions of the preceding paragraphs the judge may order, in case of urgency, any provisional or protective measures.

Article 16

When a writ of summons or an equivalent document had to be transmitted abroad for the purpose of service, under the provisions of the present Convention, and a judgment has been entered against a defendant who has not appeared, the judge shall have the power to relieve the defendant from the effects of the expiration of the time for appeal from the judgment if the following conditions are fulfilled—

a) the defendant, without any fault on his part, did not have knowledge of the document in sufficient time to defend, or knowledge of the judgment in sufficient time to appeal, and

b) the defendant has disclosed a *prima facie* defence to the action on the merits.

An application for relief may be filed only within a reasonable time after the defendant has knowledge of the judgment.

Each Contracting State may declare that the application will not be entertained if it is filed after the expiration of a time to be stated in the declaration, but which shall in no case be less than one year following the date of the judgment.

This Article shall not apply to judgments concerning status or capacity of persons.

Chapter II — Extrajudicial Documents

Article 17

Extrajudicial documents emanating from authorities and judicial officers of a Contracting State may be transmitted for the purpose of service in another Contracting State by the methods and under the provisions of the present Convention.

Chapter III – General Clauses

Article 18

Each Contracting State may designate other authorities in addition to the Central Authority and shall determine the extent of their competence.

The applicant shall, however, in all cases, have the right to address a request directly to the Central Authority.

Federal States shall be free to designate more than one Central Authority.

Article 19

To the extent that the internal law of a Contracting State permits methods of transmission, other than those provided for in the preceding Articles, of documents coming from abroad, for service within its territory, the present Convention shall not affect such provisions.

Article 20

The present Convention shall not prevent an agreement between any two or more Contracting States to dispense with —

a) the necessity for duplicate copies of transmitted documents as required by the second paragraph of Article 3,

b) the language requirements of the third paragraph of Article 5 and Article 7,

c) the provisions of the fourth paragraph of Article 5,

d) the provisions of the second paragraph of Article 12.

Article 21

Each Contracting State shall, at the time of the deposit of its instrument of ratification or accession, or at a later date, inform the Ministry of Foreign Affairs of the Netherlands of the following —

a) the designation of authorities, pursuant to Articles 2 and 18,

b) the designation of the authority competent to complete the certificate pursuant to Article 6,

c) the designation of the authority competent to receive documents transmitted by consular channels, pursuant to Article 9.

Each Contracting State shall similarly inform the Ministry, where appropriate, of —

a) opposition to the use of methods of transmission pursuant to Articles 8 and 10,

b) declarations pursuant to the second paragraph of Article 15 and the third paragraph of Article 16,

c) all modifications of the above designations, oppositions and declarations.

Article 22

Where Parties to the present Convention are also Parties to one or both of the Conventions on civil procedure signed at The Hague on 17th July 1905, and on 1st

March 1954, this Convention shall replace as between them Articles 1 to 7 of the earlier Conventions.

Article 23

The present Convention shall not affect the application of Article 23 of the Convention on civil procedure signed at The Hague on 17th July 1905, or of Article 24 of the Convention on civil procedure signed at The Hague on 1st March 1954.

These Articles shall, however, apply only if methods of communication, identical to those provided for in these Conventions, are used.

Article 24

Supplementary agreements between Parties to the Conventions of 1905 and 1954 shall be considered as equally applicable to the present Convention, unless the Parties have otherwise agreed.

Article 25

Without prejudice to the provisions of Articles 22 and 24, the present Convention shall not derogate from Conventions containing provisions on the matters governed by this Convention to which the Contracting States are, or shall become, Parties.

Article 26

The present Convention shall be open for signature by the States represented at the Tenth Session of the Hague Conference on Private International Law.

It shall be ratified, and the instruments of ratification shall be deposited with the Ministry of Foreign Affairs of the Netherlands.

Article 27

The present Convention shall enter into force on the sixtieth day after the deposit of the third instrument of ratification referred to in the second paragraph of Article 26.

The Convention shall enter into force for each signatory State which ratifies subsequently on the sixtieth day after the deposit of its instrument of ratification.

Article 28

Any State not represented at the Tenth Session of the Hague Conference on Private International Law may accede to the present Convention after it has entered into force in accordance with the first paragraph of Article 27. The instrument of accession shall be deposited with the Ministry of Foreign Affairs of the Netherlands.

The Convention shall enter into force for such a State in the absence of any objection from a State, which has ratified the Convention before such deposit, notified to the Ministry of Foreign Affairs of the Netherlands within a period of six months after the date on which the said Ministry has notified it of such accession.

In the absence of any such objection, the Convention shall enter into force for the acceding State on the first day of the month following the expiration of the last of the periods referred to in the preceding paragraph.

Article 29

Any State may, at the time of signature, ratification or accession, declare that the present Convention shall extend to all the territories for the international relations of which it is responsible, or to one or more of them. Such a declaration shall take effect on the date of entry into force of the Convention for the State concerned.

At any time thereafter, such extensions shall be notified to the Ministry of Foreign Affairs of the Netherlands.

The Convention shall enter into force for the territories mentioned in such an extension on the sixtieth day after the notification referred to in the preceding paragraph.

Article 30

The present Convention shall remain in force for five years from the date of its entry into force in accordance with the first paragraph of Article 27, even for States which have ratified it or acceded to it subsequently.

If there has been no denunciation, it shall be renewed tacitly every five years.

Any denunciation shall be notified to the Ministry of Foreign Affairs of the Netherlands at least six months before the end of the five year period.

It may be limited to certain of the territories to which the Convention applies.

The denunciation shall have effect only as regards the State which has notified it. The Convention shall remain in force for the other Contracting States.

Article 31

The Ministry of Foreign Affairs of the Netherlands shall give notice to the States referred to in Article 26, and to the States which have acceded in accordance with Article 28, of the following —

a) the signatures and ratifications referred to in Article 26;

b) the date on which the present Convention enters into force in accordance with the first paragraph of Article 27;

c) the accessions referred to in Article 28 and the dates on which they take effect;

d) the extensions referred to in Article 29 and the dates on which they take effect;

e) the designations, oppositions and declarations referred to in Article 21;

f) the denunciations referred to in the third paragraph of Article 30.

In witness whereof the undersigned, being duly authorised thereto, have signed the present Convention.

Done at The Hague, on the 15th day of November, 1965, in the English and French languages, both texts being equally authentic, in a single copy which shall be deposited in the archives of the Government of the Netherlands, and of which a certified copy shall be sent, through the diplomatic channel, to each of the States represented at the Tenth Session of the Hague Conference on Private International Law.

Appendix 2[2]

HAGUE CONVENTION ON THE SERVICE ABROAD OF JUDICIAL AND EXTRA-JUDICIAL DOCUMENTS IN CIVIL AND COMMERCIAL MATTERS

State Department Circular

DISCLAIMER: THE INFORMATION IN THIS CIRCULAR RELATING TO THE LEGAL REQUIREMENTS OF SPECIFIC FOREIGN COUNTRIES IS PROVIDED FOR GENERAL INFORMATION ONLY AND MAY NOT BE TOTALLY ACCURATE IN A PARTICULAR CASE. QUESTIONS INVOLVING INTERPRETATION OF SPECIFIC FOREIGN LAWS SHOULD BE ADDRESSED TO FOREIGN COUNSEL OR THE FOREIGN CENTRAL AUTHORITY FOR THE CONVENTION.

IN FORCE: ..ANGUILLA[3], ANTIGUA AND BARBUDA, ARGENTINA[7], ARUBA[5], BAHAMAS, BARBADOS, BELARUS, BELGIUM, *BELIZE*[1], BERMUDA[3], BOTSWANA, BRITISH VIRGIN ISLANDS[3], BULGARIA[7,13], CANADA, CAYMAN ISLANDS[3], CHINA[2,7], CYPRUS, CZECH REPUBLIC[2,7], DENMARK, *DJIBOUTI (formerly Afars and Issas)*[1], EGYPT[7], ESTONIA, FALKLAND ISLANDS AND DEPENDENCIES[3], *FIJI*[1,3], FINLAND, FRANCE (including French Overseas Departments), FRENCH POLYNESIA[4], GERMANY[7,8,9], GIBRALTAR[3], GREECE[10], GUERNSEY[3], HONG KONG SAR[3], IRELAND, ISLE OF MAN[3], ISRAEL, ITALY, JAPAN, JERSEY[3], *KIRIBATI (formerly Gilbert Islands and Central and Southern Line Islands)*[1,3], KOREA, Republic of (SOUTH KOREA)[7,14], LATVIA, LITHUANIA[7], LUXEMBOURG[11], MACAU SAR[6], MALAWI, MEXICO, MONTSERRRAT[3], NETHERLANDS, *NEVIS*[1], NORWAY[7], PAKISTAN, PITCAIRN[3], POLAND, PORTUGAL, RUSSIAN FEDERATION, *ST. CHRISTOPHER (KITTS)*[1], ST. HELENA AND DEPENDENCIES[3], *ST. LUCIA*[1], *ST. VINCENT AND THE GRENADINES*[1], SEYCHELLES, SLOVAK REPUBLIC[2,7], *SLOVENIA, SOLOMON ISLANDS*[1], SPAIN, SRI LANKA[7], SWEDEN, SWITZERLAND[7], TURKEY[7], TURKS AND CAICOS ISLANDS[3], *TUVALU (formerly Ellice Islands)*[1], UKRAINE, UNITED KINGDOM, UNITED STATES[12], VENEZUELA[7].

---

[1] This country achieved independence. No declaration has been made on the continuation in force of the Convention. We have requested the assistance of the Hague Conference on Private International Law in ascertaining from these countries whether they are applying the Convention.

[2] In accordance with Article 34(1) of the Vienna Convention on Succession of States in Respect of Treaties, the U.S. view is that when a country which is a party to a multilateral treaty or convention has dissolved, the successor state(s) inherit the treaty obligations of the former government, consistent with Article 34 of the Vienna Convention on Succession of States in Respect of Treaties. However, as a practical matter, the custom is for depositaries to expect a notice of succession to confirm that the new entity is performing its treaty obligations. Many newly independent states may not really be implementing such conventions at this time in that they may be performing the functions set forth in

the Convention. We continue to work with these governments and the depositories to obtain confirmation that the respective successor state is complying with treaty obligations.

[3] The Convention was extended to this territory, possession or other jurisdiction by the United Kingdom.

[4] The Convention was extended to this territory, possession or other jurisdiction by France.

[5] The Convention was extended to this territory, possession or other jurisdiction by the Netherlands.

[6] The Convention was extended to this territory, possession or other jurisdiction by Portugal.

[7] Argentina, China, the Czech Republic, Egypt, Germany, Greece, Latvia, Lithuania, Luxembourg, Norway, Poland, the Republic of South Korea, the Slovak Republic, Sri Lanka, Switzerland, Turkey, Ukraine, and Venezuela have notified the Hague Conference on Private International Law on accession, ratification or subsequently that they object to service in accordance with Article 10, sub-paragraph a of the Convention, via postal channels.

[8] The Hague Service Convention provision for service by a Central Authority is the exclusive method for service of process in the Federal Republic of Germany.

[9] On November 19, 1992, the Federal Republic of Germany advised the depositary for the Convention that notwithstanding the provisions of the first paragraph of Article 15, a German judge may give judgment even if no certificate of service or delivery has been received, if all the following conditions are fulfilled: the document was transmitted by one of the methods provided for in the Convention; a period of time of not less than six months, considered adequate by the judge in the particular case, has elapsed since the date of the transmission of the document; no certificate of any kind has been received, even though every reasonable effort has been made to obtain it through the competent authorities of the State addressed. In addition, Germany advised that an application for relief in accordance with Article 16 will not be entertained if it is filed after the expiration of one year following the termination of the time-limit which has not been observed.

[10] On November 23, 1989, Greece informed the depositary government for the Convention that the judges of Greece may give judgment if all the conditions in Article 15, paragraph 2(a),(b) and (c) of the Convention are fulfilled even if no certificate of service or delivery has been received.

[11] Luxembourg communicated the withdrawal of its declaration opposing service through postal channels in accordance with Article 10(a) of the Convention in a Note to the Government of the Netherlands dated June 2, 1978.

[12] As of June 28, 1978, the United States will not charge a fee for service of judicial documents which it receives from any State Party to the Convention which does not impose a charge for service of documents sent from the United States for service under the Convention. On March 31, 1994, the Government of the United States declared that the Convention shall also be extended to the Commonwealth of the Northern Mariana Islands.

[13] In accordance with Article 28, second paragraph, the Convention will enter into force for the Republic of Bulgaria in the absence of any objection from a State which has ratified the Convention before the deposit of the accession, notified to the Ministry of Foreign Affairs of the Netherlands within a period of six months after the date on which the Ministry has notified it of the accession. For practical reasons, this six months' period will run from January 31, 2000 to July 31, 2000. The Republic of Bulgaria objects to the use of channels of transmission for service mentioned in Article 10 of the Convention. The Republic of Bulgaria requires the document, which is to be served, to be written in or accompanied by a translation into the Bulgarian language. The Republic of Bulgaria designates the district courts as authorities which are competent to complete the certificate (Article 6, paragraphs 1 and 2).

[14] Ratified Convention January 13, 2000; in accordance with Article 28, second paragraph, the Convention will enter into force for the Republic of Korea in the absence of any objections from a State which has ratified the Convention before the deposit of the accession, notified to the Ministry of Foreign Affairs of the Netherlands within a period of six months after the date on which the Ministry has notified it of the accession. For practical reasons, this six month's period will run from January 31, 2000 to July 31, 2000. Pursuant to Article 10, the Republic of Korea objects to the following: **a)** the freedom to send judicial documents, by postal channels, directly to persons abroad, **b)** the freedom of judicial officers, officials or other competent persons of the State of origin to effect service of judicial documents directly through the judicial officials or other competent persons of the State of destination, **c)** the freedom

of any person interested in a judicial proceeding to effect service of judicial documents directly through judicial officers, officials or other competent persons of the State of destination.

CITATIONS

20 U.S.T. 1361

658 U.N.T.S. 163

T.I.A.S. No. 6638

28 U.S.C.A. (Appendix following Rule 4 FRCvP)

16 I.L.M. 1339 (1977)

Martindale-Hubbell Law Directory, Law Digest Volume, Selected International Conventions

U.S. CENTRAL AUTHORITY

Office of International Judicial Assistance
Civil Division
Department of Justice
1100 L Street, NW
Room 11006
Washington, D.C. 20530
(202) 307-0983

PURPOSE

The Hague Service Convention codifies service of process by international registered mail and by agent. The treaty also provides for service of process by a Central Authority (usually the Ministry of Justice) in the Convention countries pursuant to a request submitted on a form USM-94, available at the office of any United States Marshal. The text of the treaty is self-explanatory, but see the reservations and declarations each country made on accession to the treaty. Some countries made specific reservations against particular methods of service. The Convention method should be employed in all countries party to it.

SCOPE OF THE CONVENTION

This question was raised at the first Special Commission meeting on the operation of the Convention. The applicability of the Convention to administrative cases is generally decided on a case-by-case basis. See Commission Reported, cited under References.

REQUEST FOR SERVICE FORM (USM-94)

You may obtain a copy of the Request for Service form (USM-94) from the local office of the U.S. Marshal's Service. Further information on the treaty may be obtained from the Supervisory Deputy for process at the nearest U.S. Marshal's office. You may also contact Headquarters, U.S. Marshal's Service, 202-307-9110. (See also Memo No. 386, Revision

No. 3, at the U.S. Marshal's office or at Vol. 16, Intl Legal Materials, 1331, (1977) Am. Soc. Intl. Law).

COMPLETE THE FORM

The completed request form and documents to be served, with accompanying translations (2 copies of each), should be mailed directly to the foreign central authority as provided by Article 3 of the Convention.

FEDERAL AUTHORITY FOR ATTYS TO COMPLETE AND SEND FORM

Effective February 26, 1983 Public Law 97-462 amended Rule 4 of the Federal Rules of CivilProcedure regarding service of process. Pursuant to this change in Rule 4(c)2(A) the U.S. Marshal will no longer transmit Form USM-94 directly to the foreign central authority of a country party to the Hague Service Convention. Rather, the attorney representing the party seeking service should execute the portion of Form USM-94 marked "Identity and Address of the Applicant" and the "Name and Address of the Requesting Authority" portion of the Summary of the Document to be Served.

CITE AUTHORITY

A reference to the statutory authority to serve the document should appear prominently on the request, stating that "service is requested pursuant to Rule 4(c)2(A), U.S. Federal Rules of Civil Procedure" which authorizes any person who is not a party and is not less than 18 years of age to serve a summons and complaint.

STATE COURT ACTIONS

In actions pending in state courts, state law designates the person authorized to effect service. Requests pending in state courts should specify that the request is made pursuant to Rule 4(c)2(A) of the U.S. Federal Rules of Civil Procedure and any pertinent state law. See U.S. Marshal's Memo 386, [p. 14, footnote 11,] 16 I.L.M. 1331 et seq. (1977) for guidance on service requests in actions pending in state courts.

DESIGNATING METHOD OF SERVICE TO BE USED BY CENTRAL AUTHORITY

Fill in the USM-94 in duplicate, designating the method of service to be used by the foreign Central Authority.

FORMAL SERVICE

(Article 5, paragraph 1, sub-paragraph a)The Central Authority itself serves or arranges to have served "by a method prescribed by its internal law for the service of documents in domestic actions upon persons who are within its territory". Generally, documents to be served in accordance with this method must be translated into the official language of the country. See the Practical Handbook on the Convention for specific information, or consult the U.S. Central Authority.

INFORMAL DELIVERY

(Article 5, paragraph 2)Unless a particular method is requested, the document may always be served by delivery to an addressee who accepts it voluntarily. This method of informal delivery is by far the most broadly used approach in a substantial number of Contracting States. The person who delivers the document is often a police official. In most cases, the addressees accept the document voluntarily or come down to pick it up at the police station, which dispenses with the need for translation of the documents to be served.

PERSONAL SERVICE

(Article 5, paragraph 1, sub-paragraph b)If personal service is required, delete methods (a) and (c) on the Request for Service form (USM-94) and indicate method (b) on the form, noting that the documents should be served personally upon the person or company to be served.

TRANSLATIONS

Unless the party to be served will accept service voluntarily, the documents to be served must be accompanied by a translation into the official language of the foreign country. See Ristau, International Judicial Assistance (Civil and Commercial), International Law Institute, 1995, Vol. 1, Section 4-2-3(5), pp. 133-138. See Teknekron Management Inc. v. Quante Fernmeldtechnik Gmbh, 115 F.R.D. 175 (D. Nev. 1987); Vornees v. Fischer & Krecke, 697 F. 2d 574, 575 (4th Cir. 1983)

COSTS

There are generally no costs incurred in connection with service through the central authority under the Convention. However, if personal service is made and the person to be served resides in some remote location, some fees may be charged. The fees will be billed to the requester by the foreign central authority.

TIME FRAME

There is no specific time frame for serviceprovided for in the Convention. However, the Hague Conference on Private International Law advises that most Convention central authorities generally accomplish service within two months.

PROOF OF SERVICE

On the reverse side of the Request for Service form is a Certificate of Service form. The certificate, which serves as proof of service, is completed and mailed directly to the requesting party by the foreign central authority after service has been effected.

SERVICE OTHER THAN BY CONVENTION CENTRAL AUTHORITY

SERVICE THRU CONSULAR & DIPLOMATIC CHANNELS

(Articles 8 and 9)U.S. consular officers are prohibited by Federal regulations from effecting service of process in private matters. See 22 CFR 92.85.

SERVICE BY POSTAL CHANNELS

(Article 10, sub-paragraph a)American courts have consistently held that international mail service of civil summonses is not proper in the case of States party to the Hague Service Convention which have entered an appropriate reservation under Article 10 thereof. See Ristau, Vol. 1, Section. 4-1-6, pp. 121.3-121.9. See also, Epstein, International Litigation, A Guide to Jurisdiction, Practice and Strategy, 2nd., 1994, Section 4.04(3), pp. 4-14-4-19.

Argentina, China, the Czech Republic, Egypt, Germany, Greece, the Republic of South Korea, Latvia, Lithuania, Luxembourg, Norway, Poland, the Slovak Republic, Sri Lanka, Switzerland, Turkey, Ukraine, and Venezuela have notified the Hague Conference on Private International Law on accession, ratification or subsequently that they object to service in accordance with Article 10, sub-paragraph a of the Convention, via postal channels.

SELECTED CASES: Re Hunt's Pier Associates Debtor, 156 Bankr, 464 (E.D. Pa. 1993); Grand Entertainment v. Star Media Sales, 988 F. 2d 476 (3rd Cir. 1993); Peabody Holding Co. v. Lotain Group PLC, 808 F. Supp. 1425 (E.D. Mo. 1992); Perfumer's Workshop, Ltd. v. Roure Bertrand du Pont, S.A., 737 F. Supp. 785 (S.D.N.Y. 1990); Wilson v. Honda Motor Co. Ltd, 766 F. Supp. 339 (E.D. Tenn 1991); Honda Motor Co., Ltd., v. Superior Court (10 Cal. App. 4th 1043, 12 Cal. Rptr 2d 861 (1992); Sheets v. Yamaha Motor Co. Ltd., (891 F. 2d 533 (5th Cir. 1990)); Bankston v. Toyota Motor Corp. (889 Fed. Rptr, 2d Series, 172, (8th Cir. 1989; W.D. Ark., 4 Jan 1989); Suzuki Motor CO., Ltd. v. Superior Court (200 Cal. App. 3d 1476, 249 Cal. Rptr. 376 (1988); Hantover Inc. v. Omet S.N.A., 688 F. Supp. 1377 (W.D. Mo. 1988); Turick v. Yamaha, (121 F.R.D. 32 (S.D.N.Y. 1988)); Cooper v. Makita Electric Works Ltd., 117 F.R.D. 16 (1987); Ackermann v. Levine (788 F. wd 830 (2d Cir. 1986); , Pochop v. Toyota Motor Co. Ltd., 111 F.R.D. 464 (1986), Mommsen v. Toro Co., 108 F.R.D. 444 (1985); DeJames v. Magnificence Carriers, Inc., 654 F.2d 280 (3d Cir. 1981); Porsche v. Superior Court, 177 Cal. Rptr. 155 (1981); Cintron v. W&D Machinery Co. Inc., 182 N.J. Super. 126, 440 (A. 2d 76 (1981)); Kadota v. Hosogai, 608 P. 2d 68 (Ct. of Appeals, Ariz, 1980); Shoei Kako Co. v. Superior Court, 33 Cal. App. 3d 808, 109 Cal. Rptr. 402 (1973).

But see, Umbenhauer v. Woog, 959 F. 2d 25, (3rd Cir, 1992) which held that objections from foreign governments cannot justify non-compliance with the Federal Rules of Civil Procedure for service of process by international mail. It should be noted that the country in question, Switzerland, was not a party to the Hague Service Convention at that time, and thus did not file formal objection to service by postal channels under Article 10(a). Formal objections to this method of service made at the time of accession or subsequently in accordance with the Convention are honored as a Treaty obligation.

Note: With respect to the debate in the courts regarding the validity of service by mail in Japan, see our country specific flyer, Service of Process in Japan, via our autofax service or at our Internet Home Page.

BUT SEE, FTC v. Compagnie de Saint-Gobain-Pont-a-Mousson, 636 F. 2d 1327, n. 150 (D.C. Cir. 1980) on the issue of service via international registered mail when the document to be served is not compulsory or punitive when there is no treaty obligation to refrain from such methods of service. See also, Digest of United States Practice in International Law, Department of State, Office of the Legal Adviser, 1980 p. 457.

TRANSLATIONS AND SERVICE BY MAIL

Translation of documents to be served by registered mail is not strictly required by the Convention. Courts have ruled that the translation requirement of Article 5 applies only to service of documents by the foreign Central Authority, and not direct postal service. See Lemme v. Wine of Japan Import, Inc., 631 F. Supp. 456, 463-64 (E.D.N.Y. 1986). See also Greenfield v. Suzuki Motor Co., Ltd., 776 F. Supp. 698, 701-703 (E.D.N.Y. 1991). See Epstein, International Litigation: A Guide to Jurisdiction, Practice and Strategy, , 2nd, 1994, Section 4.04(1), p. 4-13. But see, Ristau, Vol 1, Section 4-3-1(2), p. 142 for a discussion of challenges which can occur if documents are not served in the language the recipient understands.

SERVICE THRU JUDICIAL OFFICERS

(Article 10, sub-paragraphs b and c)Permits the judicial officers, officials and other competent persons of the state of origin to effect service of judicial documents through the efforts of the judicial officials of the state of destination, unless the latter state objects to this method.

SEE ALSO Volkswagenwerk Aktiengesellschaft v. Schlunk, 108 S. Ct. 2104, 100 L. Ed. 2d 722, 27 I.L.M. 1093 (15 June 1988) on the issue of service on an agent for a foreign corporation in the United States.

FOREIGN CENTRAL AUTHORITIES

The Hague Conference on Private International Law Handbook on the Operation of the Hague Service Convention provides the following addresses of foreign central authorities:

ANDORRA:
1. El Ministre d'Afers Exteriors
2. El Ministre de Justícia i Interior
All legalization requests are centralized through the following address:
Ministeri d'Afers Exteriors
Prat de la Creu
Edifici del Govern
Andorra la Vella
Principat d'Andorra
Tel.: 376-875-700
Fax: 376-869-559
E-mail: exteriors.gov@andorra.ad

ANGUILLA:
The Registrar of the Supreme Court
Anguilla

ANTIGUA & BARBUDA:
(1) The Governor General Antigua and Barbuda;
(2) Registrar of the High Court
High Street
St. John's, Antigua, West Indies
tel: 809-462-3147

ARGENTINA:
Acceded to the Convention: February 2, 2001
Enters into Force: December 1, 2001
Central Authority: Ministry of Foreign Affairs, International Trade and Worship
Treaty Bureau
Esmeralda 1212—15th. Fl.
1007 Buenos Aires
Tel: (5411) 4819-7000
4819-8015

Argentina made the following declarations:
1—To Article 5, third paragraph: "The ARGENTINE REPUBLIC shall not accept documents to be served or transmitted unless they are accompanied by a translation into the Spanish language."
2—To Article 21, first paragraph, a): "The Argentine Government designates the Ministry of Foreign Affairs, International Trade and Worship as the Central Authority."
3—To Article 21, second paragraph, a): "The ARGENTINE REPUBLIC opposes to the use of methods of transmission pursuant to Article 10."
4—To Article 21, second paragraph, b): "The Argentine Government accepts declarations pursuant to second paragraph of Article 15 and third paragraph of Article 16."
5—The ARGENTINE REPUBLIC rejects the claimed extension of application of the Convention on the Service Abroad of Judicial and Extrajudicial Documents in Civil or Commercial Matters, adopted at The Hague on November 14, 1965, to the Malvinas, South Georgias and South Sandwich Islands as notified on May 20, 1970 by the UNITED KINGDOM OF GREAT BRITAIN AND NORTHERN IRELAND to the KINGDOM OF THE NETHERLANDS as Depositary of the Convention under the "Falkland Islands and dependencies" inaccurate denomination. Therefore, the ARGENTINE REPUBLIC similarly rejects the designation of the "Registrar of the Supreme Court" in the Malvinas Islands as application authority of this Convention which was made on that same opportunity, as well as any other act derived or that may be derived from this claimed territorial extension.
The General Assembly of the United Nations has recognized the existence of a dispute on the Malvinas, South Georgias and South Sandwich Islands sovereignty and has urged the ARGENTINE REPUBLIC and the UNITED KINGDOM OF GREAT BRITAIN AND NORTHERN IRELAND to hold negotiations in order to find, as soon as possible, a peaceful and definite solution to such dispute, with United Nations Secretary General's good offices mediation, who shall inform the General Assembly about the progress made (Resolutions 2065 (XX), 3160

(XXVIII), 31/49, 37/9, 38/12, 39/6, 40/21, 41/40, 42/19 and 43/25). The Special Committee on Decolonization having equally declared, has annually adopted a resolution which proclaims that to put an end to this colonial situation the negotiations must be resumed in order to peacefully and definitely solve this sovereignty dispute. The last of these resolutions was adopted on July 1, 1999.
The ARGENTINE REPUBLIC reaffirms its sovereignty on the Malvinas, South Georgias and South Sandwich Islands and its maritime surrounding areas which are an integral part of its national territory.''

ARUBA:
The Kingdom of the Netherlands declared that the application of the Convention shall extend to *Aruba* on 28 May 1986. Entry into Force for *Aruba: 27 July 1986.* Effective November 1, 2000, the Central Authority is:
Procurator General
L.G. Smith Boulevard 42-44
Oranjestad, Aruba
Tel: (279) 834-387 / 829-132
Fax: (279) 838-891

BAHAMAS:
Entered into Force: February 1, 1998. Designated Central Authority: ''The Honorable Attorney General.''
Bahamian Central Authority for the Hague Service
Rhonda Bain
The Attorney General's Office
PO Box N3007
East Hill Street
Nassau, Bahamas
Tel: (242)-502-0400

BARBADOS:
The Registrar of the Supreme Court of Barbados Law Courts, Bridgetown, Barbados
tel: 809-42-75537

BELARUS:
Ministry of Justice
Division of Execution of International Treaties
Department of Legal Provision of Foreign Relations
Kollektornaya St. 10
220048 Minsk
Belarus
Contact: Ms. Marina Zhandarova
Telephone: 375-17-211-0185

BELGIUM:
Le Ministere de la Justice
Administration de la Legislation
Place Poelaert 4
1000 Bruxelles
tel: 511-42-00
telex: 62.440 Min Jus

BELIZE:
Now Independent. No formal confirmation to depositary government that Convention applies. Government of Belize authorities have advised the U.S. Embassy that the Convention does apply and that requests for service should be sent to the following central authority:
The General Registry
Supreme Court Building
P.O. Box 87
Belize City, Belize

BERMUDA:
The Registrar of the Supreme Court
Sessions House
21 Parliament St.
Hamilton HM 12, Bermuda
tel: 809-292-1350

BOTSWANA:
The Minister of State in the Office of the President of the Republic of Botswana
Lobatse, Botswana

BRITISH VIRGIN ISLANDS:
The Registrar of the Supreme Court
British Virgin Islands

BULGARIA:
The Republic of Bulgaria designates the Minstry of Justice and European Legal Integration as Central Authority. The same authority is competent to receive the documents forwarded under Article 9, paragraph 1.

CANADA:
To save time, requests should be forwarded directly to the Central Authority of the province or territory concerned. They may, however, also be forwarded to the Federal Central Authority which will transmit them to the relevant Central Authority in the province or territory.

Federal Central Authority:
Director, Legal Advisory Division
Department of External Affairs
125 Sussex Drive
Ottawa, Ontario
Canada K1A 0G2
(613) 995-0119

For Alberta:
Attorney-General for Alberta
Attn: Executive Director—Court Services
9833-109th Street
Edmonton, Alberta
Canada T5K 2E8
tel: (403) 427-4992

For British Columbia:
Ministry of the Attorney-General for British Columbia
Office of the Deputy Minister
Fifth Floor, 910 Government Street
Victoria, British Columbia
Canada V8V 1X4
tel: (604) 387-5211

For Manitoba:
Attorney-General for Manitoba
c/o Director—Civil Legal Services
Woodsworth Building
6th Floor
405 Broadway
Winnipeg, Manitoba
Canada, R3C 0V8
tel: (204) 945-2847

For New Brunswick:
Attorney-General for New Brunswick
P.O.Box 6000
Fredericton, New Brunswick
Canada, E3B 5H1
tel: (506) 453-2208

For Newfoundland:
Department of Justice
Confederation Building
St. John's, Newfoundland
Canada A1C 5T7
tel: (709) 576-2869

For Nova Scotia:
Attorney General of Nova Scotia
Legal Services Division
P.O. Box 7
Halifax, Nova Scotia
tel: (902) 424-4024

For Ontario:
Ministry of the Attorney General for Ontario Reciprocity Office: Civil Law Division
18 King St. East
Toronto, Ontario
Canada M5C 1C5
tel: (416) 965-2570

For Prince Edward Island:
Attorney General of Prince Edward Island
Office of the Deputy Minister
P.O. Box 2000
Charlottetown, Prince Edward Island
Canada C1A 7N8
tel: (902) 368-4570

For Quebec:
Ministre de la Justice du Quebec
a/s Le service juridique
1200 route de l'Eglise
5eme etage
Ste-Foy, Quebec
Canada G1V 4M1
(418) 643-1436

For Saskatchewan:
Minister of Justice for Saskatchewan Att.
of Director of Sheriff Services
1874 Scarth St., 10th Floor
Regina, Saskatchewan
Canada S4P 3V7
(306) 787-5488

For Yukon:
Director of Court Services
Department of Justice
Box 2703
Whitehorse, Yukon Y1A 2C6
(403) 667-5942

For Northwest Territories:
Deputy Minister of Justice
Government of the Northwest Territories
Box 1320
Yellowknife, Northwest Territories
Canada X1A 2L9
tel: (613) 995-0119

CAYMAN ISLANDS:
Clerk of the Courts
Grand Cayman, Cayman Islands

CHINA:
Bureau of International Judicial Assistance
Ministry of Justice of the People's Republic of China
10 Chaoyangmen Nandajie
Chaoyang District
BEIJING, 100020
China

CYPRUS:
Ministry of Justice & Public Order
Office of Permanent Secretary
125 Athalassa Avenue
2024 Nicosia,Cyprus
Tel: 357-22-805955
Fax: 357-22-518356

CZECH REPUBLIC:
Ministerstvo Spravedlnosti Ceske Republiky/Ministry of Justice of the Czech Republic
128 10 Praha 2, Vysehradska 16
Prague, Czech Republic

DENMARK:
Ministry of Justice
Justitsministeriet
Slotsholmsgade 10
1216 Kobenhavn K.
Copenhagen, Denmark
tel: 120906
telex: 15530

DJIBOUTI:
Unknown. Now Independent. Formerly French territory of Afars and Issas.
No formal confirmation to depositary government that Convention applies.

EGYPT:
Ministry of Justice
Office of International Judicial Cooperation
New Annex Building 7th Floor
Nobar Street
Abdin, Cairo, Egypt
tel. 011-20-2-795-6059

ESTONIA:
The Ministry of Justice of the Republic of Estonia

FALKLAND ISLANDS:
The Registrar of the Supreme Court
Stanley, Falkland Islands

FIJI:
Chief Registrar of the High Court of Fiji
Government Buildings
Suva, Fiji
Fiji became an independent State October 10, 1970. Prior to that time, Fiji was a dependency of the United Kingdom which extended its accession to the Convention to Fiji. Fiji has never confirmed to the Hague Conference on Private International Law or the Government of the Netherlands whether it considers the Hague Service Convention to apply to Fiji. However, Fijian authorities have provided the U.S. Embassy with the name and address of the Central Authority noted above to whom requests for service under the Hague Convention may be transmitted.

FINLAND:
Ministry of Justice
10 Etelaesplanadi
Helsinki 13, Finland
tel: 358-0-1601

FRANCE:
Ministere de la Justice
Bureau de l'Entraide Judiciaire Internationale D4
13 Place Vendome
75042 Paris (1er), Cedex 01, France
tel: 261-80-22
telex: 211-802F

GERMANY:

For Baden-Wurttemberg:
Justizministerium Baden-Wurttemberg
Schillerplatz 4
70173 Stuttgart, Federal Republic of Germany

For Bavaria:
Bayerisches Staatsministerium der Justiz
Justizpalast
Prielmeyerstrasse 7
80335 Muenchen
Munich, Germany
(this is the street address)
(For correspondence the following address should be used):
Bayerisches Staatsministerium der Justiz
80097 Muenchen
Munich, Germany

For Berlin:
Senator fur Justiz
Salzburger Strasse 21-25
10825 Berlin, Germany

For Brandenburg:
Das Ministerium der Justiz
des Landes Brandenburg
Heinrich-Mann-Alee 107
14460 Potsdam, Germany

For Bremen:
Prasident des Landgerichts Bremen
Domsheide 16
28195 Bremen, Germany

For Hamburg:
Prasident des Amtsgerichtes Hamburg
Sievekingplatz 1
20335 Hamburg

For Hesse:
Hessischer Minister der Justiz
Luisenstrasse 13
65185 Wiesbaden, Germany

For Lower Saxony:
Niedersachsisher Minister der Justiz
Am Waterlooplatz 1
30169 Hannover, Germany

For Mecklenburg-Western Pomerania:
Der Minister fur Justiz
Bundes- und Europaangelegenheiten
des Landes Mecklenburg-Vorpommern
Demmlerplatz 14
19053 Schwerin, Germany

For Northrhine-Westphalia:
Justizminister des Landes Nordrhein-Westfalen
Cecilienallee 3
40474 Dusseldorf, Germany

For Rhineland-Palatinate:
Ministerium der Justiz
Ernst-Ludwig-Strasse 3
55116 Mainz, Germany

For Saarland:
Minister der Justiz des Saarlandes
Zahringerstrasse 12
66119 Saarbrucken, Germany

For Saxony:
Sachsisches Staatsministerium der Justiz
Archivstrasse 1
01097 Dresden, Germany

For Saxony-Anhalt:
Ministerium der Justiz
des Landes Sachsen-Anhalt
Wilhelm-Hopfner-Ring 6
39116 Magdeburg, Germany

For Schleswig-Holstein:
Der Justizminister
des Landes Schleswig-Holstein
Lorentzendamm 35
24103 Kiel, Germany

For Thuringia:
Thuringer Justizministerium
Alfred-Hess Strasse 8
99094 Erfurt, Germany

GIBRALTAR:
The Registrar of the Supreme Court
Gibraltar

GREECE:
Ministry of Foreign Affairs
Department of Administrative and Judicial Affairs
D-3 Section, Department 2
Zalakosta 1, Athens, Greece

GUERNSEY:
The Bailiff
Bailiff's Office
Royal Court House
Guernsey
Channel Islands

HONG KONG SAR (CHINA) / CHINA (HONG KONG SAR):
The Chief Secretary of Hong Kong
Central Government Offices
Lower Albert Road
Hong Kong, tel: 011-852-8102954

ISLE OF MAN:
The First Deemster and Clerk of the Rolls
Roll's Office
Douglas, Isle of Man

IRELAND:
Master of the High Court
Dublin, Ireland
or
– a practising Solicitor; or
– a Country Registrar; or
– a District County Clerk

ISRAEL:
Director of Courts
Directorate of Courts
Russian Compound
Jerusalem
tel: 246919

ITALY:
The Registry of the Court of Appeal
Rome, Italy
L'Ufficio unico degli ufficiali
giudiziari presso la corte d'appello la corte d'appello di Roma
Rome, Italy

JAPAN:
The Minister of Foreign Affairs
2-2-1 Kasumigaseki, Chiyoda-ku
Tokyo 100, Japan
tel: 81-3-3581-4015

JERSEY:
The Attorney General
Jersey, Channel Islands

KIRIBATI:
Unknown. Now Independent. No formal confirmation to depositary government that Convention applies. Former Central Authority: Registrar of the High Court

KOREA, REPUBLIC OF (SOUTH KOREA):
Ministry of Court Administration, Attn.: Director of International Affairs, 967, Seocho-dong, Seocho-gu, SEOUL 137-750, Republic of Korea

LATVIA:
Ministry of Justice
Brivibas Boulevard 34
LV—1536 Riga

LITHUANIA:
Signatory: August 2, 2000
Accession: May 15, 2001
Entry into Force: June 1, 2001
Central Authority: Ministry of Justice
Dept. of International Law
Gedimino 30
Vilnius, Lithuania.

An alternative central authority is the District Attorney, Procuracy General, Smetonos 4, Vilnius, Lithuania.
The instrument of accession of Lithuania contains the following declarations:
And whereas it is provided in Article 2 of the said Convention, the Republic of Lithuania designates the Ministry of Justice of the Republic of Lithuania as a Central Authority to receive requests for service coming from other Contracting States;
And whereas it is provided in Article 8 of the said Convention, the Republic of Lithuania declares that it opposes to the ways of service of documents provided in this Article, unless the documents are to be served upon a national of the State in which the documents originate;
And whereas it is provided in Article 10 of the said Convention, the Republic of Lithuania declares that it is opposed to the ways of service of documents provided in this Article;
And whereas it is provided in paragraph 2 of Article 15 of the said Convention, the Republic of Lithuania declares that the judge of the Republic of Lithuania may give judgment even if no certificate of service or delivery has been received, if all conditions of paragraph 2 of Article 15 are fulfilled;
And whereas it is provided in paragraph 2 of Article 16 of the said Convention, the Republic of Lithuania declares that an application for relief will not be entertained if it is filed after the expiration of one year following the date of the final judgment;. . .''.

LUXEMBOURG:
Parquet general pres la Cour superieure de Justice
12 Cote d'Eich
Luxembourg-Ville
tel: 475981 or 26765 or 41464

MACAU SAR (CHINA) / CHINA (MACAU SAR):
Portugal extended its accession to Macau. Requests for service of process in Macau may be transmitted to the Portuguese Central Authority for forwarding to the Competent Authority in Macau to effect service. See Portugal.

MALAWI:
The Registrar of the High Court of Malawi
P.O. Box 30244
Chichiri
Blantyre 3
Malawi

MEXICO:
Secretaria de Relaciones Exteriores
Direccion General de Asuntos Juridicos
Av. Ricardo Flores Magon No. 1—Anexo 2
Planta Alta
Colonia Tlatelolco
06995 Mexico, D.F.
tel: 011-52-55-5782-4144
By a Note dated 7 May 2001, the Embassy of Mexico at The Hague informed the depositary of the following: besides English and French, request forms addressed to the Mexican Central Authority should be filled in Spanish, according to Article 7 of the Convention.

MONTSERRAT:
The Registrar of the High Court
Montserrat

NETHERLANDS:
The Public Prosecutor
District Court of the Hague
Juliana van Stoleberglaan 2-4
The Hague, the Netherlands
tel: 82-40-41

NEVIS:
Ministry of Legal Affairs
P.O. Box 186
Government Headquarters
St. Kitts-Nevis, West Indies
tel: 809-465-2521

NORWAY:
Ministry of Justice
Boks 8005
Oslo/Dep
Oslo 1, Norway

PAKISTAN:
Solicitor
Ministry of Law and Justice
Islamabad, Pakistan
Other Authorities in addition to Central Authority
Within Their Respective Territorial Jurisdictions:
Registrars of:
Lahore High Court, Lahore
Peshawar High Court, Peshawar
Baluchistan High Court, Quetta
High Court of Sind, Karachi

PITCAIRN:
The Governor and Commander-in-Chief, Pitcairn
British High Commission
Reserve Bank of New Zealand Building (9th Floor)
2 The Terrace (P.O. Box 1812)
Wellington 1
New Zealand

POLAND:
Ministry of Justice
Department of International Cooperation and European Law
Al. Ujazdowskia 11
00-950 Warsaw, Poland
tel: 48-22-628-4431 (ext. 247)
fax: 48-22-628-0949

PORTUGAL:
Director General of the Judicial Service of the Ministry of the Ministry of Justice (Direccao-Geral dos Servicas Judiciarios, Ministerio de Justica)
Av. Casal Ribeiro 48
1098 Lisboa Codex
Lisbon, Portugal
tel: 351-21-315-52 82
fax: 351-21-353-87 02

RUSSIAN FEDERATION:
Accession: May 1, 2001
Entry into Force: December 1, 2001
Central Authority: Unknown. Seeking clarification from the Russian Federation and the Hague Conference on Private International Law.

SLOVENIA:
Signatory: September 18, 2000
Accession: May 15, 2001
Entry into Force: June 1, 2001
Central Authority unknown

SRI LANKA:
Signatory: August 31, 200
Accession: May 15, 2001
Entry into Force: June 1, 2001
Central Authority: Secretary/Ministry of Justice and Constitutional Affairs. Seeking clarification regarding address and phone number from Sri Lanka and Hague Conference on Private International law.

The instrument of accession of Sri Lanka contains the following declarations:
In terms of Article 2, the Secretary/Ministry of Justice and Constitutional Affairs is designated the Central Authority.
The authority competent to act upon a Letter of Request pursuant to Article 6 would be the Secretary, Ministry of Justice and Constitutional Affairs/Registrar of the Court of Appeal.
For purposes of Article 7, the documents should be in the English language.
For purposes of Article 10, Sri Lanka has no objection to the procedure set out in paragraph (b) thereof. However it does not agree to the procedure set out in paragraphs (a) and (c).
In terms of Article 15, Sri Lanka wishes to declare that the Judge may proceed to give judgement even if no certificate of service or delivery has been received, provided the conditions set out in Article 15 are fulfilled.

ST. CHRISTOPHER (St. Kitts):
Ministry of Legal Affairs
P.O. Box 186
Government Headquarters
St. Kitts-Nevis, West Indies
tel: 809-465-2521
Now Independent. No formal confirmation to depositary government that Convention applies, however local government has provided information to the U.S. Embassy regarding central authority competent to receive Hague Service Convention requests noted above.

ST. HELENA:
The Supreme Court
Saint Helena

ST. LUCIA:
Now Independent. No formal confirmation to depositary government that Convention applies, however local government has provided the following information to the U.S. Embassy regarding central authority competent to receive Hague Service Convention requests.
Registrar of the High Court
Attn: Miss Isabella Shillingford
Registry Department
Peynier Street
Castries, St. Lucia, W.I.
tel: 809-452-1257
There is no standard fee for service.

ST. VINCENT:
Now Independent. No formal confirmation to depositary government that Convention applies, however local government has provided the following information to the U.S. Embassy regarding central authority competent to receive Hague Service Convention requests.
Ministry of Foreign Affairs
St. Vincent and the Grenadines
W.I.
tel: 809-456-1111
There is no fee. The Ministry of Foreign Affairs forwards the request for service to the Registrar's Office which effects service.

SEYCHELLES:
The Registrar
Supreme Court
Victoria
Mahe, Republic des Seychelles

SLOVAK REPUBLIC:
Ministerstvo Spravodlivosti Slovenskej Republicky
Zupne namestie 13, 813 11 Bratislava
Slovak Republic
Fax: (00427) 5316035

SLOVENIA:
Signatory: September 18, 2000
Accession: May 15, 2001
Entry into Force: June 1, 2001
the Ministry of Justice of the Republic of Slovenia
Zupanciceva 3
1000 LJUBLJANA
tel.: +386 1 478 5244
fax: +386 1 426 1050

SOLOMON ISLANDS:
Unknown. Now Independent. No formal confirmation to depositary government that Convention applies. Former Central Authority: Registrar of the High Court, Honiara

SPAIN:
Secretaria General Tecnica
Subdireccion de Cooperacion Juridica Internacional
Ministerio de Justicia
San Bernardo, 45
28015 Madrid, Spain
tel: (34)(1) 390-2328

SWEDEN:
Ministry of Justice
Division for Criminal and International Judicial Cooperation
Central Authority
SE-103 33 Stockholm, Sweden
tel: (46)(8) 405-5057
fax: (46)(8) 405-4676

SWITZERLAND:
Switzerland designates the cantonal authorities listed below as Central Authorities as referred to in the respective conventions. Requests for the service of documents may also be addressed to:
The Federal Justice and Police Department
Federal Office for Police Matters
International Judicial and Extrajudicial Assistance
Bundesrain 20
3003 Bern
Switzerland
Tel. 011-41-31-322-4310
Fax 011-41-31-322-5380

That office will forward the requests for service to the Central Authority in the appropriate canton.

Requests for service under the Hague Convention may also be sent directly to the Central Authority for the appropriate Canton. The following list provides the canton, official language of the canton, address and telephone number.

(Rel.6–10/05)

Authorized Swiss Central Authorities for each Canton
Cantonal Central Authorities (list up to date as per 14 September 2001)
The competent cantonal Central Authority to whom a request may be addressed can be ascertained on-line at the following address:
<http://www.elorge.admin.ch/>

Official Language(s) (G=German F=French I=Italian)

Canton: Aargau (AG) G; Obergericht des Kantons Aargau Obere Vorstadt 40 5000 Aarau; tel.: +41.62-835.3850 fax: +41.62-835.3949

Canton: Appenzell Ausserrhoden (AR) G; Kantonsgericht Appenzell A.Rh. 9043 Trogen; tel.: +41.71-343.6399 fax: +41.71-343.6359

Canton: Appenzell Innerrhoden (AI) G; Kantonsgericht Appenzell I.Rh. 9050 Appenzell; tel.: +41.71-788.9551 fax: +41.71-788.9554

Canton: Basel-Landschaft (BL) G; Obergericht des Kantons Basel-Landschaft 4410 Liestal; tel.: +41.61-925.5111 fax: +41.61-925.6964

Canton: Basel-Stadt (BS) G; Appellationsgericht Basel-Stadt 4051 Basel; tel.: +41.61-267.8181 fax: +41.61-267.6315

Canton: Bern (BE) G/F; Justiz-, Gemeinde- und Kirchendirektion des Kantons Bern Münstergasse 2 3011 Bern; tel.: +41.31-633.7676 fax: +41.31-633.7626

Canton: Fribourg (FR) F/G; Tribunal cantonal 1700 Fribourg; tel.: +41.26-305.3910 fax: +41.26-305.3919

Canton: Genève (GE) F; Parquet du Procureur général 1211 Genève 3; tel.: +41.22-319.2797 fax: +41.22-781.4365

Canton: Glarus (GL) G; Obergericht des Kantons Glarus 8750 Glarus; tel.: +41.55-645.2525 fax: +41.55-645.2500

Canton: Graubünden (GR) G; Justiz-, Polizei- und Sanitätsdepartement Graubünden 7001 Chur; tel.: +41.81-257.2121 fax: +41.81-257.2166

Canton: Jura (JU) F; Département de la Justice Service juridique 2800 Delémont; tel.: +41.32-421.5111 fax: +41.32-421.5555

Canton: Luzern (LU) G; Obergericht des Kantons Luzern Hirschengraben 16 6003 Luzern; tel.: +41.41-228.6262 fax: +41.41-228.6264

Canton: Neuchâtel (NE) F; Département de la justice, de la santé et de la sécurité Service de la justice Châ teau 2001 Neuchâtel; tel.: +41.32-889.4110 fax: +41.32-889.6064

Canton: Nidwalden (NW) G; Kantonsgericht Nidwalden 6370 Stans; tel.: +41.41-618.7950 fax: +41.41-618.7963

Canton: Obwalden (OW) G; Kantonsgericht Obwalden Postfach 1260 6061 Sarnen; tel.: +41.41-666.6222 fax: +41.41-660.8286

Canton: St. Gallen (SG) G; Kantonsgericht St. Gallen Klosterhof 1 9001 St. Gallen; tel.: +41.71-229.3898 fax: +41.71-229.3787

Canton: Schaffhausen (SH) G; Obergericht des Kantons Schaffhausen Postfach 568 8201 Schaffhausen; tel.: +41.52-632.7422 fax: +41.52-636.7836

Canton: Schwyz (SZ) G; Kantonsgericht Schwyz 6430 Schwyz; tel.: +41.41-819.1124

Canton: Solothurn (SO) G; Obergericht des Kantons Solothurn 4500 Solothurn; tel.: +41.32-627.7311 fax: +41.32-627.2298

Canton: Tessin (TI) I; Tribunale di appello 6901 Lugano; tel.: +41.91-815.5111 fax: +41.91-815.5478

Canton: Thurgau (TG) G; Obergericht des Kantons Thurgau 8500 Frauenfeld; tel.: +41.52-722.3121 fax: +41.52-722.3125

Canton: Uri (UR) G; Landgericht Uri Am Rathausplatz 2 6460 Altdorf; tel.: +41.41-875.2244 fax: +41.41-875.2277

Canton: Valais (VS) F/G; Tribunal cantonal 1950 Sion; tel.: +41.27-322.9393 fax: +41.27-322.6351

Canton: Vaud (VD) F; Tribunal cantonal 1014 Lausanne; tel.: +41.21-316.1511 fax: +41.21-316.1328

Canton: Zug (ZG) G; Obergericht des Kantons Zug Rechtshilfe 6300 Zug; tel.: +41.41-728.3154 fax: +41.41-728.3144

Canton: Zürich (ZH)[TAB]*G*[TAB]*Obergericht des Kantons Zürich, Rechtshilfe 8023 Zürich*[TAB]*tel.: +41.1-257.9191 fax: +41.1-261.1292*

TURKEY:
General Service of Civil Affairs
Ministry of Justice
Ankara, Turkey
(Adalet Bakanligi Hukuk Isleri Genel Mudurlugu, Ankara, Turkey)

TURKS & CAICOS:
The Registrar of the Supreme Court
Turks and Caicos Islands

TUVALU:
Now Independent. No formal confirmation to depositary government that Convention applies. Former Central Authority: Registrar of the High Court.

UKRAINE:
Accession: February 1, 2001; Entry into Force: December 1, 2001.
Central Authority: Ministry of Justice of Ukraine. Seeking clarification regarding address and phone number from Ukraine and the Hague Conference on Private International Law.

The instrument of accession of Ukraine contains the following declarations and reservations:
'1) on Article 2 of the Convention: the Ministry of Justice of Ukraine is the Central Authority of Ukraine;
2) on Article 6 of the Convention: the Ministry of Justice of Ukraine and its territorial departments of justice are competent to complete the certificate of service;
3) on Article 8 of the Convention: service of judicial documents through diplomatic or consular agents of another State within the territory of Ukraine may be effected only upon nationals of the State in which the documents originate;
4) on Article 9 of the Convention: the Ministry of Justice of Ukraine is the authority competent to receive documents transmitted by consular channels or, if exceptional circumstances so require, by diplomatic channels;
5) on Article 10 of the Convention: Ukraine will not use methods of transmission of judicial documents provided for in Article 10 of the Convention;
6) on Article 15 of the Convention: if all the conditions provided for in the second paragraph of Article 15 of the Convention are fulfilled, the judge, notwithstanding the provisions of the first paragraph of Article 15 of the Convention, may give judgment

even if no certificate of service or delivery has been received;
7) on Article 16 of the Convention: application for relief will not be entertained in Ukraine if it is filed after the expiration of one year following the date of the judgment.''

UNITED KINGDOM:
Her Majesty's Principal Secretary of State for Foreign and Commonwealth Affairs
London SW1A 2AL

For England and Wales:
The Senior Master of the Supreme Court of Judicature
Royal Courts of Justice
Strand
London WC2A 2LL, United Kingdom

For Scotland:
By a Note of 21 March 2000, the British Government notified that, with effect from 1 April 2000, the designated authority for Scotland will be:
The Scottish Executive Justice Department
Civil Justice and International Division
Hayweight House
23 Lauriston Street
Edinburgh, EH3 9DQ
Telephone: +44.131.221.6815
Fax: +44.131.221.6894

For Northern Ireland:
By a Note of 10 June 1980, the British Government notified that instead of the Registrar of the Supreme Court of Northern Ireland, designated in 1967 as the additional authority for Northern Ireland in conformity with Article 18 of the Convention, the Master (Queen's Bench and Appeals) is designated as the said additional authority. The address of the Master (Queen's Bench and Appeals) is Royal Courts of Justice, Belfast 1.

VENEZUELA:
Ministry of Foreign Affairs
Caracas, Venezuela

REFERENCE

''Checklist for the Discussions of the Special Commission of April 1989 on the Operation of the Hague Convention on the Service of Process Abroad'', Preliminary Document No. 1 of March 1989, Hague Conference on Private International Law, 28 I.L.M. 1556 (1989).

''Report on the Work of the Special Commission on the Operation of the Service Convention'', 17 I.L.M. 312, 312 (1978). Practical Handbook on the Operation of the Hague Convention of 15 November 1965 on the Service Abroad of Judicial and Extrajudicial Documents in Civil or Commercial Matters, Hague Conference on Private International Law, Maarten Kluwer's Internationale Uitgeversonderneming, Antwerp 1983. U.S. Distributor: Butterworth Publishers Inc., 10 Tower Office Park, Woburn, Boston, Massachusetts 01801. Contact U.S. Central Authority for addresses of other distributors.

Cumulative Digest of United States Practice in International Law, 1981-1988, Vol. II, Department of State, Office of the Legal Adviser, pp. 1530-1547 (1994).

Digest of United States Practice in International Law, 1976, Department of State, Office of the Legal Adviser, p. 307.

Digest of United States Practice in International Law, 1977, Department of State, Office of the Legal Adviser, pp. 477-490; pp. 501-504.

Digest of United States Practice in International Law, 1980, Department of State, Office of the Legal Adviser, p. 457.

Amram, ''The Proposed International Convention on the Service of Documents Abroad'', 51 A.B.A. J. 650 (1965).

Baeck & Ginsberg, ''Service of Process Abroad'', 4 Int'l. Law. 145 (1969).

Basarrate, Note: ''International Service of Process: Reconciling the Federal Rules of Civil Procedure with the Hague Convention on the Service Abroad of Judicial and Extrajudicial Documents in Civil or Commercial Matters'', Vanderbilt Journal of Transnational Law'', Vol. 22, No. 5, pp. 1071-1096 (1988).

Beucher & Sandage, ''United States Punitive Damage Awards in German Courts: The Evolving German position on Service and Enforcement'', Vanderbilt Journal of Transnational Law, Vol. 23, No. 5, pp. 967-991 (1991).

Boyd, ''Contemporary Practice of the United States Relating to International Law—The Hague Service Convention'', 72 American Journal of International Law, 130 (1978).

Downs, ''Note: The Effect of the Hague Convention on Service Abroad of Judicial and Extrajudicial Documents in Civil or Commercial Matters'', 1 Cornell Intl L. J., 125 (1969).

Epstein, International Litigation: A Guide to Jurisdiction, Practice and Strategy, 2nd, Prentice Hall Law & Business, 1994.

Gordon, Comment: ''Service of Process by Registered Mail on a Japanese Defendant is Ineffective Under Article 10(a) of the Hague Convention of November 15, 1965 on the Service Abroad of Judicial and Extrajudicial Documents in Civil and Commercial Matters, Bankston v. Toyota Motor Corp. 889 F. 2nd 172 (8th Cir. 1989)'' Vanderbilt Journal of Transnational Law, Vol. 23, No. 4, pp. 851-869.

Horlick, ''Service of Process and other Documents Abroad, American Bar Association, Problems in Transnational Litigation, 23 (1980). Horlick, ''A Practical Guide to Service of Process Abroad'', 14 Int'l. Law. 637 (1980).

Hoyal, ''The Hague Service Convention and Agency Concepts: Lamb v. Volkswagenwerk Aktiengesellschaft'', Cornell International Law Journal, Vol. 20, pp. 391-412.

Leo, Note: ''The Interplay Between Domestic Rules Permitting Service Abroad by Mail and the Hague Convention on Service: Proposing an Amendment to the Federal Rules of Civil Procedure'', Cornell International Law Journal, Vol. 22, No. 2, pp. 335-370 (1989).

Miller and Pionk, ''The practical aspects of litigating against foreign corporations'', 54 Journal of Air Law and Commerce 123 (Fall 1988), esp. pp. 128-137.

Mitsui, ''Ratification of Convention Relating to Civil Procedure on the Service Abroad of Judicial and Extra-Judicial Documents in Civil and Commercial Matters'', 16 Japanese Annual Int'l. L. 7 (1972).

Nanda and Pansius, Litigation of International Disputes in U.S. Courts, Vol. 4, International Business and Law Series, (1996), Sec. 2.02(2), pp. 2-4—2-15.

Note, ''Closing the Chasm of International Judicial Assistance: Extraterritorial Service of Documents, 12 How. L. J. 238 (1966).

Ristau, International Judicial Assistance (Civil and Commercial), International Law Institute (1984, supp. 1990, 1995).

Schwartz, ''Obtaining Evidence Overseas: Discovery on Foreign Shores'', 9 Family Advocate 28 (1987) [includes discussion of service abroad].

Vazquez, ''Hague Service Convention—scope and application—role of internal law: Volkswagen Aktiengesellschaft v. Schlunk, 82 American Journal of International Law 816 (1988).

ADDITIONAL INFORMATION:

The Office of American Citizens Services has available general information flyers on international judicial assistance. These topics include country-specific information about service of process and obtaining evidence abroad.

Using the Internet: Many of our judicial assistance flyers are available on the Internet via the Department of State, Bureau of Consular Affairs home page. See also, the Department of State, Office of the Legal Adviser for Private International Law home page for information regarding the work of the Hague Conference on Private International Law. See also the home pages for many of our embassies. As noted above, the text of the Convention and updatedinformation concerning countries which have acceded to the Convention can be found in the Martindale-Hubbell Law Directory, Law Digest Volume.

QUESTIONS:

1. U.S. Central Authority: Additional questions regarding the operation of the Hague Service Convention should be addressed to the U.S. Central Authority, the Office of International Judicial Assistance, Civil Division, Department of Justice, tel: (202) 307-0983.

2. General questions may also be addressed to the appropriate geographic division of the Office of American Citizens Services, at telephone (202) 647-5225 or 202-647-5226.

Appendix 3

FORM OF REQUEST FOR SERVICE ABROAD OF JUDICIAL OR EXTRAJUDICIAL DOCUMENTS (HAGUE CONVENTION)

REQUEST
FOR SERVICE ABROAD OF JUDICIAL OR EXTRAJUDICIAL DOCUMENTS

Identity and addressof the applicant:	*Address of receiving authority:*

The undersigned applicant has the honour to transmit — in duplicate — the documents listed below and, in conformity with Article 5 of the above-mentioned Convention, requests prompt service of one copy thereof on the addressee, *i.e,*

(*identity and address*)

____

____

☐ *a)* in accordance with the provisions of sub-paragraph *(a)* of the first paragraph of Article 5 of the Convention*.

☐ *b)* in accordance with the following particular method (sub-paragraph *(b)* of the first paragraph of Article 5)*:

____

____

☐ *c)* by delivery to the addressee, if he accepts it voluntarily (second paragraph of Article 5)*.

The authority is requested to return or to have returned to the applicant a copy of the documents—and of the annexes*—with a certificate as provided on the reverse side.

List of documents

____

____

____

____

____

Done at __________, *the* _______

Signature and/or stamp.

____

* Delete if inappropriate.

Reverse of the request

CERTIFICATE

The undersigned authority has the honour to certify, in conformity with Article 6 of the Convention,

1) that the document has been served*

— the (*date*)____
— at (*place, street, number*) __________________________________
____

— in one of the following methods authorised by Article 5:

☐ *a)* in accordance with the provisions of sub-paragraph (a) of the first paragraph of Article 5 of the Convention*.

☐ *b)* in accordance with the following particular method*: ____________
____

☐ *c)* by delivery to the addressee, who accepted it voluntarily* .

The documents referred to in the request have been delivered to:

— (*identity and description of person*):
____
____

— relationship to the addressee (*family, business or other*):
____
____

2) that the document has not been served, by reason of the following facts*:
____
____
____

In conformity with the second paragraph of Article 12 of the Convention, the applicant is requested to pay or reimburse the expenses detailed in the attached statement*.

Annexes

Documents returned:
____
____
____

In appropriate cases, documents establishing the service:
____
____
____

Done at_____________, the________
Signature and/or stamp.
____

* Delete if inappropriate.

SUMMARY OF THE DOCUMENT TO BE SERVED

Convention on the Service Abroad of Judicial and Extrajudicial Documents in Civil or Commercial Matters, signed at The Hague, the 15th of November 1965.

(Article 5, fourth paragraph)

Name and address of the requesting authority:
____
____
____

Particulars of the parties*:
____
____
____

JUDICIAL DOCUMENT**

Nature and purpose of the document: ______________________________
____
____

Nature and purpose of the proceedings and, where appropriate, the amount in dispute: ______________________________
____
____

Date and place for entering appearance**: ______________________________
____

Court which has given judgment**: ______________________________
____

Date of judgment**: ______________________________

Time-limits stated in the document**:

EXTRAJUDICIAL DOCUMENT**

Nature and purpose of the document: ______________________________
____
____

Time-limits stated in the document**: ______________________________
____
____

* If appropriate, identity and address of the person interested in the transmission of the document.

** Delete if inappropriate.

Appendix 4

REPORT OF THE SPECIAL COMMITTEE ON THE OPERATION OF HAGUE CONVENTIONS

Conférence de La Haye de droit international privé
Hague Conference on private international law

Entraide judiciaire
Judicial co-operation
Août/August 1989

Rapport sur les travaux de la Commission spéciale d'avril 1989 sur le fonctionnement des Conventions de La Haye du 15 novembre 1965 relative à la signification et la notification à l'étranger des actes judiciaires et extrajudiciaires en matière civile ou commerciale et du 18 mars 1970 sur l'obtention des preuves à l'étranger en matière civile ou commerciale

établi par le Bureau Permanent

• • •

Report on the work of the Special Commission of April 1989 on the operation of the Hague Conventions of 15 November 1965 on the Service Abroad of Judicial and Extrajudicial Documents in Civil or Commercial Matters and of 18 March 1970 on the Taking of Evidence Abroad in Civil or Commercial Matters

drawn up by the Permanent Bureau

Bureau Permanent de la Conférence
Scheveningseweg 6, La Haye, Pays-Bas

Permanent Bureau of the Conference
Scheveningseweg 6, The Hague, Netherlands

Rapport sur les travaux de la Commission spéciale d'avril 1989 sur le fonctionnement des Conventions de La Haye du 15 novembre 1965 relative à la signification et la notification à l'étranger des actes judiciaires et extrajudiciaires en matière civile ou commerciale et du 18 mars 1970 sur l'obtention des preuves à l'étranger en matière civile ou commerciale

établi par le Bureau Permanent

• • •

Report on the work of the Special Commission of April 1989 on the operation of the Hague Conventions of 15 November 1965 on the Service Abroad of Judicial and Extrajudicial Documents in Civil or Commercial Matters and of 18 March 1970 on the Taking of Evidence Abroad in Civil or Commercial Matters

drawn up by the Permanent Bureau

Rapport sur les travaux de la Commission spéciale d'avril 1989 sur le fonctionnement des Conventions de La Haye du 15 novembre 1965 relative à la signification et la notification à l'étranger des actes judiciaires et extrajudiciaires en matière civile ou commerciale et du 18 mars 1970 sur l'obtention des preuves à l'étranger en matière civile ou commerciale

établi par le Bureau Permanent

INTRODUCTION

1 Dans l'Acte final de la Seizième session de la Conférence de La Haye de droit international privé, signé le 20 octobre 1988, figure parmi les Décisions exposées à la page 12, le texte suivant:

> "*La Seizième session,*
>
> *Se fondant sur les propositions et suggestions émises au sein de la Première commission:*
>
> ....
>
> 6 *Charge le Secrétaire général de convoquer une Commission spéciale sur le fonctionnement des* Conventions de La Haye du 15 novembre 1965 relative à la signification et la notification à l'étranger des actes judiciaires et extrajudiciaires en matière civile ou commerciale *et* du 18 mars 1970 sur l'obtention des preuves à l'étranger en matière civile ou commerciale."

2 Afin d'exécuter ces instructions, le Secrétaire général a convoqué, pour la période du 17 au 20 avril 1989, une Commission spéciale, à laquelle furent invités à participer non seulement les Etats membres de la Conférence de La Haye de droit international privé, mais aussi tous les autres Etats parties aux deux traités internationaux mentionnés ci-dessus, ou à l'un ou l'autre d'entre eux, ainsi que certaines organisations intergouvernementales et non gouvernementales internationales intéressées par l'objet de ces traités. Vingt-deux Etats ont effectivement participé à la Commission, tous Membres de la Conférence de La Haye.

3 Les organisations représentées par des observateurs étaient le Secrétariat du Commonwealth, l'International Bar Association, ainsi que l'Union internationale des huissiers de justice et officiers judiciaires. A tous les participants furent remis le Document préliminaire No 1 de mars 1989, "Récapitulation des points à discuter par la Commission spéciale d'avril 1989 sur le fonctionnement des Conventions de La Haye relative à la signification et la notification à l'étranger et sur l'obtention des preuves à l'étranger", établi par M. Adair Dyer, Premier secrétaire au Bureau Permanent, ainsi que des traductions en langue anglaise de certaines décisions rendues par la Cour Suprême des Pays-Bas en application d'une part de la Convention de La Haye du 15 novembre 1965 relative à la signification et la notification à l'étranger des actes judiciaires et extrajudiciaires en matière civile ou commerciale ("Convention-Notification") et d'autre part de la Convention du 18 mars 1970 sur l'Obtention des preuves à l'étranger en matière civile ou commerciale ("Convention- Obtention des preuves").

Report on the work of the Special Commission of April 1989 on the operation of the Hague Conventions of 15 November 1965 on the Service Abroad of Judicial and Extrajudicial Documents In Civil or Commercial Matters and of 18 March 1970 on the Taking of Evidence Abroad in Civil or Commercial Matters

drawn up by the Permanent Bureau

INTRODUCTION

1 In the Final Act of the Sixteenth Session of the Hague Conference on private international law, signed 20 October 1988, among the Decisions set out on page 13 is the following:

> "*The Sixteenth Session,*
>
> *Having regard to the proposals and suggestions advanced within the First Commission -*
>
> ....
>
> 6 *Instructs the Secretary General to convene a Special Commission on the operation of the* Hague Conventions of 15 November 1965 on the Service Abroad of Judicial and Extrajudicial Documents in Civil or Commercial Matters *and* of 18 March 1970 on the Taking of Evidence Abroad in Civil or Commercial Matters."

2 Pursuant to this instruction, the Secretary General convened during the period of 17-20 April 1989 a Special Commission, in which were invited to participate not only the Member States of the Hague Conference on private international law, but also all other States which were Parties to one or both of the international Treaties mentioned above, as well as certain intergovernmental and non-governmental international organizations having an interest in the subject-matter of these Treaties. Twenty-two States participated, all of which were Members of the Hague Conference.

3 The organizations represented by observers were the Commonwealth Secretariat, the International Bar Association and the International Union of Bailiffs and Law Officers. All participants were furnished with Preliminary Document No 1 of March 1989, "Checklist for the discussions of the Special Commission of April 1989 on the operation of the Hague Conventions on the Service of Process Abroad and on the Taking of Evidence Abroad", drawn up by Mr Adair Dyer, First Secretary at the Permanent Bureau, and with English translations of certain decisions made by the Supreme Court of the Netherlands applying the Hague Convention of 15 November 1965 on the Service Abroad of Judicial and Extrajudicial Documents in Civil or Commercial Matters ("Hague Service Convention") and the Convention of 18 March 1970 on the Taking of Evidence Abroad in Civil or Commercial Matters ("Hague Evidence Convention") respectively.

4 M. J.C.Schultsz, Président de la Commission d'Etat néerlandaise pour la codification du droit international privé ouvre la réunion et souhaite la bienvenue aux participants. M. Gustaf Möller, expert de la Finlande est élu à l'unanimité Président de la Commission spéciale et M. Justice Ronan Keane, expert de l'Irlande, est élu à l'unanimité Vice-président.

5 Il est admis que les questions énumérées dans le Document préliminaire No 1 doivent servir d'ordre du jour de la réunion, étant entendu que des questions additionnelles pourront être posées au cours de la discussion et qu'à la fin de la réunion serait abordé le problème du contenu et de l'utilité des Manuels pratiques sur la Convention-Notification et sur la Convention-Obtention des preuves, édités par le Bureau Permanent.

PREMIÈRE PARTIE - CONVENTION-NOTIFICATION

I Portée de la Convention quant à son objet

Question A: La portée de l'expression "en matière civile ou commerciale" employée dans le titre de la Convention et dans son article premier a-t-elle soulevé des difficultés?

6 Il ne semblait pas y avoir de décisions judiciaires publiées concernant l'interprétation de cette expression dans le cadre de la Convention-Notification, bien que, comme on l'a relevé dans le Document préliminaire No 1, à la page 21, deux importantes décisions aient été rendues par les Cours Suprêmes d'Etats parties (les Pays-Bas et le Royaume-Uni) concernant la portée du même terme dans le contexte de la Convention-Obtention des preuves.

7 Néanmoins, certaines demandes de signification avaient été refusées par l'Autorité centrale de l'un des *Länder* allemands dans le cas de procédures engagées devant les tribunaux des Etats-Unis en vue de l'obtention de dommages-intérêts - résultant, entre autres, d'une responsabilité du fait des produits - où il était également demandé d'importantes sommes à titre "punitif" ("*punitive damages*"). La position adoptée par cette Autorité centrale, qui n'était pas au demeurant nécessairement partagée par le Ministère de la Justice à Bonn, ni par les Autorités centrales des autres *Länder*, consistait à qualifier de pénales et non de civiles des demandes *excessives* de dommages-intérêts "punitifs"*.

8 Il ressort des discussions qu'un certain nombre d'experts étaient d'avis:

a que la qualification de la demande au regard du domaine matériel de la Convention relève de la compétence de l'Etat requérant;

b que puisque la Convention concerne l'assistance judiciaire, une attitude libérale s'impose - d'autant que les règles relatives à la reconnaissance des jugements étrangers fourniraient le moyen le plus naturel de réagir contre les anomalies procédurales affectant l'introduction de l'instance;

c que dans la mesure où il résulte des conclusions des parties que les dommages-intérêts "punitifs" doivent être versés au demandeur et non à l'Etat requérant, il semble difficile de considérer ces derniers autrement que comme faisant l'objet d'une action civile ou commerciale;

---

* *Note du Bureau Permanent*: signalons ici qu'après la Commission spéciale, soit le 9 mai 1989, l'*Oberlandesgericht* de Munich a rejeté cette thèse et a qualifié de "civils" les dommages-intérêts "punitifs" (jugement partiellement publié dans *RIW* 1989, fasc. 6, p. 483).

4 Mr J.C. Schultsz, President of the Netherlands Standing Government Committee on private international law, opened the meeting and welcomed all participants. Mr Gustaf Möller, Expert of Finland, was unanimously elected to serve as Chairman of the Special Commission, and Mr Justice Ronan Keane, Expert of Ireland, was unanimously elected to serve as Vice-Chairman.

5 The questions set out in Preliminary Document No 1 were adopted in principle as the agenda for the meeting, it being understood that additional points could be raised in the course of discussions and that at the end of the meeting a discussion would be held on the content and utility of the Practical Handbooks edited by the Permanent Bureau in loose-leaf format for the Hague Service Convention and the Hague Evidence Convention, respectively.

PART ONE - HAGUE SERVICE CONVENTION

I Scope of the Convention as to its subject-matter

Question A: Have any problems arisen as to the scope of the term "in civil or commercial matters" employed in the title and in Article 1 of the Convention?

6 There had been apparently no reported court decisions concerning the interpretation of this term in the Hague Service Convention although, as pointed out in Preliminary Document No 1, at page 20, two significant decisions had been handed down by the highest courts of different States Parties (the Netherlands and the United Kingdom) concerning the scope of the same expression used in the Hague Evidence Convention.

7 Nonetheless, some requests for service of process had been refused by the Central Authority in one of the German *Länder* involving law suits filed in the courts of the United States of America asserting claims for civil damages - for example arising from products liability - to which large claims for "punitive" damages were joined. The theory of this regional Central Authority, which was not necessarily shared by the Ministry of Justice in Bonn or by the Central Authorities of the other *Länder*, apparently was that *excessive* claims for punitive damages were penal rather than civil or commercial in nature.*

8 The discussions showed that a number of experts thought:

a that it was for the requesting State to characterize the claim in respect of the substantive scope of the Convention;

b that, since the Convention provided assistance in judicial proceedings, a liberal attitude should be taken - especially as the rules concerning recognition of foreign judgments would be used as the obvious means of counteracting procedural deficiencies at the time of service;

c that, to the extent that it is established by the pleadings that "punitive damages" are to be paid to the plaintiff and not to the requesting State, it seems difficult to characterize such damages as other than an element of a civil or commercial action; and,

* *Note by the Permanent Bureau*: It should be mentioned here that subsequently to the Special Commission, on 9 May 1989, the *Oberlandesgericht* of Munich rejected this theory and characterized punitive damages as civil in nature (decision published in part in *RIW*, 1989, Heft 6, p. 483).

d qu'il est impossible d'écarter la qualification civile ou commerciale d'une telle action sur le seul fondement du montant des sommes demandées, puisque la nature civile ou commerciale d'une action n'est pas tributaire du montant des dommages-intérêts demandés.

9 Par ailleurs, il a été souligné que:

e la signification et la notification de documents à l'étranger dans le cadre du contentieux international ne présupposent pas la validité de ces derniers;

f le but de la Convention est d'informer rapidement le défendeur de l'instance engagée contre lui; et

g le refus d'appliquer la Convention laisse la place à l'application des règles procédurales internes de l'Etat requérant, qui défavorisent fréquemment le défendeur.

10 Enfin, il a été rappelé, comme le souligne le Document préliminaire No 1 à la page 3, que la Commission spéciale réunie en novembre 1977 afin d'étudier le fonctionnement de la Convention-Notification avait conclu que les demandes de dommages-intérêts "punitifs" relèvent du domaine de la Convention (voir le Rapport sur les travaux de la Commission spéciale dans les *Actes et documents de la Quatorzième session*, 1980, tome IV, *Entraide judiciaire*, p. 381-382; Manuel pratique, p. 30.)

11 La discussion des décisions judiciaires rendues par application des Conventions concernant la portée de l'expression "en matière civile et commerciale" a été reportée. Mais certaines conclusions relatives au domaine matériel des Conventions-Notification et Obtention des preuves figurent parmi les "Conclusions sur les points les plus importants examinés par la Commission spéciale" adoptées à la réunion d'avril 1989. Celles-ci peuvent être trouvées ci-dessous aux paragraphes 25-27 ou à l'Annexe.

II Portée procédurale de la Convention

Question B: Dans quelles circonstances une société anonyme ou autre personne morale peut-elle être considérée comme se trouvant sur le territoire d'un pays aux fins de la notification d'un acte judiciaire ou extrajudiciaire dans ce pays?

12 Comme il est indiqué dans la Récapitulation, cette question a été soulevée par deux affaires tranchées par les Cours Suprêmes de deux pays différents, dans lesquelles la signification a été faite à une personne dont il était prétendu qu'elle représentait une société étrangère sur le territoire du pays concerné: *Schlunk* v. *Volkswagen Aktiengesellschaft*, décision rendue par la Cour Suprême des Etats-Unis le 15 juin 1988, et *Segers and Rufa BV.* v. *Mabanaft GmbH*, décision rendue par le *Hoge Raad* néerlandais le 27 juin 1986. L'affaire *Schlunk* concernait la signification à une filiale nationale totalement contrôlée par la société-mère étrangère; la filiale a été jugée représenter la société-mère aux fins de la signification, alors même qu'elle n'avait pas été expressément désignée à ces fins. L'affaire *Mabanaft* concernait la question de savoir si les règles procédurales en vigueur aux Pays-Bas, selon lesquelles l'avocat auprès duquel le défendeur a élu domicile reste habilité à recevoir la signification d'actes intervenant à des stades ultérieurs de la procédure (lors de l'appel notamment), devaient s'appliquer

d that it is impossible to characterize such an action as other than civil or commercial on the basis of the amounts claimed, since a civil or commercial action does not alter according to the amount of damages sought.

9 In addition, it was pointed out:

e that the service of documents abroad does not presuppose their validity in international litigation;

f that the aim of the Convention is to inform the defendant rapidly of proceedings against him; and

g that refusal to apply the Convention leads to the application of the domestic rules of procedure of the requesting State which is often disadvantageous to the defendant.

10 Finally it was recalled, as pointed out in Preliminary Document No 1 at page 2, that the Special Commission which met in November 1977 to consider the operation of the Hague Service Convention concluded that claims for punitive damages fall within the scope of the Convention (see the Report of the Special Commission in *Proceedings*, Fourteenth Session, Tome IV, *Judicial Co-operation* at pp. 381-382; Practical Handbook, page 30).

11 Discussions of the court cases decided under the Hague Evidence Convention concerning the scope of the words "civil or commercial matters" were deferred. Thereafter, certain conclusions concerning the subject-matter scope of the Hague Service and Evidence Conventions were included among the "Conclusions on the most important points considered by the Special Commission" adopted at the April 1989 meeting. For these, please refer to paragraphs nos 25-27, below, or to the Annex.

II Procedural scope of the Convention

Question B: Under what circumstances may a company with limited liability or other corporate entity be considered to be present within the jurisdiction of a country for purposes of service upon it of a judicial or extrajudicial document within the territory of that country?

12 This question was posed as indicated in the Checklist by two cases decided by the highest courts in two different countries involving service upon the purported agent of a foreign incorporated company within the territory of the respective country: *Schlunk* v. *Volkswagen Aktiengesellschaft*, decided by the Supreme Court of the United States, 15 June 1988 and *Segers and Rufa BV* v. *Mabanaft GmbH*, decided by the *Hoge Raad* of the Netherlands on 27 June 1986. The *Schlunk* case involved service upon a wholly owned domestic subsidiary of the foreign company which was deemed to be an agent to receive service of process on behalf of the parent company, even though it had not been expressly so designated. The *Mabanaft* case involved the question of whether procedural rules adopted by the Netherlands to make a lawyer a continuing agent for his client who had elected domicile at his office to receive service of process in later (appellate) stages of a legal

lorsque le destinataire de ces actes résidait à l'étranger, et ainsi exclure l'application de la Convention à la notification de l'exercice des voies de recours devant la Cour d'appel, ainsi que devant le *Hoge Raad*. Dans les deux cas, les juges s'étaient fondés sur le principe selon lequel il appartient à la juridiction saisie de décider s'il y a lieu de transmettre un acte à l'étranger pour y être signifié ou notifié.

13 Le principe aux termes duquel le for doit trancher cette question selon sa propre loi a été largement admis, bien que fût reconnu le danger de permettre la signification sur le territoire du for à une personne n'ayant pas été expressément désignée à cet effet. Car un pareil mode de signification peut ne pas réaliser les objectifs de la Convention, qui vise à assurer que le défendeur soit informé en temps utile de la procédure engagée contre lui. Il a été souligné que les tribunaux de certains pays tels que le Royaume-Uni hésiteraient davantage que les juridictions des Etats-Unis à "percer le voile" de la personnalité morale séparant la société-mère étrangère de sa filiale nationale, en raison de l'absence de tout "garde-fou" tel que celui qu'offre la Constitution des Etats-Unis assurant "*due process of law*".

14 L'opinion a été exprimée que l'incidence pratique de la décision rendue dans l'affaire *Schlunk* sur la jurisprudence ultérieure serait probablement assez limitée. Par conséquent, une attitude d'attente semblait la plus appropriée. L'affaire *Mabanaft* ne soulevait pas de difficulté dans la mesure où le *Hoge Raad* avait décidé que la modification subie par la règle nationale n'avait pas pour effet de rendre la Convention inapplicable.

III Forme de signification ou de notification

Question C: Des problèmes se sont-ils posés au sujet de demandes de formes particulières de signification ou de notification faites en vertu de l'article 5 b *de la Convention-Notification?*

15 Aucune question n'a été soulevée sur ce point.

Question D: Des décisions judiciaires ont-elles été rendues dans votre pays au sujet de l'interprétation de l'article 10 a *de la Convention-Notification, dont le texte est le suivant:*

> *"La présente Convention ne fait pas obstacle, sauf si l'Etat de destination déclare s'y opposer:*
>
> a *à la faculté d'adresser directement, par la voie de la poste, des actes judiciaires aux personnes se trouvant à l'étranger ..."*

16 Il a été souligné que la transmission d'un acte par voie postale constitue une forme de signification ou de notification qui est tout à fait distincte de celle qui a lieu par l'entremise des Autorités centrales ou entre officiers ministériels. L'article 10 *a* offre en effet aux Etats contractants la possibilité de faire une réserve quant à la transmission d'actes judiciaires par la voie de la poste, lorsqu'ils considèrent que cette forme de transmission constituerait une atteinte à leur souveraineté. Ainsi, toute hésitation relative à la nature juridique de cette procédure est sans fondement. Toutefois, certains tribunaux des Etats-Unis, dans des décisions citées dans la "Récapitulation", ont conclu que la transmission par voie postale de l'acte introductif d'instance n'était pas autorisée par la Convention.

proceeding, were intended to apply when the person to be served resided abroad, thus rendering the Convention inapplicable to notice of appeal to the intermediate appellate court or the *Hoge Raad*. The courts in both cases had started from the assumption that it was for the court before which the proceeding was pending to decide whether there was "occasion" to transmit documents abroad for service.

13 The principle that the forum is to decide this question under its own law was broadly accepted, although the danger of permitting domestic service upon a person who had not been expressly designated as an agent to receive service of process was recognized. Such service might not fulfill the purposes of the Convention which were to assure timely notice of the legal action to the person to be served. It was pointed out that courts of certain countries such as the United Kingdom would be more reluctant to "pierce the corporate veil" between a foreign parent company and its wholly owned domestic subsidiary than the courts of the United States of America had been, because of the lack of a "safety net" such as that offered by the clause of the United States Constitution's Bill of Rights guaranteeing "due process of law".

14 Some opinion was expressed that the practical impact of the *Schlunk* decision on future cases in the United States of America would probably be rather limited. Thus a wait-and-see attitude seemed appropriate. The *Mabanaft* case offered no problem since the *Hoge Raad* had concluded that the domestic rule change did not have the effect of rendering the Convention inapplicable.

III Methods of service

Question C: Have any problems arisen with requests for particular methods of service made under Article 5 b *of the Hague Service Convention?*

15 No problems were raised in connection with this question.

Question D: Have there been any court decisions in your country interpreting Article 10 a *of the Hague Service Convention which reads as follows:*

> *"Provided the State of destination does not object, the present Convention shall not interfere with -*
>
> a *the freedom to send judicial documents, by postal channels, directly to persons abroad ..."*

16 It was pointed out that the postal channel for service constitutes a method which is quite separate from service via the Central Authorities or between judicial officers. Article 10 *a* in effect offered a reservation to Contracting States to consider that service by mail was an infringement of their sovereignty. Thus, theoretical doubts about the legal nature of the procedure were unjustified. Nonetheless, certain courts in the United States of America in opinions cited in the "Checklist" had concluded that service of process abroad by mail was not permitted under the Convention.

17 La délégation japonaise a expliqué que son gouvernement souhaitait faire la déclaration de principe suivante:

> *"Position japonaise relative à l'article 10 a de la Convention de La Haye relative à la signification et la notification à l'étranger des actes judiciaires et extrajudiciaires en matière civile et commerciale:*
>
> *Le Japon n'a pas déclaré objecter à la transmission directe, par voie postale, d'actes judiciaires à des personnes résidant à l'étranger. A cet égard, cependant, il a précisé que le fait qu'il ne s'oppose pas au recours à la transmission par voie postale d'actes judiciaires à des personnes résidant au Japon n'implique pas nécessairement que pareille méthode de transmission soit considérée comme une signification valable au regard du droit japonais; il signifie seulement que le Japon ne considère pas pareille transmission comme attentatoire à sa souveraineté."*

Il a été convenu que la position du Japon telle qu'exprimée dans cette déclaration serait mentionnée dans la prochaine revision du Manuel pratique sur la Convention-Notification.

Question E: Les alinéas b *et* c *de l'article 10 de la Convention-Notification ont-ils soulevé des problèmes?*

18 L'application de ces dispositions n'a pas soulevé de difficulté. La signification d'actes transmis entre officiers ministériels est assez rare en pratique, probablement parce que pareille possibilité est insuffisamment connue. D'un autre côté, la transmission d'actes par des avocats à des officiers ministériels étrangers en vue de leur signification directe est d'une pratique fréquente aux Pays-Bas, en Belgique et en France.

19 Une décision rendue par une juridiction américaine, *the United States District Court for the Eastern District of Missouri, Tax Lease Underwriters* v. *Blackwall Green*, concernant une action civile et non une affaire fiscale, a été considérée comme constituant un précédent quant à la validité d'une signification effectuée directement en Angleterre par l'intermédiaire d'un *solicitor* anglais.

IV Autorités expéditrices

Question F: Des problèmes se sont-ils posés au sujet de la qualité de personnes transmettant des actes judiciaires ou extrajudiciaires à des Autorités centrales à l'étranger?

20 La délégation des Etats-Unis a fait valoir que certaines difficultés étaient apparues concernant l'interprétation par l'Etat requis de l'article 3 de la Convention. En particulier, certains Etats - le Royaume-Uni et Israël - avaient refusé d'accepter des demandes de signification d'actes lorsque celles-ci émanaient d'avocats des Etats-Unis. Il est apparu toutefois que d'autres Etats, notamment la République fédérale d'Allemagne, avaient montré une attitude plus libérale dans la mesure où les autorités allemandes étaient prêtes à accepter une demande de signification émanant de toute personne compétente à cet effet en vertu du droit de l'Etat requérant, à condition que les titres de cette personne soient suffisamment précisés dans la demande: par exemple, devait y figurer la référence à la règle (loi ou règlement de la Cour) habilitant à cet effet les avocats admis à exercer dans l'Etat requérant.

17 The Japanese delegation explained that their Government wished the following statement of position to be made known:

> *"Japanese position on Article 10* a *of the Hague Convention on the Service Abroad of Judicial and Extrajudicial Documents in Civil or Commercial Matters:*
>
> *Japan has not declared that it objects to the sending of judicial documents, by postal channels, directly to persons abroad. In this connection, Japan has made it clear that no objection to the use of postal channels for sending judicial documents to persons in Japan does not necessarily imply that the sending by such a method is considered valid service in Japan; it merely indicates that Japan does not consider it as infringement of its sovereign power."*

It was understood that the Japanese position as expressed in this statement would be included in the next revision of the Practical Handbook on the Hague Service Convention.

Question E: Have any problems arisen under Article 10 b *or* c *of the Hague Service Convention?*

18 The application of these provisions had not given rise to any problems. Service of documents forwarded by one process server to another occurred rather seldom in practice, probably because this option was not sufficiently known. On the other hand, the forwarding of documents by lawyers to foreign process servers for direct service was a frequent practice in the Netherlands, Belgium and France.

19 A case decided by the United States District Court for the Eastern District of Missouri, *Tax Lease Underwriters* v. *Blackwall Green*, dealing with a civil action and not with a tax matter, was found to constitute a precedent accepting the validity of service of process effected in England through direct service by an English solicitor.

IV Forwarding authorities

Question F: Have any issues arisen concerning the authority of persons forwarding judicial or extrajudicial documents to Central Authorities abroad?

20 The delegation of the United States of America mentioned that certain problems had appeared concerning the interpretation by requested States of Article 3 of the Convention. In particular certain States - the United Kingdom and Israel - had refused to accept requests for service of documents when such requests were forwarded by attorneys from the United States of America. It appeared that other States, notably the Federal Republic of Germany, had shown a more liberal attitude in that the German authorities would accept a request for service emanating from any person competent under the laws of the requesting State, provided that the authority of such person was sufficiently specified in the request: for example, by reference to the law or rule of court granting this authority to an attorney licensed to practice law in the requesting State.

21 La délégation du Royaume-Uni a indiqué qu'au regard des observations formulées par la délégation américaine, elle donnerait davantage de considération à la question de savoir si l'article 69 du Règlement de la Cour Suprême du Royaume-Uni donnait lieu à une pratique conforme à ses obligations telles qu'elles résultaient de la Convention-Notification. Toutefois, la délégation du Royaume-Uni souhaitait que les voies de signification indiquées à l'article 10 de la Convention soient employées de préférence à la transmission des actes au *Senior Master*.

V <u>Frais</u>

<u>Question G</u>: Des problèmes se sont-ils posés au sujet des frais entraînés par les significations ou notifications requises d'une Autorité centrale en vertu de la Convention?

22 Il ressort des discussions qu'aucun Etat partie à la Convention n'exigerait de taxe ni de remboursement de frais à raison d'une signification par voie normale effectuée par ses autorités. Dans certains pays, notamment en Belgique, en France et aux Pays-Bas, la transmission d'un acte à un destinataire qui l'accepte volontairement, hypothèse visée à l'article 5, paragraphe 2, de la Convention, est considérée comme une voie de signification normale. Si une signification formelle à la personne du destinataire est requise, il faut alors faire intervenir un huissier (*deurwaarder* en néerlandais) dont les émoluments sont considérés comme étant payables ou remboursables par le requérant aux termes de l'article 12, paragraphe 2.

VI <u>Protection des défendeurs</u>

<u>Question H</u>: Des décisions judiciaires ont-elles été rendues dans votre pays au sujet de l'application de l'article 15 ou de l'article 16 de la Convention-Notification?

23 L'attention de la Commission a été attirée vers l'importance et la nouveauté de l'article 15, qui empêche les tribunaux de statuer si les conditions prévues par cet article n'ont pas été remplies. En ce qui concerne l'acte introductif d'instance, l'article 15 est d'une importance particulière en Europe du fait qu'aux termes de l'article 20 de la Convention de Bruxelles du 27 septembre 1968, en vigueur dans le contexte de la Communauté économique européenne, ainsi qu'aux termes identiques de l'article 20 de la Convention de Lugano du 16 septembre 1988, établie conjointement par les Etats membres de la Communauté économique européenne et ceux de l'Association européenne de libre échange, un jugement ne sera pas exécuté dans les rapports entre pays qui sont parties à la fois à l'un de ces traités et à la Convention-Notification, si les exigences de l'article 15 n'ont pas été satisfaites.

Les délégués de certains pays ont indiqué que des décisions judiciaires y avaient été rendues impliquant l'article 15 de la Convention-Notification et le Bureau Permanent a renouvelé sa demande que des copies de telles décisions, ou des extraits pertinents, lui soient transmis par les autorités nationales.

24 Au terme de la discussion, il a été observé que l'article 14 de la Convention-Notification n'empêche pas les Autorités centrales de résoudre entre elles des difficultés soulevées en rapport avec l'application de la Convention et qu'il n'est pas nécessaire de passer systématiquement par le canal diplomatique.

21 The delegation of the United Kingdom indicated that in view of the observations by the American delegation it would institute further consideration as to whether the United Kingdom's practice under Article 69 of the Rules of the English Supreme Court was wholly consistent with its obligations under the Hague Service Convention. However, the United Kingdom delegation expressed the hope that service under Article 10 of the Convention might be used in preference to forwarding documents to the Senior Master.

V <u>Costs</u>

<u>*Question G:*</u> *Have any issues arisen concerning financial charges made for service requested through a Central Authority under the Convention?*

22 From the discussions it appeared that no State Party to the Convention would levy any taxes or costs for normal service made by its authorities. In some countries, notably Belgium, France and the Netherlands, delivery of the document to an addressee who accepts it voluntarily as described in the second paragraph of Article 5 of the Convention, was considered to be the normal method of service. If personal service in a formal manner upon the addressee was required then this involved the employment of a professional process server (referred to as a *huissier* in the French language or a *deurwaarder* in the Dutch language) and the fees of this professional were considered to be payable or reimbursable by the applicant under the second paragraph of Article 12.

VI <u>Protective provisions for defendants</u>

<u>*Question H:*</u> *Have any court decisions been rendered in your country concerning the application of Article 15 or Article 16 of the Hague Service Convention?*

23 The Commission's attention was drawn to the importance and novelty of Article 15 which prevents the courts from rendering a judgment if the conditions of Article 15 have not been fulfilled. With respect to the writ of summons, Article 15 is of special importance in Europe because under Article 20 of the Brussels Convention of 27 September 1968 drawn up within the European Economic Community and the exactly similar Article 20 of the Lugano Convention of 16 September 1988 drawn up jointly by the Member States of the European Economic Community and those of the European Free Trade Association, as between countries which are parties to one of those Conventions and to the Hague Service Convention, a judgment will not be enforced if the conditions of the Hague Convention's Article 15 have not been met.

The delegates of certain countries indicated that decisions under Article 15 of the Hague Service Convention had been rendered by their courts and the Permanent Bureau renewed its request that copies of such decisions or relevant extracts therefrom be forwarded by the national authorities to the Permanent Bureau.

24 At the end of the discussion it was observed that Article 14 of the Hague Service Convention does not prevent Central Authorities from resolving among themselves difficulties arising in connection with the Convention's application and that it is not always necessary to use diplomatic channels first.

DEUXIÈME PARTIE - CONVENTION-OBTENTION DES PREUVES

I Portée de la Convention quant à son objet

Question J: Des problèmes se sont-ils posés dans votre pays quant à la portée de l'expression "en matière civile ou commerciale" employée à l'article premier de la Convention-Obtention des preuves?

25 Ainsi qu'il est indiqué dans la "Récapitulation", deux importantes décisions ont été rendues par les Cours Suprêmes de deux Etats différents, Parties à la Convention, relatives à la portée de la notion de "matière civile ou commerciale". Pour cette raison, un examen complet de cette question avait été renvoyé à la discussion de la Convention-Obtention des preuves (v. No 11 du présent Rapport, *supra*).

26 En fin de compte, la discussion a conduit à la rédaction d'une série de conclusions relatives à la "portée des deux Conventions quant à leur objet" qui figurent parmi les "Conclusions sur les points les plus importants examinés par la Commission spéciale" adoptées le dernier jour de la Session. Ces conclusions, dans la mesure où elles concernent l'interprétation de l'expression "matière civile ou commerciale", sont reproduites ci-après:

Domaine matériel des deux Conventions

a *La Commission souhaite que l'expression "civile ou commerciale" reçoive une interprétation autonome, sans qu'une référence exclusive soit faite soit à la loi de l'Etat requérant, soit à la loi de l'Etat requis, soit aux deux cumulativement.*

b *Dans la "zone grise" des matières qui se situent entre le droit privé et le droit public, l'évolution historique devrait amener à une ouverture plus large de la notion "civile ou commerciale"; il est notamment admis que le droit de la faillite, le droit des assurances et le droit du travail puissent tomber sous la notion "civile ou commerciale".*

c *Par contre, en ce qui concerne d'autres matières considérées par la plupart des Etats comme de droit public, par exemple le droit fiscal, cette évolution ne semble pas pour l'instant conduire à les inclure dans le champ d'application des Conventions.*

d *Cependant, rien n'empêche des Etats contractants d'appliquer entre eux les deux Conventions à des matières de droit public, mais pas nécessairement d'une manière identique pour les deux Conventions.*

Question K: Des problèmes se sont-ils posés dans votre pays au sujet de l'expression "de faire tout acte d'instruction" figurant dans le premier alinéa de l'article premier de la Convention-Obtention des preuves?

27 Le Bureau Permanent a considéré que les questions essentielles étaient les suivantes:

i) une personne pouvait-elle se voir obligée de se soumettre à une analyse sanguine ou autre examen en vue d'établir sa paternité?

ii) les développements technologiques récents ont-ils des incidences sur le fonctionnement de la Convention?

PART TWO - HAGUE EVIDENCE CONVENTION

I Scope of the Convention as to its subject-matter

Question J: Have any issues arisen in your country as to the scope of the term "civil or commercial matters" as employed in Article 1 of the Hague Evidence Convention?

25 As pointed out in the Checklist, there had been two significant decisions rendered by the highest courts of two different States Parties to the Convention concerning the scope of the concept "civil or commercial matters". For this reason, the full discussion on this point had been deferred to the discussion on the Hague Evidence Convention (see no 11 of this Report *supra*).

26 This discussion ultimately lent itself to the drafting of conclusions on the "scope of the two Conventions as to their subject-matter" which were included among the "Conclusions on the most important points considered by the Special Commission" as adopted on the final day of the meeting. These Conclusions, in so far as they deal with the interpretation of the term "civil or commercial matters" are set out below:

Scope of the two Conventions as to their subject-matter

a *The Commission considered it desirable that the words "civil or commercial matters" should be interpreted in an autonomous manner, without reference exclusively either to the law of the requesting State or to the law of the requested State, or to both laws cumulatively.*

b *In the "grey area" between private and public law, the historical evolution would suggest the possibility of a more liberal interpretation of these words. In particular, it was accepted that matters such as bankruptcy, insurance and employment might fall within the scope of this concept.*

c *In contrast, other matters considered by most of the States to fall within public law, for example tax matters, would not yet seem to be covered by the Conventions as a result of this evolution.*

d *However, nothing prevents Contracting States from applying the Conventions in their mutual relations to matters of public law, though not necessarily in an identical manner for both Conventions.*

Question K: Have any issues arisen in your country concerning the expression "to obtain evidence" as employed in the first paragraph of Article 1 of the Hague Evidence Convention?

27 The Permanent Bureau considered that the following were the essential questions:

i) could a person be compelled to submit to a blood test or other test to establish paternity?

ii) did recent technological developments have implications for the operation of the Convention?

28 La délégation des Etats-Unis a fait remarquer que son Autorité centrale recevait fréquemment des demandes tendant à ce que soient effectuées des analyses en vue d'établir une paternité, émanant de la République fédérale d'Allemagne. Il ressort de la jurisprudence connue que dans la plupart des cas, les tribunaux avaient accepté qu'il soit procédé sous astreinte à l'analyse. Dans quelques cas toutefois, il a été demandé à l'autorité requérante de fournir, à l'appui de sa requête, des preuves faisant apparaître de prime abord la vraisemblance de la paternité, de façon à mettre les juges de l'Etat requis en possession des faits de la façon la plus complète possible, afin de décider du sort à réserver à la requête.

II Portée procédurale de la Convention

Question L: Quel est le rapport approprié entre les dispositions de la Convention et les dispositions relatives à la "discovery" ou à l'obtention des preuves en matière civile ou commerciale figurant dans les règles de procédure interne d'un Etat contractant?

29 Cette question a donné lieu aux discussions les plus importantes de la réunion de la Commission spéciale, dans la mesure où elle concernait le domaine d'application des procédures prévues à l'article premier de la Convention-Obtention des preuves, ainsi que leurs rapports avec la réserve autorisée par l'article 23 de la Convention. L'article 23 permet d'exclure le recours, dans le cadre de la Convention, à une partie importante des procédures prévues pour l'obtention de preuves par les règles procédurales nationales. Dans une décision rendue en 1987, la Cour Suprême des Etats-Unis a estimé que la Convention ne faisait pas obstacle à ce qu'un Etat partie se prévale de telles procédures prévues par son droit national en vue d'obtenir des preuves localisées matériellement à l'étranger ou d'interroger des témoins résidant à l'étranger, dès lors que la partie se trouvant en possession de ces preuves ou ayant à son service des témoins relevait du pouvoir juridictionnel du juge saisi.

30 Les points de vue exprimés sur cette question furent divers. Certaines délégations ont estimé en effet que la Convention s'appliquait de façon exclusive et empêchait par conséquent l'application de règles procédurales nationales chaque fois que les preuves étaient localisées matériellement à l'étranger; d'autres en revanche étaient d'avis que la Convention offrait des possibilités qui étaient parallèles et complémentaires par rapport aux procédures prévues par les règles nationales de chaque Etat contractant.

31 Certains délégués considéraient que l'emploi du verbe "pouvoir" plutôt que celui de "devoir" au début de chaque chapitre, ainsi que les arguments tirés des articles 23 et 27 de la Convention, ne suffisaient pas à fonder la conclusion de la Cour Suprême des Etats-Unis aux termes de laquelle les procédures prévues par la Convention étaient facultatives. De surcroît, les développements d'ordre historique figurant dans la décision ont été jugés partiaux, en ce qu'ils privilégiaient les sources américaines. D'autres délégations faisaient valoir qu'étant donné les principes de l'indépendance de l'ordre judiciaire ainsi que de la stricte séparation des pouvoirs consacrés par les constitutions de certains pays, il était peu opportun de se livrer à une critique détaillée du raisonnement d'une Cour Suprême dans le cadre d'une institution telle que la Commission spéciale.

28 The delegation of the United States of America noted that its Central Authority frequently received requests for tests to establish paternity from the Federal Republic of Germany. As far as was known, in most cases submission to a test under compulsion had been permitted. More rarely, the requesting authority had been asked to support its request with *prima facie* evidence of a kind that would enable the courts of the requested State to assess the request in full possession of the facts.

II Procedural scope of the Convention

Question L: What is the appropriate relationship between the provisions contained in the Hague Evidence Convention and the provisions relating to the "discovery" or the obtaining of evidence in civil or commercial matters contained in the domestic procedural rules of a Contracting State?

29 This question gave rise to the most extensive discussions of the Special Commission's meeting, involving as it did the scope of application of the procedures provided for in Article 1 of the Hague Evidence Convention and their relationship to the reservation permitted under Article 23 of the Convention. Article 23 permitted an important part of the procedures used for the obtaining of documents under the domestic procedural rules of some States to be blocked out from use under the Convention. In a 1987 decision, the Supreme Court of the United States had ruled that the Convention did not preclude a State Party from invoking such domestic procedures in order to obtain evidence physically located abroad or to examine certain witnesses residing abroad when the party possessing such documents or identified with such witness was subject to the personal jurisdiction of the court in question.

30 The views expressed on this point were varied; some delegations taking the view that the Convention occupied the field and therefore excluded application of domestic procedural rules whenever the evidence was physically located or the witness was physically residing abroad, others taking the view that the Convention offered facilities which were parallel and complementary to procedures offered by the domestic rules in each Contracting State.

31 Some delegates thought that the use of the facultative verb "may" rather than the imperative "must" at the beginning of each chapter and the arguments drawn from Articles 23 and 27 of the Convention were insufficient to support the United States Supreme Court's conclusion that the Convention's procedures were optional. Moreover, the historical review made by the court was seen as being one sided, concentrating on American sources. Other delegations pointed out that, given the principles of the independence of the courts and the strict separation of powers which were embodied in the constitutions of certain countries, detailed criticism of a superior court's reasoning in a body such as the Special Commission was inappropriate.

32 L'article 23 représente l'une des clés des discussions ainsi menées. En effet, cette réserve avait été introduite à un stade tardif des négociations en 1968 et certaines délégations pensaient que son domaine ainsi que son importance n'avaient pas été compris lors de son adoption. Que tel fut effectivement le cas ressort des déclarations faites par un certain nombre de pays tendant à limiter la portée de la réserve qu'ils avaient faite sur le fondement de l'article 23.

33 De l'avis de certaines délégations, au fait que la portée de l'article 23 avait été mal saisie à l'origine est venu s'ajouter la prise en considération insuffisante par la Convention elle-même de la question de la contrainte indirecte. Le chapitre premier de la Convention fournit en effet un cadre international pour l'application de moyens de contrainte directe destinés à l'obtention des preuves. Mais certaines règles nationales de procédure civile offrent de larges possibilités de contrainte indirecte.

34 En fin de compte, le groupe adopta une déclaration nuancée relative à la Convention-Obtention des preuves, déclaration constituant un chapitre de ces "Conclusions relatives aux points les plus importants examinés par la Commission spéciale" (dont une copie figure en annexe au présent Rapport), et dont la teneur est la suivante:

a *La Commission spéciale rappelle que l'un des buts principaux poursuivis par les auteurs de la Convention était de constituer un lien entre le système d'obtention des preuves du droit civil et celui du* common law.

b *La Commission prend acte du fait que les opinions restent divergentes sur la question de l'application exclusive de la Convention.*

c *Cependant, en raison du but de la Convention, la Commission estime que dans tous les Etats contractants, et quelle que soit leur opinion sur la question de l'application exclusive de celle-ci, priorité doit être donnée aux procédures prévues par la Convention dans leur demande d'obtention de preuves localisées à l'étranger.*

d *En vue de faciliter l'utilisation prioritaire de la Convention, la Commission encourage les Etats qui ont fait ou qui estiment devoir faire la réserve de l'article 23 de limiter la portée de celle-ci.*

e *Si néanmoins les autorités judiciaires d'un Etat contractant ont recours à leur droit de procédure interne pour l'obtention sous contrainte de preuves documentaires à l'étranger, la Commission émet le voeu que ces autorités respectent l'esprit de la réserve de l'article 23 telle que limitée par l'Etat sur le territoire duquel la preuve est localisée.*

35 En pratique, la jurisprudence des juridictions inférieures des Etats-Unis depuis la décision de la Cour Suprême rendue en 1987 dans l'affaire *Aérospatiale*, était divergente, les juges du fond tantôt obligeant à recourir aux procédures de la Convention-Obtention des preuves, tantôt autorisant à recourir aux règles nationales de procédure même lorsque les documents recherchés à des fins probatoires étaient matériellement localisés à l'étranger. Le Bureau Permanent, suivi en cela par d'autres commentateurs intéressés, avait recueilli et classé cette jurisprudence jusqu'à la date de la réunion de la Commission

32 **Article 23 was one of the keys to the issues which had arisen. This reservation had been introduced at a late stage of the negotiations in 1968 and certain delegations felt that its breadth and importance had not been understood at the time when it was adopted. This was reflected in the declarations which had been made by a number of countries limiting the scope of their reservations taken under Article 23.**

33 **In the view of certain delegations the original failure to understand the breadth of Article 23 was joined with a failure to take sufficient account in the Convention of the question of indirect compulsion. Chapter 1 of the Convention provided an international framework for the application of direct measures of compulsion in order to obtain evidence. Some domestic rules of civil procedure offered wide means of indirect compulsion.**

34 **In the end, as a chapter of its "Conclusions on the most important points considered by the Special Commission" (a copy of which is attached as an Annex to this Report), this group adopted a balanced statement concerning the Convention on the Taking of Evidence Abroad expressed as follows:**

a *The Special Commission stressed that one of the principal objects of the authors of the Convention was to create a link between the system of taking of evidence of the civil law and that of the common law.*

b *The Special Commission took note of the fact that opinions remain divided as to whether or not the Convention is of exclusive application.*

c *However, having regard to the object of the Convention, the Commission thought that in all Contracting States, whatever their views as to its exclusive application, priority should be given to the procedures offered by the Convention when evidence located abroad is being sought.*

d *With a view to facilitating the resort to the Convention as a matter of priority, the Commission encouraged any States which have made or contemplate making the reservation under Article 23 to limit the scope of such reservation.*

e *Where nonetheless the judicial authorities of a Contracting State resort to measures of compulsion under their domestic rules of procedure for the purpose of obtaining documentary evidence located in another Contracting State, the Commission expressed the wish that such judicial authorities respect the spirit of a limited Article 23 reservation made by such other State.*

35 In practice, the cases decided by the lower courts in the United States of America since the Supreme Court's opinion in the 1987 *Aérospatiale* case had brought on differing results, the trial courts sometimes ordering resort to the Hague Convention's procedures, other times permitting resort to the domestic rules of procedure even when documents sought for evidentiary purposes were physically located abroad. The Permanent Bureau, as well as other interested commentators, had collected and monitored such court decisions up to the date of the April Special Commission meeting

spéciale d'avril et comptait poursuivre ce travail dans le cadre de la revision du "Manuel pratique" sur la Convention-Obtention des preuves. Il a été reconnu que les solutions données par les juges du fond étaient largement tributaires de l'habileté des avocats représentant les parties et pouvaient également subir l'influence des opinions données par les autorités des pays intéressés, apparaissant en qualité d'*amicus curiae*. Aux Etats-Unis, juges et avocats étaient de plus en plus sensibilisés par l'abus de procédures de "*discovery*" dans les affaires civiles et commerciales; des efforts appropriés intervenant au premier stade de la procédure judiciaire en vue d'obtenir du juge à titre préventif un "*protective order*", ainsi que de faire inclure la procédure de "*discovery*" dans le déroulement des mesures d'instruction, pourraient contribuer à ce que soient canalisées par la Convention les demandes de preuves écrites ou d'auditions de témoins résidant à l'étranger.

36 Parmi les suggestions pratiques formulées à l'intention des avocats de parties étrangères impliquées dans une procédure judiciaire aux Etats-Unis, il a été rappelé que:

a en participant aux stades initiaux de la procédure, par exemple à la réunion avant l'audience au fond (*pre-trial*) prévue par les règles fédérales de procédure civile (*Federal Rules of Civil Procedure*), ils pourraient plaider de façon plus efficace en faveur de l'utilisation de la Convention-Obtention des preuves et faire incorporer le recours à la Convention dans le déroulement des mesures d'instruction;

b si l'emploi de la Convention dépend largement des efforts des parties, les gouvernements étrangers peuvent néanmoins promouvoir le recours à la Convention en faisant connaître leur position dans une opinion donnée en qualité d'*amicus curiae*;

c une procédure préventive ("*protective orders*") existe pour le cas où un avocat ferait des demandes de "*discovery*" de nature excessive ou abusive, ou impliquant la révélation d'informations confidentielles;

d les amendements apportés en 1983 aux règles fédérales (articles 11 et 26 *g* des *Federal Rules*) prévoient des sanctions pécuniaires et autres en cas de mauvaise foi de l'avocat ou autre abus des procédures de "*discovery*". Si de telles sanctions ne s'étaient pas fait sentir avant la Commission spéciale de 1985, elles commencent actuellement à exercer un effet important;

e bien que certaines décisions rendues depuis l'affaire *Aérospatiale* n'aient pas fait application de la Convention, les tribunaux américains sont en voie de se familiariser avec cette dernière et de nombreux jugements publiés ou non y ont recours. Diverses juridictions se sont déclarées très impressionnées par les modifications apportées aux règles procédurales des pays de droit civil en vue de tenir compte de procédures américaines;

f la question a été posée de savoir si, puisque la Convention-Obtention des preuves a été considérée par la Cour Suprême des Etats-Unis comme devant s'appliquer parallèlement aux règles fédérales, la charge de la preuve ne devait pas peser sur la partie désirant écarter l'application de la Convention.

and this process was expected to continue in the context of the revision of the "Practical Handbook" on the Hague Evidence Convention. It was recognized that the results in the trial courts depended very much on the advocacy of lawyers representing the parties and could be influenced by the submission of *amicus curiae* briefs by the authorities of the interested countries. Both judges and lawyers in the United States of America had become increasingly sensitized to the abuse of discovery procedures in civil and commercial cases and appropriate efforts at an early stage of a legal proceeding to obtain a protective order from the court concerning discovery, and have the discovery process included in an overall timetable for the case, could enhance the likelihood that requests for documentary evidence or for the deposition of witnesses residing abroad would be channeled through the Hague Convention.

36 Practical suggestions addressed to legal counsellors of foreign parties involved in court proceedings in the United States included the following:

a by taking part in the proceedings early, such as at the pre-trial conference envisaged by the Federal Rules of Civil Procedure, they can more effectively advocate the use of the Evidence Convention and have its use incorporated into a planned timetable for discovery;

b use of the Convention is largely dependent on the efforts of the Parties, but foreign governments can assist by making their position clear in an *amicus curiae* brief;

c a protective order procedure is available if an attorney makes discovery requests that are overboard, harassing or require confidential information to be disclosed;

d the 1983 amendments to the Federal Rules make provision for fines and other sanctions under Articles 11 and 26 *g* where attorneys act in bad faith or otherwise abuse discovery procedures. These sanctions had not made their presence felt prior to the 1985 Special Commission meeting but are beginning to have a considerable effect;

e although some decisions since *Aérospatiale* did not lead to the application of the Convention, courts in the US are undergoing a process of education, and many reported and also unreported instances of its use should be emphasized. Several courts had been most impressed by alterations made in the laws of civil law countries to accommodate American procedural methods;

f it is arguable that since the Evidence Convention was seen by the US Supreme Court as operating alongside the Federal Rules, the burden of proof should be on the party wishing to resist application of the Convention.

37 Le Canada, qui envisage l'accession de son pays à la Convention-Obtention des preuves et qui a consulté des juristes relevant de ses diverses provinces sur l'application de celle-ci, a soulevé les questions suivantes:

1) la portée de la Convention quant à l'arbitrage;

2) son application à l'égard de témoins non parties à l'instance;

3) l'expérience d'autres pays en ce qui concerne l'interprétation de l'expression "autres actes judiciaires" figurant à l'article premier.

En ce qui concerne 1), la question avait déjà été discutée en 1985 et la Commission estima qu'il n'y avait pas lieu d'effectuer semblable extension. Toutefois, le droit de certains pays prévoit une assistance judiciaire pour l'obtention de preuves en matière d'arbitrage, auquel cas la Convention pourrait éventuellement être utilisée en vue de rechercher des preuves situées à l'étranger. Bien que la rédaction de la version anglaise de l'article premier, paragraphe 2 de la Convention semble exclure cette possibilité, le texte français est plus général.

En ce qui concerne 2), la Convention était certainement applicable à l'égard de témoins non parties à l'instance.

En ce qui concerne 3), les "autres actes judiciaires" visaient tout autre acte produisant un effet juridique, tel que le consentement à un mariage devant être obtenu auprès d'une personne résidant à l'étranger.

III Formes à respecter pour l'obtention des preuves

Question M: Des problèmes se sont-ils posés à propos de demandes tendant à ce qu'il soit procédé suivant une forme spéciale?

38 Les formes spéciales d'obtention de preuves qui ont été demandées comprenaient l'enregistrement sur vidéo, ainsi que la possibilité de soumettre les témoins à un interrogatoire contradictoire (*cross-examination*). Si la plupart des délégations ne voient aucun obstacle à ce que soit accueillie une demande de preuve par vidéo, les représentants du Luxembourg, du Danemark et de la Suède estiment que de telles demandes rencontreraient des difficultés au regard de leurs droits nationaux.

39 L'interrogatoire contradictoire ("*cross-examination*") ne semble pas soulever de difficultées juridiques particulières. Plusieurs Etats parties à la Convention avaient même modifié leur droit national afin d'en tenir compte. En revanche, des difficultés pratiques pourraient survenir du fait du peu d'expérience des juristes des pays de droit civil en ce domaine. Pour cette raison, il est important que tous les intéressés soient clairement informés des règles de procédure applicables, préalablement à tout interrogatoire de ce type.

Question N: Des problèmes se sont-ils posés au sujet des frais occasionnés par des demandes de preuves présentées en vertu de la Convention?

40 La question du remboursement des frais a soulevé peu de difficultés. L'interprétation restrictive de l'article 14 par le Royaume-Uni a toutefois été mise en cause. Par ailleurs, il a été signalé que l'Autorité centrale des Etats-Unis exigeait paiement pour le recours à une commission rogatoire, mais non pour l'obtention de preuves par des commissaires.

37 Canada, which was considering accession to the Evidence Convention and had consulted practitioners in its Provinces concerning the application of the Convention, raised queries about the following three points and received the replies indicated:

1) the extension of the Convention to arbitration;

2) its use in connection with witnesses who were not parties to the action; and

3) the experience of other jurisdictions in interpreting the expression "other judicial act" in Article 1.

As to 1), the matter had been discussed in 1985 and it was felt there was no demand for making such an extension. The laws of some countries did however provide for judicial assistance in obtaining evidence for arbitration, and the Convention could then possibly be used to obtain evidence located abroad. Although the wording of the English text of Article 1, paragraph 2, of the Convention seemed to exclude this possibility, the French text was more general.

As to 2), the Convention was certainly applicable in respect of witnesses who were not parties to the action.

As to 3), "other judicial act" referred to any act which had legal effect. An example might be the need to obtain an official consent to a marriage from a party residing abroad.

III Methods of taking of evidence

Question M: Have any issues arisen from requests for special methods or procedures for the taking of evidence?

38 Particular methods or procedures for taking evidence which had been requested included video evidence, and the opportunity for cross-examination of witnesses. Most delegations did not envisage problems with requests for video recordings, but the representatives of Luxembourg, Denmark and Sweden considered that there would be difficulties with such requests under their laws.

39 Cross-examination was not felt to raise any legal problems. Several States Parties to the Convention had changed their domestic law to allow for it. Practical problems were foreseen, however, owing to the inexperience of lawyers of civil law countries in such matters. Because of this it was important that all Parties should be clearly informed of the relevant rules of procedure prior to cross-examination.

Question N: Have any issues arisen concerning the costs of carrying out requests for evidence made under the Hague Evidence Convention?

40 The question of reimbursing costs had caused few problems. The restrictive interpretation of Article 14 by the United Kingdom was questioned, and it was noted that the United States Central Authority charged for use of letters of request, but not for taking of evidence by commissioners.

IV Protection des témoins

Question P: Des problèmes se sont-ils posés au sujet des dispenses ou interdictions invoquées conformément à l'article 11 de la Convention-Obtention des preuves?

41 La délégation des Pays-Bas a fourni des éclaircissements quant à la position du droit néerlandais concernant les dispenses ou interdictions de déposer. En effet, la déclaration du gouvernement des Pays-Bas telle que rapportée dans le Manuel pratique est trop générale. Il est ainsi loisible selon ce droit, à des personnes recevant des informations confidentielles, telles que médecins, avocats, et fonctionnaires, d'exciper de la dispense de déposer.

42 La délégation américaine a relevé que les demandes de preuves sont fréquemment accompagnées de textes de droit étranger. Pareille pratique crée des difficultés pour les avocats américains lorsque ces textes ne sont pas traduits en anglais.

TROISIÈME PARTIE - SYNTHÈSE DES PROBLÈMES SOULEVÉS PAR LES DEUX CONVENTIONS

Question Q: Existe-t-il un type particulier de litige qui tende spécialement à susciter des controverses en vertu de l'une ou l'autre ou des deux Conventions?

43 Il est apparu que des demandes de preuves sont formulées dans le cadre de contentieux très variés et que la responsabilité du fait des produits ne devait pas faire l'objet d'un examen particulier à cet égard.

QUATRIÈME PARTIE - MANUELS PRATIQUES

44 L'établissement de Manuels pratiques est très vivement approuvé. Il est souvent difficile en effet pour les juristes d'obtenir à d'autres sources des informations appropriées. Les délégués espèrent par conséquent qu'il soit possible à l'avenir de diffuser les manuels de façon plus large et poussent à la parution de nouvelles éditions.

45 Le Bureau Permanent a fait savoir que la priorité serait donnée à la revision et à la mise à jour du Manuel pratique sur la Convention-Notification. Il compte à cette fin envoyer à chaque Autorité centrale désignée conformément à l'article 2 des demandes de modification ou de correction concernant l'état de son droit national tel qu'exposé par le Manuel lors de sa première publication en 1983 ou corrigé dans le supplément de mars 1985. Il sera demandé aux Etats ayant accédé à la Convention depuis mars 1985 de fournir les informations appropriées de façon à ce qu'elles soient incluses dans la nouvelle édition.

IV <u>Protective provisions for witnesses</u>

<u>Question P</u>: Have any issues arisen in respect of privileges or duties to refuse to give evidence asserted under Article 11 of the Hague Evidence Convention?

41 The Netherlands delegation clarified the position under Netherlands law regarding privileges or duties to refuse to give evidence. The declaration of the Netherlands Government reported in the Practical Handbook was too general. It was possible for persons in receipt of confidential information, such as doctors, lawyers and government officials, to invoke the defence of privilege.

42 The American delegation noted that often provisions of foreign law concerning privilege were attached to requests for evidence. Since they were frequently not translated into English this created difficulties for American attorneys.

PART THREE - SYNTHESIS OF ISSUES UNDER THE TWO CONVENTIONS

<u>Question Q</u>: Is there a particular type of litigation which tends particularly to provoke controversy under one or both of these Conventions?

43 It was felt that requests for evidence arose in many types of cases and that products liability could not be singled out for special attention.

PART FOUR - PRACTICAL HANDBOOKS

44 The preparation of Practical Handbooks was strongly supported. It was often difficult for lawyers to obtain the relevant information elsewhere. Delegates hoped that it would prove possible to circulate the Handbooks more widely in the future and pressed for the completion of new editions.

45 The Permanent Bureau indicated that it would give priority to revision and updating of the Practical Handbook on the Hague Service Convention. It intended to send out to the Central Authorities designated under Article 2 requests for any changes or corrections to the information concerning their country's practice under the Convention as set out in the Handbook when it was originally published in 1983 or as corrected in the supplement of March 1985. The States which had ratified or acceded to the Convention since March 1985 would be asked as necessary to furnish the relevant information so that it could be included in the new edition.

ANNEXE

CONCLUSIONS SUR LES POINTS LES PLUS IMPORTANTS EXAMINÉS PAR LA COMMISSION SPÉCIALE

telles que discutées et adoptées par la Commission spéciale le 20 avril 1989

I <u>Domaine matériel des deux Conventions</u>

a La Commission souhaite que l'expression "civile ou commerciale" reçoive une interprétation autonome, sans qu'une référence exclusive soit faite soit à la loi de l'Etat requérant, soit à la loi de l'Etat requis, soit aux deux cumulativement.

b Dans la "zone grise" des matières qui se situent entre le droit privé et le droit public, l'évolution historique devrait amener à une ouverture plus large de la notion "civile ou commerciale"; il est notamment admis que le droit de la faillite, le droit des assurances et le droit du travail puissent tomber sous la notion "civile ou commerciale".

c Par contre, en ce qui concerne d'autres matières considérées par la plupart des Etats comme de droit public, par exemple le droit fiscal, cette évolution ne semble pas pour l'instant conduire à les inclure dans le champ d'application des Conventions.

d Cependant, rien n'empêche des Etats contractants d'appliquer entre eux les deux Conventions à des matières de droit public, mais pas nécessairement d'une manière identique pour les deux Conventions.

II <u>Convention sur l'obtention des preuves</u>

a La Commission spéciale rappelle que l'un des buts principaux poursuivis par les auteurs de la Convention était de constituer un lien entre le système d'obtention des preuves du droit civil et celui du *common law*.

b La Commission prend acte du fait que les opinions restent divergentes sur la question de l'application exclusive de la Convention.

c Cependant, en raison du but de la Convention, la Commission estime que dans tous les Etats contractants, et quelle que soit leur opinion sur la question de l'application exclusive de celle-ci, priorité doit être donnée aux procédures prévues par la Convention dans leur demande d'obtention de preuves localisées à l'étranger.

d En vue de faciliter l'utilisation prioritaire de la Convention, la Commission encourage les Etats qui ont fait ou qui estiment devoir faire la réserve de l'article 23 de limiter la portée de celle-ci.

e Si néanmoins les autorités judiciaires d'un Etat contractant ont recours à leur droit de procédure interne pour l'obtention sous contrainte de preuves documentaires à l'étranger, la Commission émet le voeu que ces autorités respectent l'esprit de la réserve de l'article 23 telle que limitée par l'Etat sur le territoire duquel la preuve est localisée.

ANNEX

CONCLUSIONS ON THE MOST IMPORTANT POINTS CONSIDERED BY THE SPECIAL COMMISSION

as discussed and adopted by the Special Commission on 20 April 1989

I Scope of the two Conventions as to their subject-matter

a The Commission considered it desirable that the words "civil or commercial matters" should be interpreted in an autonomous manner, without reference exclusively either to the law of the requesting State or to the law of the requested State, or to both laws cumulatively.

b In the "grey area" between private and public law, the historical evolution would suggest the possibility of a more liberal interpretation of these words. In particular, it was accepted that matters such as bankruptcy, insurance and employment might fall within the scope of this concept.

c In contrast, other matters considered by most of the States to fall within public law, for example tax matters, would not yet seem to be covered by the Conventions as a result of this evolution.

d However, nothing prevents Contracting States from applying the Conventions in their mutual relations to matters of public law, though not necessarily in an identical manner for both Conventions.

II Convention on the Taking of Evidence Abroad

a The Special Commission stressed that one of the principal objects of the authors of the Convention was to create a link between the system of taking of evidence of the civil law and that of the common law.

b The Special Commission took note of the fact that opinions remain divided as to whether or not the Convention is of exclusive application.

c However, having regard to the object of the Convention, the Commission thought that in all Contracting States, whatever their views as to its exclusive application, priority should be given to the procedures offered by the Convention when evidence located abroad is being sought.

d With a view to facilitating the resort to the Convention as a matter of priority, the Commission encouraged any States which have made or contemplate making the reservation under Article 23 to limit the scope of such reservation.

e Where nonetheless the judicial authorities of a Contracting State resort to measures of compulsion under their domestic rules of procedure for the purpose of obtaining documentary evidence located in another Contracting State, the Commission expressed the wish that such judicial authorities respect the spirit of a limited Article 23 reservation made by such other State.

Appendix 5[1]

INTER-AMERICAN CONVENTION ON LETTERS ROGATORY

The Governments of the Member States of the Organization of American States, desirous of concluding a convention on letters rogatory, have agreed as follows:

I. Use of Terms

Article 1

For the purposes of this Convention the terms "*exhortos*" and "*cartas rogatorias*" are synonymous in the Spanish text. The terms "letters rogatory", "'commissions rogatoires", and "*cartas rogatórias*" used in the English, French and Portuguese texts, respectively, cover both "*exhortos*" and "*cartas rogatorias*".

II. Scope of the Convention

Article 2

This Convention shall apply to letters rogatory, issued in conjunction with proceedings in civil and commercial matters held before the appropriate authority of one of the States Parties to this Convention, that have as their purpose:

a. The performance of procedural acts of a merely formal nature, such as service of process, summonses or subpoenas abroad;

b. The taking of evidence and the obtaining of information abroad, unless a reservation is made in this respect.

Article 3

This Convention shall not apply to letters rogatory relating to procedural acts other than those specified in the preceding article; and in particular it shall not l apply to acts involving measures of compulsion.

III. Transmission of Letters Rogatory

Article 4

Letters rogatory may be transmitted to the authority to which they are addressed by the interested parties, through judicial channels, diplomatic or consular agents, or the Central Authority of the State of origin or of the State of destination, as the case may be.

Each State Party shall inform the General Secretariat of the Organization of American States of the Central Authority competent to receive and distribute letters.

IV. Requirements for Execution

Article 5

Letters rogatory shall be executed in the States Parties provided they meet the following requirements:

a. The letter rogatory is legalized, except as provided for in Articles 6 and 7 of this Convention. The letter rogatory shall be presumed to be duly legalized in the State of origin when legalized by the competent consular or diplomatic agent;

b. The letter rogatory and the appended documentation are duly translated into the official language of the State of destination.

Article 6

Whenever letters rogatory are transmitted through consular or diplomatic channels or through the Central Authority, legalization shall not be required.

Article 7

Courts in border areas of the States Parties may directly execute the letters rogatory contemplated in this Convention and such letters shall not require legalization.

Article 8

Letters rogatory shall be accompanied by the following documents to be delivered to the person on whom process, summons or subpoena is being served:

a. An authenticated copy of the complaint with its supporting documents, and of other exhibits or rulings that serve as the basis for the measure requested;

b. Written information identifying the authority issuing the letter, indicating the time-limits allowed the person affected to act upon the request, and warning of the consequences of failure to do so;

c. Where appropriate, information on the existence and address of the court-appointed defense counsel or of competent legal-aid societies in the State of origin.

Article 9

Execution of letters rogatory shall not imply ultimate recognition of the jurisdiction of the authority issuing the letter rogatory or a commitment to recognize the validity of the judgment it may render or to execute it.

V. EXECUTION

Article 10

Letters rogatory shall be executed in accordance with the laws and procedural rules of the State of destination.

At the request of the authority issuing the letter rogatory. the authority of the State of destination may execute the letter through a special procedure, or accept the observance of additional formalities in performing the act requested, provided this procedure or the observance of those formalities is not contrary to the law of the State of destination.

Article 11

The authority of the State of destination shall have jurisdiction to determine any issue arising as a result of the execution of the measure requested in the letter rogatory. Should such authority find that it lacks jurisdiction to execute the letter rogatory, it shall *ex officio* forward the documents and antecedents of the case to the authority of the State which has jurisdiction.

Article 12

The costs and other expenses involved in the processing and execution of letters rogatory shall be borne by the interested parties.

The State of destination may, in its discretion, execute a letter rogatory that does not indicate the person to be held responsible for costs and other expenses when incurred. The identity of the person empowered to represent the applicant for legal purposes may be indicated in the letter rogatory or in the documents relating to its execution.

The effects of a declaration in *forma pauperis* shall be regulated by the law of the State of destination.

Article 13

Consular or diplomatic agents of the States Parties to this Convention may perform the acts referred to in Article 2 in the State in which they are accredited, provided the performance of such acts is not contrary to the laws of that State. In so doing, they shall not perform any acts involving measures of compulsion.

VI. General Provisions

Article 14

States Parties belonging to economic integration systems may agree directly between themselves upon special methods and procedures more expeditious than those provided for in this Convention. These agreements may be extended to include other States in the manner in which the parties may agree.

Article 15

This Convention shall not limit any provisions regarding letters rogatory in bilateral or multilateral agreements that may have been signed or may be signed in the future by the States Parties or preclude the continuation of more favorable practices in this regard that may be followed by these States.

Article 16

The States Parties to this Convention may declare that its provisions cover the execution of letters rogatory in criminal, labor, and "contentious-administrative" cases, as well as in arbitrations and other matters within the jurisdiction of special courts. Such declarations shall be transmitted to the General Secretariat of the Organization of American States.

Article 17

The State of destination may refuse to execute a letter rogatory that is manifestly contrary to its public policy ("*ordre public*").

Article 18

The States Parties shall inform the General Secretariat of the Organization of American States of the requirements stipulated in their laws for the legalization and the translation of letters rogatory.

VII. Final Provisions

Article 19

This Convention shall be open for signature by the Member of the Organization of American States.

Article 20

This Convention is subject to ratification. The instruments of ratification shall be deposited with the General Secretariat of the Organization of American States.

Article 21

This Convention shall remain open for accession by any other State. The instrument of accession shall be deposited with the General Secretariat of the Organization of American States.

Article 22

This Convention shall enter into force on the thirtieth day following the date of deposit of the second instrument of ratification.

For each State ratifying or acceding to the Convention after the deposit of the second instrument of ratification, the Convention shall enter into force on the thirtieth day after deposit by such State of its instrument of ratification or accession

Article 23

If a State Party has two or more territorial units in which different systems' of law apply in relation to the matters dealt with in this Convention, it may, at the time of signature, ratification or accession, declare that this Convention shall extend to all its territorial units or only to one or more of them.

Such declaration may be modified by subsequent declarations, which shall expressly indicate the territorial unit or units to which the Convention applies. Such subsequent declarations shall be transmitted to the General Secretariat of the Organization of American States and shall become effective thirty days after the date of their receipt. This Convention shall remain in force indefinitely, but any of the States Parties may denounce it. The instrument of denunciation shall be deposited with the General Secretariat of the Organization of American States. After one year from the date of deposit of the instrument of denunciation, the Convention shall no longer be in effect for the denouncing State, but shall remain in effect for the other States Parties.

Article 25

The original instrument of this Convention, the English, French, Portuguese and Spanish texts of which are equally authentic, shall be deposited with the General Secretariat of the Organization of American States. The Secretariat shall notify the Member States of the Organization of American States and the States that have acceded to the Convention of the signatures, deposits of instruments of ratification, accession, and denunciation as well as of reservations, if any. It shall also transmit the information mentioned in the second paragraph of Article 4 and in Article 18 and the declarations referred to in Articles 16 and 23 of this Convention.

IN WITNESS WHEREOF the undersigned Plenipotentiaries, being duly authorized thereto by their respective Governments, have signed this Convention.

DONE AT PANAMA CITY, Republic of Panama, this thirtieth day of January one thousand nine hundred and seventy-five.

Appendix 5[2]

ADDITIONAL PROTOCOL TO THE INTER-AMERICAN CONVENTION ON LETTERS ROGATORY

The Governments of the Member States of the Organization of American States, desirous of strengthening and facilitating international cooperation in judicial procedures as provided for in the Inter-American Convention on Letters Rogatory done in Panama on January 30, 1975, have agreed as follows:

I. Scope of Protocol

Article 1

This Protocol shall apply only to those procedural acts set forth in Article 2 (a) of the Inter-American Convention on Letters Rogatory, hereinafter referred to as "the Convention". For the purposes of this Protocol, such acts shall be understood to mean procedural acts (pleadings, motions, orders, and subpoenas) that are served and requests for information that are made by a judicial or administrative authority of a State Party to a judicial or administrative authority of another State Party and are transmitted by a letter rogatory from the Central Authority of the State of origin to the Central Authority of the State of destination.

II. Central Authority

Article 2

Each State Party shall designate a central authority that shall perform the functions assigned to it in the Convention and in this Protocol. At the time of deposit of their instruments of ratification or accession to this Protocol, the States Parties shall communicate the designations to the General Secretariat of the Organization of American States, which shall distribute to the States Parties to the Convention a list containing the designations received. The Central Authority designated by a State Party in accordance with Article 4 of the Convention may be changed at any time. The State Party shall inform the above-mentioned Secretariat of such change as promptly as possible.

III. Preparation of Letters Rogatory

Article 3

Letters rogatory shall be prepared on forms that are printed in the four official languages of the Organization of American States or in the languages of the State of origin and of the State of destination and conform to Form A contained in the Annex to this Protocol.

Letters rogatory shall be accompanied by the following:

a. Copy of the complaint or pleading that initiated the action in which the letter rogatory was issued, as well as a translation thereof into the language of the State of destination;

b. Untranslated copy of the documents attached to the complaint or pleading;

c. Untranslated copy of any rulings ordering issuance of the letter rogatory;

d. Form conforming to Form B annexed to this Protocol and containing essential information for the person to be served or the authority to receive the documents; and

e. Certificate conforming to Form C annexed to this Protocol on which the Central Authority of the State of destination shall attest to execution or non-execution of the letter rogatory.

The copies shall be regarded as authenticated for the purposes of Article 8(a) of the Convention if they bear the seal of the judicial or administrative authority that issued the letter rogatory.

A copy of the letter rogatory together with Form B and the copies referred to in items a, b, and c of this Article shall be delivered to the person notified or to the authority to which the request is addressed. One of the copies of the letter rogatory and the documents attached to it shall remain in the possession of the State of destination; the untranslated original, the certificate of execution and the documents attached to them shall be returned to the Central Authority of the State of origin through appropriate channels.

If a State Party has more than one official language, it shall, at the time of signature, ratification or accession to this Protocol, declare which language or languages shall be considered official for the purposes of the Convention and of this Protocol. If a State Party comprises territorial units that have different official languages, it shall, at the time of signature, ratification or accession to this Protocol, declare which language or languages in each territorial unit shall be considered official for the purposes of the Convention and of this Protocol The General Secretariat of the Organization of American States shall distribute to the States Parties to this Protocol the information contained in such declarations.

IV. Transmission and Processing of Letters Rogatory

Article 4

Upon receipt of a letter rogatory from the Central Authority in another State Party, the Central Authority in the State of destination shall transmit the letter rogatory to the appropriate judicial or administrative authority for processing in accordance with the applicable local law.

Upon execution of the letter rogatory, the judicial or administrative authority or authorities that processed it shall attest to the execution thereof in the manner prescribed in their local law, and shall transmit it with the relevant documents to the Central Authority. The Central Authority of the State Party of destination shall certify execution of the letter rogatory to the Central Authority of the State Party of origin on a form conforming to Form C of the Annex, which shall not require legalization. In addition, the Central Authority of the State of destination shall return the letter rogatory and attached documents to the Central Authority of the State of origin for delivery to the judicial or administrative authority that issued it.

V. Costs and Expenses

Article 5

The processing of letters rogatory by the Central Authority of the State Party of destination and its judicial or administrative authorities shall be free of charge. However, this State Party may seek payment by parties requesting execution of letters rogatory for those services which, in accordance with its local law, are required to be paid for directly by those parties.

The party requesting the execution of a letter rogatory shall, at its election, either select and indicate in the letter rogatory the person who is responsible in the State of destination for the cost of such services or, alternatively, shall attach to the letter rogatory a check for the fixed amount that is specified in Article 6 of this Protocol for its processing by the State of destination and will cover the cost of such services or a document proving that such amount has been transferred by some other means to the Central Authority of the State of destination.

The fact that the cost of such services ultimately exceeds the fixed amount shall not delay or prevent the processing or execution of the letter rogatory by the Central Authority or the judicial or administrative authorities of the State of destination. Should the cost exceed that amount, the Central Authority of the State of destination may, when returning the executed letter rogatory, seek payment of the outstanding amount due from the party requesting execution of the letter rogatory.

Article 6

At the time of deposit of its instrument of ratification or accession to this Protocol with the General Secretariat of the Organization of American States, each State Party shall attach a schedule of the services and the costs and other expenses that, in accordance with its local law, shall be paid directly by the party requesting execution of the letter rogatory. In addition, each State Party shall specify in the above-mentioned schedule the single amount which it considers will reasonably cover the cost of such services, regardless of the number or nature thereof. This amount shall be paid when the person requesting execution of the letter rogatory has not designated a person responsible for the payment of such services in the State of destination but has decided to pay for them directly in the manner provided for in Article 5 of this Protocol.

The General Secretariat of the Organization of American States shall distribute the information received to the States Parties to this Protocol. A State Party may at any time notify the General Secretariat of the Organization of American States of changes in the above-mentioned schedules, which shall be communicated by the General Secretariat to the other States Parties to this Protocol.

Article 7

States Parties may declare in the schedules mentioned in the foregoing articles that, provided there is reciprocity, they will not charge parties requesting execution of letters rogatory for the services necessary for executing them, or will accept in complete satisfaction of the cost of such services either the single fixed amount specified in Article 6 or another specified amount.

Article 8

This Protocol shall be open for signature and subject to ratification or accession by those Member States of the Organization of American States that have signed, ratified, or acceded to the Inter-American Convention on Letters Rogatory signed in Panama on January 30, 1975.

This Protocol shall remain open for accession by any other State that accedes or has acceded to the Inter-American Convention on Letters Rogatory, under the conditions set forth in this article.

The instruments of ratification and accession shall be deposited with the General Secretariat of the Organization of American States.

Article 9

This Protocol shall enter into force on the thirtieth day following the date on which two States Parties to the Convention have deposited their instruments of ratification or accession to this Protocol.

For each State ratifying or acceding to the Protocol after its entry into force, the Protocol shall enter into force on the thirtieth day following deposit by such State of its instrument of ratification or accession, provided that such State is a Party to the Convention.

Article 10

If a State Party has two or more territorial units in which different systems of law apply in relation to matters dealt with in this Protocol, it may, at the time of signature, ratification or accession, declare that this Protocol shall extend to all its territorial units or only to one or more of them.

Such declaration may be modified by subsequent declarations that shall expressly indicate the territorial unit or units to which this Protocol applies. Such subsequent declarations shall be transmitted to the General Secretariat of the Organization of American States, and shall become effective thirty days after the date of their receipt.

Article 11

This Protocol shall remain in force indefinitely, but any of the States Parties may denounce it. The instrument of denunciation shall be deposited with the General Secretariat of the Organization of American States. After one year from the date of deposit of the instrument of denunciation, the Protocol shall no longer be in effect for the denouncing State, but shall remain in effect for the other States Parties.

Article 12

The original instrument of this Protocol and its Annex (Forms A, B and C), the English, French, Portuguese and Spanish texts of which are equally authentic, shall be deposited with the General Secretariat of the Organization of American States, which will forward an authenticated copy of the text to the Secretariat of the United Nations for registration and publication in accordance with Article 102 of its Charter. The General Secretariat of the Organization of American States shall notify the Member States of that Organization and the States that have acceded to the Protocol of the signatures, deposits of instruments of ratification, accession and denunciation, as well as of reservations, if any. It shall also transmit to them the information mentioned in Article 2, the last paragraph of Article 3, and Article 6 and the declarations referred to in Article 10 of this Protocol.

IN WITNESS WHEREOF the undersigned Plenipotentiaries, being duly authorized thereto by their respective Governments, have signed this Protocol.

DONE AT MONTEVIDEO, Republic of Uruguay, this eighth day of May, one thousand nine hundred and seventy-nine.

ANNEX TO THE ADDITIONAL PROTOCOL TO THE INTER-AMERICAN CONVENTION ON LETTERS ROGATORY

FORM A

LETTER ROGATORY[1]

1 REQUESTING JUDICIAL OR ADMINISTRATIVE AUTHORITY
Name
Address

2 CASE:
Docket No.:

3 CENTRAL AUTHORITY OF THE STATE OF ORIGIN
Name
Address

4 CENTRAL AUTHORITY OF THE STATE OF DESTINATION
Name
Address

5 REQUESTING PARTY
Name
Address

6 COUNSEL TO THE REQUESTING PARTY
Name
Address

PERSON DESIGNATED TO ACT IN CONNECTION WITH THE LETTER ROGATORY

Name
Address

Is this person responsible for costs and expenses?

YES _/ NO_ /

* If not, check in the amount of ______________is attached

* Or proof of payment is attached

The Central Authority signing this letter rogatory has the honor to transmit to you in triplicate the documents listed below and, in conformity with the Protocol to the Inter-American Convention on Letters Rogatory:

*A. Requests their prompt service on:

---

* Delete if inapplicable.

1 Complete the original and two copies of this form; if A(1) is applicable, attache the original and two copies of this item in the language of the State of destination.

The undersigned authority requests that service be carried out in the following manner:

*(1) In accordance with the special procedure or additional formalities that are described below, as provided for in the second paragraph of Article 10 of the above-mentioned Convention; or

*(2) By service personally on the identified addressee or, in the case of a legal entity, on its authorized agent; or

*(3) If the person or the authorized agent of the entity to be served is not found, service shall be made in accordance with the law of the State of destination.

*B. Requests the delivery of the documents listed below to the following judicial or administrative authority:

Authority:

*C. Requests the Central Authority of the State of destination to return to the Central Authority of the State of origin one copy of the documents listed below and attached to this letter rogatory, and an executed Certificate on the attached Form C.

Done at_________________ this____ date of______________, 19 __.

Signature and stamp of the judicial or administrative authority of the State of origin	Signature and stamp of the Central Authority of the State of origin

Title or other identification of each document to be delivered:

(Attach additional pages, if necessary.

* Delete if inapplicable.

ANNEX TO THE ADDITIONAL PROTOCOL TO THE INTER-AMERICAN CONVENTION ON LETTERS ROGATORY

FORM B

ESSENTIAL INFORMATION FOR THE ADDRESSEE[1]

To: (Name and address of the person being served)

You are hereby informed that (Brief statement of nature of service)

A copy of the letter rogatory that gives rise to the service or delivery of these documents is attached to this document. This copy also contains essential information for you. Also attached are copies of the complaint or pleading initiating the action in which the letter rogatory was issued, of the documents attached to the complaint or pleading, and of any rulings that ordered the issuance of the letter rogatory.

ADDITIONAL INFORMATION

I*

For Service

A. The document being served on you (original or copy) concerns the following:

B. The remedies sought or the amount in dispute is as follows:

C. By this service, you are requested:

D. *In case of service on you as a defendant you can answer the complaint before the judicial or administrative authority specified in Form A, Box 1 (State place, date and hour):

* You are being summoned to appear as:

* If some other action is being requested of the person served, please describe:

E. If you fail to comply, the consequences might be:

F. You are hereby informed that a defense counsel appointed by the Court or the following legal aid societies are available to you at the place where the proceeding is pending:

Name:
Address:

The documents listed in Part III are being furnished to you so that you may better understand and defend your interests.

---

[1] Complete the original and two copies of this form in the language of the State of origin and two copies in the language of the State of destination.

* Delete if inapplicable.

II*

For Information from Judicial or Administrative Authority

To: (Name and address of the judicial or administrative authority)

You are respectfully requested to furnish the undersigned judicial or administrative authority with the following information:

The documents listed in Part III are being furnished to you to facilitate your reply.

* Delete if inapplicable

III

List of Attached Documents

(Attach additional pages if necessary.)

Done at ________________ this______________day of ___________19

______________________________	______________________________
Signature and stamp of the judicial or administrative authority of the State of origin	Signature and stamp of the Central Authority of the State of Origin

ANNEX TO THE ADDITIONAL PROTOCOL TO THE INTER-AMERICAN CONVENTION ON LETTERS ROGATORY

FORM C

CERTIFICATE OF EXECUTION

To: (Name and address of judicial or administrative authority that issued the letter rogatory)

In conformity with the Additional Protocol to the Inter-American Convention on Letters Rogatory, signed at Montevideo on May 8, 1979, and in accordance with the attached original letter rogatory, the undersigned Central Authority has the honor to certify the following:

*A. That one copy of the documents attached to this Certificate has been served or delivered as follows:

Date:
At (address)

By one of the following methods authorized by the Convention.

*(1) In accordance with the special procedure or additional formalities that are described below, as provided for in the second paragraph of Article 10 of the above-mentioned Convention, or

*(2) By service personally on the identified addressee or, in the case of a legal entity, on its authorized agent, or

*(3) If the person or the authorized agent of the entity to be served was not found, in accordance with the law of the State of destination: (Specify method used)

*B. That the documents referred to in the letter rogatory have been delivered

Identity of person
Relationship to the addressee (family, business or other)

*C. That the documents attached to the Certificate have not been served or delivered for the following reason(s):

*D. In conformity with the Protocol, the party requesting execution of the letter rogatory is requested to pay the outstanding balance of costs in the amount indicated in the attached statement.

Done at ____________ the ____________ day of ______________ 19 _

____

Signature and stamp of Central Authority of the State of destination

Where appropriate, attach originals or copies of any additional documents proving service or delivery, and identify them.

---

[1] Complete the original and one copy in the language of the State of destination.

* Delete if inapplicable.

Appendix 5[3]

INTER-AMERICAN CONVENTION ON LETTERS ROGATORY AND ADDITIONAL PROTOCOL

State Department Circular

Disclaimer: THE INFORMATION IN THIS CIRCULAR RELATING TO THE LEGAL REQUIREMENTS OF SPECIFIC FOREIGN COUNTRIES IS PROVIDED FOR GENERAL INFORMATION ONLY AND MAY NOT BE TOTALLY ACCURATE IN A PARTICULAR CASE. QUESTIONS INVOLVING INTERPRETATION OF SPECIFIC FOREIGN LAWS SHOULD BE ADDRESSED TO FOREIGN COUNSEL OR THE FOREIGN CENTRAL AUTHORITY FOR THE CONVENTION.

In Force: ARGENTINA, BRAZIL, CHILE, COLOMBIA[1], ECUADOR, GUATEMALA, MEXICO, PANAMA, PARAGUAY, PERU, UNITED STATES, URUGUAY and VENEZUELA.

U.S. Central Authority: Office of International Judicial Assistance, Civil Division, Department of Justice, 1100 L St., N.W., Room 11006, Washington, D.C. 20530, tel: (202) 307-0983; fax: (202) 514-6584.

Summary: The United States has a treaty relationship only with countries which are a party to the Convention and the Additional Protocol. The treaty provides a mechanism for service of documents by a foreign central authority. Requests are prepared on a Convention form and transmitted via the U.S. Central Authority in the Department of Justice. The text of the Convention and Additional Protocol are self-explanatory, but see the reservations and declarations each country made on accession to the treaty available in the Martindale-Hubbell Law Directory, Law Digest Volume, Selected International Conventions. Despite the title of the Convention, no formal letter rogatory in the traditional sense is required. The Convention form serves that purpose.

Citations: S. Treaty Doc. 98-27, 98th Cong., 2d sess., (1984), pp. III-V, XII.; 14 Int'l Leg. Mat. 339 (March 1975); 18 Int'l Leg. Mat. 1238 (1984); Martindale-Hubbell Law Directory, Law Digest Volume, Selected International Conventions; See also, Ristau, Int'l Judicial Assistance, Civil and Commercial, Int'l Law Institute, Vol. 1, Sec. 7-1-5, p. 257-274.16; Epstein, International Litigation: A Guide to Jurisdiction, Practice and Strategy, Prentice Hall Law & Business, 1994 supp., Sec. 4.05, p. 4-24 - 4-28; Born & Westin, International Civil Litigation in United States Courts, (1989), p. 136-137; and Nash, Cumulative Digest of United States Practice in International Law, 1981-1988, p. 1555-1564 (1994).

---

[1] Colombia deposited its instruments of ratification to the Convention and Additional Protocol April 28, 1995, but has not yet designated a Central Authority to send and receive service requests. The OAS and the Colombian Ministry of Justice advise that requests for service of documents in Colombia continue to be sent through diplomatic channels (Department of State) until a Central Authority is designated. Colombia will send its requests for service directly to the U.S. Central Authority.

OAS Treaty Database: The texts of the Convention and Additional Protocol and information about recent accessions is also available through the OAS Internet Treaty Database: **gopher://oasunix1.oas.org:70/00/pub/english/treaties/series b/b36e** (Convention Text and Notes); **gopher://oasunix1.oas.org:70/00/pub/english/treaties/series b/b46e** (Additional Protocol and Notes)

Scope of the Convention: Article 2 provides that the scope of the Convention is limited to civil and commercial matters. Article 16 permits states to apply the Convention to criminal and administrative matters. Only Chile has declared that it will apply the Convention in such cases. See Ristau, Vol. 1, Sec. 7-1-4, p. 259-261 (1995 supp.). For information about the use of formal letters rogatory to effect service in criminal or administrative matters, see our general "Preparation of Letters Rogatory" and "Service of Process" flyers under "Additional Information" below. For prosecutors, in countries where a Mutual Legal Assistance in Criminal Matters (MLAT) treaty applies, the MLAT procedure may offer another alternative. Prosecutors may contact the Office of International Affairs, Criminal Division, Department of Justice for additional information (202) 514-0015 for additional information about MLATs. See our general flyer "Obtaining Evidence Abroad" for a list of MLAT treaties now in force.

Mandatory Convention Forms USM-272/272A: Submit a request for service in a foreign country party to the Convention and Additional Protocol on a form USM-272/272A, available at the office of any United States Marshal. See also, Martindale-Hubbell Law Directory, Law Digest Volume, Selected International Conventions; Ristau, Vol. 1, Sec. 7-4-5, p. 274.3 (1995 supp.); Epstein, App.-85 - App.-99, 1994 supp.; and Born & Westin, International Civil Litigation in United States Courts, (1989), Appendix E, p. 670-684. (See also, Department of Justice instructions to U.S. Marshal's Service dated 1/9/90.) According to that instruction, all requests for information regarding the treaty or completion of the forms should be directed to the U.S. Central Authority in the Department of Justice. See Ristau, Vol. 1, Sec. 7-2-3(1), p. 264 (1995 supp.) re use of the forms.

Number of Copies: The request for service includes the following: (a) the original and two copies of the USM-272 and USM 272A forms and three copies of the summons and complaint or other documents to be served. See Ristau, Vol. 1, Sec. 7-2-3(4), p. 266 (1995 supp.).

Annotating the Summons and Complaint: Article 3 of the Additional Protocol calls for the "letters rogatory" to be prepared on the Convention forms (USM 272/272A). The United States has taken the position that the USM-272/272A satisfies this requirement, and that a separate, formal letter rogatory is not/not in fact required, provided that the Convention forms are utilized and that the summons and complaint (or other comparable document) reflect that the person to be served is located in the specified foreign country. Moreover, the complaint should reflect that because the person to be served is in the specified foreign country, service is to be sought pursuant to the Inter-American Convention on Letters Rogatory and Additional Protocol to which the United States and the specified country are parties. See Ristau, Vol. 1, Sec. 7-2-3(2), p. 265 (1995 supp.).

Translations: While it is not necessary to translate responses to the USM-272, USM 272A into the language of the foreign country, the documents to be served, such as a summons and complaint, must be translated into the foreign language. Some commentaries recommend translation of the forms as well to help ensure more timely assistance. See Ristau, Vol. 1, Sec. 7-2-3(3), p. 266 (1995 Supp.).

Signature of Clerk of Court in U.S. Required: Unlike the Hague Service Convention, the Inter-American Convention requires that the Convention form bear the seal and signature of the judicial or authority of the country of origin and the signature and stamp of the U.S. Central Authority. The clerk of the court in the U.S. where the action is pending must place their seal and signature on pages 2 and 5 of the USM-272 and USM-272A on the left hand side "Signature and stamp of the judicial or other adjudicatory authority of the state of origin". The U.S. Central Authority (Department of Justice) will execute the signature/stamp on the right hand side of page 2 and 5 of the USM-272/272A. See Ristau, Vol. 1, Sec. 7-2-5, p. 267 (1995 supp.). Article 2 provides that authorities competent to request service include judicial or other adjudicatory authorities, the latter term has not been defined.

Fees: Article 5 of the Additional Protocol provides that processing of requests shall be free of charge. However, it also provides that a state party to the Convention and Additional Protocol may seek payment by parties for services in accordance with local law. Article 6 of the Additional Protocol provides that each state shall attach a schedule of services and costs to its instrument of ratification or accession. Article 7 of the Additional Protocol provides that states may charge no fees based on reciprocity. Some foreign countries charge fees of $25.00 to the foreign central authority. Mexico and Argentina have made declarations that they do not charge the fee. Other countries party to the Convention and Additional Protocol have been silent on the subject. Therefore, if service is sought in countries other than Mexico and Argentina, a certified check or money order in the amount of $25.00 made payable to the foreign central authority should be forwarded to the U.S. Authority with the USM-272/272A and the documents to be served. If no fee is charged the check will be returned. See Epstein, Sec. 4.05, p. 4-27 (1994 supp.); and Ristau, Vol. 1, Sec. 7-3-3, p. 270-271 (1995 supp.).

Proof of Service: The foreign central authority will execute page 7 of the forms as proof of service. See Ristau, Vol. 1, Sec. 7-3-4, p. 271 (1995 supp.).

Special Note Re Border States: Article 7 of the Convention provides that courts in border areas of the states parties may directly execute the letters rogatory contemplated in the Convention and such letters rogatory shall not require legalization. The U.S. Central Authority advises that border states such as Texas and even Florida have transmitted requests directly to foreign Central Authorities. The U.S. Central Authority advises that if attorneys representing clients in border states do transmit requests directly to foreign Central Authorities, proof of service is transmitted to the U.S. Central Authority. It is therefore imperative that the somewhere on the request it be stated where the executed request should be returned. The U.S. Central Authority would prefer that this information include the name and address of the attorney. Apparently, clerks of court in border states have be unable to identify the case when the executed request is returned by the U.S. Central authority. The U.S. Central Authority also advises that Article 7 notwithstanding, Mexico requires that a request transmitted from a border state to the Mexican Central Authority be fully authenticated with the seal of the Mexican embassy or consulate in the U.S.

Exclusivity of the Convention: The "Inter-American Service Convention" does reflect an effort by Inter-American countries to establish uniform procedures and may become more practically effective over time. In several reported and unreported cases, U.S. courts have held that the Convention is not the exclusive method of service for U.S. courts in countries party to the Convention. See Kreimerman v. Casa Veerkamp, S.A. 22 F 3d 634 (5th Cir. 1994); Mayztexil S.A. v. Liztez U.S.A., Inc., 1994 U.S. Dist. LEXIS 6663, S.D.N.Y. No. 92-Civ

452855, 5/19/94; Taylor v. Costa Cruises, Inc., 1992 U.S. Dist. LEXIS 11435; S.D.N.Y. No. 90, CIV 2630 (K.C.) 8/3/92; Pizzabiocche v. Vinelli, 772 F Supp. 1245, M.D. Fla. (1991). See Ristau, Vol. 1, Sec. 7-4-4, p. 274-274.2.

Time Frame: Time required to execute a Convention request is not much faster than the cumbersome letter rogatory procedure in some countries. Generally it can take 6 months to a year for a request to be executed. The U.S. Central Authority advises that Argentina and Peru have succeeded in processing requests more quickly, generally within three months.

Practical Notes on Operation of the Convention: There have been some practical problems with implementation of the Convention and Additional Protocol in certain countries. For example, some countries which have become parties to the Convention and Additional Protocol either have not designated a Central Authority or have not established the bureaucratic machinery to efficiently execute requests. Colombia is a recent example of a country which has not designated a central authority. The U.S. Central Authority advises that Venezuela is currently not executing requests forwarded to its Central Authority (April 1997). .The Departments of State and Justice are exploring these problems. In some cases foreign countries claim never to have received requests transmitted by the U.S. Central Authority. To counter this, the U.S. Central Authority began transmitting requests by registered mail, however return receipts were never returned signed. However, the U.S. Central Authority has observed some success by foreign Central Authorities in accomplishing service within a reasonable period of time and it is expected that as foreign Central Authorities become more experienced the procedure will become more efficient as time goes on.

Other Methods of Service:

Is Eventual Enforcement of a Judgment Abroad Anticipated: Generally, the decision whether or not to utilize the Convention method of serving documents depends on whether other methods of service are acceptable under international law, under the laws of the foreign country and under U.S. federal or state law. If eventual enforcement of a judgment is foreseen, it may be prudent to seek guidance from a foreign attorney regarding the best method of service to employ. Lists of foreign attorneys prepared by U.S. embassies and consulates abroad are available from this office.

Service by Mail: Neither the Convention nor the Additional Protocol expressly provide for service by mail. Local (foreign) law would determine whether service by mail is acceptable in that country. But see, FTC v. Compagnie de Saint-Gobain-Pont-a-Mousson, 636 F. 2d 1327, n. 150 (D.C. Cir. 1980) on the issue of service via international registered mail when the document to be served is not compulsory or punitive when there is no treaty obligation to refrain from such methods of service. See Ristau, Vol. 1, Sec. 7-3-5(2), p. 271 (1995 supp.).

Service by Formal Letters Rogatory—Using Diplomatic Channel: Although Article 4 of the Convention allows for the continued transmittal of formal letters rogatory requesting service of process utilizing the traditional diplomatic and consular channel, Article 1 of the Additional Protocol's provision quoted above mandates that requests must be transmitted via the central authority. See Ristau, Vol. 1, Sec. 7-3-5(3), p. 271-272 (1995 supp.). Moreover, the U.S. Central Authority advises that it has been informed when a request is sent outside the Central Authority channel, foreign authorities return the request unexecuted with instructions to submit the request through the Central Authority under the Convention. Confusion about the use of the diplomatic channel continues. The U.S. Central Authority advises, for example, that a number of countries party to the Convention require that the U.S. Central Authority transmit the request to the foreign Central Authority through the foreign embassy in Washington, D.C., although this contradicts the purpose of the Convention.

U.S. Reservation Re Obtaining Evidence: In acceding the Convention, the United States made a reservation pursuant to Article 2(b) of the Inter-American Convention on Letters Rogatory, letters rogatory that pertain to obtaining evidence are excluded from the operation of the Convention between the United States and other countries party to the Convention. Contact this office for information about obtaining evidence.

Service in the U.S. Under the Convention: For incoming requests from foreign treaty countries for service in the U.S., the Office of International Judicial Assistance in the Department of Justice will forward the requests to the appropriate U.S. Marshal's offices for service and processing in the same manner as those received under the Hague Service Convention. The U.S. is required to charge a reciprocal fee for service in the U.S. of $25.00 payable to the U.S. Treasurer for requests from any country which charges a fee for requests for service in the foreign country.

Foreign Central Authorities: According to the Organization of American States, the following are addresses of foreign central authorities:

ARGENTINA
Minister of Foreign Affairs
Reconquista 402
1405 Buenos Aires
Argentina
tel: (011) (54) (01) 3113113, 3110188, 3113999
No Fee.

BRAZIL
Ministerio da Justica
Esplanada dos Ministerios - Bloco T
70064-900 - Brasilia, DF
Brazil
tel: 011-55-61-218-3000
fax: 011-55-61-224-0954

CHILE
Ministry of Foreign Affairs
Compania Esq.
Morande, Ex edificio Deo
Congreso
Santiago, Chile

COLOMBIA
No Central Authority Designated
See Note p. 1.

ECUADOR
Ministry of Foreign Affairs
Departmento de Juridico
Carrion y Diez de Agosto
Quito, Ecuador
tel: (011) (593) (02) 230100
Contact: Sr. Diego Cordovez, Minister

GUATEMALA
Organismo Judicial
Corte Suprema de Justicia
21 Calle 7-70, Zona #1
Guatemala City, Guatemala
tel: (011) (502) (2) 53 2001
Contact: Dr. Edmundo Zasquez, President

MEXICO
Direccion General De Asuntos Juridicos
Direccion Juridicio Contenciosa
Departamento De Exhortos Y
Relaciones Con Embajadas
Secretaria De Relaciones Exteriores
Flores Magon No. 1, Col. Tlaltelolco
Mexico, D.F., Mexico
tel: (011) (905) 782 3624

No Fee. Mexico does not consider service by private individuals such as attorneys, investigators or private process servers to be valid in Mexico.

PANAMA
Ministerio de Relaciones Exteriores
Calle 24, Plaza Porras
Panama 1, Republic of Panama

PARAGUAY
Ministerio de Relacciones Exteriores
Jeoleary y Eayala
Asuncion, Paraguay
tel: (011) (595) (21) 444 457

PERU
(1) Documents can be forwarded to the Embassy of Peru in Washington, D.C.
Embassy of Peru
Consular Section (Attn: Mr. Schialer)
1700 Massachusetts Ave. N.W.
Washington, D.C. 20036

(2) Supreme Court of Justice
Paseo de la Republica
SN Lima 1, Peru
tel: (011) (51) (14) 284853, 283690

URUGUAY
Ministry of Education and Culture
(Asesoria Autoridad Central de Cooperacion Juridica Internacional)
Reconquista, #535
Montevideo, Uruguay
tel: (011) (598) (02) 46016, 403873

VENEZUELA
Herique Meier Echeverria
Ministerio de Justicia
Division de Tramites Legales
Central Simon Bolivar
Torre Norte, Piso 25
Caracas
Venezuela 1010
tel: (02) 483-1280, 483-7978 and 483-9933
fax: (02) 483-7515

Selected Bibliography:

Federal Register 31132, Vol. 53, No. 159, Wednesday, August 17, 1988 announced entry into force of the Convention and address of U.S. Central Authority.

Federal Register, Vol. 53, No. 85, Tuesday, May 3, 1988, April 28, 1988, Executive Order 12638, Delegation of Functions Relating to the Implementation of the Convention and Additional Protocol to the United States Department of Justice.

Born, International Litigation, The International Lawyer's Deskbook, Section of International Law and Practice, American Bar Association, p. 281 (1996).

Born & Westin, International Civil Litigation in United States Courts, (1989), p. 136-137; Appendix E, p. 670-684.

Carl, Service of Judicial Documents in Latin America, Vol. 53, No. 3, Denver Law Journal 455-475 (1976).

Epstein, International Litigation: A Guide to Jurisdiction, Practice and Strategy, Prentice Hall Law & Business, Sec. 4.05, p. 4-24 - 4-28 (1994 supp.).

Kearney, Developments in Private International Law, 81 Am. J. Int'l. L. 724, 737 (1987).

Low, International Judicial Assistance Among the American States: Inter-American Conventions, 18 Int'l Law. 705 (1984).

McDowell, Digest of United States Practice in International Law, Department of State, Office of the Legal Adviser, 1975, 893 (1975).

Nash, Digest, United States Practice in International Law, Department of State, Office of the Legal Adviser, 1979, 1868-1882 (1979).

Nash, Cumulative Digest of United States Practice in International Law, Department of State, Office of the Legal Adviser, 1981-1988, p. 1441, 1555-1564 (1994).

Ristau & Laguna, The Inter-American Letters Rogatory Convention, Arizona J. of Int'l. & Comp. L. 124, 138 (1985).

Ristau, International Judicial Assistance (Civil and Commercial), International Law Institute, Vol. 1, Sec. 7-1-5, p. 257-274.16 (Supp. 1995).

Additional Information: The Office of American Citizens Services has available general information flyers on international judicial assistance many of which are available through our automated fax system or via our Internet Consular Affairs Home Page. These topics include country-specific information about service of process and obtaining evidence abroad.

Using the Autofax System:

* Dial (202) 647-3000 using the phone on your fax machine.
* Follow the prompt to obtain a printed index of judicial assistance topics. There are four indexes.

Travel Information - Index of Countries - Press 1
Passports and Visas - Index of Flyers - Press 2
Judicial Assistance - General and Country Specific - Press 3
Child Custody and Adoption - Index of Flyers - Press 4

* Enter the four digit code for the document desired as listed in the index.
* When the prompt identifies the document and asks if you want that document, enter Y (9) for yes or N (6) for no.
* If you want another document, enter the four digit code, using the same procedures noted in the previous step.
* When you finish selecting, press the # key on the phone keyboard and press the start button on your fax machine.
* After a brief delay of up to a minute, the documents will print automatically on your fax machine.

Autofax General Judicial Assistance Codes:

1052 - Hague Evidence
1051 - Hague Service
1049 - Service of Process - General
1047 - Obtaining Evidence - General
1045 - Preparation of Letters Rogatory - General
1050 - Foreign Sovereign Immunities Act
1053 - Hague Legalization of Documents
1046 - Authentication - General
1208 - Inter-American Letters Rogatory Convention on Service

For Country-Specific Codes, See Autofax Index.

Using the Internet: Many of our judicial assistance flyers are also available on the Internet via the Department of State, Bureau of Consular Affairs Home Page at http://travel.state.gov/ under International Legal Assistance or through the main State Department Home Page at http://www.state.gov/ under Travel, Consular, or International Legal Assistance. See also, the Department of State, Office of the Legal Adviser for Private International Law (L/PIL) Home Page at http//www.lpil.com for information regarding the work of the OAS at Private International Law Unification. See also the Home Pages for many of our embassies which are linked to the Consular Affairs Home Page. As noted above, the text of the Convention and updated information concerning countries which have acceded to the Convention can be found in the Martindale-Hubbell Law Directory, Law Digest Volume. See the Martindale-Hubbell Home Page on the Internet at http://www.martindale.com/products/digests.html.

Treaty Databases on the Internet:

United Nations (UN): **http://www.un.org/** under Databases/Treaties at **http://www.un.org/Depts/Treaty/;**

Council of Europe (COE): **http://www.coe.fr:80/index.html** under Texts/Treaties **http://www.coe.fr.80/eng/legaltxt/treaties.htm;**

Organization of American States (OAS): **http://www.oas.org/** under Public Information/Documents/Treaties at **gopher://oasunix1.oas.org:70/11/pub/english/treaties**.

Questions: Additional questions regarding the operation of the Inter-American Service Convention should be addressed to the U.S. Central Authority, the Office of International Judicial Assistance, Civil Division, Department of Justice, tel: (202) 307-0983. General questions may also be addressed to the Inter-American Services Division of the Office of American Citizens Services at (202) 647-5118 or 202-647-5226.

CA/OCS/ACS 4/97

Appendix 6[1]

FORM OF REQUEST FOR SERVICE ABROAD OF JUDICIAL OR EXTRAJUDICIAL DOCUMENTS PURSUANT TOTHE ADDITIONAL PROTOCOL TO THE INTER-AMERICAN CONVENTION ON LETTERS ROGATORY

FORM A

LETTER ROGATORY [1]

1	2
REQUESTING JUDICIAL OR OTHER ADJUDICATORY AUTHORITY Name Address	CASE: DOCKET No.:

3	4
CENTRAL AUTHORITY OF THE STATE OF ORIGIN Name Address	CENTRAL AUTHORITY OF THE STATE OF DESTINATION Name Address

5	6
REQUESTING PARTY Name Address	COUNSEL TO THE REQUESTING PARTY Name Address

PERSON DESIGNATED TO ACT IN CONNECTION WITH THE LETTER ROGATORY	
Name Address	Is this person responsible for costs and expenses? YES ☐ NO ☐ * If not, check in the amount of ________ is attached * Or proof of payment is attached

[1] Complete the original and two copies of this form; if A(1) is applicable, attach the original and two copies of the translation of this item in the language of the State of destination.

* Delete if inapplicable.

Form USM-272
(Est. 1/89)

The Central Authority signing this letter rogatory has the honor to transmit to you in triplicate to you in triplicate the documents listed below and, in conformity with the Protocol to the Inter-American Convention on Letters Rogatory:

* A. Requests their prompt service on:

____

____

____

The undersigned authority requests that service be carried out in the following manner:

* (1) In accordance with the special procedure or additional formalities that are described below, as provided for in the second paragraph of Article 10 of the above-mentioned Convention; or

____

____

____

____

* (2) By service personally on the identified addressee or, in the case of a legal entity, on its authorized agent; or

* (3) If the person or the authorized agent of the entity to be served is not found, service shall be made in accordance with the law of the State of destination.

* B. Requests the delivery of the documents listed below to the following judicial or administrative authority:

Authority: ____________________________________

____

____

* C. Requests the Central Authority of the State of destination to return to the Central Authority of the State of origin one copy of the documents listed below and attached to this letter rogatory, and an executed Certificate on the attached Form C.

Done at ____________ this ____________ date of ____________, 19___.

________________________	________________________
Signature and stamp of the judicial or other adjudicatory authority of the State of origin	Signature and stamp of the Central Authority of the State of origin

Title or other identification of each document to be delivered:

____

____

(Attach additional pages, if necessary.)

* Delete if inapplicable.

ANNEX TO THE ADDITIONAL PROTOCOL TO THE INTER-AMERICAN CONVENTION ON LETTERS ROGATORY

FORM B

ESSENTIAL INFORMATION FOR THE ADDRESSEE [1]

To (Name and address of the person being served) ____________________
____

You are hereby informed that (Brief statement of nature of service) ____________________
____
____

A copy of the letter rogatory that gives rise to the service or delivery of these documents is attached to this document. This copy also contains essential information for you. Also attached are copies of the complaint or pleading initiating the action in which the letter rogatory was issued, of the documents attached to the complaint or pleading, and of any rulings that ordered the issuance of the letter rogatory.

ADDITIONAL INFORMATION

I *

FOR SERVICE

A. The document being served on you (original or copy) concerns the following:
____
____

B. The remedies sought or the amount in dispute is as follows:
____
____

C. By this service, you are requested:
____
____

D. * In case of service on you as a defendant you can answer the complaint before the judicial or other adjudicatory authority specified in Form A, Box 1 (State place, date and hour): ____________________
____

* You are being summoned to appear as: ____________________
____

[1] Complete the original and two copies of this form in the language of the State of origin and two copies in the language of the State of destination.

* Delete if inapplicable.

- If some other action is being requested of the person served, please describe: ______________________

E. If you fail to comply, the consequences might be: ______________________

F. You are hereby informed that a defense counsel appointed by the Court or the following legal aid societies are available to you at the place where the proceeding is pending.

Name: ______________________

Address: ______________________

The documents listed in Part III are being furnished to you so that you may better understand and defend your interests.

II *

FOR INFORMATION FROM JUDICIAL OR ADMINISTRATIVE AUTHORITY

To: ______________________

(Name and address of the judicial or administrative authority)

You are respectfully requested to furnish the undersigned authority with the following information: ______________________

The documents listed in Part III are being furnished to you to facilitate your reply.

* Delete if inapplicable.

III

LIST OF ATTACHED DOCUMENTS

____

(Attach additional pages if necessary.)

Done at ______________________ this ______________ day

of ______________, 19____

Signature and stamp of the judicial or other adjudicatory authority of the State of origin

Signature and stamp of the Central Authority of the State of Origin

ANNEX TO THE ADDITIONAL PROTOCOL TO THE INTER-AMERICAN CONVENTION ON LETTERS ROGATORY

FORM C

CERTIFICATE OF EXECUTION [1]

To: ____

____

____

(Name and address of judicial or other adjudicatory authority that issued the letter rogatory)

In conformity with the Additional Protocol to the Inter-American Convention on Letters Rogatory, signed at Montevideo on May 8, 1979, and in accordance with the attached original letter rogatory, the undersigned Central Authority has the honor to certify the following:

* A. That one copy of the documents attached to this Certificate has been served or delivered as follows:

Date: ____

At (Address) ____

By one of the following methods authorized by the Convention.

* (1) In accordance with the special procedure or additional formalities that are described below, as provided for in the second paragraph of Article 10 of the above-mentioned Convention, or

____

____

____

* (2) By service personally on the identified addressee or, in the case of a legal entity, on its authorized agent, or

* (3) If the person or the authorized agent of the entity to be served was not found, in accordance with the law of the State of destination: (Specify method used)

____

____

____

____

---

[1] Complete the original and one copy in the language of the State of destination.

* Delete if inapplicable.

* B. That the documents referred to in the letter rogatory have been delivered to:

  Identity of person ______________________________

  ____

  ____

  Relationship to the addressee ______________________________

  (Family, business or other)

  ____

  ____

* C. That the documents attached to the Certificate have not been served or delivered for the following reason(s):

  ____

  ____

  ____

* D. In conformity with the Protocol, the party requesting execution of the letter rogatory is requested to pay the outstanding balance of costs in the amount indicated in the attached statement.

Done at ______________ the ________ day of ________ 19____

____

Signature and stamp of Central Authority of the State of destination

Where appropriate, attach originals or copies of any additional documents proving service or delivery, and identify them.

* Delete if inapplicable.

Appendix 6[2]

FORM OF REQUEST FOR SERVICE ABROAD OF JUDICIAL OR EXTRAJUDICIAL DOCUMENTS PURSUANT TOTHE ADDITIONAL PROTOCOL TO THE INTER-AMERICAN CONVENTION ON LETTERS ROGATORY (SPANISH VERSION)

SOLICITUD PARA EJECUTAR EN EL EXTRANJERO DOCUMENTOS JUDICIALES O EXTRAJUDICIALES BASADO EN EL PROTOCOLO ADICIONAL A LA CONVENCION INTERAMERICANA SOBRE EXHORTOS O CARTAS ROGATORIAS

EXHORTO O CARTA ROGATORIA[1]

FORMULARIO A

1

ORGANO JURISDICCIONAL REQUIRENTE
Nombre
Dirección

2

EXPEDIENTE

3

AUTORIDAD CENTRAL REQUIRENTE
Nombre
Dirección

4

AUTORIDAD CENTRAL REQUERIDA
Nombre
Dirección

5

PARTE SOLICITANTE
Nombre
Dirección

6

APODERADO DEL SOLICITANTE
Nombre
Dirección

PERSONA DESIGNADA PARA INTERVENIR EN EL DILIGENCIAMIENTO
Nombre

Dirección

¿Esta persona se hará responsable de las costas y gastos?
SI ☐ NO ☐
* En caso contrario, se acompaña cheque por la suma de ____________
* O se agrega documento que prueba el pago

[1] Debe elaborarse un original y dos copias de este Formulario; en caso de ser aplicable el A (1) debe ser traducido al idioma del Estado requerido y se adjuntarán dos copias.

* Táchese si no corresponde.

La autoridad que suscribe este exhorto o carta rogatoria tiene el honor de transmitir a usted por triplicado los documentos abajo enumerados, conforme al Protocolo Adicional a la Convención Interamericana sobre Exhortos o Cartas Rogatorias.

* A. Se solicita la pronta notificación a: ______________________

____

____

La autoridad que suscribe solicita que la notificación se practique en la siguiente forma:

* (1) De acuerdo con el procedimiento especial o formalidades adicionales, que a continuación se describen, con fundamento en el segundo párrafo del artículo 10 de la mencionada Convención;

____

____

____

____

* (2) Mediante notificación personal a la persona a quien se dirige, o al representante legal de la persona juridica;

* (3) En caso de no encontrarse la persona natural o el representante legal de la persona jurídica que deba ser notificada, se hará la notificación en la forma prevista por la ley del Estado requerido.

* B. Se solicita que se entregue a la autoridad judicial o administrative que se identifica, los documentos abajo enumerados:

Autoridad ______________________

____

____

* C. Se ruega a la autoridad central requerida devolver a la autoridad central requirente una copia de los documentos adjuntos al presente exhorto o carta rogatoria, abajo enumerados, y un certificado de cumplimiento conforme a lo dispuesto en el Formulario C adjunto.

Hecho en ______________ el día ______________ de ______________ de 19 ____ .

______________________	______________________
Firma y sello del organo jurisdiccional requirente	Firma y sello de la autoridad central requirente

Título u otra identificación de cada uno de los documentos que deban ser entregados:

____

____

(*Agregar hojas en caso necesario*)

* Táchese si no corresponde.

ANEXO AL PROTOCOLO ADICIONAL A LA CONVENCION INTERAMERICANA SOBRE EXHORTOS O CARTAS ROGATORIAS

INFORMACION ESENCIAL PARA EL NOTIFICADO[1]

FORMULARIO B

A *(Nombre y dirección del notificado)* ______________________________

____

Por la presente se le comunica que *(explicar brevemente la que se notifica)* ______________________________

____

____

A este documento se anexa una copia del exhorto o carta rogatoria que motiva la notificación o entrega de estes documentos. Esta copia contiene también información esencial para usted. Asimismo, se adjuntan copias de la demanda o de la petición con la cual se inició el procedimiento en el que se libró el exhorto o carta rogatoria, de los documentos que se han adjuntado a dicha demanda o petición y de las resoluciones jurisdiccionales que ordenaron el libramiento del exhorto e carta rogatoria.

INFORMACION ADICIONAL

I*

PARA EL CASO DE NOTIFICACION

A. El documento que se le entrega consiste en: *(original o copia)*

____

____

B. Las pretensiones o la cuantía del proceso son las siguientes: ______________________________

____

____

C. En esta notificación se le solicita que: ______________________________

____

____

D. * En caso de citación al demandado, éste puede contestar la demanda ante el órgano jurisdiccional indicado en el cuadro 1 del Formulario A *(indicar lugar, fecha y hora)*: ______________________________

____

* Usted está citado para comparecer como: ______________________________

____

[1] Completar el original y dos copias de este Formulario en el idioma del Estado requirente y dos copias en el idioma del Estado requerido.

*Táchese lo que no corresponde.

* En caso de solicitarse otra cosa del notificado, sirvase describirla: ______

E. En caso de que usted no compareotere, las consecuencias aplicables podrian ser: ______

F. Se le informa que existe a su disposición la defensoría de oficio, o sociedad de auxilio legal en el lugar del juicio.

Nombre: ______

Dirección: ______

Los documentos enumerades en la parte III se le suministran para su mejor conocimiento y defensa.

II*

PARA EL CASO DE SOLICITUD DE INFORMACION DEL ORGANO JURISDICCIONAL

A: ______

(Nombre y dirección del órgano jurisdiccional)

Se le solicita respetuosamente proporcionar al órgano que suscribe, la siguiente información ______

Los documentos enumerados en la Parte III se le suministran para facilitar su respuesta.

*Táchese si no corresponde.

III

LISTA DE LOS DOCUMENTOS ANEXOS

______

(Agregar hojas si fuera necesario)

Hecho en ______ el día ______ de ______ de 19____.

Firma y sello del órgano jurisdiccional requirente

Firma y sello de la autoridad central requirente

ANEXO AL PROTOCOLO ADICIONAL A LA CONVENCION INTERAMERICANA SOBRE EXHORTOS O CARTAS ROGATORIAS

FORMULARIO C

CERTIFICADO DE CUMPLIMIENIO[1]

A: ____

____

____

(Identificación y dirección del órgano jurisdiccional que libro el exhorto o carta rogatoria)

De conformidad con el Protocolo Adicional a la Convención Interamericana sobre Exhortos o Cartas Rogatorias, suscrito en Montevideo ei 8 de mayo de 1979, y con el exhorto o carta rogatoria adjunto, la autoridad que suscribe tiene el honor de certificar lo siguiente:

* A. Que un ejemplar de los documentos adjuntos al presente Certificado ha sido notificado o entregado como sigue:

Fecha: ____

Lugar *(dirección)*: ____

De conformidad con uno de los siguientes métedos autorizados en la Convención:

* (1) De acuerdo con el procedimiento especial o formalidades adicionales que a continuación se describen, con fundamento en el segundo párrafo del artículo 10 de la mencionada Convención,

____

____

____

____

* (2) Mediante notificación personal a la persona a quien se dirige, o al representante legal de una persona jurídica,

* (3) En caso de no haberse encentrado la persona que debió haber sido notificada, se hizo la notificación en la forma prevista por la ley del Estado requerido: *(Sírvase describirla)*

____

____

____

____

[1] Original y una copia en el idioma del Estado requerido.

*Táchese si no corresponde.

* **B.** **Que los documentos indicados en el exhorto o carta rogatoria han sido entregados a:**
  Identidad de la persona ______________________________
  ____
  ____
  Relación con el destinatario ______________________________
  (familiar, comercial u otra)
  ____
  ____

* **C.** **Que los documentos no han sido notificados o entregados por los siguientes motivos:**
  ____
  ____
  ____

* **D.** **De conformidad con el Protocolo, se solicita al interesado que pague el saldo adeudado cuyo detaille se adjunta.**

  Hecho en __________ **el día** __________ **de** __________ **de 19**____.

____
(Firma y sello de la autoridad central requerida)

Cuando corresponda, adjuntar original o copia de cualquier documento adicional necesario para probar que se ha hecho la notificación o entrega, e identificar el citado documento.

---

*Táchese si no correspnde.

Appendix 7

DRAFT CONVENTION ON SOVEREIGN IMMUNITY

Office of the Legal Advisor
[Public Notice 1784]

Draft Convention on Sovereign Immunity; Invitation for Public Comment

AGENCY: Department of State.
ACTION: Notice.

SUMMARY: Invitation for public comment.

FOR FURTHER INFORMATION CONTACT:
Linda Jacobson, Department of State
Office of the Legal Adviser for Special Functional Problems
2201 C Street, NW
Washington DC 20520
202-6471074

SUPPLEMENTARY INFORMATION:

Draft Convention on Sovereign Immunity

Invitation for Public Comment

The International Law Commission, an organ of the United Nations has presented draft articles on the Jurisdictional Immunities of States and their Property to the General Assembly for possible adoption as a convention. The convention, a multilateral international agreement, would establish uniform rules concerning the extent to which a State may invoke sovereign immunity before the courts of another State. At the forty-seventh session of the General Assembly, a working group of the Sixth Committee met between September 25 and November 6, 1992, to study the draft articles and the written comments of governments, in order to facilitate the conclusion of a convention. The United States submitted written comments and also participated in the working group. The General Assembly decided to reestablish the working group in the Sixth Committee at its forty-eighth session in September, 1993.

In its written and oral comments, the United States supported the efforts of the International Law Commission to reflect the "restrictive theory" of sovereign immunity embodied in the United States Foreign Sovereign Immunities Act, but expressed concerns about certain articles. The U.S. concerns related *inter alia,* to: The definition of the term "State", especially with reference to "political subdivisions" and "agencies or instrumentalities" (Article 2, paragraphs 1(b) (iii) and (iv)); the subsidiary "purpose" test to determine whether a contract or transaction is "commercial" (Article 2, paragraph 2); the limitation on the ability of private parties, in exceptional circumstances, to obtain jurisdiction over a State that creates a separate State-controlled commercial entity (Article 10, paragraph 3); the operation of *in rem* proceedings and other limitations on immunity for ships and cargo (Article 16); limitations in the area of arbitration, including the absence of an exception to immunity for judicial enforcement of agreements to arbitrate and confirmation of arbitral awards (Article 17); the failure to provide adequately for immunity from pre-judgment attachments (Article 18); the requirement that State commercial property to be executed upon must be related to the underlying claim (Article 18).

The text of the draft articles is reproduced below for public comment. Comment may be addressed to the Assistant Legal Adviser for Special Functional Problems, room 5420, Department of State, Washington, DC 20520. All public comments should be received on or before July 1, 1993, to ensure consideration. The written comments of the United States, as well as the report of the working group on its meeting in the fall of 1997, are available upon request from the Office of the Assistant Legal Adviser for Special Functional Problems (202-647-1074).

Dated: March 24, 1993.
Michael Matheson,
Acting Legal Adviser

Draft Articles on Jurisdictional Immunities of State and Their Property

Part I—Introduction

Article I—Scope of the Present Articles

The present articles apply to the immunity of a State and its property from the jurisdiction of the courts of another State.

Article 2—Use of Terms

1. For the purposes of the present articles:
   (a) "Court" means any organ of a State, however named, entitled to exercise judicial functions;
   (b) "State" means:
      (i) The State and its various organs of government;
      (ii) Constituent units of a federal State;
      (iii) Political subdivisions of the State which are entitled to perform acts in the exercise of the sovereign authority of the State;
      (iv) Agencies or instrumentalities of the State and other entities, to the extent that they are entitled to perform acts in the exercise of the sovereign authority of the State;
      (v) Representatives of the State acting in that capacity;
   (c) "Commercial transaction" means:
      (i) Any commercial contract or transaction for the sale of goods or supply of services;
      (ii) Any contract for a loan or other transaction of a financial nature, including any obligation of guarantee or of indemnity in respect of any such loan or transaction;
      (iii) Any other contract or transaction of a commercial, industrial, trading or

professional nature, but not including a contract of employment of persons.

2. In determining whether a contract or transaction is a "commercial transaction" under paragraph 1(c), reference should be made primarily to the nature of the contract or transaction, but its purpose should also be taken into account if, in the practice of the State which is a party to it, that purpose is relevant to determining the non-commercial character of the contract or transaction.
3. The provisions of paragraphs 1 and 2 regarding the use of terms in the present articles are without prejudice to the use of those terms or to the meanings which may be given to them in other international instruments or in the internal law of any State.

Article 3—Privileges and Immunities Not Affected by the Present Articles

1. The present articles are without prejudice to the privileges and immunities enjoyed by a State under international law in relation to the exercise of the functions of:
   (a) Its diplomatic missions, consular posts, special missions, missions to international organizations, or delegations to organs of international organizations or to international conferences; and
   (b) Persons connected with them.
2. The present articles are likewise without prejudice to privileges and immunities accorded under international law to Heads of State *ratione personae*.

Article 4—Non-Retroactivity of the Present Articles

Without prejudice to the application of any rules set forth in the present articles to which jurisdictional immunities of States and their property are subject under international law independently of the present articles, the articles shall not apply to any question of jurisdictional immunities of States or their property arising in a proceeding instituted against a State before a court of another State prior to the entry into force of the present articles for the States concerned.

Part II—General Principles

Article 5—State Immunity

A State enjoys immunity, in respect of itself and its property, from the jurisdiction of the courts of another State subject to the provisions of the present articles.

Article 6—Modalities for Giving Effect to State Immunity

1. A State shall give effect to State immunity under article 5 by refraining from exercising jurisdiction in a proceeding before its courts against another State and to that end shall ensure that its courts determine on their own initiative that the immunity of that other State under article 5 is respected.
2. A proceeding before a court of a State shall be considered to have been instituted against another State if that other State:
   (a) Is named as a party to that proceeding; or
   (b) Is not named as a party to the proceeding but the proceeding in effect seeks to affect the property, rights, interests or activities of that other state.

Article 7—Express Consent of Exercise of Jurisdiction

1. A State cannot invoke immunity from jurisdiction in a proceeding before a court of

another State with regard to a matter or case if it as expressly consented to the exercise of jurisdiction by the court with regard to the matter or case:
(a) By international agreement;
(b) In a written contract: or
(c) By a declaration before the court or by a written communication in a specific proceeding.
2. Agreement by a State for the application of the law of another State shall not be interpreted as consent to the exercise of jurisdiction by the courts of that other State.

Article 8—Effect of Participation in a Proceeding Before a Court

1. A State cannot invoke immunity from jurisdiction in a proceeding before a court of another State if it has:
(a) Itself instituted the proceeding; or
(b) Intervened in the proceeding or taken any other step relating to the merits. However, if the State satisfies the court that it could not have acquired knowledge of facts on which a claim to immunity can be based until after it took such a step, it can claim immunity based on those facts, provided it does so at the earliest possible moment.
2. A State shall not be considered to have consented to the exercise of jurisdiction by a court of another State if it intervenes in a proceeding or takes any other step for the sole purpose of:
(a) Invoking immunity; or
(b) Asserting a right or interest in property at issue in the proceeding.
3. The appearance of a representative of a State before a court of another State as a witness shall not be interpreted as consent by the former State to the exercise of jurisdiction by the court.
4. Failure on the part of a State to enter an appearance in a proceeding before a court of another State shall not be interpreted as consent by the former State to the exercise of jurisdiction by the court.

Article 9—Counter-Claims

1. A State instituting a proceeding before a court of another State cannot invoke immunity from the jurisdiction of the court in respect of any counter-claim arising out of the same legal relationship of facts as the principal claim.
2. A State intervening to present a claim in a proceeding before a court of another State cannot invoke immunity from the jurisdiction of the court in respect of any counter-claim arising out of the same legal relationship or facts as the claim presented by the State.
3. A State making a counter-claim in a proceeding instituted against it before a court of another State cannot invoke immunity from the jurisdiction of the court in respect of the principal claim.

Part III—Proceeding in Which State Immunity Cannot be Invoked

Article 10—Commercial Transactions

1. If a State engages in a commercial transaction with a foreign natural or juridical person and, by virtue of the applicable rules of private international law, differences relating to the commercial transaction fall within the jurisdiction of a court of another State, the State cannot invoke immunity from that jurisdiction in a proceeding arising out of that

commercial transaction.

2. Paragraph 1 does not apply:
   (a) In the case of a commercial transaction between States; or
   (b) If the parties to the commercial transaction have expressly agreed otherwise.
3. The immunity from jurisdiction enjoyed by a State shall not be affected with regard to a proceeding which relates to a commercial transaction engaged in by a State enterprise or other entity established by the State which has an independent legal personality and is capable of:
   (a) Suing or being sued; and
   (b) Acquiring, owning or possessing and disposing of property, including property which the State has authorized it to operate or manage.

Article 11—Contracts of Employment

1. Unless otherwise agreed between the States concerned, a State cannot invoke immunity from jurisdiction before a court of another State which is otherwise competent in a proceeding which relates to a contract of employment between the State and an individual for work performed or to be performed, in whole or in part, in the territory of that other State.
2. Paragraph 1 does not apply if:
   (a) The employee has been recruited to perform functions closely related to the exercise of governmental authority;
   (b) The subject of the proceeding is the recruitment, renewal of employment or reinvestment of an individual;
   (c) The employee was neither a national nor a habitual resident of the State of the forum at the time when the contract of employment was concluded;
   (d) The employee is a national of the employer State at the time when the proceeding is instituted; or
   (e) The employer State and the employee have otherwise agreed in writing, subject to any consideration of public policy conferring on the courts of the State of the forum exclusive jurisdiction by reason of the subject-matter of the proceeding.

Article 12—Personal Injuries and Damage to Property

Unless otherwise agreed between the States concerned, a State cannot invoke immunity from jurisdiction before a court of another State which is otherwise competent in a proceeding which relates to pecuniary compensation for death or injury to the person, or damage to or loss of tangible property, cased by an act or omission which is alleged to be attributable to the State, if the act or omission occurred in whole or in part in the territory of that other State and if the author of the act or omission was present in that territory at the time of the act or omission.

Article 13—Ownership, Possession and Use of Property

Unless otherwise agreed between the States concerned, a State cannot invoke immunity from jurisdiction before a court of another State which is otherwise competent in a proceeding which relates to the determination of:

(a) Any right or interest of the State in, or its possession or use of, or any obligation of the State arising out of its interest in, or its possession or use of, immovable property situated in the State of the forum;
(b) Any right or interest of the State in movable or immovable property arising by way

of succession, gift or *bona vacantia*; or

(c) Any right or interest of the State in the administration of property, such as trust property, the estate of a bankrupt or the property of a company in the event of its winding-up.

Article 14—Intellectual and Industrial Property

Unless otherwise agreed between the States concerned, a State cannot invoke immunity from jurisdiction before a court of another State which is otherwise competent in a proceeding which relates to:

(a) The determination of any right of the State in a patent, industrial design, trade name or business name, trade mark, copyright or any other form of intellectual or industrial property, which enjoys a measure of legal protection, even if provisional, in the State of the forum; or

(b) An alleged infringement by the State in the territory of the State of the forum, of a right of the nature mentioned in subparagraph (a) which belongs to a third person and is protected in the State of the forum.

Article 15—Participation in Companies or Other Collective Bodies

1. A State cannot invoke immunity from jurisdiction before a court of another State which is otherwise competent in a proceeding which related to its participation in a company or other collective body, whether incorporated or unincorporated, being a proceeding concerning the relationship between the State and the body or the other participants therein, provided that the body:
   (a) Has participants other than States or international organizations; and
   (b) Is incorporated or constituted under the law of the State of the forum or has its seat or principal place of business in that State
2. A State can, however, invoke immunity from jurisdiction in such a proceeding if the States concerned have so agreed or if the parties to the dispute have so provided by an agreement in writing or if the instrument establishing or regulating the body in question contains provisions to that effect.

Article 16—Ships Owned or Operated by a State

1. Unless otherwise agreed between the States concerned, a State which owns or operates a ship cannot invoke immunity from jurisdiction before a court of another State which is otherwise competent in a proceeding which relates to the operation of that ship, if at the time the cause of action arose, the ship was used for other than government non-commercial purposes.
2. Paragraph 1 does not apply to warships and naval auxiliaries nor does it apply to other ships owned or operated by a State and used exclusively on government non-commercial service.
3. For the purposes of this article, "proceeding which relates to the operation of that Ship" means, inter alia, any proceeding involving the determination of a claim in respect of:
   (a) Collision or other accidents of navigation;
   (b) Assistance, salvage and general average;
   (c) Repairs, supplies or other contracts relating to the ship;
   (d) Consequences of pollution of the marine environment.
4. Unless otherwise agreed between the States concerned, a State cannot invoke immunity from jurisdiction before a court of another State which is otherwise competent in a

proceeding which relates to the carriage of cargo on board a ship owned or operated by that State if, at the time the cause of action arose, the ship was used for other than government non-commercial purposes.

5. Paragraph 4 does not apply to any cargo carried on board the ships referred to in paragraph 2 nor does it apply to any cargo owned by a State and used or intended for use exclusively for government non-commercial purposes.
6. States may plead all measures of defence, prescription and limitation of liability which are available to private ships and cargoes and their owners.
7. If in a proceeding there arises a question relating to the government and non-commercial character of a ship owned or operated by a State or cargo owned by a State, a certificate signed by a diplomatic representative or other competent authority of that State and communicated to the court shall serve as evidence of the character of that ship or cargo.

Article 17—Effect of an Arbitration Agreement

If a State enters into an agreement in writing with a foreign natural or juridical person to submit to arbitration differences relating to a commercial transaction, that State cannot invoke immunity from jurisdiction before a court of another State which is otherwise competent in a proceeding which relates to:

(a) The validity or interpretation of the arbitration agreement;
(b) The arbitration procedure; or
(c) The setting aside of the award, unless the arbitration agreement otherwise provides.

Part IV—State Immunity From Measures of Constraint in Connection With Proceedings Before a Court

Article 18—State Immunity From Measures of Constraint

1. No measures of constraint, such as attachment, arrest and execution, against property of a State may be taken in connection with a proceeding before a court of another State unless and except to the extent that:
   (a) The State has expressly consented to the taking of such measures as indicated:
      (i) By international agreement;
      (ii) By an arbitration agreement or in a written contract; or
      (iii) By a declaration before the court or by a written communication after a dispute between the parties has arisen;
   (b) The State has allocated or earmarked property for the satisfaction of the claim which is the object of that proceeding; or
   (c) The property is specifically in use or intended for use by the State for other than government non-commercial purposes and is in the territory of the State of the forum and has a connection with the claim which is the object of the proceeding or with the agency or instrumentality against which the proceeding was directed.
2. Consent to the exercise of jurisdiction under article 7 shall not imply consent to the taking of measures of constraint under paragraph 1, for which separate consent shall be necessary.

Article 19—Specific Categories of Property

1. The following categories, in particular, of property of a State shall not be considered as property specifically in use or intended for use by the State for other than government non-commercial purposes under paragraph 4(c) of article 18:
   (a) Property, including any bank account, which is used or intended for use for the

purposes of the diplomatic mission of the State or its consular posts, special missions, missions to international organizations, or delegations to organs of international organization or to international conferences;

(b) Property of a military character or used or intended for use for military purposes;

(c) Property of the central bank or other monetary authority of the State;

(d) Property forming part of the cultural heritage of the State or part of its archives and not placed or intended to be placed on sale;

(e) Property forming part of an exhibition of objects of scientific, cultural or historical interest and not placed or intended to be placed on sale.

2. Paragraph 1 is without prejudice to paragraph 1(a) and (b) of article 18.

Part V—Miscellaneous Provisions

Article 20—Service of Process

1. Service of process by writ or other document instituting a proceeding against a State shall be effected:
   (a) In accordance with any applicable international convention binding on the State of the forum and the State concerned; or
   (b) In the absence of such a convention:
      (i) By transmission through diplomatic channels to the Ministry of Foreign Affairs of the State concerned; or
      (ii) By any other means accepted by the State concerned, if not precluded by the law of the State of the forum.
2. Service of process referred to in paragraph 1(b)(i) is deemed to have been effected by receipt of the documents by the Ministry of Foreign Affairs.
3. These documents shall be accompanied, if necessary, by a translation into the official language, or one of the official languages, of the State concerned.
4. Any State that enters an appearance on the merits in a proceeding instituted against it may not thereafter assert that service if process did not comply with the provisions of paragraphs 1 and 3.

Article 21—Default Judgement

1. A default judgement shall not be rendered against a State unless the court has found that:
   (a) The requirements laid down in paragraphs 1 and 3 of article 20 have been complied with;
   (b) A period of not less than four months has expired from the date on which the service of the writ or other document instituting a proceeding has been effected in accordance with paragraphs 1 and 2 of article 20; and
   (c) The present articles do not preclude it form exercising jurisdiction.
2. A copy of any default judgement rendered against a State, accompanied if necessary by translation into the official language or one of the official languages of the State concerned, shall be transmitted to it through one of the means specified in paragraph 1 of article 20 and in accordance with the provisions of that paragraph.
3. The time-limit for applying to have a default judgement set aside shall not be less than four months and shall begin to run from the date on which the copy of the judgement is received or is deemed to have been received by the State concerned.

Article 22—Privileges and Immunities During Court Proceedings

1. Any failure or refusal by a State to comply with an order of a court of another State

enjoining it to perform or refrain from performing a specific act or to produce any document or disclose any other information for ht purposes of a proceeding shall entail no consequences other than those which may result from such conduct in relation to the merits of the case. In particular, no fine or penalty shall be imposed on the State by reason of such failure or refusal.

2. A State shall not be required to provide any security, bond or deposit, however described, to guarantee the payment of judicial costs or expenses in any proceeding to which it is a party before a court of another State.

Annex II—Proposal on Settlement of Disputes

Part V—Dispute Settlement

Article 23—Disputes in Respect of a Proceeding Instituted Before a Domestic Court

(1) Any dispute between two or more States Parties concerning the interpretation or application of this convention in respect of a proceeding instituted before a court of one of the parties to the dispute against the other party or parties to the dispute shall be submitted to the International Court of Justice on the application of one of the parties to the dispute or by special agreement.

(2) If the dispute is submitted to the International Court of Justice on the application of one of that parties to it, the party shall request that the case be dealt with by the chamber of summary procedure formed in pursuance of Article 29 of the Statute of the Court.

(3) The States Parties to this Convention agree that disputes to which this article applies shall be dealt with by the chamber of summary procedure formed in pursuance of Article 29 of the Statute of the International Court of Justice and that oral proceedings shall be dispensed with.

(4) A State against which a proceeding has been instituted before a court of another State shall not submit a dispute to the International Court of Justice pursuant to paragraph (2) unless:
   (a) Default judgment has been given against it by the court of the other State; or
   (b) The dispute arises out of the rejection by the court of the other State of a claim of immunity under this Convention.

(5) In a case to which paragraph (4)(b) applies, the State may not raise any question before the International Court of Justice which has not first been the subject of a decision by the court of the other State.

(6) Where a dispute is submitted to the International Court of Justice pursuant to paragraph (2), proceedings shall ber suspended pending the judgment of the International Court of Justice.

Article 24—Other Disputes

Any dispute between two or more States Parties concerning the interpretation or application of this Convention (other than a dispute to which article 23 applies) which is not settled by negotiation shall be submitted to the International Court of Justice o the application of one of the Parties to the dispute or by special agreement unless the parties agree on a different method of peaceful settlement of the dispute.

[FR Doc. 93-7276. Filed 3/29/93; 8::45 am]
BILLING CODE 4710-06-M

Appendix 8[1]
FOREIGN SOVEREIGN IMMUNITIES ACT

§ 1330. Actions against foreign states

(a) The district courts shall have original jurisdiction without regard to amount in controversy of any nonjury civil action against a foreign state as defined in section 1603(a) of this title as to any claim for relief in personam with respect to which the foreign state is not entitled to immunity either-under sections 1605-1607 of this title or under any applicable international agreement.

(b) Personal jurisdiction over a foreign state shall exist as to every claim for relief over which the district courts have jurisdiction under subsection (a) where service has been made under section 1608 of this title.

(c) For purposes of subsection (b), an appearance by a foreign state does not confer personal jurisdiction with respect to any claim for relief not arising out of any transaction or occurrence enumerated in sections 1605-1607 of this title.

§ 1332. Diversity of citizenship; amount in controversy; costs

(a) The district courts shall have original jurisdiction of all civil actions where the matter in controversy exceeds the sum or value of $75,000, exclusive of interest and costs, and is between—

(1) citizens of different States;

(2) citizens of a State and citizens or subjects of a foreign state;

(3) citizens of different States and in which citizens or subjects of a foreign state are additional parties; and

(4) a foreign state, defined in section 1603(a) of this title, as plaintiff and citizens of a State or of different States.

For the purposes of this section, section 1335, and section 1441, an alien admitted to the United States for permanent residence shall be deemed a citizen of the State in which such alien is domiciled.

(b) Except when express provision therefor is otherwise made in a statute of the United States, where the plaintiff who files the case originally in the Federal courts is finally adjudged to be entitled to recover less than the sum or value of $75,000, computed without regard to any setoff or counterclaim to which the defendant may be adjudged to be entitled, and exclusive of interest and costs, the district court may deny costs to the plaintiff and, in addition, may impose costs on the plaintiff.

(c) For the purposes of this section and section 1441 of this title—

(1) a corporation shall be deemed to be a citizen of any State by which it has been incorporated and of the State where it has its principal place of business, except that in any direct action against the insurer of a policy or contract of liability insurance, whether incorporated or unincorporated, to which action the insured is not joined as a party-defendant, such insurer shall be deemed a citizen of the State of which the insured is a citizen, as well as of any State by which the insurer has been incorporated and of the State where it has its principal place of business; and

(2) the legal representative of the estate of a decedent shall be deemed to be a citizen only of the same State as the decedent, and the legal representative of an infant or incompetent shall be deemed to be a citizen only of the same State as the infant or incompetent.

(d) The word "States", as used in this section, includes the Territories, the District of Columbia, and the Commonwealth of Puerto Rico.

§ 1391. Venue generally

(f) A civil action against a foreign state as defined in section 1603(a) of this title may be brought-

(1) in any judicial district in which a substantial part of the events or omissions giving rise to the claim occurred, or a substantial part of property that is the subject of the action is situated,

(2) in any judicial district in which the vessel or cargo of a foreign state is situated, if the claim is asserted under section 1605(b) of this title;

(3) in any judicial district in which the agency or instrumentality is licensed to do business or is doing business, if the action is brought against an agency or instrumentality of a foreign state as defined in section 1603(b) of this title; or

(4) in the United States District Court for the District of Columbia if the.action is brought against a foreign state or political subdivision thereof.

§ 1441. Actions removable generally

(d) Any civil action brought in a State court against a foreign state as defined in section 1603(a) of this title may be removed by the foreign state to the district court of the United States for the district and division embracing the place where such action is pending. Upon removal the action shall be tried by the court without jury. Where removal is based upon this subsection, the time limitations of section 1445(b) of this chapter may be enlarged at any time for cause shown.

§ 1602. Findings and declaration of purpose

The Congress finds that the determination of United States courts of the claims of foreign states to immunity from the jurisdiction of such courts would serve the interests of justice and would protect the rights of both foreign states and litigants in United States courts. Under international law, states are not immune from the jurisdiction of foreign courts insofar as their commercial activities are concerned, and their commercial property may be levied upon for the satisfaction of judgments rendered against them in connection with their commercial activities. Claims of foreign states to immunity should henceforth be decided by courts of the United States and of the States in conformity with the principles set forth in this chapter.

§ 1603. Definitions

For purposes of this chapter—

(a) A "foreign state", except as used in section 1608 of this title, includes a political subdivision of a foreign state or an agency or instrumentality of a foreign state as defined in subsection (b).

(b) An "agency or instrumentality of a foreign state" means any entity–

(1) which is a separate legal person, corporate or otherwise, and

(2) which is an organ of a foreign state or political subdivision thereof, or a majority of whose shares or other ownership interest is owned by a foreign state or political subdivision thereof, and

(3) which is neither a citizen of a State of the United States as defined in section 1332(c) and (d) of this title, nor created under the laws of any third country.

(c) The "United States" includes all territory and waters, continental or insular, subject to the jurisdiction of the United States.

(d) A "commercial activity" means either a regular course of commercial conduct or a particular commercial transaction or act. The commercial character of an activity shall be determined by reference to the nature of the course of conduct or particular transaction or act, rather than by reference to its purpose.

(e) A "commercial activity carried on in the United States by a foreign state" means commercial activity carried on by such state and having substantial contact with the United States.

§ 1604. Immunity of a foreign state from jurisdiction

Subject to existing international agreements to which the United States is a party at the time of enactment of this Act a foreign state shall be immune from the jurisdiction of the courts of the United States and of the States except as provided in sections 1605 to 1607 of this chapter.

§ 1605. General exceptions to the jurisdictional immunity of a foreign state

(a) A foreign state shall not be immune from the jurisdiction of courts of the United States or of the States in any case—

(1) in which the foreign state has waived its immunity either explicitly or by implication, notwithstanding any withdrawal of the waiver which the foreign state may purport to effect except in accordance with the terms of the waiver;

(2) in which the action is based upon a commercial activity carried on in the United States by the foreign state; or upon an act performed in the United States in connection with a commercial activity of the foreign state elsewhere; or upon an act outside the territory of the United States in connection with a commercial activity of the foreign state elsewhere and that act causes a direct effect in the United States;

(3) in which rights in property taken in violation of international law are in issue and that property or any property exchanged for such property is present in the United States in connection with a commercial activity carried on in the United States by the foreign state; or that property or any property exchanged for such property is owned or operated by an agency or instrumentality of the foreign state and that agency or instrumentality is engaged in a commercial activity in the United States;

(4) in which rights in property in the United States acquired by succession or gift or rights in immovable property situated in the United States are in issue;

(5) not otherwise encompassed in paragraph (2) above, in which money damages are sought against a foreign state for personal injury or death, or damage to or loss of property, occurring in the United States and caused by the tortious act or omission of that foreign state or of any official or employee of that foreign state while acting within the scope of his office or employment; except this paragraph shall not apply to—

(A) any claim based upon the exercise or performance or the failure to exercise or perform a discretionary function regardless of whether the discretion be abused, or

(B) any claim arising out of malicious prosecution, abuse of process, libel, slander, misrepresentation, deceit, or interference with contract rights;

(6) in which the action is brought, either to enforce an agreement made by the foreign state with or for the benefit of a private party to submit to arbitration all or any differences which have arisen or which may arise between the parties with respect to a defined legal relationship, whether contractual or not, concerning a subject matter capable of settlement by arbitration under the laws of the United States, or to confirm an award made pursuant to such

an agreement to arbitrate, if (A) the arbitration takes place or is intended to take place in the United States, (B) the agreement or award is or may be governed by a treaty or other international agreement in force for the United States calling for the recognition and enforcement of arbitral awards, (C) the underlying claim, save for the agreement to arbitrate, could have been brought in a United States court under this section or section 1607, or (D) paragraph (1) of this subsection is otherwise applicable; or

(7) not otherwise covered by paragraph (2), in which money damages are sought against a foreign state for personal injury or death that was caused by an act of torture, extrajudicial killing, aircraft sabotage, hostage taking, or the provision of material support or resources (as defined in section 2339A of title 18) for such an act if such act or provision of material support is engaged in by an official, employee, or agent of such foreign state while acting within the scope of his or her office, employment, or agency, except that the court shall decline to hear a claim under this paragraph—

(A) if the foreign state was not designated as a state sponsor of terrorism under section 6(j) of the Export Administration Act of 1979 (50 U.S.C. App. 2405(j)) or section 620A of the Foreign Assistance Act of 1961 22 U.S.C. 2371) at the time the act occurred, unless later so designated as a result of such act; and

(B) even if the foreign state is or was so designated, if—

(i) the act occurred in the foreign state against which the claim has been brought and the claimant has not afforded the foreign state a reasonable opportunity to arbitrate the claim in accordance with accepted international rules of arbitration; or

(ii) neither the claimant nor the victim was a national of the United States (as that term is defined in section 101(a)(22) of the Immigration and Nationality Act) when the act upon which the claim is based occurred.

(b) A foreign state shall not be immune from the jurisdiction of the courts of the United States in any case in which a suit in admiralty is brought to enforce a maritime lien against a vessel or cargo of the foreign state, which maritime lien is based upon a commercial activity of the foreign state: Provided, That—

(1) notice of the suit is given by delivery of a copy of the summons and of the complaint to the person, or his agent, having possession of the vessel or cargo against which the maritime lien is asserted; and if the vessel or cargo is arrested pursuant to process obtained on behalf of the party bringing the suit, the service of process of arrest shall be deemed to constitute valid delivery of such notice, but the party bringing the suit shall be liable for any damages sustained by the foreign state as a result of the arrest if the party bringing the suit had actual or constructive knowledge that the vessel or cargo of a foreign state was involved; and

(2) notice to the foreign state of the commencement of suit as provided in section 1608 of this title is initiated within ten days either of the delivery of notice as provided in paragraph (1) of this subsection or, in the case of a party who was unaware that the vessel or cargo of a foreign state was involved, of the date such party determined the existence of the foreign state's interest.

(c) Whenever notice is delivered under subsection (b)(1), the suit to enforce a maritime lien shall thereafter proceed and shall be heard and determined according to the principles of law and rules of practice of suits in rem whenever it appears that, had the vessel been privately owned and possessed, a suit in rem might have been maintained. A decree against the foreign state may include costs of the suit and, if the decree is for a money judgment, interest as ordered by the court, except that the court may not award judgment against the foreign state in an amount greater than the value of the vessel or cargo upon which the maritime lien arose. Such value shall be determined as of the time notice is served under subsection (b)(1). Decrees shall be subject to appeal and revision as provided in other cases of admiralty and maritime jurisdiction. Nothing shall preclude the plaintiff in any proper case from seeking relief in personam in the same action brought to enforce a maritime lien as provided in this section.

(d) A foreign state shall not be immune from the jurisdiction of the courts of the United States in any action brought to foreclose a preferred mortgage, as defined in the Ship Mortgage Act, 1920 (46 U.S.C. 911 and following). Such action shall be brought, heard, and determined in accordance with the provisions of that Act and in accordance with the principles of law and rules of practice of suits in rem, whenever it appears that had the vessel been privately owned and possessed a suit in rem might have been maintained. A decree against the foreign state may include costs of the suit and, if the decree is for a money judgment, interest as ordered by the court, except that the court may not award judgment against the foreign state in an amount greater than the value of the vessel or cargo upon which the maritime lien arose. Such value shall be determined as of the time notice is served under subsection (b)(1). Decrees shall be subject to appeal and revision as provided in other cases of admiralty and maritime jurisdiction. Nothing shall preclude the plaintiff in any proper case from seeking relief in personam in the same action brought to enforce a maritime lien as provided in this section.

(e) For purposes of paragraph (7) of subsection (a)—

(1) the terms "torture" and "extrajudicial killing" have the meaning given those terms in section 3 of the Torture Victim Protection Act of 1991;

(2) the term "hostage taking" has the meaning given that term in Article 1 of the International Convention Against the Taking of Hostages; and

(3) the term "aircraft sabotage" has the meaning given that term in Article 1 of the Convention for the Suppression of Unlawful Acts Against the Safety of Civil Aviation.

(f) No action shall be maintained under subsection (a)(7) unless the action is commenced not later than 10 years after the date on which the cause of action arose. All principles of equitable tolling, including the period during which the foreign state was immune from suit, shall apply in calculating this limitation period.

(g) Limitation on discovery.—

(1) In general.—

(A) Subject to paragraph (2), if an action is filed that would otherwise be barred by section 1604, but for subsection (a)(7), the court, upon request of the Attorney General, shall stay any request, demand, or order for discovery on the United States that the Attorney General certifies would significantly interfere with a criminal investigation or prosecution, or a national security operation, related to the incident that gave rise to the cause of action, until such time as the Attorney General advises the court that such request, demand, or order will no longer so interfere.

(B) A stay under this paragraph shall be in effect during the 12-month period beginning on the date on which the court issues the order to stay discovery. The court shall renew the order to stay discovery for additional 12-month periods upon motion by the United States if the Attorney General certifies that discovery would significantly interfere with a criminal investigation or prosecution, or a national security operation, related to the incident that gave rise to the cause of action.

(2) Sunset.—

(A) Subject to subparagraph (B), no stay shall be granted or continued in effect under paragraph (1) after the date that is 10 years after the date on which the incident that gave rise to the cause of action occurred.

(B) After the period referred to in subparagraph (A), the court, upon request of the Attorney General, may stay any request, demand, or order for discovery on the United States that the court finds a substantial likelihood would—

(i) create a serious threat of death or serious bodily injury to any person;

(ii) adversely affect the ability of the United States to work in cooperation with foreign and international law enforcement agencies in investigating violations of United States law; or

(iii) obstruct the criminal case related to the incident that gave rise to the cause of action or undermine the potential for a conviction in such case.

(3) Evaluation of evidence.—The court's evaluation of any request for a stay under this subsection filed by the Attorney General shall be conducted ex parte and in camera.

(4) Bar on motions to dismiss.—A stay of discovery under this subsection shall constitute a bar to the granting of a motion to dismiss under rules 12(b)(6) and 56 of the Federal Rules of Civil Procedure.

(5) Construction.—Nothing in this subsection shall prevent the United States from seeking protective orders or asserting privileges ordinarily available to the United States.

§ 1606. Extent of liability

As to any claim for relief with respect to which a foreign state is not entitled to immunity under section 1605 or 1607 of this chapter, the foreign state shall be liable in the same manner and to the same extent as a private individual under like circumstances; but a foreign state except for an agency or instrumentality thereof shall not be liable for punitive damages, except any action under section 1605(a)(7) or 1610(f); if, however, in any case wherein death was caused, the law of the place where the action or omission occurred provides, or has been construed to provide, for damages only punitive in nature, the foreign state shall be liable for actual or compensatory damages measured by the pecuniary injuries resulting from such death which were incurred by the persons for whose benefit the action was brought.

§ 1607. Counterclaims

In any action brought by a foreign state, or in which a foreign state intervenes, in a court of the United States or of a State, the foreign state shall not be accorded immunity with respect to any counterclaim—

(a) for which a foreign state would not be entitled to immunity under section 1605 of this chapter had such claim been brought in a separate action against the foreign state; or

(b) arising out of the transaction or occurrence that is the subject matter of the claim of the foreign state; or

(c) to the extent that the counterclaim does not seek relief exceeding in amount or differing in kind from that sought by the foreign state.

§ 1608. Service; time to answer; default

(a) Service in the courts of the United States and of the States shall be made upon a foreign state or political subdivision of a foreign state:

(1) by delivery of a copy of the summons and complaint in accordance with any special arrangement for service between the plaintiff and the foreign state or political subdivision; or

(2) if no special arrangement exists, by delivery of a copy of the summons and complaint in accordance with an applicable international convention on service of judicial documents; or

(3) if service cannot be made under paragraphs (1) or (2), by sending a copy of the summons and complaint and a notice of suit, together with a translation of each into the official language of the foreign state, by any form of mail requiring a signed receipt, to be addressed and dispatched by the clerk of the court to the head of the ministry of foreign affairs of the foreign state concerned, or

(4) if service cannot be made within 30 days under paragraph (3), by sending two copies of the summons and complaint and a notice of suit, together with a translation of each into the official language of the foreign state, by any form of mail requiring a signed receipt, to be addressed and dispatched by the clerk of the court to the Secretary of State in Washington, District of Columbia, to the attention of the Director of Special Consular Services—and the Secretary shall transmit one copy of the papers through diplomatic channels to the foreign state and shall send to the clerk of the court a certified copy of the diplomatic note indicating when the papers were transmitted.

As used in this subsection, a "notice of suit" shall mean a notice addressed to a foreign state and in a form prescribed by the Secretary of State by regulation.

(b) Service in the courts of the United States and of the States shall be made upon an agency or instrumentality of a foreign state:

(1) by delivery of a copy of the summons and complaint in accordance with any special arrangement for service between the plaintiff and the agency or instrumentality; or

(2) if no special arrangement exists, by delivery of a copy of the summons and complaint either to an officer, a managing or general agent, or to any other agent authorized by appointment or by law to receive service of process in the United States; or in accordance with an applicable international convention on service of judicial documents; or

(3) if service cannot be made under paragraphs (1) or (2), and if reasonably calculated to give actual notice, by delivery of a copy of the summons and complaint, together with a translation of each into the official language of the foreign state—

(A) as directed by an authority of the foreign state or political subdivision in response to a letter rogatory or request or

(B) by any form of mail requiring a signed receipt, to be addressed and dispatched by the clerk of the court to the agency or instrumentality to be served, or

(C) as directed by order of the court consistent with the law of the place where service is to be made.

(c) Service shall be deemed to have been made—

(1) in the case of service under subsection (a)(4), as of the date of transmittal indicated in the certified copy of the diplomatic note; and

(2) in any other case under this section, as of the date of receipt indicated in the certification, signed and returned postal receipt, or other proof of service applicable to the method of service employed.

(d) In any action brought in a court of the United States or of a State, a foreign state, a political subdivision thereof, or an agency or instrumentality of a foreign state shall serve an answer or other responsive pleading to the complaint within sixty days after service has been made under this section.

(e) No judgment by default shall be entered by a court of the United States or of a State against a foreign state, a political subdivision thereof, or an agency or instrumentality of a foreign state, unless the claimant establishes his claim or right to relief by evidence satisfactory to the court. A copy of any such default judgment shall be sent to the foreign state or political subdivision in the manner prescribed for service in this section.

§ 1609. Immunity from attachment and execution of property of a foreign state

Subject to existing international agreements to which the United States is a party at the time of enactment of this Act the property in the United States of a foreign state shall be immune from attachment arrest and execution except as provided in sections 1610 and 1611 of this chapter.

§ 1610. Exceptions to the immunity from attachment or execution

(a) The property in the United States of a foreign state, as defined in section 1603(a) of this chapter, used for a commercial activity in the United States, shall not be immune from attachment in aid of execution, or from execution, upon a judgment entered by a court of the United States or of a State after the effective date of this Act, if—

(1) the foreign state has waived its immunity from attachment in aid of execution or from execution either explicitly or by implication, notwithstanding any withdrawal of the waiver the foreign state may purport to effect except in accordance with the terms of the waiver, or

(2) the property is or was used for the commercial activity upon which the claim is based, or

(3) the execution relates to a judgment establishing rights in property which has been taken in violation of international law or which has been exchanged for property taken in violation of international law, or

(4) the execution relates to a judgment establishing rights in property–

(A) which is acquired by succession or gift, or

(B) which is immovable and situated in the United States: Provided, That such property is not used for purposes of maintaining a diplomatic or consular mission or the residence of the Chief of such mission, or

(5) the property consists of any contractual obligation or any proceeds from such a contractual obligation to indemnify or hold harmless the foreign state or its employees under a policy of automobile or other liability or casualty insurance covering the claim which merged into the judgment, or

(6) the judgment is based on an order confirming an arbitral award rendered against the foreign state, provided that attachment in aid of execution, or execution, would not be inconsistent with any provision in the arbitral agreement, or

(7) the judgment relates to a claim for which the foreign state is not immune under section 1605(a)(7), regardless of whether the property is or was involved with the act upon which the claim is based.

(b) In addition to subsection (a), any property in the United States of an agency or instrumentality of a foreign state engaged in commercial activity in the United States shall not be immune from attachment in aid of execution, or from execution, upon a judgment entered by a court of the United States or of a State after the effective date of this Act, if—

(1) the agency or instrumentality has waived its immunity from attachment in aid of execution or from execution either explicitly or implicitly, notwithstanding any withdrawal of the waiver the agency or instrumentality may purport to effect except in accordance with the terms of the waiver, or

(2) the judgment relates to a claim for which the agency or instrumentality is not immune by virtue of section 1605(a) (2), (3), (5), or (7) or 1605(b) of this chapter, regardless of whether the property is or was involved in the act upon which the claim is based.

(c) No attachment or execution referred to in subsections (a) and (b) of this section shall be permitted until the court has ordered such attachment and execution after having determined that a reasonable period of time has elapsed following the entry of judgment and the giving of any notice required under section 1608(e) of this chapter.

(d) The property of a foreign state, as defined in section 1603(a) of this chapter, used for a commercial activity in the United States, shall not be immune from attachment prior to the entry of judgment in any action brought in a court of the United States or of a State, or prior to the elapse of the period of time provided in subsection (c) of this section, if—

(1) the foreign state has explicitly waived its immunity from attachment prior to judgment, notwithstanding any withdrawal of the waiver the foreign state may purport to effect except in accordance with the terms of the waiver, and

(2) the purpose of the attachment is to secure satisfaction of a judgment that has been or may ultimately be entered against the foreign state, and not to obtain jurisdiction.

(e) The vessels of a foreign state shall not be immune from arrest in rem, interlocutory sale, and execution in actions brought to foreclose a preferred mortgage as provided in section 1605(d).

(f) (1) (A) Notwithstanding any other provision of law, including but not limited to section 208(f) of the Foreign Missions Act 22 U.S.C. 4308(f)), and except as provided in subparagraph (B), any property with respect to which financial transactions are prohibited or regulated pursuant to section 5(b) of the Trading with the Enemy Act (50 U.S.C. App. 5(b)), section 620(a) of the Foreign Assistance Act of 1961 22 U.S.C. §§ 2370(a)), sections 202 and 203 of the International Emergency Economic Powers Act 50 U.S.C. 1701-1702), or any other proclamation, order, regulation, or license issued pursuant thereto, shall be subject to execution or attachment in aid of execution of any judgment relating to a claim for which a foreign state (including any agency or instrumentality or such state) claiming such property is not immune under section 1605(a)(7).

(B) Subparagraph (A) shall not apply if, at the time the property is expropriated or seized by the foreign state, the property has been held in title by a natural person or, if held in trust, has been held for the benefit of a natural person or persons.

(2) (A) At the request of any party in whose favor a judgment has been issued with respect to a claim for which the foreign state is not immune under section 1605(a)(7), the Secretary of the Treasury and the Secretary of State should make every effort to fully, promptly, and effectively assist any judgment creditor or any court that has issued any such judgment in identifying, locating, and executing against the property of that foreign state or any agency or instrumentality of such state.

(B) In providing such assistance, the Secretaries—

(i) may provide such information to the court under seal; and

(ii) should make every effort to provide the information in a manner sufficient to allow the court to direct the United States Marshall's office to promptly and effectively execute against that property.

(3) Waiver.—The President may waive any provision of paragraph (1) in the interest of national security.

§ 1611. Certain types of property immune from execution

(a) Notwithstanding the provisions of section 1610 of this chapter, the property of those organizations designated by the President as being entitled to enjoy the privileges, exemptions, and immunities provided by the International Organizations Immunities Act shall not be subject to attachment or any other judicial process impeding the disbursement of funds to, or on the order of, a foreign state as the result of an action brought in the courts of the United States or of the States.

(b) Notwithstanding the provisions of section 1610 of this chapter, the property of a foreign state shall be immune from attachment and from execution if—

(1) the property is that of a foreign central bank or monetary authority held for its own account, unless such bank or authority, or its parent foreign government, has explicitly waived its immunity from attachment in aid of execution, or from execution, notwithstanding any withdrawal of the waiver which the bank, authority or government may purport to effect except in accordance with the terms of the waiver; or

(2) the property is, or is intended to be, used in connection with a military activity and

(A) is of a military character, or

(B) is under the control of a military authority or defense agency.

(c) Notwithstanding the provisions of section 1610 of this chapter, the property of a foreign state shall be immune from attachment and from execution in an action brought under section 302 of the Cuban Liberty and Democratic Solidarity (LIBERTAD) Act of 1996 to the extent that the property is a facility or installation used by an accredited diplomatic mission for official purposes.

Appendix 8[2]

FORM OF NOTICE OF SUIT UNDER THE FOREIGN SOVEREIGN IMMUNITIES ACT

* * *

22 C.F.R. § 93.2 *Notice of Suit (or of Default Judgment)*

(a) A Notice of Suit prescribed in section 1608(a) of Title 28, United States Code, shall be prepared in the form that appears in the Annex to this section.

(b) In preparing a Notice of Suit, a party shall in every instance supply the information specified in items 1 through 5 of the fom appearing in the Annex to this section. A party shall also supply information specified in item 6, if notice of a default judgment is being served.

(c) In supplying the information specified in item 5, a party shall in simplified language summarize the nature and purpose of the proceeding (including principal allegations and claimed bases of liability), the reasons why the foreign state or political subdivision has been named as a party in the proceeding, and the nature and amount of relief sought. The purpose of item 5 is to enable foreign officials unfamiliar with American legal documents to ascertain the above information.

(d) A party may attach additional pages to the Notice of Suit to complete information under any item.

(e) A party shall attach, as part of the Notice of Suit, a copy of the Foreign State Immunities Act of 1976 (Pub. L. 94-583; 90 Stat. 2891).

ANNEX

Notice of Suit (or of Default Judement)[1]

1. Title of legal proceeding; full name of court; case or docket number:

2. Name of foreign state (or political subdivision) concerned:

3. Identity of the other Parties:

Judicial Documents

4. Nature of documents served (e.g., Summons and Complaint; Default Judgment):

5. Nature and purpose of the proceedings; why the foreign state (or political subdivision) has been named; relief requested:

6. Date of default judgment (if any):

7. A response to a "Summons" and "Complaint" is required to be submitted to the court, not later than 60 days after these documents are received. The response may present jurisdictional defenses (including defenses relating to state immunity).

8. The failure to submit a timely response with the court can result in a Default Judgment and a request for execution to satisfy the judgment. If a default judgment has been entered, a procedure may be available to vacate or open that judgment.

9. Questions relating to state immunities and to the jurisdiction of United States courts over foreign states are governed by the Foreign Sovereign Immunities Act of 1976, which appears in sections 1330, 1391(f), 1441(d), and 1602 through 1611, of Title 28, United States Code (Pub. L. 94-583; 90 Stat. 2891).

---

[1] Relevant only if items 4 and 6 indicate that a default judgment has occurred.

Appendix 9[1]

HAGUE CONVENTION ABOLISHING THE REQUIREMENT OF LEGALIZATION FOR FOREIGN PUBLIC DOCUMENTS

MULTILATERAL

Judicial Procedure: Abolishing Requirement of Legalization for Foreign Public Document

Convention done at The Hague October 5, 1961;
Transmitted by the President of the United States of America to the Senate July 19, 1976 (S. Ex. L, 94th Cong., 2d Sess.);
Reported favorably by the Senate Committee on Foreign Relations November 20, 1979 (S. Ex. Rep. No. 96–17, 96th Cong., 1st Sess.);
Advice and consent to accession by the Senate November 28, 1979;
Accession approved by the President December 27, 1979;
Accession of the United States of America deposited with the Netherlands December 24, 1980;
Proclaimed by the President September 21, 1981;
Entered into force with respect to the United States of America October 15, 1981.

BY THE PRESIDENT OF THE UNITED STATES OF AMERICA

A PROCLAMATION

CONSIDERING THAT:

The Convention Abolishing the Requirement of Legalization for Foreign Public Documents was done at The Hague on October 5, 1961, a certified copy of which Convention, is hereto annexed;

The Senate of the United States of America by its resolution of November 28, 1979, two-thirds of the Senators present concurring therein, gave its advice and consent to the accession of the United States of America to the Convention;

On December 27, 1979, the President of the United States of America approved accession to the Convention;

The United States of America deposited its instrument of accession on December 24, 1980, in accordance with the provisions of the Convention;

The Convention will enter into force for the United States of America on October 15, 1981;

Now, THEREFORE, I, Ronald Reagan, President of the United States of America, proclaim and make public the Convention, to the end that it shall be observed and fulfilled with good faith on and after October 15, 1981, by the United States of America and by the citizens of the United States of America and all other persons subject to the jurisdiction thereof.

IN TESTIMONY WHEREOF, I have signed this proclamation and caused the Seal of the United States of America to be affixed.

DONE at the city of Washington this twenty-first day of September in the year of our Lord one thousand nine hundred [SEAL] eighty-one and of the Independence of the United States of America the two hundred sixth.

RONALD REAGAN

By the President:
WALTER J. STOESSEL JR.
Acting Secretary of State

CONVENTION SUPPRIMANT L'EXIGENCE DE LA LÉGALISATION DES ACTES PUBLICS ÉTRANGERS

Les Etats signataires de la présente Convention,

Désirant supprimer l'exigence de la légalisation diplomatique ou consulaire des actes publics étrangers,

Ont résolu de conclure une Convention à cet effet et sont convenus des dispositions suivantes:

Article premier

La présente Convention s'applique aux actes publics qui ont été établis sur le territoire d'un Etat contractant et qui doivent être produits sur le territoire d'un autre Etat contractant.

Sont considérés comme actes publics, au sens de la présente Convention:

a) les documents qui émanent d'une autorité ou d'un fonctionnaire relevant d'une juridiction de l'Etat, y compris ceux qui émanent du ministère public, d'un greffier ou d'un huissier de justice;

b) les documents administratifs;

c) les actes notariés;

d) les déclarations officielles telles que mentions d'enregistrement, visas pour date certaine et certifications de signature, apposées sur un acte sous seing privé.

Toutefois la présente Convention ne s'applique pas:

a) aux documents établis par des agents diplomatiques ou consulaires;

b) aux documents administratifs ayant trait directement à une opération commerciale ou douanière.

Article 2

Chacun des Etats contractants dispense de légalisation les actes auxquels s'applique la présente Convention et qui doivent être produits sur son territoire. La légalisation au sens de la présente Convention ne recouvre que la formalité par laquelle les agents diplomatiques ou consulaires du pays sur le territoire duquel l'acte doit être produit attestent la véracité de la signature, la qualité en laquelle le signataire de l'acte a agi et, le cas échéant, l'identité du sceau ou timbre dont cet acte est revêtu.

CONVENTION ABOLISHING THE REQUIREMENT OF LEGALISATION FOR FOREIGN PUBLIC DOCUMENTS

The States signatory to the present Convention,

Desiring to abolish the requirement of diplomatic or consular legalisation for foreign public documents,

Have resolved to conclude a Convention to this effect and have agreed upon the following provisions:

Article 1

The present Convention shall apply to public documents which have been executed in the territory of one contracting State and which have to be produced in the territory of another contracting State.

For the purposes of the present Convention, the following are deemed to be public documents:

a) documents emanating from an authority or an official connected with the courts or tribunals of the State, including those emanating from a public prosecutor, a clerk of a court or a process server ("huissier de justice");

b) administrative documents;

c) notarial acts;

d) official certificates which are placed on documents signed by persons in their private capacity, such as official certificates recording the registration of a document or the fact that it was in existence on a certain date and official and notarial authentications of signatures.

However, the present Convention shall not apply:

a) to documents executed by diplomatic or consular agents;

b) to administrative documents dealing directly with commercial or customs operations.

Article 2

Each contracting State shall exempt from legalisation documents to which the present Convention applies and which have to be produced in its territory. For the purposes of the present Convention, legalisation means only the formality by which the diplomatic or consular agents of the country in which the document has to be produced certify the authenticity of the signature, the capacity in which the person signing the document has acted and, where appropriate, the identity of the seal or stamp which it bears.

Article 3

La seule formalité qui puisse être exigée pour attester la véracité de la signature, la qualité en laquelle le signataire de l'acte a agi et, le cas échéant, l'identité du sceau ou timbre dont cet acte est revêtu, est l'apposition de l'apostille définie à l'article 4, délivrée par l'autorité compétente de l'Etat d'où émane le document.

Toutefois la formalité mentionnée à l'alinéa précédent ne peut être exigée lorsque soit les lois, règlements ou usages en vigueur dans l'Etat où l'acte est produit, soit une entente entre deux ou plusieurs Etats contractants l'écartent, la simplifient ou dispensent l'acte de légalisation.

Article 4

L'apostille prevue à l'article 3, alinéa premier, est apposée sur l'acte lui-même ou sur une allonge; elle doit être conforme au modèle annexé à la présente Convention.

Toutefois elle peut être rédigée dans la langue officielle de l'autorité qui la délivre. Les mentions qui y figurent peuvent également être données dans une deuxième langue. Le titre „Apostille (Convention de La Haye du 5 octobre 1961)" devra être mentionné en langue française.

Article 5

L'apostille est délivrée à la requête du signataire ou de tout porteur de l'acte.

Dûment remplie, elle atteste la véracité de la signature, la qualité en laquelle le signataire de l'acte a agi et, le cas échéant, l'identité du sceau ou timbre dont cet acte est revêtu.

La signature, le sceau ou timbre qui figurent sur l'apostille sont dispensés de toute attestation.

Article 6

Chaque Etat contractant désignera les autorités prises ès qualités, auxquelles est attribuée compétence pour délivrer l'apostille prévue à l'article 3, alinéa premier.

Il notifiera cette désignation au Ministère des Affaires Etrangères des Pays-Bas au moment du dépôt de son instrument de ratification ou d'adhésion ou de sa déclaration d'extension. Il lui notifiera aussi toute modification dans la désignation de ces autorités.

Article 7

Chacune des autorités désignées conformément à l'article 6 doit tenir un registre ou fichier dans lequel elle prend note des apostilles délivrées en indiquant:

a) le numéro d'ordre et la date de l'apostille,

b) le nom du signataire de l'acte public et la qualité en laquelle il a agi, ou, pour les actes non signés, l'indication de l'autorité qui a apposé le sceau ou timbre.

A la demande de tout intéressé l'autorité qui a délivré l'apostille est tenue de vérifier si les inscriptions portées sur l'apostille correspondent à celles du registre ou du fichier.

Article 8

Lorsqu'il existe entre deux ou plusieurs Etats contractants un traité, une convention ou un accord, contenant des dispositions qui soumettent l'attestation de la signature, du sceau ou timbre à certaines formalités, la présente Convention n'y déroge que si lesdites formalités sont plus rigoureuses que celle prévue aux articles 3 et 4.

Article 9

Chaque Etat contractant prendra les mesures nécessaires pour éviter que ses agents diplomatiques ou consulaires ne procèdent à des légalisations dans les cas où la présente Convention en prescrit la dispense.

Article 10

La présente Convention est ouverte à la signature des Etats représentés à la Neuvième session de la Conférence de La Haye de droit international privé, ainsi qu'à celle de l'Irlande, de l'Islande, du Liechtenstein et de la Turquie.

Elle sera ratifiée et les instruments de ratification seront déposés auprès du Ministère des Affaires Etrangères des Pays-Bas.

Article 3

The only formality that may be required in order to certify the authenticity of the signature, the capacity in which the person signing the document has acted and, where appropriate, the identity of the seal or stamp which it bears, is the addition of the certificate described in Article 4, issued by the competent authority of the State from which the document emanates.

However, the formality mentioned in the preceding paragraph cannot be required when either the laws, regulations, or practice in force in the State where the document is produced or an agreement between two or more contracting States have abolished or simplified it, or exempt the document itself from legalisation.

Article 4

The certificate referred to in the first paragraph of Article 3 shall be placed on the document itself or on an "allonge"; it shall be in the form of the model annexed to the present Convention.

It may, however, be drawn up in the official language of the authority which issues it. The standard terms appearing therein may be in a second language also. The title "Apostille (Convention de La Haye du 5 octobre 1961)" shall be in the French language.

Article 5

The certificate shall be issued at the request of the person who has signed the document or of any bearer.

When properly filled in, it will certify the authenticity of the signature, the capacity in which the person signing the document has acted and, where appropriate, the identity of the seal or stamp which the document bears.

The signature, seal and stamp on the certificate are exempt from all certification.

Article 6

Each contracting State shall designate by reference to their official function, the authorities who are competent to issue the certificate referred to in the first paragraph of Article 3.

It shall give notice of such designation to the Ministry of Foreign Affairs of the Netherlands at the time it deposits its instrument of ratification or of accession or its declaration of extension. It shall also give notice of any change in the designated authorities.

Article 7

Each of the authorities designated in accordance with Article 6 shall keep a register or card index in which it shall record the certificates issued, specifying:

a) the number and date of the certificate,

b) the name of the person signing the public document and the capacity in which he has acted, or in the case of unsigned documents, the name of the authority which has affixed the seal or stamp.

At the request of any interested person, the authority which has issued the certificate shall verify whether the particulars in the certificate correspond with those in the register or card index.

Article 8

When a treaty, convention or agreement between two or more contracting States contains provisions which subject the certification of a signature, seal or stamp to certain formalities, the present Convention will only override such provisions if those formalities are more rigorous than the formality referred to in Articles 3 and 4.

Article 9

Each contracting State shall take the necessary steps to prevent the performance of legalisations by its diplomatic or consular agents in cases where the present Convention provides for exemption.

Article 10

The present Convention shall be open for signature by the States represented at the Ninth session of the Hague Conference on Private International Law and Iceland, Ireland, Liechtenstein and Turkey.

It shall be ratified, and the instruments of ratification shall be deposited with the Ministry of Foreign Affairs of the Netherlands.

Article 11

La présente Convention entrera en vigueur le soixantième jour après le dépôt du troisième instrument de ratification prévu par l'article 10, alinéa 2.

La Convention entrera en vigueur, pour chaque Etat signataire ratifiant postérieurement, le soixantième jour après le dépôt de son instrument de ratification.

Article 12

Tout Etat non visé par l'article 10 pourra adhérer à la présente Convention après son entrée en vigueur en vertu de l'article 11, alinéa premier. L'instrument d'adhésion sera déposé auprès du Ministère des Affaires Etrangères des Pays-Bas.

L'adhésion n'aura d'effet que dans les rapports entre l'Etat adhérant et les Etats contractants qui n'auront pas élevé d'objection à son encontre dans les six mois après la réception de la notification prévue à l'article 15, litt. d). Une telle objection sera notifiée au Ministère des Affaires Etrangères des Pays-Bas.

La Convention entrera en vigueur, entre l'Etat adhérant et les Etats n'ayant pas élevé d'objection contre l'adhésion, le soixantième jour après l'expiration du délai de six mois mentionné à l'alinéa précédent.

Article 13

Tout Etat, au moment de la signature, de la ratification ou de l'adhésion, pourra déclarer que la présente Convention s'étendra à l'ensemble des territoires qu'il représente sur le plan international, ou à l'un ou plusieurs d'entre eux. Cette déclaration aura effet au moment de l'entrée en vigueur de la Convention pour ledit Etat.

Par la suite, toute extension de cette nature sera notifiée au Ministère des Affaires Etrangères des Pays-Bas.

Lorsque la déclaration d'extension sera faite par un Etat ayant signé et ratifié la Convention, celle-ci entrera en vigueur pour les territoires visés conformément aux dispositions de l'article 11. Lorsque la déclaration d'extension sera faite par un Etat ayant adhéré à la Convention, celle-ci entrera en vigueur pour les territoires visés conformément aux dispositions de l'article 12.

Article 14

La présente Convention aura une durée de cinq ans à partir de la date de son entrée en vigueur conformément à l'article 11, alinéa premier, même pour les Etats qui l'auront ratifiée ou y auront adhéré postérieurement.

La Convention sera renouvelée tacitement de cinq en cinq ans, sauf dénonciation.

La dénonciation sera, au moins six mois avant l'expiration du délai de cinq ans, notifiée au Ministère des Affaires Etrangères des Pays-Bas.

Elle pourra se limiter à certains des territoires auxquels s'applique la Convention.

La dénonciation n'aura d'effet qu'à l'égard de l'Etat qui l'aura notifiée. La Convention restera en vigueur pour les autres Etats contractants.

Article 15

Le Ministère des Affaires Etrangères des Pays-Bas notifiera aux Etats visés à l'article 10, ainsi qu'aux Etats qui auront adhéré conformément aux dispositions de l'article 12:

a) les notifications visées à l'article 6, alinéa 2;

b) les signatures et ratifications visées à l'article 10;

c) la date à laquelle la présente Convention entrera en vigueur conformément aux dispositions de l'article 11, alinéa premier;

d) les adhésions et objections visées à l'article 12 et la date à laquelle les adhésions auront effet;

e) les extensions visées à l'article 13 et la date à laquelle elles auront effet;

f) les dénonciations visées à l'article 14, alinéa 3.

En foi de quoi, les soussignés, dûment autorisés, ont signé la présente Convention.

Fait à La Haye, le 5 octobre 1961, en français et en anglais, le texte français faisant foi en cas de divergence entre les textes, en un seul exemplaire, qui sera déposé dans les archives du Gouvernement des Pays-Bas et dont

Article 11

The present Convention shall enter into force on the sixtieth day after the deposit of the third instrument of ratification referred to in the second paragraph of Article 10.

The Convention shall enter into force for each signatory State which ratifies subsequently on the sixtieth day after the deposit of its instrument of ratification.

Article 12

Any State not referred to in Article 10 may accede to the present Convention after it has entered into force in accordance with the first paragraph of Article 11. The instrument of accession shall be deposited with the Ministry of Foreign Affairs of the Netherlands.

Such accession shall have effect only as regards the relations between the acceding State and those contracting States which have not raised an objection to its accession in the six months after the receipt of the notification referred to in sub-paragraph d) of Article 15. Any such objection shall be notified to the Ministry of Foreign Affairs of the Netherlands.

The Convention shall enter into force as between the acceding State and the States which have raised no objection to its accession on the sixtieth day after the expiry of the period of six months mentioned in the preceding paragraph.

Article 13

Any State may, at the time of signature, ratification or accession, declare that the present Convention shall extend to all the territories for the international relations of which it is responsible, or to one or more of them. Such a declaration shall take effect on the date of entry into force of the Convention for the State concerned.

At any time thereafter, such extensions shall be notified to the Ministry of Foreign Affairs of the Netherlands.

When the declaration of extension is made by a State which has signed and ratified, the Convention shall enter into force for the territories concerned in accordance with Article 11. When the declaration of extension is made by a State which has acceded, the Convention shall enter into force for the territories concerned in accordance with Article 12.

Article 14

The present Convention shall remain in force for five years from the date of its entry into force in accordance with the first paragraph of Article 11, even for States which have ratified it or acceded to it subsequently.

If there has been no denunciation, the Convention shall be renewed tacitly every five years.

Any denunciation shall be notified to the Ministry of Foreign Affairs of the Netherlands at least six months before the end of the five year period.

It may be limited to certain of the territories to which the Convention applies.

The denunciation will only have effect as regards the State which has notified it. The Convention shall remain in force for the other contracting States.

Article 15

The Ministry of Foreign Affairs of the Netherlands shall give notice to the States referred to in Article 10, and to the States which have acceded in accordance with Article 12, of the following:

a) the notifications referred to in the second paragraph of Article 6;

b) the signatures and ratifications referred to in Article 10;

c) the date on which the present Convention enters into force in accordance with the first paragraph of Article 11;

d) the accessions and objections referred to in Article 12 and the date on which such accessions take effect;

e) the extensions referred to in Article 13 and the date on which they take effect;

f) the denunciations referred to in the third paragraph of Article 14.

In witness whereof the undersigned, being duly authorised thereto, have signed the present Convention.

Done at The Hague the 5th October 1961, in French and in English, the French text prevailing in case of divergence between the two texts, in a single copy which shall be deposited in the archives of the Government of

une copie certifiée conforme sera remise, par la voie diplomatique, à chacun des Etats représentés à la Neuvième session de la Conférence de La Haye de droit international privé, ainsi qu'à l'Irlande, à l'Islande, au Liechtenstein et à la Turquie.

Pour la République Fédérale d'Allemagne,
For the Federal Republic of Germany,

(s.) Dr. J. LONS

Pour l'Autriche,
For Austria,

(s.) Dr. GEORG AFUHS

Pour la Belgique,
For Belgium,

(s.) W. VAN CAUWENBERG
10 Maart 1970

Pour le Danemark,
For Denmark,

Pour l'Espagne,
For Spain,

Pour la Finlande,
For Finland,

(s.) H. v. KNORRING
le 13 mars 1962

Pour la France,
For France,

le 9 octobre 1961
(s.) ETIENNE COIDAN

Pour la Grèce,
For Greece,

(s.) P. A. VERYKIOS

Pour l'Irlande,
For Ireland,

Pour l'Islande,
For Iceland,

Pour l'Italie,
For Italy,

(s.) R. GIUSTINIANI
15 décembre 1961

the Netherlands, and of which a certified copy shall be sent, through the diplomatic channel, to each of the States represented at the Ninth session of the Hague Conference on Private International Law and also to Iceland, Ireland, Liechtenstein and Turkey.

Pour le Japon,
For Japan,

(s.) MASATO FUJISAKI
12 March 1970

Pour le Liechtenstein,
For Liechtenstein,

(s.) E. DE HALLER
18.IV.62

Pour le Luxembourg,
For Luxemburg,

(s.) J. KREMER

Pour la Norvège,
For Norway,

Pour les Pays-Bas,
For the Netherlands,

(s.) H.R. VAN HOUTEN
30-11-62

Pour le Portugal,
For Portugal,

(s.) CARLOS DE LIZ BRANQUINHO
20-8-65

Pour le Royaume-Uni de Grande-Bretagne et d'Irlande du Nord,
For the United Kingdom of Great Britain and Northern Ireland,

(s.) A.N. NOBLE
19th Oct. 1961

Pour la Suède,
For Sweden,

Pour la Suisse,
For Switzerland,

(s.) M. SCHERLER

Pour la Turquie,
For Turkey,

(s.) F. KEPENEK
8-5-962

Pour la Yougoslavie,
For Yougoslavia,

(s.) RADE LUKIĆ
(sous réserve de la ratification)

Appendix 9[2]

HAGUE CONVENTION ABOLISHING THE REQUIREMENT OF LEGALIZATION FOR FOREIGN PUBLIC DOCUMENTS

State Department Circular

DISCLAIMER: THE INFORMATION IN THIS CIRCULAR RELATING TO THE LEGAL REQUIREMENTS OF SPECIFIC FOREIGN COUNTRIES IS PROVIDED FOR GENERAL INFORMATION ONLY. QUESTIONS INVOLVING INTERPRETATION OF SPECIFIC FOREIGN LAWS SHOULD BE ADDRESSED TO FOREIGN COUNSEL.

IN FORCE: ANDORRA, ANGOLA[1,8], ANGUILLA[7], ANTIGUA AND BARBUDA, ARGENTINA, ARMENIA[2,3], ARUBA[6], AUSTRALIA, AUSTRIA, BAHAMAS, BARBADOS, BELARUS[2,3], BELGIUM, BELIZE, BERMUDA[7], BOSNIA-HERZEGOVINA[2,4], BOTSWANA, BRITISH ANTARCTIC TERRITORY[7], BRITISH VIRGIN ISLANDS[7], BRUNEI, CAYMAN ISLANDS[7], COMOROS ISLANDS (formerly Moroni)[1,5], CROATIA[2,4], CYPRUS, DJIBOUTI (formerly Affars and Issas)[1,5], DOMINICA[1,7], EL SALVADOR, FALKLAND ISLANDS[7], FIJI, FINLAND, FRANCE, FRENCH GUIANA[5], FRENCH POLYNESIA[5], GUADELOUPE[5], GERMANY, GIBRALTA[7], GREECE, GRENADA[1,7], GUERNSEY (Bailiwick of)[7], HONG KONG[7], HUNGARY, ISLE OF MAN[7], ISRAEL, ITALY, JAPAN, JERSEY (Bailiwick of)[7], KIRIBATI (formerly Gilbert Islands)[1,7], LATVIA, LESOTHO, LIBERIA[9], LIECHTENSTEIN, LUXEMBOURG, MACEDONIA[2,4], MALAWI, MALTA, MARSHALL ISLANDS, MARTINIQUE[5], MAURITIUS, MEXICO, MONTSERRAT[7], MOZAMBIQUE[1,8], NETHERLANDS, NETHERLANDS ANTILLES[6] (Curacao, Bonaire, St. Martin, St. Eustatius and Saba), NEW CALEDONIA[5], NORWAY, PANAMA, PORTUGAL, REUNION[5], RUSSIAN FEDERATION[2,3], ST. CHRISTOPHER (Kitts) AND NEVIS, ST. GEORGIA AND SOUTH SANDWICH ISLANDS[7], ST. HELENA[7], ST. LUCIA, ST. PIERRE AND MIQUELON[5], ST. VINCENT AND THE GRENADINES[7], SAN MARINO, SEYCHELLES, SLOVENIA[2,4], SOLOMON ISLANDS (formerly British Solomon Islands)[1,7], SOUTH AFRICA, SPAIN, SURINAME, SWAZILAND, SWITZERLAND, TONGA, TURKEY, TURKS AND CAICOS[7], TUVALU (formerly Ellice Islands)[1,7], UNITED KINGDOM, UNITED STATES, VANUATU (formerly New Hebrides)[1,5,7], WALLIS AND FUTUNA[5].

---

[1] This country achieved independence. No declaration has been made on the continuation in force of the Convention. We have requested the assistance of the Hague Conference on Private International Law in ascertaining from these countries whether they are applying the Convention.

[2] In accordance with Article 34(1) of the Vienna Convention on Succession of States in Respect of Treaties, the U.S. view is that when a country which is a party to a multilateral treaty or convention has dissolved, the successor state(s) inherit the treaty obligations of the former government, consistent with Article 34 of the Vienna Convention on Succession of States in Respect of Treaties. However, as a practical matter, the custom is for depositaries to expect a notice of succession to confirm that the new entity is performing its treaty obligations. Many newly independent states may not really be implementing such conventions at this time in that they may be performing the functions set forth in the Convention. We continue to work with these governments and the depositories to obtain confirmation that the respective successor state is complying with treaty obligations.

PURPOSE:

The Convention abolishes the requirement of diplomatic and consular legalization for public documents originating in one Convention country and intended for use in another. Documents issued in a Convention country which have been certified by a Convention apostille are entitled to recognition in any other Convention country without any further authentication. Such recognition is an obligation on the part of the United States to the other countries party to the Convention and the federal courts and state authorities have been alerted to this obligation. Consular officers in Convention countries are prohibited from placing a certification over the Convention apostille.

---

[3]On September 4, 1991, the Union of Soviet Socialist Republics (USSR) deposited an instrument of accession to the Convention. The Convention was to have entered into force for the USSR on April 1, 1992. Prior to that date, the USSR dissolved. Three members of the Newly Independent States (NIS), the Russian Federation, the Belarus Republic and Armenia have informed the depositary for the Convention that the Convention applies in those jurisdictions. We have requested the assistance of the Hague Conference on Private International Law in ascertaining from the other NIS countries whether they are applying the Convention. Even if other NIS countries were to consider the Convention to apply, it may not be operational. Each jurisdictions must designate an authority competent to issue the Convention certificate (apostille) before the Convention can be operational. It may be wise to have documents prepared for use in jurisdictions which have not yet designated an authority competent to affix the Convention apostille in two sets, one using the apostille and one using the chain authentication method, including the seal of the foreign embassy or consulate if possible. Local authorities in such jurisdictions may question the validity of the apostille due to lack of familiarity with the certificate.

In addition, the some states, for example, the Russian Federation, have declined to affix the Convention apostille to administrative or commercial documents. Such documents would have to be authenticated using the chain authentication method. See the Office of American Citizens Services general authentication flyer, available via the autofax at document #1046. See Questions for information about using the autofax service.

[4]Former Yugoslavia was a party to the Convention. Slovenia, Macedonia, Bosnia-Herzegovina and Croatia have informed the depositary that they consider the Convention to apply and have designated a competent authority to issue the Convention certificate (apostille). The names of the competent authorities designated by the remaining segments of former Yugoslavia (Serbia-Montenegro) continue to be listed in this flyer as a point of reference. See note 2 above.

[5]The Convention was extended to this territory, possession or other jurisdiction by France November 25, 1964, and a competent authority designated.

[6]The Convention was extended to this territory, possession or other jurisdiction by the Netherlands March 1, 1967, and a competent authority designated.

[7]The Convention was extended to this territory, possession or other jurisdiction by the United Kingdom February 24, 1965, and a competent authority designated October 17, 1968.

[8]The Convention was extended to this territory, possession or other jurisdiction by Portugal October 22, 1969, and competent authorities designated.

[9]The United States has declared that the Convention is not/not in force between the United States and Liberia.

WHAT ARE PUBLIC DOCUMENTS:

For the purposes of the Convention, public documents shall include:

(a) documents emanating from an authority or an official connected with the courts or tribunals of the state, including those emanating from a public prosecutor, a clerk of court or a process server;

(b) administrative documents;

(c) notarial acts; and(d) official certificates which are placed on documents signed by persons in their private capacity, such as official certificates recording the registration of a document or the fact that it was in existence on a certain date and official and notarial authentications of signatures.

CONVENTION APOSTILLE CERTIFICATE:

If you have a document which you want legalized for use in another Convention country, the Convention certification called an "apostille" must be affixed to the document by a competent authority. The apostille is a pre-printed form prescribed by the Convention.

PROCEDURE:

Since the authorities designated by the U.S. to affix the apostille can only attest to the validity of certain seals, it may be necessary for you to obtain some intermediate seals on your document, depending on the origin of the document, before the apostille can be affixed. There is no single U.S. competent authority to issue the Convention apostille. There are different authorities for documents originating in state and local jurisdictions, Federal courts and Federal government agencies. Contact the competent local authority who will affix the certification (apostille) on your document. There follows in appendix A (available in autofax form) of this flyer a chart which summarizes the process and a list of competent authorities. If it is necessary for you to obtain some intermediate seals on your document before obtaining the Convention apostille, consult the appropriate state or federal authority listed.

Hague "Apostille" Authentication Certificate:

Article 7 of the Convention provides for the use of a standardized authentication certificate called an "apostille". A sample apostille certificate is provided in Appendix B of this flyer. The apostille consists of the following: 1) name of country from which the document emanates; 2) name of person signing the document; 3) the capacity in which the person signing the document has acted; 4) in the case of unsigned documents, the name of the authority which has affixed the seal or stamp; 5) place of certification; 6) date of certification; 7) the authority issuing the certificate; 8) number of certificate; 9) seal or stamp of authority issuing certificate; 10) signature of authority issuing certificate.

Fees:

Fees charged by federal and state government authorities listed below were effective January 1, 1997. Please note that fees vary from state to state and are subject to change.

U.S. COMPETENT AUTHORITIES:

Origin of Document/Seal	Authority to Affix Apostille
Federal Executive and Administrative Agencies	Authentication Office, U.S. Department of State, 518 23rd St., N.W., Washington, D.C. 20520 (202) 647-5002 Fee: $5.00

For additional information, call the Federal Information Center: 1-800-688-9889, and choose option 6 after you press 1 for touch tone phones. Walk-in service is available from the Authentications Office from 8 a.m. to 12 noon Monday-Friday, except holidays. Walk-in service is limited to 15 documents per person per day (documents can be multiple pages). Processing time for authentication requests sent by mail is 5 working days or less. See also, the State Department Home Page: http://www.state.gov (Resources and Services) or http://www.state.gov/www/about state/infogen.html, page 5. See also in general, 22 C.F.R. 131.

U.S. Courts

Clerks and Deputy Clerks of the Federal Court System.
Fee: $5.00.

For the purposes of the Convention, clerks and deputy clerks of the U.S. Courts shall include the clerks and deputy clerks of the following: The Supreme Court of the United States, the Courts of Appeals for the First through the Eleventh Circuits and the District of Columbia Circuit, the United States District Courts, the United States Court of Claims, the United States Court of Customs and Patent Appeals, the United States Court of International Trade, the United States District Court for the District of the Canal Zone, the District Court of Guam, the District Court of the Virgin Islands, and the District Court for the Northern Mariana Islands.

States, Territories and Other Jurisdictions:

State Secretary of State or other counterpart (listed below)

STATE AUTHORITIES:

The following state authorities are authorized to issue the Convention "apostille" legalizing state documents:

Alabama:

Office of the Secretary of State, State Capitol, Bainbridge St., Montgomery, AL 36130, 334-242-7205. Fee: $5.00.

Designated Authority: Secretary of State

Alaska:

Lieutenant Governor, P.O. Box 110015, Juneau, AK 99811, 907-465-3509. Fee: $2.00.

Designated Authority: Lieutenant Governor; Attorney General; Clerk of the Supreme Court

Arizona:

Office of the Secretary of State, Public Services Department, 7th Floor, 1700 W. Washington, Phoenix, AZ 85007, 602 542-4086. Fee: $3.00.

Designated Authority: Secretary of State; Assistant Secretary of State.

Arkansas:

Office of Secretary of State, Notary Division, State Capitol, Little Rock, AR 72201-1094, 501-682-3409. Fee: $10.00.

Designated Authority: Secretary of State; Chief Deputy Secretary of State.

California:

Office of the Secretary of State, P.O. Box 942877, Sacramento, CA 94277-0001, 916-653-3595. Fee: $20.00.

Designated Authority: Secretary of State; any Assistant Secretary of State; any Deputy Secretary of State.

Colorado:

Office of Secretary of State, 1560 Broadway, Suite 200, Denver, CO 80202, 303-894-2680. Fee: By Mail: $2.00. While You Wait: $17.00.

Designated Authority: Secretary of State; Deputy Secretary of State.

Connecticut:

Office of the Secretary of State, Authentications, 30 Trinity St., Hartford, CT 06106, 203-566-5273. Fee: $20.00.

Designated Authority: Secretary of State; Deputy Secretary of State.

Delaware:

Office of Secretary of State, Notary Division, P.O. Box 898, Dover, DE 19903, 302-739-3077; 302-739-3756. Fee: $10.00.

Designated Authority: Secretary of State; Acting Secretary of State.

District of Columbia:

Office of the Secretary, D.C., Notary Commissions & Authentications Section, 717 14th St. N.W., Suite 230, Washington, D.C. 20005, 202-727-3117. Fee: $10.00.

Designated Authority: Executive Secretary; Assistant Executive Secretary; Mayor's Special Assistant and Assistant to the Executive Secretary; Secretary of the District of Columbia.

Florida:

Department of State, Bureau of Notaries Public, The Capitol Building, Suite 1801, Tallahassee, FL 32399-0250, 904-413-9732. Fee: $10.00.

Designated Authority: Secretary of State

Georgia:

Secretary of State, Notary Division, 2 Martin Luther King Drive, West Tower, Suite 820, Atlanta, GA 30334, 404-656-2899. Fee: $3.00.

Designated Authority: Secretary of State; Notary Public Division Director.

Hawaii:

Office of the Lieutenant Governor, Box 3226, Honolulu, HI 96802, 808-586-0255. Fee: $1.00.

Designated Authority: Lieutenant Governor of the State of Hawaii.

Idaho:

Office of Secretary of State, Box 83720, Boise, ID 83720, 208-334-2300. Fee: $10.00.

Designated Authority: Secretary of State; Chief Deputy Secretary of State; Deputy Secretary of State; Notary Public Clerk.

Illinois:

Office of the Secretary of State, Index Department, 111 E. Monroe St., Springfield, IL 62756, 217-782-0646. Fee: $2.00.

Designated Authority: Secretary of State; Assistant Secretary of State; Deputy Secretary of State.

Indiana:

Office of Secretary of State, Statehouse, Suite 201, Indianapolis, IN 46204, 317-232-6542. Fee: $0.50.

Designated Authority: Secretary of State; Deputy Secretary of State

Iowa:

Office of Secretary of State, Hoover Office Building, Second Floor, Des Moines, IA 50319, 515-281-5204. Fee: $5.00.

Designated Authority: Secretary of State; Deputy Secretary of State

Kansas:

Office of Secretary of State, State Capitol, Second Floor, Topeka, KS 66612, 913-296-2744. Fee: $5.00.

Designated Authority: Secretary of State; Assistant Secretary of State; any Deputy Assistant Secretary of State.

Kentucky:

Office of Secretary of State, Capitol Building, P.O. Box 718, Frankfort, KY 40602-0178, 502-564-7330. Fee: $5.00.

Designated Authority: Secretary of State; Assistant Secretary of State.

Louisiana:

Office of Secretary of State, P.O. Box 94125, Baton Rouge, LA 70804-9125, 504-342-4981. Fee: $5.00.

Designated Authority: Secretary of State.

Maine:

Office of Secretary of State, Bureau of Corporations, Elections and Commissions, Statehouse Station 101, Augusta, ME 04333, 207-287-3676. Fee: $10.00.

Designated Authority: Secretary of State; Deputy Secretary of State.

Maryland:

Office of Secretary of State, Statehouse, Annapolis, MD 21401, 410-974-5520. Fee: $5.00.

Designated Authority: Secretary of State.

Massachusetts:

Deputy Secretary of the Commonwealth for Public Records, Room 1719, Commissions, 1 Ashburton Place, Boston, MA 02108, 617-727-2795. Fee: $3.00.

Michigan:

Department of State, Office of the Great Seal, Lansing, MI 48918-1750, 517-373-2531. Fee: $1.00.

Designated Authority: Secretary of State; Deputy Secretary of State.

Minnesota:

Secretary of State's Office, 180 State Office Bldg., St. Paul, MN 55155, 612-297-9102. Fee: $5.00.

Designated Authority: Secretary of State; Deputy Secretary of State.

Mississippi:

Office of Secretary of State, P.O. Box 136, Jackson, MS 39205-0136, 601-359-1615. Fee: $5.00.

Designated Authority: Secretary of State; any Assistant Secretary of State.

Missouri:

Office of Secretary of State, Commission Division, P.O. Box 784, Jefferson City, MO 65102, 314-751-2336. Fee: $10.00.

Designated Authority: Secretary of State; Deputy Secretary of State.

Montana:

Office of Secretary of State, Room 225, Box 202801, State Capitol, Helena, MT 59602, 406-444-5379. Fee: $2.00.

Designated Authority: Secretary of State; Chief Deputy Secretary of State; Government Affairs Bureau Chief.

Nebraska:

Office of Secretary of State, Notary Division, Room 1303, Box 95104, State Capitol, Lincoln, NE 68509, 402-471-2558. Fee: $10.00.

Designated Authority: Secretary of State; Deputy Secretary of State.

Nevada:

Office of Secretary of State, State Capitol Complex, Carson City, NV 89710, 702-687-5203. Fee: $20.00.

Designated Authority: Secretary of State; Chief Deputy Secretary of State; Deputy Secretary of State.

New Hampshire:

Office of Secretary of State, Statehouse, Room 204, Concord, NH 03301, 603-271-3242. Fee: $5.00.

Designated Authority: Secretary of State; Deputy Secretary of State

New Jersey:

Department of State, Division of Commission Recording, Notary Section, CN 452, Trenton, NJ 08625, 609-530-6421. Fee: Regular Service: $25.00. Expedited Service: $35.00.

Designated Authority: Secretary of State; Assistant Secretary of State

New Mexico:

Office of the Secretary of State, State Capitol Building, Room 421, Santa Fe, NM 87503, 505-827-3600. Fee: $3.00.

Designated Authority: Secretary of State.

New York:

1. Upstate Counties: Miscellaneous Records, 162 Washington Ave., Albany, NY 12231, 518-474-4770. Fee: $10.00.

Designated Authority: Secretary of State; Executive Deputy Secretary of State; any Deputy Secretary of State; any Special Deputy Secretary of State.

2. Down State Counties: New York authorities in Albany advise that documents issued in the nine down state counties are authenticated under the Convention by the New York City office. The nine down state counties are New York, Kings, Queens, Bronx, Westchester, Nassau, Suffolk, Rockland and Richmond. The address of the New York Department of State, Certification Unit is 6th Floor, 270 Broadway, New York, New York 10007, tel: 212-417-5684. Fee: $10.00.

North Carolina:

Office of Secretary of State, Authentication Division, 300 N. Salisbury Street, Raleigh, N.C. 27603-5909, 919-733-4129. Fee: $6.25.

Designated Authority: Secretary of State; Deputy Secretary of State

North Dakota:

Office of Secretary of State, Capitol Building, Bismarck, ND 58505, 701-328-2900. Fee: $10.00.

Designated Authority: Secretary of State; Deputy Secretary of State.

Ohio:

Office of the Secretary of State, 30 East Broad St., 14th Fl., Columbus, OH 43266-0418, 614-466-2585. Fee: $5.00.

Designated Authority: Secretary of State; Assistant Secretary of State.

Oklahoma:

Office of Secretary of State, 2300 N. Lincoln, Room 101, Oklahoma City, OK 73105, 405-521-4211. Fee: $25.00 (cashiers check or money order).

Designated Authority: Secretary of State; Assistant Secretary of State; Budget Officer of the Secretary of State.

Oregon:

Office of Secretary of State, 255 Capitol St., Suite 151, Salem OR 97310, 503-986-2200. Fee: $10.00.

Designated Authority: Secretary of State; Deputy Secretary of State; Acting Secretary of State; Assistant to the Secretary of State.

Pennsylvania:

Department of State, Bureau of Commissions, Elections and Legislation, North Office Building, Room 304, Harrisburg, PA 17120, 717-787-5280. Fee: $15.00.

Designated Authority: Secretary of the Commonwealth; Executive Deputy Secretary of the Commonwealth.

Rhode Island:

Office of Secretary of State, Notary Division, 100 N. Main St., Providence, RI 02903, 401-277-1487. Fee: $5.00.

Designated Authority: Secretary of State; First Deputy Secretary of State; Second Deputy Secretary of State

South Carolina:

Office of Secretary of State, P.O. Box 11350, Columbia, SC 29211, 803-734-2119. Fee: $2.00.

Designated Authority: Secretary of State

South Dakota:

Office of Secretary of State, 500 East Capitol, Pierre, SD 57501-5077, 605-773-5004. Fee: $2.00.

Designated Authority: Secretary of State; Deputy Secretary of State

Tennessee:

Office of Secretary of State, James K. Polk Building, 18th Floor, Nashville, TN 37243-0306, 615-741-3699. Fee: $2.00.

Designated Authority: Secretary of State.

Texas:

Office of Secretary of State, P.O. Box 12079, Austin, TX 78711, 512-463-5705. Fee: $10.00.

Designated Authority: Secretary of State; Assistant Secretary of State

Utah:

Office of the Lieutenant Governor, State Capitol, Room 203, Salt Lake City, UT 84145-8414, 801-538-1040. Fee: Certifying Notary's Seal: $10.00. Apostille: $5.00.

Designated Authority: Lieutenant Governor; Deputy Lieutenant Governor; Administrative Assistant.

Vermont:

Office of Secretary of State, 109 State St., Montpelier, VT 05609-1103, 802-828-2308. Fee: $2.00.

Designated Authority: Secretary of State; Deputy Secretary of State.

Virginia:

Office of Secretary of Commonwealth, Authentications Division, P.O. Box 2454, Richmond, VA 23219, 804-786-2441. Fee: $10.00.

Designated Authority: Secretary of the Commonwealth; Chief Clerk, Office of the Secretary of Commonwealth.

Washington:

Department of Licensing, Business and Professions Division, Notary Section, P.O. Box 9027, Olympia, WA 98507-9027, 360-586-4575. Fee: $15.00.

Designated Authority: Secretary of State; Assistant Secretary of State; Director, Department of Licensing.

West Virginia:

Office of Secretary of State, 1900 Kanawha Blvd. East, Capitol Building, No. 157-K, Charleston, WV 25305-0770, 304-558-6000. Fee: $5.00.

Designated Authority: Secretary of State; Under Secretary of State; any Deputy Secretary of State.

Wisconsin:

Office of Secretary of State, P.O. Box 7848, Madison, WI 53707-7848, 608-266-5503. Fee: $5.00.

Designated Authority: Secretary of State; Assistant Secretary of State.

Wyoming:

Office of Secretary of State, The Capitol, Cheyenne, WY 82002-0020, 307-777-5342. Fee: $3.00.

Designated Authority: Secretary of State; Deputy Secretary of State.

American Samoa:

Office of the Governor, Pago Pago, AS 96799, 011-684-633-4116.

Designated Authority: Secretary of American Samoa; Attorney General of American Samoa.

Guam (Territory of):

Office of the Governor, P.O. Box 2950, Agana, GU 96910, 011-671-472-1537.

Designated Authority: Director, Department of Administration; Acting Director, Department of Administration; Deputy Director, Department of Administration; Acting Deputy Director, Department of Administration.

Northern Mariana Islands (Commonwealth of the):

Designated Authority: Attorney General; Acting Attorney General; Clerk of the Court, Commonwealth Trial Court; Deputy Clerk, Commonwealth Trial Court

Puerto Rico (Commonwealth of):

Office of the Secretary of State, Department of State, Box 3271, San Juan, PR 00902-3271, 809-723-4334.

Designated Authority: Under Secretary of State; Assistant Secretary of State for External Affairs; Assistant Secretary of State; Chief, Certifications Office; Director, Office of Protocol.

U.S. Virgin Islands:

Office of the Lieutenant Governor, 7 & 8 King St., Christiansted, St. Croix, USVI 00802, 809-774-2991. No authority designated; refer requests to the U.S. Department of State, Authentications Office, 2400 M St. N.W., Washington, D.C. 20520, (202) 647-5002.

FOREIGN COMPETENT AUTHORITIES:

If you want to have a document legalized in another Convention country for use in the United States, consult the following list of foreign authorities, or contact the nearest American embassy or consulate for the name of the competent local authority in that country who will affix the apostille. When the document is executed outside the United States and is intended for use in a non-Convention country, the American consular officer in the consular district in which the document was issued or executed can authenticate the document.

Andorra:

Unknown. The Convention entered into force for Andorra November 1, 1996.

Angola:

Unknown. Now Independent. No confirmation issued by newly independent country that Convention is deemed to apply. On October 22, 1969, Portugal extended Convention to Angola. Competent authority was declared to be the Governor General ("Les Gouverneurs generaux ("Governadores Gerais").

Anguilla:

Extended by the United Kingdom to Anguilla February 24, 1965. Competent authority declared October 17, 1968 The Governor of Anguilla

Antigua and Barbuda:

Antigua and Barbuda declared on May 1, 1985 that it considers itself bound by the Convention. On February 24, 1965 the Convention had been extended to Antigua by the United Kingdom. The effective date of accession to the Convention by Antigua and Barbuda is November 1, 1981, the date of independence.

a. Governor-General, Antigua-Barbuda

b. Registrar of the The High Court
High Street
St. John's, Antigua, West Indies
tel: 809-462-3147

Argentina:

Ministerio de Relaciones Exteriores y Culto, Reconquista 1088, 1003 Buenos Aires, Argentina

Armenia:

Ministry of Foreign Affairs and Ministry of Justice

Australia:

Secretary to the Department of Foreign Affairs and Trade of the Commonwealth

Austria:

1. Federal Ministry of Foreign Affairs (Bundesministerium fur auswartige Angelegenheiten;

2. The Presidents of any Civil Court of First Instances, with the exception of the Commercial Court (Handelsgericht) of Vienna and the Juvenile Court (Jugendgerichtshof) of Vienna, or their representatives authorized to issue the apostille;

3. The Governors of the Provinces (Landeshauptmanner);

4. Governments of the Provinces (Landesregierungen)

Bahamas:

Bahamas declared on April 30, 1976 that it considers itself bound by the Convention. On February 24. 1965, the Convention had been extended to the Bahamas by the United Kingdom. The effective date of the Bahamas accession to the Convention is July 10, 1973, the date of Bahamian independence.

1. Permanent Secretary, Ministry of Foreign Affairs.

2. Director General, Ministry of Foreign Affairs
3. Under Secretary, Ministry of Foreign Affairs
4. Senior Asst Secretary, Ministry of Foreign Affairs
5. Chief Executive Officer, Dept of Legal Affairs

Barbados:

By a note of August 1995 to the depositary, the Government of Barbados declared that it considers itself bound by the Convention which was applicable to its territory before it gained independence on November 30, 1966. On February 24, 1965, the Convention had been extended to Barbados by the United Kingdom.

1. Solicitor-General
2. Deputy Solicitor General
3. Registrar of the Supreme Court of Barbados Law Courts, Bridgetown, Barbados tel: 809-42-75537
4. The Permanent Secretary - Foreign Affairs, Ministry of Foreign Affairs, Tourism and International Transport
5. The Chief of Protocol, Ministry of Foreign Affairs, Tourism and International Transport

Belarus:

Ministry of Justice (judicial/court docs)

Ministry of National Education(educational docs)

Committee for Archives and Administration (state archives docs)

Ministry of Foreign Affairs (all other documents)

Belgium:

Ministry of Foreign Affairs, External Trade and Cooperation in Development (Ministere des Affaires Etrangeres, du Commerce exterieur et de la Cooperation au Developpement)

Belize:

Belize acceded to the Convention July 17, 1992. The Convention entered into force for Belize April 11, 1993.

The Registrar General

Bermuda:

On February 24, 1965, the Convention was extended to Bermuda by the United Kingdom. On October 17, 1968 a competent authority was declared.

The Governor and Commander-in-Chief of the Bermudas or Somers Islands or any member of his staff signing on his behalf and using his official seal

Bosnia-Herzegovina:

The Ministry of Justice and Administration of the Republic of Bosnia and Herzegovina

Botswana:

On September 16, 1968, Botswana, formerly Bechuanaland declared that it considers itself bound by the Convention. On February 24, 1965 the Convention was extended to Bechuanaland by the United Kingdom. The effective date of Botswana's accession is September 30, 1966, the date of independence.

1. Permanent Secretary;
2. Registrar of the High Court;
3. District Commissioner;
4. Any person appointed or empowered to hold a subordinate court of the first class;
5. Such other person as the President may appoint by notice in the Gazette

British Virgin Islands:

The Convention was extended to the BVI by the United Kingdom on February 24, 1965. On October 17, 1968 a competent authority was declared. The Governor of the Virgin Islands

Brunei:

Brunei acceded to the Convention February 23, 1987. The Convention entered into force for Brunei December 3, 1987.

Chief Registrar, Deputy Chief Registrar and Registrars of the Supreme Court of Brunei Darussalam;

Chief Magistrate, Magistrates and Registrars of subordinate Courts of Brunei Darussalam.

Cayman Islands:

Extended by the United Kingdom February 24, 1965. Competent authority declared October 17, 1968. The Governor of the Cayman Islands

Comoros Islands:

Now Independent. No formal confirmation that Convention is deemed to apply. When France extended its accession to the Convention to the Comoros Islands (Moroni), the competent authority to affix the Convention "apostille" certificate was the General Procecutor of the Republic at the High Court of Appeal at Moroni (le Procureur de la Republique pres le Tribunal Superieur d'appel de Moroni.)

Croatia:

Municipal courts or the Ministry of Justice and Administration of the Republic of Croatia

Cyprus:

Ministry of Justice of the Republic of Cyprus

Djibouti:

Unknown. Now Independent. No confirmation issued by newly independent country that Convention is deemed to apply. When France extended its accession to the Convention to the Affars and the Issas (now Djibouti), the competent authority to affix the Convention "apostille" certificate was the General Procecutor of the Republic at the High Court of Appeal at Djibouti (le Procureur de la Republique pres le Tribunal Superieur d'appel de Djibouti.)

Dominica:

Unknown. Now Independent. No confirmation issued by newly independent country that Convention is deemed to apply. The Convention was extended by the United Kingdom to Dominica on February 24, 1965.

El Salvador:

Ministry of Foreign Relations
General Directorate for the Foreign Service
Carretera a Santa Tecla, Km 6 1/2
San Salvador, El Salvador
tel: 503-243-3740/3776/3707
Cost: No Fee

Falkland Islands:

Extended by the United Kingdom to the Falkland Islands on February 24, 1965. Competent authority declared on October 17, 1968. The Governor of the Falkland Islands

Fiji:

Declared on March 29, 1971 that it considered itself bound by the Convention. On February 24, 1965, the Convention had been extended to Fiji by the United Kingdom. Fiji's accession to the Convention was effective October 10, 1970, the date of Fijian independence.

The Chief Registrar of the Supreme Court of Fiji

Finland:

The Notary Public of the Registry of each Jurisdictional District

France:

Departments in Europe and Overseas Departments (Guadeloupe, French Guiana, Martinique and Reunion): The General Prosecutors at the Courts of Appeal (Les Procureurs generaux pres les cours d' appel

French Overseas Territories:

New Caledonia: The General Prosecutor at the Court of Appeal of Noumea (le Procureur general pres la Cour d'appel de Noumea

Wallis and Futuna: The Judge of the Section of the Court of First Instance of Noumea at Mata Utu (le Juge de la Section du Tribunal de premiere instance de Noumea siegeant a Mata Utu)

French Polynesia: The Prosecutor of the Republic at the High Court of Appeal at Papeete (le Procureur de la Republique pres le Tribunal superieur d'appel de Papeete)

St. Pierre and Miquelon: The President of the High Court of Appeal of Saint-Pierre (le President du Tribunal Superieur d'appel de Saint-Pierre)

Germany, Federal Republic of:

(a) Federal Authorities:

1. Federal Administrative Office (Bundesverwaltungsamt in Koln); 2. President of the German Patent Office (Prasident des Deutschen Patentamtes)

(b) Authorities of the "Lander":

3. Minister of Justice (Ministerium (Senator) fur Justiz Land-, (Amts-) gerichtsprasident);

4. President of the Provincial Court (Landgerichtsprasident);

5. President of the District Court/Court of First Instance (Amtsgerichsprasident);

6. Minister of Home Affairs, Ministerium (Senator) fur Innere Regierungsprasident (Prasident des Verwaltungsbezirks);

7. Ministerium (Senator) fur Inneres Regierungsprasident (Prasident des Verwaltungsbezirks)

8. Head of the Provincial Government (Regierungsprasident);

9. Head of the Administrative District (Prasident des Verwaltungsbezirks)

With the reunification of Germany on October 3, 1990, Convention apostille certificates from the new federal Lander of Brandenburg, Mecklenburg-West Pomerania, Saxony, Saxony-Anhalt and Thuringia is the responsibility of the following Land authorities:

1. Minister of Justice, Die Ministerien fur Justiz sowie die Prasidenten der Langerichte (Bezirksgerichte)

2. Head of the Provincial Government, Die Ministerien fur Inneres sowie die Regierungsprasidenten (Bezirksregierungen) und das Landesverwaltungsamt (Thuringen)

3. Minister of Home Affairs, Die Ministerien fur Inneres;

4. Die Regierungsprasidenten (Bezirksregierungen), die Ministerien fur Justiz sowie d ie Prasidenten der Landgerichte (Bezirksgerichte)

Gibraltar:

Extended by the United Kingdom to Gibraltar on February 24, 1965. Competent authority declared on October 17, 1968. The Governor and Commander-in-Chief of the City and Garrison of Gibraltar

Greece:

The designated authority for legalization is the local nomarchy (department). Specifically, for Athens, administrative documents come from the Athens Nomarchy, Stadiou 29, Athens, Greece. All judicial documents, both penal and civil, as well as notarial deeds, are legalized by the local court of first instance, in the area where the decision or the notarial deed was issued.

Grenada:

Unknown. Now Independent. No confirmation issued by newly independent country that Convention is deemed to apply. The Convention was extended by the United Kingdom to Grenada on February 24, 1965.

Guyana:

Confirmation to U.S. Embassy in Georgetown, December, 1996 that Guyana considers itself bound by the Convention. On February 24, 1965, the Convention was extended to then British Guiana by the United Kingdom. Guyana achieved independence in 1966 and became a republic in 1970.

Legal Adviser, Ministry of Foreign Affairs
Takuba Lodge
254 South Road Bourda
Georgetown, Guyana
Tel: 011-592-2-54166 or 011-592-2-54151
Fax: 011-592-2-59192
Attn: Neveille Bissember

Guernsey:

Extended to Guernsey by the United Kingdom January 24, 1965. Competent authority declared January 17, 1968.

The Lieutenant Governor of the Bailiwick of Guernsey

Hong Kong:

Extended to Hong Kong by the United Kingdom February 24, 1965. Competent authority declared October 17, 1968. Governor of Hong Kong delegated authority 10/18/86 to the Registrar, Supreme Court; Deputy Registrar or Assistant Registrar, Supreme Court; and Deputy Chief Secretary, Supreme Court

Registrar
Hong Kong Supreme Court
38 Queensway
Hong Kong

tel: (852) 2825-4254

Hungary:

1. Minister of Justice regarding public documents and judicial documents;

2. Minister of Foreign Affairs regarding public documents and legalizations executed by other authorities

Israel:

1. Ministry of Foreign Affairs

2. Registrars of Magistrates Courts and Civil Servants appointed by the Minister of Justice under Notaries Law, 1976.

Italy:

1. The Public Prosecutor (I Procurators della Reppublica);

2. The Competent Prefetti (Heads) of the Territories for the Valley of Aosta; Il Presidente della Regione (The Head of the District for the Provinces of Trente and Bolzano; Il Commissario di Governo (The Commissioner of the Government)

Japan:

Ministry of Foreign Affairs
Authentications Division (Shomei-han)
2-1 Kasumigaseki 2-chome
Chiyoda Ku, Tokyo 100, Japan
Attn: Mr. Yamasaki.

Request an application for obtaining an apostille from the Ministry. The letter must include an explanation as to why you need this document. After you receive the application, you must complete it and send it back to the Japanese authority with the "original" document to be authenticated bearing the appropriate seal of the issuing authority. The "original" document must have been certified by the issuing office within the past six months. You should also send a photocopy of the document and a self addressed stamped envelope. You will receive the authenticated documents directly from the Ministry. There is no fee for this service. You may also contact the Japanese Embassy or Consulate in the U.S. nearest you for additional information.

Jersey:

Extended by the United Kingdom January 24, 1965. Competent authority declared October 17, 1968. The Lieutenant Governor of the Bailiwick of Jersey

Kiribati:

Unknown. Now Independent. No confirmation issued by newly independent country that Convention is deemed to apply. Convention extended to the Gilbert and Ellice Islands by the United Kingdom February 24, 1965.

Latvia:

The Ministry of Foreign Affairs, Consular Department
57 Elizbietes Street, Riga, LV 1510, Latvia
tel: 728-9505

Cost: $10.00 (for individuals, 10 day processing)
$20.00 (for individuals, one day service)
$20.00 (for organizations, 10 day processing)
$40.00 (for organizations, one day service)

Lesotho:

Extended by the United Kingdom to Basutoland on February 24, 1965. On April 24, 1972, Lesotho declared that it considers itself bound by the Convention. The effective date of Lesotho's accession is the date of independence, October 4, 1966.

1. The Attorney General;
2. The Permanent Secretary of a Ministry or Department;
3. The Registrar of the High Court;
4. A Resident Magistrate;
5. A Magistrate of the First Class;
6. By appointment of the Minister, noticed in Gazette

Liberia:

Convention Not in Force Between U.S. and Liberia as U.S. concluded Liberia cannot fulfill responsibilities of competent authority to issue Convention "apostille" at present.

Liechtenstein:

Office of the Government of the Prince at Vaduz

(Regierungskanzlei der furstlichen Regierung)

Luxembourg:

Ministry of Foreign Affairs (Ministere des Affaires Etrangeres)

Macao:

Extended to Macao by Portugal at the time of Portugal's accession to the Convention on October 22, 1969.

1. The Governor of Macau, Palacio do Governo, Av. da Praia Grande, Macau;

2. The Assistant Secretary for Justice of Macau, R. de S. Lourenco, Edificiodos Secretarios Adjuntos, 1 andar, Macau

3. The Head of the Justice Department of Macau Av. da Praia Grande, 594, Edificio BCM, 8 andar, Macau

Macedonia, the Former Yugoslav Republic of:

Ministry of Justice

Malawi:

Malawi acceded to the Convention February 24, 1967. The Convention entered into force for Malawi on December 2, 1967.

1. The Attorney General or the Solicitor General;

2. The Permanent Secretary of a Government Ministry;

3. The Registrar of the High Court;

4. The Registrar General;

5. A Government Agent;

6. A notary public;

7. A Resident Magistrate

Malta:

Ministry of Commonwealth and Foreign Affairs

Man, Isle of:

Extended by the United Kingdom on January 24, 1965. Competent Authority declared October 17, 1968. The Lieutenant Governor of the Isle of Man

Marshall Islands:

Acceded to the Convention November 18, 1991. The Convention entered into force for the RMI on August 14, 1992.

1. Minister of Foreign Affairs of the Marshall Islands;
2. Attorney General and Acting Attorney General;
3. Clerk and Deputy Clerk of the High Court;
4. Registrars and Deputy Registrars of Corporations;
5. Maritime Administrator and Special Agents thereof;
6. Commissioner and Deputy Commissioner of Maritime Affairs or Special Agents thereof.

Mauritius:

On December 20, 1968, Mautitius declared it considers itself bound by the Convention. On February 24, 1965, the Convention had been extended to Mauritius by the United Kingdom. The effective date of accession is March 12, 1968, the date of independence. In a note to the depositary dated September 17, 1973, Mauritius declared the competent authority is now:

The Permanent Secretary, or in his absence, A Principal Assistant Secretary of the Prime Minister's Office

Mexico:

A. Federal Documents

1. Direccion General de Gobierno
Bucareli No. 99, Planta Baja
06600 Mexico, D.F.

tel: 535-31-12; 535-43-92
fax: 535-26-88

2. Direccion de Coordinacion Politica
Con Los Poderes de la Union
Abraham Gonzalez No. 48, Planta Baja
06600 Mexico, D.F.

tel: 535-51-31
fax: 566-12-25

3. Subdireccion de Formalizacion Y Control
Abraham Gonzalez No. 48, Planta Baja
06600 Mexico, D.F.

tel: 535-53-84; 546-57-32
fax: 566-12-25

B. Secretaria De Gobernacion Directorio Representaciones de la Subsecretaria de Gobierno

BAJA CALIFORNIA:

Servicios Migratorios, Linea
Internacional, Agustin Melgar No. 1,
Col. Centro,
21100 Mexicali, B.C.

tel: 65-556665
fax: 65-529050

BAJA CALIFORNIA SUR:

Bravo No. 406, entre Aquiles Serdan y Guillermo Preito
23000 La Paz, B.C.S.

tel: 112-32083
fax: 112-32280

CAMPECHE:

Av. de las Palmas S/N junto al centro
Bizantino Bartimeo
24020 Campeche, Camp.

tel: 91-981-53150; 53186
fax: 91-981-53149

CHIAPAS:

Libramiento Norte S/N a un
costado de Esq. Pablo Guardado Chavez,
Tuxtla Gutierrez, Chis.

tel: 91-961-43288
fax: 91-961-899091

CHIHUAHUA:

Doblado y 3a No. 117
Despacho 2 y 3, Col. Centro,
3100 Chihuahua, Chih.
tel: 14-167499
fax: 14-370149

COAHUILA:

Victoria No. 406-1, Zona
Centro, 2500 Saltillo, Coah.

tel: 18-175506
fax: 18-175334; 178951

COLIMA:

Gabino Barrera No. 159-a,
Zona Centro, 28000 Colima, Col.

tel: 91-331-45912
fax: 91-331-45912

DURANGO:

Constitucion No. 210-1, Norte Altos,
Zona Centro, 34000, Durango, Dgo.

tel: 18-17506
fax: 18-178951

GUANAJUATO:

Agora del Baratillo Despacho 8,
Zona Centro, 36000 Guanajuato, Gto.

tel: 91-473-29446
fax: 91-473-29110; 29111

GUERRERO:

Av. Ignacio Ramirez No. 22-a
Col. Centro, 39000
Chilpancingo, Gro.

tel: 91-74-711772
fax: 91-74-721144

Calle Mina No. 120 Esq.
Morelos, Col. Centro, 39300
Acapulco, Gro.

tel: 91-74-828751
fax: 91-74-800341

HIDALGO:

Torre Coby, Art. 3 No. 97-7
piso, Fracc, Constitution, 42080 Pachuco, Hgo.

tel: 91-771-34026
fax: 91-771-34026

JALISCO:

Chesterton 184, Jardines Vallarta
45030 Guadalajara, Jal.

tel: 91-3-6732394
fax: 91-3-6732138

MEXICO:

Chaoco No. 703-8, Col. Sanchez
50140 Toluca, Mexico

tel: 91-72-134679
fax: 91-72-134768; 158325

MICHOACAN:

Av. Siervo de la Nacion S/N
Col. del Valle
58260 Morelia, Mich.

tel: 91-43-267

MORELOS:

Galeana No. 2-8 piso Edificio
Ocampo, Col. Centro, 62000
Cuernavaca, Mor.

tel: 91-73- 188594
fax: 91-73-188708

NAYARIT:

Zacatecas No. 16 sur 1 y 2
piso entre Allende y Abasolo
63000 Tepic, Nayarit

tel: 91-321-46269
fax: 91-321-46271

NUEVO LEON:

Zaragoza No. 1000 Sur,
Condominio Acero PH, 64000
Monterrey, N.L.

tel: 8-3403000
fax: 8-3403000

OAXACA:

Calzada de la Republica No. 402-B
Jalatlaco, 33606
Oaxaca, Oax.

tel: 91-951-42145
fax: 91-951-42145

PUEBLA:

Calla Italia No. 2224, Fracc.
Las Hadas entre 15 de mayo y
26 Pte., 72070 Puebla, Pue.

tel: 91-22-494082
fax: 91-22-494072

QUERETARO:

Boulevard Hernando Quintana
No. 168 Desp. 203 y 204
76050 Queretaro, Qro.

tel: 91-42-234960 or 91-42-234660
fax: 91-42-234960

QUINTANA ROO:

Av. Primo de Verdad No. 181
int. 1 Esp. Av. Heroes,
67000 Chetumal, Q. Roo

tel: 91-983-27347
fax: 91-983-22744

SAN LUIS POTOSI:

Av. Venustiano Carranza 707-402
Col. Centro 78250
San Luis Potosi, S.L.P.

tel: 91-48-144092
fax: 91-48-173988

SINALOA:

Lazaro Cardenas No. 913 Sur
Primer piso, Zona Centro
80129 Culiacan, Sin.

tel: 67-173988
fax: 67-173988

SONORA:

Blvd. Navarrete No. 125
Despacho 2, Edif. Sonmol.
Col. Valle Verde, 83200
Hermosillo, Son.

tel: 62-165044
fax: 62-165044

TABASCO:

Centro Admvo. Del Estado
Tabasco 2000, 86035
Villahermosa, Tab.

tel: 91-93-165152
fax: 91-93-165152

TAMAULIPAS:

Matamoros 11 y 12 No. 613
Cd. Victoria, Tamps.

tel: 131-20462
fax: 131-20462

TLAXCALA:

Kilometro 1 1/2 Carretera
federal Tlaxcala-Puebla S/N
90000 Tlaxcala, Tlax.

tel: 91-246-27147
fax: 91-246-27264

VERACRUZ:

Zaragoza No. 2 Esq. Miguel
Barragan, 91000 Xalapa, Ver.

tel: 91-28-189303
fax: 91-28-189395

YUCATAN:

Calle 51 No. 459 x 50, Zona
Centro, 97000 Merida, Yuc.
tel:
91-99-239142
91-99-239636
91-99-239671
91-99-240815

fax: 91-99-235535

ZACATECAS:

Calle Sabino No. 114 Fracc.
La Penuela, 98060 Zacatecas, Zac.

tel: 492-42318
fax: 492-42318

Montserrat:

Extended by the United Kingdom to Montserrat on February 24, 1965. Competent authority declared October 17, 1968: The Governor of Montserrat

Mozambique:

Unknown. Now Independent. No confirmation issued by newly independent country that Convention is deemed to apply. On October 22, 1969, Portugal extended the Convention to Mozambique. The competent authority was designated to be the Governor General ("Les Gouverneurs generaux ("Governadores Gerais")

Netherlands:

Kingdom in Europe: Registrars of the Courts of First Instance (Griffiers van de arrondissementsrechtbanken)

Netherlands Antilles:

Extended by the Netherlands March 1, 1967. Entered into force for the Netherlands Antilles April 30, 1967. Competent authority declared to be Lieutenant Governor of an Island or Group of Islands (Gezaghebber van het eilandgebied)

Curacao: the Lieutenant Governor of the Island of Curacao — has delegated his authority to: (1) the Head of the Births, Deaths and Marriages, Population and Electoral Registers of the island of Curacao, and (2) the acting Head of the Births, Deaths, Marriages, Population and Electoral Registers of the island of Curacao.

Aruba: the Head of the Births, Deaths and Marriages Register and the Population Register (het Hoofd van de Burgerlijke Stand en het Bevolkingsregister)

Nevis:

Extended by the United Kingdom February 24, 1965. Competent authority declared October 17, 1968. Now independent, Saint Kitts and Nevis (formerly Saint Christopher and Nevis) acceded to the Convention on February 26, 1994. The Convention entered into force on December 14, 1994.

1. The Attorney General.

2. The Solicitor General.

3. The Chief Secretary of the Office of the Prime Minister.

4. The Permanent Secretary in the Ministry of Foreign Affairs; or

5. The Registrar of the Supreme Court

And for the Island of Nevis, the competent authority shall be:

1. The Chief Secretary in the Office of the Premier.

2. The Legal Adviser in the Legal Department or

3. The Deputy Registrary of the Supreme Court.

Ministry of Legal Affairs
P.O. Box 186
Government Headquarters
St. Kitts-Nevis, West Indies

tel: 809-465-2521

Norway:

Royal Norwegian Ministry of Foreign Affairs;

the County Governors, namely:

Fylkesmannen i Oslo og Akershus
Postboks 8111 Dep.
N-0032 Oslo 1

tel: 02-42-90-85

Fylkesmannen i Ostfold
Postboks 325
N-1501 Moss

tel: 032-54-100

Fylkesmannen i Hedmark
Postboks 308
N-2301 Hamar

tel: 065-26-080

Fylkesmannen i Oppland
N-2600 Lillehammer

tel: 062-66-000

Fylkesmannen i Budkerud
N-3000 Drammen

tel: 03-83-81-50

Fylkesmannen i Vestfold
N-3100 Tonsberg

tel: 033-17-515

Fylkesmannen i Telemark
N-3700 Skien

tel: 03-52-70 20/52 82 74

Fylkesmannen i Aust-Agder
Postboks 55
N-4801 Arendal

tel: 041-25-860

Fylkesmannen i Vest-Agder
Tinghuset
N-4600 Kristiansand S

tel: 042-28-000

Fylkesmannen i Rogaland
Postboks 59
N-4001 Stavanger

tel: 04-52-70-60

Fylkesmannen i Hordaland
Postboks 106
N-5001 Bergen

tel: 05-23-70 00

Fylkesmannen i Sogn og Fjordane
N-5840 Hermansverk

tel: 056-55-000

Fylkesmannen i More og Romsdal
Fylkeshuset
N-6400 Molde

tel: 072-58 000

Fylkesmannen i Sor-Trondelag
N-7000 Trondheim

tel: 07-51-08 11

Fylkesmannen i Nord-Trondelag
N-7700 Steinkjer

tel: 077-66-722

Fylkesmannen i Nordland
N-8000 Bode

tel: 081-62-1000

Fylkesmannen i Troms
Postboks 595
N-9001 Tromso

tel: 083-87530

Fylkesmannen i Finnmark
N-9800 Vadso

tel: 085-51 761/53 001

Panama:

1. Concerning documents authorized by competent court authorities or officials, the Secretary of the Supreme Court or his legal substitutes;

2. Concerning deeds drawn up by a notary or private documents authenticated by a notary, the officials of the Department of Administrative Service of the Ministry of Justice;

3. Regarding documents issued by any central government bodies, any autonomous or semi-autonomous bodies, municipal or police authorities or a Public Ministry, the officials of the Consular and Legalization Department of the Ministry of Foreign Affairs;

4. Regarding all other public documents, any of the three preceeding procedures are allowed.

Portugal:

Applicable on entry into force to entire territory of the Republic of Portugal

Portugal: General Prosecutor of the Republic (Procurador General de Republica) and Prosecutors of the Republic at the Courts of Appeal (Procuradores da Republica junto dos Tribunals da Relacao)

Macau, territory of: see Macau

Angola and Mozambique: see Angola and Mozanbique

Other Overseas Departments: Les gouverneurs ("Governadores")

Russian Federation:

(1) Ministry of Justice (documents of organizations and institutions directly subordinate to the Ministry)

(2) Ministries of Justice of the Republics within the Russian Federation and judicial bodies of the administration of krais, regions and autonomous formations as well as of the towns of Moscow and St. Petersburg shall certify documents of judicial bodies subordinate to them and institutions and corresponding bodies of law of the republic, krai, region, district or town.

(3) Republican registry offices of the republics within the Russian Federation, central registry offices of krais, regions and districts as well as of the towns of Moscow and St. Petersburg shall certify certificates of civil status of the above-mentioned bodies or registry offices subordinate to them;

(4) The Department of documentary and reference work of the Archives Committee of the Russian Federation shall certify documents issued by the central state archives of Russia;

(5) Archives bodies of autonomous formations and archive departments of krais and regions shall certify documents issued by archives subordinate to them;

(6) The Department of Procurator General's Office of the Russian Federation shall certify documents made through the channels of the bodies of prosecution.

St. Christopher(St. Kitts):

Extended by the United Kingdom February 24, 1965. Competent authority declared October 17, 1968. Now independent, Saint Kitts and Nevis (formerly Saint Christopher and Nevis) acceded to the Convention on February 26, 1994. The Convention entered into force on December 14, 1994.

1. The Attorney General.

2. The Solicitor General.

3. The Chief Secretary of the Office of the Prime Minister.

4. The Permanent Secretary in the Ministry of Foreign Affairs; or

5. The Registrar of the Supreme Court

Ministry of Legal Affairs
P.O. Box 186
Government Headquarters
St. Kitts-Nevis, West Indies
Tel: 809-465-2521

St. Georgia and the South Sandwich Islands:

Competent authority declared by the United Kingdom October 17, 1968. The Commissioner for South Georgia and the South Sandwich Islands

Saint Helena:

Extended to Saint Helena by the United Kingdom February 24, 1965. Competent authority declared October 17, 1968. The Governor and Commander-in-Chief of the Island of St. Helena and its Dependencies

Saint Lucia:

Extended to Saint Lucia by the United Kingdom February 24, 1965. Achieved independence in 1979. Confirmation to U.S. Embassy in Bridgetown that country considers itself bound by Convention.

Registrar of the High Court
Registry Department
Peynier Street
Castries, St. Lucia, W.I.
tel: 809-452-1257

St. Vincent and the Grenadines:

Extended to Saint Vincent by the United Kingdom February 24, 1965. Achieved independence in 1979. Confirmation to U.S. Embassy in Bridgetown that country considers itself bound by Convention.

Ministry of Foreign Affairs
St. Vincent and the Grenadines
W.I.
tel: 809-456-1111

Ministry of Foreign Affairs forwards to Registrar's Office

San Marino:

Acceded to Convention May 26, 1994. Convention entered into force February 13, 1995.

1. The Minister for Foreign Affairs (Il Segretario di Stato per gli Affari Esteri della Repubblica di San Marino) or

2. a person delegated and officially authorized by him/her to sign and authenticate legal instruments and documents issued by the Department of Foreign Affairs and other of the Republic's public bodies.

Seychelles:

Extended by United Kingdom February 24, 1965. Achieved independence. Acceded to Convention June 9, 1978. Convention entered into force March 31, 1979.

The Registrar, Supreme Court, Victoria, Mahe

Slovenia, Republic of:

Ministry of Justice and Administration, Republic of Slovenia

Solomon Islands:

Unknown. Achieved independence 1978. No confirmation issued by country that Convention is deemed to apply. Extended to former British Solomon Islands Protectorate by United Kingdom February 24, 1965.

South Africa:

Acceded August 3, 1994. Convention entered into force April 30, 1995.

1. Any magistrate or additional magistrate.

2. Any registrar or assistant registrar of the Supreme Court of South Africa

3. Any person designated by the Director-General: Justice

4. Any person designated by the Director-General: Foreign Affairs

Spain:

Entered into force September 25, 1978. By a note to the depositary dated November 10, 1978, Spain notified a modification in the designated competent authorities:

1. For documents drawn up by competent judicial authorities or officials: the Secretaries of "Territorial Courts" (Secretarios de Gobierno de las Audiencias) or their deputies;

2. For documents authenticated by a notary public, or private documents where the signatures have been authenticated by a notary public: the President of the relevant Association of notaries public or the person legally responsible for its affairs;

3. For other public documents, excepting those issued by central administrative bodies: any of the officials referred to in paragraphs 1 and 2, above;

4. For documents issued by authorities of the central administration:

Head of the Central Section of the Ministry of Justice (Jefe de la Seccion Central de la Subsecretaria)
Ministerios de Justicia
Registro General
c/ San Bernardo 45
28015 Madrid, Spain

tel: 34-1-390-2000

Suriname:

Extended by the Kingdom of the Netherlands May 16, 1967. Achieved independence November 25, 1975. Suriname declared on October 29, 1976 that it considers itself bound by the Convention. Effective date of accession is date of independence. Registrar at the Court of Justice of Suriname (Griffier by het Hof van Justitie in Suriname)

Swaziland:

Extended to Swaziland by the United Kingdom on February 24, 1965. Achieved independence September 6, 1968. Swaziland declared on July 3, 1978 that it considers itself bound by the Convention.

1. The Deputy Prime Minister;

2. The Attorney General;

3. The Registrar of the High Court;

4. The Head of Department not specified in paragraphs 2 and 3;

5. A District Commissioner;

6. A Magistrate;

7. Such other officer as the Deputy Prime Minister may, by notice published in the Gazette, specify.

Switzerland:

(a) Federal Authorities: The Federal Office (La Chandellerie federale);

(b) Cantonal Authorities: Canton of....

State Office (Die Staatskanzlei): Aargau, Basel-Stadt, Lucerne, St. Gallen, Schaffhausen, Solothurn, Thurgau, Zug, Zurich.

State Office (Die Standeskanzlei): Nidwalden, Obwalden, Schwyz, Uri.

State Office (Die Staatskanzlei/La Chancellerie d'Etat): Bern, Freiburg, Wallis.

Government Office (Die Regierungskanzlei): Glarus.

Office of the Land (Die Landeskanslei): Basel-Landschaft.

State Office (La Chancellerie d'Etat): Geneva, Neuchatel, Vaud.

Canton Office (Die Kantonskanzlei): Appenzell Z.-Rh.

Council Office (Die Ratskanzlei): Appenzell I.-Rh.

State Office (Die Standeskanzlei/La Cancelleria dello Stato): Graubuden.

State Office (La Chancelleria dello Stato): Ticino.

Tonga:

Tonga declared on October 28, 1971 that it considers itself bound by the Convention. On February 24, 1965, the United Kingdom extended the Convention to Tonga.

The Secretary to Government

Prime Minister's Office

Nuku'alofa

Turkey:

1. Administrative documents: a. In Provinces: Governor, Deputy-Governor, Director of Juridical Matters; b. In towns: Vice-Governor;

2. Judicial Documents: Presidencies of the Judicial Commissions where the high criminal courts exist.

Turks and Caicos Islands:

The Governor of the Turks and Caicos Islands

Tuvalu:

Unknown. Now Independent. No confirmation issued by newly independent country that Convention is deemed to apply. Extended to former Ellice Islands by the United Kingdom February 24, 1965.

United Kingdom:

Her Majesty's Principal Secretary of State for Foreign and Commonwealth Affairs, Foreign and Commonwealth Office, London SW1, United Kingdom

Vanuatu:

Unknown. Now Independent. No confirmation issued by newly independent country that Convention is deemed to apply. In notes of April 1, 1970, the British and French Embassies notified the depositary that the respective governments have reached an agreement whereby he extension of the Convention to the Anglo-French Condominium of the New Hebrides with effect from February 15, 1966 has been confirmed, and the competent authorities to issue the certificate designated. The New Hebrides achieved independence on July 30, 1980 and became the Republic of Vanuatu.

Former Yugoslavia:

See Note ++++ page 4. See also Slovenia, Macedonia, Bosnia-Herzegovina and Croatia above.

Les Tribunaux communaux, qui sont d'apres la legislation yougoslave, les tribunaux de premiere instance et les organes administratifs des republiques, competents dans le domaine de la justice.

The Courts of First Instance of Orna, Gora (Montenegro) and Srbija (Serbia)

The Administrative Tribunals of the Republics:

Serbia (Srbija): Republicki sekretarijat za pravosudje i opstu upravu;

Montenegro (Orna Gora): Republicki sekretarijat za pravosudje, zakonodavstvo i organizaciju uprave

REFERENCES:

9 International Lawyer, No. 4, 55; 1975

11 Harvard International Law Journal, 476; 1970

60 American Bar Association Journal, 310, March 14, 1974

January 1982, Patent and Trademark Review 39

Ristau, International Judicial Assistance (Civil and Commercial), Vol. 1, International Law Institute, Washington, D.C. 1984, pp. 269 - 284.

California Attorney General's Opinion No. 88-802, January 5, 1989, 89 Daily Journal D.A.R. 148 (recordability of an apostille in the French language).

California Attorney General's Opinion No. 81-1213, March 19, 1982 (Convention supersedes state law).

Pfund, P.H., Chapter, "Legalization of Documents for Use Abroad" in The International Lawyer's Deskbook, edited by Lowe, Norton and Drory, ABA (Section of International Law and Practice) 1996, ISBN 1-57073-166-7.

QUESTIONS:

Persons having questions about the operation and implementation of this Convention should address their inquiries to the appropriate local state or federal authority or to the Office of American Citizens Services, Department of State, Washington, D.C. 20520, telephone (202) 647-5225.

Automated Fax Service:

Additional copies of this information flyer are available from our Automated Fax System. Use the phone on your fax machine equipped with a telephone jack. Dial (202) 647-3000. Ignore the prompts. Enter the four digit code 1053. Follow the prompts and the document will print automatically on your fax machine. An information flyer on authentication of documents in non-Hague Convention countries may be obtained from the Automated Fax System by entering the four digit code 1046.

Internet:

Information is also available on the Internet via the Department of State, Bureau of Consular Affairs Home Page at the URL: http://travel.state.gov which includes material on authentication of documents and international judicial assistance. See also, the Department of State, Office of the Legal Adviser for Private International Law (L/PIL) Home Page at the URL: http//www.lpil.com. As noted on page 1, the text of the Convention and updated information concerning countries which have acceded to the Convention can be found in the Martindale-Hubbell Law Directory, Law Digest Volume. See the Martindale-Hubbell Home Page on the Internet at the URL: http://www.martindale.com/products/digests.html.

Appendix 9[3]

State Authentication Authorities

State Department Circular

DISCLAIMER: THE INFORMATION IN THIS CIRCULAR RELATING TO THE LEGAL REQUIREMENTS OF SPECIFIC FOREIGN COUNTRIES IS PROVIDED FOR GENERAL INFORMATION ONLY. QUESTIONS INVOLVING INTERPRETATION OF SPECIFIC FOREIGN LAWS SHOULD BE ADDRESSED TO FOREIGN COUNSEL.

Summary: Documents issued in one country which need to be used in another country must be ''authenticated'' or ''legalized'' before they can be recognized as valid in the foreign country. This is a process in which various seals are placed on the document. Such documents range from powers of attorney, affidavits, birth, death and marriages records, incorporation papers, deeds, patent applications, home studies and other legal papers. The number and type of authentication certificates you will need to obtain depend on the nature of the document and whether or not the foreign country is a party to the multilateral treaty on ''legalization'' of documents. (A) If your document is intended for use in a country which is a party to a treaty called the Hague Convention Abolishing the Requirement of Legalization for Foreign Public Documents ('Hague Legalization Convention') (countries listed below), obtaining a special ''apostille'' certificate is generally all that is required. The procedure is explained in detail in our separate information flyer available via our home page on the Internet or through our automated fax service. See ''Additional Information'' below. (B) If the country where the document will be used is not a party to the Convention, you will have to begin the cumbersome, time-consuming process of obtaining a series of certifications known as the ''chain authentication method''. This is literally a paper chase in which authorities will have to attest to the validity of a succession of seals beginning with your document and ending with the seal of the foreign embassy or consulate in the United States.

Treaty Authority:

Article 5(f) and (m) of the Vienna Convention on Consular Relations, 21 U.S.T. 77; TIAS 6820; 596 U.N.T.S. 261;

Applicable bilateral consular conventions;

Hague Convention Abolishing the Requirement of Legalization for Foreign Public Documents, TIAS 10072; 33 U.S.T. 883, 527 U.N.T.S. 189; 28 U.S.C.A., appended to Rule 44; U.S. Senate Executive L., 94th Cong., 2d Sess. (1976).

Statutory Authority:

Notarial/authentication function of consuls: 22 U.S.C. Sec. 4215; 4221; 22 C.F.R. Section 92.36—92.41;

Consular refusal to perform notarial/authentication function: 22 C.F.R. Section 92.9—92.10; Attorney General's Opinion August 1, 1866, Vol. XII, Official Opinions of the Attorneys General.

Certification of documents: 22 C.F.R. Sec. 131.1;

Refusal of certification for unlawful purpose: 22 C.F.R. 131.2;

Authentication of official records of sister-states: Art. IV, Sec. 1 of the Constitution; 28 U.S.C. Sec. 1739; Rule 44(a)(1), F.R.Civ. P. and Rule 902(1) and (2), F.R. Evid.;

Admissibility of authenticated copies of consular papers: 28 U.S.C. Sec. 1740;

Admissibility of authenticated copies of foreign official documents as evidence: 28 U.S.C. Sec. 1741;

Proof of official record; authentication of foreign record: Rule 44(a)(2) Fed. R. Civ. P., 28 U.S.C. Appendix.

Self-Authentication—foreign public documents: Rule 902(3), Fed. R. Evid., 28 U.S.C. Appendix.

Chain Authentication

1. Foreign Embassy: This is the last step in the authentication chain. Usually, foreign embassies or consulates in the U.S. can only authenticate the seal of the U.S. Department of State. Check with the embassy or consulate of the foreign country to see if some of the steps can be avoided. Some foreign embassies and consulates maintain sample seals of state authorities. Remember that what is needed is only the foreign consul's authentication on the document for the document to be ''self-proving'' in the foreign country. If a foreign consul will authenticate the document without the intermediate steps, you will have saved yourself money, time and effort. See our consular information sheets via the internet or autofax for the phone number for foreign embassies in the U.S. under ''Entry Requirements'' explained under ''Additional Information'' below. Also ask the foreign embassy or consulate about any fees they may charge. If the foreign embassy informs you that you must also obtain the seal of the U.S. embassy or consulate in the foreign country, which is required very rarely, you will then need to send the document to the Consular Section, American Citizens Services of the U.S. embassy or consulate, enclosing a money order or bank check payable to U.S. Embassy/Consulate (fill in name of city). The addresses of U.S. embassies and consulates abroad are included in the final paragraph of our consular information sheets available via the Internet on our home page or via our autofax service. See ''Additional Information'' below.

2. U.S. Department of State Authentications Office: The office is located at 518 23rd St., N.W., Washington, D.C. 20520, tel: (202) 647-5002. There is a fee of $5.00 for each authentication payable in the form of a check drawn on a U.S. bank or money order made payable to the Department of State. For additional information, call the Federal Information Center: 1-800-688-9889, and choose option 6 after you press 1 for touch tone phones. Walk-in service is available from the Authentications Office from 7:30 a.m. to 11:00 a.m. Monday-Friday, except holidays. Walk-in service is limited to 15 documents per person per day (documents can be multiple pages). Processing time for authentication requests sent by mail is 5 working days or less. See also, the State Department home page at http://www.state.gov. See also in general, 22 C.F.R. 131.

3. Documents Issued by Federal Courts: Documents issued under the seal of a federal court should be sent to Justice Management Division, Security Program Staff, Physical Security Office, 9th and Pennsylvania Avenue, Room 6531, Washington, D.C. 20530, tel: (202) 514-2314 or 514-4667 for the preliminary authentication. Then forward the document(s) to the U.S. Department of State, Authentications Office as explained above. Finally, send the documents to the foreign embassy or consulate in the United States.

4. Documents Issued by Federal Agencies: Documents issued under the seal of a federal agency can be authenticated by the U.S. Department of State Authentications Office following the instructions above. Then send the documents to the foreign embassy or consulate in the United States as explained above.

5. State Documents: State documents such as documents originating with a state court or agency (birth, death, marriage, etc.) must be authenticated by the appropriate office in the state Secretary of State's office (listed below). The document may then be authenticated by the U.S. Department of State Authentications Office as explained above. The document may then be authenticated by the foreign embassy or consulate in the United States following the instructions above.

6. Notarized Documents: The procedure for authenticating documents executed before a notary public such as affidavits or acknowledgments varies from state to state. It is advisable to contact the state authentication authority listed below to learn what steps are necessary between the notary's seal and the state Secretary of State's seal. In some states, this requires contacting the clerk of the court of the county where the notary is licensed, and obtaining an authentication of the notary's seal. The state Secretary of State's office can then authenticate the seal of the clerk of the county court. After the seal of the state Secretary of State or comparable authority listed below is on the document, it may be authenticated by the U.S. Department of State Authentications Office. The final step is to obtain the seal of the foreign embassy or consulate in the United States following the instructions above.

Hague Legalization Convention Procedure

The United States is a party to the Hague Convention Abolishing the Requirement of Legalization for Foreign Public Documents. The Convention abolishes the requirement of diplomatic and consular legalization for public documents originating in one Convention country and intended for use in another. For the purposes of the Convention, public documents include: (a) documents emanating from a court, (b) documents issued by an administrative authority (such as civil records), and (c) documents executed before a notary. Such documents issued in a Convention country which have been certified by a Convention certificate called an ''apostille'' are entitled to recognition in any other Convention country without any further authentication. See TIAS 10072; U.N.T.S. 189; 28 U.S.C.A., Fed. R. Civ. P. 44, pp. 323-327 (1992 & West Supp. 1993); Martindale-Hubbell Law Directory, Law

Digest Volume, Selected International Conventions; 20 Int'l. Leg. Mat. 1405-1414 (November 1981). A detailed information flyer concerning the process is available from our home page on the Internet or via our automated fax service. See ''Additional Information'' below.

IN FORCE: ANDORRA, *ANGOLA,* ANGUILLA, ANTIGUA AND BARBUDA, ARGENTINA, ARMENIA, ARUBA, AUSTRALIA, AUSTRIA, BAHAMAS, BARBADOS, BELARUS, BELGIUM, BELIZE, BERMUDA, BOSNIA-HERZEGOVINA, BOTSWANA, BRITISH ANTARCTIC TERRITORY, BRITISH VIRGIN ISLANDS, BRUNEI, BULGARIA, CAYMAN ISLANDS, *COMOROS ISLANDS (formerly Moroni)*, CROATIA, CYPRUS, *DJIBOUTI (formerly Affars and Issas)*, *DOMINICA*, EL SALVADOR, FALKLAND ISLANDS, FIJI, FINLAND, FRANCE, FRENCH GUIANA, FRENCH POLYNESIA, GUADELOUPE, GERMANY, GIBRALTAR, GREECE, *GRENADA*, GUERNSEY (Bailiwick of), HONG KONG, HUNGARY, ISLE OF MAN, ISRAEL, ITALY, JAPAN, JERSEY (Bailiwick of), *KIRIBATI (formerly Gilbert Islands)*, LATVIA, LESOTHO, LIECHTENSTEIN, LUXEMBOURG, MACAO, MACEDONIA, MALAWI, MALTA, MARSHALL ISLANDS, MARTINIQUE, MAURITIUS, MEXICO, MONTSERRAT, *MOZAMBIQUE*, NETHERLANDS, NETHERLANDS ANTILLES (Curacao, Bonaire, St. Martin, St. Eustatius and Saba), NEW CALEDONIA, NORWAY, PANAMA, PORTUGAL, REUNION, RUSSIAN FEDERATION, ST. CHRISTOPHER (Kitts) AND NEVIS, ST. GEORGIA AND SOUTH SANDWICH ISLANDS, ST. HELENA, ST. LUCIA, ST. PIERRE AND MIQUELON, ST. VINCENT AND THE GRENADINES, SAN MARINO, SEYCHELLES, SLOVENIA, *SOLOMON ISLANDS (formerly British Solomon Islands)*, SOUTH AFRICA, SPAIN, SURINAME, SWAZILAND, SWITZERLAND, TONGA, TURKEY, TURKS AND CAICOS, *TUVALU (formerly Ellice Islands)*, UNITED KINGDOM, UNITED STATES, *VANUATU (formerly New Hebrides)*, WALLIS AND FUTUNA.

(Italics indicate country now independent, but no formal confirmation of continued applicability of Convention received.)

State Authentication Authorities: (This list of state authorities was valid effective 4/1/97. See also 28 U.S.C.A., Fed. R. Civ. P. 44, pp. 328-31 (1992 & West Supp. 1993). It is valid for chain authentication and Hague Legalization Convention ''apostille'' procedures; but see our specialized flyer on the operation of the Hague Legalization Convention since the Convention ''apostille'' certificate is affixed by different American authorities depending on the nature of the document.)

State Authentication Authorities

Alabama
Office of the Secretary of State
Authentication Section
State Capitol, Room E-204
600 Dexter Ave.
Montgomery, AL 36104
334-242-7210
http://www.sos.state.al.us/authenticate/index.htm
Fee: $5.00
Designated Authority: Secretary of State

Alaska
Notary Administrator
Office of the Lieutenant Governor
P.O. Box 110015
Juneau, AK 99811- 0015
907-465-3509
http://www.gov.state.ak.us/ltgov/notary/authentications.htm
Fee: $2.00
Designated Authority: Lieutenant Governor; Attorney General; Clerk of the Supreme Court

Arizona
Office of the Secretary of State
Business Services Division, Notary Section
1700 W. Washington, 7th Floor
Phoenix, AZ 85007-2888
602 542-4086/602 542-4758
http://www.sosaz.com/notary
Fee: $3.00
Designated Authority: Secretary of State; Assistant Secretary of State.

Arkansas
Office of Secretary of State
Corporations Division
State Capitol
Little Rock, AR 72201-1094
501-682-3409
http://www.sosweb.state.ar.us/business.html
Fee: $10.00
Designated Authority: Secretary of State; Chief Deputy Secretary of State.

California
Office of the Secretary of State
Business Programs Division
Notary Public Section
P.O. Box 942877
Sacramento, CA 94277-0001
916-653-3595
http://www.ss.ca.gov/business/notary/notary.htm
Fee: $20.00
Designated Authority: Secretary of State; any Assistant Secretary of State; any Deputy Secretary of State.

Colorado
Office of Secretary of State
1560 Broadway, Suite 200
Denver, CO 80202
303-894-2680
http://www.sos.state.co.us/pubs/infocenter/2001fees.htm
Fee: By Mail: $2.00 While You Wait: $17.00
Designated Authority: Secretary of State; Deputy Secretary of State.

Connecticut
Office of the Secretary of State
Authentication Unit
30 Trinity St.
Hartford, CT 06106
860-509-6135
http://www.sots.state.ct.us/recordslegislativeservices/authen.html#orders
Fee: $20.00
Designated Authority: Secretary of State; Deputy Secretary of State.

Delaware
Office of Secretary of State
Notary Division
401 Federal St., Suite 3
Dover, DE 19901
302- 302/739-4111
http://www.state.de.us/sos/sos.htm
Fee: $10.00
Designated Authority: Secretary of State; Acting Secretary of State.

District of Columbia
Office of the Secretary, D.C.
Notary Commissions & Authentications Section
441 4th St. N.W. (One Judiciary Square)
Washington, D.C.
202-727-3117
http://os.dc.gov/info/notary/notary.shtm#document
Fee: $10.00
Designated Authority: Executive Secretary; Assistant Executive Secretary; Mayor's Special Assistant and Assistant to the Executive Secretary; Secretary of the District of Columbia.

Florida
Department of State
Office of International Affairs
Notary Certification/Apostille Section
The Capitol Building
Suite 1902
Tallahassee, FL 32399-0250
804-488-7521
http://notaries.dos.state.fl.us/notproc7.htm
Fee: $10.00
Designated Authority: Secretary of State

Georgia
Georgia Superior Court Clerks' Cooperative Authority
Notary Division
1875 Century Boulevard, Suite 100
Atlanta, GA 30345
404-327-6023
http://www2.gsccca.org/projects/apost.html
or
Office of Secretary of State
Administrative Procedures Unit
2 Martin Luther King Jr. Drive
Suite 820—West Tower
Atlanta, Georgia 30334
404-656-2885
http://www.sos.state.ga.us/administration/notary.htm
Fee: $3.00
Designated Authority: Secretary of State; Georgia Superior Court Clerks' Cooperative Authority.

Hawaii
Office of the Lieutenant Governor
State Capitol, 5th Floor,
Honolulu, Hawaii 96813
808-586-0255
http://www.state.hi.us/ltgov/page8.html
Fee: $1.00
Designated Authority: Lieutenant Governor of the State of Hawaii.

Idaho
Office of Secretary of State
Notary Department
Box 83720
Boise, ID 83720
208- 332-2810
http://www.idsos.state.id.us/notary/apostill.htm
Fee: $10.00
Designated Authority: Secretary of State; Chief Deputy Secretary of State; Deputy Secretary of State; Notary Public Clerk.

Illinois
Office of the Secretary of State
Index Department, Notaries Public Division
111 E. Monroe St.
Springfield, IL 62756
217- 217-782-7017
http://www.sos.state.il.us/departments/index/division.html
Fee: $2.00
Designated Authority: Secretary of State; Assistant Secretary of State; Deputy Secretary of State.

Indiana
Office of Secretary of State
Statehouse
Suite 201
Indianapolis, IN 46204
317-232-6532
http://www.in.gov/sos/notary/seal.html
Fee: no charge
Designated Authority: Secretary of State; Deputy Secretary of State

Iowa
Office of Secretary of State
Lucas Building
First Floor, Public Service
Des Moines, IA 50319
515-281-5204
http://www.sos.state.ia.us
Fee: $5.00
Designated Authority: Secretary of State; Deputy Secretary of State

Kansas
Office of Secretary of State
State Capitol
Second Floor
Topeka, KS 66612
913-296-2744
http://www.kssos.org
Fee: $5.00
Designated Authority: Secretary of State; Assistant Secretary of State; any Deputy Assistant Secretary of State.

Kentucky
Office of Secretary of State
Capitol Building
P.O. Box 718
Frankfort, KY 40602-0178
502-564-7330
Fee: $5.00
http://www.kysos.com
Designated Authority: Secretary of State; Assistant Secretary of State.

Louisiana
Office of Secretary of State
P.O. Box 94125
Baton Rouge, LA 70804-9125
504-342-4981
Fee: $5.00
http://www.sec.state.la.us/comm/comm-index.htm
Designated Authority: Secretary of State.

Maine
Office of Secretary of State
Bureau of Corporations
Elections and Commissions
101 State House Station
Augusta, ME 04333-0101
207-624-7650
http://www.state.me.us/sos/cec/rcn/notary/authapos.htm
Fee: $10.00
Designated Authority: Secretary of State; Deputy Secretary of State.

Maryland
Office of Secretary of State
Statehouse
Annapolis, MD 21401
410-974-5520
http://www.sos.state.md.us/sos/certif/html/certif2c.html#apos
Fee: $5.00
Designated Authority: Secretary of State.

Massachusetts
Secretary of the Commonwealth
Public Records Division
Commissions Section
McCormack Building, Room 1719
One Ashburton Place
Boston, MA 02108
617-727-2832
http://www.state.ma.us/sec/pre/precom/comidx.htm
Fee: $3.00

Michigan
Department of State
Office of the Great Seal
7064 Crowner Boulevard
Lansing, MI 48918
517-373-2531
http://www.michigan.gov/sos/1,1607,7-127-16388734—,00.html
Fee: $1.00
Designated Authority: Secretary of State; Deputy Secretary of State.

Minnesota
Secretary of State's Office
180 State Office Bldg.
St. Paul, MN 55155
651-296-2803
http://www.sos.state.mn.us/uccd/authinfo.html
Fee: $5.00
Designated Authority: Secretary of State; Deputy Secretary of State.

Mississippi
Office of Secretary of State
P.O. Box 136
Jackson, MS 39205-0136
601-359-1615
http://www.sos.state.ms.us/busserv/notaries/notaries.html
Fee: $5.00
Designated Authority: Secretary of State; any Assistant Secretary of State.

Missouri
Office of Secretary of State
Commission Division
600 West Main, Room 367
Jefferson City, MO 65102
573-751-2783
http://www.sos.state.mo.us/business/commissions/certify.asp
Fee: $10.00
Designated Authority: Secretary of State; Deputy Secretary of State.

Montana
Office of the Secretary of State
Notary/Certification Division
State Capitol Rm 260
PO Box 202801
Helena MT 59620-2801
UPS-FedEx-DHL- etc. address: 1236 E 6th Ave Helena MT 59620
406-444-1877 (Tuesdays—Thursdays only)
http://sos.state.mt.us/css/Notary/Certifications.asp
email: sosnotary@state.mt.us
Fee: $10.00 per document
Designated Authority: Secretary of State; Any Deputy Secretary of State

Nebraska
Office of Secretary of State
Notary Division
Box 95104
State Capitol
Lincoln, NE 68509
402-471-2558
http://www.sos.state.ne.us/Notary/notauth.htm
Fee: $10.00
Designated Authority: Secretary of State; Deputy Secretary of State.

Nevada
Secretary of State
101 N. Carson Street, #3
Carson City, NV 89701-4786
775-684-5708
http://sos.state.nv.us/notary/apostille.htm
Fee: $20.00
Designated Authority: Secretary of State; Chief Deputy Secretary of State; Deputy Secretary of State.

New Hampshire
Office of Secretary of State
Statehouse
Room 204
Concord, NH 03301
603-271-3242
http://www.state.nh.us/sos/certific.htm
Fee: $5.00
Designated Authority: Secretary of State; Deputy Secretary of State

New Jersey
Department of State
Notary Public Unit
Division of Commercial Recording
PO Box 452
Trenton, NJ 08625
609-530-6421
http://www.state.nj.us/treasury/revenue/dcr/programs/notary.html
Fee: Regular Service: $25.00 Expedited Service: $35.00
Designated Authority: NJ Department of the Treasury, Division of Revenue

New Mexico
Office of the Secretary of State
State Capitol North Annex, Suite 300
Santa Fe, NM 87503
505-827-3600
http://www.sos.state.nm.us/notary-cert.htm
Fee: $3.00
Designated Authority: Secretary of State

New York
• *Upstate Counties*
Miscellaneous Records
162 Washington Ave.
Albany, NY 12231
518-474-4770
http://www.dos.state.ny.us
Fee: $10.00
Designated Authority: Secretary of State; Executive Deputy Secretary of State; any Deputy Secretary of State; any Special Deputy Secretary of State.
• *Down State Counties*
New York authorities in Albany advise that documents issued in the nine down state counties are authenticated under the Convention by the New York City office. The nine down state counties are New York, Kings, Queens, Bronx, Westchester, Nassau, Suffolk, Rockland and Richmond. The address of the New York Department of State, Certification Unit is 6th Floor, 270 Broadway, New York, New York 10007, tel: 212-417-5684. Fee: $10.00

North Carolina
Office of Secretary of State
Authentication Division
PO Box 29622
Raleigh, NC 27626-0622
919-807-2140
http://www.secretary.state.nc.us/authen
Fee: $10.00
Designated Authority: Secretary of State; Deputy Secretary of State

North Dakota
Office of Secretary of State
Capitol Building
600 E Boulevard Ave., Dept 108
Bismarck, ND 58505
701-328-2900
http://www.state.nd.us/sec
Fee: $10.00
Designated Authority: Secretary of State; Deputy Secretary of State.

Ohio
Office of the Secretary of State
30 East Broad St.
15th Fl.
Columbus, OH 43266-0418
877-767-6446
http://www.state.oh.us/sos/authenticationofdocumentsstat.htm
Fee: $5.00
Designated Authority: Secretary of State; Assistant Secretary of State.

Oklahoma
Office of Secretary of State
2300 N. Lincoln
Room 101
Oklahoma City, OK 73105
405-521-4211
http://www.sos.state.ok.us
Fee: $25.00 (cashiers check or money order)
Designated Authority: Secretary of State; Assistant Secretary of State; Budget Officer of the Secretary of State.

Oregon
Office of Secretary of State
255 Capitol St.
Suite 151
Salem OR 97310
503-986-2200.
http://www.filinginoregon.com/notary/index.htm
Fee: $10.00
Designated Authority: Secretary of State; Deputy Secretary of State; Acting Secretary of State; Assistant to the Secretary of State.

Pennsylvania
Department of State
Bureau of Commissions
Elections and Legislation
North Office Building
Room 210
Harrisburg, PA 17120
717-787-5280
http://www.dos.state.pa.us/bcel/certifications/certifications.html
Fee: $15.00
Designated Authority: Secretary of the Commonwealth; Executive Deputy Secretary of the Commonwealth.

Rhode Island
Office of Secretary of State
Notary Division
100 N. Main St.
Providence, RI 02903
401-277-1487
http://www.corps.state.ri.us/notaries/notaries.htm
Fee: $5.00
Designated Authority: Secretary of State; First Deputy Secretary of State; Deputy Secretary of State

South Carolina
Office of Secretary of State
P.O. Box 11350
Columbia, SC 29211
803-734-2119
http://www.scsos.com/notariesbc.htm
Fee: $2.00
Designated Authority: Secretary of State

South Dakota
Office of Secretary of State
500 East Capitol
Pierre, SD 57501-5077
605-773-5004
http://www.state.sd.us/sos/Notaries/apostillesandauthentications.htm
Fee: $2.00
Designated Authority: Secretary of State; Deputy Secretary of State

Tennessee
Office of Secretary of State
James K. Polk Building
Division of Business Services
312 Eighth Avenue North
6th Floor, William R. Snodgrass Tower
Nashville, TN 37243
615-741-3699
http://www.state.tn.us/sos/service.htm#apostilles
Fee: $2.00
Designated Authority: Secretary of State.

Texas
Office of Secretary of State
P.O. Box 12079
Austin, TX 78711
512-463-5705
http://txsos-7.sos.state.tx.us/authfaqs.shtml
Fee: $10.00
Designated Authority: Secretary of State; Assistant Secretary of State

Utah
Office of the Lieutenant Governor
210 State Capitol
Salt Lake City, UT 84145-8414
801-538-1040
http://governor.state.ut.us/ltgover/internationaltemplate.html
Fee: Certifying Notary's Seal: $10.00
Apostille: $5.00
Designated Authority: Lieutenant Governor; Deputy Lieutenant Governor; Administrative Assistant.

Vermont
Office of Secretary of State
109 State St.
Montpelier, VT 05609-1103
802-828-2308
http://www.sec.state.vt.us
Fee: $2.00
Designated Authority: Secretary of State; Deputy Secretary of State.

Virginia
Office of Secretary of Commonwealth
Authentications Division
830 East Main Street, 14th Floor
Richmond, VA 23219
804-786-2441
http://www.soc.state.va.us
Fee: $10.00
Designated Authority: Secretary of the Commonwealth; Chief Clerk, Office of the Secretary of Commonwealth.

Washington
Office of the Secretary of State
Corporations Division
Apostille and Certificate Program
PO Box 40228
Olympia, WA 98504-0228
360-586-2268
http://www.secstate.wa.gov/apostilles
Fee: $15.00
Designated Authority: Secretary of State; Assistant Secretary of State; Director, Department of Licensing.

West Virginia
Office of Secretary of State
Capitol Building
1900 Kanawha Blvd. East
No. 157-K
Charleston, WV 25305-0770
304-558-6000
http://www.wvsos.com/execrecords/other/authentication.htm
Fee: $10.00
Designated Authority: Secretary of State; Under Secretary of State; any Deputy Secretary of State.

Wisconsin
Office of Secretary of State
P.O. Box 7848
Madison, WI 53707-7848
608-266-3159
http://badger.state.wi.us/agencies/sos/authen.htm
Fee: $10.00
Designated Authority: Secretary of State; Assistant Secretary of State.

Wyoming
Office of Secretary of State
The Capitol
Cheyenne, WY 82002-0020
307-777-5342
http://soswy.state.wy.us/authenti/authenti.htm
Fee: $3.00
Designated Authority: Secretary of State; Deputy Secretary of State.

American Samoa
Office of the Governor
Pago Pago, AS 96799
011-684-633-4116
http://www.amsamoa.com
Designated Authority: Secretary of American Samoa; Attorney General of American Samoa.

Guam (Territory of)
Office of the Governor
P.O. Box 2950
Agana, GU 96910
011-671-472-1537
http://www.admin.gov.gu/doa
Designated Authority: Department of Administration

Northern Mariana Islands (Commonwealth of the)
Designated Authority: Attorney General; Acting Attorney General; Clerk of the Court, Commonwealth Trial Court; Deputy Clerk, Commonwealth Trial Court
http://www.saipan.com/gov

Puerto Rico (Commonwealth of)
Supreme Court of Puerto Rico
Office of Notarial Inspection
P.O. Box 190860
San Juan, PR 00919-0860
787-763-8816
http://www.lexjuris.com/lexnotaria.htm
Designated Authority: Supreme Court of Puerto Rico

U.S. Virgin Islands
Office of the Lieutenant Governor
7 & 8 King St.
Christiansted, St. Croix, USVI 00802
340-774-2991
http://www.ltg.gov.vi/Departments/Administration/index.html

No authority designated: refer requests to the U.S. Department of State, Authentications Office, 2400 M Street, NW, Washington, DC 20520. 202-647-5002

Authentication of Foreign Documents for Use in U.S.: In countries party to the Hague Legalization Convention, foreign documents are authenticated by the foreign competent authority listed in our separate information flyer on the Convention. See ''Additional

Information'' below. In non-Hague countries, documents can be authenticated by a consular officer at the U.S. embassy or consulate. Effective June 1, 2002, the consular fee for authentication is $30.00 per seal. See Federal Register, May 16, 2002, Volume 67, Number 95, Rules and Regulations, Page 34831-34838; 22 CFR 22.1; Item No. 41. Hours for authentication services may vary from one U.S. embassy to another. Contact the U.S. embassy or consulate directly for more information. See our Consular Information Sheets via our home page on the Internet or our automated fax system for the addresses, phone numbers and fax numbers for U.S. embassies and consulates abroad.

Selected Bibliography:

Addendum (Section 4, paragraphs 304.1-304.7) to Guide to Judiciary Policies and Procedures (Vol. IV, Ch. 3), by Administrative Office of the United States Courts.

Amram, Toward Easier Legalization of Foreign Public Documents, 60 A.B.A.J. 310 (1974).

Basic Documents of International Economic Law, II, 845-854 (S. Zamora & R.A. Brand eds. 1990).

Clerks Manual, United States District Courts, Vol I, Section 17.06- (Hague Convention) Apostilles.

Corr, Authentication of Foreign Conveyances of Connecticut Real Property, Connecticut Attorneys Title Insurance Company, (1986).

Cumulative Digest of United States Practice in International Law, 1981-1988, Department of State, Office of the Legal Adviser, Vol. II, 1548, 1555 (1994).

Digest of United States Practice in International Law, Department of State, Office of the Legal Adviser, 1975, 255.

Digest of United States Practice in International Law, Department of State, Office of the Legal Adviser, 1976, 780, 781.

Digest of United States Practice in International Law, Department of State, Office of the Legal Adviser, 1977, 146, 149.

Digest of United States Practice in International Law, Department of State, Office of the Legal Adviser, 1978, 397-398, 400-401.

Digest of United States Practice in International Law, Department of State, Office of the Legal Adviser, 1979, 888-891.

Epstein & Snyder, International Litigation: A Guide to Jurisdiction, Practice and Strategy, 2d ed., Prentice Hall Law & Business, Section 9.07, p. 9-16—9-20; Appendix 9 and Appendix 10, app-119—app-124 (1994 supp.).

Golding, Foreign Public Documents Proof/Authentication, 6 Estate Planning, Trust and Probate News 21 (No. 1, Spring 1984).

Griew, Hague Draft Convention on the Legalisation of Foreign Public Documents and the Form of Wills, 8 Int'l & Comp. L.Q. 559 (1959).

Hackworth, Digest of International Law, Department of State, Office of the Legal Adviser, Vol. IV, p. 847-850, 854.

Harvey, The United States and the Hague Convention Abolishing the Requirement of Legalisation for Foreign Public Documents, 11 Harv. Int'l. L.J. 476 (1970).

Hergen, How to Practice Family Law in Europe When You're Not European, Family Advocate, Vol. 3, No. 4, p. 25-27, 41-44, Spring, 1981.

Note, Authentication: Proving Your Powers, The National Notary, p. 24, January 1990.

Note, Patent and Trademark Review 39, January 1982.

Report of the Committee on the International Unification of Private Law, with Action by the ABA Section of International Law and the House of Delegates, 9 Int'l Law. 755 (1975).

Note, The Time-Saving ''Apostille'', The National Notary, p. 25, January 1990.

Note, Untangling the Red Tape of Authentication, The National Notary, p. 34-35, January/February 1981.

Opinion of John K. van de Kamp, Attorney General of the State of California, 71 Ops. Cal. Atty. Gen. 362 (1989); California Attorney General's Opinion No. 88-802, January 5, 1989, 89 Daily Journal D.A.R. 148 (recordability of an apostille in the French language).

Opinion of George Deukmejian, Attorney General of the State of California, on the Hague Convention Abolishing the Requirement of Legalization for Foreign Public Documents, 65 Ops. Cal. Atty. Gen. 205 (1982); 21 Int'l. Leg. Mat. 357 (1982); California Attorney General's Opinion No. 81-1213, March 19, 1982 (Convention supersedes state law).

Pedowitz, New Procedures for Authentication of Foreign Documents, ABA, Probate and Property, Vol. 10, No. 5, p. 9-10, Spring 1982.

Pfund, P.H., Chapter, ''Legalization of Documents for Use Abroad'' in The International Lawyer's Deskbook, edited by Lowe, Norton and Drory, ABA (Section of International Law and Practice) 1996, ISBN 1-57073-166-7.

Ristau, Ch. XII, Authenticating Foreign Official Documents, Transnational Commercial and Trade Litigation: Recent Developments, ALI-ABA Course Stury Materials, p. 245-260, November 20-22, 1986.

Ristau, International Judicial Assistance (Civil and Commercial), Vol. 1, International Law Institute, Washington, D.C., Sec. 6-1-1—6/1/3, pp. 241-254 (1995 supp.).

Sinnott, A Practical Guide to Document Authentication: Legalization of Notarized and Certified Documents, N.Y., London, Rome, Oceana Publications, Inc., 1984.

Whiteman, Digest of International Law, Department of State, Office of the Legal Adviser, Vol. 7, p. 519-520, 597-605 (1970).

Additional Information: The Office of American Citizens Services has available general information flyers on international judicial assistance many of which are available through our automated fax system or via our Internet Consular Affairs Home Page. These topics include country-specific information about service of process and obtaining evidence abroad.

Using the Internet: Many of our judicial assistance flyers are also available on the Internet via the Department of State, Bureau of Consular Affairs home page under Judicial Assistance. See also, the Authentication Office section of the Department of State home page for information. See also the home pages for many of our embassies which are linked to the Consular Affairs home page. As noted above, the text of the Convention and updated information concerning countries which have acceded to the Convention can be found in the Martindale-Hubbell Law Directory, Law Digest Volume. See the Martindale-Hubbell home page on the Internet.

Treaty Databases on the Internet:

United Nations (UN): Databases/Treaties

Council of Europe (COE) under Texts/Treaties

Organization of American States (OAS): under Documents/Treaties and Conventions.

Questions: General questions may be addressed to the Office of American Citizens Services at 202-647-5226.

Appendix 10

ANNEX TO THE CONVENTION ABOLISHING THE REQUIREMENT OF LEGALIZATION FOR FOREIGN PUBLIC DOCUMENTS: MODEL OF CERTIFICATE (APOSTILLE)

ANNEXE A LA CONVENTION

Modèle d'apostille

L'apostille aura la forme d'un carré de 9 centimètres de côté au minimum

APOSTILLE
(Convention de La Haye du 5 octobre 1961)

1. Pays: . . . .

Le présent acte public

2. a été signé par . . . .
3. agissant en qualité de . . . .
4. est revêtu du sceau/timbre de . . . .

. . . .

Attesté

5. à . . . . 6. le . . . .
7. par . . . .
8. sous N° . . . .
9. Sceau/timbre: 10. Signature:

. . . .

ANNEX TO THE CONVENTION

Model of Certificate

This certificate will be in the form of a square with sides at least 9 centimetres long

APOSTILLE
(Convention de La Haye du 5 octobre 1961)

1. County: . . . .

This public document

2. has been signed by . . . .

3. acting in the capacity of . . . .

4. bears the seal/stamp of . . . .

. . . .

Certified

5. at . . . . 6. the . . . .

7. by . . . .

8. N°. . . . .

9. Seal/stamp: 10. Signature:

. . . .

Copie Certifiée conforme à l'original

Chef du Bureau de Publication
des Traités
du Minstère des Affaires Etrangères
du Royaume des pays-Bas:

Appendix 11

OBTAINING EVIDENCE ABROAD

State Department Circular

DISCLAIMER: THE INFORMATION IN THIS CIRCULAR RELATING TO THE LEGAL REQUIREMENTS OF SPECIFIC FOREIGN COUNTRIES IS PROVIDED FOR GENERAL INFORMATION ONLY AND MAY NOT BE TOTALLY ACCURATE IN A PARTICULAR CASE. QUESTIONS INVOLVING INTERPRETATION OF SPECIFIC FOREIGN LAWS SHOULD BE ADDRESSED TO FOREIGN COUNSEL.

INDEX

C. GENERAL PROVISO

When evidence sought is in a foreign country, it is necessary to observe not only applicable state or federal rules, but also the laws and regulations of the foreign country where the evidence is located. Procedures may vary in civil, criminal and administrative cases. Some countries view the taking of any form of evidence, even voluntary depositions, as an infringement on their judicial sovereignty. This applies to party and non-party witnesses. Telephone depositions are prohibited in many countries. Many countries do not permit the pre-trial discovery of documents. Attempting to obtain evidence without following the requirements of the foreign country may result in the arrest, detention, deportation or imprisonment of participants, including American counsel. The blocking statutes of some countries even extend to informal contact (See Moore's Federal Practice, 28.16). But see ALI's Restatement (Third) of Foreign Relations Law of the United States, Sec. 442, Reporters' Note 1 (1987). Since foreign laws and practices vary considerably, consult the Department of State, Office of American Citizens Services (ACS) country-specific material available through our autofax service and on our home page on the Internet.

D. VOLUNTARY DEPOSITIONS OF WILLING WITNESSES

1. Informal Deposition Arrangements on Stipulation: Many depositions conducted abroad are taken by stipulation of the parties (Rule 29, Fed. R. Civ. P.) at a time and location of mutual convenience and frequently do not involve any participation by a U.S. consular officer. This of course presupposes that the foreign country permits a deposition taken under these circumstances. Such depositions are frequently conducted by American attorneys in the offices of a foreign attorney or solicitor who has the power to administer oaths in the foreign country, hotel or some other venue, or by telephone from the United States and involve no U.S. consular involvement. In countries where this is not permitted, it is necessary to arrange for a deposition before a U.S. consular officer. Note that the authority to administer oaths in foreign countries is a matter of foreign law. Consular conventions empower U.S. consular officers to administer oaths abroad. Certain officers of the U.S. military have authority to administer oaths abroad under Status of Forces (SOFA) agreements. This may not extend to the taking of depositions on U.S. military bases abroad, which may not be permitted by the SOFA agreement or the laws of the particular foreign country. Other persons authorized to administer oaths in the United States, such as notaries public, "cyber notaries", commissioners of deeds, or officers of the court may have no independent authority to do so abroad under the laws of the foreign country. See Wright and Miller, Sec. 277, Sec. 2462, (1995 Supp.); Blackmer v. U.S., 1932, 52 S. Ct. 252, 284 U.S. 421, 76 L. Ed. 375.

2. Consular Authority: 22 U.S.C. 4215; 22 USC 4221; 18 U.S.C. App. Fed. R. Civ. P., Rules 15 and 17; 28 U.S.C. Fed. R.Civ. P., Rules 28-31; 22 CFR 92.55 - 92.66 (general authority). Article 5(f), Vienna Convention on Consular Relations, 21 UST 77; 596 UNTS 261; TIAS 6820 (where applicable). Chapter II, Articles 15-22, Hague Convention on the Taking of Evidence Abroad in Civil or Commercial Matters, 23 U.S.T. 2555; TIAS 7444; 847 UNTS 231 (where applicable). Bilateral Consular Conventions (where applicable). The consular officer may act on the request to take the deposition on notice or commission provided that the testimony is voluntary and local (foreign) law does not preclude such action. See United States v. Paraffin Wax, 2255 Bags, 23 FRD 289 (ED NY 1959). Oral depositions and depositions on written questions may be taken before a U.S. consular officer "on notice" (Rule 28(b)(1), Fed. R. Civ. P.) or pursuant to a court order or commission (Rule 28(b)(2) Fed. R. Civ.P.). See Ristau, International Judicial Assistance Civil and Commercial, Vol. 1, International Law

Institute, Sec. 3/2/1 - 3-2-8, p. 76-93; Sec. 5-3-1 - 5-3-4, p. 232-240 (1995 Supp.); Moore's Federal Practice, 28 App. 06 (1993). Wherever possible, U.S. consular officers now simply administer oaths to the witnesses and court reporter/interpreter and withdraw, based on stipulation between the parties (See 22 C.F.R. 92.56). Questions are actually asked by attorneys from the U.S. and counsel in the foreign country.

3. Sample Notices, Orders or Commissions: A commission or notice requesting that a United States consular officer take a deposition should be addressed to "Any Consul or Vice Consul of the United States of America at (Name of Locality)." See Wright & Miller, Federal Practice & Procedure, Civ., Sec. 2131, Sec. 2083 (1996 Supp.) For a sample notice or order/commission see Ristau, International Judicial Assistance Civil and Commercial, Sec. 3-2-3 - 3-2-5, p. 82-86; 5-3-4, p. 238.4, Vol. 1 (1995 Supp.); Moore's Federal Practice, Sec. 28.03, 28.04, 28.08, 28.13-28.14 (1993); West's Federal Practice Manual, Sec. 8250, 8231, 8234, Vol. 7 (1995).

4. Arranging for Consular Depositions: When a consular officer is needed to preside at the taking of a voluntary deposition at an American embassy or consulate, obtain the applicable judicial assistance information flyer via our Internet Home Page or Autofax Service. Scheduling depositions is done directly by our embassies and consulates at a time and date of mutual convenience. Please note that for administrative and security reasons, the U.S. embassy/consulate are not available for deposition taking outside of working hours 8:30 a.m. to 5:00 p.m. or on weekends or holidays. After reviewing the procedures described, contact the U.S. embassy or consulate directly via telephone, fax, letter or telex. The addresses, telephone numbers and fax numbers of our embassies and consulates are included in our Consular Information Sheets available via our Home Page on the Internet and via our Autofax Service. See also the home pages of U.S. embassies and consulates which are linked to the Department of State, Consular Affairs home page http://travel.state.gov. U.S. federal, state and local government officials interested in obtaining evidence abroad should contact the Office of American Citizens Services (ACS) at (202) 647-5226, which assists these officials in making the necessary arrangements for testimony of foreign officials, host country clearance and can assist them in retaining the services of stenographers, interpreters and video operators, where available.

5. Contact the U.S. Embassy/Consulate: Furnish the following information to the American Services Section of the Consular Section of the American embassy or consulate.

   a. Requesting counsel's full name, address, telex, fax and telephone number;

   b. A brief description of the nature of the case and any special aspect of the proposed depostition (trial date, telephone deposition, witness incarcerated, etc.)

   c. Full name and address of the persons to be deposed as well as their citizenship and a statement that the witnesses' appearance is voluntary;

   d. Suggested dates for taking the deposition or a period within which the deposition should be taken;

   e. Proposed location for the deposition (U.S. Embassy or Consulate, hotel, solicitor's chambers, corporate offices, military base, etc.).

   f. Whether the deposition will be oral or based on written questions;

g. Who will attend the taking of the deposition (e.g., requesting counsel, opposing counsel, number of witnesses, stenographer, interpreter, video-operator, etc. (This may be important when the size of the room available to conduct the deposition is a problem.)

h. Whether the consular officer will be required to preside at the entire proceedings or may administer the appropriate oath(s) and withdraw subject to recall.

i. Include in the fax, letter, telegram, or telex authorization for a return collect cable/call from the consular officer to confirm arrangements.

j. Attach to the letter, or fax a copy of the commission or notice, or forward separately when available. For Depositions on Written Questions attach the interrogatories and any special instructions. For both oral depositions and depositions on written questions, make arrangements to forward the requisite fees before the depositions begin as explained below.

6. Arranging Appearance of Witness: Requesting counsel must make arrangements with the witness to insure his or her appearance for the deposition (travel fees, witness fees, etc.) The embassy/consulate does not arrange the appearance of witnesses for private attorneys.

7. Consular Deposition Fees: U.S. consular fees for the taking of depositions are set forth at Federal Register, January 30, 1998, Vol. 63, No. 20, pp. 5097-5103. They include the following:

SERVICES FEE Item #Non-Refundable Deposition Scheduling Fee

2 hours consular time required for scheduling, communication with counsel, and local authorities as applicable. Additional 2 hour fee charged to reschedule

$400.00 Hourly Deposition Fee

Generally $200.00 (one hour consular time) x number of days payable in advance of taking of deposition. If further consular participation required, hourly rate charged accordingly, payable in advance

$200.00 Notarial Service for Closing Certificate

$ 55.00 Postage for Return of Transcript

Deposit payable in advance prior to taking of deposition based on consular officer's estimate for usual costs

Actual Costs Packaging and Preparing Certification for Lengthy Deposition

One hour of consular time payable in advance of taking of deposition

$180.00

Fees for Government Requests: No fees are charged for depositions at the request of U.S., state or local government officials (Schedule of Fees items 38(a) and (b).)

Estimating Time Required to Take Deposition: Notify the embassy/consulate of the estimated length of time necessary to take the deposition, allowing for the additional time required for translating questions and answers. Be aware that if the witnesses will be deposed in a foreign language, the use of interpreters will approximately double the time required.

Payment of Fees: Payment should be made by international money order or certified bank check payable to the American Embassy or to the appropriate American consulate (corporate or personal checks not acceptable). Any unused portion from your deposit will be refunded. As federal regulations prohibit the performance of consular services in advance of payment of statutory consular fees, depositions cannot be convened until all the required funds have been deposited. Should the deposition require more time than anticipated, additional fees and expenses must be paid by requesting counsel before the completed deposition will be released by the U.S. embassy or consulate.

E. HOST COUNTRY CLEARANCE REQUIRED FOR CERTAIN "OFFICIAL" PARTIPANTS

1. U.S. Federal, State or Local Government Participants: If a U.S., state or local Government official is to participate in a deposition before a U.S. consular officer, special host country clearance must be obtained for the travel. Such Government officials should contact the Office of American Citizens Services, Department of State, (202) 647-5226, fax (202) 647-2835 to initiate the process of obtaining the host country clearance. A copy of the host country clearance questionnaire will be faxed to you. It will also be available via our Internet Home Page and Autofax Service. See also U.S. Attorney's Manual (USAM) Title 9, Sections 2.151 and 13.534, and Title 3, Section 3.730.

2. Special Masters: See also, Rule 53, Fed. R. Civ. P. (Role of Special Master in general). If a Special Master is to be used in taking the deposition, please advise the U.S. consular officer. In general no special host country clearance is generally required for participation of Special Masters (See Note re Judges below or U.S. or state officials above). However, if particular foreign countries have problems or questions about the practice, the Department of State, Office of American Citizens Services can assist explaining the role of the Special Master.

3. American Judges: Judges from U.S. Federal, State or Local courts, including administrative law judges, should not perform official functions in foreign countries without the express consent of the host country authorities. Such actions may violate the judicial sovereign of the host country. This proviso also applies to depositions or other proceedings conducted at U.S. embassies/consulates abroad and U.S. military bases abroad. See, Cumulative Digest of United States Practice in International Law, 1981-1988, Vol. II, 1400, 1402, Department of State (1994). But see, Administrative Office of the U.S. Courts, Guide to Judiciary Policies and Procedures, Vol. III, Judges' Manual, February 1988, trans. 2, vol. III, chap. XV, p. 3, Sec. B.1.c. which provides that "By a resolution of the Judicial Conference of the United States, a judge may not be reimbursed for expenses of travel to a foreign country to preside over the taking of depositions." This instruction cross references the Reports of the Proceedings of the Judicial Conference of the United States held at Washington, D.C. March 9-10, 1978 and Sepember 21-22, 1978, Proceedings, September 1978, p. 4-5. Those proceedings provide that "the Conference, upon consideration of the report of the Committee on Court Administration, disapproved, as a matter of policy, the practice of Federal judges traveling abroad to take testimony or depositions in cases pending before them." See also, United Kingdom: House of Lords Decision in Westinghouse Electric Corporation Uranium Contract

Litigation, 16 I.L.M. 784 (1977); Merhige, Obtaining Foreign Discovery and Evidence for Use in Litigation in the United States. The Westinghouse Uranium Case: Problems Encountered in Seeking Foreign Discovery and Evidence, 13 Int'l Law. 19 (1979). Wilkey, Symposia: Transnational Litigation, Part I: Transnational Adjudication: A View From the Bench, 18 Int'l Law. 541 (1984). For more information, contact the Office of General Counsel, Administrative Office of the U.S. Courts. The Department of State, Office of American Citizens Services will assist in attempting to obtain permission from foreign governments for such travel. See also section of this flyer regarding U.S. federal, state and local government officials participating in depositions abroad.

F. TELEPHONE/TELECONFERENCE DEPOSITIONS

If counsel desires to conduct telephone depositions, please check with the U.S. embassy or consulate first to confirm that such procedures are permitted in the foreign country and that electrical and telephonic equipment in the foreign country and at the U.S. embassy/consulate is adequate for this purpose. See, Rule 30(b)(7) F. R. Civ. P. which provides that depositions by telephone are authorized by Rule 29, upon stipulation of the parties; The final sentence added to make clear that when a deposition is taken by telephone it is taken in the district and at the place where the witness is to answer the question. See 85 F.R.D. 521, 529. For this reason, telephone depositions conducted of witnesses located abroad may only be taken where the foreign country permits telephone depositions. See Rehau, Inc. v. Colortech, Inc., D.C. Mich. 1993, 145 F.R.D. 444. See also, Moore, Moore's Federal Practice, Rule 30(b)(7); 30.09(5). But see, Cumulative Digest of United States Practice in International Law, Department of State, Vol. II, 1429, 1430 (1994).

G. RECORDING DEPOSITIONS

1. Video Operations and Other Equipment: Counsel should also be aware that video-taping is not permitted in many foreign countries. U.S. consular officers do not have professional expertise in the technical or legal aspects of recording depositions by other than stenographic means. Requesting counsel must provide video-tape operators with specific instructions on any special procedures to be followed. U.S. Consular officers can advise videotape operators that any specific instructions provided by American attorneys on stipulation by the parties/participants be included in the record of the deposition (22 C.F.R. 92.56 (special instructions). American equipment may need special adapters, generators, etc. to function on different foreign electrical currents. Consult the U.S. embassy or consulate for particulars.

2. Foreign Customs Requirements: If counsel intends to utilize video-tape equipment for the purpose of recording the deposition (Rule 30(b)(4) Fed. R. C.P.), please note that special foreign customs clearances must be obtained from the foreign country before such video equipment is transported into the foreign country or the equipment may be confiscated by the foreign authorities. Contact the embassy of the foreign country in the United States for guidance regarding customs requirements. The address and telephone number of the foreign embassies are included in our Consular Information Sheets regarding foreign travel under "Entry Requirements" which are available via our Home Page or through our Autofax Service .

3. Guidelines for Video Recording Testimony: See Guidelines for Pre-Recording Testimony on Videotape Prior to Trial, Federal Judicial Center, Washington, D.C., December 1976, 2d, FJC Pub. No. 76-3, FJC Information Service. But see, Cumulative Digest of United States Practice in International Law, Department of State, Vol. II, 1429,

1430 (1994). Selected Cases (Not Comprehensive): See Wescott v. Neeman, 55 F.R.D. 257 (D.C. Neb. 1972) (Guidelines for Recording Depositions by NonStenographic Means); Colonial Times Inc. v. Gasch, 509 F. 2d 517 (D.C. Cir. 1975); In the Matter of Daniels, 69 F.R.D. 579 (N.D. Ga. 1975); Marlboro Products Corp. v. N. Am. Phillips Corp., 54 F.R.D. 487 (S.D.N.Y. 1972); Kallen v. Nexus Corp., 54 F.R.D. 610 (N.D. Ill. 1972); Buck v. Bd. of Education of the City of New York, 16 Fed. R. Serv. 2d 112, 113 (E.D.N.Y. 1972); Carson v. Burlington Northern Inc., 52 F.R.D. 492 (D. Neb. 1971). Selected Articles: Barber & Bates, Videotape in Criminal Proceedings, 25 Hastings L.J. 1017 (1974); Cunningham, Videotape Evidence: Technological Innovation in the Trial Process, 36 Ala. Lawyer 228 (1975); Darnieder, Videotaped Depositions, a Court Reporter's View, 34 Nat's Shorthand Rep. 13 (June 1973); Kornblum, Videotape in Civil Cases, 24 Hastings L.J. 9 (1972); Miller, Videotaping the Oral Deposition, 18 Prac. Law. 45 (1972); Valentino, Practice, Procedure and Forms under the Nebraska Videotape Deposition Statute, 8 Creighton L. Rev. 314 (1975); Annot., Recording of Testimony at Deposition by Other than Stenographic Means Under Rule 30(b)(4), 16 A.L.R. Fed. 969 (1973); Case Note, Evidence — Admission of Videotape (Hendricks v. Swenson), 38 Mo. L. Rev. 111 (1973); Note, Review of Discovery Order Under F.R. Civ. P. 30(b)(4), 22 Wayne L. Rev. 179 (1975); Modernizing Trial Techniques and Management: Audio-Visual Testimony, Excerpt from Proceedings of the Judicial Conference of the Sixth Judicial Circuit of the United States, 58 F.R.D. 221 (May 1972).

4. Court Reporters/Interpreters: The U.S. Embassy/Consulate may be able to provide information concerning interpreters, translators and audio/video operators. Private counsel must make their own arrangements to retain the services of interpreters, translators and audio/video operators. Attorneys for local or state government of the U.S. government may contact the Office of American Citizens Services or contact U.S. embassies and consulates directly for assistance in retaining these services. Note: not all foreign countries have court reporters, interpreters and translators. American embassies and consulates do not have staff personnel available to perform such functions. It may be necessary to bring your own experts in these fields from the United States.

H. DEPOSITIONS ON WRITTEN QUESTIONS

U.S. consular officers can conduct depositions on written questions (22 CFR 92.58). Such depositions are scheduled at a date and time of mutual convenience to the witness and the U.S. consular officer. It is the responsibility of requesting counsel to contact the witness and the U.S. consular officer to make these arrangements, and to take necessary measures to retain a court reporter and interpreter. It is also possible, on stipulation, to arrange that the witness will write down the answers to the questions directly after having been placed under oath by the U.S. consular officer. The consular officer will prepare the deposition closing certificate and requesting counsel can arrange for the translation at a later date. A copy of the notice or commission should accompany the written questions and any translations. See Moore's Federal Practice, Chapter 28; Ch. 31 (1993).

I. COMPULSION OF EVIDENCE

When a witness is not willing to testify or produce documents or other evidence voluntarily, the assistance of foreign authorities generally must be sought. The customary method of compelling evidence is by letter rogatory or "letter of request", unless the country in question is a party to the Hague Evidence Convention. For prosecutors, bilateral Mutual Legal Assistance treaties (MLATs) are another option. (See our separate flyer on MLATs). Some foreign countries have domestic discovery laws which offer simpler, more timely solutions.

If, however, the witness or custodian of records is subject to the U.S. court's personal jurisdiction, other alternative methods of exterritorial discovery may be available. All of these procedures are discussed below.

1. Compulsion Evidence Via Letters Rogatory: A letter rogatory, now more commonly known as a "letter of request", is a formal request from a court in one country to "the appropriate judicial authorities" in another country requesting compulsion of testimony or documentary or other evidence. (28 U.S.C. 1781; 22 C.F.R. 92.66(b)&(c); 28 U.S.C. Fed. R.Civ. P., Rule 28(b); Article 5(j), Vienna Convention on Consular Relations, 21 U.S.T. 77, 596 UNTS 261; TIAS 6820 (where applicable); Bilateral Consular Conventions (where applicable). Letters rogatory or letters of request can also be used to request service of process. Most foreign countries will only accept letters rogatory from a court, and will not recognize a request from an administrative law judge. Letters rogatory can be used in civil and criminal matters, and have been used in administrative matters. The execution of a request for judicial assistance by the foreign court is based on comity between nations, unless a specific treaty obligation exists such as the Hague Evidence Convention or MLAT treaties. For additional information regarding the preparation of letters rogatory or letters of request, see our flyers on "Preparation of Letters Rogatory" and our country-specific judicial assistance flyers. See "Additional Information" below. Letters rogatory are a cumbersome, time consuming mechanism which should not be used unless there is no other alternative.

2. Hague Evidence Convention - Civil/Commercial/Administrative Matters: HAGUE CONVENTION ON THE TAKING OF EVIDENCE ABROAD IN CIVIL OR COMMERCIAL MATTERS, (23 U.S.T. 2555; T.I.A.S. 7444; 847 UNTS 231; 28 U.S.C.A. 1782 (1975 Cum. Supp.); 28 U.S.C.A. 1781 (Supp. 1979); 8 I.L.M. 37 (1969); Martindale-Hubbell Law Directory, Law Digest Volume, Selected International Conventions). It is possible to conduct depositions in countries party to the Convention. Consult our flyer on the Convention and our country specific flyers available via our Internet Home Page or Autofax Service and consult the declarations and reservations found in the Martindale-Hubbell Law Directory, Law Digest Volume, Selected International Conventions. To compel testimony under the Hague Evidence Convention, a letter of request (similar to a letter rogatory) sent directly to a foreign central authority by the court or litigant in the United States is used. Consult our flyer on the Convention for details. In Force*: ANGUILLA, ARGENTINA (excludes recognition of the extension of the Convention by the United Kingdom to the MALVINAS, SOUTH GEORGIA and SOUTH SANDWICH ISLANDS), ARUBA, AUSTRALIA, BARBADOS, CAYMAN ISLANDS, CYPRUS, CZECH REPUBLIC, DENMARK, DJIBOUTI, ESTONIA, FALKLAND ISLANDS, FINLAND, FRANCE, FRENCH GUIANA, FRENCH POLYNESIA, GERMANY, GIBRALTAR, GUADELOUPE, GUERNSEY, HONG KONG, ISLE OF MAN, ISRAEL, ITALY, JERSEY, LATVIA, LUXEMBOURG, MACAO, MARTINIQUE, MEXICO, MONACO, NETHERLANDS, NORWAY, POLAND, PORTUGAL, SAINT PIERRE AND MIQUELON, SINGAPORE, SLOVAK REPUBLIC, SOVEREIGN BASE AREAS OF AKROTIRI AND DHEKELIA, SPAIN, SWEDEN, SWITZERLAND, UNITED KINGDOM, UNITED STATES, VENEZUELA.

---

* See our specific flyer on the Hague Evidence Convention for annotations regarding extension of accession to the Convention to territories and overseas possessions which have since been declared independent, and other footnotes on particular countries, names and addresses of foreign central authorities, etc. See also the country specific flyers available on the Internet at our home page and via our automated fax service discussed below under "Additional Information".

3. Service of Federal Subpoena for Witness Abroad (28 U.S.C. 1783): The statute provides for service of a federal subpoena or order to show cause on a U.S. citizen or permanent resident alien abroad requiring the appearance of the witness before a court in the United States. See 22 CFR 92.86, 92.87, 92.88. See also, Born & Westin, 273, note 37; Moore's Federal Practice, Sec. 28.17 (1993). It is not possible to compel the testimony of a witness at a deposition abroad by service of an American subpoena.

4. Invoking Foreign Domestic Discovery Laws More Expeditious than Letters Rogatory or Hague Evidence Convention Requests: Some common law countries have domestic laws which provide for a solicitor to obtain an order from a local (foreign) court compeling a witness to appear at a solicitor's office. See also, country-specific flyers for the United Kingdom, Hong Kong, Canada, etc. for information about this process or consult local foreign counsel. See, Black, Discovery in Great Britain: The Evidence (Proceedings in Other Jurisdictions) Act, 11 Cornell Int'l L. J. 344 (1978). Lipstein, The Evidence (Proceedings in Other Jurisdiction) Act 1975: An Interpretation (Foreign Evidence in English Courts), Int'l and Comp. L. Q., 120, 135 (1990).

J. EXTRATERRITORIAL DISCOVERY

1. Restatement of Foreign Relations Law of the United States (Revised)(Third), Sec. 442 (1987). The American Law Institute (ALI)'s Restatement (Second) of the Foreign Relaitons Law of the United States (Second Restatement) sets forth a balancing test to assist courts in solving jurisdictional conflicts. Section 40 of the Second Restatement lists five nonexclusive factors that courts should consider to resolve jurisdictional conflicts. The ALI's Third Restatement restructured the Second Restatement's extraterritorial discovery balancing test in several ways. Section 442 of the Third Restatement provides five factors for the U.S. courts, under the principle of international comity, to balance when determining whether the requested documents are directly relevant, necessary, and material to an investigation conducted by a government agency or to any court discovery action. Section 442(1)(a) of the ALI's Third Restatement provides "A court or agency in the United States, when authorized by statute or rule of court, may order a person subject to its jurisdiction to produce documents, objects, or other information relevant to an action or investigation, even if the information or the person in possession of the information is outside of the United States." Sec. 442 also provides for sanctions for failure to comply with an order.

2. Selected Commentary: Robinson, Symposia: Transnational Litigation, Part I, Compelling Discovery and Evidence in International Litigation, The Int'l Law., Vol. 18, No. 3, 533 (1984). Cumulative Digest of United States Practice in International Law, 1981-1988, Vol. II, 1522 (1994); Born & Westin, 302, 305; Rosenthal & Yale-Loehr, Two Cheers for the ALI Restatement's Provisions on Foreign Discovery, 16 N.Y.U.J. Int'l L. & Pol. 1075 (1984).; Houck, Restatement of the Foreign Relations Law of the United States (Revised): Issues and Resolutions, 20 Int'l Law. 1361 (1986). Van Brauman, Foreign Evidence Gathering and Discovery for U.S. Civil Tax Determination Purposes, 30 Int'l Law. 589, 619 (1996). Plaster, The Hague Evidence Convention: The Need for Guidance on Procedures and Resolution of Conflicts in International Discovery, Vanderbilt Journal of Transnational Law, Vol. 27, No. 1, pp. 185-217 (1994).

3. Selected Illustrative Cases: (Not Comprehensive): Societe National Industrielle Aerospatiale v. U.S. District Court, 107 S. Ct. 2542 & N. 28 (1987). Grand Jury Proceedings: The Bank of Nova Scotia II, In re , 740 F.2d 817 (11th Cir. 1984), cert.

den., 469 U.S. 1106 (1985); 105 S. Ct. 778 (1985); United States v. Bank of Nova Scotia I, 691 F.2d 1384 (11th Cir. 1982), cert. denied, 103 S. Ct. 3086 (1983); Richmark Corp. v. Timber Falling Consultants, 959 F.2d 1468 (9th Cir. 1992); In re Perrier Bottled Water Litigation, 138 F.R.D. 348 (D. Conn. 1991); Reinsurance Co. v. Administratia Asigurarilor de Stat, 902 F.2d 1275 (7th Cir. 1990); In Re Grand Jury Proceedings Yanagihara, 709 F. Supp. 192 (C.D. Cal 1989); United States v. Rubin, 836 F.2d 1096 (8th Cir. 1988); Hudson v. Hermann Pfanter GmbH & Co., 117 F.R.D. 33 (N.D.N.Y. 1987); United States v. Davis, 767 F.2d 1025 (2d Cir. 1985); Graco, Inc. v. Kremlin, Inc., 101 F.R.D. 503 (N.D. Ill. 1984); Laker Airways Ltd. v. Pan American World Airways, 103 F.R.D. 42 (D.D.C. 1984); United States v. Toyota Motor Corp., 569 F. Supp. 1158 (C.D. Cal. 1983); Hong Kong and Singapore Bank Corp. v. Commissioner, 85 T.C. No. 41 (Nov. 5, 1985); United States v. First National Bank of Chicago, 699 F.2d 341 (7th Cir. 1983); United States v. Vetco, 691 F.2d 1281 (9th Cir.) cert. denied, 454 U.S. 1098 (1981); SEC v. Banca della Svizzera Italiana, 92 F.R.D. 111 (S.D.N.Y. 1981); In re Uranium Antitrust Litigation, 480 F. Supp. 1138 (N.D. Ill. 1979); In re Westinghouse Elec. Corp. Uranium, 563 F.2d 992 (10th Cir. 1977); Federal Maritime Commission v. DeSmedt, 366 F. 2d 464 (2d Cir.), cert. denied, 385 U.S. 974 (1966); Societe Internationale v. Rogers, 357 U.S. 197 (1958).

4. Direct Extraterritorial Discovery Under Subpoena Provisions of Rule 45, F.R. Civ. P.: Compulsion of documentary evidence located abroad has been sought by U.S. courts if the court has in personam jurisdiction of the person in possession or control of the material. Wright & Miller, Sec. 2209, 2454, 2462, p. 65-67 (1970). See Born & Westin, International Civil Litigation in United States Courts, 266, 273 (1989). See also, United States v. Bank of Nova Scotia, 691 F.2d 1384 (11th Cir. 1982), cert. denied, 462 U.S. 1119 (1983); In re Marc Rich & Co., 707 F.2d 663 (2d Cir), cert. denied, 463 U.S. 1215 (1983). But see, Afram Export Corp. v. Metallurgiki Halyps, S.A., 772 F.2d 1358, 1365-66 (7th Cir. 1985) regarding court's refusal to issue Rule 45(d) F.R.Civ. P. subpoena for testimony of witness located abroad, and its decision to order the deposition in the United States, not in the foreign country. See Born & Westin, 274, 276. But see, FTC v. Compagnie de Saint Gobain-Pont-a-Mousson, 636 F. 2d 1300 (D.C. Cir. 1980).

K. ADDITIONAL INFORMATION

The Office of American Citizens Services has available general information flyers on international judicial assistance many of which are available through our automated fax system or via our Internet Consular Affairs Home Page. These topics include country-specific information about service of process and obtaining evidence abroad.

Using the Autofax System:

*Dial (202) 647-3000 using the phone on your fax machine.

*Follow the prompt to obtain a printed index of judicial assistance topics.Thereare four indexes.

Travel Information - Index of Countries - Press 1

Passports and Visas - Index of Flyers - Press 2

Judicial Assistance - General and Country Specific - Press 3

Child Custody and Adoption - Index of Flyers - Press 4

* Enter the four digit code for the document desired as listed in the index.

* When the prompt identifies the document and asks if you want that document, enter Y (9) for yes or N (6) for no.

* If you want another document, enter the four digit code, using the same procedures noted in the previous step.

* When you finish selecting, press the # key on the phone keyboard and press the start button on your fax machine.

* After a brief delay of up to a minute, the documents will print automatically on your fax machine.

Using the Internet:

Many of our judicial assistance flyers are also available on the Internet via the Department of State, Bureau of Consular Affairs Home Page at the URL: http://travel.state.gov under "judicial assistance" or via the main State Department home page at http://www.state.gov/ under "travel".. See also, the Department of State, Office of the Legal Adviser for Private International Law (L/PIL) Home Page at http://his.com/~pildb/ for information about the work of the Hague Conference on Private International Law and the OAS in private international law unification. See also the home pages for many of our embassies which are linked to the Consular Affairs home page..

L. TREATY DATABASES ON THE INTERNET

Information on which countries are party to a particular treaty is available from the following databases:

United States Department of State, Office of the Legal Adviser, Treaty Affairs, List of Treaties and Other International Agreements of the United States In Force: http://www.acda.gov/state/.

United Nations (UN): http://www.un.org/ under Databases/Treaties at http://www.un.org/Depts/Treaty/;

Council of Europe (COE): http://www.coe.fr:80/index.html under Texts/Treaties http://www.coe.fr.80/eng/legaltxt/treaties.htm;

Organization of American States (OAS): http://www.oas.org/ under Public Information/Documents/Treaties at gopher://oasunix1.oas.org:70/11/pub/english/treaties.

U.S. House of Representatives Internet Law Library Treaties and International Law: http://law.house.gov/89.htm.

M. QUESTIONS

For additional information, contact the appropriate geographic division of the Office of American Citizens Services and Crisis Management at telephone (202) 647-5226.

N. SELECTED BIBLIOGRAPHY

1. Books:

Abbell & Ristau: International Judicial Assistance - Criminal, volumes 3,4, 5 (Obtaining Evidence, Prisoner Transfer and Extradition), International Law Institute (1990, 1995 supp.)

Bilateral Studies in Private International Law Series, Parker School of Foreign and Comparative Law, Columbia University, Oceana Publicaitons, 1958-1964 (Swiss, French, Dutch, German, Colombian, Greek, Danish, Australian, Brazilian, Chilean, Austrian, Japanese).

Born & Westin, International Civil Litigation in the United States Courts (2d ed. 1992).

Epstein, International Litigation: A Guide to Jurisdiction, Practice and Strategy, 2d, Prentice Hall Law & Business (1994).

Grossman, Letters Rogatory: A Symposium Before the Consular Law Society, Federal Legal Publications, Inc., New York (1956).

Hackworth, Digest of International Law, Office of the Legal Adviser, Department of State, Vol. II, (1941).

Kos-Rabcewicz-Zubkowski, International Cooperation in Civil and Commercial Procedure: American Continent, Canadian Inter-American Research Institute; U. of Ottawa Press, (1975).

Lookofsky, Transnational Litigation and Commercial Arbitration, A Comparative Analysis of American, European, and International Law, 445-89 (1992).

Lowenfeld, Int'l Litigation & Arbitration, 1993.

Nanda & Pansius, Litigation of International Disputes in U.S. Courts, Vol. 4, International Business Law Series, Sec. 2.02(2), p. 2-4, 2-25 (1996 Supp.).

Nash, Digest of United States Practice in International Law, Department of State, Office of the Legal Adviser, 1973-1988.

Ristau, International Judicial Assistance (Civil and Commercial), International Law Institute (1984, 1996 suppl.)

Smit, International Cooperation in Litigation: Europe, The Hague, Martinus Nijhoff, 1965.

Weinsten & Berger, Evidence, United States Rules, Sec. 1004(2)(01), 1004-23-26 (1983).

Whiteman, Digest of International Law, Office of the Legal Adviser, Department of State, Vol 7, 573, 605 (1970).

Wigmore, On Evidence, Sec. 2195, (1986 Supp.).

2. Articles:

Acomb, Foreign Depositions: The Problems, Pitfalls and Procedures, 14 The Forum 440 (1979).

April & Fried, Compelling Discovery and Disclosure in Transnational Criminal Litigation, A Canadian View, 16 N.Y.U. J. Int'l L. & Pol. 961, 964-65 (1984).

Baade, International Civil and Commercial Litigation: A Tentative Checklist, 8 Texas Int'l L. J. 5, No. 1, (1973).

Beckett, Transnational Litigation: Perspectives from the U.S. and Abroad: United Kingdom, 18 Int'l Law. 773 (1984).

Black, Discovery in Great Britain: The Evidence (Proceedings in Other Jurisdictions) Act, 11 Cornell Int'l L. J. 344 (1978).

Blechman, Antitrust Jurisdiction, Discovery and Enforcement in the International Sphere: An Appraisal of American Developments and Foreign Relations, 49 Antitrust L.J. 1197 (1980).

Blejec, Extraterritorial Jurisdiction of U.S. Courts Regarding the Use of Subpoenas Duces Tecum to Obtain Discovery in Transnational Litigation: The Search for a Limiting Principle, 16 N.Y.U.J. Int'l L. and Pol. 1135 (No. 5, Summer 1984).

Borel and Boyd, Opportunities for and obstacles to Obtaining Evidence in France for Use in Litigation in the United States, Int'l Law., Vol. 72, 133 (1978).

Bornstein & Levitt, Much Ado About 1782, 20 U. Miami Inter-Am. L. Rev. 429, 458-62 (1989).

Boyd, Symposium: Obtaining Foreign Discovery and Evidence for Use in Litigation in the United States, 13 Int'l Law. 1 (1979).

Boyd, Contemporary Practice of the United States Relating to International Law - The Hague Evidence Convention, 72 Am. J. Int'l Law 133 (1978).

Burke, United States v. Salim: A Harbinger for Federal Prosecutions Using Depositions Taken Abroad, Catholic U.L.R., Vol. 39, No.3, 895, 943 (1990).

Cairns, Discovery and Preservation of Evidence Under Inherent Jurisdiction (United Kingdom), Civil Justice Quarterly (C.J.Q.), 309, Oct. 1985.

Cairns, The Law of Discovery in Australia: Documents, Interrogatories and Property, Sydney, The Law Book Company Limited, 1984.

Carter, Obtaining Foreign Discovery and Evidence for Use in Litigation in the United States - Existing Rules and Procedures, 13 Int'l Law. 5 (1979).

Cayman Islands, The Narcotic Drugs (Evidence) (United States of America) Law, 1984, 24 Int'l Leg. Mat. 937, NO. 4, July 1985.

Christenson, International Judicial Assistance and Utah Practice, 7 Utah L. Rev. 478 (1961).

Cira, The Challenge of Foreign Laws to Block American Antitrust Actions, 18 Stan. J. Int'l L. 247 (1982).

Cohen, Discovery Abroad in Patent Infringement Litigation, Nordiskt Immateriellt Rattsskydd (N.I.R.), 62, No. 1, 1985.

Cohen, In Personam Jurisdiction in Federal Courts Over Foreign Corporations: The Need for a Federal Long-Arm Statute, 14 Denver J. Int'l L. & Pol'y 59, No. 1, Spring/Summer 1985.

Collins, Opportunities for and Obstacles to Obtaining Evidence in England for Use in Litigation in the United States; The Int'l Law., Vol 13, 27, (1979).

Comment, Discovery in Great Britain: The Evidence (Proceedings and Other Jurisdictions) Act, 11 Cornell Int'l L.J. 323 (1978).

Comment, Discovery of Documents Located Abroad in U.S. Antitrust Litigation: Recent Developments in the Law Concerning the Foreign Illegality Excuse for Non-Production, 14 Va. J. Int'l. L. 4 (1974).

Comment, Foreign Non-Disclosure Laws and Domestic Discovery Orders and Antitrust Litigation, 88 Yale L.J. 612 (1979).

Comment, International Law: International Judicial Assistance in Oklahoma Practice, 22 Okla. L. Rev. 217 (1969).

Comment, Judicial Cooperation in the Taking of Evidence Abroad — The Canada and Ontario Evidence Acts, 8 Tex. Int'l L.J. 57 (1973).

Comment, Judicial Notice and Deposition Practice in International Litigation, Duke L. J. 512 (1966).

Comment, Jurisdiction and Procedure — Discovery — Party Unable to Comply With Discovery Order Which Contravenes Foreign Nondisclosure Law Is Not In Contempt of Court, 11 Vand. J. Trans. Law 351 (1978).

Comment, Ordering Production of Documents From Abroad and Violation of Foreign Law, 31 U. Chi. L. Rev. 791 (1964).

Comment, Revitalization of the International Judicial Assistance Procedures of the United States: Service of Documents and Taking of Testimony, 62 Mich. L. Rev. 1375, 1387-1388 (1964).

Comment, Subpoena of Documents Located in Foreign Jurisdictions Where Law of the Situs Prohibits Removal, 37 N.Y.U.L. Rev. 295 (1962).

Comment, The International Uranium Cartel: Litigation and Legal Implications, 14 Tex. Int'l. L.J. 59 (1979).

Comment, U.S. Foreign Subpoena Power Subdued: The Case of the FTC v. Compagnie de Saint-Gobain, 8 Brooklyn J. Int;l L. 499 (1982).

Cook, Note, International Reciprocity, 4 Canadian-Am L.J. 93, 94 (1993).

Lam, Economic and Political Aspects of Extraterritoriality, 19 Int'l Law. 887 (1985).

Deutsch, Note, Judicial Assistance: Obtaining Evidence in the United States, Under 28 U.S.C. 1782 for Use in a Foreign or International Tribunal, 5 B.C. Int'l & Comp. L. Rev. 175, 190-92 (1982).

Devine & Olsen, Note, Taking Evidence Outside of the United States, Boston University L. R., 368, (1975).

Dorman, California Statutory Contributions in the Field of International Judicial Assistance, 39 L.A.B. Bull. 7 (1963).

Doyle, Taking Evidence by Deposition and Letters Rogatory and Obtaining Documents in Foreign Territory, Proc. A.B.A., Sec. Int'l & Comp. L. 37 (1959).

Edwards, Taking of Evidence Abroad in Civil or Commercial Matters, 18 Int'l. and Comp. L. Q. 646 (1969).

Ellis and Pisani, The United States Treaties on Mutual Assistance in Criminal Matters: A Comparative Analysis, 19 Int'l Law. 189 (1985).

Fedders, Policing Internationalized U.S. Capital Markets: Methods to Obtain Evidence Abroad, 18 Int'l Law. 89 (1984).

Frei, Transnational Litigation: Perspectives from the U.S. and Abroad: Switzerland, 18 Int'l Law. 789 (1984).

Friedman and Wilson, Representing Foreign Clients in Civil Discovery and Grand Jury Proceedings, 26 Va. J. of Int'l L. 327 (1986).

Gerber, Obscured Visions: Policy, Power and Discretion in Transnational Discovery, 23 Vand. J. Transnat'l L. 993, 999 (1991).

Gerber, International Discovery After Aerospatiale: The Quest for an Analytical Framework, 82 Am. J. Int'l Law 521, 551 (1988).

Gerber, Extraterritorial Discovery and the Conflict of Procedural Systems: Germany and the United States, 34 American Journal of Comparative Law 745 (1986).

Germany, Law on International Assistance in Criminal Matters, 24 Int'l Leg. Mat. 945, No. 4, July 1984).

Ginsberg, The Soviet Union and International Cooperation in Civil Matters, 53 Iowa L. Rev. 1020 (1968).

Gori-Montanelli & Botwinik, International Judicial Assistance - Italy, 9 Int'l L. 717 (1975).

Griffin & Bravin, Beyond Aerospatiale: A Commentary on Foreign Discovery Provisions, 25 Int'l Law. No. 2, 315 (1991).

Griffin, Procedures for Civil Discovery Outside the United States after Aerospatiale, 15 Int'l Bus. Law. 350 (1987).

Harada, Civil Discovery Under Japanese Law, 16 Law In Japan 21 (1983).

Hayne, Convention and the Federal Rules of Civil Procedure, 9 Hous. J. Int'l L. 333 (1987).

Heck, Transnational Litigation: Perspectives from the U.S. and Abroad: Germany, 18 Int'l Law. 793 (1984).

Heilpern, Procuring Evidence Abroad, 14 Tul. L. Rev. 29 (1939).

Herzog, The 1980 French Law on Documents and Information, American J. of Int'l L., 382, (1981).

Hindenburg, Commissions for Taking Evidence Before Foreign Tribunals, 2885 Int. Law. Ass'n Rep. 114

Hindenburg, On the Taking of Evidence of Witnesses Resident in Foreign Countries, 1901 Int'l Law. Ass'n Rep. 325.

Hindenburg, Evidence of Foreign Witnesses, 1907 Int. Law. Ass'n Rep. 234.

Hollman, Problems of Obtaining Evidence in Anti-Trust Litigation: Comparative Approaches to the Multi-National Corporation, 11 Tex. Int'l. L. J. 46 (1976).

Houck, Restatement of the Foreign Relations Law of the United States (Revised): Issues and Resolutions, 20 Int'l Law. 1361 (1986).

Issacs, U.S. Letters Rogatory and the English Courts, Lloyd's Maritime and Commercial Law Quarterly 464 (1978).

Jacobs, Extraterritorial Application of Competition Law - an English View, The Int'l Law., Vol. 13, 645 (1979).

Jones, Compulsion Over Comity: The United States' Assault on Foreign Bank Secrecy, 12 NW. J. Int'l L. & Bus. 454, 485 (1992).

Jones, International Judicial Assistance: Procedural Chaos and a Program for Reform, 62 Yale L.J. 515, 540 (1953).

Kaplan, An American Lawyer in the Queen's Courts: Impressions of English Civil Procedure, 69 Mich. L. Rev. 821, 824-26 (1971).

Knapp, Mutual Legal Assistance Treaties as a Way to Pierce Bank Secrecy, J. of Int'l L., Case Western Reserve, Vol. 20, No.2, 405, 433 (1988).

Kiely, Case Comment, Comity - Judicial Assistance, 13 Suffolk Transnat'l L.J. 355, 357 n. 13 (1989).

Koroyasu, Transnational Litigation: Perspectives from the U.S. and Abroad: Japan, 18 Int'l Law. 785 (1984).

Kos-Rabcewicz-Zubkowski, Quebec (Provincial) and Canadian (Federal) Rules on International Procedure (International Judicial Assistance in Civil and Commercial Matters) 13 Int;l & Comp. L. Q. 270 (1964).

Langbein, The German Advantage in Civil Procedure, 52 U. Chi. L. Rev. 823, 826-27 (1985).

Light, Discovery Abroad and the Consequences When It Is Not Possible, 50 Antitrust L.J. 577 (1982).

Lipstein, The Evidence (Proceedings in Other Jurisdiction) Act 1975: An Interpretation (Foreign Evidence in English Courts), Int'l and Comp. L. Q., 120, 135 (1990).

Low, International Judicial Assistance Among the American States, The Int'l Law., Vol. 18, No. 3, 705 (1984).

Lowe, Blocking Extraterritorial Jurisdiction: The British Protection of Trading Interests Act, 1980, 75 Am. J. Int'l L. 257 (1981).

Lowenfeld, Introduction: Discovering Discovery, International Style, 16 N.Y.U. J. Int'l L. & Pol. 957 (1984).

Lowenfeld, International Litigation and Arbitration (1993).

McCarthy, A Proposed Uniform Standard for U.S. Courts in Granting Requests for International Judicial Assistance, 15 Fordham Int'l L.J. 772, 781 (1991-1992).

McCawley, Compelled Production of Documents Located Abroad - Marc Rich and Co. v. U.S., 11 Tax Plan. Int'l Rev. 7 (No. 11, Nov. 1984).

McCusker, "Some United States Practices in International Judicial Assistance" (1957), 37 United States Department of State Bulletin 808.

McKay, Compelling Discovery and Disclosure in Transnational Litigation: A Selected Bibliography, 16 N.Y.U.J. Int'l L. and Pol. 1217 (No. 5, Summer 1984).

Maher, Time Uranium in the Legislative Process, 9 Fed. L. Rev. 399 (1978).

Maier, Resolving Extraterritorial Conflicts, or "There and Back Again," 25 Va. J. Int'l L. 7, 25-33 (1984).

Maier, Interest Balancing and Extraterritorial Jurisdiction, 31 Am. J. Comp. L. 579 (1983).

Maier, Extraterritorial Jurisdiction at a Crossroads, 76 Am. J. Int'l L. 280 (1982).

Mann, Mari & Lavdas, Developments in International Securities Law Enforcement and Regulation, The International Lawyer, Vol. 29, No. 4, p. 729-873 (1995).

Martens, D.H., German Civil Procedure and the Implementation of the Hague Evidence Convention, International Litigation Quarterly, Vol. 1, No. 2 (September 1985), p. 115.

Merhige, Obtaining Foreign Discovery and Evidence for Use in Litigation in the United States. The Westinghouse Uranium Case: Problems Encountered in Seeking Foreign Discovery and Evidence, 13 Int'l Law. 19 (1979).

Miller, International Cooperation in Litigation Between the United States and Switzerland: Unilateral Procedural Accommodation in a Test Tube, 49 Minn. L. Rev. 1069, 1088-1096 (1965).

Moore-Bick, Service of Process in the United Kingdom, 9 Int'l. Law. No. 4, p. 699-715 (1975).

Moore, Judicial Cooperation in the Taking of Evidence Abroad — The Canada and Ontario Evidence Acts, 8 Tex. Int'l L. J. 57 (1973).

Mori, The Difference Between U.S. Discovery and Japanese Taking of Evidence, 23 Int'l Law. 3 (1989).

Mundiya, U.S. Court Invites Foreign Litigants to Use U.S. Discovery Laws, 42 Int'l & Comp. L.Q. 356, 357 n. 3 (1993)

Myrick & Love, Obtaining Evidence Abroad for Use in United States Litigation, 18 Patent Law Annual 167, 222 (1980).

Nadelmann, Negotiations on Criminal Law Assistance Treaties, 33 Am. J. Comp. L. 467 (1985).

Note, Civil Procedure: International Judicial Assistance — In Re Letters Rogatory from the Tokyo District, Tokyo, Japan, 18 Harv. Int'l L.J. 460 (1977).

Note, Compelling Production of Documents in Violation of Foreign Law: An Examination and Reevaluation of the American Position; 50 Fordham L. Rev. 877, 879 (1982).

Note, Court Ordered Violations of Foreign Bank Secrecy and Blocking Laws: Solving the Extraterritorial Dilemma, U. Ill. L. Rev. 563 (1988).

Note, Discovery Abuse under the Federal Rules: Causes and Cures, 92 Yale L. J. 352 (1982).

Note, Discovery of Documents: Crown Privilege, 79 L. Qtly. Rev. 37 (1963).

Note, Evidence-Effect of Letters Rogatory and Claims to Privlege Against Self-Incrimination Before the English Court, 13 Tex. Int'l L.J. 365 (1978).

Note, Foreign Nondisclosure Laws and Domestic Discovery Orders in Antitrust Discovery, 88 Yale L.J. 612 (1979).

Note, International Judicial Assistance — Letters Rogatory — Tokyo District Court Aiding a Prosecutor in Criminal Investigation Qualifies for Assistance Under 28 U.S.C. 1782, 12 Tex. Int'l L.J. 104 (1977).

Note, Judicial Assistance for the Foreign "Tribunal", 1968 Duke L.J. 981, 989 (1968).

Note, Letters Rogatory — Privilege Against Self-Incrimination — Infringement of United Kingdom Sovereignty, Cambridge L.J. 244 (1978).

Note, Limitations on the Federal Judicial Power to Compel Acts Violating Foreign Law, 63 Colum. L. Rev. 1441 (1963).

Note, Marc Rich: An Explanation of United States Criminal Jurisdiction Over Foreign Defendants, 6 Nw. J. Int'l L. & Bus. 615, No. 2, Summer 1984.

Note, Obtaining International Judicial Assistance Under the Federal Rules and the Hague Convention on the Taking of Evidence Abroad: An Exposition of the Procedures and a Pratical Example — In Re Westinghouse Uranium Contract Litigation, 10 Ga. J. Int'l & Comp. L. (1980).

Note, Ordering Production of Documents Abroad in Violation of Foreign Laws, 31 U. Chi. L. Rev. 791 (1963-64).

Note, Quebec (Provincial) and Canadian (Federal) Rules of International Procedure (International Judicial Assistance) in Civil and Commercial Matters, 12 Int'l and Comp. L.Q. 70 (1964).

Note, Reciprocity for Letters Rogatory Under the Judicial Code, 58 Yale L.J. 1193, 1193-94 (1949).

Note, Rio Tinto — Zinc Corporation v. Westinghouse Electric Corporation: Extra Territorial Jurisdiction in Antigrust Matters, 5 Mont. U.L. Rev. 76 (1978).

Note, Strict Enforcement of Extraterritorial Discovery, 28 Stan. L. Rev. 841 (1986).

Note, Taking Evidence Outside the United States, 55 Boston U. L. Rev. 368 (1975).

O'Kane, Obtaining Evidence Abroad, 17 Vand. J. Transnat'l L. 233 (No. 2, 1984).

O'Kane & O'Kane, Taking Depositions Abroad, The Problem Still Remains, FIC Quarterly, Vol. 4, 343, (1981).

Onkelinx, Conflict of International Jurisdiction: Ordering the Production of Documents in Violation of the Law of the Situs, 64 NW. U.L. Rev. 487 (1969).

Oxman, The Choice Between Direct Discovery and Other Means of Obtaining Evidence Abroad: The Impact of the Hague Evidence Convention, 37 U. Miami L. Rev. 733 (1983).

Paget-Brown, Bank Secrecy and Criminal Matters: Cayman Islands and U.S. Cooperative Development, J. of Int'l L., Case 'Western Reserve, Vol. 20, No. 2, 369, 391 (1988).

Paikin, Problems of Obtaining Evidence in Foreign States for Use in Federal Criminal Prosecutions, 22 Colum. J. Transnat'l L. 233 (No. 2, 1984).

Pettit & Styles, The International Response to the Extraterritorial Application of United States Antitrust Laws, 27 Bus. Law. 697 (1982).

Pinera-Vasquez, Note, Extraterritorial Jurisdiction and International Banking: A Conflict of Interests, 43 U. Miami L. Rev. 449, 476 (1988).

Platto, C., Obtaining Evidence in Another Jurisdiction in Business Disputes, International Bar Association Series, 1988.

Platto, Taking Evidence Abroad for Use in Civil Cases in the United States, 16 Int'l Law. 575, 584 (1982).

Rafalko, Depositions, Commissions and Letters Rogatory in a Conflict of Laws Case (1965), 4 Dusquesne University Law Review 115.

Ristau, Symposia: Transnational Litigation, Part I, Overview of International Judicial Assistance, The Int'l Law, Vol. 18, No. 3, 525 (1984).

Ristau, International Cooperation in Penal Matters: The Lockheed Agreements, Transnational Aspects of Criminal Procedure, 1983 Michigan Yearbook of International Legal Studies, 85, 104 (1983).

Robinson, Symposia: Transnational Litigation, Part I, Compelling Discovery and Evidence in International Litigation, The Int'l Law., Vol. 18, No. 3, 533 (1984).

Robinson, Conflict of Jurisdiction and the Draft Restatement, 15 Law and Policy, Int'l Bus.1147 (1983).

Rosdeitcher, Foreign Blocking Statutes and U.S. Discovery: A Conflict of National Policies, 16 N.Y.U. J. Int;l L. & Pol. 1061 (1984).

Rosenberg and King, Curbing Discovery Abuse in Civil Litigation: Enough is Enough, B.Y.U. L. Rev. 579 (1981).

Rosenthal & Yale-Loehr, Two Cheers for the ALI Restatement's Provisions on Foreign Discovery, 16 N.Y.U.J. Int'l L. & Pol. 1075 (1984).

Schwartz, Obtaining Evidence Overseas: Discovery on Foreign Shores, 9 Family Advocate 28 (1987).

Shemanski, Obtaining Evidence in the Federal Republic of Germany: The Impact of the Hague Evidence Convention on German-American Judicial Cooperation, Int'l Law., Vol. 17, No. 3, 465, 487 (1983).

Sklaver, Obtaining Evidence in International Litigation, 7 Cumberland L. Rev. 233 (1976).

Smit, International Litigation Under the United States Code, 65 Colum L. Rev. 1015, 1026 (1965).

Smit, Int'l Aspects of Federal Civil Procedure, 61 Colum. L. Rev. 1031 (1961).

Springer, An Overview of International Evidence and Asset Gathering in Civil and Criminal Tax Cases, 22 Geo. Wash. J. Int'l L. & Econ. 277-330 (1988).

Stahr, Discovery Under 28 U.S.C. 1782 for Foreign and International Proceedings, 30 VA. J. Int'l L. 597, 601 (1990).

Stein, Depositions in Foreign Jurisdictions: Innocence Abroad, 7 Litigation No. 3, at 14 (1981).

Stern, International Judicial Assistance (Part I: Service and Discovery Abroad), (1968), 14 Practical Lawyer 17.

Stern, International Judicial Assistance (Part II: Depositions under Letters Rogatory) (1969), 15 Practical Lawyer 55.

Stiefel, Discovery - Probleme und Erfahrungen im Deutsch-Amerikanischen Rechtshilfeverkehr, 25 Recht der Internationalen Wirt-Schaft 509, 514-20 (1979).

Struve, Discovery from Foreign Parties in Civil Cases Before U.S. Courts, 16 N.Y.U.J. Int'l L. & Pol. 1101, 1111 (1984).

Sunderland, The Use of the Letter of Request (or Letter Rogatory) for the Purpose of Obtaining Evidence for Proceedings in England and Abroad, 31 Intl and Comp L. Q. 784 (1982).

Sutherland, Rio Tinto-Zinc Corporation v. Westinghouse Electric Corporation: Extraterritorial Jurisdiction in Antitrust Matters (1978) 5 Monash University Law Review 76.

Symposium, Compelling Discovery in Transnational Litigation, 16 N.Y.U.J. Int'l L. and Pol. 957-1156; 1217-1248 (No. 5, Summer 1984).

Tanugi, Extraterritorial Discovery Orders: Foreign Nondisclosure Laws in American Courts, Cambridge, Mass (Harvard Law Library) .

Teitelbaum, Note, Strict Enforcement of Extraterritorial Discovery, 28 Stan. L. Rev. 841, 856 (1986).

Toms, The French Response to the Extraterritorial Application of United States Antitrust Laws; The Int'l L., Vol. 15, 585, (1981).

Ulmer, Obtaining Testimony Outside the United States: Problem for the California Practitioner, Hastings L.J., Vol. 29, No.5, 1237, 1256 (1978).

Van Brauman, Foreign Evidence Gathering and Discovery for U.S. Civil Tax Determination Purposes, The International Law, Vol. 30, No. 3, pp. 589-619, (1996).

Von Mehren, Discovery of Documentary and Other Evidence in a Foreign Country, 77 Am. J. Int'l Law 896 (1983).

Von Mehren, Discovery Abroad: The Perspective of the U.S. Private Practitioner, 16 N.Y.U. J. Int'l L & Pol. 985, 993 (1984).

Walker-Sanzone, Extra Statutory Discovery Requirements - Violating the Twin Purposes of 28 U.S.C. 1782, Vanderbilt Journal of Transnational Law, Vol. 29, No. 1, pp. 117-153 (1996).

Waller, Bringing Meaning to Interest Balancing in Transnational Litigation, 23 Vand. J. of Transnat'l L., No. 5, 925, 966 (1991).

Weiner, In Search of International Evidence: A Lawyer's Guide Through the United States Department of Justice, 58 Notre Dame Law. 60 (1982).

Weir, Obtaining Evidence in Canada for Use in Courts in the United States and Other Countries, 29 Geo. Wash. L. Rev. 519 (1961).

Wilkey, Symposia: Transnational Litigation, Part I: Transnational Adjudication: A View From the Bench, 18 Int'l Law. 541 (1984).

Wilkey, Transnational Litigation: Perspectives from the U.S. and Abroad: U.S., 18 Int'l Law. 779 (1984).

Wortman, In Search of Discovery: The Split Between the Circuits Surrounding a Threshold Discoverability Requirement to Provide Assistance Under 28 U.S.C. 1782, Texas International Law Journal, Vol 30, No 3, pp. 583-602, (1995).

Appendix 12

STATE DEPARTMENT REGULATIONS ON DEPOSITIONS AND LETTERS ROGATORY

DEPOSITIONS AND LETTERS ROGATORY

§ 92.49 Deposition defined.

A deposition is the testimony of a witness taken in writing under oath or affirmation, before some designated or appointed person or officer, in answer to interrogatories, oral or written. (For the distinction between a deposition and an affidavit see § 92.22.)

§ 92.50 Use of depositions in court actions.

Generally depositions may be taken and used in all civil actions or suits. In criminal cases in the United States, a deposition cannot be used, unless a statute has been enacted which permits a defendant in a criminal case to have a deposition taken in his own behalf, or unless the defendant consents to the taking of a deposition by the State for use by the prosecution. (For exception in connection with the proving of foreign documents for use in criminal actions, see § 92.65.)

§ 92.51 Methods of taking depositions in foreign countries.

Rule 28(b) of the Rules of Civil Procedure for the District Courts of the United States provides that depositions may be taken in foreign countries by any of the three following methods:

(a) On notice before a secretary of embassy or legation, consular general, consul, vice consul, or consular agent of the United States;

(b) By commission, before such person or officer as may be appointed by the commission;

(c) Under letters rogatory, before an appropriate foreign court.

Rule 15 of the Federal Rules of Criminal Procedure provides that depositions may be taken in the same manner as in civil cases, but only upon order of court. The statutes of the States define the methods which may be employed for taking depositions in foreign countries for use in State courts and the provisions vary from one jurisdiction to another. However, provision is usually made for one or all of the aforementioned methods.

§ 92.52 "Deposition on notice" defined.

A "deposition on notice" is a deposition taken before a competent official after reasonable notice has been given in writing by the party or attorney proposing to take such deposition to the opposing party or attorney of record. Under the Federal law, diplomatic and consular officers are defined as competent officials for taking depositions on notice in foreign countries (see § 92.51). This method of taking a deposition does not necessarily involve the issuance of a commission or other court order.

§ 92.53 "Commission to take depositions" defined.

A "commission to take depositions" is a written authority issued by a court of justice, or by a quasi-judicial body, or a body acting in such capacity, giving power to take the testimony of witnesses who cannot appear personally to be examined in the court or before the body issuing the commission. In Federal practice, a commission to take depositions is issued only when necessary or convenient, on application and notice. The commission indicates the action or hearing in which the depositions are intended to be used, and the person or persons required to take the depositions, usually by name or descriptive title (see § 92.55 for manner of designating consular officers). Normally a commission is accompanied by detailed instructions for its execution.

§ 92.54 "Letters rogatory" defined.

In its broader sense in international practice, the term "letters rogatory" denotes a formal request from a court in which an action is pending, to a foreign court to perform some judicial act. Examples are requests for the taking of evidence, the serving of a summons, subpoena, or other legal notice, or the execution of a civil judgment. In United States usage, letters rogatory have been commonly utilized only for the purpose of obtaining evidence. Requests rest entirely upon the comity of courts toward each other, and customarily embody a promise of reciprocity. The legal sufficiency of documents executed in foreign countries for use in judicial proceedings in the United States, and the validity of the execution, are matters for determination by the competent judicial authorities of the American jurisdiction where the proceedings are held, subject to the applicable laws of that jurisdiction. See § 92.66 for procedures in the use of letters rogatory requesting the taking of depositions in foreign jurisdictions.

§ 92.55 Consular authority and responsibility for taking depositions.

(a) *Requests to take depositions or designations to execute commissions to take depositions.* Any United States consular officer may be requested to take a deposition on notice, or designated to execute a commission to take depositions. A commission or notice should, if possible, identify the officer who is to take the depositions by his official title only as in the following manner: "Any Consul or Vice Consul of the United States of America at (name of locality)". The consular officer responsible for the performance of notarial acts at a post should act on a request to take a deposition on notice, or should execute the commission, when the documents are drawn in this manner, provided local law does not preclude such action. However, when the officer (or officers) is designated by name as well as by title, only the officer (or officers) so designated may take the depositions. In either instance, the officer must be a disinterested party. Rule 28(c) of the Rules of Civil Procedure for the District Courts of the United States prohibits the taking of a deposition before a person who is a relative, employee, attorney, or counsel of any of the parties, or who is a relative or employee of such attorney or counsel, or who is financially interested in the action.

(b) *Authority in Federal law.* For the basic provisions of law controlling the taking of all depositions for use in either State or Federal courts, for a statement of the necessity to charge the appropriate fee, and for a statement of the penalty for the giving of false evidence, see Title 22, sections 1195 and 1203, of the United States Code. For the more detailed provisions which control particularly the taking of depositions for courts of the United States (i.e., for the Federal courts) see the Rules of Civil Procedure for the District courts of the United States, which appear in Title 28 of the United States Code, following section 2072 thereof. See also Rules of the Court of Claims of the United States, following section 2071 of Title 28. For the provisions of law which govern particularly the taking of depositions to prove the genuineness of foreign documents which it is desired to introduce in evidence in any criminal action or proceeding in a United States (i.e., Federal) court see Title 18, sections 3491 through 3496, of the United States Code.

(c) *Procedure where laws of the foreign country do not permit the taking of depositions.* In countries where the right to take depositions is not secured by treaty, consular officers may take depositions only if the laws or authorities of the national government will permit them to do so. Consular officers in countries where the taking of depositions is not permitted who receive notices or commissions for taking depositions should return the documents to the parties from whom they are received explaining why they are returning them, and indicating what other method or methods may be available for obtaining the depositions, whether by letters rogatory or otherwise.

§ 92.56 Summary of procedure for taking depositions.

In taking a deposition on notice or executing a commission to take depositions, a consular officer should conform to any statutory enactments on the subject in the jurisdiction in which the depositions will be used. He should also comply with any special instructions which accompany the request for a deposition on notice or a commission. Unless otherwise directed by statutory enactments or special instructions, the officer should proceed as follows in taking depositions:

(a) Request the witnesses, whose testimony is needed, to appear before him; or, at the request of any party to the action or proceeding, request designated persons to supply him or the requesting party with needed records or documents in their possession, or copies thereof;

(b) When necessary, act as interpreter or translater, or see that arrangements are made for some qualified person to act in this capacity;

(c) Before the testimony is taken, administer oaths (or affirmations in lieu thereof) to the interpreter or translator (if there is one), to the stenographer taking down the testimony, and to each witness;

(d) Have the witnesses examined in accordance with the procedure described in §§ 92.57 to 92.60;

(e) Either record, or have recorded in his presence and under his direction, the testimony of the witnesses;

(f) Take the testimony, or have it taken, stenographically in question-and-answer form and transcribed (see § 92.58) unless the parties to the action agree otherwise (rules 30(c) and 31(b), Rules of Civil Procedure for the District Courts of the United States);

(g) Be actually present throughout the examination of the witnesses, but recess the examination for reasonable periods of time and for sufficient reasons;

(h) Mark or cause to be marked, by identifying exhibit numbers or letters, all documents identified by a witness or counsel and submitted for the record.

§ 92.57 Oral examination of witnesses.

When a witness is examined on the basis of oral interrogatories, the counsel for the party requesting the deposition has the right to conduct a direct examination of the witness without interruption except in the form of objection by opposing counsel. The opposing counsel has the same right on cross-examination. Cross-examination may be followed by redirect and recross-examinations until the interrogation is complete. The consular officer taking the deposition should endeavor to restrain counsel from indulging in lengthy colloquies, digressions, or asides, and from attempts to intimidate or mislead the witness. The consular officer has no authority to sustain or overrule objections but should have them recorded as provided in § 92.59. Instead of taking part in the oral examination of a witness, the parties notified of the taking of a deposition may transmit written interrogatories to the consular officer. The consular officer should then question the witness on the basis of the written interrogatories and should record the answers verbatim. (Rules 30 (c) and 31 (b), Rules of Civil Procedure for the District Courts of the United States.)

§ 92.58 Examination on basis of written interrogatories.

Written interrogatories are usually divided into three parts:

(a) The direct interrogatories or interrogatories in chief;

(b) The cross-interrogatories; and

(c) The redirect interrogatories.

Recross-interrogatories sometimes follow redirect interrogatories. The consular officer should not furnish the witness with a copy of the interrogatories in advance of the questioning, nor should he allow the witness to examine the interrogatories in advance of the questioning. Although it may be necessary for the officer, when communicating with the witness for the purpose of asking him to appear to testify, to indicate in general terms the nature of the evidence which is being sought, this information should not be given in such detail as to permit the witness to formulate his answers to the interrogatories prior to his appearance before the consular officer. The officer taking the deposition should put the interrogatories to the witness separately and in order. The written interrogatories should not be repeated in the record (unless special instructions to that effect are given), but an appropriate reference should be made thereto. These references should, of course, be followed by the witness' answers. All of the written interrogatories must be put to the witness, even though at some point during the examination the witness disclaims further knowledge of the subject. When counsel for all of the parties attend an examination conducted on written interrogatories, the consular officer may, all counsel having consented thereto, permit oral examination of the witness following the close of the examination upon written interrogatories. The oral examination should be conducted in the same manner and order as if not preceded by an examination upon written interrogatories.

§ 92.59 Recording of objections.

All objections made at the time of the examination to the qualifications of the officer taking the deposition, or to the manner of taking it, or to the evidence presented, or to the conduct of any party, and any other objection to the proceedings must be noted in the deposition. Evidence objected to will be taken subject to the objections. (Rules 30 (c) and 31 (b), Rules of Civil Procedure for the District Courts of the United States.)

§ 92.60 Examination procedures.

(a) *Explaining interrogatory to witness.* If the witness does not understand what an interrogatory means, the consular officer should explain it to him, if possible, but only so as to get an answer strictly responsive to the interrogatory.

(b) *Refreshing memory by reference to written records.* A witness may be permitted to refresh his memory by referring to notes, papers or other documents. The consular officer should have such occurrence noted in the record of the testimony together with a statement of his opinion as to whether the witness was using the notes, papers or other documents to refresh his memory or for the sake of testifying to matters not then of his personal knowledge.

(c) *Conferring with counsel.* When the witness confers with counsel before answering any interrogatory, the consular officer should have that fact noted in the record of the testimony.

(d) *Examining witness as to personal knowledge.* The consular officer may at any time during the examination of a witness propound such inquiries as may be necessary to satisfy himself whether the witness is testifying from his personal knowledge of the subject matter of the examination.

(e) *Witness not to leave officer's presence.* The consular officer should request the witness not to leave his presence during the examination, except during the recesses for meals, rest, etc., authorized in § 92.56 (g). Failure of the witness to comply with this request must be noted in the record.

§ 92.61 Transcription and signing of record of examination.

After the examination of a witness is completed, the stenographic record of the examination must be fully transcribed and the transcription attached securely to any document or documents to which the testimony in the record pertains. (See § 92.63 regarding the arrangement of papers.) The transcribed deposition must then be submitted to the witness for examination and read to or by him, unless such examination and reading are waived by the witness and by the parties to the action. Any changes in form or substance desired by the witness should be entered upon the deposition by the consular officer with a statement of the reasons given by the witness for making the changes. The witness should then sign the transcript of his deposition and should initial in the margin each correction made at his request. However, the signature and initials of the witness may be omitted if the parties to the action by stipulation waive the signing or if the witness is ill, refuses to sign, or cannot be found. If the deposition is not signed by the witness, the consular officer should sign it and should state on the record the reason for his action, i.e., the waiver of the parties, the illness or absence of the witness, or the refusal of the witness to sign, giving the reasons for such refusal. The deposition may then be used as though signed by the witness except when, on the motion to suppress, the court holds that the reasons given for the refusal to sign require the rejection of the deposition in whole or in part. (Rule 30 (e) and 31 (b), Rules of Civil Procedure for the District Courts of the United States.)

§ 92.62 Captioning and certifying depositions.

The consular officer should prepare a caption for every deposition; should certify on the deposition that the witness was duly sworn by him and that the deposition is a true record of the testimony given by the witness; and should sign and seal the certification in the manner prescribed in §§ 92.15 and 92.16. (Rules 30 (f) (1) and 31 (b), Rules of Civil Procedures for the District Courts of the United States.)

§ 92.63 Arrangement of papers.

Unless special instructions to the contrary are received, the various papers comprising the completed record of the depositions should usually be arranged in the following order from bottom to top:

(a) Commission to take depositions (or notice of taking depositions), with interrogatories, exhibits, and other supporting documents fastened thereto.

(b) Statement of fees charged, if one is prepared on a separate sheet.

(c) Record of the responses of the various witnesses, including any exhibits the witnesses may submit.

(d) Closing certificate.

All of these papers should be fastened together with ribbon, the ends of which should be secured beneath the consular officer's seal affixed to the closing certificate.

§ 92.64 Filing depositions.

(a) *Preparation and transmission of envelope.* The notice or commission, the interrogatories, the record of the witnesses' answers, the exhibits, and all other documents and papers pertaining to the depositions should be fastened together (see § 92.63 regarding the arrangement of papers) and should be enclosed in an envelope sealed with the wax engraving seal of the post. The envelope should be endorsed with the title of the action and should be marked and addressed. The sealed envelope should then be transmitted to the court in which the action is pending.

(b) *Furnishing copies.* The original completed depositions should not be sent to any of the parties to the action or to their counsel. However, the consular officer may furnish a copy of a deposition to the deponent or to any party to the action upon the payment of the copying fee and if certification is desired under official seal that the copy is a true copy, the certification fee prescribed in the Tariff of Fees, Foreign Service of the United States of America (§ 22.1 of this chapter).

§ 92.65 Depositions to prove genuineness of foreign documents.

(a) *Authority to execute commission.* Under the provisions of section 1 of the act of June 25, 1948, as amended (sec. 1, 62 Stat. 834, sec. 53, 63 Stat. 96; 18 U.S.C. 3492), a diplomatic or consular officer may be commissioned by an United States court to take the testimony of a witness in a foreign country either on oral or written interrogatories, or partly on oral and partly on written interrogatories, for the purpose of determining the genuineness of any foreign document (any book, paper, statement, record, account, writing, or other document, or any portion thereof, of whatever character and in whatever form, as well as any copy thereof equally with the original, which is not in the United States) which it is desired to introduce in evidence in any criminal action or proceeding in any United States court under the provisions of section 1 of the act of June 25, 1948 (sec. 1, 62 Stat. 945; 28 U.S.C. 1732). Such testimony may also be taken to determine whether the foreign document was made in the regular course of business and whether it was the regular course of business to make such document. The term "business" includes business, profession, occupation, and calling of every kind. (Sec. 1, 62 Stat. 945, 28 U.S.C. 1732.)

(b) *Disqualification to execute commission.* Any diplomatic or consular officer to whom a commission is addressed to take testimony, who is interested in the outcome of the criminal action or proceeding in which the foreign documents in question are intended to be used or who has participated in the prosecution of such action or proceeding, whether by investigations, preparation of evidence, or otherwise, may be disqualified on his own motion or on that of the United States or any other party to such criminal action or proceeding made to the court from which the commission issued at any time prior to the execution thereof. If, after notice and hearing, the court grants the motion, it will instruct the diplomatic or consular officer thus disqualified to send the commission to any other diplomatic or consular officer of the United States named by the court, and such other officer should execute the commission according to its terms and will for all purposes be deemed the officer to whom the commission is addressed. (Sec. 1, 62 Stat. 834, sec. 53, 63 Stat. 96; 18 U.S.C. 3492.)

(c) *Execution and return of commission.* (1) Commissions issued in criminal cases under the authority of the act of June 25, 1948, as amended, to take testimony in connection with foreign documents should be executed and returned by officers of the Foreign Service in accordance with section 1 of that act, as amended (sec. 1, 62 Stat. 835; 18 U.S.C. 3493, 3494), and in accordance with any special instructions which may accompany the commission. For details not covered by such section or by special instructions, officers of the Foreign Service should be guided by such instructions as may be issued by the Department of State in connection with the taking of depositions generally. (See §§ 92.55 to 92.64.)

(2) Section 1 of the act of June 25, 1948 (sec. 1, 62 Stat. 835; 18 U.S.C. 3493) provides that every person whose testimony is taken should be cautioned and sworn to testify the whole truth and should be carefully examined. The testimony should be reduced to writing or typewriting by the consular officer, or by some person under his personal supervision, or by the witness himself in the presence of the consular officer, and by no other person. After it has been reduced to writing or typewriting, the testimony must be signed by the witness. Every foreign document with respect to which testimony is taken must be annexed to such testimony and must be signed by each witness who appears for the purpose of establishing the genuineness of such document.

(3) When counsel for all of the parties attend the examination of any witness whose testimony will be taken on written interrogatories, they may consent that oral interrogatories, in addition to those accompanying the

commission, be put to the witness. The consular officer taking the testimony should require an interpreter to be present when his services are needed or are requested by any party or his attorney. (Sec. 1, 62 Stat. 835, 18 U.S.C. 3493.)

(4) Section 1 of the act of June 25, 1948 (sec. 1, 62 Stat. 835; 18 U.S.C. 3494) provides that the consular officer, who executes any commission authorized under the same section, as amended (sec. 1, 62 Stat. 834, sec. 53, 63 Stat. 96; 18 U.S.C. 3492) and who is satisfied, upon all the testimony taken, that a foreign document is genuine, should certify such document to be genuine under the seal of his office. This certification must include a statement that the officer is not subject to disqualification under the provisions of section 1 of the act of June 25, 1948, as amended (sec. 1, 62 Stat. 834, sec. 53, 63 Stat. 96; 18 U.S.C. 3492). For purposes of assessment of fees, the issuance of this certificate shall be regarded as a part of the consular service of executing the commission, and no separate fee shall be charged for the certificate.

(5) The consular officer should then forward such foreign documents, together with the record of all testimony taken and the commission which has been executed, to the Department of State for transmission to the clerk of the court from which the commission issued. (Sec. 1, 62 Stat. 835; 18 U.S.C. 3494.) (See § 92.64 regarding the filing of depositions generally.)

(Sec. 303, 60 Stat. 1002, 62 Stat. 836; 22 U.S.C. 843, 18 U.S.C. 3496, E.O. 10307; 16 FR 11907, 3 CFR 1949-1953 Comp., page 387)

§ 92.66 Depositions taken before foreign officials or other persons in a foreign country.

(a) *Customary practice.* Under Federal law (Rule 28(b), Rules of Civil Procedure for the District Courts of the United States) and under the laws of some of the States, a commission to take depositions can be issued to a foreign official or to a private person in a foreign country. However, this method is rarely used; commissions are generally issued to U.S. consular officers. In those countries where American consular officers are not permitted to take testimony (see § 92.55(c)) and where depositions must be taken before a foreign authority, letters rogatory are usually issued to a foreign court. The Department of State has been authorized (62 Stat. 949; 28 U.S.C. 1781) directly or through suitable channels to receive a letter rogatory issued, or request made, by a tribunal in the United States, to transmit it to the foreign or international tribunal, officer, or agency to whom it is addressed, and to receive and return it after execution. In Federal practice letters rogatory to request the taking of evidence are issued only when necessary or convenient, on application and notice, and on such terms and with such directions as are just and appropriate (Rule 28(b), Rules of Civil Procedure for the District Courts of the United States). When the name of the foreign court is not known, letters rogatory are usually addressed "To the appropriate Judicial Authority in (here name the country)."

(b) *Transmission of letters rogatory to foreign officials.* Letters rogatory may often be sent direct from court to court. However, some foreign governments require that these requests for judicial aid be submitted through the diplomatic channel (i.e., that they be submitted to the Ministry for Foreign Affairs by the American diplomatic representative). A usual requirement is that the letters rogatory as well as the interrogatories and other papers included with them be accompanied by a complete translation into the language (or into one of the languages) of the country of execution. Another requirement is that provision be made for the payment of fees and expenses. Inquiries from interested parties or their attorneys, or from American courts, as to customary procedural requirements in given countries, may be addressed direct to the respective American embassies and legations in foreign capitals, or to the Department of State, Washington, D.C. 20520.

(c) *Return of letters rogatory executed by foreign officials.* (1) Letters rogatory executed by foreign officials are returned through the same channel by which they were initially transmitted. When such documents are returned to a United States diplomatic mission, the responsible officer should endorse thereon a certificate stating the date and place of their receipt. This certificate should be appended to the documents as a separate sheet. The officer should then enclose the documents in an envelope sealed with the wax engraving seal of the post and bearing an endorsement indicating the title of the action to which the letters rogatory pertain. The name and address of the American judicial body from which the letters rogatory issued should also be placed on the envelope.

(2) If the executed letters rogatory are returned to the diplomatic mission

from the Foreign Office in an envelope bearing the seals of the foreign judicial authority who took the testimony, that sealed envelope should not be opened at the mission. The responsible officer should place a certificate on the envelope showing the date it was received at his office and indicating that it is being forwarded in the same condition as received from the foreign authorities. He should then place that sealed envelope in a second envelope, sealed with the wax engraving seal of the post, and bearing the title of the action and the name and address of the American judicial body from which the letters rogatory issued.

(3) Charges should be made for executing either of the certificates mentioned in paragraphs (c) (1) and (2) of this section, as prescribed by item 67 of the Tariff of Fees, Foreign Service of the United States of America (§ 22.1 of this chapter), unless the service is classifiable in a no-fee category under the exemption for Federal agencies and corporations (item 83 of the same Tariff).

(4) The sealed letters rogatory should be transmitted by appropriate means to the court in which the action is pending. See Title 28, section 1781, of the United States Code concerning the manner of making return to a court of the United States (Federal court).

(d) *Transmission of commissions to foreign officials or other persons.* A commission to take depositions which is addressed to an official or person in a foreign country other than a United States diplomatic or consular officer may be sent directly to the person designated. However, if such a commission is sent to the United States diplomatic mission in the country where the depositions are intended to be taken, it should be forwarded to the Foreign Office for transmission to the person appointed in the commission. If sent to a United States consular office, the commission may be forwarded by that office direct to the person designated, or, if the consular officer deems it more advisable to do so, he may send the commission to the United States diplomatic mission for transmission through the medium of the Foreign Office.

[22 FR 10858, Dec. 27, 1957, as amended by Dept. Reg. 108.564, 32 FR 11775, Aug. 16, 1967]

§ 92.67 Taking of depositions in United States pursuant to foreign letters rogatory.

(a) *Authority and procedure.* The taking of depositions by authority of State courts for use in the courts of foreign countries is governed by the laws of the individual States. As respects Federal practice, the district court of the district in which a person resides or is found may order him to give his testimony or statement or to produce a document or other thing for use in a proceeding in a foreign or international tribunal. The order may be made pursuant to a letter rogatory issued, or request made, by a foreign or international tribunal or upon the application of any interested person and may direct that the testimony or statement be given, or the document or other thing be produced, before a person appointed by the court. By virtue of his appointment, the person appointed has power to administer any necessary oath and take the testimony or statement. The order may prescribe the practice and procedure, which may be in whole or part the practice and procedure of the foreign country or the interntational tribunal, for taking the testimony or statement or producing the document or other thing. To the extent that the order does not prescribe otherwise, the testimony or statement shall be taken, and the document or other thing produced, in accordance with the Federal Rules of Civil Procedure. A person may not be compelled to give his testimony or statement or to produce a document or other thing in violation of any legally applicable privilege. This does not preclude a person within the United States from voluntarily giving his testimony or statement, or producing a document or other thing, for use in a proceeding in a foreign or international tribunal before any person or in any manner acceptable to him (28 U.S.C. 1782).

(b) *Formulation of letters rogatory.* A letter rogatory customarily states the nature of the judicial assistance sought by the originating court, prays that this assistance be extended, incorporates an undertaking of future reciprocity in like circumstances, and makes some provision for payment of fees and costs entailed in its execution. As respects Federal practice, it is not required that a letter rogatory emanating from a foreign court be authenticated by a diplomatic or consular officer of the United States or that it be submitted through the diplomatic channel; the seal of the originating court suffices. When testimony is desired, the letter rogatory should state whether it is intended to be taken upon oral or written interrogatories. If the party on whose behalf the testimony is intended to be taken will not be represented by counsel, written interrogatories should be attached. Except where manifestly unneeded (e.g. a Spanish-language letter rogatory intended for execution in Puerto Rico) or dispensed with by arrangement with the court, letters rogatory and interrogatories in a foreign language should be accompanied by English translations.

(c) *Addressing letters rogatory.* To avert uncertainties and minimize possibilities for refusal of courts to comply with requests contained in letters rogatory in the form in which they are presented, it is advisable that counsel for the parties in whose behalf testimony is sought ascertain in advance if possible, with the assistance of correspondent counsel in the United States or that of a consular representative or agent of his nation in the United States, the exact title of the court, Federal or State as the case may be, which will be prepared to entertain the letter rogatory. In Federal practice the following form of address is acceptable:

The U.S. District Court for the ———
——————— (e.g. Northern, Southern)
District of ————————— (State)
————————— (City) —————————,
(State)

In instances where it is not feasible to ascertain the correct form of address at the time of preparation of the letter rogatory, and it will be left for counsel in the United States, or a consul or agent in the United States of the nation of origin of the letter rogatory to effect its transmission to an appropriate court, the following form may be used: "To the Appropriate Judicial Authority at (name of locality)."

(d) *Submitting letters rogatory to courts in the United States.* A letter rogatory may be submitted to the clerk of the court of which assistance is sought, either in person or by mail. This may be direct by international mail from the originating foreign court. Alternatively, submission to the clerk of court may be effected in person or by mail by any party to the action at law or his attorney or agent, or by a consular officer or agent in the United States of the foreign national concerned. Finally, the Department of State has been authorized (62 Stat. 949; 28 U.S.C. 1781) to receive a letter rogatory issued, or request made, by a foreign or international tribunal, to transmit it to the tribunal, officer, or agency in the United States to whom it is addressed, and to receive and return it after execution. This authorization does not preclude—

(1) The transmittal of a letter rogatory or request directly from a foreign or international tribunal to the tribunal, officer, or agency in the United States to whom it is addressed and its return in the same manner; or

(2) The transmittal of a letter rogatory or request directly from a tribunal in the United States to the foreign or international tribunal, officer, or agency to whom it is addressed and its return in the same manner.

[Dept. Reg. 108.564, 32 FR 11775, Aug. 16, 1967]

§ 92.68 Foreign Service fees and incidental costs in the taking of evidence.

The fees for the taking of evidence by officers of the Foreign Service are as prescribed by the Tariff or Fees, Foreign Service of the United States of America (§ 22.1 of this chapter), under the caption "Services Relating to the Taking of Evidence," unless the service is performed for official use, which comes under the caption "Exemption for Federal Agencies and Corporations" of the same Tariff. See § 22.6 of this chapter concerning the requirement for advance deposit of estimated fees. When the party on whose behalf the evidence is sought or his local representative is not present to effect direct payment of such incidental costs as postage or travel of witnesses, the advance deposit required by the officer shall be in an amount estimated as sufficient to cover these in addition to the fees proper. The same rule shall apply to charges for interpreting or for the taking and transcribing of a stenographic record when performed commercially rather than by staff members at Tariff of Fee rates.

§ 92.69 Charges payable to foreign officials, witnesses, foreign counsel, and interpreters.

(a) *Execution of letters rogatory by foreign officials.* Procedures for payment of foreign costs will be by arrangement with the foreign authorities.

(b) *Execution of commissions by foreign officials or other persons abroad.* Procedure for the payment of foreign costs will be as arranged, by the tribunal requiring the evidence, with its commissioner.

(c) *Witness fees and allowances when depositions are taken pursuant to commission from a Federal court.* A witness attending in any court of the United States, or before a United States commissioner, or before any person authorized to take his deposition pursuant to any rule or order of a cut of the United States, shall receive $4 for each day's attendance and for the time necessarily occupied in going to and returning from the same, and 8 cents per mile for going from and returning to his place of residence. Witnesses who are not salaried employees of the Government and who are not in custody and who attend at points so far removed from their respective residence as to prohibit return thereto from day to day shall be entitled to an additional allowance of $8 per day for expenses of subsistence, including the time necessarily occupied in going to and returning from the place of attendance (28 U.S.C. 1821, Supp. IV). Witnesses giving depositions before consular officers pursuant to a commission issued by the Federal Court are entitled to these fees and allowances, and the officer shall make payment thereof in the same manner as payment is made of other expenses involved in the execution of the commission, charging the advance deposit provided by the party at whose request the depositions are taken (see § 92.68). In any case to which the Government of the United States, or an officer or agency thereof, is a party, the United States marshal for the district will pay all fees of witnesses on the certificate of the United States Attorney or Assistant United States Attorney, and in the proceedings before a United States Commissioner, on the certificate of such commissioner (28 U.S.C. 1825).

§ 92.70 Special fees for depositions in connection with foreign documents.

(a) *Fees payable to witnesses.* Each witness whose testimony is obtained under a commission to take testimony in connection wtih foreign documents for use in criminal cases shall be entitled to receive compensation at the rate of $15 a day for each day of attendance, plus 8 cents a mile for going from his place of residence or business to the place of examination, and returning, by the shortest feasible route (18 U.S.C. 3495 and 3496, and E.O. 10307, 3 CFR, 1949-1953 Comp.). When, however it is necessary to procure the attendance of a witness on behalf of the United States or an indigent party, an officer or agent of the United States may negotiate with the witness to pay compensation at such higher rate as may be approved by the Attorney General, plus the mileage allowance stated above (5 U.S.C. 341). The expense of the compensation and mileage of each witness will be borne by the party, or parties, applying for the commission unless the commission is accompanied by an order of court (18 U.S.C. 3495(b) that all fees, compensations, and other expenses authorized by these regulations are chargeable to the United States (18 U.S.C. 3495).

(b) *Fee payable to counsel.* Each counsel who represents a party to the action or proceeding in the examination before the commissioner will receive compensation for each day of attendance at a rate of not less than $15 a day and not more than $50 a day, as agreed between him and the party whom he represents, plus such actual and necessary expenses as may be allowed by the commissioner upon verified statements filed with him. If the commission is issued on application of the United States, the compensation and expenses of counsel representing each party are chargeable to the United States under section 3495(b) of Title 18 of the United States Code (18 U.S.C. 3495 and 3496, and E.O. 10307, 3 CFR, 1949-1953 Comp.).

(c) *Fees payable to interpreters and translators.* Each interpreter and translator employed by the commissioner under these regulations shall receive an allowance of $10 a day, plus 8 cents a mile for going from his place of residence or business to the place of examination and returning, by the shortest feasible route. The compensation and mileage of interpreters and translators shall be chargeable to the United States.

(d) *Time for paying fees.* Witnesses, counsel, interpreters, and translators will be paid, in accordance with the foregoing regulations, by the commissioner at the conclusion of their services. Other expenses authorized by these regulations will be paid by the commissioner as they are incurred.

(e) *Payment of fees by the United States.* When it appears that the commission was issued on application of the United States or when the commission is accompanied by an order of court that all fees, compensation, and other expenses authorized by these regulations are chargeable to the United States under section 3495(b) of

Title 18 of the United States Code, the commissioner shall execute the commission without charge for his service as commissioner in connection therewith. The Commissioner shall pay witnesses, counsel, interpreter, or translator, and other expenses authorized by these regulations through the disbursing officer in his area in accordance with instructions which will be issued in each case.

(f) *Payment of fees by other parties.* When fees, compensation, and other expenses authorized by this section are chargeable to any party other than the United States, the commissioner shall undertake the execution of the commission only if such party deposits with the Department of State or with the appropriate Foreign Service post, in advance, an amount to be set by the court as apparently adequate to defray all fees, compensation, and other expenses authorized by this part. If the amount of the deposit is later found to be insufficient, the depositor shall be so notified, and the commissioner shall retain the commission and other papers until a sufficient supplemental amount has been deposited. If the amount of the deposit exceeds the aggregate amount of fees, compensation, and other expenses authorized by this part, the excess shall be returned to the party, or parties, entitled thereto. The commissioner shall pay witnesses, counsel, interpreter, or translator, and other expenses authorized by this section, from the proceeds of a check which the disbursing officer for his area will be authorized to draw on the Treasurer of the United States.

§ 92.71 Fees for letters rogatory executed by officials in the United States.

Arrangements for the payment of fees should be made directly with the court in the United States by the party in the foreign country at whose request the depositions are taken, either through his legal representative in the United States or through the appropriate diplomatic or consular officer of his country in the United States. (See § 92.67 regarding the execution of letters rogatory in the United States.)

Appendix 13

PREPARATION OF LETTERS ROGATORY

State Department Circular

DISCLAIMER: THE INFORMATION IN THIS CIRCULAR RELATING TO THE LEGAL REQUIREMENTS OF SPECIFIC FOREIGN COUNTRIES IS OBTAINED FROM PAST EXPERIENCE AND IS NOT NECESSARILY AUTHORITATIVE. QUESTIONS INVOLVING INTERPRETATION OF SPECIFIC FOREIGN LAWS SHOULD BE ADDRESSED TO FOREIGN COUNSEL

LEGAL AUTHORITY: 28 U.S.C. 1781(a)(2); 28 U.S.C. 1696; Rule 28(b), Fed. R. Civ. P.; Rule 4(f)(2)(B), Fed. R. Civ. P.; Rule 15d, Fed. R. Crim. P.22 C.F.R. 92.66(b)&(c); Article 5(j), Vienna Convention on Consular Relations, 21 U.S.T. 77, 596 UNTS 261; TIAS 6820 (where applicable); Bilateral Consular Conventions (where applicable). Letters rogatory have also been issued under the "All Writs Act", 28 U.S.C. 1651.

SELECTED CITATIONS: For general information about letters rogatory see:

Wright and Miller, Federal Practice and Procedure, (1970), Section 2083 and Section 1134 and 1992 Supp. pp. 206-207);

8 Wigmore, Evidence (rev. McNaughton 1961), Sec. 2195a (ii);
Restatement (Second) Foreign Relations Law of the United States, Sec. 40 (1965);
Restatement (Third) Foreign Relations Law of the United States, Sec. 403 (1988).

WHAT IS A LETTER ROGATORY: A letter rogatory is a formal request from a court in one country to "the appropriate judicial authorities" in another country requesting compulsion of testimony or documentary or other evidence or effect service of process. Although statutory authority generally refers to the instrument as a "letter rogatory", the terms "letter rogatory" and "letter of request" (which is used specifically in the Hague Evidence Convention) have come to be virtually synonymous in actual practice. (See Epstein & Snyder, International Litigation: A Guide to Jurisdictiön, Practice & Strategy, 2nd. Sec. 10.09, p. 10.13 -10.14.; Black's Law Dictionary (6th ed. 1994), Fed. R. Civ. P. 4(f)(2)(B) Advisory Committee's Note (West Supp. 1993).) In some countries which do not permit the taking of depositions of willing witnesses, letters rogatory are the only method of obtaining evidence or serve process. Letters rogatory can be used in civil and criminal matters, and have been used in administrative matters. The execution of a request for judicial assistance by the foreign court is based on comity between nations, absent a specific treaty obligation such as the Hague Evidence Convention or Mutual Legal Assistance in Criminal Matters (MLAT) treaties. See our general flyer on "Obtaining Evidence Abroad" or the "Hague Evidence Convention" for a further discussion of these subjects. Consular Conventions generally include language which authorizes transmission of letters rogatory through diplomatic channels. This does not obligate the foreign country to execute the request, but simply provides a formal avenue by which the requests may be made. If there is no Consular Convention in force between the United States and the foreign country, letters rogatory are received by foreign authorities on the basis of comity. **Letters rogatory are a time consuming, cumbersome process and should not be utilized unless there are no other options available.**

HOW IS A LETTER ROGATORY EXECUTED: The foreign court will execute a letter rogatory in accordance with the laws and regulations of the foreign country. In obtaining evidence, for example, in most cases an American attorney will not be permitted to participate in such a proceeding. Occasionally a local, foreign attorney may be permitted to attend such a proceeding and even to put forth additional questions to the witness. Not all foreign countries utilize the services of court reporters or routinely provide verbatim transcripts. Sometimes the presiding judge will dictate his recollection of the witness's responses. See Born & Westin, 305, 308; Ristau, International Judicial Assistance, Sec. 3-2-1 (4), p. 79 (1995 supp.); Epstein & Snyder, Sec. 10.09, p. 10-13 - 10-16 (1994 supp). See discussion below on drafting a letter rogatory which takes these peculiarities into account.

AUTHORITY FOR ISSUANCE OF A LETTER ROGATORY: The power of federal courts to issue letters rogatory derives from 28 U.S.C. 1781 and from the court's "inherent" authority. See De Villeneuve v. Morning Journal Ass'n., 206 F. 70 (S.D.N.Y. 1913), Zassenhaus v. Evening Star Newspaper Co., 404 F. 2d 1361 (D.C. Cir. 1968). See also 28 U.S.C. 1651 ("All Writs Act"). But see, DBMS Consultants, Ltd. v. Computer Assocs. Int'l, Inc., 131 F.R.D. 367, 369 (D. Mass. 1990); United States v. Reagan, 453 F.2d 165, 171-173 (6th Cir. 1971), cert. denied, 406 U.S. 946 (1972); United States v. Strong, 608 F. Supp. 188, 192-194 (E.D. Pa. 1985); United States v. Staples, 256 F.2d 290 (9th Cir. 1958); B & L Drilling Electric v. Totco, 87 F.R.D. 543, 545 (W.D. Okla. 1978).

Compulsion of Evidence: When a witness is not willing to testify or produce documents or other evidence voluntarily, the assistance of foreign authorities generally must be sought. The customary method of compelling evidence is by letter rogatory. See Rule 28(b), Fed. R. Civ. P.; Born & Westin, 305-308; Cumulative Digest of United States Practice in International Law, 1981-1988, Department of State, Office of the Legal Adviser, 1450, 1509-1510 (1994); and Digest of United States Practice in International Law, 1977, 498-499, Department of State, Office of the Legal Adviser. See Ristau, Sec. 3-3-2, Application for the Issuance of a Letter of Request (Letter Rogatory). Consult our flyer "Obtaining Evidence Abroad" regarding other methods of extraterritorial discovery of documents in control of persons over whom the court has in personam jurisdiction.

CRIMINAL CASES: The Federal Rules of Criminal Procedure do not provide for the issuance of requests for judicial assistance. Consequently, Rule 57, Fed. R. Crim. P., applies. Rule 57 provides in pertinent part: "In all cases not provided for by rule, the district judges and magistrates may regulate their practice in any manner not inconsistent with these rules or those of the district in which they act". Evidence, including documents and the testimony of witnesses, may properly be sought by means of a request for judicial assistance before or after formal charges have been made. United States v. Reagan, supra, 453 F2d at 173 n.4; In Re Grand Jury 81-2, 550 F. Supp. 24, 29 (W.D. Mich, 1982); United States v. Strong, supra, 608 F. Supp. at 194.

ADMINISTRATIVE CASES: Except as provided by statute, U.S. Administrative agencies do not have the power to compel persons outside the U.S. who have no contact with the U.S. (and therefore are not under a federal court's personal jurisdiction) to produce evidence for an investigation. Administrative agencies have succeeded in obtaining commissions to take depositions and letters rogatory using the "All Writs Act" (28 U.S.C. 1651). See: CFTC v. Nahas, 738 F.2d 487 (D.C. Cir. 1984); FTC v. Compagnie de Saint Gobain-Pont-a-Mousson, 636 F.2d 1300 (D.C. Cir. 1980). Congress has decided, since Saint Gobain, that the investigative demands of the FTC and the IRS are more in the nature of complaints than subpoenae. Thus, those two agencies have been expressly authorized to serve investigative demands in foreign states in a manner parallel to the service of process provisions of Rule 4 of the Rules of Federal Procedure. See 15 U.S.C. 57b-1 (F.T.C.) and 26 U.S.C. 982 (I.R.S.). All the federal securities statutes authorize the SEC to subpoena witnesses "from any place in the United States." This statutory language, commonly employed in the statutes governing most American regulatory agencies, has been construed by U.S. courts to be a broad and flexible authorization to require production of evidence from anywhere in the world, so long as service has been properly effected in the U.S. See, SEC v. Minas de Artemisa, S.A., 150 F. 2d 215 (9th Cir. 1945); Federal Maritime Commission v. DeSmedt, 366 F.2d 464 (2d Cir.), cert. denied, 385 U.S. 974 (1966); CAB v. Deutche Lufthansa A.G., 591 F.2d 951 (D.C. Cir. 1979); SEC v. Zanganeh, 470 F. Supp 1307 (D.D.C. 1978).

SERVICE OF PROCESS: 28 U.S.C. 1696 and Rule 4(f)(2)(B) Fed. R. Civ. P. provide for the use of letters rogatory for service of process. Service of a judicial summons, as set forth in Fed. R. Crim. P. 9(c) may also be effected pursuant to a letter rogatory. See Ristau, Sec. 3-1-12, p. 71 (1995 supp.) for a form for application for the issuance of a Letter of Request (Letter Rogatory) to Serve a Judicial Document. See also, In Re Letters Rogatory Out of First Civil Court of City of Mexico, 261 Fed. 652 (S.D.N.Y. 1919); 44 Colum. L. Rev. 72 (1944); Note, 58 Yale L.J. 1193 (1949); Republic Int'l Corp. v. Amco Eng'rs, 516 F.2d 161, 164 (9th Cir. 1975). In some countries service by letters rogatory is the only recognized method of service. **If the laws of the foreign country permit other methods of service, the use of letters rogatory is not recommended given the habitual time delays of up to a year or more in execution of the requests.** The letters rogatory procedure is "complex, costly and time consuming" and should be avoided where possible. (See Casad, Jurisdiction in Civil Actions, 4.06(2) (1983 & Supp. 1986); Horlick, A Practical Guide to Service of United States Process Abroad, 14 Int'l Law. 637, 642 (1980).) If the laws of the foreign country only recognize service by letter rogatory and eventual enforcement of a U.S. judgment in the foreign country is envisioned, requesting counsel may determine that service pursuant to a letter rogatory is necessary. See Born & Westin, 123-125, 133-136; In re Letters Rogatory out of First Civil Court, 261 Fed. 652 (S.D.N.Y. 1919); Service of Process on Foreign Parties by Letters Rogatory, 52 Inter Alia F1 (May/June 1987); Longley, Serving Process, Subpoenas and Other Documents in a Foreign Country, Proc. A.B.A., Sec. of Int'l & Comp. L. 34, 35 (1959); Cumulative Digest of United States Practice in International Law, 1981-1988, Department of State, Office of the Legal Adviser, 1442, 1448 (1994).

SAMPLE LETTERS ROGATORY: There is annexed a basic sample letter rogatory, but see, 4 J. Moore, Moore's Federal Practice 28.05-08 (2d ed. 1991) (Caveat: Do not draft the letter rogatory as a request from the President of the United States, but rather as a request from the requesting court.); 3 J. Moore & L. Frumer, Moore's Manual, Federal Practice Forms, Nos. 15:21; 15:22 (2d ed. 1988); 2A Bender's Federal Practice Forms, Fed. R. Civ. P. 28(b) (1991); 8 Wigmore, Evidence, rev. (McNaughton 1961) Sec. 2195a (ii); B. Ristau, International Judicial Assistance, Vol. 1, Part III, Ch. 3, Section 3-3-1/3-3-2, pp. 94-101 (1995 supp.); Epstein & Snyder, International Litigation, Section 10.09, 10-13 - 10-16 (2d ed. 1994); Born & Westin, International Civil Litigation in United States Courts, 308-309, (1989).

GUIDELINES ON DRAFTING LETTERS ROGATORY: Letters rogatory should be written in simple, non-technical English and should not include unnecessary information which may confuse court in the receiving foreign state. Avoid use of the term "discovery". Similarly, to avoid the appearance of a "fishing expedition" which may result in refusal of the foreign country to execute the request, try not to use phrases such as "any and all documents". Requests for documents should be as specific as possible. If particular procedures to be followed by the foreign court are preferable, include the specifics in the letter rogatory (for example, verbatim transcript, place witness under oath, permission for American or foreign counsel to attend or participate in proceedings if possible, etc.) For general guidance on drafting letters rogatory see Ristau, Sec. 3-3-2, 95-96; 3-3-5, p. 103 (1995 supp.); Born & Westin 308.

The letter rogatory should be addressed "To Appropriate Judicial Authority of (**Insert name of Country**). " (See The Mandu, II F. Supp. 845, EDNY 1935). The essential elements of a letter rogatory are:

(a) a request for international judicial assistance is being made in the interests of justice;

(b) a brief synopsis of the case, including identification of the parties and the nature of the claim and relief sought to enable the foreign court to understand the issues involved;

(c) type of case [civil, criminal, administrative];

(d) the nature of the assistance required [compel testimony or production of evidence; service of process];

(e) name, address and other identifiers, such as corporate title, of the person abroad to be served or from whom evidence is to be compelled, documents to be served;

(f) list of questions to be asked, where applicable, generally in the form of written interrogatories;

(g) list of documents or other evidence to be produced;

(h) the requesting court should include a statement expressing a willingness to provide similar assistance to judicial authorities of the receiving state [28 U.S.C. 1782];

(i) the requesting court should include a statement expressing a willingness to reimburse the judicial authorities of the receiving state for costs incurred in executing the requesting court's letter rogatory.

AUTHENTICATION REQUIREMENTS: Letters rogatory must be issued under the seal of the court and the signature of the judge. The clerk should not sign on behalf of the judge. (See Ristau, Sec. 3-1-13, p. 73 at note 14, (1995 supp.); Born & Westin 307.) For most countries, the seal of the court and signature of the judge is sufficient. Consult our country-specific information via our autofax service or via our home page on the Internet for guidance about procedures for particular countries. Some countries require further authentication of letters rogatory. **Do not waste time and money on these additional steps unless your local foreign counsel, this office, or some other authoritative source advises that it is necessary.** If there is no specific flyer for the country in question, consult the geographic division of the Office of American Citizens Services and Crisis Management. See "Questions" below.

TRIPLE CERTIFICATION, CHAIN AUTHENTICATION AND AUTHENTICATION BY THE FOREIGN EMBASSY IN THE UNITED STATES: As noted above, these additional authentication steps are not required by most countries. Some countries require **Triple Certification** of the letter rogatory which means that the judge signs the documents; the clerk certifies that the judge is the judge; the judge certifies that the clerk is the clerk). This is also known as an exemplification certificate (A.O. form 132). In addition to the triple certification or exemplification process, some foreign countries require that the letter rogatory be authenticated by the embassy or consulate of the foreign country in the United States. This is accomplished by "chain authentication" summarized below. (See Ristau Sec. 3-1-13, 1994 Rev., p. 73 at note 14.)

State Court Documents:

1. Seal and Signature of the Judge;

2. State Secretary of State or other authority authenticates the seal of the State Court; (*For a list of state authentication offices, see our information flyers on the "Hague Legalization Convention" (AUTOFAX document 1053) and "General Authentication Flyer" (AUTOFAX document 1046) available via our autofax service and our Consular Home Page on the Internet explained under "Additional Information" below. See also our Authentications Office Home Page at* **http://www.state.gov/www/authenticate/index.html**.

3. U.S. Department of State Authentications Office authenticates the seal of the State Secretary of State or comparable authority as explained below;

4. Embassy or Consulate or the foreign country in the U.S. authenticates the seal of the U.S. Department of State. (*For the address and telephone number of foreign embassies see our country-specific consular information sheets on our Home Page on the Internet under "entry requirement" or our brochure "visa requirements of foreign governments" which also lists the phone numbers of the foreign consulates in the U.S.)*

Federal Court Documents:

1. Seal and Signature of the Judge;

2. Seal of the U.S. Court is authenticated by the U.S. Department of Justice, Management Division, Security Program Staff, Physical Security Office, 9th and Pennsylvania Avenue, Room 6531, Washington, D.C. 20530, tel: (202) 514-2314 or 514-4667 or the Administrative Office of the U.S. Courts.

3. U.S. Department of State Authentications Office authenticates the seal of the Department of Justice or the Administrative Office of the U.S. Courts as explained below;

4. Embassy or Consulate or the foreign country in the U.S. authenticates the seal of the U.S. Department of State.

Expediting the Authentication Process: It may be possible to authenticate the documents at the foreign consulate nearest you and avoid the interim steps if the foreign consulate has the court's seal or the state Secretary of State's seal on file. This office will NOT undertake the task of obtaining the authentications of the State, the Departments of Justice and State and the foreign embassies.

U.S. State Department Authentication Office, 518 23rd St., N.W., Washington, D.C. 20520, (202) 647-5002 Fee: $5.00. For additional information, call the Federal Information

Center: 1-800-688-9889, and choose option 6 after you press 1 for touch tone phones. Walk-in service is available from the Authentications Office from 8 a.m. to 12 noon Monday-Friday, except holidays. Walk-in service is limited to 15 documents per person per day (documents can be multiple pages). Processing time for authentication requests sent by mail is 5 working days or less. An information flyer explaining the authentication process is available from the Office of American Citizens Services, either by mail or through our automated fax system or via our Internet Consular Affairs Home Page described below under "Additional Information". These topics include "General Authentication Flyer" (AUTOFAX document 1046). See also the U.S. State Department's Authentications Office Home Page at **http://www.state.gov/www/authenticate/index.html.**

Further Authenticating the U.S. State Department Seal: *Occassionally, foreign countries may request that after the embassy of the foreign country in the United States authenticates the seal of the U.S. Department of State, the documents be further authenticated in the foreign country by the U.S. embassy and/or the foreign country's Foreign Ministry. U.S. embassies abroad are authorized to authenticate the seal of the U.S. Department of State for a $10.00 fee. (See 22 C.F.R. 92.41(c); Schedule of Fees, 22 C.F.R. 22.1 item 45(f).)*

Hague Legalization Convention Countries: If the country where the documents are to be used is a party to the Hague Legalization Convention, and that country requires further authentication of the documents beyond the seal and signature of the judge, consult our information flyer on the Hague Legalization Convention for guidance on how to obtain the Convention "apostille" certificate. See "Additional Information" below. The flyer is available via our autofax service (document 1053) or via the Consular Home Page on the Internet at **http://travel.state.gov** under "international legal assistance", which can also be reached via the main State Department Home Page at **http://www.state.gov/** under "travel" or "consular affairs". See also the U.S. State Department's Authentications Office Home Page at **http://www.state.gov/www/authenticate/index.html.**

TRANSLATION REQUIREMENTS: The letters rogatory and any accompanying documents must be translated into the official language of the foreign country. The translator should execute an affidavit as to the validity of the translation before a notary. See Ristau, Sec. 2-2-2(2), p. 96-97 (1995 supp.)

NUMBER OF COPIES REQUIRED: Forward to the Department of State for transmittal to the foreign authorities: the original English version bearing the seal of the court and signature of the judge [or a certified copy]; a photocopy of the English; the original translation and a photocopy of the translation. The original documents will be served upon the designated recipient or deposited with the foreign court in connection with a request for evidence, and the copies returned to the court in the U.S. as proof of execution. See Ristau, Sec. 2-2-2(2), p. 96-97 (1995 supp.) For requests involving multiple witnesses in diverse locations, either prepare a separate letter rogatory for each witness, or provide a certified copy of the single letter rogatory (plus translation and duplicate copy noted above) for each witness. The foreign country may assign the matter to different courts. The U.S. embassy will endeavor to ensure that evidence obtained will be transmitted to the court in the U.S. as it is received from the Foreign Ministry rather than held by the Foreign Ministry until all the evidence has been obtained. The same procedures apply to requests involving service of process upon multiple persons.

SERVICE VIA LETTERS ROGATORY UNDER SECTION 1608(B) OF THE FOREIGN SOVERIEGN IMMUNITIES ACT: Letters rogatory requesting service of process on an agency or instrumentality of a foreign government pursuant to 28 U.S.C. 1608(b)(3)(A) must be transmitted to the Department of State, Office of American Citizens Services, Room 4811A, 2201 C Street, N.W., Washington, D.C. 20520.

TRANSMITTAL OF THE REQUEST: Letters rogatory generally may be transmitted to foreign judicial authorities through the "diplomatic channel". The "diplomatic channel" is a circuitous route by which the documents are sent to the foreign court. Unless the foreign country accepts transmittal directly from court-to-court or through local foreign counsel, you will be confronted with the difficulties of at least some portion of the diplomatic channel described below. See Ristau, Sec. 3-3-3, p. 102 (1995 supp.) described below. If your local counsel in the foreign country advise that letters rogatory may be transmitted directly by your foreign counsel to the foreign court you may elect to avoid the time consuming diplomatic channel. If the Department of State information about a particular country reflects that use of the diplomatic channel is required, you may wish to seek clarification of contrary guidance from other sources.

Cover Letter: The letters rogatory and accompanying documents may be submitted to the Office of American Citizens Services and Crisis Management, Room 4811A N.S., Department of State, 2201 C Street N.W., Washington, D.C. 20520. Please write the name of the foreign country on the outside of the envelope. The documents should be accompanied by a letter along the following lines:

Foreign Country:

Name of Case:

Docket Number:

Nature of Request: (Service of Process; Compulsion of Testimony; Production of Documents, etc.)

Person to be Served or from Whom Evidence is to be Obtained: (name and address mandatory, phone number if possible.)

Mailing Address of American Court to Which executed Request Should be Returned:

Special Instructions: (Example, Federal Express Account Number; U.S. hearing/trial date, etc.)

Deposit Enclosed:

Statement of Responsibility for Additional Costs incurred in excess of the required deposit which accompanies the letter.

Local Foreign Counsel (if any): (name and address, phone number)

Name, Address, telephone and fax number of requesting attorney in U.S.:

What is the Diplomatic Channel?: The documents proceed along the following lines:

1. Drafted by American attorney ...

2. Issued Under Seal of American court and Signature of Judge ...

3. Returned by Issuing Court to American Attorney ...

4. Sent by Attorney to U.S. State Department or U.S. Embassy Abroad ...
5. Received by U.S. Embassy ...

6. Sent to Ministry of Foreign Affairs under cover of a diplomatic note ...

7. Sent to foreign Ministry of Justice ...

8. Sent to by Ministry of Justice Foreign Court of Competent Jurisdiction ...

9. Executed by Foreign Court subject to Court's Calender ...

10. Returned to Ministry of Foreign Affairs ...

11. Returned to U.S. Embassy ...

12. Returned to U.S. Department of State ...

13. Returned to Requesting Court.

14. Requesting Attorney Receives Evidence from Requesting American Court.

COSTS: Effective February 1, 1998, there is a $455.00 consular fee for services related to execution of a letter rogatory (See 22 CFR 22.1, item 67). Foreign authorities may also charge fees, therefore, counsel are requested to submit a certified bank check in the amount of $500.00 payable to the U.S. Embassy (insert name of capital of the foreign country, for example, "U.S. Embassy Tokyo") as a deposit against which the U.S. consular fee, and any foreign fees may be deducted. Unexpended funds will be refunded by the U.S. Embassy. Corporate or personal checks are not acceptable. There is no consular fee for letters rogatory on behalf of federal, state or local government officials. If more than one witness or person to be served is involved, multiple fees may be charged and additional deposits may be requested. For letters rogatory for use in Taiwan, see our Taiwan specific flyer.

RETAINING LOCAL FOREIGN COUNSEL: 28 U.S.C. 1781(b)(2) permits American courts to transmit letters rogatory directly to the executing authority in the foreign country. Although many countries require that letters rogatory be transmitted to the foreign government through the "diplomatic channel" by the U.S. embassy, local counsel can be helpful in subsequent inquiries. Where the foreign government does not object to direct transmission, for example through a local foreign attorney, this can save time. While retention of the services of a foreign attorney to aid in the progress of a letter rogatory is not generally required (although some countries, such as the Bahamas mandate such assistance), requesting counsel in the U.S. may find it useful to retain local counsel to provide guidance on preparation of the request and to expedite the process. See Ristau, Sec. 3-3-3, at note 24, 102 and Sec. 3-3-5, p. 103 (1995 supp.); and Born & Westin 308.

REFUSAL TO HONOR AMERICAN LETTERS ROGATORY: Foreign countries have declined to honor American letters rogatory where a foreign domestic blocking statute prohibits release of the evidence requested. See Ristau, Sec. 3-3-4, p. 103 (1995 supp.)

REQUESTS FROM STATE OR FEDERAL GOVERNMENT OFFICIALS:

If the letter rogatory is being transmitted at the request of a state or federal official, please contact the Department of State, Office of American Citizens Services for special guidance. With respect to fees, no consular fee will be charged. However, local authorities in the foreign country may impose fees of their own which must be paid by the state or federal authority in the United States requesting the judicial assistance. You will be contacted if a federal appropriation number and fund code or remittance of monies to the Department of State are necessary.

TIME REQUIRED TO EXECUTE A LETTER ROGATORY: Generally letters rogatory worldwide, including those sent to the United States, take from six months to a year to execute. See Ristau, Sec. 3-3-3, p. 102-103 (1995 supp.) ; Born & Westin 307.

RETURN OF EXECUTED LETTER ROGATORY: When a letter rogatory is executed by the foreign authorities, it is returned to the requesting court in the United States by this office via certified mail. Requesting counsel is also notified. At the request of the court, the executed letter rogatory and proof of service/evidence can be returned directly to requesting counsel. If transmittal by commercial express delivery service is preferred, please include your account number in the covering letter.

Treaty Databases on the Internet: Information about treaties in force is available on the Internet at the following web sites:

United States Department of State, Office of the Legal Adviser, Treaty Affairs, List of Treaties and Other International Agreements of the United States In Force:
http://www.acda.gov/state/.

United Nations (UN): **http://www.un.org/** under Databases/Treaties at
http://www.un.org/Depts/Treaty/;

Council of Europe (COE): **http://www.coe.fr:80/index.html** under Texts/Treaties
http://www.coe.fr.80/eng/legaltxt/treaties.htm;

Organization of American States (OAS): **http://www.oas.org/** under Public Information/ Documents/Treaties at **gopher://oasunix1.oas.org:70/11/pub/english/treaties**.

U.S. House of Representatives Internet Law Library Treaties and International Law:
http://law.house.gov/89.htm.

SELECTED REFERENCES:

Books:

Born & Westin, International Civil Litigation in United States Courts, (1989).

Epstein & Snyder, International Litigation: A Guide to Jurisdiction, Practice and Strategy, 2d, Prentice Hall Law & Business (1994).

Grossman, Letters Rogatory: A Symposium Before the Consular Law Society, Federal Legal Publications, Inc., New York (1956).

Hackworth, Digest of International Law, Office of the Legal Adviser, Department of State, Vol. II, (1941).

Kos-Rabcewicz-Zubkowski, International Cooperation in Civil and Commercial Procedure: American Continent, Canadian Inter-American Research Institute; U. of Ottawa Press, (1975).

Lookofsky, Transnational Litigation and Commercial Arbitration, A Comparative Analysis of American, European, and International Law, 445-89 (1992).

Moore, A Digest of International Law 104 et seq., Sec. 189 - letters rogatory 1889-1890, (1906).

Nash, ed., Cumulative Digest of United States Practice in International Law, Department of State, Vol. II, 1409, 1424 (1994).

Ristau, International Judicial Assistance, Civil and Commercial, International Law Institute, (1995 supp.).

Smit, International Cooperation in Litigation: Europe, The Hague, Martinus Nijhoff, (1965).

Whiteman, Digest of International Law, Office of the Legal Adviser, Department of State, Vol 7, 573, 605 (1970).

Articles:

Doyle, Taking Evidence by Deposition and Letters Rogatory and Obtaining Documents in Foreign Territory, Proc. A.B.A., Sec. Int'l & Comp. L. 37 (1959).

Edwards, Taking of Evidence Abroad in Civil or Commercial Matters, 18 Int'l & Comp. L. Q. 646 (1969).

Heilpern, Procuring Evidence Abroad, 14 Rul. L. Rev. 29 (1939).

Houck, Restatement of the Foreign Relations Law of the United States (Revised): Issues and Resolutions, 20 Int'l Law. 1361 (1986).

Jones, International Judicial Assistance: Procedural Chaos and a Program for Reform, 62 Yale L.J. 515, 529-32 (1953).

McCawley, Compelled Production of Documents Located Abroad - Marc Rich and Co. v. U.S., 11 Tax Plan. Int'l Rev. 7 (No. 11, Nov. 1984).

McKay, Compelling Discovery and Disclosure in Transnational Litigation: A Selected Bibliography, 16 N.Y.U.J. Int'l L. and Pol. 1217 (No. 5, Summer 1984).

Maier, Extraterritorial Jurisdiction at a Crossroads: An Intersection Between public and Private International Law, 76 Am. J. Int'l L. 280 (1982).

Note, Letters Rogatory: Current Problems Facing International Judicial Assistance, 4 N.C. J. Int'l L. & Comm. Reg. 297 (1979).

Note, Reciprocity for Letters Rogatory Under the Judicial Code, 58 Yale L.J. 1193, 1193-94 (1949).

Note, Taking Evidence Outside of the United States, 55 B.U. L. Rev. 368, 374 (1975).

Plaster, The Hague Evidence Convention: The Need for Guidance on Procedures and Resolution of Conflicts in International Discovery, Vanderbilt Journal of Transnational Law, Vol. 27, No. 1, pp. 185-217 (1994).

Rafalko, Depositions, Commissions and Letters Rogatory in a Conflict of Laws Case (1965), 4 Dusquesne University Law Review 115.

Robinson, Symposia: Transnational Litigation, Part I, Compelling Discovery and Evidence in International Litigation, The Int'l Law., Vol. 18, No. 3, 533 (1984).

Rosenthal & Yale-Loehr, Two Cheers for the ALI Restatement's Provisions on Foreign Discovery, 16 N.Y.U.J. Int'l L. & Pol. 1075 (1984).;

Sklaver, Obtaining Evidence in International Litigation, 7 Cumberland L. Rev. 233 (1976).

Stern, International Judicial Assistance (Part II: Depositions under Letters Rogatory) (1969), 15 Practical Lawyer 55.

Sunderland, The Use of the Letter of Request (or Letter Rogatory) for the Purpose of Obtaining Evidence for Proceedings in England and Abroad, 31 Intl and Comp L. Q. 784 (1982).

Symposium, Compelling Discovery in Transnational Litigation, 16 N.Y.U.J. Int'l L. and Pol. 957-1156; 1217-1248 (No. 5, Summer 1984).

Symposium, Obtaining Foreign Discovery and Evidence for Use in Litigation in the United States, 13 Int'l L. 3, 46 (1979).

Van Brauman, Foreign Evidence Gathering and Discovery for U.S. Civil Tax Determination Purposes, 30 Int'l Law. 589, 619 (1996).

Von Mehren, Discovery of Documentary and Other Evidence in a Foreign Country, 77 Am. J. Int'l Law 896 (1983).

Von Mehren, Discovery Abroad: The Perspective of the U.S. Private Practitioner, 16 N.Y.U. J. Int'l L. & Pol. 985, 993 (1984).

Selected Cases:

DBMS Consultants, Ltd. v. Computer Assocs. Int'l, Inc., 131 F.R.D. 367, 369 (D. Mass. 1990); See, United States v. Zabady, 546 F. Supp. 35, 39 n. 9 (M.D. Pa. 1982); Rio Tinto Zinc Corp. V. Westinghouse Elec. Corp., (1978) 2 W.L.R. 81, 1All E.R. 434 (H.L. 1977); Reagan v. United States, 453 F.2d 165 (C.A. 6 1971); Re Raychem Corp. v. Canusa Coating Sys., Inc., (1970) 14 D.L.R. 3d 684; Zassenhaus v. Evening Star Newspaper Co., 404 F.2d 1361 (C.A.D.C. 1968); United States v. Paraffin Wax, 2255 Bags, 23 F.R.D. 298 (E.D.N.Y. 1959); Danisch, et al v. The

Guardian Life Insurance Co., 19 F.R.D. 235 (1956); Re Radio Corp of America v. Rauland Corp., (1956) 5 D.L.R. 2d 424; Uebersee Finanz-Korporation, A.G. v. Brownell, 121 F. Supp. 420 (D.D.C. 1954); Wheeler v. West India S.S. Co., 22 Fed. Rules Decisions 396 (1951); The Edmund Fanning petition of Isbrandtsen Co., Inc., 89 Fed. Supp. 282 (1950); Ali Akber Kiachif et al. v. Philco International Corporation, 10 F.R.D. 277 (1950); The Signe, 37 F. Supp. 819, 820 (E.D. La. 1941); The Mandu, 11 F. Supp. 845 (E.D.N.Y. 1935); De Villeneuve v. Morning Journal Ass'n., 206 F.70 (S.D.N.Y. 1913)., Gross v. Palmer t al, C.C.N.D. Ill. 1900, 105 F. 833; Nelson v. United States, 17 Fed. Cas. 1340 (No. 10.116) (C.C.D.Pa. 1816); Winthrop v. Union Ins. Co., 30 Fed. Cas. 376 (No. 17901) (C.C.D.Pa. 1807.)

ADDITIONAL INFORMATION: The Office of American Citizens Services has available general information flyers on international judicial assistance many of which are available through our automated fax system or via our Internet Consular Affairs Home Page.

Using the Autofax System:

* Dial (202) 647-3000 using the phone on your fax machine.

* Follow the prompt to obtain a printed index of judicial assistance topics. There are four indexes.

Travel Information - Index of Countries - Press 1
Passports and Visas - Index of Flyers - Press 2
Judicial Assistance - General and Country Specific - Press 3
Child Custody and Adoption - Index of Flyers - Press 4

* Enter the four digit code for the document desired as listed in the index.

* When the prompt identifies the document and asks if you want that document, enter Y (9) for yes or N (6) for no.

* If you want another document, enter the four digit code, using the same procedures noted in the previous step.

* When you finish selecting, press the # key on the phone keyboard and press the start button on your fax machine.

* After a brief delay of up to a minute, the documents will print automatically on your fax machine.

Using the Internet: Many of our judicial assistance flyers are also available on the Internet via the Department of State, Bureau of Consular Affairs Home Page at **http://travel.state.gov/** under International Legal Assistance or through the main State Department Home Page at **http://www.state.gov/** under Travel, Consular, or International Legal Assistance. See also, the Department of State, Office of the Legal Adviser for Private International Law (L/PIL) Home Page at **http://his.com/~pildb/** for information regarding private international law unification. See also the Home Pages for many of our embassies which are linked to the Consular Affairs Home Page.

QUESTIONS: Additional questions regarding letters rogatory should be addressed to the appropriate geographic division of the Office of American Citizens Services, Tel: (202) 647-5225 or (202) 647-5226.

EXAMPLE—LETTER ROGATORY:

SAMPLE REQUEST FOR INTERNATIONAL JUDICIAL ASSISTANCE

NAME OF COURT IN SENDING STATE REQUESTING JUDICIAL ASSISTANCE

NAME OF PLAINTIFF

V. DOCKET NUMBER

NAME OF DEFENDANT

REQUEST FOR INTERNATIONAL JUDICIAL ASSISTANCE (LETTER ROGATORY)

(NAME OF THE REQUESTING COURT) PRESENTS ITS COMPLIMENTS TO THE APPROPRIATE JUDICIAL AUTHORITY OF (NAME OF RECEIVING STATE), AND REQUESTS INTERNATIONAL JUDICIAL ASSISTANCE TO (OBTAIN EVIDENCE/ EFFECT SERVICE OF PROCESS) TO BE USED IN A (CIVIL, CRIMINAL, ADMINISTRATIVE) PROCEEDING BEFORE THIS COURT IN THE ABOVE CAPTIONED MATTER. A (TRIAL/HEARING) ON THIS MATTER IS SCHEDULED AT PRESENT FOR (DATE) IN (CITY, STATE, COUNTRY).

THIS COURT REQUESTS THE ASSISTANCE DESCRIBED HEREIN AS NECESSARY IN THE INTERESTS OF JUSTICE. THE ASSISTANCE REQUESTED IS THAT THE APPROPRIATE JUDICIAL AUTHORITY OF (NAME OF RECEIVING STATE) (COMPEL THE APPEAR OF THE BELOW NAMED INDIVIDUALS TO GIVE EVIDENCE/PRODUCE DOCUMENTS) (EFFECT SERVICE OF PROCESS UPON THE BELOW NAMED INDIVIDUALS).

(NAMES OF WITNESSES/PERSONS TO BE SERVED)

(NATIONALITY OF WITNESSES/PERSONS TO BE SERVED)

(ADDRESSED OF WITNESSES/PERSONS TO BE SERVED)

(DESCRIPTION OF DOCUMENTS OR OTHER EVIDENCE TO BE PRODUCED)

FACTS

(THE FACTS OF THE CASE PENDING BEFORE THE REQUESTING COURT SHOULD BE STATED BRIEFLY HERE, INCLUDING A LIST OF THOSE LAWS OF THE SENDING STATE WHICH GOVERN THE MATTER PENDING BEFORE THE COURT IN THE RECEIVING STATE.)

(QUESTIONS)

(IF THE REQUEST IS FOR EVIDENCE, THE QUESTIONS FOR THE WITNESSES SHOULD BE LISTED HERE).

(Rel.1-8/98)

(LIST ANY SPECIAL RIGHTS OF WITNESSES PURSUANT TO THE LAWS OF THE REQUESTING STATE HERE).

(LIST ANY SPECIAL METHODS OR PROCEDURES TO BE FOLLOWED).

(INCLUDE REQUEST FOR NOTIFICATION OF TIME AND PLACE FOR EXAMINATION OF WITNESSES/DOCUMENTS BEFORE THE COURT IN THE RECEIVING STATE HERE).

RECIPROCITY

THE REQUESTING COURT SHOULD INCLUDE A STATEMENT EXPRESSING A WILLINGNESS TO PROVIDE SIMILAR ASSISTANCE TO JUDICIAL AUTHORITIES OF THE RECEIVING STATE.

REIMBURSEMENT FOR COSTS

THE REQUESTING COURT SHOULD INCLUDE A STATEMENT EXPRESSING A WILLINGNESS TO REIMBURSE THE JUDICIAL AUTHORITIES OF THE RECEIVING STATE FOR COSTS INCURRED IN EXECUTING THE REQUESTING COURT'S LETTER ROGATORY.

SIGNATURE OF REQUESTING JUDGE

TYPED NAME OF REQUESTING JUDGE

NAME OF REQUESTING COURT

CITY, STATE, COUNTRY

DATE

(SEAL OF COURT)

Appendix 14[1]

HAGUE CONVENTION ON THE TAKING OF EVIDENCE ABROAD IN CIVIL AND COMMERCIAL MATTERS

MULTILATERAL

Taking of Evidence Abroad

Convention adopted at the Eleventh Session of The Hague Conference on Private International Law October 26, 1968;
Opened for signature at The Hague March 18, 1970;
Signed on behalf of the United States of America July 27, 1970;
Ratification advised by the Senate of the United States of America June 13, 1972;
Ratified by the President of the United States of America July 15, 1972;
Ratification of the United States of America deposited with the Ministry of Foreign Affairs of the Netherlands August 8, 1972;
Proclaimed by the President of the United States of America September 15, 1972;
Entered into force with respect to the United States of America October 7, 1972.

BY THE PRESIDENT OF THE UNITED STATES OF AMERICA

A PROCLAMATION

CONSIDERING THAT:

The Convention on the Taking of Evidence Abroad in Civil or Commercial Matters, adopted at the Eleventh Session of The Hague Conference on Private International Law on October 26, 1968, was opened for signature at The Hague on March 18, 1970, and was signed for the United States of America on July 27, 1970, the text of which in the French and English languages is annexed;

The Senate of the United States of America by its resolution of June 13, 1972, two-thirds of the Senators present concurring, gave its advice and consent to the ratification of that Convention;

The President ratified the Convention on July 15, 1972, and the instrument of ratification was deposited with the Ministry of Foreign Affairs of the Netherlands on August 8, 1972;

Article 37 of the Convention provides that it shall enter into force on the sixtieth day after the deposit of the third instrument of ratification; and

The Convention accordingly will enter into force for the United States of America on October 7, 1972, instruments of ratification having been deposited by Denmark and Norway on June 20, 1972 and August 3, 1972, respectively;

Now, Therefore, I, Richard Nixon, President of the United States of America, proclaim and make public the Convention on the Taking of Evidence Abroad in Civil or Commercial Matters, to the end that it shall be observed and fulfilled with good faith on and after October 7, 1972 by the United States of America and by the citizens of the United States of America and all other persons subject to the jurisdiction thereof.

In testimony whereof, I have signed this proclamation and caused the Seal of the United States of America to be affixed.

Done at the city of Washington this fifteenth day of September in the year of our Lord one thousand nine hundred seventy-two and of the Independence of the United States of America the one hundred ninety-seventh.

[SEAL]

Richard Nixon

By the President:
William P Rogers
Secretary of State

CONVENTION SUR L'OBTENTION DES PREUVES A L'ETRANGER EN MATIERE CIVILE OU COMMERCIALE

Les Etats signataires de la présente Convention,

Désirant faciliter la transmission et l'exécution des commissions rogatoires et promouvoir le rapprochement des diverses méthodes qu'ils utilisent à ces fins,

Soucieux d'accroître l'efficacité de la coopération judiciaire mutuelle en matière civile ou commerciale,

Ont résolu de conclure une Convention à ces effets et sont convenus des dispositions suivantes:

CONVENTION ON THE TAKING OF EVIDENCE ABROAD IN CIVIL OR COMMERCIAL MATTERS

The States signatory to the present Convention,

Desiring to facilitate the transmission and execution of Letters of Request and to further the accommodation of the different methods which they use for this purpose,

Desiring to improve mutual judicial co-operation in civil or commercial matters,

Have resolved to conclude a Convention to this effect and have agreed upon the following provisions –

CHAPITRE I—COMMISSIONS ROGATOIRES

ARTICLE PREMIER

En matière civile ou commerciale, l'autorité judiciaire d'un Etat contractant peut, conformément aux dispositions de sa législation, demander par commission rogatoire à l'autorité compétente d'un autre Etat contractant de faire tout acte d'instruction, ainsi que d'autres actes judiciaires.

Un acte d'instruction ne peut pas être demandé pour permettre aux parties d'obtenir des moyens de preuves qui ne soient pas destinés à être utilisés dans une procédure engagée ou future.

L'expression «autres actes judiciaires» ne vise ni la signification ou la notification d'actes judiciaires, ni les mesures conservatoires ou d'exécution.

ARTICLE 2

Chaque Etat contractant désigne une Autorité centrale qui assume la charge de recevoir les commissions rogatoires émanant d'une autorité judiciaire d'un autre Etat contractant et de les transmettre à l'autorité compétente aux fins d'exécution. L'Autorité centrale est organisée selon les modalités prévues par l'Etat requis.

Les commissions rogatoires sont transmises à l'Autorité centrale de l'Etat requis sans intervention d'une autre autorité de cet Etat.

ARTICLE 3

La commission rogatoire contient les indications suivantes:

CHAPTER I—LETTERS OF REQUEST

ARTICLE 1

In civil or commercial matters a judicial authority of a Contracting State may, in accordance with the provisions of the law of that State, request the competent authority of another Contracting State, by means of a Letter of Request, to obtain evidence, or to perform some other judicial act.

A Letter shall not be used to obtain evidence which is not intended for use in judicial proceedings, commenced or contemplated.

The expression 'other judicial act' does not cover the service of judicial documents or the issuance of any process by which judgments or orders are executed or enforced, or orders for provisional or protective measures.

ARTICLE 2

A Contracting State shall designate a Central Authority which will undertake to receive Letters of Request coming from a judicial authority of another Contracting State and to transmit them to the authority competent to execute them. Each State shall organize the Central Authority in accordance with its own law.

Letters shall be sent to the Central Authority of the State of execution without being transmitted through any other authority of that State.

ARTICLE 3

A Letter of Request shall specify –

a) l'autorité requérante et, si possible, l'autorité requise;

b) l'identité et l'adresse des parties et, le cas échéant, de leurs représentants;

c) la nature et l'objet de l'instance et un exposé sommaire des faits;

d) les actes d'instruction ou autres actes judiciaires à accomplir.

Le cas échéant, la commission rogatoire contient en outre:

e) les nom et adresse des personnes à entendre;

f) les questions à poser aux personnes à entendre ou les faits sur lesquels elles doivent être entendues;

g) les documents ou autres objets à examiner;

h) la demande de recevoir la déposition sous serment ou avec affirmation et, le cas échéant, l'indication de la formule à utiliser;

i) les formes spéciales dont l'application est demandée conformément à l'article 9.

La commission rogatoire mentionne aussi, s'il y a lieu, les renseignments nécessaires à l'application de l'article 11.

Aucune légalisation ni formalité analogue ne peut être exigée.

(a) the authority requesting its execution and the authority requested to execute it, if known to the requesting authority;

(b) the names and addresses of the parties to the proceedings and their representatives, if any;

(c) the nature of the proceedings for which the evidence is required, giving all necessary information in regard thereto;

(d) the evidence to be obtained or other judicial act to be performed.

Where appropriate, the Letter shall specify, inter alia –

(e) the names and addresses of the persons to be examined;

(f) the questions to be put to the persons to be examined or a statement of the subject-matter about which they are to be examined;

(g) the documents or other property, real or personal, to be inspected;

(h) any requirement that the evidence is to be given on oath or affirmation, and any special form to be used;

(i) any special method or procedure to be followed under Article 9.

A Letter may also mention any information necessary for the application of Article 11.

No legalization or other like formality may be required.

Article 4

La commission rogatoire doit être rédigée dans la langue de l'autorité requise ou accompagnée d'une traduction faite dans cette langue.

Article 4

A Letter of Request shall be in the language of the authority requested to execute it or be accompanied by a translation into that language.

Toutefois, chaque Etat contractant doit accepter la commission rogatoire rédigée en langue française ou anglaise, ou accompagnée d'une traduction dans l'une de ces langues, à moins qu'il ne s'y soit opposé en faisant la réserve prévue à l'article 33.

Tout Etat contractant qui a plusieurs langues officielles et ne peut, pour des raisons de droit interne, accepter les commissions rogatoires dans l'une de ces langues pour l'ensemble de son territoire, doit faire connaître, au moyen d'une déclaration, la langue dans laquelle la commission rogatoire doit être rédigée ou traduite en vue de son exécution dans les parties de son territoire qu'il a déterminées. En cas d'inobservation sans justes motifs de l'obligation découlant de cette déclaration, les frais de la traduction dans la langue exigée sont à la charge de l'Etat requérant.

Tout Etat contractant peut, au moyen d'une déclaration, faire connaître la ou les langues autres que celles prévues aux alinéas précédents dans lesquelles la commission rogatoire peut être adressée à son Autorité centrale.

Toute traduction annexée à une commission rogatoire doit être certifiée conforme, soit par un agent diplomatique ou consulaire, soit par un traducteur assermenté ou juré, soit par toute autre personne autorisée à cet effet dans l'un des deux Etats.

Nevertheless, a Contracting State shall accept a Letter in either English or French, or a translation into one of these languages, unless it has made the reservation authorized by Article 33.

A Contracting State which has more than one official language and cannot, for reasons of internal law, accept Letters in one of these languages for the whole of its territory, shall, by declaration, specify the language in which the Letter or translation thereof shall be expressed for execution in the specified parts of its territory. In case of failure to comply with this declaration, without justifiable excuse, the costs of translation into the required language shall be borne by the State of origin.

A Contracting State may, by declaration, specify the language or languages other than those referred to in the preceding paragraphs, in which a Letter may be sent to its Central Authority.

Any translation accompanying a Letter shall be certified as correct, either by a diplomatic officer or consular agent or by a sworn translator or by any other person so authorized in either State.

ARTICLE 5

Si l'Autorité centrale estime que les dispositions de la Convention n'ont pas été respectées, elle en informe immédiatement

ARTICLE 5

If the Central Authority considers that the request does not comply with the provisions of the present Convention, it shall

l'autorité de l'Etat requérant qui lui a transmis la commission rogatoire, en précisant les griefs articulés à l'encontre de la demande.

promptly inform the authority of the State of origin which transmitted the Letter of Request, specifying the objections to the Letter.

ARTICLE 6

En cas d'incompétence de l'autorité requise, la commission rogatoire est transmise d'office et sans retard à l'autorité judiciaire compétente du même Etat suivant les règles établies par la législation de celui-ci.

ARTICLE 6

If the authority to whom a Letter of Request has been transmitted is not competent to execute it, the Letter shall be sent forthwith to the authority in the same State which is competent to execute it in accordance with the provisions of its own law.

ARTICLE 7

L'autorité requérante est, si elle le demande, informée de la date et du lieu où il sera procédé à la mesure sollicitée, afin que les parties intéressées et, le cas échéant, leurs représentants puissent y assister. Cette communication est adressée directement auxdites parties ou à leurs représentants, lorsque l'autorité requérante en a fait la demande.

ARTICLE 7

The requesting authority shall, if it so desires, be informed of the time when, and the place where, the proceedings will take place, in order that the parties concerned, and their representatives, if any, may be present. This information shall be sent directly to the parties or their representatives when the authority of the State of origin so requests.

ARTICLE 8

Tout Etat contractant peut déclarer que des magistrats de l'autorité réquérante d'un autre Etat contractant peuvent assister à l'exécution d'une commission rogatoire. Cette mesure peut être soumise à l'autorisation préalable de l'autorité compétente désignée par l'Etat déclarant.

ARTICLE 8

A Contracting State may declare that members of the judicial personnel of the requesting authority of another Contracting State may be present at the execution of a Letter of Request. Prior authorization by the competent authority designated by the declaring State may be required.

ARTICLE 9

L'autorité judiciaire qui procède à l'exécution d'une commission rogatoire, applique les lois de son pays en ce qui concerne les formes à suivre.

ARTICLE 9

The judicial authority which executes a Letter of Request shall apply its own law as to the methods and procedures to be followed.

Toutefois, il est déféré à la demande de l'autorité requérante tendant à ce qu'il soit procédé suivant une forme spéciale, à moins que celle-ci ne soit incompatible avec la loi de l'Etat requis, ou que son application ne soit pas possible, soit en raison des usages judiciaires de l'Etat requis, soit de difficultés pratiques.

La commission rogatoire doit être exécutée d'urgence.

However, it will follow a request of the requesting authority that a special method or procedure be followed, unless this is incompatible with the internal law of the State of execution or is impossible of performance by reason of its internal practice and procedure or by reason of practical difficulties.

A Letter of Request shall be executed expeditiously.

Article 10

En exécutant la commission rogatoire, l'autorité requise applique les moyens de contrainte appropriés et prévus par sa loi interne dans les cas et dans la même mesure où elle y serait obligée pour l'exécution d'une commission des autorités de l'Etat requis ou d'une demande formulée à cet effet par une partie intéressée.

Article 10

In executing a Letter of Request the requested authority shall apply the appropriate measures of compulsion in the instances and to the same extent as are provided by its internal law for the execution of orders issued by the authorities of its own country or of requests made by parties in internal proceedings.

Article 11

La commission rogatoire n'est pas exécutée pour autant que la personne qu'elle vise invoque une dispense ou une interdiction de déposer, établies:

a) soit par la loi de l'Etat requis;

b) soit par la loi de l'Etat requérant et spécifiées dans la commission rogatoire ou, le cas échéant, attestées par l'autorité requérante à la demande de l'autorité requise.

En outre, tout Etat contractant peut déclarer qu'il reconnaît de telles dispenses et interdictions établies par la loi d'autres Etats que l'Etat requérant et l'Etat requis, dans la mesure spécifiée dans cette déclaration.

Article 11

In the execution of a Letter of Request the person concerned may refuse to give evidence in so far as he has a privilege or duty to refuse to give the evidence –

(a) under the law of the State of execution; or

(b) under the law of the State of origin, and the privilege or duty has been specified in the Letter, or, at the instance of the requested authority, has been otherwise confirmed to that authity by the requesting authority.

A Contracting State may declare that, in addition, it will respect privileges and duties existing under the law of States other than the State of origin and the State of execution, to the extent specified in that declaration.

ARTICLE 12

L'exécution de la commission rogatoire ne peut être refusée que dans la mesure où:

a) l'exécution, dans l'Etat requis, ne rentre pas dans les attributions du pouvoir judiciaire; ou

b) l'Etat requis la juge de nature à porter atteinte à sa souveraineté ou à sa sécurité.

L'exécution ne peut être refusée pour le seul motif que la loi de l'Etat requis revendique une compétence judiciaire exclusive dans l'affaire en cause ou ne connaît pas de voies de droit répondant à l'objet de la demande portée devant l'autorité requérante.

ARTICLE 13

Les pièces constatant l'exécution de la commission rogatoire sont transmises par l'autorité requise à l'autorité requérante par la même voie que celle utilisée par cette dernière.

Lorsque la commission rogatoire n'est pas exécutée en tout ou en partie, l'autorité requérante en est informée immédiatement par la même voie et les raisons lui en sont communiquées.

ARTICLE 14

L'exécution de la commission rogatoire ne peut donner lieu au remboursement de taxes ou de frais, de quelque nature que ce soit.

Toutefois, l'Etat requis a le droit d'exiger de l'Etat requérant le remboursement des indemnités payées aux experts et interprètes et des frais résultant de l'applica-

ARTICLE 12

The execution of a Letter of Request may be refused only to the extent that –

(a) in the State of execution the execution of the Letter does not fall within the functions of the judiciary; or

(b) the State addressed considers that its sovereignty or security would be prejudiced thereby.

Execution may not be refused solely on the ground that under its internal law the State of execution claims exclusive jurisdiction over the subject-matter of the action or that its internal law would not admit a right of action on it.

ARTICLE 13

The documents establishing the execution of the Letter of Request shall be sent by the requested authority to the requesting authority by the same channel which was used by the latter.

In every instance where the Letter is not executed in whole or in part, the requesting authority shall be informed immediately through the same channel and advised of the reasons.

ARTICLE 14

The execution of the Letter of Request shall not give rise to any reimbursement of taxes or costs of any nature.

Nevertheless, the State of execution has the right to require the State of origin to reimburse the fees paid to experts and interpreters and the costs oc-

tion d'une forme spéciale demandée par l'Etat requérant conformément à l'article 9, alinéa 2.

L'autorité requise, dont la loi laisse aux parties le soin de réunir les preuves et qui n'est pas en mesure d'exécuter elle-même la commission rogatoire, peut en charger le personne habilitée à cet effet, après avoir obtenu le consentement de l'autorité requérante. En demandant celui-ci, l'autorite requise indique le montant approximatif des frais qui résulteraient de cette intervention. Le consentement implique pour l'autorité requérante l'obligation de rembourser ces frais. A défaut de celui-ci, l'autorité requérante n'est pas redevable de ces frais.

CHAPITRE II—OBTENTION DES PREUVES PAR DES AGENTS DIPLOMATIQUES OU CONSULAIRES ET PAR DES COMMISSAIRES

ARTICLE 15

En matière civile ou commerciale, un agent diplomatique ou consulaire d'un Etat contractant peut procéder, sans contrainte, sur le territorie d'un autre Etat contractant et dans la circonscription où il exerce ses fonctions, à tout acte d'instruction ne visant que les ressortissants d'un Etat qu'il représente et concernant une procédure engagée devant un tribunal dudit Etat.

Tout Etat contractant a la faculté de déclarer que cet acte ne peut être effectué que noyennant l'autorisation accordée sur demande faite par cet agent ou en son nom, par l'autorité compétente désignée par l'Etat déclarant

casioned by the use of a special procedure requested by the State of origin under Article 9, paragraph 2.

The requested authority whose law obliges the parties themselves to secure evidence, and which is not able itself to execute the Letter, may, after having obtained the consent of the requesting authority, appoint a suitable person to do so. When seeking this consent the requested authority shall indicate the approximate costs which would result from this procedure. If the requesting authority gives its consent it shall reimburse any costs incurred; without such consent the requesting authority shall not be liable for the costs.

CHAPTER II—TAKING OF EVIDENCE BY DIPLOMATIC OFFICERS, CONSULAR AGENTS AND COMMISSIONERS

ARTICLE 15

In a civil or commercial matter, a diplomatic officer or consular agent of a Contracting State may, in the territory of another Contracting State and within the area where he exercises his functions, take the evidence without compulsion of nationals of a State which he represents in aid of proceedings commenced in the courts of a State which he represents.

A Contracting State may declare that evidence may be taken by a diplomatic officer or consular agent only if permission to that effect is given upon application made by him or on his behalf to the appropriate authority designated by the declaring State.

(Rel.1-8/98)

ARTICLE 16

Un agent diplomatique ou consulaire d'un Etat contractant peut en outre procéder, sans contrainte, sur le territoire d'un autre Etat contractant et dans la circonscription où il exerce ses fonctions, à tout acte d'instruction visant les ressortissants de l'Etat de résidence ou d'un Etat tiers, et concernant une procédure engagée devant un tribunal d'un Etat qu'il représente:

a) si une autorité compétente désignée par l'Etat de résidence a donné son autorisation, soit d'une manière générale, soit pour chaque cas particulier, et

b) s'il respecte les conditions que l'autorité compétente a fixées dans l'autorisation.

Tout Etat contractant peut déclarer que les actes d'instruction prévus ci-dessus peuvent être accomplis sans son autorisation préalable.

ARTICLE 16

A diplomatic officer or consular agent of a Contracting State may, in the territory of another Contracting State and within the area where he exercises his functions, also take the evidence, without compulsion, of nationals of the State in which he exercises his functions or of a third State, in aid of proceedings commenced in the courts of a State which he represents, if –

(a) a competent authority designated by the State in which he exercises his functions has given its permission either generally or in the particular case, and

(b) he complies with the conditions which the competent authority has specified in the permission.

A Contracting State may declare that evidence may be taken under this Article without its prior permission.

ARTICLE 17

En matière civile ou commerciale, toute personne régulièrement désignée à cet effet comme commissaire, peut procéder, sans contrainte, sur le territoire d'un Etat contractant à tout acte d'instruction concernant une procédure engagée devant un tribunal d'un autre Etat contractant:

a) si une autorité compétente désignée par l'Etat de l'exécution a donné son autorisation, soit d'une manière générale, soit pour chaque cas particulier; et

b) si elle respecte les conditions que l'autorité compétente a fixées dans l'autorisation.

ARTICLE 17

In a civil or commercial matter, a person duly appointed as a commissioner for the purpose may, without compulsion, take evidence in the territory of a Contracting State in aid of proceedings commenced in the courts of another Contracting State if –

(a) a competent authority designated by the State where the evidence is to be taken has given its permission either generally or in the particular case; and

(b) he complies with the conditions which the competent authority has specified in the permission.

Tout Etat contractant peut déclarer que les actes d'instruction prévus ci-dessus peuvent être accomplis sans son autorisation préalable

A Contracting State may declare that evidence may be taken under this Article without its prior permission.

Article 18

Tout Etat contractant peut déclarer qu'un agent diplomatique ou consulaire ou un commissaire, autorisé à procéder à un acte d'instruction conformément aux articles 15, 16 et 17, a la faculté de s'adresser à l'autorité compétente désignée par ledit Etat, pour obtenir l'assistance nécessaire à l'accomplissement de cet acte par voie de contrainte. La déclaration peut comporter toute condition que l'Etat déclarant juge convenable d'imposer.

Lorsque l'autorité compétente fait droit à la requête, elle applique les moyens de contrainte appropriés et prévus par sa loi interne.

Article 18

A Contracting State may declare that a diplomatic officer, consular agent or commissioner authorized to take evidence under Articles 15, 16 or 17, may apply to the competent authority designated by the declaring State for appropriate assistance to obtain the evidence by compulsion. The declaration may contain such conditions as the declaring State may see fit to impose.

If the authority grants the application it shall apply any measures of compulsion which are appropriate and are precribed by its law for use in internal proceedings.

Article 19

L'autorité compétente, en donnant l'autorisation prévue aux articles 15, 16 et 17 ou dans l'ordonnance prévue à l'article 18, peut déterminer les conditions qu'elle juge convenables, relatives notamment aux heure, date et lieu de l'acte d'instruction. Elle peut de même demander que ces heure, date et lieu lui soient notifiés au préalable et en temps utile; en ce cas,-un représentant de ladite autorité peut être présent à l'acte d'instruction.

Article 19

The competent authority, in giving the permission referred to in Articles 15, 16 or 17, or in granting the application referred to in Article 18, may lay down such conditions as it deems fit, *inter alia*, as to the time and place of the taking of the evidence. Similarly it may require that it be given reasonable advance notice of the time, date and place of the taking of the evidence; in such a case a representative of the authority shall be entitled to be present at the taking of the evidence.

Article 20

Les personnes visées par un acte d'instruction prévu dans ce chapitre peuvent se faire assister par leur conseil.

Article 21

Lorsqu'un agent diplomatique ou consulaire ou un commassaire est autorisé à procéder à un acte d'instruction en vertu des articles 15, 16 et 17:

a) il peut procéder à tout acte d'instruction qui n'est pas incompatible avec la loi de l'Etat de l'exécution ou contraire à l'autorisation accordée en vertu desdits articles et recevoir, dans les mêmes conditions, une déposition sous serment ou avec affirmation;

b) à moins que la personne visée par l'acte d'instruction ne soit ressortissante de l'Etat dans lequel la procédure est engagée, toute convocation à comparaître ou à participer à un acte d'instruction est rédigée dans la langue du lieu où l'acte d'instruction doit être accompli, ou accompagnée d'une traduction dans cette langue;

c) la convocation indique que la personne peut être assistée de son conseil, et, dans tout Etat qui n'a pas fait la déclaration prévue à l'article 18, qu'elle n'est pas tenue de comparaître ni de participer à l'acte d'instruction;

d) l'acte d'instruction peut être accompli suivant les formes prévues par la loi du tribunal devant lequel la procédure est engagée, à condition qu'elles ne soient pas interdites par la loi de l'Etat de l'exécution;

Article 20

In the taking of evidence under any Article of this Chapter persons concerned may be legally represented.

Article 21

Where a diplomatic officer, consular agent or commissioner is authorized under Articles 15, 16 or 17 to take evidence –

(a) he may take all kinds of evidence which are not incompatible with the law of the State where the evidence is taken or contrary to any permission granted pursuant to the above Articles, and shall have power within such limits to administer an oath or take an affirmation;

(b) a request to a person to appear or to give evidence shall, unless the recipient is a national of the State where the action is pending, be drawn up in the language of the place where the evidence is taken or be accompanied by a translation into such language;

(c) the request shall inform the person that he may be legally represented and, in any State that has not filed a declaration under Article 18, shall also inform him that he is not compelled to appear or to give evidence;

(d) the evidence may be taken in the manner provided by the law applicable to the court in which the action is pending provided that such manner is not forbidden by the law of the State where the evidence is taken;

e) la personnel visée par l'acte d'instruction peut invoquer les dispenses et interdictions prévues à l'article 11.

ARTICLE 22

Le fait qu'un acte d'instruction n'ait pu être accompli conformément aux dispositions du présent chapitre en raison du refus d'une personne d'y participer, n'empêche pas qu'une commission rogatoire soit adressée ultérieurement pour le même acte, conformément aux dispositions du chapitre premier.

CHAPITRE III - DISPOSITIONS GÉNÉRALES

ARTICLE 23

Tout Etat contractant peut, au moment de la signature, de la ratification ou de l'adhésion, déclarer qu'il n'exécute pas les commissions rogatoires qui ont pour object une procédure connue dans les Etats du *Common Law* sous le nom de «pre-trial discovery of documents».

ARTICLE 24

Tout Etat contractant peut désigner, outre l'Autorité centrale, d'autres autorités dont il détermine les compétences. Toutefois, les commissions rogatoires peuvent toujours être transmises à l'Autorité centrale.

Les Etats fédéraux ont la faculté de désigner plusieurs Autorités centrales.

ARTICLE 25

Tout Etat contractant, dans lequel plusieurs systèmes de droit sont en vigueur, peut désigner les

(e) a person requested to give evidence may invoke the privileges and duties to refuse to give the evidence contained in Article 11.

ARTICLE 22

The fact that an attempt to take evidence under the procedure laid down in this Chapter has failed, owing to the refusal of a person to give evidence, shall not prevent an application being subsequently made to take the evidence in accordance with Chapter I.

CHAPTER III - GENERAL CLAUSES

ARTICLE 23

A Contracting State may at the time of signature, ratification or accession, declare that it will not execute Letters of Request issued for the purpose of obtaining pre-trial discovery of documents as known in Common Law countries.

ARTICLE 24

A Contracting State may designate other authorities in addition to the Central Authority and shall determine the extent of their competence. However, Letters of Request may in all cases be sent to the Central Authority.

Federal States shall be free to designate more than one Central Authority.

ARTICLE 25

A Contracting State which has more than one legal system may designate the authorities of one of

autorités de l'un de ces systèmes, qui auront compétence exclusive pour l'exécution des commissions rogatoires en application de la présente Convention.

such systems, which shall have exclusive competence to execute Letters of Request pursuant to this Convention.

Article 26

Tout Etat contractant, s'il y est tenu pour des raisons de droit constitutionnel, peut inviter l'Etat requérant à rembourser les frais d'exécution de la commission rogatoire et concernant la signification ou la notification à comparaître, les indemnités dues à la personne qui fait la déposition et l'établissement du procès-verbal de l'acte d'instruction.

Lorsqu'un Etat a fait usage des dispositions de l'alinéa précédent, tout autre Etat contractant peut inviter cet Etat à rembourser les frais correspondants.

Article 26

A Contracting State, if required to do so because of constitutional limitations, may request the reimbursement by the State of origin of fees and costs, in connection with the execution of Letters of Request, for the service of process necessary to compel the appearance of a person to give evidence, the costs of attendance of such persons, and the cost of any transcript of the evidence.

Where a State has made a request pursuant to the above paragraph, any other Contracting State may request from that State the reimbursement of similar fees and costs.

Article 27

Les dispositions de la présente Convention ne font pas obstacle à ce qu'un Etat contractant:

a) déclare que des commissions rogatoires peuvent être transmises à ses autorités judiciaires par d'autres voies que celles prévues à l'article 2;

b) permette, aux termes de sa loi ou de sa coutume interne, d'exécuter les actes auxquels elle s'applique dans des conditions moins restrictives;

c) permette, aux termes de sa loi ou de sa coutume interne, des méthodes d'obtention de preuves autres que celles prévues par la présente Convention.

Article 27

The provisions of the present Convention shall not prevent a Contracting State from –

(a) declaring that Letters of Request may be transmitted to its judicial authorities through channels other than those provided for in Article 2;

(b) permitting, by internal law or practice, any act provided for in this Convention to be performed upon less restrictive conditions;

(c) permitting, by internal law or practice, methods of taking evidence other than those provided for in this Convention.

ARTICLE 28

La présente Convention ne s'oppose pas à ce que des Etats contractants s'entendent pour déroger:

a) à l'article 2, en ce qui concerne la voie de transmission des commissions rogatoires;

b) à l'article 4, en ce qui concerne l'emploi des langues;

c) à l'article 8, en ce qui concerne la présence de magistrats à l'exécution des commissions rogatoires;

d) à l'article 11, en ce qui concerne les dispenses et interdictions de déposer;

e) à l'article 13, en ce qui concerne la transmission des pièces constatant l'exécution;

f) à l'article 14, en ce qui concerne le réglement des frais;

g) aux dispositions du chapitre II.

ARTICLE 29

La présente Convention remplacera, dans les rapports entre les Etats qui l'auront ratifiée, les articles 8 à 16 des Conventions relatives à la procédure civile, respectivement signées à La Haye le 17 juillet 1905 et le premier mars 1954, dans la mesure où lesdits Etats sont Parties à l'une ou l'autre de ces Conventions.

ARTICLE 30

La présente Convention ne porte pas atteinte à l'application de l'article 23 de la Convention

ARTICLE 28

The present Convention shall not prevent an agreement between any two or more Contracting States to derogate from –

(a) the provisions of Article 2 with respect to methods of transmitting Letters of Request;

(b) the provisions of Article 4 with respect to the languages which may be used;

(c) the provisions of Article 8 with respect to the presence of judicial personnel at the execution of Letters;

(d) the provisions of Article 11 with respect to the privileges and duties of witnesses to refuse to give evidence;

(e) the provisions of Article 13 with respect to the methods of returning executed Letters to the requesting authority;

(f) the provisions of Article 14 with respect to fees and costs;

(g) the provisions of Chapter II.

ARTICLE 29

Between Parties to the present Convention who are also Parties to one or both of the Conventions on Civil Procedure signed at the Hague on the 17th of July 1905 [1] and the 1st of March 1954, [2] this Convention shall replace Articles 8–16 of the earlier Conventions.

ARTICLE 30

The present Convention shall not affect the application of Article 23 of the Convention of

[1] 99 *British Foreign and State Papers* 990.
[2] 286 UNTS 265.

de 1905, ni de l'article 24 de celle de 1954.

ARTICLE 31

Les accords additionnels aux Conventions de 1905 et de 1954, conclus par les Etats contractants, sont considérés comme également applicables à la présente Convention, à moins que les Etats intéressés n'en conviennent autrement.

ARTICLE 32

Sans préjudice de l'application des articles 29 et 31, la présente Convention ne déroge pas aux conventions auxquelles les Etats contractants sont ou seront Parties et qui contiennent des dispositions sur les matières réglées par la présente Convention.

ARTICLE 33

Tout Etat, au moment de la signature, de la ratification ou de l'adhésion, a la faculté d'exclure en tout ou en partie l'spplication des dispositions de l'alinéa 2 de l'article 4, ainsi que du chapitre II. Aucune autre réserve ne sera admise.

Tout Etat contractant pourra, à tout moment, retirer une réserve qu'il aura faite; l'effect de la réserve cessera le soixantième jour après la notification du retrait.

Lorsqu'un Etat aura fait une réserve, tout autre Etat affecté par celle-ci peut appliquer la même règle à l'égard de l'Etat qui a fait la réserve.

ARTICLE 34

Tout Etat peut à tout moment retirer ou modifier une déclaration.

1905, or of Article 24 of the Convention of 1954.

ARTICLE 31

Supplementary Agreements between Parties to the Conventions of 1905 and 1954 shall be considered as equally applicable to the present Convention unless the Parties have otherwise agreed.

ARTICLE 32

Without prejudice to the provisions of Articles 29 and 31, the present Convention shall not derogate from conventions containing provisions on the matters covered by this Convention to which the Contracting States are, or shall become Parties.

ARTICLE 33

A State may, at the time of signature, ratification or accession exclude, in whole or in part, the application of the provisions of paragraph 2 of Article 4 and of Chapter II. No other reservation shall be permitted.

Each Contracting State may at any time withdraw a reservation it has made; the reservation shall cease to have effect on the sixtieth day after notification of the withdrawal.

When a State has made a reservation, any other State affected thereby may apply the same rule against the reserving State.

ARTICLE 34

A State may at any time withdraw or modify a declaration.

Article 35

Tout Etat contractant indiquera au Ministère des Affaires Etrangères des Pays-Bas, soit au moment du dépôt de son instrument de ratification ou d'adhésion, soit ultérieurement, les autorités prévues aux articles 2, 8, 24 et 25.

Il notifiera, le cas échéant, dans les mêmes conditions:

a) la désignation des autorités auxquelles les agents diplomatiques ou consulaires doivent s'adresser en vertu de l'article 16 et de celles qui peuvent accorder l'autorisation ou l'assistance prévues aux articles 15, 16 et 18;

b) la désignation des autorités qui peuvent accorder au commissaire l'autorisation prévue à l'article 17 ou l'assistance prévue à l'article 18;

c) les déclarations visées aux articles 4, 8, 11, 15, 16, 17, 18, 23 et 27;

d) tout retrait ou modification des désignations et déclarations mentionnées ci-dessus;

e) tout retrait de réserves.

Article 36

Les difficultés qui s'élèveraient entre les Etats contractants à l'occasion de l'application de la présente Convention seront réglées par la voie diplomatique.

Article 35

A Contracting State shall, at the time of the deposit of its instrument of ratification or accession, or at a later date, inform the Ministry of Foreign Affairs of the Netherlands of the designation of authorities, pursuant to Articles 2, 8, 24 and 25.

A Contracting State shall likewise inform the Ministry, where appropriate, of the following –

(a) the designation of the authorities to whom notice must be given, whose permission may be required, and whose assistance may be invoked in the taking of evidence by diplomatic officers and consular agents, pursuant to Articles 15, 16 and 18 respectively;

(b) the designation of the authorities whose permission may be required in the taking of evidence by commissioners pursuant to Article 17 and of those who may grant the assistance provided for in Article 18;

(c) declarations pursuant to Articles 4, 8, 11, 15, 16, 17, 18, 23 and 27;

(d) any withdrawal or modification of the above designations and declarations;

(e) the withdrawal of any reservation.

Article 36

Any difficulties which may arise between Contracting States in connection with the operation of this Convention shall be settled through diplomatic channels.

(Rel.1-8/98)

ARTICLE 37

La présente Convention est ouverte à la signature des Etats représentés à la Onzième session de la Conférence de La Haye de droit international privé.

Elle sera ratifiée et les instruments de ratification seront déposés auprès du Ministère des Affaires Etrangères des Pays-Bas.

ARTICLE 38

La présente Convention entrera en vigueur le soixantième jour après le dépôt du troisième instrument de ratification prévu par l'article 37, alinéa 2.

La Convention entrera en vigueur, pour chaque Etat signataire ratifiant postérieurement, le soixantième jour après le dépôt de son instrument de ratification.

ARTICLE 39

Tout Etat non représenté à la Onzième session de la Conférence de La Haye de droit international privé qui est Membre de la Conférence ou de l'Organisation des Nations Unies ou d'une institution spécialisée de celle-ci ou Partie au Statut de la Cour Internationale de Justice pourra adhérer à la présente Convention après son entrée en vigueur en vertu de l'article 38, alinéa premier.

L'instrument d'adhésion sera déposé auprès du Ministère des Affaires Etrangères des Pays-Bas.

ARTICLE 37

The present Convention shall be open for signature by the States represented at the Eleventh Session of the Hague Conference on Private International Law.

It shall be ratified, and the instruments of ratification shall be deposited with the Ministry of Foreign Affairs of the Netherlands.

ARTICLE 38

The present Convention shall enter into force on the sixtieth day after the deposit of the third instrument of ratification referred to in the second paragraph of Article 37.

The Convention shall enter into force for each signatory State which ratifies subsequently on the sixtieth day after the deposit of its instrument of ratification.

ARTICLE 39

Any State not represented at the Eleventh Session of the Hague Conference on Private International Law which is a Member of this Conference or of the United Nations or of a specialized agency of that Organization, or a Party to the Statute of the International Court of Justice[1] may accede to the present Convention after it has entered into force in accordance with the first paragraph of Article 38.

The instrument of accession shall be deposited with the Ministry of Foreign Affairs of the Netherlands.

[1] TS 993; 59 Stat. 1055.

La Convention entrera en vigueur, pour l'Etat adhérant, le soixantième jour après le dépôt de son instrument d'adhésion.

L'adhésion n'aura d'effet que dans les rapports entre l'Etat adhérant et les Etats contractants qui auront déclaré accepter cette adhésion. Cette déclaration sera déposée auprès du Ministère des Affaires Etangères des Pays-Bas; celui-ci en enverra, par la voie diplomatique, une copie certifiée conforme, à chacun des Etats contractants.

La Convention entrera en vigueur entre l'Etat adhérant et l'Etat ayant déclaré accepter cette adhésion, soixante jours après le dépôt de la déclaration d'acceptation.

ARTICLE 40

Tout Etat, au moment de la signature, de la ratification ou de l'adhésion, pourra déclarer que la présente Convention s'étendra à l'ensemble des territoires qu'il représente sur le plan international, ou à l'un ou plusieurs d'entre eux. Cette déclaration aura effet au moment de l'entrée en vigueur de la Convention pour ledit Etat.

Par la suite, toute extension de cette nature sera notifiée au Ministère des Affaires Etrangères des Pays-Bas.

La Convention entrera en vigueur, pour les territoires visés par l'extension, le soixantième jour après la notification mentionnée à l'alinéa précédent.

The Convention shall enter into force for a State acceding to it on the sixtieth day after the deposit of its instrument of accession.

The accession will have effect only as regards the relations between the acceding State and such Contracting States as will have declared their acceptance of the accession. Such declaration shall be deposited at the Ministry of Foreign Affairs of the Netherlands; this Ministry shall forward, through diplomatic channels, a certified copy to each of the Contracting States.

The Convention will enter into force as between the acceding State and the State that has declared its acceptance of the accession on the sixtieth day after the deposit of the declaration of acceptance.

ARTICLE 40

Any State may, at the time of signature, ratification or accession, declare that the present Convention shall extend to all the territories for the international relations of which it is responsible, or to one or more of them. Such a declaration shall take effect on the date of entry into force of the Convention for the State concerned.

At any time thereafter, such extensions shall be notified to the Ministry of Foreign Affairs of the Netherlands. [1]

The Convention shall enter into force for the territories mentioned in such an extension on the sixtieth day after the notification indicated in the preceding paragraph.

[1] Extended to Guam, Puerto Rico, and the Virgin Islands pursuant to notification sent by the American Embassy at The Hague on Feb. 6, 1913.

ARTICLE 41

La présente Convention aura une durée de cinq ans à partir de la date de son entrée en vigueur, conformément à l'article 38, alinéa premier, même pour les Etats qui l'auront ratifiée ou y auront adhéré postérieurement.

La Convention sera renouvelée tacitement de cinq en cinq ans, sauf dénonciation.

La dénonciation sera, au moins six mois avant l'expiration du délai de cinq ans, notifiée au Ministère des Affaires Etrangères des Pays-Bas.

Elle pourra se limiter à certains des territoires auxquels s'applique la Convention.

La dénonciation n'aura d'effet qu'à l'égard de l'Etat qui l'aura notifiée. La Convention restera en vigueur pour les autres Etats contractants.

ARTICLE 41

The present Convention shall remain in force for five years from the date of its entry into force in accordance with the first paragraph of Article 38, even for States which have ratified it or acceded to it subsequently.

If there has been no denunciation, it shall be renewed tacitly every five years.

Any denunciation shall be notified to the Ministry of Foreign Affairs of the Netherlands at least six months before the end of the five year period.

It may be limited to certain of the territories to which the Convention applies.

The denunciation shall have effect only as regards the State which has notified it. The Convention shall remain in force for the other Contracting States.

ARTICLE 42

Le Ministère des Affaires Etrangères des Pays-Bas notifiera aux Etats visés à l'article 37, ainsi qu'aux Etats qui auront adhéré conformément aux dispositions de l'article 39:

a) les signatures et ratifications visées à l'article 37;

b) la date à laquelle la présente Convention entrera en vigueur conformément aux dispositions de l'article 38, alinéa premier;

c) les adhésions visées à l'article 39 et la date à laquelle elles auront effet;

d) les extensions visées à l'article 40 et la date à laquelle elles auront effet;

ARTICLE 42

The Ministry of Foreign Affairs of the Netherlands shall give notice to the States referred to in Article 37, and to the States which have acceded in accordance with Article 39, of the following –

(a) the signatures and ratifications referred to in Article 37;

(b) the date on which the present Convention enters into force in accordance with the first paragraph of Article 38;

(c) the accessions referred to in Article 39 and the dates on which they take effect;

(d) the extensions referred to in Article 40 and the dates on which they take effect;

e) les désignations, réserves et déclarations mentionnées aux articles 33 et 35;

f) les dénonciations visées à l'article 41, alinéa 3.

En foi de quoi, les soussignés, dûment autorisés, ont signé la présente Convention.

Fait à La Haye, le 18 mars 1970; en français et en anglais, les deux textes faisant également foi, en un seul exemplaire, qui sera déposé dans les archives du Gouvernement des Pays-Bas et dont une copie certifiée conforme sera remise, par la voie diplomatique, à chacun des Etats représentés à la Onzième session de la Conférence de La Haye de droit international privé.

(e) the designations, reservations and declarations referred to in Articles 33 and 35;

(f) the denunciations referred to in the third paragraph of Article 41.

In witness whereof the undersigned, being duly authorised thereto, have signed the present Convention.

Done at The Hague, on the 18th day of March 1970, in the English and French languages, both texts being equally authentic, in a single copy which shall be deposited in the archives of the Government of the Netherlands, and of which a certified copy shall be sent, through the diplomatic channel, to each of the States represented at the Eleventh Session of the Hague Conference on Private International Law.

POUR LA REPUBLIQUE FEDERALE d'ALLEMAGNE,
FOR THE FEDERAL REPUBLIC OF GERMANY,
Sous réserve de la ratification

(s.) Hans Arnold

POUR L'AUTRICHE,
FOR AUSTRIA,

POUR LA BELGIQUE,
FOR BELGIUM,

POUR LE CANADA,
FOR CANADA,

POUR LE DANEMARK,
FOR DENMARK,

POUR L'ESPAGNE,
FOR SPAIN,

POUR LES ETATS-UNIS D'AMÉRIQUE,
FOR THE UNITED STATES OF AMERICA,

POUR LA FINLANDE,
FOR FINLAND,

POUR LA FRANCE,
FOR FRANCE,

POUR LA GRÈCE,
FOR GREECE,

POUR L'IRLANDE,
FOR IRELAND,

POUR ISRAËL,
FOR ISRAEL,

POUR L'ITALIE,
FOR ITALY,

POUR LE JAPON,
FOR JAPAN,

POUR LE LUXEMBOURG,
FOR LUXEMBOURG,

POUR LA NORVÈGE,
FOR NORWAY,

(s.) G. ROGSTAD

POUR LES PAYS-BAS,
FOR THE NETHERLANDS,

POUR LE PORTUGAL,
FOR PORTUGAL,

(s.) CONSTANTINO RIBEIRO VAZ

Ad Referendum – Au moment de la ratification seront faites des réserves et déclarations jugées nécessaires et permises par la présente Convention

POUR LA RÉPUBLIQUE ARABE UNIE,
FOR THE UNITED ARAB REPUBLIC,

POUR LE ROYAUME UNI DE GRANDE-BRETAGNE ET D'IRLANDE DU NORD,
FOR THE UNITED KINGDOM OF GREAT BRITAIN AND NORTHERN IRELAND,

(s.) EDWARD TOMKINS

POUR LA SUÈDE,
FOR SWEDEN,

POUR LA SUISSE,
FOR SWITZERLAND,

POUR LA TCHÉCOSLOVAQUIE,
FOR CZECHOSLOVAKIA,

POUR LA TURQUIE,
FOR TURKEY,

POUR LA YOUGOSLAVIE,
FOR YUGOSLAVIA,

Copie certifiée conforme à l'original

Le Sous-Directeur des Traités
du Ministère des Affaires Etrangères
du Royaume des Pays-Bas:

17 APR. 1970

BOULONOIS

(F. G. Boulonois)

Appendix 14[2]

Hague Convention on Taking of Evidence Abroad in Civil or Commercial Matters

State Department Circular

DISCLAIMER: THE INFORMATION IN THIS CIRCULAR RELATING TO THE LEGAL REQUIREMENTS OF SPECIFIC FOREIGN COUNTRIES IS PROVIDED FOR GENERAL INFORMATION ONLY AND MAY NOT BE TOTALLY ACCURATE IN A PARTICULAR CASE. QUESTIONS INVOLVING INTERPRETATION OF SPECIFIC FOREIGN LAWS SHOULD BE ADDRESSED TO FOREIGN COUNSEL OR THE FOREIGN CENTRAL AUTHORITY FOR THE CONVENTION.

IN FORCE: ANGUILLA[1], ARGENTINA (excludes recognition of the extension of the Convention by the United Kingdom to the MALVINAS, SOUTH GEORGIA and SOUTH SANDWICH ISLANDS), ARUBA[2], AUSTRALIA, BARBADOS, BULGARIA, CAYMAN ISLANDS[1], CHINA[8], CYPRUS, CZECH REPUBLIC[3], DENMARK, DJIBOUTI[4,5], ESTONIA, FALKLAND ISLANDS[1], FINLAND, FRANCE, FRENCH GUIANA[5], FRENCH POLYNESIA[5], GERMANY, GIBRALTAR[1], GUADELOUPE[5], GUERNSEY[1], HONG KONG SAR[7,1], ISLE OF MAN[1], ISRAEL, ITALY, JERSEY[1], LATVIA, LUXEMBOURG, MACAO SAR[6], MARTINIQUE[5], MEXICO, MONACO, NETHERLANDS, NORWAY, POLAND, PORTUGAL, SAINT PIERRE AND MIQUELON[5], SINGAPORE, SLOVAK REPUBLIC[3], SOVEREIGN BASE AREAS OF AKROTIRI AND DHEKELIA[1], SPAIN, SWEDEN, SWITZERLAND, UNITED KINGDOM, UNITED STATES, VENEZUELA.

---

[1] The Convention was extended to this territory, possession or other jurisdiction by the United Kingdom.

[2] The Convention was extended to this territory, possession or other jurisdiction by the Netherlands.

[3] In accordance with Article 34(1) of the Vienna Convention on Succession of States in Respect of Treaties, the U.S. view is that when a country which is a party to a multilateral treaty or convention has dissolved, the successor state(s) inherit the treaty obligations of the former government, consistent with Article 34 of the Vienna Convention. However, as a practical matter, the custom is for depositories to expect a notice of succession to confirm that the new entity is performing its treaty obligations. Many newly independent states may not really be implementing such conventions at this time in that they may not be performing the functions set forth in the Convention. We continue to work with these governments and the depositories to obtain confirmation that the respective successor state is complying with treaty obligations.

[4] This country has achieved independence. No declaration has been made on the continuation in force of the Convention. We have requested the assistance of the Hague Conference on Private International Law in ascertaining from these countries whether they are applying the Convention.

[5] The Convention was extended to this territory, possession or other jurisdiction by France.

[6] The Convention was extended to this territory, possession or other jurisdiction by Portugal.

[7] Hong Kong became a Special Administrative Region (SAR) of the People's Republic of China on July 1, 1997 in accordance with the 1984 Sino-British Joint Declaration. The People's Republic of China has advised the United States that the Hague Service and Evidence Conventions remain in effect for Hong Kong and that the Hong Kong Central Authorities continue to be located in Hong Kong. See list of Central Authorities.

[8] Upon its accession to the Hague Evidence Convention, China declared that the provisions of Chapter II of the Convention except for Article 15 will not be applicable. The United States is seeking clarification from the People's Republic of China regarding its interpretation and implementation of the Convention.

CITATIONS: 23 U.S.T. 2555; T.I.A.S. 7444; 847 UNTS 231; 28 U.S.C.A. 1782 (1975 Cum. Supp.); 28 U.S.C.A. following 1781 (Supp. 1979); 8 I.L.M. 37 (1969); Martindale-Hubbell Law Directory, Law Digest Volume, Selected International Conventions; Ristau, International Judicial Assistance (Civil and Commercial), International Law Institute, (1995 supp.), Appendix C, A-50 *ff.*

PURPOSE: The Hague Evidence Convention codifies the taking of depositions on notice and commission before consuls and court appointed commissioners, providing minimum standards with which contracting states agree to comply. The Convention's primary purpose is to reconcile different, often conflictive, discovery procedures in civil and common law countries. The Convention also streamlines procedures for compulsion of evidence, utilizing a form ''letter of request'' which can be sent directly by the court in the U.S. to a foreign central authority, eliminating the cumbersome ''diplomatic channel''. (See International Soc'y for Krishna Consciousness, Inc. v. Lee, 105 F.R.D. 435, 442-443 (S.D.N.Y. 1984) and Philadelphia Gear Corp. v. American Pfauter Corp., 100 F.R.D. 58, 59 (E.D. Pa. 1983). The foreign central authorities are listed below. (Note: Rule 28(b) F.R.Cv.P. provides for depositions to be taken abroad pursuant to ''any applicable treaty or convention.') For a general discussion of the Convention, see, Restatement (Third) Foreign Relations Law of the United States Sec. 473 (2) (1987); Ristau, International Judicial Assistance (Civil and Commercial), International Law Institute, Sec. 5-1-1—5-3-4, pp. 159-237, (1995 Supp.); Epstein & Snyder, International Litigation: A Guide to Litigation, Practice & Strategy, 2nd, Prentice Hall Law & Business, Sec. 10.10—pp. 10-17—10-33 (1994 Supp.); Moore's Federal Practice, 3rd, Sec. 28.11, p. 28-9—28-22 (March 1997); Digest of United States Practice in International Law, U.S. Department of State, Office of the Legal Adviser, 1973, p. 210-213; 1976, p. 309; 1977, p. 490-492; 1978, p. 870-878, 1709; 1979, 891; 1980, 504-505; 1981-1988 Cumulative Digest, 1409, 1419, 1425-1426, 1509, 1510-1516. 1550, 1557, 1564.

DECLARATIONS AND RESERVATIONS: Each country had the opportunity of making reservations and declarations regarding the applicability of each article of the Convention. This makes the Convention different for each country, so it is important to review our country-specific judicial assistance flyers.

EXCLUSIVITY: The nonexclusivity of the Hague Evidence Convention procedures was at issue in

Societe Nationale Industrielle Aerospatiale v. U.S. District Court, 482 U.S. 522, 96 L.Ed.2d 461, 107 S.Ct. 2542 (1987), where the U.S. Supreme Court held that the Convention did not bar a district court, pursuant to the Federal Rules of Civil Procedure, from ordering a foreign litigant over which that court exercised personal jurisdiction to produce evidence located within the foreign litigant's own territory.

But see, ''Selected Cases'' below. For a discussion of the *Aerospatiale* case and the nonexclusivity of the Convention, see Cumulative Digest of United States Practice in International Law, 1981-1988,

U.S. Department of State, Office of the Legal Adviser, Vol. 2, p. 1516-1524 (1994) and Vol. 3, p. 3704-3707 (1995), Ristau, Sec. 5-2-7, pp. 229-231.5 (1995 Supp.), Born & Westin,

319,334; Epstein & Snyder, Sec. 10.11—10.12, pp. 10-20, 10-27; Wright, Miller & Marcus, Federal Practice and Procedure, Civil, Sec. 2005:1, p. 68-76 (1994) and 1996 pocket part; Moore's Federal Practice, Sec. 28.11[3], p. 28-11- 28-12, and other treatises on the subject, some of which are noted under "Selected References" below.

SCOPE OF THE CONVENTION: Article 1 of the Convention provides that assistance is to be provided in "civil and commercial" matters. The term "civil and commercial" is not defined. See Ristau, Sec. 5-1-4, p. 162-168, (1995 Supp.), Born & Westin 310,312; and the Reports of the Special Commissions on the operation of the Convention noted below.

U.S. CENTRAL AUTHORITY: Office of International Judicial Assistance, Civil Division, Department of Justice, 1100 L St., N.W., Room 11006, Washington, D.C. 20530, tel: (202) 307-0983; fax: (202) 514-6584.

TAKING DEPOSITIONS OF WILLING WITNESSES: Each country party to the Convention made specific reservations and declarations when they deposited their instruments of accession to the Convention. Some countries allow the taking of depositions of willing witnesses only under certain specific conditions. For example, some countries require case-by-case permission from the foreign central authority before a voluntary deposition can be taken. See our country-specific flyers for details. The declarations and reservations made by countries party to the Convention can be found in the Martindale-Hubbell Law Directory, Selected International Conventions (via the Internet, Martindale-Hubbell website:

http://www.martindale.com/products/intl law dir.html) and in the Practical Handbook on the Operation of the Hague Convention on the Taking of Evidence Abroad. See Ristau, Sec. 5-3-1- 5-2-4, pp. 232-238.4, (1995 Supp.) and Born & Westin, 315-317; Epstein & Snyder, Sec. 10.10[4], pp. 10.18 -10-20. Consult our country-specific flyers; see "Additional Information" below.

DEPOSITIONS TAKEN BY COURT APPOINTED COMMISSIONERS OTHER THAN CONSULAR OFFICERS: Article 17 provides for the possibility of court appointed commissioners to take depositions under restrictions similar to those confronting consular officers. To date, only Finland and thc United States have given broad permission for court appointed commissioners to take depositions. The United Kingdom approves such depositions on a reciprocal basis. But see our country specific flyers for additional details. Some countries, such as Denmark and Portugal, made specific declarations prohibiting such activities by court appointed commissioners. In other countries, specific permission must be sought from the foreign central authority for a commissioner other than a consular officer to conduct depositions. See Ristau, Sec. 5-3-3, pp. 236-238, (1995 Supp.); Born & Westin 316.

ARRANGING CONSULAR DEPOSITIONS: When a U.S. consular officer is needed to preside at the taking of a voluntary deposition at an American embassy or consulate scheduling depositions is done directly by our embassies and consulates at a time and date mutually convenience to the participants and the consular officer. The U.S. consular officer generally administers the oaths to the witnesses, court reporter and interpreter and withdraws, subject to recall. The actual questions are posed by the attorneys. (See 22 C.F.R. 92.56, consular officers will comply with special instructions which accompany the request for deposition on notice or commission.) Requesting counsel must make arrangements with the witness to insure his or her appearance for the deposition (travel fees, witness fees, etc.) The U.S. Embassy/Consulate may be able to provide information concerning interpreters, translators and audio/video operators. Private counsel must make their own arrangements to retain the services of interpreters, translators and audio/video operators. Note: not all foreign countries have court reporters, interpreters and translators. American embassies and consulates do not have staff personnel available to perform such functions. It may be necessary to bring your own experts in these fields from the United States. Consult the U.S. embassy or consulate or the embassy or consulate of the foreign country regarding foreign Customs restrictions concerning bringing video and other equipment into a the foreign country. Consult our general information flyer ''Obtaining Evidence Abroad'' for detailed information about arranging consular depositions, telephone depositions, depositions on written questions, videotaping depositions, etc. See Ristau, Sec. 5-3-2, pp. 234-236 (1995 Supp.) for a discussion of consular depositions.

U.S. FEDERAL, STATE OR LOCAL GOVERNMENT PARTICIPANTS:. U.S. federal, state and local government officials interested in obtaining evidence abroad should contact the Office of American Citizens Services (ACS) at (202) 647-5226. ACS assists these officials in making the necessary arrangements for testimony of foreign officials, host country clearance and can assist them in retaining the services of stenographers, interpreters and video operators, where available. A copy of the host country clearance questionnaire will be faxed to you. It will also be available via our Internet Home Page and Autofax Service.

PRE-TRIAL DISCOVERY OF DOCUMENTS: Most countries party to the Convention, with the exception of the Czech Republic, Israel, the Slovak Republic and the United States, made specific declarations objecting to the Article 23 provision on pre-trial discovery of documents. See Ristau, Sec. 5-2-5, p. 205-223 (1995 Supp.); Born & Westin, 313, 315.

COMPULSION OF EVIDENCE: Testimony and documentary or physical evidence may be compelled using the ''Model Letter of Request'' provided in the Hague Evidence Convention. The court in the U.S. transmits the request with appropriate translations directly to the foreign central authority. See Moore's Federal Practice, 3d, Section 28.12[8].

MODEL REQUEST FORM: Article 3 provides mandatory provisions concerning the content of the letter of request. See Ristau, Sec. 5-2-1(1), p. 173-175 (1995 Supp.). See Martindale-Hubbell Law Directory, Selected International Conventions; Ristau, Appendix C, DS-64 through DS-65 (1995 Supp.) for the model letter of request form to compel evidence. For a sample application to a U.S. court for issuance of a letter of request under the Convention, see Ristau, Sec. 5-2-1(3) p. 177-178 (1995 Supp.). For a sample completed letter of request using the recommended form see Ristau, Sec. 5-2-1(4), p. 179-184 (1995 Supp.) The request should include any specific procedures desired by the requesting court, such as verbatim transcripts or participation in the proceedings before the foreign court by American counsel or local counsel representing the American firm. See also Born & Westin, 317; Moore's Federal Practice, 3d, Sec. 28.12[4] and 28.12[9].

NUMBER OF COPIES: The Evidence Convention, unlike the Service Convention, does not require that a letter of request be submitted in duplicate. In practice, however, countries prefer that the request be prepared in duplicate (one English text bearing the seal of the court, one photocopy of the English text; two copies of a translation of the request an any accompanying documents.) If testimony is desired of two or more witnesses, separate letters of request should be issued for each witness. See Ristau, Sec. 5-2-1, p. 185, (1995 Supp.).

TRANSLATIONS: Articles 4 and 33 of the Convention concern translations. The Convention requires a letter of request in the language of the receiving state, but English or French is acceptable unless the receiving state has expressly stated to the contrary. See Moore's Federal Practice, Sec. 28.12[3], p. 28-15. See also S&S Screw Mach. Co. v. Cosa Corp., 647 F. Supp. 600, 613 n.23 (M.D. Tenn. 1986). Consult the declarations and reservations made by each country. See the Martindale-Hubbell Law Directory, Selected International Conventions, Law Digest Volume or the Practical Handbook on the Operation of the Hague Convention on the Taking of Evidence Abroad. See also, Ristau, Sec. 5-2-1(8), p. 185-187 (1995 Supp.), or Epstein, International Litigation, a Guide to Jurisdiction, Practice and Strategy, Section 10.10; Moore's Federal Practice, 3d, Sec. 28.12[3] (1997). Translations should be a notarized certification by the translator. See Ristau, Sec. 5-2-1, p. 187 (1995 Supp.).

TRANSMITTING REQUEST: The requesting court in the United States transmits the model letter of request and accompanying documents and appropriate translations, in duplicate, directly to the central authority. See Ristau, Sec. 5-1-5(2), p. 168-171, (1995 Supp); Moore's Federal Practice, 3d, Sec. 28.12[2] (1997).

EXECUTION OF THE REQUEST: Article 9 provides that letters of request will be executed in accordance with local foreign law. See Ristau, Sec. 5-2-2, p. 188-200 (1995 Supp.); Born & Westin 317-318, and Moore's Federal Practice, 3d, Sec. 28.12[7] for a discussion on how requests are executed in civil and common law countries.

TIME: Article 9 provides that requests be executed ''expeditiously.'' Requests under the Hague Evidence Convention are executed somewhat faster than letters rogatory. This is due in part to the direct channel from the U.S. court to the foreign central authority. However, the general estimate of 6 months to a year to execute the request is still used. See Ristau, Sec. 5-2-2(3), p. 192 (1995, Supp.); Born & Westin, 312 and Moore's Federal Practice, 3d, Sec. 28.12[7].

COSTS: Articles 14, 26 and 28(f) govern costs and fees for execution of letters of request. Generally speaking, there is no fee. However, if the executing country incurs expense for fees paid to ''experts and interpreters'' reimbursement can be sought in accordance with paragraph 2 of Article 14. For a discussion of fees, see Ristau, Sec. 5-2-4, p. 201-204 (1995 Supp.).

RETURN OF EXECUTED REQUEST: Article 13(1) provides that the executed request shall be returned to the issuing authority (requesting court) by the foreign central authority. See Ristau, Sec. 5-1-5(4), p. 171, (1995 Supp.).

(Rel.6–10/05)

FOREIGN CENTRAL AUTHORITIES

COUNTRY AND CENTRAL AUTHORITY

ANGUILLA
Governor of Anguilla

ARGENTINA
Ministry of Foreign Relations and Culture (Ministerio de Relaciones Exteriores y Culto)
Recoquista 1088, Buenos Aires, Argentina

ARUBA
Convention Extended by the Netherlands. Central Authority Unknown. Consult Local Counsel.

AUSTRALIA
Secretary of the Attorney General's Department
Commonwealth of Australia
Canberra, ACT, Australia

BARBADOS
Registrar of the Supreme Court of Barbados
Law Courts
Bridgetown, Barbados
tel: 809-427-5537

BULGARIA
Central Authority: Ministry of Justice and European Legal Integration

CAYMAN ISLANDS
His Excellency the Governor
Cayman Islands

CHINA
Bureau of International Judicial Assistance
Ministry of Justice of the People's Republic of China
10 Chaoyangmen Nandajie, Chaoyang District
Beijing 100020
China

CYPRUS
Ministry of Justice

CZECH REPUBLIC
Ministerstvo Spravedlnosti Ceske republicky
The Ministry of Justice of the Czech Republic
128 Praha 2, Vysehradska 16
Prague, Czech Republic

DENMARK
Justitsministeriet
Ministry of Justice
Slotsholmsgade 10
1216 Kobenhavn K.
Copenhagen, Denmark
tel: 120906; telex: 15530

ESTONIA
Ministry of Justice
Suur Karja #19
Tallinn, Estonia EE0001
tel: (6) 28-2648

FALKLAND ISLANDS
The Governor
Stanley, Falkland Islands

FINLAND
Ministry of Justice
10 Etelaesplanadi
Helsinki 13, Finland
tel: 358-0-1601

FRANCE
Ministere de la Justice
Ministry of Justice
Service Civil de L'Entraide Judiciaire Internationale
13, Place Vendome
75042 Paris Cedex 01, France
tel: 261-80-22; telex: 211802

GERMANY

For Baden-Wurttemberg
Justizministerium Baden-Wurttemberg
Justice Ministry
Schillerplatz 4
70173 Stuttgart, Germany
tel: 21931

For Bavaria
Das Bayerisches Staasministerium der Justiz
Justizpalast
Prielmayerstrasse 7
80335 Munchen
Munich, Germany
tel: 55971

For Berlin
Senatsverwaltung fur Justiz von Berlin
Salzburger Strasse 21-25
10825 Berlin, Germany
tel: 7831

For Brandenburg
Das Ministerium der Justiz
des Landes Brandenburg
Heinrich-Mann-Allee 107
14460 Potsdam, Germany

For Bremen
Der Prasident des Landgerichts Bremen
Domsheide 16
28195 Bremen, Germany
tel: 3614204

For Hamburg
Der Prasident des Amtsgerichtes Hamburg
Sievekingplatz 1
20335 Hamburg, Germany
tel: 34971

For Hesse
Der Hessische Minister der Justiz
Luisenstrasse 13
65185 Wiesbaden, Germany
tel: 321

For Lower Saxony
Der Niedersachsisher Minister der Justiz
Am Waterlooplatz 1
30169 Hannover, Germany
tel: 1901

For Mecklenburg-Western Pomerania
Der Minister fur Justiz
Bundes- und Europaangelegenheiten
des Landes Mecklenburg-Vorpommern
Demmlerplatz 14
19053 Schwerin, Germany

For Northrhine-Westphalia
Prasident des Oberlandesgerichts
Dusseldorf
Cecilienallee 3
40474 Dusseldorf, Germany
tel: 87921

For Rhineland-Palatinate
Das Ministerium der Justiz
Ernst-Ludwig-Strasse 3
55116 Mainz, Germany
tel: 161

For Saarland
Ministerium der Justiz des Saarlandes
Zahringerstrasse 12
66119 Saarbrucken, Germany
tel: 5051

For Saxony
Das Sachsische Stattsministerium
der Justiz
Archivstrasse 1
66119 Dresden, Germany

For Saxony-Anhalt
Das Ministerium der Justiz
des Landes Sachsen-Anhalt
Wilhelm-Hopfner-Ring 6
39116 Magdeburg, Germany

For Schleswig-Holstein
Der Justizminister des Landes Schleswig-Holstein
Lorentzendamm 35
34103 Kiel, Germany
tel: 51371

For Thuringia
Das Justizministerium Thuringen
Alfred-Hess-Strasse 8
99094 Erfurt, Germany

Gibraltar
The Deputy Governor
Gibraltar

Guernsey
Bailiff, Deputy Bailiff, any Jurat of the Royal Court
of Guernsey, the Chairman or a Jurat of the Court
of Alderney and the Seneschal (or deputy) of the
Court of the Seneschal of Sark
Guernsey, United Kingdom

Hong Kong SAR
Chief Secretary of Hong Kong
Central Government Offices
Lower Albert Road
Hong Kong; tel: (011) (852) 8102954

Isle of Man
1. See United Kingdom.
2. Her Majesty's First Deemster and Clerk of the
Rolls is designated as an additional authority to receive letters of request for execution in the Isle of Man

Israel
Director of the Courts
19 Jaffa Road
Jerusalem

Italy
Ministerio degliAffari Esteri
Rome, Italy

Jersey
Royal Court of Jersey

Latvia
Ministry of Justice
Brivibas Boulevard 34
LV—1536 Riga, Latvia

Luxembourg
Parquet General Pres La Cour Superieure de Justice
12 Cote d'Eich
Luxembourg-Ville, Luxembourg
tel: 475981 or 26767 or 41464

Macau SAR
On December 16, 1999, the Government of the People's Republic of China declared: ''In accordance with the Joint Declaration of the Governemnt of the People's Republic of China and the Government of the Republic of Portugal on the Question of Macau signed on 13 April 1987, the Government of the People's Republic of China will resume the exercise of sovereignty over Macau with effect from 20 December 1999. **Central Authority:** Procurator of the Procuratorate of Macau SAR, Alameda Dr. Carlos D'Assumpcao, NAPE, Edificio Comercial Tai Fung, 13, Regiao Administrativa Especial de Macau; tel: 853-797-8271, fax: 853-727-621. The official languages in Macau SAR are Chinese and Portugese. Foreign judical assistance requests pursuant to the Convention written in English will be accepted and processed, though the preference is for a copy to be submitted in one of the two official languages—Chinese or Portugese.

Mexico
Secretaria de Relaciones Exteriores
Dirreccion General de Asuntos Juridicos
Ricardo Flores Magon No. 1
Mexico City, Mexico
tel: 782-34-40
telex: 01762090

Monaco
Directorate of Judicial Services
MC 98025
Monaco Cedex, Monaco

Netherlands
De Officier van Justitie bij de Arrondissementsrechtbank te 's
Gravenhage
The Public Prosecutor With the District Court of the Hague
Juliana van Stolberglaan 2-4
The Hague, the Netherlands tel: 82-40-41

Norway
The Royal Ministry of Justice and Police
Toks 8005
Oslo Dep
Oslo 1, Norway

Poland
Ministry of Justice
Department of International Cooperation and European Law
Al. Ujazdowskie 11
Warsaw, Poland 00-950
tel: (48)(22) 628-4431
fax: (48)(22) 628-0949

Portugal
Direccao-Geral dos Servicas Judiciarios
Ministerio da Justica
The Director-General of the Judiciary Deparment
Ministry of Justice
Prace do Comercio
1194 Lisboa Codex
Lisbon, Portugal
tel: 360786

Singapore
The Registrar of the Supreme Court
St. Andrews Road
Singapore 0617, Singapore
tel: 65-3324021; fax: 65-3379450

Slovak Republic
Ministerstvo spravodlivosti Slovenskej republicky
The Ministry of Justice of the Slovak Republic
Zupne namestie 13,
813 11 Brtislava, Slovak Republic
Fax: 00427-531035

Sovereign Base Areas of Akrotiri & Dhekelia
Senior Registrar of the Judge's Court of the Sovereign Base Areas

Spain
The Ministry of Justice (El Ministerio Justicia)
La Direccion General de Codificacion y Cooperacion Juridica Internacional
Ministerio de Justicia e Interior
Technical Secretariat General (Secretaria General Tecnica)
Calle San Bernardo 62
28071 Madrid, Spain

Sweden
Ministry of Justice
Division for Criminal and International Judicial Cooperation
Central Authority
SE-103 33 Stockholm, Sweden
tel: (46)(8) 405-5048
fax: (46)(8) 405-4676

Switzerland
Federal Justice and Police Department
Federal Office for Police Matters
International Judicial and Extrajudicial Assistance
Bundesrain 20
3003 Bern, Switzerland
Fax: 011-41-31-322-5380
The Swiss Federal Justice and Police Department will forward the requests to the Central Authority in the appropriate canton. Requests for evidence may also be sent directly to the Central Authority for the appropriate Canton, as noted below.

Authorized Swiss Central Authorities for each Canton
Language: (G=German); (F=French); (I-Italian)

Canton: Appenzell Ausserhoden (G)
Kantonsgerich Appenzell A. Rh., 9043 Trogen, Switzerland
tel: 011-41-71-94-24-61

Canton: Aargau (G)
Obergericht des Kantons Aargau, 5000 Aargau, Switzerland
tel: 011-41-64-21-19-40

Canton: Basel-Landschaft (G)
Obergericht des Kantons Basel-Landschaft, 4410 Liestal, Switzerland
tel: 011-41-61-925-51-11

Canton: Basel-Stadt (G)
Apellationsgericht Basel-Stadt, 4054 Basel, Switzerland
tel: 011-41-61-267-81-81

Canton: Bern (G/F)
Justizdirektion des Kantons Bern, 3011 Bern, Switzerland
tel: 011-41-31-633-76-76

Canton: Fribourg (F/G)
Tribunal cantonal, 1700 Fribourg, Switzerland
tel: 011-41-37-25-39-10

Canton: Geneve (F)
Parquet du Procureur general, 1211 Geneve 3, Switzerland
tel: 011-41-22-319-21-11

Canton: Glarus (G)
Obergericht des Kantons Glarus, 8750 Glarus, Switzerland
tel: 011-41-58-61-15-32

Canton: Graubuenden (G)
Justiz-, Polizei- und Sanitaets- departement, Graubunden, 7001 Chur, Switzerland
tel: 011-41-81-21-21-21

Canton: Jura (F)
Department de la Justice, 2800 Delemont, Jura, Switzerland
tel: 011-41-66-21-51-11

Canton: Luzern (G)
Obergericht des Kantons Luzern, 6002 Luzern, Switzerland
tel: 011-41-41-24-51-11

Canton: Neuchatel (F)
Departement de Justice, 2001 Neuchatel, Switzerland
tel: 011-41-38-22-31-11

Canton: Nidwalden (G)
Kantonsgericht Nidwalden, 6370 Stans, Switzerland
tel: 011-41-41-63-79-50

Canton: Obwalden (G)
Kantonsgericht des Kantons, Obwalden, 6060 Sarnen, Switzerland
tel: 011-41-41-66-92-22

Canton: St. Gallen (G)
Kantonsgericht St. Gallen, 9001 St. Gallen, Switzerland
tel: 011-41-71-21-31-11

Canton: Schaffhausen (G)
Obergericht des Kantons, Schaffhausen, 8201 Schaffhausen, Switzerland
tel: 011-41-53-82-74-22

Canton: Schwyz (G)
Kantonsgericht Schwyz, 6430 Schwyz; Switzerland
tel: 011-41-43-24-11-24

Canton: Solothurn (G)
Obergericht des Kantons Solothurn, 4500 Solothurn, Switzerland
tel: 011-41-65-21-73-11

Canton: Tessin (I)
Tribunale di appello, 6901 Lugano, Switzerland
tel: 011-41-91-21-51-11
Canton: Thurgau (G)
Obergericht des Kantons Thurgau, 8500 Frauenfeld, Switzerland
tel: 011-41-54-22-31-21

Canton: Uri (G)
Gerichtskanzlei Uri, 6460 Altdorf, Switzerland
tel: 011-41-44-4-22-44

Canton: Valais (F/G)
Tribunal cantonal, 1950 Sion, Switzerland
tel: 011-41-27-22-93-93

Canton: Vaud (F)
Tribunal cantonal, 1014 Lausanne, Switzerland
tel: 011-41- 21-313-15-11

Canton: Zug (G)
Obergericht des Kantons Zug, Rechtshilfe, 6300 Zug, Switzerland
tel: 011-41-42-25-33-11

Canton: Zurich (G)
Obergericht des Kantons Zurich, Rechtshilfe, 8023 Zurich, Switzerland
tel: 011-41-1-257-91-91

United Kingdom
The Foreign and Commonwealth Office
London SW1A 2AL, United Kingdom

For England and Wales
The Senior Master of the Supreme Court of Judicature (Queen's Bench Division)
Royal Courts of Justice Strand
London WC2A 2LL, United Kingdom

For Scotland
The Crown Agent for Scotland
Lord Advocate's Department
Crown Office
5/7 Regent Road
Edinburgh EH7 5BL, Scotland

For Northern Ireland
Registrar of the Supreme Court of Northern Ireland

-or-

Master (Queens's Bench and Appeals)
Royal Courts of Justice
Belfast 1, Northern Ireland

Venezuela
el Miniterio Relaciones Exteriores the Ministry of External Relations

SEE ALSO:

– ''Checklist for the Discussions of the Special Commission of April 1989 on the Operation of the Hague Convention on the Taking of Evidence Abroad'', Hague Conference on Private International Law, Preliminary Document No. 1 of March 1989, 28 I.L.M. 1556 (1989).

– ''Report of the Second Meeting of the Special Commission on the Operation of the Hague Convention on the Taking of Evidence Abroad in Civil or Commercial Matters, July 1985'', 24 I.L.M. 1668 (1985).

– Practical Handbook on the Operation of the Hague Convention of 18 March 1970 on the Taking of Evidence Abroad in Civil Or Commercial Matters, Hague Conference on Private

International Law, Maarten Kluwer's Internationale Uitgeversonderneming, Antwerp, 1984. U.S. Distributor: Butterworth Publishers Inc., 10 Tower Office Park, Woburn, Boston, Massachusetts 01801. Contact the U.S. Central Authority for addresses of other distributors.

– ''Report on the Work of the Special Commission on the Operation of the Hague Convention on the Taking of Evidence Abroad in Civil or Commercial Matters Prepared by the United States Delegation'', 17 I.L.M. 1417 (1978).

– ''Report on the Work of the Special Commission on the Operation of the Convention of 18 March 1970 on the Taking of Evidence Abroad in Civil or Commercial Matters June 12-15, 1978 Prepared by the Permanent Bureau'', 17 I.L.M. 1425 (1978).

– ''Message from the President of the United States Transmitting the Convention on the Taking of Evidence Abroad in Civil or Commercial Matters'', S. Exec. Doc. No. A 92d Cong., 2d Sess. (1972), 12 I.L.M. 323 (1973).

– ''Letter of Submittal from Secretary of State William P. Rogers to the President Regarding the Evidence Convention'', S. Exec. Doc. No. A, 1, 92d Cong., 2d Sess. (1972), 12 I.L.M. 324 (1973).

– ''Report of the U.S. Delegation on the Taking of Evidence Abroad in Civil and Commercial Matters'', 8 I.L.M. 785, 804 (1969).

BUT SEE:

Societe Nationale Industrielle Aerospatiale, et al., v. United States District Court for the Southern District of Iowa, 1987 U.S. LEXIS 2615; 96 Law. Ed. 2d 461; 107 Sup. Ct. 2542; 55 U.S. Law Week 4842; 7 Federal Rules of Service 3d 1105; 482 U.S. (page unassigned) (1987), 26 I.L.M. 1021 (1987).

Supreme Court Proceedings in Societe Nationale Industrielle Aerospatiale, et al., v. United States District Court for the Southern District of Iowa (Hague Evidence Convention; Extraterritorial Discovery in the U.S. Courts.) 25 I.L.M. 1475 (1986).

In re Anschuetz and Company, 838 F. 2d 1362, 7 March 1988.

Anschuetz & Co. v. Mississippi River Bridge Authority, et al.; Messerschmitt Bolkow Blohm v. Virginia Walker, et al., Brief for United States as Amicus Curiae and Petitioner's Response. 25 I.L.M. 803 (1986).

Club Mediterranee v. Dorin, 469 U.S. 1019 (1984), 23 I.L.M. 1332 (1984). Brief for United States as Amicus Curiae. (Appeal Dismissed.)

Volkswagenwerk v. Falzon, 464 U.S. 811 (1983), 23 I.L.M. 412 (1984). Brief for United States as Amicus Curiae. (Appeal Dismissed).

Hudson v. Hermann Pfauter GmbH & Co., 117 F.R.D. 33, 9 September 1987.

In re Benton Graphics v. Uddeholm Corp., 118 F.R.D. 386, D.N.J. 30 November 1987.

Sandsend Financial Consultants v. Wood, 743 SW2d 364, Tex. Civ. App., 1st Dist. Houston, 7 January 1988.

Scarminach v. Goldwell GmbH, 531 N.Y.S. 2d 188, Sup., Monroe County, 22 June 1988.

Cf. Rich v. KIS California, Inc., 121 F.R.D. 254, M.D.N.C., 22 June 1988.

John Jenco v. Martech International, Inc., 1988 U.S. Dist. LEXIS 4727, E.D. La., 20 May 1988, reversing 1988 U.S. Dist. LEXIS 3991.

''Hague Evidence Convention in the U.S. Courts'', Laker Airways Ltd. v. Pan American World Airways, et al., U.S. District Court for the District of Columbia;

Graco v. Kremlin, Inc., U.S. District Court for the Northern District of Illinois (Eastern Division), 23 I.L.M. 748-781 (1984).

Laker Airways, Ltd. v. Sabena, Belgian World Airlines, 731 F. 2d 909, 937 (D.C. Cir. 1984).

In re Westinghouse Litigation, 563 F. 2d 992 (10th Cir. 1977).

In re Marc Rich & Co., A.G., 707 F. 2d 663, 667 (2d Cir.), cert. denied, 463 U.S. 1215 (1983). Marc Rich & Co., A.G. v. United States, 736 F. 2d 864 (2d Cir. 1984).

In re Grand Jury Proceedings: The Bank of Nova Scotia, 740 F. 2d 817 (11th Cir. 1984), cert. denied, U.S. , 105 S. Ct. 788 (1985).

SEE ALSO:

Alley, E.R., New Developments under the Hague Evidence and Service Conventions: 1989 Special Commission, International Business Lawyer, 380 (1989).

Amram, Explanatory Report on the Convention on the Taking of Evidence Abroad in Civil or Commercial Matters, Message from the President of the United States'', Sen. Exec. A., 92nd Cong., 2d Sess. (Feb. 1, 1972).

Amram, The Proposed Convention on the Taking of Evidence Abroad, 55 A.B.A. J. 651 (1969).

Amram, Report on the Eleventh Session of the Hague Conference on Private International Law, 63 Am. J. Int'l Law 521 (1969).

Amram, United States Ratification of the Hague Convention on the Taking of Evidence Abroad, 67 Am. J. Int'l Law 104 (1973).

Augustine, Obtaining International Judicial Assistance Under the Federal Rules and the Hague Convention on the Taking of Evidence Abroad in Civil and Commercial Matters: An Exposition of the Procedures and a Practical Example: In re Westinghouse Uranium Contract Litigation, 10 Ga. J. Int'l & Comp. L. 101 (1980).

Bailey, Stephen R., ''Depositions and Discovery—Hague Convention on the Taking of Evidence Abroad in Civil or Commercial Matters'', 54 Journal of Air Law and Commerce, 381 (1988).

Bermann, The Hague Evidence Convention in the Supreme Court: A critique of the Aerospatiale Decision, 63 Tul. L. Rev. 525 (1989).

Bishop, Significant Issues in the Construction of The Hague Evidence Convention, 1 Int'l Litigation Q. 2, 38 (1985).

Black, United States Transnational Discovery: The Rise and Fall of the Hague Evidence Convention, 40 Int'l and Comparative L.Q. 901-906 (1991).

Born, The Hague Evidence Convention Revisited: Reflections on Its Role in U.S. Civil Procedure, 57 Law & Contemp. Probs. 77, 90-96 (1994).

Boyd, Contemporary Practice of the United States Relating to International Law—The Hague Evidence Convention, 72 Am. J. Int'l Law 133 (1978).

Comment, The Hague Convention on the Taking of Evidence Abroad in Civil or Commercial Matters: The Exclusive and Mandatory Procedures for Discovery Abroad, 132 U. Pa. L. Rev. 1461 (1984)

Edwards, Taking of Evidence Abroad in Civil or Commercial Matters, 18 Int'l. and Comp. L. Q. 646 (1969)

Gerber, International Discovery after Aerospatiale: the Quest for an Analytical Framework, 82 Am, J. Int'l L. 521, 555 (1988).

Griffin & Bravin, Beyond Aerospatiale: A Commentary on Foreign Discovery Provisions, 25 Int'l Law. No. 2, 315 (1991).

Guzman, Rick, Interplay between the Discovery Provisions of the Hague Evidence Convention and the Federal Rules of Civil Procedure: Societe Nationale Industrielle Aerospatiale, 9 Hous. J. Int'l. L., 333 (1987).

Hayne, Hague Convention and the Federal Rules of Civil Procedure, 9 Hous. J. Int'l L. 333 (1987).

Heck, U.S. Misinterpretation of the Hague Evidence Convention, 24 Colum. J. Transnat'l. L. 231 (1986).

McLean, The Hague Evidence Convention: Its Impact on American Civil Procedure, 9 Loy. L.A. Int'l & Comp. J.J. 17, 62 (1986).

McLean & McLachlan, The Hague Convention on the Taking of Evidence Abroad. Explanatory Documentation prepared for Commonwealth Jurisdictions, Commonwealth Secretariat, (September 1985).

Maier, Extraterritorial Discovery: Cooperation, Coercion, and the Hague Evidence Convention, 19 Vand. J. Transnat'l L. 239, 252-255 (1986).

Martens, D.H., German Civil Procedure and the Implementation of the Hague Evidence Convention,1 International Litigation Quarterly, No. 2, 115 (September 1985).

Matthews, The Role of the Hague Convention for Gathering Evidence Abroad: Societe Nationale Industrielle Aerospatiale v. United States District Court for the Southern District of Iowa, Stanford J. Int'l. L. 309 (1987).

Minch, U.S. Obligations Under the Hague Evidence Convention, 22 Int'l Law. 511, 528 (1988).

Nadelmann, The United States Joins the Hague Conference on Private International Law: A "History" with Comments, 30 Law & Contemp. Probs 291 (1965).

Noonan, Lori A., Societe Nationale Industrielle Aerospatiale v. United States District Court for the Southern District of Iowa: The Supreme Court of the United States Adopts a Case-by-Case Standard in Applying the Hague Convention on the Taking of Evidence Abroad, 1 The Transnational Lawyer, No. 1, 367, (1988).

Note, Gathering Evidence Abroad: The Hague Evidence Convention Revisited, 16 L. & Pol'y in Int'l. Bus. 963 (1984).

Note, Hague Evidence Convention: A Practical Guide to the Convention, United States Case Law, Convention-Sponsored Review Commission (1978 & 1985), and Responses of Other Signatory Nations: With Digest of Cases and Bibliography, 16 Ga. J. Int'l & Comp. L. 73, 99, App. A (1986).

Note, The Hague Convention on the Taking of Evidence Abroad in Civil or Commercial Matters: The Exclusive and Mandatory Procedures for Discovery Abroad, 132 U. Pa. L. Rev. 1461-1485 (1984).

Note, The Hague Convention on the Taking of Evidence Abroad in Civil or Commercial Matters: The Exclusive and Mandatory Procedures for Discovery Abroad, 132 U. Pa. L. Rev. 1461-1485 (1984).

Note, Obtaining International Judicial Assistance Under the Federal Rules and the Hague Convention on the Taking of Evidence Abroad: An Exposition of the Procedures and a Practical Example – In Re Westinghouse Uranium Contract Litigation, 10 Ga. J. Int'l & Comp. L. (1980).

Note, The Securities Acts and International Discovery: The Hague Evidence Convention After Anschuetz and Messerschmitt Bolkow Blohm, 12 Syracuse J. Int'l L. and Com. 600 (1986).

Note, United States Ratification of the Hague Convention on the Taking of Evidence Abroad, 67 Am J. Int'l L. 104.

Notes & Comments, United States Ratification of the Hague Convention on the Taking of Evidence Abroad, 67 Am. J. Int'l Law 104, 105 (1973).

Oxman, The Choice Between Direct Discovery and Other Means of Obtaining Evidence Abroad: The Impact of the Hague Evidence Convention, 37 U. Miami L. Rev. 733 (1983).

Plaster, The Hague Evidence Convention: The Need for Guidance on Procedures and Resolution of Conflicts in International Discovery, Vand. J. Trans. L., Vol. 27, No. 1, pp. 185-217 (1994).

Prescott & Alley, Effective Evidence-Taking Under the Hague Convention, 22 The Int'l Law. 939 (Winter 1988).

Radvan, The Hague Convention on Taking of Evidence Abroad in Civil or Commercial Matters: Several Notes Concerning its Scope, Methods and Compulsion, 16 N.Y.U. J. Int'l L. & Pol. 1031 (1984).

Rogers, On the Exclusivity of the Hague Evidence Convention, 37 U. Miami L. Rev. 733 (1983).

Sadoff, The Hague Evidence Convention: Problems at Home of Obtaining Foreign Evidence, 20 Int'l Law. 659 (1986).

Shemanski, Obtaining Evidence in the Federal Republic of Germany: The Impact of the Hague Evidence Convention on German-American Judicial Co-operation, 17 Int'l Law. 465 (1983).

Weis, The Federal Rules and the Hague Conventions: Concerns of Conformity and Comity, 50 U. Pittsburgh L.R., 903 (1989).

Wotman, The Hague Convention on the Taking of Evidence Abroad in Civil or Commercial Matters—A Comparison with Federal Rules Procedures, 7 Brooklyn J. of Intl. L. 365 (1981).

ADDITIONAL INFORMATION: The Office of American Citizens Services has available general information flyers on international judicial assistance many of which are available via our Internet Consular Affairs home page. These topics include country-specific information about service of process and obtaining evidence abroad.

Using the Internet: Many of our judicial assistance flyers are also available on the Internet via the Department of State, Bureau of Consular Affairs home page under Judicial Assistance. See also, the Department of State, Office of the Legal Adviser for Private International Law home page for information regarding private international law unification. See also the home pages for many of our embassies. See also the Authentications Office home page.

TREATY DATABASES ON THE INTERNET:

United States Department of State, Office of the Legal Adviser, Treaty Affairs, List of Treaties and Other International Agreements of the United States In Force

United Nations (UN): Databases/Treaties

Council of Europe **(COE)** under Texts/Treaties

Organization of American States **(OAS):** under Documents/Treaties and Conventions.

QUESTIONS: Additional questions may be addressed to the appropriate geographic division of the U.S. Department of State, Bureau of Consular Affairs, Office of American Citizens Services at (202) 647-5225 or 202-647-5226. Questions regarding the operation of the Hague Evidence Convention may also be addressed to the U.S. Central Authority, the Office of International Judicial Assistance, Civil Division, Department of Justice, 1100 L St., N.W., Room 11006, Washington, D.C. 20530, tel: 202) 307-0983; fax: (202) 514-6584.

Appendix 15

CONVENTION ON JURISDICTION AND ENFORCEMENT OF JUDGMENTS IN CIVIL AND COMMERCIAL MATTERS (EEC) (BRUSSELS CONVENTION)

PREAMBLE

The High Contracting Parties to the Treaty Establishing the European Economic Community,

Being Desirous of executing Article 220 of this Treaty pursuant to which they are obliged to ensure the simplification of the formalities governing the mutual recognition and enforcement of judgments,

Striving to strengthen within the Community the legal protection of persons established therein,

Considering that, for this purpose, it is necessary to determine the international jurisdiction of their courts, to simplify the recognition of judgments, and to establish an accelerated procedure to assure enforcement of these judgments as well as public documents and judicial settlements,

Have Concluded a Convention for this purpose and have designated as their Plenipotentiaries:

His Majesty the King of the Belgians:
Mr. Pierre Harmel, Minister of Foreign Affairs;

The President of the Federal Republic of Germany:
Mr. Willy Brandt, Vice-Chancellor, Minister of Foreign Affairs;

The President of the French Republic:
Mr. Michel Debré, Minister of Foreign Affairs;

The President of the Italian Republic:
Mr. Giuseppe Medici, Minister of Foreign Affairs;

His Royal Highness the Grand Duke of Luxembourg:
Mr. Pierre Grégoire, Minister of Foreign Affairs;

Her Majesty the Queen of the Netherlands:
Mr. J. M. A. H. Luns, Minister of Foreign Affairs.

The Plenipotentiaries, meeting within the Council, having exchanged their full powers, found in good and due form,

Have agreed as follows:

TITLE I. SCOPE OF APPLICATION

Article 1. [Civil and commercial matters—Exceptions]

This Convention shall apply in civil and commercial matters regardless of the nature of jurisdiction.

It shall not apply to:

(1) the status and legal capacity as well as legal representation of natural persons, marital property systems, wills and inheritances;

(2) bankruptcy, insolvency, and similar proceedings;

(3) social security;

(4) arbitration.

TITLE II. JURISDICTION

Chapter 1. General Provisions

Article 2. [Courts of State of defendant's domicile]

Subject to the provisions of this Convention, persons domiciled in the territory of a Contracting State shall, irrespective of their nationality, be sued in the courts of that State.

Persons who are not nationals of the State in which they are domiciled shall be subject to the rules of jurisdiction applicable to nationals of that State.

Article 3. [Courts of other Contracting States]

Persons domiciled in the territory of a Contracting State may be sued in the courts of another Contracting State only under the rules set forth in Chapters 2 to 6.

The following provisions, in particular, may not be invoked against such persons:

—in Belgium:	Article 15 of the Civil Code and Articles 52, 52 *bis* and 53 of the Law of March 25, 1876, Concerning Jurisdiction;
—in the Federal Republic of Germany:	Section 23 of the Code of Civil Procedure;
—in France:	Articles 14 and 15 of the Civil Code;
—in Italy:	Articles 2 and 4(1) and (2) of the Code of Civil Procedure;
—in Luxembourg:	Articles 14 and 15 of the Civil Code;
—in the Netherlands:	Articles 126(3) and 127 of the Code of Civil Procedure.

Article 4. [Jurisdiction over persons not domiciled in Contracting State]

If the defendant is not domiciled in the territory of a Contracting State, the jurisdiction of the courts in each Contracting State shall be governed by the laws of that State, subject to the provisions of Article 16.

Any person domiciled in the territory of a Contracting State, irrespective of his nationality, may—like a national of that State—invoke the rules of jurisdiction applicable in that State, and particularly those contained in Article 3, paragraph 2.

Chapter 2. Special Jurisdiction

Article 5. [Jurisdiction in special situations]

A defendant domiciled in the territory of a Contracting State may be sued in another Contracting State:

(1) in contract matters, before the court of the place where the contract was or is to be performed;

(2) in alimony cases, before the court of the place where the alimony recipient has his domicile or usual residence;

(3) in cases of torts or quasi torts, before the court of the place where the injury occurred;

(4) in suits for damages or suits for restitution based on a tort, before the court in which a public proceeding was instituted insofar as such court has, under law, jurisdiction over civil claims;

(5) in disputes relating to the operation of a branch, agency or other establishment, before the court of the place where it is located.

Article 6. [Jurisdiction in other situations]

Such a defendant may also be sued:

(1) where there are several defendants, before the court of the domicile of one of them;

(2) in case of a guaranty claim or interpleader, before the court of the principal action, unless the suit was brought solely in order to remove the person from the court otherwise having jurisdiction;

(3) in case of a counterclaim based on the same contract or facts as the original suit, before the court in which the original suit is pending.

Chapter 3. Jurisdiction in Insurance Matters

Article 7. [Determination of jurisdiction]

In insurance matters, jurisdiction shall be determined by this chapter, subject to Articles 4 and 5, paragraph 5.

Article 8. [Choice in suit against insurer]

An insurer domiciled in the territory of a Contracting State may be sued either before the courts of such State or before the court of the place where the insured is domiciled or, if several insurers are sued jointly, before the court of a Contracting State in which one of the defendants is domiciled.

If the law of the court in which suit is brought provides for such jurisdiction, the insurer may also be sued, in a Contracting State other than that of his domicile, before the court of the place in whose district the intermediary for the insurance contract is domiciled, provided that the domicile is mentioned in the policy or in the application.

An insurer not domiciled in the territory of a Contracting State but operating a branch office or agency in one of such States shall, for disputes relating to the operation of such branch office or agency, be considered as having his domicile in the territory of such State.

Article 9. [Liability and real property insurance]

In the case of liability and real property insurance, the insurer may also be sued before the court of the place where the loss occurred. The same applies where both real and personal property are insured under the same insurance contract and are damaged by the same occurrence.

Article 10. [Interpleader in liability cases]

In liability cases, the insurer may also be brought before the court in which the injured party's action against him is pending, provided that the law of such court permits it.

Articles 7, 8, and 9 shall be applicable in case of a direct action brought by the victim against the insurer, provided that such direct action is permissible.

If the law governing such a direct action makes provision for interpleading the policy holder or the insured, the same court shall also assume jurisdiction over such persons.

Article 11. [Suit by insurer]

Subject to the provisions of Article 10, paragraph 3, the insurer may sue only in the courts of the Contracting State in whose territory the defendant has his domicile, regardless of whether the defendant is the policy holder, the insured, or the beneficiary.

The provisions of this section shall not prejudice the right to bring a counterclaim in the court before which the original suit is pending in accordance with the provisions of this chapter

Article 12. [Permissible scope of agreements on jurisdiction]

An agreement may derogate from the provisions of this chapter only if such agreement:

(1) was entered into after the dispute arose, or

(2) permits the policy holder, the insured, or the beneficiary to go to courts other than those indicated in this chapter, or

(3) was entered into between a policy holder and an insurer who are both domiciled in the same Contracting State in order to establish jurisdiction with the courts of that State even if the injury occurred in a foreign country, unless the law of such State prohibits such agreements.

Chapter 4. Jurisdiction in Matters Involving Installment Contracts

Article 13. [Determination of jurisdiction]

In suits involving installment contracts for the purchase of personal property or for installment loans to finance the purchase of such property, jurisdiction shall be determined by this chapter, subject to the provisions of Article 4 and Article 5, paragraph 5.

Article 14. [Suit against seller or lender]

A seller or lender domiciled in the territory of a Contracting State may be sued before either the courts of such State or the courts of the Contracting State where the purchaser or borrower is domiciled.

A seller may sue a purchaser, and a lender may sue a borrower, only before the courts of the State in which the defendant is domiciled.

These provisions shall not prejudice the right to bring a counterclaim in the court before which the original suit is pending in accordance with the provisions of this chapter.

Article 15. [Permissible scope of agreements on jurisdiction]

An agreement may derogate from the provisions of this chapter only if such agreement:

(1) was entered into after the dispute arose, or

(2) permits the purchaser or borrower to go to courts other than those indicated in this chapter, or

(3) was entered into between the purchaser and the seller or the borrower and the lender who are domiciled or have their usual residence in the same Contracting State in order to establish jurisdiction with the courts of that State, unless the law of such State prohibits such agreements.

Chapter 5. Exclusive Jurisdiction

Article 16. [Exclusive jurisdiction regardless of domicile]

The following courts shall have exclusive jurisdiction, regardless of domicile:

(1) in matters involving rights *in rem* in real property or concerning the leasing of real property: the courts of the Contracting State in which the real property is located;

(2) in matters involving the validity, nullity, or dissolution of a company or legal person having its seat in a Contracting State, or of decisions of its organs: the courts of that State;

(3) in matters involving the validity of entries in public registers: the courts of the Contracting State in whose territory the registers are kept;

(4) in matters involving the validity of patents, trademarks, designs and models, as well as of similar rights requiring a filing or registration: the courts of the Contracting State in whose territory the filing or registration was applied for or effected or is considered to have been applied for or effected under the terms of an international convention;

(5) in matters involving the enforcement of judgments: the courts of the Contracting State of the place of enforcement.

Chapter 6. Agreements on Jurisdiction

Article 17. [Jurisdiction of court by agreement]

If, in a written agreement or an oral agreement confirmed in writing, the parties at least one of which is domiciled in a Contracting State designate a court or courts of a Contracting State that are to decide an existing or future dispute arising out of a particular legal relationship, such court or courts shall have exclusive jurisdiction over such dispute.

Agreements as to which court shall take jurisdiction shall be of no effect if they contravene the provisions of Articles 12 and 15, or if the courts whose jurisdiction they preempt have exclusive jurisdiction under Article 16.

If the agreement on jurisdiction was entered into only for the benefit of one of the parties, that party shall retain the right to bring suit in any other court having jurisdiction under this Convention.

Article 18. [Appearance of defendant]

Aside from cases in which jurisdiction results from other provisions of this Convention, a court of a Contracting State shall have jurisdiction if the defendant enters an appearance before it. This does not apply if the defendant appears solely to challenge the court's jurisdiction or some other court has exclusive jurisdiction under Article 16.

Chapter 7. Examination of Jurisdiction and Admissibility

Article 19. [Declaration of lack of jurisdiction]

The court of a Contracting State shall *ex officio* declare that it lacks jurisdiction where it is requested to decide a suit in which a court of another Contracting State has exclusive jurisdiction under Article 16.

Article 20. [Non-appearance of defendant]

In case a defendant domiciled in the territory of a Contracting State is sued before a court of another Contracting State and does not enter an appearance, the court shall *ex officio* declare that it lacks jurisdiction if its jurisdiction is not established by this Convention.

The court shall stay proceedings until it has been determined that the defendant was afforded an opportunity to receive the summons in time to prepare his defense, or that every care was taken to ensure this.

The provisions of the preceding paragraph are superseded by Article 15 of the Hague Convention of November 15, 1965, concerning the service in a foreign country of judicial or nonjudicial documents in civil or commercial matters where the summons was to have been served on the basis of such convention.

Chapter 8. Pendency and Interrelationship

Article 21. [Pendency of concurrent suits in different States]

Where suits having the same object and the same basis between the same parties are brought before courts of different Contracting States, the court in which the later suit is brought shall *ex officio* yield jurisdiction in favor of the court where the action was first brought.

The court which would have to yield jurisdiction may stay the proceedings if the jurisdiction of the other court is contested.

Article 22. [Interrelationship between suits in different States]

Where related suits brought before courts of different Contracting States are still pending before the courts having original jurisdiction, the court in which the later suit was brought may stay the proceedings.

The court in which the later suit was brought may also, at the request of one of the parties, declare that it lacks jurisdiction if the law permits a joinder of related suits and the court in which the suit was first brought has jurisdiction over both suits.

Suits are related, within the meaning of this article, if the relationship between them is so close that there is reason to try and to decide them at the same time in order to avoid results that could be in conflict if the decisions were reached separately.

Article 23. [Exclusive jurisdiction of several courts]

Where suits are within the exclusive jurisdiction of several courts, the court in which the later suit was brought shall yield jurisdiction in favor of the court in which suit was first brought.

Chapter 9. Temporary and Protective Measures

Article 24. [Temporary measures by court lacking jurisdiction over merits]

The temporary or protective measures provided for in the law of a Contracting State may be requested in the courts of that State even where, under this Convention, a court of another Contracting State has jurisdiction over the merits of the case.

TITLE III. RECOGNITION AND ENFORCEMENT

Article 25. [Definition of "decision"]

The word "decision" within the meaning of this Convention means any decision rendered by a court of a Contracting State regardless of its designation, such as decree, judgment, order, or writ of execution, as well as a determination of the court costs by the clerk of the court.

Chapter 1. Recognition

Article 26. [Recognition without special proceedings]

Decisions rendered in one Contracting State shall be recognized in the other Contracting States, without requiring special proceedings for this purpose.

Where the recognition of a decision is contested, any party asserting recognition may, under the procedure provided by Chapters 2 and 3 of this title, request a ruling to the effect that the decision be recognized.

If recognition is asserted in a dispute before a court of a Contracting State whose decision depends upon the recognition, such court shall be competent to decide.

Article 27. [Exceptions]

A decision shall not be recognized:

(1) if it is contrary to the public policy of the State in which recognition is sought;

(2) if a defendant who did not enter an appearance in the proceedings was not properly served with a summons initiating the action or was not served in time to prepare his defense;

(3) if the decision conflicts with a decision rendered between the same parties in the State in which recognition is sought;

(4) if the court of the State where the decision was rendered, in rendering a decision on a preliminary question relating to the status, the legal capacity or legal representation of a natural person, the marital property system, or wills and inheritances, has contravened the provisions of international private law of the State in which recognition is sought, unless the same result would be reached if the international private law provisions of such State had been applied.

Article 28. [Additional grounds for denial of recognition]

A decision shall further not be recognized if it contravenes the provisions of Chapters 3, 4, and 5 of Title II or in the case set forth in Article 59.

In determining the jurisdiction referred to in the preceding paragraph, the court or authority of the State in which recognition is sought shall be bound by the factual findings on the basis of which the foreign court assumed jurisdiction.

Subject to the provisions of paragraph 1, the jurisdiction of the foreign court may not be reviewed; the provisions relating to jurisdiction do not concern public order within the meaning of Article 7, paragraph 1.

Article 29. [No examination of legality]

Under no circumstances shall a foreign judgment be subject to a review for legality.

Article 30. [Stay of proceedings]

A court of a Contracting State in which recognition of a decision rendered in another Contracting State is sought may stay the proceedings if the decision has been appealed.

Chapter 2. Enforcement

Article 31. [Writ of execution required]

Decisions rendered in a Contracting State that are enforceable therein may be enforced in another Contracting State after a writ of execution has been issued upon request of the interested party.

Article 32. [Courts to which request for writ must be made]

The request shall be addressed:

—in Belgium, to the court of first instance (*tribunal de première instance*);

—in the Federal Republic of Germany, to the presiding judge of a chamber of the district court (*Landgericht*);

—in France, to the presiding judge of the district court (*tribunal de grande instance*);

—in Italy, to the court of appeals (*corte d'appello*);
—in Luxembourg, to the presiding judge of the district court (*tribunal d'arrondissement*);
—in the Netherlands, to the presiding judge of the district court (*arrondissementsrechtbank*);

The venue shall be determined by the domicile of the judgment debtor. If he is not domiciled in the Contracting State in which enforcement is sought, the venue shall lie with the court in whose district the execution is to take place.

Article 33. [Request for enforcement]

The terms and conditions for the request shall be governed by the law of the State in which enforcement is sought.

The petitioner must establish domicile in the place where the court has jurisdiction. If, however, the law of the State in which enforcement is sought does not require the establishment of domicile, the petitioner must designate a representative *ad litem*.

The documents listed in Articles 46 and 47 shall be attached to the request.

Article 34. [Ruling on request]

The court to which the request is addressed shall rule without delay and without giving the judgment debtor an opportunity to enter his pleas at this stage of the proceedings.

The request shall be denied only for one of the grounds specified in Articles 27 and 28.

Under no circumstances shall a foreign judgment be subject to a review of the legality of the foreign decision.

Article 35. [Notification of petitioner]

The clerk of the court shall inform the petitioner without delay of the ruling on the request in the form prescribed by the law of the State in which enforcement is sought.

Article 36. [Appeal from grant of writ]

If a writ of execution is granted, the judgment debtor may appeal the execution order within one month of being served with it.

If the judgment debtor is domiciled in a Contracting State other than the one in which the execution order was issued, the appeal must be brought within two months, beginning with the day the order was served on him in person or at his domicile. No extension of this time limit because of distance shall be allowed.

Article 37. [Courts in which appeals to be brought]

The appeal shall be filed, in accordance with the rules governing adversary proceedings:

—in Belgium, with the court of first instance (*tribunal de première instance*);

—in the Federal Republic of Germany, with the court of appeals (*Oberlandesgericht*);

—in France, with the court of appeals (*cour d'appel*);

—in Italy, with the court of appeals (*corte d'appello*);

—in Luxembourg, with the Supreme Court acting in its capacity as appellate court in civil matters (*cour supérieure de justice siègeant en matière d'appel civil*);

—in the Netherlands, with the district court (*arrondissementsrechtbank*).

The decision rendered on appeal is subject only to an appeal for reversal (*pourvoi en cassation*) and, in the Federal Republic of Germany, to a *Rechtsbeschwerde*.

Article 38. [Stay pending appeal]

The appellate court may stay its decision at the request of the appellant if the foreign judgment has been appealed or if the time for such appeal has not run out; in the latter case, the court may set a period within which the appeal must be brought.

The court may also make the granting of a writ of execution subject to the deposit of security and determine the amount of such security.

Article 39. [Measures to secure execution]

During the period for appeal provided in Article 36 and so long as no decision on the appeal has been rendered, no measures may be taken against the judgment debtor's property except those necessary to secure execution.

The decision granting the writ of execution includes the authority to take such measures.

Article 40. [Courts hearing appeal from denial of request]

If the request is denied, the petitioner has remedies available:

—in Belgium, at the court of appeals (*cour d'appel*);

—in the Federal Republic of Germany, at the court of appeals (*Oberlandesgericht*);

—in France, at the court of appeals (*cour d'appel*);

—in Italy, at the court of appeals (*corte d'appello*);

—in Luxembourg, at the Supreme Court acting in its capacity as appellate court in civil matters (*cour supérieure de justice siègeant en matière d'appel civil*);

—in the Netherlands, at the court of appeals (*gerechtshof*).

The appellate court shall hear the judgment debtor. If he fails to appear, Article 20, paragraphs 2 and 3, shall apply even if he is not domiciled in one of the Contracting States.

Article 41. [Review of appellate decision]

The decision on the appeal provided in Article 40 may be contested only by an appeal for reversal (*pourvoi en cassation*) and in the Federal Republic of Germany by a *Rechtsbeschwerde*.

Article 42. [Foreign decision on several claims]

If a foreign decision covers several claims in the request, and enforcement cannot be granted as to all of them; the court shall grant enforcement of one or more of these claims.

The petitioner may also request enforcement for a portion of the judgment.

Article 43. [Decisions requiring payment of fines]

Foreign decisions requiring payment of a fine are enforceable in the State in which enforcement is sought only if the amount of these fines has been fixed by the court of the State in which the decision was rendered.

Article 44. [Right to legal aid]

If a petitioner was granted legal aid in the State in which the decision was rendered, he shall, in the State in which execution is sought, be entitled to receive, without further examination, legal aid also for the proceedings under Articles 32 to 35.

Article 45. [Foreigners not required to furnish security]

A party seeking enforcement in a Contracting State of a decision rendered in another Contracting State shall not be required, because of his status as a foreigner or because of his lack of domicile or residence, to furnish security or make a deposit, in any form or manner.

Chapter 3. Common Provisions

Article 46. [Documents required for recognition or enforcement]

A party seeking recognition or enforcement of a decision shall submit the following documents:

(1) a copy of the decision which meets all the requirements for its authenticity;

(2) if the decision was rendered by default, the original or a certified copy of the document establishing that the summons initiating the proceeding was served on the party in default.

Article 47. [Additional documents required for enforcement]

A party seeking enforcement shall also submit:

(1) all documents establishing that the decision is enforceable under the law of the State in which it was rendered and that it was served on the judgment debtor;

(2) if necessary, a document proving that the petitioner was granted legal aid in the State in which the decision was rendered.

Article 48. [Failure to submit documents]

In case of a failure to submit the documents specified in Articles 46(2) and 47(2), the court may set a period within which they shall be submitted, or it may accept equivalent documents, or waive them if it considers itself sufficiently informed on the matter.

A translation of the documents shall be submitted if the court so requests. The translation must be certified by a person authorized as translator in one of the Contracting States.

Article 49. [No legalization requirement]

The documents mentioned in Articles 46, 47 and 48, paragraph 2, and the power of attorney, if given, do not require legalization or other similar formality.

TITLE IV. PUBLIC DOCUMENTS AND JUDICIAL SETTLEMENTS

Article 50. [Prerequisites for writ of execution]

Public documents prepared and enforceable in a Contracting State shall, on request, be accompanied by a writ of execution in another Contracting State, in accordance with the procedure set forth in Articles 31 et seq. The request may be denied only if enforcement of the document contravenes the public policy of the State in which enforcement is sought.

The document submitted must meet all the conditions for its authenticity that are required in the State in which it was drawn up.

The provisions of Chapter 3 of Title III shall apply mutatis mutandis.

Article 51. [Enforcement of judicial settlements]

Settlements that were made in a proceeding before a judge and that are enforceable in the State in which they were drawn up shall, under the same conditions as public documents, be enforceable in the State in which enforcement is sought.

TITLE V. GENERAL PROVISIONS

Article 52. [Determination of domicile]

In determining whether a party is domiciled in the territory of a Contracting State before whose courts action is brought, the court shall apply its domestic law.

If a party is not domiciled in the State before whose courts an action is brought, the court, in determining whether such party is domiciled in another State, shall apply the law of that State.

However, in determining the domicile of a party, the law of his country shall be applied if, under such law, his domicile depends upon that of another person or upon the seat of some authority.

Article 53. [Domicile of companies and legal persons]

For purposes of applying this Convention, the seat of companies and legal persons is the same as the domicile. However, in determining such seat, the court shall apply the provisions of its international private law.

TITLE VI. TRANSITIONAL PROVISIONS

Article 54. [Scope of application]

The provisions of this Convention shall be applicable only to judicial actions brought and to public documents drawn up after its entry into force.

However, decisions rendered after the effective date of this Convention in actions brought prior to that date shall be recognized and enforced in accordance with the provisions of Title III, provided that the court's jurisdiction was based on rules conforming to those contained in Title II or in a convention in force at the time the action was brought between the State where the decision was rendered and the State in which enforcement is sought.

TITLE VII. RELATIONSHIP TO OTHER CONVENTIONS

Article 55. [Conventions that are superseded]

Without prejudice to the provisions of Articles 54, paragraph 2, and 56, this Convention shall supersede the following conventions concluded between two or more Contracting States:

—Convention between Belgium and France, signed in Paris on July 8, 1899, concerning the jurisdiction of courts, the recognition and enforcement of court decisions, arbitration awards, and public documents;

—Convention between Belgium and the Netherlands, signed in Brussels on March 28, 1925, concerning the territorial jurisdiction of courts, bankruptcy, recognition and enforcement of court decisions, arbitration awards, and public documents;

—Convention between France and Italy, signed in Rome on June 3, 1930, concerning the enforcement of court decisions in civil and commercial matters;

—Convention between Germany and Italy, signed in Rome on March 9, 1936, concerning the recognition and enforcement of court decisions in civil and commercial matters;

—Convention between Germany and Belgium, signed in Bonn on June 30, 1958, concerning the mutual recognition and enforcement of court decisions, arbitration awards, and public documents in civil and commercial matters;

—Convention between the Netherlands and Italy, signed in Rome on April 17, 1959, concerning the recognition and enforcement of court decisions in civil and commercial matters;

—Convention between Belgium and Italy, signed in Rome on April 6, 1962, concerning the recognition and enforcement of court decisions and other enforceable instruments in civil and commercial matters;

—Convention between Germany and the Netherlands, signed at The Hague on August 30, 1962, concerning mutual recognition and enforcement of court decisions and other enforceable instruments in civil and commercial matters;

and, if it has entered into force:

—Treaty between Belgium, the Netherlands, and Luxembourg, signed in Brussels on November 24, 1961, concerning the jurisdiction of courts, bankruptcy, recognition and enforcement of court decisions, arbitration awards, and public documents.

Article 56. [Extent to which prior conventions remain in force]

The Treaty and Conventions listed in Article 55 remain in force for matters to which this Convention does not apply.

They continue to remain in force also for decisions rendered and documents drawn up prior to the effective date of this Convention.

Article 57. [Conventions remaining unaffected]

This Convention shall not affect conventions which, for particular areas of the law, set forth rules on the jurisdiction of courts and the recognition and enforcement of decisions.

Article 58. [French-Swiss convention not affected]

This Convention shall not affect the rights accorded to Swiss nationals under the Convention of June 15, 1869, between France and Switzerland on the jurisdiction of courts and the enforcement of civil judgments.

Article 59. [No obstacle to treaties with third countries]

This Convention shall not prevent a Contracting State from entering into agreements with third countries on the recognition and enforcement of decisions that would require it not to recognize decisions of the courts of another Contracting State against defendants having their domicile or usual place of abode in that third country if, in the case provided in Article 4, the decision could have been rendered only by one of the courts listed in Article 3, paragraph 2.

TITLE VIII. FINAL PROVISIONS

Article 60. [Territorial scope of application]

This Convention shall apply to the European territories of the Contracting States as well as to the French overseas departments and territories.

The Kingdom of the Netherlands may, at the time of the signing or ratification of this Convention or at any later date, declare, by notifying the Secretary General of the Council of the European Communities, that this Convention shall also apply to Surinam and the Dutch Antilles. If such declaration is not given with respect to the Dutch Antilles, proceedings pending in the European territories of the Kingdom as a result of appeals [*pourvoi en cassation*] brought against decisions rendered by courts in the Dutch Antilles are deemed to be pending before such courts.

Article 61. [Ratification]

This Convention shall be ratified by the Signatory States. The instruments of ratification shall be deposited with the Secretary General of the Council of the European Communities.

Article 62. [Effective date]

This Convention shall enter into force on the first day of the third month following the deposit of the instrument of ratification by the last Signatory State to perform this formality.

Article 63. [Obligations of new EEC members]

The Contracting States recognize that any State becoming a member of the European Economic Community shall be obligated to agree that this Convention shall serve as a basis for such negotiations between the Contracting States and that State as are necessary to assure the implementation of Article 220, last paragraph, of the Treaty Establishing the European Economic Community.

The necessary adjustments may be made in a special convention between the Contracting States on the one hand and that State on the other.

Article 64. [Notices to be given by Council]

The Secretary General of the Council of the European Communities shall notify the Signatory States of:

(a) the deposit of all instruments of ratification;
(b) the date on which this Convention enters into force;
(c) the declarations received in application of Article 60, paragraph 2;
(d) the declarations received in application of Article IV of the Protocol;
(e) the communications under Article VI of the Protocol.

Article 65. [Protocol as integral part of Convention]

The Protocol annexed to this Convention by common accord of the Contracting States shall be an integral part of the Convention.

Article 66. [Effective period]

This Convention shall remain in force for an indefinite period of time.

Article 67. [Revision]

Each Contracting State may request a revision of this Convention. In such case, a revision conference shall be called by the President of the Council of the European Communities.

Article 68. [Authenticity of texts]

This Convention is drawn up in a single copy in the German, French, Italian and Dutch languages, and each text is equally authentic. It shall be deposited with the archive of the Secretariat of the Council of the European Communities; the Secretary General shall transmit a certified copy to the government of each Signatory State.

In Witness Whereof, the undersigned Plenipotentiaries have affixed their signatures to this Convention.

Done at Brussels, September 27, 1968.

[Signatures]

PROTOCOL

The High Contracting Parties have agreed to the following provisions, which are a part of the Convention.

Article I. [Certain suits against persons domiciled in Luxembourg]

Any person domiciled in the Grand Duchy of Luxembourg who is being sued before a court of another Contracting State under Article 5, paragraph 1, may assert such court's lack of jurisdiction. Unless the defendant enters an appearance in the proceeding, that court shall *ex officio* declare that it lacks jurisdiction.

Any agreement relating to court jurisdiction within the meaning of Article 17 shall be effective with respect to a person domiciled in Luxembourg only if expressly and especially accepted by such person.

Article II. [Proceedings before criminal courts]

Without prejudice to more favorable domestic provisions, persons domiciled in a Contracting State who are being prosecuted for a negligent crime in the criminal courts of another Contracting State of which they are not nationals may be defended by persons authorized to do so, even if they do not appear personally.

The criminal court may, however, order such persons to appear in person. If they fail to do so, the decision rendered in the civil action in which the defendant was unable to defend himself cannot be either recognized or enforced in the other Contracting States.

Article III. [Fees, etc., for writ of execution]

No stamp tax, duty, or fee, graduated according to the value of the matter in dispute, shall be imposed in the State in which enforcement is sought in proceedings for the issuance of a writ of execution.

Article IV. [Service of papers in other Contracting State]

Judicial or nonjudicial papers drawn up in a Contracting State and to be served upon persons in another Contracting State shall be transmitted in accordance with the conventions or agreements in effect between the Contracting States.

Unless the State of destination objects by a declaration to the Secretary General of the Council of the European Communities, these papers may also be transmitted directly by the court officials of the State in which they originate to the court officials of the State of the person for whom the papers are intended. In such case, the court official of the State of origin shall send a copy of the papers to a court official of the requested State who is competent to transmit it to the recipient. This transmittal shall be carried out in the forms prescribed by the law of the requested State. It shall be verified by a certificate which shall be sent directly to the court official of the State of origin.

Article V. [Guaranty claims and interpleaders in Germany]

The jurisdiction over guaranty claims or requests for interpleader provided for in Article 6, paragraph 2, and Article 10 may not be invoked in the Federal Republic of Germany. In that State, anyone domiciled in another Contracting State may be summoned before a court pursuant to the provisions on *Streitverkündung* [*] (Sections 68 and 72-74 of the German Code of Civil Procedure).

Decisions rendered in other Contracting States under Article 6, paragraph 2, and Article 10 shall be recognized and enforced in the Federal Republic of Germany in accordance with Title III. The effects on third parties of decisions rendered in that State pursuant to Sections 68 and 72-74 of the Code of Civil Procedure shall be recognized also in the other Contracting States.

Article VI. [Obligation to communicate legislative changes]

The Contracting States shall communicate to the Secretary General of the Council of the European Communities the texts of new legislation that modifies their provisions mentioned in this Convention or modifies court jurisdiction as set forth in Chapter 2 of Title III of this Convention.

[Signatures]

COMMON DECLARATION

The Governments of the Kingdom of Belgium, the Federal Republic of Germany, the French Republic, the Italian Republic, the Grand Duchy of Luxembourg, and the Kingdom of The Netherlands,

At the time of signing the Convention concerning the jurisdiction of courts and the recognition and enforcement of court decisions in civil and commercial matters,

Desirous to assure the most effective application of this Convention,

Striving to avoid impairment of the uniformity sought with this Convention by diverging interpretations,

Recognizing that positive and negative jurisdictional conflicts might arise in applying this Convention,

Declare their readiness:

(1) to examine these questions, particularly whether the Court of Justice of the European Communities should be given jurisdiction over certain matters and, if so, to negotiate a convention for this purpose;

(2) to arrange periodic contacts between their representatives.

[Signatures]

[* Third-party intervention.—CCH.]

Appendix 16

CONVENTION ON JURISDICTION AND ENFORCEMENT OF JUDGMENTS IN CIVIL AND COMMERCIAL MATTERS (EEC/EFTA) (LUGANO CONVENTION)

CONVENTION

on jurisdiction and the enforcement of judgments in civil and commercial matters

Done at Lugano on 16 September 1988

(88/592/EEC)

PREAMBLE

THE HIGH CONTRACTING PARTIES TO THIS CONVENTION,

ANXIOUS to strengthen in their territories the legal protection of persons therein established,

CONSIDERING that it is necessary for this purpose to determine the international jurisdiction of their courts, to facilitate recognition and to introduce an expeditious procedure for securing the enforcement of judgments, authentic instruments and court settlements,

AWARE of the links between them, which have been sanctioned in the economic field by the free trade agreements concluded between the European Economic Community and the States members of the European Free Trade Association,

TAKING INTO ACCOUNT the Brussels Convention of 27 September 1968 on jurisdiction and the enforcement of judgments in civil and commercial matters, as amended by the Accession Conventions under the successive enlargements of the European Communities,

PERSUADED that the extension of the principles of that Convention to the States parties to this instrument will strengthen legal and economic cooperation in Europe,

DESIRING to ensure as uniform an interpretation as possible of this instrument,

HAVE in this spirit DECIDED to conclude this Convention and

HAVE AGREED AS FOLLOWS:

TITLE I
SCOPE

Article 1

This Convention shall apply in civil and commercial matters whatever the nature of the court or tribunal. It shall not extend, in particular, to revenue, customs or administrative matters.

The Convention shall not apply to:

1. the status or legal capacity of natural persons, rights in property arising out of a matrimonial relationship, wills and succession;
2. bankruptcy, proceedings relating to the winding-up of insolvent companies or other legal persons, judicial arrangements, compositons and analogous proceedings;
3. social security;
4. arbitration.

TITLE II

JURISDICTION

Section 1

General provisions

Article 2

Subject to the provisions of this Convention, persons domiciled in a Contracting State shall, whatever their nationality, be sued in the courts of that State.

Persons who are not nationals of the State in which they are domiciled shall be governed by the rules of jurisdiction applicable to nationals of that State.

Article 3

Persons domiciled in a Contracting State may be sued in the courts of another Contracting State only by virtue of the rules set out in Sections 2 to 6 of this Title.

In particular the following provisions shall not be applicable as against them:

— in Belgium: Article 15 of the civil code (Code civil — Burgerlijk Wetboek) and Article 638 of the judicial code (Code judiciaire — Gerechtelijk Wetboek),

— in Denmark: Article 246 (2) and (3) of the law on civil procedure (Lov om rettens pleje),

— in the Federal Republic of Germany: Article 23 of the code of civil procedure (Zivilprozeßordnung),

— in Greece: Article 40 of the code of civil procedure (Κώδικας πολιτικής δικονομίας),

— in France: Articles 14 and 15 of the civil code (Code civil),

— in Ireland: the rules which enable jurisdiction to be founded on the document instituting the proceedings having been served on the defendant during his temporary presence in Ireland,

— in Iceland: Article 77 of the Civil Proceedings Act (lög um meðferð einkamála í héraði),

— in Italy: Articles 2 and 4, Nos 1 and 2 of the code of civil procedure (Codice di procedura civile),

— in Luxembourg: Articles 14 and 15 of the civil code (Code civil),

— in the Netherlands: Articles 126 (3) and 127 of the code of civil procedure (Wetboek van Burgerlijke Rechtsvordering),

— in Norway: Section 32 of the Civil Proceedings Act (tvistemålsloven),

— in Austria: Article 99 of the Law on Court Jurisdiction (Jurisdiktionsnorm)

— in Portugal: Articles 65 (1) (c), 65 (2) and 65A (c) of the code of civil procedure (Código de Processo Civil) and Article 11 of the code of labour procedure (Código de Processo de Trabalho),

— in Switzerland: le for du lieu du séquestre/Gerichtsstand des Arrestortes/foro del luogo del sequestro within the meaning of Article 4 of the loi fédérale sur le droit international privé/Bundesgesetz über das internationale Privatrecht/legge federale sul diritto internazionale privato,

— in Finland: the second, third and fourth sentences of Section 1 of Chapter 10 of the Code of Judicial Procedure (oikeudenkäymiskaari/rättegångsbaiken),

— in Sweden: the first sentence of Section 3 of Chapter 10 of the Code of Judicial Procedure (Rättegångsbalken),

— in the United Kingdom: the rules which enable jurisdiction to be founded on:

(a) the document instituting the proceedings having been served on the defendant during his temporary presence in the United Kingdom; or

(b) the presence within the United Kingdom of property belonging to the defendant; or

(c) the seizure by the plaintiff of property situated in the United Kingdom.

Article 4

If the defendant is not domiciled in a Contracting State, the jurisdiction of the courts of each Contracting State shall, subject to the provisions of Article 16, be determined by the law of that State.

As against such a defendant, any person domiciled in a Contracting State may, whatever his nationality, avail himself in that State of the rules of jurisdiction there in force, and in particular those specified in the second paragraph of Article 3, in the same way as the nationals of that State.

Section 2

Special jurisdiction

Article 5

A person domiciled in a Contracting State may, in another Contracting State, be sued:

1. in matters relating to a contract, in the courts for the place of performance of the obligation in question; in matters relating to individual contracts of employment, this place is that where the employee habitually carries out his work, or if the employee does not habitually carry out his work in any one country, this place shall be the place of business through which he was engaged;

2. in matters relating to maintenance, in the courts for the place where the maintenance creditor is domiciled or habitually resident or, if the matter is ancillary to proceedings concerning the status of a person, in the court which, according to its own law, has juridiction to entertain those proceedings, unless that jurisdiction is based solely on the nationality of one of the parties;

3. in matters relating to tort, delict or quasi-delict, in the courts for the place where the harmful event occurred;

4. as regards a civil claim for damages or restitution which is based on an act giving rise to criminal proceedings, in the court seised of those proceedings, to the extent that that court has jurisdiction under its own law to entertain civil proceedings;

5. as regards a dispute arising out of the operations of a branch, agency or other establishment, in the courts for the place in which the branch, agency or other establishment is situated;

6. in his capacity as settlor, trustee or beneficiary of a trust created by the operation of a statute, or by a written instrument, or created orally and evidenced in writing, in the courts of the Contracting State in which the trust is domiciled;

7. as regards a dispute concerning the payment of remuneration claimed in respect of the salvage of a cargo or freight, in the court under the authority of which the cargo or freight in question:

   (a) has been arrested to secure such payment,

   or

   (b) could have been so arrested, but bail or other security has been given;

   provided that this provision shall apply only if it is claimed that the defendant has an interest in the cargo or freight or had such an interest at the time of salvage.

Article 6

A person domiciled in a Contracting State may also be sued:

1. where he is one of a number of defendants, in the courts for the place where any one of them is domiciled;

2. as a third party in an action on a warranty or guarantee or in any other third party proceedings, in the court seised of the original proceedings, unless these were instituted solely with the object of removing him from the jurisdiction of the court which would be competent in his case;

3. on a counterclaim arising from the same contract or facts on which the original claim was based, in the court in which the original claim is pending;

4. in matters relating to a contract, if the action may be combined with an action against the same defendant in matters relating to rights *in rem* in immovable property, in the court of the Contracting State in which the property is situated.

Article 6A

Where by virtue of this Convention a court of a Contracting State has jurisdiction in actions relating to liability arising from the use or operation of a ship, that court, or any other court substituted for this purpose by the internal law of that State, shall also have jurisdiction over claims for limitation of such liability.

Section 3

Jurisdiction in matters relating to insurance

Article 7

In matters relating to insurance, jurisdiction shall be determined by this Section, without prejudice to the provisions of Articles 4 and 5 (5).

Article 8

An insurer domiciled in a Contracting State may be sued:

1. in the courts of the State where he is domiciled; or

2. in another Contracting State, in the courts for the place where the policy-holder is domiciled; or

3. if he is a co-insurer, in the courts of a Contracting State in which proceedings are brought against the leading insurer.

An insurer who is not domiciled in a Contracting State but has a branch, agency or other establishment in one of the

Contracting States shall, in disputes arising out of the operations of the branch, agency or establishment, be deemed to be domiciled in that State.

Article 9

In respect of liability insurance or insurance of immovable property, the insurer may in addition be sued in the courts for the place where the harmful event occurred. The same applies if movable and immovable property are covered by the same insurance policy and both are adversely affected by the same contingency.

Article 10

In respect of liability insurance, the insurer may also, if the law of the court permits it, be joined in proceedings which the injured party has brought against the insured.

The provisions of Articles 7, 8 and 9 shall apply to actions brought by the injured party directly against the insurer, where such direct actions are permitted.

If the law governing such direct actions provides that the policy-holder or the insured may be joined as a party to the action, the same court shall have jurisdiction over them.

Article 11

Without prejudice to the provisions of the third paragraph of Article 10, an insurer may bring proceedings only in the courts of the Contracting State in which the defendant is domiciled, irrespective of whether he is the policy-holder, the insured or a beneficiary.

The provisions of this Section shall not affect the right to bring a counterclaim in the court in which, in accordance with this Section, the original claim is pending.

Article 12

The provisions of this Section may be departed from only by an agreement on jurisdiction:

1. which is entered into after the dispute has arisen; or

2. which allows the policy-holder, the insured or a beneficiary to bring proceedings in courts other than those indicated in this Section; or

3. which is concluded between a policy-holder and an insurer, both of whom are at the time of conclusion of the contract domiciled or habitually resident in the same Contracting State, and which has the effect of conferring jurisdiction on the courts of that State even if the harmful event were to occur abroad, provided that such an agreement is not contrary to the law of the State; or

4. which is concluded with a policy-holder who is not domiciled in a Contracting State, except in so far as the insurance is compulsory or relates to immovable property in a Contracting State; or

5. which relates to a contract of insurance in so far as it covers one or more of the risks set out in Article 12A.

Article 12A

The following are the risks referred to in Article 12 (5):

1. any loss of or damage to:

   (a) sea-going ships, installations situated off shore or on the high seas, or aircraft, arising from perils which relate to their use for commercial purposes;

   (b) goods in transit other than passengers' baggage where the transit consists of or includes carriage by such ships or aircraft;

2. any liability, other than for bodily injury to passengers or loss of or damage to their baggage;

   (a) arising out of the use or operation of ships, installations or aircraft as referred to in (1) (a) above in so far as the law of the Contracting State in which such aircraft are registered does not prohibit agreements on jurisdiction regarding insurance of such risks;

   (b) for loss or damage caused by goods in transit as described in (1) (b) above;

3. any financial loss connected with the use or operation of ships, installations or aircraft as referred to in (1) (a) above, in particular loss of freight or charter-hire;

4. any risk or interest connected with any of those referred to in (1) to (3) above.

Section 4

Jurisdiction over consumer contracts

Article 13

In proceedings concerning a contract concluded by a person for a purpose which can be regarded as being outside his trade or profession, hereinafter called 'the consumer', jurisdiction shall be determined by this Section, without prejudice to the provisions of Articles 4 and 5 (5), if it is:

1. a contract for the sale of goods on instalment credit terms; or

2. a contract for a loan repayable by instalments, or for any other form of credit, made to finance the sale of goods; or

3. any other contract for the supply of goods or a contract for the supply of services, and

(a) in the State of the consumer's domicile the conclusion of the contract was preceded by a specific invitation addressed to him or by advertising, and

(b) the consumer took in that State the steps necessary for the conclusion of the contract.

Where a consumer enters into a contract with a party who is not domiciled in a Contracting State but has a branch, agency or other establishment in one of the Contracting States, that party shall, in disputes arising out of the operations of the branch, agency or establishment, be deemed to be domiciled in that State.

This Section shall not apply to contracts of transport.

Article 14

A consumer may bring proceedings against the other party to a contract either in the courts of the Contracting State in which that party is domiciled or in the courts of the Contracting State in which he is himself domiciled.

Proceedings may be brought against a consumer by the other party to the contract only in the courts of the Contracting State in which the consumer is domiciled.

These provisions shall not affect the right to bring a counterclaim in the court in which, in accordance with this Section, the original claim is pending.

Article 15

The provisions of this Section may be departed from only by an agreement:

1. which is entered into after the dispute has arisen; or

2. which allows the consumer to bring proceedings in courts other than those indicated in this Section; or

3. which is entered into by the consumer and the other party to the contract, both of whom are at the time of conclusion of the contract domiciled or habitually

resident in the same Contracting State, and which confers jurisdiction on the courts of that State, provided that such an agreement is not contrary to the law of that State.

Section 5

Exclusive jurisdiction

Article 16

The following courts shall have exclusive jurisdiction, regardless of domicile:

1. (a) in proceedings which have as their object rights *in rem* in immovable property or tenancies of immovable property, the courts of the Contracting State in which the property is situated;

   (b) however, in proceedings which have as their object tenancies of immovable property concluded for temporary private use for a maximum period of six consecutive months, the courts of the Contracting State in which the defendant is domiciled shall also have jurisdiction, provided that the tenant is a natural person and neither party is domiciled in the Contracting State in which the property is situated;

2. in proceedings which have as their object the validity of the constitution, the nullity or the dissolution of companies or other legal persons or associations of natural or legal persons, or the decisions of their organs, the courts of the Contracting State in which the company, legal person or association has its seat;

3. in proceedings which have as their object the validity of entries in public registers, the courts of the Contracting State in which the register is kept;

4. in proceedings concerned with the registration or validity of patents, trade marks, designs, or other similar rights required to be deposited or registered, the courts of the Contracting State in which the deposit or registration has

been applied for, has taken place or is under the terms of an international convention deemed to have taken place;

5. in proceedings concerned with the enforcement of judgments, the courts of the Contracting State in which the judgment has been or is to be enforced.

Section 6

Prorogation of jurisdiction

Article 17

1. If the parties, one or more of whom is domiciled in a Contracting State, have agreed that a court or the courts of a Contracting State are to have jurisdiction to settle any disputes which have arisen or which may arise in connection with a particular legal relationship, that court or those courts shall have exclusive jurisdiction. Such an agreement conferring jurisdiction shall be either:

(a) in writing or evidenced in writing, or

(b) in a form which accords with practices which the parties have established between themselves, or

(c) in international trade or commerce, in a form which accords with a usage of which the parties are or ought to have been aware and which in such trade or commerce is widely known to, and regularly observed by, parties to contracts of the type involved in the particular trade or commerce concerned.

Where such an agreement is concluded by parties, none of whom is domiciled in a Contracting State, the courts of other Contracting States shall have no jurisdiction over their disputes unless the court or courts chosen have declined jurisdiction.

2. The court or courts of a Contracting State on which a trust instrument has conferred jurisdiction shall have exclusive jurisdiction in any proceedings brought against a

settlor, trustee or beneficiary, if relations between these persons or their rights or obligations under the trust are involved.

3. Agreements or provisions of a trust instrument conferring jurisdiction shall have no legal force if they are contrary to the provisions of Article 12 or 15, or if the courts whose jurisdiction they purport to exclude have exclusive jurisdiction by virtue of Article 16.

4. If an agreement conferring jurisdiction was concluded for the benefit of only one of the parties, that party shall retain the right to bring proceedings in any other court which has jurisdiction by virtue of this Convention.

5. In matters relating to individual contracts of employment an agreement conferring jurisdiction shall have legal force only if it is entered into after the dispute has arisen.

Article 18

Apart from jurisdiction derived from other provisions of this Convention, a court of a Contracting State before whom a defendant enters an appearance shall have jurisdiction. This rule shall not apply where appearance was entered solely to contest the jurisdiction, or where another court has exclusive jurisdiction by virtue of Article 16.

Section 7

Examination as to jurisdiction and admissibility

Article 19

Where a court of a Contracting State is seised of a claim which is principally concerned with a matter over which the courts of another Contracting State have exclusive jurisdiction by virtue of Article 16, it shall declare of its own motion that it has no jurisdiction.

Article 20

Where a defendant domiciled in one Contracting State is sued in a court of another Contracting State and does not enter an appearance, the court shall declare of its own motion that it has no jurisdiction unless its jurisdiction is derived from the provisions of this Convention.

The court shall stay the proceedings so long as it is not shown that the defendant has been able to receive the document instituting the proceedings or an equivalent document in sufficient time to enable him to arrange for his defence, or that all necessary steps have been taken to this end.

The provisions of the foregoing paragraph shall be replaced by those of Article 15 of the Hague Convention of 15 November 1965 on the service abroad of judicial and extrajudicial documents in civil or commercial matters, if the document instituting the proceedings or notice thereof had to be transmitted abroad in accordance with that Convention.

Section 8

Lis Pendens – related actions

Article 21

Where proceedings involving the same cause of action and between the same parties are brought in the courts of different Contracting States, any court other than the court first seised shall of its own motion stay its proceedings until such time as the jurisdiction of the court first seised is established.

Where the jurisdiction of the court first seised is established, any court other than the court first seised shall decline jurisdiction in favour of that court.

Article 22

Where related actions are brought in the courts of different Contracting States, any court other than the court first seised may, while the actions are pending at first instance, stay its proceedings.

A court other than the court first seised may also, on the application of one of the parties, decline jurisdiction if the law of that court permits the consolidation of related actions and the court first seised has jurisdiction over both actions.

For the purposes of this Article, actions are deemed to be related where they are so closely connected that it is expedient to hear and determine them together to avoid the risk of irreconcilable judgments resulting from separate proceedings.

Article 23

Where actions come within the exclusive jurisdiction of several courts, any court other than the court first seised shall decline jurisdiction in favour of that court.

Section 9

Provisional, including protective, measures

Article 24

Application may be made to the courts of a Contracting State for such provisional, including protective, measures as may be available under the law of that State, even if, under this Convention, the courts of another Contracting State have jurisdiction as to the substance of the matter.

TITLE III

RECOGNITION AND ENFORCEMENT

Article 25

For the purposes of this Convention, 'judgment' means any judgment given by a court or tribunal of a Contracting State, whatever the judgment may be called, including a decree, order, decision or writ of execution, as well as the determination of costs or expenses by an officer of the court.

Section 1

Recognition

Article 26

A judgment given in a Contracting State shall be recognized in the other Contracting States without any special procedure being required.

Any interested party who raises the recognition of a judgment as the principal issue in a dispute may, in accordance with the procedures provided for in Section 2 and 3 of this Title, apply for a decision that the judgment be recognized.

If the outcome of proceedings in a court of a Contracting State depends on the determination of an incidental question of recognition that court shall have jurisdiction over that question.

Article 27

A judgment shall not be recognized:

1. if such recognition is contrary to public policy in the State in which recognition is sought;

2. where it was given in default of appearance, if the defendant was not duly served with the document which instituted the proceedings or with an equivalent document in sufficient time to enable him to arrange for his defence;

3. if the judgment is irreconcilable with a judgment given in a dispute between the same parties in the State in which recognition is sought;

4. if the court of the State of origin, in order to arrive at its judgment, has decided a preliminary question concerning the status or legal capacity of natural persons, rights in property arising out of a matrimonial relationship, wills or succession in a way that conflicts with a rule of the private international law of the State in which the recognition is sought, unless the same result would have been reached by the application of the rules of private international law of that State;

5. if the judgment is irreconcilable with an earlier judgment given in a non-contracting State involving the same cause of action and between the same parties, provided that this latter judgment fulfils the conditions necessary for its recognition in the State addressed.

Article 28

Moreover, a judgment shall not be recognized if it conflicts with the provisions of Sections 3, 4 or 5 of Title II or in a case provided for in Article 59.

A judgment may furthermore be refused recognition in any case provided for in Article 54B (3) or 57 (4).

In its examination of the grounds of jurisdiction referred to in the foregoing paragraphs, the court or authority applied to shall be bound by the findings of fact on which the court of the State of origin based its jurisdiction.

Subject to the provisions of the first and second paragraphs, the jurisdiction of the court of the State of origin may not be reviewed; the test of public policy referred to in Article 27 (1) may not be applied to the rules relating to jurisdiction.

Article 29

Under no circumstances may a foreign judgment be reviewed as to its substance.

Article 30

A court of a Contracting State in which recognition is sought of a judgment given in another Contracting State may stay the proceedings if an ordinary appeal against the judgment has been lodged.

A court of a Contracting State in which recognition is sought of a judgment given in Ireland or the United Kingdom may stay the proceedings if enforcement is suspended in the State of origin by reason of an appeal.

Section 2

Enforcement

Article 31

A judgment given in a Contracting State and enforceable in that State shall be enforced in another Contracting State when, on the application of any interested party, it has been declared enforceable there.

However, in the United Kingdom, such a judgment shall be enforced in England and Wales, in Scotland, or in Northern Ireland when, on the application of any interested party, it has been registered for enforcement in that part of the United Kingdom.

Article 32

1. The application shall be submitted:

— in Belgium, to the tribunal de première instance or rechtbank van eerste aanleg,

— in Denmark, to the byret,

— in the Federal Republic of Germany, to the presiding judge of a chamber of the Landgericht,

— in Greece, to the μονομελές πρωτοδικείο,

— in Spain, to the Juzgado de Primera Instancia,

— in France, to the presiding judge of the tribunal de grande instance,

— in Ireland, to the High Court,

— in Iceland, to the héraðsdómari,

— in Italy, to the corte d'appello,

— in Luxembourg, to the presiding judge of the tribunal d'arrondissement,

— in the Netherlands, to the presiding judge of the arrondissementsrechtbank,

— in Norway, to the herredsrett or byrett as namsrett,

— in Austria, to the Landesgericht or the Kreisgericht,

— in Portugal, to the Tribunal Judicial de Círculo,

— in Switzerland:

(a) in respect of judgments ordering the payment of a sum of money, to the juge de la mainlevée / Rechtsöffnungsrichter / giudice competente a pronunciare sul rigetto dell'opposizione, within the framework of the procedure governed by Articles 80 and 81 of the loi fédérale sur la poursuite pour dettes et la faillite / Bundesgesetz über Schuldbetreibung und Konkurs / legge federale sulla esecuzione e sul fallimento;

(b) in respect of judgments ordering a performance other than the payment of a sum of money, to the juge cantonal d'exequatur compétent / zuständiger kantonaler Vollstreckungsrichter / giudice cantonale competente a pronunciare l'exequatur,

— in Finland, to the ulosotonhaltija / överexekutor,

— in Sweden, to the Svea hovrätt,

— in the United Kingdom:

(a) in England and Wales, to the High Court of Justice, or in the case of a maintenance judgment to the Magistrates' Court on transmission by the Secretary of State;

(b) in Scotland, to the Court of Session, or in the case of a maintenance judgment to the Sheriff Court on transmission by the Secretary of State;

(c) in Northern Ireland, to the High Court of Justice, or in the case of a maintenance judgment to the Magistrates' Court on transmission by the Secretary of State.

2. The jurisdiction of local courts shall be determined by reference to the place of domicile of the party against whom enforcement is sought. If he is not domiciled in the State in which enforcement is sought, it shall be determined by reference to the place of enforcement.

Article 33

The procedure for making the application shall be governed by the law of the State in which enforcement is sought.

The applicant must give an address for service of process within the area of jurisdiction of the court applied to. However, if the law of the State in which enforcement is sought does not provide for the furnishing of such an address, the applicant shall appoint a representative *ad litem*.

The documents referred to in Articles 46 and 47 shall be attached to the application.

Article 34

The court applied to shall give its decision without delay; the party against whom enforcement is sought shall not at this stage of the proceedings be entitled to make any submissions on the application.

The application may be refused only for one of the reasons specified in Articles 27 and 28.

Under no circumstances may the foreign judgment be reviewed as to its substance.

Article 35

The appropriate officer of the court shall without delay bring the decision given on the application to the notice of the applicant in accordance with the procedure laid down by the law of the State in which enforcement is sought.

Article 36

If enforcement is authorized, the party against whom enforcement is sought may appeal against the decision within one month of service thereof.

If that party is domiciled in a Contracting State other than that in which the decision authorizing enforcement was given, the time for appealing shall be two months and shall run from the date of service, either on him in person or at his residence. No extension of time may be granted on account of distance.

Article 37

1. An appeal against the decision authorizing enforcement shall be lodged in accordance with the rules governing procedure in contentious matters:

— in Belgium, with the tribunal de première instance or rechtsbank van eerste aanleg,

— in Denmark, with the landsret,

— in the Federal Republic of Germany, with the Oberlandesgericht,

— in Greece, with the εφετείο,

— in Spain, with the Audiencia Provincial,

— in France, with the cour d'appel,

— in Ireland, with the High Court,

— in Iceland, with the héraðsdómari,

— in Italy, with the corte d'appello,

— in Luxembourg, with the Cour supérieure de justice sitting as a court of civil appeal,

— in the Netherlands, with the arrondissements-rechtsbank,

— in Norway, with the lagmannsrett,

— in Austria, with the Landesgericht or the Kreisgericht,

— in Portugal, with the Tribunal da Relação,

— in Switzerland, with the tribunal cantonal Kantonsgericht / tribunale cantonale,

— in Finland, with the hovioikeus / hovrätt,

— in Sweden, with the Svea hovrätt,

— in the United Kingdom:

(a) in England and Wales, with the High Court of Justice, or in the case of a maintenance judgment with the Magistrates' Court;

(b) in Scotland, with the Court of Session, or in the case of a maintenance judgment with the Sheriff Court;

(c) in Northern Ireland, with the High Court of Justice, or in the case of a maintenance judgment with the Magistrates' Court.

2. The judgment given on the appeal may be contested only:

— in Belgium, Greece, Spain, France, Italy, Luxembourg and in the Netherlands, by an appeal in cassation,

— in Denmark, by an appeal to the højesteret, with the leave of the Minister of Justice,

— in the Federal Republic of Germany, by a Rechtsbeschwerde,

— in Ireland, by an appeal on a point of law to the Supreme Court,

— in Iceland, by an appeal to the Hæstiréttur,

— in Norway, by an appeal (kjæremål or anke) to the Hoyesteretts Kjæremålsutvalg or Hoyesterett,

— in Austria, in the case of an appeal, by a Revisionsrekurs and, in the case of opposition proceedings, by a Berufung with the possibility of a Revision,

— in Portugal, by an appeal on a point of law,

— in Switzerland, by a recours de droit public devant le tribunal fédéral / staatsrechtliche Beschwerde beim Bundesgericht / ricorso di diritto pubblico davanti al tribunale federale,

— in Finland, by an appeal to the korkein oikeus / högsta domstolen,

— in Sweden, by an appeal to the högsta domstolen,

— in the United Kingdom, by a single further appeal on a point of law.

Article 38

The court with which the appeal under Article 37 (1) is lodged may, on the application of the appellant, stay the proceedings if an ordinary appeal has been lodged against the judgment in the State of origin or if the time for such an appeal has not yet expired; in the latter case, the court may specify the time within which such an appeal is to be lodged.

Where the judgment was given in Ireland or the United Kingdom, any form of appeal available in the State of origin shall be treated as an ordinary appeal for the purposes of the first paragraph.

The court may also make enforcement conditional on the provision of such security as it shall determine.

Article 39

During the time specified for an appeal pursuant to Article 36 and until any such appeal has been determined, no measures of enforcement may be taken other than protective measures taken against the property of the party against whom enforcement is sought.

The decision authorizing enforcement shall carry with it the power to proceed to any such protective measures.

Article 40

1. If the application for enforcement is refused, the applicant may appeal:

— in Belgium, to the cour d'appel or hof van beroep,

— in Denmark, to the landsret,

— in the Federal Republic of Germany, to the Oberlandesgericht,

— in Greece, to the εφετείο,

— in Spain, to the Audiencia Provincial,

— in France, to the cour d'appel,

— in Ireland, to the High Court,

— in Iceland, to the héraδsdómari,

— in Italy, to the corte d'appello,

— in Luxembourg, to the Cour supérieure de justice sitting as a court of civil appeal,

— in the Netherlands, to the gerechtshof,

— in Norway, to the lagmannsrett,

— in Austria, to the Landesgericht or the Kreisgericht,

— in Portugal, to the Tribunal da Relação,

— in Switzerland, to the tribunal cantonal / Kantonsgericht / tribunale cantonale,

— in Finland, to the hovioikeus / hovrätt,

— in Sweden, to the Svea hovrätt,

— in the United Kingdom:

(a) in England and Wales, to the High Court of Justice, or in the case of a maintenance judgment to the Magistrates' Court;

(b) in Scotland, to the Court of Session, or in the case of a maintenance judgment to the Sheriff Court;

(c) in Northern Ireland, to the High Court of Justice, or in the case of a maintenance judgment to the Magistrates' Court.

2. The party against whom enforcement is sought shall be summoned to appear before the appellate court. If he fails to appear, the provisions of the second and third paragraphs of Article 20 shall apply even where he is not domiciled in any of the Contracting States.

Article 41

A judgment given on an appeal provided for in Article 40 may be contested only:

— in Belgium, Greece, Spain, France, Italy, Luxembourg and in the Netherlands, by an appeal in cassation,

— in Denmark, by an appeal to the højesteret, with the leave of the Minister of Justice,

— in the Federal Republic of Germany, by a Rechtsbeschwerde,

— in Ireland, by an appeal on a point of law to the Supreme Court,

— in Iceland, by an appeal to the Hæstiréttur,

— in Norway, by an appeal (kjæremål or anke) to the Hoyesteretts kjæremålsutvalg or Hoyesterett,

— in Austria, by a Revisionsrekurs,

— in Portugal, by an appeal on a point of law,

— in Switzerland, by a recours de droit public devant le tribunal fédéral / staatsrechtliche Beschwerde beim Bundesgericht / ricorso di diritto pubblico davanti al tribunale federale,

— in Finland, by an appeal to the korkein oikeus / högsta domstolen,

— in Sweden, by an appeal to the högsta domstolen,

— in the United Kingdom, by a single further appeal on a point of law.

Article 42

Where a foreign judgment has been given in respect of several matters and enforcement cannot be authorized for all of them, the court shall authorize enforcement for one or more of them.

An applicant may request partial enforcement of a judgment.

Article 43

A foreign judgment which orders a periodic payment by way of a penalty shall be enforceable in the State in which enforcement is sought only if the amount of the payment has been finally determined by the courts of the State of origin.

Article 44

An applicant who, in the State of origin, has benefited from complete or partiyl legal aid or exemption from costs or expenses, shall be entitled, in the procedures provided for in Articles 32 to 35, to benefit from the most favourable legal aids or the most extensive exemption from costs or expenses provided for by the law of the State addressed.

However, an applicant who requests the enforcement of a decision given by an administrative authority in Denmark or in Iceland in respect of a maintenance order may, in the State addressed, claim the benefits referred to in the first paragraph if he presents a statement from, respectively, the Danish Ministry of Justice or the Icelandic Ministry of Justice to the effect that he fulfils the economic requirements to qualify for the grant of complete or partial legal aid or exemption from costs or expenses.

Article 45

No security, bond or deposit, however described, shall be required of a party who in one Contracting State applies for enforcement of a judgment given in another Contracting

State on the ground that he is a foreign national or that he is not domiciled or resident in the State in which enforcement is sought.

Section 3

Common provisions

Article 46

A party seeking recognition or applying for enforcement of a judgment shall produce:

1. a copy of the judgment which satisfies the conditions necessary to establish its authenticity;

2. in the case of a judgment given in default, the original or a certified true copy of the document which establishes that the party in default was served with the document instituting the proceedings or with an equivalent document.

Article 47

A party applying for enforcement shall also produce:

1. documents which establish that, according to the law of the State of origin, the judgment is enforceable and has been served;

2. where appropriate, a document showing that the applicant is in receipt of legal aid in the State of origin.

Article 48

If the documents specified in Articles 46 (2) and 47 (2) are not produced, the court may specify a time for their production, accept equivalent documents or, if it considers that it has sufficient information before it, dispense with their production.

If the court so requires, a translation of the documents shall be produced; the translation shall be certified by a person qualified to do so in one of the Contracting States.

Article 49

No legalization or other similar formality shall be required in respect of the documents referred to in Articles 46 or 47 or the second paragraph of Article 48, or in respect of a document appointing a representative *ad litem*.

TITLE IV

AUTHENTIC INSTRUMENTS AND COURT SETTLEMENTS

Article 50

A document which has been formally drawn up or registered as an authentic instrument and is enforceable in one Contracting State shall, in another Contracting State, be declared enforceable there, on application made in accordance with the procedures provided for in Articles 31 *et seq*. The application may be refused only if enforcement of the instrument is contrary to public policy in the State addressed.

The instrument produced must satisfy the conditions necessary to establish its authenticity in the State of origin.

The provisions of Section 3 of Title III shall apply as appropriate.

Article 51

A settlement which has been approved by a court in the course of proceedings and is enforceable in the State in which it was concluded shall be enforceable in the State addressed under the same conditions as authentic instruments.

TITLE V

GENERAL PROVISIONS

Article 52

In order to determine whether a party is domiciled in the Contracting State whose courts are seised of a matter, the Court shall apply its internal law.

If a party is not domiciled in the State whose courts are seised of the matter, then, in order to determine whether the party is domiciled in another Contracting State, the court shall apply the law of that State.

Article 53

For the purposes of this Convention, the seat of a company or other legal person or association of natural or legal persons shall be treated as its domicile. However, in order to determine that seat, the court shall apply its rules of private international law.

In order to determine whether a trust is domiciled in the Contracting State whose courts are seised of the matter, the court shall apply its rules of private international law.

TITLE VI

TRANSITIONAL PROVISIONS

Article 54

The provisions of this Convention shall apply only to legal proceedings instituted and to documents formally drawn up or registered as authentic instruments after its entry into force in the State of origin and, where recognition or enforcement of a judgment or authentic instrument is sought, in the State addressed.

However, judgments given after the date of entry into force of this Convention between the State of origin and the State addressed in proceedings instituted before that date shall be recognized and enforced in accordance with the provisions of Title III if jurisdiction was founded upon rules which accorded with those provided for either in Title II of this Convention or in a convention concluded between the State of origin and the State addressed which was in force when the proceedings were instituted.

If the parties to a dispute concerning a contract had agreed in writing before the entry into force of this Convention that the contract was to be governed by the law of Ireland or of a part of the United Kingdom, the courts of Ireland or of that part of the United Kingdom shall retain the right to exercise jurisdiction in the dispute.

Article 54A

For a period of three years from the entry into force of this Convention for Denmark, Greece, Ireland, Iceland, Norway, Finland and Sweden, respectively, jurisdiction in maritime matters shall be determined in these States not only in accordance with the provisions of Title II, but also in accordance with the provisions of paragraphs 1 to 7 following. However, upon the entry into force of the International Convention relating to the arrest of sea-going ships, signed at Brussels on 10 May 1952, for one of these States, these provisions shall cease to have effect for that State.

1. A person who is domiciled in a Contracting State may be sued in the courts of one of the States mentioned above in respect of a maritime claim if the ship to which the claim relates or any other ship owned by him has been arrested by judicial process within the territory of the latter State to secure the claim, or could have been so arrested there but bail or other security has been given, and either:

   (a) the claimant is domiciled in the latter State; or

   (b) the claim arose in the latter State; or

   (c) the claim concerns the voyage during which the arrest was made or could have been made; or

   (d) the claim arises out of a collision or out of damage caused by a ship to another ship or to goods or persons on board either ship, either by the execution or non-execution of a manoeuvre or by the non-observance of regulations; or

   (e) the claim is for salvage; or

(f) the claim is in respect of a mortgage or hypothecation of the ship arrested.

2. A claimant may arrest either the particular ship to which the maritime claim relates, or any other ship which is owned by the person who was, at the time when the maritime claim arose, the owner of the particula ship. However, only the particular ship to which the maritime claim relates my be arrested in respect of the maritime claims set out under 5. (o), (p) or (q) of this Article.

3. Ships shall be deemed to be in the same ownership when all the shares therein are owned by the same person or persons.

4. When in the case of a charter by demise of a ship the charterer alone is liable in respect of a maritime claim relating to that ship, the claimant may arrest that ship or any other ship owned by the charterer, but no other ship owned by the owner may be arrested in respect of such claim. The same shall apply to any case in which a person other than the owner of a ship is liable in respect of a maritime claim relating to that ship.

5. The expression 'maritime claim' means a claim arising out of one or more of the following:

(a) damage caused by any ship either in collision or otherwise;

(b) loss of life or personal injury caused by any ship or occurring in connection with the operation on any ship;

(c) salvage;

(d) agreement relating to the use or hire of any ship whether by charterparty or otherwise;

(e) agreement relating to the carriage of goods in any ship whether by charterparty or otherwise;

(f) loss of or damage to goods including baggage carried in any ship;

(g) general average;

(h) bottomry;

(i) towage;

(j) pilotage;

(k) goods or materials wherever supplied to a ship for her operation or maintenance;

(l) construction, repair or equipment of any ship or dock charges and dues;

(m) wages of masters, officers or crew;

(n) master's disbursements, including disbursements made by shippers, charterers or agents on behalf of a ship or her owner;

(o) dispute as to the title to or ownership of any ship;

(p) disputes between co-owners of any ship as to the ownership, possession, employment or earnings of that ship;

(q) the mortgage or hypothecation of any ship.

6. In Denmark, the expression 'arrest' shall be deemed as regards the maritime claims referred to under 5. (o) and (p) of this Article, to include a 'forbud', where that is the only procedure allowed in respect of such a claim under Articles 646 to 653 of the law on civil procedure (lov om rettens pleje).

7. In Iceland, the expression 'arrest' shall be deemed, as regards the maritime claims referred to under 5. (o) and (p) of this Article, to include a 'lõgbann', where that is the only procedure allowed in respect of such a claim under Chapter III of the law on arrest and injunction (lõg um kyrrsetningu og lõgbann).

TITLE VII

RELATIONSHIP TO THE BRUSSELS CONVENTION AND TO OTHER CONVENTIONS

Article 54B

1. This Convention shall not prejudice the application by the Member States of the European Communities of the Convention on Jurisdiction and the Enforcement of Judgments in Civil and Commercial Matters, signed at Brussels on 27 September 1968 and of the Protocol on interpretation of that Convention by the Court of Justice, signed at Luxembourg on 3 June 1971, as amended by the Conventions of Accession to the said Convention and the said Protocol by the States acceding to the European Communities, all of these Conventions and the Protocol being hereinafter referred to as the 'Brussels Convention'.

2. However, this Convention shall in any event be applied:

(a) in matters of jurisdiction, where the defendant is domiciled in the territory of a Contracting State which is not a member of the European Communities, or where Article 16 or 17 of this Convention confer a jurisdiction on the courts of such a Contracting State;

(b) in relation to a *lis pendens* or to related actions as provided for in Articles 21 and 22, when proceedings are instituted in a Contracting State which is not a member of the European Communities and in a Contracting State which is a member of the European Communities;

(c) in matters of recognition and enforcement, where either the State of origin or the State addressed is not a member of the European Communities.

3. In addition to the grounds provided for in Title III recognition or enforcement may be refused if the ground of jurisdiction on which the judgment has been based differs from that resulting from this Convention and recognition or enforcement is sought against a party who is domiciled in a Contracting State which is not a member of the European

Communities, unless the judgment may otherwiese be recognized or enforced under any rule of law in the State addressed.

Article 55

Subject to the provisions of Articles 54 (2) and 56, this Convention shall, for the States which are parties to it, supersede the following conventions concluded between two or more of them:

— the Convention between the Swiss Confëderation and France on jurisdiction and enforcement of judgments in civil matters, signed at Paris on 15 June 1869,

— the Treaty between the Swiss Confederation and Spain on the mutual enforcement of judgments in civil or commercial matters, signed at Madrid on 19 November 1896,

— the Convention between the Swiss Confederation and the German Reich on the recognition and enforcement of judgments and arbitration awards, signed at Berne on 2 November 1929,

— the Convention between Denmark, Finland, Iceland, Norway and Sweden on the recognition and enforcement of judgments, signed at Copenhagen on 16 March 1932,

— the Convention between the Swiss Confederation and Italy on the recognition and enforcement of judgments, signed at Rome on 3 January 1933,

— the Convention between Sweden and the Swiss Confederation on the recognition and enforcement of judgments and arbitral awards signed at Stockholm on 15 January 1936,

— the Convention between the Kingdom of Belgium and Austria on the reciprocal recognition and enforcement of judgments and authentic instruments relating to maintenance obligations, signed at Vienna on 25 October 1957,

— the Convention between the Swiss Confederation and Belgium on the recognition and enforcement of judgments and arbitration awards, signed at Berne on 29 April 1959,

— the Convention between the Federal Republic of Germany and Austria on the reciprocal recognition and enforcement of judgments, settlements and authentic instruments in civil and commercial matters, signed at Vienna on 6 June 1959,

— the Convention between the Kingdom of Belgium and Austria on the reciprocal recognition and enforcement of judgments, arbitral awards and authentic instruments in civil and commercial matters, signed at Vienna on 16 June 1959,

— the Convention between Austria and the Swiss Confederation on the recognition and enforcement of judgments, signed at Berne on 16 December 1960,

— the Convention between Norway and the United Kingdom providing for the reciprocal recognition and enforcement of judgments in civil matters, signed at London on 12 June 1961,

— the Convention between the United Kingdom and Austria providing for the reciprocal recognition and enforcement of judgments in civil and commercial matters, signed at Vienna on 14 July 1961, with amending Protocol signed at London on 6 March 1970,

— the Convention between the Kingdom of the Netherlands and Austria on the reciprocal recognition and enforcement of judgments and authentic instruments in civil and commercial matters, signed at The Hague on 6 February 1963,

— the Convention between France and Austria on the recognition and enforcement of judgments and authentic instruments in civil and commercial matters, signed at Vienna on 15 July 1966,

— the Convention between Luxembourg and Austria on the recognition and enforcement of judgements and authentic instruments in civil and commercial matters, signed at Luxembourg on 29 July 1971,

— the Convention between Italy and Austria on the recognition and enforcement of judgments in civil and commercial matters, of judicial settlements and of authentic instruments, signed at Rome on 16 November 1971,

— the Convention between Norway and the Federal Republic of Germany on the recognition and enforcement of judgments and enforceable documents, in civil and commercial matters, signed at Oslo on 17 June 1977,

— the Convention between Denmark, Finland, Iceland, Norway and Sweden on the recognition and enforcement of judgments in civil matters, signed at Copenhagen on 11 October 1977,

— the Convention between Austria and Sweden on the recognition and enforcement of judgments in civil matters, signed at Stockholm on 16 September 1982,

— the Convention between Austria and Spain on the recognition and enforcement of judgments, settlements and enforceable authentic instruments in civil and commercial matters, signed at Vienna on 17 February 1984,

— the Convention between Norway and Austria on the recognition and enforcement of judgments in civil matters, signed at Vienna on 21 May 1984, and

— the Convention between Finland and Austria on the recognition and enforcement of judgments in civil matters, signed at Vienna on 17 November 1986.

Article 56

The Treaty and the conventions referred to in Article 55 shall continue to have effect in relation to matters to which this Convention does not apply.

They shall continue to have effect in respect of judgments given and documents formally drawn up or registered as authentic instruments before the entry into force of this Convention.

Article 57

1. This Convention shall not affect any conventions to which the Contracting States are or will be parties and which in relation to particular matters, govern jurisdiction or the recognition or enforcement of judgments.

2. This Convention shall not prevent a court of a Contracting State which is party to a convention referred to in the first paragraph from assuming jurisdiction in accordance with that convention, even where the defendant is domiciled in a Contracting State which is not a party to that convention. The court hearing the action shall, in any event, apply Article 20 of this Convention.

3. Judgments given in a Contracting State by a court in the exercise of jurisdiction provided for in a convention referred to in the first paragraph shall be recognized and enforced in the other Contracting States in accordance with Title III of this Convention.

4. In addition to the grounds provided for in Title III, recognition or enforcement may be refused if the State addressed is not a contracting party to a convention referred to in the first paragraph and the person against whom recognition or enforcement is sought is domiciled in that State, unless the judgment may otherwise be recognized or enforced under any rule of law in the State addressed.

5. Where a convention referred to in the first paragraph to which both the State of origin and the State addressed are

parties lays down conditions for the recognition or enforcement of judgments, those conditions shall apply. In any event, the provisions of this Convention which concern the procedures for recognition and enforcement of judgments may be applied.

Article 58

(None)

Article 59

This Convention shall not prevent a Contracting State from assuming, in a convention on the recognition and enforcement of judgments, an obligation towards a third State not to recognize judgments given in other Contracting States against defendants domiciled or habitually resident in the third State where, in cases provided for in Article 4, the judgment could only be founded on a ground of jurisdiction specified in the second paragraph of Article 3.

However, a Contracting State may not assume an obligation towards a third State not to recognize a judgment given in another Contracting State by a court basing its jurisdiction on the presence within that State of property belonging to the defendant, or the seizure by the plaintiff of property situated there:

1. if the action is brought to assert or declare proprietary or possessory rights in that property, seeks to obtain authority to dispose of it, or arises from another issue relating to such property, or

2. if the property constitutes the security for a debt which is the subject-matter of the action.

TITLE VIII

FINAL PROVISIONS

Article 60

The following may be parties to this Convention:

(a) States which, at the time of the opening of this Convention for signature, are members of the European Communities or of the European Free Trade Association;

(b) States which, after the opening of this Convention for signature, become members of the European Communities or of the European Free Trade Association;

(c) States invited to accede in accordance with Article 62 (1) (b).

Article 61

1. This Convention shall be opened for signature by the States members of the European Communities or of the European Free Trade Association.

2. The Convention shall be submitted for ratification by the signatory States. The instruments of ratification shall be deposited with the Swiss Federal Council.

3. The Convention shall enter into force on the first day of the third month following the date on which two States, of which one is a member of the European Communities and the other a member of the European Free Trade Association, deposit their instruments of ratification.

4. The Convention shall take effect in relation to any other signatory State on the first day of the third month following the deposit of its instrument of ratification.

Article 62

1. After entering into force this Convention shall be open to accession by:

(a) the States referred to in Article 60 (b);

(b) other States which have been invited to accede upon a request made by one of the Contracting States to the depositary State. The depositary State shall invite the State concerned to accede only if, after having communicated the contents of the communications that this State intends to make in accordance with Article 63, it has obtained the unanimous agreement of the signatory States and the Contracting States referred to in Article 60 (a) and (b).

2. If an acceding State wishes to furnish details for the purposes of Protocol 1, negotiations shall be entered into to that end. A negotiating conference shall be convened by the Swiss Federal Council.

3. In respect of an acceding State, the Convention shall take effect on the first day of the third month following the deposit of its instrument of accession.

4. However, in respect of an acceding State referred to in paragraph 1 (a) or (b), the Convention shall take effect only in relations between the acceding State and the Contracting States which have not made any objections to the accession before the first day of the third month following the deposit of the instrument of accession.

Article 63

Each acceding State shall, when depositing its instrument of accession, communicate the information required for the application of Articles 3, 32, 37, 40, 41 and 55 of this Convention and furnish, if need be, the details prescribed during the negotiations for the purposes of Protocol 1.

Article 64

1. This Convention is concluded for an initial period of five years from the date of its entry into force in accordance with Article 61 (3), even in the case of States which ratify it or accede to it after that date.

2. At the end of the initial five-year period, the Convention shall be automatically renewed from year to year.

3. Upon the expiry of the initial five-year period, any contracting State may, at any time, denounce the Convention by sending a notification to the Swiss Federal Council.

4. The denunciation shall take effect at the end of the calendar year following the expiry of a period of six months from the date of receipt by the Swiss Federal Council of the notification of denunciation.

Article 65

The following are annexed to this Convention:

— a Protocol 1, on certain questions of jurisdiction, procedure and enforcement,

— a Protocol 2, on the uniform interpretation of the Convention,

— a Protocol 3, on the application of Article 57.

These Protocols shall form an integral part of the Convention.

Article 66

Any Contracting State may request the revision of this Convention. To that end, the Swiss Federal Council shall issue invitations to a revision conference within a period of six months from the date of the request for revision.

Article 67

The Swiss Federal Council shall notify the States represented at the Diplomatic Conference of Lugano and the States who have later acceded to the Convention of:

(a) the deposit of each instrument of ratification or accession;

(b) the dates of entry into force of this Convention in respect of the Contracting States;

(c) any denunciation received pursuant to Article 64;

(d) any declaration received pursuant to Article Ia of Protocol 1;

(e) any declaration received pursuant to Article Ib of Protocol 1;

(f) any declaration received pursuant to Article IV of Protocol 1;

(g) any communication made pursuant to Article VI of Protocol 1.

Article 68

This Convention, drawn up in a single original in the Danish, Dutch, English, Finnish, French, German, Greek, Icelandic, Irish, Italian, Norwegian, Portuguese, Spanish and Swedish languages, all fourteen texts being equally authentic, shall be deposited in the archives of the Swiss Federal Council. The Swiss Federal Council shall transmit a certified copy to the Government of each State represented at the Diplomatic Conference of Lugano and to the Government of each acceding State.

In witness whereof, the undersigned Plenipotentiaries have signed this Convention.

Done at Lugano on the sixteenth day of September in the year one thousand nine hundred and eighty-eight.

PROTOCOL 1

on certain questions of jurisdiction, procedure and enforcement

THE HIGH CONTRACTING PARTIES HAVE AGREED UPON THE FOLLOWING PROVISIONS, WHICH SHALL BE ANNEXED TO THE CONVENTION:

Article I

Any person domiciled in Luxembourg who is sued in a court of another Contracting State pursuant to Article 5 (1) may refuse to submit to the jurisdiction of that court. If the defendant does not enter an appearance the court shall declare of its own motion that it has no jurisdiction.

An agreement conferring jurisdiction, within the meaning of Article 17, shall be valid with respect to a person domiciled in Luxembourg only if that person has expressly and specifically so agreed.

Article Ia

1. Switzerland reserves the right to declare, at the time of depositing its instrument of ratification, that a judgment given in another Contracting State shall be neither recognized

nor enforced in Switzerland if the following conditions are met:

(a) the jurisdiction of the court which has given the judgment is based only on Article 5 (1) of this Convention; and

(b) the defendant was domiciled in Switzerland at the time of the introduction of the proceedings; for the purposes of this Article, a company or other legal person is considered to be domiciled in Switzerland if it has its registered seat and the effective centre of activities in Switzerland; and

(c) the defendant raises an objection to the recognition or enforcement of the judgment in Switzerland, provided that he has not waived the benefit of the declaration foreseen under this paragraph.

2. This reservation shall not apply to the extent that at the time recognition or enforcement is sought a derogation has been granted from Article 59 of the Swiss Federal Constitution. The Swiss Government shall communicate such derogations to the signatory States and the acceding States.

3. This reservation shall cease to have effect on 31 December 1999. It may be withdrawn at any time.

Article Ib

Any Contracting State may, by declaration made at the time of signing or of deposit of its instrument of ratification or of accession, reserve the right, notwithstanding the provisions of Article 28, not to recognize and enforce judgments given in the other Contracting States if the jurisdiction of the court of the State of origin is based, pursuant to Article 16 (1) (b), exclusively on the domicile of the defendant in the State of origin, and the property is situated in the territory of the State which entered the reservation.

Article II

Without prejudice to any more favourable provisions of national laws, persons domiciled in a Contracting State who are being prosecuted in the criminal courts of another Contracting State of which they are not nationals for an offence which was not intentionally committed may be defended by persons qualified to do so, even if they do not appear in person.

However, the court seised of the matter may order appearance in person; in the case of failure to appear, a judgment given in the civil action without the person concerned having had the opportunity to arrange for his defence need not be recognized or enforced in the other Contracting States.

Article III

In proceedings for the issue of an order for enforcement, no charge, duty or fee calculated by reference to the value of the matter in issue may be levied in the State in which enforcement is sought.

Article IV

Judicial and extrajudicial documents drawn up in one Contracting State which have to be served on persons in another Contracting State shall be transmitted in accordance with the procedures laid down in the conventions and agreements concluded between the Contracting States.

Unless the State in which service is to take place objects by declaration to the Swiss Federal Council, such documents may also be sent by the appropriate public officers of the State in which the document has been drawn up directly to the appropriate public officers of the State in which the addressee is to be found. In this case the officer of the State of origin shall send a copy of the document to the officer of the State applied to who is competent to forward it to the addressee. The document shall be forwarded in the manner specified by the law of the State applied to. The forwarding shall be recorded by a certificate sent directly to the officer of the State of origin.

Article V

The jurisdiction specified in Articles 6 (2) and 10 in actions on a warranty or guarantee or in any other third party proceedings may not be resorted to in the Federal Republic of Germany, in Spain, in Austria and in Switzerland. Any person domiciled in another Contracting State may be sued in the courts:

— of the Federal Republic of Germany, pursuant to Articles 68, 72, 73 and 74 of the code of civil procedure (Zivilprozeßordnung) concerning third-party notices,

— of Spain, pursuant to Article 1482 of the civil code,

— of Austria, pursuant to Article 21 of the code of civil procedure (Zivilprozeßordnung) concerning third-party notices,

— of Switzerland, pursuant to the appropriate provisions concerning third-party notices of the cantonal codes of civil procedure.

Judgments given in the other Contracting States by virtue of Article 6 (2) or 10 shall be recognized and enforced in the Federal Republic of Germany, in Spain, in Austria and in Switzerland in accordance with Title III. Any effects which judgments given in these States may have on third parties by application of the provisions in the preceding paragraph shall also be recognized in the other Contracting States.

Article Va

In matters relating to maintenance, the expression 'court' includes the Danish, Icelandic and Norwegian administrative authorities.

In civil and commercial matters, the expression 'court' includes the Finnish ulosotonhaltija / överexekutor.

Article Vb

In proceedings involving a dispute between the master and a member of the crew of a sea-going ship registered in

Denmark, in Greece, in Ireland, in Iceland, in Norway, in Portugal or in Sweden concerning remuneration or other conditions of service, a court in a Contracting State shall establish whether the diplomatic or consular officer responsible for the ship has been notified of the dispute. It shall stay the proceedings so long as he has not been notified. It shall of its own motion decline jurisdiction if the officer, having been duly notified, has exercised the powers accorded to him in the matter by a consular convention, or in the absence of such a convention has, within the time allowed, raised any objection to the exercise of such jurisdiction.

Article Vc

(None)

Article Vd

Without prejudice to the jurisdiction of the European Patent Office under the Convention on the grant of European patents, signed at Munich on 5 October 1973, the courts of each Contracting State shall have exclusive jurisdiction, regardless of domicile, in proceedings concerned with the registration or validity of any European patent granted for that State which is not a Community patent by virtue of the provision of Article 86 of the Convention for the European patent for the common market, signed at Luxembourg on 15 December 1975.

Article VI

The Contracting States shall communicate to the Swiss Federal Council the text of any provisions of their laws which amend either those provisions of their laws mentioned in the Convention or the lists of courts specified in Section 2 of Title III.

PROTOCOL 2

on the uniform interpretation of the Convention

PREAMBLE

THE HIGH CONTRACTING PARTIES,

HAVING REGARD to Article 65 of this Convention,

CONSIDERING the substantial link between this Convention and the Brussels Convention,

CONSIDERING that the Court of Justice of the European Communities by virtue of the Protocol of 3 June 1971 has jurisdiction to give rulings on the interpretation of the provisions of the Brussels Convention,

BEING AWARE of the rulings delivered by the Court of Justice of the European Communities on the interpretation of the Brussels Convention up to the time of signature of this Convention,

CONSIDERING that the negotiations which led to the conclusion of the Convention were based on the Brussels Convention in the light of these rulings,

DESIRING to prevent, in full deference to the independence of the courts, divergent interpretations and to arrive at as uniform an interpretation as possible of the provisions of the Convention, and of these provisions and those of the Brussels Convention which are substantially reproduced in this Convention,

HAVE AGREED AS FOLLOWS:

Article 1

The courts of each Contracting State shall, when applying and interpreting the provisions of the Convention, pay due account to the principles laid down by any relevant decision delivered by courts of the other Contracting States concerning provisions of this Convention.

Article 2

1. The Contracting Parties agree to set up a system of exchange of information concerning judgments delivered pursuant to this Convention as well as relevant judgments under the Brussels Convention. This system shall comprise:

— transmission to a central body by the competent authorities of judgments delivered by courts of last instance and the Court of Justice of the European Communities as well as judgments of particular importance which have become final and have been delivered pursuant to this Convention or the Brussels Convention,

— classification of these judgments by the central body including, as far as necessary, the drawing-up and publication of translations and abstracts,

— communication by the central body of the relevant documents to the competent national authorities of all signatories and acceding States to the Convention and to the Commission of the European Communities.

2. The central body is the Registrar of the Court of Justice of the European Communities.

Article 3

1. A Standing Committee shall be set up for the purposes of this Protocol.

2. The Committee shall be composed of representatives appointed by each signatory and acceding State.

3. The European Communities (Commission, Court of Justice and General Secretariat of the Council) and the European Free Trade Association may attend the meetings as observers.

Article 4

1. At the request of a Contracting Party, the depositary of the Convention shall convene meetings of the Committee for the purpose of exchanging views on the functioning of the Convention and in particular on:

— the development of the case-law as communicated under the first indent of Article 2 (1),

— the application of Article 57 of the Convention.

2. The Committee, in the light of these exchanges, may also examine the appropriateness of starting on particular topics a revision of the Convention and make recommendations.

PROTOCOL 3

on the application of Article 57

THE HIGH CONTRACTING PARTIES HAVE AGREED AS FOLLOWS:

1. For the purposes of the Convention, provisions which, in relation to particular matters, govern jurisdiction or the recognition or enforcement of judgments and which are, or will be contained in acts of the institutions of the European Communities shall be treated in the same way as the conventions referred to in Article 57 (1).

2. If one Contracting State is of the opinion that a provision contained in an act of the institutions of the European Communities is incompatible with the Convention, the Contracting States shall promptly consider amending the Convention pursuant to Article 66, without prejudice to the procedure established by Protocol 2.

DECLARATION

by the representatives of the Governments of the States signatories to the Lugano Convention which are members of the European Communities on Protocol 3 on the application of Article 57 of the Convention

Upon signature of the Convention on jurisdiction and the enforcement of judgments in civil and commercial matters done at Lugano on 16 September 1988,

THE REPRESENTATIVES OF THE GOVERNMENTS OF THE MEMBER STATES OF THE EUROPEAN COMMUNITIES,

taking into account the undertakings entered into *vis-à-vis* the member states of the European Free Trade Association,

anxious not to prejudice the unity of the legal system set up by the Convention,

declare that they will take all measures in their power to ensure, when Community acts referred to in paragraph 1 of Protocol 3 on the application of Article 57 are being drawn up, respect for the rules of jurisdiction and recognition and enforcement of judgments established by the Convention.

In witness whereof the undersigned have signed this Declaration.

Done at Lugano on the sixteenth day of September in the year one thousand nine hundred and eighty-eight.

[This declaration was signed by representatives of Belgium, Denmark, Greece, Italy, Luxembourg, and Portugal.]

DECLARATION

by the Representatives of the Governments of the States signatories to the Lugano Convention which are members of the European Communities

Upon signature of the Convention on jurisdiction and the enforcement of judgments in civil and commercial matters done at Lugano on 16 September 1988,

THE REPRESENTATIVES OF THE GOVERNMENTS OF THE MEMBER STATES OF THE EUROPEAN COMMUNITIES

declare that they consider as appropriate that the Court of Justice of the European Communities, when interpreting the Brussels Convention, pay due account to the rulings contained in the case-law of the Lugano Convention.

In witness whereof the undersigned have signed this Declaration.

Done at Lugano on the sixteenth day of September in the year one thousand nine hundred and eighty-eight.

[Signatures same as above.]

DECLARATION

by the Representatives of the Governments of the States signatories to the Lugano Convention which are members of the European Free Trade Association

Upon signature of the Convention on jurisdiction and the enforcement of judgments in civil and commercial matters done at Lugano on 16 September 1988,

THE REPRESENTATIVES OF THE GOVERNMENTS OF THE MEMBER STATES OF THE EUROPEAN FREE TRADE ASSOCIATION

declare that they consider as appropriate that their courts, when interpreting the Lugano Convention, pay due account to the rulings contained in the case law of the Court of Justice of the European Communities and of courts of the Member States of the European Communities in respect of provisions of the Brussels Convention which are substantially reproduced in the Lugano Convention.

In witness whereof the undersigned have signed this Declaration.

Done at Lugano on the sixteenth day of September in the year one thousand nine hundred and eighty-eight.

[This declaration was signed by representatives of Iceland, Norway, Switzerland, and Sweden.]

Appendix 17

CONVENTION ON THE RECOGNITION AND ENFORCEMENT OF FOREIGN ARBITRAL AWARDS (NEW YORK CONVENTION)

MULTILATERAL

Recognition and Enforcement of Foreign Arbitral Awards[1]

Convention done at New York June 10, 1958;[2]
Accession, with declarations, advised by the Senate of the United States of America October 4, 1968;
Accession, with said declarations, approved by the President of the United States of America September 1, 1970;
Accession of the United States of America, with said declarations, deposited with the Secretary-General of the United Nations September 30, 1970;
Proclaimed by the President of the United States of America December 11, 1970;
Entered into force with respect to the United States of America December 29, 1970.

---

[1] For note by the Department of State, see p. 2561.
[2] Texts as certified by the Secretary-General of the United Nations.

CONVENTION ON THE RECOGNITION AND ENFORCEMENT OF FOREIGN ARBITRAL AWARDS

Article I

1. This Convention shall apply to the recognition and enforcement of arbitral awards made in the territory of a State other than the State where the recognition and enforcement of such awards are sought, and arising out of differences between persons, whether physical or legal. It shall also apply to arbitral awards not considered as domestic awards in the State where their recognition and enforcement are sought.

2. The term "arbitral awards" shall include not only awards made by arbitrators appointed for each case but also those made by permanent arbitral bodies to which the parties have submitted.

3. When signing, ratifying or acceding to this Convention, or notifying extension under article X hereof, any State may on the basis of reciprocity declare that it will apply the Convention to the recognition and enforcement of awards made only in the territory of another Contracting State. It may also declare that it will apply the Convention only to differences arising out of legal relationships, whether contractual or not, which are considered as commercial under the national law of the State making such declaration. [1]

Article II

1. Each Contracting State shall recognize an agreement in writing under which the parties undertake to submit to arbitration all or any differences which have arisen or which may arise between them in respect of a defined legal relationship, whether contractual or not, concerning a subject matter capable of settlement by arbitration.

2. The term "agreement in writing" shall include an arbitral clause in a contract or an arbitration agreement, signed by the parties or contained in an exchange of letters or telegrams.

3. The court of a Contracting State, when seized of an action in a matter in respect of which the parties have made an agreement within the meaning of this article, shall, at the request of one of the parties, refer the parties to arbitration, unless it finds that the said agreement is null and void, inoperative or incapable of being performed.

Article III

Each Contracting State shall recognize arbitral awards as binding and enforce them in accordance with the rules of procedure of the territory where the award is relied upon, under the conditions laid down in the following articles. There shall not be imposed substantially more onerous conditions or higher fees or charges on the recognition or enforcement of arbitral awards to which this Convention applies than are imposed on the recognition or enforcement of domestic arbitral awards.

Article IV

1. To obtain the recognition and enforcement mentioned in the preceding article, the party applying for recognition and enforcement shall, at the time of the application, supply:

(*a*) The duly authenticated original award or a duly certified copy thereof;

(*b*) The original agreement referred to in article II or a duly certified copy thereof.

2. If the said award or agreement is not made in an official language of the country in which the award is relied upon, the party applying for recognition and enforcement of the award shall produce a translation of these documents into such language. The translation shall be certified by an official or sworn translator or by a diplomatic or consular agent.

Article V

1. Recognition and enforcement of the award may be refused, at the request of the party against whom it is invoked, only if that party furnishes to the competent authority where the recognition and enforcement is sought, proof that:

(*a*) The parties to the agreement referred to in article II were, under the law applicable

---

[1] For note by the Department of State, see p. 2561.

to them, under some incapacity, or the said agreement is not valid under the law to which the parties have subjected it or, failing any indication thereon, under the law of the country where the award was made; or

(*b*) The party against whom the award is invoked was not given proper notice of the appointment of the arbitrator or of the arbitration proceedings or was otherwise unable to present his case; or

(*c*) The award deals with a difference not contemplated by or not falling within the terms of the submission to arbitration, or it contains decisions on matters beyond the scope of the submission to arbitration, provided that, if the decisions on matters submitted to arbitration can be separated from those not so submitted, that part of the award which contains decisions on matters submitted to arbitration may be recognized and enforced; or

(*d*) The composition of the arbitral authority or the arbitral procedure was not in accordance with the agreement of the parties, or, failing such agreement, was not in accordance with the law of the country where the arbitration took place; or

(*e*) The award has not yet become binding on the parties, or has been set aside or suspended by a competent authority of the country in which, or under the law of which, that award was made.

2. Recognition and enforcement of an arbitral award may also be refused if the competent authority in the country where recognition and enforcement is sought finds that:

(*a*) The subject matter of the difference is not capable of settlement by arbitration under the law of that country; or

(*b*) The recognition or enforcement of the award would be contrary to the public policy of that country.

Article VI

If an application for the setting aside or suspension of the award has been made to a competent authority referred to in article V (1) (*e*), the authority before which the award is sought to be relied upon may, if it considers it proper, adjourn the decision on the enforcement of the award and may also, on the application of the party claiming enforcement of the award, order the other party to give suitable security.

Article VII

1. The provisions of the present Convention shall not affect the validity of multilateral or bilateral agreements concerning the recognition and enforcement of arbitral awards entered into by the Contracting States nor deprive any interested party of any right he may have to avail himself of an arbitral award in the manner and to the extent allowed by the law or the treaties of the country where such award is sought to be relied upon.

2. The Geneva Protocol on Arbitration Clauses of 1923 and the Geneva Convention on the Execution of Foreign Arbitral Awards of 1927[1] shall cease to have effect between Contracting States on their becoming bound and to the extent that they become bound, by this Convention.

Article VIII

1. This Convention shall be open until 31 December 1958 for signature on behalf of any Member of the United Nations and also on behalf of any other State which is or hereafter becomes a member of any specialized agency of the United Nations, or which is or hereafter becomes a party to the Statute of the International Court of Justice,[2] or any other State to which an invitation has been addressed by the General Assembly of the United Nations.

2. This Convention shall be ratified and the instrument of ratification shall be deposited with the Secretary-General of the United Nations.

Article IX

1. This Convention shall be open for accession to all States referred to in article VIII.

2. Accession shall be effected by the deposit of an instrument of accession with the Secretary-General of the United Nations.

Article X

1. Any State may, at the time of signature, ratification or accession, declare that this Convention shall extend to all or any of the territories for the international relations of which

[1] 27 LNTS 157; 92 LNTS 301.
[2] TS 993; 59 Stat. 1055.

it is responsible. Such a declaration shall take effect when the Convention enters into force for the State concerned.

2. At any time thereafter any such extension shall be made by notification addressed to the Secretary-General of the United Nations and shall take effect as from the ninetieth day after the day of receipt by the Secretary-General of the United Nations of this notification, or as from the date of entry into force of the Convention for the State concerned, whichever is the later.

3. With respect to those territories to which this Convention is not extended at the time of signature, ratification or accession, each State concerned shall consider the possibility of taking the necessary steps in order to extend the application of this Convention to such territories, subject, where necessary for constitutional reasons, to the consent of the Governments of such territories.

Article XI

In the case of a federal or non-unitary State, the following provisions shall apply:

(*a*) With respect to those articles of this Convention that come within the legislative jurisdiction of the federal authority, the obligations of the federal Government shall to this extent be the same as those of Contracting States which are not federal States;

(*b*) With respect to those articles of this Convention that come within the legislative jurisdiction of constituent states or provinces which are not, under the constitutional system of the federation, bound to take legislative action, the federal Government shall bring such articles with a favourable recommendation to the notice of the appropriate authorities of constituent states or provinces at the earliest possible moment;

(*c*) A federal State Party to this Convention shall, at the request of any other Contracting State transmitted through the Secretary-General of the United Nations, supply a statement of the law and practice of the federation and its constituent units in regard to any particular provision of this Convention, showing the extent to which effect has been given to that provision by legislative or other action.

Article XII

1. This Convention shall come into force on the ninetieth day following the date of deposit of the third instrument of ratification or accession.

2. For each State ratifying or acceding to this Convention after the deposit of the third instrument of ratification or accession, this Convention shall enter into force on the ninetieth day after deposit by such State of its instrument of ratification or accession.

Article XIII

1. Any Contracting State may denounce this Convention by a written notification to the Secretary-General of the United Nations. Denunciation shall take effect one year after the date of receipt of the notification by the Secretary-General.

2. Any State which has made a declaration or notification under article X may, at any time thereafter, by notification to the Secretary-General of the United Nations, declare that this Convention shall cease to extend to the territory concerned one year after the date of the receipt of the notification by the Secretary-General.

3. This Convention shall continue to be applicable to arbitral awards in respect of which recognition or enforcement proceedings have been instituted before the denunciation takes effect.

Article XIV

A Contracting State shall not be entitled to avail itself of the present Convention against other Contracting States except to the extent that it is itself bound to apply the Convention.

Article XV

The Secretary-General of the United Nations shall notify the States contemplated in article VIII of the following:

(*a*) Signatures and ratifications in accordance with article VIII;

(*b*) Accessions in accordance with article IX;

(*c*) Declarations and notifications under articles I, X and XI;

(*d*) The date upon which this Convention enters into force in accordance with article XII;

(*e*) Denunciations and notifications in accordance with article XIII.

Article XVI

1. This Convention, of which the Chinese, English, French, Russian and Spanish texts shall be equally authentic, shall be deposited in the archives of the United Nations.

2. The Secretary-General of the United Nations shall transmit a certified copy of this Convention to the States contemplated in article VIII.

Note by the Department of State

List of countries parties to the convention as of December 29, 1970, with texts of declarations and reservations made at the time of signature of the convention or deposit of the instrument of ratification or accession.

Country	Date of deposit of ratification or accession (a)
Austria	May 2, 1961(a)
The Republic of Austria will apply the Convention, in accordance with the first sentence of article I(3) thereof, only to the recognition and enforcement of arbitral awards made in the territory of another Contracting State. [Translation]	
Bulgaria	October 10, 1961
Bulgaria will apply the Convention to recognition and enforcement of awards made in the territory of another contracting State. With regard to awards made in the territory of non-contracting States it will apply the Convention only to the extent to which these States grant reciprocal treatment. [Translation]	
Byelorussian Soviet Socialist Republic	November 15, 1960
The Byelorussian Soviet Socialist Republic will apply the provisions of this Convention in respect to arbitral awards made in the territories of non-contracting States only to the extent to which they grant reciprocal treatment. [Translation]	
Cambodia	January 5, 1960(a)
Central African Republic	October 15, 1962(a)
Referring to the possibility offered by paragraph 3 of article I of the Convention, the Central African Republic declares that it will apply the Convention on the basis of reciprocity, to the recognition and enforcement of awards made only in the territory of another contracting State; it further declares	

Country	Date of deposit of ratification or accession (a)
that it will apply the Convention only to differences arising out of legal relationships, whether contractual or not, which are considered as commercial under its national law. [Translation]	
Ceylon	April 9, 1962
Czechoslovakia	July 10, 1959
"Czechoslovakia will apply the Convention to recognition and enforcement of awards made in the territory of another contracting State. With regard to awards made in the territory of non-contracting States it will apply the Convention only to the extent to which these States grant reciprocal treatment."	
Ecuador	January 3, 1962
Ecuador, on the basis of reciprocity, will apply the Convention to the recognition and enforcement of arbitral awards made in the territory of another contracting State only if such awards have been made with respect to differences arising out of legal relationships which are regarded as commercial under Ecuadorean law. [Translation]	
Finland	January 19, 1962
France [1]	June 26, 1959
Referring to the possibility offered by paragraph 3 of article I of the Convention, France declares that it will apply the Convention on the basis of reciprocity, to the recognition and enforcement of awards made only in the territory of another contracting State; it further declares that it will apply the Convention only to differences arising out of legal relationships, whether contractual or not, which are considered as commercial under its national law. [Translation]	
Germany, Federal Republic of [2]	June 30, 1961
"With respect to paragraph 1 of article I, and in accordance with paragraph 3 of article I of the Convention, the Federal Republic of Germany will apply the Convention only to the recognition and enforcement of awards made in the territory of another Contracting State."	
Ghana	April 9, 1968(a)
Greece	July 16, 1962(a)

1 Extended to all territories of the French Republic.

2 Applicable to Land Berlin.

Country	Date of deposit of ratification or accession (a)
Hungary	March 5, 1962(a)
"... the Hungarian People's Republic shall apply the Convention to the recognition and enforcement of such awards only as have been made in the territory of one of the other Contracting States and are dealing with differences arising in respect of a legal relationship considered by the Hungarian law as a commercial relationship."	
India	July 13, 1960
"In accordance with Article I of the Convention, the Government of India declare that they will apply the Convention to the recognition and enforcement of awards made only in the territory of a State, party to this Convention. They further declare that they will apply the Convention only to differences arising out of legal relationships, whether contractual or not, which are considered as commercial under the Law of India."	
Israel	January 5, 1959
Italy	January 31, 1969(a)
Japan	June 20, 1961(a)
"... it will apply the Convention to the recognition and enforcement of awards made only in the territory of another Contracting State."	
Malagasy Republic	July 16, 1962(a)
The Malagasy Republic declares that it will apply the Convention on the basis of reciprocity, to the recognition and enforcement of awards made only in the territory of another Contracting State; it further declares that it will apply the Convention only to differences arising out of legal relationships, whether contractual or not, which are considered as commercial under its national law. [Translation]	
Morocco	February 12, 1959(a)
The Government of His Majesty the King of Morocco will only apply the Convention to the recognition and enforcement of awards made only in the territory of another contracting State. [Translation]	

Country	Date of deposit of ratification or accession (a)
Netherlands [1]	April 24, 1964
Referring to paragraph 3 of article I of the Convention on the Recognition and Enforcement of Foreign Arbitral Awards, the Government of the Kingdom declares that it will apply the Convention to the recognition and enforcement of awards made only in the territory of another Contracting State. [Translation]	
Niger	October 14, 1964(a)
Nigeria	March 17, 1970(a)
"In accordance with paragraph 3 of article I of the Convention, the Federal Military Government of the Federal Republic of Nigeria declares that it will apply the Convention on the basis of reciprocity to the recognition and enforcement of awards made only in the territory of a State party to this Convention and to differences arising out of legal relationships, whether contractual or not, which are considered as commercial under the Laws of the Federal Republic of Nigeria."	
Norway	March 14, 1961(a)
"1. We will apply the Convention only to the recognition and enforcement of awards made in the territory of one of the Contracting States." "2. We will not apply the Convention to differences where the subject matter of the proceedings is immovable property situated in Norway, or a right in or to such property."	
Philippines	July 6, 1967
". . . the Philippines, on the basis of reciprocity, will apply the Convention to the recognition and enforcement of awards made only in the territory of another Contracting State and only to differences arising out of legal relationships, whether contractual or not, which are considered as commercial under the national law of the State making such declaration."	
Poland	October 3, 1961
"With reservations as mentioned in article I, par. 3."	

[1] Applicable to the Kingdom in Europe, Surinam and the Netherlands Antilles.

Country	Date of deposit of ratification or accession (a)
Romania	September 13, 1961(a)
The Romanian People's Republic will apply the Convention only to differences arising out of legal relationships, whether contractual or not, which are considered as commercial under its legislation. The Romanian People's Republic will apply the Convention to the recognition and enforcement of awards made in the territory of another Contracting State. As regards awards made in the territory of certain non-contracting States, the Romanian People's Republic will apply the Convention only on the basis of reciprocity established by joint agreement between the parties. [Translation]	
Switzerland	June 1, 1965
Referring to the possibility offered by paragraph 3 of article I, Switzerland will apply the Convention to the recognition and enforcement of awards made only in the territory of another Contracting State. [Translation]	
Syria	March 9, 1959(a)
Tanzania	October 13, 1964(a)
"The Government of the United Republic of Tanganyika and Zanzibar will apply the Convention, in accordance with the first sentence of article 1(3) thereof, only to the recognition and enforcement of awards made in the territory of another Contracting State."	
Thailand	December 21, 1959(a)
Trinidad and Tobago	February 14, 1966(a)
"In accordance with Article I of the Convention, the Government of Trinidad and Tobago declares that it will apply the Convention to the recognition and enforcement of awards made only in the territory of another Contracting State. The Government of Trinidad and Tobago further declares that it will apply the Convention only to differences arising out of legal relationships, whether contracted or not, which are considered as commercial under the Law of Trinidad and Tobago."	

Country	Date of deposit of ratification or accession (a)
Tunisia	July 17, 1967(a)

. . . with the reservations provided for in article I, paragraph 3, of the Convention, that is to say, the Tunisian State will apply the Convention to the recognition and enforcement of awards made only in the territory of another Contracting State and only to differences arising out of legal relationships, whether contractual or not, which are considered as commercial under Tunisian law. [Translation]

Ukranian Soviet Socialist Republic	October 10, 1960

The Ukrainian Soviet Socialist Republic will apply the provisions of this Convention in respect to arbitral awards made in the territories of non-contracting States only to the extent to which they grant reciprocal treatment. [Translation]

Union of Soviet Socialist Republics	August 24, 1960

The Union of Soviet Socialist Republics will apply the provisions of this Convention in respect to arbitral awards made in the territories of non-contracting States only to the extent to which they grant reciprocal treatment. [Translation]

United Arab Republic	March 9, 1959(a)
United States of America [1]	September 30, 1970(a)

"The United States of America will apply the Convention, on the basis of reciprocity, to the recognition and enforcement of only those awards made in the territory of another Contracting State."

"The United States of America will apply the Convention only to differences arising out of legal relationships, whether contractual or not, which are considered as commercial under the national law of the United States."

[1] Extended to all the territories for the international relations of which the United States of America is responsible, with effect from Feb. 1, 1971.

Appendix 18

SERVICE OF PROCESS IN JAPAN

State Department Circular

DISCLAIMER: THE INFORMATION IN THIS CIRCULAR RELATING TO THE LEGAL REQUIREMENTS OF SPECIFIC FOREIGN COUNTRIES IS PROVIDED FOR GENERAL INFORMATION ONLY AND MAY NOT BE TOTALLY ACCURATE IN A PARTICULAR CASE. QUESTIONS INVOLVING INTERPRETATION OF SPECIFIC FOREIGN LAWS SHOULD BE ADDRESSED TO FOREIGN COUNSEL.

Summary of Methods of Service: (1) Hague Service Convention service by Japanese Central Authority; (2) Service by International Registered Mail (but see note regarding Japanese Statement to the Hague Conference on this Subject and case law) below; (3) Direct Personal Service by an Agent generally is not permitted in Japan; (4) Waiver of Service: Persons willing to waive service may execute an acknowledgement or affidavit before a U.S. consul in Japan. Note: the use of methods (2), (3) or (4) is not recommended if eventual enforcement of an American judgment in Japan is contemplated.

Hague Convention on the Service Abroad of Judicial and Extrajudicial Documents in Civil and Commercial Matters (20 UST 361; TIAS 6638). Japan and the U.S. are parties to the treaty. The text of the treaty, which is largely self-explanatory, is also published in the Law Digest Volume of the Martindale-Hubbell Law Directory under the heading, "Selected International Conventions". See Rule 4(f), F.R. Cv. P. and Commentaries and C4-25 - C4-34 p. 152-168 C4-24, and Pocket Part p. 63-71 (1996). See also, Ristau, Int'l Judicial Assistance, Civil and Commercial, Int'l Law Institute, Vol. 1, Sec. 4-1-1 - 4-5-2, pp. 107-156 (1995 supp.); Epstein, International Litigation: A Guide to Jurisdiction, Practice and Strategy, Prentice Hall Law & Business, 1994 supp., Sec. 4.04, p. 4-10 - 4-24; and Born & Westin, International Civil Litigation in United States Courts, (1989), p. 136-169.

How the Convention Works: The Hague Service Convention provides a convenient method of obtaining service by a foreign judicial authority. Article 5 of the Convention also permits service by a method requested by the applicant, provided that it is compatible with local law. Article 10 provides for service by mail and for service by local foreign judicial officers. See Martindale-Hubbell for declarations and reservations of countries party to the Convention.

Japanese Central Authority: Ministry of Foreign Affairs, 2-2-1 Kasumigaseki, Chiyoda Ku, Tokyo 100, Japan; tel: 011-81-3-3580-3311 ext. 2306; fax: 011-81-3-3581-7209 (direct fax to attn: Division for the Protection of Japanese Nationals Overseas, Consular and Migration Affairs Department.)

Completing the Convention Forms: Obtain two copies of the "Request for Service" form (USM-94) from any U.S. Marshal's office. The form is also reprinted as an annex to the Convention in Martindale-Hubbell; Ristau, Vol. 1, Sec. 4-2-3, p. 127-129 (1995 supp.); Epstein, App. 33-35; and Born & Westin, Appendix C. See also Memo No. 386, Revision No. 3, at the U.S. Marshal's office or at 16 Int'l Leg. Mat. 1331, (1977). Service by the foreign central authority is requested by sending in duplicate (one original, one copy) the completed forms, the documents to be served and any appropriate translations of the documents to be served directly to a foreign central authority. See also "Methods of Service" below regarding completing the forms.

Page 1, Identity and Address of the Applicant: Effective February 26, 1983, pursuant to Public Law 97-462 (96 Stat. 2527, 28 U.S.C. Fed. R. Civ. P., Rule 4(c)(2), West, 1996 Pocket Part) the U.S. Marshal no longer transmits Form USM-94 directly to the foreign central authority. Rather, the attorney representing the person seeking service should execute the portion of Form USM-94 marked "Identity and Address of the Applicant" and the portion of the "Summary of the Document to be Served". (Department of Justice Memo dtd 2/15/83 to all United States Marshals.) In addition to the name and address of applicant, it is useful to include a telephone and fax number, see Ristau, Vol. 1, Sec. 4-2-3, p. 131 (1995 supp.).

Annotate Form Re Statutory Authority of Applicant: Foreign central authorities have been advised that private American lawyers are authorized generally by U.S. law to effect service, and that Article 3 of the Convention permits counsel to complete the Convention request forms. See Report of U.S. Delegation, reprinted in 17 Int'l Leg. Mat. at 316 (1978); U.S. Department of Justice Memorandum No. 386 at 14, reprinted in 16 Int'l Leg. Mat. 1331, 1335 (1977); excerpted in Digest of U.S. Practice in International Law, Department of State, Office of the Legal Adviser, 1977, pp. 484, 485-490. Nevertheless, some foreign central authorities continue to reject requests completed by attorneys unless the request form cites the specific U.S. or state law authorizing attorneys to serve process. See Report of the Special Commission on the Operation of Hague Conventions, August 1989, 28 Int'l. Leg. Mat. 1556 (1989); Epstein, App-52 (IV. Forwarding Authorities). A reference to the statutory authority to serve the document should appear prominently on the request form (there is no designated space for this), stating that "service is requested pursuant to Rule 4(c)(2), U.S. Federal Rules of Civil Procedure" which authorizes any person who is not a party and is not less than 18 years of age to serve a summons and complaint. Requests for service in matters pending in state courts should specify that the request is made pursuant to Rule 4(c)(2) of the U.S. Federal Rules of Civil Procedure and any pertinent state law.

Page 1, Address of Receiving Authority: **The receiving Authority is the Japanese central** authority listed above.

Page 1, Signature, Done at: The applicant dates and signs the signature block on the Request form. No seal/stamp needed.

Page 2, Certificate: Do not complete this part of the USM-94. This is the proof of service which will be completed by the Japanese central authority after service is effected. This page should be forwarded blank, together with the completed portion of the USM-94 to the Japanese Central Authority.

Page 3, Summary of the Document to be Served: The applicant should also complete this part of the USM-94. Name and address of the requesting authority is that of the applicant, generally the attorney (Rule 4(c)(2) F.R. Cv. P.) as explained above. For a sample completed form, see the U.S. Marshal's Memo 386, 16 I.L.M. 1331 et seq. (1977) and Epstein, App. 37-339.

Transmitting the Request: The completed request form and documents to be served and accompanying translation of the documents to be served, in duplicate (one original, one copy), should be mailed directly to the foreign central authority as provided by Article 3. No translation of the form itself is required. See note below regarding translation requirements.

Time Frame: The U.S. at Tokyo advises that service by the Government of Japan is generally accomplished within approximately one month from the date of receipt of the request by the central authority when the person or entity to be served resides in the Tokyo area. If outside the Tokyo area, service is generally made within about two months after receipt by the Ministry of Foreign Affairs. The Convention does not impose an obligatory time frame. Most countries take 30-90 days to effect service. Article 15, second full paragraph, sub-para (b) implies that the maximum time frame is 6 months. See Ristau, Vol. 1, Sec. 4-3-2, p. 145, 146, (1995 supp.).

Status Reports: Two months after the request was sent to the Japanese central authority, you may call the Ministry directly to inquire about the status of the request. Faxing a status inquiry in Japanese attaching a copy of the original request form may expedite a status report. Include your phone and fax numbers and address. In addition, you may wish to contact the Japanese Embassy or Consulate nearest you in the United States to learn if the executed requested has received from the Ministry for forwarding to the applicant (see below, Proof of Service). The Consular Section of the Embassy of Japan is located at 2520 Massachusetts Avenue, N.W., Washington, D.C. 20008, tel: 202-939-6700. There are Japanese Consulates in Anchorage, Los Angeles, San Francisco (http://www.infojapan.com:80/cgjsf/), Miami, Atlanta (http://cgjapanatlanta.org/), Guam, Honolulu, Chicago,New Orleans, Boston, Detroit, Kansas City, New York (http://ny.cgj.org:80/index.html), Portland, Houston, and Seattle. For a list of the state jurisdictions of Japanese Consulates in the U.S. see http://ny.cgj.org:80/gi/gi 2.html.

Proof of Service: On the reverse of the "Request for Service" form is a "Certificate of Service". After service has been effected, the certificate, which constitutes proof of service, is completed by the Japanese central authority and returned to the applicant through the nearest Japanese consulate in the United States noted above. See Ristau, Vol. 1, Sec. 4-3-4, p. 147-148 (1995 Supp.), Epstein, Sec. 4.04(2), p. 4-14 (1994 ed.), and Born & Westin, 142.

Translations: The Convention does not require that the "Request for Service" form itself be translated so long as it is completed in English or French. See Taylor v. Uniden Corp. of American, 622 F. Supp. 1011 (E.D. Mo. 1985). However, some applicants have found it useful to translate the request form together with the documents to be served to expedite service. This is not required, so applicants may wish to use their own judgment in this matter. The Convention is more specific on the matter of translation of the actual documents to be served (for example, summons and complaint). Japan did not make a specific reservation regarding translations at the time it deposited its instruments of accession to the Convention. However, in response to a questionnaire circulated in 1978 by the Secretariat of the Hague Conference on Private International Law to all Central Authorities as to internal law or practice concerning language requirements, Japan replied that a translation is required. Unless the party to be served will accept service voluntarily, the documents to be served must be accompanied by a translation into Japanese. A document not accompanied by a translation will be returned to the applicant with the request to attach the required translation. See Hague Convention Handbook, 1992 edition, p. 84.1.

See Ristau, Vol. 1, Sec. 4-2-3(5), p. 133-138 (1995 supp.); Epstein, Sec. 4.04(1), p. 4-13 (1994 ed.).; and Born & Westin, 140. See, Greenfield v. Suzuki, 776 F. Supp. 698 (E.D.N.Y. 1991).

1 Practical Handbook on the Operation of the Hague Convention of 15 November 1965 on the Service Abroad of Judicial and ExtraJudicial Documents in Civil or Commercial Matters, 2d, 1992, p. 42-43 (Special Positions of the United States and Japan); p. 134 (Japan - Transmission Through Postal Channels). Publisher: MAKLU Uitgevers, N.V., Koninginnelaan 96, Postbus 960, 7301 BE Apeldoorn, Netherlands. U.S. Distributor: Butterworth Publishers Inc., 10 Tower Office Park, Woburn, Boston, Massachusetts 01801 (also Newton Upper Falls, MA; Austin, TX; Redmond, WA, St. Paul, MN; and D & S Publishers, Clearwater, FL.

Several lower U.S. courts have quashed service abroad under Article 5(a) of the Convention due to lack of translations, see Vorhees v. Fischer & Krecke, 697 F. 2d 574 (4th Cir. 1983); Harris v. Browning-Ferris Indus. Chem. Serv., 100 F.R.D. 775 (MD. La. 1984). Courts also have held that the translation requirement only applied when the document was served by the Central Authority and not direct postal service or other method of service (Lemme v. Wine of Japan Import, Inc., 631 F. Supp. 456, 463-64 (E.D.N.Y. 1986); but see Teknekron Management, Inc., v. Quante Ternmeldetechnik, 115 F.R.D. 175 (D. Nev. 1987), service in Germany was held defective where plaintiff failed to translate a lengthy contract which was attached an exhibit to the complaint.)

Costs: There are generally no costs incurred in connection with service through the central authority under the Convention. However, if personal service is made and the person to be served resides in some remote location, some fees may be charged. The fees will be billed to the applicant. See Ristau, Vol. 1, Sec. 4-3-3, p. 146-147 (1995).

Service on the U.S. Military in Japan: It is possible to effect service on members of the U.S. Armed Forces in Japan through the Japanese central authority. See also our general flyer, "Service of Process Abroad" (See "Additional Information" below). Service by mail may also be used if state law permits (APO and FPO are U.S. mail). Also, contact the Judge Advocate General's (JAG) Office at the Pentagon for the particular branch of the service (tel: 703-545-6700).

Methods of Service

1. Article 5(a) - Service in Accordance with Japanese Internal Law: To effect service under Article 5 (a) of the Convention, delete methods (b) and (c) of the Request for Service form (USM-94) and indicate method (a).

2. Article 5, paragraph 2 - Voluntary Service: Useful only if the person to be served is willing to be served. The local court clerk in Japan will notiry the person to be served who may then pick up the documents at the court or request that they be forwarded by registered mail. This method of service may be requested by striking out methods (a) and (b) and indicating method (c) on the "Request for Service" form (USM-94). See Greenfield v. Suzuki, 776 F. Supp. 698 (E.D.N.Y. 1991). Translation of the documents to be served is not required using this method.

3. Article 5(b) - Personal Service: Strike out methods (a) and (c) on the "Request for Service" form and indicate method (b), noting that the documents should be served personally upon the person or company to be served.

4. Articles 8 and 9 - Service by Diplomatic or Consular Channels: While Japan has not declared that it objects to service by consular or diplomatic channels on its territory (Articles 8 and 9), U.S. Foreign Service officers are prohibited by Federal regulation (22 CFR 92.85) from serving process on behalf of private litigants or appointing others to do so, notwithstanding state law to the contrary.

5. Article 10(b) and (c) - Service By Judicial Officer in Requested Foreign State: On ratification, Japan declared that it objects to the use of the methods of service referred to in Article 10, sub-paragraphs b and c.

6. Article 10(a) - Service by Mail: At a meeting of the Hague Conference on Private International Law Special Commission April 17-20, 1989 the Japanese delegation issued a statement regarding service by postal channels. See 28 Int'l Leg. Mat. 1556 (1989)and Hague Service Convention Practical Handbook, 1992 ed., p. 134. The text of the Japanese statement to the Special Commission is as follows:

"Japanese position on Article 10(a) of the Hague Convention on the Service Abroad of Judicial and Extrajudicial Documents in Civil or Commercial Matters" Japan has not declared that it objects to the sending of judicial documents, by postal channels, directly to persons abroad. In this connection, Japan (in the statement by its representative to the Special Commission of April 1989 on the operation of the Conventions on the Service of Documents Abroad and on the Taking of Evidence Abroad) has made it clear that no objection to the use of postal channels for sending judicial documents to persons in Japan does not necessarily imply that the sending by such a method is considered valid service in Japan; it merely indicates that Japan does not consider it as an infringement of its sovereign power."

Based on this statement of the Japanese Government, it appears that service by mail is possible, but that persons wishing to enforce a judgment issued by a court in the United States might encounter problems in Japan if service were accomplished by mail. (See March 14, 1991, the Department of State, Office of the Legal Adviser ltr to the Administrative Office of the U.S. Courts and the National Center for State Courts regarding this case, 30 Int'l Leg. Mat. 260 (1991).)

But see, FTC v. Compagnie de Saint Gobain-Pont-a-Mousson, 636 F.2d 1300 (D.C. Cir. 1980) on the issue of service via international registered mail when the document to be served is compulsory or punitive and when there is a treaty obligation to refrain from such methods of service. See also, Nash, Digest of United States Practice in International Law, Department of State, Office of the Legal Adviser, 1980 p. 452, 457 (1986).

Historical Background: In 1970, when Japan became a party to the Hague Service Convention it did not formally object to, or make any reservation or declaration concerning Article 10(a) in the manner prescribed by the Convention. See Ristau, Vol. 1, Sec. 4-1-6, p. 121.6 (1995 Supp.). This gave rise to numerous questions regarding the sufficiency of such service and the ability to enforce a judgment in Japan. See 12 International Lawyer 503 (1978) for a copy of correspondence from the Legal Attache of the Embassy of Japan to the Chairman, Publication Committee, Section of International Law of the American Bar Association on the subject of service of documents in Japan.

On April 15, 1983, the Embassy of Japan informed the U.S. Department of State that the Japanese Government considers that the service of documents directly upon a person residing within the territory of Japan constitutes an exercise of the jurisdiction of the United States within the territory of Japan, and that the U.S. Government is required to seek approval of the Government of Japan before taking such measures. The Government of Japan does not recognize any legal effect of the unauthorized service. (Embassy of Japan Note No. E-29 dtd 4/15/83, to be found at Department of State File No. P830057-0145.)

Over the past several years several cases in the United States have been decided in which the courts, noting the use of the verb "to send" in Article 10(a) whereas other provisions of the Convention including Article 10(b) and (c) refer to "service" of documents. Some courts have concluded that the Convention does not permit "service of judicial documents by mail". Other courts have concluded that the Convention does permit such service. See Ristau, Vol. 1, Sec. 4-3-5, p. 150,151.1, (1995 Supp.); Born & Westin, p. 156-160; and Epstein, p. 4-14-4-18. Courts in the U.S. continue to confront this issue.[2]

2 Selected Cases: Gapanovich v. Komori Corp., Superior Court of New Jersey, Appellate Division, No. Z-1045-91T3, April 14, 1992). Anabe v. Kikuchi, 141 F.R.D. 498 (D. Hawaii 1992). Fleming v. Yamaha Motor Corp. USA, 744 F. Supp. (W.D. Va. 1991). Greenfield v. Suzuki, 776 F. Supp. 698 (E.D.N.Y. 1991). Patty v. Toyota Motor Corp, 777 F. Supp. 956 (N.D. Ga. 1991). Wilson v. Honda Motor Co. Ltd., 776 F. Supp. 339 (E.D. Tenn. 1991). Cintron v. W. & D. Machinery Co., 182 N.J. Super. 126, 440 A. 2d 1242 (1990). Bankston v. Toyota Motor Corp., 889 Fed. Rptr, 2d Series, 172 (8th Cir. 1989). McClenon v. Nissan Motor Corp., 726 F. Supp. 822 (N.D. Fla. 1989). Nicholson v. Yamaha Motor Co., 80 Md. App. 695, 702, 566 A. 2d 135, 139 (Md. Ct. Spec. App. 1989), cert. denied, 318 Md. 683, 569 A. 2d 1242 (1990). Meyers v. ASICS Corp., 711 F. Supp. 1001 (C.D. Cal. 1989). Montgomery, Zukerman, Davis, Inc., v. Diepenbrock, 698 F. Supp. 1453 (S.D. Ind. 1988). Smith v. Dainichi Kinzoku Koguy Co., 680 F. Supp. 847 (W.D. Tex 1988). Truick v. Yamaha Motor Corp. 121 F.R.D. 32 (S.D.N.Y. 1988). Hantover, Inc. v. Omet, 688 F. Supp 1377 (W.D. Mo. 1988). In re Mandukich, 87 Bankr. 296 (Bankr. S.D.N.Y. 1988). Suzuki Motor Co. v. Superior Court, 200 Cal. App. 3d 1476, 249 Cal. Rptr. 376 (1988). Rissew v. Yamaha Motor Co., 129 A.D. 2d 94, 515 N.Y.S. 2d 352 (N.Y. App. Div. 1987). Sandoval v. Honda Motor Co., 364 Pa. Super. 136, 527 A. 2d 564 (1987). Prost v. Honda Motor Co., 122 F.R.D. 215 (E.D. Mo. 1987). Newport Components, Inc., v. NEC Home Electronics, Inc., 671 F. Supp. 1525, 1541 (C.D. Cal. 1987). Cooper v. Makita Electric Works Ltd., 117 F.R.D. 16, (1987). Lemme v. Wine of Japan Import, Inc., 631 F. Supp. 456 (E.D.N.Y. 1986). Ackermann v. Levine, 788 F. 2d 830, 839 (2d Cir. 1986). Zisman v. Sieger, 106 F.R.D. 194 (N.D. Ill. 1985). Pochop v. Toyota Motor Co. Ltd., 111 F.R.D. 464 (1986). Reynolds v. Woosup Koh, 109 A.D. 2d 97, 490 N.Y.S. 2d 295 (N.Y. App. Div. 1985). Mommsen v. Toro Co., 108 F.R.D. 444, 446 (S.D. Iowa 1985). Ormandy v. Lynn, 472 N.Y.S. 2d (NY.S. Sup. Ct. 1984). Weight v. Kawasaki Heavy Ind., 597 F. Supp. 1082 (E.D. Va. 1984). Chrysler Corp v. General Motors Corp., 589 F. Supp. 1182 (D.D.C. 1984). Russello v. United States, 464 U.S. 16, 23, 104 S. Ct. 296, 300, 78 L. Ed. 2d (1983). Dr. Ing H.C.F. Porsche A.G. v. Superior Court, 123 Cal. App. 3d 755, 177 Cal. Rptr. 155 (1981). Consumer Prod. Safety Comm'n v. GTE Sylvania, Inc., 447 U.S. 102, 108, 100 S. Ct. 2051, 2056, 64 L. Ed. 2d 766 (1980). Kadata v. Hosogai, 125 Ariz. 131; 608 P. 2d 68, 74 (Ariz. App. 1980). Tamari v. Bache & Co. (Lebanon) S.A.L., 431 F. Supp. 1226 (N.D. Ill.), aff'd, 565 F. 2d 1194 (7th Cir. 1977), cert. denied, 435 U.S. 905 (1978). Shoei Kako v. Superior Court, 33 Cal. App. 3d 810; 109 Cal. Rptr. 402 (1973).

Selected Bibliography

Ehrenzweig, Ikehara & Jensen, American-Japanese Private International Law, Bilateral Studies in Private International Law, Parker School of Foreign and Comparative Law, Columbia University, Oceana Publications, 34-40 (1964).

Fujita, Service of American Process Upon Japanese Nationals by Registered Airmail and Enforceability of Resulting American Judgments in Japan, 12 Law in Japan 68, 73 (1985).

Gordon, Service of Process by Registered Mail on a Japanese Defendant is Ineffective Under Article 10(a) of the Hague Convention of November 15, 1965 on Service Abroad of Judicial and Extrajudicial Documents in Civil and Commercial Matters, Bankston v. Toyota Motor Corp., 889 F. 2d 172 (8th Cir. 1989), Vand. J. Transnat'l L., Vol. 23, No. 4, p. 851, (1990).

Hamilton, An Interpretation of the Hague Convention on the Service of Process Abroad of Judicial and Extra-Judicial Documents Concerning Personal Service in Japan, 6 Loy. L.A. Int'l & Comp. L.J. 143 (1983).

Harada, Civil Discovery Under Japanese Law, 16 Law In Japan 21 (1983).

Hattori & Henderson, Civil Procedure in Japan, Sec. 11.02(1), (1985).

Jorden, Beyond Jingoism: Service By Mail to Japan and the Hague Convention on the Service Abroad of Judicial and Extrajudicial Documents in Civil or Commercial Matters, 16 Law in Japan 69 (1983).

Kenadjian, R. Wohl, S. Chemtob, & G. Fukushima, Practice By Foreign Lawyers in Japan, Fordham International Law Journal, Vol. 13, No. 3, pp. 390-404, (1989-1990).

Kim & Sisneros, Comparative Overview of Service of Process: United States, Japan and Attempts at International Unity, 23 Vand. J. Transnat'l L. 299, 319 (1990).

Koroyasu, Transnational Litigation: Perspectives from the U.S. and Abroad: Japan, 18 Int'l Law. 785 (1984).

MacMullin, Foreign Attorneys in Japan: Past Policies, The New Special Measures Law and Future Expectations, Florida International Law Journal, Vol. 4, No. 1, pp. 51-84, (1988).

Matsuo, Jurisdiction in Transnational Cases, Int'l Law., Vol. 23, No. 1, p. 6, (1989).

Mitsui, "Ratification of Convention Relating to Civil Procedure on the Service Abroad of Judicial and Extra-Judicial Documents in Civil and Commercial Matters", 16 Japanese Annual Int'l. L. 7 (1972).

Mori, The Difference Between U.S. Discovery and Japanese Taking of Evidence, 23 Int'l Law. 3 (1989).

McDowell, Digest of United States Practice in International Law, Department of State, Office of the Legal Adviser, 1976, p. 318-320 (1977).

Nash, Digest of United States Practice in International Law, Department of State, Office of the Legal Adviser, 500-501, (1977).

Nash, Digest of United States Practice in International Law, Department of State, Office of the Legal Adviser, 1978, pp. 856, 857; 865-870, (1980).

Nash, Cumulative Digest of United States Practice in International Law, 1981-1988, Vol. II, Department of State, Office of the Legal Adviser, p. 1430-1441, (1994).

Note, Recognition and Enforcement of Foreign Judgment (First District Court, Munich, Federal Republic of Germany) - Judgment Rendered by Munchen Landgericht I - Conditions for Recognition of Foreign Judgment (Art. 200, C.C.P.) - Jurisdiction of the Foreign Court - Proper Law to Determine the Validity of Jurisdictional Agreement - Interpretation of "as long as" Clause - Foreign Judgment by Default - Public Order - Guarantee for Reciprocal Recognition, Nagoya District Court, Judgment, February 6, 1987; H.J. (1236) 113 (1987), H.T. (627) 244 The Japanese Annual of International Law, 1990, No. 33, p. 189, (1987).

Note, Effect of Foreign Judgment - Divorce between Japanese Spouses - Pronounced by a California Court (Superior Court, Los Angeles County, California, U.S.A.) - Service by Mail from California Court and Article 200(2), Code of Civil Procedure - Recognition (Denied), Tokyo District Court, Judgment, November 11, 1988; H.T. (703) 271, The Japanese Annual of International Law, 1990, No. 33, p. 208, (1989).

Note, Private International Law - Enforcement of Foreign (U.S. District Court, District of Columbia, U.S.A.) Judgment - Public Order - Reciprocity (Mutual Guarantee), Supreme Court of Japan, June 7, 1983, Supreme Court Civil Reports, Vol. 37, No. 5, pp. 611 et seq., The Japanese Annual of International Law, No. 27, p. 119, (1984).

Note, Private International Law - Enforcement of Foreign (U.S. District Court, District of Columbia, U.S.A.) Judgment - Public Order - Reciprocity (Mutual Guarantee), Tokyo High Court, March 31, 1982, The Japanese Annual of International Law, No. 27, p. 136, (1984).

Note, Private International Law - The Requisites for Recognition of a Foreign Judgment (U.S. District Court, District of Columbia, U.S.A.), Tokyo District Court, September 17, 1979, The Japanese Annual of International Law, No. 24, p. 196, (1981).

Note, Execution of Foreign Judgment (Paris Commercial Court) - Jurisdiction of Foreign Court - Place Where Obligation Performable Not Sufficient Connection to Establish Jurisdiction, Tokyo District Court, May 2, 1972, The Japanese Annual of International Law, No. 18, p. 209, (1974).

Note, Foreign Judgment of Divorce - Invalidity - Compliance with Requirements regarding Enforcement of Foreign Judgment (First Civil Court of Bravos District, Chihuahua, Republic of Mexico), Tokyo District Court, December 17, 1971, The Japanese Annual of International Law, No. 17, p. 212, (1973).

Note, International Law - Contracts - Judgment of Foreign Court (Superior Court of Los Angeles County, California, U.S.A.) - Compatibility with Public Order or Good Morals, Tokyo District Court, September 6, 1969, The Japanese Annual of International Law, No. 15, p. 181, (1971).

Note, Private International Law - Enforcement of New York Arbitral Award - The New York Convention on the Recognition and Enforcement of Foreign Arbitral Awards of 1958 (Article 5) - Burden of Proving Conditions to deny Recognition, Osaka District Court, April 22, 1983, The Japanese Annual of International Law, No. 27, p. 184, (1984).

Ohara, Judicial Assistance for Proceedings in the U.S., Int'l. Law., Vol. 23, No. 1, p. 10 (1989).

Peterson, Jurisdiction and the Japanese Defendant, 25 Santa Clara L. Rev. 555, 576-79 (1985).

Ramseyer, Lawyers, Foreign Lawyers, and Lawyer-Substitutes: The Market for Regulation in Japan, Harvard International Law Journal, Vol. 27, pp. 499-539, (1986).

Routh, Litigation Between Japanese and American Parties, in Current Legal Aspects of Doing Business in Japan and East Asia 188, 190-91 (J.O. Hailey ed. 1978).

Sakai & Pickard, Service of Process on a Japanese Defendant to Commence a Foreign Lawsuit, Yuasa and Hara Patent News, Summer 1978, at 5 (English Ed.)

Sawaki, Recognition and Enforcement of Foreign Judgments, Int'l Law., Vol. 23, No. 1, p. 29, (1989).

Sheeney, Japan's New Foreign Lawyer Law, Law and Policy in International Business, Vol. 19, No. 2, p. 361-383, (1987).

Symposium: Japanese Law and Practice in Transnational Litigation, Int'l Law., Vol. 23, No. 1, p. 1, (1989).

Tada, Role of Corporate Legal Departments in Japan, Int'l. Law., Vol. 22, No. 4, pp. 1141-1144, (1988).

Takaishi, Hirakawa and Tomatsu, International Civil Litigation Over Securities-Related Disputes in Japan, Hastings International and Comparative Law Review, Vol. 14, No. 2, 423, (1991).

Takakuwa, A. - Service of documents and taking of evidence in transnational civil cases in Japan; Hoso Jiho, Vol. 37, No. 4, p. 1.

Yamaoka, Address, Letters Rogatory, A Symposium Before the Consular Law Society, (Bernard Grossman, ed.), p. 22-34, (1956).

Yamanouchi and Cohen, Understanding the Incidence of Litigation in Japan: A Structural Analysis, Int'l Law., Vol. 25, No. 2, p. 443, (1991).

Additional Information: We have general flyers and other country specific flyers on judicial assistance many of which are available through our automated fax system or via our Home Page on the Internet.

Using the Autofax System: Dial (202) 647-3000 using the phone on your fax machine. If you know the number of the document you want, simply enter the four digit code immediately after you are connected to the service, then follow the prompts and you will receive the document. If you do not know the number of the document you need, follow the initial prompt to obtain a printed index of judicial assistance topics. There are four indexes.

1. Travel Information - Index of Countries - Press 1;
2. Passports and Visas - Index of Flyers - Press 2;
3. Judicial Assistance - General/ Country Specific - Press 3;
4. Child Custody and Adoption - Index of Flyers - Press 4.

* Enter the four digit code for the document desired as listed in the index.;

* When the prompt identifies the document and asks if you want that document, enter Y (9) for yes or N (6) for no;

* If you want another document, enter the four digit code, using the same procedures noted in the previous step;

* When you finish selecting, press the # key on the phone keyboard and press the start button on your fax machine;

* Hang up the phone; After a brief delay of up to a minute, the documents will print automatically on your fax machine.

Autofax General Judicial Assistance Codes:

1051 - Hague Service
1049 - Service of Process - General
1045 - Preparation of Letters Rogatory - General
1069 - Service in Japan
1068 - Obtaining Evidence in Japan
1053 - Hague Legalization of Documents

Using the Internet: Many of our judicial assistance flyers are also available on the Internet via the Department of State, Bureau of Consular Affairs Home Page **http://travel.state.gov** under the heading "International Legal Assistance". This is also accessible through the main State Department Home Page at **http://www.state.gov/** under Consular, Travel or International Legal Services. See also, the Department of State, Office of the Legal Adviser for Private International Law (L/PIL) Home Page **http//www.lpil.com**. See also the Home Pages for many of our embassies which are linked to the Consular Affairs Home Page. As noted above, the text of the Convention and updated information concerning countries which have acceded to the Convention can be found in the Martindale-Hubbell Law Directory, Law Digest Volume. See the Martindale-Hubbell Home Page **http://www.martindale.com/products/digests.html**. For the United Nations Treaty Database via the Internet see **http://www.un.org/Depts/Treaty/** or **http://www.un.org/**.

Questions: Contact our East Asia and Pacific Division at (202) 647-5226 or (202) 647-6769. Questions may also be addressed to the U.S. Central Authority: Office of International Judicial Assistance, Civil Division, Department of Justice, Washington, D.C. 20530, (202) 307-0983.

Appendix 19

OBTAINING EVIDENCE IN JAPAN

State Department Circular

DISCLAIMER: THE INFORMATION IN THIS CIRCULAR RELATING TO THE LEGAL REQUIREMENTS OF SPECIFIC FOREIGN COUNTRIES IS PROVIDED FOR GENERAL INFORMATION ONLY AND MAY NOT BE TOTALLY ACCURATE IN A PARTICULAR CASE. QUESTIONS INVOLVING INTERPRETATION OF SPECIFIC FOREIGN LAWS SHOULD BE ADDRESSED TO FOREIGN COUNSEL.

PROVISO: THE PURPOSE OF THIS FLYER IS TO PROVIDE GENERAL INFORMATION ABOUT PROCEDURES FOR OBTAINING EVIDENCE IN JAPAN. THE INFORMATION IN THIS FLYER IS BASED ON EXTENSIVE DISCUSSIONS BETWEEN THE STATE DEPARTMENT AND THE JAPANESE EMBASSY REGARDING JAPAN'S INTERPRETATION OF APPLICABLE TREATIES AND OTHER INTERNATIONAL CONVENTIONS, AND JAPANESE LAW AND REGULATIONS. THIS IS AN INFORMATIONAL FLYER, NOT A LEGAL OPINION, AND IS NOT INTENDED TO TAKE A POSITION ON ANY ASPECT OF LITIGATION.

General Summary: It is our understanding that Japanese law permits the taking of a deposition of a willing witness for use by a court in the United States only if the deposition is presided over by a U.S. consular officer pursuant to a court order or commission, and is conducted on U.S. consular premises, Rule 28 Federal Rules of Civil Procedure; Rule 15, Federal Rules of Criminal Procedure notwithstanding. This understanding is based on extensive discussions between the Department of State and the Japanese Embassy in Washington, and between the American Embassy in Tokyo and the Japanese Ministry of Justice.

Persons travelling from the United States to Japan to participate in depositions must obtain a special Japanese deposition visa from the Japanese Embassy or Consulate in the United States. Any effort to conduct a deposition in Japan in any other way could be viewed as a violation of the judicial sovereignty of Japan and might result in the arrest and/or deportation of the person attempting to take a deposition in Japan outside these procedures. These procedures have been established pursuant to the U.S. - Japan Consular Convention, as a result of extensive discussions between the Department of State and the Embassy of Japan.

Please inform all attorneys, for both the plaintiff and the defense of the above requirements, particularly the special deposition visa.

Special Note for Official Travellers: Any local, state or federal prosecutor, attorney, investigator, etc. attempting to obtain evidence in Japan should contact the Office of American Citizens Services, Department of State for additional, specific assistance. General requirements for local, state and federal government officials are summarized in this flyer. This office will be pleased to assist local, state and federal government officials in making the necessary arrangements to obtain evidence in Japan. Officials travellers are required to obtain their own passports and visas and must obtain the necessary court orders or letters rogatory explained in this information flyer.

Special Note Regarding American Attorneys Residing in Japan: In Note Verbale Hokubei 1 No. 220 dated October 31, 1996, the Japanese Ministry of Foreign Affairs provided additional clarification regarding the visa status of American Attorneys Residing in Japan who wish to participate in depositions at the U.S. Embassy or consulate in Japan. American lawyers residing in Japan under the status of "legal/accounting services" (as "gaikokuhu jimubengoshi"), permanent residents, or their spouses may participate in depositions under their current visa status, that is, without the special deposition visa under certain circumstances. They must notify the Ministry of Foreign Affairs through the U.S. Embassy in Tokyo of their proposed participation. When submitting the note verbale notification to the Ministry, the Embassy will need to provide the names of such lawyers, their company affiliation in Japan, their address, telephone number, and the type and validity of their visa, in addition to a copy of the requisite commission or court order issued by the court in the United States for the taking of the deposition before the U.S. consular officer on U.S. consular premises. In order to facilitate the notification procedures, the Embassy has prepared a worksheet which each lawyer resident in Japan will need to fill out in order for the Embassy to submit the requisite note verbale. Questions may be addressed to the Consular Section of the U.S. Embassy in Tokyo directly.

Authority: The taking of depositions of willing witnesses in Japan is governed by:

Article 5(f) and 5(j) of the Vienna Convention on Consular Relations (to which Japan and the United States are parties);

Article 17(1)(e)(ii) of the U.S. - Japan Consular Convention, 15 U.S.T. 768;

22 U.S.C. 4215; 22 USC 4221; 18 U.S.C. App. Fed. R. Civ. P., Rules 15 and 17; 28 U.S.C. Fed. R.Civ. P., Rules 28-31; 22 CFR 92.55 - 92.66 (general authority)

It is our understanding that **Articles 3 and 72 of the Japanese Lawyer Law may prohibit the taking of depositions in Japan by private attorneys not admitted to practice law in Japan.**

Depositions of Willing Witnesses

Article 17 of the Japan-United States Consular Convention authorizes American consular officers to take depositions in Japan, "on behalf of the courts or other judicial tribunals or authorities of the sending state (United States), voluntarily given, in accordance with the laws of the sending state (U.S.) and in a manner not inconsistent with the laws of the receiving state (Japan)". This general reference to the authority of consular officers to take depositions has been interpreted by the Government of Japan very strictly. Japanese law and practice, and the mutually agreed upon interpretation of the U.S. - Japan Consular Convention concerning obtaining evidence in Japan permits the taking of a deposition of a willing witness for use in a court in the United States only

(a) if the deposition is presided over by a U.S. consular officer;

(b) is conducted on U.S. consular premises

(c) is taken pursuant to an American court order or commission;

(d) and if any non-Japanese participant travelling to Japan applies for and obtains a Japanese Special Deposition visa.

The Japanese Ministry of Foreign Affairs and Ministry of Justice have advised the United States that these requirements apply in civil, criminal and administrative cases. The Japanese requirement for a court order and special deposition visas would apply in all cases, even though the depositions began in the United States initially. Japan will not accept orders issued by administrative law judges. Examples of court orders obtained from U.S. courts under the All Writs Act, 28 U.S.C. 1651, by various administrative agencies for the taking of depositions in Japan are available from this office upon request. The Ministry of Foreign Affairs has informed the U.S. Embassy that Japan does not permit telephone depositions.

Therefore, depositions may be taken in Japan:

(1) pursuant to a commission (28 U.S.C. App. Fed. R. Civ. P. Rule 28(b)(2)) to take a deposition issued by a court to any Consul or Vice-Consul of the United States at (Tokyo, Naha, Osaka-Kobe, Sapporo, Fukuoka) or

(2) on notice, provided an order issued by a court in the United States specifically authorizes an U.S. consular officer to take the deposition on notice.

Sample Suggested Text for Court Order or Commission

Japanese authorities have requested that the court order or commission contain the following information:

NAME OF COURT

CAPTION)
)
)
)

TO ANY CONSUL OR VICE CONSUL OF THE UNITED STATES

UNITED STATES (EMBASSY/CONSULATE) (NAME OF CITY)

UPON THE APPLICATION OF (PLAINTIFF, DEFENDANTS), AND PURSUANT TO ARTICLE 17 OF THE UNITED STATES - JAPAN CONSULAR CONVENTION,

YOU HAVE BEEN DULY APPOINTED AND YOU ARE HEREBY AUTHORIZED TO TAKE ORAL DEPOSITIONS AT THE UNITED STATES (EMBASSY/CONSULATE) IN (NAME OF CITY), JAPAN, OF THE FOLLOWING WITNESSES WHO WILL APPEAR VOLUNTARILY:

OR

IT IS ORDERED THAT THE DEPOSITIONS ON NOTICE OF THE FOLLOWING WITNESSES BE TAKEN AT THE UNITED STATES (EMBASSY/CONSULATE) IN (NAME OF CITY), JAPAN

(NAMES, ADDRESSES, AND EMPLOYER OF WITNESSES) COMMENCING ON OR ABOUT (DATE), (TIME) AND TERMINATING ON OR ABOUT (DATE), (TIME), AND TO MARK ANY DOCUMENTARY EXHIBITS IN CONNECTION THEREWITH.

COUNSEL FOR DEFENDANTS WHO WILL PARTICIPATE IN SAID DEPOSITIONS ARE (NAMES); AND COUNSEL FOR PLAINTIFFS WHO WILL PARTICIPATE IN SAID DEPOSITIONS ARE (NAMES). THE PROCEEDINGS WILL BE REPORTED BY (NAME OF AMERICAN COURT REPORTER, IF ONE IS TRAVELLING FROM UNITED STATES TO JAPAN). PLEASE CAUSE THE TESTIMONY OF SAID

WITNESSES TO BE REDUCED TO WRITING AND THE DEPOSITIONS SIGNED BY SAID WITNESSES AND ANNEX SAID DEPOSITION TESTIMONY TO YOUR COMMISSION AND CLOSE THE SAME UNDER YOUR SEAL AND MAKE RETURN THEREOF TO THIS COURT WITH ALL CONVENIENT SPEED.

DATE SIGNATURE OF JUDGE

NAME OF JUDGE

SEAL

Voluntary Oral Depositions: American attorneys may travel to Japan to participate in depositions on U.S. consular premises (as described in 22 CFR 92.57) provided they have obtained the "special deposition visa" required by Japan. Any effort to conduct a deposition in Japan in any other way might be viewed as a violation of the judicial sovereignty of Japan and could result in the arrest, detention or deportation of the participants. The procedure for scheduling a deposition at the U.S. Embassy or one of the U.S. Consulates in Japan and obtaining the "special deposition visa" is outlined below.

U.S. Federal, State or Local Government Participants: If a U.S., state or local Government official is to participate in a deposition before a U.S. consular officer in Japan, special host country clearance (in addition to the deposition visa) must be obtained for the travel. Such Government officials should contact the Office of American Citizens Services, Department of State, (202) 647-6769, fax (202) 647-2835 to initiate the process of obtaining the host country clearance. The Japanese Government requires 7-10 days to consider such a formal request before host country clearance is answered by the Ministry of Foreign Affairs. Some U.S. Government agencies find it preferable to bring their own court reporters and interpreters to Japan to ensure confidentiality and availability/flexibility.

Voluntary Depositions on Written Questions: Voluntary depositions on written questions may be taken in Japan (28 USC Fed. R. Civ. P., Rule 31, 22 C.F.R. 92.58). Requesting counsel should contact the U.S. Embassy or Consulate to arrange a mutually convenient day or days when the deposition may be conducted. The requirements for an American court order, consular fees and scheduling the Embassy special deposition room based on space availability still apply. Counsel must make all the arrangements for the witness to appear and for stenographic or video services and translators if necessary. The U.S. consular officer will administer the oath to the witness, and if necessary to the stenographer, video tape operator or interpreter/translator, and withdraw, subject to recall. If the witness does not speak or read English adequately, a Japanese translation of the English text should be provided. The questions should be sent directly to the U.S. consular officer at the U.S. Embassy or Consulate. If preferred, the witness may write down the answers to the questions, rather than dictate the answers to the stenographer or video tape operator. The U.S. consular officer will affix a closing certificate after the deposition is completed.

Arranging the Deposition

(1) Scheduling With the U.S. Embassy/Consulate: Contact the U.S. Embassy or Consulate and make arrangements to schedule the availability of U.S. consular premises and a U.S. consular officer to conduct the deposition. Note: The American Embassy in Tokyo is generally booked six months in advance.

Please note that for administrative and security reasons, the embassy/consulate's deposition room and consular staff are not available for deposition taking outside of working hours 8:30 a.m. to 5:00 p.m. or on weekends or holidays.

The Embassy/consulate can tentatively schedule a deposition, and hold the dates reserved for three weeks. If the non-refundable scheduling fee ($410.00) is not received at the Embassy/consulate within three weeks, the dates tentatively reserved will be released to others. In addition, the Embassy/consulate cannot confirm a scheduled deposition until both the court order/commission and deposit for the prescribed deposition fee are received at the Embassy/consulate. We suggest that the court order be worded "on or about" a date for maximum flexibility in scheduling. The court order/commission should be addressed to "any consul or vice consul at (Tokyo; Naha; Osaka Kobe; Fukuoka; Sapporo), Japan".

The embassy/consulate does not schedule the appearance of deponents or make arrangements for court reporters/stenographers or interpreters for private attorneys.

(2) Court Order/Commission: Obtain a Commission or Court Order as noted above. The Commission or Court Order should include the name of the case, docket number, names of the witnesses to be deposed, the fact that they are willing (voluntary) witnesses, the dates on which the depositions will be conducted and the fact that the depositions will be attended by counsel before "any consul or vice consul of the United States, at the (United States Embassy (Consulate) in (name of city), Japan. Send the original order, or a certified copy to the U.S. Embassy or Consulate where the deposition is to be conducted by the fastest available means. In addition, names of lawyers and other participants should be provided to the U.S. Embassy in Tokyo since the Japanese Foreign Ministry checks with the Embassy before approving visa issuance.

(3) Special Deposition Visa: Apply for a "special deposition visa" at the Japanese Embassy or Consulate in the United States nearest you. The Consular Section of the Japanese Embassy is located at 2520 Massachusetts Avenue, N.W., Washington, D.C. 20008, tel: (202) 939-6700. Japanese consulates are also located in Anchorage, Atlanta, Boston, Chicago, Detroit, Guam, Honolulu, Houston, Kansas City, Los Angeles, Miami, New Orleans, New York, Portland, San Francisco and Seattle. You will be required to present a photocopy of the commission or court order to the Japanese consular officer when you apply for the "special deposition visa". This special visa must be applied for at least two weeks before departure for Japan. The request should be made on letterhead stationery and include the following information: (a) the name and location of the court; (b) name and occupation of each witness; and (c) a summary of the case. Travellers will also be required to present their U.S. passport, complete Japanese Embassy/consulate visa application forms and to provide the requisite photographs. A photocopy of the commission or order for a U.S. consular officer to take the deposition must accompany the request. Special visas may also be required of deposition participants other than attorneys (American stenographers, interpreters, parties, etc.). Inquiries should be made of the appropriate Japanese consular officer in the United States.

(4) The Japanese Embassy or Consulate in the United States will contact the Japanese Foreign Ministry for permission to issue the "special deposition visa".

(5) The Japanese Foreign Ministry will contact the U.S. Embassy or Consulate to confirm whether the U.S. consular officer has received a photocopy of the American court order and whether the deposition has been scheduled.

(6) The Japanese Foreign Ministry will authorize the Japanese Embassy or Consulate in the United States to issue the "special deposition visa".

Consular Fees for Voluntary Depositions: The prescribed statutory fee for consular services in connection with depositions (22 CFR 22.1, item 69, as amended 11/1/91) is 140 dollars per hour for consular officer time plus 65 dollars per hour for consular clerical time. A flat fee of $410.00 must be paid to the embassy or consulate before a deposition can be scheduled. **The fee is not refundable if the deposition is later canceled**. The fee covers consular officer and staff time in scheduling the deposition, communicating with requesting counsel by telephone or fax, and coordinating with Japanese authorities to confirm the scheduling of a deposition before Japanese authorities will issue the special deposition visa to persons travelling to Japan to participate in a deposition.

Pre-paid Hourly Rate for Consular Time During the Deposition: In addition to the non-refundable scheduling fee, there is a fee of $140.00 per hour for consular officer time plus $65.00 per hour for consular clerical time for the length of the deposition. You should notify the embassy/consulate of the estimated length of time necessary to take the deposition, allowing for the additional time required for interpreter/translator services questions and answers. Be aware that the use of interpreters will approximately double the time required. The Embassy or consulate must receive a deposit ($140.00 x the number of hours required for the deposition plus $65.00 clerical fee), which must be deposited in full prior to the taking of the deposition. (22 CFR 22.5(c))

Deposition Closing Certificate Fee and Postage: In addition, the U.S. Embassy/consulate requires a 65 dollar deposit to cover clerical time involved in consular certification of the completed deposition and for postage. Any unused portion from your deposit will be refunded. As federal regulations prohibit the performance of consular services in advance of payment of statutory consular fees, depositions cannot be convened until all the required funds have been deposited.

Payment of Fees: Payment should be made by international money order or certified bank check payable to the American Embassy, Tokyo, Japan or to the appropriate American consulate. Personal or corporate checks are not acceptable.

Court Reporters/Stenographers/Interpreters: The U.S. Embassy/consulate does not provide interpreters or stenographers. American attorneys must arrange directly with such persons for their services and payment of their fees. (As noted previously, the Office of American Citizen Services and the U.S. Embassy/consulate can make these arrangements on behalf of U.S. Government officials or state and local Government officials. Contact the Office of American Citizens Services for more information.) At least a week to ten days advance notice or more is desirable so that the assigned interpreter/translator may have time to familiarize himself/herself with the subject concerned. If lengthy depositions are envisioned, arrangements should be made weeks or months in advance.

In accordance with the guidelines for interpreters of the Administrative Office of the U.S. Courts, when taking the testimony of a non-English speaking witness, generally the question is posed in English, the interpreter translates the English question into Japanese; the witness answers in Japanese; the interpreter translates the answer into English and the stenographer records the answer in English. Not all interpreter/stenographer services have the capacity to provide simultaneous translations. The U.S. Embassy/consulate will attempt to accommodate any special instructions which accompany the request for a deposition pursuant to a commission or court order (22 CFR 92.56).

Participants may wish to bring their own court reporters/interpreters from the U.S. with this capability. They must have the Japanese Special Deposition visas and be included in the American court order. If any participant (not a witness) is a Japanese citizen travelling to Japan from the U.S. or residing in Japan, they are not eligible for a Japanese visa, but must be included in the American court order.

Video Tape Equipment: The embassy/consulate does not provide tapes, taping equipment or equipment operators. The embassy/consulate also does not provide commercial rates for tapes, taping equipment or equipment operators. Participants must make all arrangements directly with the service providers. Participants are responsible for obtaining their own clearances from Japanese Customs authorities for bringing equipment into Japan. Check with the Consular Section of the Japanese Embassy or Consulate in the U.S. for details. If you intend to bring equipment to Japan for the deposition, it is advisable to provide the U.S. Embassy/Consulate with details via fax or phone regarding that equipment to ensure that it is compatible to the electrical equipment at the U.S. Embassy/Consulate. After the advance arrangements are completed, please so notify the U.S. Embassy a few days in advance of the actual deposition, so that the Embassy can obtain the necessary clearance from the Security Office for the entry of the equipment and the operators into the Embassy premises.

Fees for Interpreters/Stenographers: Fees for interpreters in Japan range from 90,000 to 100,000 yen per day and stenographic services from 70,000 to 80,000 yen per day plus transcript fees of 3,000 to 3,500 yen per page. The exchange rate fluctuates daily. See also the U.S. Embassy Tokyo, Commercial Section Home Page: http://www.csjapan.doc.gov at the heading, "Doing Business in Japan".

Signing, Certifying and Mailing Depositions: Participants to a deposition may stipulate regarding the manner in which the transcript of the deposition (any exhibits) should be signed, certified and mailed. The transcript may be forwarded to counsel rather than to the clerk of court which requested the deposition. Moreover, participants may stipulate that after the deposing of witnesses is completed and the stenographer transcribes the testimony, the transcript may be sent directly to the witness for signature or to counsel for the participants who will make arrangements directly with the witness for signature of the transcript. If required by local or federal rules in the United States, the witness may bring the transcript to the American embassy or consulate for signature before a consular officer, making any necessary corrections in the presence of a consular officer. If required, a consular certification of the deposition may be made at this time.

If you plan to have the deposition taped without subsequent transcription, the embassy/consulate asks that the court order or commission specify whether audio or video tape is to be used. Tapes may be sent directly by the video operator or by the embassy/consulate via registered air mail to either the person stipulated by the participants or directly to the court clerk immediately following completion of the deposition. Any change in the above procedures would have to be agreed to by both parties in the dispute and, if necessary, covered by an amended court order.

List of Interpreters, Stenographers and Video Operators

Disclaimer: The Department of State and the U.S. Embassy in Tokyo and Consulate General in Osaka Kobe assume no responsibility for the professional ability and integrity of the interpreters, stenographers and video operators whose names appear in this list from the consular districts.

Internet Resources

For additional lists of interpreters/stenographers, see the U.S. Embassy Tokyo, Commercial Section Home Page: http://www.csjapan.doc.gov at the heading, "Doing Business in Japan".

Tokyo

Interpreters:

Alpha Corporation, 5-7 Hirakawa-cho 2 chome, Chiyoda Ku, Tokyo 102, tel: 011-81-3-3230-0090; fax: 011-81-3-3234-5336

English Services, c/o Hotel Okura, South Wing Arcade, 2-10-4 Toranomon, Minato Ku, Tokyo 107. tel: 011-81-3-3585-8578 (Mrs. Sei Ghoda). Fax: c/o Hotel Okura: 011-81-3-3582-3707

Inter Group Corporation, 7-5-17 Akasaka, Minato Ku, Tokyo 107, tel: 011-81-3-5570-6161

Interlanguage Service System (ISS), Nihon Seimei Ichibancho Bldg., 7F, 23-3 Ichibancho, Chiyoda Ku, Tokyo 102. tel: 011-81-3-3230-4391; fax: 011-81-3-3262-6633

International Institute of Japan (IIJ), Belaire Gardens Bldg., 4-2-11 Jingumae, Shibuya Ku, Tokyo 150, tel: 011-81-3-3405-0754; fax: 011-81-3-3405-0754

Man-Friday Co, Ltd., Shin Aoyama Bldg., West 13th Floor, 1-1-1 Minami Aoyama, Minato Ku, Tokyo 107, tel: 011-81-3-3408-7196

Manpower, Japan Co., Ltd., CS Tower, 1-11-30 Akasaka, Minato Ku, Tokyo 107 tel: 011-81-3-5570-4781

Multilingua Inc., Kawamura Bldg., 5F, 21-6 Akasaka 3-chome, Minato Ku, Tokyo 107, tel: 583-0791;

Okawara, Taji & Associates, 3-26-1-B1 Ekoda, Aoba-ku, Yokohama-shi, Kanagawa-ken 225, tel: 011-81-45-904-4503; fax: 011-81-45-904-4502

Sansei International Inc., Fukide Bldg., No. 2, 4-1-21 Toranomon, Minato Ku, Tokyo 105, tel: 011-81-3-3433-1560; fax: 011-81-3-3433-1612

Simul International Inc., No. 9 Kowa Bldg., 1-8-10 Akasaka Minato Ku, Tokyo 107, tel: 011-81-3-3586-8911; fax: 011-81-3-3583-8336

Mrs. Kaoru Ikeda, 5-3-11 Kinuta, Setagaya Ku, Tokyo 157, tel: 011-81-3-3417-7949

Mr. William Lise, New-Tech, Ltd., Room 1101 Seven Star Mansion Higashiyama, 1-5-9 Higashiyama, Meguro-ku, Tokyo 153. tel: 011-81-3-3791-6870; fax: 011-81-3-3715-2748

Mr. Osamu Takagi, Tokyo: 1-403-10, Sunnywell Kosugi Nakahara-ku, Kawasaki-shi Kanagawa-ken 211; Okazaki: 301 Kura Bldg. Syouda Miai, Okazaki-shi, Aichi-ken 441, tel: 011-81-564-55-8844; fax: 011-81-564-2308

Stenographers:

Alpha Corporation: See Interpreting Services.

English Services: See Interpreting Services.

International Institute of Japan: See Interpreting Services.

Ralph Rosenberg Court Reporters: 2460 Pacific Tower, 1001 Bishop st., Honolulu, Hawaii 96813, tel: 808-524-2090; fax: 808-524-2596.

Sansei International Inc.: See Interpreting Services.

Simul International Inc.: See Interpreting Services.

Ms. Tomoko Ito, 2-37-18 Nakamachi, Setagaya Ku, Tokyo 158, tel: 011-81-3-3701-1961; fax: 011-81-3-3704-2325

Mrs. Mary Regan Kagami, Apt. 605, 1-9-11 Meguro Honcho, Meguro Ku, Tokyo 152, tel: 011-81-3-3712-3176

Mrs. Kimiko Seki, 2-31-5 Matsugaoka, Nakano Ku, Tokyo 165, tel: 011-81-3-3952-1542.

Video Operators:

Eizo Kiroku Service, Yamazaki Bldg., 302, 6-12-12 Honcho, Nakano Ku, Tokyo 164, tel: 011-81-3-3384-5551; fax: 011-31-3-3384-5333

ELCOM, 1-4-1 Shibaura, Minato Ku, Tokyo 105, tel: 011-31-3-3453-5551; fax: 011-81-3-3453-5428

Hawaii Video Productions, Inc., Pioneer Plaza, 900 Fort Street Mall, Suite 210, Honolulu, Hawaii 96813; tel: 808-538-0005; fax: 808-538-7627

Ichinohashi Studio, Ai Square 3F, 2-10-3 Azabu Juban, Minato Ku, Tokyo 106, tel: 011-31-3-5443-6382; fax: 011-81-3-5443-6395

Rise Video 80, 2-12-5 Ikebukuro, Toshima Ku, Tokyo 170, tel: 011-81-3-3988-0804; fax: 011-81-3-3987-3670

Spot Shokai, 1-2-saki Nishi, Ginza, Chuo Ku, Tokyo 104, tel: 011-31-3-3567-5021; fax: 011-81-3-3561-7305

Videobank, 6-6-16 Akasaka, Minato Ku, Tokyo 107, Tel: 011-81-3-3588-1011; fax: 011-81-3-3589-0054

Visual Information Systems Inc., 3-20-7 Nishidai Itabashi Ku, Tokyo 105, Office tel: 011-81-3-3933-2358; Studio Tel: 011-81-3-3505-1271; fax: 011-81-3-3505-1272

Heidi Vorwidk, Holcombe Video Service, 1734 N. McCadden Place, Suite B, Los Angeles, California 90028, tel: 213-385-3315

Osaka Kobe

Disclaimer: The American Consulate General in Osaka-Kobe assumes no responsibility for the professional ability or integrity of the under-mentioned interpreters, stenographers and video recorders. They will provide a cost estimate upon receipt of a direct request. There is no significance to the order in which they are listed.

Inter Osaka (interpreter)
Shohaku Bldg 2-12
Kakuto-cho
Kita-ku
Osaka 530, Japan
Tel: 011-81-6-372-8048
Fax: 011-81-6-372-6127

Mrs. Yasuko Kawakami (interpreter)
2-10-1 Takakuradai,
Suma-ku, Kobe 650
Tel: 011-81-78-734-0515

Rainbow Network
1750 Kalakaua Ave. No. 116,
Honolulu, Hawaii 96826
Tel: 808-955-5257
Fax: 808-946-7025

Kokusai Communication Service (interpreter)
IB Center Bldg. No. 505
1-13 Isogami-dori, 4-chome
Chuo-ku
Kobe 650, Japan
Tel: 011-81-78-251-8821
Fax: 011-81-78-251-8694

Nihon Convention Service, Inc. (interpreter)
Sumitomo Seimei Midosuji Bldg. 13th Floor
14-3 Nishitenma, 4-chome
Kita-ku
Osaka, Japan
Tel: 011-81-6-311-2131
Fax: 011-81-6-311-2130

Simul International, Inc. (interpreter)
Kogin Bldg., Annex 8F
4-2-7 Koraibashi, Chuo-ku, Osaka 541
Tel: 011-81-6-231-2441
Fax: 011-81-6-231-2447

Stenographers: The following deposition stenographers are located in Tokyo, but willing to travel to Osaka for depositions.

Mrs. Mary Regan KAGAMI
1-9-11 Meguro Honcho Apt 605
Meguro-ku
Tokyo 152, Japan
Tel: (81) (3) 3712-3176

Mrs. Kimiko Keki
2-31-5 Matsugaoka
Nakano-ku
Tokyo 165, Japan
Tel: (81) (3) 3952-1542
Fax: (81) (3) 3223-0313

Naha, Sapporo, Fukuoka

A list of interpreters and stenographers outside the Tokyo and Osaka Kobe consular districts is available directly from the U.S. consulates.

U.S. Consular Offices in Japan

American Embassy
ATTN: Consular Section/American Citizen Services
10-1, Akasaka 1-chome
Minato-ku (107)
Tokyo, Japan
tel: 011-81-3-3224-5000
fax: 011-81-3-3224-5856
telex: 2422118 AMEMB J

Internet: http://www.csjapan.doc.gov for the Commercial Service Home Page.

American Consulate General
ATTN: Consular Section/American Citizen Services
11-5 Nishitenma
2-chome
Kita Ku
Osaka 530
Osaka, Japan
tel: 011-81-6-315-5900
fax: 011-81-6-315-5914
telex: 5233037 AMCONJ

Internet: http://www.senri-i.or.up/amcon/usa 01.html for the American Citizens Services home page. This includes a segment on taking depositions under "Other Topics" which can be downloaded.

American Consulate ATTN: Consular Section, American Citizen Services
5-26 Ohori 2-chome
Chuo Ku,
Fukuoka 810
Fukouka, Japan
tel: 011-81-92-751-9331
fax: 011-81-92-713-9222
telex: 725679

Internet: http://www.city.kitakyushu.jp/amconsul/consvc.html

American Consulate General
ATTN: Consular Section/American Citizen Services
2564 Nishihara
Urasoe City
Okinawa 901-21
Naha, Okinawa, Japan
tel: 011-81-98-876-4211
fax: 011-81-98-876-4243

Internet: None

American Consulate General
ATTN: Consular Section/American Citizen Services
Kita 1-Jo
Nishi 28-chome
Chuo Ku
Sapporo 064
Sapporo, Japan
tel: 011-81-11-641-1115
fax: 011-81-11-643-1283
telex: 935338 AMCONS J

American Consulate
Nishiki SIS Building 6l, 10-33
Nishiki 3-chome
Naka-ku
Nagoya 460, Japan
tel: 011-81-52-203-4011
fax: 011-81-52-201-4612

Internet: None, but see Osaka-Kobe Home Page, http://www.senri-i.or.jp/amcon/usa 03.html, Consular Services for Americans, Nagoya Text.

(BECAUSE OF ITS LIMITED STAFF, THE NAGOYA CONSULATE PROVIDES NOTARIAL AND EMERGENCY SERVICES FOR AMERICAN CITIZENS ONLY, AND GENERALLY IS NOT AVAILABLE TO CONDUCT DEPOSITIONS.)

Other Informal Evidence Gathering

Conducting Informal Interviews: While the taking of depositions, under the conditions explained above, is a right secured under the U.S.-Japan Consular Convention, 15 U.S.T. 768, conducting interviews and other informal evidence gathering or investigation techniques are entirely subject to the discretion of the Japanese government. The Japanese Ministry of Foreign Affairs has advised the U.S. Embassy in Tokyo that it considers the conducting of information interviews by in Japan to constitute formal evidence gathering and therefore to be subject to the Japanese law on international investigative assistance. Private litigants may need to obtain a special visa for travel to Japan to conduct informal interviews, inspections or other investigations. Contact the Japanese Embassy or consulate in the U.S. for information. Japanese authorities may require that the request to conduct such interviews be made in the form of a letter rogatory, or in criminal cases, on behalf of the U.S. Government, a formal letter of request. Local, state and federal prosecutors/attorneys seeking to conduct such interviews/inspections should contact the Office of American Citizens Services for additional information.

Compulsion of Evidence

Japan is not a party to the Hague Convention on the Taking of Evidence Abroad in Civil or Commercial Matters. There is not in force between the United States and Japan any other treaty or international agreement on judicial assistance.

Compulsion of evidence in Japan from an unwilling witness can only be achieved on the basis of comity, pursuant to a letter rogatory. See Rule 28(b), Fed. R. Civ. P.; 4 Moore's Federal Practice 28.05-28.8 (2d ed. 1950); Ristau, International Judicial Assistance (Civil and Commercial), Vol. I, 3-36 et seq., International Law Institute, 1984; Article 5(j) of the Vienna Convention on Consular Relations [1963], 21 UST 77 to which the United States and Japan are both parties.

Preparation of Letter Rogatory for Use in Japan: A letter rogatory is a request from a court in one country for assistance from a court in another country. Such requests are executed by Japanese district courts in accordance with the laws of Japan and generally take six months to a year to execute. The Japanese court will compel the witness to appear before a Japanese judge to respond to written questions annexed to the letter rogatory. All proceedings will be conducted in the Japanese language. The letter rogatory should be written in clear, simple language and should be written in the form of a request, not a demand for assistance. Japan requires that requests for international judicial assistance be processed through the diplomatic channel. This means that a request must be transmitted to the Department of State by the requesting court, or by counsel. The Department of State understands that the following conditions must be met before such a request will be honored:

A. The request must be made through diplomatic channels (as mentioned);

B. The letter rogatory should have attached documents showing parties to be examined, the type of evidence to be examined, the name, nationality and address of the persons to be examined and the items with respect to which they should testify [Law W relating to Reciprocal Judicial Aid to be Given at the Request of Foreign Courts - Law 63 of March 13, 1905, as amended];

C. The letter rogatory and all attachments must be translated into Japanese. Japanese courts often reject a letter rogatory if the documents including all attachments are not completely translated into Japanese, or if the quality of the translation is poor;

D. The letter rogatory must assure the Japanese court that compensation for all expenses incurred by the Japanese court will be paid;

E. The letter rogatory must assure the Japanese court that the requesting court will honor similar requests from the Japanese court.

Moreover, Japan requires that any document annexed to the letter rogatory must bear the seal of the requesting court and the signature of the judge. Japan will reject a request if the letter rogatory or accompanying documents bear the signature of the clerk of the court. Japanese authorities do not honor amendments to a letter rogatory which are not under the seal of the requesting court. A separate information flyer regarding preparation and transmittal of letters rogatory is available from the Department of State, Office of American Citizens Services autofax service by dialing (202) 647-3000 from the phone on your fax machine, entering the code 1045, followed by Y followed by *, then pressing the start button on your fax machine. A copy of this flyer can also be mailed to you if you contact our office at (202) 647-3675.

Fees for Letters Rogatory:

The consular fee for transmittal of letters rogatory (22 CFR 22.1 item 67) is $32.00. Japanese authorities may charge additional fees. The U.S. Embassy in Tokyo requests that a check in the amount of $200.00 accompany letters rogatory for use in Japan, payable to American Embassy Tokyo in the form of a money order or certified bank check. A personal check or corporate check is not acceptable. ($200 is the estimate based on compulsion of testimony of one witness.) Any unused funds will be refunded.

Participation of American Counsel in Japanese Court Proceedings Regarding Execution of Letters Rogatory: Most American attorneys would prefer to participate in the proceeding before the Japanese court. This may well pose a problem in that it appears generally prohibited by Articles 3 and 72 of the Japanese Lawyer Law. The Japanese judge, however, may permit American counsel to participate on a case-by-case basis. For this reason, it may be preferable for you to prepare the letter rogatory in a way which offers the Japanese court alternative ways of executing the request. For example, the letter rogatory could request that:

(a) American counsel be permitted to participate in the proceedings before the Japanese court;

(b) If this is not possible, the letter rogatory could ask that local Japanese counsel representing the American client be permitted to participate in the proceedings;

(c) Finally, if this alternative is not possible, the letter rogatory could enclose written questions to be put to the witness by the Japanese court.

Retaining a Foreign Attorney: You may wish to retain local Japanese counsel for more detailed information about Japanese procedures. Lists of attorneys in Japan are available from the Department of State, Office of American Citizens Services and from the U.S. Embassy and consulates in Japan. See also, the Martindale-Hubbell Law Directory, available via the Internet at: http://www.martindale.com/products/intl law dir.html.

Transmittal of Letter Rogatory: The letter rogatory and any accompanying documents should be translated into Japanese and transmitted in duplicate (a certified original in English and a photocopy; a certified translation in Japanese and a photocopy) to the Office of American

Citizens Services, East Asia and Pacific Division, Department of State, Room 4811A, 2201 C Street N.W., Washington, D.C. 20520. The Department will transmit the request to the American Embassy in Tokyo, which will transmit the request to the Japanese Ministry of Foreign Affairs. The Ministry of Foreign Affairs will forward the request to the Japanese Supreme Court which will send the letter rogatory to the appropriate Japanese District Court. The Japanese District Court will execute the letter rogatory and send the evidence back through the same channel to the American Embassy in Tokyo which will forward the evidence to the Department of State for transmittal to the requesting court in the United States. Requesting counsel in the United States will be advised by the Department of State when the evidence is forwarded to the court in the United States.

Criminal Cases: Requests for compulsion of evidence (testimony or production of documents) on behalf of the U.S. Government (including local, state and federal prosecutors) are made in the form of a formal letter of request. These requests constitute formal evidence gathering and therefore to be subject to the Japanese law on international investigative assistance. Preparation of the formal letter of request is coordinated with the Office of International Affairs, Criminal Division, Department of Justice, 202-514-0005. Japan does not permit direct transmission of judicial assistance requests to agencies or instrumentalities of the Government of Japan, but rather requires formal transmission through established diplomatic channels. Requests on behalf of defense counsel are prepared in the form of a letter rogatory, using the general instructions noted in the previous discussion of letters rogatory. Department of Justice assistance is only available to local, state and federal prosecutors and other government attorneys, not to private litigants or defense counsel generally.

Compulsion of Documents and Other Physical Evidence: As in the taking of depositions United States consular officials have no authority to compel the production of any document or other article. Japan has advised the United States that Japanese law does not include any provision for compulsion of documents or other physical evidence except in criminal cases. The Department of State continues to explore this issue with Japanese authorities. In the interim, while the Department is prepared to transmit such requests, be aware that attempts to compel such evidence by means of letters rogatory in civil cases have proven unsuccessful. However, production of documents and other physical evidence may be compelled through the Japanese courts by letters rogatory in criminal cases.

References

T. Hattori & D. Henderson, Civil Procedure in Japan, 1985.

Kenadjian, R. Wohl, S. Chemtob, & G. Fukushima, Practice By Foreign Lawyers in Japan, Fordham International Law Journal, 1989-1990, Vol. 13, No. 3, pp. 390-404.

Koroyasu, Transnational Litigation - Part II: Perspectives from the U.S. and Abroad: Japan, The International Lawyer, Fall 1984, Vol. 18, No. 4, pp. 785-787.

MacMullin, Foreign Attorneys in Japan: Past Policies, The New Special Measures Law and Future Expectations, Florida International Law Journal, Fall 1988, Vol. 4, No. 1, pp. 51-84.

Matsuo, Jurisdiction in Transnational Cases, The International Lawyer, Spring 1989, Vol. 23, No. 1, pp. 6-9.

Mori, Discovery and Taking Evidence (in Japan), The International Lawyer, Spring 1989, Vol. 23, No. 1, pp. 3-5.

Ohara, Judicial Assistance to be Afforded by Japan for Proceedings in the United States, The International Lawyer, Spring 1989, Vol. 23, No. 1, pp. 10-28.
Peterson, Jurisdiction and the Japanese Defendant, 25 Santa Clara L. Rev. 555, 576-79 (1985)

Ramseyer, Lawyers, Foreign Lawyers, and Lawyer-Substitutes: The Market for Regulation in Japan, Harvard International Law Journal, 1986, Vol. 27, pp. 499-539.

Sawaki, Recognition and Enforcement of Foreign Judgments, The International Lawyer, Spring 1989, Vol. 23, No. 1, p. 29.

Sheehey, Japan's New Foreign Lawyer Law, Law and Policy in International Business, Vol. 19, No. 2, 1987, pp. 361-383.

Symposium: Japanese Law and Practice in Transnational Litigation, The International Lawyer, Spring 1989, Vol. 23, No. 1.

Tada, Role of Corporate Legal Departments in Japan, The International Lawyer, Winter 1988, Vol. 22, No. 4, pp. 1141-1144.

Takaishi, Hirakawa and Tomatsu, International Civil Litigation Over Securities-Related Disputes in Japan, Hastings International and Comparative Law Review, Winter 1991, Vol. 14, No. 2, 423.

Yamanouchi and Cohen, Understanding the Incidence of Litigation in Japan: A Structural Analysis, The International Lawyer, Summer 1991, Vol. 25, No. 2, pp. 443-454.

Recognition and Enforcement of Foreign Judgment (First District Court, Munich, Federal Republic of Germany) - Judgment Rendered by Munchen Landgericht I - Conditions for Recognition of Foreign Judgment (Art. 200, C.C.P.) - Jurisdiction of the Foreign Court - Proper Law to Determine the Validity of Jurisdictional Agreement - Interpretation of "as long as" Clause - Foreign Judgment by Default - Public Order - Guarantee for Reciprocal Recognition, Nagoya District Court, Judgment, February 6, 1987; H.J. (1236) 113 (1987), H.T. (627) 244 (1987), The Japanese Annual of International Law, 1990, No. 33, p. 189.

Effect of Foreign Judgment - Divorce between Japanese Spouses - Pronounced by a California Court (Superior Court, Los Angeles County, California, U.S.A.) - Service by Mail from California Court and Article 200(2), Code of Civil Procedure - Recognition (Denied), Tokyo District Court, Judgment, November 11, 1988; H.T. (703) 271 (1989), The Japanese Annual of International Law, 1990, No. 33, p. 208.

Private International Law - Enforcement of Foreign (U.S. District Court, District of Columbia, U.S.A.) Judgment - Public Order - Reciprocity (Mutual Guarantee), Supreme Court of Japan, June 7, 1983, Supreme Court Civil Reports, Vol. 37, No. 5, pp. 611 et seq., The Japanese Annual of International Law, 1984, No. 27, p. 119.

Private International Law - Enforcement of Foreign (U.S. District Court, District of Columbia, U.S.A.) Judgment - Public Order - Reciprocity (Mutual Guarantee), Tokyo High Court, March 31, 1982, The Japanese Annual of International Law, 1984, No. 27, p. 136.

Private International Law - The Requisites for Recognition of a Foreign Judgment (U.S. District Court, District of Columbia, U.S.A.), Tokyo District Court, September 17, 1979, The Japanese Annual of International Law, 1981, No. 24, p. 196.

Execution of Foreign Judgment (Paris Commercial Court) - Jurisdiction of Foreign Court - Place Where Obligation Performable Not Sufficient Connection to Establish Jurisdiction, Tokyo District Court, May 2, 1972, The Japanese Annual of International Law, 1974, No. 18, p. 209.

Foreign Judgment of Divorce - Invalidity - Compliance with Requirements regarding Enforcement of Foreign Judgment (First Civil Court of Bravos District, Chihuahua, Republic of Mexico), Tokyo District Court, December 17, 1971, The Japanese Annual of International Law, 1973, No. 17, p. 212.

International Law - Contracts - Judgment of Foreign Court (Superior Court of Los Angeles County, California, U.S.A.) - Compatibility with Public Order or Good Morals, Tokyo District Court, September 6, 1969, The Japanese Annual of International Law, 1971, No. 15, p. 181.

Private International Law - Enforcement of New York Arbitral Award - The New York Convention on the Recognition and Enforcement of Foreign Arbitral Awards of 1958 (Article 5) - Burden of Proving Conditions to deny Recognition, Osaka District Court, April 22, 1983, The Japanese Annual of International Law, 1984, No. 27, p. 184.

Additional Information: The Office of American Citizens Services has available general information flyers and country specific flyers on international judicial assistance many of which are available through our automated fax system or via our Internet Consular Affairs Home Page.

Using the Autofax System:

* Dial (202) 647-3000 using the phone on your fax machine.

* Follow the prompt to obtain a printed index of judicial assistance topics.

Index of Topics: There are four indexes.

Travel Information - Index of Countries - Press 1

Passports and Visas - Index of Flyers - Press 2

Judicial Assistance - General and Country Specific - Press 3

Child Custody and Adoption - Index of Flyers - Press 4

* If you know the code for the document you want, simply enter it and follow the prompts. If you do not know the code, follow the prompts to request an index and then select index 3 for judicial assistance.

* Enter the four digit code for the document desired as listed in the index.

* When the prompt identifies the document and asks if you want that document, enter Y (9) for yes or N (6) for no.

* If you want another document, enter the four digit code, using the same procedures noted in the previous step.

* When you finish selecting, press the # key on the phone keyboard and press the start button on your fax machine.

* Hang up the phone.

* After a brief delay of up to a minute, the documents will print automatically on your fax machine.

These topics include:

"Obtaining Evidence in Japan" (AUTOFAX document 1068)

"Preparation of Letters Rogatory" (AUTOFAX document 1045)

"Hague Legalization Convention" (AUTOFAX document 1053)

"Hague Service Convention" (AUTOFAX document 1051)

Using the Internet: Many of our judicial assistance flyers are also available on the Internet via the Department of State, Bureau of Consular Affairs Home Page at the URL: http://travel.state.gov. See also, the Department of State, Office of the Legal Adviser for Private International Law (L/PIL) Home Page at the URL: http//www.lpil.com. See also the Home Pages for our Embassy in Tokyo (Commercial Section Only); the Consulate General in Osaka-Kobe and the Consulate in Fukuoka which are linked to the Consular Affairs Home Page. As noted above, the text of the Convention and updated information concerning countries which have acceded to the Convention can be found in the Martindale-Hubbell Law Directory, Law Digest Volume. See the Martindale-Hubbell Home Page on the Internet at the URL: http://www.martindale.com/products/digests.html.

Questions: Should you have further questions about the procedures obtaining evidence in Japan not addressed in this material, please contact the Office of American Citizens Services, East Asia and Pacific Division, Department of State, 2201 C Street, N.W., Room 4811A, Washington, D.C. 20520, tel: 202-647-6769; or 202-647-5226; fax: 202-647-2835.

Appendix 20

Mutual Legal Assistance Treaties (MLATs) and Other Agreements

Start Department Circular

DISCLAIMER: THE INFORMATION IN THIS CIRCULAR RELATING TO THE LEGAL REQUIREMENTS OF SPECIFIC FOREIGN COUNTRIES IS PROVIDED FOR GENERAL INFORMATION ONLY AND MAY NOT BE TOTALLY ACCURATE IN A PARTICULAR CASE. QUESTIONS INVOLVING INTERPRETATION OF SPECIFIC FOREIGN LAWS SHOULD BE ADDRESSED TO FOREIGN COUNSEL.

Criminal Cases Mutual Legal Assistance in Criminal Matters Treaties: Since the first U.S. bilateral Mutual Legal Assistance Treaty (MLAT) entered into force with Switzerland in 1977, our MLATs have become an increasingly important. They seek to improve the effectiveness of judicial assistance and to regularize and facilitate its procedures. Each country designates a central authority, generally the two Justice Departments, for direct communication. The treaties include the power to summon witnesses, to compel the production of documents and other real evidence, to issue search warrants, and to serve process. Generally, the remedies offered by the treaties are only available to the prosecutors. The defense must usually proceed with the methods of obtaining evidence in criminal matters under the laws of the host country, which usually involve *letters rogatory.* See also general information in *Obtaining Evidence Abroad.*

PROSECUTORS: contact the *Office of International Affairs,* Criminal Division, Department of Justice, Washington, D.C. 20530, tel: (202) 514-0015.

CRIMINAL DEFENSE COUNSEL: For additional information about the letters rogatory process or other non-MLAT procedures, see our *judicial assistance home page* and *judicial assistance country specific page.* If the information you require is not available there, contact the appropriate geographic division of the Office of American Citizens Services and Crisis Management at (202) 647-5226.

TREATY NEGOTIATION ISSUES: Contact the Office of the Legal Adviser, Department of State, Law Enforcement and Intelligence (L/LEI), Washington, D.C. 20520, tel: (202) 647-5111.

OTHER U.S. GOVERNMENT WEB MATERIALS:
9 Criminal Resource Manual 276 Treaty Requests
U.S. Department of Justice, Tax Division Reading Room—*Obtaining Foreign Evidence and Other Types of Assistance in Criminal Tax Cases*
Internal Revenue Manual 9.13.2 International Investigations: Treaties, Mutual Assistance Laws

BILATERAL MUTUAL LEGAL ASSISTANCE TREATIES IN FORCE

The United States now has the following MLATs in force, unless otherwise noted as being signed but not in force. This list is subject to change. See *Treaties in Force* and *Treaty Actions* for the most recent information.

Country	Entered Into Force (or signed, not yet in force, where noted)	Citations
Antigua and Barbuda	July 1, 1999	Treaty Doc. 105-24 105th Cong., 1st Sess. Exec. Rept. 105-22, 105th Cong., 2nd Sess.
Argentina	February 9, 1993	Treaty Doc. 102-18, 102nd Cong., 1st Sess., Exec. Rept. 102-33, 102nd Cong., 1st Sess.
Australia	September 30, 1999	Treaty Doc. 105-27, 105th Cong., 1st Sess. Exec. Rept. 105-22, 105th Cong., 2nd Sess.
Austria	August 1, 1998	Treaty Doc. 104-21, 104th Cong., 1st Sess., Exec. Rept. 104-24, 104th Cong., 2nd Sess.
Bahamas	July 18, 1990	Treaty Doc. 100-17, 100th Cong. 2nd Sess. Exec. Rept. 100-30, 100th Cong. 2nd Sess.
Barbados	March 3, 2000	Treaty Doc. 105-23, 105th Cong., 1st Sess., Exec. Rept. 105-22, 105th Cong. 2nd Sess
Belize	January 7, 2003	Treaty Doc. 107-13 *U.S. Belize MLAT Press Release*
Belgium	January 1, 2000	Treaty Doc. 100-16, 100th Cong., 2nd Sess., Exec. Rept. 100-29, 100th Cong., 2d Sess. Exec. Rept. 101-11, 101st Cong., 1st Sess.
Brazil	February 21, 2001	Treaty Doc. 105-42 105th Cong. 2nd Sess., Exec. Rept 105-22, 105th Cong, 2nd Sess.
Canada	January 24, 1990	Treaty Doc. 100-14; 100th Cong., 2nd Sess. Exec. Rept. 100-28; 100th Cong, 2nd Sess. Exec. Rept

Country	Entered Into Force (or signed, not yet in force, where noted)	Citations
		101-10; 101st Cong., 1st Sess. XXIV ILM No. 4, 7/85, 1092-1099. *Canada Mutual Legal Assistance in Criminal Matters* (OAS) *Canadian Central Authorities (RCMP)* *MLATs: Investigator's Guide to Seeking Assistance Through the Department of Justice (RCMP)* *Alternative Approaches to Combating Transnational Crime*
Colombia	Signed August 20, 1980 **(Not in Force)**	Treaty Doc. 97-11, 97th Cong. 1st Sess. Exec Rept 97-35
Cyprus	September 18, 2002	Treaty Doc. 106-35, 106 Cong. 2nd Sess. Exec. Rept 106-24, 106 Cong. 2nd Sess.
Czech Republic	May 7, 2000	Treaty Doc. 105-47, 105th Cong., 2nd Sess., Exec. Rept. 105-22, 105th Cong. 2nd Sess.
Dominica	May 25, 2000	Treaty Doc. 105-24, 105th Cong., 1st Sess., Exec. Rept. 105-22; 105th Cong. 2nd Sess.
Egypt	November 29, 2001	Treaty Doc. 106-19, 106th Cong. 2nd Sess., Exec. Rept. 106-24, 106th Cong, 2nd Sess.
Estonia	October 20, 2000	Treaty Doc. 105-52, 105th Cong., 2nd Sess., Exec. Rept. 105-22, 105th Cong. 2nd Sess.
European Union	Signed June 25, 2003 **(Not in Force)**	
		Agreement on Mutual Legal Assistance Between European Union and United States of America (EU site) *U.S. Signs Pacts With Three European Nations* *U.S. Mission to EU—U.S. Signs Accords with Sweden, Finland, Belgium*
Finland	Signed December 16, 2004 **(Not in Force)**	

Country	Entered Into Force (or signed, not yet in force, where noted)	Citations
France	December 1, 2001	Treaty Doc. 106-17, 106th Cong. 2nd Sess., Exec. Rept 106-24, 106th Cong. 2nd Sess.
Germany	Signed October 14, 2003 **(Not in Force)**	
Greece	November 20, 2001	Treaty Doc. 106-18, 106th Cong. 2nd Sess., Exec. Rept. 106-24, 106th Cong, 2d Sess.
Grenada	September 14, 1999	Treaty Doc. 15-24, 105th Cong. 1st Sess., Exec. Rept. 105-22, 105th Cong., 2d Sess.
Hong Kong SAR	January 21, 2000	*Treaty Doc. 105-6,* 105th Cong., 1st Sess., Exec. Rept. 105-22; 105th Cong., 2d Sess.
Hungary	March 18, 1997	Treaty Doc. 104-20, 104th Cong., 1st Sess. Exec Rept. 104-25, 104th Cong. 2d Sess.
India	Signed October 17, 2001 **(Not in Force)**	*Treaty Doc. 107-3,* 107th Cong., 2d Sess.
Ireland	Signed January 18,2001 **(Not in Force)**	Treaty Doc. 107-9, 107th Cong., 2d Sess.
Israel	May 25, 1999	Treaty Doc. 105-40, 105th Cong., 2d Sess., Exec. Rept. 105-22, 105th Cong., 2d Sess.
Italy	November 13, 1985	Sen. Ex. 98-25, Exec. Rept. 98-36, 98th Cong., 2d Sess.
Jamaica	July 25, 1995	Treaty Doc. 102-16, 102d Cong., 1st Sess., Exec. Rept. 102-32, 102d Cong., 1st Sess.
Japan	Signed August 5, 2003 **(Not in Force)**	*Treaty Doc. 108-12.* *Japanese Ministry of Foreign Affairs, Signing of MLAT with United States*
Korea	May 23, 1997	Treaty Doc. 104-1, 104th Cong., 1st Sess., Exec. Rept. 104-22; 104th Cong. 2d Sess.
Latvia	September 17, 1999	Treaty Doc. 105-34, 105th Cong., 2d Sess., Exec. Rept. 105-22; 105th Cong., 2nd Sess.
Liechtenstein	August 1, 2003	*Treaty Doc. 107-16*

Country	Entered Into Force (or signed, not yet in force, where noted)	Citations
Lithuania	August 26, 1999	Treaty Doc. 105-41, 105th Cong., 2d Sess., Exec. Rept. 105-22, 105th Cong., 2d Sess. *U.S. Lithuania Sign Extradition MLAT Accords* (June 5, 2005)
Luxembourg	February 1, 2001	Treaty Doc. 105-11, 105th Cong., 1st Sess., Exec. Rept. 105-22, 105th Cong., 2d Sess.
Mexico	May 3, 1991	Treaty Doc. 100-13, Exec. Rept. 100-27, 100th Cong., 2 Sess., Exec. Rept. 101-09, 101st Cong. 1st Sess., XXVII ILM, No. 2, 3/88, 447.
Morocco	June 23, 1993	Sen. Ex. 98-24, Exec. Rept. 98-35, 98th Cong., 2d Sess.
Netherlands	September 15, 1983	TIAS 10734
Panama	September 6, 1995	Treaty Doc. 102-15, 102 Cong., 1st Sess., Exec. Rept. 104-3, 102 Cong., 2d Sess.
Philippines	November 22, 1996	Treaty Doc. 104-18, 104th Cong., 1st Sess., Exec. Rept. 104-26, 104th Cong., 2d Sess. *Treaty With the Philippines on MLAT*
Poland	September 17, 1999	Treaty Doc. 105-12, 105th Cong., 1st Sess., Exec. Rept. 105-22, 105th Cong., 2d Sess.
Romania	October 17, 2001	Treaty Doc. 106-20, 106th Cong. 2d Sess., Exec. Rept. 106-24, 106th Cont, 2d Sess.
Russian Federation		*Fact Sheet Mutual Legal Assistance Treaty Between the U.S. and Russia January 31, 2002* *DOJ Overseas Prosecutorial Development*
Saint Kitts & Nevis	February 23, 2000	Treaty Doc. 105-37, Exec. Rept. 105-22, 105th Cong., 2d Sess.
Saint Lucia	February 2, 2000	Treaty Doc. 105-24, 105th Cong., 1st Sess., Exec. Rept. 105-22; 105th Cong., 2d Sess.

Country	Entered Into Force (or signed, not yet in force, where noted)	Citations
Saint Vincent & the Grenadines	September 8, 1999	Treaty Doc. 105-44, Exec. Rept. 105-22, 105th Cong., 2d Sess.
South Africa	June 25, 2001	Treaty Doc. 106-36, 106th Cong., 2d Sess. Exec. Rept. 106-24, 106th Cong. 2d Sess. *South Africa Department of Justice, MLATs*
Spain	June 30, 1993	Treaty Doc. 102-21, 102d Cong., 2d Sess., Exec. Rept. 102-35, 102d Cong., 2d Sess.
Sweden	Signed December 17, 2001 **(Not in Force)**	Treaty Doc. 107-12, 107th Cong., 2d Sess. *U.S.—Swedish MLAT*
Switzerland	January 23, 1977	TIAS 8302, 27 UST 2019 *Swiss Division for International Legal Assistance* *Swiss MLAT Fact Sheet* *U.S. Embassy Bern Judicial Assistance Criminal Matters*
Thailand	June 10, 1993	Treaty Doc. 100-18, Exec. Rept. 100-31, 100th Cong., 3d Sess., Exec. Rept. 101-13, 101st Cong., 1st Sess.
Trinidad and Tobago	November 29, 1999	Treaty Doc. 105-22, 105th Cong., 1st Sess., Exec. Rept. 105-22, 105th Cong., 2d Sess. *Mutual Legal Assistance in Criminal Matters In Trinidad and Tobago (OAS)*
Turkey	January 1, 1981	TIAS 9891
United Kingdom	December 2, 1996	Treaty Doc. 104-2, 104th Cong., 1st Sess., Exec. Rept. 104-23, 104th Cong., 2d Sess. *Foreign and Commonwealth Office MLATs*
United Kingdom (Cayman Islands)	March 19, 1990	Treaty Doc. 100-8; 100th Cong., 1st Sess., Exec. Rept. 100-26, 100th Cong., 1st Sess., Exec. Rept. 100-26; 100th Cong., 2d Sess., Exec. Rept. 101-8, 101st Cong., 1st Sess., XXVI ILM 536, 3/87.

Country	Entered Into Force (or signed, not yet in force, where noted)	Citations
United Kingdom (Anguilla)	November 9, 1990	Treaty with U.K. on Cayman Islands extended to Anguilla.
United Kingdom (British Virgin Islands)	November 9, 1990	Treaty with U.K. on Cayman Islands extended to British Virgin Islands.
United Kingdom (Montserrat)	April 26, 1991	Treaty with U.K. on Cayman Islands extended to Montserrat.
United Kingdom (Turks and Caicos Islands)	November 9, 1990	Treaty with U.K. on Cayman Islands extended to Turks and Caicos.
Uruguay	April 15, 1994	Treaty Doc. 102-19, 102d Cong., 1st Sess., Exec. Rept. 102-34, 102d Cong., 2d Sess.
Venezuela	Signed October 12, 1997 **(Not in Force)**	Treaty Doc. 105-38, 105th Cong., 2d Sess., Exec. Rept. 105-22, 105th Cong., 2d Sess.

OTHER INTERNATIONAL AGREEMENTS

SEC Arrangements: The Securities and Exchange Commission (SEC) has developed informal, case-by-case understandings that facilitate the production of information from other countries. These range from Memoranda of Understanding to frameworks for cooperation to less specific exchanges and undertakings. See Mann, Mari & Lavdas, International Agreements and Understands for the Production of Information and Other Mutual Assistance, The Int'l Law, Vol. 29, No. 4, 780, 838 (1995). See also, Transnational Initiatives, Cumulative Digest of United States Practice in International Law, 1981-1988, Department of State, Vol. II, 1495, 1510 (1994); Mann and Mari, Developments in International Securities Law Enforcement and Regulation, Securities Regulation Seminar, October 24, 1990, Los Angeles, California. For information about SEC Understandings with foreign securities officials, contact the *Securities and Exchange Commission, Office of International Affairs*.

Narcotics Agreements: *United Nations Convention Against Illicit Traffic in Narcotic Drugs and Psychotropic Substances* with annex and final act. Done at Vienna December 20, 1988. Entered into force November 11, 1990. Article 7 of this Convention to obtain evidence from other countries party to it without the need to use the cumbersome, time-consuming letters rogatory process. For information, contact the Office of the Legal Adviser for Law Enforcement and Intelligence of the Department of State or the *Office of International Affairs, Criminal Division, Department of Justice*.

SELECTED REFERENCES:

Ellis & Pisani, The United States Treaties on Mutual Assistance in Criminal Matters: A Comparative Analysis, 19 Int'l Law. 189 (1985).

Harris, *Mutual Legal Assistance Treaties: Necessity, Merits, and Problems Arising in the Negotiation Process,* Asia Crime Prevention Foundation (ACPF) Lecture, 2000.

Knapp, Mutual Legal Assistance Treaties as a Way to Pierce Bank Secrecy, 20 J. of Int'l L. 405, 434 (1988).

Nadelmann, Negotiations on Criminal Law Assistance Treaties, 33 Am. J. Comp. L. 467 (1985).

Nash, Cumulative Digest of United States Practice in International Law, 1981-1988, Department of State, Vol. II, 1449, 1488 (1994).

Ristau & Abbell, Vol. 3, International Judicial Assistance (Criminal), Sec. 12-4-1—12-4-8 (1995).

Snow, Symposium: Prosecuting White-Collar Crime: The Investigation and Prosecution of White Collar Crime: International Challenges and the Legal Tools Available to Address Them, 22 Wm. & Mary Bill of Rts. J. 209, (2002).

Swartz, *Statement of Bruce Swartz Deputy Assistant Attorney General Criminal Division Senate Foreign Relations Committee Multilateral Law Enforcement Treaties June 17, 2004*

United Nations Office for Drug Control and Crime Prevention, *Report UNDCP Informal Expert Working Group on Mutual Legal Assistance Casework Best Practice*, Vienna, December 3-7, 2001

United Nations Office for Drug Control and Crime Prevention, *Report of the Expert Working Group on Mutual Legal Assistance and Related International Confiscation*, Vienna, February 15-19, 1993

United Nations Economic and Social Council, *Resolution 1998/15, Mutual Assistance and International Cooperation in Criminal Matters*

United States, *Mutual Legal Assistance in Criminal Matters and Extradition,* OAS

Winer, *Statement Of Jonathan Winer, Deputy Assistant Secretary, Bureau For International Narcotics And Law Enforcement Affairs, House Committee On Banking And Financial Services, June 11, 1998*

Appendix 21

International Judicial Assistance, Notarial Services and Authentication of Documents

State Department Circular

SPECIAL NOTICE: Change in the Service of Process Function

Effective June 1, 2003, the U.S. Department of Justice is delegating the service of process function to a private contractor, Process Forwarding International of Seattle, Washington. The contractor will be handling requests under the multilateral Hague and Inter-American Service Conventions, and requests from countries not party to either treaty. This procedural change does not imply the formal designation of a new central authority for either the Hague Service Convention or the Inter-American Convention on Letters Rogatory and Additional Protocol, but simply reflects the outsourcing of certain activities conducted by the central authority, which formally remains in the U.S. Department of Justice. Contact: Process Forwarding International, 910 5th Avenue, Seattle, WA98104 USA, telephone: (206) 521-2979; fax: 206-224- 3410; e-mail: info@hagueservice.net; website: http://www.hagueservice.net. Process Forwarding International will be the only private process server company authorized to act on behalf of the United States under the Hague Service Convention and Inter-American Convention to receive requests for service, proceed to serve the documents, and complete the certificate of service. For the Inter-American Convention, Process Forwarding International will also have the exclusive authority to act on behalf of the United States in transmitting outgoing requests for service of process abroad. The U.S. Department of State, Bureau of Consular Affairs materials about the Hague and Inter-American Service Conventions, and country-specific flyers are being updated accordingly.

DISCLAIMER: THE INFORMATION IN THIS SITE RELATING TO THE LEGAL REQUIREMENTS OF SPECIFIC FOREIGN COUNTRIES IS PROVIDED FOR GENERAL INFORMATION ONLY AND MAY NOT BE TOTALLY ACCURATE IN A PARTICULAR CASE. QUESTIONS INVOLVING INTERPRETATION OF SPECIFIC FOREIGN LAWS SHOULD BE ADDRESSED TO FOREIGN COUNSEL.

This is an official U.S. Government source. Inclusion of non-U.S. Government links does not imply endorsement of contents.

COUNTRY-SPECIFIC INFORMATION

- Australia
- Belgium
- Taking Depositions in Brazil
- Canada
- China
- Croatia
- Cyprus
- Czech Republic
- Denmark
- El Salvador
- Fiji
- Finland
- France
- Germany
- Greece
- Honduras
- Hong Kong, S.A.R., China
- Indonesia
- Ireland
- Israel
- Service of Documents in Israel
- Italy
- Obtaining Evidence in Japan
- Service of Process in Japan
- Jordan
- Luxembourg
- Malaysia
- Mexico
- The Netherlands
- New Zealand
- Norway
- Service of Documents in Pakistan
- Philippines
- Portugal
- Russia (update in progress)
- Singapore
- Slovak Republic
- Slovenia
- Spain
- Sweden
- Switzerland
- Taiwan
- Thailand
- United Kingdom

GENERAL INFORMATION

SERVICE OF PROCESS ABROAD

- U.S. Department of State Circular: Service of Process Abroad: General Overview
- U.S. Department of State Circular: Preparation of Letters Rogatory
- Service Provisions of the Foreign Sovereign Immunities Act (FSIA), 28 USC 1608, for service on a foreign state, political subdivision, agency or instrumentality
- Checklist for Plaintiffs- Service of Process upon a Foreign State
- Prohibition against service of process by consular officers: 22 CFR 92.85
- Consular responsibility for serving subpoeneas: 22 CFR 92.86
- Consular procedures for service of subpoeneas: 22 CFR 92.88

Treaties on Service of Documents

Hague Convention of the Service Abroad of Judicial and Extra-Judicial Documents in Civil and Commercial Matters

- U.S. Department of State Circular on Operations of the Hague Service Convention
- Hague Service Convention Text
- Hague Service Convention Explanatory Report
- Hague Service Convention Bibliography

Inter-American (Service) Convention on Letters Rogatory and Additional Protocol

- U.S. Department of State Circular on Operations of the Inter-American Convention
- Link to Treaty Text on the Organization of American States (OAS) web site (1975)
- Link to Additional Protocol to Inter-American Convention on Letters Rogatory on the Organization of American States (OAS) web site (1975)

OBTAINING EVIDENCE ABROAD

- U.S. Department of State Circular: Obtaining Evidence Abroad: General Overview

- U.S. Department of State Circular: Preparation of Letters Rogatory

Treaties on Obtaining Evidence Abroad

Hague Convention on Obtaining Evidence Abroad in Civil and Commercial Matters

- U.S. Department of State Circular on Hague Evidence Convention Operations
- Hague Evidence Convention Text
- Hague Evidence Convention Explanatory Report
- Hague Evidence Convention Bibliography
- Hague Evidence Convention Country Status Report
- Mutual Legal Assistance in Criminal Matters Treaties

ENFORCEMENT OF JUDGMENTS

- U.S. Department of State Information: Enforcement of Judgments

TRAVEL ABROAD FOR JUDICIAL ASSISTANCE PURPOSES

- Host Country Clearance - Travel of Government Officials
- Travel Warnings, Public Announcements and Consular Information Sheets

NOTARIAL AND AUTHENTICATION SERVICES

- Notarial Functions of Consuls
- Notaries Public Abroad
- Refusals of Requests for Notarial Services: 22 CFR 92.9
- U.S. Department of State, Bureau of Consular Affairs: General Circular on Authentication of Documents
- Authentication of Academic Credentials
- Go to the U.S. Department of State Authentications Office.

Treaties on Authentication/Legalization of Documents

Hague Convention Abolishing the Requirements for Legalization of Foreign Public Documents

- U.S. Department of State Circular: Hague Legalization Convention Operations
- Legalization Text Treaty
- Legalization Convention Apostille Certificate
- Legalization Convention Explanatory Report
- Legalization Convention Country Status Report
- Legalization Convention Country Status Report

CRIMINAL MATTERS

- Mutual Legal Assistance in Criminal Matters Treaties (MLATs)
- U.S. Department of Justice, U.S. Attorney's Manual
- Prisoner Transfer Treaties
- Consular Notification and Access
- National Criminal Justice Reference Service: Anti-Crime Training and Technical Assistance Program
- National Criminal Justice Reference Service: International Resources
- National Institute of Justice, International Center, U.N. Activities: Crime Prevention Program
- National Institute of Justice, International Center
- Federal Law Crime and Justice

FAMILY LAW AND CHILD PROTECTION ISSUES

- Child Protection Services
- Child Support Enforcement
    - U.S. Department of Justice, Criminal Division, Child Support Recovery Act
    - Passport Restrictions for Child Support
    - International Child Support Enforcement
    - U.S. Department of Health and Human Services (HHS): A Caseworker's Guide to Child Support Enforcement and Military Personnel
    - Uniform Inter-State Family Support Act (1996)
- Marriage and Divorce
    - For information on Marriage and Divorce Abroad, go to the Services for American Citizens Abroad page.
    - Parental Child Abduction
    - International Adoption
    - U.K. Foreign and Commonwealth Office - Forced Marriage: Your Rights Abroad
    - U.K. Home Office - Forced Marriage: A Choice by Right

- Trafficking in Women and Children
    - U.S. State Department's Office of Global Affairs - Trafficking in Women and Children
    - U.S. Department of Justice, Violence Against Women Office
    - U.S. DOJ, Violence Against Women Office - Laws and Regulations
    - Steps Taken to Stop the Trafficking in Women and Children - January 2000
    - President's Interagency Council on Women
    - Executive Memorandum: March 11, 1998 - Steps to Combat Violence Against Women and Trafficking in Women and Girls
    - Violence Against Women
- Child Abuse, Neglect and Exploitation
    - U.S. Department of Justice, Child Exploitation and Obscenity Section
    - U.S. Department of Justice, International Aspects of Child Exploitation

Child Labor

- Fact Sheet on Child Labor

Other Children's Issues

- Refugee Children
- Children in Armed Conflict
- FBI: A Parent's Guide to Internet Safety
- FBI Director, Congressional Statement: Child Pornography, 1997
- Department of Justice, Office for Victims of Crime - Child Sexual Exploitation: Improving Investigations and Protecting Victims - A Blueprint for Action
- Department of Justice, Office for Victims of Crime - Breaking the Cycle of Violence: Recommendations to Improve the Criminal Justice Response to Child Victims and Witnesses
- Department of Justice, Office for Victims of Crime - Children Exposed to Violence: Criminal Justice Resources

Treaties in Progress and International Initiatives

- Hague Convention of October 19, 1996 on Jurisdiction, Applicable Law, Recognition, Enforcement and Cooperation in Respect of Parental Responsibility and Measures for the Protection of Children: Project Objectives

Other Family Related Issues

- Hague Convention on the International Protection of Adults: Status

Other Family Related Links

- U.S. State Department's Office of the Legal Adviser for Private International Law: Family Law

- Department of Justice, Office for Victims of Crime - Improving the Police Response to Domestic Elder Abuse

FOREIGN ATTORNEYS

- Retaining a Foreign Attorney
- Prohibition against recommending attorneys: 22 CFR 92.82

U.S. Embassies Abroad - Lists of Attorneys

- Martindale-Hubbell Law Directory
- Other Useful Judicial Links
- New South Wales and Australian Capital Territory, Australia
- Queensland, Australia
- New South Wales, Australia - specializing in criminal law
- Austria
- Bangladesh
- Belgium
- Belize
- Botswana
- Brazil
- Bulgaria
- Burkina Faso
- Chad
- China
- Colombia
- Costa Rica
- Côte d'Ivoire
- Estonia
- Ethiopia
- France
- Georgia
- Germany
- Greece
- Guatemala
- Guyana
- Honduras
- Hungary
- Calcutta, India
- Chennai, India
- Mumbai, India
- New Delhi, India (Scroll down to list of attorneys)
- Ireland
- Tel Aviv, Israel
- Italy - Attorneys in Rome
- Italy - Legal Advisors in Rome
- Italy - Attorneys in Florence
- Italy - Attorneys and Notaries in Milan
- Italy - Attorneys in Naples
- Jamaica
- Japan
- Fukuoka, Japan
- Seoul, Korea
- Lebanon
- Macedonia
- Malaysia
- Malta
- Mexico
- Ciudad Juarez, Mexico
- Guadalajara, Mexico
- Moldova
- Morocco
- Nepal
- Netherlands Antilles (Aruba, Bonaire, Curacao, St. Maarten)
- Nicaragua
- Poland
- Portugal and the Azores
- Philippines
- Yekaterinburg, Russia
- Saudi Arabia
- Singapore
- Spain
- Sudan
- Syria
- Switzerland
- Taiwan
- Thailand
- Turkey
- Turkmenistan
- Venezuela

OTHER LINKS

DIPLOMATIC AND CONSULAR SPECIFIC TREATY LINKS

- Vienna Convention on Consular Relations
- Vienna Convention on Diplomatic Relations

TREATY DATABASES

U.S. Department of State

- Treaties in Force
- Current Treaty Actions
- Treaty Actions
- Office of the Legal Adviser for Private International Law
- Office of the Legal Adviser

U.S. House and Senate

- Government Printing Office
- Library of Congress

International Organizations

- United Nations under Databases/Treaties
- Hague Conference on Private International Law
- U.S. Department of State Circular on Operations of the Inter-American Convention
- Link to Treaty Text on the Organization of American States (OAS) web site (1975)
- Link to Additional Protocol to Inter-American Convention on Letters Rogatory on the Organization of American States (OAS) web site (1975)
- Council of Europe (COE) under Texts/Treaties, COE press releases including treaty action
- United Nations Commission on International Trade Law

U.S. DEPARTMENT OF JUSTICE

- Foreign Claims Settlement Commission
- Office for Victims of Crime

PRIVATE ORGANIZATIONS

- American Society for International Law (ASIL)
- ASIL Guide to Electronic Resources for International Law
- Center for Comparative and Foreign Law Studies

FOREIGN LAW LINKS

- European Union Law
- Council of Europe
- European Union
- OAS Department of Legal Cooperation and Information

NOTARIAL AND AUTHENTICATIONS LINKS

- Department of State Authentications Office
- American Society of Notaries
- National Notary Association
- United States Notary Association

COMPARATIVE CHART ON SELECTED PRIVATE INTERNATIONAL LAW TREATIES

Country	Hague Evidence Convetion	Hague Service Convention	New York Convention on Arbitration	Inter-American Convention on Letters Rogatory		Legalization Convention	Inter-American Convention on International Commercial Arbitration
				Convention	Protocol		
Albania						*	
Algeria			*				
Andorra						*	
Anguilla	*	*					
Antigua and Barbuda		*	*			*	
Argentina	*	*	*	*	*	*	*
Armenia			*			*	
Aruba	*	*					
Australia	*		*			*	
Austria			*			*	
Azerbaijan			*				
Bahamas		*				*	
Bahrain			*				
Bangladesh			*				
Barbados	*	*	*			*	
Belarus	*	*	*			*	
Belgium		*	*			*	
Belize						*	
Benin			*				
Bermuda		*					
Bolivia			*	*			*
Bosnia Herzegovina			*			*	
Botswana		*	*			*	
Brazil				*	*	*	*
British Virgin Islands		*					
Brunei			*			*	
Bulgaria	*	*	*			*	
Burkina Faso			*				
Cambodia			*				

*FB (The treaties listed in this Chart are in force in the enumerated countries.
Source: Depart of State, Office of the Assistant Legal Advisor for Treaty Affairs.

Country	Hague Evidence Convetion	Hague Service Convention	New York Convention on Arbitration	Inter-American Convention on Letters Rogatory		Legalization Convention	Inter-American Convention on International Commercial Arbitration
				Convention	Protocol		
Cameroon			*				
Canada		*	*				
Cayman Islands	*	*					
Central African Republic			*				
Chile			*	*	*		*
China	*	*	*				
Colombia			*	*	*	*	*
Costa Rica			*	*			*
Cote d'Ivoire			*				
Croatia			*			*	
Cuba			*				
Cyprus	*	*	*			*	
Czech Republic	*	*	*			*	
Denmark	*	*	*				
Djibouti	*		*				
Dominica			*			*	
Dominican Republic							*
Ecuador			*	*	*		*
Egypt		*	*				
El Salvador			*	*		*	*
Estonia	*	*	*			*	
Falkland Islands	*	*					
Fiji		*				*	
Finland	*	*	*			*	
France	*	*	*			*	
French Polynesia		*					
French Guiana	*						
Germany	*	*	*			*	
Georgia			*				
Ghana			*				
Gilbraltara	*	*					
Granada						*	
Greece		*	*			*	
Guatemala			*	*	*		*

TREATIES CHART

Country	Hague Evidence Convetion	Hague Service Convention	New York Convention on Arbitration	Inter-American Convention on Letters Rogatory		Legalization Convention	Inter-American Convention on International Commercial Arbitration
				Convention	Protocol		
Guinea			*				
Haiti			*				
Holy See			*				
Honduras			*	*			*
Hong Kong	*	*				*	
Hungary			*			*	
Iceland			*				
India			*				
Indonesia			*				
Iran			*				
Ireland		*	*			*	
Isle of Man	*	*					
Israel	*	*	*			*	
Italy	*	*	*			*	
Japan		*	*			*	
Jersey	*	*					
Jordan			*				
Kazakhstan			*			*	
Kenya			*				
Kiribati		*					
Korea		*	*				
Kuwait			*				
Kyrgyzstan			*				
Lao			*				
Latvia	*	*	*			*	
Lebanon			*				
Lesotho			*			*	
Liberia						*	
Liechtenstein						*	
Lithuania	*		*			*	
Luxembourg	*	*	*			*	
Macao	*	*				*	
Macedonia			*			*	
Madagascar			*				
Malaysia			*				
Malawi		*				*	
Mali			*				
Malta						*	
Marshall Islands						*	

Country	Hague Evidence Convetion	Hague Service Convention	New York Convention on Arbitration	Inter-American Convention on Letters Rogatory		Legalization Convention	Inter-American Convention on International Commercial Arbitration
				Convention	Protocol		
Martinique	*						
Mauritania			*				
Mauritius			*			*	
Mexico	*	*	*	*	*	*	*
Moldova			*				
Monaco	*		*			*	
Mongolia			*				
Montserrat		*					
Morocco			*				
Mozambique			*				
Namibia						*	
Nepal			*				
Netherlands	*	*	*			*	
New Zealand			*			*	
Nicaragua				*		*	*
Niger			*				
Nigeria			*				
Niue						*	
Norway	*	*	*			*	
Oman			*				
Pakistan		*	*				
Panama			*	*	*	*	*
Paraguay			*	*	*		*
Peru			*	*	*		*
Philippines			*				
Pitcairn Island		*					
Poland	*	*	*				
Portugal	*	*	*			*	
Romania			*			*	
Russian Federation		*	*			*	
St. Christopher		*					
St. Helena		*					
St. Kitts & Nevis						*	
St. Lucia		*				*	
St. Pierre & Miquelon	*						

TREATIES CHART

Country	Hague Evidence Convetion	Hague Service Convention	New York Convention on Arbitration	Inter-American Convention on Letters Rogatory		Legalization Convention	Inter-American Convention on Inter-national Commercial Arbitration
				Convention	Protocol		
St. Vincent & Grenadines			*			*	
Samoa						*	
San Marino			*			*	
Saudi Arabia			*				
Senegal			*				
Serbia & Montenegro						*	
Seychelles		*				*	
Singapore	*		*				
Slovak Republic	*	*	*			*	
Slovenia	*		*			*	
Soloman Islands		*					
South Africa	*		*			*	
Spain	*	*	*			*	
Sri Lanka	*		*				
Suriname	*	*				*	
Swaziland						*	
Sweden	*	*	*			*	
Switzerland	*	*	*			*	
Syrian Arab Republic			*				
Tanzania			*				
Thailand			*				
Tonga						*	
Trinidad and Tobago			*			*	
Tunisia			*				
Turkey	*	*	*			*	
Turks & Caico Islands		*					
Tuvalu		*					
Uganda			*				
Ukraine	*	*	*			*	
United Kingdom	*	*	*			*	
United States	*	*	*	*	*	*	*
Uruguay			*	*	*		*
Uzbekistan			*				

Country	Hague Evidence Convetion	Hague Service Convention	New York Convention on Arbitration	Inter-American Convention on Letters Rogatory		Legalization Convention	Inter-American Convention on International Commercial Arbitration
				Convention	Protocol		
Venezuela	*	*	*	*	*	*	*
Vietnam			*				
Yugoslavia			*			*	
Zimbabwe			*				
Sovereign Base Areas of Akrotiri & Dhekelia	*						

TABLE OF CASES

A

B

(Rel.6–10/05)

C

D

E

F

G

I

(Rel.6–10/05)

J

(Rel.6–10/05)

K

L

M

N

O

P

Q

R

(Rel.6–10/05)

WEBSITE INDEX

American Arbitration Association (AAA), www.adr.org

Cornell University, www.law.cornell.edu

Emory University, www.law.emory.edu

Europa, providing information on the laws and institutions of the European Union, http://europa.eu.int/index.htm

Findlaw, devoted entirely to legal research and containing "LawCrawler" search engine, http://www.findlaw.com/

Hague Conference on Private International Law, http://www.hcch.net/e/conventions/index.html

Hieros Gamos, containing information, forums, and links to other sites regarding international law, http://www.hg.org

International Chamber of Commerce (ICC), www.iccwbo.org.

U.S. House of Representatives Internet Law Library Treaties and International Law, http://law.house.gov/52.htm

U.S. State Department, Bureau of Consular Affairs, http://travel.state.gov/fsia.html

U.S. State Department Private International Law Database, http://www.his.com/~pildb/

YAHOO!, containing search engine and links to law Web sites, http://www.yahoo.com/

See also supra Appendix 20, at page APP 20-5, listing internet treaty sites of certain non-governmental entities (NGOs)

INDEX

A

B

C

D

E

(Rel.4–7/02)

(Rel.2–8/99)

G

H

I

J

M

N

O

TRANSNATIONAL DISCOVERY .... § 3.09, § 10.02, § 10.04

S

T

(Rel.6–10/05)

U

V

(Rel.6–10/05)

W

X

Y

TABLE OF STATUTES

BIBLIOGRAPHY

A

ABA *Model Code of Professional Responsibility* Canon 6 (1980) .... § 2.07

ABA *Model Code of Professional Responsibility* DR 6-101(A)(2) (1980) .... § 2.07

ABA, Section of Antitrust Law, *Task Force Report: The Antitrust Guide for International Operations Revisited*, 54 Antitrust L.J. 839 (1985) .... § 8.03

Comment, *The Act of State Doctrine: A History of Judicial Limitations and Exceptions*, 18 Harv. Int'l L.J. 677 (1977) .... § 8.04, § 8.09, § 8.10

Note, *The Act of State Doctrine: Resolving Debt Situs Confusion*, 86 Colum. L. Rev. 594 (1986) .... § 8.06[2]

Note, *Alien Corporations and Aggregate Contacts: A Genuinely Federal Jurisdictional Standard*, 95 Harv. L. Rev. 470 (1981) .... § 6.01, § 6.03

47 Am. Jur. 2d *Jury* § 10 (1969) .... § 3.02

Note, *An Analysis of the Act of State Doctrine*, 22 N.Y.L. Sch. L. Rev. 995 (1977) .... § 8.10

Tom Arnold, et. al., *Patent Litigation 1990: Alternative Dispute Resolution*, 300 PLI/Pat 213 (1990) .... § 12.02[5]

Tom Arnold, *Suggested Form of Contract to Arbitrate a Patent or Other Commercial Dispute, Annotated*, 2 Tex. Intell. Prop. L.J. 205, 207 (1994) .... § 12.02[5]

Note, Asahi Metal Indus. Co. v. Superior Court: *Effect of State Court Jurisdiction on International Trade*, 3 Am. U. J. Int'l L. & Pol'y 197 (1988) .... § 6.04[1]

Asencio & Dry, *An Assessment of the Service Provisions of the Foreign Sovereign Immunities Act of 1976*, 8 J. Legis. 237 (1981) .... § 7.14[2]

Ask and You May Receive, Int'l Comm. Lit. 14–23 (Mar. 1998) .... § 10.03

Timothy B. Atkeson & Stephen D. Ramsey, *Proposed Amendments to the Foreign Sovereign Immunities Act*, 79 Am. J. Int'l L. 770 (1985) .... § 7.07

B

Charles S. Baldwin, *Protecting Confidential and Proprietary Commercial Information in International Arbitration*, 31 Tex. Int'l L.J. 451 (1996) .... § 12.02[5]

Bazyler, *Abolishing the Act of State Doctrine*, 134 U. Penn. L. Rev. 325 (1986) .... § 8.03

2A BENDER'S FEDERAL PRACTICE FORMS .... § 10.09

George Bermann, *The Use of Anti-Suit Injunctions in International Litigation*, 28 Colum. J. Transnat'l L. 589 (1990) .... § 5.08[3]

BLACK'S LAW DICTIONARY (6th ed. 1994) .... § 4.05, § 10.09

Jacques Borel & Stephen M. Boyd, *Opportunities for and Obstacles to Obtaining Evidence in France for Use in Litigation in the United States*, 13 Int'l Law. 35 (1979) .... § 10.03

Gary B. Born, *International Commercial Arbitration in the United States* (1994) .... § 12.02[4], § 12.04

Gary B. Born, *Whole World in Their Hands*, Int'l Legal Times, Aug. 29, 1988 .... § 4.04[5]

Gary B. Born, *Reflections on Judicial Jurisdiction in International Cases*, 17 Ga. J. Int'l & Comp. L. 1 (1987) .... § 6.01

Gary B. Born & Scott Hoing, *Comity and the Lower Courts: Post* Aerospatiale *Applications of the Hague Evidence Convention*, 24 Int'l Law. 393 (1990) .... § 1.04, § 3.09

Ronald A. Brand, *Enforcement of Foreign Money-Judgments in the United States: In Search of Uniformity and International Acceptance*, 67 Notre Dame L. Rev. 253 (1991) .... § 11.09

Charles N. Brower, *Jurisdiction Over Foreign Sovereigns: Litigation v. Arbitration*, 17 Int'l Law. 681 (1983) .... § 7.02[1]

John R. Brown, *44.1 Ways to Prove Foreign Law*, 9 Mar. Law. 179 (1984) .... § 9.03

Lenore B. Browne, *Extraterritorial Discovery: An Analysis Based on Good Faith*, 83 Colum. L. Rev. 1320 (1983) .... § 10.23[1]

C

Carl, *Suing Foreign Governments in American Courts: The United States Foreign Sovereign Immunities Act in Practice*, 33 Sw. L.J. 1009 (1979) .... § 8.10

1 R. Casad, Jurisdiction in Civil Actions (2d ed. 1983)........ § 6.02[2], § 6.04[2], § 6.04[3]

Cohen, How to Find the Law (1976) .... § 2.02, § 2.03, § 2.04

Michael Collins, *Privacy and Confidentiality in Arbitration Proceedings*, 30 Tex. Int'l L.J. 121 (1995) .... § 12.02[5]

Committee on International Law, the Hague Convention on the Service Abroad of Judicial and Extrajudicial Documents on Civil or Commercial Matters, 22 Rec. Ass'n Bar of City of N.Y. 280 (1967) .... § 4.07

Comprehensive Guide to Bar Admission Requirements, American Bar Association National Conference of Bar Examiners (1993) .... § 2.08, § 2.09

Emily Couric, *Foreign Firms Invade the U.S.: An Asset to Bar?*, Nat'l L.J., Oct. 29, 1984, at 1 .... § 2.09

Crawford, *Execution of Judgments and Foreign Sovereign Immunity*, 75 Am. J. Int'l L. 820 (1981) .... § 7.16

Richard W. Cutler, *Executing Judgments Under the FSIA: Winning Isn't Everything*. N.Y. Law Journal (Aug. 17, 1995) .... § 7.16

D

Veronica Ann Deberadine, *Foreign Corrupt Practices: Creating An Exception to the Act of State Doctrine*, Am. U.L. Rev., vol. 34:203, 203 (1984) .... § 8.13

Georges R. Delaume, *The Foreign Sovereign Immunities Act and Public Debt Litigation: Some Fifteen Years Later*, 88 Am. J. Int'l L. 257 (1994) .... § 7.05[2], § 7.06[3]

Georges R. Delaume, *Long-Arm Jurisdiction Under the Foreign Sovereign Immunities Act*, 74 Am. J. Int'l L. 640 (1980) .... § 7.06[2]
Georges R. Delaume, *Public Debt and Sovereign Immunity: Some Considerations Pertinent to S. 556*, 67 Am. J. Int'l L. 745 (1973) .... § 7.01
Joseph W. Dellpenna, *Transnational Litigation Today*, A.B.A. Section of Int'l Law & Practice, Fall/Winter Section Meeting, Panel on Resolving Commercial Disputes in the North American Market (Jan. 20, 1994) .... § 5.08[1]
Joseph W. Dellpenna, *Suing Foreign Governments and Their Corporations*, Com. L.J. 298 (Aug./Sept. 1980) .... § 7.16
Dodd, *A Comparative Analysis of Selected Rules of International Arbitration*, Currents (Summer 1993) .... § 12.02[4]
Maureen A. Dowd & Theodore B. Eichelberger, *Recent Decision: International Law—Act of State Doctrine: An Emerging Corruption Exception In Antitrust Cases?*, 59 Notre Dame L. Rev. 455 (1984) .... § 8.13
Jacqueline Duval, Major, *One Way Ticket Home: The Federal Doctrine of Forum Non Conveniens and the International Plaintiff*, 77 Cornell L. Rev. 650 (1992) .... § 5.06

E

Note, *Effects Jurisdiction Under the Foreign Sovereign Immunities Act: How Far Does the Long Arm Reach?*, 20 L. & Pol'y Int'l Bus. 463 (1988) .... § 7.06[1]
Note, Environmental Tectonics Corp. v. W.S. Kirkpatrick, Inc.: *The Act of State Doctrine and the Problem of Judicial Inconsistency*, 14 N.D.J. Int'l L. & Com. Reg. 495 (1989) .... § 8.02[3]
Extraterritorial Application of American Law After the Insurance Trust Case: A Reply to Professors Lowenfeld and Tribble, 89 A.J. Twill 750 (1995) .... § 5.08

F

Richard Fairbanks, Letter from, Asst. Sec'y of State, (Oct. 2, 1981), *reprinted in* S. Rep. No. 211, 97th Cong., 1st Sess. 4-5 (1981) .... § 7.07

Eric C. Fastiff, *The Proposed Hague Convention on the Recognition and Enforcement of Civil and Commercial Judgments: A Solution to Butch Reynold's Jurisdiction and Enforcement Problems*, 28 Cornell Int'l L.J. 469 (1995) .... § 11.01

Feldman, *Foreign Sovereign Immunity in the United States Courts 1976–1986*, 19 Vand. J. Transnat'l L. 19 (1986)... § 7.16

Alfred G. Feliu, Discovery in Arbitration: How Much Is Enough?, ADR Currents (Mar. 1999), *reprinted in* N.C. Lawyers Weekly, pp. 11–12 (Sept. 13, 1999)..... § 12.05[3]

Andre R. Fiebig, *The Recognition and Enforcement of Punitive Damages in Germany: Recent Developments.* 22 Ga. J. Int'l & Comp. L. 635 (1992) .... § 1.02

Filzer, *The Continued Validity of the Act of State Doctrine in Foreign Branch Bank Expropriation Cases*, 3 Am. U.J. Int'l L. & Pol'y 99 (1988) .... § 8.06[2]

Note, *Foreign Branches of Law Firms: The Development of Lawyers Equipped to Handle International Practice*, 80 Harv. L. Rev. 1284 (1967) .... § 2.10

Form USM 94, U.S. Marshals .... § 3.08

Form USM 272, 272A, U.S. Marshals .... § 3.08

Fox, *Reexamining the Act of State Doctrine: An Integrated Conflicts Approach*, 33 Harv. Int'l L.J. 521 (1992) .... § 8.02[3]

Charles A. Friedrich, Note, *Jurisdiction: Personal Jurisdiction Over an Alien Corporation*, 26 Harv. Int'l L.J. 630 (1985) .... § 6.04[2]

Fuerstman and Thomas, *Implications of the* Technostroyexport *Decision*, Int'l Bus. Law. (Sept. 1994) .... § 12.05

G

H

Convention on the Taking of Evidence Abroad in Civil or Commercial Matters, May 28–31, 1985, 24 I.L.M. 1668 .... § 4.04[3]
Sabbatino Halberstam, *Resurrected: The Act of State Doctrine in the Revised Restatement of Foreign Relations Law*, 79 Am. J. Int'l L. 68 (1985) .... § 8.03
Henkin, *Act of State Today: Recollections in Tranquility*, 6 Colum. J. Transnat'l L. 175 (1967) ....§ 8.03, § 8.06[1], § 8.11
Brigette Ecolivet Herzog, *The 1980 French Law on Documents and Information*, 75 Am. J. Int'l L. 382 (1981) .... § 10.23[2]
Danny A. Hoek, *Foreign Sovereign Immunity and Saudi Arabia v. Nelson: A Practical Guide*, 18 Hastings Int'l & Comp. L. Rev. 617 (1995) ....§ 7.06[3]
Michael F. Hoellering, *Administering International Arbitration Proceedings*, Dispute Resolution J. 64, 67 (American Arbitration Assoc., Feb. 1998) .... § 12.05[1]
Howard M. Holtzmann, ''Balancing the Need for Certainty and Flexibility in International Arbitration Procedures'' *International Arbitration in the 21st Century: Towards ''Judicialization'' and Uniformity?* (Transnational Publishers, Inc., 1994)... § 12.05[1]
H.R. Rep. No. 94-1487, 94th Cong. 2d Sess. 5 (1976), *reprinted in*, 1976 U.S.C.C.A.N. 6604 ....§ 3.07, § 7.01, § 7.03[1], § 7.03[2], § 7.03[3], § 7.04[1], § 7.04[3], § 7.05[1], § 7.05[2], § 7.05[3], § 7.06[1], § 7.06[3], § 7.06[5], § 7.07, § 7.08, § 7.09, § 7.11, § 7.12, § 7.13, § 7.14[1], § 7.14[2], § 7.14[3], § 7.15, § 7.16

I

Jenia Iontcheva, Note, *Sovereignty on Our Terms,* 110 Yale L.J. 885 (2001) ....§ 10.12

J

Janis, *The Lawyer's Responsibility for Foreign Law and Foreign Lawyers*, 16 Int'l Law. 693 (1982) .... § 2.07

Jones, *International Judicial Assistance: Procedural Chaos and a Program for Reform*, 62 Yale L.J. 515 (1953) .... § 3.02
Note, *Jurisdiction Over Foreign Governments: A Comprehensive Review of the Foreign Sovereign Immunities Act*, 19 Vand. J. Transnat'l L. 119 (1986) .... § 7.06[1], § 7.06[3]
Note, *Jurisdiction: Personal Jurisdiction Over Alien Corporations*, 29 Harv. Int'l L.J. 207 (1988) .... § 6.04[1]
U.S. DEPARTMENT OF JUSTICE, ANTITRUST GUIDE FOR INTERNATIONAL OPERATION (1977) .... § 8.03
U.S. DEPARTMENT OF JUSTICE, GUIDELINES FOR INTERNATIONAL OPERSTIONS (1988) .... § 8.06[1]

K

Richard A. Kaplan, Jay N. Fastow and Lawrence J. Reina, *A Foreign Company Can Be A Sovereign State, If the Timing is Right*, Nat'l L.J. (June 13, 1994) .... § 7.03[1]
Keyes, *Encyclopedic Dictionary of Contract and Procurement Law*, vol. 20 (1987) .... § 3.04
Frederic L. Kirgis, *Act of State Exceptions and Choice of Law*, 44 U. Colo. L. Rev. 173 (1972) .... § 8.03, § 8.06[1]
Frederic L. Kirgis, *Alien Tort Claims, Sovereign Immunity and International Law in U.S. Courts*, 82 Am. J. Int'l L. 323 (1988) .... § 7.04[2]
Frederic L. Kirgis, *Editorial Comment: Understanding the Act of State Doctrine's Effect*, 82 Am. J. Int'l L. 58 (1988) .... § 8.01[3], § 8.02[2]
Julie A. Klein, *Arbitration Law: Agreeing or Refusing to*
Hear Evidence, N.Y.L.J. (Feb. 2, 1998) .... § 12.02[3]
Knight, *International Debt and the Act of State Doctrine: Judicial Abstention Reconsidered*, 13 N.C.J. Int'l L. & Com. Reg. 35 (1988) .... § 8.06[2]
Knoppke-Wetzel, *Employment Restrictions and the Practice of Law By Aliens in the United States and Abroad*, 1974 Duke L.J. 871 .... § 2.08

Kosagi, *Regulation of Practice by Foreign Lawyers*, 27 Am. J. Comp. L. 678 (1979) .... § 2.09

L

J. Lacey, Act of State and Extraterritorial Reach (1983) .... § 8.08[2]

Dieter Lange Gary Born, The Extraterritorial Application of National Laws (1989) .... § 5.08[1], [2]

Leacock, *The Commercial Activity Exception to the Act of State Doctrine Revisited: Evolution of a Concept*, 13 N.C.J. Int'l L. & Com. Reg. 1 (1988) .... § 8.03, § 8.10

Ronald D. Lee, Note, *Jurisdiction Over Foreign States for Acts of Their Instrumentalities: A Model for Attributing Liability*, 94 Yale L.J. 394 (1984) .... § 7.03[1]

Office of the Legal Advisor, *Draft Convention on Sovereign Immunity*, 58 Fed. Reg. 16729 (Mar. 30, 1993) .... § 7.01

Marian N. Leich, *Judicial Determinations of Immunity and the Department of State's Role*, 81 Am. J. Int'l L. 643 (1987) .... § 7.15

Marian N. Leich, Contemporary Practice of the United States Relating to International Law, *Unrecognized Governments: Access to U.S. Courts*, 90 A.J. Tull L. 263 (1996) .... § 5.04

Monroe Leigh, Sabbatino's *Silver Anniversary and the Restatement: No Cause for Celebration*, 24 Int'l L. 1 (1990) .... § 8.03, § 8.11

Monroe Leigh, *Sovereign Immunity—The Case of the* Imias, 68 Am. J. Int'l L. 280 (1974) .... § 7.01

Leigh & Sandler, Dunhill: *Toward a Reconsideration of* Sabbatino, 16 Va. J. Int'l L. 685 (1976) .... § 8.03, § 8.05, § 8.08[2]

Lex Mundi Directory of Law Firm Associations, Alliances, Clubs, and Other Affiliations, Int'l Law. Newsl., vol. xv, § no. 6, 1993 .... § 2.10

Lillich, *Requiem for Hickenlooper*, 69 Am. J. Int'l L. 97 (1975) .... § 8.11

Graham C. Lilly, *Jurisdiction Over Domestic and Alien Defendants*, 69 Va. L. Rev. 85 (1983)................. § 5.03
A. V. LOWE, EXTRATERRITORIAL JURISDICTION (1983).. § 5.08[2]
Lowenfeld, *The Sabbatino Amendment—International Law Meets Civil Procedure*, 59 Am. J. Int'l 89 (1965)... § 8.11
Robert A. Lusardi, *Nationwide Service of Process: Due Process Limitations on the Power of the Sovereign*, 33 Vill. L. Rev. 1 (1988)........................... § 6.03

M

Harold G. Maier, *Resolving Extraterritorial Conflicts, or "There and Back Again,"* 25 Va. J. Int'l L. 7 (1984).. § 5.08[2]
Harold G. Maier, *Extraterritorial Jurisdiction at a Crossroads: An Intersection Between Public and Private International Law*, 76 Am. J. Int'l L. 280 1982).. § 5.08[2]
Stanley J. Marcus, *Jurisdiction with Respect to Foreign Branches and Subsidiaries: Judicial Power in the Foreign Affairs Context Under Section 414 of the Foreign Relations Restatement*, 26 Int'l Law. 1 (1992).. § 6.01
MARTINDALE-HUBBELL INTERNATIONAL LAW DIRECTORY, vols. I & II (1994)................................ § 2.10
MARTINDALE-HUBBELL INTERNATIONAL LAW DIGEST, ARGENTINA–VENEZUELA SELECTED INTERNATIONAL CONVENTIONS (1994)...............§ 2.02, § 3.08, § 3.09, § 4.02, § 4.04, § 9.07, § 10.10[4]
Luis M. Martinez, *International Groups Report ADR Caseload Rise*, Disp. Resol. Times (Am. Arb. Ass'n, Winter 1997–98).................................... § 3.01
Ramona Martinez, "Recognition and Enforcement of International Arbitral Awards Under the United Nations Convention of 1958: The 'Refusal' Provisions," 24 Int'l Law. 487, 501–02 (1990)................................12.06

Karl M. Meesen, *Antitrust Jurisdiction Under Customary International Law*, 78 Am. J. Int'l L. 783 (1984) .... § 5.08[2]

Roger Miner, *The Reception of Foreign Law in the U.S. Federal Courts*, 43 Am. J. Comp. L. 581 (1995) .... § 9.03

JAMES W. MOORE ET AL., MOORE'S FEDERAL PRACTICE (2d ed. 1991).................... § 10.06, § 10.09

Murphy, *The Four Languages of Charles V, Resolving Commercial Disputes Without Trial*, Houston, (Mar. 1992, *reprinted in* Int'l Q.).............. § 12.02[4]

N

Courts Stress Importance of Clear [Arbitration] Clauses,
Nat'l L.J. (Sept. 22, 1997) at B23............ § 5.10[2], § 12.02[4]

2d Circuit Bars Suits by ''Offshore'' Corporations, Nat'l L.J. (Aug. 25, 1997) at B9 .... § 5.06[1], [2]

War Crimes Suits on Tap in NYC, Nat'l L.J. (Dec. 29, 1997) at A6 .... § 5.06[1]

A.D. NEALE M.L. STEPHENS, INTERNATIONAL BUSINESS and NATIONAL JURISDICTION
Clarendon Press 94–98 (1988).................... § 8.03

Carroll E. Neeseman, *Outside Counsel: More Certainty*
Comes to Arbitration, N.Y.L.J. (Mar. 26, 1998)............ § 12.06

Steven C. Nelson, *Alternatives to Litigation of International Disputes*, 23 Int'l Law. 187 (1989)...§ 3.01, § 3.03
§ 3.11, § 3.12, § 12.02[3]

Theodore Newcomb & Christian Kohler, *''Coping with Secrecy and Blocking Laws,''* Transnational Litigation: Practical Approaches to Conflicts and Accommodations, (Sections of Litigation and Int'l Law and Practice), A.B.A. Nat'l Inst. 631 (1984)....... § 10.23[1]

Lawrence W. Newman, *Service of Process in Latin America: Potential Pitfalls*, NEW YORK LAW JOURNAL (Sept. 27, 2002).................... § 4.05

O

Linda Karr O'Connor, *International and Foreign Legal Research: Tips, Tricks, and Sources*, 28 Cornell Int'l L.J. 417 (1995) .... § 2.02
L. OPPENHEIM, I INTERNATIONAL LAW (8th ed. 1955) .... § 5.08[1]
Bernard H. Oxman, *The Choice Between Direct Discovery and Other Means of Obtaining Evidence Abroad: The Impact of the Hague Evidence Convention*, 37 U. Miami L.R. 733 (1983) .... § 10.02

P

Gerald W. Palmer, *Enforcing Arbitral Decisions*, Nat'l L.J. (Feb. 7, 1994) ....§ 5.08[2], § 12.06
Patrikis, *Foreign Central Bank Property: Immunity From Attachment in the United States*, 1982 U. Ill. L. Rev. 265 .... § 7.16
Joel R. Paul, *Comity in International Law*, 32 Harv. Int'l L.J. 1 (1991) .... § 5.08[1]
Brian Pearce, *The Comity Doctrine as a Barrier to Judicial Jurisdiction; A U.S.–E.U. Comparison*, 30 Stant. J. Int'l L. 525 (1994) .... § 5.08[1]
Milton Pollack, *Proof of Foreign Law*, 26 Am. J. Comp. L. 470 (1978) .... § 9.03
Comment, *Providing Legal Services in Foreign Countries: Making Room for the American Attorney*, 83 Colum. L. Rev. 1767 (1983) ....§ 2.08, § 2.10
Publication 42, United States Postal Service ....§ 7.14[2]

R

Charles R. Ragan, *Arbitration in Japan: Caveat Drafter and Other Lessons from an American Perspective on Trans-Pacific Dispute Resolution, Private Investments Abroad*, at 12–20 (Matthew Bender & Co., Inc. 1996) .... § 12.02[4]
Prakash Rajamani, *International Litigation: Act of State*, 32 Int'l Lawyer 223, 252 (1998) .... § 8.01[3]

Recognition and Enforcement in Switzerland of U.S. Judgments Containing an Award of Punitive Damages, Int'l Bus. Law (June 1994) .... § 11.07
Reese, *Depacage: A Common Phenomenon in Choice of Law*, 73 Colum. L. Rev. 58 (1974)............... § 9.06
Report on the Second Meeting of the Special Commission on the Operation of the Hague Convention of 18 Mar., 1970, on the Taking of Evidence Abroad in Civil or Commercial Matters, 24 I.L.M. 1668 (1985)................................ § 10.04
Report of United States Delegation to Eleventh Session of Hague Conference on Private International Law, 8 I.L.M. 785 (1969)....................... § 10.10
RESTATEMENT (SECOND) OF CONFLICTS OF LAW (1971):
§ 6 .... § 9.06
§ 10 .... § 9.06
§ 98 .... § 11.06
§ 117 cmt. c .... § 11.03, § 11.07
RESTATEMENT (SECOND) OF FOREIGN RELATIONS LAW § 18 (1965) .... § 7.06[6]
RESTATEMENT (SECOND) OF FOREIGN RELATIONS LAW § 40 (1971) .... § 10.16
RESTATEMENT (REVISED) OF FOREIGN RELATIONS LAW§ 437(1)(c) .... § 10.11
RESTATEMENT (THIRD) OF FOREIGN RELATIONS LAW (1987):
Part IV, introductory note .... § 5.02
§ 401(1)(c)... § 5.04[2]
§ 402 ....§ 5.02, § 5.03, § 5.03[1], § 5.08, § 7.06[6]
§ 403 ....§ 1.01, § 3.06, § 5.08[2], § 7.06[6]
§ 414 .... § 6.01
§ 421 ....§ 1.01, § 3.05,§ 3.06, § 6.01, § 6.03, § 6.04, § 6.04[1], § 6.04[2], § 6.04[3], § 6.05
§ 437 .... § 12.05
§ 441 .... § 8.03
§ 442 .... § 8.03
§ 442 ....§ 1.01, § 1.04, § 10.16, § 10.17, § 10.23[1]
§ 442(1)(a)... § 10.22
§ 442(1)(c).................................... § 1.04, § 10.11, § 10.16

INTERNATIONAL COMMERCE: THE PROBLEM OF EXTRATERRITORIALITY (1982).. § 5.08[2]
Philip Rothman, *PSSST, Please Keep it Confidential*, 49 Disp. Resol. J. 69, 69 (1994)........... § 12.02[5]
David Rubenstein, *Foreign Firms Offer Quality Work at Bargain Rates*, Corp. Legal Times (Nov. 1992)... § 2.10

S

Stephen L. Sass, *Foreign Law in Federal Courts*, 29 Am. J. Comp. L. 97 (1981)....................................... § 9.03
Sawaki, *Recognition and Enforcement of Foreign Judgments in Japan*, Int'l Law. 29 (1989)..................... § 11.04
John R. Schmertz, *A Modern Procedural Framework for Establishing the Law of a Foreign Country*, 28 Prac. Law., vol. 6, 63 (1982)..................... § 9.03
S. Exec. Rep. 95, 92nd Cong., 2d Sess. 1 (1972) § 10.10
S. Rep. No. 1188, Part I, 88th Cong., 2d Sess. 24 (1964)... § 8.11
S. Rep. No. 21, 98th Cong., 1st Sess. 6–7 (1983) (Permanent Subcommittee on Investigation of the Committee on Governmental Affairs, *Staff Study of Crime and Secrecy: The Use of Offshore Banks and Companies)* .... § 10.16
Donald R. Shemanski, *Obtaining Evidence in the Federal Republic of Germany: The Impact of the Hague Evidence Convention on German–American Judicial Cooperation*, 17 Int'l Law. 465 (1983).. § 10.04
Hans Smit, *International Litigation Under the United States Code*, 65 Colum. L. Rev. 1015, 1026 n.71 (1965).. § 12.05
Hans Smit, *The Proposed United States—United Kingdom Convention on Recognition and Enforcement of Judgments: A Prototype for the Future?*, 17 Va. J. Int'l L. 443 (1977)........................ § 11.01

Robert M. Smith, *Saving Ourselves From Being Lawyered to Death*, Washington Post (Sept. 24, 1995) at C4 .... § 12.02[5]

James P. Springer, *An Overview of International Evidence and Asset Gathering in Civil and Criminal Tax Cases*, 22 Geo. Wash. J. Int'l L. & Econ. 277 (1988)..§ 10.19

Margaret G. Stewart, *Forum Non Conveniens: A Doctrine in Search of a Role*, 74 Cal. L. Rev. 1259 (1986).. § 5.07

Swanson, *A Threshold Test for Validity: The Supreme Court Narrows the Act of State Doctrine*, 23 Vand. J. Transnat'l L. 889 (1991)............§ 8.02[3], § 8.03

SWEENEY, OLIVER LEECH, THE INTERNATIONAL LEGAL SYSTEM (1981)... § 8.11

Symposium, *Compelling Discovery in Transnational Litigation*, 16 N.Y.U.J. Int'l L. & Pol. 957 (1984)..§ 10.10

T

Letter from Jack B. Tate, Acting Legal Advisor of Department of State, to Phillip Perlman, Acting U.S. Attorney General (May 19, 1952), *reprinted in*, 26 Dep't State Bull. 984 (1952)..................§ 7.01, § 7.08

Louise Ellen Teitz, *International Litigation, I. Parallel Proceedings: Treading Carefully*, 32 Int'l Law. 223, 223 (1998)................................§ 5.08[3]

Christine Lecuyer-Thieffry & Patrick Thieffry, *Negotiating Settlement of Disputes Provisions in International Business Contracts: Recent Developments in Arbitration and Other Processes*, 45 Bus. Law. 581 (1990)................§ 3.01, § 3.02, § 3.04, § 3.11

Bate C. Toms, *The French Response to Extraterritorial Application of United States Antitrust Laws*, 15 Int'l Law. 585 (1981)................ § 10.23[2]

TREATIES IN FORCE, U.S. DEPARTMENT OF STATE (1993)...§ 4.04, § 4.05, § 8.07

Peter D. Trooboff, *International Decisions*, 84 Am. J. Int'l L. 550 (1990) .... § 8.02[3]
Peter D. Trooboff, *International Decisions*, 83 Am. J. Int'l L. 565 (1989) .... § 7.04[2]
Mary Twitchell, *The Myth of General Jurisdiction*, 101 Harv. L. Rev. 610 (1988) .... § 6.04[2]
Note, *Two Faces of the Trader: Guidelines for Distinguishing Between Governmental and Commercial Acts Under the Foreign Sovereign Immunities Act of 1976*, 23 Tex. Int'l L.J. 465 (1988) .... § 7.06[1]

V

Detlev F. Vagts, *Senate Materials and Treaty Interpretation: Some Research Hints for the Supreme Court*, 83 Am. J. Int'l L. 546 (1989) .... § 2.05
Darryl Van Duch, *When Does a Sovereign State Control a Company?* National Law Journal, April 1, 1996 .... § 7.03[1]
Von Mehren, *The Foreign Sovereign Immunities Act of 1976*, 17 Colum. J. Transnat'l L. 33 (1978) .... § 7.01, § 7.06[1], § 7.07
Von Mehren & Trautman, *Jurisdiction to Adjudicate, A Suggested Analysis*, 79 Harv. L. Rev. 1121 (1966) .... § 6.04[2]
Victor & Hood, *Personal Jurisdiction, Venue, and Service of Process in Antitrust Cases Involving International Trade: Amenability of Alien Corporations to Suit*, 46 Antitrust L.J. 1063 (1978) .... § 6.07, § 6.08

W

Don Wallace, Jr. & Joseph P. Griffin, *The Restatement and Foreign Sovereign Compulsion: A Plea for Due Process*, 29 Int'l Law. 63–74 (1989) .... § 8.03
Mary Beth West & Sean D. Murphy, *The Impact on U.S. Litigation of Non-Recognition of Foreign Governments*, 26 Stan. J. Int'l L. 435 (1990) .... § 5.06

Z